These paintings represent a schizophrenic girl's gropings toward sanity. As she painted them, she did not know what they meant. Yet there was a message in them, and through gradually identifying the symbols in which it was "coded," Dr. Ainslie Meares, the psychiatrist who treated her, was able to establish communication with her. Then, by talking in the same symbols, he was able to help her slowly find her way out of her frightening world. Dr. Meares tells her story in *The Door of Serenity* (Thomas, 1958)

When Dr. Meares first saw Jennifer, she was 19 and living alone in a boarding house on a small annuity. She was entirely withdrawn and shunned all offers of friendship; terror and confusion were her only companions. It was virtually impossible to communicate with her, and Dr. Meares soon discovered that he must not touch her, talk to her, or even look at her. Only through such passive offers of friendship as staying quietly with her, moving her chair a little closer to the fire, and helping her light a cigarette was he able to establish rapport with her. Many times he felt clumsy and bungling, as when he tried to give her a cup of tea to calm her when her hands were shaking so that she could not hold it. Insulin and electroshock were tried, to no avail, as was a series of group therapy sessions. For a long time he saw no hope; he feared she might commit suicide, yet was reluctant to commit her to a mental hospital.

D

E

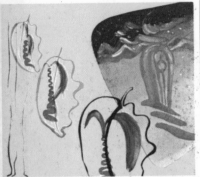

Painting *D* shows a stage in her improvement. The tree at the left is carelessly drawn, but a leg can be clearly distinguished. Its leaves are falling, leaves with red and black in them. Men are becoming less evil, less sexual. As Jennifer realizes this, she is permitted a vision both of the gateway through which she now may be able to pass and of what lies beyond—the clear, cool, moonlit mountains of serenity. For the first time Jennifer had hope that serenity might one day be for her.

The gateway in this painting illustrates the danger of confusing "universal" symbols—symbols used with the same meaning by many people in their dreams and fantasies—with "individual" symbols, which carry a unique meaning for one person. A doorway is a characteristic female symbol, much as the rod and the snake are characteristic phallic symbols. But if Jennifer's door is interpreted in this way, the whole meaning of her paintings is lost.

Dr. Meares was still puzzled by the third wing that continually appeared on the bird, but something Jennifer said finally provided the clue—a clue

which he might have missed had it not been for the paintings. She was recalling an incident when she was a child, when she and her foster brother had been bathed together. "I saw the difference between me and little boys. I felt I was wrong." Could this fear of her own deformity have tormented her through childhood and persisted, as a conviction that she was evil, into adulthood? Painting *E*, provided confirmation. The bird symbol and the tree symbol are merged: the third wing is an attempt to make the bird male. But it is crossed off. Jennifer should not have a phallus after all. Realizing this she is able to feel the rays of the "anesthetic moon," another of her symbols for serenity.

Increasingly, Dr. Meares was able to communicate with Jennifer in her own symbolic language. He found that the statement, "The door is opening," usually had a deep effect on her, while the equivalent statement in ordinary language, "You are getting better," had none. References to the tree losing its red, to the blue mountains, or to the fact that there was a road to the mountains would calm her.

Finally came a day of triumph when she brought him painting *F*. The bird no longer has the third wing, which lies lifeless—no longer threatening. Jennifer was free. And suddenly she was no longer able to paint. But she continued to improve and at 26 was well enough to take her first job.

There is much to be learned from this case history. From the constriction, confusion, and turmoil of Jennifer's earlier paintings we can feel something of what it is like to be schizophrenic; from the freedom and lyricism of the later ones we can experience with her the glorious feeling of approaching safety and order. We see the patience and imagination and empathy needed by those who work with the mentally ill and the frustration they often feel. But above all we learn the necessity for flexibility and perceptiveness in dealing with mental patients. They live in worlds of their own which often are filled with symbols they cannot understand. If they cannot speak our language, we must learn to understand theirs.

Abnormal Psychology and Modern Life • Third Edition

Third Edition

James C. Coleman
Professor of Psychology, The University of California at Los Angeles

Scott, Foresman and Company

ABNORMAL PSYCHOLOGY AND MODERN LIFE

Preface to the Third Edition

Eight years have gone by since the second edition of *Abnormal Psychology and Modern Life* was published. They have been years of rapid change in which the world has been shaken by major social crises, political realignments, and rumblings of war. These years have contained many tragic events, but they have also seen the emergence of new hopes for man's future.

In part, these new hopes and visions rest upon scientific advances which have added greatly to our understanding of human behavior and ability to control it. For example, the clear delineation of the role of sociocultural deprivation in mental retardation has both increased our understanding of this disorder and opened the way for a reduction in its incidence. It is our task in this new revision to bring our presentation up to date in the light of such new findings.

Throughout this third edition, new research findings have been reported; much new case material has been introduced; and numerous new summary charts have been added. A number of topics have received more comprehensive treatment, including (a) human genetics and neurophysiology—to encompass the new breakthroughs in molecular genetics and in electrical brain stimulation, (b) the effects of early sociocultural deprivation on personality development, (c) the role of learning in both the development and the amelioration of abnormal behavior, (d) the influence of the individual's interpersonal relationships—particularly pathogenic family patterns—on his development and functioning, (e) the new roles of chemotherapy, behavior therapy, and family therapy in treatment, (f) the nature of the stresses which characterize contemporary life, and (g) the critical importance of meaning, choice, responsibility, and values in man's existence. The sections dealing with schizophrenia, mental retardation, juvenile delinquency, and adult crime have been greatly amplified in accordance with the extreme importance of these disorders. New sections have been added on compulsive gambling, the "new" criminal, and military and space psychiatry.

Also new with this edition is a brief Appendix summary of psychoanalytic and other major personality theories. The effects of different basic assumptions about personality are evident in the different explanations of abnormal behavior that are advanced and the different methods of treatment that are chosen. Hence it seemed desirable to clarify for the student several of these basic patterns of assumptions, but without making a detour into personality theory in the main body of the text—whose focus is abnormal behavior.

Throughout the text, an attempt has been made to achieve a rigorous approach appropriate to the increased sophistication of today's students and the higher academic standards being set in our colleges and universities. This has included a critical, and it is hoped challenging, concern with research questions in our discussion of various forms of abnormal behavior. We have retained our conceptual framework based on the integration of relevant biological, psychological, and sociological data. It is felt that such a framework is essential for organizing the large and unwieldy mass of knowledge that has accumulated so rapidly in the behavioral sciences. Such a framework also enables us to see how the contributions of several scientific fields fit together to make a more complete picture, and it helps us to see the full complexity and richness of human behavior. Although no attempt has been made to avoid complex and difficult concepts and topics, every effort has been made to avoid unnecessary complexities and to keep the exposition as clear and direct as possible.

This third edition of *Abnormal Psychology and Modern Life* follows the same sequence as the previous edition:

Part I (two chapters) sets the stage, defining

L. C. Catalog Card #64-20449
Copyright © 1964 by Scott, Foresman and Company, Glenview, Illinois 60025. Previous copyright 1956, 1950.
All rights reserved. Printed in the United States of America. Regional offices of Scott, Foresman and Company are located in Atlanta, Dallas, Glenview, Palo Alto, and Oakland, N. J.

The family therapy case on pages 574-575 is from *Clinical Psychology* by Norman D. Sundberg and Leona E. Tyler. Copyright © 1962, MeredithPublishing Company. Reprinted by permission of the publisher Appleton-Century-Crofts. The anxiety hierarchy and case excerpt on pages 597 and 598 are reprinted from *Psychotherapy by Reciprocal Inhibition* by Joseph Wolpe with the permission of the publishers, Stanford University Press. © Copyright 1958 by the Board of Trustees of the Leland Stanford Junior University.

the problem and showing its magnitude, laying to rest certain common misconceptions about abnormal behavior, and tracing the historical changes in theories and methods of treatment since ancient times.

Part II (two chapters) lays the theoretical groundwork for an understanding of the dynamics of personality development and adjustment, both normal and abnormal. All behavior is seen as a function of (a) the individual's adjustive capacity, which in turn depends on his psychobiological make-up, and (b) the stress situation he faces. With this framework it becomes apparent to the student that any illness is an illness of the whole individual occurring in a given stress setting—and must be so regarded to be fully understood.

Parts III and IV (eight chapters) detail the symptoms, dynamics, therapy, and prognosis of the various abnormal reaction patterns. Part III considers the "functional" disorders—those in which brain pathology is not considered of primary etiological significance or is not apparent. Part IV takes up the mental disorders associated with brain pathology. The syndromes described conform essentially to the classification adopted by the American Psychiatric Association. Thus the student who goes on for further work in this field will find that the terms and categories he learns here will be the ones he will be using later. While organizing our discussion around these agreed-upon categories, however, we have put our main emphasis on the dynamics of the various types of abnormal behavior and not on classification *per se*.

Part V (three chapters) deals with modern concepts and methods of diagnosis, treatment, and prevention of abnormal behavior. Included here is a full report on the modern mental health movement and an appraisal of the role of psychiatry[1]—actual and potential—in our modern world.

As in the previous edition there is a comprehensive glossary, a brief bibliography of modern writings that deal with abnormal behavior, and a list of sources for further information and psychological help.

To provide flexibility and depth in the teaching of the abnormal psychology course, three other publications are available with this revision: (a) a study guide for the text, prepared by Dr. and Mrs. Dewey Moore, Indiana State College, can be used to focus and guide the student's reading and provide a concise summary of each chapter for review purposes; (b) a series of tapes of actual therapy sessions, collected by Dr. Stewart Shapiro, Western Psychological Center, will let students listen in on six different types of therapy with patients suffering from different types of mental disorders; and (c) a brief book of readings, edited by Dr. Walter Nunokawa, Portland State College, will provide students with deeper roots in primary source materials relating to the scientific study and treatment of abnormal behavior in our society. These are described more fully in the *Instructor's Guide for Abnormal Psychology and Modern Life*. This *Instructor's Guide* also contains an annotated list of appropriate films, and a complete battery of test items. It will be supplied on request without charge to instructors using the text.

The author is greatly indebted to many colleagues in the biological and social science fields whose conscientious research is helping to conquer the still new frontier of abnormal behavior. Although his general orientation is not that of any one school, his thinking relative to dynamic concepts has been strongly influenced by many men, including Freud, Meyer, Sullivan, the Menningers, Dorcus, Rogers, Syngg, Combs, Maslow, Allport, Cantril, Murphy, Guthrie, Tolman, Eysenck, Skinner—and many others. For this third edition, he wishes especially to express his appreciation to Mrs. Marguerite Clark, the directing editor, who has worked closely with the author on all phases of the revision. His thanks go to Mrs. Frances Berres, Miss Ann Davy, Miss Rita Mann, and Miss Janis Stone for critical reading suggestions. Finally, he is most grateful to Drs. H. David Archibald, Andrew Comrey, Gunnar Dybwad, Molly Gorelick, Evelyn Hooker, Newell Jones, Donald Lindsley, Roger Russell, Elliot Rodnick, Joseph Sheehan, and Marion Wenger for help in clarifying various systematic and technical points and related assistance.

James C. Coleman

---

[1]*Psychiatry* as used here designates not simply the specialty of that name but the disciplined application of research from the biological and social sciences in understanding and dealing with mental illness.

PART ONE

INTRODUCTION

contents

15 *Action for Mental Health*   612

APPENDIX

INTRODUCTION

part one

ABNORMAL BEHAVIOR IN OUR TIMES

chapter 1

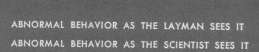

ABNORMAL BEHAVIOR AS THE LAYMAN SEES IT

ABNORMAL BEHAVIOR AS THE SCIENTIST SEES IT

The seventeenth century has been called the Age of Enlightenment; the eighteenth, the Age of Reason; the nineteenth, the Age of Progress; and the twentieth, the *Age of Anxiety*. With the conquest of many of the physical ills which have afflicted him throughout his history, man has become increasingly aware of the role of psychological factors in human existence. No longer are civilized men—at least the fortunate majority—the victims of famines and epidemics. The black plague has been replaced by a host of subtler psychological plagues—worry, value conflicts, loneliness, disillusionment, and doubts as to whether one can weave a successful course through the complex maze of freeways and blind alleys that make up modern existence.

Modern man's path to happiness is not an easy one. It is beset by seemingly endless personal and social problems. Wars have disrupted personal life and left their wake of mutilations, grief, and social unrest. Periodic breakdowns and runaways of the economic machinery—as well as automation and other technological innovations—have taken their toll in the millions of victims of unemployment and dislocation. The human population explosion is creating difficult political and social problems and tensions. Racial discrimination, with its unreasoned feelings of superiority, hatred, and resentment, hurts both the individual and the community. Homes broken by divorce leave emotional scars upon parents and children alike. Excessive competition, conflicting pressure groups, impersonal bureaucracy, rapid social change, and the ever present threat of global atomic war further aggravate modern man's anxieties.

Ours is an age of tremendous growth of knowledge. More scientific and technological discoveries have been made in the past fifty years than in all previous recorded time, and science is having an increasingly profound effect on all phases of our life. In a short time man will set foot on a planet other than the one on which he was born. Yet paradoxically, his scientific advances have led to a shrinking of his world, so that he must daily face international problems as well as national and local ones. And as man ventures into the vast universe, he is increasingly and inescapably confronted with the finiteness of his own individual existence and with questions as to its meaning. At the same time traditional values and beliefs no longer seem

self-evident, and he lacks the comforting absolutes that gave security to his forebears. Unfortunately, advances in the understanding of man have lagged far behind those in the physical sciences. We know much about the atom but not nearly enough about love or the values needed for a meaningful and fulfilling life. With all his uncertainties and anxieties, modern man has few moral beliefs to guide him. As a consequence, he stumbles around among a myriad of religions, philosophies, and social programs, seeking answers that will satisfy him.

Small wonder that on every side we see anxious, unhappy, bewildered people who are missing the fulfillment of their best potential because they cannot achieve a satisfactory adjustment to problems that seem just too great. Instead of smooth, effective functioning, we see widespread symptoms of personality maladjustment. In this Age of Anxiety, Americans spend over 10 billion dollars a year on liquor, books on personality adjustment have become best sellers, and the volume of tranquilizing drugs sold is measured in hundreds of tons.

In most cases the symptoms we see merely hinder the best potential adjustment of the individual; he worries along and solves his problems after a fashion. But in many cases the stress of modern life proves too much for him, and he becomes a psychiatric casualty. It is startling to note that mental illness incapacitates more people than all other health problems combined, that mental patients occupy almost one half of the country's hospital beds, and that approximately one out of ten persons now living in the United States will at some time be hospitalized for mental illness if present trends continue. And for each of those currently hospitalized for mental illness, there are at least twenty more who are not so severely maladjusted but nevertheless need psychiatric aid. Furthermore, these figures say nothing of the many kinds of organic illness brought on by emotional conflict or of delinquency and crime.[1]

[1]Statistics used in this chapter are conservative estimates based on the following sources: Battista (1960), California Commission of Higher Education (1960), Fein (1958), Leighton (1956), Los Angeles Organization for Mentally Ill Children (1961), Macmillan (1957), Metropolitan Life Insurance Company (1960), National Association for Mental Health (n.d.), National Committee Against Mental Illness (1959), Pasamanick, 1962; Rainie (1960), Srole *et al.* (1962), U.S. Children's Bureau; (1961), U.S. Public Health Service (1963).

Abnormal behavior is thus the country's Number One health problem. This does not mean that there are not many well-adjusted persons or that effective personality adjustment is not possible in modern life. It does mean, however, that many of us encounter serious difficulties in dealing with life's problems—particularly problems centering around values and questions of how one should live. Thus the study of abnormal behavior may be of great value in bettering individual adjustment and in reducing the great toll of misery and lost productivity which maladjustment and mental illness are exacting in our modern society.

Abnormal Behavior As the Layman Sees It

When we think of abnormal behavior, we are most likely to think of extreme, spectacular examples, because, as in every other field, it is the bizarre and sensational things that command attention. The many examples of mental illness that have come down to us from history and those described in literature are apt to be extreme cases which, isolated and lumped together, give us a "chamber-of-horrors" picture of mental illness rather than the truer picture, in which less spectacular minor maladjustments are far more common. Undoubtedly, most of the popular present-day beliefs about mental illness have been shaped by these extremely interesting but often quite unscientific historical and literary descriptions. This has been inevitable, because it is only recently that scientific research has entered the field of human behavior.

Nevertheless, despite their shortcomings, a brief review of a few cases from the past and from literature will be of value in giving us a broader perspective of our problem, for most of the forms of severe mental illness we see today have been observed and reported in other ages too.

IDEAS CARRIED OVER FROM HISTORY

Some of the earliest writings of man—Chinese, Egyptian, Hebrew, and Greek—provide striking "case histories" of disturbed individuals.[1] Saul, King of Israel in the eleventh century B.C., suffered from recurrent manic-depressive episodes. During an attack of mania (excitement) he stripped off all his clothes in a public place. On another occasion he tried to kill his son Jonathan.

Cambyses, King of Persia in the sixth century B.C., was one of the first alcoholics on record. His alcoholic excesses were apparently associated with periods of uncontrollable rage during which he behaved "as a madman not in possession of his senses." (Whitwell, 1936, p. 38) On one occasion, without making any provision for the feeding of his army, he set out against the Ethiopians, who had greatly enraged him by calling the Persians "dung eaters." He was shortly forced to return to Memphis, where he found the people celebrating the feast of Apis. Furious at what he took to be rejoicing at his failure, he ordered all the people taking part in the feast to be killed. Cambyses also defied Persian law by marrying one of his sisters and later killed his other sister by kicking her during pregnancy. On another occasion he used his friend's son as a target for his arrows to demonstrate that his excessive drinking had not affected his skill or mental stability. His aim was true and he killed the boy, thus proving his point, at least to his own satisfaction.

Greek mythology contains many descriptions of mentally ill persons which afford us some insight into the nature of the real-life cases from which the descriptions must have been drawn. For example, Hercules seems to have been afflicted with convulsive seizures accompanied by a homicidal fugue-type reaction. His attacks are graphically described by Euripides in the

---

[1] Sources drawn on in this section include the following: Bluemel (1948), Born (1946), Lombroso (1891), Marks (1925), Sewell (1943), Whitwell (1936), and Zilboorg and Henry (1941).

Nebuchadnezzar, King of ancient Babylon, suffered from lycanthropy, a form of disorder in which he believed himself to be a wolf. Contemporaries regarded this as a punishment for the king's boastfulness.

Above, King Saul is depicted beginning to suspect David. The biblical account relates that at first David's music soothed Saul "when the evil spirit was upon him" but that later he became increasingly fearful and jealous of David and eventually tried to kill him.

"Phrenzy of Hercules": his eyes rolled, his consciousness clouded, he frothed at the mouth, showed violent fury, and attacked persons in his way, then fell, writhed, and finally fell into a deep sleep. Upon awakening he had complete amnesia for the seizure. During the course of several attacks, Hercules killed two of his own children, two of his brother's children, his best friend, and his teacher. Ajax, too, became mentally disordered and slew a flock of sheep under the impression that he was attacking his enemies. On regaining his senses, he was so overcome with remorse that he committed suicide by throwing himself on his sword.

Many of the notables of later Greece and Rome, including Socrates, Democritus, and Alexander the Great, apparently suffered from mental disorders of one kind or another, and the ensuing period of the Middle Ages contains innumerable instances of abnormal behavior. The great oriental conqueror, Tamerlane (1336-1405), for example, was particularly fond of building pyramids of human skulls. One of his architectural achievements is reported to have contained some forty thousand of them.

In more recent times, George III of England suffered from severe manic-depressive reactions. During periods of manic excitement he showed the typical unregal symptoms of this disorder: he jumped rapidly from one topic to another; asked precipitate questions without waiting for an answer; ate his food so rapidly that the members of his court had to bolt their food or leave the table hungry; raced up and down stairs; rode his horse to death; indulged in obscene language; and displayed the tireless energy typical of the manic who is just too busy to sleep.

The French philosopher Jean Jacques Rousseau (1712-1778) developed marked paranoid symptoms during the latter part of his life. He was obsessed with fears of secret enemies and thought that Prussia, England, France, the king, priests, and others were waging a terrible war against him. He believed that these enemies caused him to have all kinds of internal troubles, but that their chief artifice was to torture him by overwhelming him with benefits and praise, even going so far as to corrupt vegetable peddlers so that they would sell him better vegetables more cheaply. According to Rousseau, this was undoubtedly designed to prove his baseness and their generosity. It would be interesting here to know whether this behavior was related to the fact that he and his wife had left each of their five children at a foundling hospital.

Rousseau became panicky during a visit to London and fled leaving all his luggage and money at the hotel. On his arrival at the coast the winds were not favorable for his departure, and in this he saw another indication of the plot against him. After his return to France, his invisible enemies apparently stepped up their persecution. They corrupted his coffee merchant, his hairdresser, and his landlord; the shoeblack had no more blacking when Rousseau needed him; the boatman had no boats when this unfortunate man wished to cross the Seine; his enemies even prevented his front door from opening. He demanded to be put in prison, but even this was prevented by his imaginary foes. No longer able to trust man, he turned to God, to whom he addressed a very tender and familiar letter. To ensure the arrival of the letter at its proper destination, he tried to place it on the altar of Notre Dame at Paris. Finding the railing closed, he believed that Heaven, too, was conspiring against him. Finally he even came to distrust his dog.

The list of philosophers, painters, writers, and musicians who might also be mentioned in our discussion is a long and celebrated one. During the composition of the *Requiem* Mozart labored under the delusion that he was being poisoned. Beethoven, although miserably poor, was constantly changing his living quarters and sometimes had to pay for lodgings at three or four different places at once. Robert Schumann, in later life, was pursued by turning-tables which knew everything, and heard spirit voices and melodies and harmonies which developed into entire compositions.

On one occasion Van Gogh cut off his ear and sent it to a prostitute, an action apparently performed in a state of clouded consciousness resulting from his epileptic condition. Schopen-

hauer, Chopin, and John Stuart Mill suffered from attacks of depression. Rabelais, Tasso, Samuel Butler, Burns, and Byron used alcohol excessively. Coleridge's "Kubla Khan" and Poe's "Fall of the House of Usher" show the unmistakable effects of having been written under the influence of opiates.

As we approach contemporary times, the names of Mussolini, Hitler, Goering, and other notorious figures of modern history enter our discussion. Certain of these figures will come under scrutiny in connection with our discussion of particular abnormal patterns.

In reviewing these historical instances of abnormal behavior, it should be made clear that we are to some extent evaluating this behavior in the light of our present-day concepts of mental illness. In their own day, some of these men were looked upon as perfectly normal and others as only eccentric or unusual. It should also be emphasized that although many mentally ill individuals have played important roles in the shaping of history, it has been those men and women of more effective personality adjustment who have carried the major burden, particularly in the achievement of social progress.

IDEAS CARRIED OVER
FROM LITERATURE

Since long before the development of modern psychiatry, the masters of the novel, the epic, and the drama have written brilliant and moving characterizations of abnormal behavior, which they have developed not through systematic clinical or experimental study but through their sensitive, keen observations of human behavior. Their primary purpose, of course, has been artistic rather than scientific: they have obviously not been interested in developing a systematic body of scientific principles. But their descriptions of human abnormality in all its infinite subtleties of degree and variety often have a lifelike vividness and an emotional force that science cannot achieve. *Othello,* for example, gives us an unforgettable insight into the subjective quality of obsessive, violent jealousy.

Unfortunately, literature cannot provide either the theoretical or the practical basis for understanding and curing specific cases of abnormal behavior. A court psychiatrist familiar with *Othello* may feel deep sympathy with a patient who has become irrationally convinced of his wife's infidelity and has killed her in a fit of jealous rage. But this insight and sympathy will not alone determine the sanity or insanity of the accused or indicate what treatment will be most effective. The psychiatrist must perform examinations and systematically search for factors like those that have been observed to operate in thousands of cases of similar abnormal behavior.

Literature and psychology, then, give different kinds of understanding of abnormal behavior; they can and should complement each other. In fact, "Quite apart from the enjoyment of literature, the reader cannot fail to learn something genuine about psychopathology. . . . And the psychiatrist will learn what he will not find in the textbooks. For if he knows only psychiatry, he does not know psychiatry." (Aswell, 1947, p. 371) Let us glance briefly at a few classical illustrations.

The writings of the Greek poets and dramatists contain many allusions to abnormal behavior. In his play *Medea,* Euripides (480-406 B.C.) described and analyzed the emotions of jealousy and revenge as displayed by a mother who murders her children. Sophocles (495-406 B.C.) in *Oedipus Rex* and *Electra* has given us the first intimation of incest motives in the shaping of human behavior. And in *Orestes* he clearly described delusional and hallucinatory symptoms arising out of severe feelings of remorse and guilt.

Many of the characters in the plays of Shakespeare (mostly written and produced between 1590 and 1610) portray the development of abnormal behavior with almost clinical accuracy. The intense guilt reaction of Lady Macbeth, after planning and participating in the bloody murder of King Duncan, is well brought out in her uneasy sleepwalking and symbolic handwashing:

"It is an accustomed action with her, to seem thus washing her hands: I have known her continue in this a quarter of an hour."—*Macbeth,* Act V, Scene 1

That her compulsive handwashing has failed, however, to "cleanse" her of her feelings of un-cleanliness and guilt is shown in her admission that

"Here's the smell of the blood still: all the perfumes of Arabia will not sweeten this little hand. Oh, oh, oh!"—Act V, Scene 1

Can anyone who has passed through the idealistic period of early adolescence fail to see the humor and pathos in the adventures of Don Quixote in Cervantes' famous novel of that name? Don Quixote becomes so overwhelmed by reading the most famous books of chivalry that he believes them to be true. How natural it seems for him to accept his "mission" as a knight errant and to sally forth into the world to defend the oppressed and to right injustice like the heroes of his romances. Even when his excited imagination turns windmills into giants, solitary inns into castles, and galley slaves into oppressed gentlemen, he does not completely lose us. And finally when he is restored to his "right" mind through a severe illness and is made to renounce

In one of his hallucinations Don Quixote imagines two flocks of sheep to be opposing armies and rushes to the rescue of the weaker group.

the follies of knight errantry, most of us probably feel a tinge of disappointment that he must give up his dreams and his noble "mission."

Many of the expressions found in literature not only yield valuable information about the concepts of personality dynamics and mental illness prevalent during a particular historical period but also tell us a great deal about the inner experiences of the author.

Man has long been puzzled by irrational motivations and images that seem to lie deeply buried in his unconscious and come to light only under the most unusual circumstances—delirium, the influence of drugs, or severe mental illness—when inner restraints are lowered and perceptions are distorted. The opium dreams of De Quincey reveal something of this "world within."

". . . I brought together all creatures, birds, beasts, reptiles, all trees and plants, usages and appearances, that are found in all tropical regions, and assembled them together in China or Indostan. From kindred feelings, I soon brought Egypt and all her gods under the same law. I was stared at, hooted at, grinned at, chattered at, ran into pagodas: and was fixed for centuries at the summit, or in secret rooms; I was the idol; I was the priest; I was worshipped; I was sacrificed. I fled from the wrath of Brama through all the forests of Asia: Vishnu hated me: Seeva laid wait for me. I came suddenly upon Isis and Osiris: I had done a deed, they said, which the ibis and the crocodile trembled at. I was buried for a thousand years in stone coffins, with mummies and sphinxes, in narrow chambers at the heart of eternal pyramids. I was kissed, with cancerous kisses, by crocodiles; and laid, confounded with all unutterable slimy things, amongst reeds and Nilotic mud."—*Confessions of an English Opium Eater*

In still other cases it is interesting to speculate concerning the motivation that prompted the writings. Vicarious sadism, for example, seems to have been behind the fantasies of Jonathan Edwards when he pictured the brutal torturings in hell of those considered by him as sinners. When he preached on "Sinners in the Hands of an Angry God," his congregation received a terrifying warning:

"The wrath of God burns against them; their damnation does not slumber; the pit is prepared; the fire is made ready; the furnace is now hot, ready to receive them; the flames do now rage and glow. . . . The devils watch them; they are ever by them, at their right hand; they stand waiting for them, like greedy, hungry lions that see their prey, and expect to have it, but are for the present kept back; if God should withdraw His hand, by which they are restrained, they would in one moment fly upon their poor souls. The old serpent is gaping for them; hell opens its mouth wide to receive them; and if God should permit it, they would be hastily swallowed up and lost. . . .

"The God that holds you over the pit of hell, much as one holds a spider or some loathsome insect over the fire, abhors you, and is dreadfully provoked; His wrath towards you burns like fire; He looks upon you as worthy of nothing else, but to be cast into the fire; He is of purer eyes than to bear to have you in His sight; you are ten times so abominable in His eyes, as the most hateful and venomous serpent is in ours. . . .

"If we knew that there was one person, and but one, in the whole congregation, that was to be the subject of this misery, what an awful thing it would be to think of! If we knew who it was, what an awful sight would it be to see such a person. How much all the rest of the congregation might lift up a lamentable and bitter cry over him! But alas! instead of one, how many is it likely will remember this discourse in hell! And it would be a wonder, if some that are now present should not be in hell in a very short time, before this year is out. And it would be no wonder if some persons that now sit here in some seats of this meeting-house in health, and quiet, and secure, should be there before to-morrow morning. These of you that finally continue in a natural condition, that shall keep out of hell longest, will be there in a little time!" (Edwards, 1809, pp. 489-502)

Many modern writers have attempted to capture, often from their own experience, the pattern of thought processes underlying various types of abnormal behavior. Subjects so treated have included schizophrenia, alcoholism, paresis, manic-depressive psychoses, homosexuality —in fact, almost the entire gamut of abnormal reaction patterns.[1]

Because of their popular appeal, such narratives are often widely read, and in some cases disseminated even more widely through tele-

---

[1]A list of modern writings concerned with abnormal behavior will be found in the Appendix.

vision and motion-picture adaptations. In general, their influence on the public has probably been beneficial, assisting in a better understanding of abnormal behavior by removing some of the mystery and dread associated with it and by promoting public interest in the improvement of facilities for the treatment and prevention of mental illness. In many cases, however, authors have taken quite atypical cases or have lacked sufficient understanding of the dynamic factors to present mental illness as anything but a mysterious, weird, horrible thing.

Even the biographer, historian, and political scientist have inevitably become psychiatrically minded. The biographer tries to explain personality development and odd or peculiar behavior in historical persons in the light of present psychiatric knowledge. And the historian can no longer afford to ignore psychiatric principles in his attempt to understand historical events. For example, psychiatric evaluations of Nazi leaders have added much to our insight into the events that shocked the world during their period of power. More recently the World Health Organization Expert Committee on Mental Health has expressed the opinion that the stresses on persons in high positions are often too great for normal people. One consequence is that individuals with psychopathic personality make-up— who tend to exploit power for selfish purposes and have little concern for ethical values or social progress—often become leaders (WHO, 1960). Obviously such a possibility has profound social implications.

ABNORMAL BEHAVIOR
IN EVERYDAY LIFE

One cannot read a metropolitan newspaper without encountering murder, sexual pathology, suicide, robbery, and a variety of other incidents involving personality difficulties. Likewise, television, movie, and radio dramas— "psychological thrillers"—in which abnormal behavior is a central theme have become extremely popular. How often in encountering these themes have we wished that we understood more about the dynamics of crime, of sexual deviations, of suicide, of "nervous breakdowns," and other abnormal behavioral patterns. The study of abnormal behavior has become an indispensable tool in understanding many of the events in modern life.

Although anxiety and maladjustment are so widespread in our culture, the cases which we encounter in current newspapers and drama, like those we find in history and literature, are apt to be the extreme ones. The typical, more prevalent, maladjustments we experience and see around us are usually milder, involving ineffective approaches to problems rather than more severe incapacitating mental disorders.

Perhaps we can best clarify this picture by describing several somewhat arbitrarily defined levels of seriousness. In the least extreme cases, the individual is regarded as "odd" or "eccentric" but still within the bounds of ordinary, understandable human experience: here, for example, is the boy of brilliant intelligence who complains that he "just can't concentrate" on his studies and does inferior college work; the secretary who has persistent headaches for which the doctors can find no organic explanation; the painfully self-conscious young man who blushes crimson whenever he becomes the center of attention; the middle-aged Don Juan who centers his life around the conquest of women.

The difficulties may be more serious and may bring a recognition that "there's definitely something wrong," as, for example, with the 25-year-old bachelor who will not accept a promotion because it involves an occasional business trip away from his mother; the college girl who is so depressed, anxious, and tearful, for no reason she can name, that she cannot study or go to class and eventually has to drop out of school entirely; the young husband who cruelly mistreats his wife and then threatens suicide when she decides to leave him; the successful professional man who insists that he is a "miserable failure" and can't continue his work; the adolescent girl who forges checks to pay for her shopping tours; the father who wanders away from his family and is found months later in a strange community—the victim of amnesia.

Finally, there are individuals whom everyone recognizes as obviously abnormal—the 14-year-old boy who steals a car and deliberately runs down a young girl; the young mother who kills her illegitimate baby; the indignant young man who insists that his enemies have set up an electrical device that "controls his thoughts"; the middle-aged man who molests children; the alcoholic who cringes in terror before an "invasion of cockroaches"; and the "persecuted" paranoid who kills several innocent people he believes are "plotting" against him.

POPULAR BELIEFS AND MISCONCEPTIONS

It is probably inevitable that through the ages people should have held many erroneous beliefs and misconceptions about abnormal behavior as a result of their fragmentary acquaintance with it through history and literature and their attempts to cope with it in everyday life without benefit of scientific understanding. Some of these misconceptions are still popular today.

Personal fears of becoming mentally ill. Fears of possible mental illness are quite common and cause much needless unhappiness. Other people seem so self-assured and capable. They cannot possibly have the inconsistent impulses or unreasonable fantasies we do, or feel

the hostility or anxiety or discouragement that plague us. There are times when most of us feel "Everyone is normal but me."

Especially since psychiatry has become popularly known and accepted, people worry about any of their behavior or attitudes that do not fit into their concept of "normality." Most people occasionally feel anxious, discouraged, and inadequate for periods of days or weeks; they may notice with alarm that they are irritable and restless, seem unduly fatigued, and suffer from sleeplessness and loss of appetite—in short, that they have almost every neurotic symptom described in magazine articles. When psychological stresses become especially great, they may develop physical ailments, find themselves unable to concentrate, feel that they are "going to pieces," and even contemplate suicide. They may become convinced they are going insane, and if, like most of us, they have a relative who was either "odd" or in a mental hospital, their fears are only strengthened.

One effective way of allaying these unnecessary fears is to realize that most, if not all, other people share these experiences at some time during their lives. Almost anyone, if pressed,

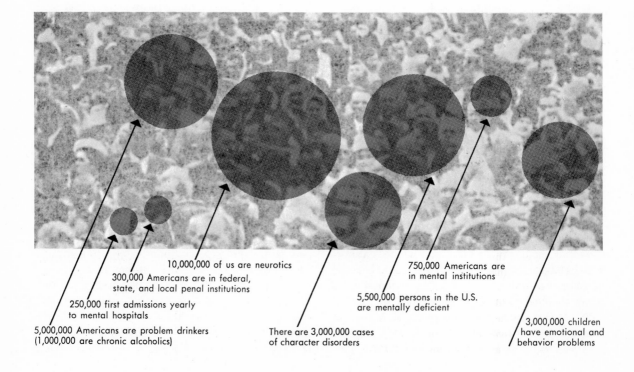

10,000,000 of us are neurotics

300,000 Americans are in federal, state, and local penal institutions

250,000 first admissions yearly to mental hospitals

5,000,000 Americans are problem drinkers (1,000,000 are chronic alcoholics)

There are 3,000,000 cases of character disorders

750,000 Americans are in mental institutions

5,500,000 persons in the U.S. are mentally deficient

3,000,000 children have emotional and behavior problems

would admit to feelings of insecurity and anxiety and some worry about his future; many students state freely that they fear they are headed for a "nervous breakdown." In a recent study, a representative sample of Americans were asked if they had ever felt they were going to have a "nervous breakdown." One out of five people interviewed replied, "Yes." (Gurin, Veroff, and Feld, 1960) In this connection it should perhaps be mentioned that students of medicine and psychology are especially prone, in reading about organic and mental illness, to imagine that they have almost every symptom of the various disorders described.

We should not be misled by the apparent self-confidence, efficiency, and happiness of other people into thinking that we alone are unhappy in our struggles with life's problems. Often we are surprised, when we are going through a particularly difficult period, that other people do not seem to notice our unhappiness; we may even be rather annoyed when they belittle our problems and declare, "You're perfectly normal." In the same way, other people have acquired a social façade, have learned to conceal their true feelings and to present to the world a reasonably happy and confident exterior. The fact that even the outwardly most successful person may have serious inner difficulties is dramatically illustrated in a poem by E. A. Robinson (1943):

RICHARD CORY

Whenever Richard Cory went down town,
We people on the pavement looked at him:
He was a gentleman from sole to crown,
Clean favored, and imperially slim.

And he was always quietly arrayed,
And he was always human when he talked;
But still he fluttered pulses when he said,
"Good morning," and he glittered when he walked.

And he was rich—yes, richer than a king—
And admirably schooled in every grace:
In fine, we thought that he was everything
To make us wish that we were in his place.

So on we worked and waited for the light,
And went without the meat, and cursed the bread;
And Richard Cory, one calm summer night,
Went home and put a bullet through his head.

A realization that others share our difficulties helps to destroy the feelings of isolation and of "being different," which usually play such a large part in fears of mental illness. Likewise, through studying the dynamics of abnormal behavior and becoming familiar with the concrete known factors which can precipitate or allay abnormal trends, we become more confident of our ability to assure our mental health.

And finally an examination of some of the other popular misconceptions of abnormal behavior, which most of us share to some extent, should be of help in dispelling unnecessary, agonizing fears about mental illness.

The belief that mental illness is a disgrace. Many people are reluctant to go to psychiatrists or psychologists with their problems, though they usually do not hesitate to consult an ophthalmologist, a dentist, or any other kind of medical specialist. This attitude causes many cases of mild abnormal behavior to develop to the "breaking point"; in other cases, it prevents the sufferer from receiving treatment that could alleviate his difficulties in less time and with less suffering than if he "worried it out" alone. It also may lead to the concealment of a mentally ill relative when treatment or institutionalization may be essential to his own happiness or safety as well as to that of his family. And when concealment is impossible, the family often feels disgraced in the eyes of the community.

Actually, it is no more disgraceful to become mentally ill than to become physically ill. We do not blame an individual for succumbing to disease germs. Why should we blame him for succumbing to overpowering stress? Everyone has his breaking point, and we all face stresses from time to time which tax our adjustive resources. It is fortunate that, for most of us, these stresses are not so severe or long continued that we become psychiatric casualties.

The Joint Commission on Mental Illness and Health (1961) has pointed out that, despite the attempt to educate people to a better understanding of mental illness, in our society we still tend to reject the mentally ill. Even the majority of general practitioners, as well as other medical personnel, are both uninformed and unsympathetic when they are confronted with cases of mental illness. Whereas most people are sympathetic toward a crippled child or an adult with a dread disease, they turn away from the person suffering from incapacitating mental illness. Yet the great majority of persons who fall prey to mental illness are doing the best they know how and desperately need understanding and help.

The concept of mental illness as weird, unnatural, and incomprehensible.   There is a popular notion that the inmates of mental hospitals are a weird lot who spend their time cutting out paper dolls, posing as Napoleon, or ranting and raving. The majority of patients are well aware of what is going on around them and can discuss their condition in much the same way that we might tell our doctor about severe indigestion. Only a minority of patients present a picture of severely disturbed or deviant behavior.

If mentally disordered individuals are thought to be entirely different from individuals more successful in their life adjustments, then of course their behavior cannot be understood in the same way that we understand the behavior of normal people. But if both normal and abnormal behavior are regarded as *attempts by individuals to adjust to life situations,* with different methods and different degrees of success, then fundamental dynamic principles of behavior can be discovered which apply both to the normal and to the abnormal, however unusual the latter may seem. It was in the same way that the understanding of physical disease took a tremendous spurt when, during the Renaissance, men recognized at last that disease was subject to the same laws of causation and development that govern other natural phenomena—that it was not an affliction brought on by evil spirits or witches whose influence was "super"-natural and thus incomprehensible and beyond control.

The widespread assumption that abnormal behavior is weird and basically different from normal behavior is also related to the common failure to recognize it in its milder forms. Actually, the clientele of the average psychiatrist or clinical psychologist is made up of people from all situations of life: "They are in practically all respects average American citizens, undistinguishable from any others. Their only common denominators are nervous symptoms or emotional problems which they cannot handle themselves and for which they seek professional help." (Rickles *et al,* 1950, p. 849)

We have probably all known and sympathized with someone who became embittered after an unhappy love affair, or someone who became deeply depressed following a serious failure. The important thing is to recognize that these individuals were showing behavior which differed only in degree from that of mental patients, on the one hand, and from that of "normal, well-adjusted" people, on the other. Mental illness, however strange it may appear, is quite within the range of our potential understanding.

Sharp differences between "normal" and "abnormal."   A sharp dividing line between "normal" and "abnormal" behavior simply does not exist, contrary to popular belief. As we have already seen, there are not "normal" people on one hand and "madmen" on the other, two different and distinct kinds of beings. Success in adjustment seems to follow what is called a "normal" distribution, with most people clustering around a central point or average, and the rest spreading out toward the two extremes. Most people are moderately well adjusted; a few at one extreme enter mental hospitals and a few at the other extreme lead unusually happy, efficient, and useful lives.

Not only does the behavior of different individuals range by imperceptible degrees from the normal to the abnormal, but one individual may shift at different times to different positions along the range. Common observations show that a person's success in adjustment is subject to change from many different causes. For example, an individual may be making a satisfactory adjustment when some change in his environment—such as disappointment in love, loss of money, illness, an accident, or the death of a loved one—may so greatly increase the severity of his adjustment problems that he is no longer able to cope with them satisfactorily. In the same way, a business promotion or an improvement in physical health can lead to better adjustment.

Mental illness as a hereditary taint.   Most families have one or more mentally ill individuals in their histories, and the relatives—especially close relatives—often live in fear of becoming mentally ill themselves, or are reluctant to marry because they fear their children may be victims of their "tainted" heredity. In general, such fears are unfounded, according to our present knowledge. It has been shown that certain forms of mental retardation and congenital malformations result from chromosomal irregularities on the part of one or both of the parents, but new advances in genetics now make it possible to tell whether a prospective parent has a normal chromosomal pattern.

Undoubtedly, hereditary factors sometimes play a role in the development of schizophrenia and other disorders, but the nature of this role is unknown (it probably varies according to the type of mental disorder and the interaction of other etiological factors). In most cases where "insanity runs in families," the children probably "inherit" the mental illness through *learning,* not through the germ plasm. Often the adults are too disturbed to provide the child with the proper environment of affection, security, and consistent discipline, so that as he is growing up he does not develop healthy patterns of adjustment. Here the mental illness is due to *social* rather than *genetic* heredity.

This is not to say, of course, that mental illness is inevitable where there is an undesirable family background or that in every case of mental illness the child has simply "learned" his family's poor adjustment patterns, for there is usually an interaction of many factors. In any case a psychiatrist or clinical psychologist can advise whether fears of mental illness through heredity are well founded. In most cases they are not.

The belief that sex causes mental illness. The belief that mental illness is caused by sexual practices is especially widespread with regard to masturbation, but since masturbation is almost universal, especially among boys during early adolescence, any direct relation between insanity and masturbation would long ago have destroyed the mental health of the whole human race. The belief takes superficial support from the fact that some mental patients masturbate openly and excessively and that disturbances in sexual functions are common in psychopathology. No doubt that is why, until recent times, special wards were set aside for patients whose illness presumably resulted from sexual practices.

In the past few decades the relation between sexual activity and abnormal behavior has been given a different interpretation. It is recognized that sexual activity is very often accompanied by guilt, worry, and feelings of sin and unworthiness, which may place such great stress upon the individual that he no longer is able to adjust adequately even to everyday life problems. Thus it is not the sexual behavior itself, but the way the individual evaluates it that is now believed to be sometimes responsible for the development of abnormal patterns. But conflicts and guilt centering around sexual problems are only *one* cause of abnormal behavior; some of the many other complex, interacting causes will be discussed at length in later chapters.

Genius as akin to mental illness. People regarded as geniuses in the arts and sciences have often been looked upon as especially prone to mental illness. Lombroso (1891), Nisbet (n.d.), and other writers fostered this misconception by compiling long lists of historical personages who did suffer from mental illness, in an attempt to prove genius related to insanity.

Experimental studies, however, have found no such relationship. After a seventeen-year study of heredity and physical and mental health conditions of 294 highly gifted personalities in the arts and sciences, Juda (1949) concluded that there is "no evidence to support the assumption that the genesis of highest intellectual ability depends on psychic abnormalities." (p. 306) In an even more comprehensive study, Terman (1940) followed the lives of over 1300 California school children who had obtained I.Q.'s of 140 or above in the early 1920's. A tally when most of the "children" had reached their midforties, showed that their death rate, divorce rate, and mental illness rate were all lower than those for the general population (Terman and Oden, 1959). Similarly, MacKinnon (1962), in an intensive study of architects, writers, and other professional personnel considered to be highly creative, failed to find a significant relationship between creative talent and psychopathology. Rather, he emphasized the tendencies of these creative people toward self-acceptance, lack of defensiveness, openness to new experience, and complexity and richness of personality. Such findings effectively explode the old notion that creativity and genius are "akin to insanity."

Mental illness as always incurable. There is a common belief that mental illness is incurable and that persons who have been discharged from mental hospitals as recovered are to be viewed with suspicion. This belief is erroneous and can do great damage. It cannot but impede the social adjustment of a person who has recovered from some type of mental illness to have his family, employer, and colleagues continue to regard him with suspicion, and often it keeps people from seeking psychiatric treatment in the first place because the individual or his relatives do not believe he can be cured. While it is true that persons with certain forms of mental illness (such as psychoses associated with severe senile brain damage) will never recover completely, most mental patients respond well to treatment. If treatment is adequate and is received in time, some 70 to 80 per cent of all hospitalized mental patients can recover and make a satisfactory adjustment within society. And in many cases the individual achieves a higher level of personality integration and mental health than before his illness.

Abnormal Behavior As the Scientist Sees It

In order to diagnose, treat, and eventually prevent abnormal behavior, a scientist must start with clear definitions of what he means by "normal" and "abnormal" and work out criteria for distinguishing one from the other in actual clinical cases.

WHAT DO WE MEAN BY "ABNORMAL"?

Since the word *abnormal* means "away from the normal," it implies deviation from some clearly defined norm. In the case of physical illness, the norm is the structural and functional integrity of the body and the boundary lines between normality and pathology can usually be clearly delineated by medical science. On a psychological level, however, we have no "ideal model" of man to use as a base of comparison, nor are we entirely clear as to just what behavior is or is not normal. As a consequence, the problem of defining abnormal behavior has proved to be a most difficult one. However, several criteria have been proposed.

Statistical norms. If we were to use the word *abnormal* in a strictly literal sense, statistical norms would be sufficient. Any deviation from the majority would be, by definition, abnormal. A genius would be as abnormal as a mentally retarded person; a Christian among head-hunters would be as abnormal as a head-hunter among us; an honest person in a dishonest society would be abnormal. And what was normal today might become abnormal tomorrow.

Clearly such use of the term, however accurate literally, would be sterile for our purposes. What we are after is a definition of *abnormality* more in the sense of *pathology,* a norm that can be applied in different cultures and can distinguish between desirable and undesirable deviations.

Personal adjustment (adaptation). Another norm which is often suggested is personal adjustment. Life is a continuous process of adjusting, in which we strive to meet our own needs and maintain harmonious relations with our environment. When an individual deals with his problems effectively, he is said to be *well adjusted*—to be adapting successfully to both the inner and outer demands being made upon him. Conversely, when his problems prove too much for him—as shown by anxiety, inefficiency, unhappiness, or more serious symptoms—he is referred to as *maladjusted.*

This norm is very popular and has the added advantage of being applicable to biological as well as psychological levels of adjustment. However, personal adjustment as a norm has several serious limitations. It makes no reference to self-actualization—the extent to which the individual develops and utilizes his potentialities. But a genius who is content to spend all his time on routine tasks is not showing healthy behavior from either a personal or social viewpoint. In addition, personal adjustment makes no reference to the individual's role in the group. For example, how are we going to classify a crooked politician or an unethical businessman? Either might be a successful, happy, and well-adjusted personality. Obviously, the welfare of the group as well as that of the individual must be considered.

Personality integration. The criterion of integration refers to the "wholeness" of the individual, to the harmonious working together of the components of the human system and of this system, in turn, with its environment. On a psychological level, the effectiveness of integration is evaluated in terms of the coordination of thought, feeling, and action; of freedom from disruptive inner conflicts and rigid defenses; of "openness" to new experience; and of adequacy of adjustment to the environment.

Often the terms *adjustment* and *integration* are used synonomously. There is a difference, however, for a person may show a low level of personality integration and still be well adjusted if the environment makes minimal demands upon him. Thus an immature and poorly integrated young adult may adjust adequately as long as he lives at home with a mother who protects him from having to meet the usual demands of adulthood. Here we see again the inadequacy of the concept of personal adjustment as a criterion of normality, since such an individual can hardly be considered healthy.

But integration, too, is an inadequate criterion, since a variety of forms of integration have been considered effective under different conditions. The emotional detachment that makes survival and sanity possible in a concentration camp would be abnormal in more usual circumstances. It is difficult even to say what level of integration really is the most "normal" form of adaptation in our complex and stressful world. Evidently some other criterion is necessary for deciding what type of personality integration is effective in given circumstances.

Personal maturity and growth. A criterion which has received a good deal of emphasis is that of personal maturity. Behavior is considered mature when it is appropriate to the age level, the problems, and the adjustive resources of the individual and contributes to his long-range growth and actualization. Personal maturity is thus an index of how "grown-up" an individual

is and of the extent to which he is fulfilling himself as a human being.

Although personal maturity is a very useful concept, it does not by itself provide us with a standard for evaluating either normal or abnormal behavior. We must decide what "grown-up" and "self-actualizing" behavior is. Of course, where an adult has temper tantrums, is very dependent on others, and is impulsive in making crucial decisions, we can generally agree that he is showing *immature* behavior. Unfortunately, however, delineating what we mean by *maturity* is a much more difficult task. Often we arbitrarily stipulate certain characteristics as typical of "mature" people—characteristics like achieving a realistic view of oneself and one's world, developing problem-solving and other competencies for meeting the demands of living, and showing responsible self-direction. But not all people have the same concept of maturity. Again we must fill in the details according to our own definition.

Group well-being and progress. A large part of the normality or abnormality of a person's behavior depends on whether it furthers or blocks the needs and purposes of the society of which he is a part. The behavior of the successful criminal is considered abnormal, since it hurts the group. So our norms must include the factor of social adjustment: individuals should fit in with and contribute to the values, purposes, and activities of the group.

But what if the group condones concentration camps, or slavery, or racial prejudice? With the increasing knowledge of group behavior supplied by the social sciences, we have come to realize that a society can be as "sick" as an individual. But there still are differences of opinion as to what constitutes the most desirable form of social organization and what types of individual behavior are most conducive to group well-being and progress.

A tentative definition. Until the social sciences have evolved a more adequate theoretical structure, both general and specific criteria of abnormality will of necessity remain somewhat arbitrary and will be influenced by the theoretical orientation of the person trying to define them. Several kinds of attempts at defining *normality* and *abnormality* are summarized in the chart on pages 16-17.

THE PROBLEM OF DEFINING "NORMAL" AND "ABNORMAL"

Unfortunately, we have no "ideal model" of man to help us in distinguishing mental health from mental disorder. Attempts to delineate what we mean by mental health or normality have taken the following forms:

FRONTAL ATTACK—DEFINITIONS

The following are representative of many of the definitions of mental health that have been proposed:

World Health Organization. Health is "a state of complete physical, mental, and social well-being and not merely the absence of disease or infirmity."

H. B. English, a psychologist. Mental health is "a relatively enduring state wherein the person is well adjusted, has a zest for living, and is attaining self-actualization or self-realization. It is a positive state and not mere absence of mental disorder."

Karl Menninger, a psychiatrist. "Let us define mental health as the adjustment of human beings to the world and to each other with a maximum of effectiveness and happiness. Not just efficiency, or just contentment—or the grace of obeying the rules of the game cheerfully. It is all of these together. It is the ability to maintain an even temper, an alert intelligence, socially considerate behavior, and a happy disposition. This, I think, is a healthy mind."

W. W. Boehm, a social worker. Mental health is "a condition and level of social functioning which is socially acceptable and personally satisfying."

These and other definitions suffer from a lack of specificity and of scientific grounding, but they are helpful in pointing up various dimensions of what we think of as "mental health." In general, such definitions emphasize both the individual and the social setting in which he functions.

MULTIPLE CRITERIA APPROACH

This approach involves listing a number of personality traits considered essential to mental health. In general, six categories of traits appear to emerge:

Attitudes toward self. Emphasizing self-acceptance, adequate self-identity, realistic appraisal of one's assets and liabilities.

Perception of reality. A realistic view of oneself and the surrounding world of people and things.

Integration. Unity of personality, freedom from disabling inner conflicts, good stress tolerance.

Competencies. Development of essential physical, intellectual, emotional, and social competencies for coping with life problems.

Autonomy. Adequate self-reliance, responsibility, and self-direction—together with sufficient independence of social influences.

Growth, self-actualization. Emphasizing trends toward increasing maturity, development of potentialities, and self-fulfillment as a person.

Delineating such personality traits is helpful in filling in our picture of mental health but is still not a completely satisfactory approach since different investigators emphasize different traits and the entire structure lacks an adequate scientific base.

THEORETICAL SYSTEMS APPROACH

This approach is based on different systematic views of man's nature and functioning. Five such viewpoints are:

Naturalism. Emphasis on man's basic instinctual drives, such as hunger and sex. Health seen as the ability to gratify these basic needs and adapt within the limits imposed by environment. Mental disorder seen as failure in adaptation.

Humanism. Emphasis on view that man is essentially rational by nature with tendencies toward responsible self-direction and actualization under favorable circumstances. Abnormal behavior seen as stemming from the blocking or distortion of man's tendencies toward mental health and self-fulfillment as a person.

Culturalism. Emphasis on man's social nature and the importance of "adjusting" to social requirements. Mental health and mental disorder seen as closely related to the individual's ability to establish satisfying relationships with others in a healthy society.

Existentialism. Emphasis on breakdown of traditional values and beliefs and necessity for the individual to find a self-identity and fulfilling way of life within the personal experience of his own existence. Abnormality seen as inability to find adequate self-identity, values, and meaning.

Theism. Emphasis on man's dependence on God and the view that the ultimate solution to his problems is a religious faith to give meaning to his existence and provide guides for his behavior.

These viewpoints represent different ways of ordering our information about man's nature and functioning. The assumption is that as our knowledge increases, many differences will be resolved. Meanwhile, many psychologists and psychiatrists maintain what may be called an "eclectic" approach, incorporating concepts from several approaches.

RESEARCH APPROACH

Here the attempt is made to increase our fund of scientific information by applying research techniques to relevant problems concerning man's nature and behavior. Three general areas of research are of particular significance:

Biological. Aimed at a better understanding of genetic processes, brain functioning, and the effects of various drugs and other physical agents and conditions on physical and psychological functioning.

Psychological. Aimed at a better understanding of human behavior, including problems related to learning, perception, emotions, motivation, and thinking. Included here too is research on the effects of various types of stress on behavior.

Sociological. Aimed at a better understanding of the role of sociocultural processes in personality development, of the social patterns best suited to man's nature, and of the effects of disturbed interpersonal relationships, pathogenic family constellations, and other social conditions on human behavior.

The research approach represents the best long-range solution for delineating the conditions essential for effective functioning and for distinguishing between mental health and mental disorder for the species. Until needed research data become available, however, definitions and criteria of mental health will of necessity depend heavily upon pragmatic considerations.

Chart based on material from Allport (1960), Boehm (1955), English and English (1958), Jahoda (1958), Knutson (1963), Lowe (1959), Menninger (1945), Rogers (1959), Scott (1961), Shoben (1957), Smith (1961), Sundberg and Tyler (1962), and Szasz (1960).

But although the social sciences have not yet provided a sufficiently comprehensive and integrated picture of man's nature and behavior to allow us to see just what a "model man" would be like, most social scientists would agree that normal behavior will represent the *optimal development and functioning of the individual consistent with the long-term well-being and progress of the group*. This norm gives us a broad framework into which we can gradually fit a more precise definition of man as his unique characteristics and requirements are increasingly identified. Such a norm also includes the concepts of adjustment, integration, maturity, fulfillment, and social well-being, with the obvious implication that our province extends beyond the individual's adjustment to the fostering of those social conditions which science and experience recommend—for example, conditions which respect the worth and dignity of the individual and provide opportunities for personal freedom, choice, and self-fulfillment. Our definition of *normal* is not what is most prevalent but what is in keeping with the available knowledge concerning the individual and social needs of man. From this point of view "abnormal behavior" encompasses a wide range of maladjustive reactions—including alcoholism, unethical business practices, juvenile delinquency, racial discrimination, psychoneuroses, psychoses, drug addiction, peptic ulcers, and sexual deviations. All are indicative of some sort of biological, psychological, or sociological maladjustment which impairs the functioning and actualization of the individual and/or the well-being and progress of the group.[1]

The broad norm which we have adopted has many important implications for the diagnosis, treatment, and prevention of abnormal behavior. For example, we no longer treat the maladjusted individual solely with the idea of getting him adjusted to existing social conditions regardless of their nature. We may attempt to restructure and strengthen his personality and to promote personal growth but at the same time attempt to correct abnormal family relationships as well as broader social conditions which are making a satisfactory adjustment difficult or impossible. Thus in treating an emotionally disturbed child, we may treat his parents too in order that conditions may be established in the home which are more likely to foster normal growth and behavior; similarly, while treating the juvenile delinquent, we also strive to eradicate economic deprivation, illiteracy, and other conditions which breed delinquency. This norm also makes it mandatory that as new and relevant scientific information concerning human behavior becomes available we make indicated modifications in our concepts and practices.

CLINICAL EVALUATION OF ADJUSTIVE REACTIONS

In actual clinical practice theoretical definitions must be translated into usable criteria for evaluating an individual case. Needless to say, this is not an easy matter. We have an accepted psychiatric classification which describes the various types of abnormal behavior, but it is far more useful for distinguishing serious mental disorders than it is for evaluating the less severe maladjustive patterns common in everyday life. As W. C. Menninger astutely pointed out some years ago: "One might seriously question if our world condition does not now place many of us in a continuously abnormal situation to which we are having normal reactions, even though these by all previous standards are pathological. To such a turbulent world, one might legitimately ask, what is a normal reaction?" (1947, p. 156) Certainly this question is even more pertinent today. In addition, many individuals have to function in life situations which are far from satisfactory and are not amenable to change. Again one may ask, what is a normal reaction under such circumstances?

Probably the most we can do is to suggest three types of questions to which a clinician gives attention in attempting to assess the normality or abnormality of a patient's behavior.

1.   What degree of harmony do the individual's adjustive reactions enable him to maintain among his various needs, goals, and values?

---

[1]Terms used to indicate abnormal behavior are many: *mental illness, mental disorders, psychiatric disorders, neuropsychiatric disorders, psychopathology,* and *abnormal behavior* will be used interchangeably in the present discussion. It may be noted that this is a more inclusive usage of these terms than has often been customary. (See Glossary for other terms, such as *mental disease, insanity, lunacy, madness, possessed,* etc.)

Are his goals realistic? Does he feel reasonably self-confident in coping with his problems? Does he show adequate self-acceptance? Is his sexual adjustment satisfactory? Has he worked out a satisfactory value system? Is he open to new experience? Or is he weakened by feelings of inferiority, lack of self-acceptance, excessive defensiveness and rigidity, sexual problems, or other severe inner conflicts or sources of lowered integration? If he devalues himself as a person, is a "house divided" by severe conflicts, or relies too heavily on rationalization and other such defense mechanisms in coping with his problems, his reactions fall into the category of abnormal behavior.

2. What degree of harmony do his adjustive reactions enable him to maintain with his environment? Is his view of this environment reasonably accurate? Does he have the occupational and other skills requisite for effective participation in the group? Does he feel he is an essential and wanted member of the group? Is he able to establish satisfying relationships with others? Is he able to give and receive affection? Does he conform adequately to group demands while at the same time being emancipated to the extent of thinking and acting independently without excessive need for social approval? If he feels isolated and rejected, or if his group relationships are chronically torn by serious and unnecessary friction, we would say that his reactions are abnormal.

3. Do the individual's adjustive reactions contribute to his own self-actualization and to social welfare and progress? Is he growing and maturing as a person? Does he have an adequate sense of self-identity? Is he capable of responsible self-direction? Is he using his potentialities in a constructive way in his own interests and those of society? If he is immature, if he has high potentialities which are not being effectively utilized, or if his abilities are directed toward socially undesirable goals, then his behavior is abnormal.

Negative answers to questions such as these mean inadequate adjustment and are often accompanied by other characteristics—anxiety, tension, unhappiness, and so on—which we refer to as "symptoms." In severe personality maladjustment there are further symptoms, such as delusions or hallucinations.

A later chapter will be devoted to the special medical, psychological, and sociological techniques of diagnosis that have been worked out for making specific evaluations of adjustive reactions and their etiology in individual cases.

CLASSIFYING ABNORMAL BEHAVIOR

Classification is a necessary first step in clarifying relationships and introducing some order into our discussion of the symptoms, dynamics, and causes of abnormal behavior. However, the task of classifying abnormal behavior is a formidable one. Not only must we deal with a wide range of maladjustive reactions, but the clinical symptoms of two patients may be very similar —anxiety, inability to concentrate, irritability, lowered efficiency, and fatigue, for example— yet the causes may be very different. In addition, two individuals with a brain tumor—the same essential "cause"—may react very differently, one becoming depressed, the other becoming expansive.

To cope with these difficulties, various classification schemes have been worked out, but none has been completely satisfactory. The current classification accepted by the American Psychiatric Association (1952) is based largely on the classification worked out by the United States Army during World War II and subsequently used by the Veterans Administration. This scheme, though still far from satisfactory, provides a comprehensive coverage of abnormal reaction patterns and differentiates reasonably well among specific mental disorders. It has been widely accepted and is used here with minor modifications.

A complete outline of this classification appears on the endsheets at the back of the book. The two main divisions and the most important subgroups are summarized here. They form the basis for the chapter divisions in Parts III and IV of the present text.

Disorders of psychogenic origin. Disorders in which there is no apparent physical cause or brain pathology include:

1. *Transient situational personality disorders.* Under conditions of great or unusual stress—being trapped in a burning building, seeing one's husband or child killed, experienc-

INCIDENCE OF ABNORMAL BEHAVIOR IN THE UNITED STATES

CONSERVATIVE ESTIMATE OF INCIDENCE (in millions)	ABNORMAL BEHAVIOR
300,000	TRANSIENT DISORDERS (civilian, each year)
10,000,000	PSYCHONEUROSES
20,000,000	PSYCHOPHYSIOLOGIC DISORDERS
700,000	PSYCHOTIC DISORDERS (functional)
3,000,000	CHARACTER DISORDERS (psychopathic, criminal)
5,000,000	PROBLEM DRINKING
1,000,000	CHRONIC ALCOHOLISM
60,000	DRUG ADDICTION
100,000	ACUTE BRAIN DISORDERS
1,000,000	CHRONIC BRAIN DISORDERS
5,500,000	MENTAL RETARDATION (mental deficiency)

ing the combat conditions of modern war—individuals may show panic, severe grief, neurotic or psychotic symptoms, or other behavior indicative of personality maladjustment. These reactions differ from neuroses and psychoses in that they are precipitated by acute or special stress and involve previously normal individuals who show good recoverability.

2. *Psychoneurotic disorders.* A number of types of psychoneuroses are commonly distinguished. The chief characteristic of all of them is *anxiety,* which may be either "free floating" and directly felt, or unconsciously and automatically controlled through the use of various psychological defense mechanisms, such as repression and dissociation. The patient's happiness and efficiency are usually seriously lowered, but there is no gross disorganization of the personality or loss of contact with reality, and he does not ordinarily require hospitalization.

3. *Psychophysiologic autonomic and visceral disorders.* This category includes migraine headaches, hypertension, dermatitis, peptic ulcers, and other reactions in which emotional factors play a causative role.

4. *Functional psychoses.* These reactions involve severe degrees of personality disorganization and a loss of adequate contact with reality. Ordinarily, hospitalization is required for both protection and treatment. This category includes schizophrenic reactions, affective reactions, and paranoid reactions.

5. *Personality disorders (character disorders).* The reactions included in this category seem to result from developmental defects rather than from personality disorganization due to excessive stress. In most cases the individual has little or no feeling of anxiety or distress, and his disorder represents a lifelong pattern of socially undesirable behavior ("acting-out"). Such diverse patterns as inadequate personality, antisocial reactions, sexual deviations, alcoholism, and drug addiction are included in this group of disorders.

Disorders associated with organic brain disturbance. Disorders in which organic causes are apparent include:

1. *Acute brain disorders.* In cases of temporary impairment of brain-tissue function (as in high fever, vitamin deficiency, hyperthyroidism, or acute alcoholic intoxication) there may be hallucinations, delusions, or other behavior disturbances resulting from brain pathology or the lowering of cortical adaptive controls. These symptoms are temporary, and the patient ordinarily recovers.

2. *Chronic brain disorders.* Where a brain tumor, head injury, arteriosclerosis, or other acute condition results in lasting damage to cerebral tissue, some impairment of judgment, memory, orientation, and emotional responses can be expected to occur and persist.

Mental retardation (mental deficiency). An additional major category in this APA classification includes mild, moderate, or severe mental retardation where the defect of intelligence has existed since birth without demonstrable brain disease. In our discussion of mental retardation, we shall include also cases in which organic pathology is present. Often in a given case, an accurate distinction is difficult or impossible.

It should be emphasized that the adjustive reactions of each individual are somewhat unique and that the behavior of a given patient may not fit well into any of the above categories. Frequently there is disagreement as to whether a given patient should be classified as neurotic or psychotic, or whether his reactions are predominantly manic-depressive or schizophrenic. Not infrequently two psychiatric conditions are present, such as both an antisocial personality and a psychosis. In the latter case, both conditions are ordinarily recorded in the diagnosis, and the treatment is planned accordingly.

Parts III and IV will be a detailed study of these various disorders. There we shall take up typical symptoms and developmental patterns, investigate the biological, psychological, and sociological factors involved, and indicate the most fruitful methods of treatment and the prognosis for each disorder.

HELPING THE MALADJUSTED

What is involved in helping people who are poorly adjusted? With disorders so diverse and, until recently, so little understood, it is inevitable that conflicting theories of causation and methods of treatment should have developed. In the next chapter we shall trace the historical development of modern psychiatric thought and procedures.

At the present time there are several distinct but closely related scientific fields, all professionally concerned with abnormal behavior. The distinction among them is often hard to draw precisely; although each has its own function and its own area of work, the contributions of one field are constantly influencing the work in others.

Abnormal psychology is the field of psychology which specializes in the development and integration of psychological principles for the understanding of abnormal behavior—that is, it probes the dynamics of abnormal behavior. *Clinical psychology* is inextricably bound up with abnormal psychology but is more directly concerned with the application of psychological principles to the practical diagnosis and treatment of maladjustive reactions. A worker in this field holds a Ph.D. degree in clinical psychology and receives internship training in psychological assessment, counseling, and psychotherapy. *Counseling psychology,* overlapping clinical psychology, is concerned with helping essentially normal individuals with problems related to educational, occupational, and marital decisions. The counseling psychologist has a Ph.D. in counseling psychology and related internship training.

Psychiatry specializes in the understanding, diagnosis, treatment, and prevention of mental illness and is thus closely related to clinical psychology. Unlike the clinical psychologist, however, the psychiatrist holds a degree in medicine and may prescribe drugs and employ medical techniques in therapy. We may note here that while psychiatry is a specialized field

While the population has increased about fourfold since 1880, the number of patients in mental hospitals has become over 18 times greater. Although new facilities and attitudes toward mental illness account for the hospitalization of many patients who would formerly have been cared for at home, the increase still appears to be significant.

PATIENTS IN HOSPITALS FOR MENTAL ILLNESS FROM 1880 TO 1964

POPULATION (in millions)					PATIENTS (in 100,000's)								
200	150	100	50	0	0	1	2	3	4	5	6	7	8
			50,155,783	1880	40,942								
		110,705,086		1923		267,617							
190,000,000				1964								750,000	

of medicine, the term *psychosomatic medicine* refers to a comprehensive approach to bodily disorders which weighs the influence of biological, psychological, and sociocultural factors. This approach has been found useful in dealing with all types of human ailments and indispensable to the accurate diagnosis and treatment of certain disorders, such as peptic ulcers. *Psychoanalysis* is a particular school of psychiatry. Psychoanalysts are distinguished from other psychiatrists in that their approach is based on the work of Sigmund Freud, implies a particular theory of personality development and functioning, and emphasizes a particular method of psychotherapy. (Some of the current theories of personality underlying the various approaches to treatment are summarized in the Appendix.) *Psychiatric nursing* is the field of nursing which specializes in the care of mental patients. Personnel in this field are registered nurses with additional training in psychology and psychiatry. *Psychiatric social work* is the field of sociology which specializes in the analysis of social data and the adjustment of the patient in his family and social setting. The psychiatric social worker holds a master's degree in social work and receives special training in carrying treatment procedures into the home and community. Finally, the *mental health* field is concerned with the development of well-integrated, healthy personalities, in the interest of preventing mental illness. Scientists and laymen alike are vitally concerned with mental health problems.

Of these fields, psychiatry is the most inclusive in its actual practice, which extends into almost all life activities. In drawing up theories, principles, case materials, diagnoses, and treatment programs, it utilizes research findings and concepts from many other sciences: genetics, anatomy, physiology, biochemistry, neurology, psychology, sociology, and anthropology. This "team" approach, which integrates medical, psychological, and sociological data in approaching the understanding of human behavior, is carried over into the diagnosis and treatment of individual mental patients, with psychiatrists, clinical psychologists, psychiatric social workers, psychiatric nurses, occupational therapists, and other specialists working together as the needs of each case warrant. And since psychiatry, of practical necessity, has come to include the prevention as well as the treatment of abnormal behavior, it has had to interest itself in the study of the economic and social conditions which are most conducive to the mental health of society as a whole.

Throughout this volume we shall be trying to acquire a perspective on abnormal behavior and its place in our society. Most of our space will be devoted to the dynamics (etiology) of mental disorders—to gaining a picture of the symptoms, causes, and developmental sequences in the various abnormal behavioral patterns. Later we shall devote two chapters to a detailed study of the techniques of diagnosis and treatment which are helping maladjusted individuals to greater personal maturity, integration, and effectiveness. At the end, we shall discuss the problem of preventing mental illness and the potentialities of modern psychology and psychiatry for helping mankind to a more sane and harmonious world.

REFERENCES

The reference list includes not only the sources from which the author has drawn material, but acknowledgments of the permissions granted by authors and publishers to quote directly from their works.

ALLPORT, G. W. *Personality and personal encounter.* Boston: Beacon Press, 1960.

American Psychiatric Association. *Diagnostic and statistical manual, mental disorders.* Washington, D.C.: Author, 1952.

ASWELL, MARY L. (Ed.) *The world within.* New York: McGraw-Hill, 1947.

BATTISTA, O. A. *Mental drugs: chemistry's challenge to psychotherapy.* Philadelphia: Chilton, 1960.

BLUEMEL, C. S. *War, politics, and industry.* Denver: World Press, 1948.

BOEHM, W. W. The role of psychiatric social work in mental health. In A. M. Rose (Ed.), *Mental health and mental disorder.* New York: Norton, 1955.

BORN, W. Great artists who suffered from mental disorders. *Ciba Symposia,* 1946, 7, 225-233.

California Commission of Higher Education. *California higher education news briefs.* April, 1960, 1, 2.

EDWARDS, J. Sinners in the hands of an angry God. *The works of President Edwards in eight volumes,* Vol. 7. Worcester: Isaiah Thomas, 1809.

ENGLISH, H. B., & ENGLISH, AVA C. *A comprehensive dictionary of psychological and psychoanalytical terms.* New York: Longmans, Green, 1958.

FEIN, R. *Economics of mental illness.* Joint Commission on Mental Illness and Health, Monograph Series No. 2. New York: Basic Books, 1958.

GURIN, G., VEROFF, J., & FELD, SHEILA. *Americans view their mental health; a nationwide survey.* Joint Commission on Mental Illness and Health, Monograph Series No. 4. New York: Basic Books, 1960.

JAHODA, MARIE. *Current concepts of positive mental health.* New York: Basic Books, 1958.

Joint Commission on Mental Illness and Health. *Action for mental health.* New York: Basic Books, 1961.

JUDA, ADELE. The relationship between highest mental capacity and psychic abnormalities. *Amer. J. Psychiat.,* 1949, 106, 296-307.

KNUTSON, A. L. New perspectives regarding positive mental health. *Amer. Psychologist,* 1963, 18, 300-306.

LEIGHTON, DOROTHEA C. The distribution of psychiatric symptoms in a small town. *Amer. J. Psychiat.,* 1956, 112, 716-723.

LOMBROSO, C. *Man of genius.* New York: Scribner's, 1891.

Los Angeles Organization for Mentally Ill Children. *The Quarterly,* 1961, 2, 1.

LOWE, C. M. Value orientations—an ethical dilemma. *Amer. Psychologist,* 1959, 14, 687-693.

MAC KINNON, D. W. The nature and nurture of creative talent. *Amer. Psychologist,* 1962, 17, 484-495.

MAC MILLAN, A. M. The health opinion survey: technique for estimating prevalence of psychoneurotic and related types of disorder in communities. *Psychol. Rep.,* 1957, 3, 325-339.

MARKS, JEANNETTE. *Genius and disaster.* New York: Greenberg, 1925.

MENNINGER, K. *The human mind.* (3rd ed.) New York: Knopf, 1945.

MENNINGER, W. C. The role of psychiatry in the world today. *Amer. J. Psychiat.,* 1947, 104, 155-163.

Metropolitan Life Insurance Company. *Statist. Bull. 41,* 1960, 41.

The National Association for Mental Health. *12 Facts about mental illness.* New York: Author, n.d.

National Committee Against Mental Illness, *Facts about mental illness in the U.S.* Washington, D.C.: Author, 1959.

NISBET, J. F. *The insanity of genius.* (5th ed.) London: Alexander Moring, n.d.

PASAMANICK, B. A survey of mental disease in an urban population. VII. An approach to total prevalence by race. *Amer. J. Psychiat.,* 1962, 119, 299-305.

RAINIE, R. C. Alcoholism, a local and national problem. *N. Hamp. Bull. on Alcoholism,* 1960, IX, 1, 6-15.

RICKLES, N. K., KLEIN, J. J., & BASSAN, M. E. Who goes to a psychiatrist? *Amer. J. Psychiat.,* 1950, 106, 845-850.

ROBINSON, E. A. Richard Cory. In G. D. Sanders, & J. H. Nelson (Eds.) *Chief modern poets of England and America.* (3rd ed.) New York: Macmillan, 1943. Reprinted by permission of Charles Scribner's Sons and Macmillan.

ROGERS, C. R. A theory of therapy, personality, and interpersonal relationships, as developed in the client-centered framework. In S. Koch (Ed.), *Psychology: a study of a science,* Vol. 3. *Formulations of the person and the social context.* New York: McGraw-Hill, 1959. Pp. 184-256.

SCOTT, WILLIAM A. Research definitions of mental health and mental illness. In T. R. Sarbin (Ed.) *Studies in behavior pathology.* New York: Holt, Rinehart, & Winston, 1961. Pp. 8-22.

SEWELL, W. S. (Ed.) *Famous personalities.* Philadelphia: Blakiston, 1943.

SHOBEN, E. J., JR. Toward a concept of the normal personality. *Amer. Psychol.,* 1957, 12, 183-189.

SMITH, M. B. "Mental health" reconsidered: a special case of the problem of values in psychology. *Amer. Psychologist,* 1961, 16, 299-306.

SROLE, L., LANGER, T. S., MICHAEL, S., OPLER, M. K., & RENNIE, T. A. C. *Mental health in the metropolis: the midtown Manhattan study,* Vol. 1. New York: McGraw-Hill, 1962.

SUNDBERG, N. D., & TYLER, LEONA E. *Clinical psychology: an introduction to research and practice.* New York: Appleton-Century-Crofts, 1962.

SZASZ, T. S. The myth of mental illness. *Amer. Psychologist,* 1960, 15, 113-118.

TERMAN, L. M. Psychological approaches to the biography of genius. *Science,* 1940, 92, 293-301.

TERMAN, L. M., & ODEN, M. H. *The gifted group at mid-life.* Vol. 5. *Genetic studies of genius.* Stanford, Calif.: Stanford Univer. Press, 1959.

U. S. Children's Bureau. *Juvenile court statistics 1960.* Washington, D. C.: Statistical Series No. 65, 1961.

U. S. Public Health Service. *Patients in mental institutions, 1960. Part II: Public hospitals for the mentally ill.* (Public Health Service Publication No. 963). Washington, D.C.: Government Printing Office, 1963.

WHITWELL, J. R. *Historical notes on psychiatry.* London: H. K. Lewis, 1936.

World Health Organization. Wide research needed to solve the problem of mental health. *World ment. Hlth,* 1960, 12.

ZILBOORG, G., & HENRY, G. W. *A history of medical psychology.* New York: Norton, 1941.

EMIL KRAEPELIN

IVAN PETROVICH PAVLOV

SIGMUND FREUD

CARL JUNG

ADOLF MEYER

DEVELOPMENT
OF OUR
MODERN
VIEWS

chapter 2

With our modern research methods, "psychiatric teams," and scientifically equipped mental hospitals and clinics, we feel that we have come a long way from the superstitious and often cruel treatment of the mentally ill of earlier times. The story of this journey is a fascinating one, and it is a story which will help us to understand better our modern views of abnormal behavior. For not only do our popular misconceptions about mental disorders have their roots in the dim historical past, but even our modern scientific concepts are the result of a long developmental process. For example, electroshock treatment is antedated by flogging, immersing the patient in cold water, and other crude "shock" treatments worked out by the ancients. Even modern brain surgery, as we shall shortly see, had its early precursor many thousands of years ago. Let us turn, then, to an examination of some of the earlier beliefs and practices and the steps by which they have changed and developed through the centuries up to the present time. In this way we shall gain a better perspective for understanding our modern views, and shall also get a "feel" for the trends of thought and the directions in which psychology and psychiatry seem to be moving at the present time.

Demonology among the Ancients

The earliest "psychiatry" of which we have any knowledge was that practiced by Stone Age cave men some half million years ago. For certain forms of mental illness, probably those where the patient complained of severe headaches and developed convulsive attacks, the early medicine man treated the disorder by means of an operation now called *trephining.* This operation was performed with crude stone instruments and consisted of chipping away one area of the skull in the form of a circle until the skull was cut through. This opening, called a *trephine,* presumably permitted the evil spirit which was causing all the trouble to escape, and incidentally may have relieved a certain amount of pressure on the brain. In some cases trephined skulls of primitive men show healing around the opening, indicating that the individual survived the operation and lived for many years afterwards (Selling, 1943). This early brain surgery left much to be desired in terms of technique, but it was even more inadequate in terms of the naïve, unscientific theory of demonology upon which it rested.

References to mental disorders in the early writings of the Chinese, Egyptians, Hebrews, and Greeks make it clear that they too attributed such disorders to demons which had taken possession of the individual. This is not surprising when we remember that "good" and "bad" spirits were widely used to explain lightning, thunder, earthquakes, storms, fires, sickness, and many other events which primitive men did not understand. It was probably a very simple and logical step to extend this theory to peculiar and incomprehensible behavior in their fellows.

The decision as to whether the "possession" involved good spirits or evil spirits usually depended upon the patient's symptoms. If the possessed person's speech or behavior appeared to have a religious or mystical significance, it was usually thought that the person was possessed by a good spirit or god. Such individuals were often treated with considerable awe and respect, for it was thought that they had supernatural powers. In the Bible story, David took advantage of this popular belief when he simulated "madness" in order to escape from Achish, the king of Gath (Samuel 21:12-14).

Most possessions, however, were considered to be the work of evil spirits, particularly when the patient became excited and overactive and engaged in behavior contrary to the teachings of the priests and temple worshipers. Among the ancient Hebrews, such possessions were thought to represent the wrath and punishment of God. Moses is quoted in the Bible as saying, "The Lord shall smite thee with madness. . . ." Apparently this primarily involved the withdrawal of God's protection, and the abandonment of the individual to the forces of evil. For example, Saul presumably disobeyed God with the result that the spirit of the Lord left him and an evil spirit was thereby permitted to enter. In such cases every effort was made to rid the patient of the evil spirit. Christ reportedly cured a man with an "unclean spirit" by casting out the devils that plagued him into a herd of swine who in turn became possessed and "ran violently down a steep place into the sea" (Mark 5:1-13).

The primary type of treatment for demoniacal possession was *exorcism,* which included various techniques that were developed for casting the evil spirit out of the body of the afflicted one. These varied considerably but typically included prayer, incantation, noisemaking, and the use of various horrible-tasting concoctions such as purgatives made from sheep's dung and wine. In extreme cases flogging, starving, and other more severe measures were often used in an attempt to make the body of the afflicted one such an unpleasant place that the evil spirit would be driven out.

Such treatment was originally in the hands of

medicine men, or shamans, but was eventually taken over in Greece, China, and Egypt by the priests, who were apparently a curious mixture of priest, physician, psychologist, and magician. Although these priests were dominated in the main by beliefs in demonology and established exorcistic practices, they did make a beginning in the more humane and scientific treatment of the mentally ill. For example, as early as 860 B.C. in the temples of Asclepius in Greece, the priests supplemented the usual prayer and incantation with kindness, suggestion, and recreational measures such as theatricals, riding, walking, and harmonious music. However, despite this modern note, treatment was not free of its barbaric aspects, and starving, flogging, and chains were still advocated for recalcitrant patients.

Membership in the medical priesthood of these Greek temples of healing was originally hereditary, but in time, as their influence started to wane, outsiders were admitted and various "schools" were formed. In one of these groups the celebrated Greek physician Hippocrates received his early training. As we shall see, however, Hippocrates was to stray far from the fold of demonology.

Early Medical Concepts of Mental Illness

Against this background of primitive superstition, there occasionally appeared an outstanding figure or group who approached mental illness on a more scientific basis. Especially during the Golden Age of Greece we find considerable progress being made in the understanding and treatment of mental illness.

HIPPOCRATES

The great Greek physician Hippocrates (460-357 B.C.) has been called the "father of modern medicine." He denied the intervention of deities and demons in the development of disease, and insisted that mental disorders had natural causes and required treatment like other diseases. His position was unequivocal: "For my own part, I do not believe that the human body is ever befouled by a God." (Lewis, 1941, p. 37) As the basic explanation of mental illness, Hippocrates emphasized the view, earlier set forth by Pythagoras, that the brain was the central organ of intellectual activity and that mental illness was due to brain pathology. Hippocrates also emphasized the importance of heredity and predisposition and pointed out that injuries to the head could cause sensory and motor disorders.

All mental disorders were classified by Hippocrates into three general categories—mania, melancholia, and phrenitis—and he gave detailed clinical descriptions of the specific disorders included in each category, such as alcoholic delirium and epilepsy. Hippocrates relied heavily upon clinical observation, and his descriptions, which were based upon the daily clinical records of his patients, were surprisingly thorough in their coverage. It is interesting to note that Hippocrates realized the clinical importance of dreams for understanding the personality of the patient. On this point he anticipated one of the principal concepts of contemporary psychoanalysis.

Although crude, Hippocrates' notions of treatment were far in advance of the prevalent exorcistic practices. For the treatment of melancholia, he prescribed: a regular and tranquil life, sobriety and abstinence from all excesses, a vegetable diet, continence, exercise short of fatigue, and bleeding if indicated. For hysteria,[1] which was thought to be restricted to women and caused by the wandering of the uterus to various parts of the body because of its pining for children, Hippocrates recommended marriage as the best remedy. He also believed in the importance of environment, and not infrequently removed the patients from their families.

Hippocrates' emphasis upon natural causes, clinical observations, and brain pathology in relation to mental disorders was truly revolutionary. Unfortunately, however, he was handi-

---

[1]For the psychiatric meaning of *hysteria,* see Glossary.

capped by inadequate anatomical and physiological knowledge. (Greek physicians were poor anatomists because they deified the human body and dared not dissect it.) Thus in his concept of the "four humors" (blood, black bile, yellow bile, and phlegm), Hippocrates apparently conceived the notion of a balance of physiological processes as essential to normal brain functioning and mental health. In his work *On Sacred Disease,* he stated that when the humors were adversely mixed or otherwise disturbed, physical or mental disease resulted: "depravement of the brain arises from phlegm and bile; those mad from phlegm are quiet, depressed and oblivious; those from bile excited, noisy and mischievous." Although this concept went far beyond demonology, it was too crude physiologically to be of any great value. Medical treatment based upon such inadequate anatomical and physiological knowledge was to continue for many centuries, often proving both humorous and tragic.

PLATO AND ARISTOTLE

The problem of dealing with mentally disturbed individuals who committed criminal acts was studied by the great philosopher Plato (429-347 B.C.). He made it clear that such persons were obviously not responsible for their acts and should not receive punishment in the same way as normal persons: ". . . someone may commit an act when mad or afflicted with disease . . . let him pay simply for the damage; and let him be exempt from other punishment." Plato also made provision for mental cases to be cared for in the community as follows: "If anyone is insane, let him not be seen openly in the city, but let the relatives of such a person watch over him in the best manner they know of; and if they are negligent, let them pay a fine. . . ." (Plato, n.d., p. 56) In addition to this emphasis on the more humane treatment of the mentally ill, Plato contributed to a better understanding of human behavior by pointing out that man, as well as all other forms of life, was motivated by physiologic needs or "natural appetites." He also seems to have anticipated Freud's insight into the functions of fantasies and dreams as substitutive satisfactions, concluding

that in dreams, desire tended to satisfy itself in imagery when the higher faculties no longer inhibited the "passions." In his *Republic* (on the ideal type of state), Plato emphasized the importance of individual differences in intellectual and other abilities, and pointed out the role of sociocultural influences in shaping the thinking and behavior of the individual. Despite these modern ideas, however, Plato could not transcend the ignorance and superstition of his time and considered mental illness as partly organic, partly moral, and partly divine.

The question of whether mental disorders could be caused by psychological factors like frustration and conflict was discussed and rejected by the celebrated systematist Aristotle (384-322 B.C.), who was a pupil but not a follower of Plato. In his extensive writings on mental illness, Aristotle generally followed the Hippocratic theory of disturbances in the bile. For example, he believed that very hot bile generated amorous desires and loquacity, and was also responsible for suicidal impulses. This rejection of psychological causes for mental disorders undoubtedly retarded the development of modern psychopathology.

LATER GREEK AND ROMAN THOUGHT

Work along the more scientific lines established by Hippocrates was continued by some of the later Greek and Roman physicians. Particularly in Alexandria, Egypt, which, after its founding in 332 B.C. by Alexander the Great, became the center of Greek culture, medicine developed to a high level, and the temples dedicated to Saturn were first-rate sanatoriums. Pleasant surroundings were considered of great therapeutic value for the mentally ill, and the patients were provided with constant occupation, entertainment, and exercise. These activities included parties, dances, walks in the temple gardens, rowing along the Nile, and musical concerts. The later Greek and Roman physicians also utilized a wide range of other kinds of therapeutic measures, including dieting, massage, hydrotherapy, gymnastics, hypnotism, and education, as well as certain less desirable measures such as bleeding, purging, and mechanical restraints (R. W. Menninger, 1944).

Among the Roman physicians who continued in the Hippocratic tradition were Asclepiades, Aretaeus, and Galen. Asclepiades (*c.* B.C. 124) was well versed in the medical ideas and philosophy of his day and made notable contributions to psychiatry (Zilboorg and Henry, 1941). He was the first to note the difference between acute and chronic mental illnesses, and to distinguish between illusions, delusions, and hallucinations. In addition, he invented various ingenious devices designed to make the patients more comfortable. One of these was a suspended hammock-like bed whose swaying was considered very beneficial for disturbed patients. Asclepiades' progressive approach to mental illness was also evidenced by his vigorous opposition to bleeding, mechanical restraints, and dungeons.

The first hint that certain mental diseases are but an extension of normal psychological processes was given by Aretaeus near the end of the first century A.D. People who were irritable, violent, and easily given to joy and pleasurable pursuits were thought to be prone to the development of manic excitement, while those who tended to be serious were thought to be more apt to develop melancholia. Aretaeus was the first to describe the various phases of mania and melancholia, and to consider these two pathological states as expressions of the same illness. His insight into the importance of emotional factors and of the pre-psychotic personality of the patient was quite an achievement for the day in which he lived.

Galen (130-200 A.D.) did not contribute much that was new to the therapy or clinical description of mental disorders, although he did make many original contributions concerning the anatomy of the nervous system and maintained a scientific approach to mental illness, performing a major service in compiling and integrating the existing material in this field (Guthrie, 1946). In the latter connection, he divided the causes of mental illness into physical and mental. Among the causes he named were injuries to the head, alcoholic excess, shock, fear, adolescence, menstrual changes, economic reverses, and, disappointment in love.

Although historians divide ancient history from medieval by the fall of Rome to the barbarians in the latter part of the fifth century, the Dark Ages in psychiatric history began with the death of Galen in 200 A.D. For the contributions of Hippocrates and the later Greek and Roman physicians (which anticipated so many of our modern concepts of mental illness) were shortly lost in the welter of popular superstition, and most of the medical men of later Rome returned to some sort of demonology. One notable exception to this, however, was Alexander Trallianus (525-605 A.D.), who followed the works of Galen rather closely but placed a great deal of emphasis on constitutional factors, stating, for example, that people with dark hair and a slim build were more likely to be affected by melancholia than persons with light hair and a heavy build. Worthy of note also are some of the clinical cases he recorded (Whitwell, 1936). Among his patients he cited the case of a woman who had the delusion that her middle finger was fixed in such a way that it held the whole world within its power. This caused her great distress for fear she should bend her finger, thus overthrowing the world and destroying everything. Another interesting case was that of a man who was greatly depressed because he was convinced that his head had been amputated. Trallianus reported that he cured this case by suddenly placing a close-fitting leaden cap on the patient's head so that he could feel the weight and thought his head had been replaced.

SURVIVAL OF GREEK THOUGHT IN ARABIA

During medieval times it was only in Arabia that the more scientific aspects of Greek medicine survived. Here the mentally ill received much more humane treatment than in Christian lands. The outstanding figure in Arabian medicine was Avicenna (*c.* A.D. 980-1037), called the "Prince of Physicians" (Campbell, 1926). The case below will show his unique treatment of a mental patient.

"A certain prince . . . was afflicted with melancholia, and suffered from the delusion that he was a cow. . . . he would low like a cow, causing annoyance to everyone, . . . crying, 'Kill me so that a good stew may be made of my flesh,' finally . . . he would eat nothing. . . . Avicenna was persuaded to take the case.

. . . First of all he sent a message to the patient bidding him be of good cheer because the butcher was coming to slaughter him, whereat . . . the sick man rejoiced. Some time afterwards Avicenna, holding a knife in his hand, entered the sickroom saying, 'Where is this cow that I may kill it?' The patient lowed like a cow to indicate where he was. By Avicenna's orders he was laid on the ground, bound hand and foot. Avicenna then felt him all over and said, 'He is too lean, and not ready to be killed; he must be fattened.' Then they offered him suitable food of which he now partook eagerly, and gradually he gained strength, got rid of his delusion, and was completely cured." (Browne, 1921, pp. 88-89)

Unfortunately, most medical men of Avicenna's time were approaching the problems of the mentally ill in a very different way.

Demonology in the Middle Ages

With the collapse of Greek and Roman civilization, medicine as well as other scientific pursuits suffered an almost complete eclipse in Europe. There was a tremendous revival of the most ancient superstition and demonology with only a slight modification to conform to current theological demands. Man now became the battleground of demons and spirits who waged eternal war for the possession of his soul. Mental disorders were apparently fairly frequent during the Middle Ages, and there is reason to believe that their incidence was considerably greater than in ancient times.

"MASS MADNESS"

During the latter part of this period, there was a peculiar trend in mental illness, involving the widespread occurrence of group mental disorders which were apparently mainly cases of hysteria. Whole groups of people were affected simultaneously.

Dance manias, taking the form of epidemics of raving, jumping, dancing, and convulsions, were reported as early as the tenth century. One such episode, occurring in Italy early in the thirteenth century, was recorded by physicians of the time whose records have been reviewed by the medical historian H. E. Sigerist. He has written:

"The disease occurred at the height of the summer heat. . . . People, asleep or awake, would suddenly jump up, feeling an acute pain like the sting of a bee. Some saw the spider, others did not, but they knew that it must be the tarantula. They ran out of the house into the street, to the market place, dancing in great excitement. Soon they were joined by others who like them had been bitten, or by people who had been stung in previous years. . . .

"Thus groups of patients would gather, dancing wildly in the queerest attire. . . . Others would tear their clothes and show their nakedness, losing all sense of modesty. . . . Some called for swords and acted like fencers, others for whips and beat each other. . . . Some of them had still stranger fancies, liked to be tossed in the air, dug holes in the ground, and rolled themselves into the dirt like swine. They all drank wine plentifully and sang and talked like drunken people. . . ." (1943, pp. 103, 106-107)

Actually, the behavior was very similar to the ancient orgiastic rites by which people had worshiped the Greek gods. These had been banned with the advent of Christianity, but were deeply imbedded in the culture and were apparently kept alive by secret gatherings. Probably considerable guilt and conflict were engendered; then, with time, the meaning of the dances changed, and the old rites appeared as symptoms of disease. The participants were no longer sinners but the poor victims of the tarantula (Gloyne, 1950).

Known as *tarantism* in Italy, the dancing mania later spread to Germany and the rest of Europe where it was known as *St. Vitus' dance*. Other peculiar manifestations also appeared. In the fifteenth century, a member of a German convent was overcome with a desire to bite her fellow nuns. The practice was taken up by her companions, and the mania spread to other con-

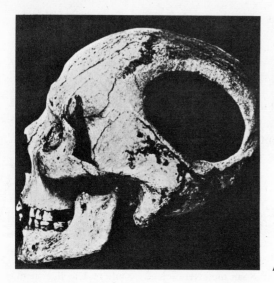

A

B

C

DEMONOLOGY

Mental illness has often been attributed to supernatural powers. Archaeological evidence indicates that Stone Age men performed trephining operations (A), in which an opening was made in the skull of the patient, presumably on the theory that this would allow the evil spirit to escape.

With modifications, this "evil spirit" theory endured for centuries. Naturally, it influenced attempts to treat mental illness, but even though the theory was false, it did not always lead to entirely unrealistic therapy. Even the trephining operation may have had beneficial results in some cases by removing pressure on the brain. And in some

vents in Germany, Holland, and Italy (A. D. White, 1896).

Isolated rural areas were also afflicted with outbreaks of *lycanthropy*—a form of mental illness in which the patient imagined himself a wolf and imitated its actions. In 1541 a case was reported wherein the lycanthrope told his captors, in confidence, that he was really a wolf but that his skin was smooth on the surface because all the hairs were on the inside (Stone, 1937). To cure him of his delusions, his extremities were amputated, following which he died, still unconvinced.

These epidemics continued into the seventeenth century, but apparently reached their peak during the fifteenth and sixteenth centuries

—a period noted for oppression, famine, and pestilence. During this period, Europe was ravaged by an epidemic known as the "Black Death," which spread across the continent, destroying millions of human lives and severely disrupting social organization. Undoubtedly many of the peculiar manifestations during this period, including the Children's Crusade, in which thousands of children left their homes to liberate the Holy Sepulcher, were related to the depression, fear, and wild mysticism engendered by the terrible events of the time. People did not dream that such frightening catastrophes were attributable to natural causes and thus would some day be within man's power to control, prevent, and even create.

places the tendency was toward kindness, with treatment involving such gentle practices as prayer, visits to holy places, and the laying on of hands. A bas-relief of the fourth or fifth century (B) illustrates an attempt to drive out a devil by applying the cross.

Unfortunately, later techniques concentrated on making the possessed person's body an undesirable place for a devil to inhabit. Scourging exorcisms were attempts to wound the devil's pride by insulting him. Torture became an acceptable method for driving the devil out. Then, in the fifteenth century, it began to be thought that although some persons were possessed unwillingly, others had made a bargain with the devil. Such a belief seemed to justify all manner of cruel practices.

The sixteenth and seventeenth centuries saw both the reappearance of critical thought and the full development of the demonological view. Illustrations of the time depict witches with their attending demons (C) and a group of witches raising a storm against the ship of James I (D). Sympathetic treatment was not unknown, as can be seen in the seventeenth-century engraving "St. Clara healing an epileptic woman" (E), but the period was characterized by its extreme practices, such as the burning of those thought to be witches (F).

TREATMENT IN MEDIEVAL TIMES

The treatment of the mentally ill was now left largely to priests, and the monasteries served as refuges and places of confinement for many patients. During the early medieval period, the mentally ill, when not too difficult to manage, were treated with considerable kindliness. Much store was set by prayer, holy water, sanctified ointments, the breath or spittle of the priests, the touching of relics, visits to holy places, and mild forms of exorcism. In some monasteries and shrines exorcism was performed by the gentle "laying on of hands." Such methods were often intermixed with vague ideas of medical treatment derived mainly from Galen, which gave rise to such prescriptions as the following: "For a fiend-sick man: When a devil possesses a man, or controls him from within with disease, a spew-drink of lupin, bishopswort, henbane, garlic. Pound these together, add ale and holy water." (Cockayne, n.d.)

As exorcistic techniques became more fully developed, it was emphasized that it was Satan's pride which had led to his original downfall. Hence, in treating persons possessed by a devil, the first thing to do was to strike a fatal blow at the devil's pride—to insult him. This involved calling the devil some of the most obscene epithets that the worst imaginations could devise, and the foul insults were usually supplemented by long litanies of cursing:

". . . May all the devils that are thy foes rush forth upon thee, and drag thee down to hell! . . . May God set a nail to your skull, and pound it in with a hammer, as Jael did unto Sisera! . . . May . . . Sother break thy head and cut off thy hands, as was done to the cursed Dagon! . . . May God hang thee in a hellish yoke, as seven men were hanged by the sons of Saul!" (From *Thesaurus Exorcismorum*)

This procedure was considered highly successful in the treatment of possessed persons. A certain bishop of Beauvais claimed to have rid a person of five devils, all of whom signed an agreement stating that they and their subordinate imps would no longer persecute the possessed individual (A. D. White, 1896).

Had this been the worst treatment the mentally ill received during the Middle Ages, the world would have been spared some of the most terrible and tragic chapters in its history. Unfortunately, however, as theological beliefs concerning mental illness became more fully developed and were endorsed by the secular world, mildness and gentle treatment began to disappear. It came to be generally believed that cruelty to "madmen" was punishment of the devil residing within them, and when "scourging" proved ineffective, the authorities felt justified in driving out the demons by less pleasant methods. Flogging, starving, chains, immersion in hot water, and other torturous methods were devised in order to make the body such an unpleasant place of residence that no self-respecting devil would remain in it. Undoubtedly many men and women who might have been restored to health by more gentle and kindly measures were driven into hopeless mental illness by these brutal methods.

WITCHCRAFT

Today it is almost unbelievable that sober and pious townspeople could gather in the village square and cheer the burning or torturing of a woman who was so demented as obviously not to know what she was doing. Yet only three hundred years ago people not only cheered but felt that in such practices they were doing their sacred duty.

For during the latter part of the fifteenth century, beliefs concerning demoniacal possessions took a horrible turn for the worse. It now became the accepted theological belief that demoniacal possessions were of two general types: (1) possessions in which the victim was unwillingly seized by the devil as a punishment by God for his sins, and (2) possessions in which the individual was actually in league with the devil. The latter persons were supposed to have made a pact with the devil, consummated by signing in blood a book presented to them by Satan which gave them certain supernatural powers. They could cause pestilence, storms, floods, sexual impotence, injuries to their enemies, and ruination of crops, and could rise through the air, cause milk to sour, and turn themselves into animals. In short, they were witches.

These beliefs were not confined to simple serfs but were held and elaborated upon by most of the important clergymen of this period. No less a man than Martin Luther (1483-1546) came to the following conclusions:

"The greatest punishment God can inflict on the wicked . . . is to deliver them over to Satan, who with God's permission, kills them or makes them to undergo great calamities. Many devils are in woods, water, wildernesses, etc., ready to hurt and prejudice people. When these things happen, then the philosophers and physicians say it is natural, ascribing it to the planets.

"In cases of melancholy . . . I conclude it is merely the work of the devil. Men are possessed by the devil in two ways; corporally or spiritually. Those whom he possesses corporally, as mad people, he has permission from God to vex and agitate, but he has no power over their souls." (*Colloquia Mensalia*)

Those who were judged to have been unwillingly seized by the devil as punishment by God were treated initially in accordance with the established exorcistic practices of the time. As time went on, however, the distinction between the two types of possessions became somewhat obscured, and by the close of the fifteenth century, the mentally ill were generally considered heretics and witches.

More and more concern was expressed in official quarters over the number of witches roaming around and the great damage they were doing by pestilences, storms, sexual depravity, and other heinous crimes. Consequently, on December 7, 1484, Pope Innocent VIII sent forth his bull *Summis Desiderantes Affectibus* in which he exhorted the clergy of Europe, especially Germany, to leave no means untried in the detection of witches. This papal bull was theologically based upon the scriptural command "Thou shalt not suffer a witch to live" (Exodus 22:18), and although it was not intended as an endorsement of the torture or persecution of innocent people, it was to lead to one of the most tragic periods of all human history.

To assist in this great work, a manual, *The Witch Hammer, Malleus Maleficarum,* was prepared by two Dominican monks, Johann Sprenger and Heinrich Kraemer, both Inquisitors appointed by the Pope to act in northern Germany and territories along the Rhine. This manual, revered for centuries in both Catholic and Protestant countries as being almost divinely inspired, was complete in every detail concerning witchcraft and was of great value in witchhunting. It was divided into three parts. The first confirmed the existence of witches and pointed out that those who did not believe in them were either in honest error or polluted with heresy. The second part contained a description of the clinical symptoms by which witches could be detected, such as red spots or areas of anesthesia on the skin, which were thought to resemble the claw of the devil ("devil's claw") and were presumably left by the devil to denote the sealing of the pact with him. The third part dealt with the legal forms of examining and sentencing a witch.

In accordance with the precepts laid down in the *Malleus,* the accepted way to gain sure proof of witchcraft was to torture the person until a confession was obtained. This method was eminently effective. The victims of these inhuman tortures—writhing in agony and viewed with horror by those they loved—confessed to anything and everything. Frequently they were forced to give the names of alleged accomplices in their evil doings, and these unfortunate persons were in turn tortured until a satisfactory confession of their evil activities was elicited.

Confessions were often weird, but this seldom deterred the learned judges. For example, James I of England proved, through the skillful use of unlimited torture, that witches were to blame for the tempests which beset his bride on her voyage from Denmark. A Dr. Fian, whose legs were being crushed in the "boots" and who had wedges driven under his fingernails, confessed that more than a hundred witches had put to sea in a sieve to produce the storms (A. D. White, 1896).

Further impetus to these persecutions was undoubtedly given by many of the suspects themselves, who, although obviously ill by our present standards, participated so actively in the beliefs of the time that they often freely "confessed" their transactions with the devil, almost gleefully pointed out the "marks" he had left on their bodies, and claimed great powers as a result of their evil doings. Others, suffering from severe depressions, elaborated on their terrible sins and admitted themselves to be beyond redemption. This sort of basis for the iron-bound logic of the Inquisitors is well illustrated in the following case of a woman who was probably suffering from involutional melancholia.

"A certain woman was taken and finally burned, who for six years had an incubus devil even when she was lying in bed at the side of her husband . . . the homage she has given to the devil was of such a sort that she was bound to dedicate herself body and soul to him forever, after seven years. But God provided mercifully for she was taken in the sixth year and condemned to the fire, and having truly and completely confessed is believed to have obtained pardon from God. For she went most willingly to her death, saying that she would gladly suffer an even more terrible death if only she would be set free and escape the power of the devil." (Stone, 1937, p. 146)

Probably the majority of these unfortunate persons were so ill mentally that they were delusionally convinced of their powers or sins and had little realization of the fate that lay in store for them. (Even today many psychotics are convinced of their hopeless guilt and damnation.) For to be convicted of witchcraft was a most serious matter. The penalty usually followed one of three general forms. There were those who were beheaded or strangled before being burned; those who were burned alive; and those who were mutilated before being burned. The treatment accorded a mentally disordered man

B

A

C

ATTEMPTS TO TREAT MENTAL ILLNESS

It was not only demonology that led to extremes of inhumane treatment of mental illness. Even a belief in
natural causes was no guarantee against cruelty and
foolishness. Some medieval quacks taught that mental
disorders were caused by stones developed in the head.
They performed operations to remove the stones, but in
fact made only superficial cuts (A).

Before the reforms begun by Pinel, it was commonly
thought that violence of some kind was appropriate treatment. Doctors at St. Medard, Paris, jumped on patients
in order to remove "mental obstructions" (B). In the asylum

caught in the wrong period of history is illustrated in the following case:

"In Königsberg in 1636 a man thought he was God
the Father; he claimed that all the angels and the devil
and the Son of God recognized his power. He was convicted. His tongue was cut out, his head cut off, and
his body burned." (Zillboorg and Henry, 1941, p. 259)

There seems to have been little distinction between the Roman and the Reformed churches
in their attitudes toward witchcraft, and large
numbers of people were put to death in the latter
part of the fifteenth century.

"A French judge boasted that he had burned 800

women in sixteen years on the bench; 600 were burned
during the administration of a bishop in Bamberg. The
Inquisition, originally started by the Church of Rome,
was carried along by protestant churches in Great
Britain and Germany. In protestant Geneva 500 persons were burned in the year 1515. In Trèves some
7000 people were reported burned during a period of
several years." (Bromberg, 1937, p. 61)

However, the full horror of the witch mania
and its enthusiastic adoption by other countries
including some American colonies took place
during the sixteenth and seventeenth centuries.
And though medical thought began to change
gradually, the basic ideas of mental illness as
representing punishment by God or deliberate

E

D

at Leyden, hot irons were applied to the head to bring patients to their senses (C). Even in the early nineteenth century, English asylums used rotating devices in which the mentally ill were whirled around (D).

Understandably enough, the beginnings of our modern methods were shrouded in mystic and fanciful theories. Mesmer's use of hypnotism, for example, involved the baquet (E) and was based on notions of a universal magnetic fluid. Later investigations of hypnotism, divorced from these trappings, showed the importance of psychological factors in mental illness while other investigations demonstrated the influence of organic pathology.

With the awareness that mental illness could be traced to organic and psychological causes, the scientific approach to the problem was firmly established. Scientific investigation led to increased understanding—understanding on which effective treatment procedures could be based. Modern methods of treatment are a result of this continuing search for better understanding.

association with the devil, which were developed in such elaborate detail during the Middle Ages, were to continue to dominate popular thought until well into the nineteenth century.

Reappearance of Scientific Questioning in Europe

Any criticism or questioning of the theological doctrine of demonology during the Middle Ages was made at the risk of life itself. Yet even during the early part of the sixteenth century we find the beginnings again of more scientific intellectual activity. The concepts of witchcraft and demonology, which had acted for centuries as a drag upon medical science and especially psychiatry, began to be challenged and attacked by men greater than their time—men from the fields of religion, physics, medicine, and philosophy.

In the early part of the sixteenth century, Paracelsus (1490-1541) pointed out that the "dancing mania" was not a possession but a form of disease and that it should be treated as such

(Zilboorg and Henry, 1941). He also formulated the idea of psychic causes for mental illness and advocated "bodily magnetism," which later became hypnosis, in treatment. Although Paracelsus rejected demonology, his views of mental illness were confused by belief in astral influences (*lunatic* is derived from the Latin word "luna" or moon): he was convinced that the moon exercised a supernatural influence over the brain. Paracelsus paid a heavy price for his unconventional ideas and was hounded and persecuted until his death.

Johann Weyer (1515-1588), a physician and man of letters who wrote under the Latin name of Joannus Wierus, was so deeply impressed by the scenes of imprisonment, torture, and burning of persons accused of witchcraft that he made a careful study of the entire problem of witchcraft and about 1563 published a book on the subject. In it he pointed out that a considerable number, if not all, of those imprisoned, tortured, and burned for witchcraft were really sick mentally or bodily, and consequently that great wrongs were being committed against innocent people.

Weyer's work received the approval of a few outstanding physicians and theologians of his time. In the main, however, it met with vehement protest and condemnation. Father Spina, the author of a polemical book against Weyer, stated: "Recently Satan went to a Sabbath[1] attired as a great prince, and told the assembled witches that they need not worry since, thanks to Weyer and his followers, the affairs of the Devil were brilliantly progressing." (Castiglioni, 1946, p. 253)

Weyer was one of the first physicians to specialize in mental disorders, and his wide experience and progressive views on mental illness justify his being regarded as the true founder of modern psychiatry. Unfortunately, however, he was too far ahead of his time. His works were banned by the Church and remained so until the twentieth century.

Perhaps there is no better illustration of the developing skepticism than the works of the Oxford-educated Reginald Scot (1538-1599), who devoted his life to exposing the fallacies of witchcraft and demonology. In his book *Discovery of Witchcraft,* published in 1584, he convincingly and daringly denied the existence of demons, devils, and evil spirits as the cause of mental disorders.

"These women are but diseased wretches suffering from melancholy, and their words, actions, reasoning, and gestures show that sickness has affected their brains and impaired their powers of judgment. You must know that the effects of sickness on men, and still more on women, are almost unbelievable. Some of these persons imagine, confess, and maintain that they are witches and are capable of performing extraordinary miracles through the arts of witchcraft; others, due to the same mental disorder, imagine strange and impossible things which they claim to have witnessed." (Castiglioni, p. 253)

King James I of England, however, came to the rescue of demonology, personally refuted Scot's advancement of science, and ordered his book seized and burned.

Churchmen too were beginning to question the practices of the time. The wise and far-seeing

---

THE
Difcovery of Witchcraft:
PROVING,

That the Compacts and Contracts of Witches with *Devils* and all *Infernal Spirits* or *Familiars*, are but Erroneous Novelties and Imaginary Conceptions.

Alfo difcovering, How far their Power extendeth in Killing, Tormenting, Confuming, or Curing the bodies of Men, Women, Children, or Animals, by Charms, Philtres, Periapts, Pentacles, Curfes, and Conjurations.

WHEREIN LIKE WISE

The Unchriftian Practices and Inhumane Dealings of *Searchers* and *Witch-tryers* upon *Aged, Mellancholly,* and *Superftitious* people, in extorting Confeffions by Terrors and Tortures, and in devifing falfe Marks and Symptoms, are notably Detected.

And the Knavery of *Juglers, Conjurers, Charmers, Soothfayers, Figure-Cafters, Dreamers, Alchymifts* and *Philterers;* with many other things that have long lain hidden, fully Opened and Deciphered.

ALL WHICH

Are very neceffary to be known for the undeceiving of *Judges, Juftices,* and *Jurors,* before they pafs Sentence upon Poor, Miferable and Ignorant People; who are frequently Arraigned, Condemned, and Executed for *Witches* and *Wizzards.*

IN SIXTEEN BOOKS.

By R E G I N A L D S C O T *Efquire.*

Title Page of Reginald Scot's Discoverie of Witchcraft

---

[1]The word *Sabbath* has no relation to the Biblical Sabbath, but refers to witches' gatherings in which orders were supposedly received from Satan.

St. Vincent de Paul (1576-1660), surrounded by every opposing influence and at the risk of his life, declared: "Mental disease is no different to bodily disease and Christianity demands of the humane and powerful to protect, and the skilful to relieve the one as well as the other."

From concerted attacks, which continued through the next two centuries, demonology was forced to give ground, and the way was gradually paved for the triumph of observation and reason, culminating in the development of modern experimental science and psychopathology.

Establishment of Mental Hospitals

Demonology slowly gave way to the belief that the mentally ill were sick people. From the sixteenth century on, monasteries and prisons gradually relinquished the care of mental patients to asylums which were being established in increasing numbers. The care of patients in these asylums, however, left much to be desired.

EARLY ASYLUMS

In 1547, the monastery of St. Mary of Bethlehem at London was officially made into a mental hospital by Henry VIII. Its name soon became contracted to "Bedlam," and it became widely known for the deplorable conditions and practices that prevailed. The more violent patients were exhibited to the public for one penny a look, and the more harmless inmates were forced to seek charity on the streets of London as did the "Bedlam Beggars" described by Shakespeare.

"Bedlam beggars, who, with roaring voices . . .
Sometime with lunatic bans, sometime with prayers
Enforce their charity."—*King Lear,* Act II, Scene 3

Such hospitals, or "asylums" as they were called, were gradually established in other countries (Lewis, 1941). The San Hipolito, established in Mexico in 1566 by the philanthropist Bernardino Alvares, was the first hospital for the care and study of mental disorders to be established in the Americas. The first mental hospital in France, La Maison de Charenton, was founded in 1641 in the suburbs of Paris. A mental hospital was established in Moscow in 1764

and the notorious Lunatics' Tower in Vienna was constructed in 1784. This was a show place in Old Vienna and the description of the edifice and its practices makes interesting reading. It was an ornately decorated round tower within which were square rooms. The doctors and "keepers" lived in the square rooms, while the patients were confined in the spaces between the walls of the square rooms and the outside of the tower. The patients were put on exhibit to the public for a small fee, and were in general treated like animals and criminals—a practice which, as we shall see, was characteristic of these early hospitals.

The Pennsylvania Hospital at Philadelphia, completed under the guidance of Benjamin Franklin in 1756, provided some cells or wards for the mentally ill, but the first hospital in the United States devoted exclusively to mental patients was constructed in Williamsburg, Virginia, in 1773.

These early asylums, or hospitals, were primarily modifications of penal institutions, and the inmates were treated more like wild animals than sick human beings. Selling gives a striking account of the treatment of the chronic insane in La Bicêtre Hospital in Paris. This treatment was typical of the asylums of this period and continued through most of the eighteenth century.

The patients were ordinarily shackled to the walls of their dark, unlighted cells by iron collars which held them flat against the wall and permitted little movement. Ofttimes there was also an iron hoop around the waist of the patient and both his hands and feet were chained. Although these chains usually permitted enough movement so that the patient could feed himself out of a bowl, they often did not permit him to lie down at night. Since little was known about dietetics, and the patients were presumed to be animals anyway, little attention was paid to whether the patient was adequately fed or to whether the food was good or bad. The cells were furnished only with straw and were never swept or cleaned; the patient was permitted to remain in the midst of all the accumulated ordure. No one visited him except at feeding time, no provision was made to keep him warm, and even the most elementary gestures of humanity were lacking. (Modified from Selling, 1943, pp. 54-55)

Treatment of mental patients in the United States was little if any better. The following is a vivid description of the plight of those mentally ill in this country during colonial times:

"The mentally ill were hanged, imprisoned, tortured, and otherwise persecuted as agents of Satan. Regarded as sub-human beings, they were chained in specially devised kennels and cages like wild beasts, and thrown into prisons, bridewells and jails like criminals. They were incarcerated in workhouse dungeons or made to slave as able-bodied paupers, unclassified from the rest. They were left to wander about stark naked, driven from place to place like mad dogs, subjected to whippings as vagrants and rogues. Even the well-to-do were not spared confinement in strong rooms and cellar dungeons, while legislation usually concerned itself more with their property than their persons." (Deutsch, 1946, p. 53)

Some insight into the prevalent forms of treatment in the early American hospitals may be gained from a thesis on "Chronic Mania," written by a medical student in 1796 at the New York Hospital, in which cells or wards were provided in the cellar for the mentally ill patients. He considered that restraint should be avoided as long as possible, "lest the strait jackets, and chains and cells should induce a depression of spirits seldom surmounted." He also doubted the propriety of "unexpected plunging into cold water," of "two to six hours in spring water or still colder," of the "refrigerant plan," of bleeding, purging, vomiting, streams of cold water on the head, blisters, and similar procedures (Russel, 1941, p. 230).

Even as late as 1830, new patients had their heads shaved, were dressed in strait jackets, put upon a low diet, compelled to swallow some active purgative, and placed in a dark cell. If these measures did not serve to quiet unruly or excited patients, more severe measures such as starvation, solitary confinement, cold baths, and other methods of torture were used (Bennett, 1947).

THE GHEEL SHRINE

There were a few bright spots in this otherwise tragic situation. Out of the more humane Christian tradition of prayer, the laying on of hands, or holy touch, and visits to shrines for help in cases of mental illness, there arose several great shrines where treatment by kindness and love stood out in marked contrast to generally prevailing conditions. The one at Gheel in Belgium, visited since the thirteenth century, is probably most famous.

"Somewhere in the dim past there lived a king in Ireland who was married to a most beautiful woman and who sired an equally beautiful daughter. The good queen developed a fatal illness, and at her death bed the daughter dedicated herself to a life of purity and service to the poor and the mentally bereft. The widowed king was beside himself with grief and announced to his subjects that he must at once be assuaged of sorrow by marrying the woman in his kingdom who most resembled the dead queen. No such paragon was found. But the devil came and whispered to the king that there was such a woman—his own daughter. The devil spurred the king to propose marriage to the girl, but she was appropriately outraged by this incestuous overture and fled across the English Channel to Belgium. There the king overtook her and with Satan at his elbow, slew the girl and her faithful attendants. In the night the angels came, recapitated the body and concealed it in the forest near the village of Gheel. Years later five lunatics chained together spent the night with their keepers at a small wayside shrine near this Belgian village. Overnight all the victims recovered. Here indeed must be the place where the dead girl, reincarnated as St. Dymphna, was buried, and here was the sacred spot where her cures of the insane are effected. In the 15th century pilgrimages to Gheel from every part of the civilized world were organized for the mentally sick. Many of the pilgrims remained in Gheel to live with the inhabitants of the locality, and in the passing years it became the natural thing to accept them into the homes and thus the first 'colony' was formed and for that matter the only one which has been consistently successful." (Karnosh and Zucker, 1945, p. 15)

The colony of Gheel has continued its work to the present day. Some 2400 certified patients live in private homes, work with the inhabitants, and suffer few restrictions except to refrain from using alcohol and visiting public places (Barton, 1959; Dumont and Aldrich, 1962). Many mental disorders are represented in this colony including schizophrenia, manic-depressive psychoses, psychopathic personality, mental retardation, and various types of organic brain disorders. Approximately one in every ten persons in the community of some 20,000 people is a mental patient. Each patient reports regularly to a supervising psychiatrist and ordinarily stays in Gheel until the medical commission considers him recovered. It is unfortunate that the great humanitarian work of this colony has received so little recognition, and that economic and other factors appear to be leading to a gradual but steady decline in resident patients (Hewitt, 1962).

HUMANITARIAN REFORM

Despite the fact that the age of skepticism had undermined the old beliefs, the early asylums, as we have noted, were no better than concentration camps where the unfortunate inmates lived and died amidst the most incredible filth and cruelty. But as modern experimental science gradually emerged, there was an increasingly more scientific and humane approach to the mentally ill. In the year 1792, this new approach received its first great impetus from the work of Philippe Pinel (1745-1826) in France, and William Tuke in England.

Shortly after the French Revolution, Pinel was placed in charge of La Bicêtre (the hospital for the insane in Paris to which we have previously referred). In this capacity he received the grudging permission of the Revolutionary Commune to remove the chains from some of the inmates as an experiment to test his views that the mentally ill should be treated with kindness and consideration—as sick people and not as vicious beasts or criminals. Had his experiment proved a failure, Pinel might well have lost his head, but, fortunately for all, it proved to be a great success. Chains were removed, sunny rooms were provided instead of dungeons, patients were permitted to exercise on the hospital grounds, and kindliness was extended to these poor creatures, some of whom had been chained in dungeons for thirty years or more. The effect was almost miraculous. The previous noise, filth, and abuse were replaced by order and peace. As Pinel said: "The whole discipline was marked with regularity and kindness which had the most favorable effect on the insane themselves, rendering even the most furious more tractable." (Selling, 1943, p. 65)

The reactions of these patients when all their chains were removed for the first time is a pathetic story. One patient, an English officer who had years before killed a guard in an attack of fury, tottered outside on legs weak from lack of use, and for the first time in some forty years saw the sun and sky. With tears in his eyes he exclaimed, "Oh, how beautiful!" (Zilboorg and Henry, 1941, p. 323) Finally when night came, he voluntarily returned to his cell, which had been cleaned during his absence, to fall peacefully asleep on his new bed. After two years of orderly behavior, including helping to handle other patients, he was pronounced cured and was permitted to leave the hospital. It is a curious and satisfying fact of history that Pinel was saved from the hands of a mob who suspected him of antirevolutionary activities by a soldier whom he had freed from asylum chains.

Pinel was later given charge of the Salpêtrière Hospital, where the same reorganization in treatment was carried out with similar gratifying results, the Bicêtre and Salpêtrière hospitals thus becoming the first modern hospitals for the care of the insane. Pinel's successor, Jean Esquirol (1772-1840), continued his good work at the Salpêtrière and, in addition, helped in the establishment of some ten new mental hospitals, which helped to put France in the forefront of modern psychiatry.

While Pinel was reforming the Bicêtre Hospital, an English Quaker named William Tuke established the "York Retreat," a pleasant country house where mental patients lived, worked, and rested in a kindly religious atmosphere. This

A   B

D

C

represented the culmination of a noble battle against the brutality, ignorance, and indifference of his time. Some insight into the difficulties and discouragements he encountered in the establishment of the York Retreat may be gleaned from a simple statement he made in a letter regarding his early efforts: "All men seem to desert me." This is not surprising when we remember that demonology was still widespread, and that as late as 1768 we find the Protestant John Wesley's famous declaration that "The giving up of witchcraft is in effect the giving up of the Bible." The belief in demonology was too strong to be conquered overnight.

As word of the amazing results obtained by Pinel spread to England, Tuke's small force of Quakers gradually gained support from John Connolly, Samuel Hitch, and other great English medical psychologists. In 1841 Hitch intro-

duced trained women nurses into the wards at the Gloucester Asylum and put trained supervisors at the head of the nursing staffs. These innovations, regarded as quite revolutionary at the time, were of utmost importance, for they not only improved the care of mental patients but engendered a better public attitude, because mental illness was put on the same footing as physical illness. At last the mystery and ignorant fear which had always surrounded the mental patient was being dispelled.

EARLY MENTAL HOSPITALS IN AMERICA

The success of Pinel's and Tuke's experiments in more humanitarian methods revolutionized the treatment of the mentally ill throughout the

INSTITUTIONAL CARE OF THE MENTALLY ILL

Since the mentally ill are often unable to care for themselves and are sometimes dangerous to themselves and others, society has usually made special provision for their care and confinement. Consistent with the views of Hippocrates—that mental disorders had natural causes—some temples in the Greek and Roman periods provided excellent care. But with the revival of superstition during the Middle Ages, humane treatment became the exception.

In the sixteenth century, belief in demonology began to wane. In increasing numbers, patients were cared for in asylums rather than in prisons and monasteries. Early asylums (A) left much to be desired, however: chains, cells, and other physical restraints were still thought necessary. Patients of all types were often crowded together and were objects of public curiosity. An engraving by Hogarth (B) shows two ladies of fashion visiting the St. Mary of Bethlehem asylum. It remained for Pinel to demonstrate, by removing the chains from the patients in La Bicêtre Hospital in Paris (C), that more humane treatment was not only possible but in fact beneficial.

Despite Pinel's dramatic success, reform was a slow process. Devices like Dr. Rush's "tranquillizer" (D) and the "crib" (E) were still used for violent patients. But in the next hundred and fifty years the trend was toward clean, light surroundings, with a minimum of restraint (F). In the best modern hospitals today, providing a pleasant environment is a major consideration, and patients are encouraged to keep busy in interesting activities.

E

F

civilized world. In the United States, this was reflected in the work of Benjamin Rush (1745-1813), "the father of American psychiatry," at the Pennsylvania Hospital, where he began his duties in 1783. Rush encouraged more humane treatment of the mentally ill, wrote the first systematic treatise on psychiatry in America, *Medical Inquiries and Observations upon the Diseases of the Mind* (1812), and was the first American to organize a course in psychiatry. But even he did not escape entirely from the established beliefs of his time. His medical theory was tainted with astrology and his principal remedies were bloodletting and purgatives. In addition, he invented and used a torturelike device called "the tranquillizer." Despite these limitations, however, we may consider Rush an important transitional figure between the old era and the new.

The early work of Benjamin Rush was followed through by an energetic New England schoolteacher, Dorothea Dix (1802-1887). Miss Dix was retired early from her teaching job because of recurring attacks of tuberculosis, and in 1841 began to teach in a Sunday school for female prisoners. Through this contact she soon became acquainted with the deplorable conditions prevalent in jails, almshouses, and asylums. In a "Memorial" submitted to the Congress of the United States in 1848, she stated that she had seen "more than 9000 idiots, epileptics and insane in the United States, destitute of appropriate care and protection . . . bound with galling chains, bowed beneath fetters and heavy iron balls attached to drag-chains, lacerated with ropes, scourged with rods and terrified beneath storms of execration and cruel blows; now subject to jibes and scorn and torturing tricks; now

abandoned to the most outrageous violations."
(Zilboorg and Henry, 1941, pp. 583-584)

As a result of her findings, Miss Dix carried
on a zealous campaign between 1841 and 1881,
which aroused the people and the legislatures to
an awareness of the inhuman treatment accorded the mentally ill. Through her efforts
many millions of dollars were raised to build
suitable hospitals, and some twenty states responded directly to her appeals. Not only was
she instrumental in improving conditions in the
United States, but she directed the opening of
two large institutions in Canada and completely
reformed the asylum system in Scotland and several other countries. She is credited with the establishment of some thirty-two modern mental
hospitals, an astonishing record considering the
ignorance and superstition which still prevailed
in the field of mental illness. She rounded out
her amazing career by organizing the nursing
forces of the Northern armies during the Civil
War. A resolution presented by the United
States Congress in 1901 characterized her as
"among the noblest examples of humanity in all
history." (Karnosh and Zucker, 1945, p. 18)

Most of the early American asylums had been
under the direction of a warden or steward who
was not medically trained, and medical attention
was not provided on a continuous basis. Gradually, however, the superintendence of the institutions was placed in the hands of medical men,
and in 1844 thirteen superintendents formed the
Association of Medical Superintendents of
American Institutions for the Insane (Lowrey,
1946), which was to develop into the American
Psychiatric Association of today.

PUBLIC EDUCATION
AND MENTAL HYGIENE

During the latter half of the nineteenth century the asylum, "the big house on the hill,"
with its high turrets and fortresslike appearance
became a familiar landmark in America. In it
the mentally ill lived under semiadequate conditions of comfort and freedom from abuse. To
the general public, however, the asylum was an
eerie place, and its occupants a strange and
frightening lot. Little was done by the resident
psychiatrists to educate the public along lines

that would reduce the general fear and horror of
insanity. One principal reason for this, of course,
was that the early psychiatrist had very little
actual information to impart. Even as late as
1840, no clear-cut classification of mental disorders had been worked out, and a German
teacher, Dr. Heinroth, was still advancing the
theory that sin produced insanity and repentance a cure, and that piety constituted mental
health (Lewis, 1941). Until approximately the
turn of the twentieth century, progress centered
around the more humanitarian treatment of the
mentally ill.

In America, attention to the importance of
public education regarding mental illness was
soon to be initiated by Clifford Beers, whose
famous book, *A Mind That Found Itself,* was
published in 1908. Beers, a Yale graduate, described his own mental collapse and told of the
bad treatment he received in three typical institutions of the day, and of his eventual recovery
in the home of a friendly attendant. Although
chains and other torture devices had long since
been given up, the strait jacket was still widely
used as a means of "quieting" excited patients.
Beers experienced this treatment and supplied
a vivid description of what such painful immobilization of the arms means to an overwrought
mental patient in terms of further intensification
of inner excitement. He resolved that something
should be done to make people realize that this
was no way to handle the sick. In his effort, he
was successful in arousing the interest and aid
of many public-spirited citizens and scientists,
including the eminent psychologist, William
James, and the great psychiatrist, Adolf Meyer.
In fact, it was the latter who suggested the term
mental hygiene as the appropriate name for the
movement about to be launched to educate the
people in an understanding of mental illness and
away from the prevalent attitudes of fear and
horror. The first Society for Mental Hygiene was
founded in 1908; later this local society developed into the National Committee for Mental
Hygiene. Under the energetic leadership of
Clifford Beers, this movement became world
wide, and in 1919 the International Committee
for Mental Hygiene was formed. The mental-
hygiene movement has played an important
role in the development of modern psychiatry.
However, we are getting ahead of our story.

Emergence of Scientific Theories and Practices

With the emergence of modern experimental science, tremendous advances were made in psychiatric theory and practice. These may be conveniently thought of as centering around the development of organic, psychological, and sociological viewpoints—eventually culminating in the holistic viewpoint.

DEVELOPMENT OF THE ORGANIC VIEWPOINT

From the early part of the eighteenth century, knowledge of anatomy, physiology, neurology, chemistry, and general medicine increased rapidly. These advances led to the gradual uncovering of organic pathology underlying many physical ailments, and it was only another step for these early workers to look upon mental illness as a definite sickness based upon organic brain pathology. This concept of mental illness is called the *organic viewpoint;* it represents the first great advance of modern science in the understanding and treatment of mental illness.

As early as 1757, Albrecht von Haller (1708-1777) in his *Elements of Physiology* emphasized the importance of the brain in psychic functions and advocated studying the brains of the insane by post-mortem dissection. The first systematic presentation of the organic viewpoint, however, was made by the German psychiatrist William Griesinger (1817-1868). In his textbook, *The Pathology and Therapy of Psychic Disorders,* published in 1845, Griesinger insisted that psychiatry should proceed on a physiological and clinical basis and emphasized his belief that all mental illness could be explained on the basis of brain pathology.

Although the work of Griesinger received considerable attention, it was his follower, Emil Kraepelin (1856-1926), who played the dominant role in the establishment of the organic viewpoint. Kraepelin, whose textbook *Lehrbuch der Psychiatrie* was published in 1883, not only emphasized the importance of brain pathology in mental illness but also made several related contributions which helped establish this viewpoint. The most important of these was his system of classification. Kraepelin noted that certain groups of symptoms of mental illness occurred together with sufficient regularity to be regarded as specific types of mental disease, in much the same way that we think of measles, smallpox, and other distinct physical ailments. He then proceeded to describe and clarify these types of mental disorders, working out the scheme of classification which is the basis of our present categories. The integration of the clinical material underlying this classification was a herculean task and represented a major contribution to the growing field of psychiatry.

Kraepelin looked upon each type of mental illness as separate and distinct from the others, and thought that its course was as predetermined and predictable as the course of measles. Such conclusions led to widespread interest in the accurate description and classification of mental disorders, for by this means the outcome of a given type of mental illness could presumably be predicted even if it could not yet be controlled.

The subsequent period in psychiatry, during which description and classification were so heavily emphasized, has been referred to as the "descriptive era." During this period tremendous strides were being made in the study of the nervous system by such now famous men as Golgi, Ramón y Cajal, Broca, Jackson, and Head, and the brain pathology underlying many mental disorders was gradually being uncovered. The syphilitic basis of general paresis (syphilis of the brain) was finally established as the result of the brilliant contributions of a series of medical scientists. Similarly, the brain pathology in cerebral arteriosclerosis and in the senile psychoses was established by Alzheimer and other investigators. One success was followed by another, and eventually the organic pathology underlying the toxic psychoses, certain types of mental retardation, and other "organically" caused mental illness was discovered.

These discoveries were not made overnight but resulted from the combined efforts of many scientists. For example, at least ten different steps can be traced in the discovery of the organic pathology underlying general paresis and the development of appropriate therapy. Prior to this discovery, organic pathology had been suspected in many mental disorders but had not been demonstrated systematically and completely enough to allow for effective therapy. The sequence of events in this long search shows graphically the way in which scientists working independently can utilize research by others in the field in advancing knowledge bit by bit and developing a theory that will fit all the known facts. The major steps involved were:

1. Differentiation of general paresis as a specific type of mental illness by the Frenchman A. L. J. Bayle in 1825. Bayle gave a very complete and accurate description of the symptom pattern and convincingly presented his reasons for believing paresis to be a separate type of mental illness.

2. Report by Esmarch and Jessen in 1857 of cases of paresis who were known to have had syphilis and their conclusion that the syphilis caused the paresis.

3. Description by the Scotchman Argyll-Robertson in 1869 of the failure of the pupillary reflex to light (failure of the pupil of the eye to narrow under bright light) as diagnostic of the involvement of the central nervous system in syphilis.

4. Experiment by the Viennese psychiatrist Richard Krafft-Ebing in 1897, involving the inoculation of paretic patients with matter from syphilitic sores. None of the patients developed the secondary symptoms of syphilis, which led to the conclusion that they must previously have been infected. This was a crucial experiment which definitely established the relationship of general paresis to syphilis.

5. Discovery of the *Spirochaeta pallida* by Schaudinn in 1905 as the cause of syphilis.

6. Development by von Wassermann in 1906 of a blood test for syphilis. Now it became possible to check for the presence of the deadly spirochetes in the blood stream of a man who would not otherwise realize he was infected.

7. Application by Plant in 1908 of the Was-sermann test to the cerebrospinal fluid, to indicate whether or not the spirochete had invaded the patient's central nervous system.

8. Development by Paul Ehrlich in 1909, after 605 failures, of the arsenical salvarsan (which he thereupon called "606") for the treatment of syphilis. Although "606" proved effective in killing the syphilitic spirochetes in the blood stream, it was not effective against the spirochetes which had penetrated into the central nervous system.

9. Verification by Noguchi and Moore in 1913 of the syphilitic spirochete as the brain-damaging agent in general paresis. They discovered these spirochetes in the post-mortem study of the brains of patients who had suffered from paresis.

10. Introduction in 1917 by Julius Wagner-Jauregg, chief of the psychiatric clinic of the University of Vienna, of the malarial fever treatment of syphilis and paresis. He inoculated nine of the paretic patients in his clinic with the blood of a soldier who was ill with malaria and found marked improvement in three patients and apparent recovery in three of the others.

Thus the organic brain pathology underlying one of the most serious mental disorders was uncovered and scientific measures for its treatment developed. True, the complete understanding of paresis—why one patient becomes expansive and another depressed with the same general organic brain pathology—involves an understanding of certain psychological concepts yet to be discussed. Also, of course, progress in treatment has continued, and penicillin has become the preferred method of treatment, avoiding the complications of malaria. But the steps outlined above show the way in which, *for the first time in all history, a clear-cut conquest of a mental disorder was made by medical science.* And this had been one of the most serious of all mental illnesses, for prior to the development of fever therapy, the result of paresis had been a general mental and physical deterioration, ending in the patient's death in from two to five years.

These discoveries of the brain damage underlying paresis and certain other types of mental illness were greatly encouraging to the early investigators, and it is not surprising that during the early part of the twentieth century, the great majority of medical men accepted the organic point of view and were convinced that some underlying organic pathology of the brain or nervous system must be the cause of all mental illness.

So impetus was given to intensive research in anatomy, physiology, biochemistry, neurology, and other allied medical fields in an attempt to isolate the brain pathology presumably underlying the various other types of mental illness. Such researches are still under way, based now upon the holistic rather than the organic viewpoint, and have led to the gradual delineation of the various organic psychoses; to most remarkable advances in treatment, which we shall presently discuss; and to a better understanding of the role of organic factors in all human behavior, both normal and abnormal.

Let us pause for a moment, then, to examine the important advances that had been made in psychiatry up to the year 1915, which we may set as the last year that psychiatric theory and practice were to be almost completely dominated by the organic viewpoint.

1. The early concepts of demonology had finally been destroyed, and the organic viewpoint of mental illness as based upon brain pathology was well established.

2. For general paresis and certain other mental disorders, definite underlying brain pathology had been discovered and appropriate methods of treatment developed.

3. Mental illness had finally been put on an equal footing with physical illness, at least in medical circles, and for the first time the mentally ill were receiving humane treatment based upon scientific medical findings.

4. A workable, though not yet completely satisfactory, scheme of classification had been set up.

5. A great deal of research was under way in anatomy, physiology, biochemistry, and other allied medical sciences in an attempt to ascertain the brain pathology (or other bodily pathology which might be affecting the brain) in other types of mental illness and to clarify the role of organic processes in all behavior.

6. Emphasis had finally been placed upon the importance of public education for the understanding, early detection, and prevention of mental illness.

These were truly remarkable achievements and represented the first great breakthrough in modern psychiatry.

DEVELOPMENT OF THE PSYCHOLOGICAL VIEWPOINT

Despite the great advances that had been made by the organic approach, there still remained many extremely puzzling aspects of this problem of mental illness. For one thing, repeated clinical examinations and research studies failed to reveal any organic pathology in over one half of the patients. True, a given patient might show some minor deviation in bodily chemistry, but then so did a great many normal people; furthermore, many other patients with the same symptoms of psychic disorder did not show the same organic deviation.

To some scientists this was only a challenge to intensify their research, for they felt certain that organic pathology must be there and that refinement of their laboratory techniques would reveal it. Other workers, however, became discouraged and decided that a disordered mind was lost forever. Many of the latter workers justified their conclusions by falling back upon a *hereditary approach,* assuming that mental disease represented a genetic deficiency which could not as yet be understood and about which nothing could be done.

As early as the turn of the twentieth century, however, a new current of psychiatric thought had been emerging and challenging the dominance of the belief in brain pathology as the sole cause of mental illness. This was the "revolutionary" view that certain types of mental illness might be caused by *psychological* rather than organic factors.

According to this new view, the frustrations and conflicts common to everyday living might become so overwhelming that the individual would resort to the use of unhealthy responses in his efforts to adjust. For example, the individual who felt he had failed miserably in life might become chronically discouraged and depressed, or he might project the blame for his difficulties onto other people who were supposedly working against him. In other instances, the individual might simply have learned patterns of behavior—such as irrational fears or phobias —which were maladaptive. Presumably the accumulation of such faulty response patterns could lead to more extreme types of abnormal behavior. Thus mental disorders might result from faulty learning or from the use of unhealthy reactions to everyday problems of adjustment.

It might at first be assumed that the role of these psychological factors in mental illness would have been already discovered and formulated by psychologists. But this was not the case. In 1900, psychology as an accepted science was still in its infancy, its inception dating back only some twenty-one years to the establishment of the first experimental psychology laboratory at the University of Leipzig in 1879 by Wilhelm Wundt. In addition, early psychology was rather naïve in its approach to an understanding of human behavior and consisted primarily of experimental studies of the physiology of sense perception. True, William James (1890) had published his monumental work, *Principles of Psychology,* in which he attempted to explain emotion, memory, reasoning, habits, consciousness of self, hysteria, and other aspects of human behavior. However, he was handicapped because little experimental work had been done in these areas, and his brief allusions to abnormal behavior were mainly descriptive and speculative.

This is not to disparage the contributions of the early workers who helped psychology through its infant period or to minimize the importance of physiological studies as a foundation for what came next. The fact remains, however, that psychology was still in its early stages; and there was little systematic knowledge regarding the role of psychological processes in adaptive behavior.

Mesmerism. Strangely enough, we find the origin of the psychological point of view in a somewhat unexpected place—in the study of hypnosis, especially in its relation to hysteria. Our story begins with one of the most notorious figures in psychiatry, Anton Mesmer (1734-1815), who further developed Paracelsus' notion of the influence of the planets on the human body. Their influence was believed to be caused by a universal magnetic fluid, and it was the distribution of this fluid in the body that presumably determined health or disease. In attempting to find a cure for mental disorders, Mesmer came to the conclusion that all persons possess magnetic forces which can be used to influence the distribution of the magnetic fluid in other persons, thus effecting cures.

Mesmer attempted to put his theory into practice in Vienna and in various other towns, but it was not until he came to Paris in 1778 that he achieved success. Here he opened a clinic in which he treated all kinds of diseases by "animal magnetism." The patients were seated around a tub (the *baquet*) that contained various chemicals and from which protruded iron rods which were applied to the portions of the body affected; the room was darkened, appropriate music was provided, and Mesmer appeared in a lilac robe, passing from one patient to another and touching each one with his hands or his wand. By this means Mesmer was apparently able to remove hysterical anesthesias and paralyses and to demonstrate most of the phenomena discovered later by the use of hypnosis.

Finally branded as a charlatan by his medical colleagues, Mesmer was forced to leave Paris and shortly faded into obscurity. However, his methods and results were the center of controversy in scientific circles for many years—in fact, mesmerism in the early part of the nineteenth century was as much a source of heated discussion as psychoanalysis was to be in the early part of the twentieth century. This discussion eventually led to a revival of interest in the hypnotic phenomenon as itself an explanation of the cures that took place. James Braid in England, for example, concluded that the removal of hysterical anesthesias and paralyses, which had been ascribed to the action of magnetism, was actually due to the suggestive effect of ideas aroused in the patient's mind by the doctor's words and gestures. Braid referred to these effects of suggestion as "hypnotism" and explained them in purely psychological terms. Investigation of hypnotism lagged after the time of Braid, but during the latter part of the nineteenth century, hypnosis was used more or less successfully by some physicians in their medical practice.

The Nancy school. One of the most successful of these physicians was the Frenchman Liébeault (1823-1904), who practiced at Nan-

At first Charcot strongly opposed the view that hysterical ailments could be directly caused by psychological factors. As a result of extensive study, however, he later reversed his position. He is shown above conducting a demonstration in one of his classes.

cy. Also in Nancy at this time was a professor of medicine, Bernheim (1840-1919), who became interested in the relationship between hysteria and hypnosis primarily as a result of Liébeault's success in curing by hypnosis a patient whom Bernheim had been unsuccessfully treating by more conventional methods for some four years (Selling, 1943). Bernheim and Liébeault worked together on the problem and developed the concept that hypnotism and hysteria were related and that both were due to suggestion (Brown and Menninger, 1940). Their theory was based upon two lines of evidence: (a) phenomena observed in hysteria, such as paralysis of an arm, inability to hear, anesthetic areas in which the individual could be stuck with a pin without feeling pain—all of which occurred when there was apparently nothing organically wrong with the patient—could be produced in normal subjects by means of hypnosis; and (b) symptoms such as these could be removed in hysterical subjects by means of hypnosis so that the patient could use his arm, or hear, or feel in the previously anesthetized areas. Thus

it seemed likely that hysteria was a sort of self-hypnosis. The physicians who accepted this view were known as the Nancy school.

Meanwhile, Jean Charcot (1825-1893), who was head of the Salpêtrière Hospital in Paris and the leading neurologist of his time, had been experimentally investigating some of the phenomena described by the old mesmerists. As a result of his research, Charcot disagreed with the findings of Bernheim and Liébeault and insisted that there were factors of an organic degenerative nature in hysteria in addition to suggestion. In this Charcot proved to be wrong, but work on the problem by so outstanding a scientist did much to awaken medical and scientific interest.

In one of the major medical debates of history, in which many harsh words were used on both sides, the viewpoint of the Nancy school finally triumphed. The recognition of one psychologically caused mental illness spurred research, and it was not long before the role of psychological factors in morbid anxiety, phobias, and other mental illnesses was being uncovered. Eventually Charcot himself, a man of great scientific honesty, was won over to the new point of view, and subsequently did much to promote an understanding of the role of psychological factors in various mental disorders. Pierre Janet (1859-1947) was another Frenchman whose extensive research on hysteria further served to popularize the psychological viewpoint. He also worked out a psychological theory of psychoneurosis which, though not accepted today, was a great step forward. He believed that a certain level of psychological tension was necessary for adequate unification and integration of mental processes, and that as a consequence of nervous exhaustion this energy level could be lowered to the point where mental synthesis would be disrupted and neurotic symptoms might appear.

Toward the end of the nineteenth century, then, it was clear to many that there were mental disorders with a psychological as well as an organic basis, but one major question still remained to be answered: How do these psychologically caused mental illnesses come about?

Psychoanalytic thought and its offshoots. The first steps toward an understanding of psychodynamics came about through the astounding contributions of one man—Sigmund Freud (1856-1939). Freud was a brilliant young Viennese physician who at first specialized in neurology and received an appointment as lecturer on nervous diseases at the University of Vienna. On one occasion, however, he introduced to his audience a psychoneurotic patient suffering from a persistent headache and mistakenly diagnosed the case as chronic localized meningitis. As a result of this error in diagnosis, he lost his job, although, as he pointed out in his autobiography, greater authorities than he were in the habit of diagnosing neurasthenia as cerebral tumor. Freud went to Paris in 1885 to study under Charcot, and later became acquainted with the work of Liébeault and Bernheim at Nancy. He was greatly impressed by their use of hypnosis on hysterical patients and came away convinced that powerful mental processes may remain hidden from consciousness.

On his return to Vienna, Freud worked in collaboration with an older physician, Joseph Breuer, who had introduced an interesting innovation in the use of hypnosis on his neurotic patients, chiefly women. He let the patient under hypnosis talk about her problems and tell what had oppressed her. The patient usually talked rather freely under these circumstances, displayed considerable emotion, and on wakening from the hypnotic state felt considerably relieved. Because of the regular discharge of emotions, this method was called the "cathartic method." This simple innovation in the use of hypnosis proved to be of great significance, for not only did it help the patient to discharge her emotional tensions by discussion of her problems, but it revealed the nature of the difficulties which had brought about her neurotic symptoms. The patient saw no relationship between her problems and her hysterical symptoms but the therapist could usually see it quite readily.

Thus was made the discovery of the "unconscious"—the realization of the important role played by unconscious processes in the determination of behavior. In 1893, Freud and Breuer published their joint paper *On the Psychical Mechanisms of Hysterical Phenomena* which constituted one of the great milestones of psychodynamics.

Freud soon discovered, moreover, that he could dispense with the hypnotic state entirely. For by encouraging the patient to say freely whatever came into her mind without regard to logic or decency, Freud found that she would eventually overcome inner obstacles to remembering and would discuss her problem freely. The new method was called *free association,* and the term *psychoanalysis* was given to the principles involved in analyzing and interpreting what the patient said and did, and in helping her to gain insight and achieve a more adequate adjustment.

Freud devoted the remainder of his long and energetic life to the development and elaboration of psychoanalytic doctrines.[1] In the present context it must suffice to point out the direct effects of Freud's concepts on the development of the psychological viewpoint in relation to mental illness. It may be noted that it was not only his specific findings and concepts but his general dynamic orientation which proved so significant in implementing and expanding this viewpoint.

1.   The development of techniques—free

---

[1] Psychoanalytic and other major personality theories are discussed in some detail in the Appendix.

association and dream analysis—for becoming acquainted with both conscious and unconscious aspects of the mental life of the patient. The data thus obtained led Freud to emphasize (a) the dynamic role of unconscious processes in determining behavior, (b) the importance of early childhood experiences in later personality adjustment and maladjustment, and (c) the importance of sexual factors in mental illness. Although Freud used the term *sex* in a much broader sense than it is ordinarily used, the idea caught the popular fancy, and the role of sexual factors in human behavior was finally brought out into the open and made the subject of scientific study.

2. The demonstration that abnormal mental phenomena were simply exaggerations of normal phenomena, and that the patient's symptoms represented the outcome of his attempts to meet his problems as best he could. The gap between normal and abnormal behavior was thus bridged at last. With the realization that the same fundamental psychological principles are basic to both, much of the mystery and fear surrounding mental illness was dispelled, and the mental patient was thus helped to regain his human dignity. These concepts are the basis of modern psychopathology.

3. The development of a therapeutic technique—psychoanalysis—for the psychological treatment of the mentally ill. Psychoanalytic therapy is an intensive and long-range therapeutic program which attempts a restructuring of the patient's personality in the direction of greater integration and more effective methods of coping with life's problems.

4. The development of a dynamic and systematic theoretical framework which recognized the role of biological, psychological, and social factors in personality development and functioning. Particular emphasis was given here to conflicts arising within the individual as a result of social demands and prohibitions which are incompatible with the individual's basic biological needs. The comprehensive nature of psychoanalytic theory made possible the integration of material from various research areas (notably physiology, neurology, psychology, sociology, and anthropology) which, in turn, led eventually to *the holistic approach*—the consideration of man as a unified organism.

Psychoanalysis was formally introduced to America's scientists in 1909, when Freud, together with his disciple C. G. Jung, delivered a now-famous series of lectures at Clark University, Worcester, Massachusetts, at the invitation of G. Stanley Hall, the eminent American psychologist who was then president of the University. These *Introductory Lectures on Psychoanalysis* led to a great deal of controversy which helped to publicize the concepts of psychoanalysis to both scientists and the general public.

Freud's path was not an easy one, and for many years he worked alone in the face of great opposition. In England and America his theories received widespread criticism and condemnation by psychologists and psychiatrists alike. In fact, the English-speaking world did not take official cognizance of Freud until he was close to death. In 1936, on his eightieth birthday, he was elected an honorary member of the American Psychiatric Association, and in 1939, during his last illness, he was apprised of his election as a Foreign Fellow in the Royal Society (Zilboorg and Henry, 1941).

As Freud's work gradually received recognition, an increasing number of now well-known names appeared among his special students and supporters. As early as 1906 the great Swiss psychiatrist, E. Bleuler, who is remembered for his epoch-making discoveries on the dynamics of schizophrenia, had become interested in Freud's ideas (Bleuler, 1912). In 1910 Freud, Bleuler, and Jung founded the International Psychoanalytic Association, which played an important role in the development and dissemination of psychoanalytic doctrines (Zilboorg and Henry, 1941).

In the course of time some of these students found themselves in serious disagreement with various aspects of Freud's system and set up modified systems of their own. Among the more prominent of the dissenters were C. G. Jung and Alfred Adler, who both left Freud in 1911.

Jung thought that Freud overemphasized the importance of sexual factors in motivation and neuroses; accordingly, he developed his own systematic approach—the Zurich school of Analytic Psychology. Jung's personality theory is comprehensive in scope and different in many fundamental respects from psychoanalytic theory. Three of its most distinctive concepts are the "collective unconscious," "inner self experience," and "psychological types."

In addition to the personal unconscious—consisting of the individual's experiences which once were conscious but have been forgotten, suppressed, or repressed—Jung believed that the individual also has a collective unconscious consisting of "racial" memories established through the thousands of years of man's existence and inherited in the brain structure in the form of "primordial images" or "archetypes." An archetype is a universal image or idea which contains a large element of emotion and is elicited by some aspect of the individual's life situation. Thus the archetype of the mother, the primordial image of the mother figure, is elicited by the child's own mother. Such "collective" memories were used by Jung to account for similarities in folklore, symbols, and other aspects of culture found among diverse peoples throughout the world.

In emphasizing the importance of inner self experience, Jung held that everything within the unconscious seeks outward manifestation, and that the individual achieves true "wholeness" only as fantasies, images, and dreams from the personal and racial unconscious become accessible to the conscious self. When he is cut off or alienated from his unconscious, it may erupt into consciousness, taking various irrational forms such as phobias, delusions, and hallucinations.

Perhaps Jung's most popular, although not his most valuable, contribution was his distinction between *extrovert* and *introvert* personality types, a distinction which has been of practical value in our understanding of adjustive behavior. Jung devoted many active years to research into the deep-lying processes of the human personality and is acknowledged to have been one of the most profound thinkers of the twentieth century.

Alfred Adler developed the school of Individual Psychology, which holds that man is inherently a social being and that his most basic motivation is to belong to and participate in the group. Adler did not submerge the individual in the group, however; on the contrary he emphasized an active, creative "self" that plays a central role in the individual's attempts to organize his experiences and fulfill himself as a human being. The individual personality is unique and each person develops a "style of life" which reflects his basic pattern of motives, values, and action patterns. Inferiority feelings arise whenever the individual feels a sense of incompleteness or lack of fulfillment in any life area. Such inferiority feelings are normal driving forces which push him toward improvement and superiority. Inferiority feelings, however, may be exaggerated into an *inferiority complex* which leads to unhealthy overcompensation. Thus the neurotic person may strive for power and self-aggrandizement in order to compensate for underlying feelings of inadequacy and inferiority. Out of such concepts Adler fashioned a humanistic view of man's nature emphasizing tendencies toward "social interest" and self-direction—a view directly in contrast to Freud's more gloomy concept of man's irrationality and continual battle with his socially disapproved instincts.

Others of Freud's students and followers stayed more within the general theoretical framework developed by Freud, further elaborating and modifying established psychoanalytic doctrine. It has been these men and women, both American and European, who have played the prominent role in shaping psychoanalytic thought. Here we find such well-known names as Karl Abraham, Franz Alexander, A. A. Brill, S. E. Jellife, Otto Fenichel, Anna Freud, Frieda Fromm-Reichmann, H. Hartman, David Rapaport, William A. White, and the Menningers.

Freud's theories met opposition, criticism, and sometimes violent condemnation because of their conflict with religious ideas and because of Freud's emphasis on sexual factors in mental illness, his failure to give adequate consideration to cultural differences in personality development, and the lack of rigorous experimental verification of his clinical concepts. But despite the opposition, and despite the fact that many of his concepts have had to be rejected or revised in the light of later findings, his ideas have made themselves felt with tremendous force throughout the world, and his influence has probably been greater than that of any other man in the shaping of modern psychiatric and psychological thought.

Experimental neuroses. Another major contribution to the establishment of the psychological viewpoint stems from the work of the great Russian physiologist, Ivan Pavlov (1849-1936). While performing a series of studies on the salivary response in dogs, Pavlov discovered the phenomenon of the "conditioned reflex" which was to become a fundamental concept in modern psychology. In 1914, while pursuing the study of conditioned reflexes in dogs, one of Pavlov's students reported an unusual and dramatic incident. He had conditioned a dog to distinguish between a circle and an ellipse. The ellipse was then altered in shape so that it became more and more like the circle, until the dog could no longer distinguish accurately between the two. During three weeks of subsequent experimentation, the dog's ability to discriminate between the two similar figures not only failed to improve, but became considerably worse, and finally disappeared altogether. At the same time the behavior of the dog underwent an abrupt change. The previously quiet and cooperative animal began to squeal and squirm in its stand and tore off the experimental apparatus with its teeth. In addition, when taken into the experimental room, the dog now barked violently, instead of going quietly as it had before. On testing, even the cruder differentiations between the circle and the ellipse which the dog had previously mastered could not be elicited. This change in the dog's behavior was considered by Pavlov to be equivalent to an acute neurosis (Pavlov, 1927).

Following this initial lead, later investigators have conducted similar experiments with rats, cats, dogs, sheep, pigs, monkeys and chimpanzees with comparable results. When the animals were forced by the experimental conditions to make discriminations which were beyond their capacities, they seemed to suffer the equivalent of a "nervous breakdown"—usually referred to as an "experimental neurosis."

Thus an unusual incident in laboratory routine, which might have been overlooked as merely trivial and annoying by a less astute observer than Pavlov, led to a whole new method of attack in the study of abnormal behavior. On the basis of subsequent experimental findings, Pavlov went on, after the age of eighty, to attempt a rather comprehensive formulation of human psychopathology (Pavlov, 1941). This formulation was based on the assumption that the different reaction patterns shown by dogs to the conditioned-reflex techniques would be reflected on the human level, also, in reactions to life stresses. Among dogs Pavlov had found three general reaction, or constitutional, types: an excitatory group, an inhibitory group, and a central group. Each reaction type was found to develop a somewhat different kind of experimental neurosis. For example, when an animal of the excitatory type was forced beyond the limits of his discriminatory ability, he developed periods of depression or excitement comparable to manic-depressive reactions in humans. Under similar conditions, the inhibitory type developed schizophrenic-like reactions, whereas the central group developed what appeared to be mixed reactions.

In applying these findings to human beings, Pavlov made certain modifications in order to take into account the factor of language. Thus he distinguished two personality types: (a) the artistic type, intense, vivid, and highly responsive to external stimulation, and (b) the thinking type, quiet, ruminative, and responsive to verbal concepts and ideas rather than to sensory stimulation. In the event of mental illness, the artistic type would presumably be prone to hysterical and manic-depressive reactions, while the thinking type would be more prone to obsessive-compulsive and schizophrenic reactions.

Although Pavlov's concept of reaction types is still undergoing evaluation (Wortis, 1962), his conditioning techniques and concepts of excitation and inhibition have paved the way for a vast amount of experimental work—particularly on the role of learning in maladjustment.

Behaviorism. Pavlov's principle of conditioning was seized upon by an American psychologist, J. B. Watson (1919, 1924), as a procedure for studying human behavior more objectively and avoiding the pitfalls of introspection implicit in psychoanalytic theory. Combining the principle of conditioning with certain ideas of his own, Watson formulated a point of view which he called "behaviorism." As might be expected, this approach placed heavy emphasis upon the role of the social environment in "conditioning" personality development and upon the importance of assessing the effects of given stimuli upon learning and behavior.

Watson used the conditioning technique in a dramatic demonstration of the role of learning in *abnormal* behavior. In his famous experiment with little Albert, an eleven-month-old boy who was fond of animals, Watson demonstrated the learning of an irrational fear or phobia through simple conditioning. His procedure was simple: he stood behind the boy and struck a steel bar with a hammer whenever Albert reached for the animal. The loud noise elicited a fear response on the boy's part and made him cry. After several repetitions of this experience Albert became greatly disturbed at the sight of a white rat even without the loud noise, and his fear spread to include other furry animals and objects as well. Watson's demonstration of the development and spread of this irrational fear suggested that other types of abnormal behavior might also be the result of learning (Watson and Rayner, 1920).

Following the lead of Pavlov and Watson, many psychologists have utilized conditioning techniques for the study of learning and have evolved a cluster of somewhat divergent viewpoints known as *behavior* or *learning theory*.[1] And on the assumption that both normal and abnormal behavior are at least in part a product of learning and subject to the same principles, some experimenters have applied learning theory concepts directly to a study of the development and alleviation of psychopathology. Such studies have contributed greatly to our understanding of abnormal behavior, and a number of them will be referred to at later points in our discussion.

Self theory. In his *Principles of Psychology,* published in 1890, William James had a famous chapter on the concept of *self* which set the stage for later contemporary theorizing. In his discussion, James viewed the self much as we do today: (a) the self as object—the individual's perception and evaluation of himself as an object, and (b) the self as process—as a reference point and integrative center for evaluating new experiences and coordinating adjustive behavior.

Both Jung and Adler emphasized the concept of a creative self striving toward wholenss and fulfillment, and the social psychologist George Mead (1934) elaborated on the social origins of self and the importance of the self-concept in understanding human behavior. The advent of behaviorism, however, with its emphasis on stimulus and response and disregard for cognitive processes, diverted attention for a time from the study of the self. Eventually it became apparent that psychologists were losing sight of a crucial process in human experience and behavior, and the self again became a reputable subject for scientific inquiry.

Currently there are two mainstreams in self theory: existentialism and client-centered psychology. In contrast to Freud's essentially deterministic view of the individual as the prisoner of primitive urges, mental mechanisms, and past experiences, the existentialists view the individual as essentially free with the capability of finding and being himself and taking responsibility for his own existence. To flee from this freedom and responsibility or to be unable to find a meaningful and fulfilling way of life is to experience existential frustration, anxiety, and despair—in extreme form, to become neurotic or psychotic.

The most clearly worked out and systematized self theory is the client-centered psychology of Carl Rogers (1951, 1959, 1961), which is based largely on his pioneering research into the nature of the psychotherapeutic process. Rogers' approach (a) views the individual as having one basic striving—to maintain and actualize himself, (b) is phenomenological in character—emphasizing that the individual always reacts to situations in terms of *his* unique perceptions of himself and his world, (c) assumes that most of the individual's reactions are consistent with his self-concept, (d) emphasizes the self as the unifying and directing force in behavior, and (e) stresses man's potential for self-growth and fulfillment. Experiences which are perceived as incongruent and devaluating to the self are seen as threats; they arouse anxiety and force the self to undertake defensive measures. If the self cannot defend itself against such threats—particularly those relating to adequacy and worth—the result is disintegration and catastrophic psychological breakdown.

---

[1]Distinguished American psychologists who have contributed to the development and extension of learning theory include E. C. Tolman, E. R. Guthrie, Clark Hull, R. R. Sears, B. F. Skinner, J. Dollard, N. E. Miller, and O. H. Mowrer.

We have traced the development of the psychological viewpoint on into contemporary psychological theory. For the moment, let us retrace our steps and note that although by the onset of World War I the psychological dynamics in hysteria and other mental disorders had been worked out, the battle for the psychological viewpoint had not yet been completely won. There were still strongholds of organicists who were bitterly opposed to the newer theories. During World War I, however, so many cases of psychologically induced mental illness occurred (hysteria was the most frequently occurring mental illness in the American armed forces in World War I and incapacitated almost as many men as combat wounds) that it finally came to be generally admitted, even by the most adamant, that at least certain cases of mental illness could have a psychological origin, explanation, and cure. Thus by the end of World War I the psychological viewpoint was firmly established although its particular formulations were to keep evolving and changing right up to the present time.

DEVELOPMENT OF THE SOCIOLOGICAL VIEWPOINT

By the beginning of the twentieth century, sociology and anthropology had emerged as independent scientific disciplines and were making rapid strides in understanding the role of sociocultural factors in man's development and behavior.[1] Soon it became apparent that man is almost infinitely malleable and that his personality development is largely a product of the society in which he lives—of its institutions, traditions, values, ideas, and technology—and of the specific family and other interpersonal relationships to which he is exposed. Eventually, too, it became apparent that there is a relationship between sociocultural factors and mental disorders—that the stressful social and cultural factors in a society are related to the incidence and types of mental illness that occur in it.

Gradually these sociocultural findings began to permeate psychology and psychiatry, adding a third dimension to modern thinking concerning abnormal behavior. Among the psychiatrists who early recognized these findings and were to give personality theory a new more socially oriented look were Alfred Adler, Karen Horney, Harry Stack Sullivan, and Erich Fromm. We shall examine the findings of a number of sociocultural studies in our later discussion of abnormal behavior. Suffice it for the moment to point out that with the acceptance of the sociological viewpoint, the almost exclusive concern with the individual's biological and/or psychological functioning now broadened to include a concern with the role of the family and community context and other sociocultural factors in mental disorders.

THE HOLISTIC VIEWPOINT[2]

As the research engendered by the organic, psychological, and sociological viewpoints gradually led to a better understanding of the role of these factors in mental illness, it became increasingly apparent that each was incomplete in itself. Even in the organic disorder *paresis,* the pride and joy of the organicists, it was observed that some patients became depressed and others expansive and happy with approximately the same underlying organic brain damage. Similarly, in psychoses associated with senile and arteriosclerotic brain damage, it was found that some patients became severely ill mentally with only a small amount of brain damage, whereas others showed only mild symptoms despite relatively extensive brain damage. Investigators gradually realized that the patient's psychological reaction to the brain damage and to the resulting change in his life situation was of

[1]Prominent early contributors to this field were Ruth Benedict, Ralph Linton, Abram Kardiner, Margaret Mead, and Franz Boas.

[2]The terms *holistic* and *psychosomatic* both refer to a unified view of the individual as a psychobiological organism inextricably immersed in a physical and sociocultural environment. Implied by either term is an interdisciplinary approach to both research and practice involving the application of various scientific fields and personnel to the solution of a common problem. The term *holistic* is used here in preference to *psychosomatic* because, as Karl A. Menninger (1945) has pointed out, the term *psychosomatic* tends to perpetuate the outmoded dualistic view of mind and body which is the exact opposite of what is intended. In addition, the term has often been restricted to "psychosomatic disorders"—physical illnesses such as peptic ulcers—in which emotional factors play an important role in the onset and course of physiological disorders. Here it may be emphasized that the holistic viewpoint is as applicable to "physical" as to "mental" illness—as appropriate to the field of general medicine as to psychiatry.

vital importance in determining his overall symptom pattern. It also became apparent that the emotional support of family members and the kind of family situation to which he would be returning on leaving the hospital were significant factors in determining the prognosis. Finally, in certain functional psychoses, in which the patient's illness was apparently the result of psychological rather than organic factors, it was nevertheless found that the use of organic therapies—such as electroshock and tranquilizing drugs—produced dramatic results.

Thus, with the realization that psychological and sociological factors play an important role in mental disorders formerly considered purely organic in nature, and conversely that organic processes are of significance in many functional mental disorders formerly considered purely psychological in nature, there was a fusion of organic, psychological, and sociological viewpoints into a holistic approach. From this newer point of view, every disorder becomes a medical problem, a psychological problem, and a sociological problem in diagnosis, understanding, and treatment.

In dealing with a particular disorder, of course, we may be concerned primarily with one or another aspect. But every disorder is a disorder of the whole individual and it will both affect and be affected by his life situation. What we must do is to evaluate the role of organic, psychological, and sociological factors in each case.

The fusion of the organic, psychological, and sociological viewpoints into the holistic approach was a long, hard struggle. We have mentioned the systematic contributions that psychoanalysis and several other theories made toward one or another aspect of it. In passing, we should mention also a great psychiatrist, Adolf Meyer

(1866-1950), who tirelessly promoted the holistic point of view (Lief, 1948; Bleuler, 1962). Meyer came to the United States in 1892 from Zurich and after working in several mental hospitals became a professor of psychiatry at Johns Hopkins in 1910. His broad, eclectic approach to mental illness was formulated under the heading of *psychobiology* and rests essentially on the holistic assumptions that:

1. The study of the total personality of the patient is the only basis for an understanding of his behavior.

2. The determinants of the patient's behavior are pluralistic and interactional, and all the many relevant factors—biological, psychological, sociological—must be investigated and coordinated into our understanding of the developmental pattern of mental illnesses.

Meyer's broad approach attracted a large number of outstanding students and followers including Samuel Kraines, Edward Strecker, F. G. Ebaugh, Wendell Muncie, Jules Masserman, Hardin Branch, and Roy Dorcus, to name only a few. Meyer played a prominent role in the development of American psychological and psychiatric thought and has appropriately been called the "dean of American psychiatry."

Although the holistic point of view was fairly well established in psychological and psychiatric circles prior to World War II, there were still many who were opposed to it. In much the same way that World War I established a psychological viewpoint, we find World War II establishing the holistic one. For the incidence of "psychosomatic" disorders in the form of gastrointestinal disturbances (which were the leading medical problem of World War II) as well as the problem of "combat fatigue" finally led to the realization that human behavior can be approached adequately only in this broad way.

Psychiatry Today

Psychiatry has come a long way since its hospital isolation at the turn of the twentieth century. New methods of diagnosis and treatment—biological, psychological, and sociological—have been developed. A more dynamic and

flexible classification scheme has been worked out which is useful for guiding therapy and coordinating research rather than merely pigeonholing patients in the Kraepelinian tradition. A healthy research orientation has developed which has led to many new findings and to the continual evaluation and modification of existing concepts and procedures in the light of new information. At the present time over forty scientific journals dealing with various aspects of mental illness bring the more important new findings to the attention of the various personnel in the field.

CURRENT ADVANCES AND TRENDS

A most spectacular new research development on the *biological* (organic) level has been in the field of chemotherapy—in the discovery of tranquilizing and energizing drugs which have proven highly effective in the treatment of mental disorders. These drugs have made it possible for more patients to function in the community and receive treatment outside a mental hospital setting; they have led to the earlier discharge of patients who do require hospitalization; they have reduced the severity of symptoms and made locked wards, restraint, and seclusion almost a thing of the past; and they have outmoded such drastic forms of treatment as insulin shock and psychosurgery. As R. W. White (1959) pointed out, it is interesting to reflect that Pinel's mission in striking the chains from the mentally ill is now close to its ultimate fulfillment. On the biological level we can also point to recent dramatic breakthroughs in the field of genetics and to the vigorous experimental work in neurophysiology and neurobiochemistry, which is gradually unlocking the secrets of the human brain and helping us to understand how damage to the brain or changes in bodily chemistry can lead to disturbances in our thought processes.

On the *psychological* level great advances have been made in our understanding of human nature and behavior. The old view of man's nature as basically evil and irrational is giving way to a newer view which emphasizes man's tendencies toward goodness and rationality under favorable circumstances. Many studies in the field of perception have shown the importance of the individual's "frame of reference"—the assumptions he makes about himself and his world—in determining the way he views and reacts to various types of stressful situations.

The new concepts centering around man's tendencies toward personal growth or self-fulfillment have broadened our concepts of motivation. Studies of how man learns and of the relation of learning to other psychological processes have contributed greatly to our understanding of personality development and maladjustive reactions. The delineation of "task-oriented" as contrasted with "ego defensive" reactions has proved of great value in understanding effective and ineffective behavior. Investigations dealing with conflict and other types of stress have demonstrated the relationship between severe stress and the disorganization of behavior. The reintroduction of the concept of the "self" as the core of man's psychological being, around which his attitudes and behavior are organized, has proved highly useful in understanding many facets of behavior. The application of such research findings and concepts to practical problems in personality assessment and psychotherapy has greatly increased the effectiveness of these procedures. Currently, too, there is active experimentation with "behavior therapy" —an attempt to correct maladaptive responses by applying the principles of conditioning developed in laboratory research.

Advances are also evident on the sociological level. A concept receiving increasing research emphasis is that of the "pathogenic family structure," in which unhealthy interpersonal relationships among family members foster mental disorders so that treatment of the other family members as well as of the patient may be required. Other research efforts are concerned with (a) assessing the nature and extent of mental disorders in our society, (b) ascertaining the effects of social class, cultural patterns, and other sociological factors on mental disorders, (c) a comparison of mental disorders in different societies, (d) the effect of mental disorders on society and culture as well as the effect of culture on mental illness, and (e) the concept of the mental hospital as a "therapeutic community"—a society in its own right—and the coordination of hospital and general community facilities.

From both an administrative and a sociological viewpoint, there is a movement toward establishing small community in-patient hospital facilites, perhaps as part of a general hospital, instead of large state hospitals which may have several thousand patients. Patients can go to such community hospitals more informally and for brief periods with less disruption of their lives than that caused by going to a large, distant, impersonal institution.

Coupled with these advances have been the establishment of the "team approach" involving the coordinated efforts of psychiatrists, psychologists, psychiatric social workers, and related personnel; the establishment of outpatient clinics directed toward treating the patient in his family and community setting rather than sending him to a mental hospital, often far removed from his family and ordinary life situation; the expansion of psychiatry into diverse areas of modern life including children's problems, industrial problems, and penal problems; and the application of research findings to public mental health programs.

DISAGREEMENT AND POINTS OF AGREEMENT

Despite all these advances, we still have a long way to go. There are many aspects of the dynamics of abnormal behavior which we do not fully understand, and our methods of treatment and prevention leave much to be desired. The newer drugs, useful as they are, do not represent the ultimate treatment of mental disorders, since they lead only to the alleviation and masking of symptoms. As Barsa (1960) has pointed out, the neurotic whose anxieties have been dissipated with tranquilizers still retains his unhealthy personality structure, and the schizophrenic whose delusions and hallucinations have disappeared through the influence of drugs still retains his schizophrenic make-up. In fact, R. W. White somewhat facetiously states that drugs have a curious double action— "that of calming the patient and elating the physician." (1959, p. 273) But we no longer expect that the final answers to man's problems will be found in the "test tube" alone for we realize that biological advances must be integrated with those of psychology, sociology, and allied scientific fields.

A complicating factor has been, and still is, the welter of controversy and disagreement that

has attended the gradual growth of our knowledge concerning the dynamics of human behavior. Research findings can be interpreted and organized to fit different "models" of man. Inevitably this has led to the emergence of several different "schools" of thought, such as psychoanalysis, behavior theory, and self theory.

Often the warfare among these schools has been more destructive than constructive; ultimately, of course, only new research findings can settle the points of difference. Yet a body of fundamental principles has gradually gained general acceptance. Among the more important of these fundamental points of agreement which may be said to underlie contemporary psychiatric and psychological thought are the following:

1. Acceptance of the holistic approach to the diagnosis, understanding, treatment, and prevention of mental illness.

2. Agreement that the same fundamental dynamic principles underlie both normal and abnormal behavior.

3. Emphasis on dynamics rather than symptoms. Symptoms are viewed as signs that something has gone wrong with the adjustive efforts of the individual. Although the alleviation of symptoms may be extremely important, it is usually the underlying nature and etiology of the illness rather than the symptoms *per se* which receive emphasis.

4. Agreement on the staff or "team" approach to the diagnosis, understanding, and treatment of abnormal behavior. This involves the integrated teamwork of psychiatrists, clinical psychologists, psychiatric social workers, and other specialized personnel.

5. Emphasis on the utilization of material from varied research approaches. This includes the integration and use of material from genetics, anatomy, biochemistry, neurology, physiology, psychology, sociology, anthropology, clinical medicine, and other relevant scientific disciplines.

6. Emphasis on both social and individual pathology in understanding and treating abnormal behavior and a realization that society as well as the individual may be sick.

7. Emphasis on the importance of public education and the early detection and prevention of abnormal behavior.

The preceding historical review has traced the development of modern psychiatry from its early beginnings in demonology through medieval theological concepts to the development of the organic, the psychological, and eventually the holistic point of view. Of necessity this review has been sketchy, and much interesting and relevant historical material has been omitted. However, it is hoped that the present review has broadened the reader's general perspective of abnormal behavior and has prepared him for a more adequate understanding and evaluation of the data and concepts in this dynamic, expanding field of abnormal behavior.

The task now remains of integrating the varied vocabularies, clinical data, research findings, and theoretical concepts of modern psychiatry into a meaningful and coherent picture. We shall approach this task from an eclectic point of view, and the remainder of the book will be devoted to a presentation of what seems to be the core of more generally accepted psychological and psychiatric thought on the dynamics of abnormal behavior.

REFERENCES

The reference list includes not only the sources from which the author has drawn material, but acknowledgments of the permissions granted by authors and publishers to quote directly from their works.

BARSA, J. A. Combination drug therapy in psychiatry. *Amer. J. Psychiat.*, 1960, 117, 448-449.

BARTON, W. E. Family care and outpatient psychiatry. *Amer. J. Psychiat.*, 1959, 115, 642-645.

BENNETT, A. E. Mad doctors. *J. nerv. ment. Dis.*, 1947, 106, 11-18.

BLEULER, E. *The theory of schizophrenic negativism*, William A. White (Tr.). Washington, D. C.: Nervous and Mental Disease Publishing Co., 1912.

BLEULER, M. Early Swiss sources of Adolf Meyer's concepts. *Amer. J. Psychiat.*, 1962, 119, 193-196.

BROMBERG, W. *The mind of man: the story of man's conquest of mental illness*. New York: Harper, 1937.

BROWN, J. F., & MENNINGER, K. A. *Psychodynamics of abnormal behavior*. New York: McGraw-Hill, 1940.

BROWNE, E. G. *Arabian medicine*. New York: Macmillan, 1921.

CAMPBELL, D. *Arabian medicine and its influence on the Middle Ages*. New York: Dutton, 1926.

CASTIGLIONI, A. *Adventures of the mind*. New York: Knopf, 1946.

COCKAYNE, T. O. *Leechdoms, wort cunning, and star craft of early England*. London: Longman, Green, Longman, Roberts, & Green, 1864-1866.

DEUTSCH, A. *The mentally ill in America*. New York: Columbia Univer. Press, 1946. Copyright by the American Foundation for Mental Hygiene and used with their permission.

DUMONT, M. P., & ALDRICH, C. K. Family care after a thousand years—a crisis in the tradition of St. Dymphna. *Amer. J. Psychiat.*, 1962, 119, 116-121.

GLOYNE, H. F. Tarantism: mass hysterical reaction to spider bite in the Middle Ages. *American Imago*, 1950, 7, 29-42.

GUTHRIE, D. J. *A history of medicine*. Philadelphia: Lippincott, 1946.

HEWITT, R. T. Critique of M. P. Dumont & C. K. Aldrich. Family care after a thousand years—a crisis in the tradition of St. Dymphna. *Amer. J. Psychiat.*, 1962, 119, 120-121.

JAMES, W. *The principles of psychology*, Vols. 1 & 2. New York: Holt, 1890.

KARNOSH, L. J. & ZUCKER, E. M. *Handbook of psychiatry*. St. Louis: C. V. Mosby, 1945.

KRAEPELIN, E. *Clinical psychiatry*. (2nd ed.) A. R. Diefendorf (Tr.). New York: Macmillan, 1907.

LEWIS, N. D. C. *A short history of psychiatric achievement*. New York: Norton, 1941.

LIEF, A. (Ed.) *The commonsense psychiatry of Dr. Adolf Meyer*. New Jersey: McGraw-Hill, 1948.

LOWREY, L. G. *Psychiatry for social workers*. New York: Columbia Univer. Press, 1946.

MENNINGER, K. A. *The human mind*. (3rd ed.) New York: Knopf, 1945.

MENNINGER, R. W. The history of psychiatry. *Dis. nerv. System*, 1944, 5, 52-55.

PAVLOV, I. P. *Conditioned reflexes; an investigation of the physiological activity of the cerebral cortex*, G. V. Anrep (Ed. & Tr.). London: Oxford Univer. Press, 1927.

PAVLOV, I. P. *Lectures on conditioned reflexes*. Vol. 2. *Conditioned reflexes and psychiatry*, W. H. Gantt (Ed. & tr.). New York: International Publishers, 1941.

PLATO, *The Laws*, Vol. 5. G. Burges (Tr.). London: George Bell & Sons, n. d.

ROGERS, C. R. *Client-centered therapy*. Boston: Houghton Mifflin, 1951.

ROGERS, C. R. A theory of therapy, personality, and interpersonal relationships, as developed in the client-centered framework. In S. Koch (Ed.), *Psychology: a study of a science*, Vol. 3. New York: McGraw-Hill, 1959.

ROGERS, C. R. *On becoming a person: a therapist's view of psychotherapy*. Boston: Houghton Mifflin, 1961.

RUSSELL, W. L. A psychopathic department of an American general hospital in 1808. *Amer. J. Psychiat.*, 1941, 98, 229-237.

SELLING, L. S. *Men against madness*. New York: Garden City Books, 1943.

SIGERIST, H. E. *Civilization and disease*. Ithaca, N.Y.: Cornell Univer. Press, 1943.

STONE, S. Psychiatry through the ages. *J. abnorm. soc. Psychol.*, 1937, 32, 131-160. Reprinted by permission of the American Psychological Association.

WATSON, J. B. *Psychology from the standpoint of a behaviorist*. Philadelphia: Lippincott, 1919.

WATSON, J. B. *Behaviorism*. New York: Norton, 1924.

WATSON, J. B. & RAYNER, ROSALIE. Conditioned emotional reactions. *J. exp. Psychol.*, 1920, 3, 1-14.

WHITE, A. D. *A history of the warfare of science with theology in Christendom*. New York: Appleton, 1896.

WHITE, R. W. Abnormalities of behavior. *Annu. Rev. Psychol.*, 1959, 10, 265-286.

WHITWELL, J. R. *Historical notes on psychiatry*. London: H. K. Lewis, 1936.

WORTIS, J. (Ed.) Pavlovianism and clinical psychiatry. *Recent advances in biological psychiatry*, Vol. 4. New York: Plenum Press, 1962. Pp. 13-23.

ZILBOORG, G., & HENRY, G. W. *A history of medical psychology*. New York: Norton, 1941. Reprinted by permission of W. W. Norton and Company and George Allen and Unwin, Ltd.

DYNAMICS OF NORMAL AND ABNORMAL BEHAVIOR

part two

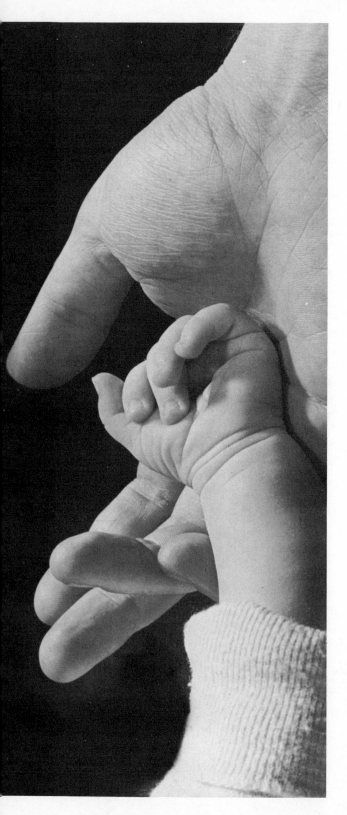

PERSONALITY DEVELOPMENT AND ADJUSTMENT

chapter 3

Why do some people become homosexuals and others heterosexuals, some alcoholics and others teetotalers, some criminals and others law-abiding citizens, some mentally ill and others well adjusted? What are the principles underlying personality development and functioning which will enable us to understand such extremes of behavior?

The answers to these questions will require a review of the influences of heredity and environment, of the role of the "ego," or "self," and of the essentials of motivation, stress, and adjustive reactions.

Determinants of Personality

The basic sources of personality development are heredity and environment. However, as our genetic inheritance interacts with and is shaped by environmental factors, a unique individual emerges who early becomes an agent in his own development.

HEREDITY

What interests us here is not the mechanics of heredity but the unique characteristics of our genetic inheritance and the ways in which they influence personality development. At conception each new individual receives a genetic endowment from his parents which provides for physical equipment—muscles, glands, sense organs, nerves, and so on—essential for his development into an adult human being. The specific characteristics of this equipment, of course, vary widely from one individual to another. Thus heredity not only provides the potentialities for development but is an important source of individual differences.

Heredity influences the determination of some traits more than others. We see its influence perhaps most clearly in physical features and in various constitutional factors such as sensitivity, vigor, vulnerability to disease, and intelligence. Even during the first few weeks of life, infants differ in "generalized sensitivity." Some startle at even slight sounds or cry if sunlight hits their faces; others are seemingly insensitive to such stimulation. Thus conditions which one baby can tolerate may be quite upsetting to another. Differences in physical vigor predispose some infants to energetic activity and self-assertion; others are more passive and prone to fantasy pursuits. Similarly, some infants react to sudden changes in routine by developing a fever; others develop a digestive disorder, a skin irritation, or a sleeping disturbance. Presumably, the most vulnerable bodily system is the first to develop "symptoms" if the overall functioning of the organism is disturbed.

Genetic factors may also lower the individual's resistance to physical diseases, such as tuberculosis and cancer, as well as to various mental disorders.

Probably the most unique aspect of man's inheritance is his superior brain. It has been described as the most highly organized apparatus in the universe. It consists of some 10 billion nerve cells, or *neurons,* with countless interconnecting fibers as well as generous connections with the other parts of the body, thus producing a fantastic communication network with tremendous capabilities for integrating the overall functioning of the human organism, for interpreting and "storing" new experience, and for reasoning, imagining, and problem solving. As with other constitutional traits, individuals vary widely in intellectual level.

Through such constitutional differences, heredity appears to be an important factor in providing basic equipment for development and in determining how the individual reacts to his environment and thus how it influences his development.

ENVIRONMENT

Our psychobiological development is constantly being shaped by forces in our environment. Different *physical* environments foster somewhat different characteristics, even among people with similar inheritance. Each setting is unique in its constellation of favorable and unfavorable conditions and in the special demands it makes on organisms living within it.

Our *sociocultural* environment influences our development even more dramatically. Through our contacts with it we learn the language we speak, the customs we follow, the values we believe in, and the competencies necessary for dealing with life problems.

Each group of people fosters its own cultural patterns by the systematic teaching of the younger members of the group. Such practices tend to make all members of the group somewhat alike, or as Linton (1945) has put it, to establish "the basic personality types." Individuals reared among head-hunters will become head-hunters; individuals reared in societies which do not sanction violence will settle their differences in nonviolent ways. In New Guinea two tribes of similar racial origin, living in the same general geographical area, were found to have developed diametrically opposed characteristics: the Arapesh were a kindly, peaceful, cooperative people; the Mundungumor were warlike, suspicious, competitive, and vengeful. Such differences are clearly social in origin (Mead, 1949).

The more uniform and thorough the education of the younger members, the more alike they will become. Thus in a society where children meet a limited and consistent point of view, we do not find the wide individual differences typical in a society like ours, where children have contact with many divergent beliefs and values.

Besides participating in a general sociocultural environment, we are members of subgroups existing within it, such as family, sex, age, social class, occupational, and religious groups. Each of these subgroups fosters its own values and ways of behavior—largely by means of establishing *social roles* which its members learn to adopt. Men are expected to behave and dress in certain ways identified as "masculine." In our society this usually includes preparing for an occupation, taking the initiative in courtship, and supporting one's family. The masculine role does not permit the wearing of nail polish or lipstick or other actions which are regarded as feminine.

Similarly, we could delineate the role behavior expected of the army officer, the minister, and the members of different age and religious groups. And because any individual is a member of various subgroups, he is subject to various role expectations. When his social roles are conflicting or when any role is unclear or uncomfortable, his personality development may be handicapped.

In addition to his group memberships, each individual is exposed to various interpersonal relationships beginning with the members of his family and gradually extending to his peer group and the other important people in his world. Much of his personality development reflects his experiences with these key people. For example, the child who is rejected and mistreated by his parents is likely to develop differently from the one who is accepted and encouraged. Similarly, the values and behavior patterns children learn depend heavily upon whether their parents are mature or impulsive, selfish or considerate, tolerant or bigoted, spiritually or materialistically oriented.

Since each individual belongs to a somewhat unique pattern of subgroups and experiences a unique pattern of interpersonal relationships, he participates in the sociocultural environment in an individual way. As a consequence of such "differential participation," no two of us live in quite the same world. Thus the sociocultural environment is the source of differences as well as commonalities in personality development.

In summary so far, we may say that our genetic endowment provides the essential basis and sets the limits for both physical and psychological development, but the shaping of our potentialities into actualities depends on our physical and sociocultural environment.

SELF (EGO)

As the infant grows and learns to distinguish between himself and other people and things, a part of his total perceptual field gradually becomes delineated as the "me," "I," "ego," or "self."[1] As this *self-structure* emerges, it becomes the essential integrating core of his personality—the reference point around which his experiences and reaction patterns are organized.[2]

---

[1] In the present discussion we are using the concepts of the *ego* and *self* as synonymous. Many social scientists make various distinctions between them. An excellent summary of pertinent research literature relating to the self-concept may be found in Wylie (1961). The term *self* or *self-concept* is often used in reference to the way the individual views himself, while the term *self-structure* is more likely to be used when an observer is viewing the individual.

[2] The self-structure, like gravity, cannot be observed directly but is inferred from the finding that various psychological functions appear to operate in terms of some unifying principle. As Hebb (1960) has pointed out, "The self is neither mythical nor mystical, but a complex mental process." (p. 743) It has a developmental course, is influenced by learning in both structure and degree of differentiation, and can be studied by various experimental procedures.

When a problem arises, it is perceived, thought about, and acted upon in relation to the self.

Fundamental to the individual's self-structure are the assumptions he develops about himself and the world. These assumptions are of three kinds: (a) *reality* assumptions—his view of things as he thinks they really are, of the kind of person he is and the nature of the world he lives in, (b) *value* assumptions—his view of the way things should be, of right and wrong, good and bad, desirable and undesirable, and (c) *possibility* assumptions—his concept of how things could be, of possibilities for change, of opportunities for personal growth and social progress. These three sets of assumptions provide the individual with a *frame of reference*— a consistent view of himself in relation to his environment—essential for guiding his behavior.

Several aspects of the individual's frame of reference are of interest in understanding his self-structure and behavior. For one thing, the individual's assumptions about reality, value, and possibility provide him with a sense of *self-identity*—of who and what he is. They also give him a *self-ideal*—a picture of what he could and should be. As we shall see, a marked discrepancy between his "real" and "ideal" self can lead to serious inner conflict. Second, the individual's pattern of assumptions leads to consistent ways of perceiving, thinking, and acting —to a characteristic *modus operandi* or *life style*. Third, the individual's assumptions serve not only as guides to behavior but also as *inner controls*. For example, value assumptions may prevent the individual from stealing or behaving in other ways he considers unethical. In fact, his value assumptions are often referred to as his *conscience,* or *superego.*

When the individual's inner controls are sufficient to direct his behavior in accordance with the value patterns of the group, he is said to be socialized. In some cases, for reasons we shall examine, these inner controls do not develop to an adequate degree; and under certain conditions, such as alcoholic intoxication, they may give way. However, society does its best to see that they are well developed and maintained, for without them, civilized living would be impossible.

The individual's assumptions may be valid or invalid; they may be held with varying degrees of conviction; and they may be more or less explicit and conscious. Since they are learned, they are subject to continual modification, though usually new learning is consistent with ideas already held. Sharply divergent or contradictory assumptions are not usually learned. In fact, such contradictions and discrepancies make us uncomfortable, and we actively— though often unconsciously—try to protect ourselves from them. From the barrage of incoming stimulation, we tend to select the messages that corroborate our assumptions and to reject or distort those that do not. Thus our idea of the kind of person we are may be as important as objective "reality" in determining what we perceive and hence what we can learn.

Regardless of how accurate or inaccurate, clearly defined or vague an individual's frame of reference may be, it provides his only basis for evaluating new experiences and coping with the world. As a consequence, he tends to defend his existing assumptions—particularly those concerning the adequacy and worth of the self. For this purpose, as we shall see, he develops a system of *ego defense mechanisms.*

As the individual achieves a sense of selfhood, he becomes an increasingly important force in directing his own behavior. He perceives and responds to each new situation in the light of *his* motives, assumptions, and feelings— and he achieves an increasing sense of his own identity and of *self-direction.* If we view the individual as a striving, organizing, adjusting system in his own right—not simply as the passive result of heredity and environment—we may consider the "self" as our third and final determinant of personality development.

In viewing the interaction of genetic, environmental, and self determinants in the shaping of personality development, it may be pointed out that the tremendous advances of modern science are adding a new dimension to this pattern. As man transforms his physical and sociocultural environment, he is also changing himself— physiologically and psychologically. Breakthroughs in genetics, brain research, communication, learning theory, and other areas are steadily increasing his power to mold, change, and control human behavior. The value problems and other implications of this new power will be discussed in Chapter 15.

DEVELOPMENTAL TASKS OF DIFFERENT LIFE PERIODS

Infancy and early
    childhood
    0-6 years

Learning to walk and talk. Learning to take solid foods and to control the elimination of body wastes. Achieving physiological stability. Developing a sense of trust in oneself and in others. Learning to relate oneself emotionally to parents, siblings, and other people. Forming an identification with one's own sex. Developing simple concepts of social and physical reality. Mastering simple safety rules. Learning to distinguish right from wrong and to respect rules and authority.

Middle childhood
    6-12 years

Gaining wider knowledge and understanding of the physical and social world. Building wholesome attitudes toward oneself. Learning an appropriate masculine or feminine social role. Developing conscience, morality, and a scale of values. Learning to read, write, and calculate, and learning other fundamental intellectual skills. Learning physical skills. Developing attitudes toward social groups and other institutions. Learning to win and maintain a place among one's age-mates. Learning to give and take and to share responsibility. Achieving increasing personal independence.

Adolescence
    12-18 years

Developing self-confidence and a clear sense of identity. Accepting one's physique and adjusting to body changes. Achieving a masculine or feminine social role. Developing new, mature relations with age-mates. Achieving emotional independence from parents and other adults. Developing concern beyond oneself; achieving mature values and social responsibility. Selecting and preparing for an occupation. Preparing for marriage and family life. Learning to make choices and take responsibility. Building a conscious value system in harmony with an adequate world picture.

Early adulthood
    18-35 years

Completing formal education. Getting started in an occupation. Selecting and learning to live with a mate. Starting a family and providing for the material and psychological need of one's children. Finding a congenial social group. Taking on civic responsibility. Developing a satisfying philosophy of life.

Middle age
    35-60 years

Accepting greater civic and social responsibility. Achieving personal growth with one's mate, and relating to one's mate as a person. Establishing a standard of living and developing adequate financial security for remaining years. Developing adult leisure-time activities and extending interests. Helping teen-age children become responsible and happy adults. Adjusting to aging parents. Accepting and adjusting to the physiological changes of middle age.

Later life

Adjusting to decreasing physical strength. Adjusting to retirement and reduced income, and establishing satisfactory living arrangements. Adjusting to the death of spouse or friends. Meeting social and civic obligations within one's ability. Establishing an explicit affiliation with one's own age group. Maintaining active interests and concerns beyond oneself.

Tasks at
    all periods

Developing and using one's physical, social, and emotional competencies. Accepting oneself and developing basic self-confidence. Accepting reality and building valid attitudes and values. Participating creatively and responsibly in family and other groups. Building rich linkages with one's world.

Adapted in part from Erikson (1950), Havighurst (1952), Kagan and Moss (1962), and Witmer and Kotinsky (1952).

Patterning of Development

In studying the development of the individual, it is useful to distinguish three levels of analysis: (a) the biological system—the closely coordinated physiological interactions within the body; (b) the psychological system, or "personality"—the organized interaction of motives, abilities, assumptions, and defenses integrated around the self; and (c) sociological, or group, systems—the interactions of the individual in his family or broader group contexts.

In our discussion throughout the book, we shall continually refer to biological, psychological, and sociological factors or levels of analysis as we strive to gain a complete view of the individual and his functioning. But we will also emphasize the transactions among them and the fact that the individual functions as a unit. Thus it is important here to keep in mind that development or change of an organism is always *patterned* change: all the interactive component systems may be affected.

DEVELOPMENTAL SCHEDULE (SEQUENCING)

Intensive studies of thousands of infants and children have shown that human development tends to follow a definite schedule not only in physical and motor development but also in emotional, intellectual, and social development (Gesell and Amatruda, 1947; Gesell, 1953; Ilg and Ames, 1955; Piaget, 1952). The infant crawls and sits up before he begins to walk; his early diffuse emotional reactions become differentiated into love, humor, grief, and other specific patterns; his language behavior progresses from random vocalization to words which eventually become vehicles for thinking.

In this timetable of development, both *maturation* and *learning* play decisive roles. Maturational processes guide the development of our bodily structure and pave the way for learning, but what we can learn in any situation depends both on maturational readiness and on what we have learned in the past. Each new phase of development is limited by previous development, and, in turn, influences and remains a part of successive stages of development.

Particularly during early life, any factors (either genetic or environmental) which interfere with the normal scheduling of growth processes are likely to have serious consequences. In extreme cases this can be seen in the birth of babies without arms or with other serious deformities as well as in the mental retardation often seen in children who have undergone extreme sensory and emotional privation in infancy. But with adequate heredity and a favorable environment, development follows a schedule which is characteristic for the human species.

DEVELOPMENTAL TASKS

In the present context, it is not necessary to discuss the stages of human development—prenatal, infancy, childhood, adolescence, adulthood, and old age—or to delineate the details of development in intellectual or other specific areas. But it is important for our purposes to know that at each stage maturational or social pressures, or both, impose certain specific tasks which the individual must master if he is to maintain a normal course of development. For example, learning to walk and talk are key tasks of infancy and early childhood. When the various tasks are not mastered during the appropriate developmental period, the individual suffers from immaturities and incompetencies which persist and handicap his adjustment on later developmental levels. Developmental tasks of six broad life periods are shown in the chart on page 64.

Implicit in these developmental tasks are several specific pathways toward maturity. Among the most important of these are the following:

1. *Dependence to self-direction.* One of the most obvious pathways toward maturity is from the dependency of fetus, infant, and child

B

C

A

G

H

CHILDREN WHO ARE "SHY"

Stills from the film *Shyness*, produced by the National Film Board of Canada

It is a commonplace that people differ. What is often not realized, however, is that the same trait, as observed or measured on a test, may mean very different things in the context of different personalities. Thus the same overt behavior may reflect quite different needs and motives in different children. For example, according to a class sociogram (A), Anna, Jimmy, and Robert are all isolates, not sought out by their classmates. All are described by

their teacher as shy." But a closer look reveals three quite different dynamic patterns.

Anna is eager to join in but hangs back because she fears rebuff (B). An overdemanding, critical mother kept her from developing confidence in herself as a little child (C); now she sees herself as one who fails and is "different." Teachers who repeat her mother's mistakes and try to force Anna out of her shyness only add more failure and more shame, making her more timid than ever (D). When instead she is given jobs at which she succeeds, she gains confidence. One teacher, for example, notices that she is naturally graceful and loves to dance. Here is something she does so well that the others can admire and learn from her (E). Left to herself, she never volunteers for anything, but when she is assigned to cooperative

D

E

F

I

J

projects like decorating the valentine box (F), she finds that the others are not so unkind and frightening as she has thought. From class discussion she learns that even the confident and cocky ones have fears and moments of insecurity. Feeling more confident and no longer "different" she at last sees herself as "one of them." She can join freely in group activities, and when she fails, she can rally and try again.

The second child, Jimmy, is shy because he is afraid. For him, the playground is a hostile, terrifying place, and he has no desire to join the other children (G). Overprotected by a doting, possessive mother he has never had a chance to develop even the most simple emotional and social competencies and now sees himself as totally inadequate to cope with the world around him (H). So he

shrinks from it. He will need psychiatric help to overcome his "shyness."

Robert, too, spends a great deal of time alone, but for different reasons. He is full of curiosity about so many things that he just would rather be hunting out answers than playing with others (I). But he has no difficulty in responding to others (J), and he is not fearful or lacking in self-confidence. No one need worry about Robert.

So one cannot make a blanket statement that shyness is unhealthy or even, conversely, that a usually commendable trait, such as desire to excel or careful attention to detail, is always healthy. Whether a trait is healthy or unhealthy depends on the overall personality context within which it occurs and the particular purpose it is serving for that individual.

to the independence of adulthood. Inextricably bound up with growth toward independence and self-direction is the development of an integrated frame of reference and of competencies essential for the assumption of adult responsibilities. Implicit here, too, is sufficient emancipation from family and social groups to be a person in one's own right.

2. *Pleasure to reality.* Freud postulated the *pleasure principle*—the tendency to seek pleasure and to avoid pain and discomfort—as fundamental in governing early behavior. However, he thought this principle was in time subordinated to the *reality principle*—the realization that we must learn to perceive and face reality if we are to meet our needs. This means achieving a realistic view of oneself and one's world, delaying immediate need gratification in the interests of long-range goals, and learning to take in stride the inevitable hurts, disappointments, and frustrations of living.

3. *Ignorance to knowledge.* The human infant is born in a state of what might be called total ignorance but rapidly begins to acquire information about himself and his world. With time, this information is organized into a coherent pattern of assumptions concerning reality, value, and possibility which provides him with a stable frame of reference for guiding his behavior. If this frame of reference is to prove adequate, it needs to be realistic, to be relevant to the kinds of problems he must deal with, and to be one in which he has faith. Also, it needs to be flexible and "open-ended" so that it can be modified by new experiences.

4. *Incompetence to competence.* The entire preadult period from infancy through adolescence is directed toward the mastery of intellectual, emotional, social, and other competencies essential for adulthood. The individual acquires skills in problem solving and decision making, learns to control his emotions and to use them for the enrichment of living, and learns to deal with others and to establish satisfying interpersonal relationships. Included here, too, is preparation for marital, sexual, and other problems likely to be met in adult living.

5. *Diffuse sexuality to heterosexuality.* The psychoanalysts have emphasized the importance of sexual development in the person's growth toward maturity. Initial expressions of sexuality, while relatively diffuse and generalized, are found at an early age: even infants have been observed to experience pleasure from genital stimulation, and childhood "crushes" often have a high degree of sexual involvement. In later childhood the individual may go through a period of so-called normal homosexuality in which his interests and emotional feelings are directed toward other members of the same sex. With the advent of puberty, heterosexual differentiation progresses rapidly. However, maturity in sexual behavior involves more than directing one's desires toward a member of the opposite sex. In marriage, adequate sexual adjustment requires the establishment of an intimate and satisfying personal relationship. Thus the individual's sexual maturity is limited by his maturity in other life areas.

6. *Amoral to moral.* The newborn infant has no concept of "right" and "wrong," but very early he learns that certain forms of behavior are approved and "good" while other patterns are disapproved or "bad." Gradually he learns a pattern of value assumptions which operate as inner guides or controls of behavior and which we have referred to as his *conscience,* or *superego.* Initially, he accepts these value assumptions blindly; with increasing maturity, he learns to evaluate them critically and works out a pattern which bears the stamp of his individuality.

7. *Self-centered to other-centered (capacity to care beyond the limited self).* One of the most important pathways to maturity involves the individual's gradual transition from exclusive preoccupation with himself and his needs to an understanding and acceptance of social responsibilities and an involvement in the "human enterprise." This includes the ability to give love in one's family setting and to be concerned about and contribute to the welfare of one's group and of society in general.

Although these goals characterize normal development, there are widespread individual differences in success in reaching them.

VARIATIONS IN DEVELOPMENT

All of us go through the same stages of growth, but the general pattern leaves ample room for individual variation in the traits that emerge. In measuring various kinds of individual differences, it has been found that most traits are distributed among the population along a continuum, with most measures clustering around a midpoint and the number of cases falling off rapidly toward either extreme of the range.[1] For example, most people fall in the intermediate or average range of intelligence, while a few at one extreme are geniuses and a few at the other extreme are mentally retarded. Thus very few people possess a very large or a very small degree of a given trait. This is an important point, since we often tend to think of people erroneously as falling into "either-or" categories—introvert or extrovert, creative or uncreative, and well-adjusted or maladjusted.

Although the distribution of traits tends to follow the pattern we have described, it is also relevant to note that variation may occur from one individual to another in (a) the *nature* of a given trait, such as blood type or skin color, (b) the *differentiation* or extent to which a given trait is developed, (c) the *integration* of traits or harmony among them, and (d) the overall *pattern* of traits, which we call *personality.* Variation within a considerable range is normal and to be expected in all these aspects. It is abnormal only when it becomes extreme enough to impair one's adjustive capacities seriously.

The significance of variation in a particular trait depends on a number of factors. If the individual's position with respect to the trait is very much above or below the average, the trait is likely to play a more important role in his development and behavior than if he is near the average. If the trait in question is an inclusive trait like general intelligence, it is likely to be more important than less inclusive traits, such as perceptual speed. The significance of a given trait depends, too, on the total trait pattern. A girl with low intelligence but outstanding physical beauty will probably not develop in the same way as will a girl with low intelligence plus a severe physical handicap.

When we consider the unique pattern of interactive determinants—genetic, environmental, and self—which shape a given individual, we can readily see that the potentialities for individual differences are beyond human calculation. However, it may be emphasized that these determinants produce commonalities as well as differences in development. On a *universal level,* we share an inheritance which distinguishes man from all other living things, and we are born into a kind of sociocultural environment unlike that of any other species. On a *communal* level, we share an inheritance with our particular group which tends to produce similar physical characteristics and a sociocultural environment which tends to produce uniformities among the members of our society. On an *individual level,* each of us has a unique genetic inheritance (except for identical twins) and a pattern of experiences different from anyone else's. An understanding of both the uniqueness of each individual and the commonalities among human beings is essential for an understanding of development and adjustment.

In concluding our discussion of personality development, it may be emphasized that the general pattern of human development is toward health and normality. However, a number of things may go wrong: (a) Development may be *arrested* at some point along the pathway from infancy to maturity. Thus we see adults who still throw temper tantrums when they fail to get their way, and aging Don Juans whose sexual behavior resembles that of the adolescent. (b) The developmental sequence may be reversed, as in *regression,* where the individual reverts from more mature to less mature behavior. This may occur when severe stress disrupts more recently learned and complex patterns of functioning. It may also be seen in some older people who become increasingly self-centered and preoccupied with their bodily processes. (c) Trauma and other conditions which adversely affect development may lead to *"weak spots"*—areas of special vulnerability. Thus a serious illness, such as pneumonia, may reduce the individual's resistance to all respiratory infections; or the divorce of his parents may leave the child sensitized to conflicts which later threaten the stability of his own marriage. (d) There may be a *distortion* of development, as we see in physical malformations or in the deviant and undesirable value assumptions of professional criminals. In the next chapter we shall examine the causes underlying such faulty patterns of development.

[1]The term *trait* is used to refer to any distinguishable and relatively enduring characteristic of the individual.

Motivation of Human Behavior

Underlying the apparently limitless diversity of human behavior are certain basic strivings which are common to people the world over. It is this common motivational core which enables us to understand such divergent behavior as that of the student cramming for an examination, the hate-monger fanning fear and prejudice, and the priest performing the last rites for a dying man. In our discussion of motivation we shall emphasize its role in determining the *direction* and the *activation* of human behavior.

MAINTENANCE AND ACTUALIZATION STRIVINGS

The motivation of all living organisms is based on their fundamental tendencies toward maintenance and the actualization of their potentialities. We see this principle operating on biological, psychological, and sociological levels. The individual resists disintegration or decay and tends to develop and behave in accordance with his genetic potentialities.[1]

Although we do not fully understand the processes involved, it is apparent that digestive, circulatory, and other body functions operate in such a way as to maintain the physiological equilibrium and integration of the body. In the mechanisms for combating invading microorganisms, for ensuring normal blood chemistry, and for maintaining constant body temperature, we see this continuous endeavor of the body to maintain conditions within the limits necessary for survival—an endeavor known as *homeostasis* (Bernard, 1859; Cannon, 1939). And the tendency toward fulfillment of potentials on the biological level can be seen in our physical growth and in sexual and parental behavior, which perpetuates the race.

If we do not fully understand the forces underlying biological motivation, we understand still less the forces related to psychological motivation. However, they appear to be an extension of the maintenance and actualization strivings we see operating on the biological level. On the psychological level this striving becomes an attempt to maintain and enhance the self. Damage to the self—as in the case of severe feelings of inferiority and guilt—can disable a man just as surely as can the failure of physiological homeostatic mechanisms, as we can readily see by studying patients in mental hospitals. The individual strives to protect the self from damage or devaluation and to develop his potentialities and grow as a person.

It is in relation to maintenance and actualization strivings that the terms *adjustment* and *maladjustment* become meaningful, for they refer to the outcome of these strivings. The term *treatment,* too, becomes meaningful only in this context. For if it were not for our basic tendencies toward wholeness, neither medical nor psychological treatment could help us. What physicians, psychiatrists, and clinical psychologists do is aid our existing tendencies toward integration and health.

In attempting to further our understanding of human motivation, it is useful to think in terms of certain basic needs which the individual must meet if he is to maintain and actualize himself. After delineating these needs, we will proceed to an examination of the drive forces which subserve them.

Biological needs.   On a biological level, the needs which appear most relevant to an understanding of human motivation are:

1. *Visceral*—for food, water, oxygen, sleep, the elimination of wastes, and other substances and conditions necessary for life.

2. *Safety*—relating to the avoidance of bodily harm or damage.

---

[1]The tendency of living matter to preserve itself is dramatically illustrated in Wilson's (1925) experiment with a sponge. He reduced the sponge to a pulp, squeezed and rolled it flat, and centrifuged it so that no trace of its original form remained. He then allowed the remains to stand overnight. Slowly and in orderly fashion, the material reconstituted itself into the organized sponge it had been before its mistreatment. More recently, scientists have demonstrated that completely scrambled cells taken from the liver or kidney of chick embryos can reconstruct the same organ (Weiss and Taylor, 1960).

3. *Sex*—basic to the perpetuation of the species and important to individual fulfillment.

4. *Sensory and motor*—for sensory stimulation and motor activity in order for our bodily equipment to develop and function properly.

Of these various needs, that of sensory stimulation requires special comment. The effects of experimental sensory deprivation, as well as the personal accounts of explorers, have demonstrated that mental stability is dependent on adequate contact with the outside world (Solomon *et al.,* 1961). When the incoming stimulation is greatly reduced under experimental conditions for a period of several hours, the individual's thought processes undergo some measure of disorganization (Lilly, 1956; Heron *et al.,* 1956; Grunebaum *et al.,* 1960; Vernon *et al.,* 1961; Kubzansky and Leiderman, 1961). Individuals react differently to such situations depending on their personality make-up, but typically there is some disorientation, impairment of problem-solving ability, and other symptoms of lowered integration. In some instances, subjects develop delusions and hallucinations. In addition, the individual becomes prone to accept any information that is "fed in" —a tendency which suggests why "brainwashing" may be effective after long periods of solitary confinement.

Further evidence of the need for stimulation comes from the experience of Dr. Alain Bombard, who sailed alone across the Atlantic Ocean for 65 days on a life raft to prove that shipwrecked people could survive for an indefinite length of time. He subsisted solely on the food he could get from the sea. During this period of isolation, Bombard stated that he "wanted terribly to have someone . . . who would confirm my impressions, or better still, argue about them. . . . I began to feel that . . . I would be incapable of discerning between the false and the true." (Bombard, 1954)

Recently J. G. Miller (1960) has demonstrated that "information input overloading" may also lead to impaired problem solving and lowered integration. When messages come in too fast, we cannot handle even the usual number effectively. On the other hand, we often strive to increase the level of incoming stimulation, as in the case of activities which we refer to as "exciting" or which involve elements of novelty or surprise

(Prentice, 1961). Such seeking for stimulation appears to be closely related to the fact that constancy of stimulation leads to monotony and boredom, also an unhealthy state. Varied and meaningful environmental stimulation is apparently needed for the maintenance of stability and efficiency of behavior (Davis *et al.,* 1960; Kubzansky and Leiderman, 1961).

Thus it would appear that there is an optimal level and heterogeneity of stimulation which varies with the individual and with time. The individual evidently strives to maintain the level and type of stimulation within the limits essential for his normal integration. In the course of our discussion, we shall examine in more detail the significance of sensory deprivation, constancy of stimulation, and overstimulation for abnormal behavior.

Psychological needs. The organism must also meet a number of psychological requirements. These are more influenced by learning and by social processes than are biological requirements, and the goals relating to their gratification are capable of greater variation. Leadership, for example, so highly valued and sought after in our society as a means of meeting needs for adequacy and worth, is considered a nuisance and a burden among the Arapesh and is gladly avoided whenever possible (Mead, 1949). But despite wide individual and group differences in the development of such needs and in the goals sought in order to meet them, they play an important part in human motivation in any culture. Failure to meet them impairs psychological integration and growth. Men in all cultures seem to need the following:

1. *Order and meaning.* Man strives to achieve a meaningful picture of his world and of himself in relation to it.[1] Such a frame of reference is essential for evaluating new situations and anticipating the outcome of his actions. Human beings do not like ambiguity, lack of structuring, chaos, or events which seem beyond their understanding and control and which place them at the mercy of alien forces. Even the most primitive peoples develop explanations for lightning, thunder, death, and other events. Accurate or not, explanations provide order and meaning and a sense of potential prediction and

---

[1]This point is elaborated by Cantril (1957), Bruner (1959), and Harvey *et al.* (1961).

control. Modern science is simply a more sophisticated attempt in the same direction. But in his quest for meaning, man is ultimately confronted with the baffling question of the meaning of his own existence. Here science, too, falls short of providing full answers. It can tell how but not why.

Our perceptual and thought processes operate in ways which maintain the consistency and stability of our frame of reference. New experiences are "screened" and interpreted in relation to our existing assumptions. Contradictory reality, value, and possibility assumptions would lead to confusion in evaluating and coping with life's problems. Therefore, when new information contradicts our assumptions, we experience *cognitive dissonance,* and we are uncomfortable until we can somehow reconcile the differences or convince ourselves they are not there (Festinger, 1958; Brehm, 1962).

To say that man strives for order, meaning, and constancy in his world does not mean that he always acts rationally. But curiously enough, he strives to prove to himself and others that his motives and actions *are* rational. As Fromm (1955) has pointed out: "However unreasonable or immoral an action may be, man has an insuperable urge to rationalize it—that is, to prove to himself and to others that his action is determined by reason, common sense, or at least conventional morality." (p. 65) To face the fact that one's behavior may be irrational arouses anxiety, for it implies a lack of order and dependability in oneself, comparable to what one would experience in a world lacking in order and stability.

2. *Adequacy and competence.* When we see our adjustive resources as inadequate for coping with a stressful situation, we tend to become confused and disorganized. This pattern is dramatically demonstrated in stage fright or in panic reactions, but felt inadequacy in any situation can interfere with integrated and effective behavior.

We have seen how "experimental neuroses" can be produced by placing animals in problem situations in which they are forced to act although their adjustive capacities are inadequate. We do not put human beings into comparable experimental situations, but life often does, and the results seem much the same.

To achieve and maintain feelings of adequacy, the individual must acquire workable assumptions about his world and develop the physical, intellectual, emotional, and social competencies he will need for dealing with the tasks of life. R. W. White (1959) pointed out that motivation toward competence is evident even in the early playful and investigatory behavior of children. Children appear to be innately curious and attempt to explore and manipulate everything within reach. This process of "reality testing" brings into play learning, reasoning, and other integrative abilities and enables the child to acquire practical knowledge and essential skills. Where reality testing leads to injury, social disapproval, or other unpleasant results, however, feelings of inadequacy and fear may block normal exploratory activities and prevent the development of needed knowledge and competencies.

3. *Security.* The need for security develops with and is closely related to the need for adequacy. The growing individual soon learns that failure to meet his biological or psychological needs leads to acutely unpleasant results. Consequently he learns to strive toward the maintenance of whatever conditions can be counted on to assure gratification of his needs.

This need for security is reflected in the common preference for jobs with tenure, in social security legislation, in insurance against disability and other contingencies, and in society's emphasis on law and order. Feelings of insecurity may have widely differing effects on behavior, but typically they lead to a restriction in activities, to fearfulness and apprehension, and to failure to participate fully in one's world. As a consequence, the individual is denied many enrichment and growth experiences.

4. *Social approval (belongingness, status).* The growing infant is completely dependent for his existence on the assistance and approval of others. He rapidly learns that when he behaves in socially approved ways he is rewarded, whereas socially disapproved behavior brings punishment. At first, this pattern involves only the family group, but later he finds that being accepted and approved by other individuals and groups becomes increasingly essential if he is to meet many of his physical and psychological needs. So he learns to strive for positive regard from other persons who play an important role in his life and tries to become and remain an approved member of the social groups with which he identifies himself.

Failure to achieve interpersonal and group acceptance and the loneliness that results are particularly difficult problems in the group-conscious, group-oriented society in which we live (Fromm-Reichman, 1959). Especially is this true for the person who depends heavily upon others for his feelings of self-identity and worth. Eloquent testimony to man's need for social approval, acceptance, and relatedness was provided by the experience of small groups of scientists, officers, and enlisted personnel who voluntarily subjected themselves to isolated antarctic living for the better part of a year. During this period, troublesome individuals were occasionally given the "silent treatment": the man was completely ignored by the group as if he did not exist. This "isolation" procedure resulted in a syndrome called the "long eye," which was characterized by varying combinations of sleeplessness, spontaneous bursts of crying, hallucinations, a deterioration in habits of personal hygiene, and a tendency for the man to move aimlessly about or lie in his bunk staring into space. These symptoms cleared up when he was again accepted by the group and permitted to interact with others in it (Rohrer, 1961).

5. *Self-esteem* (*worth*).   Closely related to our needs for feelings of adequacy and social approval is our need to feel good about ourselves, to feel that we are worthy of the respect of others. Usually we judge our personal worth largely in terms of the values and standards of those around us. If we measure up to these standards—for example, in terms of physical appearance, economic status, achievement—we can approve of ourselves and feel worth while. If we see ourselves as falling short, we tend to feel inferior, guilty, and insecure. Also, of course, other people indicate their evaluation of us in various direct or subtle ways, and this too enters into our feelings of worth.

Self-esteem has its early grounding in parental affirmation of our worth and in our own mastery of developmental tasks and successful problem solving; it receives continual nourishment from a feeling of competency in areas that gain us

social approval. Most of us try to make ourselves attractive to others, to identify ourselves with accepted social groups, and to achieve goals that gain us approval and status. In such ways we enhance our feelings of worth and self-esteem. Self-approval is hard to achieve or maintain without the confirmation of social approval—especially the approval of the people most important to us.

6. *Love and relatedness.*   The need to love and be loved is crucial for healthy personality development and functioning. In an intensive study of 158 well-adjusted children, Langdon and Stout (1951) concluded that the most important single factor—in fact the only factor common to all the cases studied—was satisfaction of the child's need for love and acceptance. Human beings appear to be so constructed that they need and strive to achieve warm, loving relationships with others. The longing for intimacy with others remains with us throughout our lives, and separation from or loss of loved ones usually presents a difficult adjustment problem.

Most of us meet our needs for love and affection in the relationships of marriage, family, and friends. Children reared in homes which do not provide adequate warmth and affection often experience difficulties later in giving and receiving love. Sometimes such individuals are overly possessive of the persons they love and are almost insatiable in their need to be assured that others love them. More typically, they become "insulated" or "frosted" and tend to remain aloof and self-contained, but usually they admit to underlying feelings of loneliness, isolation, and frustration.

Often the need for love is thought of simply as a need to be loved, but our need to love is fully as great. We need to relate to and care about people and things outside ourselves if we are to grow and function properly as human beings. Christianity and other religions see such an outgoing love as basic to man's fulfillment. Such love goes beyond the love of family and friends to a brotherly love—a basic orientation of concern for others and for one's world. Without such "psychological roots" we are likely to feel like strangers in a foreign land.

7. *Self-enhancement and growth.*   Motivation theory has long been dominated by the concept of maintenance, with man's actions seen as meeting any deficiency that arises and returning to a state of equilibrium. But this is only part of our motivational structure. Maintenance strivings cannot explain the mountain climber or the explorer, the scientist or the inventor, the great artist or the composer. Man strives to grow, to improve, to become more capable—to actualize his potentialities and fulfill himself as a human being. Huxley (1953) emphasized this point in his statement that:

"Human life *is* a struggle—against frustration, ignorance, suffering, evil, the maddening inertia of things in general; but it is also a struggle *for* something. . . . And fulfillment seems to describe better than any other single word the positive side of human development and human evolution—the realization of inherent capacities by the individual and of new possibilities by the race; the satisfaction of needs, spiritual as well as material; the emergence of new qualities of experience to be enjoyed; the building of personalities." (pp. 162-163)

Strivings toward fulfillment take different forms with different people, depending upon their abilities, values, and life situations. On a simple level, we see attempts at self-enhancement through the use of cosmetics, the wearing of stylish clothes, and the seeking of higher social status. On a more complex level, fulfillment strivings may take the form of being a good wife and mother, of writing poetry, or of other activities that contribute to personal growth and add meaning to one's existence.

Whatever the form our activities take, we appear to share tendencies toward creative self-expression, toward finding increased satisfactions, toward building richer linkages with our world, toward developing and using our potentialities, and toward "becoming a person." Here the terms *self-enhancement, self-actualization,* and *self-fulfillment* are roughly synonymous.

Many psychologists have been impressed with man's search for identity—with his striving to find and to be his "real self." Rogers (1958) has put it this way:

"As I follow the experience of many clients in the therapeutic relationship which we endeavor to create for them, it seems to me that each one has the same problem. Below the level of the problem situation about which the individual is complaining—behind the trouble with studies, or wife, or employer, or with his own uncontrollable or bizarre behavior, or with his frightening feelings lies one central search. It seems to me that at bottom each person is asking: 'Who am I, really? How can I get in touch with this real self, underlying all my surface behavior? How can I become myself?' . . . It appears that the goal the individual most wishes to achieve, the end which he knowingly or unknowingly pursues, is to become himself." (pp. 9-10)

Our actualization strivings receive no automatic fulfillment, and their expression may be difficult or impossible in some situations. The neurotic is too busy defending himself to be free to grow; the person who must struggle hard for mere physical survival has little time or energy for personal growth; the individual in a regimented culture may find many of his growth tendencies blocked. People in such situations usually experience a sense of frustration and dissatisfaction. Life seems meaningless and incomplete, for they are missing the fulfillment of themselves as human beings.

The preceding needs represent the basic core of psychological requirements which typically emerge through normal interaction with the physical and sociocultural world and which contribute heavily to the direction of man's behavior. Given needs may, of course, vary considerably in intensity from one person to another. The individual who has failed repeatedly may show strong needs for adequacy and security, while the person who was spoiled as a child and has always had his way may show very little need for social approval. It can also be seen that our psychological needs are closely interrelated and that maintenance strivings merge imperceptibly into actualization strivings.

ACTIVATION (ENERGY MOBILIZATION)

The human organism is a going concern which stores energy and releases it in the various forms of activity required for the meeting of its needs and the pursuit of its goals. The activation of the organism is made possible by a complex combination of mechanisms in which various body systems participate in different and changing degrees.[1]

Mechanisms of activation (drive forces). To ensure the adequate meeting of body needs, we have certain homeostatic mechanisms, ranging from immunological defenses against disease to biological drives and emotions. Their function is to maintain internal conditions within the range essential for the healthy functioning of the organism. Some, like the mechanisms involved in maintaining an even body temperature, take place automatically and without our awareness; others, like the hunger drive, involve not only awareness but reasoning, learning, and voluntary activity. When the homeostatic mechanisms are unable to maintain or restore equilibrium, ill health or death results.

Some of our homeostatic mechanisms involve the mobilization of energy for needed action of the organism in relation to its environment, as when food or water must be found and ingested. It is these that chiefly concern us here. As we shall see, certain of these mechanisms subserve psychological as well as biological needs.

1. *Biological drives.* When biological needs are not being adequately met, equilibrium is disturbed and various internal changes take place in the organism. In the case of several biological needs, these changes in turn lead to energy mobilization and goal-seeking activity. For example, when the individual is deprived of water for a period of time, the thirst drive comes into operation. Although the precise nature of this drive is not fully understood, it usually appears to involve both the unpleasant sensation of dryness of the mouth and throat tissues and changes in the salt concentration of the blood stream that lead to energy mobilization through a direct sensitizing action on specific neural centers. Such changes thus appear to "drive" the organism to action toward meeting the need and restoring equilibrium. This is the basis of our various biological drives, which are the provision nature has taken to ensure the satisfaction of visceral needs, to protect the organism against injury, and to stimulate activities favorable to reproduction and infant care.

Since our psychological needs are so heavily dependent upon learning, we do not have any built-in psychological drives which go into action when a particular psychological need is not being met. However, emotions, pain and pleasure, and tension serve as driving forces in meeting psychological as well as biological needs.

2. *Emotions.* Like biological drives, emotions may arouse, sustain, and direct activity and thus play an energizing role in behavior. Whereas biological drives are initially activated by tissue needs of the organism, however, emotional arousal depends upon the perceived significance of a given situation to the individual. Emotions also serve as emergency sources of power, particularly in stressful situations where habitual reaction patterns are not appropriate or adequate. Strong emotions make maximum energy resources available to the organism for meeting such emergencies.

Particularly important in subserving both biological and psychological needs are fear, anger, and anxiety. Fear tends to protect the organism by leading it to withdraw from dangerous situations; it may also reinforce behavior initiated by biological drives. For example, fear of starving to death may reinforce the hunger drive. Anger and hostility are aroused by obstacles blocking need gratification. Circumstances permitting, they lead to a direct attack on such obstacles and efforts to remove them. Perhaps most important from a psychological viewpoint is the emotion we call *anxiety,* which is aroused by a threat to the adequacy or worth of the self. Anxiety is often referred to as "psychic pain" and is acutely unpleasant. It operates as a powerful driving force toward maintenance on a psychological level.

Although we have emphasized the role of emotions in increasing energy mobilization, certain emotions may have little effect upon activation level or may actually lower it. Under normal conditions, love appears to have little direct effect on activation level, although it markedly influences the direction of behavior. Of course, if the loved object is endangered, love may lead to strong emotional mobilization and sustained effort. Depression typically leads to an actual

[1]Some social scientists prefer to think of motivation simply in terms of the activation level of an ongoing energy system rather than in terms of needs and goals. As Duffy (1962) has pointed out, the emphasis here is on fluctuations in activation level (energy mobilization), in the parts of the body maximally activated, and in the direction of activity in relation to the environment. The terms *activation, arousal,* and *energy mobilization* are used interchangeably. The term *motive* is used to indicate an internal condition that initiates or regulates behavior toward a goal. Thus it implies a need-goal relationship.

DRIVE CENTERS IN THE BRAIN

In recent years the motivational functions of various brain centers have been studied by electrically stimulating various areas in the brains of chickens, rats, cats, and monkeys. The stimulating current is administered by means of fine wire electrodes which are implanted in the desired areas. The animal subjects are essentially undamaged by these procedures; they remain healthy even during experiments extending over a number of years.

The effect of brain stimulation varies with the area stimulated. Apparently, stimulation in certain areas is extremely pleasurable. An animal will learn to perform various tasks if he is rewarded by stimulation in these areas; he will press a bar hundreds of times an hour—as long as the reward continues. Other locations evidently function as pain centers, and still other areas are associated with other emotions. Rage and aggression, friendly behavior, fear, or anxiety can be produced by stimulation of appropriate brain areas.

These pictures show still another response to brain stimulation. With no electrical stimulation, the moderately thirsty rat drinks from a tube. Stimulation eliciting the hunger drive causes him to leave the tube and push aside a door to obtain food. If no food is available, he will gnaw inedible objects while the stimulation continues (Miller, 1958).

In other investigations, stimuli have been administered to two or more different areas at the same time in a preliminary effort to study the way drives interact. This is an important next step, for the identification of particular brain areas with certain impulses does not in itself show how these areas normally interact in the production of behavior, or how these drives are activated in the absence of an interfering investigator with electrodes.

lowering of activation level and to decreased effort and energy expenditure. Thus in relating emotions to activation, it is relevant to consider the specific effects of a given emotion.

3. *Pain and pleasure.* Of key importance in determining the level of activation as well as the direction of behavior are *pain* and *pleasure*.[1] Man's drive to avoid pain—physical or psychic —is a strong one. Examples of its effects are seen in the search for better anesthetics as well as in the development of tranquilizing drugs to dull the painful anxieties of everyday life. Similarly, the strength of drive forces may be strong-

---

[1] Some investigators consider pain and pleasure as biological drives whereas others consider them to be emotions. It would appear that they can be viewed as either drives or emotions or as additional mechanisms of activation.

ly reinforced by actual or anticipated pleasure. A hungry man may look forward eagerly to a delicious steak; an actor may be spurred on by hopes of recognition and acclaim. Most people devote considerable energy to making their lives more pleasurable.

In recent years, techniques making possible the electrical stimulation of specific brain areas in man and other animals have revealed so-called "pain" and "pleasure" centers. If permitted, white rats will avoid the stimulation of certain brain areas presumably associated with unpleasant or painful sensations, while they will avidly press a lever which stimulates other areas until hunger, thirst, or fatigue forces an interruption. The limited research on human beings indicates that the correlation between animal and human responses is very high. Thus the old hedonistic doctrine that pleasure and pain are important in human motivation appears to be supported by modern brain research.

4. *Tension.* With the mobilization of energy that follows disturbances in the equilibrium of the organism, we experience some measure of tension. When immediate action is inhibited, this increased tension is experienced as unpleasant—the degree of tension and its unpleasantness being generally proportional to the degree of activation. The feeling of tension appears to stem both from the sensation of increased muscle tension and from the conflict between excitatory and inhibitory processes in the central nervous system (McConaghy, 1962). In any event, tension is a stimulus which calls for action, because it can be discharged and its accompanying unpleasantness relieved only by some type of activity. In this sense, tension functions as a powerful drive force in its own right.

The activation of the organism thus involves changes in neural, glandular, muscular, and other bodily systems. In man, the nervous system —particularly the brain—seems to exercise ultimate control. Since the specific neural, glandular, and other components involved in different states of arousal may vary considerably—for example, the components involved in fear differ from those in anger, and the components in pleasure differ from those in pain—the pattern of activation as well as the level is important.

Level of activation. Our level of activation at a given time may be influenced by a wide range of individual and situational factors including activity cycles (such as eating and sleeping), noxious or painful stimuli, drugs, fantasies, memories, dangers, and incentives. In general, the more *ego involved* we are in a situation—the more we perceive it as related to our essential purposes and satisfactions in living— the more likely the situation is to raise our level of activation.[1] For example, the individual who is strongly ego involved in becoming a physician is willing to make more sacrifices and devote more energy and effort to his studies than the individual who is going into medicine because his parents want him to do so. Of course, there are marked individual differences in the degree of activation elicited by a given situation, depending upon the way the situation is perceived.

Situations which are perceived as dangerous or threatening usually lead to a high level of activation. The father who is told that his son is critically ill or an aspiring actress who is trying out for a key role in a television series may both evidence a high degree of activation.

The level of activation is also influenced by metabolic conditions such as fatigue, by personal tempo or pace, by the sensitivity or excitability of the individual, and by his speed of recovery from prior activation.

As a consequence of experience and learning, the individual usually responds to situations with an appropriate level of activation. For most tasks, this means a moderate degree of activation (Duffy, 1962). With too low a level, the individual may fail to expend the energy and effort essential for task achievement, whereas too high a level of activation leads to impulsive and poorly coordinated activity. Abnormal behavior often is accompanied by inappropriate degrees of activation, by extreme fluctuations in activation, and by slow recovery from the effects of prior activation.

SOCIAL FORCES IN MOTIVATION

In our discussion up to this point, we have viewed motivation in terms of activation and striving on the part of the human system. How-

[1]For a critical review of some of the findings and issues relating to the role of ego involvement in behavior, the reader is referred to Ferguson (1962).

ever, environmental factors are of great importance in inhibiting or eliciting given strivings, in determining the goals we work toward in meeting our needs, and in determining the extent to which our needs are gratified. Furthermore, not all adjustive demands originate within us: activation and behavior can also be initiated by environmental demands.

Social inhibition and facilitation of motives. Often increased activation and goal-directed behavior are initiated by environmental incentives rather than by actual need deprivation. Thus social requirements or the odor of food may lead to the individual's eating even when he is not hungry; or an individual may engage in sexual activity because the opportunity presents itself rather than because of deprivation. The individual is continuously scanning and evaluating his environment in relation to the availability of desirable goals as well as the presence of dangers and threats.

A crucial aspect of the group's maintenance and actualization is the exercise of some measure of control over the motive patterns of its members. By its system of values and by the manipulation of rewards and punishments, society encourages the gratification of certain needs while it attempts to inhibit others. In most societies, sexual desires and patterns of gratification are brought under many social regulations, and in general such desires are inhibited. Conversely, other needs, such as the need for social approval, may be strongly encouraged.

The rewards and punishments controlled by the group and its value patterns also influence the goals we seek in attempting to meet our needs and the means we learn to use in working toward these goals. In our society, there are strong incentives to strive toward such goals as athletic prowess, academic excellence, creative accomplishment, financial success, and the achievement of leadership. And although a wide range of means for achieving these goals is approved, there are limitations, and the use of socially disapproved means subjects the individual to possible punishment. In other societies, the goals and means which are encouraged may be considerably different from ours. In any society, however, failure to achieve socially approved goals can be self-devaluating and can lead to abnormal behavior.

Needs of society.   Social groups strive for maintenance and actualization in much the same sense that individuals do. To maintain themselves, social groups too must meet certain needs such as the maintenance of law and order and defense against attack by other groups—which in turn require the development of various "homeostatic" mechanisms such as police forces and armies.

When normal group functioning or organizational structure is disrupted, groups strive to restore a state of equilibrium. This applies to small groups as well as larger ones. If a general is killed in battle, another officer moves up to take his place; if the father of a small family dies, there are changes in relationships and responsibilities as other family members attempt to establish a new organizational equilibrium. Stresses that upset the equilibrium of a group also result in an increase in activation as resources are mobilized to deal with the danger.

Groups, like individuals, must set goals and develop and mobilize their resources if they are to fulfill their purposes and actualize themselves. When the primary resources of the group are directed toward maintenance, as in wartime, actualization strivings are apt to suffer.

The needs of society are important forces in the determination of the individual's behavior. Usually, the meeting of society's needs also promotes the welfare of most individual members. Sometimes, however, the needs of society take precedence over the needs of the individual, as when the soldier is called upon to risk and, if need be, sacrifice his life in combat.

MOTIVATION AND BEHAVIOR

In the preceding discussion, we have been concerned primarily with the nature and direction of man's strivings and with the processes involved in energy mobilization, or activation. Now let us add a few additional details to our overall picture of motivation.

Motivational sequences.   On a *maintenance* level, the sequence of events in meeting our needs involves three basic elements: (a) need deprivation, resulting in energy mobilization, (b) choice of some goal and of means for attaining it, and (c) goal-directed behavior, leading,

HIERARCHY OF NEEDS

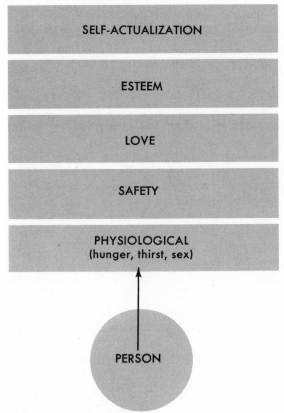

SELF-ACTUALIZATION

ESTEEM

LOVE

SAFETY

PHYSIOLOGICAL
(hunger, thirst, sex)

PERSON

According to Maslow, needs on the "lower" levels are prepotent as long as they are unsatisfied. When they are adequately satisfied, however, the "higher" needs occupy the individual's attention and effort.

if successful, to gratification of the need. All three elements in this sequence are important. Energy mobilization is essential for action, but action will bring satisfaction only if it is directed toward an appropriate goal and if the action utilizes means suitable for attaining the goal. Many times our adjustive efforts prove ineffective because we pursue inappropriate goals or utilize unsuitable means. Usually, need gratification is pleasurable and leads to a reduction in activation.

On an *actualization* level, the motivational sequence is more complex. Instead of trying to alleviate unpleasant tension and/or emotion—as in the case of intense hunger or a threat to the worth of the self—there is a welcoming of stimulation, tension, and effort. The scientist may

go without food and sleep in the excitement of a crucial experiment; the mountain climber may risk his life to conquer some dangerous peak; the writer may isolate himself from others and devote seemingly endless hours and effort to his work. Even when the effort promises to be tedious, painful, or otherwise unpleasant, human beings are often willing to give up comfort and security in their efforts to express and fulfill themselves. The attainment of goals associated with actualization strivings usually leads to a temporary lowering of activation and to pleasurable feelings of self-enhancement and perhaps elation.

There are, however, conditions under which need gratification can be distinctly unpleasant, as in the case of a vegetarian who violates religious values and eats meat in order to keep from starving, or in the case of a person who finds sexual relations repugnant. Both pleasurable and unpleasurable aspects of need gratification are important to an adequate understanding of motivation.

Interaction of needs.   Although a particular need may predominate, behavior is usually *multineed* determined—which is simply another way of saying that motivational sequences involve the complex interaction of many needs. In addition, there is a high degree of interdependency among our needs, and the satisfaction or frustration of one need may strengthen or weaken others. For example, a child who feels lonely and rejected may develop a craving for sweets which in some way are partial compensation for the important psychological satisfactions he is being denied.

Hierarchy of needs.   Although changes in motivational patterns are closely tied in with the rhythm or periodicity of biological drives, Maslow and Murphy (1954) have suggested that there is a fundamental ordering to this structure—that our needs arrange themselves in a hierarchy from the most basic biological needs to self-esteem and actualization needs, which represent the higher development of the personality. Unless food and other basic needs are reasonably well gratified, behavior will be dominated by them. With their gratification, however, the individual is free to devote his energies to meeting his needs on higher levels.

This hierarchy concept tends to be borne out

by observations of behavior under extreme conditions. Friedman (1949) found that: "In all survivors of the Nazi camps, one might say the self-preservation instinct became so dominant that it blotted out all other instincts." Similarly Wolf and Ripley (1947) reported that Allied prisoners subjected to imprisonment and torture by the Japanese manifested a general lowering of moral standards and often obtained food by devious means at the expense of other prisoners.

Under experimental conditions, too, the tremendous driving force of hunger has been demonstrated dramatically.

During World War II, a study of semistarvation was carried on at the University of Minnesota with 36 young conscientious objectors who volunteered for the experiment. Among the dramatic personality changes observed over the prolonged period of semistarvation were a constant preoccupation with thoughts of food and inability to concentrate on anything else, easy fatigability and preference for sedentary rather than active behavior, reduction and practical disappearance of sex drive coupled with a loss of interest in their girl friends, replacement of a sense of humor by a feeling of depression and gloom, and a marked decrease in sociability together with irritability toward others. By the end of the 25th week, *the hunger drive had become the dominant influence in the behavior of the subjects.* Food dominated their thoughts, their conversations, their leisure-time activities, and their daydreams (Keys *et al.,* 1950).

Although this hierarchy of needs presumably is characteristic of the motivational structure of most people, Maslow leaves room for exceptions. For some individuals, other values become more important than the meeting of food or safety needs, as shown by the countless people who have sacrificed their lives or suffered physical torture for the sake of ethical, social, or religious values. In the face of severe and prolonged frustration, however, biological needs seem most likely to predominate.

From this point of view the effects of gratification are as important as the effects of deprivation. For only through gratification of basic needs can higher-level needs become dominant, and only through efforts to meet these higher-level needs can the individual actualize his full potentialities as a human being. As Maslow

et al. (1954) put it: "I should say simply that a healthy man is primarily motivated by his needs to develop and actualize his fullest potentialities and capacities. If a man has any other basic needs in any active, chronic sense, he is simply an unhealthy man." (p. 105)

Preferred motive patterns. As we have noted, each individual develops a relatively stable self-structure and a consistent life style. An essential element in this consistent life style is the individual's preferred pattern of motives —the needs, goal objects, and means which characterize his strivings. For example, the key motives of some individuals are in the direction of love, relatedness, and self-actualization, while other persons are concerned primarily with security, material possessions, and creature comforts. Any individual's pattern is in part an outgrowth of his assumptions concerning reality, value, and possibility and in part a reflection of the demands, limitations, and opportunities of his environment.

Implicit in the individual's preferred motive pattern is his *level of aspiration.* Well-adjusted people tend to have a reasonably accurate evaluation of themselves in relation to their world and hence have a fairly realistic level of aspiration. Maladjusted people, on the other hand, tend to be unrealistic—to set their aspirations either too high or too low—leading to inevitable failure or to wasted opportunities and, in either case, to unhappiness.

Although the individual tends to show a relatively consistent pattern of motives, changes do occur. Some of these are short-term changes stemming from the attainment of given goals. This is often illustrated when we achieve some important goal such as college graduation only to find that instead of relaxation and peace a whole new set of motives comes into operation. Other changes are more basic and represent major changes in the individual's overall motive pattern. These may result from experience and learning, from changes in purposes and requirements at different life stages, or from radical modifications in the individual's environment which markedly enlarge or restrict his opportunities.

Motivational selectivity. Our motives are constantly influencing our perceiving, reasoning, learning, and other psychological processes.

It is commonplace that we tend to perceive the aspects of the environment which are related to the gratification of our long-term or immediate needs. The man looking for the television section in the newspaper ignores the political columns and the sports section. The social climber is constantly alert for signs of approval from those he is seeking to impress. On a more dramatic level, we could predict that a man lost on the desert and suffering from intense thirst would ignore the vivid colors of the sunset and keep scanning his surroundings for some indication of water. This influence of motives on perceptual processes is well delineated in the concept of *selective vigilance:* "In any given situation, the organism singles out what it considers to be the environment's most relevant aspects—relevant to adaptation in the situation." (Bruner and Postman, 1947, p. 305)

Motivation also influences what we learn—and how rapidly and how much; and despite our attempts to be logical, we often tend to believe what we *want* to believe and to subvert our thought processes to justify our assumptions and behavior. However, this is a two-way road, and motives may themselves be encouraged or ignored, expressed or denied expression in keeping with our assumptions. For example, the assumption that sex is evil may lead to the inhibition of one's sex drive. Our motives are constantly being affected by what we believe is possible, worthwhile, and admirable.

Dreaming, another important form of thought, is also influenced by our motives. Children who live in orphanages commonly dream—both in daydreams and during sleep—about being adopted into a happy family. Similarly, the dreams of prisoners tend to be about freedom. We have all probably had dreams about revenge, sexual activities, and other experiences in which we could readily see the influence of motivational factors. Therapists often utilize a patient's dreams in attempting to understand his problems.

CONSCIOUS AND UNCONSCIOUS ASPECTS OF MOTIVATION

Some years ago, W. A. White (1947) pointed out that our failure to take unconscious motiva-

tion into consideration was ". . . probably the cause of more inadequacies in the understanding of human behavior than any other one thing." Although there is still considerable controversy among psychologists concerning the nature and importance of unconscious processes in human behavior, there is abundant evidence that the individual is often unaware or only partially aware of what his needs and goals really are.[1]

Many physiological needs operate on an unconscious level; others enter awareness as conscious desires or wishes only when they become pressing. We are not ordinarily aware of our need for air until breathing is hindered in some way. Even then, the degree of awareness may vary. We may mutter something about how stuffy it is and proceed to loosen our collars or open a window. But if all air is cut off and we are in danger of suffocation, then the awareness is immediate and vivid, and more drastic action may be undertaken to restore our equilibrium.

Psychological needs such as those for security, adequacy, social approval, and self-esteem may also operate on relatively unconscious levels. Thus we may show off, join exclusive clubs, and even get married for reasons of which we are unaware. Of course we may think of good reasons to justify our behavior, but these may not be the real reason at all.

The degree of our awareness of our motivation varies considerably from one behavior pattern to another and from person to person. Usually individuals who are seriously maladjusted lack insight into many key facets of their motivational patterns. The following illustration demonstrates the action of unconscious motivation and is especially revealing because here we know the exact motivational pattern, which is not usually the case.

"During profound hypnosis the subject was instructed to feel that smoking was a bad habit, that he both loved

---

[1]A number of investigators have pointed to certain misconceptions commonly associated with the term *unconscious*, such as the notions that (a) it possesses a "will" and organization of its own, and (b) it ensures that nothing is ever forgotten. To avoid the pitfalls of a conscious-unconscious dichotomy, Cameron and Magaret (1951) have suggested the use of the concept *accessibility to awareness*. Perhaps the simplest solution to this problem is to think of "conscious" and "unconscious" as a continuum, with degrees of awareness or accessibility to consciousness.

and hated it, that he wanted to get over the habit but that he felt it was too strong a habit to break, that he would be very reluctant to smoke and would give anything not to smoke, but that he would find himself compelled to smoke; and that after he was awakened he would experience all of these feelings.

"After he was awakened the subject was drawn into a casual conversation with the hypnotist who, lighting one himself, offered him a cigarette. The subject waved it aside with the explanation that he had his own and that he preferred Camels, and promptly began to reach for his own pack. Instead of looking in his customary pocket, however, he seemed to forget where he carried his cigarettes and searched fruitlessly through all of his other pockets with a gradually increasing concern. Finally, after having sought them repeatedly in all other pockets, he located his cigarettes in their usual place. He took them out, engaged in a brief conversation as he dallied with the pack, and then began to search for matches, which he failed to find. During his search for matches he replaced the cigarettes in his pocket and began using both hands, finally locating the matches too in their usual pocket. Having done this, he now began using both hands to search for his cigarettes. He finally located them but then found that he had once more misplaced his matches. This time however he kept his cigarettes in hand while attempt-

ing to locate the matches. He then placed a cigarette in his mouth and struck a match. As he struck it, however, he began a conversation which so engrossed him that he forgot the match and allowed it to burn his finger tips whereupon, with a grimace of pain, he tossed it in the ash tray. . . .

"This behavior continued with numerous variations. He tried lighting a cigarette with a split match, burned his fingers, got both ends of one cigarette wet, demonstrated how he could roll a cigarette, kept stopping to converse or tell a joke, and so on. Several cigarettes were ruined and discarded. When he finally got one going successfully, he took only a few good puffs with long pauses in between and discarded it before it was used up." (Erickson, 1939, pp. 342-345)

In summary, motivation is an important determinant of the direction and intensity of human behavior. Man strives to maintain and actualize himself—on both biological and psychological levels. To succeed, he must meet certain basic needs on both levels, and his performance is heavily dependent upon both activation processes and environmental conditions. Each individual tends to show a relatively consistent motive pattern, although he may be aware, partially aware, or unaware of his motives.

Problems of Adjustment (Stress)

Life would be simple indeed if our needs were immediately and automatically satisfied. But as we know, there are many obstacles, both environmental and internal, which interfere with need gratification and complicate our efforts to maintain and actualize ourselves. Such obstacles place adjustive demands or *stress* on the organism. They require extra effort and a change in ongoing activity if the organism is to cope with them and meet its needs. When the stress is excessive, it overtaxes our resources and leads to a breakdown of integrated functioning.

LEVELS OF STRESS

Stress may occur on a biological or a psychological level. For example, pneumonia viruses produce stress on a biological level in that the basic adjustive demand involves primarily the biological defenses of the body. Guilt, on the other hand, is a source of psychological stress in that mainly ego defenses are involved. Stress may also occur on group as well as individual levels. Economic depressions and wars are examples of situations which place adjustive demands both on individuals and on the group as a unit.

SOURCES OF STRESS

Problems of adjustment, or stress, situations can be classified as frustrations, conflicts, or pressures.

Frustration. Frustration results when our

motives are thwarted, either by some obstacle that blocks or impedes our progress toward a desired goal, or by the absence of an appropriate goal. For example, overly restrictive parents would be a source of frustration to an adolescent girl who wanted to go to a school party, while a lack of water would be a source of frustration to a man lost in the desert. Frustrations may be minor, or they may be serious threats to our welfare; they may arise from outer or inner sources.

1. *External frustrations.* There is a wide range of environmental obstacles, both physical and social, which can lead to frustration of our needs and efforts. Famines, droughts, storms, fires, earthquakes, injuries, accidents, and the death of loved ones are major sources of thwarting in the physical environment. In addition, there are the more commonly experienced minor frustrating situations such as car trouble when we are in a hurry, or rain when we wish to play tennis or golf.

Social obstacles are found in the various restrictions and regulations which society places upon behavior and in the punishments imposed for breaking these rules. To meet our needs we must direct our energies toward socially approved goals and use only socially approved means. Deviation from these social rules, as in stealing, homosexuality, or physical violence, means risking social disapproval and punishment. Such punishment may take a variety of forms—withdrawal of affection, lowering of our social status, loss of a job, or confinement in jails or prisons—all of which are severely frustrating in their own right.

On the other hand, abiding by social mores also subjects us to a wide range of frustrations, prominent among which are delay and the concentration of effort in one direction. Delay may take the form of postponing sexual relations until marriage or of waiting until our educational requirements are completed before we can be admitted to some professional field. Concentration of effort is often frustrating because it means giving up many things we would like to do and directing our energies—no matter how pleasant or unpleasant the task—toward one particular goal to the exclusion of others.

Other major external obstacles include wars, economic depressions, excessive competition, lack of opportunity, racial and religious intoler-ance, rapid change, and general social uncertainty. Such conditions place a great deal of stress upon many of us and evoke feelings of inadequacy, isolation, and insecurity. We shall consider certain of these in more detail in discussing the causes of abnormal behavior.

2. *Internal frustrations.* Personal limitations in the form of physical handicaps, insufficient ability, or lack of social charm, may all become sources of frustration in the fiercely competitive struggle for social recognition, success, marital partners, and status. Failures resulting from personal limitations and mistakes are likely to be serious sources of self-devaluation and frustration, particularly when such failures involve our key motives and purposes.

Many internal frustrations arise out of psychological barriers in the form of reality and ethical controls. The individual may refrain from premarital sexual relations because of fear of pregnancy or because of moral attitudes which make such behavior unacceptable. And if reality and ethical restraints break down, self-recrimination and guilt may follow. We all do things which we later regret and condemn ourselves for, and the resulting self-devaluation is extremely unpleasant and frustrating to our important need for self-esteem.

Biological conditions such as fatigue and disease are common and important sources of stress. Fatigue may be frustrating in its own right and in addition is often important in lowering our general psychobiological resistance to other types of stress. Disease may tax or even exceed our adjustive capacities.

Conflict. Often the frustration comes not from a single obstacle but from a conflict between two needs or valued goals, in which choosing either alternative means frustration with regard to the other. Complete sexual gratification may involve lowered self-esteem and social disapproval, or an early marriage may mean foregoing a college degree. Such incompatible action systems usually require a decision on the part of the individual and, as we shall see, may play an important part in the development of mental illness.

Although we are discussing frustration and conflict as if they were distinct sources of stress, the essential element of conflict is the anticipated frustration entailed in the choice of either alternative. Conflicts with which all of us have to cope may be conveniently classified into approach-avoidant, double-approach, and double-avoidant conflicts.

1. In *approach-avoidant* conflicts there are strong tendencies both to approach and to avoid the same goal. A person may want to marry for sexual, social, and security reasons, while at the same time he fears the responsibilities and loss of personal freedom. He has tendencies both to approach and to avoid marriage. In a similar way his desires may conflict with his inner reality or ethical restraints or with fear of failure.

2. *Double-approach* conflicts involve competition between two or more desirable goals. On a simple level the individual may have to decide between two movies or two makes of automobiles, or between steak and fish for dinner. In more complex cases he may be torn between duty and ambition, between loyalty to his mother and to his wife, between a legal and a medical career, or between present satisfactions and future ones.

3. In *double-avoidant* conflicts the individual is completely hemmed in—he is caught "between the Devil and the deep blue sea." He may have to choose between unemployment and a job which he dislikes, between marrying someone he does not love and the possibility that he will be unable to find anyone else. In wartime, he may have to choose between fighting, with the possibility of being killed, and social disapproval, with feelings of being a coward.

Conflicts are important sources of stress and frequently lead to such tension and inner turmoil that the individual's adjustive capacities are seriously impaired. In our society, adjustive difficulties are particularly common in the handling of conflicts centering around dependence vs. self-direction, contradictory values, and sexual desires vs. restraints. We shall consider these in more detail in the next chapter.

Pressure. Problems of adjustment may stem not only from frustrations and conflicts but also from pressures that complicate our strivings. Parents who have made sacrifices to send their son to college may exert a great deal of pressure on him for high achievement, and he may feel under considerable pressure not to let them down. Similarly, a business executive may be under heavy and sustained pressure by virtue of the sheer number of important decisions he has to make each day. Such pressures force us to intensify our efforts and to speed up our activity —often to an uncomfortable degree. Even minor pressures can build up to a point where they involve severe stress. Pressures, like frustrations, may stem from inner or outer sources.

1. *Inner pressures.* Inner pressures typically involve our self-ideal and level of aspiration. Often we strive to live up to unrealistically high standards of ethical behavior, courage, and social responsibility—to fit our picture of ourselves as we think we could and should be. Many of us drive ourselves mercilessly toward high levels of achievement. We are determined to get to the top, to be the best, to "succeed." In our highly competitive society, such aspirations can subject us to continuous and severe pressure and considerable discomfort.

2. *Outer demands.* Many pressures arise from environmental demands. Parents may exert pressure on their children to get good grades; wives may exert pressure on their husbands to make more money; children may make severe demands on their parents' time and energy. Education, marriage, parenthood, occupation, and civic responsibilities all exert pressures. Sometimes the sheer details of living subject us to considerable pressure, and we feel confronted by a never ending stream of problems to be solved, decisions to be made, and deadlines to be met.

It may be emphasized that a given stress situation may involve elements of frustration, conflict, and pressure. For example, a serious financial loss not only may lead to lowered living standards but also may confront the individual with the problem of reconciling his picture of himself as a shrewd businessman with the reality that he was impulsive and used poor judgment in making his investment. Such "cognitive dissonance," arising from information contradictory to our existing assumptions about ourselves and our world, adds to the complexity of many stress situations. And although a particular stress may predominate, we rarely deal with an isolated stress situation, but usually with a continuously changing complex of interrelated and sometimes contradictory demands. Thus we speak of stress patterns rather than simply a given stress situation.

SEVERITY OF STRESS

In much the same sense that we refer to the amount of stress placed on a bridge, we speak of the severity of stress placed on the adjustive capacities of the organism. The actual severity of stress is determined by a number of objective and subjective factors.

Duration, importance, multiplicity of demands. Ordinarily, the longer a stress lasts, the more severe it is. Prolonged fatigue is a more severe stress than temporary fatigue. Often stress also appears to have a cumulative effect. A husband or wife may maintain composure through a long series of minor irritations or frustrations only to "explode" in the face of the "final straw."

Encountering a number of stresses at the same time makes a difference too. If a man has a heart attack, loses his job, and is deserted by his wife all at the same time, the resulting stress will obviously be more severe than if these events occurred separately.

The importance of a demand made on the individual depends on the degree of need deprivation and disruption in the system that will occur if he fails to cope with the demand. Simply telling an employee that he *may* lose his job *if* his work does not improve may be a severe stress when it directly involves his feelings of security. Here, too, dissonant cognitions will increase the severity of the stress. The employee who considers himself highly capable and efficient may be very upset emotionally by such a warning, since the experience is dissonant with his self-concept and expectations.

Strength and equality of conflicting forces. Conflicts between weak motives or motives with little ego involvement involve minimal stress, for neither choice would involve serious loss. On the other hand, conflicts between strong motives which are important to the individual—such as having to choose between self-esteem and social approval—are likely to subject the individual to considerable stress. Of course, the more nearly equal the strength of the opposing needs or goals, the greater the stress.

Curiously enough, in approach-avoidance conflicts, the relative strength of the opposing forces is likely to shift as the goal draws near. For example, if a young man is ambivalent about getting married, both his eagerness and his fear will become greater as the wedding date approaches. But typically, as the goal draws near, the avoidance tendency increases in strength more sharply (N. E. Miller, 1959). This helps to explain why many people experience a feeling of near panic on their wedding day.

Individual's evaluation of the problem. One factor usually crucial in determining the severity of stress is the individual's evaluation of the stress situation. Two girls in love may view a broken engagement in quite different ways. For one, it may represent a humiliating failure and may induce severe feelings of inadequacy and insecurity. The other may view it as hurtful but fortunate, in that the incompatibility became apparent before rather than after marriage.

This point is particularly important in our understanding of mental illness. We may see no stresses in a patient's life situation severe enough to have brought on his illness. Yet to him the situation may have been intolerable. An individual always reacts not simply to the situation but *to the situation as he evaluates it*—especially in relation to his feelings about his own ability to cope with it.

Stress tolerance of individual. The severity of a given stress depends, too, on the individual's resources for withstanding stress. If he is marginally adjusted, the slightest frustration or pressure may place him under severe stress. The term *stress tolerance,* or *frustration tolerance,* refers to the amount of stress he can tolerate before his integrated functioning is seriously impaired. Both biologically and psychologically, we vary greatly in our general vulnerability to stress as well as in the types of stress to which we are most vulnerable. Emergencies, disappointments, and other life problems that one individual can take in stride may prove incapacitating to another.

Sometimes, as we have seen, early traumatic experiences (psychological wounds) leave the individual especially vulnerable to certain kinds of stress. The hurt felt by a little girl whose father has divorced her mother may later make it difficult or impossible for her to accept the possibility of divorce as a solution to her own unhappy marriage. Such a "weak spot" in our stress tolerance is often referred to as our "Achilles heel."

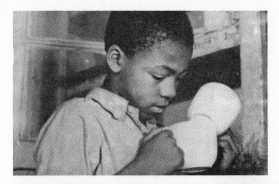

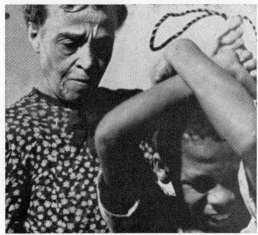

THE QUIET ONE

Stills from the film produced by Film Documents, Inc.

When the external stresses are severe, as when a boy lives in squalid surroundings and is unwanted and unloved, the role of the individual's evaluation of his situation and himself would seem to be of little importance: one might be tempted to say that the objective conditions "caused" the almost inevitable abnormal behavior and faulty development. Yet even here the behavior is a function of both the stress and the individual's self- and environmental-evaluations, as shown by the fact that with wise counsel and the experience of friendship, a much better adjustment may be possible even without changing the life situation. We see this in Donald's story.

Donald lives in the Harlem slums, is unloved, unwanted by the grandmother with whom he lives and by his mother, now living with another man. Without the love and acceptance so necessary for feelings of self-esteem and confidence, Donald does not develop in a normal, healthy way. Sometimes his unsatisfied needs for affection and security make him rebel with a hatred neither he nor his grandmother can understand.

Running away or playing hooky from school has only one consequence: a beating. Such added stress results in increased resentment, for always he seems to be rejected or punished. Nowhere is he really accepted; nowhere does he find a feeling of belonging and being wanted. Sometimes he steals coins from the cupboard and wanders, lonely, through the neighborhood, seeking to "buy" friends, who flatter or tolerate him only while the money lasts.

Once he seeks out his mother, his shy longing for her love showing in his face, but she is too insecure and

maladjusted in her own life to give him the affection he so desperately needs. Seemingly unable to find any place in the world where he "belongs," this final rejection by his mother is too hurtful to bear, and Donald's resentment at last bursts out in one hostile, antisocial act. He hurls a stone through a shopwindow and is apprehended and sent to the Wiltwyk School for Boys.

Here Donald joins other unwanted children, many with severe personality problems and long delinquency records. Although Donald has been badly scarred emotionally, he is still able to respond, gradually, to the kindness of a young counselor. But he is so starved for affection and so afraid of being rejected and hurt again that he cannot share his friend with others. His final sense of loss comes when he makes a piece of ceramics for his mother and finds that she has disappeared, leaving no address. Hurt, bewildered, resentful, he steals a cigarette lighter

from the counselor and runs away, going aimlessly down the railroad track.

A narrow escape from death by a train passing through a narrow cut is the crisis for Donald. In a few seconds he sees in a realistic way the experiences in the past that have made him afraid and unsure. Illusions about his home, his mother, and the recent counselor give way to a reluctant but more healthful acceptance of the present, and a birth of a new self-reliance. His adjustment will be slow, and many wounds may never heal entirely, but he is now able to join in the play with other boys like himself and will someday find it possible to take a constructive place in society.

Unfortunately, most boys like Donald are not able to find the complete emotional acceptance and security they need as a first step toward developing feelings of worth and becoming participating members of society.

STRESS AND THREAT

Related to both the individual's perception of the situation and his tolerance for it is the matter of threat. Many stress situations do not carry any major threat to biological or psychological needs. A cold is not the threat that pneumonia is; similarly, an individual isolated during recovery from a communicable disease may be lonely but does not experience the threat evidently experienced by the individuals who were given the "silent treatment" in the antarctic. (See page 73.) In the latter case, there was a direct threat to important psychological needs.

Stress situations which we perceive as physically damaging or threatening to our survival—such as having a limb amputated or being given a diagnosis of cancer—carry a high degree of threat. Similarly, stress situations which threaten the adequacy and worth of the self—such as loss of social status, failure in one's chosen occupation, or desires which the individual considers highly immoral and incompatible with his self-concept and self-ideal—involve a strong element of threat. The individual is also likely to feel threatened in situations which place demands on him that he perceives as important but beyond his power to meet. Thus the person who deeply doubts his adequacy and worth is constantly experiencing threat, whereas a more secure person, even in the face of severe stress, may not feel serious threat. In general, a situation perceived as threatening is much more stressful than one perceived as presenting a difficult but manageable problem. Threat arouses anxiety which, as we shall see, has many implications for adjustive behavior.

STRESS PATTERNS ARE UNIQUE AND CHANGING

Each individual faces a unique pattern of adjustive demands. This is true partly because of differences among people in the interpretation of the same situation. But objectively, too, no two people are faced with exactly the same pattern of demands. Each individual's age, sex, occupation, economic status, personality make-up, and other factors help to determine the demands made on him: the stress pattern a child faces differs in many respects from that of an older person, and the stress pattern faced by a carpenter will differ from that of a business executive. Stress patterns change with time too—both predictably, as the individual enters different life periods, and unpredictably, as an accident, a death in the family, or some other unforeseen event makes new demands.

WE MAY BE UNAWARE OF STRESS

Although we are often acutely aware of our frustrations and conflicts, they can also operate below the level of consciousness. We saw in the hypnosis experiment a subject who was unaware of the conflict dominating his behavior. The rejected boy who shows off and the insecure girl who boasts of her wealthy relatives may be quite unaware of the frustrations that lead to their behavior. Similarly, an individual may have severe conflicts centering around homosexual desires and yet be unaware that he even has such impulses. We shall shortly see how our ego defense mechanisms make this possible.

Reactions to Stress—Some General Principles

The effects of stress depend heavily upon the severity of the stress: mild stress may actually improve the performance and functional efficiency of the organism, whereas severe stress tends to impair integration and effectiveness, and excessive stress eventuates in a breakdown of the system. In our immediate discussion, we shall be thinking primarily of *severe* stress.

Stress leads to automatic, persistent attempts at its resolution—it forces us to do something about it. What we do depends on a host of factors, including our frame of reference, our motives, our competencies, our stress tolerance, environment limitations, and momentary conditions like prior mental set or fatigue. Sometimes inner factors play the dominant determining role; at other times, outer factors are of primary importance. Any stress reaction, of course, reflects the interplay of a combination of determinants—some more influential than others, but all working together to make the individual react as he does. In the rest of this chapter we shall see what sorts of things we do and what happens when the stress is so great that it overtaxes our adjustive capacities.

REACTIONS ARE HOLISTIC

We have seen that living organisms tend to maintain their integrity—their "wholeness"— and that this tendency appears on biological, psychological, and sociological levels. Of course, conflicting needs, as in the case of social approval vs. sex, may lead to the sacrifice of satisfaction on one level, but even here the organism reacts *as a whole* and the action offering the least disturbance in psychobiological equilibrium is the one chosen.

Although we shall continually emphasize this unity of the organism—its reaction to stress as an integrated whole—we again find it convenient to utilize our concept of three interactional levels in our examination of adjustive reactions. In this context we shall refer to biological, psychological, and sociological *levels of defense.*

Biological defenses. We are particularly concerned with three types of biological defenses. First there are the cellular or immunological processes involved in protecting the organism against disease. When these defenses fail to hold, there is impairment in the biological and often the psychological functioning of the organism. Particularly when the central nervous system is affected, as in brain tumors or in syphilitic infection of the brain, we are likely to find disturbances in psychological functioning. In later chapters, we shall elaborate upon the known relations between such disease processes and mental illness.

Second are the emergency emotional processes. Strong unexpected stimuli, injuries, and situations evaluated as threatening lead to marked physiological changes designated by Cannon (1939, 1953) as *emergency emotional reactions,* for they represent the total mobilization of body resources to deal with the stress sit-uation. These changes are effected largely through the autonomic nervous system and include increased muscle tonus, the dumping of stored sugar into the blood stream, the speeding up or deepening of breathing, faster beating of the heart, and the secretion of adrenalin. At the same time, physiological processes not crucial for the immediate action, such as digestion, may be stopped. In essence, the individual is placed on a "war footing." Although such emergency measures contribute to the adaptive potential of the organism, they may overshoot their mark, and behavior disorganization may result.

Third are the neural defenses, which range from alerting the organism to extra vigilance and sensitivity in the face of danger to actually protecting it from excessive stimulation and disorganization. Of significance here is the concept of *protective inhibition.* On a simple neural level, protective inhibition takes place when stimulation exceeds the working capacity of given cells

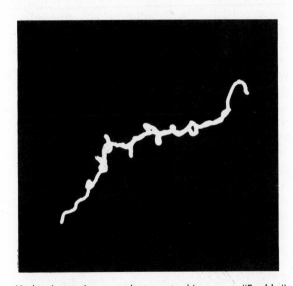

Under hypnosis, a student wrote his name, "Freddy," linked to the name "Jean." Upon awaking, he was greatly embarrassed and explained that he wanted to marry Jean but was engaged to another girl. He had for some time wanted to break the engagement but had not had courage to tell either the girl or his parents. Interestingly enough, "Freddy" was a childhood diminutive which he particularly hated. His linking of these names reveals the conflict between his dependence on parental approval and his love for Jean. (Adapted from Harriman, 1942, p. 181.)

(Bykov, 1959). Here the normal reaction of the nerve cell to stimuli is inhibited to protect the life of the cell. On a more complex level, we can see a comparable inhibition when the individual avoids an overwhelmingly traumatic experience by fainting.

Psychological defenses.   For purposes of discussion, we may distinguish two types of psychological defenses: (a) task-oriented reactions, involving our cognitive abilities in fairly direct attempts to solve problems and gratify needs, and (b) ego defense-oriented reactions, involving numerous ego defense mechanisms—largely unconscious devices by which we protect the self from hurt.

The way in which we perceive, learn, and reason will be markedly influenced by the frame of reference we have developed—our assumptions about both ourselves and our world. When our frame of reference is fairly consistent with reality, we can organize effective adjustive reactions. But when we are reacting to a "world that isn't there," our behavior cannot help but be maladjustive. And unfortunately our tendencies to maintain our existing assumptions operate as persistently for inaccurate assumptions as for accurate ones. New experiences which are incompatible with these assumptions are often denied symbolization (rejected) or given a distorted meaning to minimize the disturbance to our existing structure of assumptions (Rogers, 1957).

The individual's pattern of ego defensive reactions, like his pattern of assumptions, tends to be relatively consistent and enduring. Under severe stress, there is often an exaggeration of the ego defensive reactions that the individual customarily relies upon. The latter point is well illustrated in a study by Cappon (1961) of the behavior of 20 dying patients. He found that "The hostile became more hostile, the fearful more fearful, the weak weaker. They each clung to their habitual defenses—regression, denying, withdrawing, projecting, as before. . . ." (p. 36) We shall shortly discuss in greater detail the actual types of psychological defenses we muster—both the direct, deliberate ones and the unconscious, "automatic" ones.

Sociological defenses.   The individual adjusts not only as a unit but also by means of groups or organizations such as the family, the church, and the army. The author once heard a noted speaker refer to democracy as an "unstable equilibrium of pressure groups." Banding together in social groups for united action to benefit the constituent members is a major adjustive reaction in a democracy. Furthermore, a social group, like an individual, may use adaptive or maladaptive means to protect itself.

Up to this point, we have briefly noted that the individual has several types of coping mechanisms and lines of defense for maintaining his integrity—immunological, emergency emotional, cerebrally controlled adaptive, ego defensive, and group or sociological. It should be re-emphasized that these levels of defense are categorized only for convenience and that the individual reacts to stress as a psychobiological unit.

EXCITATION AND INHIBITION

Basic to the integration of human behavior—on both biological and psychological levels—are the neural processes of inhibition and excitation. Through these processes some activities are held in abeyance while others are facilitated, thus making possible the overall coordination of the organism and providing considerable flexibility in dealing with stress.

The activity of muscles, glands, and other bodily organs and systems is regulated largely by means of nerve impulses which exert either an excitatory or an inhibitory influence. On a simple level, we observe the reciprocal innervation of body muscles—one set relaxing while another contracts in the bending of joints and the movement of limbs. On a more complex level, we have noted the interaction of the various processes in the activation of the organism. These same processes are operative in highly complex patterns of thought and action. The human brain not only receives, filters, digests, and assigns meaning to new experience but regulates all thoughts and actions. Thus impulses may be permitted direct action, suppressed until a more appropriate time and place, or completely repressed. In general, action needs to be inhibited until relevant factors in a problem situation have been taken into account. Impulsive behavior is usually not well integrated or effective (Duffy, 1962).

We can also see excitatory and inhibitory processes on social levels. Laws and mores tend to inhibit certain types of behavior while financial and other incentives are used to facilitate behavior considered desirable by the group. In fact, as we have previously noted, the individual's own inner psychological controls are largely a reflection of social assumptions concerning reality and value which he has learned and accepted from his group for the guidance of his own behavior.

Although the human brain has certain built-in safeguards—for example, the activity of the lower brain centers is subject to regulation by the higher and more distinctively human cerebral cortex—excitatory and inhibitory mechanisms may be defective in development or they may break down under excessive stress. Developmental defects in inhibitory neuronal fields or in learned reality and value controls may lead to impulsive, aggressive, antisocial behavior. Similarly, brain pathology as well as various functional mental disorders may lead to an imbalance in either excitatory or inhibitory processes with a resulting disorganization of behavior.

REACTIONS ARE ECONOMICAL

Not only does the individual react to stress as an integrated unit, but he reacts in a way which is economical, involving a minimal expenditure of energy. This, of course, is what we might expect in view of his tendencies toward self-maintenance. Man's needs and goals are many, but his resources, while impressive, are limited. On both biological and psychological levels, the individual tries to meet his needs and reach his goals in the simplest way that he can—he is always doing his best in relation to the way he evaluates the problem.

As J. G. Miller (1957) has pointed out, organisms that survive tend to employ the least expensive defenses against stress first and increasingly more expensive ones later. If a continuously increasing amount of acid is injected into a dog's veins, the first defense mechanism which appears is overbreathing. If this does not prove effective, more drastic protective mechanisms, such as biochemical changes in the blood, are brought into operation.

A person unable to achieve an important goal may reveal a comparable patterning of defenses on the psychological level. First he may lower his level of aspiration. This is relatively inexpensive. Then he may rationalize his behavior by saying that he could have accomplished more if he had been given more time. This is a little more expensive since he runs the risk of being given more time and still being unable to achieve the goal. With continuing failure, repression may be his next line of defense, and in time the unresolved stress may lead to psychological or somatic symptoms—an expensive consequence. Finally, to avoid extreme self-devaluation, he may develop a schizophrenic reaction and deny the reality of the situation—an extremely expensive defense.

The principle of economy is also relevant in a slightly different context. Reaction patterns, whether mental or physical, tend to involve less conscious effort and less energy with repetition. This is readily apparent in the formation of habits, such as driving an automobile. Although less obvious, the same principle holds in relation to habitual ways of perceiving and thinking. As a consequence, the individual tends to maintain his existing patterns of thought and action not only because they provide his basic source of security in dealing with the world but because it requires less effort to follow established patterns than it does to modify them or adopt new ones. This tendency to resist change in established ways of perceiving and acting has been referred to as "inertia" on the individual level and as "cultural lag" on the social level. It is one of the big blocks to successful therapy and helps us to understand the tendency of maladaptive behavior patterns to persist long after new, more efficient patterns have become available.

REACTIONS MAY BE CONSCIOUS OR UNCONSCIOUS

Reactions to stress situations may fall anywhere on the conscious-unconscious continuum: they may be undertaken with conscious intent, with only partial awareness, or with no conscious involvement at all. In general, our potentials for conscious and unconscious functioning represent complementary resources for adjustive action.

Automatic functioning. On a biological level, corrective and defensive processes go into operation automatically when our equilibrium is disturbed. This can be seen in the regulation of body temperature, the repair of damaged tissue, and other routine maintenance operations as well as in our cellular and immunological defenses against invading microörganisms. Biological drives, energy mobilization, and emergency emotional processes also go into operation automatically, although conscious problem solving may be required before the individual's needs are met.

On the psychological level, automatic functioning may take the form of habits, in which reactions which were once conscious no longer require our attention. Another kind of automatic functioning is the use of unconscious defense mechanisms against threats to our self-structure. Seeing what we want to see, screening out or distorting threatening ideas, and repressing painful experiences are all examples of automatic and largely unconscious processes. Although potentially a boon in taking care of routine problems so that our attention is freed for solving new problems, it is apparent that automatic functioning can also lead to irrational and ineffective behavior.

Conscious efforts to adjust. In our complicated and changing environment we must constantly change our behavior to meet new demands. On a biological level, as we have noted, the organism adjusts automatically to many kinds of change, but on a psychological level adjustment to change usually requires conscious processes involving reasoning, imagination, and learning of new behavior.

Despite a great deal of research, we know relatively little about what goes on in the human brain as it "processes" a stress situation and directs our adjustive action. Some theoreticians have likened the operation of the brain to that of a complex electronic computer. The analogy, of course, is far from complete, and our self-aware "human computer" is both more and less efficient in handling problems than is the machine. On the one hand, it is more inventive and creative; on the other, more subject to error. We often come up with wrong answers not only because of a lack of information or wrong assumptions, but also because of urgent time pressures, emotional involvement, our need to defend our self-structure, and other limiting conditions which are peculiarly human.

STRESS AROUSES EMOTION

The particular emotional states accompanying reactions to stress vary greatly, but where the stress is severe, it typically leads to emotional mobilization for emergency action. Three emotional patterns are of special significance in our present discussion.

Frustration arouses anger (hostility). The immediate reaction of the organism to frustration is typically one of anger. Physiological arousal in anger seems to energize the attack response and to intensify aggressive action—to help the organism meet its needs through attack upon and removal of the obstacle.

Where the frustration continues or the individual is confronted with a succession of frustrating situations stemming from the same source, anger gradually blends into hostility (Buss, 1961). In a general sense, hostility may be viewed as prolonged anger. It involves increased drive toward destruction, damage, or hurt to the object viewed as the source of frustration.

In many respects, anger and hostility are difficult emotions to deal with. Both involve tension which demands discharge, yet the conditions of civilized living permit few direct outlets. Consequently, such tension is often discharged in fantasy and other indirect and deviant but "safe" ways which we shall presently examine.

Danger arouses fear. Specific dangers tend to arouse fear. Ordinarily, fear elicits withdrawal or flight reactions. However, the nature of the stress situation and the degree of fear elicited will have much to do with the direction and quality of behavior induced.

The individual who fears that he has cancer may go in immediately for a general medical checkup or may put it off because he fears facing the real possibility of an affirmative diagnosis. In the face of intense fear, the individual may panic or freeze and become unable to function in an organized manner. Such behavior can be readily observed in fires and other disasters.

Threat arouses anxiety. Although closely

related to fear, anxiety is a subjective warning of threat in which the specific nature of the danger is not known. Many stress situations—the possibility of global atomic warfare, for example—give rise to both fear and anxiety. But in general we may conceive of fear as directly related to perceived dangers, while the sources of anxiety are perceived vaguely or not at all.

Stress situations inducing anxiety are often difficult to cope with—as in the case of repressed homosexual desires that threaten to break through existing ego defenses—since the nature of the threat is usually unclear to the individual, yet the anxiety or psychic pain demands some sort of protective action. As we shall see, the defenses mustered to cope with anxiety may run the entire gamut of abnormal behavior.

Hostility, fear, and anxiety may be aroused singly or in various combinations. Where fear or anxiety is aroused, hostility is likely to follow, for the things we fear are actual or potential sources of frustration. Also, when intense hostility threatens to produce overt behavior, anxiety may be elicited at this possibility.

ADAPTATION TO STRESS IS EXPENSIVE

Severe stress, even when it is not excessive, is expensive. Particularly is this true of stress which continues over long periods.

Lowering of adaptive efficiency. Under severe stress there is a narrowing of the perceptual field and an increased rigidity of cognitive processes. As a consequence, it is difficult and often impossible for the individual under severe stress to reinterpret a situation or see new factors or relationships in it. Studies with animal subjects have shown that even when the stress situation is changed and new possibilities of solution are made available, the animal that has been under stress is likely not to see the new possibilities but instead to continue to follow a rigid, stereotyped adjustive pattern (Maier, 1949).

In human subjects, reasoning is often further impaired by the emotional processes that typically accompany severe stress. For example, people with a high level of anxiety tend to be rigid and inflexible and to approach new problems in a stereotyped way (Cowen, 1952a, 1925b; Jones, 1954; Longenecker, 1962). In

fact, we may generalize to the extent of saying that as stress increases beyond a minimal level, reasoning, problem solving, and adaptive efficiency progressively decrease.

Reduction in resistance to other stresses. In building defenses for coping with one stress, the organism typically suffers a lowering of tolerance to other stresses (Selye, 1956). For example, mice exposed to extremes of cold develop increased resistance to the cold but become unusually sensitive to X rays. Similarly, soldiers who develop resistance to combat may show a lowering of tolerance for other stresses, such as virus infections or bad news from home. It appears that the defensive resources of the system are limited and that if they are mobilized against one stress, they are not available for coping with others. This helps to explain how sustained psychological stress can lower biological resistance to disease, and how sustained bodily disease can lower resistance to psychological stress. Sustained stress of any kind may lead to a serious reduction in the overall adaptive capacity of the organism.

Wear and tear on the system. With sustained or very severe stress there may be a considerable amount of irreversible wear and tear on the system. Many people believe that after undergoing very stressful experiences, rest can completely restore them. Selye (1956) has pointed to evidence that this is a false assumption:

"Experiments on animals have clearly shown that each exposure leaves an indelible scar, in that it uses up reserves of adaptability which cannot be replaced. It is true that immediately after some harassing experience, rest can restore us almost to the original level of fitness by eliminating acute fatigue. But the emphasis is on *almost*. Since we constantly go through periods of stress and rest during life, just a little deficit of adaptation energy every day adds up—it adds up to what we call *aging*.

"... Due to the great advances made by classic medicine during the last half century, premature death caused by specific disease producers (microbes, malnutrition, etc.) has declined at a phenomenal rate. ... [But] an ever-increasing proportion of the human population dies from the so-called wear-and-tear diseases, or degenerative diseases, which are primarily due to stress." (pp. 274-275)

It may also be pointed out that in some individuals sustained or very severe stress appears to lead to chemical changes in the blood that interfere with brain functioning and seriously impair the individual's ability to think, feel, and act in an integrated manner. In fact, a disorganization of thought processes similar to that observed in various severe mental disorders can be induced temporarily in normal people by the injection of certain drugs such as lysergic acid or mescaline. We shall examine later the implications of such chemical changes.

Types of Psychological Stress Reactions

When we feel competent to handle a stress situation, our behavior tends to be *task-oriented*—aimed primarily at dealing with the requirements of the situation. But when our feelings of adequacy and worth are threatened by the stress situation, our reactions tend to be *ego defense-oriented*—aimed primarily at protecting ourselves from devaluation and relieving painful tension and anxiety. In the face of continued demands that exceed our adjustive resources, we undergo personality *decompensation*—our behavior becomes increasingly disorganized and disintegrative.

TASK-ORIENTED REACTIONS

Task-oriented reactions are aimed at realistically meeting the demands of the stress situation. They tend to be based on an objective appraisal of the situation and to be constructive, rational, and consciously directed. The task may involve meeting an inner demand or an outer one or a combination of both, and task-oriented behavior can mean making changes in oneself or one's surroundings or both—whatever the situation warrants. It can involve attack, withdrawal, or compromise, and the reaction may be overt or covert. For example, lowering one's level of aspiration in the face of failure may be as much a task-oriented reaction to stress as increasing one's efforts to achieve the original goal.

Attack. In attack behavior we attempt to remove or surmount obstacles to need satisfaction. Such attack responses are apparently based on fundamental tendencies of living organisms toward increased activity and variation in mode of attack when obstacles are encountered. The possible ways of directly attacking problems are

legion, and they range from obvious techniques such as physical assault or learning new skills to subtle means such as patience or passive resistance.

The most typical emotional reinforcement of attack behavior is anger or hostility. Many stress situations cannot be dealt with adequately by means of direct aggression. When attack is unsuccessful, the individual is subjected to unpleasant or painful frustration which typically elicits anger or hostility—directed toward the object or persons viewed as the obstacle. Thus attack responses which at first involve only a tendency toward increased activity may come to have strong emotional reinforcement. In many instances, of course, the initial stress situation may elicit anger which acts as a powerful driving force toward attack behavior.

When appropriate to the situation and the individual, an attack approach usually offers the best channel for using and coordinating abilities in constructive action. However, attack behavior may be destructive as well as constructive. With hostility, there is a tendency to destroy as well as attack. For example, if an adolescent feels unwanted, unjustly treated, and deprived of opportunities afforded to others, he may build up a high level of hostile tension which is discharged in delinquent behavior. Stealing, destruction of property, fire setting, sexual misbehavior, and assault frequently represent attack patterns involving defiant, hostile reactions of this sort.

Withdrawal. Simple withdrawal is a second fundamental type of reaction to stress. Many animals seem capable of fairly well-coordinated withdrawal or flight reactions shortly after birth, but the human infant has no such complex pattern. However, he is able to withdraw a hand or foot from a painful stimulus such as a hot object, and when subjected to sudden, unexpected stimuli, he may tend to curl up into a ball, apparently a type of primitive fear reaction.

In addition to withdrawing physically, the individual may withdraw in various psychological ways—such as admitting defeat, reducing his ego involvement in the situation, lowering his aspirations, restricting the situations with which he attempts to cope, curtailing energy and effort, or becoming apathetic. Resistance and protective inhibition are common forms of avoidance or withdrawal in the face of excessive pressure.

As the individual learns to associate certain objects and situations with frustration and hurt, he may avoid rather than attack them. His tendency to withdraw in the face of such dangerous situations is typically reinforced by fear. With time, his fears may involve a wide range of real and imagined dangers. Hostility, too, may be aroused, since withdrawal usually involves some measure of frustration. And when withdrawal is incompatible with one's ego ideal, there may be guilt feelings—a complicated admixture of apprehension, anxiety, and self-devaluation which we shall examine later.

So just as simple aggression becomes complicated by anger or hostility, we find simple withdrawal becoming complicated by fear and perhaps hostility and guilt as well. In both cases, the individual's reaction tendencies are reinforced by emotional processes leading to a high degree of tension which demands discharge. But here again, social living provides few situations in which such mobilized energy can be utilized effectively in direct physical action. Taking final examinations, being interviewed for jobs, coping with excessive competition—these stress situations cannot ordinarily be met by direct physical withdrawal but must usually be faced despite fears.

There are, of course, many stress situations in which the most realistic solution is simply to withdraw. Many college students find themselves majoring in areas not well suited to their interests or abilities. In such cases, withdrawal and the pursuit of an alternative area of training may be the most appropriate action.

Compromise. Since most situations cannot be dealt with successfully by either direct attack or withdrawal, it usually becomes necessary to work out some sort of compromise. Compromise may mean changing one's method of operation, accepting substitute goals, or resorting to normally unacceptable means. An individual faced with starvation may compromise with his conscience and steal "just this one time" or he may eat worms, bugs, spiders, or even human flesh.

Often, too, we resort to symbolic satisfactions under conditions of severe frustration. Thus a soldier may gain some substitutive satisfaction from pin up pictures or from wish-fulfilling daydreams. In fact, Masserman (1961) has shown that under sustained frustration the individual usually becomes increasingly willing to accept substitute goals—both symbolic and nonsymbolic ones.

Making a decision that resolves a conflict is usually a compromise reaction, for a decision in either direction inevitably involves some measure of frustration. As a consequence, such decisions are difficult to make, and the individual may feel considerable anxiety and hesitation. The girl who feels she must decide between two suitors may procrastinate, vacillate from one possibility to the other, and feel increasingly anxious as she tries to avoid the inevitable frustration which either decision would entail.

When compromise reactions succeed in meeting the essential requirements of the stress situation, the problem is resolved and the individual can go on to other activities. Often, however, we make compromises which we cannot fully accept and live with because important needs continue to go unmet. In such instances, additional adjustive action is required. Perhaps the most common emotions accompanying compromise reactions are fear, anxiety, and guilt.

Task-oriented reactions of all three types—attack, withdrawal, and compromise—involve the same steps: (a) seeing and defining the problem, (b) working out alternative solutions to the problem, (c) deciding upon the safest and most rewarding course of action, and (d) evaluating the "feedback" or results of the action to see if possible errors can be compensated for or corrected. Perhaps the most difficult step in this sequence is that of decision making, or choice, for here we are concerned with weighing values, predicting outcomes, and balancing risk against potential reward, none of which can be a matter of complete certainty. In essence, we "play the probabilities" as we see them.

Under conditions of severe and sustained stress which cannot be resolved with the resources available, the individual often develops various "strategies" for coping with the situation. For example, under experimental conditions of "information input overloading"—where the individual is forced to process more bits of information than he can handle efficiently—J. G. Miller (1961) noted the following strategies:

omission—not processing part of the information

error—processing incorrectly and not making corrections

queuing—delaying responses during peak overloads and then trying to catch up during lulls

filtering—systematically omitting certain categories of information according to some priority scheme

approximation—responding in less accurate or precise ways because of time pressure

escape—leaving the situation or taking other measures to cut off the flow of information

At high rates of information input, filtering and omission were the strategies used most. At very high rates, as much as 98 per cent of all information input was not responded to. In this way the individual was able to keep functioning even though his efficiency was markedly impaired. Students who have experienced "overloading" in their academic work are likely to be familiar with these strategies.

Although task-oriented behavior has a better chance of meeting our needs than does ego defense-oriented behavior, it obviously is not always successful in coping with the stress situation. A faulty frame of reference, for example, can lead to unrealistic and maladjustive solutions. Where feedback is available, however, and is used in a task-oriented way, it is often possible to correct faulty initial assumptions and change ongoing behavior.

EGO DEFENSE MECHANISMS

As we have seen, the self is the integrating core of the personality and any threat to its worth or adequacy is a threat to the individual's very center of existence. Consequently, various defense mechanisms are gradually learned for protecting the self. These are called into play whenever we find ourselves in a situation in which threat to the integrity of the self is present.

All of us use these ego defense mechanisms. They are essential for softening failure, reducing cognitive dissonance, alleviating anxiety, protecting ourselves against trauma, and maintaining our feelings of adequacy and personal worth. Thus we must consider them normal adjustive reactions unless they are used to such an extreme degree that they interfere with the maintenance of self-integrity instead of being an aid. Like a nation devoting its major energies to armaments, the self can break down under too heavy a load of defensive activities.

These mechanisms, necessary as they are, have certain drawbacks. They involve a high degree of self-deception and reality distortion and usually are not adaptive in the sense of realistically coping with the adjustment problem. The individual who continually rationalizes away his mistakes is not apt to profit from them. Because defense mechanisms operate on relatively unconscious levels, they are not subject to normal conscious checks and evaluations. In fact, the individual usually resents having his attention called to them, for once they become conscious, they do not serve their defensive purposes so well.

Ego defense mechanisms take many forms. Like task-oriented reactions, they may involve primarily attack, withdrawal, or compromise. For example, the individual may defend himself by a good offense—perhaps blaming others for mistakes or unacceptable desires that are really his own. Or he may escape from the painful truth by denying it or by unconsciously pushing it out of his consciousness. Or he may work out a compromise in which a painful idea is admitted to consciousness but distorted in such a way that it is no longer hurtful. The more common defense mechanisms are discussed in the next several pages.

Denial of reality (escapism). Probably the simplest and most primitive of all ego defense mechanisms is denial of reality. We evade many disagreeable realities simply by ignoring or refusing to acknowledge them. Very few of us, for example, accept the full inevitability of death. Of course, we act as if we were quite resigned to the idea, but the full realization of the actual physical decay of our bodies is usually mercifully obscured by vague feelings of our omnipotence—everybody else dies but not us—and by various religious and philosophical convictions about continuation of life after death.

This tendency to avoid or deny unpleasant reality is related to the concept of *perceptual defense*. Not only do we become increasingly sensitive to stimuli that appear useful in adaptation or enhance the self, but we tend to avoid those aspects of a situation which are traumatic or self-devaluating or contradictory to our assumptions. We turn away from unpleasant sights, we refuse to discuss unpleasant topics, we ignore or deny criticism, we refuse to face many of our real problems, and even in old age we are prone to deny to ourselves the evidence of physical decline. Proud parents are notoriously blind when it comes to perceiving the defects of their offspring. One mother, whose nine-year-old son had been diagnosed by several psychologists and psychiatrists as mentally retarded, developed the firm belief that her son was a member of a new species which matured at a slower rate and would in the long run achieve a higher level of mental development. Under extreme conditions —such as imprisonment—the individual may experience the feeling that "This isn't really happening to me." Here the defensive reaction appears, at least temporarily, to protect the individual from the full impact of his traumatic situation.

Some of the methods commonly used for avoiding unpleasant reality are referred to as *escapism*. These include such strategies as procrastination, refusal to face unpleasant situations, and preoccupation with work, social engagements, or other activities to such an extent that the individual is just too busy with seemingly important matters to face his real problems. The latter is sometimes referred to as "escape into reality." Other commonly used methods of escapism are "not being in the mood" or getting "sick."

By means of this mechanism of ignoring or denying unpleasant reality, we do protect ourselves from a great deal of stress. But like the proverbial ostrich who buries his head in the sand when danger approaches, we may fail to take cognizance of many things which are essential for effective adjustment.

Fantasy. Not only do we often deny un-

pleasant outer or inner realities, but we also tend to construct the world in fantasy as we would like it to be. We fall for various "get rich quick" schemes, we accept flattery eagerly, and we are highly susceptible to selling techniques based on telling us what we want to hear about the merchandise.

Fantasy is stimulated by frustrated desires and grows essentially out of mental images associated with need gratification. In fantasy the person achieves his goals and gratifies his needs, although in substitute fashion. Such fantasies may take many forms. Starving men commonly have mental images of food; the would-be business tycoon has fantasies of wealth, success, and high social standing.

Of course, fantasy may be either productive or nonproductive. Productive fantasy is used constructively in maintaining motivation and in the solution of immediate problems, as in creative imagination. Nonproductive fantasy is merely a wish-fulfilling activity, compensating for lack of achievement or need gratification rather than stimulating or promoting achievement.

Two common varieties of wish-fulfilling fantasy are the "conquering hero" and the "suffering hero" patterns. In the first, the individual pictures himself a great and courageous soldier, an athlete, a surgeon, or some other remarkable figure who performs incredible feats and wins the admiration and respect of all, the essential idea being that he is rich, powerful, and respected. James Thurber used this theme as the basis for his *Secret Life of Walter Mitty*. Hostility is frequently dissipated safely and conveniently through conquering hero fantasies in which the individual destroys or punishes all who stand in his way. Most students report fantasies involving the physical injury or destruction of others, such as hitting, shooting, machine-gunning, and even running over people in tanks. Undoubtedly these fantasies act as safety valves for the release of hostility and provide some measure of compensatory gratification.

The suffering hero does not have to admit any personal inferiority because he imagines that he may be suffering from some terrible affliction, handicap, or visitation from unjust fate. When others find out about his difficulties and realize how nobly and with what courage he has carried on, they will accord him the sympathy and admiration he deserves. Thus inferior performance is explained away without any threat to the individual's feeling of adequacy or basic worth.

Many of our fantasies are ready-made for us in the form of movies, television dramas, magazine stories, and books. In these we can escape from our own status and identify ourselves in fantasy with the hero or heroine, bravely facing and surmounting their problems with them, and sharing in their adventures and triumphs.

The ability to escape temporarily from unpleasant reality into a more pleasant fantasy world has considerable adjustive value. It may add the dash of excitement and interest which enables us to bear up under an otherwise drab and uninteresting existence, or our fantasy achievements and their rewards may spur us on to greater efforts toward our goals in real life. We often return to work with increased vigor and enthusiasm after seeing a movie. Purely wish-fulfilling fantasies, however, are divorced from reality, and thus present a danger for adequate personality adjustment. For it may become increasingly easy to retreat to a dream world when the going gets tough. Particularly under conditions of extreme frustration our fantasies are apt to get out of hand. For example, in a study of 19 men awaiting death by execution, Bluestone and McGahee (1962) noted that many of the men took it for granted that their appeals for clemency would be successful. In one extreme case, the prisoner developed the delusional belief that a pardon had been granted. In the case of these men, we can see both fantasy and denial of reality at work.

Rationalization. Rationalization has two major defensive values: (a) it helps us to justify what we do and what we believe, and (b) it aids us in softening the disappointment connected with unattainable goals.

Typically, rationalization involves thinking up logical, socially approved reasons for our past, present, or proposed behavior. With a little effort we can soon justify to ourselves the absolute necessity of purchasing a new car, of watching television instead of studying, or even of marrying someone with whom we are not in love. Carrying matters a step further, we may find it equally easy to justify most selfish and antisocial behavior. "Why should we yield the right of way to an oncoming motorist? He

wouldn't yield it to us if he could help it, so why should we show him any consideration?" "Suppose we did misrepresent the facts in making a sale—the other fellow has to learn sometime not to be so gullible and this provided a cheap lesson."

Often we manage not only to *justify* our behavior, but actually to feel righteous about it. Even callous brutality can be reinterpreted through rationalization as noble and praiseworthy. Thus Hitler saw the liquidation of the Jews not as reprehensible but as a noble crusade. One of the most notorious bootleggers and gangsters of American history, when finally caught and imprisoned, insisted that the government was persecuting him—that all he was trying to do was bring people the "lighter pleasures of life." By such rationalizations it is possible to feel admirable and righteous instead of ashamed and guilty.

In protecting ourselves from the disappointment of failure to reach unattainable goals, we often resort to two additional types of rationalization—the so-called sour grapes and sweet lemon mechanisms. The "sour grapes" mechanism is based upon the fable of the fox who, unable to reach clusters of luscious grapes, decided that they were sour and not worth having anyway. A new automobile may not be desirable because it costs more than it is worth, the insurance on it is exorbitant, it would lead to increased driving and increased possibility of accidents, and besides if people don't like you well enough to enjoy riding in your old car, they aren't worth having as friends. Similarly, we may view business success as requiring too much effort or point out that the girl we couldn't get talks too much and will probably lose her figure at an early age. As Aronson and Carlsmith (1962) have pointed out, one way of reducing the discrepancy between our assumptions of what is desirable and our failure to take action is to convince ourselves that the particular goal object is not really desirable after all.

The "sweet lemon" attitude is in a sense an extension of the "sour grapes" mechanism. Not only is the unattainable not worth while, but what we have is remarkably satisfactory. The disadvantages of a new car are obvious and the many virtues of our old one would make such an exchange extremely silly. We find comfort in our poverty, for money is the root of all evil and would probably distort our political and economic views. Such "sweet lemon" mechanisms may involve more generalized "Pollyanna" attitudes so that "Every dark cloud has a silver lining" and "Everything happens for the best."

Frequently, of course, it is difficult to tell where an objective consideration of facts and problems leaves off and rationalization begins. Rather conclusive indications of rationalization are (a) hunting for reasons to justify our behavior or beliefs, (b) being unable to recognize inconsistencies or contradictory evidence, and (c) becoming upset when our "reasons" are questioned. The questioning of our rationalizations, of course, is a threat to the defenses we have managed to construct against self-devaluation, and anxiety would be aroused if we were to permit these defenses to be destroyed.

Even the young child soon learns to justify questionable behavior by advancing reasons for it which he has learned are socially approved. And as he internalizes the value attitudes of society he follows the same procedures in justifying his behavior to himself. In this way rationalization becomes an important adjustive reaction in helping us to avoid unnecessary frustrations and to maintain a reasonable degree of self-integrity in a dangerous world. The price of this defensive reaction, however, is self-deception, for we accept reasons for our behavior which are not the true ones. As a result, we are less likely to profit from our errors, and may instead spend our energy in trying to justify them or in proving that they were not really errors or misdeeds at all. When used to an extreme degree, rationalization may lead to the development of false beliefs or delusions which are maintained despite contradictory objective evidence.

Projection. Projection is a defensive reaction by means of which we (a) transfer the blame for our own shortcomings, mistakes, and misdeeds to others, and (b) attribute to others our own unacceptable impulses, thoughts, and desires.

Projection is perhaps most commonly evidenced in our tendency to blame someone or something outside ourselves for our own mistakes and shortcomings. The student who fails an examination may feel sure the teacher was unfair; the erring husband may blame his moral lapse on "the girl who led me on"; the boy being punished for fighting may protest, "It wasn't my fault—he hit me first." Fate and bad luck are particularly overworked objects of projection. Even inanimate objects are not exempt from blame. The three-year-old boy who falls off his hobby horse may attack it with blows and kicks; the tennis player who misses the ball may look at his racquet with a puzzled expression as if there must be a hole in it; and the basketball player who slips may return to inspect the imaginary slippery spot. In extreme cases the individual may become convinced that other persons or forces are systematically working against him. Such ideas may develop into delusions of persecution involving the supposed plots and conspiracies of his enemies.

In other projective reactions we attribute to others our own unacceptable desires and wishes and thoughts. On an elementary level, this is evidenced by our tendency to see others in the light of our own personality make-up. If we are honest, we tend to think others are too, whereas if we are deceitful, we are prone to attribute this characteristic to others. In more extreme degrees of projection, the individual with guilt-arousing homosexual leanings may accuse other men of trying to seduce him—while he remains unaware of his own homosexual inclinations. It is common for mental patients who are obsessed by ethically unacceptable sexual ideas to accuse others of "pouring filth into their minds."

Projections probably develop from our early realization that putting the blame on others for our own failures, unethical thoughts, and misdeeds helps us to avoid social disapproval and punishment. And as we internalize society's values, such projections protect us from self-devaluation. Again, however, we may pay an exorbitant price for our ego defenses.

Repression. Repression is a defensive reaction by means of which the individual's own painful or dangerous thoughts and desires are excluded from his consciousness without his awareness of what is happening. It has often been referred to as selective forgetting, but it is more in the nature of selective remembering. For although the material is denied admission to consciousness, it is not really forgotten. The soldier who has seen his best friend killed by shrapnel may find this experience so terribly painful that it is excluded from consciousness and he becomes "amnesic" for the battle experience. However, by means of hypnosis or sodium pentothal interviews, the repressed experience may be brought into consciousness.

It is of value to distinguish repression from *suppression*. Suppression differs from repression in that here the individual consciously "puts the idea out of his mind" and thinks of other things. Thus it is not as dangerous to his mental health as repression is apt to be, for it is deliberate—the individual knows what he is doing.

Repression is by no means always complete: often desires and thoughts are only partially excluded from consciousness. Repressed desires are frequently revealed in dreams, reveries, jokes, and slips of the tongue, as well as under the influence of alcohol or drugs. Vague feelings of unworthiness, insecurity, and guilt also may indicate incomplete repression. With continued frustration, repressed desires may increase in strength and threaten to break through into consciousness and overt action. Such threats lead to the arousal of anxiety and additional defenses.

Repression is an extremely important ego defense mechanism and in varying degrees enters into most, if not all, of the other ego defense mechanisms. In helping the individual to control dangerous desires and in minimizing the disruptive effects of painful experiences, it plays an important role. In the case of sudden, traumatic experience, it may operate as a temporary defense until time and other factors have somewhat desensitized the individual to the shock. Like other defensive reactions, however, repression is self-deceptive and may be used to an exaggerated degree or to protect the individual from problems that could be met better by a realistic facing and working through than by evasion. The repression of dangerous desires also ties up considerable energy which then is not available for direct attempts to solve life's problems.

Reaction formation.   Sometimes we protect ourselves from dangerous desires by not only repressing them but actually developing conscious attitudes and behavior patterns which are just the opposite. In this way we erect obstacles or barriers to reinforce our repression and keep our real desires from being carried out in overt behavior.

Usually reaction formation can be easily rec-ognized by its extreme intolerance, which is out of all proportion to the importance of the situation. The most militant crusaders against vice are often fighting their own repressed impulses as well as condemning the outcome of such impulses in others. Self-appointed protectors of the public's morals who voluntarily devote their lives to reading obscene literature, attending burlesque shows, and investigating the younger generation and who obsessively condemn homosexuality, alcohol, and other alleged vices are usually found to have dangerously strong impulses in the same directions themselves. By making such activities their "duty," they partially satisfy their repressed desires and at the same time hold them in check by their energetic condemnations.

In everyday behavior, reaction formation may take the form of developing a "don't care" attitude to conceal feelings of rejection and a craving for affection, of assuming an air of bravado when we are fearful, of developing a puritanical attitude toward sexual and other pleasures, of being excessively polite to a person we don't like—so much so that we make him uncomfortable. In more extreme form, the individual may develop various exaggerated fears, as for example of syphilis, which may help him to keep his dangerous impulses in check. Reaction formation in extreme form is well illustrated by excerpts from an interesting and self-diagnostic letter which Masserman (1961) received from a "kind-hearted" antivivisectionist:

". . . I read [a magazine article] . . . on your work on alcoholism . . . I am surprised that anyone who is as well educated as you must be to hold the position that you do would stoop to such depths as to torture helpless little cats in the pursuit of a cure for alcoholics. . . . A drunkard does not want to be cured—a drunkard is just a weak minded idiot who belongs in the gutter and should be left there. Instead of torturing helpless little cats why not torture the drunks or better still exert your would-be noble effort toward getting a bill passed to *exterminate* the drunks. They are not any good to anyone or themselves and are just a drain on the public, having to pull them off the street, jail them, then they have to be fed while there and it's against the law to feed them arsenic so there they are. . . . If people are such weaklings the world is better off without them.

". . . My greatest wish is that you have brought home to you a torture that will be a thousand fold greater than what you have, and are doing to the little animals. . . . If you are an example of what a noted psychiatrist should be I'm glad I am just an ordinary human being without a letter after my name. I'd rather be just myself with a clear conscience, *knowing I have not hurt any living creature,* and can sleep without seeing frightened, terrified dying cats—because I know they must die after you have finished with them. No punishment is too great for you and I hope I live to read about your mangled body and long suffering before you finally die—and I'll laugh long and loud." (p. 38)

Reaction formation, like repression, has adjustive value in helping us to maintain socially approved behavior and to avoid facing our unacceptable desires with the consequent self-devaluation that would be involved. But because this mechanism, too, is self-deceptive, it often results in exaggerated and rigid fears or beliefs which may complicate the individual's adjustive reactions and may lead to excessive harshness or severity in dealing with the lapses of others.

Undoing (atonement). Undoing is designed to negate or annul some disapproved thought, impulse, or act. It is as if the individual has spelled a word wrong and used an eraser to clear the paper and start over. Apologizing for wrongs committed against others, penance, repentance, and undergoing punishment are all forms of undoing.

Undoing apparently develops out of our early training in which we are made to apologize or to make some restitution, or are punished in some way commensurate with our socially disapproved behavior. Once the apology or restitution or punishment has taken place, our misdeed is negated and we can start with a clean slate and with renewed parental approval and affection. In this sequence of events, we also learn that repentance, penance, or restitution may enable us to avoid more serious punishment—by returning Johnny's toys with considerable alacrity, we may avoid being spanked, although we may of course be scolded. By saying we are sorry and offering to do something to make up for our misdeed, we may escape punishment and rejection.

Since we have been taught that wrong-doing inevitably leads to punishment, we have all developed various methods of atoning for or undoing our misdeeds—methods designed to avoid or ameliorate the punishment that would otherwise accrue. The unfaithful husband may bring his wife presents; the unethical businessman may give huge sums of money to charity.

Sometimes we feel that the only atonement for our misdeeds is punishment itself, and we may confess them in order that we may be punished and thereby pay for and erase our sins. Not infrequently people who have committed crimes years earlier will confess to the police in order to be punished and regain their self-esteem and security. Where sins seem so great that the individual sees no hope of atoning for them, he may suffer such intense guilt, anxiety, and self-devaluation that suicide seems the only way out.

Since undoing is fundamental to the maintenance of ethical human relations, as well as to our self-esteem, it is one of our most valuable ego defenses. Particularly in combination with rationalization and projection it is a potent defense against self-devaluating guilt feelings. As we shall see, however, in our study of psychotic patterns, undoing is subject to exaggerated and unhealthy usage.

Regression. Regression is a defensive reaction involving a retreat to the use of reaction patterns which were appropriate at an earlier level of development. It involves a modification of behavior in the direction of more primitive, infantile modes of behavior. When a new addition to the family has seemingly undermined his status, a child may revert to bed-wetting, baby talk, thumb-sucking, and other infantile behavior which once brought him parental attention. The frustrated adult may return to the temper tantrums which were useful during childhood. The bride may run home to Mother at the first sign of trouble. Perhaps regression is best typified by the tendency of older people to live more and more in the past. In fact, regression has been called the "old oaken bucket" delusion because of its emphasis on the superior joys of "the good old days."

Regression can be readily understood if we remember the child's gradual shift from a position of helplessness and dependence on the parents to one of independent action and responsibility. This developmental process from dependence to independence is by no means an easy

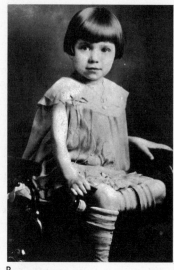
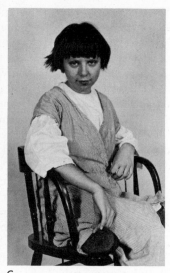

A B   C

An extreme example of regression. The patient looked like any other seventeen-year-old girl. (A) until she found the photograph of herself taken at the age of five (B). Thereafter, she tried to look as much as she could like the pictured child (C).

accomplishment, and it is common for all of us in the face of adult difficulties to yearn for the carefree, sheltered days of childhood. Consequently, it is not surprising that in the face of severe stress we may retreat from adult reaction patterns to a less mature level of adjustment. We might expect something akin to regression to occur merely on the basis of the frequent failure of more recently learned reactions to bring satisfaction. In looking for other, more successful modes of adjustment it would be only natural that we should try out discarded patterns which previously brought satisfaction (Barthol and Ku, 1959).

However, regression is a more comprehensive reaction than merely trying out older modes of response when new ones have failed. For in regression the individual retreats from reality to a less demanding personal status—one which involves lowered aspirations and more readily accomplished satisfactions. This point is well illustrated by Bettelheim's reference to a general "regression to infantile behavior" seen in nearly all the prisoners at Dachau and Buchenwald.

"The prisoners lived, like children, only in the imme-

diate present; . . . they became unable to plan for the future or to give up immediate pleasure satisfactions to gain greater ones in the near future. . . . They were boastful, telling tales about what they had accomplished in their former lives, or how they succeeded in cheating foremen or guards, and how they sabotaged the work. Like children they felt not at all set back or ashamed when it became known that they had lied about their prowess." (1943, p. 443)

The disorganization and collapse of adult behavior and the emergence of developmentally lower levels of functioning is a very common form of ego breakdown. In its most dramatic form; it is seen in mentally ill adults who show such extreme regression to infantile levels of behavior that they are unable to wash, dress, or feed themselves or take care of their eliminative needs. In some cases, they even curl up in a position similar to that of the fetus in the womb.

The defensive function of regression is readily apparent in this severe case.

"A seventeen-year-old girl was brought to a psychiatric clinic by her mother with the complaint that for the preceding five months her behavior had become increasingly destructive and irrational. The history revealed that after the patient was about four years old her parents had begun to quarrel violently, making her early environment extremely contentious and unstable.

"At about this age she first developed various neurotic traits: nail-biting, temper-tantrums, enuresis and numerous phobias. When the patient was seven the mother refused further sexual relations with the father and left the marital bed, but the patient continued to sleep with the father until she was thirteen. At this time the mother suspected that the patient was being incestuously seduced, obtained legal custody of the girl and moved away with her to a separate home. The patient resented this, quarreled frequently with her mother, became a disciplinary problem at home and at school and acquired a police record for various delinquencies. Three years later, at the patient's insistence, she and her mother paid an unexpected visit to the father and found him living with a girl in questionable circumstances. In a violent scene, the mother denounced the father for unfaithfulness and, again contrary to the patient's wishes, took her home. There the patient refused to attend school and rapidly became sullen, withdrawn, and non-communicative. During her mother's absence at work she would throw the house into disorder, destroy clothes her mother had made for her, and throw her mother's effects out of the window. During one of these forays she discovered a photograph of herself at the age of five, which, incidentally, was so poorly lighted and faded that, for one detail, it did not show her eyebrows. Using this as a pattern, she shaved off her own eyebrows, cut her hair to the same baby bob, and began to affect the facial expression and sitting posture of the pictured child. When brought to the hospital her general behavior was correspondingly childish; she was untidy and enuretic, giggled incessantly or spoke in simple monosyllabic sentences, spent most of her time on the floor playing with blocks or paper dolls, and had to be fed, cleaned, and supervised as though she were an infant. In effect, she appeared to have regressed to a relatively desirable period in life antedating disruptive jealousies and other conflict; moreover, she acted out this regression in unconsciously determined but strikingly symbolic patterns of eliminating the mother as a rival and regaining the father she had lost in her childhood." (Masserman, 1961, pp. 70-71, case of Dr. John Romano)

Identification. The growing child soon realizes that other people's evaluation of him is to a large extent dependent upon his family and other group memberships. The position of his father, the size of his house, the importance of his relatives all help to determine his personal prestige and status, and his sense of identity comes to include these external sources of strength and prestige. Exaggerating the strength, importance, and wealth of his father early becomes a common means of enhancing his own prestige.

This mechanism of identification is expanded in later life to include a wide variety of situations and persons and enables the individual to experience vicarious achievements, feelings of adequacy, and other satisfactions through his various identifications. Not only does society evaluate him in terms of his group identifications, but he comes to evaluate himself in the light of them. College students bask in the reflected glory of their football team—"We won today." Fraternity and sorority members enjoy the social prestige of their groups; adults identify themselves with their occupations, the size of their homes, their membership in exclusive clubs, the size of their bank accounts, and the cars they drive. Parents identify themselves with the accomplishments of their children. Most employees identify themselves with the power and prestige of the company for which they work. By so doing, the individual takes as his own some of the desirable attributes of the groups and institutions to which he belongs.

We are probably all prone to a certain amount of fantasy identification in which we gain vicarious satisfaction through identifying ourselves with the leading characters in novels, movies, and television dramas. It is interesting to note that in those rare pictures in which the hero dies, some members of the audience slump down in their seats and figuratively or symbolically die themselves. Such identifications, particularly in the form of "hero worship," may play an important role in shaping the personality development of the child, who strives to be like his hero in dress and manner. He shapes his own values after those of his hero.

Most people identify themselves with the hero or winner and thus achieve increased feelings of adequacy or worth. However, sometimes identification backfires, as when we identify ourselves with a group that does not accept us or when our football team continues to lose games and is scoffed at by sports writers and friends. In such cases our identification leads to self-devaluation rather than self-enhancement. This is one important reason why it is difficult for a coach to hold his job if his team loses consistently.

In general, individuals tend to identify themselves with others who are most like themselves or who possess the qualities which they most desire. The high-school athlete identifies himself with the athletic hero, the scholar with the great scientist, the coed with the glamorous cinema beauty. Where there is compensatory identification, the meek, timid individual may become the great and brave detective, or the uneducated man the renowned scholar and scientist, but all identifications conform to the individual's values and ego ideal.

We all use identification. But like the other ego defense mechanisms it is potentially dangerous. We see identification in extreme form in certain psychotic reactions, where there is a complete loss of personal identification and the firm belief that one is some famous person such as Jesus Christ or Abraham Lincoln.

Introjection. Introjection is, in a way, a primitive form of identification in which the individual internalizes aspects of the threatening situation. This is exemplified early in life when the child gradually learns and accepts as his own various social regulations and value attitudes. He can then control his own behavior in the light of his internalized values, thus protecting himself from possible infractions of regulations and avoiding social retaliation.

The use of introjection under extreme conditions is well described by Bettelheim (1943) in his report of his experiences at the German concentration camps of Dachau and Buchenwald. Under the insidious camp experiences, previous values and identifications were broken down and new norms were introjected—Nazi norms.

"A prisoner had reached the final stage of adjustment to the camp situation when he had changed his personality so as to accept as his own the values of the Gestapo. . . . old prisoners were sometimes instrumental in getting rid of the unfit, in this way making a feature of Gestapo ideology a feature of their own behavior." (pp. 447-449)

In revolutions leading to dictatorial forms of government, many people introject the new values and beliefs as a protection against behavior which might get them into trouble.

Introjection is thus a defensive reaction which seems to follow the general idea, "If you can't beat 'em, join 'em." Apparently from an ego-defensive point of view it is better to be good or bad oneself than to be continually at the mercy of good or bad objects or forces from without.

Compensation. Compensatory reactions are defenses against feelings of inferiority and inadequacy growing out of real or imagined personal defects or weaknesses as well as out of our inevitable failures and setbacks. Such reactions may take many forms and may even represent deliberate, task-oriented behavior, as in the case of a physical handicap where the individual attempts to overcome his handicap directly through increased effort and persistence. Demosthenes, the great orator, had to overcome his early stuttering, and Theodore Roosevelt waged a valiant fight against early ill-health to become noted for his physical daring and robustness. Compensatory reactions of this type may be a deciding factor in success, as biographers are quick to point out.

More commonly, compensatory reactions are indirect: there is an attempt to substitute for the defect in some way or to draw attention away from it. The physically unattractive boy or girl may develop an exceptionally pleasing personality, the puny boy may turn from athletics to scholarship, and the mediocre nobody may become the Grand Imperial Potentate of some secret order. A whole science of dress has developed which centers around the concealing of undesirable physical features and the emphasizing of desirable ones. The short girl is made to look tall, the fat girl thin, the colorless one glamorous.

Unfortunately, not all compensatory reactions are desirable or useful. The child who feels insecure may show off to try to get more attention and raise his status in the eyes of others and himself; the boy who feels inferior and unpopular may become the local bully; the person who feels unloved and frustrated may eat too much or resort to excessive fantasy satisfactions. Some people brag about their illustrious ancestors and exaggerate their own accomplishments, while others resort to criticism or innuendoes in an attempt to cut others down to their own size. In extreme cases, the individual may engage in antisocial behavior or develop marked eccentricities in an unconscious attempt to get some attention and evidence of interest and concern from others.

Compensatory reactions are greatly stimulated by our highly competitive society. We constantly compare ourselves with others and too often measure our worth and that of others largely by status, achievements, and possessions. Such social values lead to the development of strong psychological motivation toward at least average, and if possible superior, achievement. In meeting these conditions, compensatory reactions may be of great adjustive value, but when they result in increased anxiety or become exaggerated or take antisocial forms, they hinder rather than help us.

Displacement. In displacement there is a shift of emotion, symbolic meaning, or fantasy from a person or object toward which it was originally directed to another person or object. Typically it involves the discharge of aroused emotions toward neutral or less dangerous objects. A child who has been spanked or thwarted by his mother may kick his little sister or a young playmate or may break up his toys. Many times a minor situation acts as a sort of trigger which releases the pent-up emotional feelings in a torrent of displaced anger and abuse surprising to everyone involved and out of all proportion to the immediate incident.

Through a process of symbolic association, displacement may become extremely complex and deviant. Swearing is commonly used as a means of discharging pent-up feelings. "Beating" a disliked rival at bridge or golf may symbolically represent his destruction. Destructive criticism and vindictive gossip are frequently only disguised methods of expressing hostility. Repressed fears of murdering a hated husband may be displaced to fear of all sorts of dangerous weapons such as guns, knives, or poison. Such apparently irrational fears, or *phobias,* act as additional defenses by protecting the individual from situations in which his dangerous impulses might be carried out in action.

Frequently, displacement is combined with projection, as in Nazi Germany, where the blame for all the country's ills was projected upon the Jews and the Communists, and pent-up feelings of frustration and hostility were displaced onto these two groups. This scapegoating is common in dictatorships, where hostility is likely to be aroused by the stern, repressive measures of the government but where any opposition or direct expression of the hostility is extremely dangerous.

Displacement is of considerable adjustive value because it enables the individual to discharge dangerous emotional tensions without even knowing to whom such feelings were originally directed, hence avoiding the risk of loss of love and possible retaliation. In this way, it enables the individual to avoid the conflict of ambivalent feelings toward some powerful or loved person. By displacing his pent-up hostility onto his wife, the little clerk maintains relatively pure feelings, consciously, of respect and cordiality toward his domineering boss. The boy who displaces his hostility onto his toys or playmates can maintain relatively pure feelings of love toward the mother who has just punished or frustrated him. In such instances, displacement is often accompanied by repression (particularly where hostility is directed toward some loved person such as the mother), and this combination is an extremely potent ego defense.

Unfortunately, however, displacement may exact a heavy price in terms of the efficiency with which stress situations are handled. The clerk who displaces onto his wife the hostility aroused by his boss may avoid certain problems in his job but only at the expense of his marriage. Similarly, the use of minority groups as scapegoats for the frustrations and hostilities of the dominant group is not likely to contribute to social progress. When feasible, it is much more healthful to face and work through hostility-arousing situations than to avoid them through displacement.

Emotional insulation. In emotional insulation the individual reduces his degree of emotional involvement in situations that might prove disappointing or hurtful.

Since we all undergo many disappointments in life, we usually learn to keep our hopes and anticipations within bounds until a hoped-for event actually occurs. We are careful to avoid premature celebrations or to let our hopes get too high. The student who is looking forward to a date with a very attractive girl may not let himself get too excited or enthusiastic for fear that something will happen to prevent it or that she will not like him. Such reactions are well expressed in the common saying, "I didn't dare to even hope."

In more extreme conditions of long-continued frustration, as in chronic unemployment or prison confinement, many persons lose hope, become resigned and apathetic, and adapt themselves to a restricted way of living devoid of hope and ego involvement. Such "broken" individuals protect themselves from the bitter hurt of sustained frustration and disappointment by giving up and becoming passive recipients of whatever life brings them. Similarly, in certain forms of mental illness, such as chronic schizophrenia, there is often an extreme use of emotional insulation which protects the individual from ego involvement in a world which he has found unbearably hurtful.

Up to a point, emotional insulation is an important means of defense against unnecessary disappointment and hurt. But life involves calculated risks, and most of us are willing to take our chances on active participation. Although we occasionally get badly hurt, we have the resiliency to recover and try again. Unfortunately, some individuals who have been badly bruised by life's blows thereafter restrict any further involvement by which they might again be hurt. The sensitive youth who has been hurt by a broken love affair may insulate himself to such an extent that he finds it impossible to achieve a close affectional relationship again. Emotional insulation provides a protective shell of aloofness and detachment which prevents a repetition of previous pain, but it reduces the individual's healthy, vigorous participation in life.

Isolation (intellectualization, dissociation). Isolation is a form of emotional insulation in which the emotional charge in a hurtful situation is distorted or cut off. The hurt over Mother's death is reduced by saying that she lived a full life or that she died mercifully without pain. Catastrophes are interpreted within the framework of, "It is the will of the Lord." Cynicism may become a convenient means of withdrawing emotional support from our ideals. We may reduce guilt feelings over unethical behavior by

emphasizing the cultural relativity of ideas of right and wrong. Often the glib admission that "we should work harder" or that "we should be less selfish and more interested in the welfare of others" seems to cut off a good deal of guilt and relieve us of the necessity of positive action.

Intellectualization, a form of isolation, may be utilized under extremely stressful conditions as well as in dealing with the milder stresses of everyday life. Bluestone and McGahee have found that this defense mechanism was often utilized by prisoners awaiting execution. They have described the pattern as follows: " 'So they'll kill me; and that's that'—this said with a shrug of the shoulders suggests that the affect appropriate to the thought has somehow been isolated." (1962, p. 395) In such reactions, rationalization and other ego defense mechanisms may play a prominent role, but it is the cutting off of the normal affective (emotional) charge by means of intellectualization which primarily concerns us here.

Another form of isolation involves the dissociation of certain conflicting attitudes or of normal thought-affect relationships. The confirmed believer in democracy may also believe in racial discrimination. The ruthless and dishonest businessman may be a kind father and a "pillar" of the church.

The individual may resort to rationalization to make such incompatible values seem more consistent, but usually he is even unaware of his inconsistency. The essential process seems to be one of unconscious isolation in which one attitude is dissociated from the other. A passage from Sheila Cousins (1938), a London prostitute, well illustrates this type of dissociation or isolation reaction. She wrote:

"The act of sex I could go through because I hardly seemed to be taking part in it. It was merely something happening to me, while my mind drifted inconsequentially away. Indeed, it was scarcely happening even to me; it was happening to something lying on a bed that had a vague connection with me, while I was calculating whether I could afford a new coat or impatiently counting sheep jumping over a gate." (pp. 150-151)

In this way situations which would ordinarily give rise to strong emotional conflicts are kept isolated from each other in our minds. In more

SUMMARY CHART OF EGO DEFENSE MECHANISMS

Denial of reality	Protecting self from unpleasant reality by refusal to perceive or face it, often by escapist activities like getting "sick" or being preoccupied with other things
Fantasy	Gratifying frustrated desires in imaginary achievements
Rationalization	Attempting to prove that one's behavior is "rational" and justifiable and thus worthy of self and social approval
Projection	Placing blame for difficulties upon others or attributing one's own unethical desires to others
Repression	Preventing painful or dangerous thoughts from entering consciousness
Reaction formation	Preventing dangerous desires from being expressed by exaggerating opposed attitudes and types of behavior and using them as "barriers"
Undoing	Atoning for and thus counteracting immoral desires or acts
Regression	Retreating to earlier developmental level involving less mature responses and usually a lower level of aspiration
Identification	Increasing feelings of worth by identifying self with person or institution of illustrious standing
Introjection	Incorporating external values and standards into ego structure so individual is not at their mercy as external threats
Compensation	Covering up weakness by emphasizing desirable trait or making up for frustration in one area by overgratification in another
Displacement	Discharging pent-up feelings, usually of hostility, on objects less dangerous than those which initially aroused the emotions
Emotional insulation	Reducing ego involvement and withdrawing into passivity to protect self from hurt
Intellectualization	Cutting off affective charge from hurtful situations or separating incompatible attitudes by logic-tight compartments
Sublimation	Gratifying or working off frustrated sexual desires in nonsexual activities
Sympathism	Striving to gain sympathy from others thus bolstering feelings of self-worth despite failures
Acting-out	Reducing the anxiety aroused by forbidden desires by permitting their expression

extreme cases, we may find the isolation or dissociation of entire sections of the ego, as in multiple personality or certain psychotic reactions where the patient looks up from scrubbing the floor to tell you in a detached way that he is a multimillionaire.

Sublimation. Sublimation, as it has been traditionally conceived, involves the acceptance of a socially approved substitute goal for a drive whose normal channel of expression or normal goal is blocked. Presumably, the girl who fails to marry may find a substitute emotional outlet in teaching or nursing. The chronically hostile individual may become a mortician.

There is considerable doubt, however, as to whether any real process of sublimation actually takes place. For example, can a desire as basic as the sexual desire actually be sublimated? Kinsey *et al.* (1948) found evidence of repression but hardly any evidence of sublimation in sexual behavior. Apparently sublimation, in so far as it does occur, is based upon the utilization of general body energy in constructive activities which indirectly reduce the tension built up around frustrated sexual or other drives.

Sympathism and acting-out. Other ego defense mechanisms have been delineated, such as *sympathism* and *acting-out*. In the former the individual strives to gain the sympathy of others by telling about his "tough breaks," illnesses, and other difficulties. In this way, his feelings of self-worth are bolstered, despite his failures, by the expressions of concern and sympathy of others who realize how difficult it must be for one who is in ill-health or has had such bad luck.

Acting-out is a mechanism in which the individual reduces the anxiety aroused by forbidden desires by actually permitting their expression. Thus rather than trying to repress immoral sexual or hostile desires which are anxiety arousing, he simply engages in the behavior. Obviously, this is not likely to be possible under ordinary circumstances unless the individual has very weak ethical and reality controls, since he would otherwise subject himself to the possibility of subsequent guilt feelings, social disapproval, and punishment. There are times, however, when particular conflicts or situations build up to such high levels of tension and anxiety that almost any action is welcomed as a relief in order "to get it over with."

In the preceding discussion we have dealt with the major ego defense mechanisms. It is worth re-emphasizing that these defense mechanisms are learned adjustive reactions, that they are motivated by the driving force of anxiety aroused by threats to the self, that they function in both individual and group behavior, that they operate on relatively habitual and unconscious levels, and that they involve self-deception and reality distortion. However, these mechanisms are essential for the maintenance of ego integrity and we all use them in various degrees and ways. Consequently, they may be considered quite normal and even desirable except in cases where they are used to an extreme degree, at the expense of the ultimate adaptive efficiency and happiness of the individual.

Excessive Stress and Decompensation

When the individual's biological and psychological defenses result in a relatively smooth and appropriate adjustment to stress, we call his behavior healthy or normal—it is adjustive, effective, good. When these normal defenses fail, however, the individual is forced to more extreme measures in his struggle to maintain his integrity—often to the extent of exaggerated and inappropriate defensive measures which we refer to as "abnormal." He now becomes ill—physically, mentally, or both.

As we now enter the realm of abnormal behavior proper, it is helpful to note Menninger's (1947) generalization that "What we call disease is an exaggeration of the defensive measures of the personality against any disturbance of its total adjustment homeostasis." When the stress becomes too great and the normal defenses fail to hold, the individual is forced to resort to exaggerated and deviant defensive patterns with a resultant lowering in integration referred to as *decompensation*. This process occurs on biological, psychological, and sociological levels.

BIOLOGICAL DECOMPENSATION

Decompensation on a biological level has been described by Selye (1953, 1956), following his extensive investigations of the hormonal defenses mediated by the autonomic nervous system. Selye found three stages in the physiological decompensation of the pituitary-adrenal system in the face of excessive stress: (a) the "alarm-reaction"—a "call to arms" of the body's defense forces, (b) the "stage of resistance" in which the adaptation is optimal in terms of bodily resources, and (c) the "stage of exhaustion" in which the hormonal defenses break down so that further exposure to stress leads to disintegration and death. Even in the second stage, however, the defensive reactions may overshoot their mark, leading to the disruption of homeostasis—the excessive hormonal secretions may result in ulcers or other pathology which Selye refers to as the "diseases of adaptation."

Where decompensation does not run its entire course leading to the exhaustion and death of the organism, maintenance mechanisms attempt to repair damage and reorganize functions. If the stress has resulted in extensive damage, this is often a matter of the reorganization of "remaining parts" with a permanent lowering of the previous level of integration and functioning.

PSYCHOLOGICAL DECOMPENSATION

The overall course of personality decompensation in the face of excessive stress seems to follow somewhat similar stages. First comes "alarm and mobilization," typically involving increased sensitivity and alertness (vigilance), emotional arousal and increased tension, determined efforts at self-control, and the intensified use of various ego defense mechanisms. Here the individual may show symptoms of maladjustment, such as continuous anxiety, somatic manifestations, and lowered efficiency —indications that the mobilization of adaptive resources is not proving adequate to cope with the stress. Next comes the "stage of resistance," in which new and deviant defensive measures are brought into operation. These include the exaggerated use of ego defense mechanisms like denial and projection and the gradual introduction of neurotic and eventually psychotic patterns. Neurotic reactions usually enable the individual to stabilize his defenses on this level, but in the face of continued severe stress, neurotic defenses may also prove inadequate, and the individual may resort to even more deviant defenses in the form of psychotic reactions, characterized by a break with reality and the introduction of delusional and hallucinatory defenses which attempt to restructure reality in such a way as to protect what remains of his psychological integrity. Thus he may hallucinate voices which tell him that he has been appointed to save mankind. Developing the delusional belief that he is a great religious savior may help him to maintain some semblance of inner integration and some feeling of adequacy though at a heavy price. If these exaggerated and abnormal defensive measures still fail to hold, then the process of decompensation continues to the "stage of exhaustion," with complete ego disintegration and continuous, uncontrolled violence or stupor ending in physical exhaustion and death.

Under continued excessive stress then, psychological decompensation will follow a progressive course from normal alarm and mobilization reactions through neurotic and psychotic defenses to eventual exhaustion and death. Of course, this process of decompensation may stop at any of the stages, if the individual's defensive reactions hold up against the stress or if the stress decreases. Actually, psychotic defenses usually hold up well enough that the individual does not decompensate further to the stage of exhaustion. The following case of a young college girl illustrates the course of decompensation from the "alarm and mobilization" stage through a neurotic to a psychotic level of decompensation.

A sensitive, highly intelligent college girl . . . had a personal history of being rather shy, withdrawn, philosophically minded and overly given to daydreaming. During her sophomore year . . . she was informed by her parents that they were unhappy and planning a divorce. This served to undermine her precarious security further and precipitated the following reaction:

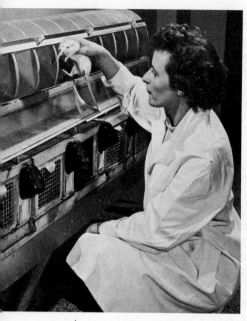

A

B

In Dr. Selye's laboratory, several groups of rats were exposed to different types of stress. Some were tumbled in a rotating drum (A). Some had to swim to the point of exhaustion to keep from drowning (B). Others were exposed to extreme cold. Still others were injected with an overdose of a hormone. Dr. Selye discovered that whatever the particular stress, and regardless of the body system most directly attacked, there was the same overall "stress reaction" of the body as a whole, involving the pituitary-adrenal system. Furthermore, as the animals developed resistance to one type of stress, they became more vulnerable to other types.

On the human level, too, it is apparent that the reaction to stress is not only a specific reaction of the body system most directly threatened but also a reaction of the whole organism. Severe, prolonged stress on any level takes its toll in overall adjustive resources. This means that stress on one level may lead to symptoms on another: thus an ulcer may reflect largely psychological stresses, whereas hallucinations may reflect physiological stress.

"I decided that I would start with a clean slate, study hard, look into and revise some of my views and avoid the unhappiness that seemed to saturate the world. The main trouble was that I could find no one else who wanted to be sensible and mature. This led to a rather hermitic existence in which I studied and philosophized most of the time.

". . . I set certain people, who I thought were leading the perfect life, up on little pedestals and completely worshipped them and devoted myself to them. Since I wanted so to please them and was under such tension, I could hardly speak and was soaked with perspiration while with them. Each remark they had made, no matter how trivial, was indelibly impressed in my mind. It was during this period that I somehow seemed to get completely off the track. In my desperate attempts to find security, I planned a strict schedule which I must adhere to each day. I would figure out my plan, enter it whole-heartedly, and then something would go wrong. One rung off the perfect ladder would send me plunging into the depths. During this period I began to experience obsessive ideas of suicide. I felt so terribly alone and isolated and such a miserable failure. With my attempts at building security I developed grasping, clutching feelings. I wanted to grab people, or trees, or buildings, whenever I felt emotional.

"During this period I was enrolled in a course in biology. My biology teacher was a wonderful person but he did not believe in God as I had been taught to. He knocked the props right out from under my blind faith in God. I could find no immediate substitute which would show clearly which way my life's course should turn. Now I began to experience depressions and as time went on they became more severe and lasted longer. The world seemed a terrible place, and I had no hope for the future. I would spend an average of two to three hours in daydreams each day, and would talk to myself and other imaginary persons whenever I was alone.

"It seems that during this period I somehow lost control. I would hear voices and see persons who weren't really there but they seemed real."[1]

Severe decompensation brings anxiety and exaggerated ego defenses, a predominance of irrational and involuntary reactions, and a generally lowered integration of behavior. As defense piles on defense, the individual's main efforts are toward maintaining some semblance of inner integration and his primary concern becomes the maintenance of his defensive structures. These efforts lead to further distortions in his frame of reference and thus lessen still further his already meager chances of solving his problems realistically. Breaking out of such a vicious circle usually requires therapy.

Certain individuals seem able to maintain effective defenses on a neurotic level in the face of extreme stress, whereas others seem unable to utilize neurotic defensive reactions and go almost directly from normal to psychotic reactions. This has led many investigators to conclude that individuals become either neurotic or psychotic —that the individual utilizes either one or the other of these defense systems but not both. It would appear, however, that we are dealing with differences in the degree to which neurotic defenses are utilized rather than any either-or differences. Some individuals utilize such defenses to a marked degree; others, only slightly. Each of us would eventually become psychotic under sustained, excessive stress.

Usually decompensation is a gradual, long-range process, particularly where it progresses to psychotic reactions, even though the psychotic symptoms themselves may appear suddenly. As we shall see, however, acute neurotic and even psychotic reactions may be precipitated in fairly well-adjusted individuals by sudden and extreme stress which is beyond their stress tolerance. Here the decompensation proceeds rapidly.

If treatment measures increase the individual's adaptive capacities or if the stress decreases, the process of decompensation may be reversed —*recompensation*. The outcome here depends heavily upon the previous level of personality integration and on the degree and length of the ego disorganization. Without adequate treatment, long-continued neurotic or psychotic reactions do not usually reverse themselves with decreasing stress, although there may be a gradual restructuring of defenses within a neurotic or psychotic framework in terms of what remains of normal defensive patterns. This may lead to more effective adjustive reactions and to the *spontaneous remission* of more disabling symptoms.

An excellent summary of the concepts of decompensation outlined in the preceding pages was afforded by Marmor and Pumpian-Mindlin (1950). Their chart, adapted and reproduced on page 112, shows the twofold nature of causation in mental disorder. They stated:

". . . we see now that mental health can be hypothecated as that state in the interrelationship of the individual and his environment in which the personality structure is relatively stable, and the environmental stresses are within its absorptive capacity. . . . If the level of the environmental stresses are increased beyond a certain point, however, neurotic symptoms will develop in the most stable individual, and in cases of extreme stress even psychotic symptoms. . . .

"When . . . the individual personality structure is unstable owing to unfavorable hereditary or early environmental influences, the amount of environmental stress necessary to produce abnormal symptoms is correspondingly less. Thus at one end of our scale we have our theoretically perfectly integrated individual whom only realistic threats of greatest severity and duration can succeed in unsettling; while at the other extreme we have individuals whose personality structure is so poorly equilibrated . . . that the simplest routine of everyday living is too much for it. . . . Between these two extremes there are infinite gradations." (pp. 20-24)

It should be emphasized that personality decompensation may be brought on by biological stresses—such as extreme fatigue or organic disturbances involving the nervous system, which

---

[1]Unless otherwise indicated, the cases cited in this text are from the author's files.

lower the individual's adjustive capacity and hence his stress tolerance—as well as by psychological stress. It is perhaps of value also to note that some writers use *regression* and *decompensation* more or less synonymously. We shall use the concept of decompensation more broadly, however, to include any lowering of ego integration under stress.

SOCIOLOGICAL DECOMPENSATION

Although science is only beginning to make inroads into the understanding of social pathology, it would appear that the concept of decompensation is just as applicable here as on biological and psychological levels. In the face of wars, economic problems, and other internal and external pressures that surpass the adjustive ca-

pacity of the group, it too may undergo varying degrees of decompensation, often resorting to extreme measures as it attempts to maintain its organization and resist disintegration. This process has been depicted by Toynbee and other writers in their description of the decline and fall of Greece, Rome, and other societies which were unable to cope effectively with their internal and external problems.

Although we have separated the biological, psychological, and sociological aspects of adjustment for purposes of discussion, it may be reemphasized that they are mutually interactive factors which are relatively meaningless by themselves—man functions as a psychobiological organism immersed in a physical and social environment. In short, "illness" can be understood in terms of stresses which activate physiological, psychological, and sociological coping

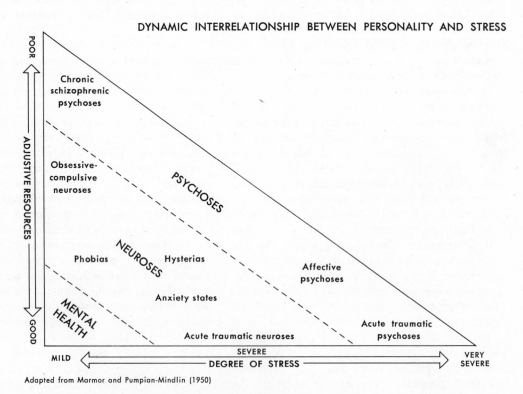

DYNAMIC INTERRELATIONSHIP BETWEEN PERSONALITY AND STRESS

Adapted from Marmor and Pumpian-Mindlin (1950)

Level of adjustment depends on the interaction of two variables: the severity of the stress and the adjustive resources of the individual. Immaturity, a distorted frame of reference, low stress tolerance, or lack of competencies, for example, would lower the individual's resources for dealing with stress and make him vulnerable to stresses that stronger personalities could easily cope with. On the other hand, even a mature, stable personality is vulnerable to very severe stress. Mental disorder appears when the stress—however mild or severe—is too great for one's adjustive resources.

mechanisms and defenses. The outcome depends on (a) the effectiveness of the adjustive action in coping with the stress, (b) the extent to which any damage can be repaired and remaining resources reorganized, and (c) the level of integration and functioning which can be achieved. In some instances the functional level may be permanently lowered following severe stress; in other cases the system—biological, psychological, or sociological—may attain a higher level of integration and functioning than existed previously.

Development and Adjustive Reactions—Summary

We are now in a position to summarize the major points in the dynamic framework which we have constructed in the present chapter.

1. *Personality development.* We may view personality development and functioning in terms of the interaction of biological, psychological, and sociological processes.

a. Since these three sets of processes differ for each person, we have the basis for wide individual differences.

b. The "ego" or "self" develops out of this interactional pattern and functions as the psychological integrating core of the personality. This includes the integration of perceiving, thinking, and acting.

c. Personality development normally follows a patterned sequence or schedule.

2. *Motivation.* The direction and activation of behavior are determined largely by our strivings toward maintenance and actualization.

a. Maintenance and actualization require the meeting of various needs (requirements) on both biological and psychological levels.

b. Among the drive forces which subserve our needs are physiological drives, emotions, pain or pleasure, and tensions.

c. The degree of activation at a given time is determined by a wide range of inner and outer conditions.

d. Pleasure, pain, and ego involvement are important in the reinforcement of motivation.

e. Psychobiological needs are organized in a hierarchical pattern in relation to prepotency (strength).

f. Motivation greatly influences cognitive processes—perceiving, learning, reasoning, remembering, and imagining.

g. The individual is frequently unaware or only partially aware of his needs and goals.

h. Society inhibits or facilitates given strivings and also makes additional demands stemming from the group's needs.

3. *Stress.* The individual is continually faced with adjustive demands of varying degrees of difficulty which place him under stress.

a. Frustration, conflict, and pressure represent the major types of adjustment problems.

b. Stress may occur on biological, psychological, or sociological levels and may stem from either external or internal sources.

c. The greater the threat to psychobiological needs, the greater the stress.

d. The severity of a given stress situation depends to a large extent upon the individual's evaluation of it.

e. Each person faces a unique and changing pattern of stress.

f. The individual is often unaware or only partially aware of many of his frustrations and conflicts.

4. *Adjustive reactions.* Since the individual strives to maintain his psychobiological integrity, he automatically and persistently attempts to cope with stress.

a. Reactions to stress are holistic and economical.

b. Reactions to stress may involve varying degrees of emotional reinforcement, consciousness, and facilitation or inhibition.

c. Stress reactions have both inner and outer determinants. Psychological stress reactions are heavily influenced by the individual's assumptions concerning reality, value, and possibility.

d. In general, the individual deals with stress by attack, withdrawal, or compromise reactions. Such reactions may be primarily task-oriented or primarily ego defense-oriented.

e. Where the stress involves a threat to the integrity of the self, anxiety is aroused and ego defense mechanisms are brought into play.

f. Under severe frustration, reactive behavior tends toward substitutive and symbolic satisfactions; under severe conflict, toward procrastination, vacillation, and anxiety; under severe pressure, toward resistance and various defensive strategies.

g. Adaptation to severe stress is expensive in terms of lowered adaptive efficiency, re-duced resistance to other stresses, and wear and tear on the system.

h. An upset in the excitation-inhibition balance leads to impulsive or overinhibited behavior

i. When the individual's stress tolerance is exceeded, he undergoes some degree of personality disorganization, or decompensation.

j. The course of severe decompensation proceeds from alarm and mobilization, through neurotic and psychotic reactions (stage of resistance), to the stage of exhaustion and death.

k. This course may be arrested at any point and in some cases is reversed even without therapy.

REFERENCES

The reference list includes not only the sources from which the author has drawn material, but acknowledgments of the permissions granted by authors and publishers to quote directly from their works.

ARONSON, E., & CARLSMITH, J. M. The effect of the severity of threat on the devaluation of forbidden behavior. *Amer. Psychologist*, 1962, 17, 300.

BARTHOL, R. P., & KU, N. D. Regression under stress to first learned behavior. *J. abnorm. soc. Psychol.*, 1959, 59, 134-136.

BERNARD, C. *Leçons sur les propriétés physiologiques et les altérations pathologiques des liquides de l'organisme.* Paris: J. B. Baillère et Fils, 1859.

BETTELHEIM, B. Individual and mass behavior in extreme situations. *J. abnorm. soc. Psychol.*, 1943, 38, 417-452. Reprinted by permission of the American Psychological Association.

BLUESTONE, H., & MC GAHEE, C. L. Reaction to extreme stress: impending death by execution. *Amer. J. Psychiat.*, 1962, 119, 393-396.

BOMBARD, ALAIN. *The voyage of the Hérétique.* New York: Simon and Schuster, 1954.

BREHM, J. W. Motivational effects of cognitive dissonance. In M. R. Jones (Ed.), *Nebraska symposium on Motivation.* Lincoln: Univer. Nebraska Press, 1962. Pp. 51-77.

BRUNER, J. S. The cognitive consequences of early sensory deprivation. *Psychosom. Med.*, 1959, 21, 89-95.

BRUNER, J. S., & POSTMAN, L. Tension and tension release as organizing factors in perception. *J. Pers.*, 1947, 15, 300-308.

BUSS, A. H. *The psychology of aggression.* New York: Wiley, 1961.

BYKOV, K. M. Pavlovian contemporary psychiatry in the USSR. *Amer. J. Psychiat.*, 1959, 116, 203-207.

CAMERON, N. A., & MAGARET, ANN. *Behavior pathology.* Boston: Houghton Mifflin, 1951.

CANNON, W. B. *The wisdom of the body.* (Rev. ed.) New York: Norton, 1939.

CANNON, W. B. *Bodily changes in pain, hunger, fear and rage.* (2nd ed.) Newton Centre, Mass.: Charles T. Branford, 1953.

CANTRIL, H. Perception and interpersonal relations. *Amer. J. Psychiat.*, 1957, 114, 119-126.

CAPPON, D. The psychology of dying. *Pastoral Psychol.*, 1961, 12, 35-44.

COUSINS, SHEILA (pseud.). *To beg I am ashamed.* New York: Vanguard Press, 1938.

COWEN, E. L. The influence of varying degrees of psychological stress on problem-solving rigidity. *J. abnorm. soc. Psychol.*, 1952a, 47, 512-519.

COWEN, E. L. Stress reduction and problem-solving rigidity. *J. consult. Psychol.* 1952b, 16, 425-428.

DAVIS, J., MC COURT, W. F., & SOLOMON, P. Effect of visual stimulation on hallucinations and other mental experiences during sensory deprivation. *Amer. J. Psychiat.*, 1960, 116, 889-892.

DUFFY, ELIZABETH. *Activation and behavior.* New York: Wiley, 1962.

ERICKSON, M. H. Experimental demonstrations of the psychopathology of everyday life. *Psychoanal. Quart.*, 1939, 8, 338-353.

ERIKSON, E. H. *Childhood and society.* New York: Norton, 1950.

FERGUSON, EVA. Ego involvement: a critical examination of some methodological issues. *J. abnorm. soc. Psychol.*, 1962, 64, 407-417.

FESTINGER, L. The motivating effect of cognitive dissonance. In G. Lindzey (Ed.), *Assessment of human motives.* New York: Rinehart, 1958.

FRIEDMAN, P. Some aspects of concentration camp psychology. *Amer. J. Psychiat.*, 1949, 105, 601-605.

FROMM, E. *The sane society.* New York: Rinehart, 1955.

FROMM-REICHMANN, FRIEDA. Loneliness. *Psychiatry*, 1959, 22, 1-15.

GESELL, A. Human infancy and the embryology of behavior. In A. Weider (Ed.), *Contributions toward medical psychology.* New York: Ronald, 1953. Pp. 51-74.

GESELL, A., & AMATRUDA, CATHERINE S. *Developmental diagnosis: normal and abnormal child development.* (2nd ed.) New York: Harper, 1947.

GRUNEBAUM, H. U., FREEDMAN, S. J., & GREENBLATT, M. Sensory deprivation and personality. *Amer. J. Psychiat.*, 1960, 116, 878-882.

HARRIMAN, P. L. The experimental induction of a multiple personality. *Psychiatry*, 1942, 5, 179-186.

HARVEY, O. J., HUNT, D. E., & SCHRODER, H. M. *Conceptual systems and personality organization.* New York: Wiley, 1961.

HAVIGHURST, R. J. *Developmental tasks and education.* (2nd ed.) New York: Longmans, 1952.

HERB, D. O. The American revolution. *Amer. Psychologist,* 1960, 15, 735-745.

HERON, W., DOANE, B. K., & SCOTT, T. H. Visual disturbances after prolonged perceptual isolation. *Canad. J. Psychol.,* 1956, 10, 13-18.

HUXLEY, J. *Evolution in action.* New York: Harper, 1953.

ILG, FRANCES L., & AMES, L. B. *Child behavior.* New York: Harper, 1955.

JONES, L. C. T. Frustration and stereotyped behavior in human subjects. *Quart. J. exp. Psychol.,* 1954, 6, 12-20.

KAGAN, J., & MOSS, H. A. *Birth to maturity.* New York: Wiley, 1962.

KEYS, ANCEL, BROŽEK, J., HENSCHEL, A., MICKELSON, O., & TAYLOR, H. L. *The biology of human starvation.* Minneapolis: Univer. Minn. Press, 1950.

KINSEY, A. C., POMEROY, W. B., & MARTIN, C. E. *Sexual behavior in the human male.* Philadelphia: W. B. Saunders, 1948.

KUBZANSKY, P. E., & LEIDERMAN, P. H. Sensory deprivation. An overview. In P. Solomon, *et al.* (Eds.), *Sensory Deprivation: A symposium held at Harvard Medical School.* Cambridge, Mass.: Harvard Univer. Press, 1961. Pp. 221-238.

LANGDON, GRACE, & STOUT, I. *These well-adjusted children.* New York: John Day, 1951.

LILLY, J. C. Mental effects of reduction of ordinary levels of physical stimuli on intact, healthy persons. *Psychiat. Res. Rep.,* 1956, 5, 1-9.

LINTON, R. *The cultural background of personality.* New York: Appleton, 1945.

LONGENECKER, E. D. Perceptual recognition as a function of anxiety, motivation, and the testing situation. *J. abnorm. soc. Psychol.,* 1962, 64, 215-221.

MC CONAGHY, N. The inhibitory index in relation to extroversion-introversion. *Amer. J. Psychiat.,* 1962, 119, 527-533.

MAIER, N. R. F. *Frustration.* New York: McGraw-Hill, 1949.

MARMOR, J., & PUMPIAN-MINDLIN, E. Toward an integrative conception of mental disorder. *J. nerv. ment. Dis.,* 1950, 111, 19-29.

MASLOW, A. H., & MURPHY, G. (Eds.) *Motivation and personality.* New York: Harper, 1954.

MASSERMAN, J. H. *Principles of dynamic psychiatry.* (2nd ed.) Philadelphia: W. B. Saunders, 1961.

MEAD, MARGARET. *Male and female.* New York: Morrow, 1949.

MENNINGER, K. A. Changing concepts in medicine and their effect upon medical education. *J. Kans. Med. Soc.,* 1947, 48, 353-355.

MILLER, J. G. Mental health implications of a general behavior theory. *Amer. J. Psychiat.,* 1957, 113, 776-782.

MILLER, J. G. Information input overload and psychopathology. *Amer. J. Psychiat.,* 1960, 116, 695-704.

MILLER, J. G. Sensory overloading. In B. E. Flaherty (Ed.), *Psychophysiological aspects of space flight.* New York: Columbia Univer. Press, 1961. Pp. 215-224.

MILLER, N. E. Central stimulation and other new approaches to motivation and reward. *Amer. Psychol.,* 1958, 13, 100-108.

MILLER, N. E. Liberalization of basic S-R concepts: extensions to conflict behavior, motivation, and social learning. In S. Koch (Ed.), *Psychology: a study of a science.* Vol. 2. *General systematic formulations, learning, and special processes.* New York: McGraw-Hill, 1959.

MORGAN, C. T. Physiological mechanisms of motivation. In M. R. Jones (Ed.), *Nebraska symposium on motivation.* Lincoln, Neb.: Univer. of Nebraska Press, 1957. Pp. 1-35.

PIAGET, J. *The origins of intelligence in children.* New York: International Univer. Press, 1952.

PRENTICE, W. C. H. Some cognitive aspects of motivation. *Amer. Psychologist,* 1961, 16, 503-511.

ROGERS, C. R. Roger's self theory. In C. S. Hall, & G. Lindzey (Eds.), *Theories of personality.* New York: Wiley, 1957. Pp. 467-502.

ROGERS, C. R. *Becoming a person.* Austin: Hogg Found. Ment. Hlth., Univer. Texas, 1958.

ROHRER, J. H. Interpersonal relations in isolated small groups. In B. E. Flaherty (Ed.), *Psychophysiological aspects of space flight.* New York: Columbia Univer. Press, 1961. Pp. 263-271.

SELYE, H. *The physiology and pathology of exposure to stress.* Montreal: Acta, Inc., 1950.

SELYE, H. The general-adaptation-syndrome in its relationships to neurology, psychology, and psychopathology. In A. Weider (Ed.), *Contributions toward medical psychology.* New York: Ronald, 1953. Pp. 234-274.

SELYE, H. *The stress of life.* New York: McGraw-Hill, 1956.

SOLOMON, P., KUBZANSKY, P. E., LEIDERMAN, P. H., MENDELSON, J. H., TRUMBUL, R., & WEXLER, D. (Eds.) *Sensory deprivation: a symposium held at Harvard Medical School in 1958.* Cambridge, Mass.: Harvard Univer. Press, 1961.

VERNON, J., MARTON, T., & PETERSON, E. Sensory deprivation and hallucinations. *Science,* 1961, 133, 1808-1812.

WEISS, P. A., & TAYLOR, A. C. Shuffled cells can reconstruct same organs. *Sci. Newsletter,* 1960, 78, 263.

WHITE, R. W. Motivation reconsidered: the concept of competence. *Psychol. Rev.,* 1959, 66, 297-333.

WHITE, W. A. Medical philosophy from the viewpoint of a psychiatrist. *Psychiatry,* 1947, 10, 77-98, 191-210.

WILSON, E. B. *The cell in development and heredity.* (3rd ed.) New York: Macmillan, 1925.

WITMER, H. L., & KOTINSKY, R. (Eds.) *Personality in the making.* New York: Harper, 1952.

WOLF, S., & RIPLEY, H. S. Reactions among Allied prisoners of war subjected to three years of imprisonment and torture by the Japanese. *Amer. J. Psychiat.,* 1947, 104, 180-193.

WYLIE, RUTH C. *The self concept; a critical survey of pertinent research literature.* Lincoln, Neb.: Univer. of Nebraska Press, 1961.

CAUSES
OF ABNORMAL
BEHAVIOR

chapter 4

FAULTY BIOLOGICAL DEVELOPMENT
FAULTY PSYCHOLOGICAL DEVELOPMENT
SOCIOLOGICAL FACTORS IN FAULTY DEVELOPMENT
SEVERE BIOLOGICAL STRESS
SEVERE PSYCHOLOGICAL STRESS
SEVERE SOCIOLOGICAL STRESS

In discussing the dynamics of personality development and adjustment, and in describing what happens when stress becomes too great, we have paved the way for an examination of the causes of abnormal behavior—faulty development and excessive stress. So far we have been dealing largely with general principles; now we must consider particular developmental factors which determine our adaptive resources and stress tolerance and the kinds of stress which are likely to be too great.

The type of adjustment that we are achieving at any time is always a function of both our *psychobiological development* and the *stress situation* confronting us. Anything that leads to faulty development or increases stress may bring trouble. In some instances, as in combat situations, it is the overwhelming stress which plays the dominant role; in other instances, as in the case of a withdrawn, fearful child who becomes a seriously maladjusted young adult and gradually slips into schizophrenia, early and continued faulty personality development seems to be chiefly responsible for the abnormal behavior. These may be considered extreme cases, however; much more commonly, both developmental and stress factors play important parts.

It is often helpful in understanding causation to divide causative factors into biological, psychological, and sociological categories.[1] Mental disorders known to be based on brain pathology, such as syphilitic infection of the brain or senile brain degeneration, are called *organic* or *biogenic*. Where there is no known brain pathology and the disorder is presumably based on faulty assumptions, inadequate competencies, and other conditions which lead to maladjustive reactions to stress, the disorder is called *functional* or *psychogenic*. Finally, there are disorders which are primarily *sociogenic* in nature—in which sociological factors, such as economic and cultural deprivation, induce distortions in development or create stresses which are too great for healthy adjustment. But whether biological, psychological, or sociological factors appear to play the dominant role, we are always dealing with an interaction of determinants that contribute in varying degree to the mental disorder. Even in such a specific disease as syphilis of the brain, sociological factors may have contributed to the contraction of the disease, and psychological factors affect the degree of personality decompensation that takes place.

Causative factors are also often divided into *predisposing* and *precipitating* causes. Predisposing factors go before and pave the way for later psychopathology by lowering the individual's adjustive ability, as, for example, in the case of fatigue or parental overprotection. Precipitating causes represent the particular condition, such as brain disease or disappointment in love, which proved too much for the individual and precipitated the symptoms. In a given case the exact pattern of predisposing and precipitating causes may be far from clear, and what precipitates today's symptoms may become a predisposing factor in tomorrow's behavior. But we can attempt to show the part various factors play in lowering our adjustive ability or in increasing stress.

This problem can be approached in many ways, with many different kinds of tools. In some instances we shall see more with an electronic microscope, in others with a chemical analysis, and in still others with a psychological test or sociological survey. Throughout we shall attempt an integration of biological, psychological, and sociological data.

Faulty Biological Development

In our discussion of the patterned sequence of psychobiological development, we noted that any disruption might lead to developmental defects and deviations. In a highly simplified sense this sequence can be likened to an assembly line in an automobile plant, except that in biological development there is no way to stop the assembly line, and a lack of necessary materials or impaired timing may lead to irreparable damage. Since our behavior is based upon the quality and functional intactness of our nervous system and other body equipment, any factors which can interfere with normal physical development must be considered as potential causes of abnormal behavior. Either hereditary or environmental factors may be responsible for such interference in normal development.

HEREDITY

At one time or another most mental disorders have been attributed to heredity, but at present schizophrenia and other functional psychoses are the major area of dispute. Since man, like other animals, remains the product of his biological inheritance, it seems probable that genetic factors do play some role in psychopathology.

---

[1] As Ruesch (1961) has pointed out, the concept of causality in the behavioral sciences is a complex one. Rarely, except under extreme conditions like severe brain damage or prolonged sleep deprivation, can it be demonstrated that event A always lead to effect B. Since mental disorders usually seem to involve the contribution and interaction of biological, psychological, and sociological determinants, we shall use the terms *causation* and *etiology* as roughly synonymous with the term *dynamics*, which implies this interaction of factors.

BREAKING THE GENETIC CODE

One of nature's best kept secrets has been how a single fertilized egg cell can develop into an adult human being with billions of highly differentiated cells and complex organ systems and functions. In a series of epic research studies, scientists have traced the secret to DNA (deoxyribonucleic acid), which is the substance that genes are made of.

The DNA molecule is a helix, a spiral that looks like a coiled ladder (A). The sides of this "ladder" are chains of alternating sugar and phosphate; the rungs are formed between the sugar groups by combinations of four basic control chemicals—adenine, thymine, guanine, and cytosine—a given rung being formed by a pair of these chemicals (adenine-thymine, thymine-adenine, cytosine-guanine, or guanine-cytosine). It is in the sequence of these rungs (B) that the specific hereditary instructions of the growing organism are encoded. DNA molecules are present not only in germ cells but in the nucleus of every living cell. Each living thing resembles the stock from which it descended because of the DNA which it inherits. And interestingly enough, the same four "letters" appear to be present in the DNA codes of all living creatures—demonstrating the oneness of the whole living world.

Just as the uniqueness of each word in the dictionary depends upon a specific arrangement of the 26 letters in our alphabet, the uniqueness of each gene in a DNA ladder depends upon the specific linear arrangement of the four chemical "letters." Spelling with a four-letter alphabet might appear to limit the number of possible words, but each word (gene) contains hundreds or thousands of these "letters," leaving ample room for great diversity in hereditary information.

A

B

The instructions of the DNA make provision for two main functions—the reproduction of itself, by making exact copies, and the direction of the metabolic activities in each cell, including the building of proteins. Both processes start with a splitting apart of the two halves of the helix (C). To replicate itself, each half then picks up appropriate loose nucleotides available near it until two complete helixes are formed.

To direct metabolic activities in the cell, an intermediary chemical is made by the DNA in the nucleus of the cell. Here various sections of the divided ladder gather groups of nucleotides complementary to them, which they then send to various sites in the cell with specific instructions. These intermediaries are called *ribonucleic acid* (RNA) because, though chemically similar to DNA, they contain a sugar called *ribose* which is not present in DNA. Since there are many tasks to be performed, DNA makes several kinds of RNA. One kind is called messenger-RNA; messenger-RNA forms alongside the DNA ladder and when it has received its instructions passes into the cell cytoplasm, where it acts as a sort of template in assembling the amino acid building blocks used in the manufacture of a given protein. Another kind of intermediary is transfer-RNA, which is equipped to recognize a given type of amino acid and bring it to the messenger-RNA assembly line.

If any detail of the DNA instructions is missing or garbled—as we might misspell *cat* as *cot*—the human organism may be in for trouble. For example, people become ill and die with inherited cycle-cell anemia, in which a single amino acid is wrong out of the 574 that make up a hemoglobin molecule of the blood.

Identifying the exact nature of the communication between the DNA and RNA and between the RNA and the sequence of amino acids manufactured in the cell is known as the "coding problem." Once this genetic code is broken, it will be potentially possible for man either to correct the faulty DNA ladder itself or to bypass the faulty DNA instructions by modifying the RNA, thus giving the cell the correct instructions for normal growth and functioning. This third great breakthrough in modern genetics will influence virtually every facet of man's life. For it will pave the way for a fantastic new power for man to correct and prevent genetic pathology and to control his own growth.

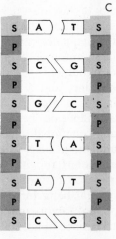

C

Diagrams redrawn, with permission, from Sonnenborn (1962). Chart also based on material from Crick (1962, 1963), Hurwitz and Furth (1962), and Nirenberg (1963).

However, despite exciting new scientific breakthroughs in molecular genetics, the precise role of genetic factors in most mental disorders remains to be delineated.[1]

Chromosomal aberrations. Perhaps the first great breakthrough in modern genetics was the identification of the normal complement of 46 chromosomes in the human cell. The chromosomes are the structures in the cell nucleus which encode the hereditary plan—which contain the *overall* strategy or information for guiding development.

When fertilization takes place, the normal inheritance of the new individual consists of 23 pairs of chromosomes—one of each pair being derived from the mother and one from the father. Twenty-two of these chromosome pairs are called *autosomes;* they determine body characteristics. The remaining pair, the *sex chromosomes,* determine the individual's sex and certain other characteristics. In the female, both of these sex chromosomes, one from each parent, are of a large type designated as *X chromosomes.* In the male, the chromosome from the mother is an *X* but that from the father is called a *Y.* Recent studies in developmental genetics have shown that abnormalities in the number or structure of the chromosomes are associated with a wide range of congenital malformations and hereditary diseases. In mongolism, for example—a type of mental retardation in which the individual has slanting eyes, a flat face, and other characteristics that produce a superficial resemblance to mongoloids—investigators have discovered an extra chromosome, involving a trisomy (three instead of two) of one chromosome pair (Lejeune *et al.,* 1959). Similarly, *Turner's syndrome*—characterized by short stature, "webbing" of the neck, and sexual infantilism—has been shown to result from an abnormal number of sex chromosomes. Disorders that are associated with the sex chromosomes are said to be sex-linked, meaning that the genetic defect is present only in the sex chromosomes. Interestingly enough, females are less susceptible to aberrations involving the sex chromosomes, since they have two X chromosomes: if one is faulty, the other will ordinarily do the work of development. But the male has only one X and one Y chromosome, and if either is defective, he is in for trouble.

The causes of chromosomal anomalies are not fully understood. In most cases they probably are transmitted by faulty recessive genes from one or both parents, but they can reflect gene mutations in the fertilized—ovum for example, as the result of ionizing radiation (Rugh, 1962). However, it may be emphasized that most gene mutations do not result in gross and observable chromosomal irregularities. In fact, chromosomal aberrations usually lead to the death of the embryo. Here it may also be pointed out that every human cell formed after fertilization contains a replication of the original chromosomal pattern. By studying cells taken from the gonads, bone marrow, or other bodily parts, it is possible to make a "chromosomal map" for a child or adult which is useful in understanding and predicting certain types of pathology.

In general, chromosomal irregularities appear to result in defective body structure rather than in mental disorders. Kallmann (1960) has concluded that since gross defects in the chromosomes are usually lethal, a search for chromosomal irregularities in functional psychoses like schizophrenia would probably not be fruitful. However, the microscopic study of the chromosomes is still in its infancy, and much yet remains to be learned concerning the role of chromosomal aberrations in faulty development and psychopathology.

Mutant genes. The second breakthrough in modern genetics was the development of ultramicroscopic techniques—for example, the combined use of the electron microscope and X-ray diffraction—which make it possible to study the actual structure of the genes making up the chromosomes. A gene looks like a flexible ladder which has been twisted to include 10 rungs within each complete spiral. Each gene is made up of DNA (deoxyribonucleic acid), which is the very essence of life. Encoded in the DNA are the *specific* hereditary instructions—the secret information—which provide for eye color, pigmentation, and other traits of the growing or-

---

[1] The role of genetic factors in human pathology may be investigated in two ways: (1) by the direct study of the chromosomes and their component genes—an approach referred to as *cytogenetics* or *biochemical genetics,* and (2) by the statistical analysis of characteristics transmitted from one generation to the next—an approach referred to as *population genetics* or *transmission genetics.*

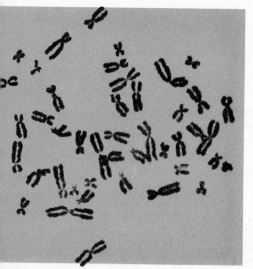

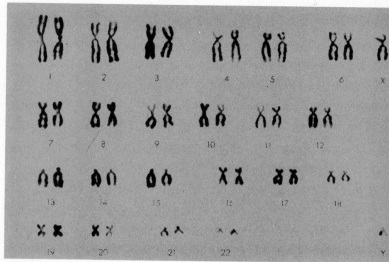

A

B

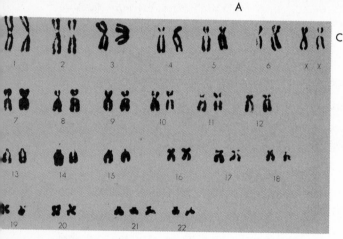

C

A chromosome count can now be made by treating a cell with a colchicine derivative to stop cell division at the point where the chromosomes are most visible and then applying a salt solution that swells and disperses the chromosomes (A). Treated in this way, chromosomes can then be arranged in pairs. The sample here (B) shows the normal complement of chromosomes for a boy. Such an arrangement also makes it easy to identify certain chromosomal aberrations, such as the trisomy of chromosome 21 common in mongolism (C).

ganism. Thus a second approach to relating genetic factors to mental disorders involves the study of gene mutations—losses, gains, or changes of material in the gene itself. Gene mutations have played an important role in human evolution, and man's genes continue to mutate as they have since he first appeared on earth. As Dobzhansky (1960) has pointed out:

"Every one of the tens of thousands of genes inherited by the individual has a tiny probability of changing in some way during his generation. Among the small, and probably atypical, sample of human genes for which very rough estimates of the mutation frequencies are available, the rates of mutation vary from one in 10,000 to one in about 250,000. For example, it has

been calculated that approximately one sex cell in every 50,000 produced by a normal person carries a new mutant gene that causes *retinoblastoma*, a cancer of the eye affecting children." (p. 206)

These frequencies are "spontaneous," occurring in people not exposed to special mutagens—agents that can induce mutations, such as ionizing radiations and X rays.

Geneticists agree that the effects of mutations are usually detrimental, and that mutations may produce a wide variety of hereditary diseases, congenital malformations, and constitutional weaknesses. It has also been demonstrated that gene mutations resulting from exposure of the fertilized ovum to ionizing radiation can produce abnormalities (Rugh, 1962). During the past decade ionizing radiations from nuclear weapons tests have become a major source of gene mutations. On the basis of figures published by the United States Federal Radiation Council (1962), it has been estimated that the number of deaths or gross physical or mental defects in all future generations as a result of weapons testing through 1962 will approximate 1.2 million from radioactive fall-out and 16 million from carbon-14 (Pauling, 1962).[1]

Mutant or defective genes have been identified in the case of rare biochemical disorders associated with mental deficiency. Perhaps the best known of these disorders is phenylketonuria (PKU). This disorder occurs in infants who lack an enzyme needed to break down phenylalanine, an amino acid found in protein foods. When this condition is undetected and dietary treatment is not undertaken early, the phenylalanine builds up in the blood and damages the brain. This biochemical disorder is assumed to be transmitted via a recessive gene, and 1 person in 70 is thought to be a carrier (Hsia, 1959; Kalter, 1962).[2]

Attempts have also been made to delineate the role of genetic factors in Huntington's chorea and other relatively rare degenerative diseases of the central nervous system which appear to follow a Mendelian pattern of inheritance. As in the case of chromosome studies, however, studies of mutant genes have thus far been concerned primarily with specific structural defects rather than with neuroses, functional psychoses, and other mental disorders.

Family history and twin studies. So far, most of the knowledge we have as to the contribution of heredity to mental disorders has been gained from studies of family histories and of twins. It has long been observed, for example, that mental illness tends to run in families. The notorious Kallikaks and Jukes have provided ample statistics to show this. Such findings have led many investigators to a belief that mental disorders must be inherited in some sort of Mendelian ratio—usually in the form of recessive genes.

In using the family history method, the investigator observes a large sample of relatives of each *proband* or *index case* (carrier of the trait in question, such as schizophrenia) in order to see whether the incidence increases in propor-

tion to the degree of hereditary relationship. In addition, the incidence of the trait in a normal population is compared with the incidence among the relatives of the index cases. This approach is illustrated in Kallmann's (1953, 1958) figures for schizophrenia.[3]

DEGREE OF RELATIONSHIP TO SCHIZOPHRENIC	PER CENT WHO DEVELOP SCHIZOPHRENIA
Identical (one-egg) twins	86.2%
Fraternal (two-egg) twins	14.5%
Siblings	14.2%
Half-siblings	7.1%
General population	0.85%

These figures indicate that the incidence of schizophrenia is much higher for all degrees of blood relationship than in the general population, and that with an increasing degree of blood relationship there is an increasing incidence of schizophrenia—from 7.1 per cent in half-siblings of schizophrenics to 86.2 per cent in identical twins. Kallmann at first concluded from his findings that schizophrenia must be transmitted via recessive genes.

Unfortunately, family history studies, including those of Kallmann, have suffered from various methodological limitations which make their findings difficult to interpret. Typically such studies have failed to take into account the importance of early environmental conditions in the production of abnormal behavior. For example, Jackson (1960) has pointed out that even physical diseases may run in families without necessarily having a genetic basis. Beriberi, a vitamin deficiency disease, tends to do so. What is apparently "inherited" is the preference

---

[1]Since these figures represent rough estimates, Pauling suggests a range of 80,000 to 18 million for radioactive fallout, and 320,000 to 800 million for carbon-14. All preceding figures refer to the world population. Statistics for the U.S. are about 1/10 of world population figures for radioactive fallout, and about 1/20 for carbon-14.

[2]In general, undesirable mutant genes are weeded out in the process of natural selection—especially in a reproductive manner. For example, in *achondroplastic dwarfism*, caused by a gene mutation that results in people with normal heads and trunks, but short arms and legs, the reproduction ratio is about 1 in 5. That is, these dwarfs produce, on the average, only some 20 surviving children for every 100 produced by their normal brothers and sisters (Dobzhansky, 1960).

[3]Schizophrenia has long been a proving ground in the evaluation of hereditary influences in mental illness, and we shall consider other studies relating to it in our later discussion.

for vitamin-poor foods, a preference acquired from the parents through learning rather than genetic transmission. Nevertheless, family history studies cannot be summarily dismissed; they definitely point to the probability that genetic factors are important in mental disorders.

Studies of identical and fraternal twins have also yielded somewhat controversial results. As Kallmann found in schizophrenia, mental disorders seem to occur considerably more often in both identical twins, who of course have identical genetic endowment, than in both fraternal twins, whose inheritance is no more similar than that of siblings. However, it is a complicated task to determine whether twins are identical or fraternal, and in some of the earlier studies questions have been raised as to the validity of the methods used.[1] And even with identical twins, the rate is not 100 per cent.

Here, too, the effect of a similar early environment is not completely clear. In the few cases studied where twins were reared in separate environments, the development of mental illness in one twin was much less often accompanied by mental illness in the other. Another study found that where twins differed markedly in personality adjustment there usually had been some definitely pathologic feature in the early environment of the twin who had the poorer mental health (Fields, 1958).

There also are studies like those of Hobbs (1941), in which mental disorders occurred in only one of each of five pairs of identical twins, an impossibility if the twins were actually identical and mental illness were caused directly by something in the germ plasm. Such findings raise serious doubts about whether mental disorders follow a simple dominant or recessive genetic pattern. The only neuropsychiatric disorders that appear to follow a definite Mendelian ratio are Huntington's chorea, certain other relatively rare disorders of the central nervous system, and a few kinds of mental retardation.

The apparent failure of functional mental disorders to follow such patterns has led many geneticists to retreat to the more tenable concept of *inherited predisposition*. Here it is held that inferior or mutant genes cause a distortion of one or more biochemical systems in the body, which, in turn, reduces the individual's resistance to various physical and mental disorders.

Thus certain individuals presumably are more prone to develop mental illness if placed under stress, but their inherent weakness may not show up in a favorable life situation.

This position is bolstered by medical evidence of inherited predisposition to tuberculosis, cancer, and a wide range of other diseases. In fact, the borderline between genetic and environmental diseases is becoming blurred as medicine inclines more and more to the belief that hereditary factors are important in determining resistance or susceptibility to almost all forms of disease. However, for both physical disease and mental disorders it is necessary to demonstrate the precise genetic and physiological nature of these predispositions and to relate them to the various stress patterns which may also play an important part in lowering resistance. This is not easily done; it is further complicated by the fact that environmental forces begin to influence and change the individual even during prenatal life. As the field of molecular cytogenetics progresses, however, the study of ultramicroscopic rearrangements and alterations in genetic material will undoubtedly shed new light on the role of genetic processes in psychopathology. (The third great breakthrough in modern genetics—the breaking of the *genetic code*—and the significance of this breakthrough for understanding and controlling human behavior are described in the chart on page 118.)

CONSTITUTION

The term *constitution* is generally used to denote the biological make-up of the individual, including both innate and acquired assets and liabilities. Physique, sex, temperament, endocrine function, and blood type are some of the characteristics included in this category. Certain constitutional traits change, of course, as the

---

[1]Formerly the "fetal-membrane" method was used, based on the assumption that identical twins are born with only one placenta. This required a precise medical check at the time of birth, and in the case of many twins who later became mentally ill this evidence was not available. It is now known that not all identical twins are born with only one placenta, and consequently the "similarity method" is now used. This involves a comparison of such characteristics as facial features, ear lobe form, dental specifications, pigmentation of hair and eyes, and fingerprint and blood-group data. Reciprocal skin grafts can be used where the preceding measures are indecisive (Kallmann, 1959).

THE SHELDON THEORY OF CONSTITUTIONAL TYPES

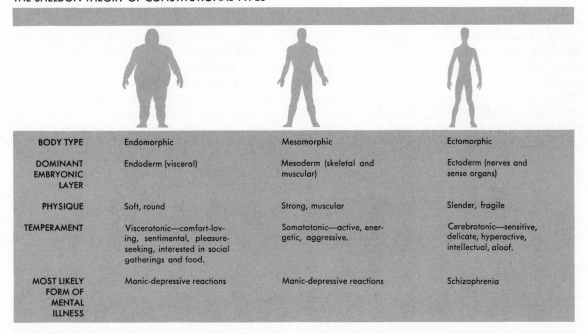

BODY TYPE	Endomorphic	Mesomorphic	Ectomorphic
DOMINANT EMBRYONIC LAYER	Endoderm (visceral)	Mesoderm (skeletal and muscular)	Ectoderm (nerves and sense organs)
PHYSIQUE	Soft, round	Strong, muscular	Slender, fragile
TEMPERAMENT	Viscerotonic—comfort-loving, sentimental, pleasure-seeking, interested in social gatherings and food.	Somatotonic—active, energetic, aggressive.	Cerebrotonic—sensitive, delicate, hyperactive, intellectual, aloof.
MOST LIKELY FORM OF MENTAL ILLNESS	Manic-depressive reactions	Manic-depressive reactions	Schizophrenia

individual goes through the human life cycle.

Since ancient times, attempts have been made to classify people into *types* in terms of constitutional factors and to use these classifications for predicting general personality and behavior patterns.

Physique and personality. When Shakespeare's Julius Caesar exclaims:

Let me have men about me that are fat;
Sleek-headed men and such as sleep o'nights:
Yond Cassius has a lean and hungry look;
He thinks too much: such men are dangerous.
(Act I, Scene ii)

he expresses the age-old popular belief that fat men are more likely to be good-natured and reliable.

Perhaps the best known of modern scientific attempts to relate physique to personality and psychopathology is that of Sheldon and his associates (1954). Sheldon concluded that there are three types of body build corresponding to the predominant development of one of the three embryonic layers and that corresponding to these three types of physique are three types of temperament, as shown in the chart. Accord-

ing to Sheldon, the type of physique and temperament presumably has nothing to do with the individual's becoming mentally ill, but influences the type of illness he will develop should he become psychotic.

Sheldon has worked out a scale with values ranging from 1 to 7 for each of the three categories. This makes it possible to describe an individual's somatotype (body type) precisely by a three-digit number. For example, 1-1-6 would be low in endomorphy, low in mesomorphy, and high in ectomorphy. Such an individual would incline toward the typical ectomorphic traits as listed in the chart. If he became mentally ill, he would most likely develop schizophrenia.

The origin of the individual's somatotype (body type) has been attributed by Sheldon to heredity, glandular functioning, and various early environmental experiences. In connection with the latter, he points out that it is the vigorous-bodied somatotonics who take the lead in childhood enterprises. The viscerotonics tend to join in with good fellowship and conviviality, while the cerebrotonics seem to want to stay on the sidelines and constitute a watchful but unsocialized periphery. In this context, it is interesting to note that Davidson *et al.* (1957), in a study of seven-year-old children, found that boys with above-average fatty tissue were more self-confident, stocky boys showed superior abilities to communicate and greater aggressiveness, and boys with less than average muscular development tended to display more anxiety and "showing-off" behavior. These investigators concluded that during childhood there are consistent temperament correlates with physique similar to those hypothesized by Sheldon.

Similarly, Parnell (1957) compared somatotypes of 405 healthy college students with those of 208 students advised by general practitioners to seek psychiatric help. It was found that the student with a linear build, poor muscular development, and below-average fatty tissue was six times more common in the maladjusted group, while the rather short, muscular person with an average amount of fatty tissue was found to be five times more common in the healthy group. On the other hand, both Sheldon (1949) and Glueck and Glueck (1961, 1962) have reported a disproportionately high incidence of mesomorphs among juvenile delinquents and adult criminals—perhaps indicating simply that mesomorphs are more vigorous and aggressive than average and, in a high-delinquency area, more likely to find delinquency rewarding. Certainly vigor and aggressiveness could be channeled in either desirable or undesirable directions.

Although Sheldon's findings have been supported by some investigators, others have failed to replicate his findings. This is true also of the claims of the other somatotype theories.[1] However, we have only to look at everyday life situations to realize that physique does play an important role in personality development and adjustment. Beauty, for example, is at a premium in our society. One need only attend a social gathering, watch television and motion pictures, or note the billions of dollars spent each year on cosmetics and beauty treatments to observe its importance in determining behavior. Similarly tallness and shortness and various other variations in physique (we shall consider physical impairments in the next section) influence the adjustive reactions of the individual and other people's reactions to him. When we stop to realize the unique problems introduced into the life of a person who is very tall—endless remarks about the "climate up there," frustrating encounters with standard beds and doorways, scarcity of ready-made clothes, being expected to be big in spirit as well as stature, and so on—we may conclude with Barker *et al.* (1946) that "very tall men are in many respects in quite a different sociopsychological situation from persons of normal height." (p. 13)

Similarly, changes in body proportions during adolescence or old age may force a major revision in one's self-image. Where such changes are extreme and devaluating in nature, they can create a serious adjustment problem for the individual. This is especially true for the young adolescent when his perception of his body image is discrepant with what he sees as the current cultural ideal.

Although its significance may vary greatly from one person to another and we still lack needed scientific information, it is apparent that physique cannot be ignored as one factor in the determination of personality development and adjustment.

Physiology and personality.   Over two thousand years ago, Hippocrates, the most famous of the ancient Greek physicians, developed a fourfold classification of personality types based upon the "humors," or fluids of the body, as they were then understood. Although his theory has long since been discarded in the light of later evidence, it was the forerunner of later attempts to relate physiological factors to personality make-up.

Since there are constitutional differences in all the body organs and systems upon which growth and behavior depend—sense organs, effectors, endocrine glands, respiratory system, nervous system, and so on—it seems apparent that such physiological differences contribute to unique reaction tendencies and vulnerabilities in each individual. Of particular significance in our present discussion have been attempts to delineate the role of biological energy level, autonomic reactivity, resistance to stress, and the quality and stability of the central nervous system in determining basic reaction tendencies and adjustive behavior.

---

[1] An excellent critical evaluation of findings concerning the role of constitutional factors in abnormal behavior is that of L. Rees (1961).

An individual's constitutional energy level may have an important bearing on the way he typically discharges tension. Persons with a high energy level appear inclined to discharge tension through neuromuscular activity, whereas persons with a low energy level appear more inclined to use ideomotor or fantasy discharge. Relevant here is the finding that even in infants a mildly disturbing stimulus tends to produce either striped-muscle behavior or visceral behavior—but not both (Jones, 1930). Carrying this point a step further, McFarland and Huddelson (1936) have suggested that "internalizing" infants—those who react to disturbing stimuli by developing circulatory, gastrointestinal, and other visceral symptoms—are often relatively free of overt behavior symptoms, whereas those inclined to an overt muscular discharge are more apt to be free of inner disturbance. It would appear that such reaction tendencies may predispose an individual to one or another type of pathology if he should later become a psychiatric casualty.[1]

The role of autonomic reactivity in faulty development and functioning has been strongly emphasized by Eysenck (1960), who has suggested that either an excess or a deficit of autonomic reactivity may lead to trouble. The more autonomically reactive the child (the more prone to react emotionally to stress), the more likely he is to develop conditioned fears and anxieties which are resistant to extinction and color his later stress reactions. Although certain conditioned fears and anxieties are considered essential for normal socialization, the child who is too reactive autonomically presumably forms "surplus conditioned reactions," many of which are maladaptive and lower his stress tolerance.

On the other hand, the child who is deficient in emotional reactivity presumably lacks the capacity to form quick and strong conditioned responses and is likely to suffer from "deficient conditioned reactions." In this case the result is inadequate socialization, characterized by impulsivity, antisocial behavior, and a lack of inner controls. Although marked deviation from the average in autonomic reactivity may prove disadvantageous or even disastrous, details in this area still remain to be worked out and verified.

Another factor receiving intensive study to-day is the role of constitutional defects in the body's defenses against disease and other stresses. Normally the body produces antibodies to defend itself against invading viruses and bacteria. Faulty functioning of the antibody-producing system leaves the body vulnerable to certain diseases, and it may be that degenerative diseases of the nervous system are among them. Likewise, it has been established that constitutional inadequacies in the chemistry of hormone or enzyme production or in the disposal of toxic by-products from the incessant metabolic processes of living may show up under stress and disrupt the delicate biochemistry of the brain.[2] It would also appear that under biological or psychological stress, certain individuals are more vulnerable than others to disruptions in various biochemical systems which are involved in brain functioning, but further research is needed in biochemistry and neurophysiology to delineate the precise nature and effects of these constitutional vulnerabilities.

The possible role of these and other constitutional factors in faulty development is summarized in the chart on page 127. The effect of a specific factor will vary depending upon the total interactional growth pattern and make-up of the individual. Here it is of value to emphasize again both the individuality and the continuity of psychobiological development. As Gesell and Amatruda (1945) have concluded:

"Every embryo is unique. The uniqueness is so fundamental that it pervades the whole life cycle. It expresses itself in psychic constitution, temperament, motor demeanors, and distinctive modes of growth. . . . Certain qualities of equableness, poise, self-contained-ness, and responsiveness manifest themselves so early and so consistently in the first year of life that they must be ascribed to inborn determinants. Culture organizes personality, but does not transcend the individuality inherent in every growth complex." (p. 248)

[1] For a more intensive review of findings concerning somatic reactivity to stress, the reader is referred to Martin (1961) and Wenger *et al.* (1961).

[2] The role of faulty genes, metabolic imbalances, or other vicissitudes in producing alterations in enzymes leading, in turn, to disruptions in cellular functioning is well described by Ham (1963). Such abnormalities may be so minimal that under normal conditions a given organ or system can still carry out its necessary function, as in the case of subclinical diabetes. Resistance is lowered, however, and under increased stress the system may fail, with far-reaching consequences for the total organism.

CONSTITUTIONAL FACTORS AND ABNORMAL BEHAVIOR

CONSTITUTIONAL FACTOR	RELATION TO ABNORMAL DEVELOPMENT
Physique	Role not clear but bodily disproportions, frailty, and ugliness appear to be associated more commonly with psychopathology than do robustness and physical attractiveness.
Energy and activity level	Apparently related to whether individual develops aggressive or more internalized reactions to stress; thus related to type of mental disorder shown if the individual becomes mentally ill.
Autonomic reactivity	High emotional reactivity possibly related to overreaction to minor stresses and formation of unnecessary conditioned fears; deficient emotional reactivity presumably leads to inadequate socialization via too few conditioned reactions.
Bodily resilience, resistance to infection	Help determine biological and psychological stress tolerance and which organ system is most vulnerable. Some individuals apparently highly vulnerable to disturbances in bodily systems related to brain functioning.
Sensitivity	Determines in part the types of stress to which child is most vulnerable and the degree of stress that he can tolerate without behavioral disorganization. Influences way child perceives world.
Intellectual endowment, other aptitudes	Influence child's opportunities for success in competition and thus for self-confidence based on achievement.

Similarly Escalona and Heider (1959) have found that:

"As one notes behavioral alterations from infancy to —in the case of our study—later preschool ages, one knows that not a single behavior has remained the same, yet one is struck with the inherent continuity of behavioral style and of the child's pattern of adaptation." (p. 9)

Although the individual's constitutional make-up is determined largely by his genetic inheritance, it can be changed by environmental factors before and after birth. For example, environmental influences operating before birth— such as toxins, viruses, and ionizing radiation— can produce damage ranging from temporary minor disturbances to death of the child. Studies of prenatal development are yielding increasing evidence of influences operating during this period that are important in shaping later develop-

ment. Both before and after birth there appear to be "critical periods" in the developmental scheduling or "sequencing" of biological systems when a lack of needed growth materials or other disruptive conditions may do maximal damage. With time, too, there appears to be less flexibility in biochemical systems, and the constitution of the individual becomes relatively defined and more resistant to further change (Eiduson *et al.*, 1962).

CONGENITAL AND ACQUIRED DEFECTS

Robert Burton (1577-1640), in his *Anatomy of Melancholy,* wrote these poignant words: "Deformities and imperfections of our bodies, as lameness, crookedness, deafness, blindness, be they innate or accidental, torture many men. . . ."

In the United States today there are some 20 million people with chronic diseases or permanent physical impairments which substantially limit their activity—and as many more who suffer from chronic but less handicapping conditions (National Health Education Committee, 1961). Approximately half of the more severely handicapped persons are under 50 years of age; 20 per cent are under 25 years of age. Such defects place the individual under special stress and are likely to increase the difficulties of his marital, occupational, and social adjustments.

Except in the case of defects which are almost totally disabling, however, such as severe mental retardation, the significance of these impairments in the development of psychopathology depends primarily upon the way the individual evaluates and adjusts to his unusual or changed life situation. Among the great obstacles for the handicapped person to overcome are resignation and the tendency to accept the role of a recluse which society often seems to expect him to play (Hughes, 1960). Other common undesirable reactions to such handicaps are feelings of inferiority, self-pity, fear, and hostility. In an intensive study of children hospitalized as a consequence of the severe crippling effects of poliomyelitis, Bernabeu (1958) emphasized the core reactions of frustration, anxiety, and rage. These feelings were handled by defenses which were considered pathogenic in nature or intensity or inappropriate to a given stage of development.

Parental attitudes toward the child's impairment are often of critical importance. Too often, parents of handicapped children develop attitudes of extreme overprotection or rejection or expect performance beyond the child's abilities. In such cases, the child is unnecessarily handicapped psychologically in meeting life's problems.

Particularly during adolescence, when physical appearance becomes so important in attaining group status, overt physical defects are apt to become highly stressful. Even in fairly stable adults, however, the loss of vision, of hearing, or of limbs presents a serious adjustment problem. In a study of amputation cases in the Armed Forces, it was found that immediately following the injury, over 60 per cent showed evidence of serious emotional maladjustment (Randall *et al.*, 1946). A follow-up study of comparable cases six months or more after the loss of a limb revealed that some 50 per cent manifested psychological reaction patterns likely to interfere with satisfactory adjustment (J. R. Rees, 1945). In general, personality maladjustment is more common among physically disabled persons than among physically normal persons, although there is no necessary causal connection between the handicap and the maladjustment. It is the individual's attitudes, not the dis-

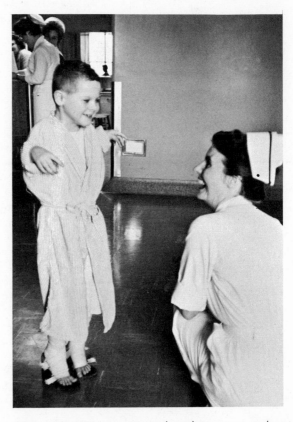

Often well-meaning parents and teachers are so anxious about a handicapped child or a child who has suffered a serious accident that they teach him to be anxious and unsure of himself or to demand that others do everything for him. Then, even if the physical handicap is overcome, the psychological handicap remains. This delighted child is the only patient known to have survived after suffering third-degree burns over 85 per cent of his body. Despite fourteen months of inactivity and painful treatment in a hospital, he has not become a passive, dependent, or complaining child. He is proving—literally—that he intends to stand on his own two feet.

IONIZING RADIATION OF FETUS AND CONGENITAL DEFECTS

Seven out of 100 American babies who survive one month after birth have some relatively severe birth defect such as club foot, cleft palate, or extra fingers. An additional 2 per cent have severe birth defects which threaten to destroy life or actually do so. A high percentage of these defects are inherited from parents with defective genes. However, an appreciable percentage would appear to be due to penetrating ionizing radiations of the fetus during prenatal development. Sources of such exposure include background radiation, diagnostic X rays of the pregnant mother, and radiation from nuclear weapons. The effects of such ionizing radiations have been summarized by Rugh (1962):

1. Penetrating ionizing radiation occurring at any time after fertilization may interfere with normal development and result in congenital anomalies. The majority of such anomalies involve the nervous system.

2. The effects of ionizing radiations at different stages of embryonic development depend both on the level of exposure and on the particular tissues and organs actively differentiating at the time:
    a) Irradiation during very early stages of development is most likely to be lethal.
    b) Irradiation during organogenesis (15-42 days for the human fetus) is most likely to result in gross congenital anomalies, particularly of the central nervous system.
    c) Exposure during the later stages of fetal development is most likely to result in functional rather than gross structural anomalies.

3. Ionizing radiations produce their effects by maiming or killing cells and by producing mutations. When maimed cells persist, they may interfere with development, resulting in structural and/or functional defects. The gonads and germ cells of the child can accumulate the mutations induced by ionizing radiations.

4. The terms *survival, recovery,* and *normality* have often been confused in radiobiological literature. These terms are not synonymous. An irradiated embryo may survive and even appear to have recovered but in fact may exhibit structural and/or functional deviations from the normal during the postnatal life of the individual.

Information contained in the preceding summary by Rugh is based on the study of individuals exposed to radiation accidentally or in medical treatment, on studies of the populations of Hiroshima and Nagasaki, and on experiments with animals. The following references are also relevant: Medical Research Council (1960), International Atomic Energy Agency (1961), National Academy of Sciences (1961), National Radiation Advisory Committee (1960), Pauling (1962), World Health Organization (1959).

ability itself, that are the primary determinants of his mode and level of adjustment.[1]

We are now in a position to see how there may be good adjustment despite a severe handicap and widespread personality difficulties with only very slight physical defects. A long nose, skin blemishes, tallness, shortness, crooked teeth, glasses, and any number of other minor impairments may be extremely traumatic for certain individuals. In a society as conscious of physical appearance as ours, even slight physical devia-

tions or impairments may pose difficult adjustment problems.

In summary, then, both defective genes and a wide range of prenatal and postnatal environmental factors can result in defective bodily machinery. Some defects, such as physical handicaps, are apparent, while others, such as distorted biochemical systems, are more subtle and difficult to assess. Defective bodily machinery may directly impair biological or psychological functioning or lower resistance to stress.

Faulty Psychological Development

The importance of the early years for later personality development has long been recognized, as evidenced by the common sayings, "As the twig is bent, the tree is inclined" and "The child is father to the man." However, it remained for Sigmund Freud and later twentieth-century investigators to grasp the full significance of the early years for later adjustment. For it is during this period that the foundations are laid for our adult environmental evaluations and self-evaluations, habits of thinking, and patterns of reaction. Yet it may be emphasized that as we mature and become capable of critical reflection and evaluation, we may make major changes in our patterns of thinking and action. We are not forever doomed by or limited to conditioned responses established in childhood.

In general, faulty psychological development involves (a) immaturities or fixations, in which the individual fails to develop one or more of the dimensions of maturity listed on pages 67-68, (b) "weak spots," as when traumatic experiences leave him sensitized and vulnerable to certain types of stress, or (c) distortions, as when he develops inappropriate attitudes or reaction patterns or fails to achieve normal personality integration. We shall examine some factors in unhealthy psychological development.

EARLY DEPRIVATION

Evidence is accumulating that either biological or psychological deprivation during the early

months of life can do irreversible damage to the developing organism.

Maternal deprivation. Abnormal development has often been observed in infants deprived of adequate maternal care as a consequence of either (a) separation from the mother and placement in an institution or (b) lack of adequate "mothering" in the home.[2]

In an institution, as compared with an ordinary home, there is likely to be less mothering contact, less intellectual, emotional, and social stimulation, and a lack of encouragement and help in positive learning (Yarrow, 1961). Bakwin (1949) has summarized the clinical picture for young infants in such institutional settings:

"Infants under six months of age who have been in an institution for some time present a well-defined picture. The outstanding features are listlessness, emaciation and pallor, relative immobility, quietness, unresponsiveness to stimuli like a smile or a coo, indifferent appetite, failure to gain weight properly despite ingestion of diets which are entirely adequate, frequent stools, poor sleep, and an appearance of unhappiness,

---

[1]See chart on reactions to blindness, page 182.

[2]"Mothering" refers to emotional warmth and stimulation. It can be supplied by a mother surrogate—perhaps an aunt or foster mother—as well as by the real mother. And of course a father who spends a good deal of time with the infant may help to counteract maternal deprivation. Excellent critical reviews of the research findings and issues in maternal deprivation may be found in Yarrow (1961) and WHO (1962). In our discussion of maternal deprivation, we shall include "insufficiencies," "distortions," and "discontinuities" in mother-infant interactions.

proneness to febrile episodes, absence of sucking habits."

Additional descriptive data have been supplied by Provence and Lipton, who have compared the behavior of infants living in institutions with that of infants living in families. At one year of age, the institutionalized infants showed a general impairment in their relationship to people—rarely turning to adults for help, comfort, or pleasure and showing no signs of a strong attachment to any person. These investigators also emphasized a marked retardation of speech and language development, an impaired ability to delay the immediate gratification of needs, and emotional apathy together with impoverished and repetitive play activities. In comparison with the babies living in families, the institutionalized infants failed to show the personality differentiation and learning which "can be thought of both as accomplishments of the first year of life and as the foundation upon which later learning is built." (1962, p. 161)

Institutions vary, of course, and some institutions provide more stimulation and affection than some families. But the difficulty of providing adequate personal contact for infants "en masse" is a very real one. In fact, as late as 1919 about half of the mortality in institutionalized infants under one year was attributed to *marasmus*, a condition in which, despite adequate physical care, infants seemed to "waste away" for lack of warm, personal contact and the meeting of other psychological needs—another example of physiological symptoms as a result of psychological stress. Since then, an effort has been made to provide more individualized and personal care for infants in institutions, but even the best institution can hardly provide the continuing close affectional relationships, variety of challenge, and individualized teaching and guidance that a good family can offer to children in the critical early years.

As Bowlby (1951) has pointed out, the "extent and quality of the damage . . . vary with the age at which the deprivation occurs, with the length of time it persists, and with the quality of substitute care that is provided." (p. 11) Vulnerability seems to be maximum during early infancy (3 to 6 months), and decreases up to about seven years (Gray, 1958). As the child

grows older, of course, the effects of prolonged institutionalization are likely to be complicated by feelings of rejection and remaining unwanted. Certain growth processes appear to be more affected by maternal deprivation than others. Particularly vulnerable are (a) intellectual processes, including language development and the ability to abstract; (b) emotional processes, including the ability to form warm affectional ties with other persons; and (c) control processes, including the ability to control inner impulses in the interests of long-range goals (Ainsworth, 1962).

The long-range effect of severe early deprivation of maternal love and stimulation is suggested by the findings of Beres and Obers (1950) in a study of 38 adolescents who had been institutionalized between about three weeks and three years of age. At the time of the study, 16 to 18 years after discharge from the orphanage, 4 were diagnosed as psychotic, 21 as having a character disorder, 4 as mentally retarded, and 2 as psychoneurotic. Only 7 were judged to have achieved a satisfactory personality adjustment.

By far the greatest number of infants subjected to maternal deprivation are not separated from their mothers. Rather they suffer from inadequate maternal care and distorted mother-infant relationships. Prugh and Harlow (1962) have pointed out that the effects of such "masked deprivation" are fully as devastating. Even a negative attitude on the part of the mother toward pregnancy may be reflected in deviant behavior—excessive crying, sleep disturbances, and irritability—on the part of the infant during the first few days after birth (Ferreira, 1960).

The early work of Ribble (1944, 1945) has shown that rejecting, indifferent, or punishing mothers may cause tense, unsatisfied, and negativistic behavior on the part of the infant even at a very early age. There may even be a refusal to nurse, and the infant may fall into a semi-stuporous condition from which it is extremely difficult to arouse him. In a later study of 379 mothers of 5-year-olds, Sears *et al.* (1957) found that "cold" mothers reported a background of feeding problems, persistent bed-wetting, aggressiveness, and slow conscience development in their children.

Monkeys separated from their mothers at birth and raised in isolation with artificial mothers—wire frames covered with terry cloth—treated them like real mothers, spent hours clinging to them (left), and apparently developed normally. At maturity, however, they failed to establish normal sexual relations, and those that bore young were helpless and dangerous mothers. Other monkeys, raised by pseudomothers but allowed to play together (right), later showed normal adult behavior. Preliminary studies of monkeys growing up with their real mothers but without contact with other young monkeys suggests that interaction with peers is necessary for normal development.

Conditions of nursing, weaning, and toilet training also have long been considered important in "masked deprivation" and the shaping of personality development. For example, where parental demands are beyond the infant's level of development, constant failure and reproof may lead to emotional reactions and behavioral disturbances. It would appear, however, that it is the warm or rejecting context rather than the age at which these early learning experiences occur that is of most importance (Chess *et al.,* 1960). It is also relevant to note that discontinuities in maternal care—for example, a series of separations from the mother or substitute mother figure to whom the infant has formed an attachment—represent another form of maternal deprivation which has been shown to affect emotional development adversely (Ainsworth, 1962).

A number of investigators have pointed out that the effects of maternal deprivation vary considerably from infant to infant and that infants in other societies appear to thrive under widely differing conditions of maternal care. Despite such differences, however, available evidence leaves no doubt that maternal deprivation in infancy can adversely affect intellectual, emotional, social, and even physiological development. In severe cases these effects may be irreversible or only partially reversible despite later corrective experiences.[1]

General environmental deprivation. The human infant, like any other organism, is not a self-contained unit. He is dependent on his environment for a wide range of materials and conditions. Hence it is not surprising that deprivation of any of these needed elements or conditions in early life may have lasting adverse effects. Bruner (1959) summarized the effects of

[1] Studies of *imprinting*—the tendency of the young of certain species to follow and remain near adults of their own kind—appear to be of value in helping to understand the pathogenic effects of deprivations during early development. For example, in a study of mallard ducklings, Hess (1959) found that imprinting occurred only between 9 and 20 hours after birth—that the ducklings followed a moving "model" only if it was made available to them at that time. When no model was available, the following response did not develop. Thus although this following response is evidently based on maturation, the individual's early experience determines whether the response will occur and if so what type of object will be followed. For a good summary of the basis for and significance of imprinting, the reader is referred to Gray (1958), Moltz (1960), and Riesen (1961).

EFFECTS OF EARLY EXPERIENCES ON ADULT BEHAVIOR OF ANIMALS

BEHAVIOR AREA	EARLY EXPERIENCES	ADULT BEHAVIOR
Sensory discrimination and perception	Infant animal raised in darkness	Inability to respond adaptively to visual cues (fish, birds, some but not all mammals)
	Animals restrained from usual touch and proprioceptive stimulation by use of such devices as cardboard tubes encasing the limbs	Retarded use of limbs, abnormal sitting and walking posture, absence of grooming behavior (chimpanzees)
Feeding behavior	Amount of nursing behavior reduced by using bottle with large-holed nipple	Exhibition of sucking movements after feeding time and sucking noises while asleep. Tendency to suck own bodies (puppies)
	Partial starvation in infancy	Increased hoarding and a faster eating rate (rats)
Reproduction	Animals raised in isolation or with members of another species	Attempts to mate indiscriminately with males or females or only with species with which they have been raised (fish and birds)
	Animals raised in cages which contained no nest-building materials or transportable objects	Failure to build nests at parturition even though appropriate types of materials made available (rats)
Gregariousness and filial behavior	Birds raised with other types of songbirds	Acquisition of the song of other birds or some modification of own song
	Mammals raised by humans	Preference for human company over own species (chimpanzee, lamb of wild sheep)
	Infant animals imprinted to human adult	Difficulty in adjusting to own kind, following of human (birds, guinea pigs)
	Infant goats deprived of mother but raised with each other	Highly vigilant and very low in dominance
Emotion and temperament	Hungry infant mice trained to fight over food; others trained in noncompetitive or cooperative behavior	Fighting over food by aggressively trained mice even when not hungry. Other mice far less aggressive
	Infant mice subjected to trauma-producing noise	Greater emotionality and possible timidity in wide range of situations
Learning	Wide range of experiences compared with restricted opportunities	Better learning with wide range of early experience (rats and dogs)
	Differing amounts of physical stimulation and handling	Handling tends to improve performance in learning tasks (rats)

The material in this chart is based in part on the excellent summary of earlier literature in this field by Beach and Jaynes (1954) and also on Eiduson et al. (1962), Gray (1958), Harlow (1962), Hersher et al. (1962), Lindzey et al. (1960), and Moltz (1960). Although these findings cannot be applied directly to human behavior, they help us to understand the behavior of lower animals and provide interesting leads for exploration of more complex human behavior.

early deprivation of needed growth elements in the infant's environment:

"In general, an impoverished environment, one with diminished heterogeneity and a reduced set of opportunities for manipulation and discrimination, produces an adult organism with reduced ability to discriminate, with stunted strategies for coping with roundabout solutions, with less taste for exploratory behavior, and with a notably reduced tendency to draw inferences that serve to cement the disparate events of its environment." (p. 91)

In this context it is of interest to note that extreme deprivation of stimulation during early infancy has been shown to be associated with mental retardation (Yarrow, 1961).

Early frustrations or deprivations may also lead to "weak spots" and distortions as well as to arrested development. This is well illustrated in Hunt's (1941) experiment with four equated groups of rats. Two groups were fed normally during the developmental period; a third was fed normally in infancy, scantily during the prepubertal period, and then normally again; a fourth group was subjected to feeding frustration during the infant period, but received ample food later. In adulthood an interesting behavioral difference was observed. The fourth group, which had been frustrated in infancy, showed gross hoarding, laying up large quantities of unneeded food, whereas the others hoarded much less. Similarly, it would appear that inadequate food, security, approval or love, or other acute frustrations in infancy may have long-term consequences on the human level.

As in the case of physiological development, there would appear to be *critical periods* during which stimulation and associated learning experiences as well as the gratification of various needs are essential for the normal scheduling of intellectual, emotional, and social development. And although the damage accomplished by early deprivations may often be modified by later experiences, the desired results may be slower in making their appearance or may be only partially achievable (Riesen, 1961; Riese, 1962). The effects of several kinds of early deprivation on animal development are summarized in the caption on page 131 and in the chart on page 132.

PATHOGENIC FAMILY PATTERNS

As the infant progresses into childhood, his physical and sociocultural environments become increasingly varied and complex and a wide range of new conditions enters into the shaping of his developing personality. Now he has to deal with other people as well as family members. He must learn new competencies, develop usable assumptions about himself and his world, and increasingly control his behavior to avoid social disapproval and punishment.

During this period, the family remains the crucial guiding influence in the child's personality development, and faulty parent-child relations or pathogenic family interactions are a fertile source of maladjustment. Sometimes parents do too much, not letting a child do his own growing. Sometimes they do too little, not providing him with a stimulating environment or giving him the encouragement and guidance that he needs. And sometimes they teach him inappropriate reaction patterns. Whatever they do, their methods tend to be fairly consistent during the child's growing years (Schaefer and Bayley, 1960).

Unfortunately, there is a lack of adequate evidence concerning the effects of specific types of pathogenic family patterns, partly because the effect of a given child-rearing procedure depends upon the total social context in which it occurs. Also, different children respond somewhat differently to similar practices, and not all effects are permanent: early damage is often corrected to some extent by later experiences. However, several types of parent-child relationships are quite consistently found in the backgrounds of disturbed children.

Rejection. It is particularly important that the child feel loved, wanted, and accepted by his all-powerful parents, for they are his main source of security. The family unit represents the child's base of operations, from which he ventures into the outer world of people and things and to which he returns with his triumphs, problems, and disappointments. Without a secure and adequate "home base," the child's personality may suffer serious and lasting distortion.

Since the child's self-concept is largely a reflection of the way "significant others" react to him, it also becomes apparent that parental rejection fosters a distorted and devaluated self-image. If his parents do not see him as being of worth or significance, it is difficult for the child to think of himself in a positive way. It also becomes difficult for the child to discriminate between approved and disapproved behavior, since he is not appropriately rewarded for desirable behavior by praise and acceptance. If the child becomes discouraged and gives up striving for parental approval, his parents then lose control of an important means of guiding his development.

The effects of parental rejection vary considerably, depending upon whether both parents are involved, how much affection is shown by the nonrejecting parent, how the rejection is expressed, whether the child was accepted at first and rejected later, and other aspects of the child's total life situation. In general, however, rejected children tend to be fearful, insecure, attention-seeking, jealous, aggressive, hostile, and lonely (Pepitone and Wilpizeski, 1960; Sears *et al.,* 1957; Bandura and Walters, 1959). Many of these children are slow in conscience development and have difficulty in later life expressing and responding to affection. In the course of our discussion we shall examine the insidious damage which parental rejection often accomplishes and the diverse etiological roles it may play in mental disorders.

Overprotection. Maternal overprotection, or "momism," involves the "smothering" of the child's growth. The mother may watch over him constantly, prevent him from taking the slightest risk, protect him from all outsiders, overly clothe and medicate him, and make up his mind for him at every opportunity. Often there is excessive mother-child contact in which the mother may sleep with the child for years and fondle him excessively.

Children of overly protective mothers usually lack self-reliance and the ability to cope realistically with their problems. In protecting the child from every danger, the mother denies him opportunities for needed reality testing and for developing essential competencies. In a general sense, life is a series of choice points or problem situations scaled from simple choices of little importance to complex problems of crucial importance. It is only through learning to deal with the simpler problems and choices that we prepare ourselves for the more complex ones. In addi-

tion, the mother's extreme overprotection keeps telling him, in effect, that she regards him as incapable of fending for himself, an evaluation he is likely to accept. It is not surprising that such children often tend to be passive and to feel helpless in the face of a dangerous world. Interestingly enough, overprotection is likely to be more harmful to the development of boys than to that of girls (Kagan and Moss, 1962).

It would be of interest to go into the parental motivations that lead to overprotection, but this would take us too far afield. We may note in passing, however, that Levy (1945) found that 75 per cent of a group of abnormally protective mothers had little in common with their husbands. Such maternal reactions thus may represent a compensatory type of behavior in which the mother attempts, through her contact with the child, to gain satisfactions that should normally be obtained in her marriage. It is not uncommon in such cases for the mother to call the child her "lover" and actually to encourage the child in somewhat typical courting behavior.

It should be noted that not all overly dependent children are the product of overprotective mothers. In fact, in one study of 20 children judged overly dependent by teachers and parents, it was found that over two thirds of the children had not been overly protected. As a group, however, they had had to make about four times as many critical adjustments in early childhood, such as adjustment to a physical disability or to loss of a father (Stendler, 1954). Overly dependent behavior in boys has also been found to follow early and severe emotional deprivation (McCord *et al.,* 1962).

Overindulgence. Although less common than is popularly believed, one or both of the parents may cater to the child's slightest whims (Watson, 1957; Whiting and Child, 1953). Overly indulged children are characteristically spoiled, selfish, and demanding. Unlike the rejected, emotionally deprived child who finds it difficult to enter into warm, human relationships, the indulged child enters readily into such relationships but exploits them for his own purposes in the same way that he has learned to exploit his parents. Such a child is usually rebellious toward authority, having had his own way for so long, and typically approaches his problems with an aggressive, demanding attitude. The overly indulged child also tends to be impatient and to find it difficult to accept present frustrations for the sake of long-range goals. Often he has little sense of appreciation of the value of objects or conditions since he has never had to work for them himself. The fact that his important and pampered status in the home does not transfer automatically to the outside world may come to him as a great shock and result in widespread personality repercussions, as "reality" forces him to a reassessment of his assumptions concerning himself and his world.

Perfectionistic demands. Some parents demand that their children excel in school and other activities. When the child has the capacity for exceptionally high-level performance, things may work out, but often the child is never quite able to live up to parental demands and aspirations. If he improves his grade from a C to a B, he is asked why he didn't get an A. If he gets an A, the next step is to get the highest A in his class. No matter how hard he tries, he somehow seems to fail in the eyes of his parents and ultimately in his own eyes as well, with attendant frustration and self-devaluation.

One need only observe a child's eager "Watch me, Mommy," as he demonstrates some new achievement, to understand the importance of success and recognition in healthy development. Although some failure is inevitable, parents who promote failures by their excessive demands undermine the child's sense of adequacy and worth and discourage further effort on his part. Almost inevitably he comes to feel, "I can't do it, so why try?" Even where the child has the ability to live up to parental expectations, he is under such sustained pressure that little room is left for spontaneity or for development as a person in his own right.

Rigid, unrealistic moral standards. In other instances, parents insist on unrealistic moral standards. When everything from sex to dancing, smoking, and card playing is considered terribly sinful, the child is forced to face many guilt-arousing and self-devaluating conflicts. The internalization of extremely rigid parental values leads the child to be critical and severe in evaluating his own behavior—to develop a severe conscience. Often, too, the result is an "infantile conscience," in that the individual blindly accepts the moral rubrics he has been taught and

dares not attempt an evaluation of their merits. The frequent self-condemnation and guilt feelings which then arise out of the most minor infractions are highly detrimental to his feelings of self-confidence and general worth.

Sometimes the child rebels against severe moral restrictions and goes to the other extreme. As we shall see, this conflict between violent rebellion and submission is not infrequently reflected in the sexual behavior of delinquent girls. Rebellion, however, usually leads to anxiety and feelings of guilt and so does not satisfactorily solve the problem. In general, excessively high standards lead to the development of rigid, restricted personalities.

With boys of extreme moral sensitivity, conflicts centering around masturbation may assume serious proportions. They may feel that it is sinful, or that it will undermine their manhood and lead to all manner of horrible afflictions, or simply that it proves their lack of self-control and moral strength. In any case, despite their repeated attempts to control themselves, they cannot seem to help masturbating. Such anxiety-tinged failures, of course, are devastating to feelings of self-esteem. In our later discussion of sexual disturbances, we shall again consider this frequent relationship between sexual pathology and early sexual miseducation combined with perfectionistic standards.

Faulty discipline. Parents have been particularly confused during recent years with respect to appropriate forms of discipline. Sometimes a general misinterpretation of psychological and educational concepts has led to the notion that the child must not be frustrated or disciplined in any way. But the importance of firm, consistent discipline and guidance for adequate development is emphasized by virtually all modern psychiatrists and psychologists. In a study of twelve-year-old children, Sears (1961) found that antisocial aggressive behavior was related positively to high permissiveness and low punishment, particularly during middle and later childhood. In general, an overly permissive home produces a spoiled, inconsiderate, antisocially aggressive child, and an insecure one as well.

On the other hand, overly severe discipline may have a variety of harmful effects, among which are fear and hatred of the punishing person and a tendency to be overly rigid and severe in punishing oneself for mistakes or misdeeds. Watson (1957) found very strict parental discipline associated with less initiative, less spontaneity, and less friendly feelings toward others on the part of the child. Socially deviant behavior is also common among boys subjected to restrictiveness and punitiveness (Winder and Rau, 1962). Where overly severe discipline is accompanied by rigid moral standards, it is likely to result in a highly repressed, rigid child who lacks spontaneity and warmth and spends much of his energy controlling his own unacceptable impulses and desires.

Similarly, inconsistent discipline will make it difficult for the child to establish stable values for guiding his behavior. When he is punished one time and ignored or rewarded the next for the same behavior, he is at a loss to know what behavior is appropriate. In an intensive study of child-rearing patterns, Sears *et al.* (1957) found that intermittent punitiveness and permissiveness commonly resulted in highly aggressive behavior on the part of the child. Similar findings have been reported by Rosenthal (1962).

If the child is to develop healthy inner reality and value controls, it seems essential that he have a clear view of the behavior that is expected of him, and that consistent and positive methods be worked out for dealing with infractions. Caution must also be exercised, however, to avoid forcing the child into rigid conformity with parental views at the expense of his own individuality and development as a person. In general, clear structuring and freedom commensurate with the child's maturity appear essential for healthy development.

Sibling rivalry. When a child feels that more parental attention and love are directed to a brother or sister than to himself, or when a new arrival in the family replaces him as the center of attention, personality difficulties may ensue. Many times such children threaten to kill or injure their brothers and sisters and often actually do kick and pinch them. However, they usually learn that such direct and open aggression leads to a further deterioration of parental relations and consequently adopt more indirect and covert methods of expressing their hostility, such as belittling, tattling, or referring to siblings with contempt.

Such sibling jealousy and rivalry for parental affection may lead to marked feelings of insecurity. Often the child who feels unloved will resort to disapproved behavior in an attempt to obtain some evidence of parental affection and concern, even if it is only in the form of punishment. Not infrequently, older children show regressive behavior in an attempt to maintain their central position in the mother's affection. The child may wet himself, resort to baby talk, develop feeding difficulties, show off by crawling on the floor, and so on. Such behavior, of course, is a defensive reaction to what the child evaluates as a disturbing and threatening condition. Hence his behavior cannot be dealt with directly or corrected by punishment. Both the hostile and the regressive behavior, however, will tend to disappear if the parents make him feel that he is important and precious to them.

Faulty parental models. Children observe and imitate the patterns of behavior they see around them. Bandura (1962) found in an interesting study that children who watched aggressive models were themselves more aggressive later when frustrated than were a control group. A third group, who had watched nonaggressive models, made the most nonaggressive responses to frustration.

As Bandura has pointed out, learning of coping techniques can be considerably accelerated by the provision of adult models with whom the child can identify. Ordinarily the child's key models are his parents, and their behavior can have a highly beneficial or detrimental effect on the way the child learns to perceive, think, feel, and act. Often the imitative behavior of the child is reinforced by subtle or obvious approval by the parents. When parental behavior is based upon undesirable moral values or when parents are themselves emotionally disturbed or mentally ill, they provide faulty models for the child to follow. This is undoubtedly an important factor in the tendency for delinquency and crime as well as mental illness to run in families.

Marital discord and broken homes. Parental quarreling, bickering, nagging, and general tension are unfortunate conditions for the growing child. They represent a threat to his base of operations and he responds to family tension by developing tension himself. Somewhat typical here is the case of a college student who told of his severe feelings of insecurity during childhood

IMITATIVE LEARNING

The extent to which children may pattern their behavior on the actions of adults was graphically illustrated in a study by Bandura *et al.* (1963). In this study, as in the one described in the text (p. 136), children watched aggressive models. The children, aged three to six, were divided into four groups but observed individually. Members of one group saw a film in which an adult model performed aggressive acts on a large inflated doll, as shown in the pictures in the top row above: the model sat on the doll and struck it repeatedly on the nose, battered its head with a mallet, and kicked it. Half of this group saw the female model; half saw a male model. The second group saw the same models do the same things in person, rather than on film. Again, half the children saw the female model, half saw the male. The third group saw a cartoon in which a cat performed the aggression. The control group saw no aggressive models.

After seeing the models, each child underwent mild frustration and was then observed in a playroom. Some toys in the room—a mallet, a dart gun, and an inflated doll, for example—could be used in aggressive play; others, such as tea sets, crayons, and balls, were more suitable for nonaggressive play. The children were rated on the amount of aggression they displayed in the playroom. The influence of the model was strikingly demonstrated by some children who, as shown in the pictures above, imitated the model's actions almost exactly. Total aggression scores, based on aggressive acts that were not imitative as well as those that were, showed that the experimental groups were nearly twice as aggressive as the control group. Boys were more aggressive than girls, and both appeared to be more strongly influenced by the male than the female model. The three experimental groups did not differ significantly.

In the film *Angry Boy*, Tommy sees himself being used by his mother as a weapon against his father. His hurt and resentment are expressed in stealing and other forms of hostile, aggressive behavior at home and at school.

because of the periodic quarrels of his parents. He stated that he would sit outside on the porch apprehensively biting his nails and anticipating the breaking up of his home. Often, too, parental tensions are displaced in part onto the child through unusually severe or capricious discipline, or the parents may come to resent the child as the only reason for maintaining the unhappy marriage.

Broken homes similarly lead to feelings of insecurity, often aggravated by conflicting loyalties, by the tensions of long, involved legal suits, and by the spoiling that the child may receive while staying with one or the other parent. Perhaps even more important is the lack either of maternal or of paternal care and influence. The boy who is brought up by only a mother suffers a definite lack in his dealings with other children who have protecting father figures. In addition, he suffers from the lack of a model to help him in patterning his behavior along masculine lines. If other male models are available, the damage may be minimal. However, if the mother tends to be the dominant figure in his life, he may model his behavior after her and develop femi-

nine rather than masculine characteristics. The scope of this problem is suggested by the finding that about one ninth of our children now live in homes broken by death, divorce, or desertion (White House Conference, 1960).

Pathogenic interaction in the family as a group.   A great deal of emphasis is being placed today on the family as a social group, and on pathogenic patterns of interaction involving all of the family members. In studies of the families of schizophrenic patients, for example, investigators have pointed to rigidity of role structure within the family, to tendencies of family members to disqualify each other's statements, to underlying tension and hostility concealed by seemingly normal surface interactions, to severe parental discord in which the children are often used as pawns, and to a general social isolation and irrational atmosphere of the family setting. Fisher *et al.* (1959) have concluded that (a) normal adjustment of the child is fostered by parents who are individually well adjusted and form harmonious relationships with each other, (b) neurotic adjustment is fostered by parents who are maladjusted individually but still able to maintain moderately good relationships with each other, and (c) the possibility of later schizophrenic breakdown is greatest where parents are individually disturbed and also relate to each other very inharmoniously.[1] We shall examine this new approach in more detail in our later discussion of the dynamics of schizophrenic reactions and other types of psychopathology.

Many other pathogenic family patterns may lead to adjustment difficulties. Inadequate physical care—for example, failure to see that the child receives adequate nutrition and rest—may lead to unnecessary colds and other ailments and to a lack of normal energy. Contradictory demands made on the child may constantly place him in situations where he "can't win" and thus impair his developing personality. Bateson (1960) has developed the concept of the "double-bind" to refer to such situations. For example, the mother may complain of the child's lack of affection but then freeze up or punish him when he tries to be affectionate. Bateson found this sort of parent-child relationship com-

---

[1] The "successful family" is well described in the report of the White House Conference on Children and Youth (1960).

mon in the background of the schizophrenics he studied.

On page 141 is a summary of the typical effects of some of these undesirable conditions. Although we have emphasized the influence of parental behavior on the development of the child, it is important to remember that the parent-child relationship is always an interaction—not just a one-way influence of the parent on the child. Even at birth and increasingly thereafter, the child comes to the interaction not as a blank tablet but as an active organism with certain reaction tendencies, vulnerabilities, and unique needs. Thus in assessing the results of given conditions, we cannot assume that the parents' behavior is always the independent variable and the child's behavior and development dependent variables.

EARLY PSYCHIC TRAUMAS

Most of us have had accidents or other acute traumatic experiences that temporarily shattered our feelings of security and adequacy and were important in influencing our later environmental evaluations and self-evaluations. The following illustrates such an incident.

"I believe the most traumatic experience of my entire life happened one April evening when I was eleven. I was not too sure of how I had become a member of the family, although my parents had thought it wise to tell me that I was adopted. That much I knew, but what the term *adopted* meant was something else entirely. One evening after my step-brother and I had retired, he proceeded to explain it to me—with a vehemence I shall never forget. He made it clear that I wasn't a 'real' member of the family, that my parents didn't 'really' love me, and that I wasn't even wanted around the place. That was one night I vividly recall crying myself to sleep. That experience undoubtedly played a major role in making me feel insecure and inferior."

Such traumas are apt to leave psychological wounds that never completely heal. As a result, later stress which reactivates these early wounds is apt to be particularly difficult for the individual to handle and often explains why one person has difficulty with a problem that is not highly stressful to other people.

Three points may aid further understanding of this process:

1. Conditioned responses are readily established in anxiety-provoking situations and are highly resistant to extinction or change (Gantt, 1960; Mednick, 1957; Sweetbaum, 1963). Thus one traumatic experience with a vicious dog may be sufficient to establish a conditioned fear response which endures over a long period of time. If, in the experience, the individual feels acutely inadequate or guilty—as in certain cases of sexual assault where the person is too frightened to resist—his self-concept may undergo considerable devaluation. Hence a traumatic experience may continue to influence behavior long after the original event.

2. Conditioned emotional responses stemming from traumatic experiences may generalize to other objects, events, and persons. On a simple level, this process was demonstrated in an early experiment in which a group of subjects were asked for their associations to a list of words. The word *red* occurred six times in the list, each time being followed by the word *barn,* after which the subject was given a rather painful electric shock. Later, the subjects were asked to recall as many of the words as possible and their emotional responses to each word were recorded by means of galvanic skin responses. Interestingly enough, the subjects now showed emotional responses not only to the word *barn* but also to the word *red* and to all other words on the list associated with farm life, such as *hay, cow,* and *pasture* (Diven, 1937). In the same way, the child who has been severely frightened by one vicious dog may be afraid of dogs in general and even of other furry animals. This mechanism was illustrated in Watson's experiment with little Albert, cited in Chapter 2. Under heightened anxiety, our ability to discriminate decreases while our tendency to generalize increases (Mednick, 1957).

3. Traumatic situations result in emotional conditioning rather than in responses learned through reasoning and problem solving. As a consequence, a repetition or similar situation reactivates an emotional response rather than a consciously formulated one which would be more subject to modification and more likely to be adaptive (Mowrer, 1950).

The ease of formation, tendency to generalization, and extreme durability of conditioned emotional responses stemming from traumatic situations all tend to make them maladaptive. Thus when a child is exposed to repeated early traumas, their net effect may be highly pathogenic. Although subsequent experiences may have a corrective effect on the wounds made by early traumas, the scars may never be completely obliterated.

Although we have emphasized the importance of early traumas in unhealthy personality development, such stressful experiences at any age may adversely affect development and adjustive behavior beyond that point. In general, however, early traumas seem to have more far-reaching consequences, largely because reflection, critical evaluation, and self-defenses are not yet present in the young to a degree comparable to that in adulthood. In many instances a traumatic experience in adulthood may actually tend to immunize the individual to later similar experiences because it is now a familiar phenomenon, its limits have been perceived, the individual has equated it with other known experiences, and self-defenses have been developed (West, 1958).

INADEQUATE PREPARATION FOR ADOLESCENCE

Adolescence has long been looked upon as a critical period in personality development. Writers on adolescent psychology emphasize the emotional upheavals, conflicts, and maladjustments characteristic of this period of "storm and stress."

During adolescence the individual is faced with rapid growth, changes in his body proportions, and the physiological changes of sexual maturing. At the same time, the criteria by which his social status is determined are undergoing modification and his formerly dependent position is changing to one of independence and responsibility which will bring with it marital, occupational, and general social-status problems.

These changes inevitably entail modifications in his previous self-concept. Erikson (1950) has described late adolescence as the stage of "identity crisis" where the individual is involved in a final definition of his self-identity. It is dur-

ing this period that he must establish himself as a person apart from his family and work out such problems as further education, marriage, work, and life in a community setting. All of these require increased self-definition, which is not always easily achieved. Many an adolescent goes through a traumatic state of "identity diffusion" in which he experiences uncertainty as to just "who he is" and "what life is all about." As Spivack (1957) has pointed out, many emotionally disturbed adolescents are not rebelling but rather searching for self-definition and meaningful standards of conduct to follow.

Since a variety of texts and other books contain comprehensive treatments of the vicissitudes of adolescence, we shall not deal with the subject at length here. However, it may be pointed out that the stresses of this period are to a large extent rooted in our particular form of sociocultural organization. In certain societies, the adolescent reaches adult status without any undue emotional disturbances.

Apparently, where the child has been adequately prepared to face the problems of sex and changing status and where there are well-structured social roles for young people, there is no reason to anticipate any unusual difficulties during this period of physical and emotional change. Too often in our society, however, there is a paucity of social roles for adolescents, or the adolescent finds the role assigned to him uncomfortable and perhaps devaluating, or there is a conflict between the roles for which the teen-age culture rewards him and those which his parents and society expect him to assume. Frequently lacking in preparation for the inevitable changes in his "self" and life situation, it is not surprising that an adolescent in our society often has trouble resolving his conflicts.

LACK OF COMPETENCIES FOR ADULTHOOD

During the adolescent and early adult period, the individual is acquiring various competencies essential for adult living—for earning a living, marriage, parenthood, citizenship, and getting along with other people. Failure to achieve these competencies is an important factor in the etiology of mental illness.

SUMMARY CHART OF FAULTY PARENT-CHILD RELATIONSHIPS

UNDESIRABLE CONDITION	TYPICAL PERSONALITY DEVELOPMENT OF CHILD
Rejection	Feelings of insecurity and isolation. Attention-seeking, negativistic, hostile behavior. Unable to give and receive affection.
Overprotection—domination	Submission, inadequate, lack of initiative, tendency to passive dependency in relations with others.
Overindulgence	Selfish, demanding, with inability to tolerate frustration. Rebellious to authority, excessive need of attention, lack of responsibility.
Perfectionism—unrealistic ambitions for child	Child internalizes parents' unrealistic standards. Inevitable failure leads to continual frustration, guilt, and self-devaluation.
Rigid, unrealistic moral standards	Extreme conscience development. Tendency to rigidity, severe conflicts, guilt, self-condemnation, and self-devaluation.
Faulty discipline	Overpermissiveness associated with insecurity, antisocial aggressiveness. Severe discipline typically leads to excessive condemnation of self for socially disapproved behavior, anxiety over aggressive behavior. Inconsistent discipline commonly results in lack of stable values for guiding behavior with tendency to inconsistency and vacillation in meeting problems.
Sibling rivalry	Direct or indirect hostility, insecurity, lack of self-confidence, regression.
Marital discord and broken homes	Anxiety, tension, insecurity, lack of secure home base, tendency to evaluate world as a dangerous and insecure place. Conflicting loyalties, lack of adequate models for proper ego development.
Faulty parental models	Internalization of unethical and socially undesirable value attitudes which frequently lead to difficulties with the law.
Contradictory demands ("double-bind")	Lack of integrated frame of reference; confusion and self-devaluation.

The exact effects of faulty parent-child relationships on later behavior depend on many factors, including the age of the child, the constitutional and personality make-up of the child at the time, the duration and degree of the unhealthy relationship, his perception of the relationship, and the total family setting and life context, including the presence or absence of alleviating conditions and whether or not subsequent experiences tend to reinforce or correct early damage. There is no uniform pattern of pathogenic family relationship underlying the development of later psychopathology, but the conditions we have discussed often act as predisposing factors.

Inadequate physical competencies. Here we are basically concerned with keeping physically fit and protecting the body against disease. Maintaining a healthy and attractive body contributes to a sense of well-being and adequacy and enhances our attractiveness to others. Conversely a lack of physical fitness tends to entail chronic fatigue, impaired efficiency in learning and problem solving, and lowered resistance to disease. Problems that seem difficult when we are in good physical condition may seem insurmountable when we are "run-down." Unquestionably, the failure of many emotionally upset people to maintain proper nutrition and rest contributes to their eventual breakdown.

Inadequate emotional competencies. Although our emotions are important resources in our adjustive arsenal, they may also present many problems in expression and control. Anxiety, fear, anger, depression, guilt, and grief are all difficult emotions to handle effectively. Often we overreact to minor anxieties and fears, give way to chronic hostility, or suffer from exaggerated feelings of guilt. Realistic anxiety and worry are adaptive mechanisms which help us to deal with threats and dangers, but when they are inappropriate to the stress situation, they become maladaptive. Anger and hostility are often constructive forces in helping us to overcome obstacles through aggressive action, but unbridled anger and sustained hostility complicate interpersonal relations and tend to isolate the individual from others. In some instances, chronic hostility leads to criminal or other antisocial behavior (Buss, 1961). Chronic hostility may also lead to a variety of psychosomatic ailments, as we shall see in Chapter 7. Similarly, normal feelings of guilt can help us to make needed changes in our attitudes and behavior, but exaggerated and morbid guilt leads to pervasive feelings of devaluation and despair. Thus each individual needs to work out appropriate and effective patterns of emotional response.

Here too, it may be emphasized that a sense of humor and the ability to receive and give love are emotional competencies which are not given to us as gifts but must be developed. Both are essential for healthy adjustment; love in particular is fundamental to the achievement of a meaningful and fulfilling life.

Inadequate social competencies. Most of our needs can be met only through relationships with other people; thus the nature of our interpersonal relationships has much to do with the satisfactions we gain in living. Whether we are attempting to attract a desired mate, achieve a happy marriage, promote a new idea or civic enterprise, or simply make friends, the outcome is heavily dependent on the competencies we have developed for give-and-take with other people. If we antagonize people, or try to lean on them, or seek to dominate them, we are likely to find some of our deepest psychological needs going unsatisfied.

Inadequate social competencies may both stem from and result in a lack of adequate group participation and identification. In his growing-up period the individual usually tries out various social roles, and the reactions of others to the roles he adopts are extremely important in helping him to clarify his self-identity and find the role most satisfactory for him as an individual. The individual who feels ill at ease in the group may withdraw from social participation as much as possible or even compensate with an exaggerated independence in which he belittles the group as stupid and confining, appropriate only for the slaves of convention. Cut off from group interactions, he then has reduced opportunities for clarifying the possibilities and limitations of the social environment in relation to himself. He also is likely to feel that no one cares about him, that he is unimportant and worthless, and that he stands alone without anyone to help him in time of need. Those who feel isolated, left out, and without any place in the group are vulnerable to many stresses which they could perhaps handle readily if they were assured of the interest and emotional support of those around them.

A lack of essential social competencies may also contribute to excessive group identification and overconformity to group standards. Fearful of losing his group status and approval, the individual may blindly follow the dictates of the group without question. This is often observed in the gangs and secret societies of adolescence, and of course in dictatorships. Such overidentification hinders the development of individuality and self-direction. In addition, it is actually unhealthy for the group itself, since an effective social group needs the reasoned participation of each member in shaping its activities and directing them to productive and worth-while channels.

Inadequate intellectual competencies. Despite man's great potentialities for thinking, he is often very inefficient in solving his personal problems and those of his group. It is not necessary to go into the factors involved in efficient learning, problem solving, and decision making or the common errors in reasoning, which are well covered in elementary psychology texts. However, it may be emphasized that effective thinking is a highly skilled process involving adequate information, training in methodology, accurate assumptions, and continual reality checks. Failure to fulfill these requirements is a major reason why man, with the best brain that has ever been evolved, often uses it so ineffectively.

We have emphasized that perceiving, learning, and reasoning occur in the context of our existing motives, feelings, and assumptions. Fear and anxiety have been shown to impair perceptual discrimination and the ability to learn and reason. And where reality conflicts with our needs or assumptions, cognitive distortion is likely to result. This is readily apparent in rationalization, projection, and other ego defense mechanisms. Here cognitive processes are used primarily to protect our feelings of adequacy and worth rather than for the objective evaluation and solution of problems—resulting in reality distortion, self-deception, and lowered adaptive efficiency.

In a broad sense, essential competencies include an adequate "briefing" on the nature of various crucial life problems, such as marriage, parenthood, occupation, and old age. In addition to general competencies—physical, emotional, social, and intellectual—we need preparation for the specific problems we are all likely to encounter in different life periods.

FAULTY FRAME OF REFERENCE

We have noted that the individual gradually builds a frame of reference—a set of basic assumptions concerning fact, value, and possibility —which provides him with a meaningful picture of himself and his world. Without such a frame of reference he would be incapable of consistent or purposeful action. His basic assumptions may

be accurate or inaccurate, conscious or unconscious, rigidly maintained or held tentatively. In any case, they are the only guides he possesses for evaluating and responding to new situations. If they are warped, his perceiving and thinking are distorted accordingly.

All the factors in faulty psychological development so far discussed contribute in one way or another to inaccuracies and distortions in the individual's views of himself or the surrounding world on which his adjustive reactions are based. Such distortions have two important implications for his adjustive behavior. First, he is put in a position of following an erroneous map. He may bristle at nonexistent bogeymen and be unaware of real hazards. To the extent that his view is distorted, he is adjusting to a world that does not exist, and he inevitably makes miscalculations which lead to failure and self-devaluation. This is especially true when he grossly overestimates or underestimates either his own abilities or the environmental opportunities.

Below is an example of a faulty environmental evaluation which is likely to lead to serious adjustment difficulties.

"I think the world is a pretty crumby place. Everybody is trying to take advantage of you if they can. The only way to get ahead is to be tougher and stronger than the other guy and strike first. I have always admired the way that notorious criminals manage to put the jerks in the world in their place. Of course the small ones get caught and sent up, but believe me there are plenty of successful big shots. I was the toughest guy in a pretty tough neighborhood as a kid, and I have learned plenty since then. First I am going to get a degree in law which will help me get the contracts I need for really being a success. Then watch me go!"

Second, the individual's assumptions concerning reality, value, and possibility determine what behavior he will avoid as likely to lead to frustration and hurt. For example, if he sees the world as a dangerous, threatening place, he will restrict his self-investment only to the safest areas of activity and will have a generally defensive orientation to life. Or if he has perfectionistic moral values, he may spend considerable energy fighting impulses he considers dangerous and may become a rigid person who cannot afford the luxury of spontaneity or flexibility. In a rapidly changing society like ours, which requires a good deal of flexibility, such an individual is constantly in danger of being thrown off balance.

Whether our views are accurate or distorted, rigid or flexible, they tend to be perpetuated. The individual who sees the world as a jungle will be selectively sensitive to dishonesty, selfishness, and other characteristics which tend to support his point of view. Similarly, the individual with rigid views concerning the evilness of sex will find ample incidents to support his contentions. We do not easily become aware of our errors in perception because new situations, seen through distorted lenses, seem to keep validating our earlier perceptions. For this reason, faulty assumptions and other developmental defects tend to produce *vicious circles* unless corrective measures are undertaken. That is, they tend to perpetuate themselves with a cumulative effect on the individual's adjustment.

INADEQUATE SELF-DIFFERENTIATION AND INTEGRATION

We have noted that one of the pathways to maturity is from outer direction by parents and others to self-direction. To achieve adequate self-direction requires not only the mastery of essential competencies and a realistic frame of reference but sufficient self-differentiation to have a clear sense of one's own identity. Differentiation of the self makes possible greater determination of behavior from within and is essential if the individual is to experience himself as the originator of his actions with some measure of freedom, choice, and control in directing his life.

In modern life there appear to be two key dangers to adequate self-direction. One stems from the difficulty of achieving and maintaining a stable self-identity amid complexity and rapid change. Our self-identity is dependent on many factors, including our possessions, social status, social roles, frame of reference, interpersonal relationships, and group identifications. But all these factors are undergoing continual change. Often we hear people make such statements as "I am a different person from what I was 5 years ago." To achieve and maintain a stable sense of

self-identity in the face of constant inner and outer change is not an easy task.

A second danger to adequate self-differentiation and direction stems from the courage it takes to "be oneself." Not only may this often place the individual in conflict with group opinion but it requires seeking values, making choices, and taking responsibility for the consequences of one's actions. The inconsistency of adolescent behavior often reflects a very real ambivalence: the adolescent wants to be self-directing but hesitates to give up his security for the responsibilities that go with independence. Even in adulthood the individual may attempt to "escape from freedom" by immersing himself in the group. The sociologist David Riesman (1950) has emphasized the tendency of modern man to be "outer-directed"—to be a sort of "radar man" who lives as though he wore a receiving set on his head in order to get signals from everyone else as to what he should believe and how he should live. Such a man is sensitive to social situations in the sense of wanting to do what is expected, to conform, to avoid ideas or role behavior that might be disapproved. He is dependent on society in much the same way that a child is dependent on his parents—but in this case at the expense of his own self-differentiation and actualization as a person.

The "inner-directed" man, by contrast, does not blindly accept established social values and practices but is critical, evaluating, and searching. Neither does he passively accept the identity which the group may assign him in relation to his status and roles. Rather he attempts to formulate a frame of reference and a style of life which are appropriate for him while still contributing to the group. To the extent that a basic feeling of security is possible in our society, it stems from the individual's knowledge of himself and his confidence that he can cope with most situations successfully—that he can guide and take the responsibility for his own life. It is, of course, for this purpose—to achieve better self-differentiation and more effective self-direction—that many people undertake psychotherapy.

Important as is adequate differentiation, healthy development is dependent also upon the *integration* of the various components of the personality system. Serious conflicts, discrepancies, and imbalances among components—for example, marked differences between one's self-concept and one's ego ideal, an imbalance between task- and defense-oriented behavior, discrepancies between goals and the competencies needed to achieve them, or confusion over values—may impair personality integration and contribute to faulty development. Of course, such conditions need not be permanent, and their resolution may contribute to personal growth and effectiveness.

Sociological Factors in Faulty Development

In looking for genetic factors and psychological influences, we sometimes forget the profound influence of the cultural setting in determining development and behavior. The well-known anthropologist Margaret Mead (1953) has shown vividly how even physiological functioning and physical development are shaped by sociocultural factors.

"During this process of socialization, a certain pattern of behavior is built into the growing organism and becomes a part of him, in the same sense that a certain pattern of capillary behavior is a part of a patient with Raynaud's disease. Culture is seen not as a set of external impacts and catastrophes to which an organism . . . is subjected, but as a principal element in the development of the individual, which will result in his having a structure, a type of functioning, and a pattern of irritability different in kind from that of individuals who have been socialized within another culture [p. 378] . . . the functioning of every part of the human body is moulded by the culture within which the individual has been reared—not only in terms of diet, sunlight, exposure to contagious and infectious diseases, overstrain, occupational disease hazards, catastrophes, and traumatic experiences, but also by the way that he, born into a society with a definite culture, has been fed and disciplined, fondled and put to sleep, punished and rewarded. . . . [p. 377] .

"We may take Graves' disease as an example. It is recognized that the incidence of Graves' disease is related to the amount of anxiety under which the individual lives . . . [consequently] . . . a type of culture which systematically exerts upon the developing organism . . . anxiety-producing pressure at critical stages in maturation . . . [may produce] . . . an alteration in thyroid metabolism which would become chronic and to which many other homeostatic systems would make a systematic adjustment. The average representative of such a culture would show a consistent variation in homeostatic pattern in the same direction as that in patients suffering from disturbances of thyroid metabolism. In the light of this approach (holistic) every socialized individual is seen as so profoundly moulded by his culture that the most fundamental life processes will have systematically different patterns even though these patterns may all lie within the margin of safety for human functioning." (pp. 389-390)

In addition to biological changes induced by the cultural setting, anthropological studies have shown that varying patterns of social organization seem to breed somewhat different types of psychological disorders. In other societies trends in mental illness have been found which are considerably different from ours, apparently reflecting differences in sociocultural conditions rather than biological differences. Even within our society investigators have found differences between rural and urban areas and between different socioeconomic levels. We shall examine these differences in some detail in our discussion of neuroses, psychoses, and other mental disorders.

Society as well as the individual can develop in unhealthy ways, as evidenced by police states, racial discrimination, and other social pathology. Such faulty development both lowers the stress tolerance of the group and provides a pathological social climate for the rearing of its members. And in much the same way that the individual may show decompensation in response to excessive stress, society may undergo decompensatory changes which, in turn, affect the individuals in the group. Thus from the standpoint of the individual, the influence of sociocultural factors is a double one, since they play a large part in shaping both the kinds of attitudes and stress reactions he develops and the kinds of stress he must face. Later in the chapter we shall examine some of the sociological conditions in our culture which place us under special stress.

We have considered some of the factors that can prevent healthy development and hence predispose individuals and social groups to abnormal functioning. Now we are ready to examine some of the most frequent sources of excessive stress on biological, psychological, and sociological levels.

Severe Biological Stress

Many biological conditions—infections, intoxications, physical traumas, malnutrition, emotional strain, fatigue—either may lower the individual's stress tolerance and act as predisposing causes in mental illness or may themselves be the precipitating factor.

FATIGUE AND DIETARY DEFICIENCIES

In order to survive and have the capacity for meeting adjustive demands, the organism must constantly renew itself through rest and through taking in the various nutrients needed to replace the materials being used up in the process of living. Prolonged interference with such renewal weakens the organism's resources for coping with even normal adjustive demands and makes it highly vulnerable to special stresses. Prisoners have sometimes been "broken" by nothing more persuasive than repetitive questioning and systematic prevention of sleep over a period of several days.

In one experimental study, army volunteers underwent sleep deprivation ranging from 72 to 98 hours. As sleep loss increased, the subjects showed increased visual misperceptions, temporal disorientation, and cognitive disorganization. Other anomalies included tactual illusions and feelings of depersonalization. A few reported the "hat illusion"—feeling a band of pressure around the head—and were observed making repeated efforts to remove the nonexistent hat (Morris, *et al.*, 1960). Under conditions of combat or other special stress where strong anxiety, fear, or pain may be added to the extreme fatigue, even the most mature, well-integrated personality may break down.

Studies of dietary deficiencies have also pointed to marked changes in psychological functioning, the exact change depending in large part on the type and extent of the deficiency (Dean *et al.,* 1955; Brožek, 1955; Brožek and Guetzkow, 1957; McIlwain, 1955). Pantothenic acid deficiency, induced in normal human volunteers, produced such symptoms as profound apathy and depression, neuromotor disorders with tingling and burning sensations, and complaints of clumsiness, dizziness, and weakness (Dean *et al.,* 1955).

In everyday life we are rarely subject to such excessive physical demands, but many of us lower our general resistance to stress through insufficient rest, inadequate diet, or trying to carry a full work load under the handicap of a bad cold, an emotional strain, or a generally rundown condition. In so doing, we deprive ourselves of needed adjustive resources and make ourselves more vulnerable to whatever stresses we are facing.

ACCIDENTS AND DISEASE

Accidents and disease may also prove highly stressful. It is startling to note that over 90,000 persons are killed each year in accidents and a hundred times as many are injured, many seriously (National Safety Council, 1962). Such accidents are highly stressful in their own right in terms of painful and often permanent injuries and may involve the death or injury of loved ones too.

Many millions of people also suffer from heart conditions and other ailments which place serious restrictions on their life activities and in some instances pose a continual threat to life itself (National Health Education Committee, 1961). Chronic disease may be both painful and debilitating and may confront the individual with a reduction in his expected life span. In some instances, the individual may be forced to undergo operations which are disfiguring as well as highly anxiety arousing. Such conditions reduce adjustive capacity and augment the total stress load with which the individual has to deal. They also may call for changes in one's self-evaluation, level of aspiration, and value patterns—changes that are not easy to make.

The actual role of physical pain as a stress has never been clearly delineated. Certainly, pain is itself an acute adjustive demand; when pain is severe and long continued, it may gradually wear down adjustive resources and lead the individual to overwhelming feelings of hopelessness and despair.

TOXIC AND ORGANIC BRAIN PATHOLOGY

Another set of biological factors, whose role in psychopathology has been better delineated, are the more typical organic disturbances that directly affect the central nervous system.

About one half of all patients in mental hospitals are suffering from mental disorders associated with toxic or organic brain pathology—that is, conditions which result in the destruction of brain tissue or otherwise interfere with the normal functioning of the brain. Brain pathology may be temporary, as in the delirium of fever, or it may involve permanent damage to the brain tissues, as in syphilitic infection.

Again it should be emphasized that both brain damage and the personality organization of the individual play important parts in the associated mental disorder. As we have noted, certain individuals become severely disordered with only slight brain damage, whereas more stable individuals are able to compensate successfully for much more extensive damage. In addition, the clinical picture—whether the patient becomes depressed or euphoric or perhaps develops hypochondriacal tendencies—is determined largely by the pre-illness personality of the patient rather than by the brain pathology. In Part IV, we shall devote two chapters to the various mental disorders in which there is demonstrable brain pathology.

A great deal of current research is directed toward (a) delineating the precise nature and role of excitatory and inhibitory centers and processes in the brain and (b) identifying faulty chemical reactions that occur in connection with mental disorders. This research has received encouragement from the finding that minute amounts of certain drugs can seriously disturb brain functioning, resulting in what are called "model psychoses." For example, the injection of small amounts of the drug LSD leads to feelings of unreality and confusion which approximate some of the symptoms of schizophrenia. It is possible that severe stress—either biological or psychological—may lead to similar biochemical distortions in certain predisposed individuals.

DISRUPTIVE EMOTIONAL PROCESSES

We have noted that emotional processes like fear and anger represent the mobilization of body resources to meet emergency situations. Ideally, of course, this total mobilization of resources would be utilized in the direction of the greatest advantage to the threatened organism, helping it either to fight or to flee more effectively. In our civilized life, however, we are rarely confronted with situations that can be adequately met by simple physical attack or flight. But man has not experienced a comparable reduction in emotional excitability; we still become mobilized for physical flight or attack when we feel threatened even though such actions are now socially inappropriate. Our fear and anger may thus be maladaptive when we have no adequate channel of discharge for the increased energy and tension.

Even mild fear, anger, or anxiety can adversely affect the accuracy of perception and thought. However, such mild emotions may reinforce and concentrate adjustive behavior on given goals—and hence be integrative in their overall effect. But as we get into the intermediate range of intensity, emotions are typically detrimental to problem solving and task performance. For example, Worchel (1957) showed that angry subjects had difficulty in concentrating and scored lower on a digit symbol task than did subjects who had been allowed to dissipate their anger.

As the level of emotional tension increases, it

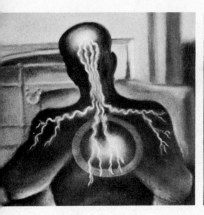  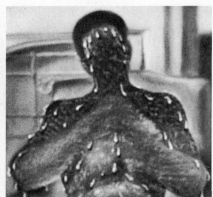

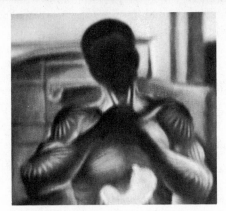

Emergency emotional mobilization means widespread changes in bodily functioning. From the brain go messages speeding the action of the heart and alerting both central and autonomic nervous systems, which in turn activate the adrenal glands and cause stored sugar to be dumped into the blood. Muscles tense for action and we perspire; palms become moist; digestion stops. These conditions, designed for emergency fight or flight, often hinder the ordinary adjustments of modern life. Insecure or fearful individuals often maintain this state of physiological mobilization constantly as a habitual reaction, because they see their life situation as a constant threat and emergency. Such long-continued emergency mobilization may seriously lower the individual's stress tolerance and even eventuate in various "psychosomatic" ailments, which we will examine in Chapter 7.

becomes increasingly disruptive to organized behavior. Extreme fear, for example, leads to serious behavior disorganization such as the panic reactions we see during fires and other dangerous emergency situations: individuals may be paralyzed by fright or may trample each other in blind attempts to escape. Intense anger may lead to blind rage and aggression with resulting physical attack on another person, which may later lead to punishment and extreme remorse.

The typical effects of mild, intermediate, and intense levels of anxiety have been well summarized:

"At low levels of anxiety there is a general alerting of the organism, an increase in vigilance. . . . In this state there is an increased sensitization to outside events and an increased ability to cope with danger.

The organism is in the state of preparedness. . . . The threshold for potentially noxious stimuli particularly is lowered as the alert and apprehensive organism seeks the sources of danger in its world. This sensitivity continues at higher levels of anxiety, but the ability to differentiate the dangerous from the trivial becomes reduced. . . .

"As stress increases . . . or anxiety mounts, the organism becomes less capable of mastery. Behavior loses its spontaneity and flexibility. There is a general rigidification and individuals respond in terms of the more habitual and hence safer response tendencies. Anything novel is threatening and the ability to improvise is reduced (Ausubel *et al.*, 1953). Increased effort has been expended in order to maintain adequate behavior.

"At higher levels of free anxiety there is no longer the ability for effective action. The organization of behavior breaks down. Regression to simpler and more primitive modes of response occurs. All aspects of psychological functioning are affected; coordination and integration are greatly reduced. In this state the organism can no longer adequately differentiate between dangerous and harmless stimuli, nor respond in a differentiated way. Clinically, this is manifest in the great distractibility, generalized irritability, and the random-appearing behavior of the anxiety patient. It is as if the central control mechanisms were disordered." (Basowitz *et al.*, 1955, pp. 12-13)

Thus it would appear that severe emotional upheavals actually defeat their emergency functions. Even on a biological level coordination is upset: Gellhorn (1943) has shown that when emotion reaches a high level of intensity or continues over a sustained period, there is a disturbance in coordination between sympathetic and parasympathetic nervous systems resulting in *autonomic disorganization* comparable to the psychological disorganization.

As we noted earlier, Selye (1953, 1956) has shown that during prolonged emotional mobilization, changes occur which are not only useless but actually harmful. During such prolonged emotional reactions to stress, Selye found that all organs of the body except the adrenal cortex show involutive or degenerative changes. In fact, the production of certain hormones—ACTH and the corticoids, mediated primarily by the anterior pituitary and the adrenal cortex—actually become excessive. Selye considers this a useful part of the mobilization of body resources during the "alarm reaction"—a sort of nonspecific adaptive reaction to severe stress.

When continued over a long period, however, these excessive hormonal secretions lead to various pathological changes in the brain and other organs—for example, such reactions as edema, hemorrhages, and rise in intracranial pressure with increased formation of cerebrospinal fluid. This resulting encephalopathy is capable of producing epileptoid seizures, acute excitation, confusional states, pronounced depression, or coma.

During the "stage of resistance," the ability of the nervous system to adapt to new or different stresses is lowered. Presumably it exhausts its adaptive resources in dealing with the original stress and lacks resiliency for coping with new ones (Selye, 1956; Selye and Fortier, 1950).

The work of Selye and other investigators has eventuated in what may be termed the "stress theory of disease" and has led to intensive research in an effort to relate severe or chronic stress to the onset and course of various body ailments (Simon, 1960). In Chapter 7 we shall discuss psychosomatic, or psychophysiologic, disorders—peptic ulcers, arthritis, and many other physical ailments in which chronic emotional mobilization typically plays a major role. Even those of us who do not develop psychosomatic ailments are likely to experience some degree of worry or anxiety much of the time in the face of the constant pressures, frustrations, and uncertainties of modern life and the pace at which it must be lived. A chronic state of emotional mobilization is the price too often paid for "high pressure" living.

Severe Psychological Stress

Many kinds of frustrations, conflicts, and pressures are associated with modern living. Although we shall consider several of them singly, they occur as parts of a total stress pattern.

FRUSTRATIONS LEADING TO SELF-DEVALUATION

In the preceding chapter we saw that feelings of adequacy and worth are basic psychological needs, and that we develop a system of ego defense mechanisms to meet these needs and to prevent self-devaluation. We must think well of ourselves and feel adequate to deal with our problems if we are to maintain our psychological integration. Again and again in tracing the development of mental illness, we find severe self-devaluation playing a crucial role.

In contemporary life there are a number of common frustrations that lead to self-devaluation and hence are particularly difficult to cope with.

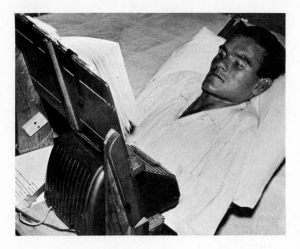

One common obstacle faced by the handicapped person is a form of resignation which the patient confuses with self-acceptance. Here the individual *resigns* himself to his fate and assumes the role of the helpless cripple (Hughes, 1960). Unfortunately, society often encourages the handicapped person to play this role instead of helping him to regard himself as an essentially normal, competent person with a handicap. Pictured above is a man who though paralyzed from the neck down as a result of an auto accident, is still accepting life's challenge to make a useful, happy life. He is continuing his studies via TV; his book is held by a mechanical holder where he can read it comfortably.

Among the most important of these are failure, losses, envious status comparisons, personal limitations, guilt, and unrelatedness and lack of meaning.

Failure. In our highly competitive society many of us fail to reach the goals we set for ourselves—to live up to our ego ideal. Often this results from setting our goals unrealistically high, so that even though we do make good progress, we feel that we have failed. In other cases our failure is more than a matter of *feeling* we have failed. We actually lose a job or are beaten out by a rival. Such failures have been experienced by all of us in one area of life or another.

Since our society places such a high premium upon success, failures lead to strong feelings of inferiority and self-devaluation. Successive failures are especially frustrating, as is failing in an undertaking we consider especially important.

If failures are not to leave an individual with permanent feelings of inferiority and fearfulness, it is important that the failure experiences be "worked through" and used constructively for avoiding similar mistakes in the future. In this connection it is interesting to note that the Eskimos at Cape Prince of Wales conduct a primitive form of psychodrama in their community igloo during the six-month winter. Accompanied by an orchestra of drums, they stage a pantomime of the failure experiences in their lives and laugh at their own mistakes thus objectively viewed (Harmeling, 1950).

Losses. Closely related to failure are the many losses which we inevitably experience—losses involving objects we treasure or individuals with whom we strongly identify who are in real measure parts of ourselves. The pain of most losses is enhanced by the fact that there is nothing we can do about them once they have occurred.

Among the most distressing physical losses are those of money and status. Money gives its owner security and self-esteem in our society, and an appreciable financial loss is apt to lead to severe self-recrimination. Similarly, loss of social status tends to self-devaluation in one's own eyes as well as in the eyes of others.

Other losses relate to human rather than material objects. We may lose the friendship of a person whom we esteem very highly or the love and respect of our mate. In other instances loss may involve the death of loved ones. Bereavement is a highly traumatic experience for most people and one which all of us are likely to experience at one time or another. Many older persons never fully recover from the death of the mate with whom they have shared their life. In some cases, they even seem to lose the will to live and die themselves within a short time. It is interesting to note that in one study the key reasons given by normal individuals who felt they were about to "go to pieces" were a death, an illness, or separation from a loved one (Gurin *et al.,* 1960).

Envious status comparisons. Few of us ever attain the personal status in society that we should like to have. Our job, our home, our social position, our material possessions may, in our opinion, compare unfavorably with those of other persons. Often we daydream of how wonderful it would be to be some famous movie actor or four-star general, or to be extremely wealthy or a great genius, or to have a beautiful and thrilling wife. Such fantasies are, of course, stimulated by movies, radio and television programs, and romantic novels in which we identify with the heroes and heroines who actually enjoy such wished-for status.

In large part, too, such fantasies are the outcome of our tendency to compare our achievements and status continually with those of others and with the norms on which those around us seem to place value. Many of us try to "keep up with the Joneses" and evaluate our own status in relation to that of others rather than in terms of its actual merits. In fact, our status often comes to seem synonymous with our basic worth: if our status is something less than we think it should be, we feel "worthless" or "no good."

Personal limitations. Closely related to these status considerations are the more personal factors—physical appearance, sex, age, intelligence, special abilities—which influence our status in society and are an essential part of our self-evaluation. Personal characteristics which are admired by our group are valuable assets in raising our feelings of adequacy and self-esteem; conversely, characteristics which the group ignores or disapproves of are likely to lead to self-devaluation.

Here too, of course, we tend to compare ourselves with others, and few of us find such comparisons highly satisfactory. We are likely to be acutely aware of our big nose, freckles, or other alleged inferiorities while we ignore and fail to make the most of the assets we do have.

For an individual who has serious physical handicaps—loss of vision, hearing, limbs, and so on—the problem of self-acceptance, as we have seen, is likely to be a very difficult one.

Guilt. Guilt is one of the chief sources of self-devaluation and one that operates in all cultures. We may take advantage of our friends, engage in immoral sexual behavior, show selfishness or hostility toward those we love, lack the courage to take a stand on an important social issue, or in other ways fail to live up to our ethical values. Such behavior leads to feelings of guilt and self-devaluation which are extremely unpleasant and frustrating.

In our society many social prohibitions and highly emotional moral attitudes center around the expression of hostility and sexual desires. Most people feel especially guilty over infractions in these areas. They dare not admit feelings of hostility toward parents or children or close friends; yet occasional feelings of hostility toward loved ones are probably universal and to be expected.

Sometimes early sexual experiences, such as incest or mutual sex play among boys, are evaluated as terribly sinful in the light of ethical and moral values learned much later. The results are often devastating.

A college student had engaged in mutual masturbation with boys during his early youth and had had occasional homosexual experiences during his army life. He had later married, but his homosexual fantasies and past behavior, which he considered unpardonable, made his sexual adjustment in marriage quite hopeless and led to attempts to seduce practically every woman he met in an attempt to demonstrate his masculinity. Like so many patients, he had also become convinced that he was different from other people, that they might be able to tell that he had homosexual inclinations, and that he deserved to fail because he was fundamentally no good. The improvement in this patient was startling once he realized the nature of his problem and could understand that his homosexual fantasies and past experiences were not unusual and would probably cease to bother him as his marital adjustment became better established.

Severe and continued self-recrimination over wasted opportunities or past unethical behavior plays havoc with feelings of security and adequacy and may even predispose the individual to fear success because he feels he does not deserve it and sooner or later will be punished. In understanding such guilt feelings, it is important to remember that (a) we learn and accept various assumptions concerning right and wrong which we then apply to the evaluation of our own behavior and impulses, and (b) we have been taught, often by hard experience, that wrongdoing or "sin" leads to punishment. Thus when we behave in ways which we view as immoral, we experience self-devaluation and apprehension. As a consequence of this orientation, we often become reaction-sensitive to immediate failures and search back through our past life locating and exaggerating misdeeds which have presumably led to our present difficulties. This process is especially obvious among depressed mental patients who even react to present unethical desires as if they had actually been carried out in action—a severe and pathological type of guilt reaction.

Unrelatedness and lack of meaning. Feelings of isolation and loneliness are another potent source of self-devaluation and discouragement. Many individuals experience a painful sense of being alone in the world—of somehow not belonging. They feel like strangers in a strange world. Others seem not to understand or care about them. Such feelings of loneliness may become extremely painful when the individual suffers the loss of some loved person who provided him with his main source of interpersonal intimacy—as often happens in the case of divorce or the death of one's mate. Frieda Fromm-Reichmann (1959) has commented on the disintegrative effect of feeling alone, unappreciated, and unloved; she considers this feeling a particularly difficult stress in the group-conscious culture in which we live. Only as we build rich linkages with our world—warm and satisfying relationships with others and a basic orientation of concern for our group and for mankind in general—are we likely to overcome feelings of alienation.

Related to feelings of loneliness, and equally destructive of morale, is an inability to find meaning in one's life. As Becker (1962) has pointed out: "Let it be stressed emphatically that the most difficult realization for man is the possibility that *life has no meaning.*" (p. 30) Without meaning, life is wasted, futile, empty. There is little reason to try, to be concerned, or even to hope. Rather we are confronted with the doctrine of despair so dramatically portrayed in the familiar lines of Shakespeare's Macbeth that life

> . . . is a tale
> Told by an idiot, full of sound and fury,
> Signifying nothing.
>
> *(Act V, Scene v)*

Thus again we sense man's great need for a sense of identity, for relatedness, and for values which help him to find meaning and to live a fulfilling life.

CORE CONFLICTS OF CONTEMPORARY LIFE

In the preceding chapter we discussed conflicts as an important source of frustration and hence of potential maladjustment. Numerous experiments have shown that animals will develop typical neurotic symptoms if they are forced to choose between two undesired alternatives or to make discriminations that are beyond the range of their sensory ability. In human beings, overwhelming conflicts produce comparable, though far more complex, results. In general, it is conflicts, rather than privations or mere frustrations, that tear us apart and prove so disruptive to our adjustive efforts. Thus if we are to gain an adequate understanding of mental disorders in our contemporary society, we must know what kinds of conflicts are most prevalent.

In assessing common sources of trouble, we find that the core conflicts which place a burden upon our adjustive abilities center around avoiding vs. facing reality, dependence vs. self-direction, integrity vs. self-advantage, fear vs. positive action, love vs. hate, sexual desires vs. restraints, and conflicts concerning values. In each case there is considerable ego involvement. Thus anxiety and a feeling of threat are important elements in these conflicts.

Avoiding vs. facing reality. Perhaps the first requisite of personal maturity is the development of the ability to see ourselves and the world around us as objectively as possible and to face and make the best of realities. But this is no simple task. Reality is often unpleasant and anxiety arousing and may undermine our constant efforts to feel good about ourselves. For example, facing the reality that our failure in some important venture such as marriage has resulted from certain stupidities on our part would be self-devaluating. Hence we tend to avoid facing this reality by rationalizing, projecting, or using other defense mechanisms.

Most of us entertain an image of ourselves which enhances some of the virtues that we admire. Thus we may view ourselves as more reasonable or patient or conscientious or unselfish than we really are. Such an image may, of course, help us to accept ourselves and to feel adequate in dealing with life's problems—but it may also keep us from facing our limitations realistically and making needed changes in our aspirations or modes of adjustment.

We all have a tendency to see and believe what we want to see and believe both about ourselves and about our world. We do not search out evidence that contradicts our pet theories. We close our eyes and ears to social injustices that might otherwise make us uncomfortable. We avoid thinking about many unpleasant realities by filling every waking moment with activity and stimulation. It is much easier to avoid reality than to face it, and the ways are legion, but when we do so, we are operating with an inaccurate map and should not be surprised if we get lost.

Dependence vs. self-direction. All of us have to make the transition from the dependent, protected status of childhood to adult status and responsibility, with all that this implies in terms of independence and self-directed activity. For most of us this transition is a difficult one, and when problems accumulate and the going gets tough, we may wish, consciously or unconsciously, that we could return to the security and protected status of our childhood. Sometimes we even seek to re-establish a dependency relationship with a mate or a close friend.

Some persons manage to maintain a somewhat dependent position all their lives by marrying older women or men, who take care of them in much the same way that their parents did. Others become lifelong inmates of mental hospitals, where their needs are taken care of and where they do not have to face the responsibilities and problems of normal adult life. But for most of us a retreat to dependency is not practical, for it would play havoc with our feelings of adequacy and self-esteem and would only lead to further frustration. So our retreat may take a fantasy or symbolic form in which we imagine a secure and carefree life on some remote South Sea island.

Usually this dependence-independence conflict is most severe during late adolescence and young adulthood when we are expected to begin to assume adult responsibilities. Its importance is indicated by the finding of Lloyd (1952) that almost half of a group of 1000 college students had failed to attain adequate emotional emancipation from their parents. With further emotional maturity and successful achievement,

the conflict is usually diminished and resolved in favor of independence and self-direction. However, underlying dependency needs may still remain, revealing themselves at times of setback and failure.

Integrity vs. self-advantage. There are often times when it appears that our needs might be served best by actions strongly in conflict with our ethical attitudes. Thus we may be tempted to cheat on examinations, to flatter people when we are trying to get them to do something for us, to be unfaithful to our spouse, to be slightly devious in our business transactions, or to fail to stand up for values in which we believe because of possible social disapproval or retaliation. We are particularly likely to be tempted by such behavior when we note that others engage in it with seemingly successful results.

Of course, individuals who are very limited in their conscience development or whose ethical attitudes make such behavior acceptable will experience little conflict, nor will they have guilt feelings afterwards. In fact, they may feel that the successful completion of their objective is a far more important consideration than the means used in achieving it. But most of us have been taught that such means are unethical and consequently we experience conflict over the temptation to use them and serious guilt feelings if we give in. The idealistic adolescent in particular may find it both disillusioning and self-devaluating to learn that the adult world does not always abide by the standards he has been taught in school and that he himself is tempted to use means which he does not consider to be entirely honest. He may experience considerable conflict in the process of working out and adhering to his own standards.

Fear vs. positive action. May has pointed out that ". . . living without fear in the twentieth century shows weakness of mind, or more accurately, insensitivity, atrophy of mind . . . a certain amount of anxiety in people is the expected, normal reaction." (1951) But many of us overreact to the real dangers with disproportionate fear, and our fear leads to feelings of inadequacy, exaggerations of threat, and often an unreasoned and self-defeating "lashing out" at our problems.

The effects of fear are illustrated by the person who is afraid to go out in the dark alone after watching a terrifying murder mystery on television. If he goes out anyway, he is prone to jump at the slightest sound. This increased sensitivity is characteristic of the many frightened, insecure individuals who go through life overreacting to the slightest threat. Their fears rob them of courage and cripple their reasoning and other adjustive capacities. Also, as we have seen, we tend to hate the things we fear. Fear and hate combined are, of course, not conducive to reasoned positive action.

Although most of us have experienced fear often enough to be familiar with the increased tension, desire to flee, and other common manifestations of it, few of us realize that fatigue, worry, sensitivity to criticism, indecision, and the centering inward of one's concerns may be disguised effects of fear. Actually such symptoms are probably more common in modern civilization than the more direct manifestations.

Another aspect of fear which is commonly overlooked is the distinction between feeling, showing, and reacting to it. We all experience fear although most of us learn to conceal it rather effectively. But the key factor in dealing with fear is how we act when we are afraid. The brave soldier is not the one who experiences no fear, but the one who performs courageously despite it. Not realizing this, many people expend their efforts fighting the *feeling* of fear and trying to deny or conceal it instead of learning to function effectively in spite of it. To the extent that we allow fear or worry to inhibit positive actions, we block our own progress.

Love vs. hate. Love and hate are two powerful and conflicting emotional forces in human existence. Both may give rise to adjustive difficulties in their own right, and an admixture of love and hostility complicates most of our relationships with others.

Hostility is difficult for many of us to handle for three reasons: (a) we have been taught, as already noted, that hostility is unethical—particularly when directed toward parents, brothers or sisters, or mates, for whom we should presumably feel only pure affection, (b) we have learned through experience that to express hostility is to invite social retaliation and loss of love, and (c) high levels of hostility tend to block love and other positive emotions.

Since the mixture of love and hate which we call *ambivalence* complicates most of our relationships with loved ones, the adequate channeling and discharge of hostility becomes an important problem in human relations. This is especially true where the parent-child relationships evoke continued hostility on the part of the child. A dominating, authoritative, or brutal father usually arouses considerable hostility which is especially difficult for the child to handle because he is likely to fear such a parent. Similarly, an overly possessive mother usually elicits hostility, since the child may dimly realize that he is being used by the mother to meet her own needs. Such hostility toward parents may arouse guilt feelings and may complicate the child's adjustments in later intimate relationships.

Thwarting of the need to love and be loved is a common source of unhappiness and maladjustment. Love is perhaps the strongest positive force in human behavior, and to love and be loved promotes feelings of adequacy, worth, and self-fulfillment. However, love also has its dangers, for to love others is to take a "calculated risk" in that the love may not be permanently returned or the loved one may be lost through death. Consequently, many individuals tend to insulate themselves emotionally to avoid the risk of being hurt. Others who love but feel they are not loved enough in return feel frustrated and thus tend to have strong ambivalent feelings toward the loved one.

Despite the dangers involved, however, most people strive to establish warm, loving relationships with others. The alternative is to invite feelings of estrangement, loneliness, and unrelatedness.

Sexual desires vs. restraints. As a result of the social prohibitions centering around the expression of the sex drive, we may experience severe conflicts. Initially, sexual conflicts usually are related to masturbation and, as we have seen, may become a running battle between strong sexual impulses and a belief that masturbation is a vile habit that will undermine our health and is engaged in only by those who lack moral fiber and will power.

Often, too, the early sexual picture is complicated by an overattachment to the mother or father. Freudian theory has placed great emphasis on the importance of the "Oedipal situation."[1] According to this theory, a male child initially desires the entire attention and affection of his mother and has difficulty in orienting himself to her as a woman and to his father as her husband. Normally, the boy becomes chiefly attached to his mother and the girl to her father. Generally, this situation is resolved as the boy gradually comes to identify with his father and the girl with her mother, and latent sexual desires give way to harmless tender affection. In some instances, however, the individual never satisfactorily resolves his Oedipal conflict, and later personality development may be seriously affected.

With later adolescence and young adulthood, sexual conflicts are likely to be aroused by questions of petting, premarital sexual relations, and infidelity after marriage—patterns of sexual behavior which are in conflict with established social mores and often with the individual's moral convictions. In addition, various considerations such as the possibility of pregnancy may enter the picture. Thus conflicts of high intensity may be generated.

When the individual has a background of rigid training regarding the "evils" of sex, he may find it very difficult to accept his sex drive as a part of himself or to accept himself as a worthwhile person in view of his sexual desires. Such attitudes, however, only create inner conflict without reducing the sex drive, and the individual has to devote considerable energy to holding his "immoral" desires in check, disguising them, or channeling them into substitute activity of one kind or another. To complicate matters further, such individuals often retain the undifferentiated sexual desires characteristic of preadolescence. Their sexual fantasies are often directed toward both males and females, leading to bewilderment and self-devaluation. They do not realize that such fantasies are common as youngsters are growing up and are usually outgrown later.

So again we have a severe inner conflict as the individual battles against his own "evil" nature. And here, too, various ego defense mechanisms may be called on. In severe cases, an individual unable to accept sexual desires as part of himself may project his desires outward to preserve his equilibrium; now he may feel other men are making homosexual advances toward him. Small wonder, then, that sexual conflicts are frequently found as major factors in mental illness.

Value conflicts. Values enter into all the conflicts which we have discussed, for our values ultimately determine the choices we make. In selecting goals, in choosing means for achieving these goals, and in resolving conflicts, we are influenced at every turn by our conception of what is desirable or undesirable. Where the individual's value assumptions are unclear or contradictory, he is likely to experience difficulties in making choices and directing his behavior.

Often a distinction is made between *conceived* and *operative* values. Conceived values are conceptions of the ideal which the individual may hold with considerable conviction but may not follow in his actual behavior; operative values are the assumptions concerning desirable and undesirable, good and bad, right and wrong, which the individual actually uses in making choices. Sometimes the discrepancy between an individual's conceived and operative values indicates an alarming schism between his "idealized" and "real" self.

Several writers of our time—Riesman (1950), Fromm (1955), Getzels (1957), and Maslow (1959)—have pointed to the tendency of many people in our age of anxiety to surrender to the blind security of authority the task of thinking through their values and prescribing rules for their behavior. They guide their behavior and judge themselves as worthy or unworthy, successful or unsuccessful, in terms of the standards of this "outer" authority. Where such standards run counter to their own perceptions of value, inner turmoil and self-devaluation are the inevitable result.

Psychologists have become increasingly aware of the importance of values both in guiding our choices and in determining the satisfactions and meaning we find in living. In fact, it has become apparent that problems centering around values, choice, and responsibility—of how we should live—are crucial factors in many mental disorders (Mowrer, 1960; Szasz, 1960).

---

[1]The term is derived from the name of a Greek king, Oedipus, who according to mythological accounts unknowingly killed his father and married his mother.

PRESSURES

Stress involves not only frustrations and conflicts but also pressures of various types. In general, pressures force us to change the direction of our activity, to intensify our efforts, or to speed up our activities. Pressures may stem from inner or outer sources, and we may react to them either by changing ourselves or by changing the external situation. In some instances, we learn to live with them without undue strain; in other instances they are acutely uncomfortable; in still other instances they become excessive and lead to a breakdown of organized behavior.

Each of us faces a somewhat unique pattern of pressures, but in a general way we all face the pressures of competing with others, meeting educational, occupational, and marital demands, and coping with the complexity and rapid pace of modern living.

Competition (achievement). We live in a highly competitive society in which we compete for grades, athletic honors, leadership, jobs, marital partners, social status, and almost everything else we value. In these competitive endeavors we are encouraged to surpass others, to excel, to "get to the top." As a consequence, we often drive ourselves mercilessly toward high levels of achievement, and in the process subject ourselves to sustained and severe pressure.

Whatever we may say in defense of such values, they are bound to lead to much disappointment and frustration, especially in a materialistic society such as ours. For statistically there is not room at the top for everyone, and the inculcation of such unrealistic goals can lead only to excessive competition and to widespread feelings of inferiority, failure, and frustration for the many who do not come in first. It is small wonder that many people come to view the world as a "forest primeval," subject only to the law of the "survival of the fittest." Such attitudes, of course, hinder the development of healthy ego structures in winners and losers alike.

Educational, occupational, and marital demands. Many pressures stem from demands made on us in connection with our education, career, and marriage. The long hours of study, the tension of examinations, and the sustained concentration of effort over many years result in considerable stress for most students—particularly those who go beyond the high-school level. Where the individual is handicapped by inefficient study skills, financial problems, or other difficulties, the competition for grades and for advanced training may become highly stressful. With the recent shift in American schools toward more emphasis on academic excellence and less on personality adjustment, the stress of educational competition can be expected to increase. Impetus to this trend is also given by automation, which is rapidly eliminating semi-skilled jobs and making advanced training a prerequisite to adequate occupational and economic status.

Occupational demands are often highly stressful, especially when the individual is very ambitious or feels under pressure from family or friends to get to the top. Many jobs make severe demands in terms of responsibility, time, and performance standards. If the individual is not really interested in or well suited to his work, occupational demands are likely to be highly stressful regardless of the actual demands of the work situation.

Marriage also makes many demands on both partners—demands that may be stressful if either individual is immature and poorly prepared for the responsibilities of marriage, if there are basic incompatibilities between the marital partners, or if financial or other problems make the external situation unfavorable. Marriage calls on the individual to adjust to intimate relationships with another person, to take responsibilities, and to resolve value conflicts. With the arrival of children, the problems of parenthood may further complicate marital adjustment problems.

Complexity and pace of modern living. One interesting series of studies showed that when a colony of rats were given adequate food and nesting materials but confined in an area at about twice the normal population density, many forms of abnormal social and sexual behavior appeared. Maternal behavior was so disrupted that few of the young survived, and there was evidence that in time the colonies would have died out. Even when a few of the healthiest males and females were moved to uncrowded surroundings, they continued to produce fewer than normal litters, and none of their offspring survived to maturity (Calhoun, 1962).

No generalizations can be drawn from these studies, of course, as to the likely effects of severe overcrowding at the human level. We would expect any stressful condition to be more disruptive to members of a species whose normal patterns are largely dependent on instinctive mechanisms than to man, with his great capacity for adaptability. It has been suggested, however, that on the human level, too, the multiplicity of social and other stimulation in a crowded setting can produce abnormality by starting many action patterns that are never completed because new stimuli keep interrupting to start new actions (Spitz, 1963).

It has been established, as we have seen, that either understimulation or overstimulation can impair normal development and functioning. The mere complexity and pace of modern living tend to "overload" the organism, and the strain of living under such highly complicated and demanding conditions can play havoc on both biological and psychological levels. Increasing research evidence is pointing to the role of "overloading" in heart attacks and physical disorders. On a psychological level, "overloading" leads to lowered efficiency and irritability; in extreme degree, there may be a complete breakdown of organized behavior (J. G. Miller, 1961).

Many of the demands made on us are contradictory in nature, such as the problem of insufficient time to meet combined family, civic, and occupational demands. Thus the need to make choices and bear responsibility for them adds to the stress of the demands themselves. Where the individual is immature, has no clear sense of his own identity, and lacks an adequate value system, he may find it extremely difficult or impossible to cope with such demands satisfactorily.

Many other frustrations, conflicts, and pressures could of course be mentioned in our present discussion. Disappointments in love are probably experienced by most of us at one time or another and often leave us terribly hurt. Delays in need gratification—delaying marriage until we have completed school, or waiting to buy a new automobile or home until we have saved sufficient money—are often difficult to cope with, especially when we see others enjoying the things we want and when we are stimulated by advertisements which make waiting more difficult. Many people suffer the handicapping effects of poverty and/or cultural deprivation. Painful conflicts between self-expression and conformity, cooperation and competition, duty and pleasure are ever present for most of us. Although affecting fewer people, terrifying accidents, loss of social status, and imprisonment are highly stressful for those who have to face them. To persons whose status or feelings of worth are largely dependent upon physical attractiveness, the deteriorating effects of aging may present particularly difficult problems. Finally, the prospect of our own inevitable death is an extremely traumatic reality which we all must face.

Severe Sociological Stress

Some of the psychological stresses common to many individuals in our society have already been discussed. Other stresses especially characteristic of our time and place in history and exerting an influence on all who live in the United States today are war and threat of war, occupational difficulties and economic fluctuations, widespread family instability, racial discrimination, and rapid social change.

In an intensive study of both American and Chinese subjects, Hinkle *et al.* (1957) found that the individual's relation to his social environ-

ment, as he perceived it, had a profound effect not only on his peace of mind but even on his general physical health. As a group, those who had had serious difficulty in adapting to their social environment had had a disproportionate amount of all of the illness reported.

WAR AND THREAT OF WAR

Any study of the history of the United States —or of the world in general—is devoted largely

RELATIONSHIP BETWEEN LIFE SITUATIONS AND CLUSTERS OF ILLNESS

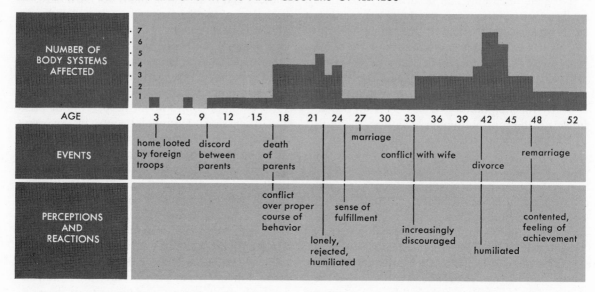

An extensive study of the lifetime illnesses and adjustment difficulties of three groups of subjects (two American, one Chinese) disclosed consistent patterns of relationship between them. Not all the subjects, of course, had the same amount of illness, but even those who had a great deal of it had long periods during their lifetimes without illness. The interesting thing was that there frequently were clusters of illnesses, in which several body systems were affected, and that these clusters tended to occur at times reported by the subjects to have been especially stressful—times when they were trying to adapt to unusually difficult life situations, such as conflict with family members, threats to social position, loss of important psychological supports, or excessive demands or pressures.

Above is a chart showing for one subject the relationships between actual life events, the individual's perceptions, and the amount of physical illness he suffered. The first illness cluster involved hemorrhoids, irritable colon, respiratory difficulties, and severe depression, as well as development of myopia. The second cluster included gout, hepatitis, hypertension, hay fever, frequent colds, and deep depression with an episode of alcoholism. During the interval between the two clusters, the patient's only physical complaint was his myopia (Hinkle et al., 1957).

to a consideration of wars. Although wars have sometimes been necessary to achieve or maintain freedom and human rights, the conditions of warfare have placed great stress upon large numbers of people. Privation, mutilation, death, grief, and social disorganization have been inevitable accompaniments of warfare.

Today most of mankind lives in fear of the new and incredibly destructive instruments of modern warfare—thermonuclear, chemical, and bacteriological. Unless some solution can be found to the problem of war, the world will be engulfed in a holocaust that will affect all of us and destroy civilization as we know it. Fear growing out of this threat has led some of us to overaggressive attitudes, intellectualization, apathy, or other irrational, defense-oriented behavior rather than a task-oriented search for a solution. The crucial challenge facing us today—one which we cannot ignore—is to find some effective means of controlling the use of military force while at the same time preserving our freedom and values.

OCCUPATIONAL PROBLEMS AND ECONOMIC FLUCTUATIONS

Satisfactory employment is an important source of economic well-being and feelings of self-worth. Perhaps nothing adds more to a man's sense of competence and to the meaningfulness of his life than work that he can do well and feels is of value. In fact, there is an old saying to the effect that "to destroy a man, it is only necessary to make his work seem inept and useless." And since the individual spends most of his waking hours on the job, the quality of his personal relationships with supervisors and other employees is also of vital importance in his occupational satisfaction or dissatisfaction. If he feels inadequate or cannot take pride in his work or is in constant friction with others, his work becomes a problem instead of a source of strength. Yet it is conservatively estimated that well over one third of all employees have jobs with which they are dissatisfied.

Even more demoralizing than unsatisfying work is inability to find work at all. The history of the United States has been dotted by a series of widespread depressions. Undoubtedly, these depression periods have brought increases in certain types of abnormal behavior, such as apathy resulting from chronic unemployment, suicides, crime, and marital unhappiness. Inflation is another economic factor that has placed a hardship on many people, particularly older people who have retired and must live on a fixed income. Fortunately, the trend is toward broad social legislation which ensures at least minimal standards of housing, nutrition, and medical care for the unemployed as well as for older people whose income has been depleted by inflation.

However, there are many people today who face serious occupational problems. Older people who are still capable and productive are being forced to retire at an arbitrary age; they must adjust to a reduced income and to feelings of being no longer useful. Many people today—especially unskilled and semiskilled workers—are being displaced by automation. Such dislocations bring both physical hardships and self-devaluation. Many young people who lack technological skills are either unable to find employment or forced to accept jobs which they consider unsatisfactory. Most of us have at one time or another worked at jobs which we found boring and dissatisfying; it is not difficult to imagine how unpleasant it would be to see nothing else ahead.

MARITAL UNHAPPINESS AND FAMILY INSTABILITY

Although our divorce rate has dropped from a postwar high of one divorce for every three marriages, it still has frightening implications as to the extent of personal disappointment, disillusionment, and hurt which many of today's marriages entail.

It has been conservatively estimated that a third of all marriages continue in the face of deep dissatisfaction. Heartache, bickering, feelings of wasted opportunity, of being tied down, of marking time, and so on are very common, especially when children are the only bond holding the marriage together. Here marital partners are denied the emotional support and positive sharing of experience which are such important values in marriage, and they often feel that they have been trapped and are wasting their lives. It is thought-provoking to note that estimates indicate approximately one half of all married partners would not pick the same mate if they had it to do over again.

On the more hopeful side, Burgess (1954) feels that the present symptoms of family breakdown are an outgrowth of the transition from a rural to an urban, industrial society and that a new, healthier form of family is emerging. Whereas authority was formerly vested in the father and the ties that bound the family together were duty, convention, and conformity to law, religion, and custom and in some cases the survival needs of the family group, all family members now share in the responsibility and decision making, and the emphasis is on affection, personal development, and the happiness of family members. In the current stage of transition, however, there are special hazards to the family. For example, the new family constellation gives adolescents far more freedom, and often they lack the maturity to use it wisely. Similarly, the complexity and pace of modern living places a heavy strain upon the family as a "team," while rapid social change often leads to problems unknown to previous generations. As a consequence, a new need has arisen for help from "experts" in solving family problems.

In discussing family instability as a cause of maladjustment, it is relevant to emphasize the crucial role of the family in meeting the needs of the individual and in determining the satisfactions he finds in living not only during childhood but throughout the life span. As Ackerman has pointed out: "The interrelations of individual and family contribute to the determinants of mental health at every stage of maturation, infancy, childhood, adolescence, adulthood, and old age. Such relations influence the precipitation of illness, its course, the likelihood of recovery, and the risk of relapse." (1958, pp. 727-728)

RACIAL DISCRIMINATION

Racial discrimination is an aspect of our culture that is almost universally decried in theory; yet it seems to be among our most ingrained habits. All of society suffers as a result of this prejudice, but it is of course the victims of the prejudice who lose most by it. In addition to the increased stress and tendencies toward hostility and self-devaluation engendered by racial discrimination, the victims may also be subjected to lower economic and educational opportunities. The resulting effects upon personality development are widespread both individually and socially (Lief and Stevenson, 1958).

Adjustments are particularly difficult for those who do not have definite, accepted status in any group, as in the case of light-complexioned northern Negroes or the children of immigrant parents who are not readily accepted because of foreign mannerisms and attitudes. Children in minority groups often tend to be ashamed of their parents and hostile toward them.

As Kenworthy (1959) has pointed out, people everywhere are rebelling against discrimination. For centuries people have more or less blindly accepted inequality, but today the idea of equality has reached the most isolated parts of the world. No matter who they are or where they live, people want to be treated and respected as human beings.

RAPID SOCIAL CHANGE AND EXISTENTIAL ANXIETY

All life involves change—we grow up, marry, have children, shift social roles, face the death of parents, undergo operations, and adjust to numerous other major and minor changes as we go through life. Change *per se* need not cause difficulty. In fact, we have long since grown accustomed to the frequent changes brought about in our lives by advances in modern science and technology—and in the main we regard these changes as beneficial.

However, rapid social change has also created serious problems for man. It has played havoc with traditional mores and value patterns and with many of our assumptions concerning the meaning of human existence. With the advent of the space age, man is confronted with a new perspective of time and space and the problem of finding the meaning of his existence in a universe in which the earth and even the whole solar system may be no larger in relation to the whole than an atom is to the earth. At the same time, materialistic values—based upon the belief that scientific progress would automatically lead to man's happiness and fulfillment—have proved sadly disillusioning. As a result, many people are groping about, bewildered and bitter, unable to find any enduring faith or to develop a satisfying philosophy of life. Despite their fine automobiles, well-stocked refrigerators, and other material possessions and comforts, the meaning of life seems to be evading them. In essence, they are suffering from *existential anxiety* —deep concern about finding values which will enable them to live satisfying, fulfilling, and meaningful lives.

Rapid changes are taking place in other parts of the world as well as in our own country. In fact, we are living in a period of world unrest and tension in which vast social changes seem to be the order of the day. Few are the places in the world where people still follow as a matter of course the ways of their fathers and grandfathers. As Cantril (1958) has pointed out, people are seeing the more abundant way of life that can be provided by modern technology; they are becoming aware of the inadequacies of many existing forms of political and social organization; and they are feeling both hope for a better way of life and frustration that they themselves may not experience it. Unfortunately, all these changes are accompanied by considerable turmoil and conflict as old patterns and values give way to new ones.

In summary, we have emphasized adjustment as a function of the level and types of stress in relation to the person's adjustive resources. We found that for convenience the various factors operating in any maladjustive behavior could be classified as: (a) predisposing factors—such as heredity and pathogenic family patterns—which have eventuated in inadequate personality development and/or lowered stress tolerance, and (b) precipitating factors involving excessive stress, such as loss of loved ones, extreme and sustained pressure, or severe conflicts. Either predisposing or precipitating factors may be predominantly biological, psychological, or sociological. Usually factors on all three levels are involved, sometimes reinforcing each other, sometimes counterbalancing each other, but each playing a part in our behavior.

REFERENCES

The reference list includes not only the sources from which the author has drawn material, but acknowledgments of the permissions granted by authors and publishers to quote directly from their works.

ACKERMAN, N. W. Toward an integrative therapy of the family. *Amer. J. Psychiat.,* 1958, 114, 727-733.

AINSWORTH, MARY D. The effects of maternal deprivation: a review of findings and controversy in the context of research strategy. In World Health Organization. *Deprivation of maternal care: a reassessment of its effects.* Geneva: WHO, 1962. Pp. 97-165.

AUSUBEL, D. P., SCHIFF, H. M., & GOLDMAN, M. Qualitative characteristics in the learning process associated with anxiety. *J. abnorm. soc. Psychol.,* 1953, 48, 537-547.

BAKWIN, H. Emotional deprivation in infants. *J. Pediatrics,* 1949, 35, 512-521.

BANDURA, A. Social learning through imitation. In M. R. Jones (Ed.), *Nebraska symposium on motivation.* Lincoln: Univer. Nebraska Press, 1962. Pp. 211-269.

BANDURA, A., ROSS, D., & ROSS, S. A. Imitation of film-mediated aggressive models. *J. abnorm. soc. Psychol.,* 1963, 66, 3-11.

BANDURA, A., & WALTERS, R. H. *Adolescent aggression.* New York: Ronald, 1959.

BARKER, R. G., WRIGHT, BEATRICE A., & GONICK, MOLLIE R. Adjustment to physical handicap and illness: a survey of the social psychology of physique and disability. *Soc. Sci. Res. Council Bull.,* 1946, 55, 1-372.

BASOWITZ, H., KORCHIN, S. J., PERSKY, H., & GRINKER, R. R. *Anxiety and stress.* New York: McGraw-Hill, 1955.

BATESON, G. Minimal requirements for a theory of schizophrenia. *AMA Arch. gen. Psychiat.,* 1960, 2, 477-491.

BEACH, F. A., & JAYNES, J. Effects of early experience upon the behavior of animals. *Psychol. Bull.,* 1954, 51, 239-263.

BECKER, E. Toward a comprehensive theory of depression: a cross-disciplinary appraisal of objects, games and meaning. *J. nerv. ment. Dis.,* 1962, 135, 26-35.

BERES, D., & OBERS, S. J. The effects of extreme deprivation in infancy on psychic structure in adolescence: a study in ego development. In R. S. Eissler, *et al.* (Eds.), *The psychoanalytic study of the child.* Vol. 5. New York: International Univer. Press, 1950. Pp. 212-235.

BERNABEU, EDNITA P. The effects of severe crippling on the development of a group of children. *Psychiatry,* 1958, 21, 169-194.

BOWLBY, J. *Maternal care and mental health.* World Health Organization. Monograph Series No. 2, 1952.

BROŽEK, J. Nutrition and behavior: psychologic changes in acute starvation with hard physical work. *J. Amer. Dietet. Ass.,* 1955, 31, 703-707.

BROŽEK, J., & GUETZKOW, H. Psychological effects of thiamine restriction and deprivation in normal young men. *Amer. J. clin. Nutrit.,* 1957, 5, 109-118.

BRUNER, J. S. The cognitive consequences of early sensory deprivation. *Psychosom. Med.,* 1959, 21, 89-95.

BURGESS, E. W. Economic, cultural, and social factors in family breakdown. *Amer. J. Orthopsychiat.,* 1954, 24, 462-470.

BUSS, A. H. *The psychology of aggression.* New York: Wiley, 1961.

BUYTENDIJK, F. J. J. *Pain: its modes and functions.* Chicago: Univer. Chicago Press, 1962.

CALHOUN, J. B. Population density and social pathology. *Scientif. Amer.,* 1962, 206, 139-150.

CANTRIL, H. *Politics of despair.* New York: Basic Books, 1958.

CHESS, STELLA, THOMAS, A., BIRCH, H. G., & HERTZIG, MARGARET. Implications of a longitudinal study of child development for child psychiatry. *Amer. J. Psychiat.,* 1960, 117, 434-441.

CRICK, F. H. C. The genetic code. *Scientif. Amer.,* 1962, 207 (4), 66-74.

CRICK, F. H. C. On the genetic code. *Science,* 1963, 139, 461-464.

DAVIDSON, M. A., MC INNES, R. G., & PARNELL, R. W. The distribution of personality traits in seven-year-old children: a combined psychological, psychiatric and somatotype study. *Brit. J. educ. Psychol.,* 1957, 27, 48-61.

DEAN, W. B., HODGES, R. E., & DAUM, K. Pantothenic acid deficiency induced in human subjects. *J. clin. Invest.,* 1955, 34, 1073-1084.

DIVEN, K. Certain determinants in the conditioning of anxiety reactions. *J. Psychol.*, 1937, 3, 291-308.

DOBZHANSKY, T. The present evolution of man. *Scientif. Amer.*, 1960, 203 (3), 206-217.

EIDUSON, BERNICE T., EIDUSON, S., & GELLER, E. Biochemistry, genetics, and the nature-nurture problem. *Amer. J. Psychiat.*, 1962, 119, 342-350.

ERIKSON, E. H. Growth and crises of the "healthy personality." *Symposium on the healthy personality.* New York: Josiah Macy, Jr. Found., 1950.

ESCALONA, SIBYLLE K., & HEIDER, G. M. *Prediction and outcome.* New York: Basic Books, 1959.

EYSENCK, H. J. *Behaviour therapy and the neuroses.* London: Pergamon Press, 1960.

FERREIRA, A. J. The pregnant woman's emotional attitude and its reflection on the newborn. *Amer. J. Orthopsychiat.*, 1960, 30, 553-561.

FIELDS, J. Twins brought up apart. *Eugen. Rev.*, 1958, 50, 115-123.

FISHER, S., BOYD, INA, WALKER, D., & SHEER, DIANNE. Parents of schizophrenics, neurotics, and normals. *AMA Arch. gen. Psychiat.*, 1959, 1, 149-166.

FROMM, E. *The sane society.* New York: Rinehart, 1955.

FROMM-REICHMANN, FRIEDA. Loneliness. *Psychiatry*, 1959, 22, 1-15.

GANTT, W. A. Pavlov and Darwin. In Jax, Sol (Ed.), *Evolution after Darwin.* Vol. 2. *Evolution of man.* Chicago: Univer. Chicago Press, 1960.

GELLHORN, E. *Autonomic regulations; their significance for physiology, psychology and neuropsychiatry.* New York: Interscience Publishers, 1943.

GESELL, A. L., & AMATRUDA, CATHERINE. *The embryology of behavior.* New York: Harper, 1945.

GETZELS, J. W. A stable identity in a world of shifting values. *Educ. Leadership*, 1957, 14, 237-240.

GLUECK, S., & GLUECK, ELEANOR. *Family environment and delinquency.* Boston: Houghton Mifflin, 1962.

GRAY, P. H. Theory and evidence of imprinting in human infants. *J. Psychol.*, 1958, 46, 155-166.

GURIN, G., VEROFF, J., & FELD, SHEILA. *Americans view their mental health; a nationwide survey.* New York: Basic Books, 1960.

HAM, G. C. Genes and the psyche: perspectives in human development and behavior. *Amer. J. Psychiat.*, 1963, 119, 828-834.

HARLOW, H. F. The heterosexual affectional system in monkeys. *Amer. Psychologist*, 1962, 17, 1-9.

HARMELING, PEGGY C. Therapeutic theater of Alaska Eskimos. *Group Psychother.*, 1950, 3, 74-76.

HERSHER, L., MOORE, U., RICHMOND, J. B., & BLAUVELT, HELEN. The effects of maternal deprivation during the nursing period on the behavior of young goats. *Amer. Psychologist*, 1962, 17, 307.

HESS, E. H. Imprinting. *Science*, 1959, 130, 133-141.

HINKLE, L. E., JR., et al. Studies in human ecology. *Amer. J. Psychiat.*, 1957, 114, 212-220.

HOBBS, G. E. Mental disorder in one of a pair of identical twins. *Amer. J. Psychiat.*, 1941, 98, 447-450.

HSIA, D. Y. *Inborn errors of metabolism.* Chicago: Year Book Publishers, 1959.

HUGHES, G. R. Self-resignation: a mighty foe. *J. Rehabilit.*, 1960, 265, 18-19.

HUNT, J. M. The effects of infant-feeding frustration upon adult hoarding in the albino rat. *J. abnorm. soc. Psychol.*, 1941, 36, 338-360.

HURWITZ, J., & FURTH, J. J. Messenger RNA. *Scientif. Amer.*, 1962, 206 (2), 41-49.

International Atomic Energy Agency. *Diagnosis and treatment of acute radiation injury.* New York: International Documents Service, 1961. Proceedings of a scientific meeting jointly sponsored by the International Atomic Energy Agency and the World Health Organization.

JACKSON, D. *Etiology of schizophrenia.* New York: Basic Books, 1960.

JONES, H. E. The galvanic skin reflex. *Child Develpm.*, 1930., 1, 106-110.

KAGAN, J., & MOSS, H. A. *Birth to maturity.* New York: Wiley, 1962.

KALLMANN, F. J. Heredity and eugenics. *Amer. J. Psychiat.*, 1960, 116, 577-581.

KALLMANN, F. J. *Heredity in health and mental disorder.* New York: Norton, 1953.

KALLMANN, F. J. Psychogenetic studies of twins. In S. Koch (Ed.), *Psychology: a study of a science.* Vol 3. *Formulations of the person and the social context.* New York: McGraw-Hill, 1959. Pp. 328-362.

KALLMANN, F. J. The use of genetics in psychiatry. *J. ment. Sci.*, 1958, 104, 542-549.

KALTER, H. Paper delivered at symposium on phenylketonuria. Inst. for post-graduate education, Cincinnati, Nov. 16, 1961. Reported by Ross Laboratories: Currents in Public Health, 1962, 2.

KENWORTHY, L. S. Human aspirations are changing our world. *Childh. Educ.*, 1959, 36, 55-57.

LEJEUNE, J., TURPIN, R., & GAUTIER, M. *Ann. de Génétique*, 1959, 1, 41.

LEVY, D. M. Maternal overprotection. In N. D. C. Lewis & B. L. Pacella (Eds.), *Modern trends in child psychiatry.* New York: International Univer. Pr., 1945.

LIEF, H. I., & STEVENSON, I. P. Psychological aspects of prejudice with special reference to desegregation. *Amer. J. Psychiat.*, 1958, 114, 816-823.

LINDZEY, G., LYKKEN, D. T., & WINSTON, H. D. Infantile trauma, genetic factors, and adult temperament. *J. abnorm. soc. Psychol.*, 1960, 61, 7-14.

LLOYD, R. G. Parent-youth conflicts of college students. *Sociol. soc. Res.*, 1952, 36, 227-230.

MARTIN, IRENE. Somatic reactivity. In H. J. Eysenck (Ed.), *Handbook of abnormal psychology.* New York: Basic Books, 1961. Pp. 417-456.

MASLOW, A. H. (Ed.) *New knowledge in human values.* New York: Harper, 1959.

MAY, R. Anxiety. *Psychol. Bull.*, 1951, 48, 166-167.

MC CORD, W., MC CORD, JOAN, & VERDEN, P. Familial and behavioral correlates of dependency in male children. *Child Develpm.*, 1962, 33, 313-326.

MC FARLAND, R. A., & HUDDELSON, J. H. Neurocirculatory reactions in the psychoneuroses studied by the Schneider method. *Amer. J. Psychiat.*, 1936, 93, 567-599.

MC ILWAIN, H. *Biochemistry and the central nervous system.* Boston: Little, Brown, 1955.

MEAD, MARGARET. The concept of culture and the psychosomatic approach. In A. Weider (Ed.), *Contributions toward medical psychology.* Vol. 1. New York: Ronald, 1953. Pp. 368-397.

Medical Research Council, Gt. Brit. *The hazards to man of nuclear and allied radiations: a second report.* London: H. M. Stat. Off., 1960.

MEDNICK, S. A. Generalization as a function of manifest anxiety and adaptation to psychological experiments. *J. consult. Psychol.*, 1957, 21, 491-494.

MILLER, J. G. Sensory overloading. In B. E. Flaherty (Ed.), *Psychophysiological aspects of space flight.* New York: Columbia Univer. Press, 1961. Pp. 215-224.

MOLTZ, H. Imprinting: empirical basis and theoretical significance. *Psychol. Bull.*, 1960, 57, 291-314.

MORRIS, G. O., WILLIAMS, H. L., & LUBIN, A. Misperception and disorientation during sleep deprivation. *Arch. gen. Psychiat.*, 1960, 2, 247-254.

MOWRER, O. H., *Learning theory and personality dynamics.* New York: Ronald, 1950.

MOWRER, O. H. "Sin": the lesser of two evils. *Amer. Psychologist*, 1960, 15, 301-304.

National Academy of Sciences. National Research Council. Report of the Subcommittee on long-term effects of ionizing radiations from external sources and of the Committee on pathologic effects of atomic radiation. Publication 849. Washington, D. C.: National Research Council, National Academy of Sciences, 1961.

National Health Education Committee. *Facts on the major killing and crippling diseases in the United States today.* New York: Author, 1961.

National Radiation Advisory Committee. Third Annual report to the Prime Minister. *Med. J., Austral.,* 1960, 750-752.

National Safety Council. *Accident facts.* Chicago: Author, 1962.

NIRENBERG, M. W. The genetic code: II. *Scientif. Amer.,* 1963, 208 (3), 80-95.

PARNELL, R. W. Physique and mental breakdown in young adults. *Brit. Med. J.,* 1957, 1, 1485-1490.

PAULING, L. Genetic effects of weapons tests. *Bull. atom. Scientists,* 1962, 18 (10), 15-18.

PEPITONE, A., & WILPIZESKI, C. Some consequences of experimental rejection. *J. abnorm. soc. Psychol.,* 1960, 60, 359-364.

PROVENCE, SALLY, & LIPTON, ROSE C. *Infants in institutions.* New York: International Univer. Press, 1962.

PRUGH, D. G., & HARLOW, R. G. "Masked deprivation" in infants and young children. In World Health Organization. *Deprivation of maternal care: a reassessment of its effects.* Geneva: WHO, 1962. Pp. 9-29.

RANDALL, G. C., EWALT, J. R., & BLAIR, H. Psychiatric reaction to amputation. *Res. Publ. Ass. nerv. ment. Dis.,* 1946, 25, 94-115.

REES, L. Constitutional factors and abnormal behavior. In H. J. Eysenck (Ed.), *Handbook of abnormal psychology.* New York: Basic Books, 1961. Pp. 344-392.

REES, J. R. *Shaping of psychiatry by war.* New York: Norton, 1945.

RIBBLE, MARGARETHA A. Anxiety in infants and its disorganizing effects. In N. D. C. Lewis & B. L. Pacella (Eds.), *Modern trends in child psychiatry.* New York: International Univer. Press, 1945.

RIBBLE, MARGARETHA A. Infantile experience in relation to personality development. In J. McV. Hunt (Ed.), *Personality and the behavior disorders.* Vol. 2. New York: Ronald, 1944. Pp. 621-651.

RIESE, HERTHA. *Heal the hurt child.* Chicago: Univer. Chicago Press, 1962.

RIESEN, A. H. Critical stimulation and optimum period. Symposium, Division 7, APA Convention, New York, September 1, 1961.

RIESMAN, D. (in collaboration with R. Denney, & N. Glazer). *The lonely crowd: a study of the changing American character.* New Haven: Yale Univer. Press, 1950.

ROSENTHAL, M. J. The syndrome of the inconsistent mother. *Amer. J. Orthopsychiat.,* 1962, 32, 637-644.

RUESCH, J. Psychosomatic medicine and the behavioral sciences. *Psychosom. Med.,* 1961, 23, 277-286.

RUGH, R. Ionizing radiations and congenital anomalies of the nervous system. *Military Med.,* 1962, 127, 883-907.

SCHAEFER, E. S., & BAYLEY, NANCY. Consistency of maternal behavior from infancy to preadolescence. *J. abnorm. soc. Psychol.* 1960, 61, 1-6.

SEARS, R. R. Relation of early socialization experiences to aggression in middle childhood. *J. abnorm. soc. Psychol.,* 1961, 63, 466-492.

SEARS, R. R., MACCOBY, ELEANOR E., & LEVIN, H. *Patterns of child rearing.* Evanston, Ill.: Row, Peterson, 1957.

SELYE, H. The general-adaptation-syndrome in its relationships to neurology, psychology, and psychopathology. In A. Weider (Ed.), *Contributions toward medical psychology.* New York: Ronald, 1953. Pp. 234-274.

SELYE, H. *The stress of life.* New York: McGraw Hill, 1956.

SELYE, H., & FORTIER, C. Adaptive reaction to stress. *Psychosom. Med.,* 1950, 12, 149-157.

SHELDON, W. H. *Varieties of delinquent youth: an introduction to constitutional psychiatry.* New York: Harper, 1949.

SHELDON, W. H. *et al.* *Atlas of men: a guide for somatotyping the adult male at all ages.* New York: Harper, 1954.

SIMON, A. J. Illness and the psychodynamics of stressful life situations as seen in a children's clinic. *J. Hlth. human Behav.,* 1960, 1, 13-17.

SONNENBORN, T. M. The new genetics. *Int. Sci. Technol.,* 1962, 1, (9), 66-74.

SPITZ, RENE A. The derailment of dialogue. Paper read at Amer. Psychiat. Ass., St. Louis, May, 1963.

SPIVACK, G. Child-rearing attitudes of emotionally disturbed adolescents. *J. consult. Psychol.,* 1957, 21, 178. (Abstract)

STENDLER, CECILIA B. Possible causes of overdependency in young children. *Child Develpm.,* 1954, 25, 125-146.

SWEETBAUM, H. A. Comparison of the effects of introversion-extraversion and anxiety on conditioning. *J. abnorm. soc. Psychol.,* 1963, 66, 249-254.

SZASZ, T. S. The myth of mental illness. *Amer. Psychologist,* 1960, 15, 113-118.

U. S. Federal Radiation Council. *Health implications of fallout from nuclear weapons testing through 1961.* Washington, D. C.: Author, 1962.

WATSON, GOODWIN. Some personality differences in children related to strict or permissive parental discipline. *J. Psychol.,* 1957, 44, 227-249.

WENGER, M. A., CLEMENS, T. L., COLEMAN, D. R., CULLEN, T. D., & ENGEL, B. T. Autonomic response specificity. *Psychosom. Med.,* 1961, 23, 185-193.

WEST, LOUIS J. Psychiatric aspects of training for honorable survival as a prisoner of war. *Amer. J. Psychiat.,* 1958, 115, 329-336.

White House Conference on Children and Youth (Golden Anniversary). *The nation's children.* Vols. 1, 2, 3. E. Ginzberg (Ed.) Washington, D. C.: Columbia Univer. Press, 1960.

WHITING, J. W. M., & CHILD, I. L. *Child training and personality.* New Haven: Yale Univer. Press, 1953.

WINDER, C. L., & RAU, LUCY. Parental attitudes associated with social deviance in preadolescent boys. *J. abnorm. soc. Psychol.,* 1962, 64, 418-424.

WORCHEL, P. Catharsis and the relief of hostility. *J. abnorm. soc. Psychol.,* 1957, 55, 238-243.

World Health Organization. *Effect of radiation on human heredity.* (Technical report series, No. 166.) Geneva: Author, 1959.

World Health Organization. *Deprivation of maternal care: a reassessment of its effects.* Geneva: WHO, 1962.

YARROW, L. J. Maternal deprivation: toward an empirical and conceptual re-evaluation. *Psychol. Bull.,* 1961, 58, 459-490.

DISORDERS OF PSYCHOGENIC ORIGIN

part three

TRANSIENT SITUATIONAL PERSONALITY DISORDERS

chapter 5

As we have previously noted, any one of us may develop psychiatric symptoms if the going gets tough enough. In most studies of neurotic and psychotic behavior we are dealing with long-term trends of maladjustment which are central to the whole personality organization of the individual. There are, however, certain situations such as terrifying accidents, assault or rape, and the combat conditions of war which can induce a sudden ego decompensation in even stable, normally well-integrated individuals. Although physical injury may be involved, it is the psychological aspects of the stress which are of prime importance in such disorders.

The resulting symptoms may be similar to those of typical neurotic and psychotic reactions, but they usually clear up rapidly with only mild therapy. Perhaps the special value of starting our discussion with these transient personality reactions, particularly reactions to the acute stress of combat, lies in the perspective they can give us on the development of more "typical" cases of mental illness which occur in less extreme stress situations.

World War II and the Korean War furnished psychiatry with a laboratory in which the effects of severe environmental stresses upon the personality organization of thousands of men could be immediately evaluated. Here ego decompensation as well as recovery was telescoped in time so that the basic dynamic pattern stood out in clear relief. This was a research opportunity that could perhaps never be duplicated in civilian life. As a result of this unique situation, plus the pressure of military necessity growing out of the large number of psychiatric casualties, great strides were made in the understanding and treatment of mental illness.

These forward strides in military psychiatry led in turn to a better understanding of mental disorders by the general public. For the first time, millions of people became aware of the potential effects of extreme stress upon the personality. They learned that such stress could seriously impair adjustive behavior or even incapacitate the individual, and they learned that this was not necessarily a disgrace—it could happen to anyone.

We shall begin our discussion with the psychiatric casualties of World War II and the Korean conflict, particularly those cases involving army personnel subjected to combat; then we shall attempt to show the implications of our findings for military psychiatry in the event of future warfare. Next, we shall examine transient personality reactions to civilian catastrophes and to other situations of unusual and severe stress. Finally, we shall discuss some of the psychological problems associated with man's conquest of space.

Traumatic Reactions to Combat

During World War I traumatic reactions to combat conditions were called "shell shock," a term coined by a British pathologist, Col. Frederick Mott, who regarded them as organic conditions produced by minute hermorrhages of the brain. It was gradually realized, however, that only a very small percentage of such cases represented physical injury from concussion of exploding shells or bombs. Most of the these men were suffering instead from the general combat situation with its physical fatigue, the ever present threat of death or mutilation, and severe psychological shocks. During World War II, traumatic reactions to combat passed through a number of classifications, such as "operational fatigue" and "war neuroses," before finally being termed "combat exhaustion" in the army's official classification.[1]

Even this term was none too aptly chosen since it implied that physical exhaustion played a more important role in such reactions than is actually the case. However, it did serve to distinguish for purposes of diagnosis and therapy between (a) temporary neuropsychiatric reactions to combat which could progress to more clearly defined neuroses or psychoses but which more typically cleared up with mild therapy, and (b) neurotic or psychotic reactions which happened to occur under war conditions but might equally well have occurred in civilian life —cases usually showing a history of neurotic or psychotic tendencies which were only aggravated by the increased stress of military life. In the great majority of cases men who became psychiatric casualties under combat conditions belonged to the first type. They were men who had adjusted satisfactorily to civilian life and to prior military experiences.

Although an estimated 10 per cent or less of men in combat developed combat exhaustion, the actual incidence is not known since many received therapy at their battalion aid station and were returned to combat within a matter of hours. Records were kept only on men evacuated from the front lines; these were the more seriously disturbed patients. The available statistics combine both the combat exhaustion cases and the regular neurotic and psychotic ones. In all, the army accepted slightly over 10,000,000 men for military service during World War II. Of this number approximately

---

[1]The newer American Psychiatric Association classification has adopted the term *gross stress reaction* with subheadings (1) combat and (2) civilian catastrophe to refer to transient disorders due to these conditions.

1,363,000 were given medical discharges, 39 per cent (approximately 530,000) of which were for neuropsychiatric disorders. In contrast, only 27 per cent of the medical discharges in the Korean War during 1953 (the only year for which statistics are available) were for neuropsychiatric disorders. Such a difference would appear to indicate improvement in psychiatric management and treatment although more effective screening at the time of induction cannot be ruled out (Bell, 1958). Since World War II about half a million veterans have received compensation for service-connected neuropsychiatric disabilities, and over half of all patients in Veterans Administration hospitals have been psychiatric cases.

SYMPTOMS

The clinical picture in combat exhaustion varied considerably depending upon the branch of the service, the severity and nature of the traumatic experience, and the personality make-up of the individual. Common symptoms among combat troops were dejection, weariness, hypersensitivity, sleep disturbances, and tremors. In air-corps personnel, after long combat flying, the more typical symptoms were anxiety, frequently with accompanying dejection and depression, phobias toward combat missions, irritability, and startle reactions (Levy, 1945). In addition, where the stress was cumulative, symptoms often differed from those brought on by a sudden and particularly intense combat situation. Despite such variations, however, there was surprising uniformity in the general clinical symptoms—both in World War II and the Korean War.

A good picture of preliminary symptom development is furnished in a report made by a commission of civilian psychiatrists who were sent to the European Theater of Operations during World War II to study combat cases.

"There is almost unanimous agreement that the first symptoms of the failure to maintain psychological equilibrium are increasing irritability and disturbances of sleep.

"The irritability is manifested externally by snappishness, over-reaction to minor irritations, angry reactions to innocuous questions or incidents, flare-ups with profanity and even tears at relatively slight frustrations. The degree of these reactions may vary from angry looks or a few sharp words to acts of violence.

"Subjectively, the state of irritation is perceived by the soldier as an unpleasant 'hypersensitiveness' and he is made doubly uncomfortable by a concomitant awareness of his diminishing self-control. One patient put this very vividly by saying—'The first thing that brought home to me the fact that I was slipping was this incident: A fellow next to me took some cellophane off a piece of hard candy and crumpled it up, and that crackling noise sounded like a forest fire. It made me so mad I wanted to hit him. Then I was ashamed of being so jumpy.'

"In association with this 'hypersensitiveness' to minor external stimuli, the 'startle reaction' becomes manifest (increasingly so as time goes on). This is a sudden leaping, jumping, cringing, jerking or other form of involuntary self-protective motor response to sudden, not necessarily very loud noises, and sometimes also to sudden movement or sudden light.

"The disturbances of sleep, which almost always accompany the symptom of increased irritability, consist mainly in the frustrating experience of not being able to fall asleep even upon those occasions when the military situation would permit. Soldiers have to snatch their rest when they can. They expect a rude and sudden awakening at any time. Opportunities for sleep become very precious and an inability to use them very distressing. Difficulties were experienced also in staying asleep because of sudden involuntary starting or leaping up, or because of terror dreams, battle dreams and nightmares of other kinds.

"This triad of increased 'sensitivity,' irritable reactions and sleep disturbances represents the incipient state of 'combat exhaustion.' It usually does not lead to referral.[1] It may exist without much change for days, weeks or even months. Sooner or later, often upon the occasion of some incident of particularly traumatic significance to the soldier, the marginal and very unstable equilibrium is upset and the soldier becomes a casualty." (Bartemeier *et al.*, 1946, pp. 374-375)

When these combat casualties reached the physician in the aid station or the psychiatrist at the clearing station, they presented a somewhat typical pattern of symptoms differing only in the degree of personality decompensation.

---

[1] Referral to a psychiatrist for treatment.

"In the majority of cases they followed a stereotyped pattern: 'I just can't take it any more'; 'I can't stand those shells'; 'I just couldn't control myself.' They varied little from patient to patient. Whether it was the soldier who had experienced his baptism of fire or the older veteran who had lost his comrades, the superficial result was very simliar. Typically he appeared as a dejected, dirty, weary man. His facial expression was one of depression, sometimes of tearfulness. Frequently his hands were trembling or jerking. Occasionally he would display varying degrees of confusion, perhaps to the extent of being mute or staring into space. Very occasionally he might present classically hysterical symptoms."[1] (Menninger, 1948, p. 143)

The following diary covers a period of about six weeks and illustrates the cumulative effect of combat stresses on a normal personality.

"Aug. 7, 1942. Convoy arrived at Guadalcanal Bay at approximately 4 A.M. in the morning. Ships gave enemy a heavy shelling. At 9 A.M. we stormed the beach and formed an immediate beachhead, a very successful landing, marched all day in the hot sun, and at night took positions and rested. Enemy planes attacked convoy in bay but lost 39 out of 40 planes.

"Aug. 8, 1942. Continued march in the hot sun and in afternoon arrived at airport. Continued on through the Jap village and made camp for the night. During the night, Jap navy attacked convoy in battle that lasted until early morning. Enemy had terrific losses and we lost two ships. This night while on sentry duty, I mistook a horse for a Jap and killed it.

"Aug. 19, 1942. Enemy cruiser and destroyer came into bay and shelled the beach for about two hours. The cruiser left and the destroyer hung around for the entire morning. We all kept under shelter for the early afternoon a flying fortress flew over, spotting the ship and bombed it, setting it afire we all jumped and shouted with joy. That night trouble again was feared and we again slept in foxholes.

"Aug. 21, 1942. The long awaited landing by the enemy was made during the night 1500 troops in all and a few prisoners were taken and the rest were killed. Bodies were laying all over beach. In afternoon planes again bombed the Island. [Here the writing begins to be shaky, and less careful than previously.]

"Aug. 28, 1942. The company left this morning in higgins Boats to the end of the Island, landed and started through thick Jungle and hills. It was hot and we had to cut our way through. In afternoon we con-

tacted the japs. our squad was in the assault squad so we moved up the beach to take positions the enemy trapped us with machine gun and rifle fire for about two hours. The lead was really flying. Two of our men were killed, two were hit by a hand greade and my corporal received a piece of shrampnel in back,—was wounded in arm, out of the squad of eight we have five causitry. We withdrew and were taken back to the Hospital.

"Sept. 12, 1942. Large jap squadron again bombed Island out of 35 planes sent over our air force knocked down 24. During the raid a large bomb was dropped just sevety yards from my fox hole.

"Sept. 13, 1942. At on o'clock three destroyers and one cruiser shelled us contumally all night The ships turned surch lights all up and down the beach, and stopped one my foxhole seveal time I'm feeling pritty nervese and scared, afraid I'll be a nervas reack be for long. slept in fox hole all night not much sleep. This morning at 9:00 we had a nother air raid, the raid consisted of mostly fighter planes. I believe we got several, this afternoon. we had a nother raid, and our planes went out to met them, met them someplace over Tulagi, new came in that the aircraft carrier wasp sent planes out to intersept the bombers. This eving all hell broke lose. Our marines contacted enemy to south of us and keep up constant fire all night through.

"Sept. 14, 1942. This morning firing still going on my company is scaduted to unload ships went half ways up to dock when enemyfire start on docks, were called back to our pososeion allon beach, company called out again to go after japs, hope were lucker than we were last time [part of this illegible.] Went up into hills at 4:00 P.M. found positions, at 7:00 en 8 sea planes fombed and strifed us, 151942 were strifed biy amfibious planes and bombed the concussion of one through me of balance and down a 52 foot hil. I was shaking likd a leaf. Lost my bayanut, and ran out of wathr. I nearves and very jumpy, hop I last out until morning. I hope sevearly machine s guns ore oping up on our left flank there going over our heads

"Sept. 16. this morning we going in to take up new possissons we march all moring and I am very week and nerves, we marched up a hill and ran in to the affaul place y and z company lost so many men I hardly new what I was doing then I'm going nuts.

"Sept. 17. don't remember much of this day.

"Sept. 18. Today I'm on a ship leaving this awful place, called Green Hell. I'm still nearves and shakey." (Stern, 1947, pp. 583-586)

---

[1]A hysterical symptom is an ailment such as blindness or paralysis for which there is no organic basis.

In some instances the personality decompensation was more immediate and acute as a result of some particularly overwhelming combat experience. Although the symptoms varied from one soldier to another, the common core was usually overwhelming anxiety. An exception was noted in the case of the troops from India to whom admission of fear was unacceptable. They rarely showed anxiety reactions, instead resorting occasionally to self-mutilation and other "honorable" ways of avoiding further combat (Williams, 1950).

It is interesting to note that wounded soldiers were apt to show less anxiety and other combat-exhaustion symptoms: in general, the more disabling the wound, the less the anxiety, except in cases of permanent mutilation (Noble, Roudebush, and Price, 1952). In fact, anxiety states with major wounds were exceptionally rare (McElroy, 1945). Apparently the wound, in providing an escape from the stressful combat situation, at the same time removed the source of the anxiety states. It was not unusual for a soldier to admit that he had prayed to be hit or to have something honorable happen to remove him from battle. When they were approaching full recovery and the necessity of returning to combat, injured men sometimes showed a prolongation of their symptoms or a delayed traumatic reaction with nervousness, insomnia, and other such symptoms which were nonexistent during the initial period of hospitalization.

In some cases soldiers who had stood up exceptionally well under intensive combat experience developed delayed combat reactions upon their return home—often in response to relatively minor stresses in the home situation which they had previously been capable of handling. Evidently there had been underlying damage to their adaptive ability (Karpe and Schnap, 1952).

DYNAMICS

In a combat situation, with the continual threat of injury or death and repeated narrow escapes, one's ordinary adjustive reactions are relatively useless. The adequacy and security feelings the individual has known in a relatively safe and dependable civilian world are completely undermined. Furthermore, the ever present threat can be neither overcome nor escaped. And so, to meet it, there is an emergency mobilization of emotional resources accompanied by severe and increasing anxiety as the threat continues and no adequate response pattern can be found. The resulting symptoms reflect (a) the disorganizing effects of the anxiety itself (hypersensitivity, tremors), (b) the unconscious devices by which the individual tries to defend himself against the anxiety (stupor, amnesia), and (c) the effects of other factors such as extreme fatigue.

The hypersensitivity shown in the startle reaction follows directly from the continued fear and anxiety. Consequently, the buzz of a fly or the striking of a match may produce marked overreactions. This hypersensitivity is, of course, intensified when the stimulus bears a direct association with the original traumatic situation. A soldier who has been strafed by attacking planes may be terrified by the sight of approaching aircraft. As continued emotional mobilization and fatigue take their toll of adjustive resources, the common symptom of irritability makes its appearance and adds to the soldier's anxiety by making him aware of his diminishing self-control. Even in our normal lives, prolonged emotional stress and fatigue tend to keep our nerves "on edge" and to increase irritability.

Difficulties in falling asleep and other sleep disturbances are common accompaniments of anxiety and sustained emotional arousal. Most of us have difficulty in sleeping when we are emotionally upset. However, the dynamic significance of the recurrent nightmares is not fully understood. How and why does the traumatic material become reactivated during sleep, when the soldier desperately needs quiet and rest? In some cases the repeated dreams are so terrifying that the soldier is even afraid to go to sleep. Apparently, however, the continual reliving of the battle experience in dreams gradually serves to discharge the anxiety associated with it and to desensitize the individual to the point where he can assimilate the experience without undue disruption.

In severe combat exhaustion cases, the stupor or amnesia results from temporary repression which enables the individual to avoid consciousness of the traumatic experience until its emotional intensity has cooled down to the point where he can tolerate memory of it. Here the defensive function of repression is clearly demonstrated since the repressed material can be brought to consciousness in full detail under the influence of hypnosis or various drugs such as sodium pentothal. When the individual's entire past life and personal identity are repressed along with the battle experience, it is probably because the inhibitory and repressive defenses overshoot their mark.

So far, we have spoken only of excessive stress as a precipitating cause in combat exhaustion. However, we must not overlook the fact that some 90 per cent of the men came through combat without becoming psychiatric casualties, although most of them evidenced severe fear reactions and other symptoms of ego disorganization which were not serious enough to be incapacitating. In addition, many men tolerated almost unbelievable stress before they broke, while others became casualties under conditions of relatively slight combat stress. Consequently, other factors—such as possible biological predisposition, personal immaturity, individual differences in the evaluation of combat stress, lack of confidence in officers, and confusion about war goals—must be examined for their contribution to the total picture.

Biological predisposing factors. Do constitutional differences in sensitivity, vigor, and temperament affect one's resistance to the stress of combat? The probabilities are that they do, but there is a dearth of actual evidence. Similarly, the importance of a family history of mental illness is not clear. Hastings *et al.* (1944) reported a history of psychoses in 6 per cent of the families of 100 American fliers who had completed a tour of combat duty without psychiatric mishap. Thus a family history of mental illness is not necessarily disqualifying for military service. Army investigators did find, however, a relatively lower incidence of pathological conditions in the family background of successful soldiers, although this cannot be taken as conclusive evidence of the importance of hereditary predispositions (Hirschberg, 1944; McNeel and Dancey, 1945; Sheps, 1944).

The conditions of battle place a tremendous strain upon a soldier's physical stamina. Grinker and Spiegel describe this vividly:

"Battle conditions are notoriously destructive to health. Frequently men must go for days without adequate sleep or rest. . . . The purely physiological effects of nearby blasts are also a factor. Many men are repeatedly subjected to minimal doses of blast. They are knocked over by the compression wave, or perhaps blown slightly off the ground, if they are lying prone. In some instances they are temporarily numbed or even stunned. . . . Lastly, the continued auditory irritation of constant explosions, bangs, snaps of machine guns, whines of artillery shells, rustle of mortars . . . wears down resistance." (1945, pp. 68-70)

Add other factors, such as severe climatic conditions and the terrific drain upon body resources from continual emotional mobilization, and the result is a general lowering of the individual's resistance to all stress.

Psychological predisposing factors. Some of the personal and situational factors that can predispose a soldier to break down are emotional immaturity, separation from home and loved ones, sacrifice of personal freedom, frustrations of all sorts, domestic difficulties, and anxiety built up by prior combat experiences. Letters from home which create worries add to the soldier's already difficult adjustive burden—particularly since he is far away and is helpless to take any action. A soldier who has withstood months of combat may break when he finds that his wife has been unfaithful, when she stops writing, or when she writes that she is suing for divorce. The death of a buddy may lead to a sudden loss of emotional support which the buddy has provided, or to a weakening of ego organization due to identification with him, or to feelings of guilt for not having saved him.

Several other psychological predisposing factors deserve special discussion:

1. Strangeness of the situation is a strong factor in the overwhelming of the ego. When the individual knows what to expect and what to do, he has a much better chance of coming through with a minimum of ego disorganization. But no training can fully prepare the soldier for all the conditions of battle. The factor of strangeness also partly explains the effectiveness of innovation in armaments for which enemy soldiers are not properly prepared.

2. Immobilization in the face of acute danger makes men especially vulnerable. Saul

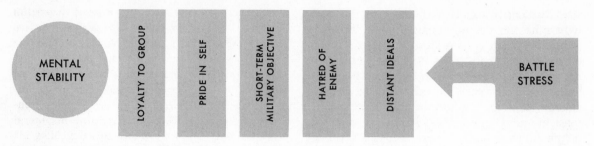

In studying the eventual breakdowns of the army personnel who had been most resistant to personality decompensation, Sobel (1949) found that such individuals seemed to have been protected by five "defensive layers." These were surrendered progressively in the face of too-severe stress and threat. Distant ideals like "democracy" and "the four freedoms" went first. Loyalty to the group was the last to be given up.

(1945), for example, cites the case of an enthusiastic volunteer who appeared to enjoy combat. He stood up well until an enemy plane was hit and came hurtling to earth, as it seemed, directly at the patient. Crouched in a watery foxhole, he could neither fight nor run. Immobilized and forced to "sweat it out," his anxiety mounted to such a degree as to be overwhelming. Some activity or duty to perform, even though it does not lessen the actual danger, provides some outlet for tension and helps the individual to keep his fear and anxiety within manageable limits (Shaffer, 1947).

3.   The necessity of killing enemy soldiers is also an important predisposing factor in combat reactions. Most of us have strong attitudes against any physically hostile behavior and especially against killing. It is psychologically almost impossible for some men to become overtly hostile and to engage in ruthless killing. In extreme cases such men are unable even to defend themselves when attacked. Men who feel extremely guilty about their belligerency and hostility cannot engage in killing without an automatic fear of retaliation and punishment.

A good fighter, a machine gunner, one day killed five of the enemy almost simultaneously. "His first reaction was elation—but suddenly he felt that it was wrong to enjoy this and thereupon developed anxiety with some depression, so severe that he was incapacitated." (Saul, 1945, p. 262)

To such a man, further combat may come to mean fulfillment of dreaded retaliation and pun-

ishment. Thus anxiety growing out of combat often reflects not only simple fear of physical injury and death but also emotional conflicts, fears, and guilt feelings generated by killing or by feeling relieved that others have been killed instead of oneself.

4.   After a soldier has been in combat for a long time and has seen many of his buddies killed and wounded as well as having had narrow escapes himself, he usually loses whatever feelings of invulnerability he may have had. Particularly where a soldier has almost completed the number of missions or duration of duty necessary for rotation, he is likely to feel that his "luck has run out" and that each new shell he hears coming "has his name on it."

5.   We have seen that with prolonged acute stress and long-continued emotional mobilization there may be a gradual undermining or weakening of the ego and a lowering of stress tolerance. This was exemplified in World War II by "the old sergeant syndrome" in which men of established bravery exhibited anxiety, depression, tremulousness, and impairment of self-confidence and judgment after prolonged combat experience—usually 150 to 350 days of combat (Bell, 1958). Thus fear and anxiety are important as both psychological and biological predisposing factors. Their importance is frequently intensified by the soldier's conflict between a desire to run away or give up, and his devotion to duty or his fear of what the other men in the outfit would think of such cowardice.

6.   Traits which lower the individual's general resistance to stress or to a particular type of

stress are important in determining his reactions to combat. Personal immaturity—often stemming from maternal overprotection—has often been cited as making the individual more vulnerable to combat stress. In an analysis of 200 neuropsychiatric cases occurring under combat conditions in the South Pacific, the most important predisposing factor was judged to be an unfortunate home background, resulting in a personality too immature to deal with the problems of war (Henderson and Moore, 1944).

Interestingly enough, a history of personality maladjustment was not necessarily disqualifying for combat service—excluding, of course, seriously immature or marginally adjusted personalities. In a study of 17 highly neurotic soldiers with 60 or more days of combat, Needles (1945) found the presence of powerful compensating mechanisms—determination, fear of disobedience, effort to live up to lifelong patterns of conscientiousness, attachment to comrades, and externally directed aggression—which enabled these men to remain in combat despite their neuroses. In a study of 72 neurotic veterans who had fulfilled military obligations satisfactorily, Valenstein *et al.* (1953) reported similar findings, emphasizing especially the importance of good conscience development, perseverance, and self-discipline. Anxiety neurotics may be so accustomed to anxiety that they can cope with it more or less automatically, whereas men who are feeling severe anxiety for the first time are often terrified by the experience, lose their self-confidence, and go to pieces. Thus in some cases it would appear that a neurosis may actually be beneficial to a man's adjustment to combat. It has also been observed that psychopathic personalities, though frequently in trouble in the armed services during peacetime, as a consequence of disregarding rules and regulations, often demonstrated good initiative and effective combat aggression against the enemy.

In general, however, the more adequate the individual's personality integration prior to combat, the more stress he can stand before breaking. The best soldiers seem to be men recruited from family backgrounds which have fostered emotional maturity, acceptance of responsibility, self-reliance, and ready adjustment to new situations (Knight, 1943; Nardini, 1962b).

Sociological predisposing factors. Although many factors included in the preceding section are social as well as psychological in nature, we may particularly emphasize here such factors in army life as a lack of group solidarity, crowded conditions, poor leadership or lack of confidence in leaders, and a lack of clearly understood and accepted goals. Where such conditions prevail, they contribute to poor general morale.

It has been found particularly important to maintain good group identification and *esprit de corps* in combat troops. Where the soldier is unable to identify himself with or take pride in his group, he lacks the feeling of "we-ness." He stands alone, psychologically isolated and less able to withstand stress. The spirit of the group as a whole seems to be a contagious thing. When the group is generally optimistic and confident prior to battle, the individual is also apt to show good morale. If the unit has a reputation for efficiency in battle, the individual soldier is challenged to exhibit his maximum efficiency. On the other hand, when the unit is demoralized prior to battle or is defeated in battle or resorts to disordered flight, the individual, too, succumbs more easily to anxiety and panic.

Confidence in leaders is also of vital importance. When the individual respects his leaders, has confidence in their judgment and ability, and can accept them as relatively strong father or brother figures, his morale and resistance to stress are bolstered. On the other hand, lack of confidence or actual dislike of leaders is highly detrimental to morale and to combat stress tolerance.

Where the individual is fighting only because he is forced to, or to "get the damned war over with," he is not as effective and does not stand stress as well as the soldier who knows what he is fighting for and is convinced of its importance. Time and again men who feel strongly the rightness of their cause and its vital importance to themselves and their loved ones have shown incredible endurance, bravery, and personal sacrifice under combat conditions. The more concretely and realistically war goals can be integrated into the ego values of the individual in terms of "his stakes" in the war, the greater will be their stabilizing effect on him.

Prisoners of war subjected to "brainwashing" by the Chinese Communists were systematically isolated from these sources of ego strength. Leaderless and alone, encouraged to be suspicious of each other and to question America's war goals, and systematically made to choose between ethical values and satisfaction of minimum body needs, their will to resist was often broken. The brainwashing techniques used and their short-term effects are summarized in the chart on pages 186-187.

Thus the terrifying nature of the combat situation is actually only one of the causes of combat reactions. We must also consider a complex of other factors such as the morale of the group, the attitudes of buddies, the competency of leaders, the individual's motivation, his degree of physical fatigue, the adequacy of his training, his family problems, and his ego strength. All such factors may raise his stress tolerance to combat situations or predispose him to be especially vulnerable to the stresses of combat.

THERAPY

In most cases the decompensation brought on by the acute stress of battle conditions was quickly reversed when the men were taken out of combat and given psychiatric treatment. In both World War II and the Korean War, an attempt was made to give treatment as near to the battle front or combat group as was practical (Menninger, 1948; Glass, 1954). Treatment usually consisted of mild supportive psychotherapy, warm food, and sedation to help the soldier gain needed sleep. Many men were able to return to combat after a night or two of such relief.

In the Korean War, marked emphasis was placed on (a) a "duty-expectant" attitude—the attitude that every soldier, despite his anxieties, was expected to perform his combat duties, and (b) the removal, insofar as possible, of the factor of gain in psychiatric illness—the attitude that anxiety, fear, and tension were not illnesses of sufficient severity to require permanent removal from battle. Such an approach on the part of psychiatric personnel—who were themselves in the forward area and under enemy fire—implied that "the soldier was a morally responsible individual who either could fold up as the situation became more hazardous or could

go on in spite of the multiplicity of symptoms which he might develop due to his fear and anxiety." (Bell, 1958, p. 285) The decision was his to make. It was felt that most men found themselves able to bear much more anxiety and tension than they would have believed possible and that the number of psychiatric casualties who were declared unfit for duty was markedly reduced by this approach.

In severe or resistant cases where the therapeutic goal was recovery for noncombat status or the relief of grossly incapacitating symptoms, such as mutism and amnesia, a short cut was found in which psychotherapy was carried out under the influence of some sedative such as sodium pentothal. Under the influence of the drug the repressed material could be brought to consciousness in full detail. By reliving a traumatic experience in this condition, the patient could discharge much of the emotional tension connected with it and, with the aid of suggestions from the therapist, learn to view his experience in a less traumatic light and to assimilate or "synthesize" it into his ego structure. Sometimes this involved repeated narcosis interviews in which there was a gradual release of the repressed emotions.

This pattern is well brought out in the following case of an infantry officer who had been under severe mortar fire in the Kairouan Pass:

"The patient was agitated and trembled constantly. His face betrayed persistent fright and bewilderment. He was unable to talk, producing only syllables in a whisper or a low voice. He could not give his name and was apparently unable to recall what had happened to him, or even to make the effort to recall. His only word was 'Who?' He started with terror at any sudden noise or any unexpected motion made toward him by attendants." (Grinker and Spiegel, 1945, pp. 7-8)
[In his first narcosis interview the patient was told that he was in the Kairouan Pass, and that mortar shells were dropping about him.]
"At the mention of the word 'shells,' he shuddered. . . . He then spat on the floor—i.e. the battlefield—and got out of bed, crying 'Steve! Steve, are you all right?' He knelt on the floor and passed his hands over it, as if examining a body. Standing up suddenly, he looked as if he were going to cry, and buried his face in his hands. Then he clenched his fists and, assuming a belligerent attitude, he smiled grimly and said, 'Never mind, I'll

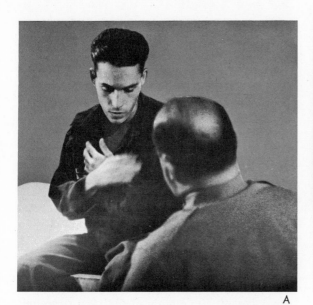

A   B

These pictures show a soldier who suffered from hysterical lameness (A) during World War II, partly as a result of conflicts related to his family situation. Given an injection of sodium pentothal, he was directed by the psychiatrist to walk, which he found himself able to do, much to his own surprise. A few days later, he was well enough to take part in a baseball game (B).

get even with those bastards. Those bastards! I'll kill them!' He began pacing up and down, and then suddenly looked up and said, 'Got to find Steve. Got to find Steve and Davey.' He then lurched about the room, looking for something; from time to time he cowered, as if hearing an approaching shell; and then, trembling with fear, crouched on the ground, as he might in his foxhole. He did not appear to find what he was looking for, and eventually began the whole scene over again with the two-people-killed episode." (p. 98)

[Although the therapist kept talking to the patient in an attempt to maintain contact, the patient appeared bewildered by his failure to find his friends and was taken back to the ward still puzzled and amnesic. However, speech had been recovered and considerable emotional catharsis had taken place, leading to a reduction in anxiety. In his second interview, he again began to talk of his battle experience but now in the past tense with awareness that he was telling the therapist a story.]

"We'd been pinned down in our foxholes all day. Jerry had us spotted, and was throwing mortars at us. I was terribly frightened, but I tried not to show it in front of the men. I had trouble keeping them in their foxholes. They wanted to get out and stretch every few hours. When anyone stood up, five or six mortar shells

came over in a few seconds. We didn't know where the German batteries were located, couldn't find out. The shells came from nowhere; not a sign of a gun, not even a flash. I saw two men standing up out of their foxholes. I climbed out of mine to order them back into their hole. Just then a mortar came over and landed in a foxhole near me. Oh, that explosion! It knocked me down, but I got right up, and went over to the hole. Two men were in there, our First Sergeant and a Staff Sergeant. I could hardly look at them. The First Sergeant was on top. He was dead, with his head blown open. There wasn't any top to his head. The other man was underneath. He was still alive, but the side of his chest was open, and I could see part of the lung. He was crying: God, I can still hear him crying. I felt sick, and my mind was funny; I couldn't think. I was shaking so I could hardly move. I don't know how I did it, but I helped take care of them. I told myself I had to hang on. I tried to get a grip on myself. The shells were falling all around us. Then I saw a gunflash. I knew where the German batteries were by the gunflash. Stevie was at the Command Post. I had to go find him, to tell him about the position so he could phone the artillery. I went down the road to look for him. But I had to keep ducking down on the ground because the shells kept falling near me. I think the Germans could see me going down the road. But I couldn't find Steve. I never got to the Command Post. What happened to me? I remember. While I was going down the road, I heard three shells coming. I jumped into the ditch; it was a good ditch. One of the shells, the first one, landed on the road. I can still hear the sound of the shells: whirr . . . Don't you hear it? Oh, what a sound! I don't want to ever hear that sound again. I can't go back to the front! I can't take it again. I remember the second shell landing behind me, off the side of the road. I don't remember the third. I don't remember what happened after that. Oh, those shells! They weren't mortars: you can hear mortars tumbling over and over. This was a whirr." At this point the patient covered his eyes with his hands, and buried his head on the medical officer's shoulder. Then he suddenly smiled and said, "I remember my name: it's F——, I remember where I live. God, what a miracle that I can talk. I thought I'd never be able to, but I tried. I tried right along to talk and remember, but I couldn't. They must think I'm an awful baby. I am a baby to be like this." (pp. 99-101)

The men evacuated to rear-area hospitals were usually individuals with incipient neurotic or psychotic tendencies which had been precipitated by the traumatic combat experience. Neurotic patients typically evidenced hysterical or hypochondriacal reactions which were unconsciously maintained because of their value in protecting the patient from return to combat. Following therapy, however, the great majority of these patients were able to return to noncombat and in many instances to combat duty. It is interesting to note that where decompensation had progressed to the stage of psychosis, the psychotic symptoms were often replaced by neurotic reactions in the course of therapy (Mulinder, 1945). The effectiveness of psychiatric treatment in the Korean War is indicated by the fact that the few patients requiring evacuation to the United States were almost all seriously psychotic cases.

The treatment of neurotic and psychotic cases followed standard civilian methods, except, perhaps, for the more widespread use of group therapy. Since group therapy made possible the treatment of several patients at the same time, it became of necessity an important treatment method in the armed forces. Its success there, in turn, has led to its increasing use in many other settings. (See Chapter 14.)

PROGNOSIS

Gross stress reactions in combat usually cleared rapidly or developed into one of the familiar neurotic or psychotic patterns. For a given case, the prognosis depended upon a combination of factors. In general the following indicated a favorable outcome and their reverse a less favorable one:

1. Evidence of good personality adjustment and ego strength prior to combat.

2. A severe precipitating stress or combat experience.

3. Anxiety, fatigue, and dejection with a lack of severe guilt or hostility.

4. A short time lapse between appearance of symptoms and treatment.

5. Treatment as close to the front lines as possible with a minimum of time lost from unit and no suggestion that his symptoms might remove the individual from combat.

A prolonged delay between the occurrence of symptoms and therapy tended to fixate the decompensatory pattern, making it much more resistant to therapy. Similarly, the removal of a patient from the zone of combat to an interior zone seemed · to encourage the unconscious maintenance of symptoms in order to prevent a return to combat. During the first combat engagements of the American forces in North Africa, psychiatric casualties were transported from the fighting area to base hospitals, often some 300 to 500 miles behind the lines. Less than 10 per cent of these men were able to return to duty (Menninger, 1948).

With immediate, intensive treatment within 15 to 20 miles of the front lines, approximately 60 per cent of combat exhaustion cases in World War II were sent back to combat duty, and apparently the majority of these men readjusted successfully to combat conditions (Ludwig and Ranson, 1947). Such statistics varied, however, from 80 to 90 per cent for men from units with only a month or so of combat to 30 to 35 per cent for "old" divisions. Comparable statistics were obtained in the Korean War with 50 to 90 per cent of the men returnable to combat, and only some 10 per cent of those returned showing up as repeaters (Peterson and Chambers, 1952).

In addition, an attempt was made in the Korean campaign to reclaim for combat duty earlier psychiatric casualties who had been assigned to noncombat positions in Japan (Glass, 1954). All such cases were re-evaluated after 3 months, and 40 per cent were considered sufficiently recovered to return to combat duty. Most of these men were able to carry on without further difficulty. In a minority of cases, the combat syndrome persisted for a sustained period. In one group of 57 combat patients studied 15 years after their combat experience, Archibald et al. (1962) found a high incidence of symptoms such as tension, irritability, depression, diffuse anxiety, headaches, insomnia, nightmares, and avoidance of situations involving exposure to loud noises or reminders of combat. These appear to be severe and atypical cases in which the combat experience contributed to a chronic state of "overvigilance" and impaired ego functioning.

Where the combat reaction was complicated by permanent physical disability or mutilation, the prognosis was less favorable, but the eventual outcome depended upon the way the individual reacted to the change in his life situation and reshaped his self-evaluation. In a study of orthopedic cases seriously wounded in the Korean War, Noble, Roudebush, and Price (1952) found psychiatric symptoms present in about half the cases, but available statistics indicate that the great majority of such combat casualties showed consistent improvement and made successful civilian readjustments.

CURRENT MILITARY PSYCHIATRY

Current military psychiatry is concerned with many problems including the screening of inductees, the training and utilization of personnel, the maintenance of morale and personal effectiveness in the performance of duties, training for survival in the event of capture, and the prevention and treatment of combat reactions. For the moment we are concerned with the latter three tasks.

There has been an increasing awareness among military psychiatrists that noneffective military behavior stems more often from difficulties in the environment and interpersonal relationships than from individual psychopathol-

ogy (Glass et al., 1961). As a consequence, there has been a gradual displacement of psychiatric personnel from their usual role and location in the clinic and hospital setting to the military community. This has resulted in a close working relationship between psychiatrists, officers, and other administrative personnel which permits utilization of the "milieu" (the setting in which the soldier functions) for the prevention and treatment of ineffective behavior.

This new orientation has fostered three kinds of help: (a) primary prevention—involving attempts to influence favorably the conditions under which soldiers work, live, or fight in order to decrease the likelihood of a disabling maladjustment; (b) secondary prevention—emphasizing the early recognition and prompt management of maladjustive behavior on an outpatient basis while the soldier is still a member of his unit; and (c) tertiary prevention—employing "milieu" and other therapeutic tools for severe mental disorders which require hospitalization, the hope here being to head off the development of chronically disabling mental conditions. In recent years this program has been expanded to include disciplinary offenders as well as other psychiatric categories and has resulted in a marked reduction in recorded psychiatric hospitalization and psychiatric discharge rates as well as in the military prisoner population (Glass et al., 1961).

In the preparation of personnel for honorable survival as prisoners of war the following points have been emphasized: (a) a clear understanding of what to expect as a prisoner and what is expected of him in the way of resisting collaboration, (b) a clear understanding of the futility and genuine hazards of collaboration, including the effects of ostracism by his own group, and (c) a strong identification with the military group and commitment to the civilian community for which he is fighting (Wolff, 1960). It also appears that simulated capture and interrogation is a highly useful training procedure in preparing the soldier more realistically for what to expect and what to do in the event of capture.

Prevention of combat reactions in any future war would seem even more than in the past to require preparing the soldier to know what to expect and what to do, fostering his pride in his nation and what it stands for, encouraging deep identification with his unit and the broader military community, and emphasizing his role as a self-reliant and morally responsible individual. Soldiers of the future must be prepared for eventualities which man has never before had to face—at least not on the same scale—such as the probable killing or wounding of hundreds of millions of people during the first few hours of warfare and the widespread social disorganization that would follow. Also, with the dispersion of troops necessitated by atomic warfare, soldiers would be more isolated and probably subjected to many occasions when they would have to function alone in the face of tremendous stress. All these conditions would demand great adaptability, self-reliance, and moral responsibility. Both individual soldiers and their officers need to understand the stresses likely to be en-

gendered in the event of future war and the best ways of meeting them (Weiss, 1958).

Since the stresses in any future global war—and presumably the combat reactions—would differ from those of past wars, methods of treatment would have to be adapted accordingly. Where conditions were comparable with those of the past, however, treatment methods would probably not differ greatly from those used in the Korean War and would center around immediate emergency measures—including rest and mild supportive psychotherapy—while emphasizing a "duty-expectant" attitude and the removal of gain from psychiatric illness. It is also probable that some of the newer psychopharmaceutic drugs might prove useful in both prevention and treatment of combat reactions. But psychological factors would still play the key role.

Reactions to Civilian Catastrophes

In civilian life, people exposed to plane crashes, automobile accidents, explosions, fires, earthquakes, tornadoes, sexual assault, or other terrifying experiences frequently show "shock" reactions—transient personality decompensation. Over half the survivors of the disastrous Cocoanut Grove fire in Boston, for example, required treatment for severe psychological shock (Adler, 1943). Other events, such as the sudden loss of loved ones, social disgrace, or severe financial losses, may also prove extremely traumatic. However, for our immediate purposes, we may confine ourselves to a consideration of reactions to terrifying experiences. These will serve as models for understanding the general dynamics in all types of transient personality disorders in civilian life and will keep the discussion parallel to that of combat exhaustion.

SYMPTOMS

Such "shock" cases may develop a wide range of symptoms, depending upon the severity and nature of the terrifying experience, the degree of surprise, and the personality make-up of the in-

dividual. Among victims of tornadoes, explosions, and similar catastrophes, a "disaster syndrome" has been delineated. This syndrome, which appears to characterize most of the people in the disaster area, may be described in three stages:

1. "Shock stage" in which the victim is stunned, dazed, and apathetic. Frequently he is unaware of the extent of his injuries, tends to wander about aimlessly until guided or directed by someone else, and is unable to make more than minimal efforts at aiding himself or others. In extreme cases the individual may be stuporous, disoriented, and amnesic for the traumatic event.

2. "Suggestible stage" in which the individual tends to be passive, suggestible, and willing to take directions from rescue workers or others less affected than himself. Here the individual often expresses extreme concern over the welfare of others involved in the disaster and attempts to be of assistance; however, his behavior tends to be highly inefficient even in the performance of routine tasks.

3. "Recovery stage" in which the individual gradually regains his psychological equilibrium, often with the help of mild supportive psycho-therapy at a hospital or other aid center. Here he may repetitively tell about the catastrophic event, become critical of rescue and relief workers, and show symptoms of generalized anxiety. Often he is tense, jumpy, and apprehensive, shows difficulty in concentrating and sleeping, and tires easily. In about half of the cases there are recurrent nightmares which usually re-enact or are closely related to the traumatic experience. Usually with mild psychotherapy there is rapid recovery (adapted from Raker *et al.,* 1956).

These three stages are well illustrated in the *Andrea Doria* disaster.

"On July 25, 1956, at 11:05 P.M., the Swedish liner *Stockholm* smashed into the starboard side of the Italian liner *Andrea Doria* a few miles off Nantucket Island, causing one of the worst disasters in maritime history. . . . During the phase of initial shock the survivors acted as if they had been sedated . . . as though nature provided a sedation mechanism which went into operation automatically." During the phase of suggestibility "the survivors presented themselves for the most part as an amorphous mass of people tending to act passively and compliantly. They displayed psycho-motor retardation, flattening of affect, somnolence, and in some instances, amnesia for data of personal identification. They were nonchalant and easily suggestible." During the stage of recovery, after the initial shock had worn off and the survivors had received aid, "they showed . . . an apparently compulsive need to tell the story again and again, with identical detail and emphasis." (Friedman and Linn, 1957, p. 426)

In cases where loved ones have been lost in the catastrophe, the disaster syndrome may be complicated by intense feelings of grief and depression. Where the patient feels he bears some responsibility for the disaster—as, for example, in automobile or plane accidents—or feels he failed loved ones who perished in the disaster, the picture may be further complicated by strong feelings of guilt. This pattern is well brought out in the following case of a man who had failed in his attempt to save his wife but had been saved himself.

A man aged 35 had received only minor burns from the Cocoanut Grove fire. By the end of the fifth day of hospitalization he was apparently well on the road to recovery and was informed that his wife had died in the fire. He seemed to accept the news quite well and appeared somewhat relieved of his worry about her fate. Shortly after his return home, however, he became restless and agitated, and was rehospitalized. On admission he was apprehensive and unable to concentrate. He would attempt to read only to drop it; he would start conversations and break them off abruptly. He repeatedly muttered to himself statements such as, "Nobody can help me. When is it going to happen? I am doomed, am I not?" With great effort it was possible to establish enough rapport to carry on interviews. He complained about extreme tension, inability to breathe, generalized weakness and exhaustion, and his frantic fear that something terrible was going to happen. "I'm destined to live in insanity or I must die. I know it is God's will. I have this awful feeling of guilt." With intense morbid guilt feelings he reviewed incessantly the events of the fire. When he had tried to save his wife, he had fainted and was shoved out by the crowd. She was burned while he was saved. "I should have saved her or I should have died too." He complained about feelings of incredible hostility and violence and did not know what to do about them. The rapport established with him lasted only for brief periods of time, and then he would fall back into his state of intense agitation and muttering. He slept poorly even with large sedation. However, in the course of four days he became somewhat more composed, had longer periods of contact with the psychiatrist, and seemed to feel that he was making progress in coping with his morbid guilt. On the sixth day of his hospital stay, however, after skillfully distracting the attention of his special nurse, he jumped through a closed window to a violent death. (Adapted from Lindemann, 1944, p. 146)

As in combat cases, some civilians who undergo terrifying accidents reveal a somewhat typical post-traumatic syndrome which may last for days, weeks, or months and includes the following symptoms (Modlin, 1960): (a) anxiety varying from mild apprehension to episodes of panic, (b) chronic muscular tension with tremor, restlessness, insomnia, and inability to relax, (c) repetitive nightmares reproducing the traumatic incident directly or symbolically, (d) irritability, often accompanied by a startle reaction, and (e) withdrawal from and avoidance of any experience that might increase ex-

One woman cannot bear to look—it is her house that is on fire. Sometimes people react to sudden, overwhelming stress by more severe forms of denial, such as refusing to believe that the event has occurred.

citation—most commonly manifested in avoidance of social contacts, poor concentration, loss of sexual interest, and unwillingness to discuss symptoms or the traumatic incident. Modlin suggests that this syndrome "may be a fundamental, nonspecific, organismic reaction to severe external stress of a frightening or life-threatening kind." (1960, p. 51)

A delayed traumatic neurosis may also occur in cases involving physical injury, with the realization of personal mutilation and/or of necessary changes in one's life situation. This syndrome is often complicated by the psychological effects of damage suits and workmen's compensation laws. Somewhere between 10 and 25 per cent of the applicants for industrial compensation suffer from post-traumatic reactions. The assurance or even possibility of compensation may also lead to a prolongation of symptoms, especially in the case of involved legal suits which require months or even years to settle. For this reason, it is considered advisable to have early settlements of claims involving physical injuries.

DYNAMICS

The dynamics in civilian traumatic reactions seem basically similar to the reactions to the stress of combat. Here, too, the world, which has seemed relatively secure and safe, suddenly becomes a terrifying place, in which one's adjustive abilities are completely inadequate. In the face of this catastrophic threat, the individual is overwhelmed by intense anxiety and is unable to function in an integrated and efficient manner. The symptoms of being stunned, dazed, and apathetic stem in part from the disorganization of behavior; they also appear in part to be defense mechanisms protecting the individual from the full impact of the catastrophic experience.

The stage of suggestibility apparently results from the individual's temporary inability to deal with the situation himself plus a tendency to regress to a passive-dependent position in which he is grateful to have the direction and help of others. During the stage of recovery, the recurrent nightmares and the typical need to tell about the disaster again and again with identical detail and emphasis appear to be mechanisms for reducing anxiety and desensitizing the individual to the traumatic experience. The tension, apprehensiveness, and hypersensitivity which often accompany the recovery stage appear to be residual effects of the shock reaction and to reflect the individual's realization that the world can become overwhelmingly dangerous and threatening.

Feelings of guilt are often intense in civilian casualties, largely because responsibility can frequently be more directly assigned. But except for some accidents, most disasters result from natural causes over which the individual could have had no control. Here guilt typically centers around feelings of having failed to protect loved ones who perished or were seriously injured in the disaster.

Contrary to popular opinion, panic reactions are not common among people in the impact area of a disaster. Panic, defined as acute fear followed by flight behavior, tends to occur only under fairly specific conditions: (a) when a group of persons is directly threatened, for example, by fire, (b) when the situation is viewed as one in which escape is possible at the moment but maybe only for a few minutes or not for everyone, and (c) when the group is taken by surprise and has no prearranged plan for dealing with such a disaster (Fritz, 1957).

Under such conditions there may be a complete disorganization or demoralization of the group with each individual striving to save himself. Here the emotional, panic-stricken behavior of others seems to be highly contagious and a person may be completely overwhelmed by fear. In such cases behavior may be extremely irrational and nonadaptive and may actually result in needless loss of life. For example, in the Co-

coanut Grove fire the exits were jammed by a rush of panic-stricken people so that many were trampled and those behind them could not get out. And in the well-known Iroquois Theatre fire in Chicago, the only deaths that took place were due to panic rather than to burns.

Both precipitating and predisposing conditions in combat situations are apt to differ considerably from those in civilian life, for in the latter the individual is not typically separated from home, extremely fatigued, or exposed to prolonged fear and conflict over physical danger. But here, too, predisposing factors may determine which survivors develop traumatic reactions and which do not and why some recover much more rapidly than others. Prior trauma, immaturity, sensitivity to anxiety-provoking experience, mutilation, and other biological, psychological, and sociological conditions may be important predisposing factors. It may be pointed out also that the civilian is usually less prepared psychologically for the traumatic experience than is the soldier since he is not in a situation of acute stress to begin with but is subjected to acute stress with little or no warning or preparation for coping with it.

THERAPY AND PROGNOSIS

The treatment of shock reactions in civilian life is little different from that in the army except that there is no need to prepare the individual to face the traumatic situation again. Proper rest (induced by sedatives if necessary) and reassuring psychotherapy usually lead to the rapid alleviation of symptoms. In some accident cases the patient may be encouraged to continue with his activities—for example, to go swimming again after a narrow escape from drowning. This can help to re-establish the patient's confidence in himself and to prevent the fixation of anxiety in relation to this kind of activity.

Accurate statistics on the general recovery of civilian shock cases are not available. In general, it would appear that the great majority of cases clear up very rapidly. However, in a minority of cases various pathological symptoms become fixed after the shock symptoms themselves have cleared up. Where an injury serves to remove the patient from disliked occupational

PSYCHOLOGICAL REACTIONS TO LOSS OF VISION

Any permanent loss that necessitates the reorganization of one's life pattern and especially of one's self-concept may be very difficult to cope with. Reactions of adults to loss of vision, as analyzed by Cholden (1954), provide a fairly typical example of the stages through which successful readjustment must proceed, thus giving helpful clues to those who suffer such a loss as well as to relatives and friends who are anxious to help.

Shock

At first there is a numbness, an emergency constriction of the ego as a defense against imminent disintegration. Patient is "frozen," may be unable to think or even to feel physical pain. The longer this state lasts, the more difficult is the individual's readjustment.

Depression

As the shock reaction wanes, it is replaced by deep depression, with self-recrimination, self-pity, and feelings of hopelessness. Recognizing his loss, the individual is beginning a period of mourning. This phase of reorganization—dying as a sighted person in order to be reborn as a blind one—is considered necessary, and no attempts should be made to abort it.

Readjustment

The patient is now a different person; hence the primary task of readjustment is internal reorganization. His capacities, interests, social position, and aspirations must be woven into a new self-picture and a new body image. Until he accepts himself as a different person, his readjustment cannot proceed. Thus, instead of fostering unrealistic hopes, friends and relatives should help him to accept his blindness and to see that he can lead a full life even as a blind man.

responsibilities or where there are other pronounced secondary gains, as in compensation cases, the patient may be predisposed to delayed recovery. In general, the more stable and better integrated the personality and the more favorable the life situation, the quicker the recovery.

The importance of therapy in preventing a post-traumatic syndrome is highlighted by a follow-up study of 34 experienced seamen who had survived a highly traumatic explosion and fire on board a gasoline tanker. Despite their success in lowering a lifeboat and getting away from the inferno without leadership, an investigation 3½ to 4½ years later showed that 12 of the men had never returned to sea work or had been forced to give it up as a result of post-traumatic symptoms. Of those who had continued to work at sea all showed similar post-traumatic symptoms—tension, fearfulness, and anxiety aboard

ship. The investigators concluded that with prompt psychotherapy at the time of the accident these conditioned fears could have been prevented from building up (Leopold and Dillon, 1963).

It may be pointed out again that many other crises in addition to terrifying experiences may produce these transient personality reactions. Such emotional experiences as having a loved one die, going through a divorce, finding one's wife or husband in an intimate relationship with another person, and undergoing severe social disgrace may all lead to some measure of ego disorganization. Typical stages in reactions to the trauma of losing one's sight are summarized in the chart above. Unfortunately, there has been little scientific material available concerning such traumatic experiences, and the need for additional study in this general area is clearly indicated.

Reactions to Chronic Situational Stress

In addition to the transient reactions to acute stress seen in combat exhaustion and civilian "shock" reactions, transient reactions may also build up when the individual continues for an extended time in a situation where he feels threatened, seriously dissatisfied, or inadequate. The stress may be a part of the person's life situation for as far ahead as he can see. Regimentation may make army life intolerable for some. A lifetime farmer may be unable to feel at home in the city. Even unhappy marriages may offer examples of what is meant by situational maladjustment. We will limit our discussion to adult situational reactions, but the chart on page 184 summarizes transient maladjustive reactions of several other life periods.

In civilian life, chronic fatigue, poor efficiency, and excessive drinking are typical symptoms of adult situational maladjustment. In army life, where many usual behavioral restraints are reduced or removed, gambling, drinking, and frequenting of prostitutes are common means of reducing anxiety and feelings of boredom and isolation. Some soldiers develop a particularly embittered attitude and are resistant, irritable, fault-finding, and highly resentful about being "shoved around"; others, particularly those in isolated outposts, show a loss of interest in their environment and become apathetic. For example, studies of submarine confinement for periods up to 83 days have revealed a progressive decline in personal motivation and group morale, an increase in homesickness, and a disturbance of time perception (Weybrew, 1961).

REACTIONS OF PRISONERS OF WAR

The symptoms of acute situational maladjustment under extreme conditions are illustrated by prisoner-of-war and concentration-camp experiences. One of the best descriptions is that of Commander Nardini, himself an eyewitness and participant, who depicts the effects of imprisonment and mistreatment on American soldiers following the fall of Bataan and Corregidor.

"Our national group experience accustoms us to protection of individual rights and recourse to justice. The members of this group found themselves suddenly deprived of name, rank, identity, justice, and any claim to being treated as human beings. Although physical disease and the shortages of food, water, and medicine were at their highest during this period, emotional shock and reactive depression . . . undoubtedly contributed much to the massive death rate during the first months of imprisonment.

"Conditions of imprisonment varied from time to time in different places and with different groups. In general there was shortage, wearisome sameness, and deficiency of food; much physical misery and disease; squalid living conditions; fear and despair; horrible monotony . . . inadequate clothing and cleansing facilities; temperature extremes; and physical abuse.

". . . Hungry men were constantly reminded of their own nearness to death by observing the steady, relentless march to death of their comrades. . . . Men quibbled over portions of food, were suspicious of those who were in more favored positions than themselves, participated in unethical barter, took advantage of less clever or enterprising fellow prisoners, stole, rummaged in garbage, and even curried the favor of their detested captors. There was a great distortion of previous personality as manifested by increased irritability, unfriendliness, and sullen withdrawal. . . . Hungry, threatened men often found it difficult to expand the horizon of their thinking and feeling beyond the next bowl of rice. . . .

"Disease was abundant . . . fever, chills, malaise, pain, anorexia, abdominal cramps from recurrent malaria (acquired in combat), and dysentery plagued nearly all and killed thousands. . . . most men experienced bouts of apathy or depression. These ranged from slight to prolonged deep depressions where there was a loss of interest in living and lack of willingness or ability to marshal the powers of will necessary to combat disease. An ever-present sign of fatal withdrawal occurred 3 to 4 days before death when the man

TYPICAL SITUATIONAL REACTIONS OF DIFFERENT LIFE PERIODS

LIFE PERIOD	MALADJUSTIVE REACTIONS
Infancy	Undue apathy or excitability, feeding or sleeping difficulties, excessive crying or "fussing," or other indications of psychic disturbances in infants. In most instances these are outgrowths of stressful interaction with parents or other significant persons in the environment or lack of interaction with such persons.
Childhood	(a) Habit disturbances such as nail-biting, thumb-sucking, enuresis, masturbation, and tantrums; (b) conduct disturbances such as truancy, stealing, destructiveness, cruelty, sexual offenses, and use of alcohol; (c) symptomatic reactions such as tics, habit spasms, somnambulism, stammering, and phobias where these are transient reactions of children to some immediate situation or emotional conflict. More prolonged and definitive disturbances in all three groups are classified elsewhere.
Adolescence	Rebelliousness, extremes in dress and manner, slavish conformity to peer standards, "identity diffusion." Oversensitivity, painful self-consciousness, self-abnegation. Antisocial behavior stemming from boredom, frustration, and hostility.
Adulthood	Unemployment, chronic fatigue, drifting (from job to job or mate to mate), psychological withdrawal from unrewarding marriage or job, alcoholism, affiliation with extreme political or religious group in attempt to find meaning.
Later life	Petulance, overconcern with bodily functions, apathy and withdrawal from active participation in life. Tendency to be overdemanding, overcritical, self-centered, suspicious of others. Chronic poor health, marked lowering of living standards, regret over "wasted life."

pulled his covers up over his head and lay passive, quiet, and refusing food.

". . . One of the most distressing features was the highly indefinite period of imprisonment. The future offered only visions of continued hunger, cold, disease, forced labor, and continued subservence in the face of shoutings, slappings, and beatings. . . . Strong hostility naturally arose from the extreme frustration. . . . Little could be done with these hostile feelings. . . . It was not possible to demonstrate recognizable signs of hostility to the captors for obvious reasons. Therefore, where there were mixed groups of Allied prisoners, much hostility was turned from group to group and in other instances to individuals within the group. . . . In many cases hostile feelings were obviously turned in-

ward and joined with appropriate feelings of frustration to produce serious waves of depression. . . . Self pity, in which some indulged, was highly dangerous to life. . . ." (Nardini, 1952, pp. 241-244)

Similar reactions were observed among prisoners held by the North Koreans and Chinese Communists during the Korean War (Lifton, 1954; Segal, 1954; Strassman *et al.,* 1956). Here, however, the picture was further complicated by "brainwashing" techniques which are described in the chart on pages 186-187.

Descriptions of prisoners in concentration camps, where even more sadistic methods of treatment were often utilized, emphasize approximately the same symptomology (Bettel-heim, 1943; Federn, 1951; Friedman, 1948). Inmates of concentration camps also showed greater use of the mechanism of denial—"This isn't really happening to me"—and tended to form unrealistic hopes of deliverance via miraculous events, possibly because their situation was even more hopeless from a long-range point of view than that of the POW's and any hope would have had to be rather unrealistic (Eitinger, 1961, 1962).

DYNAMICS OF CHRONIC SITUATIONAL REACTIONS

The overall clinical picture encountered in ordinary situational maladjustment almost fills in its own dynamics. As in the other types of transient personality reactions, the individual finds himself in a situation which does not meet his needs and where certain things are required of him which he feels do not correspond with what he is able to give. He feels like a "fish out of water." Frustrations, tension, and anxiety mount, leading to apathy, feelings of hopelessness and despair, hostile acting-out behavior, or other maladjustive patterns. In the prisoner-of-war experiences the stress situation was greatly complicated by fear, physical hardship, and often torture or the threat of it.

Just as in the case of traumatic reactions, there are wide individual differences—some individuals adjust readily to changes in their life situation, whereas others find even relatively minor changes terribly upsetting. Here, again, the reaction of a particular individual depends upon a host of predisposing factors, biological, psychological, and sociological.

In more severe situations, as in POW camps, the degree of personality decompensation may be severe. The reaction of apathy, which appeared common among men in POW and concentration camps, utilized the defense mechanism of emotional insulation—withdrawal from emotional involvement with the current situation—in this way partially depriving it of the power to hurt them. This apathy syndrome helped the individual to maintain personality integration in the face of sustained stress, which, as far as he knew, might continue indefinitely.

As conditions in the POW camps improved somewhat and the threat of death from malnutrition and disease decreased, the problem for the men was no longer merely to survive but to avoid collaboration with their captors. Here the pattern of "playing it cool"—being cautious, noncommittal, and minimally communicative, and of holding back strong feelings—came into increasing prominence as a means of avoiding major collaboration while at the same time not getting "on the wrong side" of their captors.

The success of the Chinese Communists in obtaining false "confessions" from some prisoners depended upon a number of techniques including the forced choice between "cooperation" and possible starvation, torture, and death. In some instances the extreme use of isolation served to "soften" the prisoner and break his will to resist. Hinkle and Wolff have emphasized the importance of isolation as a major technique of "brainwashing":

"When the initial period of imprisonment is one of total isolation . . . the complete separation of the prisoner from the companionship and support of others, his utter loneliness, and his prolonged uncertainty have a further disorganizing effect upon him. Fatigue, sleep loss, pain, cold, hunger, and the like, augment the injury induced by isolation. . . . With the passage of time, the prisoner usually develops the intense need to be relieved of the pressures put upon him and to have some human companionship. He may have a very strong urge to talk to any human and to be utterly dependent on anyone who will help him or befriend him. At about this time he also becomes mentally dull and loses his capacity for discrimination. He becomes malleable and suggestible. . . ." (1956, p. 173)

The interrogator would then exploit the prisoner's dependence, need for human companionship, suggestibility, and impaired thinking—by scolding, threatening, and punishing him when he did not "cooperate," and by approving and rewarding him when he did.

THERAPY AND PROGNOSIS FOR CHRONIC SITUATIONAL REACTIONS

In the great majority of cases, mild situational reactions clear up very rapidly when the in-

BRAINWASHING OF AMERICAN PRISONERS BY CHINESE COMMUNISTS

The men captured by the North Koreans during the early part of the war were subjected to conditions similar to those of American prisoners of the Japanese. These included forced "death marches," inadequate diet, exposure to freezing weather without adequate clothing or shelter, vicious beatings for minor or alleged transgressions, and seeing fellow prisoners shot in cold blood. All suffered from malnutrition, dysentery, and exposure, and only a minority survived. After the Chinese Communists took charge of all United Nations prisoners, physical conditions were somewhat improved, but with these improvements came the emotional assault of "brainwashing" aimed at undermining American cultural values, indoctrinating prisoners in communist values, and achieving collaboration. This general approach can be broken down into 3 phases which were in simultaneous and constant operation: isolation, thought control, and political conditioning.

PHASE	HOW CARRIED OUT	RESULTS
Isolation	Removal of leaders: officers transferred to a separate camp and natural leaders, as they emerged, removed silently to "reactionary" camps. Informers rewarded to discourage personal ties and interaction. Home ties cut—pessimistic, complaining letters delivered while other mail withheld.	Creation of a group of "isolates" with low morale and no *esprit de corps*. Social and emotional isolation robbed soldier of usual sources of strength and prevented him from validating his beliefs and values through discussion with others. Led to loss of strength to resist, increased suggestibility, and vulnerability to both threats and bribes.
Thought control	Prisoners forced to choose between "cooperation" and possible starvation, torture, and death. Ethical values, loyalty to country, religion, and self-identity placed in direct opposition to self-preservation and meeting of bodily needs: resistees subjected to threat, punishment, and marginal living conditions; cooperators rewarded with increased food, privileges in camp, and promises of early repatriation. Guilt feelings concerning prior behavior stimulated by mandatory "confessions" and self-criticism. Alternate harshness and friendliness by "inscrutable authority."	Fear, anxiety, guilt, confusion, and conflict about how to behave. "Playing it cool"—being inconspicuous, holding back strong feelings, being minimally communicative and noncommittal on everything, "cooperating" a little when necessary but avoiding major collaboration. Withdrawal of emotional involvement, marked apathy. Listlessness and apparent indifference.

dividual is removed from the stressful situation. Yet such a simple therapeutic procedure is often impossible or undesirable. For example, a child who is having great difficulty in adjusting to his first year of school cannot be allowed to stay home—at least not indefinitely. Such a procedure would only undermine his self-confidence and further complicate his adjustment problems. In cases where it is impossible or inadvisable to remove the individual from his cur-

rent situation, psychotherapy is often of value in helping him to modify inappropriate attitudes, to develop more effective coping techniques, and to make the best of a stressful situation.

In the case of former prisoner-of-war and concentration-camp survivors, there is often persistent organic as well as psychological damage and a generally lowered tolerance to stress of any kind. In the observation and treatment of large numbers of former prisoners of war, the

| Political conditioning | Daily "instruction" with repetitious teaching of communist catch phrases and principles. Appeals to be "openminded" and to "just listen to our side of the story." Only anti-American books and newspapers available stressing inequalities and injustices in U.S. Communists portrayed as "peace seekers," prisoner offered "opportunity to work for peace." Intensive pressure applied to those who seemed most susceptible, those already convinced used to indoctrinate others. Constant use of reward for cooperation and punishment for resistance. | Little actual conversion to communism but considerable confusion and doubt about America's role in war; poor morale and discipline; breakdown of group loyalty. Men turned against each other—"progressives" versus "reactionaries." Difficulty in relating to others even after release. Five per cent later won commendation as resisters, 15 per cent were judged to have complied unduly; the remaining 80 per cent were relatively passive. |

When prisoners were first released, they were apathetic, detached, dazed, without spontaneity, and at the same time tense and suspicious of their new surroundings. Large memory gaps were present, particularly for the period of their capture and for so-called "death marches." They were ambivalent in their feelings about the Chinese Communists, showed strong guilt about all phases of their POW experience, and were not anxious to return home to the U.S. This "zombie reaction" wore off after three to five days and was followed by a period of greater spontaneity. However they still appeared "suspended in time"—confused by their newly acquired status and incapable of making decisions concerning future courses of action. All of the men felt alienated from others who had not shared their POW experience and were apprehensive about homecoming; they tended to band together in small, uneasy groups and maintained isolation from nonrepatriates.

On their return home, some got into difficulty over indiscriminate outbursts of misdirected long pent-up hostility. Expecting at last to be free of stress, some became disillusioned and discouraged in their efforts to adjust to economic and other changes and to communicate with others. Physical disabilities, chronic fatigue, and a confused self-picture complicated the adjustment problems of many. But although some drank too much or managed other escape measures, the majority of these men eventually made adequate adjustments. In a few cases, their weathering of the prison experience seemed to have given them increased inner strength and greater capacity for achievement.

Material for this chart taken from Lifton (1954), Segal (1954), Strassman et al. (1956), and West (1958). For information on the application of similar techniques to the civilian population in Russia and Red China see Hinkle and Wolff (1956) and Hunter (1954).

following clinical pattern has been emphasized:

"With relatively few exceptions the presenting complaints[1] are usually as follows: fatigability, lack of ability to withstand frustration, frequent resort to alcohol and sedative drugs, low resistance to physical illness, neurotic-type pains in feet and hands and frequently edema of the ankles and feet, irritability and other manifestations in varying degree of emotional instability, and a need for preferential duty assign-

ments. . . . On physical examination remarkably little is found in the way of structural pathology." (Chambers, 1952, pp. 247-348)

Similarly, a recent follow-up study of 100 Norwegian survivors of German concentration camps found 96 per cent continuing to experience symptoms resulting from their stay in the concentration camps. Predominant symptoms included fatigue, nervousness, irritability, restlessness, impairment of memory, sleep disturbances, anxiety, feelings of inadequacy, loss of initiative, headaches, depressions, and abuse of alcohol. All but three of these survivors were found to have lived a normal life up to the time of their arrest. Of these 100 former prisoners, 84 could cope with their work but only with the greatest effort. These residual symptoms were attributed not only to the psychological stresses of the concentration-camp experience but also to biological stresses, such as head injuries suffered during interrogation, prolonged malnutrition, and serious infectious diseases—all of which were common in the concentration camps (Eitinger, 1961, 1962).

It should be pointed out that in analyzing the reactions of those who survived, we are dealing with a select group, for about half of the Japanese and Korean War prisoners and an even higher proportion of concentration-camp inmates died during their imprisonment (Eitinger, 1962).[1] Optimal qualities for survival in such settings have never been studied systematically. Undoubtedly chance factors often played a crucial role. Nardini (1962b) has suggested the following qualities as being positive factors in both physical and psychological survival of POW experiences: a philosophical, fatalistic, yet nondefeatist attitude; intense application of life energies to the present; an ability to retain hope in the face of the greatest hardships; the ability to manage hostility and fight depression; personality maturity and ego strength; a strong sense of self-identity and self-respect; and the intangible but all-inclusive determination to live.

Nardini observed that some passive-dependent individuals did fairly well in POW camps because they could accept a passive role and follow instructions. The aggressive psychopath almost invariably developed a depressive reaction when he finally realized the inevitable and final restrictions of confinement. Prisoners with mild paranoid trends often made a fair adjustment since they were very persevering in their determination not to let the enemy win. Immature individuals did not fare well because they were most vulnerable to temptations to collaborate with the enemy for which, in turn, they suffered the serious consequences of ostracism.

In general, the eventual outcome for the survivors of POW camps seems to have depended on the individual's psychobiological stress tolerance, the length and severity of the traumatic experience, and his ability to devise defenses to protect his integrity. Some men adjusted well to combat but not to POW camps; some adjusted well to POW camps but not to their return home. In some instances after their return home they had trouble with indiscriminate outbursts of hostility. Evidently, underlying the apathy so prevalent in the POW situation there were often intense pent-up feelings of hostility which proved to be a problem to the individual once he was no longer in the stressful situation. Despite a wide variation in adjustment, however, follow-up studies indicate that the majority of Korean and World War II Pacific Area POW's made adequate postwar adjustments (Schein *et al.,* n.d.; Nardini, 1962b).

SPACE PSYCHIATRY

The psychological problems of space travel are becoming of increasing interest to military scientists. Present knowledge of psychological stress in space flight is based partly on man's limited experience and partly on inference. However, it would appear that key stresses are separation from earth, prolonged exposure to danger, adjustment of the individual to the group, sameness of the environment, and the absence of many accustomed sources of emotional gratification. Some of these hazards, such as loneliness and a sense of ever present danger, can be anticipated but not simulated.

Problems relating to the adjustment of the individual to the group, to monotony, and to absence of many accustomed sources of gratification were studied among a small group of scientists, officers, and enlisted personnel who voluntarily subjected themselves to isolated Antarctic living for almost a year. Typical reactions to this experience are summarized in the chart on page 190. From an overall viewpoint, the navy found that the most important single factor in successful adjustment in the Antarctic was work efficiency, in the sense that the effective functioning of the small group depended on each

---

[1]Over 10,000,000 people died in Hitler's concentration camps.

individual's performing his assigned task efficiently. The next most important factor was the individual's adjustment to the small isolated group.

In space flights, the smaller crews, more confined quarters, more alien environment, and greater danger can be expected to render problems of technical proficiency, adjustment to the group, and adaptability to diverse stresses even more crucially significant.

In connection with the problem of assembling a crew who can function effectively as a team, experimental studies have been made of small groups of men placed in confined compartments over a period of several days. Before and after each experiment the subjects are put through psychological assessment procedures and a detailed record is kept of their reactions in the experimental situations. Findings indicate marked individual differences in reactions to such situations depending upon the subject's personality make-up, background, motivation, and mental set. Of key importance is the way the individual perceives or evaluates the stress situation. Some subjects adapt successfully while others show various symptoms of personality decompensation.

The development of an artificial environment which can support effective human functioning during relatively long periods of time poses many physiological and psychological problems. Experimental studies are being undertaken to investigate the problems of reduced atmospheric pressure, oxygen supply, radiation, acceleration, noise, extreme temperature changes, isolation, confinement, and prolonged exposure to danger. Under conditions which simulate orbital flight, the combined stresses of confinement, restricted perceptual field, and fatigue have commonly resulted in thought disturbances such as distortions of space and time dimensions, hypnagogic-like imagery, and illusions of body image. Negative reactions of a few subjects have required termination of the simulated flight. For example, one subject, after twenty-two hours of "flight," suddenly shouted that there was a fire inside the chamber, and believed he had seen the flame and smelled the smoke." (Flinn, 1961, pp. 93-94)

Even mild thought disturbances, of course, might have serious consequences if they occurred during a space mission. In general, it would appear that both variety and meaningfulness of sensory input (stimulation and information) are essential for preventing the disorganization of perception and thought. As Ruff and Levy point out:

"Our tentative formulation is that subjects react to isolation by structuring their experience in some meaningful fashion. As long as the structure is maintained, the individual preserves his sense of continuity and sameness. This enables him to function in the absence of accustomed sources of information. For isolation is stressful not only because fewer physical stimuli impinge upon receptors, but also because the meanings they ordinarily convey to the subject are lost." (1959, p. 796)

Another approach to the problem of effective human functioning in space is directed toward the modification of the human system itself. As White (1958-1959) has pointed out, "Man is a sea-level, low-speed, one-g, 12-hour animal." For greater adaptability in functioning under various extraterrestrial conditions, chemical and electrical techniques are being developed to implement the body's own homeostatic controls—both on physiological and psychological levels (Kline and Clynes, 1961). For example, it might be possible to use drugs or other techniques to have the pilot or other crew members sleep twenty-three hours out of the day. Of course, there would be procedures for wakening them in the event of an emergency. It may also be that we can reduce the amount of "earth environment" which crew members must take with them by controlling their cardiovascular rate, body temperature, metabolic systems, and even thought processes.

In the man-machine system required for space flight, it becomes apparent that limitations of the human organism are the baseline which determines the efficiency of the total system (Flaherty, 1961). However, it would appear that physiological and psychological stresses analogous to those likely to be encountered in most space flights have been adapted to successfully on earth; that with experience man will find ways of coping with the hazards of space flight; and that as habitable spaceships are constructed, effective crews will be found to man them.

REACTIONS TO "WINTERING OVER" IN THE ANTARCTIC

Problems related to the individual's adjustment to close group interdependence, monotony of environment, and absence of accustomed sources of emotional gratification have been studied among groups of volunteers subjected to isolated antarctic living for 6 to 8 months at isolated U.S. Bases. Scientists, officers and enlisted personnel lived in groups of 12 to 40, with each man assigned a specific job and hence dependent on every other man. Technical competence, responsibility, and stability in job performance thus became key factors in determining group acceptance and status. Reactions such as those cited below, are of special interest in terms of their possible relationship to reactions to the conditions of space travel.

SYMPTOMS OBSERVED

Intellectual inertia	Lack of energy for intellectual pursuits, especially during winter. Earlier plans to catch up on reading or learn a foreign language rarely realized.
Impaired memory and concentration	Varied from absent-mindedness and poor concentration to marked lowering of intellectual acuity and periods of amnesia. Most pronounced during winter months.
Insomnia	Varying degrees of sleeplessness, again mostly in winter. Individual felt tired but unable to relax.
Headaches	Frequent headaches, more common among officer-scientist group than among enlisted men. Appeared to be of psychogenic origin and possibly related to repression and control of hostility.
Hostility	Relatively little overt hostility expressed, probably because of the tremendous need for relatedness and group acceptance in these small, isolated groups. Social censure, in the form of the "silent treatment," inflicted on the occasional troublesome individual; resulted in "long-eye" syndrome—varying degrees of sleeplessness, crying, hallucinations, deterioration in personal hygiene, and a tendency to move aimlessly about or to lie in bed staring blankly into space until man was again accepted by group.
Depression	Low-grade depression prevalent, particularly during winter months. Of 6 men who became psychiatric casualties, 3 diagnosed as cases of relatively severe neurotic depression.
Appetite	Appetite for food greatly increased, possibly because of absence of other gratifications. Weight gains of 20 to 30 pounds not unusual.

This program was initiated during the International Geophysical Year, 1957-1958, and is still continuing on a reduced scale. The chart is based on material from Mullin (1960), Nardini (1962a), and Rohrer (1961).

REFERENCES

The reference list includes not only the sources from which the author has drawn material, but acknowledgments of the permissions granted by authors and publishers to quote directly from their works.

ADLER, ALEXANDRA. Neuropsychiatric complications in victims of Boston's Cocoanut Grove disaster. *J. Amer. Med. Ass.*, 1943, 123, 1098-1101.

ARCHIBALD, H. C., LONG, DOROTHY M., MILLER, CHRISTINE, & TUDDENHAM, R. D. Gross stress reaction in combat—a 15-year follow-up. *Amer. J. Psychiat.*, 1962, 119, 317-322.

BARTEMEIER, L. H., KUBIE, L. S., MENNINGER, K. A., ROMANO, J., & WHITEHORN, J. C. Combat exhaustion. *J. nerv. ment. Dis.*, 1946, 104, 358-389, 489-525.

BELL, E., JR. The basis of effective military psychiatry. *Dis. of nerv. Sys.*, 1958, 19, 283-288.

BETTELHEIM, B. Individual and mass behavior in extreme situations. *J. abnorm. soc. Psychol.*, 1943, 38, 417-452. Reprinted by permission of The American Psychological Association, Inc.

CHAMBERS, R. E. Discussion of "Survival Factors . . . ." *Amer. J. Psychiat.*, 1952, 109, 247-248.

CHOLDEN, L. Some psychiatric problems in the rehabilitation of the blind. *Bull. Menninger Clin.*, 1954, 18, 107-112.

EITINGER, L. Pathology of the concentration camp syndrome. *Arch. gen. Psychiat.*, 1961, 5, 371-379.

EITINGER, L. Concentration camp survivors in the postwar world. *Amer. J. Orthopsychiat.*, 1962, 32, 367-375.

FEDERN, E. The endurance of torture. *Complex*, 1951, No. 4, 34-41.

FLAHERTY, B. E. (Ed.) *Psychophysiological aspects of space flight.* New York: Columbia Univer. Press, 1961.

FLINN, D. E. Psychiatric factors in astronaut selection. In B. E. Flaherty (Ed.), *Psychophysiological aspects of space flight.* New York: Columbia Univer. Press, 1961. Pp. 87-95.

FRIEDMAN, P. The effects of imprisonment. *Acta Med. Orientalia, Jerusalem,* 1948, 163-167.

FRIEDMAN, P., & LINN, L. Some psychiatric notes on the Andrea Doria disaster. *Amer. J. Psychiat.,* 1957, 114, 426-432.

FRITZ, C. E. Disasters compared in six American communities. *Human Organization,* 1957, 16, (2), 6-9.

GLASS, A. J. Psychotherapy in the combat zone. *Amer. J. Psychiat.,* 1954, 110, 725-731.

GLASS, A. J., ARTISS, K. L., GIBBS, J. J., & SWEENEY, V. C. The current status of Army psychiatry. *Amer. J. Psychiat.,* 1961, 117, 673-683.

GRINKER, R. R., & SPIEGEL, J. P. *War neuroses.* Philadelphia: Blakiston, 1945.

HASTINGS, D. W., WRIGHT, D. G., & GLUECK, B. C. *Psychiatric experiences of the Eighth Air Force.* New York: Josiah Macy, Jr. Found., 1944.

HENDERSON, J. L., & MOORE, M. The psychoneuroses of war. *New England J. Med.,* 1944, 230, 273-278.

HINKLE, L. E., JR., & WOLFF, H. G. Communist interrogation and indoctrination of "enemies of the states." *AMA Arch. neurol. Psychiat.,* 1956, 76, 115-174.

HIRSCHBERG, C. Neurology and psychiatry: psychoneuroses in military personnel. *Amer. J. med. Sci.,* 1944, 208, 119-132.

HUNTER, E. *Brain-washing in Red China.* New York: Vanguard, 1954.

KARPE, R., & SCHNAP, I. Nostopathy—a study of pathogenic homecoming. *Amer. J. Psychiat.,* 1952, 109, 46-51.

KLINE, N. S., & CLYNES, M. Drugs, space, and cybernetics: evolution of cyborgs. In B. E. Flaherty (Ed.), *Psychophysiological aspects of space flight.* New York: Columbia Univer. Press, 1961.

KNIGHT, R. P. The treatment of the psychoneuroses of war. *Bull. Menninger Clin.,* 1943, 7, 148-155.

LEOPOLD, R. L., & DILLON, H. Psychoanatomy of a disaster: a long term study of post-traumatic neuroses in survivors of a marine explosion. *Amer. J. Psychiat.,* 1963, 119, 913-921.

LEVY, N. A. *Personality disturbances in combat fliers.* New York: Josiah Macy, Jr. Found., 1945.

LIFTON, R. J. Home by ship: reaction patterns of American prisoners of war repatriated from North Korea. *Amer. J. Psychiat.,* 1954, 110, 732-739.

LINDEMANN, E. Symptomatology and management of acute grief. *Amer. J. Psychiat.,* 1944, 101, 141-148.

LUDWIG, A. O. & RANSON, S. W. A statistical follow-up of the effectiveness of treatment of combat-induced psychiatric casualties. I and II. *Milit. Surgeon,* 1947, 100, 51-62, 169-175.

MC ELROY, R. B. Psychoneuroses, combat-anxiety type. *Amer. J. Psychiat.,* 1945, 101, 517-520.

MC NEEL, B. H., & DANCEY, T. E. The personality of the successful soldier. *Amer. J. Psychiat.,* 1945, 102, 337-342.

MENNINGER, W. C. *Psychiatry in a troubled world.* New York: Macmillan, 1948. Copyright by The Macmillan Co. and used by their permission.

MODLIN, H. C. The trauma in "traumatic neurosis." *Bull. Menninger Clin.,* 1960, 24, 49-56.

MULINDER, E. K. Psychotic battle casualties. *Brit. Med. J.,* 1945, 1, 733.

MULLIN, C. S., JR. Some psychological aspects of isolated antarctic living. *Amer. J. Psychiat.,* 1960, 117, 323-5.

NARDINI, J. E. Survival factors in American prisoners of war of the Japanese. *Amer. J. Psychiat.,* 1952, 109, 241-248.

NARDINI, J. E. Navy psychiatric assessment program in the antarctic. *Amer. J. Psychiat.,* 1962a, 119, 97-105.

NARDINI, J. E. Psychiatric concepts of prisoners of war confinement. The William C. Porter Lecture—1961. *Mil. Med.,* 1962b, 127, 299-307.

NEEDLES, W. The successful neurotic soldier. *Bull. U.S. Army Med. Dept.,* 1945, 4, 673-682.

NOBLE, D., ROUDEBUSH, MARION E., & PRICE, D. Studies of Korean War casualties. Part I: Psychiatric manifestations in wounded men. *Amer. J. Psychiat.,* 1952, 108, 495-499.

PETERSON, D. B. & CHAMBERS, R. E. Restatement of combat psychiatry. *Amer. J. Psychiat.,* 1952, 109, 249-254.

RAKER, J. W., WALLACE, A. F. C., & RAYMER, JEANETTE F. *Emergency medical care in disasters: a summary of recorded experiences.* Disaster Study No. 6, National Academy of Sciences, National Research Council, Publication No. 457, Washington, D. C., 1956.

ROHRER, J. H. Interpersonal relations in isolated small groups. In B. E. Flaherty (Ed.), *Psychophysiological aspects of space flight.* New York: Columbia Univer. Press, 1961.

RUFF, G. E., & LEVY, E. Z. Psychiatric research in space medicine. *Amer. J. Psychiat.,* 1959, 115, 793-797.

SAUL, L. J. Psychological factors in combat fatigue. *Psychosom. Med.,* 1945, 7, 257-272.

SEGAL, H. A. Initial psychiatric findings of recently repatriated prisoners of war. *Amer. J. Psychiat.,* 1954, 111, 358-363.

SHAFFER, L. F. Fear and courage in aerial combat. *J. consult. Psychol.,* 1947, 11, 137-143.

SHEPS, J. G. A psychiatric study of successful soldiers. *J. Amer. Med. Ass.,* 1944, 126, 271-273.

SOBEL, MAJ. R. Anxiety-depressive reactions after prolonged combat experience—the old sergeant syndrome. *Bull. U.S. Army Med. Dept., Combat Psychiat. Suppl.,* Nov. 1949, 137-146.

STERN, R. L. Diary of a war neurosis. *J. nerv. ment. Dis.,* 1947, 106, 583-586.

STRASSMAN, H. D., THALER, MARGARET B., & SCHEIN, E. H. A prisoner of war syndrome: apathy as a reaction to severe stress. *Amer. J. Psychiat.,* 1956, 112, 998-1003.

VALENSTEIN, A. F., MICHAELS, J. J., & EVJE, MARGARET. Aspects of character in the neurotic veteran. *J. nerv. ment. Dis.,* 1953, 117, 445-451.

WEISS, J. M. A conceptual framework for preventive psychiatry programs in military centers. *Milit. Med.,* 1958, 122, 231-232.

WEST, L. J. Psychiatric aspects of training for honorable survival as a prisoner of war. *Amer. J. Psychiat.,* 1958, 115, 329-336.

WEYBREW, B. B. Human factors and the work environment. II. The impact of isolation upon personnel. *J. occup. Med.,* 1961, 3, 290-294.

WHITE, GEN. T. D. The inevitable climb to space. *Air Univer. quart. Res.,* 1958-59, 10, (4)

WILLIAMS, A. H. A psychiatric study of Indian soldiers in the Arakan. *Brit. J. med. Psychol.,* 1950, 23, 130-181.

WOLFF, H. G. Every man has his breaking point? The conduct of prisoners of war. *Milit. Med.,* 1960, 125, 85-104.

PSYCHO-NEUROTIC DISORDERS

chapter 6

THE NEUROTIC NUCLEUS

SPECIFIC REACTION PATTERNS AND DYNAMICS

GENERAL ETIOLOGY OF THE NEUROSES

THERAPY OF THE NEUROSES

PROGNOSIS FOR THE NEUROSES

In our discussion of transient situational disorders, both acute and chronic, we have been dealing for the most part with stable and well-adjusted personalities who have been subjected to excessive stress. In psychoneurotic disorders[1] we will find pathological development trends within the personality of the individual which lead to misevaluations of environmental problems, to severe conflicts, and to inefficient personal and social adjustments. Almost invariably these pathological trends show a long developmental history, usually beginning in faulty parent-child relations that have led to immature and distorted attitudes toward the self and toward the surrounding world. Consequently, in the face of stress situations which most of us could handle successfully, these individuals experience severe anxiety and resort to the use of unhealthy neurotic defense patterns. The neurotic response to these stresses may take many forms, such as anxiety attacks, phobias, and compulsions. Several psychoneurotic patterns

[1]The terms *psychoneuroses* and *neuroses* may be used interchangeably; likewise, *psychoneurotic* and *neurotic*.

have been delineated; we shall consider them individually in the present chapter.

Although neurotics are mentally ill, the illness does not involve gross falsification of external reality in the sense of delusions or hallucinations, nor is it likely to cause them to engage in violent behavior with respect either to society or to themselves. Rather they are unhappy, anxious, inefficient individuals who do not ordinarily require hospitalization, but who are, nevertheless, badly in need of psychiatric assistance.

The actual incidence of psychoneurotic disorders is difficult to determine, but it has been conservatively estimated that 10,000,000 or more people in the United States today could be classified as psychoneurotic (Cattell and Scheier, 1961; Macmillan, 1957). We have noted already that over one half of all persons who go to doctors with physical complaints are found to be suffering from neurotic or other emotional disorders rather than organic pathology. Psychoneurotic disorders are more frequent among females than among males and are more common in early adulthood than during any other life period (Bahn *et al.*, 1961). However, they are no respecters of intelligence or economic status and are found among all segments of the general population.

The Neurotic Nucleus

The essential sequence in the development of the psychoneurotic disorders is typically: (a) faulty personality development—immaturities, distortions—resulting in specific weaknesses in personality structure, (b) evaluation of certain common life stresses as terribly dangerous and threatening, (c) arousal of severe anxiety, (d) development of neurotic defensive patterns to cope with the threats and anxiety, and finally (e) vicious circles with lowered efficiency and a myriad of secondary symptoms such as chronic fatigue and dissatisfaction.

The same sequence is found whether the life stresses come from the outside, like a failure in some task, or from within, perhaps from repressed hostility or sexual desires. The key factor in either case is the intolerable anxiety aroused when vulnerable aspects of the personality are placed under stress and the basic adequacy and worth of the self are threatened.

Although their specific symptoms vary widely, neurotics have a number of personality characteristics in common, stemming from immaturities, weaknesses, and faulty evaluations of themselves and their problems.

1. *Inadequacy and low stress tolerance.* The neurotic sees himself as basically inadequate. This is commonly indicated by a need to cling to others for support. In some instances, however, he shows an exaggerated independence in which he refuses help from everyone, or he attempts to deny his inadequacy by striving to triumph over and dominate others. Often his underlying feelings of inadequacy are manifested in a desperate search for a strong and vital marital partner who will make his life seem secure and meaningful. Needless to say, such hopes are usually destined to disillusionment as a result of the neurotic's own personal insufficiencies.

In a study of a group of 201 clinically judged neurotics, Cattell and Scheier (1961) found a much lower than normal ego strength or stress tolerance, which they attributed primarily to "badly organized personalities" and to abnormal emotionality—for example, a consistently depressive mood. As a consequence of lower stress tolerance and feelings of inadequacy, the neurotic perceives many situations as threatening which would not be so perceived by normal individuals. In short, he evidences a high degree of "threat vulnerability." This is often revealed in a dread of competing with others. Even when he does enter into competitive activities, he is often unduly elated by victory and discouraged by defeat.

2. *Anxiety and fearfulness.* Since the neurotic is confronted by various stresses which he perceives as threatening, anxiety is a pervasive factor underlying all neuroses. Sometimes the anxiety is felt acutely, as in anxiety attacks, but more typically the neurotic develops various defenses for reducing his anxiety. These defenses are rarely adequate, however, and a considerable amount of anxiety and fearfulness usually remains.

The neurotic's anxiety is often intensified by his symptoms, which he recognizes as irrational but cannot control. Furthermore, underlying fears and conflicts held in check by neurotic defenses may flare up from time to time and raise the terrifying possibility of a breakdown of the whole defensive structure. Often this is symbolically represented in irrational fears of accident, illness, death, or insanity.

3. *Tension and irritability.* Since the neurotic is chronically anxious and fearful, he is continually mobilized for defensive action and is prone to overreact to minor reverses and annoyances which the normal person would take in stride. His continued emotional mobilization also leads to an increase in general body tension, which itself is unpleasant and disturbing.

On the basis of factor-analytic studies of a large number of neurotics, Guilford (1959) has pointed to the characteristics of "neurotic emotionality" and "neurotic hostility." These terms refer to the neurotics' emotional overresponsiveness to minor irritations and to their tendency to have a morbidly hostile and suspicious attitude toward a world which they view as dangerous and threatening. It would also appear that neurotics tend to deal with their problems in rigid and emotional rather than rational ways—a pattern which only augments tension and irritability.

4. *Egocentricity and disturbed interpersonal relationships.* The neurotic is chronically and painfully aware of himself. He is primarily concerned with his own feelings, his own hopes, and his own ambitions. Since he typically faces life with such a heavy burden of helplessness and insecurity, he often feels he is fighting for his very life, and it is not surprising that in such a fight he should be extremely self-centered.

The essential inadequacy, egocentricity, and irritability of the neurotic prevent him from forming satisfying relationships with other people—and make him blind to the feelings of others and to his own part in these unsatisfactory relationships. Often he makes unrealistic demands upon those around him—trying to find in their sympathy, affection, and approval the

security which he lacks within himself. But because his demands are insatiable, they place an impossible burden on others and eventually tend to alienate them. This rejection, in turn, augments the neurotic's insecurity, hostility, and suspiciousness.

5. *Persistent nonintegrative behavior.* As a consequence of the neurotic's overreaction to his stress situation, he either experiences disorganizing anxiety or resorts to the use of defenses which alleviate the anxiety but fail to cope with the stressful situation. In either event his behavior is nonintegrative. He is like a motorist on a mountain road who is terrified by signs warning of dangerous curves. By shutting his eyes to such warnings, he protects himself from anxiety but at the expense of lowering his driving efficiency and making himself more liable to accidents.

The neurotic's defenses, though self-defeating, tend to be self-perpetuating because they reduce his anxiety. If his defenses are somehow weakened or eliminated, the anxiety returns. In general, his defenses become stable according to the degree to which they reduce his anxiety.

6. *Lack of insight and rigidity.* Although the neurotic may complain about his symptoms, he typically has little insight into the causes of his difficulties or the inadequacy of his reactions. He may agree that his fear of social gatherings is an irrational nuisance, yet he doesn't know why he has it nor can he seem to get rid of it. In occasional instances, the neurotic may show good insight into his problems and defenses, but he still is anxiety-ridden and unable to change. Since his neurotic defensive organization is the only protection he has been able to erect to ward off terrifying dangers, he clings to it. This, in turn, requires that the rest of his life activities be geared in such a way as not to endanger this defensive structure. Thus the neurotic is a rigid person—he cannot modify his defenses or appraise and deal with his problems in a flexible manner. For this reason the neurotic is said to be a driven, compulsive, and restricted personality.

The neurotic's rigidity and lack of insight also lead to a reduced sense of reality. This is reflected not only in his inability to appraise his situation objectively and discriminate more effective ways of coping with it but also in an unclear sense of self. Since he finds himself consistently reacting in ways he does not understand but is unable to avoid, it is not surprising that he experiences some confusion in his sense of self-identity.

7. *Dissatisfaction and unhappiness.* Because of their fears, apprehensions, conflicts, and general life orientation, neurotics are prone to be tense, pessimistic, and generally dissatisfied with their life situation. They usually have vague feelings that something is missing or that something is wrong, but they are unable to locate the source of their difficulty.

Since the neurotic suffers from pervasive feelings of inadequacy, he tends to avoid the challenges and struggles essential for zestful living, normal productivity, and self-growth. As a consequence, he is denied the enhancement of self-esteem and confidence which can come from surmounting obstacles and achieving worthwhile goals. It is probably the vague awareness of his inner confusion and lack of self-fulfillment that generates the feeling that something is missing—that he is not a complete person.

8. *Psychological and somatic symptoms.* Neurotics manifest a wide range of psychological and somatic symptoms. On a psychological level these include anxiety, apprehension, phobias, obsessions, compulsions, and other symptoms which we shall shortly describe. Here it may be pointed out that neurotic defensive maneuvers like phobias and compulsions are also symptoms.

Somatic symptoms include tension, fatigue, indigestion, increased frequency of micturition, muscular twitchings, excessive sweating, heart palpitations, tension headaches, choking sensations, and an assortment of vague aches and pains. Medical examination ordinarily reveals no organic basis for these complaints, but the neurotic often interprets them as evidence of organic pathology and focuses a good deal of hypochondriacal concern on them. Perhaps the most common of these symptoms is fatigue. The neurotic's sustained anxiety, tension, and dissatisfaction eventually exact a high toll in energy and morale, with the result that fatigue in one form or another tends to be a common problem. This situation may be further augmented by insomnia, nightmares, or other sleep disturbances which interfere with needed rest. In some instances, the neurotic shows normal bodily energy but is so discouraged by a seemingly hopeless life situation that he becomes listless and apathetic. Here his fatigue is clearly psychologically based.

It may be emphasized that not all the characteristics of this neurotic nucleus are found in any given case. Neuroses are the result of a complex interaction of personality and stress factors, and the specific determinants and expressions of neurotic reactions are somewhat different for each individual. In addition, it may be borne in mind that most of us evidence some neurotic symptoms in coping with the stresses of modern civilization and that none of us can escape times of anxiety and unhappiness. As Cattell and Scheier (1961) have pointed out: ". . . a neurotic is only a person with an excess of the external and internal difficulties and inadequacies from which everyone suffers in some degree." (p. 392) He chronically overreacts to life stresses and resorts to exaggerated defensive measures which are ineffective in coping with his problems.

Specific Reaction Patterns and Dynamics

In this section we shall examine the specific neurotic reaction patterns and their individual dynamics in more detail. We shall be concerned with both the personality factors and the types of stress situations commonly associated with given neurotic reactions. Then we will proceed to a consideration of general etiological factors and the problems of treatment and prognosis for psychoneurotic disorders as a group.

Several neurotic symptom patterns have been delineated. Those we shall consider are:

1. *Anxiety reaction*—diffuse but often severe anxiety not referable to any particular situation or threat.

2. *Asthenic reaction (neurasthenia)*[1]—weakness, fatigue, lack of enthusiasm, and a variety of complaints of aches and pains.

3. *Conversion reaction*—various physical illness symptoms, such as paralysis or loss of hearing, without underlying organic pathology.

4. *Dissociative reaction*—amnesia, fugue, somnambulism, and multiple personality.

5. *Phobic reaction*—various fears which the individual realizes are irrational but from which he cannot rid himself.

6. *Obsessive-compulsive reaction*—thoughts and impulses which the individual recognizes as irrational but which still persist.

7. *Neurotic depressive. reaction*—extreme and abnormally prolonged dejection and discouragement following some environmental setback.

It may be pointed out that the individual may adopt more than one defensive reaction at a given time and that defenses may shift with time. Consequently, there is often a mixture of symptoms in which no single neurotic reaction type predominates. The diagnostic category *psychoneurotic reaction* is reserved for such patterns.

ANXIETY REACTION

This is the most common of the various psychoneurotic reaction patterns, constituting about 30 to 40 per cent of all neurotic disorders.[2] It is characterized by chronic anxiety and apprehensiveness which may be punctuated by recurring episodes of acute anxiety. Neither the anxious expectation nor the acute anxiety attacks appear to stem from any particular threat. This reaction differs from other neurotic reactions in that the anxiety is experienced directly—hence the anxiety is said to be "free-floating." In other neurotic reactions the anxiety is ameliorated by the development of phobias, compulsions, and other defensive reactions. The anxiety neurotic is largely without these defenses and so is at the mercy of his anxiety.

Symptoms. In anxiety reactions there is a relatively constant state of tension, restlessness, and diffuse uneasiness. The individual exhibits generalized irritability, has difficulty concentrating, and suffers from insomnia. Usually he has difficulty making decisions and dreads the possibility that he may make a mistake. There may be mild nausea, loss of appetite, and some loss of weight. He may have heart palpitations for no apparent reason, and there may be cardiovascular changes such as elevated blood pressure and an increased pulse rate (Gunn, 1962). In essence, the individual is suffering from a chronic state of alarm and mobilization.

Often patients suffering from anxiety reactions experience recurring attacks of acute panic that last anywhere from a few seconds to an hour or more. These attacks usually come on suddenly, mount to high intensity, then subside. During the attack, the patient's heart pounds, he has difficulty breathing, his hands and lips tremble, and he perspires excessively. As the attack mounts in intensity, he may become dizzy or unsteady on his feet and complain of unbearable tension. He may feel he is suffocating and may gasp for breath.

Accompanying these physiological symptoms are subjective feelings of excitement, apprehension, and impending catastrophe. Commonly the patient feels that he is going to die or that some terrible calamity is going to overtake him. Strangely enough, however, he usually has not the vaguest idea as to what he is going to die from or what the impending calamity will be. But the subjective feelings are nonetheless acute.

Usually the attack subsides after a few minutes. If it continues, the patient may frantically implore someone around him to summon a doctor. After medical treatment has been administered, usually in the form of reassurance and a sedative, the patient gradually quiets down. Such attacks vary in frequency from several times a day to once a month or even less often. They may occur during the day, or the patient may awaken from a sound sleep with a strong feeling of apprehension which rapidly develops into an attack. Between attacks he may appear relatively

---

[1]While the asthenic reaction is not included in the current American Psychiatric Association Classification, it is a neurotic reaction pattern which has been clearly delineated by factor-analytic studies (Guilford, 1959). Also it is a commonly observed neurotic pattern in certain foreign countries—for example, Russia (Wortis, 1961). For these reasons, it is included here for instructional purposes.

[2]Incidence statistics relative to the various neurotic patterns are rough estimates, since they are based only on patients diagnosed in clinics and hospitals.

normal, but closer examination usually reveals persistent mild anxiety and tension.

In general, anxiety neurotics are chronically apprehensive no matter how well things seem to be going. Their vague fears and general sensitivity keep them continually upset, uneasy, and discouraged. Not only do they have difficulty making decisions, but after decisions have been made, they worry excessively over possible errors and unforeseen circumstances which may lead to disaster. The lengths to which they go to find things to worry about is remarkable; as fast as one cause for worry is removed, they find another, until relatives and friends lose all patience with them.

Even after going to bed, the anxiety neurotic is not likely to find relief from his worries. Often he reviews each mistake, real or imagined, recent or remote. When he is not reviewing and regretting the events of the past, he is anticipating all the difficulties that are going to arise in the future. Then, after he has crossed and recrossed most of his past and future bridges and has managed to fall asleep, he frequently has anxiety dreams—dreams of being choked, falling off high places, being shot, or being chased by murderers, with the horrible sensation that his legs will move only in a sort of slow-motion fashion and that his pursuers, try as he will, are gradually overtaking him.

The anxiety neurotic's high level of tension is often reflected in strained postural movements, overreaction to sudden or unexpected stimuli, continual nervous movements of one sort or another, and gastrointestinal upsets. Frequently, he complains of muscular tightness, especially in the neck and upper shoulder region, chronic mild diarrhea, frequent urination, and difficulties in digestion, concentration, and sleep. The excessive use of alcohol, tranquilizing drugs, or sleeping pills may further complicate the clinical picture.

Dynamics. Anxiety reactions reflect the individual's acute feelings of inadequacy in the face of inner or outer stresses which he evaluates as threatening. Such reactions may be perfectly normal, provided the stress situation is sufficiently severe to justify them. In our present highly disturbed world, many of us feel uneasy a good deal of the time and may even experience occasional mild anxiety attacks. Similarly, severe financial reverses, loss of employment, and other acute stresses may activate rather severe but perfectly normal anxiety reactions. Thus it is not the anxiety *per se* but the type of stress situation eliciting it that determines its normality or abnormality. In neurotic reactions the anxiety is considered pathological because it tends to be chronic and is elicited by stress situations which the average individual handles without too much difficulty.

Both personality and stress factors are relevant for an understanding of neurotic anxiety reactions. The anxiety neurotic tends to be introverted, sensitive, suspicious, and persistent; usually he has an unrealistically high level of aspiration and experiences strong guilt feelings when he fails to live up to his standards (Cattell and Scheier, 1961; Portnoy, 1959). By virtue of his personality make-up, he also appears especially prone to the development of conditioned fear responses (Eysenck, 1960). As a consequence, he tends to be chronically mobilized for defensive action and to overreact to a wide range of stress situations. Five kinds of situations are especially likely to augment his anxiety and precipitate acute anxiety attacks.

1. *Threats to status or goals.* Often the chronic apprehensiveness and anxiety of the neurotic stem from the necessity of assuming adult responsibilities, meeting demands for achievement, and competing with others in the face of underlying feelings of inadequacy and inferiority. Such chronic mild anxiety may be intensified by new demands or dangers which augment the total stress load. Thus the individual may function more or less adequately despite his anxious expectations until a change in his life situation increases the pressures upon him. A promotion at work may involve the necessity of increased self-assertiveness and raise the possibility of serious friction with others. As a consequence, his anxiety level rises even though he is unable to pinpoint the relationship between his new position and his increased anxiety. In essence, he is reacting to vague danger signals stemming from deeply imbedded experiences and attitudes rather than to realistic dangers in relation to his personal resources. This is one of the reasons why success experiences may augment rather than alleviate anxiety in this type of personality. An actual failure or loss, of course, whether real or potential, is even more traumatic.

After 10 years of very successful practice, a 34-year-old dentist noted that his practice had declined very slightly during the closing months of the year. Shortly after this he began to experience mild anxiety attacks and complained of continual worry, difficulty in sleeping, and a vague dread that he was "failing." As a result, he increased his hours of practice during the evenings from one to five nights and began driving himself beyond all reason in a desperate effort to "insure the success of his practice." Although his dental practice now increased beyond what it had been previously, he found himself still haunted by the vague fears and apprehensions of failure. These, in turn, became further augmented by frequent heart palpitations and pains which he erroneously diagnosed as at least an incapacitating if not a fatal heart ailment. At this point his anxiety became so great that he voluntarily came for assistance.

In the course of psychological diagnosis and treatment, a somewhat typical pattern was revealed. The patient had a history of early and chronic emotional insecurity. No matter what his accomplishments, his parents continued to reject and belittle him, which led him to feel inferior and to anticipate failure. When he once proudly told them that the school counselor had informed him he had a very high IQ, the parents demanded to know why he didn't make better grades. He remembered occasionally receiving presents, such as a model airplane set, which were always beyond his age level so that his father would have to help him assemble the kit. Tied in with his continual failure and inferiority was a very high level of aspiration—demanded by the parents and developed by the patient himself as he tried desperately to accomplish something that would gain for him badly needed parental approval and support.

As a result of this early background, the patient was unable to enjoy the successes which he did achieve, for he always felt he should be accomplishing more. Even the mild suggestion of failure in his professional work as an adult was met by exaggerated fear and anxiety and a frantic redoubling of effort, with increasing imbalance in his daily living as more and more time was taken from other activities and devoted to his excessively long hours of work. Finally, the distressing symptoms led to worry about his own health as well as about his professional status and the realization that he was badly in need of help.

The preceding case seems to be somewhat typical of the many overly ambitious, conscientious, insecure individuals who have habitually driven themselves toward well-defined material goals. Usually such individuals have a history of feeling inadequate and inferior, and of reacting to the slightest threat of failure by a frantic redoubling of effort, which only upsets their pattern of living and augments the total stress pattern.

2. *Threatened breakthrough of dangerous desires.* Sometimes hostility or sexual desires may threaten to break through the individual's defenses into consciousness or even into behavior which would lead to serious self-devaluation or would endanger his relationship with others.

The handling of hostility is often a very real problem for the neurotic, who typically feels forced to take a compliant, subservient, self-suppressing attitude toward others as the price for security, love, and acceptance. The blocking of his own strivings to be a person inevitably leads to strong feelings of aggression and hostility, yet these dangerous feelings must be controlled and denied at all costs to avoid possible rejection by others and to maintain an image of himself as a worthy person. Sometimes such repressed hostility reveals itself in indirect ways, such as in fantasies of killing or injuring other people, perhaps even someone he loves or feels dependent upon for acceptance and security.

An eighteen-year-old male student developed severe anxiety attacks just before he went out on dates. Analysis revealed that he came from a very insecure home in which he was very much attached to an anxious, frustrated, and insecure mother. He was not particularly attractive and had considerable difficulty getting dates, especially with the girls of his choice. The girl he had been dating recently, for example, would not make any arrangements to go out until after 6:00 P.M. of the same day, after her chances for a more preferable date seemed remote. This had increased his already strong feelings of inferiority and insecurity and had led to the development of intense hostility toward the opposite sex, mostly on an unconscious level.

He had begun to have fantasies of choking the girl to death when they were alone together. As he put it, "When we are alone in the car, I can't get my mind off her nice white throat and what it would be like to choke her to death." At first he put these thoughts out of his mind, but they returned on subsequent nights with increasing persistency. Then, to complicate the matter, he experienced his first acute anxiety attack. It occurred in his car on the way over to pick up his date and lasted only a few minutes, but the patient was panic-stricken and thought that he was going to die. After that he experienced several additional attacks under the same conditions.

The relationship of the repressed hostility to the patient's persistent fantasies and anxiety attacks is apparent in this case. Yet it was not at all apparent to him. He was at a complete loss to explain either the fantasies or the attacks.

Similarly, repressed sexual desires may threaten to break through existing defenses and elicit intense anxiety. For the male neurotic, concern over masturbation and homosexuality appears to be most common (Guilford, 1959). Thus the individual may repress homosexual impulses which he considers highly immoral and completely incompatible with his self-concept as a male. For a time the repression protects him, but repression is rarely if ever complete, and the individual is likely to experience periodic flare-ups of anxiety even though he may be unaware of the reason for their occurrence. In addition, some change in his life situation—perhaps a friendly relationship with an effeminate man—may intensify his homosexual impulses, posing a major threat to his repressive defenses and eliciting intense anxiety.

3. *Anxiety-arousing decisions.* We have noted that anxiety neurotics tend to have difficulty in making decisions. Under certain conditions—such as conflicts involving moral values or possible loss of security and status—there may be acute anxiety and paralyzing indecision.

A college sophomore, Mary ——, wanted very much to marry a young man she had met in school. However, he insisted on having premarital sex relations "to be sure that they would be sexually compatible." This was contrary to her ethical and religious training, yet she found herself strongly attracted to him physically as well as very much in love. As a consequence, the thought of giving in to his demands persisted, but she was unable to make up her mind. Eventually, she began to experience periodic anxiety attacks, had serious difficulty in concentrating on her studies, and suffered from insomnia during which she would go over and over the conflict situation.

In this case the anxiety was apparently elicited by the conflict between her guilt-arousing desire for sexual relations, which she considered highly immoral, and her fear of losing the man she loved if she continued to refuse. The situation was also fraught with other anxiety-arousing uncertainties. Even if she did yield to his demands, she had to face the possibility that he was only trying to seduce her or that even if he were sincere, he might not find her sexually compatible. In addition, she had vague feelings of apprehension that she would somehow be punished if she indulged in such behavior, perhaps by becoming pregnant or causing him to lose his respect for her. The end result was indecision and anxiety.

In cases where the neurotically insecure person has achieved some degree of real success and consequently of security, anxiety attacks may develop when his proposed behavior jeopardizes this security.

A successful business executive developed acute anxiety attacks which occurred about once every two or three months. The patient's wife was eight years older than he, and he was no longer physically attracted to her. He had found himself increasingly interested in younger women and had begun to think how much more enjoyable it would be to have a younger, more companionable wife. During this period, he met a girl with whom he was sure he had fallen in love. It was shortly thereafter that the anxiety attacks began to occur. They were preceded by a period of several days of increased tenseness and anxiety, but the attacks came on suddenly and were very intense.

This man, too, was at a complete loss to explain his attacks. But the explanation was not difficult to find. The patient had had a poverty-stricken and inse-cure childhood and felt basically inferior, insecure, and threatened by a hard world. These feelings had been intensified when he had failed college courses in his second year, even though the failure had resulted pri-marily from excessive outside work. He had been able to achieve some security, however, by marrying an older and very strong woman who had instilled con-siderable self-confidence and initiative in him. The relationship had proved very fruitful financially, and the patient was living in a style which as a youth, "I hadn't dared to imagine in my wildest dreams!" His persistent thoughts about divorcing his wife, on whom he felt dependent for his security and style of life, thus represented a severe threat to the moderately successful adjustment he had been able to achieve. The anxiety attacks followed.

Life often poses problems in which the pursuit of increased satisfactions involves giving up present hard-won security and taking new risks. For the neurotic, this is likely to prove an anxiety-arousing conflict situation.

4. *Reactivation of prior trauma.* Although practically all anxiety reactions based on situational stresses could be included here, we are concerned primarily with those stresses which reopen earlier personality wounds and hence are particularly difficult to handle. The following are the initial comments of a patient who had been absent from his job for three days as a result of "sickness."

"I've just reached the point where I can't go on. Got no fight left. And not enough guts to end it here. Best damn job I ever had. Almost can see my way out of debt. And it's all going to hell, and I'm getting so I don't care about anything, except not going back to work. I can't kid myself, I just can't take it anymore. And I'll have to confess I have no faith left in anything including your profession. Or faith in myself. Maybe if I can tell someone how I feel, how balled up I am, I can see the light. I can't afford to take time off work. I can't afford to relax a couple of weeks on some warm beach, or forget my troubles with some floozy blonde. Hell, that's for the books on the best seller's list. I've just got to go about acting like my normal stupid self and something's got to blow. It goes in waves. Sometimes, I'm alright and then I get anxiety feelings, and my heart pounds. I get to shaking all over, and think I'm going to die. God, it's awful!"

Interestingly enough, the primary cause of the intense anxiety reactions in this case was found to be associated with a new and rather critical supervisor at work. In response to criticisms which may have annoyed but did not completely disrupt the behavior of other employees, the patient became a psychiatric casualty. His reaction was traced to his relationship with his father, who had died some five years before. Since his earliest memory, the patient had idolized his father and had practically lived for the occasional hard-won compliments which he received from him. Conversely, when his father had criticized him, the patient had been so upset that he would go to his room completely distraught and cry for hours at a time. Now, as an adult, this dependent, insecure individual had transferred these same feelings and attitudes to his supervisor. The prior supervisor had apparently been much more understanding and had generously praised and rarely criticized the patient. The new supervisor evidently had reactivated his old "weak spot" and had precipitated the anxiety reaction.

5. *Guilt and fear of punishment.* Occasionally, anxiety reactions develop as an aftermath of behavior which arouses acute guilt feelings and fear of punishment. Darling (1952) has cited the case of a university student who suffered from severe anxiety attacks which showed no abatement during three months of psychiatric treatment until his family disclosed that he had been in an accident in which a child had been killed. He had repressed his acute feelings of guilt and could not even recall the accident. The repressive defense was not entirely adequate, however, and his feelings of self-devaluation and apprehension of punishment revealed themselves in his anxiety attacks.

Sometimes guilt and apprehension of punishment are consequences of trying to escape from an unsatisfactory marital or other life situation by way of compensatory sexual gratifications. Here we most often find lonely, insecure women with a history of having been popular and sought-after in their youth who now find themselves neglected by critical, undemonstrative, indifferent husbands. Hungry for admiration and attention, these women reach out toward the storybook romance of extramarital affairs. Unfortunately, their clandestine affairs usually augment their insecurities and create distressing conflicts, feelings of guilt, and apprehensiveness that they will somehow be punished for their immoral behavior. As a result, they develop anxiety reactions, often complicated by periods of depression. Those who have a fairly strong conscience development and who feel that marital infidelity is highly immoral are particularly likely to experience severe guilt and self-devaluation.

Although we have emphasized the inadequacy, oversensitivity, and low ego strength of the anxiety neurotic, it may also be pointed out that he often puts up a good battle in view of his faulty evaluations of himself and his environment. As Portnoy (1959) has pointed out: "To the picture of an anxious individual apprehensively coping with life in the face of inner and outer dangers must also be added the picture of a human being with courage, able to endure this much anxiety without the more massive defenses and character distortions which characterize the other psychiatric syndromes." (p. 320)

Curiously enough, the anxiety neurotic may function well and show less anxiety when confronted with a situation that presents an actual danger which both demands and permits definitive action (Cattell and Scheier, 1961). Thus the anxiety neurotic may rise to the challenge of emergency situations. It was pointed out previously that anxiety neurotics tended to perform well in combat situations, possibly because they were accustomed to functioning under a heavy load of anxiety.

Anxiety neurotics often find some immediate relief in tranquilizing drugs and usually respond well to psychotherapy, although their general anxiety is seldom completely removed (Tobin and Lewis, 1960). Typically, however, the anxiety can be reduced to the point where they make a satisfactory adjustment. In view of the fact that most of us in this troubled world suffer from recurrent anxieties and fears, this is probably all that can be expected for the anxiety neurotic.

ASTHENIC REACTION (NEURASTHENIA)

An asthenic reaction is characterized by chronic mental and physical fatigue and an assortment of vague aches and pains. Exact estimates as to incidence disagree, but asthenic reactions, at least in milder form, are relatively common, probably accounting for 10 per cent or more of neurotic disorders. In general, middle-aged adults—particularly frustrated housewives—seem to be those most commonly subject to them. Neurasthenic reactions are also most common on lower socioeconomic levels (Rennie *et al.,* 1957).

Symptoms. The patient's primary complaint in asthenic reactions is that of physical and mental fatigue. He has difficulty concentrating, is easily distracted, and lacks the vigor required to carry activities through to successful completion. Even minor tasks seem to require herculean effort. He usually spends a good deal of time sleeping in an attempt to counteract his fatigue, yet regardless of the amount of sleep he gets, he still awakens unrefreshed.

Typically, he sleeps poorly and feels "just rotten" when he drags himself out of bed in the morning. On the rare occasions when he does feel refreshed, he is completely upset by minor emotional setbacks, such as some criticism of his behavior, and his fatigue and listlessness return. Even when things seem to be going relatively well, the fatigue tends to get worse as the day wears on, although by evening he may feel somewhat better and may go to a movie or a party without experiencing anything like his usual exhaustion. In fact, one of the most significant things about the neurasthenic's fatigue is its selective nature. He often shows relatively good energy and endurance in playing tennis, golf, or bridge or in doing anything else which really interests him. In the face of family, occupational, and other routine activities, however, he is usually a monument of listlessness, lack of enthusiasm, and general tiredness.

In addition to chronic fatigue, the neurasthenic usually has a variety of other somatic complaints, among which are headaches or stuffiness of the head, indigestion, pain in the small of the back, dizzy spells, hypersensitivity to minor irritations, and feelings of weakness. Sometimes the complaints involve a particular organ and are clear-cut and specific, but usually the neurasthenic experiences vague, general discomfort and has difficulty giving a precise description of his ailment. Thus he may complain of uncomfortable and peculiar sensations in the general area of the stomach, the chest, the head, the genitals, or elsewhere in the body. He may at first describe these sensations as painful, but on further questioning decide that they are more like pressure or perhaps a feeling of heat. The neurasthenic typically evidences a good deal of hypochondriacal concern about his fatigue and other somatic symptoms. In some instances, this extends to a morbid preoccupation with digestive and excretory functions and a tendency to keep abreast of the latest fads in special diets, laxatives, vitamins, and tranquilizing pills.

Asthenic reactions are especially common among so-called nervous housewives who feel neglected by their husbands and frustrated and cheated by life. Frequently, such women reveal a history of delicate health and parental overprotection in childhood and now feel completely dependent upon but highly resentful of their indifferent husbands. Although television soap operas, romantic novels, and movie magazines may provide some vicarious satisfaction, their life situations seem hopeless to them, and they react with discouragement, listlessness, and preoccupation with various somatic complaints.

The following excerpts are taken from an interview with a middle-aged married woman who felt, and with good reason, that her husband was no longer interested in her. Often he failed to come home for several days at a time, and when he was home, he showed little evidence of interest or affection. Although the patient had completed high school, she had no occupational skills and felt completely dependent upon her husband for support and protection. She was self-pitying in her attitude, prone to relating her symptoms almost endlessly, and very demanding in her attitude toward the therapist.

Pt.: I used to talk rather fluently, but now I'm more nervous than I've ever been and my tongue seems to catch on my teeth so that I don't speak plainly. Everything seems such an effort . . . like I had an anchor tied to me or something. I no longer care to play cards or even talk to people any more. . . . Even the simplest things are too much for me.

Dr.: Even the simplest things . . .

Pt.: Ah, hm, I mean, the phone is there and I'm lonesome and yet I don't even phone. . . . I don't even talk to my neighbors much any more even though I know that I should be with people and I like people, but I've gotten so that . . . (long pause) . . . that . . . (sigh) . . . I feel too bad to even talk or do anything (voice breaks and tears).

I've tried so many things to get well, but it's just awful . . . I mean . . . sometimes I can just barely live . . . I mean just listen to the radio or read, or eat . . . I mean just like being in a daze or some-

thing . . . I don't know . . . I just feel so horribly tired and sick.

Two months ago I felt better than I had been. I mean I was able . . . well I went to several shows and I actually even went to a dance. Often I would begin to get tired, and I was very frightened that I would break down, but I would go on . . . I mean like some people would go to a battle or to a battlefront (proud tone of voice). But . . . now . . . well I am just so tired and run-down that I can't even go to a show . . . if I do go . . . I have to leave in the middle because I am not strong enough . . . I mean I don't have enough strength to sit through it.

Dr.: Two months ago you felt better?

Pt.: Well, yes . . . you see my husband's brother came to visit us . . . and he would talk to me and he had such a way of diverting me and he was very interesting, and you'd be amazed, within a few minutes or a few hours I'd be just different . . . and he took me to several shows and to the dance. I felt so much better and I had a really good time. So I can see it isn't sleeping or eating. I mean . . . I need someone who'd give me something different to think about . . . someone who'd show you some affection . . . enough interest in you so that you would improve. But my husband . . . well I just can't understand how he can treat a woman who is ill . . . and trying her best . . . well (tears) . . . I have just sort of withdrawn . . . he has really made me sick . . .

Dynamics. Historical attempts to explain the dynamics of asthenic reactions centered around the concept of "nerve weakness," which is the literal meaning of the older term *neurasthenia*. Beard (1905), an early American psychiatrist who first applied the term to the fatigue syndrome, attributed the condition to prolonged conflict and overwork, which presumably depleted the nerve cells of essential biochemical elements.[1] This conception later gave rise to the Weir Mitchell method of treatment for "nervous exhaustion," which involved a long period of complete rest and relaxation for the

---

[1]At one time certain cases of neurasthenia were thought to be the outcome of unsolved sexual problems. Masturbation, for example, was presumed to result in depletion of bodily energy and chronic fatigue. Where sexual practices do constitute a problem, they are now considered to be merely the focal point of a much more general maladjustment.

patient. Asthenic patients, however, rarely reveal a history of overwork, nor is the condition corrected by prolonged rest.

Today neurasthenia is looked upon primarily as a psychological rather than a physical fatigue reaction. It is not overwork but prolonged frustration, discouragement, and hopelessness which reduce motivation and lead to the characteristic listlessness and fatigue (Cattell and Scheier, 1961; Guilford, 1959). In addition, there are likely to be sustained emotional conflicts centering around hostility toward one's mate and guilt over the abandonment of cherished goals.

We all feel tired and listless when we are discouraged and forced to do something that does not interest us. Those of us who have worked at jobs which were boring and frustrating can readily understand how feelings of listlessness and tiredness can arise in such situations. In the neurasthenic these feelings are elaborated into a chronic fatigue reaction similar to the fatigue reaction commonly found in acute situational maladjustment. Of course, the chronic anxiety, disturbed sleep, and overreactivity of the neurasthenic may eventually lead to a very real depletion of bodily reserves. Although such somatic conditions may complicate the clinical picture and require treatment in their own right, they are a result of the neurasthenic reaction—not the basic cause.

Since the asthenic does not understand why he feels tired all the time, he is continually searching for bodily ailments which can account for his fatigue and indirectly relieve him of the responsibility of coping with a hopeless life situation. If he is tired and sick, one cannot expect too much of him. Neurasthenics often feel relieved when medical examination does reveal some organic pathology (Chrzanowski, 1959).

As in anxiety reactions, asthenic symptoms may have important secondary gains. Symptoms tend to force others to show sympathy and concern and may even be used aggressively to control others' behavior. For example, the patient's obvious difficulties and complaints may prevent her husband from obtaining a contemplated divorce, may force additional attention and time from him, such as any sick person would merit, and may largely control the family's social life.

These patterns are developed unconsciously, of course. The asthenic often gets credit for putting up a noble battle against heavy odds. In general, however, asthenics eventually wear out the patience of their family and friends because of their essentially negative personalities. Their listlessness, morbid outlook, self-centered attitudes, and continual complaining are not conducive to the maintenance of happy social relationships. Poorly repressed hostility toward their mate or other loved ones—whom they hold accountable for their difficulties—may further augment their disturbed interpersonal relationships.

In understanding the etiology of neurasthenic reactions, it may be emphasized that feeling tired and being concerned about one's health are common in our high-pressure culture. In contrast to the normal individual, however, the neurasthenic is an immature individual who lacks self-confidence, is overly dependent on others for security, and feels completely inadequate in the face of a frustrating and seemingly hopeless life situation (Guilford, 1959). His symptoms enable him to escape the necessity of dealing with his problems, for he is just too tired and sick to solve them. However, they exact a heavy toll in the restriction of his life activities, in blocked self-fulfillment, and in reduced satisfactions in living.

Asthenic reactions are frequently very pernicious because it may not be possible to relieve the unsatisfactory life situation, and it is difficult for the patient to accept the fact that his difficulties are psychological and not somatic. To face this fact would confront him again with the problem of striving toward seemingly hopeless goals. Also, it would remove the compensatory gratification he is likely to have achieved through increased attention and concern from others. Where there are strong hypochondriacal trends in the clinical picture, the treatment problems are usually intensified. The following letter, written by a hospitalized neurotic to her anxious relatives, is a classic illustration of a neurasthenic reaction complicated by hypochondriacal trends and provides some indication of the difficulties likely to be encountered in treating such a patient.

"Dear Mother and Husband:

"I have suffered terrible today with drawing in

throat. My nerves are terrible. My head feels queer. But my stomach hasn't cramped quite so hard . . . I've been on the verge of a nervous chill all day, but I have been fighting it hard. It's night and bedtime, but, Oh, how I hate to go to bed. Nobody knows or realizes how badly I feel because I fight to stay up and outdoors if possible.

"I haven't had my cot up for two days, they don't want me to use it.

"These long afternoons and nights are awful. There are plenty of patients well enough to visit with but I'm in too much pain.

"The nurses ignore any complaining. They just laugh or scold.

"Eating has been awful hard. They expect me to eat like a harvest hand. Every bite of solid food is agony to get down, for my throat aches so and feels so closed up. . . .

"With supper so early, and evening so long, I am so nervous I can't sleep until so late. I haven't slept well since I've been here. My heart pains as much as when I was at home. More so at night. I put hot water bottle on it. I don't know if I should or not. I've been wanting to ask some Dr.

"I had headache so badly in the back of my head last night and put hot water bottle there. My nurse said not to.

"They don't give much medicine here. Mostly Christian Science it seems! Well I must close or I never will get to sleep. My nurse gets off at 8:15 so she makes me go to bed by then.

"My eyes are bothering me more.

"Come up as soon as you can. My nose runs terrible every time I eat.

"The trains and ducks and water pipes are noisy at night.

ANNIE"
(K. A. Menninger, 1945, pp. 139-140)

Tranquilizing drugs have not proved effective in the treatment of neurasthenic reactions although they may, of course, allay some of the anxiety (Chrzanowski, 1959). In general, treatment involves helping the patient to gain some insight into his reactions, to develop more effective coping techniques, and to foster growth toward personal maturity—thus enabling him to re-evaluate his problems, goals, and adjustive reactions and to gain enough self-confidence and courage to stop feeling sorry for himself and get back into the "battle of life."

CONVERSION REACTION (HYSTERIA)

Conversion reaction is a neurotic defense in which symptoms of some physical illness appear without any underlying organic pathology. It is one of the most intriguing and baffling of all the psychopathological syndromes. This reaction is still sometimes referred to as *hysteria*—the latter term being derived from the Greek word meaning "uterus." It was thought by Hippocrates and other ancient Greeks that this disorder was restricted to women and was caused by the wandering of a frustrated uterus to various parts of the body because of its pining for children. For example, the uterus might lodge in the throat and cause choking sensations, or in the spleen, resulting in temper tantrums. Hippocrates thought there was a frequent relationship of hysterical symptoms to sexual difficulties and considered marriage the best remedy for the affliction.

This concept of the relationship of sexual difficulties to hysteria was later advanced in modified form by Freud. He used the term *conversion hysteria* to indicate that the hysterical symptoms were an expression of repressed and deviated sexual energy—that is, the psychological-sexual conflict was *converted* into a bodily disturbance. A sexual conflict over masturbation might be solved by developing a paralyzed hand. This is not done consciously, of course, and the meaning of the symptoms is completely lost on the patient. This dynamic concept of conversion has been largely retained in modern psychiatry, but many other types of psychological conflicts in addition to sexual conflicts are now seen as important factors contributing to the development of conversion reactions.

In World War I, conversion reactions were the most frequent neuropsychiatric conditions, and in World War II they were relatively common among service personnel. In contemporary life, however, with our increasing medical and psychiatric sophistication, conversion reactions have become relatively rare, probably constituting about 5 per cent of all neurotic reactions (Cattell and Scheier, 1961). Reactions that do occur are found mainly among adolescents and young adults and are much more frequent among women than among men (Purtell *et al.*, 1951; Ziegler *et al.*, 1960). In general, these patients are slightly lower than other neurotic types in intelligence, educational level, and socioeconomic status.

Symptoms. In a medical age which no longer believes in being "struck" dumb, blind, or with paralysis, patients are developing fewer of these symptoms and more of the vague aches and pains which are harder to diagnose as functional. However, conversion reactions may simulate a wide range of organic illnesses, and the specific symptoms that may occur are legion.

1. *Sensory symptoms.* Any one of the senses may be involved in sensory conversion reactions. The most common forms are:

anesthesia—loss of sensitivity
hypesthesia—partial loss of sensitivity
hyperesthesia—excessive sensitivity
analgesis—loss of pain sensitivity
paresthesia—exceptional sensations, such as tingling

Anesthesias, formerly so common in hysteria, are now quite rare. For the adaptive value of the symptoms is lost if they can be readily shown on superficial medical examination to have no organic basis. This does not necessarily mean that the patient himself is particularly impressed by such evidence, but society is no longer so impressed—with the result that the symptoms lose the various primary and secondary gains associated with social acceptance.

Blindness, deafness, and loss of touch and pain sensitivity in various areas of the body are the most common of the anesthesias still found. Occasionally the patient may lose his sense of smell, but this is rare. In a rather interesting case of this type, an elderly lady lost her sense of smell when her only son began to drink excessively and came home repeatedly with the odor of alcohol on his breath.

Despite the fact that there is no actual organic pathology in these cases, the loss of sensitivity is quite real. Yet it may be selective. In cases of hysterical blindness, the patient may carefully avoid bumping into people or objects in his path. He also usually dodges objects thrown at him.

Some idea of the range of sensory symptoms which may occur in conversion reactions can be gleaned from Ironside and Batchelor's (1945) study of hysterical visual symptoms of airmen.

They found blurred vision, photophobia, diplopia, night blindness, intermittent visual failure combined with amnesia, deficient stereopsis, the tendency to look past an object which the subject is attempting to fixate, intermittent loss of vision in one eye, jumbling of print when the subject attempts to read, and failing day vision. It was also found that the symptoms of each patient were closely related to his performance duties. Night fliers, for example, were more subject to night blindness, while day fliers more often developed failing day vision.

Still other visual symptoms include triplopia, "tunnel vision" (involving various degrees of restriction of the visual field), micropsia (in

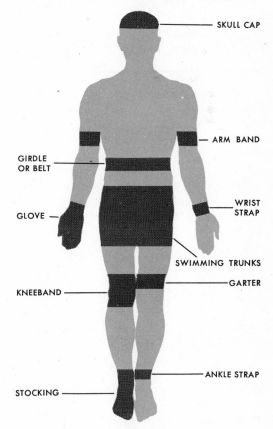

COMMON AREAS OF HYSTERICAL ANESTHESIA

SKULL CAP
ARM BAND
GIRDLE OR BELT
WRIST STRAP
GLOVE
SWIMMING TRUNKS
GARTER
KNEEBAND
ANKLE STRAP
STOCKING

Adapted from Karnosh and Zucker (1945)

These are the typical areas for which hysterical anesthesias are developed. Their correspondence with articles of clothing rather than with nerve pathways is clear evidence that their origin is psychological rather than neurological.

These pictures show a patient before and after psychotherapy for a hysterical bent back. In this case the hysterical symptoms were superimposed on a previous actual injury which X rays and careful examination showed had healed. Upon induction into the Army the patient began to feel a constant low back pain before the onset of acute symptoms and was excused from long hikes. He did not adjust well to his robust outfit; the pain became worse, and five months after his induction he was hospitalized. He complained that he could not stand straight because the pain pulled him forward. However, he was able to lie flat on his back without pain. He became emotional on slight provocation and sometimes displayed a tremor. Within a week after psychotherapy commenced, the patient stood erect and had only a slight limp, which was apparent only when he thought he was being observed. Within two weeks all the symptoms had disappeared (Adapted from Hamlin, 1953, pp. 297-299).

which objects appear unusually small), macropsia (in which they seem unusually large), and in rare cases even color blindness. Despite the fact that such symptoms show up clearly in direct clinical testing, patients are usually able to drive a car or fly a plane without any difficulty.

2. *Motor symptoms.* Hysterical motor disturbances, too, cover such a wide range of symptoms that only the most common of them can be mentioned here.

Hysterical paralyses are usually confined to a single limb, such as an arm or a leg, although occasionally the entire right or left side of the body may be affected. There may be various degrees of the paralysis too: the movement of the limb may be completely lost or only diminished. Here, too, the loss of the function may be selective. For example, in writer's cramp the patient cannot write but may be able to use the same muscles perfectly well in shuffling a deck of cards or playing the piano.

Tremors (muscular shaking or trembling) and tics (unconscious localized muscular twitches) are common. Occasionally, there are contractures, which usually involve the flexion of fingers and toes or rigidity of the larger joints, such as the knees and elbows. Paralyses and contractures frequently lead to walking disturbances. A patient with a rigid knee joint may be forced to throw his leg out in a sort of arc as he walks. Another walking disturbance worthy of mention is *astasia-abasia,* in which the patient can usually control his leg movements when sitting or lying down, but can hardly stand and has a very grotesque, disorganized walk, with his legs wobbling about in every direction.

The most common hysterical disturbances of speech are *aphonia,* in which the patient is able to talk only in a whisper, and *mutism,* in which the patient is unable to speak at all. Often, interestingly enough, a patient who can speak only in a whisper will be able to cough in a perfectly normal manner. In true laryngeal paralysis both the cough and the voice are affected. Aphonia is a common symptom in hysteria and frequently occurs suddenly after some emotional shock. Hysterical mutism is relatively rare.

Occasionally, patients evidence hysterical convulsions or "fits" similar to epileptic convulsions. However, the conversion patient shows few of the usual characteristics of true epilepsy —he rarely if ever injures himself, his pupillary reflex to light remains unaffected, and he is not incontinent. In addition, hysterical convulsions almost always take place in the presence of other people. Similarly, hysterical fainting attacks occur occasionally but rarely take place when the patient is alone.

3. *Visceral symptoms.* Hysterical visceral symptoms include headache, "lump in the throat" and choking sensations, coughing spells, difficulty in breathing, cold and clammy extremities, belching, nausea, vomiting, and so on. Occasionally, there is persistent hiccoughing or sneezing.

Another rare condition sometimes classified under conversion reactions is *anorexia nervosa.* Here there is loss of appetite and refusal of some types of food. Bond (1949) has described the case of an adolescent girl who developed anorexia nervosa following a sexual advance by a senile neighbor. She refused all foods that reminded her of sexual things by their shape, color, texture, or smell. At first this included only a few foods, but gradually almost everything edible became associated with sex and was rejected. Unless successfully treated, such patients may actually die of starvation.[1]

The ability of hysterics to simulate actual disease symptoms is almost unbelievable. In a pseudo attack of acute appendicitis, not only may the patient evidence pain in the lower abdominal region and other typical symptoms of acute appendicitis, but his temperature may also shoot up far above normal. Even cases of psychogenic malaria and tuberculosis have been cited in the psychiatric literature in which patients showed all the usual symptoms—coughing, loss of weight, recurrent fever, and night sweats—without actual organic disease. Thus it is not surprising that hysterical symptoms have led to a great many unnecessary operations.

Since hysterical symptoms are capable of simulating almost every known disease, differential diagnosis can be a problem. However, in addition to specialized medical techniques of diagnosis, there are several criteria which are commonly used for distinguishing between hysterical and organic disturbances, most of which have already been suggested:

a) A certain *belle indifference* of the hysteric. Although these patients occasionally show some concern over their ailments, they usually make their complaints in a rather matter-of-fact way, with little of the anxiety and fear that would be expected in an individual with a paralyzed arm or loss of hearing.

b) The frequent failure of the hysterical dysfunction to follow a feasible anatomical pattern in terms of actual nerve distribution. Also, in hysterical paralyses there is no atrophy or wasting away of the paralyzed limb except in very rare and long-standing cases.

c) The selective nature of the dysfunction —the fact, for example, that in hysterical blindness the patient does not ordinarily bump into people or objects, or the fact that paralyzed muscles can be used for some activities and not others. Hysterical contractures also disappear during sleep.

d) The interesting fact that under hypnosis or narcosis the symptoms can usually be induced, removed, or shifted by the suggestions of a skilled therapist. Similarly, if the patient is suddenly awakened from a sound sleep, he may be tricked into talking or into using a "paralyzed" limb.

Where hysterical symptoms are intermingled

---

[1]Wall (1959) presents a good discussion of diagnosis, treatment, and results in cases of anorexia nervosa.

with actual organic pathology, the difficulty in making an accurate diagnosis may, of course, be considerably increased.

It is usually fairly easy to distinguish between hysteria and *malingering*. The malingerer is voluntarily perpetrating a fraud, and this fact is reflected in his demeanor. Whereas the hysteric is usually dramatic, effusive, and apparently naïve, the malingerer is inclined to be defensive, surly, evasive, and suspicious. When inconsistencies in his behavior are pointed out, the hysteric is usually unperturbed, the malingerer immediately defensive. Finally, the hysteric is concerned mainly with his symptoms and willingly discusses them, whereas the malingerer is apt to be reluctant to be examined and slow to talk about his symptoms lest his pretense be discovered.

Dynamics. In conversion reactions the patient avoids or solves some problem by getting sick. As in the other neurotic reactions, the symptoms protect him from having to face the traumatic situation and at the same time bring him secondary gains in extra sympathy and attention as well as some control over the people around him. These points are well illustrated in the following classic example of a conversion reaction.

"Since a child, this young woman cherished vague and beautiful ideas of her own charm, refinement and artistic ability. Her ambitions were stimulated and fostered by an admiring family circle, a protected life, and a group of friends whose admittance to friendship, consciously or unconsciously, depended on their uncritical admiration. The more or less deliberate purpose of her striving was to insure and magnify the admiration and uncritical affection of her friends through the talented use of a great voice.

"Now the day approaches when her voice is to be tested, not by the admiring circle, but by a critical professional teacher who is to determine the course of her vaguely planned career. This day has approached before, but she has always had a severe headache or a bad throat or some other rather sudden but not infectious ailment which has prevented her meeting the test. . . .

"Finally, an act of will, or perhaps an access of ambition . . . and she actually goes to the test. She passes the earlier and simpler parts of the audition with fair credit, though with some trepidation. Then

comes a more crucial, a more important, and far more difficult step in the trial, involving an uncompromising test of real quality of voice and real ability of technique. Something happens. Her voice cracks at the very beginning of this important step, her throat hurts, she has suddenly become hoarse. It is impossible to carry the test further. She explains quite honestly to the teacher that she has a very delicate throat and that she did not realize it was in such shocking condition; furthermore, she ought not to have attempted the test. She goes home to much genuine and deserved sympathy. She becomes voiceless for several days or weeks.

". . . and she rationalizes the episode as follows: The test, because she took it when her throat was in poor condition, has strained her voice. Of course, the teacher should have known better. Ever after she refers to it sadly as the time when her voice was strained by an injudicious and premature test to which she was led by her inexorable courage and ambition. Furthermore, she says now, that because of this accident she is unable ever to sing well, the inference being that she did sing well before, which is probably not the fact, as her voice, though apparently quite normal, is of very small calibre and mediocre quality. However, the automatism of escape has 'saved her face.' It has saved the pretty picture of her great artistic ability, and has transferred the vision of her powerful and charming performance from the future to the past, and, furthermore, it has given her a perfectly satisfactory explanation and justification in perpetuity for the manifest discrepancy between the greatness of her talent and the hopeless mediocrity of her best possible performance." (Coon and Raymond, 1940, pp. 224-225)

In the history of conversion reactions there is usually the following chain of events: first, a desire to escape from some unpleasant situation; second, a fleeting wish to be sick in order to avoid the situation (this wish, however, is suppressed as unfeasible or unworthy); third, under additional or continued stress the appearance of the symptoms of some physical ailment. At this point the original wish has been repressed and the symptoms have been substituted for it. Thus the patient sees no relation between his symptoms and the stress situation. The particular symptoms that occur are usually those of a previous illness or are copied from other sources —such as illness symptoms observed among relatives or on television or read about in magazines. However, they may also be superimposed on an existing organic ailment, be associated with anticipated secondary gains, or be symbolically related to the neurotic conflict. Unfortunately, the neurological processes involved in the simulation of various disease symptoms, such as malarial fever, are not well understood.

What can be said about the personality of the individual who attempts to solve serious problems by getting sick? It should be remembered in this connection that most of us at one time or another have probably solved some problem or avoided something we didn't want to do by pleading sickness. In fact, the common saying, "I don't feel like doing it," shows the prevalence of this type of reaction. The hysteric, however, is the individual who unconsciously commits himself to this sort of reaction even though it disrupts his entire pattern of everyday activities. This means an emotionally immature, inadequate, individual.

The hysteric tends to be highly suggestible and dramatic—to be what is called a "histrionic personality." Recent investigators also emphasize the dependent and demanding behavior of these patients and their difficulties in assuming adult responsibilities. In relation to other neurotic reaction types, hysterics typically show a special need for attention, tend to be excitable but shallow in emotional responsiveness, are often seductive but frigid sexually, and are dependently demanding and manipulative in interpersonal relationships (Chodoff and Lyons, 1958; Miller *et al.,* 1960; Ziegler *et al.,* 1960).

Moss *et al.* (1962) describes this pattern lucidly in his description of Alice M., a 31-year-old divorcée diagnosed as a hysteric. She is characterized as:

". . . naïve and suggestible, unreflective and impulsive, and in her relationships she is childishly clinging, affect-laden and unstable. There is a powerful capacity for dramatization, and aggressive impulsives are repressed and displaced. A prominent feature of Alice's pathology is an intense and protracted autonomy-dependency conflict. She vascillates perpetually between a childish dependency and a façade of responsible adulthood, wallowing in indecision and ambivalence, resulting in perpetual indecision. . . . Alice's intense frustration of early dependency needs is re-flected in her life's task of searching for another person who will assume responsibility for solving her problems."

Although the general dynamic process in conversion reactions is getting sick to avoid some painful stress situation, there are a number of somewhat specific dynamic patterns.

1. Often a conversion reaction is used directly as a means of removing the individual from some unpleasant or dangerous situation. An acquaintance of the author fainted on the way to the altar on two occasions, each time with the same girl. Halpern (1944) reported fifteen cases of hysterical amblyopia[1] in the armed forces which developed at a port of embarkation and cleared up when the patients were removed from the conflict situation by hospitalization. These reactions have sometimes been called "gangplank fever." The same pattern is apparent in the case history of the would-be singer whose throat could not stand the strain. By getting sick, the patient diverts attention from his failure, provides himself with a convenient excuse, and in the process fools both himself and others—all quite unconsciously, of course: his symptoms are real and he has no conscious control over them.

2. Sometimes hysterical illness represents an attempt to regain or achieve some desired goal. In one case a ten-year-old boy developed irregular, patternless twitching movements. It was found that he had been the center of attention for years until his father met with an accident and developed severe convulsive seizures. As a result, a considerable amount of attention and care which had formerly been given to the boy was now directed toward his father. By the development of a somewhat similar pattern, the child was apparently attempting to regain his lost position as the center of affection and attention.

Occasionally, conversion symptoms may represent an attempt to gain both revenge and lost love by making another person feel that his harsh or cruel treatment has made the patient sick. Here, of course, there are likely to be strongly ambivalent feelings toward the individual involved.

3. Conversion reactions may also represent

---

[1] See Glossary.

defenses against dangerous impulses. Abse (1959) has cited the case of a middle-aged male patient who suffered total paralysis of his legs after his wife left him for another man. During the course of the treatment it became apparent that he had a strong wish to pursue his wife and kill her and her lover. Although this wish had been repressed, it was quite intense, and the paralysis apparently represented a massive defense against the possibility that this vengeful wish might be carried out in action.

Where forbidden wishes have actually broken through ego defenses and have found expression in overt behavior, conversion reactions may stem from feelings of guilt and the necessity for self-punishment. In one case, for example, a patient developed a marked tremor and partial paralysis of the right arm and hand after an attack upon her father during which she clutched and tore open his shirt with her right hand. Apparently the paralysis in this case represented a sort of symbolic punishment of the "guilty party."

4. In some instances conversion symptoms develop following some actual physical illness or an accident in which the individual may or may not have been injured. If pneumonia temporarily enables the patient to avoid highly unpleasant occupational responsibilities, he may unconsciously prolong his invalidism. An injury may lead to the same pattern.

Not uncommonly, conversion symptoms develop following some accident or injury as a result of which the patient hopes to receive some monetary compensation (Cohen *et al.*, 1953; Robins *et al.*, 1952). These reactions usually occur after accidents in which the patient might have been seriously injured but is actually only shaken up or slightly injured. Later, in relating the experience to friends, it may be agreed that the patient would have had a strong legal case if he had been injured. Is he sure that he is all right? Could he possibly have injured his back? After a few careful exploratory movements, the patient may actually notice that he does seem to be a little "stiff." Perhaps there *is* something wrong with his back. With the aid of a sympathetic lawyer, the patient may proceed to file suit for his alleged injuries.

Here it is especially hard to distinguish between the malingerer's deliberate simulation of injury and the unconscious deception of a hysteric. Apparently in many hysterical cases there is an admixture of the two, in which conscious acting is superimposed on unconscious acting. In these cases the patient shows an amazingly rapid recovery once he has been properly compensated for his "injuries."

The relationship between compensation and hysterical illness symptoms has been graphically demonstrated in the case of writer's cramp. This was formerly thought to be an occupational disease brought on by too much writing and has been relatively common in England, where the disorder is recognized as a compensable disease under the British Workman's Compensation Act. In one study of psychoneurotic British soldiers, it was found that 171 (out of 1880) had writer's cramp but that only 6 of these had done much writing. Apparently the others simply developed their symptoms in the face of uncongenial jobs (Pai, 1947). In the United States, where this disorder is not a compensable disease, writer's cramp is practically unknown.

Hysterical patients are very suggestible and can frequently be made to evidence almost any symptoms that are suggested to them. Many times in the course of examining patients who complain of vague aches or pains, physicians inadvertently suggest symptoms of a suspected disease which are then readily picked up by the patient. As might be expected, the ability of the patient to simulate such symptoms accurately tends to be commensurate with his medical sophistication (Ziegler *et al.*, 1960).

There are diverse personality and stress determinants in conversion reactions, and a given case may be far more complicated than the relatively simple illustrations we have used. However, the basic dynamic pattern involves regression and the avoidance or reduction of anxiety-arousing stress by getting sick—thus converting an intolerable emotional problem into a face-saving physical-medical one in which the responsibility for corrective action is shifted from the patient to others. The secondary gains which often ensue then tend to perpetuate the neurotic reaction.

As in the case of other neurotic reactions, having to give up the illness symptoms would bring the hysterical patient face to face again with his real problems. Consequently, despite the fact that such patients often have a conscious verbalized desire to be "cured," they unconsciously resist treatment and rarely enter into the therapeutic situation with full cooperation.

Conversion symptoms have sometimes been removed by various "miracle" cures. Such cures are apparently based in part upon the suggestibility of the hysteric and in part upon the implicit promise that he will be relieved from all problems and conflicts if he simply has "faith." But unless there is also an acceptance of some philosophical or religious way of life which enables the patient to avoid or solve his problems, such "cures" are usually short-lived and the hysteric soon redevelops the same or other illness symptoms.

As in neurasthenia, tranquilizing drugs do not appear to be particularly effective although they may reduce diffuse anxiety and tension. Hypnosis and narcosis have proved to be helpful adjuncts to therapy, especially in removing illness symptoms. (Both these techniques will be discussed at greater length in Chapter 14.) As in the case of "miracle" cures, however, removal of symptoms does not necessarily mean a cure, since this procedure alone does not ordinarily get at the root of the problem. For a lasting cure, the patient must achieve a more mature and adequate personality adjustment and greater social and emotional competence.

Group conversion reactions. In our historical introduction in Chapter 2, it was pointed out that outbreaks of mass hysteria (St. Vitus' dance and biting manias) were common during the Middle Ages. In recent times such outbreaks have become a rarity. Schuler and Parenton, however, reported an interesting case of an epidemic of hysteria in a high school.[1] This episode is of particular significance because it demonstrates quite clearly the dynamics underlying the development of a hysterical conversion reaction in one high-school girl and its subsequent spread to others.

All of the students involved in this epidemic of hysteria were girls ranging in age from 16 to 18, who at the time were sophomores, juniors, or seniors in the high school. They were all normally attractive, intelligent, well informed, and apparently free from superstitious beliefs. The chronological sequence of events was somewhat as follows:

Saturday, January 28. Helen A., one of the more popular girls in the senior class, developed a spasmodic twitching and jerking of her right leg while watching the dancing at the annual Alumni Homecoming Dance.

Tuesday, February 21 (Mardi Gras). Public dance attended by Millie and Frances, two of the girls who subsequently developed the hysterical symptoms. About one o'clock Wednesday morning, after returning to her friend's home from the dance, Millie suddenly developed an involuntary convulsive jerking in the diaphragm, chest and neck.

Wednesday, February 22. Millie's disturbance continued during the day, but she attended all her classes. After returning home that afternoon, she was examined by the family's physician, who prescribed rest at home for a few days.

Thursday, February 23. The morning was rainy, and the pupils gathered in the assembly hall before the beginning of classes. At this time Helen was observed by many of the students while experiencing one of her attacks, which, by this time, had become a common occurrence.

Apparently nothing unusual took place during the first class period, but during the second hour in a French class, Frances began her involuntary spasmodic movements, which continued for some time without interruption and soon became noticeable to the class. She was then taken to the infirmary, where some of the older students attempted to care for her. In the meantime her friend Geraldine P., who sat at the next desk, had been getting increasingly nervous. In her own words: "First I trembled a little. Then everybody kept saying, 'Look at Geraldine.' And then I started jumping. Then they carried me upstairs to the infirmary and I started crying. They gave me ammonia, but that didn't help. Plenty of girls tried to hold me down, but they couldn't."

During the course of the preceding events another unusual development was taking place. A greatly agitated and poorly informed mother drove up in the family truck and loudly demanded her children. Over the public address system, which reached every room and the playground and was clearly audible for blocks around, the principal requested the specified children to report to his office immediately. Shortly thereafter these children returned to their respective rooms to get their belongings, and then left precipitately. Soon more cars and trucks began to stream in, and more and more

---

[1] Taylor and Hunter (1958) also have described a hysterical epidemic—in this case among female neurotic patients in a hospital ward.

children were called from their classes. With these further unexplained departures, coupled with the sounds of nervous crying, and hurried running to and fro in the halls, the curiosity and anxiety of the school children were tremendously activated. The principal, in a vain attempt to reassure the panicky students as well as the nervous and fearful parents, called a special assembly—but to no avail. For in the meantime news and rumors of the "strange goings-on" at the Bellevue High School were being spread by the returning parents and children, and the noise and confusion of arriving and departing cars were increasing. With the break-up of the assembly and the beginning of recess, the children scurried around and pressed forward in an attempt to see and hear as much as possible of the hysterical subjects. Some of the latter were to be seen in the principal's office, some were being administered ammonia water by a practical nurse in the infirmary, and still others, who had not developed the hysterical motor symptoms but who were making a material contribution to the general confusion by uncontrolled fearful crying, had been taken to the nearby teachers' residence. One of the witnesses described it as a "stampede."

By this time the confusion and disorganization had reached such proportions that the school bus drivers were assembled and school was dismissed by authority of the Parish Health Office. The children who remained were then taken home, and the last reported case of hysteria appeared in one of the girls during her bus ride home. The children had been talking and joking about the morning's developments, and this reaction was apparently precipitated by a chance remark of the driver, who reportedly said, "If you want to talk about the jerks, why don't you practice them?" Whereupon Mildred W. began to jerk and twitch in the same manner as the other cases.

During the same afternoon the director of the Parish Health Unit, together with other physicians, including two representatives of the State Board of Health, investigated several of the cases. The possibility that the epidemic might have had a bacteriological basis was explored and eliminated. Sedatives, rest, and staying at home from school for one or two weeks were prescribed, together with the suggestion that the less attention called to the hysterical symptoms, the sooner they would probably disappear. School reopened the following Monday but despite official measures of reassurance, a full week was required for attendance to return to normal (Adapted from Schuler and Parenton, 1943, pp. 221-235).

In attempting to explain this hysterical outbreak, the authors pointed out that it seemed to display the characteristic pattern of hysteria as an escape mechanism—in this case an unconscious attempt by the first patient, Helen, to avoid an unpleasant situation. Helen did not know how to dance and was apparently somewhat fearful of learning, yet the social events of the high school were compelling her to participate in this activity. The jerking of her leg muscles obviously made it impossible for her to dance, and so the painful conflict situation was resolved with no discredit to her. In addition, the attack brought her the attention and sympathy which she probably unconsciously desired, since the affections of a former admirer were being alienated by a vivacious freshman newcomer.

The second phase of the outbreak involved a number of other girls who were apparently unconsciously influenced by the repeated suggestion of the initial case and who were possibly rendered more suggestible by the strain and fatigue of social events of the preceding days and nights. Finally, the third phase involved the contribution of the more easily excited and less informed parents of the community, who, fearing that the malady was contagious and dangerous, rushed to save their children from a fate not clearly understood and therefore all the more fearful.

DISSOCIATIVE REACTIONS

Dissociative reactions, often classified as one type of hysteria, include amnesia, fugue, multiple personality, and somnambulism. In each case, the patient successfully blocks off part of his life from conscious recognition. Although these conditions are closely interrelated and follow dynamic patterns similar to those of the conversion reactions, they merit separate consideration in some detail. Dissociative reactions —excluding somnambulism—account for less than 5 per cent of all neurotic disorders.

Amnesia and fugue. Amnesia is a partial or total inability to recall or identify past experience. It may occur in a psychoneurosis, in a psychosis, or in connection with any of a variety of organic conditions, including delirium, head injury, and diseases of the nervous system. Where the amnesia is based upon brain pathology, it is generally complicated by an actual failure of retention and registration—the material is truly lost. Psychogenic amnesia, on the other hand, is usually limited to a failure to recall—the "forgotten" material is still there beneath the level of consciousness, as becomes apparent under hypnosis or in cases where the amnesia clears up. As we have noted, amnesia is also common in reactions to intolerably traumatic experiences, such as those which occur under the combat conditions of warfare and the "shock" conditions of civilian life.

Amnesia is sometimes feigned by individuals trying to avoid some stressful situation. In fact, in one study of 98 amnesia cases, mostly military personnel, it turned out that 41 were feigned (Kiersch, 1962).

Symptoms. In the typical psychoneurotic amnesic reaction, the patient cannot remember his name, does not know how old he is or where he resides, and does not recognize his parents, relatives, or friends. Yet his basic habit patterns, such as the ability to write, talk, and so on, remain intact, and he seems quite normal aside from the amnesia.

In this amnesic state the individual may retreat still further from his problems by going away in what is called a "fugue state." A fugue reaction, as its name implies, is a defense by actual flight. The patient wanders away from home, and then days, weeks, or sometimes even years later he suddenly finds himself in a strange place, not knowing how he got there and with complete amnesia for the period of the fugue. His activities during the fugue may vary from merely going on a round of motion pictures to traveling across the country, entering a new occupation and starting a new way of life.

Dynamics. The pattern in psychogenic amnesia is essentially the same as in conversion reactions except that instead of avoiding some unpleasant situation by getting sick the patient does it by forgetting (repressing or suppressing) certain traumatic events or stresses. Dissociative reactions involving repression, of course, take place on an unconscious level. In those involving suppression, on the other hand, the individual apparently consciously tells himself that he will not remember some traumatic event

or situation and subsequently believes and behaves as though he were amnesic for it (Kiersch, 1962).

In psychogenic amnesia, we typically find an egocentric, immature, highly suggestible personality faced with an acutely unpleasant situation from which he sees no escape. There is often a conscious impulse to run away from it all, but this solution is too cowardly to be accepted. Eventually, however, the stress situation becomes so intolerable that large segments of the personality and the stress situation itself are repressed, while more congenial patterns carry on in an amnesic or fugue reaction. In such dissociative reactions the patient appears quite normal and is able to engage in complex activities, which are often of a wish-fulfilling or compensatory nature. This is well illustrated in an interesting case described by Masserman.

"Bernice L., a forty-two-year-old housewife, was brought to the Clinics by her family, who stated that the patient had disappeared from her home four years previously, and had recently been identified and returned from R———, a small town over a thousand miles away. On rejoining her parents, husband and children she had at first appeared highly perturbed, anxious, and indecisive. Soon, however, she had begun to insist that she really had never seen them before, that her name was not Bernice L— but Rose P— and that it was all a case of mistaken identity; further, she threatened that if she were not returned to her home in R——— immediately, she would sue the hospital for conspiracy and illegal detainment. Under treatment, however, the patient slowly formed an adequate working rapport with the psychiatrist, consented to various ancillary anamnestic procedures such as amytal interviews and hypnosis, and eventually dissipated her amnesias sufficiently to furnish the following history:

"The patient was raised by fanatically religious parents, who despite their evangelical church work and moralistic pretenses, accused each other of infidelity so frequently that the patient often questioned her own legitimacy. However, instead of divorcing each other, the parents had merely vented their mutual hostility upon the patient in a tyrannically prohibitive upbringing. In the troubled loneliness of her early years the patient became deeply attached to her older sister, and together they found some security and comfort; unfortunately, this sister died when the patient was seventeen and left her depressed and unconsolable for over a year. After this, at her parents' edict, the patient entered the University of A—— and studied assiduously to prepare herself for missionary work. However, during her second semester at the University, she was assigned to room with an attractive, warm-hearted and gifted girl, Rose P—, who gradually guided the patient to new interests, introduced her to various friendships, and encouraged her to develop her neglected talent as a pianist. The patient became as devoted to her companion as she had formerly been to her sister, and was for a time relatively happy. In her Junior year, however, Rose P— became engaged to a young dentist, and the couple would frequently take the patient with them on trips when a chaperone was necessary. Unfortunately, the patient, too, fell 'madly in love' with her friend's fiancé, and spent days of doubt and remorse over her incompatible loves and jealousies. The young man, however, paid little attention to his fiancé's shy, awkward and emotionally intense friend, married Rose P— and took her to live with him in Canada. The patient reacted with a severe depression, the cause of which she refused to explain to her family, but at their insistence, she returned to the University, took her degree, and entered a final preparatory school for foreign missionaries.

"On completion of her work she entered into a love-less marriage with a man designated by her parents and spent six unhappy years in missionary outposts in Burma and China. The couple, with their two children, then returned to the United States and settled in the parsonage of a small midwest town. Her life as a minister's wife, however, gradually became less and less bearable as her husband became increasingly preoccupied with the affairs of his church, and as the many prohibitions of the village (e.g., against movies, recreations, liberal opinions and even against secular music) began to stifle her with greater weight from year to year. During this time the patient became increasingly prone to quiet, hazy reminiscences about the only relatively happy period she had known—her first two years in college with her friend, Rose P——and these years, in her day-dreaming gradually came to represent all possible contentment. Finally, when the patient was thirty-seven, the culmination of her disappointments came with the sickness and death of her younger and favorite child. The next day the patient disappeared from home without explanation or trace, and her whereabouts, despite frantic search, remained unknown to her family for the next four years.

"Under treatment in the Clinics, the patient recollected that, after a dimly remembered journey by a devious route, she finally reached A——, the college town of her youth. However, she had lost all conscious knowledge of her true identity and previous life, except that she thought her name was Rose P—. Under this name she had begun to earn a living playing and teaching the piano, and was so rapidly successful that within two years she was the assistant director of a conservatory of music. Intuitively, she chose friends who would not be curious about her past, which to her remained a mysterious blank, and thereby eventually established a new social identity which soon removed the need for introspections and ruminations. Thus the patient lived for four years as though she were another person until the almost inevitable happened. She was finally identified by a girlhood acquaintance who had known both her and the true Rose P— in their college years. The patient at first sincerely and vigorously denied this identification, resisted her removal to Chicago, where her husband was now assigned, and failed to recognize either him or her family until her treatment in the Clinics penetrated her amnesia. Fortunately, her husband proved unexpectedly understanding and cooperative, and the patient eventually readjusted to a fuller and more acceptable life under happily changed circumstances." (Masserman, 1961, pp. 35-37)

In his analysis of this case, Masserman pointed out that the patient's behavior enabled her to flee from an intolerable mode of living as Mrs. Bernice L—, the unhappy wife, and to substitute an intensely desired way of living, personified by Rose P—, the loved and successful artist. Her "new personality" was in no sense completely novel, but represented an unconscious selection and integration of certain patterns of the old.

It is interesting to note that a patient rarely engages in activities which would have been morally incompatible with his pre-fugue personality. Thus, in her identity as Rose P—, the patient neither married again nor engaged in any direct sexual activity, since "bigamy or unfaithfulness, conscious or not, would have been untenable." (Masserman, 1961, p. 37)

Multiple personality.   Dual and multiple personalities have received a great deal of attention and publicity in fiction, television, and motion pictures. Actually, however, they are rare in clinical practice. Only slightly more than

THE FOUR FACES OF EVE

A dramatic example of multiple personality was the widely publicized case of Eve White, a 25-year-old woman who sought therapy because of "severe and blinding headaches" often followed by "blackouts." Eve had been having serious marital conflicts and was separated (and subsequently divorced) from her husband. For financial reasons, her 4-year-old daughter lived with grandparents some 100 miles away from where Eve worked. Concern about the happiness of her daughter and fear of becoming a stranger to her added to Eve's stresses.

In therapy, Eve gave the appearance of a demure, retiring, and gently conventional person trying somewhat stoically to cope with severe personal frustrations. Then one day, during an early therapy session she appeared to be seized by a sudden pain and put both hands to her head. "After a tense moment of silence, her hands dropped. There was a quick, reckless smile and, in a bright voice that sparkled, she said, 'Hi there, Doc!' . . . there was in the newcomer a childishly daredevil air, an erotically mischievous glance, a face marvelously free from the habitual signs of care, seriousness, and underlying distress, so long familiar in her predecessor. This new and apparently carefree girl spoke casually of Eve White and her problems, always using *she* or *her* in every reference, always respecting the strict bounds of a separate identity. When asked her own name she immediately replied, 'Oh, I'm Eve Black.'" (Thigpen and Cleckley, 1957, p. 137).

The traits of the two personalities, as they continued to present themselves in ensuing therapy hours, may be summarized as follows:

	EVE WHITE	EVE BLACK
Appearance	Face: quiet sweetness, sadness Movements: careful, dignified Voice: gently modulated Dress: neat, conservative, inconspicuous No allergy to nylon	Face: pixie-like, mischievous, seductive Movements: suggested light-heartedness Voice: coarse, mirthful, teasing Dress: a little provocative, expensive Skin reacted to nylon by breaking out
Personality	Industrious worker and good housekeeper, literary tastes, not spontaneous, not deceitful, devoted to child, passive strength of character, admired by others	Attractive, likable, heedless, unthinking, quick, vivid, a rowdy wit, ready for any adventure, enjoyed teasing Eve White
Role	Role involved unspoken pathos; one felt she was doomed to be overcome.	Seemed strangely secure from stresses of everyday life and from grief.

After about 8 months of therapy, a third personality, Jane, appeared. Jane was more mature and capable than the retiring Eve White and had a much more vivid personality. Unlike Eve Black, Jane had wholesome attitudes both toward herself and toward cultural values. She remained conscious when either of the two Eves was in control, but for a long time had no memory of her past.

At last, after recalling and working through a highly traumatic experience—in which she had been forced by her mother to kiss her dead grandmother—a somewhat new personality emerged who was like Jane but more complete. This personality appeared to represent a resolution of the separate entities of Eve White and Eve Black and decided to call herself Evelyn (Eve's full legal name). Evelyn remarried and at last report had managed to establish a stable marriage and family life (Thigpen and Cleckley, 1954, 1957; Lancaster and Poling, 1958).

a hundred cases can be found all together in psychiatric records.

Symptoms. Multiple personality is a dissociative reaction to stress in which the patient manifests two or more complete systems of personality. Each system has distinct, well-developed emotional and thought processes and represents a unique and relatively stable personality. The patient may change from one personality to another at periods varying from a few minutes to several years. The personalities are usually dramatically different; one may be gay, carefree, and fun-loving, and another quiet, studious, and serious.

Various types of organization may exist between the different personalities. Usually the patient alternates from one personality to the other, and cannot remember in one what happened in the other. Occasionally, however, while one personality is dominant and functions consciously, the other continues to function subconsciously and is referred to as a *co-conscious* personality. In these cases the co-conscious personality is usually intimately aware of the thoughts of the conscious personality and of things going on in the world, but indicates its awareness through automatic writing or in some other roundabout way. On the other hand, the conscious personality usually knows nothing of the co-conscious personality.

Relationships may become highly complicated when there are more than two personalities, as in the famous Beauchamp case (Prince, 1930), which involved five different and distinct personalities. Some of the personalities may be mutually amnesic while others are only one-way amnesic.

Dynamics. In a sense we are all multiple personalities in that we have many conflicting and warring tendencies and frequently do things that surprise both ourselves and others. This is illustrated by many common sayings, such as "I don't know why I did it" or "I didn't think he had it in him." It is also illustrated by the peculiar behavior many men indulge in at conventions when they are away from their families and associates and "cut loose." In pathological cases, there is evidently such a deep-seated conflict between contradictory impulses and beliefs that a resolution is achieved through separation of the conflicting parts from each other and elaboration of each into a more or less autonomous personality system. In this way, the patient is able to realize incompatible systems of behavior without the stress, conflict, and guilt that would otherwise occur. As Murphy (1947) has pointed out, "the main dynamics in most cases of double and multiple personality seems to be an exaggeration of a conflict situation which is present in nearly all of us, namely, a conflict between a conforming and a guilty non-conforming trend." (p. 443)

This dynamic pattern is well brought out in Lipton's comprehensive and excellent analysis of the case of Sara and Maud K., excerpts of which are given below.

". . . in general demeanor, Maud was quite different from Sara. She walked with a swinging, bouncing gait contrasted to Sara's sedate one. While Sara was depressed, Maud was ebullient and happy, even though suicidal. Suicide and death meant nothing to Maud, and she saw nothing wrong or depressing in them.

". . . in so far as she could Maud dressed differently from Sara. Sara had two pairs of slippers. One was a worn pair of plain gray mules; the other, gaudy, striped, high-heeled, open-toed sandals. Sara always wore the mules. Maud would throw them aside in disgust and don the sandals. Sara used no make-up. Maud used a lot of rouge and lipstick, painted her fingernails and toenails deep red, and put a red ribbon in her hair. She liked red and was quickly attracted by anything of that color. Sara's favorite color was blue.

"Sara was a mature, intelligent individual. Her mental age was 19.2 years, I.Q., 128. A psychometric done on Maud showed a mental age of 6.6, I.Q., 43. Sara's vocabulary was larger than Maud's, and she took an intelligent interest in words new to her. When Maud heard a new word, she would laugh and mispronounce it, or say, 'That was a twenty-five cent one.' In sharp contrast to Sara, Maud's grammar was atrocious. A typical statement was, 'I didn't do nuttin'.' Sara's handwriting was more mature than Maud's.

"Sara did not smoke and was very awkward when she attempted it. Maud had a compulsion to smoke. At times she insisted she 'had to' and would become agitated and even violent if cigarettes were denied her. She would smoke chain fashion as many cigarettes as were permitted but two would satisfy her for a while. . . .

"Maud had no conscience, no sense of right and wrong. She saw no reason for not always doing as she pleased. She felt no guilt over her incestuous and promiscuous sexual relationships. Sara on the other hand had marked guilt feelings over her previous immoral sexual behavior.

"It seemed that Sara changed to Maud at the point when Sara's feeling of guilt was greatest." (1943, pp. 41-44)

Judging from the previous history of this patient, it would appear that the development of a dissociated personality in the form of Maud, had, among other things, enabled Sara to gratify her sexual desires by engaging in promiscuous sexual relations without conscious knowledge and hence without guilt feelings. Apparently Sara reverted to Maud when her guilt feelings over her own previous promiscuous sexual behavior became too intense and self-devaluating.

Further light is cast on Sara's background by the report of two of her previous high-school friends that "she was 'boy crazy' and was always chasing after some boy, often being rude to her girl friends, that she dyed her hair red, and that she smoked and used Listerine to deceive her mother about smoking. Sara denied all this but Maud readily recalled it." (Lipton, 1943, p. 47) It is interesting to note that this patient later became psychotic, apparently as a result of the failure of the dissociative reaction to solve her inner conflicts satisfactorily.

Because multiple personalities can be induced experimentally, the question has been raised as to whether perhaps all cases are only artificial creations produced inadvertently by suggestions of the therapist. This seems extremely unlikely, although undoubtedly some of the cases reported would fall in this category.

Somnambulism. Somnambulism is another neurotic dissociative reaction in which the ideas blocked off from consciousness are strong enough to determine the patient's behavior, though only during sleep. The episodes may occur nightly or only irregularly. They are most common in adolescence, but may occur in childhood or during adult life. Statistics on incidence are meager, but in an early study Jenness and Jorgensen (1941) reported that 5 per cent of a group of 1808 college freshmen admitted walking in their sleep. Sleepwalking is much more common among males than among females.

Symptoms. The patient usually goes to sleep in a normal manner, but sometime during the night arises and carries out some act. This may take him to another room in the house or even outside and may involve rather complex activities. He finally returns to his bed and to sleep and in the morning remembers nothing that has taken place. During the sleepwalking the patient's eyes are usually partially or fully open, he avoids obstacles, hears when spoken to, and ordinarily responds to commands such as to return to bed. Shouting or shaking the patient will usually awaken him, and he will be surprised and perplexed at finding himself in his strange and unexpected position. Usually such sleepwalking episodes last from fifteen minutes to a half-hour.

Contrary to popular opinion, many sleepwalkers injure themselves, sometimes quite seriously, as a result of activities they undertake in their sleep. In one case the patient was struck by a car while crossing the street in front of her home. There is also a popular belief that it is dangerous to awaken a sleepwalker. There is no evidence for this belief, unless, of course, violent measures are used which unduly startle him.

These patients usually evidence other neurotic symptoms in addition to their somnambulism. In a study of 22 successive cases of somnambulism reported in the armed forces, Sandler (1945) reported that 18 had been referred for psychiatric attention because of somatic complaints rather than because of their sleepwalking. He also noted that as sleepwalking episodes were reduced in the course of treatment, this symptom was often replaced by anxiety, hypochondriacal concern over alleged ailments, and other neurotic symptoms.

Dynamics. As Kessen and Mandler (1961) have pointed out, anxiety may be reduced not only by a flight from trauma but also by the action of specific inhibitors, such as the sucking response of the newborn. For some individuals, sleepwalking appears to fall into both categories as an anxiety inhibitor—to be both a symbolic escape from a stressful situation and an act that itself discharges and inhibits tension. Here it is important to note that sleepwalking occurs in individuals prone to the motor discharge of tensions rather than to nightmares or fantasy discharge (Anthony, 1959).

In personality make-up, somnambulists vary

considerably but typically manifest many of the characteristics found among conversion reaction patients—immaturity, suggestibility, and an exaggerated need for approval and security.

During adolescence, sleepwalking is often related to sexual conflicts, dependence-independence struggles, or other problems characteristic of this life period. In adulthood, somnambulism also appears to be precipitated by anxiety-arousing stress, such as that involved in assuming adult responsibilities and making decisions for oneself. Sadler (1945) reported that the precipitating cause in the cases he studied was usually some traumatic experience that had just occurred or was expected to occur in the near future.

Sometimes in somnambulism the patient attempts to carry out during sleep desires which are effectively suppressed or repressed from consciousness during the waking state. For example, in one case the patient would arise, walk to her mother's bedroom and kiss her on the cheek, and then return to her own room. It was found here that the patient and her mother had had a serious quarrel and, even though they had lived in the same house, had not spoken to each other for some four months. The sleepwalking apparently represented the patient's suppressed desire for an exchange of affection with her mother.

Treatment for all these types of dissociative reactions is essentially the same as for conversion reactions. Some amnesias clear up following methodical questioning, free association, hypnosis, and narcosis methods, and in occasional cases recovery is spontaneous. More extensive psychotherapy is ordinarily required, however, to deal with the underlying personality problems.

PHOBIC REACTION

A phobic reaction is a persistent fear of some object or situation which presents no actual danger to the patient or in which the danger is magnified out of all proportion to its actual seriousness. The following list of the common phobias and their objects will give some hint of the wide variety of situations and objects around which phobias may be centered:

acrophobia—high places
agoraphobia—open places
algophobia—pain
astraphobia—storms, thunder, and lightning
claustrophobia—closed places
hematophobia—blood
mysophobia—contamination or germs
monophobia—being alone
nyctophobia—darkness
ocholophobia—crowds
pathophobia—disease
pyrophobia—fire
syphilophobia—syphilis
zoophobia—animals or some particular animal

Some of these phobias involve an exaggerated fear of things which most of us fear to some extent, such as darkness, fire, and disease; others, such as phobias of open places or crowds, involve situations which elicit no fear in most people.

Phobic reactions occur most frequently among young adults and are much more common among women than men. Possibly the higher incidence among women relates to the fact that in our society strong fears are more acceptable among women than they usually are among men.

Symptoms. Most of us have minor irrational fears, but in phobic reactions such fears are intense and interfere with the everyday activities of the patient. For example, a patient with claustrophobia may go to great lengths to avoid entering a small room or passageway, even when it is essential for him to do so. Patients usually admit that they have no real cause to be afraid of the object or situation but say they cannot help themselves. If they fail to give in to the fear and do not avoid the phobic situation, they are overcome with anxiety, which may vary from mild feelings of uneasiness and distress to a full-fledged anxiety attack.

In addition to their phobias, patients usually show other symptoms, such as headaches, back pains, stomach upsets, dizzy spells, feelings of inferiority, fear of having a serious organic disease, and worry about "cracking up." In some cases phobic reactions may also be obsessive in nature, as when the patient has a persistent obsessive fear of contamination which dominates his consciousness. Fears of this type will be considered in the next section under "obsessive-compulsive" reactions.

Terhune (1961) has pointed out that the particular phobias patients develop are often influenced by the current culture. This is well brought out in a study by Kerry (1960) of four patients who had a phobia of outer space. The following are excerpts taken from the records of one of these patients—a tall, burly, married schoolteacher who was 33 years of age.

"He felt unsafe 'because the earth is a ball spinning around and I am on it.' Occasionally the horizon seemed to tilt and if he looked at a picture he felt it was about to turn over. He became completely incapacitated and had to be admitted to a hospital with the fear 'of going to disappear into outer space.' He felt that his feet were on the ground and that the sky was above and he had to keep reminding himself that the force of gravity was keeping him down—'otherwise I would float into space.' At this time he blamed his illness on his resentment of changes at work. Phrases which commonly occurred included: 'It's outer space that's getting me—the curvature of the globe makes everything insecure.' 'We are surrounded by a hostile envelopment—if I think about it I want to run for cover. . . .' If he went outside and saw other people he would say, 'Do these other people realize what danger they're in on this spinning ball we call a globe?' His fear was summed up by himself as follows: 'Primitive man had a fear of the sun and the moon and the stars, and I am the same.' " (1960, p. 1383)

Kerry's other three patients also

"felt the gravity of the globe and its movements to be precarious. They were preoccupied with fears of the earth deviating from its course and being destroyed in a collision in outer space. Artificial satellites were felt to increase this danger. In all four patients, the sight of the setting sun touching the horizon exacerbated the phobia. They were aware that the frightening character of this sight was due to the globe and the sun meeting within the visual field." (p. 1386)

Dynamics. Phobic reactions may occur in the context of a wide range of personality patterns and clinical syndromes. For this reason it is useful to understand their dynamic origins. Typically, phobias are attempts to cope with internal or external dangers by preventing their occurrence or carefully avoiding them. Thus phobias are considered simple defensive reactions. The patient *has* to give in to them because otherwise the threat will return and with it the anxiety. Three dynamic patterns have been emphasized in the development of phobic reactions.

1. *Displacement of anxiety.* A phobia may represent a displacement of anxiety from the stress situation which elicited it to some other object or situation. This mechanism is strongly emphasized in psychoanalytic theory and derives largely from Freud's case history of little Hans, published in 1909. On the basis of this case and subsequent clinical experience, Freud concluded that phobias represent displaced anxiety associated with the Oedipus complex. According to this theory, the child desires to possess his mother sexually and is jealous and hostile toward the father. The child therefore fears his father—and in particular dreads being castrated. The fear of the avenging father may then be displaced to some external and formerly innocuous object. In the case of the little five-year-old Hans, according to Freud, the fear was displaced to horses; now fear of being bitten by horses replaced fear of castration by the father. Freud concluded that phobias in adults develop only in people with disturbed sexual relationships—who, for example, have failed to resolve their oedipal problems.

Later investigators have pointed out that many kinds of stress situations may lead to phobic reactions through the mechanism of displacement. For example, a person who fears that he will be discharged from his job for inefficiency may develop an elevator phobia, which makes it impossible for him to get to the office where he works and hence protects him from embarrassment and anxiety-arousing self-devaluation. The following case shows the same mechanism.

A young man had started his first business venture by renting a very small store near the entrance to a large building and stocking it exclusively with neckties. He managed to make ends meet over a trial period of several months, but it was becoming obvious that his business venture was doomed to failure. About this time he noticed that the shop "seemed stuffy," that he didn't have any "elbow room." It seemed as if the walls were closing in on him, and he would feel compelled to go outside and get his "lungs full of fresh air." These feelings increased in frequency and intensity until he was forced to close the shop.

Here the protective function of the phobic reaction is easily seen. The patient did not have to admit failure or poor business ability. He had to close the shop for other reasons, and he was completely unaware of the real source of his anxiety and fear.

Arieti (1961) has also noted that many phobias may indicate a more generalized anxiety situation. Thus intense guilt feelings over immoral behavior may lead to phobias of objects or situations which are symbolically associated with anticipated punishment; a phobia of speaking in public may relate to the individual's more generalized fear that other people will detect his insufficiencies and "see him for what he really is"; or a phobia of traveling may hide a bigger fear of making excursions into life.

2. *Defense against dangerous impulses (internal threats).* A phobia may represent a defensive reaction which protects the individual from situations in which his repressed aggressive or sexual impulses might become dangerous. Here, too, the anxiety is displaced; the thing feared consciously is not the basic cause of his anxiety. Thus a husband may develop a phobia of lakes, swimming pools, and other bodies of water because on previous occasions he had persistent ideas of drowning his wife. Or a housewife may develop a phobia of sharp knives and refuse to keep one in the house because of repressed impulses to cut her husband's throat.

Similarly the individual may protect himself from unacceptable sexual impulses by developing phobic reactions. For example, 24-year-old Herbert S. sought psychological assistance because of a "morbid fear of syphilis which makes it impossible for me to have sexual relations." In the course of psychotherapy, it became apparent that this patient's syphilophobia represented a displacement of a fear of engaging in homosexual relations. His fear of contracting syphilis helped him to maintain sexually moral behavior. That it also prevented him from engaging in heterosexual relations—which he

viewed as moral—apparently stemmed from the fact that during intercourse his "mind was completely dominated by homosexual fantasies." These fantasies were highly anxiety-arousing and on a number of occasions had terminated in impotency, which he had found acutely embarrassing. Thus the syphilophobia was in the nature of a reaction formation which helped the patient to control his threatening inner impulses.

3. *Conditioning.* A phobia may develop out of a simple conditioned fear reaction. This mechanism is strongly emphasized in "learning theory." It has been established that a neutral stimulus which makes an impact on the individual at about the same time a fear response is evoked may acquire the ability to evoke fear on subsequent occasions. If the initial fear is intense or if the conditioning experience is repeated many times, the conditioned fear will show the persistence that is characteristic of neurotic fear (Wolpe and Rachman, 1960). In addition, there will be a generalization of fear reactions to stimuli resembling the conditioned stimulus.

Most of us probably have mild phobias based upon trauma, partially or wholly forgotten, or upon undesirable examples set by phobic parents. A child who has been attacked and bitten by a vicious dog may feel vaguely uneasy around dogs even though the original traumatic event has been forgotten and some reconditioning experiences have intervened. A mother who becomes terror-stricken at the sight of spiders may communicate her fears to her children. One patient with astraphobia traced his fear to a phobic mother who would take him into an inner room of the house when a storm was approaching and cower in terror each time a clap of thunder was heard. In such instances, of course, the phobia may occur in a personality context which does *not* involve immaturity, inability to adjust to adult responsibilities, fear of competition, or other factors commonly found in the neurotic nucleus. It is simply an isolated maladaptive response that has been learned.

As with other neurotic reactions, phobias may lead to various secondary gains, such as increased attention, sympathy, assistance, and some control over the behavior of others. If the individual does not want to go on a mountain trip, he may point out regretfully that he has acrophobia, or if he wants to avoid seeing a particular movie, he may discover from reviews or other sources that this particular picture contains many scenes which would activate his phobia. Of course, in many cases the patient is ridiculed for his apparently silly fears and finds interpersonal difficulties and social disapproval complicating his already difficult adjustment.

The treatment in phobic reactions depends upon the particular dynamic pattern underlying the phobia. If the phobic reaction is the result of a severe traumatic experience, therapy usually involves a program directed toward desensitization and extinction. This may involve reassuring the patient and encouraging him to enter into the phobic situation either alone or with someone in whom he has a great deal of confidence. Thus an individual who has almost drowned may be encouraged to go swimming again, or a pilot who has survived a crash unhurt may be encouraged to fly again as soon as it is feasible. This procedure is repeated until the specific phobia has been extinguished. In other instances active deconditioning procedures may be utilized in which the feared object or situation is associated with something pleasant rather than dangerous. The basic model for this type of approach is the now-famous experiment of Mary Cover Jones (1924) with a three-year-old boy who had acquired exaggerated fears centering around furry objects. These fears were eliminated by introducing a white rabbit in a wire cage at the end of the room when Peter was eating. Each day the rabbit was brought a little closer until Peter could eat with one hand while stroking the rabbit with the other. Interestingly enough, the newly conditioned positive response to the rabbit generalized to a large number of other objects, such as white rats, frogs, and rugs, which he had formerly feared. In a more recent study, Lazarus (1960) reported the case of John, an 8-year-old boy who developed a phobia of moving vehicles after having been involved in a motor accident. The first step was to reward the boy with a piece of his favorite chocolate whenever he made a positive comment concerning vehicles. By the third interview the boy could talk freely about all types of moving vehicles. Then a series of "accidents" with toy motor cars was demonstrated, and after each accident John was

given chocolate. Next John was seated in a non-moving vehicle. In this way slow progress was made, using chocolate reinforcement, until John was able to enjoy motor travel without anxiety. The proper handling of fears immediately after the traumatic experience can, of course, do much to prevent the development of phobias of this type.

Where the phobic reactions represent a symbolic displacement of anxiety centering around external or internal dangers, there is ordinarily a more widespread pattern of personality maladjustment. Essentially the patient is being passive and submissive and attempting to avoid rather than to cope with his problem on a more active and effective plane. Although certain reconditioning techniques may be used here to alleviate immediate handicapping symptoms, more extensive psychotherapy is ordinarily indicated.

Perhaps the need for a flexible and integrated therapeutic approach can best be illustrated by reference to school phobias. Such phobias—which occur among some 3 children per 1000 in the primary grades—may be associated with a combination of conditions: (a) fear of being separated (separation anxiety) from a dominant and overly protective mother, (b) pervasive feelings of inadequacy and anxiety when forced to function alone in peer-group situations, (c) communication of anxiety from the mother to the child concerning his entrance in school, and (d) traumatic events, such as being beaten up by the school bully (Eisenberg, 1958a, 1058b; Rachman and Costello, 1961; Leton 1962). Here it is evident that the particular pattern of etiological factors will determine what therapy will be most effective.

OBSESSIVE-COMPULSIVE REACTIONS

In obsessive-compulsive reactions, as with phobias, the patient recognizes the irrationality of his behavior, but seems compelled to think about something that he wishes not to think about or to carry out actions that he does not want to carry out. These irrational obsessive and compulsive reactions are many and varied and appear to constitute some 20 to 30 per cent of all pyschoneurotic disorders.

Symptoms. Most of us have experienced

thoughts of a somewhat obsessional nature, such as persistent thoughts about a coming trip or date, or a haunting melody that we cannot seem to get out of our mind. In the case of obsessive reactions, however, the thoughts are much more persistent, appear irrational to the patient, and interfere with his everyday behavior.

Obsessive thoughts may center around a wide variety of topics, from concern over bodily functions to suicide or to the solution of some scientific problem. Particularly common are obsessive fears of uncontrollable impulses. The patient may fear that he is going to shout some obscene word, or a father may have the obsessive idea of bashing in his son's head with a hammer, a wife of stabbing or poisoning her husband, a daughter of pushing her mother down a flight of stairs. Many times the thoughts are in the nature of fantasies rather than impulses to action on the part of the patient: the patient may find himself persistently wishing that his mother would die. To the patient such thoughts may appear not only irrational but also immoral, disgusting, or horrifying.

These obsessive thoughts usually begin with occasional ruminations which can at first be easily dismissed from the mind. Even at this stage the patient may experience some anxiety at the immoral or antisocial nature of the thoughts and may make a determined effort to get rid of them. But they continue to recur, and the more desperately he tries to rid himself of them the greater their persistence.

Even though obsessive ideas are not carried out in action, they remain a source of torment to the patient. Often the patient feels that he is going insane or that he is not fit to live. This pattern is illustrated in the case of a girl who

"complained of having 'terrible thoughts.' When she thought of her boy-friend she wished he were dead; when her mother went down the stairs, she 'wished she'd fall and break her neck'; when her sister spoke of going to the beach with her infant daughter, the patient 'hoped that they would both drown.' These thoughts 'make me hysterical. I love them; why should I wish such terrible things to happen? It drives me wild, makes me feel I'm crazy and don't belong to society; maybe it's best for me to end it all than to go on thinking such terrible things about those I love.'" (Kraines, 1948, p. 183)

In compulsive reactions the patient feels compelled to perform some act which, even during the process, seems absurd and strange to him. Compulsive acts vary from relatively mild, tic-like rituals, such as running the finger around under the collar, to more complicated ritualistic acts, such as tying one's tie exactly seven times before feeling satisfied. In many cases, the compulsive behavior seriously disrupts the individual's everyday behavior, as in the case of a patient who finds it necessary to wash himself as often as fifty times a day. The performance of the compulsive act usually brings a feeling of satisfaction, however, whereas if he tries to restrain the compulsion, he is overcome with anxiety and tension.

Actually, most of us show some compulsive behavior, such as touching fence posts, stepping over cracks in sidewalks, doodling while phoning, walking around ladders instead of under them, or turning away when a black cat crosses our path—but without the persistence or sense of compulsion of the neurotic. A public speaker often shows mild compulsive reactions—like licking his lips or hunching his shoulders—which are not characteristic of his behavior in a more secure situation.

Most of us also resort to minor obsessive-compulsive patterns under severe pressure or when trying to achieve goals which we consider of critical importance. Many historical figures have shown an "obsessive-compulsive" adherence to their goals despite discouragement and ridicule—Columbus persisted for eighteen years in his efforts to secure financial backing for his expedition to "India," and Darwin assembled evidence for twenty-two years before he would present his ideas on evolution.

Adaptive temporary obsessive-compulsive patterns under particularly difficult stress situations are described in the following excerpts from an analysis of the autobiographical reports of explorers.

"Admiral Byrd wanted 'to taste peace . . . quiet and solitude long enough to find out how good they really are.' He spent 6 months alone in the Antarctic. Dr. Alain Bombard, who wished to prove that shipwrecked people could survive at sea for an indefinite length of time, sailed alone across the Atlantic Ocean for 65 days on a life raft, subsisting solely on what food he could get from the sea. Both men, dedicated scientists, reacted to their isolation and loneliness in almost identical fashion.

"Both explorers found that while their lives were threatened daily by the hazards of their milieu, it was the constancy of their surroundings which seemed like a force which would destroy them. Both men felt that they could control themselves and their environment only by thoroughly organizing their days, assigning themselves to a strict routine of work, and spending no more than one hour at a time doing a task. In this way, each felt he proved to himself that he could control both himself and his environment. . . . Both men used the same mechanisms to fight off depression: controlling their thoughts, dwelling only on pleasant past associations and experiences and refusing to allow themselves to think about the anxiety-producing aspects of their situations." (Solomon *et al.,* 1957)

Neurotic obsessive-compulsive reactions, by contrast, are considered faulty adjustive techniques because they represent exaggerated defenses in the face of stresses which are not unduly upsetting to the normal person and because they make for rigidity of behavior and restriction of the individual's personality.

Dynamics. Either the obsessive thoughts or the compulsive actions may predominate in a given case, but both are parts of a total reaction pattern, and their dynamics are essentially the same. Several dynamic patterns have been delineated.[1]

1. *Substitutive thoughts and activities.* The obsessive-compulsive may defend himself from anxiety by persistently thinking of or doing something else each time threatening thoughts or impulses make their appearance. A person walking in a lonely place late at night might find the following thought continually persisting in his mind: "There is nothing to be afraid of—I am not afraid." In this way he attempts to allay his underlying fear. Similarly an individual who has severe inadequacy feelings in a given situation may "think positively" and persistently review the success he has achieved in other situations. In essence, "safe" obsessive thoughts are subtsituted for more unpleasant or dangerous ones.

The same dynamic pattern may underlie compulsive preoccupation with some activity, such as working on a new invention, writing the "truly

great" novel, or developing a system to beat the horses. The task may never be completed, but by working on it so hard the individual is kept too busy to deal with unpleasant problems, and he is too engrossed to think dangerous thoughts. In many cases the compulsive behavior may, of course, be directed toward a constructive task. It is judged neurotic because it is used as an escape from marital, sexual, interpersonal, or other problems with which the individual must cope if he is to achieve adequate personality integration and realize his potential as a person.

2. *Reaction formation.* Often obsessive-compulsive reactions represent more than avoidance by substitution. The individual may think or act in ways which are directly contradictory to his dangerous thoughts or impulses. For example, he may unconsciously attempt to cope with inner hostility by persistently thinking of brotherly love, or he may defend himself from underlying homosexual desires by developing a strong attitude of condemnation toward such behavior. In the case below, the patient defended himself against his hostile impulses toward his family by becoming obsessively concerned for their safety.

"A successful executive who, for various reasons, hated the responsibility of marriage and fatherhood, was obsessed many times a day with the idea that his two children were 'somehow in danger,' although he knew them to be safe in a well-run private day-school to which he himself brought them every morning. As a result, he felt impelled to interrupt his office routine thrice daily by personal calls to the school principal who, incidentally, after several months began to question the sincerity of the patient's fatherly solicitude. Similarly, the patient could not return home at night without misgivings unless he brought some small present to his wife and children, although, significantly, it

---

[1]Obsessive thoughts and compulsive actions may, of course, occur as part of other clinical syndromes. Masserman (1961) has cited the case of a soldier who in an acute fatigue state kept throwing out his arms in a peculiar gesture. This gesture could not be explained until the patient recalled under narcosis that in the heat and excitement of a night battle, he had machine-gunned a friend, and had suffered a remorse so great that he had an overpowering desire to throw away his gun and run blindly from the unbearable horror of the situation. In our later discussion of psychotic disorders, we shall see how obsessive-compulsive reactions may be related to delusional and hallucinatory behavior.

was almost always something they did not want." (Masserman, 1961, p. 43)

Here the patient's repressive defense was strengthened by preoccupation with attitudes and behavior directly opposed to his underlying hostility.

3. *Isolation of fantasy from affect.* In some cases, the dangerous desires may become conscious, but the individual is not aware that they represent fulfillment of his own wishes.

A farmer developed obsessive thoughts of hitting his three-year-old son over the head with a hammer. The patient was completely unable to explain his "horrible thoughts." He stated that he loved his son very much and thought he must be going insane to harbor such thoughts. Analysis of this case revealed that the patient's wife had suffered great pain in childbirth and has since refused sexual relations with the patient for fear of again becoming pregnant. In addition, she lavished most of her attention on the son, and their previously happy marriage was now torn with quarreling and bickering.

This patient's obsessive thoughts of violence toward his son had apparently developed out of a combination of repressed hostility toward the son, who had replaced him in his wife's affection, and wishful thinking in the direction of a return to their previously happy marital state, once the son was out of the way. However, the wish-fulfillment element remained unconscious; the patient vigorously and sincerely denied it when it was suggested to him. Although his unacceptable desires were not repressed, the mechanism of denial enabled him to avoid severe self-devaluation by freeing him of responsibility for the violent thoughts—they did not really seem to be his thoughts at all. Also, the affective element underlying his fantasies had been cut off through the defense mechanism of isolation, further helping to ensure that his fantasies would not be carried out in overt action.

4. *Guilt and fear of punishment.* Obsessive-compulsive reactions sometimes grow out of feelings of guilt and self-condemnation for ethically unacceptable desires or forbidden acts. In such cases there is usually considerable fear of possible punishment for the unforgivable thoughts or behavior. The resulting obsessive

thoughts usually reveal considerable self-devaluation, as well as symbolic attempts toward expiation and atonement.

A thirty-two-year-old high-school cooking teacher developed marked feelings of guilt and uneasiness, accompanied by obsessive fears of hurting others by touching them or by their handling something she had touched. She dreaded to have anyone eat anything she had prepared, and if students in her cooking class were absent, she was certain they had been poisoned by her cooking. In addition, she developed the obsessive notion that a rash at the base of her scalp was a manifestation of syphilis, which would gnaw at her brain and make a "drooling idiot" of her.

Accompanying the obsessive fears were compulsions consisting primarily in repeated hand-washings and frequent returns to some act already performed to reassure herself that the act had been done right, such as turning off the gas or water.

Analysis of this case revealed that the patient was a self-centered but highly sensitive and conscientious person. She had graduated from college with high honors and considered herself highly intelligent. About three years before her present difficulties she had married a noncollege man of whom she had been very much ashamed because of his poor English, table manners, and other characteristics which she thought led to a very poor social showing. As a result she had rejected him in her thinking and behavior and had treated him in what she now considered a very cruel manner. On one occasion she had also been unfaithful to him, which was very much against her moral training.

Over a period of time however, she came to realize that he was a very fine person and that other people thought highly of him despite his lack of social polish. In addition, she gradually came to the realization that she was very much in love with him. At this point she began to reproach herself for her cruel treatment of him. She felt that he was a truly wonderful husband, and that she was completely unworthy of him. She was sure her past cruelty and unfaithfulness could never be forgiven. "Heaven knows that every word he says is worth fifty words I say. If I were real honest and truthful I would tell my husband to leave me."

In this case the patient's obsessive fears of contaminating others and of having syphilis apparently grew out of her intense guilt feelings, self-devaluation, and fear of punishment as a result of her unethical behavior. These obsessive fears were also augmented by and designed to protect her from occasional returns of her forbidden sexual desires for relations with other men.

5. *"Undoing" or counteracting forbidden desires.* In some instances the individual may attempt to counteract forbidden desires or cleanse himself of guilt by means of compulsive rituals. For example, a young mother's hostile fantasies toward her daughter were so acutely traumatic that she repressed them. This repression was an extremely precarious defense, however, and the dangerous hostility often threatened to break through into consciousness. As a result, the patient unconsciously developed a compulsive defensive reaction: at crucial moments she felt compelled to make the sign of the cross, repeating "God protect my dearly beloved little daughter." Yet she had not the vaguest idea why she had to say it. It seemed senseless and silly to her and was interfering with her social relationships.

Compulsive hand-washing rituals often represent an attempt to cleanse oneself of guilt relating to sexual or other immoral behavior. In the case of the high-school cooking teacher, the hand-washing compulsion was a symbolic effort to cleanse herself of both her past and present sins and make herself worthy of her husband. Lady Macbeth's symbolic and compulsive hand-washing after participating in the bloody murder of King Duncan is another well-known example.

The following case is that of a fourteen-year-old boy whose compulsive actions were interpreted as an attempt to counteract or undo forbidden behavior.

". . . This boy's excessive cleanliness first showed itself at the age of thirteen, when it was noticed that he washed his hands many times during the day. Later he began to bathe frequently. Frequently he stayed two or three hours in the bathtub. On a number of occasions he daubed iodine on his hands and face. He told his parents that he had scratched himself and wanted to prevent infection. In addition to iodine, he had bought mercurochrome and other antiseptics for use in 'emergencies.' He also used a boric acid solution to wash his eyes every evening. The parents stated that he refused to play ordinary games with other children because he did not want to soil his hands. When asked to explain his concern regarding cleanliness, he stated that he realized that he washed more than other boys, but that in his case there were real reasons. He believed that his skin was of such a texture that it retained dirt and germs, and he therefore was forced to wash and scrub himself.

"No amount of persuasion was successful in deterring the boy from this until his original conflicts began to be solved. He stated that he had been greatly worried about his guilt regarding his previous activities with other boys. His parents discovered that he took part in sex play and punished him. They had frequently lectured him on the evils of 'immoral' behavior and on one occasion, when he was nine, made him sign a pledge never to smoke or drink even beer. They also told him how some terrible diseases result from masturbation. . . . He stated that he had 'sworn off' masturbating on many occasions, and after each time he masturbated he felt thoroughly ashamed of himself. He also believed that he was deficient in character and will-power because he could not stop. He stated, 'I know it's a dirty habit and if anyone finds me out they will think terrible things about me.' After many interviews and much discussion, he began to change his attitude regarding the immorality of his past behavior and the possible consequences of his supposed moral transgressions. His excessive cleanliness gradually decreased and he was able to take part in the activities of other boys without feelings of unpleasantness from soiling his hands and clothes." (Sherman, 1938, pp. 226, 227)

Unfortunately sex, dirt, and guilt are commonly associated, and many individuals are much better indoctrinated in the sinfulness of sex than in accurate information concerning it. Thus it is not surprising that attempts at symbolic cleansing in relation to sexual fantasies or behavior are often found in obsessive-compulsive reactions.

6. *Only way out of a catastrophic situation.* Sometimes an obsessive-compulsive pattern emerges in the face of a specific stress situation which the individual views as potentially overwhelming. This is probably an exaggeration of the process at work in the case of the two explorers (page 222).

A college girl was engaged to a naval officer. After returning from several months in the South Pacific, he broke off the engagement on the grounds that she had been unfaithful to him while he was gone. Her tears and violent protestations of innocence were of no avail—he was firmly convinced she had been unfaithful.

The patient was "terribly in love" with him, had centered all her future hopes and plans around him, and felt that she could not live without him. Consequently, in desperation she went around to her friends and acquaintances requesting that they talk to her fiancé and substantiate her innocence. She even had some of them make out affidavits to the same effect. She considered her actions somewhat peculiar and inappropriate but told them that "it seems to be the only thing I can do." Despite all this evidence, however, her fiancé refused to believe in her. At this point the patient took a leave of absence from her secretarial position to devote herself full time to proving her innocence. In the course of this pursuit she sought psychological assistance to find out how she might better prove her faithfulness. She was sure that she must have overlooked something—that there must be some way to convince him.

The possibility that her fiancé was using this as a subterfuge to break off their engagement she could not admit, for such an admission would leave her face to face with a catastrophic situation—the irrevocable loss of her fiancé and the crumbling of all her hopes and plans. Consequently, she compulsively held onto this one possible solution to her problem—to prove her innocence to his satisfaction. The only alternative was catastrophic stress and a complete breakdown, which in fact took place when subsequent events finally forced her to the realization that her task was hopeless and that she had lost her fiancé to another girl.

In this case the stress situation was admittedly a difficult one. However, the rigid and exaggerated defensive pattern which followed and the eventual nervous breakdown indicated that it had hit a particularly vulnerable spot in the patient's personality.

7. *Security and predictability.* Confronted with a world that seems highly complex and dangerous, the inadequate neurotic may attempt to maintain some semblance of order and control by becoming unduly meticulous and methodical. A rigid pattern provides some security and predictability and helps to prevent anything from going wrong. But if the slightest detail gets out of order, the entire structure is endangered and the individual feels threatened and anxious.

A case which illustrates this pattern is that of a patient who, prior to hospitalization, had his life ordered in the most minute detail. He arose in the morning precisely at 6:50, took a shower, shaved, and dressed. His wife had breakfast ready precisely at 7:10 and followed a menu which he worked out months in advance. At exactly 7:45 he left for the office where he worked as an accountant. He came home precisely at 5:55, washed and read the evening paper, and had dinner precisely at 6:30, again as per menu. His schedule was equally well worked out for evenings and week ends, with a movie on Tuesday, reading on Wednesday, rest on Monday and Thursday, and bridge on Friday. Saturday morning he played golf and Sunday morning and evening he attended church. Saturday evening usually involved having guests or visiting others. He was fastidious in his dress. Each shirt had to be clean and unwrinkled, his suit pressed every two days, and so on. His demands, of course, also included his wife, who was inclined to be easy-going and was upset when he "blew up" at the smallest variation from established routine.

By means of his carefully ordered existence the patient managed to make a reasonably successful adjustment until he became involved in a business deal with a friend and lost a considerable sum of money. This proved too much for him and precipitated a severe anxiety reaction with considerable agitation and depression necessitating hospitalization.

In other instances such a compulsive following of a daily routine, particularly a socially desirable and ethical one, helps the neurotic to establish automatic control over dangerous inner desires. He avoids situations which might stimulate such desires as well as situations which might permit their expression. For example, an exhausting schedule of daily activities, involving rigid adherence to conditions which make sexual behavior impossible, prevents the individual from engaging in sexual behavior he considers immoral.

Research studies dealing with the personality make-up of obsessive-compulsives have not been entirely consistent in their findings. It would appear, however, that they tend to have unhealthy attitudes toward sex and to be rigid, methodical, conventional, conscientious, and submissive in social situations (Stengel, 1951; Ingram, 1961; Clancy and Norris, 1961; Cattell and Scheier, 1961). In addition, they share with other neurotics the characteristic feelings of inadequacy, guilt proneness, and threat susceptibility in the face of a seemingly dangerous world.

These characteristics make the obsessive-compulsive highly sensitive to both inner and outer threats. His primary means of defense against *external* threats is to try to impose rigid order, thus making the world safer and more predictable. As Goldstein (1940) has demonstrated in the case of brain-injured patients, a compulsive and careful ordering of one's world keeps a handicapped individual from being overwhelmed by complexities and dangers' and enables him to make some sort of adjustment. The more careful and precise the order, the less likely is there to be a slip-up. And the greater the degree of threat and consequently of aroused anxiety, the more likely is a repetitive, obsessive-compulsive pattern to become "fixed" or "frozen."

The semimagical signs and rituals common in obsessive-compulsive reactions are part of this ordering of a dangerous world and are probably comparable to the repetitive and rigid rituals long used by primitives as a means of warding off evil forces and ensuring the cooperation of supernatural powers. If they are to be effective, such rituals must be faithfully observed and performed in rigidly prescribed ways. Even such a simple act as knocking on wood after bragging is really a ritual designed to ward off bad luck. Similarly, as we have noted, compulsive rituals such as making the sign of the cross may be designed to ward off the effects of evil thoughts.

Anything that might threaten the order of his precariously structured world is viewed as a serious menace by the neurotic. As in any well-planned military operation, failure of any detail may threaten the entire operation. For this reason, decisions of any magnitude represent serious threats and lead to vacillation and uneasiness.

Impulses which are considered unacceptable or dangerous are also perceived as a threat to this carefully ordered world. Consequently, the patient tries desperately to suppress these impulses, but in so doing, a strange paradox develops: the more he tries to suppress them, the more they return to haunt him, partly because of the immediate threat they present to

his precariously structured world and partly because of the emotional motive power of sex, guilt, or pent-up hostility. The whole situation is aggravated, too, by the patient's overly rigid conscience. He exaggerates the seriousness of the most minor unethical impulses and actions, which everyone experiences sometimes but which most people handle easily and do not take so seriously.

The patient attempts to defend himself against such *inner* threats by substitution, isolation, undoing, and other ego-defensive measures which form part of his total obsessive-compulsive reaction pattern. Even though hostile, sexual, or other dangerous impulses may manage to enter consciousness, they are cut off from their emotional base. And by means of compulsive rituals, he may undo or atone for his guilt-arousing fantasies. In this way, however injurious they are to the individual's peace of mind, they are safely contained and are not carried out in antisocial action.

The obsessive-compulsive individual pays a high price for his neurotic defenses in rigidity, lack of openness to new experience, and restriction of his "life space." Although such individuals are likely to remain basically rigid and restricted in their personality make-up, psychotherapy can often be of marked assistance in clearing up their more disabling symptoms and removing blocks to long-range personal growth.

NEUROTIC DEPRESSIVE REACTION

In neurotic depressive reactions,[1] the individual reacts to some distressing stress situation with more than the usual amount of sadness and dejection and often fails to return to normal after a reasonable period of time. Although such reactions may last for weeks or even months, they do eventually clear up. In some cases a mildly depressed mood remains after more severe symptoms have abated. Neurotic depressive reactions appear to constitute some 20 to 30 per cent of psychoneurotic disorders.

Symptoms. The general appearance of the

---

[1]The term *neurotic depressive reaction* is synonymous with *reactive depression* and is to be ·distinguished from psychotic depressions, which are much more severe both in degree and in duration.

SUMMARY CHART OF PSYCHONEUROTIC DISORDERS

REACTION	MAJOR SYMPTOMS	BASIC DYNAMICS
Anxiety	"Free floating" anxiety, usually punctuated by acute attacks	Handling of internal or external threats by simple repression. Anxiety not yet "bound" or controlled by ego defenses
Asthenic	Feelings of weakness, fatigue, lack of enthusiasm; somatic complaints	Protection of self from anxiety aroused by unsatisfactory life situation in which individual feels trapped. Utter discouragement—feels too tired and sick to continue fight
Conversion	Simulation of actual organic illness—may involve varied sensory, motor, or somatic illness symptoms	Getting sick to escape from anxiety-arousing stress situation
Dissociative	Amnesia, fugue, multiple personality, somnambulism	Escape from anxiety-arousing conflicts by isolating or dissociating opposite poles of the conflict; in fugue reaction, for example, the conflict between fighting and withdrawal is solved by becoming amnesic and running away
Phobic	Irrational fears which individual realizes are irrational but which lead to anxiety if not heeded	Persistent conditioned fear or defensive reaction to protect self from anxiety-arousing stress by displacing anxiety from the actual danger to some symbolically related aspect of it which then protects patient from having to face the stress situation itself
Obsessive-compulsive	Persistent thoughts or impulses which the individual realizes are irrational but which he cannot avoid	Defensive reactions which protect the individual against internal and external threats by substitutive activities, reaction formation, isolation of anxiety-arousing desires from their affective base, counteracting of fears by compulsive rituals and by an obsessive "ordering" of the situation so that everything is under control and nothing can go wrong
Neurotic depressive	Feelings of dejection, discouragement, self-depreciation	Extreme discouragement resulting from environmental setbacks with part of the anxiety aroused by these setbacks allayed by intropunitiveness (self-punishment)

patient is one of dejection, discouragement, and sadness. Typically there is a high level of anxiety and apprehensiveness, together with diminished activity, lowered self-confidence, constricted interests, and a general loss of initiative (Gutheil, 1959). The patient usually complains of difficulty in concentrating, although his actual thought processes are not slowed up. Often he experiences difficulty in going to sleep and during the night he may awaken and be unable to go back to sleep. In many cases he has somatic complaints and feelings of tension, restlessness, and vague hostility.

The following is typical of a conversation with a neurotic depressive and illustrates the characteristic feeling tone.

Pt.: Well, you see, doctor, I just don't concentrate good, I mean, I can't play cards or even care to talk on the phone, I just feel so upset and miserable, it's just sorta as if I don't care any more about anything.

Dr.: You feel that your condition is primarily due to your divorce proceedings?

Pt.: Well, doctor, the thing that upset me so, we had accumulated a little bit through my efforts—bonds and money—and he (sigh) wanted one-half of it. He said he was going to San Francisco and get a job and send me enough money for my support. So (sigh) I gave him a bond, and he went and turned around and went to an attorney and sued me for a divorce. Well, somehow, I had withstood all the humiliation of his drinking and not coming home at night and not knowing where he was, but *he* turned and divorced me and this is something that I just can't take. I mean, he has broken my health and broken everything, and I've been nothing but good to him. I just can't take it doctor. There are just certain things that people—I don't know—just can't accept. I just can't accept that he would turn on me that way.

The neurotic depressive's symptoms make the performance of his everyday tasks difficult but usually not impossible. His major difficulty seems to lie in his inability to concentrate and in lowered levels of activity and initiative. However, in very severe reactive depressions the patient may be unable to work and may sit alone hopelessly staring into space, able to see only the dark side of life. In such cases he is likely to need hospitalization for adequate treatment and safeguard against possible suicide.

Dynamics. All of us have the blues sometimes and may become greatly depressed at the death of a loved one, a disappointment in love, an accident, some occupational setback, or feelings of guilt concerning failure or unethical desires or behavior. Neurotic depressive reactions occur in a personality predisposed to overreact to such stresses and lacking in the resiliency most people show.

Typically the neurotic depressive reveals low ego strength together with rigid conscience development and a proneness to guilt feelings (Cattell and Scheier, 1961; Cattell *et al.,* 1962). Common also are tendencies toward introversion and marked mood swings. When additional stress comes, it tends to overwhelm an already precariously adjusted individual.

Often the clinical picture in neurotic depressive reactions is complicated by hostility toward loved ones. This hostility is typically repressed because of its dangerous and unethical implications but may manifest itself in hostile fantasies that arouse feelings of guilt. Now if the loved person is killed or critically injured, the patient's normal feelings of grief are augmented by intense guilt, as if his hostile fantasies somehow had brought about the tragedy. Where the neurotic was actually partially responsible for the tragedy, as in an automobile accident, his feelings of guilt and self-condemnation may be extremely severe. Here his intropunitive self-condemnation may be a means of allaying his guilt by punishing himself for his behavior.

Neurotic depressives often use their symptoms to force support and sympathy from others for their predicament. One patient telephoned her therapist and told him that she was going to commit suicide. Special precautions were taken, although the patient made no serious effort of a suicidal nature. In a later therapeutic session, the therapist asked the patient why she had called him and threatened suicide. The patient explained that she thought the doctor was not taking her symptoms and hopeless situation seriously enough and was not showing proper sympathy and appreciation for her desperate plight. By her threat of suicide she hoped to make him realize that he "just had to do something for her immediately."

Most persons suffering from reactive depressions can describe the traumatic situation which led to their depression although they may not be able to explain their overreaction to the situation. Usually antidepressant drugs, supportive measures, and short-term psychotherapy are effective in alleviating the depression and helping the patient toward better adjustment. Elec-troshock therapy may be used as an emergency measure in clearing up the depressive symptoms, although newer drug therapies have made this more drastic procedure largely unnecessary. Only effective psychotherapy is likely to change the neurotic personality structure.

General Etiology of the Neuroses

In our preceding discussion we have reviewed several specific types of neurotic reactions and the key dynamic factors in each. Now let us turn to an evaluation of the role of biological, psychological, and sociological factors in the neuroses in general.

BIOLOGICAL FACTORS

In the neuroses, as in other types of psychopathology, the precise role of inherited predispositions and constitutional factors has not been delineated. Ample evidence from army records and from civilian studies indicates that the incidence of psychoneurotic disorders in the family history of neurotics is much higher than that for the general population (McNeel and Dancey, 1945; Sheps, 1944; Shields and Slater, 1961; Slater and Woodside, 1951). But the extent to which such findings reflect the effect of heredity is not known.

Slater and Woodside (1951) compared 100 neurotic soldiers and their wives with a control sample of 100 normal soldiers and their wives. In both groups there was a high degree of similarity between husbands and wives in height, intelligence, and level of education. In addition, the wives of the neurotic soldiers showed significantly more neurotic disorders than did the wives of the control sample. These investigators concluded that assortive mating might lead to a disturbed family environment which would perpetuate neurotic patterns from generation to generation. This conclusion is supported by later findings indicating that the family structure set up by neurotic parents tends to foster neurotic development in children (Ehrenwald, 1960; Fisher *et al.,* 1959).

Sex, age, glandular functioning, and other physiological factors have been investigated in relation to the neuroses without illuminating the etiological pattern. However, the interaction of biological and psychological factors in the production of neuroses can readily be seen. Faulty attitudes and psychological reactions lead to biological malfunction with very real somatic symptoms (heart palpitations, high blood pressure, and so on) which themselves become a cause of worry. This fearfulness, in turn, further augments the somatic symptoms. And if apparent or real illness helps to free the individual from having to face an unpleasant life situation, the stage is set for the maintenance of neurotic illness.

In addition, the loss of sleep, poor appetite, fatigue, and irritability resulting from prolonged emotional tension lower the general level of *both* biological and psychological stress tolerance. In severe cases, this may include some degree of impairment of higher neural functioning, particularly in relation to the balance between excitatory and inhibitory processes (Beliaeva, 1962; Wortis, 1962). Cattell and Scheier (1961) refer to these end results of chronic emotional mobilization as *low adaptation energy* and *neurotic debility;* it is important to remember that they are results of the neurotic reaction, not the primary cause of it.

Several constitutional factors, such as dispositional timidity and ease of conditioning, have been studied for possible relationship to neurotic disorders. Cattell and Scheier (1961) have concluded that dispositional timidity acts to magnify anxiety in relation to both inner and outer threats. Studies of the relationship between neuroses and ease of conditioning will be examined in the next section. However, on the basis of research findings so far, it is apparent that the role of constitutional factors in neurotic disorders is neither simple nor obvious.

PSYCHOLOGICAL FACTORS

Several psychological theories of the neuroses have been advanced. Although these are by no means mutually exclusive, they may be categorized under three headings for convenience in discussion: (a) learned maladaptive behavior, (b) stress and decompensation, and (c) immaturity and guilt.

Learned maladaptive behavior. A number of investigators take the view that all neurotic reactions constitute unadaptive responses learned according to the usual principles of reinforcement. For example, they see any phobic reaction as a simple conditioned fear response; an anxiety reaction is regarded as a conditioned "alarm neurosis" with a habitual attitude of anxiety in relation to life stresses; obsessive-compulsive reactions are seen as learned ways of coping with anxiety-generating situations. Once established, a given reaction may then come to be elicited by a wide range of situations through the process of stimulus generalization. It is thought that these neurotic reaction patterns usually arise out of early conditioning experiences although they may also be learned during later life periods.

In many cases, such conditioned neurotic responses are extinguished over a period of time as a result of a lack of reinforcement or subsequent "deconditioning" experiences. Thus a traumatic experience leading to a cat phobia may not be repeated, or subsequent pleasant associations with furry animals may dissipate the earlier fear. In many instances, however, phobias persist despite a lack of repetition of the traumatic experience. Here Eysenck (1963) has concluded that the phobia is reinforced because it does reduce anxiety and tension. For example, each time the child sees a cat, she may become anxious and run away. Since this response reduces her anxiety, it reinforces her phobic reaction. It also tends to preserve the original conditioned fear by making reality testing and desensitization impossible. It can readily be seen that either repeated trauma or rein-

A study reported by Eysenck (1961) measured a group of normal subjects and six groups of neurotics on a battery of objective tests. Statistical analysis of the scores yielded two major factors, introversion-extroversion and neuroticism. As the graph shows, the groups were well differentiated along these dimensions. Eysenck's interpretation of these results is described in the text.

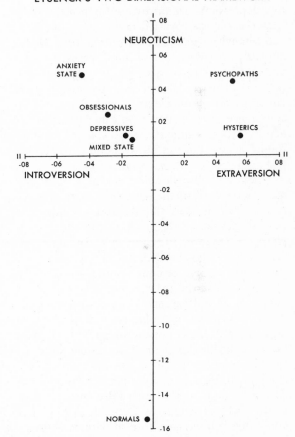

EYSENCK'S TWO-DIMENSIONAL FRAMEWORK

forcement through the reduction of anxiety can lead to maintenance of other neurotic reactions as well as phobias.

Eysenck (1960, 1963), whose writing has championed the behavioristic approach to neuroses, has also emphasized the role of ease of conditioning in neurotic disorders. Because of greater autonomic reactivity, introverts presumably form quick and strong conditioned reactions and are hence prone to "surplus conditioned reactions" involving fears and anxieties which leave them vulnerable to diverse environmental stresses. On the other hand, extroverts presumably are deficient in the capacity to form conditioned reactions, fail to acquire many needed adaptive responses, and are deficient in socialization—are weak in conscience development and unwilling to take responsibility. On the basis of their studies Eysenck and Claridge (1962) concluded that anxiety reactions, phobic reactions, obsessive-compulsive reactions, and reactive depressions are introverted neuroses, while hysteria is an extroverted neurosis.

Although Eysenck's formulation would appear to be borne out in many cases, its general applicability is questionable. Cattell and Scheier (1961) did not find hysterics to be either predominantly extroverted or weaker in conscience development than other neurotic reaction types. Similarly, Sweetbaum (1963) found anxiety but not introversion-extroversion to be related to ease of conditioning.

Unquestionably, however, learning does play an important role in the development of neurotic reactions in the sense that they are not inherited but are developed by the individual in his attempts to cope with life situations. And although further research is needed, it also appears highly probable that ease of conditioning—aside from introvertive or extrovertive tendencies—is an important etiological factor in many neurotic reactions. However, a simple conditioning model of learning does not appear adequate to explain the complexities of neurotic reaction patterns. In fact, conditioning principles have proved inadequate to explain many aspects of animal behavior, let alone that of man (Breland and Breland, 1961). To state, as Eysenck (1963) has done, that "all we have to deal with in neurosis is conditioned maladaptive behavior" (p. 868) is to ignore the relevance and utility of neurotic symptoms for meeting the patient's particular current needs and problems. Random responses reinforced in the past would hardly just happen to suit present defensive and protective purposes so well.

Most often, neurotic reactions seem to be exaggerations of ego defensive techniques we all learn for coping with threatening situations. Sometimes we learn these techniques through imitation of parental models (Bandura, 1962); sometimes they have no counterpart in the individual's immediate situation but seem more in the nature of "provisional tries" (Hilgard, 1950)

or "plans" (Miller *et al.,* 1960). And though often undertaken unconsciously, they are in keeping with the individual's assumptions about his world. There is a consistency in his life style: he is not a bundle of independent responses. Once adopted, of course, neurotic reactions may be continually reinforced and maintained. But aside from relatively simple conditioned fears, it would appear that neurotic reactions reflect immaturities and faulty assumptions and evaluations and stem primarily from desperate attempts to deal with seemingly insurmountable problems.

Stress and decompensation. Neurotic reactions may be precipitated by diverse types of stress situations. In general, the key stresses center around (a) failure to live up to unrealistic aspirations, with feelings of self-devaluation and inferiority; (b) unacceptable desires and "weak spots" arising from early trauma; (c) seemingly impossible choices or decisions; (d) dissonant cognitions in relation to one's self-structure; and (e) a frustrating life situation which robs one of meaning and hope. For the most part, the neurotic reaction pattern which results seems to be determined primarily by the personality make-up of the individual rather than by the stress situation, although there is some evidence that asthenic reactions are more apt to appear as defenses against frustrating and seemingly hopeless life situations and dissociative reactions as defenses against internal threats. Again it should be emphasized that we are dealing here with stress situations which may be relatively severe but which are met by most individuals without resort to neurotic defenses.

1. *Unrealistic aspirations.* The individual's failure to live up to his aspirations, with resulting self-devaluation and feelings of inferiority, has been emphasized by a number of eminent personality theorists. Adolf Meyer (1948) emphasized the neurotic's unrealistic level of aspiration and lack of self-acceptance. He felt that many people get into difficulty because they are unable to "accept their own nature and the world as it is, and to shape their aims according to their assets." (p. 539) Rather they seem to suffer from a false sense of competition which makes them set unrealistic goals. Then when they fail, they develop feelings of inferiority, apprehensiveness, and other faulty emotional attitudes which eventually lead to a "break in compensation" and the use of neurotic defensive measures.

Alfred Adler (1935), too, emphasized the importance of deep-seated feelings of inferiority in relation to the abilities and accomplishments of others. He believed that in the neurotic such underlying feelings are exaggerated into an *inferiority complex* which leads the individual to overcompensate for his feelings of inferiority by striving to triumph over others and dominate them in order to prove his superiority, or to avoid competition and comparison with others by getting "sick." Although Adler's approach may not be applicable to all neurotic reactions, it does contribute to the understanding of many neuroses in our highly competitive society.

A related way of describing this stress situation and its neurotic aftermath is in terms of a marked discrepancy between the individual's real and idealized self-image—between his view of himself as he is and his view of what he thinks he could and *should* be. To maintain an inner sense of unity and to protect himself from the devaluation elicited by these conflicting self-images, the individual resorts to neurotic or other pathological defensive reactions.

2. *Unacceptable desires and "weak spots."* Conflicts centering around dangerous desires and childhood trauma have been emphasized by the psychoanalytically oriented theorists. The major origin of the neuroses is assumed to be the frustration of instinctual desires by social experience and the resulting conflict between instinctual demands and learned social restraints.

In addition to conflicts, later analytically oriented writers, including Fenichel (1944) and Horney (1945, 1950), have emphasized childhood emotional experiences which lead to "weak spots" and faulty self- and environmental evaluations as the nucleus on which later neurotic reactions are built. Fenichel has pointed out that situational stresses which reactivate childhood traumas are particularly potent in the production of neurotic reactions in psychologically predisposed individuals. We saw this pattern in the case of the man who adjusted satisfactorily in adult life until he had a critical supervisor who reactivated his old fears of rejection by an authority figure and precipitated a neurosis.

The child's hostile reaction toward rejecting parents has been particularly emphasized by Horney as a basic nucleus for later neurotic reactions. Since this hostility is too dangerous to express openly, it must be repressed. If he is to be loved, he must submit to parental injustices and conform rigidly to parental standards. Thus he submerges many of his own desires and needs and spends much of his energy fighting his own dangerous impulses. Such neurotic individuals usually reveal an underlying lack of self-acceptance and a tendency to identify with and strive toward an immature and unrealistic "ego-ideal."

3. *Impossible choices.* The importance of life situations involving seemingly insoluble conflicts has been emphasized by many investigators. Combs and Snygg (1959) cited the case of a middle-aged schoolteacher who had failed to marry due to overattachment to her mother and who now found herself in a romantic relationship with her married principal. Although she felt guilty and was running the risk of social exposure and loss of employment, she also felt the need to grasp what she considered her last possibility of romance. To continue the relationship was threatening, but to give up her man was equally intolerable. Now under the pressure of external events which required some sort of decision on her part—either to accept the guilt and risk involved or to discontinue the relationship—her ability to discriminate other possibilities in her life situation was impaired.

Combs and Snygg considered her subsequent neurotic behavior—constant tension, inability to sleep, vague aches and pains, emotional lability, inability to concentrate—directly comparable to "experimental neuroses" manifested by animals placed in situations which elicit opposing conditioned reflexes or force them to make discriminations beyond their range of adjustive adequacy. Such animals lose their previously developed ability to make even simple discriminations, show an irrational generalization of response, and reveal evidence of tension and labile emotional responsivity. Some of these studies are described on pp. 234-235.

Conflicts between incompatible drives have also been emphasized by Dollard and Miller (1950). They have used the analogy of a very hungry man confronting food which he knows is poisoned, so that he is driven on the one

A   B

C

THE EXPERIMENTAL INDUCTION OF NEUROSES

An unusual series of experiments on "neurotic" behavior in animals has been carried out by Dr. Jules Masserman. Although we do not know how far the findings of such studies can be applied on the human level, there clearly are many parallels between human reactions to conflict and those observed in Masserman's animal subjects. Masserman's studies were carried out with both cats and monkeys.

The first step in Dr. Masserman's procedure was to condition the animals to respond to a food signal—a light, a bell, or an odor—by pressing a treadle which was connected to a switch. A proper response opened the plastic lid of a food box in which the animal found the reward (A). When this behavior had been learned, conflict was introduced by associating a noxious stimulus with the feeding situation. Cats were subjected to a brief electric shock or had a strong puff of air directed at their heads when they tried to obtain the food. Monkeys were commonly exposed to a toy snake, which was presented in the food box or through the wall of the apparatus. These stimuli all produced strong avoidance reactions when initially presented. After a few experiences with the noxious stimulus the basic conflict was well established: the animal faced the choice of resisting his fear in order to satisfy his hunger or withdrawing and remaining hungry in order to avoid the fear.

Under these conditions many apparently neurotic reactions were observed. Cats displayed typical symptoms of anxiety: they crouched and trembled; their hair stood on end and their pupils dilated; their breathing was rapid,

E

D

F

shallow, and irregular; their pulses were rapid; their blood pressure was markedly increased. They showed severe startle reactions and phobic aversions to sudden lights or sounds, to constricted spaces or to restraint, and to any sensory stimulation in the modality associated with the traumatic experience. Some refused to take any food even when it was presented outside the food box on the floor of the cage. Animals that had willingly entered the cage and had resisted removal during the initial learning period became eager to escape after conflict had been established. Often they would crouch near the sliding glass door of the experimental cage, waiting to be removed (B, C).

Monkeys, in addition to anxiety and phobic reactions like those shown by the cats, displayed even more profound disturbances. Somatic and motor dysfunctions in-

cluded diarrhea and gastrointestinal disorders resulting in rickets and severe neuromuscular weakness. In contrast to their previous behavior, some monkeys after experimental treatment spent long periods in stereotyped, repetitive activity, such as "pacing" back and forth in the experimental cage (D). Sometimes this behavior alternated with states of tense, apprehensive immobility (E). Some animals would stare fixedly for hours if left undisturbed (F). Often these monkeys would sleep or lie immobile in their home cages until mid-afternoon. Homosexual and autoerotic activity increased markedly, even in the presence of receptive females. One monkey attempted coitus only once in six months. "Neurotic" animals also lost their former positions of dominance in relation to other animals and were frequently attacked by other members of the colony.

hand by hunger and on the other by fear and is unable to reduce either of the conflicting drives. Many of us face comparable conflicts which could become the nucleus for full-fledged neurotic reactions.

Still another kind of conflict suggested as an important cause of neurotic reactions is an intra-psychic conflict between various subselves in a poorly differentiated and poorly integrated individual (Shapiro, 1962). For example, the individual may try to be the self his mother expects, the self his father expects, the self other people expect, the real self he thinks he is, and the ideal self he thinks he should be. Conflict among these subselves may make choices and decisions both difficult and anxiety-arousing and lead to vacillation, indecision, and various neurotic manifestations.

4. *Dissonant cognitions.* We have previously noted that dissonant cognitions—experiences that yield information contradictory to the individual's assumptions and self-concept—lead to various defensive maneuvers designed to reduce or eliminate the dissonance. In the development of neurotic behavior, this process has been well delineated by Carl Rogers (1961). Rogers has placed emphasis on the self-concept as an explanatory principle in personality dynamics and pointed to the screening from consciousness of experiences which threaten the adequacy and worth of the self. The greater the degree of perceived threat, the greater the tendency to defend oneself against the threatening experience by denying it to consciousness—either by actually denying it symbolization or by giving it a distorted symbolization—and the more rigid the organization of the self-structure becomes. As a consequence, the individual's self-image becomes less congruent with reality, and more defenses, accordingly, must be brought into operation to maintain it. The self thereby loses contact with large segments of inner and outer experience, and the increasing opposition between reality and self leads to tension, anxiety, and a lowered sense of self-identity and self-direction.

Under the sustained threat of dissonant cognitions, the individual lives in perpetual jeopardy, and in his desperate efforts to protect his self-structure and alleviate his anxiety, he may resort to various neurotic defensive maneuvers. In

some instances the neurotic reaction may take the form of a continuous, belligerent, aggressive seeking of self-enhancement as the individual tries desperately to demonstrate that what he suspects about himself is not so. Here he seems to be trying to cope with cognitive dissonance by increasing the number or importance of consonant cognitions (Brehm, 1962).

5. *Lack of meaning and hope.* In the studies of former prisoners of war and inmates of concentration camps, we have seen how stressful a frustrating life situation, devoid of hope and meaning, can be. In the less physically traumatic conditions of civilian life, Harry Stack Sullivan (1953) has emphasized the importance of disturbances in interpersonal relations which have elicited anxiety and resulted in an exaggeration or breakdown of an individual's system of self-defenses. We have noted in our discussion of neurasthenic reactions how pathogenic marital interactions which bring hostility and disillusion may rob life of meaning and hope and take a heavy toll in morale and effort. With the depersonalization characteristic of our urban society, an increased burden is placed on all the interpersonal relationships which are available to the individual.

In this context, Erich Fromm (1955, 1962) and other writers have emphasized the alienation of modern man from nature, from other men, and from himself in a vast impersonal bureaucratic society—a process of dehumanization which exacts a high price in loss of meaning, self-identity, and involvement. As Ferry (1963) has pointed out, "The danger today is not so much that machines will learn to think and feel but that men will cease to do so." Thus both individual situational factors and the broader sociological setting may contribute to neurotic behavior.

It has also been suggested that imagined or real failure in any important life area generates existential anxiety—is threatening to the existential motive of living a meaningful and fulfilling life (Thorne, 1963). When the ratio of success to failure is consistently unfavorable or when the individual is confronted with a seemingly hopeless life situation, the outcome may be incapacitating neurotic symptoms. In this process, the loss of hope and meaning appear to be of critical significance. Richter (1957) observed that when wild Norway rats were made to swim under circumstances that made the situation seem "hopeless," they died rapid deaths; whereas after elimination of the hopeless element from the situation, they continued to try and did not die. Becker (1962) has pointed out that in difficult stress situations the individual has two central tasks: (a) to maintain the continuity of his own self-identity and (b) to continue to try to cope with the situation. When meaning and hope are taken away, these tasks become almost insurmountable, and it is not surprising that personality decompensation ensues.

We have previously emphasized the importance of man's assumptions—particularly his assumptions concerning value—in guiding his behavior and providing meaning for his existence. And we have pointed to modern man's difficulties in finding an adequate value system. This general orientation is well summarized in Szasz's (1960) viewpoint that mental illness —including neurosis—is essentially the outcome of man's struggles to solve the problem of how he should live. Since the neuroses involve problems in living, they also involve problems in values—a failure to find the values necessary for adapting satisfactorily to a complex, changing, and stressful world.

Immaturity and guilt. The view that neurosis is practically synonymous with personal immaturity has been emphasized by O. H. Mowrer (1950, 1960). He has traced this immaturity to a failure of the family situation to complete the socialization of the child, particularly with respect to ethical and conscience development. Instead of a too severe conscience which conflicts with instinctual drives, as Freud emphasized, Mowrer has blamed an immature conscience development based on underlearning. The conscience is strong enough to leave the individual with unresolved guilt and self-devaluation but not strong enough to control his immature, egocentric behavior. To protect himself from the resulting self-devaluation and anxiety, he tries to repress his conscience. Neurotic symptoms, Mowrer believes, reflect unacknowledged sin—the neurotic's unwillingness to confess his sins and expiate his guilt. In his efforts to evade social responsibilities and to defend himself against guilt and anxiety, the neurotic thus becomes the victim of his own devious and exaggerated ego defenses. Mowrer has tied this viewpoint in with a basic trend he sees in our society.

"In becoming amoral, ethically neutral, and 'free,' we have cut the very roots of our being; lost our deepest sense of self-hood and identity; and, with neurotics themselves, find ourselves asking: Who *am* I? What is my *destiny*? What does living (existence) *mean*?

"In reaction to the state of near limbo into which we have drifted, we have become suddenly aware, once again, of the problem of *values* and of their centrality in the human enterprise." (1960, p. 303)

". . . Just so long as a person lives under the shadow of real, unacknowledged, and unexpiated guilt, he *cannot* (if he has a character at all) 'accept himself'; and all our efforts to reassure and accept him will avail nothing. He will continue to hate himself and to suffer the inevitable consequences of self-hatred. But the moment he (with or without assistance) begins to accept his guilt and his sinfulness, the possibility of radical reformation opens up; and with this, the individual may legitimately, though not without pain and effort, pass from deep, pervasive, self-rejection and self-torture to a new freedom, of self-respect and peace." (p. 304)

Approaching the problem of neuroses from a different orientation, Carl Jung described the role of personality immaturity in this way:

". . . there appears upon the psychological stage a man living regressively, seeking his childhood and his mother, fleeing from a cold and cruel world which denies him understanding. Often a mother appears beside him who apparently has no slightest concern that her little son should become a man, but who, with tireless and self-immolating effort, neglects nothing which might hinder him from growing up and marrying. One sees the hidden conspiracy between mother and son, and how the one assists the other to betray life." (1950, pp. 3-4)

Jung believed that the achievement of maturity and selfhood requires great courage and resolution but that failure to develop one or more essential components of the personality or the attempt to deny the deep unconscious instead of relating to it dooms the individual to a one-sided and unfulfilling life and often to neuroses or other mental disorders.

The importance of immaturity and guilt in the development of psychoneurotic disorders has also been emphasized by Rollo May (1961) and other existential theorists. Confronted with the problems of freedom, choice, and responsibility, the immature individual lacks the courage to follow the course that leads to self-definition and actualization. By means of neurotic defenses, he holds back and lives in a narrow and shrunken life space or escapes anxiety by blind conformity and immersion in the group so that his self is diffused and empty. But as a consequence of his "flight from freedom" and his lack of courage to be himself and shape his own destiny, he suffers guilt and despair.

Despite differing points of emphasis, all these personality theorists appear to agree on (a) the importance of early childhood development in predisposing the individual to later healthy or neurotic behavior, (b) the importance of various types of stress as precipitating factors in the neuroses, and (c) the tendency of neurotic reactions to maintain and augment rather than solve the individual's problems.[1] Feeling that security comes from the outside rather than from within himself, the neurotic concentrates on trying to establish a secure life situation or on finding emotional crutches for protection.

In general, it would appear that neurosis represents a complicated system of maneuvers designed to enable the individual to function under life conditions which are highly stressful for him. Although these maneuvers do alleviate anxiety and protect him from various internal and external dangers, they result in rigidity, restricted life activities, a lowered sense of identity, disturbances in interpersonal relationships, and lack of meaning and direction. The difference between normals and neurotics, then, is the difference between individuals who are on the whole integrated, flexible, and self-directing and individuals who are panicked by the stresses of life into adopting defensive armaments which are self-defeating.

SOCIOLOGICAL FACTORS

Neurotic reactions are found among all peoples and among all economic groups. Prostitutes, criminals, delinquents, successful businessmen, college professors, politicians—no group is without its proportion of neurotics. But there are wide differences among cultural groups in incidence and type of neurotic reaction.

Hysteria, for example, is more common among primitive peoples and among patients from lower economic and educational levels, whereas obsessive-compulsive reactions and anxiety reactions are more common among the wealthier and better educated. In World War II, hysteria was relatively more common among noncommissioned men, while anxiety reactions were more common among officers. Freedman and Hollingshead (1957) studied a large number of neurotic patients in a New England city of 250,000 and concluded that (a) upper-class neurotics are characterized by subjective symptoms of discomfort—anxiety, unhappiness, and dissatisfaction with themselves; (b) lower-class neurotics reveal more friction with other people and far more aches, pains, and other somatic symptoms; and (c) middle-class neurotics show some of the symptoms of both upper- and lower-class patients and tend to be less effective in their work. On the basis of the limited evidence available, Pasamanick (1963) has estimated that psychoneurotic disorders may be twice as common among whites as among nonwhites.

Certain regional differences also appear related to the incidence and nature of neurotic reactions. Perkins (1946), in an analysis of neuropsychiatric draft rejectees from the state of Tennessee, found that psychoneuroses, neurotic traits, and psychosomatic disorders were quite rare among the hill people, whereas poverty of affective response and a type of emotional immaturity were common. Similarly Wiesel and Arny (1952), in a study of coal miners in eastern Kentucky, have described a "miner's syndrome" commonly found in miners past forty. This is characterized by numerous bodily complaints, a passive, dependent attitude, and a marked lack of anxiety with rationalizations based upon having been exposed to "bad air" and "nerves being run down."

Data on the incidence of psychoneurotic disorders in other societies are very meager. Tsung-yi Lin (1953) found the general incidence of psychoneurotic disorders low and obsessive-

---

[1]Several of the personality theories mentioned in this section are described in greater detail in the Appendix.

compulsive neuroses very rare on the island of Formosa. He has pointed out that individuals there derive support from the close-knit family system and from the large number of rituals already present in the social structure. Likewise, Carothers (1953, 1959) found few obsessive-compulsive reactions among Kenya Africans. He attributed this largely to an absence there of mystery or feelings of shame about sex and to the fact that the African, as part of a rigidly structured social organization, does not have to set up his own controls and standards or bear economic trials alone but draws upon the strength and stability of the group. Thus he does not develop the tension and anxiety that come with individual responsibility for one's actions. Although the reasons are not clear, it would appear that neurasthenia is by far the most common type of psychoneurotic disorder in the Soviet Union (Wortis, 1961).[1]

Thus it would appear that both the family setting and the broader social context in which the individual lives exert important influences on his adjustive behavior. As life conditions—particularly those involving interpersonal relationships—become more complex, conflictful, and precarious, the incidence of neuroses increases.

Therapy of the Neuroses

Many medical, psychological, and sociological treatment procedures may enter into the therapy of a neurotic disorder; the exact treatment must, of course, be individualized to fit the needs of the patient.

On a biological level, many drugs have proved highly effective in dealing with depression, anxiety, and tension in neurotic patients (Giffen, 1961; Lehmann, 1961; Reusch, 1963; Wortis, 1962, 1963). Antidepressant drugs have largely replaced electroshock in the treatment of reactive depressions; where shock therapy is used, it can be greatly shortened by combination with drug therapy. Tranquilizing drugs have achieved striking results in stabilizing emotional reactivity and in reducing anxiety and tension. Available statistics indicate that 70 per cent or more of neurotic patients show a marked alleviation of symptoms following use of antidepressant and/or tranquilizing drugs, and that most of these patients are able to function more effectively in their life situations (Wortis, 1962, 1963; Stanfield, 1961; Giffen, 1961).

It may be pointed out, however, that these drugs may have undesirable side effects—ranging from minor symptoms, such as drowsiness and nasal congestion, to more serious symptoms, such as gastrointestinal bleeding and hepatitis. In some cases they are habit forming. Also, many patients expect too much of drug medication and the masking of their symptoms may prevent them from seeking needed treatment. Although such medication may relieve anxiety, tension, and depression, it cannot be expected to replace psychotherapy where personality changes are necessary or sociotherapy where factors in the life situations are conducive to neurosis. Drug therapies are viewed as extremely important but as part of a more global approach involving psychological and sociological treatment as well.

On a psychological level, therapy varies considerably in terms of objectives and procedures. Recently a good deal of interest has centered on "behavior therapy," which emphasizes the view that the maladaptive responses, being learned, can be unlearned. In the treatment of neurotic reactions, behavior therapy has been limited primarily to the use of deconditioning procedures such as reciprocal inhibition. Wolpe (1958) describes the principle of reciprocal inhibition psychotherapy as follows:

"If a response antagonistic to anxiety can be made to occur in the presence of anxiety-evoking stimuli so that it is accompanied by a complete or partial suppression of the anxiety responses, the bond between these

---

[1]Cross-cultural estimates of the prevalence of psychoneurotic disorders are complicated by variations in classification, theoretical orientation, case diagnosis, and methods of sampling. Consequently, it is difficult to make definitive comparisons.

stimuli and the anxiety responses will be weakened." (Wolpe, 1958, p. 71)

We have noted the prototype of this approach in the classic experiment of Mary Cover Jones (1924) in treating 3-year-old Peter's phobia of furry objects by introducing a white rabbit in a cage at the end of the room when Peter was eating and bringing the rabbit a little closer each day until Peter's phobia was extinguished.

More recent reports on the effectiveness of deconditioning procedures in treating neurotic disorders have been made by a number of investigators. Wolpe has reported the apparent recovery of 188 out of 210 neurotic cases in an average of 35 sessions. Although a wide range of neurotic reaction types were represented, the great majority of these cases (135) were diagnosed as anxiety reactions. Lazarus (1961), utilizing group desensitization procedures, has reported the recovery of 13 out of 18 severely phobic patients, although 3 of the 13 subsequently relapsed. Although the precise advantages and limitations of behavior therapy remain to be worked out, it appears to have most promising implications for the treatment of neurotic reactions.

In this context, it may be pointed out that it has been unfashionable in recent years to attack symptoms directly and to rely upon relief of symptoms as the primary criterion of improvement. As Eysenck (1959) has noted, however, the disappearance of very annoying symptoms breaks the vicious circle and often allays anxiety, promotes peace in the home, and fosters all-round improvement in behavior.

There are a number of more "dynamic" and widely utilized approaches to the treatment of neuroses, such as psychoanalysis, psychobiology, and client-centered psychotherapy. These approaches vary somewhat in therapeutic goals and procedures, depending in part upon the personality theory on which they are based.[1] In the past, strong emphasis was placed upon helping the patient to gain insight into his problems and defenses with the expectation that this would automatically lead to desirable changes in his behavior. Today this has given way to increased emphasis on modifying patterns of behavior which are disturbing the patient and impairing his immediate adjustment. In this process, an attempt is made to help the patient correct faulty assumptions about himself and his world, to perceive the full range of possibilities in his situation, to develop more effective coping techniques, and to attain greater personality integration. In short, insight must be implemented by appropriate new learning experiences if it is to be of maximal therapeutic value (Hobbs, 1962).

These objectives look deceptively easy to achieve; actually there are a number of common stumbling blocks. First is the problem of creating a therapeutic situation in which (a) the patient feels safe and comfortable enough to lower his defenses and explore his innermost feelings, thoughts, and assumptions—and his problems as he perceives them—and (b) the patient is provided with opportunities and encouragement for learning new ways of perceiving himself and his world, new ways of responding, and new ways of relating to others. Involved here is a process of exploration and re-education in which the patient comes to realize that his previous assumptions and behavior are neither as necessary nor as desirable as he had assumed—that new patterns are possible and would yield greater satisfaction and self-fulfillment. Unfortunately, the problem is often complicated by conditions in the patient's life situation which tend to maintain neurotic reactions. Thus an overly protective and possessive mother may complicate or even block therapeutic efforts.

Second is the problem of dealing with the patient's own resistance to being "cured." Often what the neurotic really wants is to be relieved of his symptoms without having to face his problems or assume the responsibilities of adulthood. As Weiss and English (1943) have pointed out, the neurasthenic

"presents himself and his story in such a way as to put the whole responsibility for his health, happiness, and success on the physician without himself wanting to participate in any way. He seems to say, 'There's my story, doctor' (after taking plenty of time to tell it in detail). 'Now you pat me and rub me and feed me medicine and take my pains away and give me a good appetite and an easy bowel movement and a good night's sleep, and give me inspiration and happiness and tell me how to be successful, and while you are

---

[1]Chapter 14 deals in greater detail with objectives, procedures, and other key dimensions of psychotherapy.

about it, get my mother-in-law out of the house and I'll pay you when I get a job.' " (p. 119)

Thus the neurotic patient may discuss his symptoms at great length, seemingly in a sincere attempt to help the therapist get a clear view of them. However, when it becomes apparent that he can improve only by making certain changes in his life style, he may become defensive and discontinue therapy. In some cases, the patient's symptoms temporarily disappear so that he is convinced it is unnecessary to return for further treatment; for this reason the immediate disappearance of symptoms is often looked upon as a poor prognostic sign. In still other cases, the symptoms may seemingly be intensified and the patient may report that he is becoming worse and has decided to consult another therapist.

Usually, it is not enough to treat symptoms only and ignore the individual's underlying personality difficulties. Hysterical symptoms, for example, may be removed through hypnosis and many phobic fears through deconditioning. But unless the underlying personality immaturities are modified, the same or other neurotic symptoms designed to protect the patient from what he perceives as threatening stress are likely to appear. Of course, where the symptoms are seriously interfering with the patient's life activities—as in the case of certain phobias and conversion reactions—their alleviation may be an important early step in the therapeutic process. However, except in cases where neurotic symptoms are isolated conditioned reactions, unrelated to the broader personality pattern and life situation of the individual, the removal of the symptoms is not sufficient because the neurotic personality make-up and unfavorable life situation remain.

Psychotherapy is often a painful experience for the neurotic patient and requires courage and persistence if it is to be successful. Although the basic tendency of the human organism is toward integration and health, it is by no means easy to examine one's assumptions, action patterns, and interpersonal relations objectively. Nor is it always easy to put new-found insights into actual practice. Furthermore, as the individual does grow and become a more mature person, he is confronted with problems of choice and responsibility from which he was partially protected before by his neurotic defenses. Here it may be pointed out that many individuals expect psychotherapy to relieve them from all anxiety, worry, and guilt, whereas, of course, realistic anxiety, worry, and guilt are normal and essential aspects of man's existence.

Despite these obstacles, there are powerful forces aligned on the side of psychotherapy. The obtaining of professional assistance usually gives new hope to the discouraged neurotic patient. The concrete delineation of his problems which usually occurs in psychotherapy is likely to help him submerge his vague fears and apprehensions and exert his efforts toward overcoming real problems about which he now feels he can do something (Scheier, 1962). And the individual's underlying strivings toward self-differentiation and actualization appear stronger than is often assumed. Thus, as the patient experiences some measure of improvement and sees the possibilities for increased adequacy and a more satisfying and fulfilling life, the courage to "become a person" is usually forthcoming (Rogers, 1961).

It is perhaps for the preceding reasons that even relatively superficial psychotherapy does help many neurotic patients. This is especially true of patients who have considerable insight into their problems and seriously desire to achieve a more adequate self-definition and life adjustment. Thus various forms of brief psychotherapy as well as group therapy are being increasingly used in the treatment of psychoneurotic disorders.

Statistics are not available for an adequate evaluation of the effectiveness of psychotherapy when used as the only treatment procedure or for a comparison of different types of psychotherapy. Apparently, psychoanalytic results differ little from those of other psychotherapeutic methods. Probably the qualifications of the individual therapist are more important than his "school of psychology."

Sociological aspects of treatment focus on the modification of circumstances in the patient's life situation that are tending to perpetuate his neurosis. Often there are pathogenic family interactions which keep the neurotic patient in a continually "sick situation." As the psychiatrist in T. S. Eliot's *The Cocktail Party* says:

A

B

C

D

OVERDEPENDENCY

Stills from the film *Overdependency*, produced by the National Film Board of Canada

A neurotic reaction pattern such as overdependency usually has its roots in earliest childhood. So it was with Jim Howard, whose development is portrayed in this film. For as long as he could remember, he had been "delicate." His overprotective mother and older sister watched over him anxiously, magnifying every slight illness and keeping him from school, where he might have learned to meet his problems instead of escaping from the need to face them by not feeling well. His family failed to realize that their attitudes did not give him the emotional security he needed but only convinced him that he was weak, inadequate, unable to stand on his own feet.

His father could have helped Jim gain confidence in himself, but he accepted the fact that his son was "frail."

Jim would watch wistfully as his father prepared for a fishing trip; then he would be impatiently brushed aside. Because of the false role in which his family had placed him, Jim could never hope to be a companion to his father. His older brother, on the other hand, was a "regular fellow" whose assurance and competence only accentuated Jim's feelings of inadequacy.

Only the little girls in the neighborhood accepted him as a playmate, and Jim had to content himself with "playing store" and other "sissy" games with them. He was acutely conscious that he was not like other boys and rebelled under their taunts. But when he made eager attempts to join their rough-and-tumble games, he was jeeringly rejected. This rejection was spurred on by his older brother, who was thus unconsciously compensating for the lack of attention given him at home. Jim's only refuge was his mother, who comforted and petted him after every rebuff.

Quite naturally, adulthood did not bring maturity. The

E

F

G

H

many habits of dependency, normal for a child, continued long past childhood. Jim's wife, Marion, was an older girl who carried on where mother and sister had left off. She was strong and capable and enjoyed treating him as her "little boy," who was indulgently allowed to sleep past his worktime because he was "so tired." She sympathetically aided in pampering his vague aches and weaknesses. So Jim was only physically adult. Faced with decisions, even the small one of choosing a tie, he was helpless. His dependency on others showed in many ways—borrowing a nickel for a phone call, expecting someone else to light his cigarette, letting other people make his apologies for jobs not done or appointments not kept.

Every minor crisis at work drove him deeper into self-pity and apparent ill health until his wife at last made an appointment for him to see a doctor. Surprised and disappointed in the doctor's diagnosis that nothing was physically wrong, he turned as usual to his mother. True to form, she reassured him that the doctor was wrong and that he of course was "not strong."

Through psychotherapy over a period of time the doctor helped Jim to understand the train of events that had led to his neurotic pattern, and the unconscious purposes for which he was using it. The doctor also talked to Jim's wife and helped her to understand how she had unwittingly fostered Jim's dependence on others. Fortunately she was able to continue to give him the love and encouragement he needed while at the same time not letting him lean on her as before. It was hard for Jim to learn to rely upon himself instead of others and to meet his problems instead of avoiding them by getting sick, and it required adroitness on Marion's part to keep his mother from undoing the doctor's work. But with the help of wife and doctor, Jim slowly and after many setbacks learned to respect and stand by his own decisions. Successful at last in his work, he found he no longer needed his neurotic defenses.

"Indeed it is often the case that my patients
Are only pieces of a total situation
Which I have to explore. The single patient
Who is by himself is rather the exception."

Relevant here is a study by Kohl (1962) of 39 patients hospitalized for neuroses as well as for other types of psychopathology. Kohl found that at the time of hospitalization both patients and spouses denied that marital conflict was of etiologic significance. Interestingly enough, however, the marital partner often responded to the patient's improvement with resentment, threats of divorce, and in some instances personality decompensation. Kohl describes the following case.

A successful inventor was hospitalized for a severe neurotic depression. Although both marital partners described their marriage as "ideal," it became apparent that there was an unconscious struggle for dominance between them. Little progress was accomplished in therapy until this conflict was brought out in the open and the patient became able to express his feelings of resentment freely. Then, as the patient improved, the wife, in turn, became depressed and for the first time defiantly participated in an extramarital affair. At this point, she also revealed long-standing resentment toward her husband, whom she considered overly dependent. Treatment of both marital partners was then undertaken and stabilization of the marriage was eventually achieved.

On a broader plane, biological, psychological, and sociological approaches to treatment are also concerned with the alleviation of culture-induced stresses which foster the production of neuroses and other psychopathology. We shall consider some of these problems and procedures in Chapters 14 and 15.

Prognosis for the Neuroses

The general prognosis for psychoneurotic disorders is good.[1] Some neurotics—estimates range from 40 to 60 per cent—recover spontaneously in the sense that they eventually resolve their problems and gain in adequacy and maturity *without* professional help. Apparently such individuals are fortunate in undergoing life experiences which permit them to unlearn their maladaptive responses and learn more adaptive ones. In a study of some 20 cases of spontaneous improvement, Stevenson (1961) found that the following processes facilitated recovery: (a) desensitization to past painful experiences through recall, verbalization, and assimilation or through association of such experiences with new, pleasurable experiences; (b) increased respect, reassurance, and affection from other significant persons; (c) entrance into the patient's life of new behavioral models from whom he could learn more effective behavior; (d) new situations requiring different responses—for example, the death of an overly protective and possessive mother, forcing the individual to adapt new attitudes and respon-

sibilities; and (e) shifts in motivation stemming from fear, shame, or desperation.

For those who do receive treatment, there is a dearth of statistics relative to the actual therapeutic benefits. Differences in the methods used, differences in the interpretation of such words as *recovered* or *markedly improved,* differences in the type and severity of the neurotic reactions in the first place, and failure to distinguish between immediate and long-range improvement make it difficult to evaluate the somewhat meager statistics that are available at this time. However, with an integrated medical, psychological, and sociological treatment approach, it would appear that 90 per cent or more of psychoneurotics show apparent recovery or marked improvement as a result of treatment. Patients with reactive depressions, phobic reactions, and anxiety reactions appear to respond more readily to treatment than do patients with neuras-

---

[1]This statement appears justified on the basis of available evidence though Chapman (1963) has pointed out that there are no definitive studies which clarify what the psychiatric status of the young adult neurotic can be expected to be 10 to 20 years later.

thenic, obsessive-compulsive, and conversion reactions. Although conversion and dissociative symptoms can usually be cleared up rapidly, the patient's achievement of a more integrated and mature personality is often a difficult therapeutic task.

Several additional points are relevant in our discussion of the neuroses. Fear of committing suicide is a common psychoneurotic symptom, but the actual incidence of successful suicides among neurotics appears relatively low. Nor does the life span of the neurotic appear adversely affected by his chronic tension and somatic disturbances. In an early study, Denker (1939) found that the life expectancy of a group of insured neurotics was greater than average. His statistics involve a special group, however, (those carrying insurance), and do not necessarily apply to all psychoneurotics. More recent statistics on this point are not presently available.

How does neurosis affect productiveness and occupational adjustment? Many authors have proclaimed neurotics the "salt of the earth" and have believed that they should "be glad they are neurotic." Although many great persons in history could be counted as neurotics, there is considerable question as to whether their success in making worth-while artistic and scientific contributions occurred because of or in spite of their neuroses. In general, the evidence indicates that neurotics are sick people whose full potentialities for productive accomplishment cannot be achieved until they have worked through their conflicts and achieved a more effective personality adjustment.

Will neurotic reactions decompensate further into psychoses? The answer to this question is a controversial one. Many psychiatrists and psychologists maintain that the two types of disorders are fundamentally different and that neurotics rarely, if ever, become psychotic. In point of fact, few neurotics do apparently become psychotic, estimates centering around 5 per cent. It may be that neurotic defenses are sufficient to deal with most of the stresses these individuals face. If the stress demands were to increase markedly, however, most neurotics might eventually become psychotic (Karon and Karon, 1959).

Certainly many psychotics reveal neurotic patterns prior to the onset of their psychoses, and many neurotics evidence mild delusions which belong in the realm of psychotic symptomatology. This often leads to difficulties in classification of borderline cases. Thus it would appear most profitable to think of a continuum from neuroses to psychoses with increasing personality decompensation.

REFERENCES

The reference list includes not only the sources from which the author has drawn material, but acknowledgments of the permissions granted by authors and publishers to quote directly from their works.

ABSE, D. W. Hysteria. In S. Arieti (Ed.), *American handbook of psychiatry*, Vol. 1. New York: Basic Books, 1959. Pp. 272-292.

ADLER, A. The fundamental views of individual psychology. *Int. J. indiv. Psychol.*, 1935, 1, 5-8.

ANTHONY, J. An experimental approach to the psychopathology of childhood: sleep disturbances. *Brit. J. med. Psychol.*, 1959, 32, 19-37.

ARIETI, S. A re-examination of the phobic symptoms and of symbolism in psychopathology. *Amer. J. Psychiat.*, 1961, 118, 106-110.

BAHN, ANITA, CHANDLER, CAROLINE A., & EISENBERG, L. Diagnostic and demographic characteristics of patients seen in outpatient psychiatric clinics for an entire state (Maryland): implications for the psychiatrist and the mental health program planner. *Amer. J. Psychiat.*, 1961, 117, 769-778.

BANDURA, A. Social learning through imitation. In M. R. Jones (Ed.), *Nebraska symposium on motivation*. Lincoln: Univer. Nebraska Press, 1962. Pp. 211-269.

BEARD, G. M. *A practical treatise on nervous exhaustion (neurasthenia), its symptoms, nature, sequences, treatment.* (5th ed.) New York: E. B. Treat, 1905.

BECKER, E. Toward a comprehensive theory of depression: a cross-disciplinary appraisal of objects, games and meaning. *J. nerv. ment. Dis.*, 1962, 135, 26-35.

BELIAEVA, Z. V. On characteristics of major nervous processes in neurasthenia. *Psychol. Abstr.*, 1962, 36, 376.

BOND, D. D. Anorexia nervosa. *Rocky Mountain med. J.*, 1949, 46, 1012-1019.

BREHM, J. W. Motivational effects of cognitive dissonance. In M. R. Jones (Ed.), *Nebraska Symposium on Motivation*. Lincoln: Univer. Nebraska Press, 1962. Pp. 51-77.

BRELAND, K., & BRELAND, MARIAN. The misbehavior of organisms. *Amer. Psychologist*, 1961, 16, 681-684.

CAROTHERS, J. C. The African mind in health and disease. *A study in ethnopsychiatry*. Geneva: World Organization, 1953, No. 17.

CAROTHERS, J. C. Culture, psychiatry, and the written word. *Psychiatry*, 1959, 22, 307-320.

CATTELL, R. B., & SCHEIER, I. H. *The meaning and measurements of neuroticism and anxiety.* New York: Ronald, 1961.

CATTELL, R. B., SCHEIER, I. H., & LORR, M. Recent advances in the measurement of anxiety, neuroticism, and the psychotic syndrome. *Ann. N. Y. Acad. Sci.,* 1962, 93, 840-850.

CHAPMAN, A. H. The problem of prognosis in psychoneurotic illness. *Amer. J. Psychiat.,* 1963, 119, 768-770.

CHODOFF, P., & LYONS, H. Hysteria, the hysterical personality, and "hysterical" conversion. *Amer. J. Psychiat.,* 1958, 114, 734-740.

CHRZANOWSKI, G. Neurasthenia and hypochondriasis. In S. Arieti (Ed.), *American handbook of psychiatry,* Vol. 1. New York: Basic Books, 1959. Pp. 258-271.

CLANCY, J., & NORRIS, A. Differentiating variables: obsessive-compulsive neurosis and anorexia nervosa. *Amer. J. Psychiat.,* 1961, 118, 58-60.

COHEN, M. E., *et al.* Excessive surgery in hysteria. *J. Amer. Med. Ass.,* 1953, 151, 977-986.

COMBS, A. W., & SNYGG, D. Individual behavior. (Rev. ed.) New York: Harper, 1959.

COON, G., & RAYMOND, ALICE. *A review of the psychoneuroses at Stockbridge.* Stockbridge, Mass.: Austin Riggs Found., 1940.

DARLING, C. D. The management of anxiety: a case study. *Pastoral Psychol.,* 1952, 2, 18-22.

DENKER, P. G. The prognosis of insured neurotics. *N. Y. St. J. Med.,* 1939, 39, 238-247.

DOLLARD, J., & MILLER, N. E. *Personality and psychotherapy.* New York: McGraw-Hill, 1950.

EHRENWALD, J. Neurosis in the family. *Arch. gen. Psychiat.,* 1960, 3, 232-241.

EISENBERG, L. School phobia: diagnosis, genesis, and clinical management. *Pediatr. Clin. N. Amer.,* 1958a, 5, 645-666.

EISENBERG, L. School phobia: a study in the communication of anxiety. *Amer. J. Psychiat.,* 1958b, 114, 712-718.

EYSENCK, H. J. Learning theory and behavior therapy. *J. ment. Sci.,* 1959, 105, 61-75.

EYSENCK, H. J. (Ed.) *Behaviour therapy and the neuroses.* London: Pergamon Press, 1960.

EYSENCK, H. J. Classification and the problem of diagnosis. In H. J. Eysenck (Ed.) *Handbook of abnormal psychology.* New York: Basic Books, 1961. Pp. 1-31.

EYSENCK, H. J. Behavior therapy, spontaneous remission and transference in neurotics. *Amer. J. Psychiat.,* 1963, 119, 867-871.

EYSENCK, H. J., & CLARIDGE, G. The position of hysterics and dysthymics in a two-dimensional framework of personality description. *J. abnorm. soc. Psychol.,* 1962, 64, 46-55.

FENICHEL, O. Remarks on the common phobias. *Psychoanalytic Quart.,* 1944, 13, 313-326.

FERRY, W. H. Personal correspondence, 1963.

FISHER, S., BOYD, INA, WALKER, D., & SHEER, DIANNE. Parents of schizophrenics, neurotics, and normals. *AMA Arch. gen. Psychiat.,* 1959, 1, 149-166.

FREEDMAN, L. Z., & HOLLINGSHEAD, A. B. Neurosis and social class. I: social interaction. *Amer. J. Psychiat.,* 1957, 113, 769-775.

FROMM, E. *The sane society.* New York: Rinehart, 1955.

FROMM, E. *Beyond the chains of illusion; my encounter with Marx and Freud.* New York: Simon & Schuster, 1962.

GIFFEN, M. B. Emotional dysfunction and the use of psychopharmacological drugs in a military theater. *Military Med.,* 1961, 126, 199-203.

GOLDSTEIN, K. *Human nature in the light of psychopathology.* Cambridge: Harvard Univer. Press, 1940.

GUILFORD, J. P. *Personality.* New York: McGraw-Hill, 1959.

GUNN, D. R. Psychiatric recognition of anxiety and depression. *Canad. Psychiat. Ass. J.,* 1962, 7, Special Suppl., 1-3.

GUTHEIL, E. A. Reactive depressions. In S. Arieti (Ed.), *American handbook of psychiatry,* Vol. 1. New York: Basic Books, 1959. Pp. 345-352.

HALPERN, H. J. Hysterical amblyopia. *Bull. U. S. Army Med. Dept.,* 1944, No. 72, 84-87.

HAMLIN, P. G. Camptocormia: hysterical bent back of soldiers: report of two cases. *Military Surgeon,* March 1943, 295-300.

HILGARD, E. R. *Theories of learning.* New York: Appleton-Century-Crofts, 1950.

HOBBS, N. Sources of gain in psychotherapy. *Amer. Psychologist,* 1962, 17, 741-747.

HORNEY, KAREN. *Our inner conflicts.* New York: Norton, 1945.

HORNEY, KAREN. *Neurosis and human growth.* New York: Norton, 1950.

INGRAM, I. M. The obsessional personality and obsessional illness. *Amer. J. Psychiat.,* 1961, 117, 1016-1019.

IRONSIDE, R., & BATCHELOR, I. R. C. The ocular manifestations of hysteria in relation to flying. *Brit. J. Ophthalmol.,* 1945, 29, 88-98.

JENNESS, A., & JORGENSEN, A. P. Ratings of vividness of imagery in the waking state compared with reports of somnambulism. *Amer. J. Psychol.,* 1941, 54, 253-259.

JONES, MARY C. A laboratory study of fear: the case of Peter. *Pedagog. Sem.,* 1924, 31, 308-315.

JUNG, C. G. *Shadow, animus, and anima.* New York: Analyt. Psychol. Club N. Y., Inc., 1950.

KARNOSH, L. J., & ZUCKER, E. M. *Handbook of psychiatry.* St. Louis: Mosby, 1945.

KARON, E. S. & KARON, B. P. Differentiation and differential counsel of some neurotic personalities. *J. Psychol.,* 1959, 47, 231-234.

KERRY, R. J. Phobia of outer space. *J. ment. Sci.,* 1960, 106, 1383-1387.

KESSEN, W., & MANDLER, G. Anxiety, pain, and the inhibition of distress. *Psychol. Rev.,* 1961, 68, 396-404.

KIERSCH, T. A. Amnesia: a clinical study of ninety-eight cases. *Amer. J. Psychiat.,* 1962, 119, 57-60.

KOHL, R. N. Pathologic reactions of marital partners to improvement of patients. *Amer. J. Psychiat.,* 1962, 118, 1036-1041.

KRAINES, S. H. *The therapy of the neuroses and psychoses.* (3rd ed.) Philadelphia: Lea & Febiger, 1948.

LANCASTER, EVELYN, & POLING, J. *Final face of Eve.* New York: McGraw-Hill, 1958.

LAZARUS, A. A. The elimination of children's phobias by deconditioning. In H. J. Eysenck (Ed.), *Behaviour and the neuroses.* London: Pergamon Press, 1960. Pp. 114-122.

LAZARUS, A. A. Group therapy of phobic disorders by systematic desensitization. *J. abnorm. soc. Psychol.,* 1961, 63, 504-510.

LEHMANN, H. E. New drugs in psychiatric therapy. *Canad. Med. Ass. J.,* 1961, 85, 1145-1151.

LETON, D. A. Assessment of school phobia. *Ment. Hyg.,* 1962, 46, 256-264.

LIPTON, S. Dissociated personality: a case report. *Psychiat. Quart.,* 1943, 17, 35-56.

MC NEEL, B. H., & DANCEY, T. E. The personality of the successful soldier. *Amer. J. Psychiat.,* 1945, 102, 337-342.

MACMILLAN, A. M. The health opinion survey: technique for estimating prevalence of psychoneurotic and related types of disorder in communities. *Psychol. Report,* 1957, 3, 325-339.

MASSERMAN, J. H. *Principles of dynamic psychiatry.* (2nd ed.) Philadelphia: W. B. Saunders, 1961.

MAY, R. (Ed.) *Existential psychology (studies in psychology).* New York: Random House, 1961.

MENNINGER, K. A. *The human mind.* (3rd ed.) New York: Knopf, 1945.

MEYER, A. *Commonsense psychiatry.* A. Lief (Ed.) New York: McGraw-Hill, 1948.

MILLER, G. A., GALANTER, E., & PRIBRAM, K. H. *Plans and the structure of behavior.* New York: Holt, 1960.

MOSS, C. S., THOMPSON, MARY M., & NOLTE, J. An additional study in hysteria: the case of Alice M. *Int. J. clin. exp. Hypnosis,* 1962, 10 (2), 59-74.

MOWRER, O. H. *Learning theory and personality dynamics.* New York: Ronald, 1950.

MOWRER, O. H. "Sin": the lesser of two evils. *Amer. Psychologist,* 1960, 15, 301-304.

MURPHY, G. *Personality.* New York: Harper, 1947.

PAI, M. N. The nature and treatment of "writer's cramp." *J. ment. Sci.,* 1947, 93, 68-81.

PASAMANICK, B. Some misconceptions concerning differences in the racial prevalence of mental disease. *Amer. J. Orthopsychiat.,* 1963, 33, 72-86.

PERKINS, O. C. Analysis of neuropsychiatric rejectees from the state of Tennessee. *Dis. nerv. System,* 1946, 7, 9-18.

PORTNOY, I. The anxiety states. In S. Arieti (Ed.), *American handbook of psychiatry,* Vol. 1. New York: Basic Books, 1959. Pp. 307-323.

PRINCE, M. *The dissociation of a personality.* (2nd ed.) New York: Longmans, Green, 1930.

PURTELL, J. J., ROBINS, E., & COHEN, M. E. Observations on clinical aspects of hysteria. *J. Amer. Med Ass.,* 1951, 146, 902-909.

RACHMAN, S., & COSTELLO, C. G. The aetiology and treatment of children's phobias: a review. *Amer. J. Psychiat.,* 1961, 118, 97-105.

RENNIE, T. A. C., SROLE, L., OPLER, M. K., & LANGNER, T. S. Urban life and mental health. *Amer. J. Psychiat.,* 1957, 113, 831-837.

RICHTER, C. P. On the phenomenon of sudden death in animals and man. *Psychosom. Med.,* 1957, 19, 191-198.

ROBINS, E., PURTELL, J. J., & COHEN, M. E. "Hysteria" in men. *N. Eng. J. Med.,* 1952, 246, 677-685.

ROGERS, C. R. *On becoming a person: a therapists view of psychotherapy.* Boston: Houghton Mifflin, 1961.

RUESCH, J., BRODSKY, C., & FISCHER, A. The acute nervous breakdown. *Arch. gen. Psych.,* 1963, 8, 197-207.

SADLER, W. S. *Modern psychiatry.* St. Louis: Mosby, 1945.

SANDLER, S. A. Somnambulism in the armed forces. *Ment. Hygiene,* 1945, 29, 236-247.

SCHEIER, I. H. Experimental results to date from the standpoint of the clinician. In R. B. Cattell, I. H. Scheier, & M. Lorr. Recent advances in the measurement of anxiety, neuroticism, and the psychotic syndrome. *Ann. N. Y. Acad. Sci.,* 1962, 93, 840-850.

SCHULER, E. A., & PARENTON, V. J. A recent epidemic of hysteria in a Louisiana high school. *J. soc. Psychol.,* 1943, 17, 221-235.

SHAPIRO, S. B. A theory of ego pathology and ego therapy. *J. Psychol.,* 1962, 53, 81-90.

SHEPS, J. G. A psychiatric study of successful soldiers. *J. Amer. Med. Ass.,* 1944, 126, 271-273.

SHERMAN, M. *Mental conflicts and personality.* New York: Longmans, Green, 1938.

SHIELDS, J., & SLATER, E. Heredity and psychological abnormality. In H. J. Eysenck (Ed.), *Handbook of abnormal psychology.* New York: Basic Books, 1961. Pp. 298-343.

SLATER, E., & WOODSIDE, MOYA. *Patterns of marriage.* London: Cassell, 1951.

SOLOMON, P., LEIDERMAN, P. H., MENDELSON, J., & WEXLER, D. Sensory deprivation. *Amer. J. Psychiat.,* 1957, 114, 357-363.

STANFIELD, C. E. Clinical experience with chlordiazepoxide (Librium). *Psychosomatics,* 1961, 2, 179-183.

STENGEL, E. The diagnosis and treatment of obsessional states. *Med. Practitioner,* 1951, 113, 134-146.

STEVENSON, I. Processes of "spontaneous" recovery from the psychoneuroses. *Amer. J. Psychiat.,* 1961, 117, 1057-1064.

SULLIVAN, H. S. *The interpersonal theory of psychiatry,* Helen S. Perry, *et al.* (Ed.). New York: Norton, 1953.

SWEETBAUM, H. A. Comparison of the effects of introversion-extraversion and anxiety on conditioning. *J. abnorm. soc. Psychol.,* 1963, 66, 249-254.

SZASZ, T. S. The myth of mental illness. *Amer. Psychol.* 1960, 15, 113-118.

TAYLOR, F. K., & HUNTER, R. C. A. Observations of a hysterical epidemic in a hospital ward. *Psychiat. Quart.,* 1958, 52, 821-839.

TERHUNE, W. B. The phobic syndrome—its nature and treatment. *J. Ark. Med. Soc.,* 1961, 58, 230-236.

THIGPEN, C. H., & CLECKLEY, H. A case of multiple personality. *J. abnorm. soc. Psychol.,* 1954, 49, 135-151.

THIGPEN, C. H., & CLECKLEY, H. M. *Three faces of Eve.* New York: McGraw-Hill, 1957.

THORNE, F. C. An existential theory of anxiety. *J. clin. Psychol.,* 1963, 19, 21-23.

TOBIN, J. M., & LEWIS, N. D. C. New psychotherapeutic agent, chlordiazepoxide. *J. Amer. Med. Ass.,* 1960, 174, 1242-1249.

TSUNG-YI LIN. A study of the incidence of mental disorders in Chinese and other cultures. *Psychiatry,* 1953, 16, 313-336.

WALL, J. H. Diagnosis, treatment, and results in anorexia nervosa. *Amer. J. Psychiat.,* 1959, 115, 997-1001.

WEISS, E., & ENGLISH, O. S. *Psychosomatic medicine.* Philadelphia: W. B. Saunders, 1943.

WIESEL, C., & ARNY, M. Psychiatric study of coal miners in Eastern Kentucky area. *Amer. J. Psychiat.,* 1952, 108, 617-624.

WOLPE, J. *Psychotherapy by reciprocal inhibition.* Stanford: Stanford Univer. Press, 1958.

WOLPE, J., & RACHMAN, S. Psychoanalytic "evidence": a critique based on Freud's case of little Hans. *J. nerv. ment. Dis.,* 1960, 131, 135-148.

WORTIS, J. A psychiatric study tour of the USSR. *J. ment. Sci.,* 1961, 107, 119-156.

WORTIS, J. Physiological treatment. *Amer. J. Psychiat.,* 1962, 118, 595-599.

WORTIS, J. Psychopharmacology and physiological treatment. *Amer. J. Psychiat.,* 1963, 119, 621-626.

ZIEGLER, F. J., IMBODEN, J. B., & MEYER, E. Contemporary conversion reactions: a clinical study. *Amer. J. Psychiat.,* 1960, 116, 901-909.

PSYCHOPHYSIOLOGIC DISORDERS

chapter 7

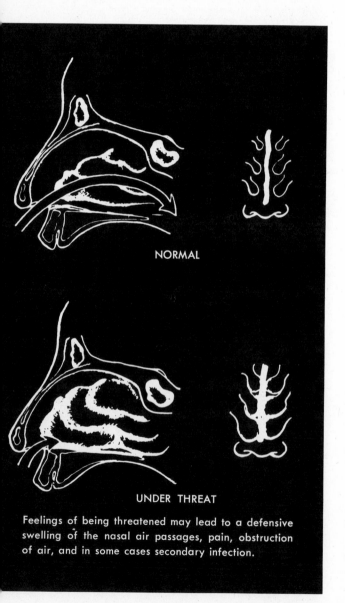

NORMAL

UNDER THREAT

Feelings of being threatened may lead to a defensive swelling of the nasal air passages, pain, obstruction of air, and in some cases secondary infection.

Traditionally, the medical profession has been concerned with physical illness and has concentrated its research on understanding and controlling the organic factors in disease. Psychiatry, on the other hand, emerged as a new profession devoted to the study and treatment of mental illness. Organic pathology was recognized as a causal factor in some cases, but interest centered on uncovering the important mental and emotional factors involved.

Now we realize that both of these viewpoints are limited—that although an illness may be primarily mental or primarily physical, it is always a disorder of the whole person, not just of his arms or lungs or mind. Thus fatigue or a bad cold may lower our tolerance for psychological stress; an emotional upset may lower our resistance to physical disease. As Seguin has stated it, this new holistic approach to medicine "has as its aim the study of man as a whole, a totality, considered as such in health and in disease, and the application of the conclusions of such study to diagnosis, prognosis, and treatment." (1950, p. 28)

Gradually, too, the holistic approach has come to include relevant sociological data, for many variations can readily be observed in the types and incidence of diseases in different groups. The ailments to which we are most subject depend in no small part on when and where we live. Likewise, the life situation to which a patient must return after an illness has much to do with the speed of his recovery. If he is eager to resume his usual activities, recovery is apt to be more rapid than if he faces a return to combat, an unpleasant home, or a frustrating job.[1]

This holistic approach to all illness—fitting relevant biological, psychological, and sociological data into the picture—is also called the *psychosomatic* approach. It now permeates medical thinking not only in treating diseases brought on by emotional tension but also in cases where no causes other than physical ones are apparent. Did emotional factors lower the resistance of the tuberculosis patient and hence contribute to the onset of the disease? How will the patient react to the changes in his life situation brought about by the disease? Will he fail to cooperate in treatment and welcome death as a way out of his problem, or will he fight the disease with a determination to get well? Some patients apparently give up and die when medically the chances seem good that they will recover. Others with more serious organic pathology get well or survive for long periods of time. In fact, Dunbar (1943) has concluded that it is often "more important to know what kind of patient has the disease than what kind of disease the patient has." (p. 23)

Since this is a book on abnormal psychology, we cannot go deeper into emotional factors in primarily physical diseases like tuberculosis, pneumonia, and cancer. We are concerned, however, with organic pathology brought on in large part by mental and emotional factors—by chronic emotional tension stemming from difficulties in adapting to stress. In these ailments, as contrasted with psychoneurotic reactions, we find (a) the repression of emotional tension and its discharge through visceral organ systems, (b) the tendency in a given patient for a single organ system to be involved, such as the respiratory, cardiovascular, or gastrointestinal system, and (c) the frequent production of structural pathology which may even become so severe as to threaten life.

In our modern civilization, psychophysiologic disorders have become a major health problem. As we have seen, at least one out of every two patients seeking medical aid is suffering from an illness related to emotional stresses. According to available statistics, over 5 million people in this country suffer from peptic ulcers, over 7 million from arthritis, and over 10 million from migraine headaches—only three of the disorders in this group (Rennie and Srole, 1956; Pasamanick *et al.,* 1960; Pasamanick, 1962; Commission on Chronic Illness, 1956-1959.[2] Although psychophysiologic disorders are most frequent during the periods of young and middle adulthood, they may occur in any period from early childhood to old age (Erfmann, 1962).

Types of Psychophysiologic Reactions

Psychophysiologic disorders are classified according to the organ system affected.[3] No part of the body seems to be immune. The present classification distinguishes ten groups.

1. *Psychophysiologic skin reaction,* including various so-called neurodermatoses, allergic eczema, some cases of hives and acne, and related disorders where emotional factors play a causative role.

2. *Psychophysiologic musculoskeletal reaction,* including such reactions as backache, muscle cramps, psychogenic rheumatism, and arthritis.

3. *Psychophysiologic respiratory reaction,* including bronchial spasms, asthma, hay fever, sinusitis, and recurring bronchitis.

4. *Psychophysiologic cardiovascular reaction,* including abrupt attacks of excessive heart action, high blood pressure, vascular spasms, and migraine headaches.

---

[1]The role of family, job, economic security, religion, and so on in the treatment of physical illness is well described in Simmons and Wolff (1954). The concept of culture in relation to disease is discussed by Margaret Mead (1953).

[2]Not all ulcers, migraine headaches, and so on are psychophysiologic, of course. In some cases, these disorders are apparently attributable largely or entirely to physiological factors. Just what proportion would fall in this category is not known, but in the preponderance of cases emotional factors appear to play an important role. For example, even though there are over fifty causes of headaches, one investigator found that out of a total of 100 cases in which headaches were the major presenting symptom, only 4 could be explained on an organic basis (Shapiro, 1955).

[3]In the American Psychiatric Association classification these are called *psychophysiologic autonomic and visceral disorders.* They also are often called *psychosomatic disorders.*

TYPICAL PATTERNS IN PSYCHOPHYSIOLOGIC DISORDERS

DISORDER (REACTION)	COMMON PERSONALITY AND STRESS PATTERNS
Asthma (About three times more common among males)	In children appears to involve an appeal for maternal help and protection. In later life may be activated by overdependency and guilt-arousing hostility toward loved ones or by environmental and/or inner conflicts which make individual feel oppressed and restrict his freedom of living. Constitutional predisposition a key factor, whether resulting from heredity, allergies, or respiratory infections.
Stomach ulcer (Three to four times more common among males)	Ambitious, driving individuals with underlying dependency problems; overemphasis on independence and tendency to react to obstacles with anxiety and sustained hostility. Often a history of severe stress involving chronic insecurity. Much more common among "career women" than other women.
Colitis (Four to five times more common among females)	Preponderantly thin, pale persons with marked muscular tension. Often obsessive trends, hypersensitivity, a tendency to be intropunitive in handling hostility, and depressive trends. Constitutional predisposition a key factor in ulcerative colitis in children. Often anxiety and hostility, following lack of needed maternal care.
Neurodermatitis (Two or more times more common among males)	Strong conflicts involving authority figures toward whom the patient feels both hostile and dependent. Often a feeling of being unfairly treated with helplessness to do anything about it. May be precipitated by relatively diverse anxiety-arousing stress situations. Frequent family history of skin disease. Eczema most prevalent during childhood and again after 35.
Migraine (Found almost exclusively among females)	Meticulous, obsessional, scrupulous, perfectionistic, rigid, intelligent with strong conscience development. Headaches usually precipitated by emotional tension stemming from problems relating to financial or social position and by unacceptable hostilities generated in frustrating interpersonal relationships. History of convulsive seizures more common than in general population.
Hypertension (Slightly more common among females)	Person tends to feel continual threat and need to be on guard. Stress may involve chronic hostility and/or anxiety stemming from dependency needs and feelings of insecurity. In many instances appears to result from sustained striving toward high goals with unbalanced life activities that do not permit a "change of pace." Incidence rises rapidly with age, especially between 34 and 64.
Rheumatoid arthritis (About twice as common among females as males)	Chronic inhibited hostility, resentment, and smoldering discontent, often allayed to some extent by self-sacrifice and serving of others. Strong dependency needs and further hostility when such activities thwarted. Often obsessive tidiness, overconscientiousness, and adherence to routine.
Obesity (Sex ratio about equal in childhood but about twice as common among females in adulthood)	Lifelong overeating, which seems to provide compensatory pleasures for frustrations and relief from unbearable tensions. May also serve as a defense; for example, individual too fat to have dates and face problem of marriage, about which he feels inadequate. Also may stem from cultural patterns, metabolic disorders, hereditary tendencies, or brain damage. Obesity appears directly proportional to age.

This chart is based on material from Bram (1950), Crile (1960), Daniels et al. (1962), Dorfman (1961), Fitzelle (1959), Furmanski (1952), Gelhorn and Loofborrow (1962), Kalis et al. (1957), Kenyon (1962), Malone (1962), Marquis et al. (1952), Margolis (1961), Miller (1952), Mohr et al. (1958), Roessler and Greenfield (1958), Stunkard (1962), Weiner et al. (1957), Weiss (1953), Wolf and Wolff (1953), Wolff (1953), and Wolpaw (1960).

5. *Psychophysiologic hemic and lymphatic reaction,* including any disturbances in the blood and lymphatic systems in which emotional factors play a causative role.

6. *Psychophysiologic gastrointestinal reaction,* including such disorders as duodenal ulcer, mucous colitis, chronic gastritis, constipation, hyperacidity, "heartburn," and loss of appetite.

7. *Psychophysiologic genitourinary reaction,* including some types of menstrual disturbances, painful urination, and painful constriction of the vagina (involved in some types of frigidity).

8. *Psychophysiologic endocrine reaction,* including enlargement of the thyroid gland with accompanying symptoms of glandular imbalance, hyperthyroidism, obesity, and related disorders in which emotional factors are prominent.

9. *Psychophysiologic nervous system reaction,* including loss of strength with fatigue and muscle pains, anxiety reaction, and some convulsive disorders.

10. *Psychophysiologic reaction of organs of special sense,* including disorders like chronic conjunctivitis (inflammation of the delicate membrane that lines the eyelids).

For most of these disorders the course of the illness tends to be phasic—there are periods of upsurgence of the symptoms, followed by a waning or disappearance of them. The sequence of their appearance and disappearance seems to be related to the amounts of tension the individual experiences at different times. Although we do not understand the reasons, it is also of interest to note that there are marked sex differences in the incidence of specific psychophysiologic disorders. For example, peptic ulcers are much more common among men while rheumatoid arthritis and mucous colitis are much more common among women.

The following case illustrates some of the interacting factors in these disorders.

"A short, young man with close-cropped, blond hair, shabby, collegiate clothes, a drawn, mask-like facial expression, and downcast eyes came for analysis because of lifelong feelings of inferiority and shyness. He had a hideous facial skin eruption diagnosed as eczema. Lesions also were present on the flexor surfaces of the forearm, the dorsum of the hands, and on the scalp, as well as occasional spots on the legs.

"His analysis brought out the following facts about his life history: He had been much loved by his mother, a gentle person of esthetic temperament who, he felt, idolized him in preference to his two younger brothers; at the same time she was apparently unconsciously seductive. For instance he recalled his anxiety in response to his mother's often putting vaseline on his penis when he was 4. When he was 7 years old she began to have a series of pulmonary hemorrhages, and when he was 8 years old she died of pulmonary tuberculosis. During the months of her final illness he spent hours with her, but would scurry away when he heard his father returning home.

"He remembered with great bitterness his father's warnings to remain out of his mother's bedroom. Her death produced such an intense emotional shock in him that he never really recovered from it. He believed that he and his father were somehow implicated in his mother's death. His father was a domineering, hard-driving, very successful business man of the 'Napoleonic' type. Toward him, especially after his mother's death, the patient felt a mixture of admiration for his success, and antagonism. . . . From early childhood the patient felt inferior to other boys in athletics, and succeeded in compensating for this feeling by brilliance in the classroom. However, when, at the age of 15, he entered an exclusive preparatory school, he found it impossible to adjust. . . . He felt his inequality with the other boys so keenly that for the first time he was not able to outshine them in the classroom. That year, marked by so much tension and frustration, was followed by a stay at camp. While there, following an inoculation of smallpox vaccine, his skin broke out over his head and face. He became acutely disturbed and expressed his guilt over masturbation to everyone in camp. . . .

"He spent the next four years at a western university of high standing, where he become associated with a group of eccentric, brilliant, neurotic young men who indulged themselves in 'esthetic' experiences and obscenities, and might be said to have majored in schizophrenia. He managed to maintain a good scholastic standing, particularly in literary and writing courses. Very often, however, around examination time, his skin would break out, he would contract a cold and spend a few days in the hospital. On several occasions these attacks were precipitated by dates with girls. . . .

"In the early part of his analysis and in his daily life he tried to display himself constantly as a literary genius, a Rabelaisian cynic, and a defeated eccentric with macerated skin—or else a tragic, ruined nonentity bringing humiliation on himself and his father. He was in a constant state of frustration. He never could write successfully, he was impotent with women, and his exhibitionism failed to impress. . . . His job, his friendship and love affairs he permitted to have no real claims upon him or meaning to him. Reality, with its demands for conformity and sublimation, he could not accept. He was constantly impelled to attack weak, depreciated women, who were the only ones who bothered about him—and to attack himself, lacerate his own skin. At the culmination of intense periods of self-destruction, when this conflict was brought to a peak by the demands of external reality—as, for instance, when he had to make his way as a member of a boy's camp, or when he graduated from college and had to get a job—he consciously desired, and actually carried out, the solution of his conflicts by being brought home to his father sick and helpless, with severely infected skin, weeping. . . .

"During analytic hours he moved about on the couch, waved his arms continuously, and spent a good deal of time trying to make an impression with his knowledge of music, art, and literature, identifying himself with Van Gogh. . . .

"It soon became clear that his exhibitionism served many purposes. It could be turned . . . into a defense against, or an expression of, his passive homosexual tendencies. He also used his intellectual exhibitionism as the solace for his wounded narcissism, since he could never expect to become a successful industrialist like his father. . . .

"He began to see, more and more, that his main conflict centered around the urge to compete with his father, an ambition doomed always to failure. . . ." (M. L. Miller, 1948, pp. 405-407, 412)

On page 257 we will examine some of the possible causal factors in this clinical picture.

Dynamics of Psychophysiologic Reactions

In psychophysiologic disorders, the psychological and the physiological variables are so intermeshed that it is difficult to separate them for special study. Perhaps the simplest starting point is to note that the normal person is not chronically anxious or hostile and is able to discharge emotional tensions that do arise through appropriate verbal, fantasy, or physical activities. If he is angry, he may not go so far as striking another person but may be frank in expressing his feelings, or he may gain relief by discussing his frustrations and feelings with a close friend, or he may find some discharge of tension in sports and other competitive activities. Even most psychoneurotic reactions permit some overt discharge of emotional tensions, although usually in an indirect way that is not entirely satisfying.

In the disorders being considered in this chapter, however, the usual channels of emotional outlet are largely blocked; the tension is discharged instead through the visceral organs. Typically this process takes place on an unconscious level: the anxiety or other emotion associated with the stress situation is partly or completely cut off from conscious experience by the defense mechanism of repression. In essence, emotional tensions are "short-circuited" through the autonomic system and discharged through visceral organs. Because these disorders represent a failure to adapt to stress, they are often referred to as "diseases of adaptation." Although much remains to be learned about them, it is especially clear here that an understanding of the dynamics will require a consideration of the interaction of biological, psychological, and sociological factors.

BIOLOGICAL FACTORS

The physical symptoms associated with these disorders are the result of an exaggeration of the normal physiology of emotion—over- or under-reactions of organ systems to sustained stress and chronic emotional mobilization. In a general sense, this takes us back to the stress theory of disease outlined by Hans Selye in his general-adaptation-syndrome, as discussed in Chapter 3. Physiological mechanisms are illustrated for stomach and duodenal ulcers on page 253 and for migraine on pages 256-257.

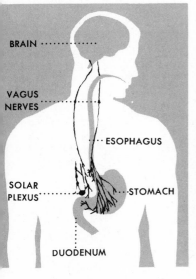

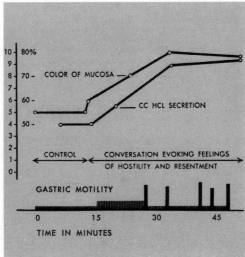

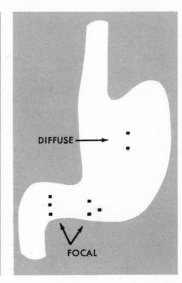

PEPTIC ULCERS

A peptic ulcer usually results from the excessive flow of the stomach's acid-containing digestive juices, which eat away the lining of the stomach or duodenum, leaving a crater-like wound. It is now recognized that nervous tension, worry, repressed anger, and general emotional strain, even more than food and drink, stimulate the flow of these juices. In a historic experiment Wolf and Wolff (1946) demonstrated that feelings of strong resentment, hostility, and anxiety result in a measurable increase of acid production and the engorgement of the stomach with blood, as shown in the chart above (center).

That excessive excitation of certain brain centers leads to ulcers was demonstrated by French et al. (1957), who subjected 19 monkeys to hypothalamic stimulation several times daily for several weeks by means of implanted electrodes. The animals showed signs of bewilderment, fear, or agitation during the stimulation, and 8 of them developed ulcerative changes, in the areas shown above at the right. These animals had also showed increased restlessness and irritability and higher gastric secretion.

More recently, Feld (in press) found that almost half of a group of chronic ulcer patients had abnormal EEG's, as compared with only a sixth of a control group. Such electrical disturbances, of course, might be caused either by earlier brain injury or by prolonged psychological stress. Thus the typical tense, hard-driving ulcer patient may be tense and hard driving because of overexcitation of certain brain centers, or he may have developed chronic overexcitation of certain brain centers because he is tense and hard driving. Probably in most cases the relationship—eventually, at least—is a circular one.

As we might expect, individuals whose life situation and/or personality organization make them prone to chronic anxiety and resentment are also prone to the development of peptic ulcers. Gosling (1957) has found a low incidence of peptic ulcers among psychotics, especially schizophrenics, but a higher than normal incidence among neurotics, alcoholics, and asthmatics.

According to Hartman (n.d.), certain Indians of Latin America never suffer from peptic ulcers; and Steigmann (1936) found that the incidence among urban Negroes in the southern United States was fairly low, though for Negroes who had lived more than five years in Chicago it was the same as that for whites. Thus there is evidence that sociocultural differences play a role in the incidence of ulcers.

Peptic ulcers first came into prominence in our Western culture between 1820 and 1840. During this period they were primarily confined to young women, but in the second half of the nineteenth century there was a shift, and now the incidence of ulcers is some three to four times higher among men than women. Modern civilization is apparently especially conducive to the chronic emotional reactions which lead to the development of peptic ulcers, and it is estimated that about 1 in every 10 Americans now living will at some time develop a peptic ulcer.

Peptic ulcers are most effectively approached from the psychosomatic point of view. If the ulcer is located in the duodenum, as most peptic ulcers are, the physician can reassure the patient who fears cancer, for the duodenal ulcer is rarely, if ever, cancerous. The condition can be controlled and alleviated through diet and various modern drugs but a cure usually requires adequate psychotherapy to correct chronic emotional overreaction.

Comparable physiological patterns have been worked out for endocrine abnormalities, high blood pressure, and various other disorders.

One of the major physiological factors which is still not understood is *organ specificity*. Why does one individual react with bronchial spasms, another with hives, and still another with migraine headaches? Three general theories have been advanced to account for this variation in specific symptoms.

The first theory assumes that various personality characteristics are associated with particular psychophysiological disorders—for example, that persons suffering from hypertension tend to be rigid, highly sensitive to threat, and prone to chronic underlying hostility (Kalis *et al.,* 1957; Kaplan *et al.,* 1961). Such personality profiles stem largely from some of the earlier work of Flanders Dunbar (1954) which raised the hope that the differentiation of accident-prone personalities, ulcer types, hypertensive characters, and so on would be of great value in understanding, diagnosis, and treatment. More recent experimental evidence suggests that this approach is overly simplified and points to the importance of constitutional factors, situational stresses, and the concept of multiple causes (Bandler, 1958; Kaplan and Kaplan, 1959; Pasamanick, 1960).

The second theory asserts that emotional tension may influence practically any physiological process and that the particular symptoms depend upon the history and constitutional make-up of the patient. Wolff (1950b) has pointed out that some people react to emotional strain with a quickened pulse but no change in blood pressure, whereas for others the reverse is true. He has suggested that people can be characterized as "stomach reactors," "pulse reactors," "nose reactors," and so on. It follows that a person who reacts to any stress with a rise in blood pressure, for example, perhaps as a result of a genetic factor, would then be particularly vulnerable to hypertension if exposed to sustained stress (Katz, 1962). Similarly, the person who has inherited a "weak" stomach presumably will be especially prone to stomach upsets when he becomes angry or anxious. Or if a person has had a respiratory infection, his lungs or nasal passages may remain especially vulnerable, and emotional stress may bring on attacks of bron-

chitis or asthma. In still other cases, early conditioning may develop individualized neurophysiological responses to stress which tend to involve one organ system to a greater extent than others and result in pathology in this organ system under sustained and exaggerated emotional tension (Grinker, 1956; Grossman and Greenberg, 1957; Richmond and Lustman, 1955). Essentially, the individual's "physiological Achilles' heel" will be the organ affected, whether this vulnerability is due to heredity, previous disease, or early conditioning.

The third theory emphasizes differences in the physiological changes accompanying various emotional states (Grace *et al.,* 1951; Wolff, 1950a; Cattell, 1963). For example, fear is associated with the release of adrenalin, whereas anxiety is not; fear dries the mouth and reduces gastric secretion, whereas anxiety produces increased salivation and secretion of stomach acid. If such changes in normal bodily function are maintained over long periods of time, they presumably lead to organ pathology—the nature of the pathology depending on the organ system and type of emotional state involved. In eliciting different emotions in the first place, the type of stress is also a contributing factor.

Most investigators apparently take an approach involving all three theories but with emphasis on the last two: special vulnerability of the affected organ system, specific emotional reactions, and the nature of the stress situation are all thought to play key roles in the etiology of psychophysiologic disorders. Personality make-up is by no means ruled out, however, for individuals view and react to particular stress situations in quite different ways—both psychologically and physiologically.

PSYCHOLOGICAL FACTORS

The role of psychological factors in psychophysiologic disorders is still somewhat unclear, but their importance is undeniable. In Chapter 4, we reported a study by Hinkle *et al.* (1957) showing the direct relationship between problems of adjustment, as perceived by the individual, and the incidence of physical illness. Throughout an individual's lifetime, the amount and timing of physical illness as well as the number of body systems involved are closely related to his life stresses.

Available studies of patients' family backgrounds emphasize the role of dominant, overly protective mothers who were uncomfortable with the child's emotions and tended to be unduly restrictive of his activities, thus arousing considerable covert hostility on the part of the child (Wenar *et al.*, 1962; Goldberg, 1959; Szyrynski, 1960). The father has been described as typically passive and an inadequate male model for the child. Individuals coming out of such a family background often have problems of dependency and insecurity, do not know how to handle hostility and anxiety, and tend to overreact with chronic emotional mobilization to stresses which the normal person handles effectively.

Evidently, however, there is a wide variation in personality make-up among individuals suffering from psychophysiologic disorders—both in general and in relation to specific reactions such as peptic ulcers. And even where "typical" personality traits are found among these patients, we are left with the problem of why many other people with similar personality traits show psychoneurotic or other reactions instead of psychophysiologic ones.

Another factor often emphasized is the inability of these individuals either to discharge their emotions adequately by the verbal and various other means most of us use every day or to erect psychological defenses for the alleviation of emotional tension (Kaplan and Kaplan, 1959). Though their awareness of their chronic and exaggerated emotion may be repressed, the physiological components of the emotion continue and eventually lead to structural damage. From this viewpoint, many psychophysiologic disorders are a consequence of the individual's vulnerability to particular stresses and continuing inability to handle the emotional tensions that are aroused.

This viewpoint is supported by the findings of Hokanson and Burgess (1962) with individuals subjected experimentally to frustrating situations. Those given an opportunity afterwards to show physical or verbal aggression against the frustrater showed a rapid return to normal of systolic blood pressure and heart rate whereas those who were permitted only fantasy ag-

gression or none at all returned to normal physiological functioning much more slowly. It may be noted, too, that psychophysiologic disorders are rare among psychotics, who as a group show little anxiety, but common among neurotics, a group typically high in anxiety (Appel and Rosen, 1950; Cattell *et al.*, 1963; Gosling, 1957; Ehrentheil and Marchand, 1960).

Another common psychological factor in the development of psychophysiologic disorders is learning through conditioning or imitation. Halliday (1953) has reported that the proportion of patients reporting the same or similar disorders in close relatives is significantly higher than would be expected for the general population. Although this could result either from a common hereditary predisposition or from their common sociocultural setting, it is also possible that such a way of dealing with emotional tensions could be learned from other family members through imitation.

Turnbull (1962) has also shown that "asthma-like" reactions can be learned by animals via conditioning procedures. By rewarding or reinforcing certain breathing behavior, the experimenter can elicit respiratory patterns which are progressively closer approximations of asthmatic breathing. Presumably, human beings might also learn asthmatic breathing as a means of reducing anxiety. For example, if an infant experienced anxiety in the absence of the mother, he might get no attention from crying, but his sighing, gasping, wheezing, or coughing —reactions which often follow crying spells— might lead to the return of the mother and the alleviation of anxiety. If this pattern were repeated, the infant might learn an asthma-like response as a means of obtaining parental attention and reducing his anxiety.

Initially, the respiratory pattern might only remotely resemble clinical asthma, but with time and continued reinforcement, it could increase in amplitude and specificity. In this way an asthmatic reaction, which is uncomfortable or even painful, might be learned through instrumental conditioning and used to deal with the still more painful experience of anxiety. In addition, through generalization the asthmatic reaction might come to be used as a means of reducing anxiety elicited by other types of stressful situations. By virtue of its anxiety-reducing qual-

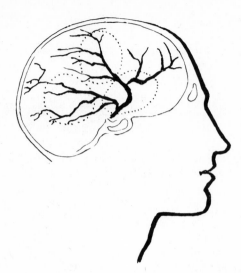

Migraine Headaches

About 12 million Americans, approximately 8 per cent of the total population, suffer from chronic headaches. Although a wide range of organic conditions such as brain tumors, high blood pressure, and fevers associated with infectious diseases are capable of producing headaches, the overwhelming majority (at least 99 out of 100) are psychophysiologic. Many are of a migraine type.

Migraine is a periodic or recurrent headache. It usually occurs on one side of the head, though it may be more generalized and may shift from side to side. Migraine is by no means new in the history of man; it was extensively described by Galen and other early medical writers. The cause of the pain remained a mystery until recently, however, when interest was focused on the pain-sensitive arteries of the head. By dilating these arteries with an injection of histamine, it was found possible to reproduce the pain of migraine.

Turning then to actual cases of migraine, researchers discovered that the onset of the headaches was accompanied by progressive dilation of the cranial arteries. In addition, patients with unilateral headaches showed dilation of the cranial artery only on the side where the pain occurred. As the attack subsided, either spontaneously or following the administration of drugs, the pain diminished, and the arteries returned to their normal size.

The side-view drawing of the head above shows the location of these pain-sensitive arteries: the shaded areas mark the places where the headache is felt as various parts of the arteries dilate and thicken.

Effort has been extended in recent years to discover the conditions which bring about vascular dilation. Since this condition seemed to run in families, heredity was assumed to be a major causative factor; but this did not account for the specific onset and recurrent nature of the pain. Further study has revealed that a variety of experimentally

---

ity, it would be continually reinforced and hence would tend to persist.

Turnbull has also noted that when more adaptive ways of coping with anxiety are later acquired, the individual still may regress to asthmatic responses under severe stress. Although constitutional factors would not be essential for the learning of a psychophysiologic reaction, sensitization or allergies to certain types of inhalants could act as predisposing influences in the etiological pattern.

Finally, it has been observed that a particular kind of stress situation often elicits similar psychophysiologic reactions in individuals exposed

to it. This is true particularly for stomach ulcers and other gastrointestinal disorders. Brady (1958) demonstrated the development of gastrointestinal lesions in "executive monkeys" exposed to a particular type of experimental stress situation. There is a similar high incidence of ulcers among human executives who work under conditions of chronic pressure and job insecurity. Likewise, as we have seen, gastrointestinal disorders were especially prevalent among combat personnel in both World War II and the Korean War. In most clinics, it is an accepted practice to investigate the stress factors in the life situation of the patient and to attempt to alleviate

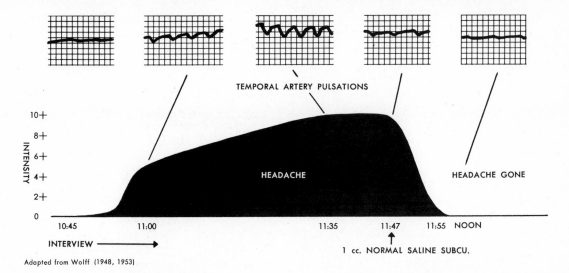

Adapted from Wolff (1948, 1953)

induced stresses—frustrations, excessive work demands, and threatening interviews—cause vascular dilation among migraine sufferers but not among other persons.

The graph traces the course of a headache induced during a discussion which evoked feelings of hostility in a patient. Both the changes in the amplitude of the artery pulsations and the corresponding increase and diminution in the intensity of the pain are shown. The headache was "cured" by means of an injection which the patient believed would end the suffering but which actually could have had no physical effect.

In general, migraine patients have been found to be ambitious, rigid perfectionists, who like to live "according to plan." While overly sensitive to criticism themselves, they are prone to be overly critical of others and feel the need to outdo them. They frequently react to frustrations in interpersonal relations with sustained anger and resentment which are not given adequate outlets.

It is now thought that the emotional tensions generated by the ambitious strivings and repressed hostilities of such persons are channeled through the vascular system in such a way that the cranial arteries are dilated, causing the painful headaches. Why the emotional reaction should affect the cranial arteries rather than result in spasms of the bronchial muscles or oversecretion of stomach acids is not known.

Cross-cultural comparisons of the incidence of migraine and comparisons among diverse groups in our own society are lacking. About the only information available at present is that there is apparently a higher incidence of migraine among women than among men and among city dwellers than among farmers.

Some temporary relief from migraine may be obtained through the administration of sedatives, but permanent recovery requires the modification of the nonadaptive reaction pattern.

those stresses which appear relevant to the etiology of the particular psychophysiologic disorder observed (Simon, 1960).

In other cases, the stress situation apparently does not determine the kind of disorder that appears but merely serves to precipitate or maintain a psychophysiologic disorder in a person already predisposed to a particular pattern. For example, the patient who already is allergic to a particular protein may have his resistance further lowered by emotional tension (J. Miller, 1960; Taub, 1961).

In the case of the young man with the psychophysiologic skin reaction, there appeared to be

several possible relationships between his emotional conflicts and his skin lesions: (a) the lesions were a relatively direct somatic expression of anxiety since his psychological defenses were highly inadequate, (b) the lesions were a defense against feelings of inadequacy and failure since they represented a physical handicap, (c) the lesions had value for exhibitionistic purposes, yielding some compensatory attention, and (d) the lesions were a means of self-punishment for failure and guilt. In addition, however, we cannot overlook the fact that his first outbreak came after an inoculation. Perhaps the skin lesions would have appeared without the inoculation. Or perhaps if he had eaten some poisoned food just then, his outbreaks then and later would have involved his digestive system instead of his skin. There had been no previous evidence of organ vulnerability.

In psychophysiologic disorders, the etiological pattern is by no means a simple one to unravel. Neurophysiological and psychological factors are so interwoven that they can hardly be separated; undoubtedly they are constantly interacting. The reaction pattern we see in a given case may be part cause and part effect. Crile (1960) has pointed out that the patient suffering from ulcerative colitis may react with acute distress to his intractable diarrhea; similarly, hyperthyroidism may be in part precipitated by a nervous, irritable temperament and itself the cause of further irritability and nervousness. Such vicious circles are also augmented by the adverse effects of the patient's symptoms on his interpersonal relationships, his efficiency at work, and his other life activities.

SOCIOLOGICAL FACTORS

We are far from an understanding of the role of sociological factors in these disorders, although we have considerable evidence of their importance. Trends in the incidence of specific diseases vary in different societies and in different strata of the same society. Migraine headaches are more common among city dwellers than among the rural population. Peptic ulcers are unheard of among certain primitive groups in South America; in our own society, the incidence varies considerably for different occupational groups.

In an extensive study of the prevalence and socioeconomic distribution of psychophysiologic disorders in a depressed midtown residential area of New York City, Rennie and Srole (1956) found that these disorders were most highly concentrated at the two extremes of the socioeconomic scale. Certain patterns for particular psychophysiologic reactions were also noted. Arthritis and hypertension were most commonly found in the lower socioeconomic strata, while colitis, rashes, and hay fever were most commonly found in the upper strata. Asthma showed the highest incidence at both extremes, being relatively infrequent in between. Stomach ulcers did not follow any socioeconomic pattern, but individuals who had fathers who were apparently "strivers," in the sense that they had less education than their occupational peers, had a higher rate of ulcers than those whose fathers' education was appropriate to their occupational level.

Reporting on an equally comprehensive study in Baltimore, Md., Pasamanick (1960, 1962) found a somewhat comparable socioeconomic distribution of psychophysiologic disorders, although hypertension was much more prevalent on middle and upper than on lower socioeconomic levels.[1] These investigators also noted that obesity, hypertension, and arthritis were more common among nonwhites, while migraine, hay fever, and other allergies were more common among the white population.

The overall incidence of psychophysiologic disorders has been reported as being more than twice as high for whites as nonwhites. Pasamanick (1963), however, cautions that this apparent discrepancy may result partly from the fact that nonwhite members of the lower class appear less concerned with such symptoms and thus are somewhat less likely to report them to interviewers.

Trends in the incidence of disease within a given society may be affected by sociological conditions such as economic recessions, political and social disorganization or change, and increasingly stressful conditions of living. In this context, it is interesting to note that in the last twenty years the incidence of cardiovascular-renal diseases and peptic ulcers has increased over 30 per cent for men but declined over 30 per cent for women (Bowman, 1958). In general, sociocultural conditions which markedly increase the stressfulness of living tend to play havoc with the human organism and lead to the increased incidence of psychophysiologic disorders as well as other physical and mental ills (Montagu, 1961).

---

[1] It is difficult to compare the findings of these two investigations since they differed widely in methodology—the New York study utilizing an interview method of trying to ascertain the "lifetime" incidence of various psychophysiologic conditions while the Baltimore study relied heavily on actual clinical evaluation of the subjects at the time of the study. These methodological differences are reviewed by Pasamanick (1962).

Treatment and Prognosis

The treatment of psychophysiologic disorders necessitates the full integration of medical, psychological, and sociological approaches. Medical procedures may involve the use of special diets, medication, and surgery, depending upon the requirements of the particular patient. Although the evidence is limited, it would appear that tranquilizing drugs are of great value in the treatment of these disorders—contributing to some alleviation of symptoms in 50 to 80 per cent of the cases (Evans, 1960; Lester *et al.*, 1962; Merlis and Turner, 1961; J. Miller, 1960; Stanfield, 1961; Taub, 1961; Tuteur, 1963; Wortis, 1962, 1963).

The treatment of psychophysiologic disorders by means of conditioning techniques also appears to show promise (Eysenck, 1960; Lesse, 1958). The basic objective here is to bring the functions of the stomach, bladder, skin, colon, and other bodily organs innervated by the autonomic nervous system under systematic control, avoiding hypo- or hyperfunction of these systems. In most cases, however, the abatement of symptoms achieved by medical or conditioning treatment will be permanent only if there is also a change in the patient's personality pattern or in his stress situation. Thus psychotherapy and sociotherapy are usually essential aspects of the treatment program. The precise treatment required, of course, depends on all the organic, personality, and stress components in the case and varies as much with the individual as with the type of disorder.

Although the prognosis is generally favorable for patients who receive appropriate therapy, a great many people continue to suffer chronically from psychophysiologic disorders because they receive only superficial treatment and the causes of their excessive, unrelieved emotional tensions are not eliminated. In some cases, too, the patient does not really want to be cured because his symptoms have important secondary gains in eliciting concern from others and enabling him to some extent to dominate their behavior. Thus a husband with peptic ulcers may use his "sickness" to control many aspects of his marital relationship. The importance of early diagnosis and treatment of these disorders cannot be overemphasized—particularly from a medical viewpoint. Delay may mean irreversible tissue change and in some instances internal hemorrhaging or other conditions threatening to life itself.

In completing our discussion of psychophysiologic disorders, we may emphasize again the tremendous potentialities that the holistic approach holds for man's eventual conquest of all disease. For as researchers have probed into diverse disease processes, the crucial importance of biological, psychological, and sociological factors in their inception and course has become increasingly apparent.

REFERENCES

The reference list includes not only the sources from which the author has drawn material, but acknowledgments of the permissions granted by authors and publishers to quote directly from their works.

APPEL, J., & ROSEN, S. R. Psychotic factors in psychosomatic illness. *Psychosom. Med.*, 1950, 12, 236-243.

BANDLER, B. Some conceptual tendencies in the psychosomatic movement. *Amer. J. Psychiat.*, 1958, 115, 36-43.

BOWMAN, K. M. Alcoholism and geriatrics. *Amer. J. Psychiat.*, 1958, 114, 621-623.

BRADY, J. V. Ulcers in "executive" monkeys. *Scientif. Amer.*, 1958, 199 (4), 95-98, 100.

BRAM, I. Psychic factors in obesity; observations in over 1,000 cases. *Arch. Pediatr.*, 1950, 67, 543-552.

CATTELL, R. B. The nature and measurement of anxiety. *Scientif. Amer.*, 1963, 208 (3), 96-104.

CATTELL, R. B., SCHEIER, I. H., & LORR, M. Recent advances in the measurement of anxiety, neuroticism, and the psychotic syndrome. *Ann. N. Y. Acad. Sci.*, 1962, 93, 840-850.

COMMISSION ON CHRONIC ILLNESS. *Chronic illness in the United States.* Cambridge: Harvard Univer. Press, 1956-59.

CRILE, G., JR. Personality traits in organic diseases. *Psychosomatics*, 1960, 1, 26-28.

DANIELS, G. E., O'CONNOR, J. F., KARUSH, A., MOSES, L., FLOOD, C. A., & LEPORE, M. Three decades in the observation and treatment of ulcerative colitis. *Psychosom. Med.*, 1962, 24, 85-93.

DORFMAN, W. The enigma of obesity. *Psychosomatics*, 1961, 2, 187-193.

DUNBAR, FLANDERS. *Psychosomatic diagnosis.* New York: Harper, 1943.

DUNBAR, FLANDERS. *Emotions and bodily changes.* (4th ed.) New York: Columbia Univer. Press, 1954.

EHRENTHEIL, O. F., & MARCHAND, W. E. *Clinical medicine and the psychotic patient.* Springfield, Ill.: Charles C. Thomas, 1960.

ERFMANN, IRMGARD. Age and manifestation of psychosomatic disorders. *Vita humana*, Basel, 1962, 5, 161-166.

EVANS, W. L. The effect of phenelzine in psychosomatic and psychophysiologic illnesses. *Psychosomatics*, 1960, 1, 263-269.

EYSENCK, H. J. (Ed.) *Behaviour therapy and the neuroses.* New York: Pergamon Press, 1960.

FELD, M. In J. Wortis, & A. Mandell (Eds.), *Recent advances in biological psychiatry.* Vol. 6., in press. New York: Plenum Press.

FITZELLE, G. T. Personality factors and certain attitudes toward child rearing among parents of asthmatic children. *Psychosom. Med.*, 1959, 21, 208-217.

FRENCH, J. D., PORTER, R. W., CAVANAUGH, E. B., & LONGMIRE, R. L. Experimental gastroduodenal lesions induced by stimulation of the brain. *Psychosom. Med.*, 1957, 19, 209-220.

FURMANSKI, A. R. Dynamic concepts of migraine: a character study of one hundred patients. *AMA Arch. Neurol. Psychiat.*, 1952, 67, 23-31.

GELLHORN, E., & LOOFBOURROW, G. N. *Emotions and emotional disorders.* New York: Harper, 1963.

GOLDBERG, ELSA M. *Family influences and psychosomatic illness.* London: Tavistock Publ. Ltd., 1959.

GOSLING, R. H. Peptic ulcer and mental disorder, Part II. *J. psychosom. Res.*, 1957, 2, 284-301.

GRACE, W. J., WOLF, S., & WOLFF, H. G. *The human colon.* New York: Harper, 1951.

GRINKER, R. R. Psychosomatic approach to anxiety. *Amer. J. Psychiat.*, 1956, 113, 443-447.

GROSSMAN, H. J., & GREENBERG, N. H. Psychosomatic differentiation in infancy: I. Autonomic activity in the newborn. *Psychosom. Med.*, 1957, 19, 293-306.

HALLIDAY, J. L. Concept of a psychosomatic affection. In A. Weider (Ed.), *Contributions toward medical psychology*, Vol. 1. New York: Ronald, 1953. Pp. 173-186.

HINKLE, L. E., JR. *et al.* Studies in human ecology. *Amer. J. Psychiat.*, 1957, 114, 212-220.

HOKANSON, J. E., & BURGESS, M. The effects of three types of aggression on vascular process. *J. abnorm. soc. Psychol.*, 1962, 64, 446-449.

KALIS, BETTY L., HARRIS, R. E., SOKOLOW, M., & CARPENTER, L. G. Response to psychological stress in patients with essential hypertension. *Amer. Heart J.*, 1957, 53, 572-578.

KAPLAN, H. I., & KAPLAN, HELEN S. Current theoretical concepts in psychosomatic medicine. *Amer. J. Psychiat.*, 1959, 115, 1091-1096.

KAPLAN, S. M., GOTTSCHALK, L. A., MAGLIOCCO, E. B., ROHOVIT, D. D., & ROSS, W. D. Hostility in verbal productions and hypnotic dreams of hypertensive patients. *Psychosom. Med.*, 1961, 23, 311-322.

KATZ, L. N. Newer concepts in relation to hypertension. *Calif. Med.*, 1962, 97, 201-205.

KENYON, F. E. A psychiatric survey of a random sample of out-patients attending a dermatological hospital. *J. Psychosom. Res.*, 1962, 6, 129-135.

LESSE, S. Current clinical and research trends in Soviet psychiatry. *Amer. J. Psychiat.*, 1958, 114, 1018-1022.

LESTER, EVA P., WITTKOWER, E. D., KALZ, F., & AZIMA, H. Phenotropic drugs in psychosomatic disorders (skin). *Amer. J. Psychiat.*, 1962, 119, 136-143.

MALONE, J. P. Migraine. *J. Irish Med. Ass.*, 1962, 51, 36-38.

MARGOLIS, M. The mother-child relationship in bronchial asthma. *J. abnorm. soc. Psychol.*, 1961, 63, 360-367.

MARQUIS, DOROTHY P., SINNETT, E. R., & WINTER, W. D. A psychological study of peptic ulcer patients. *J. clin. Psychol.*, 1952, 8, 266-272.

MEAD, MARGARET. The concept of culture and the psychosomatic approach. In A. Weider (Ed.), *Contributions toward medical psychology*, Vol. 1. New York: Ronald, 1953. Pp. 368-397.

MERLIS, S., & TURNER, W. J. Drug evaluation and practical psychiatric therapeutics. *J. Amer. Med. Ass.*, 1961, 177, 38-43.

MILLER, J. Treatment of emotional problems in allergic disorders: a double-bind placebo-controlled study. *Psychosomatics*, 1960, 1, 338-341.

MILLER, M. L. A psychological study of a case of eczema and a case of neurodermatitis. In F. Alexander & T. M. French (Eds.), *Studies in psychosomatic medicine.* New York: Ronald, 1948.

MILLER, M. L. Emotional conflicts in asthma. *Dis. nerv. System*, 1952, 13, 298-302.

MOHR, G. J., JOSSELYN, IRENE M., SPURLOCK, JEANNE, & BARRON, S. H. Studies in ulcerative colitis. *Amer. J. Psychiat.*, 1958, 114, 1067-1076.

MONTAGU, A. Culture and mental illness. *Amer. J. Psychiat.*, 1961, 118, 15-23.

PASAMANICK, B. Prevalence and distribution of psychosomatic conditions in an urban population according to social class. *Psychosom. Med.*, 1962, 24, 352-356.

PASAMANICK, B. Some misconceptions concerning differences in the racial prevalence of mental disease. *Amer. J. Orthopsychiat.*, 1963, 23, 72-86.

PASAMANICK, B., LEMKAU, P., ROBERTS, D. W., & KRUEGER, D. E. A survey of mental disease in an urban population: III. Prevalence and demographic distribution of some "psychosomatic" disorders. In J. S. Gottlieb, & G. Tourney (Eds.), *Scientific papers and discussion.* Chicago: American Psychiatric Ass., 1960. Pp. 245-253.

RENNIE, T. A. C., SROLE, L. Social class prevalence and distribution of psychosomatic conditions in an urban population. *Psychosom. Med.*, 1956, 18, 449-456.

RICHMOND, J. B., & LUSTMAN, S. L. Autonomic function in the neonate: I. Implications for psychosomatic theory. *Psychosom. Med.*, 1955, 17, 269-275.

ROESSLER, R., & GREENFIELD, N. S. *Physiological correlates of psychological disorder.* Madison, Wis.: Univer. Wisconsin Press, 1962.

SEGUIN, C. A. *Introduction to psychosomatic medicine.* New York: International Univer. Press, 1950.

SHAPIRO, M. F. Problem of psychogenic tension headache. *N. Y. St. J. Med.*, 1955, 55, 2347-2351.

SIMMONS, L. W., & WOLFF, H. G. *Social science in medicine.* New York: Russell Sage Found., 1954.

SIMON, A. J. Illness and the psychodynamics of stressful life situations as seen in a children's clinic. *J. Hlth. & Human Behav.*, 1960, 1, 13-17.

STANFIELD, C. E. Clinical experience with chlordiazepoxide (Librium). *Psychosomatics*, 1961, 2, 179-183.

STUNKARD, A. Research on a disease: strategies in the study of obesity. In R. Roessler, & N. S. Greenfield (Eds.), *Physiological correlates of psychological disorder.* Madison, Wis.: Univer. Wisconsin, 1962. Pp. 211-220.

SZYRYNSKI, V. Defective "psychological weaning" in psychosomatic pathology. *Psychosomatics*, 1960, 1, 22-25.

TAUB, S. J. The management of anxiety in allergic disorders—a new approach. *Psychosomatics*, 1961, 2, 349-350.

TURNBULL, J. W. Asthma conceived as a learned response. *J. psychosom. Res.*, 1962, 6, 59-70.

TUTEUR, W. Tranquilizers and psychosomatic illness. *Amer. J. Psychiat.*, 1963, 119, 787-788.

WEINER, H., THALER, M., REISER, M. F., & MIRSKY, I. A. Etiology of duodenal ulcer. I. Relation of specific psychological characteristics to rate of gastric secretion (serum pepsinogen). *Psychosom. Med.*, 1957, 10, 1-10.

WEISS, E. Psychosomatic aspects of essential hypertension. *Acta Psychother., psychosom. Orthopaedagogy*, 1953, 1, 13-21.

WENAR, C., et al. *Origins of psychosomatic and emotional disturbances; a study of mother-child relationships.* New York: Harper, 1962.

WOLF, S., & WOLFF, H. G. Psychosomatic aspects of peptic ulcers. *Scope*, 1946, 11, 4-9.

WOLF, S., & WOLFF, H. G. *Headaches: their nature and treatment.* Boston: Little, Brown, 1953.

WOLFF, H. G. *Headache and other head pain.* Cambridge: Oxford Univer. Press, 1948.

WOLFF, H. G. Life stress and bodily disease—a formulation. *Res. Publ. Ass. Nerv. Ment. Dis.*, 1950(a), 29, 1059-1094.

WOLFF, H. G. Life stress and cardiovascular disorders. *Circulation*, 1950(b), 1, 187-203.

WOLFF, H. G. Life stress and bodily disease. In A. Weider (Ed.), *Contributions toward medical psychology*, Vol. 1. New York: Ronald, 1953.

WOLFF, H. H. Bronchial asthma, physical and psychological aspects. *J. Irish Med. Ass.*, 1962, 51, 31-35.

WOLPAW, R. The arthritic personality. *Psychosomatic*, 1960, 1, 195-197.

WORTIS, J. Physiological treatment. *Amer. J. Psychiat.*, 1962, 118, 595-599.

WORTIS, J. Psychopharmacology and physiological treatment. *Amer. J. Psychiat.*, 1963, 119, 621-626.

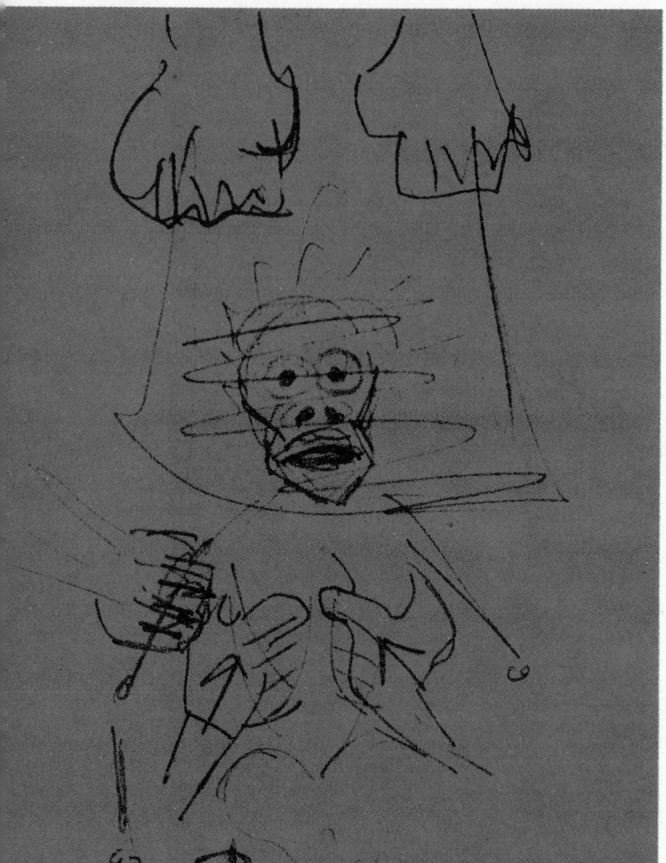

This drawing is a psychotic patient's portrayal of her feelings of disintegration. She feels she is being torn apart.

THE FUNCTIONAL PSYCHOSES

chapter 8

CLASSIFICATION AND SYMPTOMS

GENERAL ETIOLOGICAL CONSIDERATIONS

GENERAL PROGNOSIS

SCHIZOPHRENIC REACTIONS

PARANOID REACTIONS

AFFECTIVE PSYCHOTIC REACTIONS

INVOLUTIONAL PSYCHOTIC REACTIONS

In psychotic disorders, the patient manifests a severe personality decompensation with a marked distortion and loss of contact with reality. He is unable to relate himself effectively to other people or to his work and usually has to be hospitalized. Thus, in general, the psychoses are much more severe and disabling than are the psychoneuroses although it may be re-emphasized that there is no sharp dividing line between them: the neuroses blend imperceptibly into the psychoses with increasing degrees of personality disorganization or decompensation. The chart on page 264 provides a more detailed comparison of neuroses and psychoses.

The term *insanity* is frequently used in reference to psychotic patients. This is a social and legal term rather than a medical one and denotes mental disorder so severe that the individual is judged to be unable to manage his affairs, perform his social duties and responsibilities, or be held accountable for his actions.

There are an estimated 1,000,000 persons

suffering from psychotic disorders in the United States at any one time. Of these, about two thirds are hospitalized in state, veterans', county, city, or private hospitals. A limited but increasing number of psychotic patients receive treatment in day-care hospital centers and return home in the evenings and for week ends. The remainder are cared for at home for one reason or another.

Are psychoses on the increase? We have noted that mental patients (mostly psychotics) occupy almost one half of all the hospital beds in the United States. This figure requires some explanation, however, as psychotic patients may be hospitalized for several months or even years, whereas nonpsychiatric patients are hospitalized on the average for about two weeks. Were patients in general medicine hospitalized for an equivalent period, they would occupy more than ten times as many beds as do mental patients.

As we noted in Chapter 1, while the population has roughly quadrupled since 1880, the number of patients in mental hospitals now is about 18 times as high. This is largely a reflection of increased hospital facilities, changes in public attitudes toward mental illnesses (so that patients are not as reluctant as they once were to receive treatment), and marked increases in the mental disorders of old age, but the long-range trend does seem to involve a slight but continuous increase. Interestingly enough, however, this is not true for all the psychotic syndromes. The rate for schizophrenia, for example, has apparently been constant for many years, whereas that for manic-depressive reactions, paresis, and involutional psychotic reactions has actually declined. But these decreases have been more than canceled out by increases in other types, such as old-age psychoses.

Before taking up the specific syndromes, it will help the student to get an overall picture of psychotic reactions if we briefly review (a) the main types of psychoses, (b) some of the general factors that they have in common, and (c) the present prognosis for psychotic patients as a group.

Classification and Symptoms of Psychoses

Psychotic symptoms may originate from either psychological stresses or organic brain pathology or from the interaction of both. For this reason psychotic disorders are divided into two general categories—*functional* and *organic* psychoses—depending on whether or not there is some demonstrable associated brain pathology. The functional psychoses are in turn divided into four main groupings or types:

1. *Schizophrenic reactions,* a group of psychotic disorders in which there is a strong tendency to retreat from reality, with emotional "blunting" and disharmony and marked disturbances in thought processes. Delusions, hallucinations, and stereotypies are common.

2. *Paranoid reactions,* in which the patient (a) has delusions, usually of persecution and/or grandeur, but maintains in other respects a relatively intact personality structure, or (b) manifests a transient paranoid state with delusions and hallucinations but without the more severe deterioration of paranoid schizophrenics.

3. *Affective reactions,* involving extreme fluctuations in mood, with related disturbances in thought and behavior. There are two major subgroups here: manic-depressive reactions and psychotic depressive reactions.

4. *Involutional psychotic reactions,* denoting abnormal depression, agitation, and anxiety during the involutional period without previous history of psychosis.

The organic psychoses also have several subgroups. They will be discussed in Part IV but are mentioned here because many of the introductory concepts having to do with psychotic behavior apply to both types.

Although each psychotic reaction type represents a unique *cluster* of symptoms, there are many *individual* symptoms which may occur in almost any type. An overview of the range and categories of specific symptoms in psychotic reactions, as identified by the Lorr Psychiatric Scale (a rating scale), is shown in the chart on page 267. Grouping the symptoms

COMPARISON OF NEUROTIC AND PSYCHOTIC DISORDERS		
FACTOR	PSYCHONEUROSES	PSYCHOSES
General behavior	Mild degree of personality decompensation; reality contact and social functioning impaired	Severe degree of personality decompensation; reality contact markedly impaired; patient incapacitated in social functioning
Nature of symptoms	Wide range of psychological and somatic symptoms but no hallucinations or other extreme deviations in thought, feeling, or action	Wide range of symptoms with delusions, hallucinations, emotional blunting, and other severely deviate behavior
Orientation	Patient rarely loses orientation to environment	Patient frequently loses orientation to environment
Insight	Patient often has some insight into nature of his behavior	Patient rarely has insight into nature of his behavior
Social aspects	Behavior rarely injurious or dangerous to patient or to society	Behavior frequently injurious or dangerous to patient or to society
Treatment	Patient rarely needs institutional care	Patient usually needs institutional care

as has been done in this chart, is useful for descriptive purposes, but it should be remembered that each patient develops a unique pattern of symptoms and that the same symptoms may have quite different meanings in different cases.

Furthermore, a patient's symptoms may change considerably from time to time. Acute symptoms may reach a high level of intensity involving delirium and extreme disorientation and then abate to such an extent that the patient seems fairly rational and in good contact with his surroundings. The symptom picture in psychoses of long standing is usually more constant, but even here there may be episodes of intensification of symptoms.

In psychotic reactions there is a lowering of adaptive controls, which leads to thoughts, feelings, and actions that have not been characteristic of the individual's behavior. Thus he may become assaultive, ignore personal hygiene, make immoral advances, or become convinced that he has committed unpardonable sins. Although obsessive-compulsive, phobic, and other neurotic patterns are often present in these reactions, psychosomatic reactions, such as peptic ulcers, are relatively rare. Here it is of interest to note that according to Scheier (1962) psychotics in general are slightly above average in free anxiety (60th percentile)—as contrasted with psychosomatic cases, who have an average level of free anxiety (50th percentile), and neurotics, who have a high level (85th percentile).

We shall discuss the various symptoms as we take up the different psychotic reaction patterns, but it may be of value to elaborate briefly first upon two symptoms—delusions and hallucinations—which are commonly found in psychoses.

DELUSIONS

Delusions are false beliefs which the individual defends vigorously despite logical absurdity or proof to the contrary and despite their serious interference with his social adjustment. Among the most common delusions to be found are:

1. *Delusions of sin and guilt*—delusional beliefs about having committed unforgivable sins which have brought calamity to others.

2. *Hypochondriacal delusions*—delusional beliefs relating to various horrible disease conditions, such as emitting bad odors, "rotting," and being "eaten away."

3. *Nihilistic delusions*—delusional beliefs that nothing exists. Patient may insist he is living in a "shadow world" or that he died several years ago and now only his spirit in a sort of vaporous form remains.

4. *Delusions of persecution*—delusional beliefs of being deliberately interfered with, discriminated against, plotted against, threatened, and otherwise mistreated.

5. *Delusions of reference*—delusional belief that other people are talking about him, referring to him, portraying his life in cartoons, movies, or television, or otherwise making references to him in their activities.

6. *Delusions of influence*—delusional beliefs that "enemies" are influencing him in various ways, perhaps with complicated electrical gadgets which send out waves that interfere with his thoughts or "pour filth" into his mind.

7. *Delusions of grandeur*—delusional beliefs that he is some great and remarkable person, such as a great economist, physicist, religious savior, or historical figure.

The degree of delusional systematization varies from the fragmentary disorientation accompanying delirium to the logically consistent delusional system of the paranoiac. Delusions commonly center around sexual and religious topics and around ideas of personal worth. Most psychotic delusions are silly and illogical, though in some cases paranoid delusions may on first acquaintance be quite convincing. The origin of delusions will be dealt with in our subsequent consideration of the various psychotic reaction patterns.

We may note in passing, however, that many delusions grow out of elaborations of our ego defense mechanisms. We have previously observed that most of us are prone to project the blame for our mistakes upon others, and it is only an additional step to excuse our failures by insisting that we have not been given a fair chance—that other people are "working against us." Similarly, we may project our own unac-

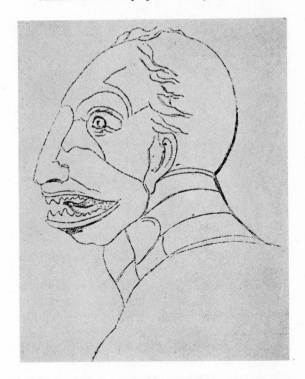

"Ghost of a Flea," based on a hallucination portrayed by William Blake. According to Blake, this flea was in the room and told him that fleas contained the damned souls of bloodthirsty men. Blake, in both his poetry and his etchings, gave many evidences of schizophrenic and paranoid ideation and religious delusions (Born, 1946).

ceptable desires to other people so that it is they who are hostile and wish to harm us, while our thoughts remain pure and quite devoid of any hostility.

HALLUCINATIONS

In hallucinatory reactions, the patient perceives various kinds of strange objects and events without any appropriate "external" sensory stimuli. He may hear voices telling him what to do or commenting upon or criticizing all of his actions. Occasionally messages are received from God or from some organization telling the patient of great powers that have been conferred upon him or of his mission to save mankind.

In some instances the voices are ascribed to specific persons such as God, some relative or friend, or "enemies." In other cases the patient insists that he has not the vaguest idea as to the identity of the person or persons talking. Similarly, the voices may be well localized—they may come from the light fixture, or the window, or an imaginary telephone receiver which the patient holds to his ear—or they may seem to come from all directions.

Although auditory hallucinations are most common, visual, olfactory, gustatory, and tactual hallucinations also occur. The patient may see angels in heaven, or smell poison gas that has been ejected into his room, or taste poison in his food, or feel small bugs crawling around under his skin.

Hallucinations may result from a variety of biological and psychological conditions. Among these are extreme fatigue, drugs, delirium accompanying fever, brain pathology, sensory deprivation, and the exaggeration of ego defense mechanisms. Even where biological conditions are primary determinants, the personality of the patient usually plays an important role in the development of hallucinations. This is brought out in Good's (1943) description of the behavioral condition of five survivors from a sunken ship who spent fifteen days adrift on a raft. Although all of these survivors reported periodic irrational thoughts while adrift (the most common being that they could walk off the raft upon the water), only one of the survivors showed such a severe reaction to the exhaustion and exposure that he turned from the rescuers to talk to an imaginary person.

The elaboration of projection, wishful thinking, and other ego defense mechanisms may lead to hallucinations as well as to delusions. Probably most of us talk to other persons in fantasy and conjure up their replies. In dreams this process is vividly illustrated. Thus it is not surprising that individuals intensely preoccupied in fantasy with their conflicts and problems should sometimes find these voices and events so real that they seem to come from external sources. Sherman (1924), for example, concluded from a study of 19 children who experienced hallucinations that the hallucinations were a simple projection of some inner difficulty and took the form of either an explanation or a compensation for the difficulty. One child who had a strong conflict between a tendency to conform and a tendency to rebel saw a person on each side of him—one saying "Be good," and the other saying "Be bad." These persons were further elaborated through symbolic fantasy so that one became a "good man" and the other "the devil." The hallucinations of many psychotic patients appear to follow a similar pattern.

General Etiological Considerations

Our knowledge of the etiological factors in the functional psychoses is still far from complete. Consequently, there is considerable difference of opinion in this matter. Some investigators emphasize unidentified genetic and constitutional factors, while others point to psychological and sociological determinants. In the present chapter we shall attempt an evaluation and integration of these divergent viewpoints.

Although most of the evaluation of specific evidence for various causal factors will be given in the context of one or another of the particular syndromes, we shall here mention briefly several factors that apply to the psychoses as a group.

CORRELATIONAL STUDIES

Many studies have been carried out in an attempt to see whether psychotic disorders are statistically related to factors such as age, sex, intelligence, marital status, and socioeconomic level.

1. *Age.* The median age of all first admissions to mental hospitals approximates 44 years. However, there is wide variation in the age at which specific psychoses tend to occur. Schizophrenia is more apt to occur during early adulthood, psychotic depressive reactions during middle adulthood, and senile psychoses during later life. For psychoses in general, the age range

SYNDROMES OF PSYCHOTIC SYMPTOMS

EXCITEMENT
Unrestrained
Hurried speech
Elevated mood
Attitude of superiority
Self-dramatization
Loud and boisterous
Overactive
Excess of speech
Dominates interview

PERCEPTUAL DISTORTION
Hallucinatory voices
Accusing voices
Threatening voices
Ordering voices
Visions
Other hallucinations
Ideas of change

MOTOR DISTURBANCE
Rigid postures
Overt tension
Slovenly appearance
Giggling
Grimacing
Repetitive movements
Talks to self
Startled glances

HOSTILE BELLIGERENCE
Verbal hostility
Attitude of contempt
Hostile attitude
Irritability
Blames others
Bitter and resentful
Complains and gripes
Suspicious of people

RETARDATION AND APATHY
Slowed speech
Lack of goals
Fixed faces
Slowed movements
Memory deficit
Speech blocking
Apathy
Whispered speech
Failure to answer

ANXIOUS INTROPUNITIVENESS
Blames self
Anxiety (specific)
Vaguely apprehensive
Self-depreciating
Depressed in mood
Guilt and remorse
Shows insight
Suicidal thoughts
Recurring thoughts
Morbid fears
Ideas of sinfulness

PARANOID PROJECTION
Delusional beliefs
Ideas of reference
Ideas of persecution
Ideas of conspiracy
People controlling
Forces controlling
Ideas of body destruction

DISORIENTATION
As to hospital
As to state
Knows no one
As to season
As to year
As to age

GRANDIOSE EXPANSIVENESS
Attitude of superiority
Voices extoll
Unusual powers
Great person
Divine mission

CONCEPTUAL DISORGANIZATION
Irrelevant answers
Incoherent answers
Rambling answers
Neologisms
Stereotyped speech

These ten syndromes have been identified in a multiple group factor analysis of the ratings of 296 psychotic patients' behavior on the Inpatient Multidimensional Psychiatric Scale. Each syndrome is regarded as a unitary pattern of response which may be present to a greater or lesser extent in a given patient (Lorr, 1962).

RELATIONSHIP FOUND IN 103 CASES
OF FOLIE A DEUX

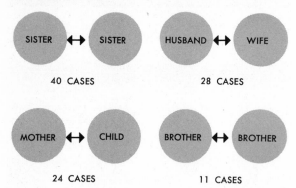

A relatively neglected phenomenon in the functional psychoses is that of *folie a deux*—a form of psychological "contagion" in which one person copies and incorporates into his own personality structure the delusions and other psychotic patterns of another person. In an extensive analysis of 103 cases, Gralnick (1942) emphasized the following explanatory factors, all environmental: (a) length of association, (b) dominance-submission, (c) type of familial relationship, (d) pre-psychotic personality, and (e) homosexual desires. The high incidence in the husband-wife category is particularly striking since common heredity would appear to be minimized as an etiological factor in these cases.

is wide: cases have been reported before the age of 5 and after the age of 80.

2. *Sex.* Males outnumber females among the first admissions to mental hospitals in about the ratio of 4 to 3. However, the females outnumber the males in several diagnostic groups, such as manic-depressive, involutional, and senile psychotic reactions.

In view of the fact that women, on the average, live about seven years longer than men, it is not surprising that women outnumber men in senile psychoses. Their predominance in manic-depressive and involutional psychotic reactions probably reflects cultural stresses to which women are particularly exposed. We shall endeavor to bring out these factors in our later discussion of manic-depressive and involutional reactions.

3. *Intelligence and education.* Mental illness is no respecter of level of intelligence, and psychotic disorders are found among geniuses as well as among the mentally retarded. In general, the range of intelligence and educational background is the same for psychotic patients as for the general population (Hardt and Feinhandler, 1961; Jaco, 1960).

There are certain group differences among patients showing particular types of psychotic reactions. Paranoiacs, as a group, tend to be brighter and better educated than other reaction types, while paretics tend to be below average in these characteristics. There is much overlapping, however, and such generalizations cannot be applied to a given patient.

4. *Marital status.* Married persons appear to be considerably less susceptible to psychosis than do the divorced, single, separated, or widowed (Jaco, 1960). But this is not to say that being married is necessarily a factor in preventing mental illness. In fact, an unhappy marriage may materially decrease the individual's stress tolerance. Other factors are probably also operative here. Unstable, maladjusted persons are less acceptable as mates in the first place and thus probably not so likely to marry or to remain married as are more adequately adjusted persons.

In a healthy marriage, however, the individual's stress tolerance is undoubtedly strengthened by the teamwork, group identification, and mutual emotional support. Family life can bring interesting and stable social relations that alleviate feelings of isolation, make the individual feel needed, and help make life meaningful.

5. *Urban-rural.* In terms of their relative populations, urban areas contribute over twice as many first admissions to mental hospitals as rural areas (Jaco, 1960). These figures, too, are somewhat deceiving, for the mentally ill in rural areas are more apt to be cared for by their families. In addition, a mental illness which is quite apparent and handicapping in city life may be tolerated in the country as long as the individual is able to do his work.

In general, however, it appears that cities do have higher rates than rural areas for psychoses, as well as for most other types of abnormal behavior. There are so many complicating factors here that we shall have to await further

FIRST ADMISSIONS TO PUBLIC MENTAL HOSPITALS IN THE UNITED STATES IN 1960

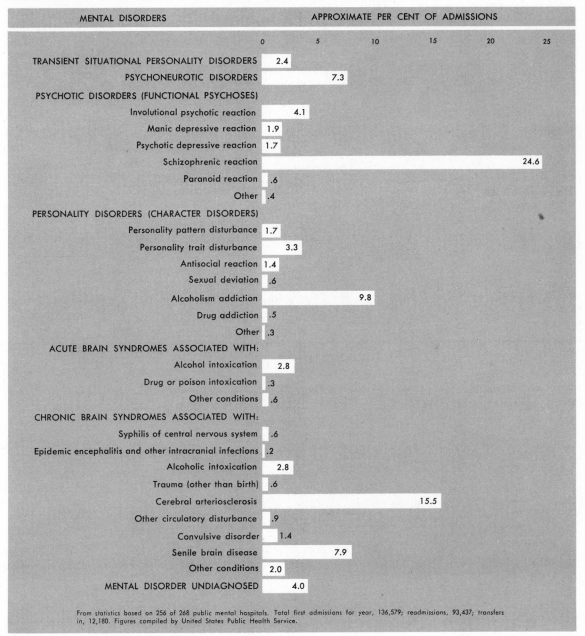

MENTAL DISORDERS	APPROXIMATE PER CENT OF ADMISSIONS
TRANSIENT SITUATIONAL PERSONALITY DISORDERS	2.4
PSYCHONEUROTIC DISORDERS	7.3
PSYCHOTIC DISORDERS (FUNCTIONAL PSYCHOSES)	
Involutional psychotic reaction	4.1
Manic depressive reaction	1.9
Psychotic depressive reaction	1.7
Schizophrenic reaction	24.6
Paranoid reaction	.6
Other	.4
PERSONALITY DISORDERS (CHARACTER DISORDERS)	
Personality pattern disturbance	1.7
Personality trait disturbance	3.3
Antisocial reaction	1.4
Sexual deviation	.6
Alcoholism addiction	9.8
Drug addiction	.5
Other	.3
ACUTE BRAIN SYNDROMES ASSOCIATED WITH:	
Alcohol intoxication	2.8
Drug or poison intoxication	.3
Other conditions	.6
CHRONIC BRAIN SYNDROMES ASSOCIATED WITH:	
Syphilis of central nervous system	.6
Epidemic encephalitis and other intracranial infections	.2
Alcoholic intoxication	2.8
Trauma (other than birth)	.6
Cerebral arteriosclerosis	15.5
Other circulatory disturbance	.9
Convulsive disorder	1.4
Senile brain disease	7.9
Other conditions	2.0
MENTAL DISORDER UNDIAGNOSED	4.0

From statistics based on 256 of 268 public mental hospitals. Total first admissions for year, 136,579; readmissions, 93,437; transfers in, 12,180. Figures compiled by United States Public Health Service.

evidence before we can adequately evaluate such differences.

6. *Occupation.* Psychotic reactions are found among all occupational groups, and there is little information about the types of reactions most prevalent in given occupations. In an early study, Fuson (1943) analyzed the occupations of 1496 male first admissions to Kansas state hospitals and found relatively more schizophrenics in lower socioeconomic occupations and more manic-depressives in upper ones. In a more recent study of psychotic disorders in Texas, Jaco (1960) obtained similar findings for males but not for females. Here it is interesting to note that depressive reactions and suicide appear to be particularly high among dentists, lawyers, and physicians (Blachly *et al.*, 1963).

Within a given occupation, of course, a wide range of mental disorders occur. In a study of 40 male teachers with mental disorders, Allen (1942) found schizophrenics, manic-depressives, alcoholics, psychopaths, a variety of psycho-neurotics, and patients with involutional reactions. Similarly, Jaco (1960) found a wide range of functional and organic psychoses among all occupational groups investigated in the Texas study.

7. *Socioeconomic status.* Hyde and Kingsley (1944) correlated the mental disorders of 60,000 selectees rejected at the Boston Armed Forces Induction Station with the socioeconomic level of the community from which the selectees came. They found that the total incidence of major mental disorders increased gradually from 7.3 per cent in communities with the highest socioeconomic status to 16.6 per cent in those with the lowest.

In a more recent investigation, Rennie *et al.* (1957) made an intensive study of a residential area of New York City which covered all ranges of socioeconomic status. They found severe mental and emotional disturbances among 28 per cent of the lower class, 18 per cent of the middle class, and 9 per cent of the upper class. Actual psychotic disorders were found in 13 per cent of the lower social stratum and in 3.6 per cent of the upper—a ratio of more than 3 to 1. Cause and effect relationships here are not clear, however, since severe mental disorders often lead to a downward adjustment of occupation and living standards.

8. *Ethnic and religious differences.* Psychotic reactions are found among all races and religious groups, but the incidence and types of abnormal behavior vary considerably from one group to another. For example, there is a proportionately higher rate of mental hospital first admissions for Negroes than whites in the United States (Dreger and Miller, 1960). One reason, of course, may be the fact that a greater proportion of the Negro population lives under adverse economic and social conditions which augment the stresses they face and also make it more difficult for them to care for a disturbed person at home. In a survey of the *total* incidence of psychoses in Baltimore—including both hospitalized and nonhospitalized cases—no significant difference was found in rates between Negroes and whites (Pasamanick, 1962). In this context, it is of interest to note that the incidence of first admissions to the Territorial (Mental) Hospital in Hawaii is significantly higher for Japanese and Filipinos than for part Hawaiians or Caucasians (Kimmich, 1960).

Psychotic reactions appear to be more prevalent among Protestants than among Catholics or Jews (Frumkin and Frumkin, 1957; Hollingshead and Redlich, 1958). The incidence of particular disorders also varies for different religious groups. For example, psychoses associated with alcoholism are relatively rare among the Jews, presumably as a result of cultural prohibitions against excessive drinking. Similarly, Eaton and Weil (1955) found that no psychoses associated with drugs, syphilis, or alcoholism were known to have occurred among a Hutterite population of over 8000 persons. Interestingly enough, manic-depressive reactions were much more frequent than schizophrenia among this religious group, whereas for the general population in the United States the situation is reversed.

In the course of our discussion we shall examine cross-cultural findings relating to the incidence and types of psychotic reactions in other societies. It would appear that differences in psychoses among cultural and ethnic groups are directly related to the values, customs, and life conditions of the group. As sociocultural conditions become more similar, variations in abnormal behavior tend to disappear.

INTERACTION OF FACTORS

No single etiological pattern seems to underlie the functional psychoses in general or even a particular reaction type, such as schizophrenia. In each case we see an interaction of biological, psychological, and sociological factors which varies with both the type of psychotic reaction and the individual in question.

Biological factors. Even though there is no known organic pathology underlying the functional psychoses, many biological conditions have been championed as being of etiological significance. Genetic inheritance in some form has received particular emphasis. As we noted in Chapter 4, however, mental illness does not follow any simple dominant or recessive genetic pattern. Currently, the focus of attention is being placed on the possible role of mutant genes and early environmental conditions (especially prenatal) in predisposing the individual to a given type of psychotic reaction. It is thought that such conditions may lead to subtle but permanent deficiencies in brain structure and/or to the distortion of biochemical systems which affect brain functioning—resulting in a lowering of adaptive resources. Under favorable life con-

ditions such defects might not show up, but under stress the individual would presumably be more prone to disturbances in neurophysiological processes and hence to the development of a psychotic reaction.

Since most studies of genetic and constitutional factors have been concerned with schizophrenia, we shall wait until our discussion of this reaction pattern to evaluate specific findings.

Psychological factors. There appears to be a continuity of abnormal and atypical experiences in the life histories of those individuals who become psychotic (Simmons, 1960), although this fact does not explain how one child is seemingly able to surmount undesirable early conditions while another is not. The pyscho-

COMPARISON OF BACKGROUND FACTORS IN NORMAL AND PSYCHOTIC CHILDREN

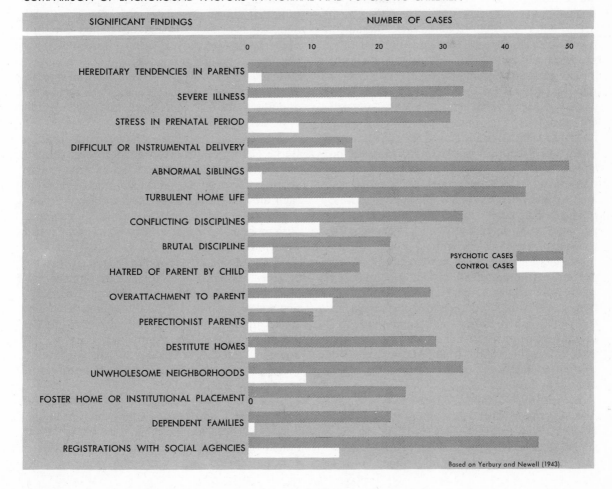

Based on Yerbury and Newell (1943)

logical factors that seem to play a major role in the development of psychotic reactions are (a) pathogenic family patterns, early psychic trauma, and other conditions tending to foster faulty personality development and inadequate adjustive resources and (b) a variety of pressures, frustrations, and conflicts which place the individual under excessive stress and lead to the exaggeration of ego defenses and eventual personality decompensation. Both developmental and stress factors vary considerably with the type of psychosis and the given individual involved. The precipitating stresses in psychotic reactions are not always readily apparent since they may stem from the subjective experiences and evaluations of the individual rather than from objectively observable conditions or events.

Although no uniform developmental pattern has been identified for psychotics as a group, recent research findings are helping to delineate patterns that often are involved and the particular patterns characteristic of different reaction types. We shall examine these findings in our discussion of schizophrenia and the other specific reactions.

The particular symptoms typical of the functional psychoses result primarily from (a) the extreme exaggeration and distortion of self-defenses, (b) the marked lowering of inner reality and ethical controls, and (c) the increased distortion of "input"—of incoming information. This does not rule out the possibility, of course, that the sustained emotional stress may also lead to disturbances in neurophysiological functioning which then contribute heavily to—or perhaps even determine—the salient characteristics of the clinical picture.

As in other forms of psychopathology, the patient's symptoms lead to vicious circles. Of particular relevance here in augmenting the total stress situation is the terrifying experience of ego decompensation—of realizing that one is losing control of his thoughts and impulses, that he is "losing his mind." Many patients state that this experience was one of the most traumatic of their entire lives.

Sociological factors. The role of sociocultural factors in the development of psychotic reactions is even more obscure—if that is possible—than are the roles of biological and psychological factors. Although the major types of

psychotic reactions are found to some extent in all societies, it appears that sociological processes affect the development of psychoses in three ways: (a) in terms of the content of symptoms, (b) in terms of actual incidence, and (c) in terms of the particular types of psychotic reactions that develop.

It is inevitable that the content of symptoms will vary with sociocultural conditions. The rural African may think a particular witch doctor is trying to bewitch him, whereas the American may be convinced that the FBI or some other organization is after him.

The rates of psychotic disorders are evidently not as high in primitive societies as in European and American groups. In an extensive study of the total incidence of psychoses—both hospitalized and nonhospitalized—among Kenya Africans, Carothers (1953) arrived at a figure of only 37 per 100,000 population compared to an incidence of approximately 880 per 100,000 population for us in the United States (Pasamanick, 1962). Carothers also cited proportionately low figures for other parts of Africa. Despite various limitations of his data, Carothers concluded, "However much the African figures may vary among themselves, they are clearly of a different order from those in England and America." (1953, p. 126)

In a psychiatric census of the South Pacific, Berne (1960) concluded that the prevalence of psychotic disorders bore a direct relation to the hospital facilities and medical practitioners in each area. In areas with few facilities and personnel he found the rates low, while in areas with more adequate treatment facilities the rates were much higher.

From an overall viewpoint, it seems that as facilities become available, the number of patients also increases. And as primitive societies are progressively exposed to modern civilization and technology, the rate of mental illness increases until earlier group differences are all but obliterated. The "reservoir" of psychopathology" seems to be of the same order for peoples the world over.

There are many examples of differences in the types of psychotic reactions which occur in different cultural groups. Japanese male patients, taught submissiveness and suppression of interpersonal conflict, rarely become violent (Mal-

INCIDENCE OF MENTAL DISORDERS AMONG KENYA AFRICANS AND MASSACHUSETTS NEGROES

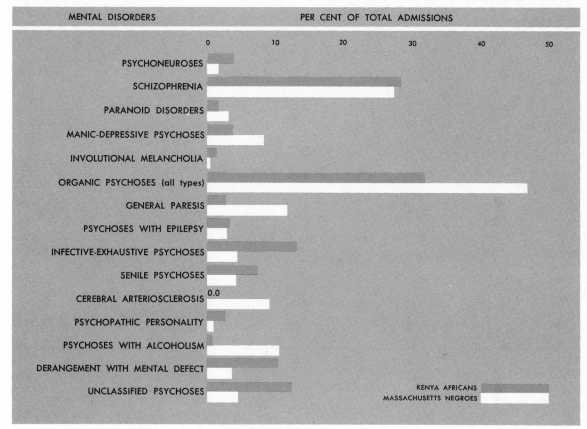

oney, 1951; Kimmich, 1960). Especially interesting is the reaction of "frenzied anxiety," relatively unknown in our culture but fairly common among the African group studied by Carothers (1947, 1953). It is a state in which the patient is excited, noisy, incoherent, and often dangerously violent. The condition is associated with some source of anxiety which is real to the patient, but the homicidal behavior is often misdirected and the alleged author of the patient's problems may or may not be among the victims. There is usually recovery in a matter of hours followed by amnesia for the event. The following example is adapted from Carother's (1947) report:

The patient was a Mkamba (Bantu) man about 30 years of age. Before and after the attack he seemed quite normal.

One afternoon he was observed doing odd things such as picking grass and placing it on the fire, and putting stones on the cooking pot. Next morning he chased his family out of the house, brandishing his bow and arrows and a hammer. All escaped except his wife and youngest son, both of whom he battered to death.

He had complete amnesia for the event, but later made this statement: "I would not have killed my wife and child had I not been ill; if I had not killed my wife and child I would have died. All my troubles have come from an old man called X with whom I had a quarrel. There was another man who wished to marry my sister and he brought beer to my father as a preliminary to the marriage. X wished to drink this beer, but I refused to allow this . . . . X then said, 'You may drink the beer today but this will be the last time.' He meant that he would bewitch me and cause my death. . . ." X's threat had apparently been made about two weeks previously. Two days before the crime the patient found some charms beside his door, presumably placed there by X. (adapted from pp. 577-578)

Carothers said of this case:

"His manner is at all times mild and amenable, and he shows none of the truculence and resentment so characteristic of aggressive psychopaths, nor has he exhibited any aggressive outbursts, although frustration must have been frequent during this period.

"Like the other cases that fall into this category he arrived at Mathari long after he had recovered his mental equilibrium, but the history is sufficiently complete to support the diagnosis of frenzied anxiety. An interesting point that emerges in this case is his remark,

'If I had not killed my wife I would have died.' It appears most probable from the evidence that he would have killed anyone he caught up with, and that the fact that he killed his wife was merely due to her being the last to reach the river." (p. 578)

Carothers has pointed out that such states of frenzied anxiety are usually due to feelings that the patient has been bewitched by someone and will die unless he kills someone. Interestingly enough, the death of *anyone* will presumably appease the gods and save his own life. Again we see the important role that sociocultural processes may play in the form that psychotic reactions take.

General Prognosis for Psychotic Reactions

Contrary to popular opinion some 80 per cent or more of all first admissions to mental hospitals—organic and functional—are later discharged as recovered or improved. Of these patients over half are returned to their communities within one to two months after admission and most of the remainder within one year.

Prognosis varies greatly, however, with the type of psychotic disorder. In general, organic psychoses have a less favorable prognosis than functional psychoses. This would be expected, especially in the case of senile psychoses, in which we are dealing with degenerative and irreversible brain pathology. Within the category of functional psychoses, schizophrenic reactions are typically more resistant to treatment than manic-depressive reactions.

The given patient is also a critically important factor in the outcome of treatment. In general, the pre-psychotic personality and life adjustment of the patient are a good gauge for predicting outcome—assuming a lack of extensive brain damage. Those who were fairly stable to begin with do not have so far to go in their recovery.

The nature of the life situation to which the patient returns also has a marked effect on his immediate and long-range prognosis. An unhappy marriage or other unfavorable conditions at home or work make for a less favorable prognosis. And of course the maintenance of pre-

scribed medication after returning home is often of crucial significance.

As with cancer and many other general medical disorders, early detection and treatment are essential. In general, the longer the duration prior to hospitalization or the longer the period of hospitalization without improvement, the less favorable the prognosis. Although some patients do recover sufficiently to be discharged even after ten or more years of hospitalization, most recoveries take place during the first year.

Needless to say, the adequacy of treatment is an important factor to the outcome. Understaffed, poorly equipped state hospitals and clinics are frequently restricted to routine types of medical treatment. Where hospitals are well staffed and offer adequate medical, psychological, and sociological therapy to their patients, there is a decidedly higher rate of recovery for all types of patients. In fact, patients undergoing such an integrated treatment program often achieve a better personal and life adjustment than they had made before their illness.

So far we have been concerned with factors that are applicable in large part to both the organic and the functional psychoses. The remainder of the present chapter will be devoted to an examination of the specific symptoms, dynamics, therapy, and prognosis of the various functional psychoses.

Schizophrenic Reactions

The Belgian psychiatrist Morel in 1860 described the case of a thirteen-year-old boy who had formerly been the most brilliant pupil in his school but who, over a period of time, lost interest in his studies, became increasingly withdrawn, seclusive, and taciturn, and appeared to have forgotten everything that he had learned. He talked frequently of killing his father and evidenced a kind of inactivity bordering on stupidity. Morel thought that the boy's intellectual, moral, and physical functions had deteriorated as a result of hereditary causes and hence were irrecoverable. He used the term *démence précoce* (meaning "mental deterioration at an early age").

This term was later adopted by the German psychiatrist Kraepelin to refer to a group of rather dissimilar conditions which all seemed to have the common feature of mental deterioration beginning early in life. Actually, however, most of these cases do not develop during childhood or adolescence but during adulthood and there is no conclusive evidence of permanent mental deterioration. Thus *dementia praecox* proved an unfortunate term.

It remained for a Swiss psychiatrist, Bleuler, to introduce in 1911 a more acceptable descriptive term for this disorder. He used the term *schizophrenia* (splitting of the personality) because he thought the disorder was characterized primarily by lack of coherence in associative and thought processes, emotional blunting, and an inward orientation away from reality. Unfortunately, the term *schizophrenia* implies a splitting or dissociation of the self, which is also inaccurate. Nevertheless, it has largely replaced the term *dementia praecox* in psychiatric usage.

The term *schizophrenia* is now used to include a group of psychotic reactions in which there are fundamental disturbances in reality relationships and in emotional and intellectual processes. Although the specific symptoms are legion and vary greatly from one individual to another, the types of symptoms in schizophrenia may be summarized as follows:[1]

1. *Withdrawal from reality.* A loss of interest in and concern with the people and events in patient's world.

2. *Autism.* A condition characterized by preoccupation with inner fantasies and by private modes of thought.

3. *Emotional blunting and distortion.* Shallowness of affect and emotional reactions which are inappropriate to the situation or the event which elicits them.

4. *Delusions and hallucinations.* Especially common are delusions of influence and persecution and auditory hallucinations in which patient hears voices talking *about* him.

5. *Anomalies of behavior.* Peculiarities of movement, gesture, posture, and expression, such as silly giggling, mutism, and various repetitive motor acts.

6. *Disorganization and lowering of inner controls.* Reflected in thought disturbances, such as inability to pursue a sustained train of thought, in deterioration in habits of personal hygiene, and in lowering of moral standards.

Often the disorder develops slowly and the early symptoms are not at all obvious. Thus the early clinical picture may be dominated by neurotic symptoms, such as continual somatic complaints for which there is no related organic pathology. As the more malignant features of the disorder make their appearance, the patient may complain that some external force seems to be controlling his thoughts and actions, that it is difficult for him to communicate with his family or other people, and that nothing seems to interest or concern him. Perhaps the most striking characteristic of the schizophrenic is his emotional withdrawal and the rupture of the bonds that ordinarily bind an individual to human society.

Schizophrenia is the most common of the

---

[1] Adapted from Report of World Health Organization Study Group on Schizophrenia, 1959.

psychotic reactions; its expected incidence in the population is about 1 per cent. Schizophrenics account for approximately 24 per cent of all first admissions to mental hospitals and 30 per cent of readmissions. The sex ratio is about equal, and the average age of first admission is 34 years. The intelligence and educational level of schizophrenic patients approximates that of the general population. Since many of these patients require prolonged hospitalization, they tend to accumulate in the hospital, usually constituting about one half of the patient population. Because of its complexity, relatively long duration, and high rate of incidence, schizophrenia has proved one of the most serious and baffling of all the psychopathological syndromes.

TYPES

Nine types of schizophrenic reactions are distinguished in the American Psychiatric Association classification of mental disorders.

Simple type. In the simple type of schizophrenic reaction, the patient evidences a gradual narrowing and waning of interests, loss of ambition, emotional indifference, and withdrawal from social relations. He no longer cares whether he passes or fails in school and is no longer concerned about his friends or family. He may show episodes of irritability and even overt aggression but becomes increasingly indifferent and seclusive. Conversation becomes scant and trivial, personal appearance and hygiene are neglected, there is little or no interest in the opposite sex, and the patient has difficulty in concentrating on anything outside his fantasy world. He makes no effort to work or to assume responsibility and seems content to lead a simple, irresponsible, indifferent, parasitic existence.

Lecturing, pleading, and encouragement by well-meaning family members are of no avail and often lead to obstinate, negativistic, evasive behavior. But despite the patient's intellectual and emotional withdrawal, his mental functions may not be markedly impaired or disintegrated.

Although simple schizophrenic reactions are infrequent in terms of hospital first admissions, this is no doubt partly because many simple schizophrenics are able to get by outside of mental hospitals. Such persons may be cared for by their families, particularly in later adolescence and early adulthood, or they may be able to care for themselves by means of simple clerical or manual work. They usually make little or no progression in their work and resist efforts to change or complicate their routine. They usually impress others as being rather queer or stupid persons who are curiously inaccessible and isolated and seem colorless and uninteresting. Undoubtedly there are many simple schizophrenics among vagrants, prostitutes, psychopaths, and criminals.

One of the best pictures of the symptomatology in the simple type of schizophrenic reaction comes from a study of 64 patients by Kant (1948). He gave special attention to six aspects:

1. *Loss of contact.* Only about one fifth showed a marked loss of superficial contact with reality. The other four fifths showed a relatively good contact with their surroundings although all but two had had delusions or hallucinations. Many patients were surprisingly eager to be interviewed and to discuss their problems.

2. *Age at onset.* The age range varied from 12 to 40 but in over two thirds of the cases the onset of illness fell in the period between 17 and 24 years.

3. *Type of onset.* In all but 2 cases, the schizophrenic changes occurred gradually. In these 2 cases endocrine factors were considered of precipitating importance.

4. *Hereditary "tainting."* About a third of the patients had family histories of functional psychoses of various types of which schizophrenia was by far the most common.

5. *Pre-psychotic personality characteristics.* All but one showed a lack of sexual adjustment and 56 of the 64 a lack of normal aggressiveness. Other common characteristics were "reaching out for contact," difficulties in holding jobs, and subnormal intellectual functioning.

The characteristic of reaching out for contact is worthy of additional comment. Many schizophrenics attempt to approach other people, but in a shy, awkward, immature way. Kant mentioned one patient who would never approach him directly but "would occasionally stand up and, with his face averted, ask the writer if he had been wanting to see him" (p. 145). One cannot help but be impressed by the need for love and affection almost pathetically evident in many of these patients, lacking as they are in adequate means of expression and apparently very much inhibited by fear.

6. *Outstanding behavioral reactions at the time of onset.* The following table shows the relative frequency of the most common behavioral reactions.

TYPE OF BEHAVIOR	PER CENT INCIDENCE
Aggressive behavior	65.0
Delusional and/or hallucinatory experiences	42.9
Sexual and/or alcoholic indulgence	39.7
Pronounced disintegrative behavior	34.9
Hypochondriacal experiences	30.2
Withdrawal (pronounced)	22.2

Aggressive behavior was manifested in either threats or attempts at assault, usually on a family member, or in the destruction of property. Sexual behavior was of a crude, aggressive variety, such as attempted rape in several instances. Sexual play with children and voyeurism were also noted in several cases. Sexual misbehavior and alcoholic indulgence were both considered evidence of the "opening up" of personality controls and for that reason were evaluated together. All patients had shown disintegrative behavior of psychotic proportions; this was particularly pronounced in about a third of the cases.

The following interview with a male patient diagnosed as schizophrenic reaction, simple type, will serve to bring out the emotional apathy and indifference typical of such patients without serious loss of contact with reality.

Dr.: Do you know who I am?
Pt.: A doctor, I suppose.
Dr.: How do you feel?
Pt.: Oh—OK, I guess.
Dr.: Do you know where you are?
Pt.: It's a hospital.
Dr.: Why are you here?
Pt.: I don't know. . . . I don't think I should be here. I'm all right.
Dr.: Where would you rather be?

Pt.: I don't care, just out . . . I don't know. Maybe with some fellows or something. I don't care. There were some guys I used to know.
Dr.: What did you do with those fellows?
Pt.: I don't know—just go around.
Dr.: How do you like it here?
Pt.: I don't know, I don't care. It's all right, I guess. I liked the boys though. I used to know them.
Dr.: And you used to like them?
Pt.: Yes,—they were all right, I guess.
Dr.: Who is "they"?
Pt.: Some men. I don't know them by name.
Dr.: Can you think of any reason why you should be here?
Pt.: No, I'm all right. I feel all right. I'd like to be with the fellows I used to know.
Dr.: Are there any fellows here you like?
Pt.: I don't know. They're all right, I guess.
Dr.: Do you think the men who brought you here had it in for you?
Pt.: No. They were nice to me. They were all right. They didn't have it in for me or hate me or anything.
Dr.: Do you ever hear strange noises?
Pt.: No, I never do that. I'm not crazy.

This patient was hospitalized on the complaint of his sister-in-law, who stated that he had tried to force her at the point of a gun to have sexual relations with him. On admission to the hospital the patient appeared rather indifferent about the whole matter and explained that it must have been some "temporary impulse" which overcame him.

Although 30 years of age, the patient had been living with his parents and was completely dependent upon them. His educational background was good. He made an A average in high school, but during his first year of college he lost interest in his studies and refused to attend classes despite his parents' pleadings. His parents then did their best to help him achieve some vocational adjustment, but the patient seemed indifferent to their efforts and hopes for him. After leaving college he did take several part-time jobs, including one in a grocery store, which he lost soon after because of his listless attitude and indifference to his duties. Thereafter he would neither look for nor accept work and was quite content to remain dependent upon his parents. Although rather handsome, he had never gone out with girls. When questioned on this subject he stated that "I'm not interested in girls. All they ever do is get you in trouble."

Hebephrenic type.   Hebephrenic reactions usually occur at an earlier age and represent a more severe disintegration of the personality than the other types. Typically the patient has a history of oddness, overscrupulousness about trivial things, and preoccupation with religious and philosophical issues. Frequently he broods excessively over the dire results of masturbation and the most minor infractions of social conventions. While his schoolmates are enjoying normal play and social activities, he is gradually becoming more seclusive and more preoccupied with his fantasies.

As the disorder progresses, the individual becomes emotionally indifferent and infantile in his reactions, with much silliness and incoherence of thought, speech, and action. A silly smile and inappropriate shallow laughter with little or no provocation often evidence the beginning of the actual mental breakdown. If asked why he laughs in this peculiar way, the patient may state that he doesn't know or volunteer some wholly irrelevant and unsatisfactory explanation. Speech becomes incoherent and there may be considerable baby talk and childish giggling.

Hallucinations, particularly auditory, are common. The "voices" may accuse the patient of immoral practices, "pour filth" into his mind, and call him vile names. Delusions are usually of a sexual, religious, hypochondriacal, or persecutory nature and are changeable and fantastic. For example, the patient may insist not only that he is being followed by enemies but that he has already been killed a number of times. In occasional cases, the patient becomes hostile and aggressive on the basis of his belief that his enemies are using complicated electrical machines to influence his thoughts. Peculiar mannerisms and other bizarre forms of behavior appear. These may take the form of verbigeration (meaningless, stereotyped repetition of words or sentences), facial grimaces, talking and gesturing to himself, sudden inexplicable laughter and weeping, and in some cases an abnormal interest in urine and feces, which the patient may smear on walls and even on his person. Obscene behavior and a frank absence of any modesty or sense of shame are characteristic. Although outbursts of anger and temper tantrums may occur in connection with his fantasy life, the patient is indifferent to real-life situations, no matter how horrifying or gruesome.

The overall picture in hebephrenic reactions is that of a young person who has retreated from the stresses of life by regressing to a silly, childish level of behavior and by withdrawing into a fantasy world of his own, with accompanying emotional distortion and blunting. Apparently the typical inappropriate laughter and silliness serve to relieve a feeling of tension. Both are reactions to frustration and imply a conviction on the part of the patient that any active solution to his difficulties is impossible. As he abandons all resistance, there appears the happy silliness in which only the occasional impression of deliberate clowning, or a grim, ironical note to the laughter, may tell of the original conflict and the patient's vague realization of the disintegration of his own personality. The author is reminded here of a hebephrenic girl who when first brought to the hospital was markedly excited, hyperactive, and completely inaccessible. She seemed completely preoccupied with silly giggling and showed an animated preoccupation with her fantasies and hallucinations. However, when the psychiatrist became slightly discouraged and made some deprecatory remark about her, the apparently inaccessible patient very slowly and distinctly thumbed her nose at him.

The general pattern in hebephrenic reactions is illustrated in the following interview with a hebephrenic patient. In addition to a shallowness of affect, which we saw in the case of the simple schizophrenic, the hebephrenic affect is distorted and inappropriate to the mental content. A further distinction lies in the extreme degree of personality disintegration in hebephrenic reactions.

The patient was a divorcée, 32 years of age, who had come to the hospital with bizarre delusions, hallucinations, and severe personality disintegration and with a record of alcoholism, promiscuity, and possible incestuous relations with a brother. The following conversation shows typical hebephrenic responses to questioning.

Dr.: How do you feel today?

Pt.: Fine.

Dr.: When did you come here?

Pt.: 1416, you remember, doctor (silly giggle).

Dr.: Do you know why you are here?

Pt.: Well, in 1951 I changed into two men. President Truman was judge at my trial. I was convicted and hung (silly giggle). My brother and I were given back our normal bodies five years ago. I am a police-woman. I keep a dictaphone concealed on my person.

Dr.: Can you tell me the name of this place?

Pt.: I have not been a drinker for sixteen years. I am taking a mental rest after a "carter" assignment or "quill." You know, a "penwrap." I had contracts with Warner Brothers Studios and Eugene broke phonograph records but Mike protested. I have been with the police department for thirty-five years. I am made of flesh and blood—see, doctor (pulling up her dress).

Dr.: Are you married?

Pt.: No. I am not attracted to men (silly giggle). I have a companionship arrangement with my brother. I am a "looner" . . . a bachelor.

Catatonic type. Catatonic reactions often develop much more suddenly than other forms of schizophrenia, but the patient's history usually shows the typical pattern of gradual withdrawal from reality and some degree of emotional apathy. In catatonic reactions the patient typically alternates between stupor and excitement. In the stupor there is a sudden loss of all animation and a tendency to remain motionless in a stereotyped position or posture. This position may be maintained for hours or even days, and the hands and feet may become blue and swollen because of the immobility.

Some of these patients are highly suggestible and will automatically obey commands or imitate the actions of others (*echopraxia*) or repeat phrases in a stereotyped way (*echolalia*). If the patient's arm is raised to an awkward and uncomfortable position, he may maintain it in this position for minutes or even hours. This is known as *cerea flexibilitas* (waxy flexibility). Ordinarily, however, in catatonic stupor the patient is extremely negativistic. He is apt to resist stubbornly any effort to change his position and may become mute, resist all attempts to feed him, and refuse to comply with even the slightest request. He pays no attention to bowel or bladder control and saliva may drool from his mouth. The patient's facial expression typically becomes vacant, and the skin waxy in appearance. Threats and painful stimuli have no effect, and

he has to be dressed and washed and have his eliminative processes taken care of.

His experiences while in the catatonic stupor often involve vivid hallucinations and grandiose delusions which may explain the personal symbolic significance of his postures and behavior. It is interesting to note that despite his apparent lack of attention to his environment while in this condition, he may later relate in detail events that were going on around him.

Without warning and for no apparent reason the patient may pass from this stuporous condition to one of great excitement, during which he seems to be under great "pressure of activity." He may talk or shout excitedly and incoherently, pace rapidly back and forth, openly indulge in sexual activities such as masturbation, mutilate himself or commit suicide, or impulsively attack and attempt to kill other persons. The suddenness and the extreme frenzy of these attacks make such patients very dangerous both to themselves and to others. One patient in a frenzy of excitement gouged his left eye, and while attendants were attempting to restrain him, he managed to injure his right eye seriously. The excitement may last a few hours or several days or even weeks.

Many catatonics alternate between these periods of stupor and excitement while other patients show a predominance of one or the other reaction. The prognosis is much more favorable in general for catatonics than for other types of schizophrenic reactions, particularly where the catatonic reactions have had an acute onset. The following case shows some of the typical symptoms in catatonic reactions.

On admission, the patient, a 35-year-old male, appeared apathetic and withdrawn. He would answer questions only after they had been repeated several times and then his speech was so indistinct that it was difficult to understand what he said. After a period of three weeks on the ward, his behavior underwent a rather dramatic shift and he became mildly excited, heard the voice of God talking to him, and spent a good deal of time on his knees praying aloud. He occasionally turned to other patients and beseeched them to "get religion" before the devil got them. During this period the following conversation occurred with the ward doctor:

Dr.: How are you today, Mr. ____?

The woman at the left is showing the typical catatonic symptom of rigidity and the holding of one pose. She stares at the ceiling and sometimes sees strange animals coming out of the light fixture. The gestures shown below were those of another catatonic patient and were found to have the following symbolic meanings: the fingers spread wide depicted the Ten Commandments; clenched fists with arms tense, muscles quivering, and arms pulling apart symbolized Unity; clenched fists and lateral motion of the arms symbolized Power; hands clasped symbolized Physical Brotherhood; hands held in receptive position depicted the Spirit of God Coming In; hands held together with head bowed was position usually following that of Ten Commandments.

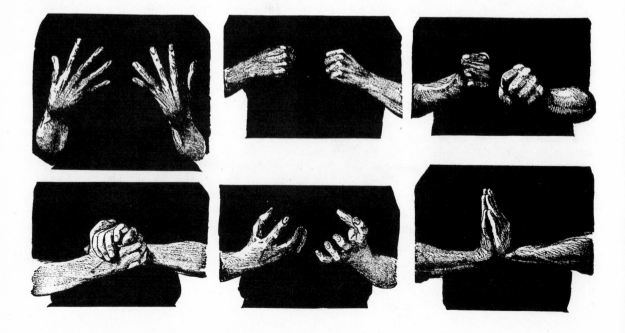

Pt.: I am fighting, doctor—fighting sin and evil.

Dr.: Sin and evil?

Pt.: Yes, sin and evil. You know what sin and evil are, and you should be down here praying with me for your salvation. . . . God knows the answers. He has imparted some of his knowledge to Churchill. He knows but others are confused. He is the true hero of the British Empire. The Bible states that "By a man's actions ye shall judge him," and he is a man of action.

Dr.: Do you feel that you have found any answers?

Pt.: I am fighting, doctor. The devil tries to confuse you, but I am fighting. Why do people die, doctor? Why did my mother have to die? That's the crucial point, how can you beat sin and evil, how can you keep from moral and physical decay? God has all the answers!

On one occasion the patient impulsively attacked another patient on the ward who had asked him if he was trying to polish the ward floor with his knees. Afterwards, he blamed the devil for his behavior, stating that it was the devil who directed the attack.

Paranoid type. This type is by far the most common, constituting over half of all schizophrenic first admissions. It usually develops between the ages of 25 and 40. Often there is a history of suspiciousness and difficulties in interpersonal relations. The eventual symptom picture is dominated by absurd, illogical, and changeable delusions. Persecutory delusions are the most frequent and may involve a wide range of ideas involving all sorts of plots. The patient may become highly suspicious of his relatives or associates and may complain of being watched, followed, poisoned, talked about, or influenced by electrical devices rigged up by his enemies.

All the attention which he is receiving may lead him to the belief that he must possess remarkable qualities or be some great person. For why else would his enemies persecute him? Consequently, he may develop delusions of grandeur in which he may believe that he is the world's greatest economist or philosopher, or that he is Napoleon, Caesar, or Lincoln.

These delusions are frequently accompanied by vivid auditory, visual, and other hallucinations. The patient may hear singing, or God speaking, or the voices of his enemies, or he may see angels or feel electric rays piercing his body at various points.

The patient's behavior becomes centered around these delusions and hallucinations, resulting in a loss of critical judgment and erratic, unpredictable, and even dangerous actions. In response to a command from a "voice" he may break up furniture or commit other violent acts. Similarly, he may attack someone who he is sure is persecuting him. As the condition progresses, there may be considerable disintegration of the emotional and intellectual capacities with utterly fantastic delusions. The illogical, delusional picture in a chronic case of paranoid schizophrenia is brought out in the following conversation.

Dr.: What's your name?

Pt.: Who are you?

Dr.: I'm a doctor. Who are you?

Pt.: I can't tell you who I am.

Dr.: Why can't you tell me?

Pt.: You wouldn't believe me.

Dr.: What are you doing here?

Pt.: Well, I've been sent here to thwart the Russians. I'm the only one in the world who knows how to deal with them. They got their spies all around here though to get me, but I'm smarter than any of them.

Dr.: What are you going to do to thwart the Russians?

Pt.: I'm organizing.

Dr.: Whom are you going to organize?

Pt.: Everybody. I'm the only man in the world who can do that, but they're trying to get me. But I'm going to use my atomic bomb media to blow them up.

Dr.: You must be a terribly important person then.

Pt.: Well, of course.

Dr.: What do you call yourself?

Pt.: You used to know me as Franklin D. Roosevelt.

Dr.: Isn't he dead?

Pt.: Sure he's dead, but I'm alive.

Dr.: But you're Franklin D. Roosevelt?

Pt.: His spirit. He, God, and I figured this out. And now I'm going to make a race of healthy people. My agents are lining them up. Say, who are you?

Dr.: I'm a doctor here.

Pt.: You don't look like a doctor. You look like a Russian to me.

Dr.: How can you tell a Russian from one of your agents?

Pt.: I read eyes. I get all my signs from eyes. I look into your eyes and get all my signs from them.

Dr.: Do you sometimes hear voices telling you someone is a Russian?

Pt.: No, I just look into eyes. I got a mirror here to look into my own eyes. I know everything that's going on. I can tell by the color, by the way it's shaped.

Dr.: Did you have any trouble with people before you came here?

Pt.: Well, only the Russians. They were trying to surround me in my neighborhood. One day they tried to drop a bomb on me from the fire escape.

Dr.: How could you tell it was a bomb?

Pt.: I just knew.

Most paranoid schizophrenic reactions are acute rather than chronic and clear up after several weeks or months with appropriate treatment. Consequently, the following case—which represents a typical acute paranoid schizophrenic reaction—will help to fill in the symptom picture for this reaction type. It is also a particularly interesting case since it involves an officer in the United States Air Force where rigorous selection and training serve to screen out individuals with conspicuous emotional difficulties. In addition, the patient had had an excellent service record as a pilot and had tolerated severe stress which had apparently proved his stability.

"The case to be reported occurred in a 41-year-old command pilot with 7,500 hours, who had flown 135 combat missions in World War II and Korea. At the time of his illness, he was a chief pilot in a command headquarters. He was an excellent pilot and had consistently received superior ratings because of his conscientious and dependable performance. The overt onset of his illness was related to a period of TDY at a conference where flight procedures on a new type aircraft were being drafted. However, in retrospect, it was learned that for several weeks he had been preoccupied and upset, had sensed that he could read other people's minds by radio waves, and suspected those with whom he worked of being 'queer.'

"While at the conference, he developed ideas of reference, believing that certain comments which his companions made, or which he heard over the radio, had hidden meanings and were directed toward him. For example, when the conferees spoke of 'take-off,' he did not know whether they were referring to an airplane or a woman, and suspected they were suggesting he should have an illicit sexual relationship. He developed the delusional idea that his associates were trying to 'teach' him something, and puzzled them several times when he confronted them with a demand that they tell

him openly whatever they wanted him to learn. They became further concerned when he became increasingly upset, tearful and incoherent, and when he did not improve after several days of 'rest' at his brother's home, he was admitted to the hospital.

"On admission, he was suspicious of those about him, wondering whether they were dope-peddlers or communists, and he refused to talk to people who could not assure him they were cleared for top secret. He believed that he was accused of taking dope, that there were concealed microphones about the ward, and he had hallucinations consisting of voices which accused him of being 'queer.' He was often apprehensive and tearful, but this alternated with periods when he was inappropriately jovial. He was oriented in all spheres, and physical and neurological exams were entirely normal.

"A review of the patient's past history revealed no other evidence of emotional disturbance. He was the second of four children of a strict, moralistic, financially successful farm family. He did well in school and one year of college, but always felt inadequate in comparison with his peers. He entered the Air Corps and flew 32 B-17 missions in World War II, was separated, then recalled in 1950 and flew 103 combat missions in Korea. He had been married for 18 years and had five children. He used alcohol only rarely, and there was no evidence that toxic or exogenous factors could have been implicated in his psychosis.

"The patient received psychotherapy and began to improve within a few days after admission. For this reason, no drug or other somatic treatment was instituted. He continued to improve over the course of the next several weeks and seemed greatly relieved after telling of an isolated extramarital adventure during the TDY. He gradually gained insight into the unreality of his experiences and was discharged from the hospital after one month.

"Following his discharge, the patient was given duties in supply and ground training which he handled without difficulty. However, he had always enjoyed flying immensely and taken pride in his outstanding proficiency, and he made repeated visits to his flight surgeon and psychiatrist to try and get back on flying status. He was referred to the School of Aerospace Medicine for evaluation and recommendations regarding return to flying status.

"When seen at the School, he was found to be very well integrated, although some underlying anxiety was apparent. Despite his apparently satisfactory remission, some residuals of his previous thinking disorder were evident. He wondered at times whether he had not been partly right about the events on TDY, and whether his fellow conferees had not been playing a practical joke on him. He had recently considered going to his Wing Commanding Officer to ask whether the experiences had been part of some kind of 'test' of his mental stability, but had decided against this because it might create an unfavorable impression if he were being tested. He had decided that whatever had happened, it was best forgotten, and through the use of this suppressive mechanism had continued to function effectively. Because of his clear-cut history of a psychotic disorder without an underlying organic basis, as well as the evidence of a continuing minimal thinking disorder, return to flying status was not considered to be consistent with flying safety." (Enders and Flinn, 1962, pp. 730-731)

In commenting on this case, Enders and Flinn emphasized the patient's lifelong rigid, moralistic code, which made him unable to tolerate an impulse toward promiscuous behavior. As a result, this unethical impulse was projected to outside agencies; comments heard on the radio or made by his companions were now misconstrued by the patient as suggesting illicit activities.

It is also of interest to note that both Freud and current investigators have pointed to the role of homosexual conflicts in paranoid schizophrenia. Klaf and Davis (1960) found homosexual preoccupations seven times as frequent in a group of 150 male paranoid schizophrenics as in a control group consisting mainly of psychoneurotics and persons with character disorders. Previous homosexual experiences were recorded almost twice as often as in the control group. In addition, approximately 85 per cent of the paranoid schizophrenics felt they had male persecutors, whereas only 5 per cent reported female persecutors, and 10 per cent reported persecutors of both sexes. Similarly, Moore and Selzer (1963) found a significantly greater incidence of past homosexual acts, preoccupation with homosexuality during psychotherapy, and latent homosexual trends among a group of 128 male paranoid schizophrenics than among a control group of 77 nonparanoid schizophrenics. The significance of such conflicts in the development of paranoid schizophrenic reactions among male patients remains to be clarified, however.

Interestingly enough, Klaf (1961) failed to find a high incidence of homosexual preoccupation or past homosexual experiences among a group of 75 female paranoid schizophrenics. In comparison to the males, 61 per cent of the female patients thought they had male persecutors, 27 per cent reported female persecutors, and 12 per cent thought they had persecutors of both sexes.

Childhood type. In schizophrenic reactions occurring during early childhood, typical symptoms include lack of relatedness to others, an obsessive desire for sameness, distortion and disorganization of thought processes, an unclear or distorted body image, extremely low frustration tolerance, and relatively unrestrained eruptions of erotic and aggressive impulses. Almost uniformly, these children show severe disturbances in language functions, such as mutism, delayed onset of speech, and distortion of the meaning of words and their use with little intent to communicate with others. Often there is an obsession with space and motion and stereotyped motor behavior such as rocking back and forth, spontaneous whirling, and toe-walking.

The following case shows the irrational aggressiveness often seen in such children.

Robert was diagnosed as a mental retardate and hospitalized at the age of 30 months. Upon admission he was mute and appeared oblivious to human contact. His eating, sleeping, and other habit patterns were very disturbed, and he was not toilet trained. He spent a great deal of time rocking back and forth in a sitting position. His responses to those around him took the form of generalized irritability and temper tantrums, which changed to extreme aggression when any attempt was made to interfere with his activities. In time, his symptoms became more psychotic than retarded. Although he had learned to understand words, he would grunt rather than speak. His frustration tolerance was so low that he responded to minor frustrations by banging his head against the wall.

In a study of over 600 schizophrenic children, aged 2 to 13, Bender (1953, 1955, 1961) emphasized retarded and irregular development. She found that the schizophrenic child typically has difficulty in developing a sense of self-identity, is unable to make adequate identification with parental or other role models, shows

Hiding behind the drape while his mother tries to get his attention by reading (A) is only one of this boy's mechanisms for trying to withdraw from a terrifying world. He has many fears; a moving cloud may send him running frantically in circles. During the day he attends a special school for schizophrenic children; his father is a scientist, his mother a teacher. The other picture (B) shows another schizophrenic boy, who spends much time standing and rocking back and forth. Four years ago, at the age of 5, he stopped talking after a tonsillectomy and has been mute ever since.

impairment in obtaining a structured view of reality, and lacks adequate development of ego defenses to deal effectively with anxiety. Weil (1953) has reported similar findings with schizophrenic children, emphasizing marked delays or irregularities in ego development, overintensity or underintensity of reactions from earliest infancy, disturbances in eating, sleeping, and other habit patterns, and the anxiety and rigidity typical of threatened persons.[1]

Acute undifferentiated type. This reaction type includes cases with a wide variety of schizophrenic symptoms which appear suddenly, often without apparent precipitating stress. They may clear up in a matter of weeks but often recur or progress to one of the other reaction types.

Chronic undifferentiated type. As its name suggests, this is a reaction with mixed symptoms, but here they persist. This category includes the so-called "latent," "incipient," and "pre-psychotic" schizophrenic reactions in which the individual shows mild schizophrenic

thought, affect, and behavior but may be able to make a marginal adjustment.

Schizo-affective type. This category is used for cases shading over into affective reactions. The mental content may be predominantly schizophrenic but accompanied by pronounced elation or depression. Or the affective coloring may predominate, accompanied by schizophreniclike thinking or bizarre behavior.

Residual type. This category includes those patients who have improved sufficiently to be discharged from the hospital but who continue to manifest mild schizophrenic symptoms.

Many personnel in the psychiatric field also use the terms *ambulatory schizophrenia, pseudoneurotic schizophrenia,* and *pseudopsychopathic schizophrenia. Ambulatory schizophrenia* refers

---

[1]For a more detailed discussion of childhood schizophrenia and differences between schizophrenic reactions in childhood, adolescence, and young adulthood, the reader is referred to Bender (1947, 1953, 1955, 1961), Colbert and Koegler (1961), Kaufman *et al.* (1962), Meyers and Goldfarb (1962), Pollack (1960), and Weil (1953).

to individuals who are definitely schizophrenic in their thinking and behavior but manage to make an adjustment in the community. *Pseudoneurotic schizophrenia* refers to patients whose symptoms initially appear to be neurotic—who, for example, show obsessions, compulsions, phobias, depression, or hypochondriacal complaints which under careful scrutiny are found to involve serious thought disturbances and to be severely disabling. *Pseudopsychopathic schizophrenia* refers to individuals who manifest pervasive antisocial traits—such as physical aggression, pathological lying, and incorrigibility—which prove to be part of a schizophrenic reaction. The two latter categories tend to bridge the gap between psychotic disorders on the one hand and psychoneurotic and character disorders, respectively, on the other.

The terms *process schizophrenia* and *reactive schizophrenia* are also used to distinguish between cases in which constitutional factors are presumed to play the primary role and cases in which environmental stresses appear of greater importance. In cases designated as *process schizophrenia* the illness apparently begins early in life with social withdrawal and excessive fantasy in the absence of strong precipitating stresses, and deterioration tends to be progressive once the schizophrenic break occurs. In cases identified as *reactive schizophrenia,* on the other hand, the individual reveals a more adequate background of early socialization, becomes ill in the face of discernible precipitating stresses, and shows good recoverability.

Although this distinction may be useful for prognostic purposes, it is difficult to say whether a case classified as process schizophrenia actually is more the result of constitutional predisposition than of a long-term inner struggle against seemingly overwhelming odds. In addition, the presumed differences in constitutional make-up between these two reaction types remain to be confirmed and delineated.

GENERAL DYNAMICS

Despite a tremendous amount of research, the dynamics underlying the development of schizophrenic reactions are still far from clear. In fact, there is some question as to whether we are not dealing with such a diversity of reaction patterns that any general dynamic formulation would be of limited value in a particular case of schizophrenia. Several quite widely divergent positions are now held on the problem of dynamic factors.

Since schizophrenia has become the primary "testing ground" for etiological concepts in the functional psychoses, we shall deal with the problem of dynamics in some detail. In our approach we shall review some of the biological, psychological, and sociological factors which have been emphasized. Although we shall attempt a preliminary evaluation and integration of various findings, this is an admittedly risky venture in view of the present state of our knowledge.[1]

Biological factors. Responsibility for the development of schizophrenia has been attributed at one time or another to numerous biological factors, among them heredity, constitution, malfunctioning of the endocrine glands or other bodily systems, and various types of brain pathology.

1. *Heredity.* In view of the disproportionate incidence of schizophrenia in the family background of schizophrenic patients, it is hardly surprising that so many investigators have emphasized the importance of genetic factors in this psychotic reaction.[2]

As we saw in Chapter 4, Kallmann (1953, 1958) has pointed out that an individual's statistical expectancy of becoming schizophrenic varies directly with the closeness of his blood relationship to a schizophrenic patient. Children of one schizophrenic parent have a probability of developing this disorder which is 19 times that of the general population; grandchildren, nephews, and nieces of schizophrenics are 5 times more likely to develop schizophrenia than the average person. When both parents are schizophrenic, the expectancy rate for their children is 80 times that of the average person. Interestingly enough, this increased probability

---

[1]In an excellent review of research problems and methodology in schizophrenia, Rodnick (1963) has pointed to the difficulties inherent in integrating research findings from diverse fields of science—each with its own terminology, frame of reference, style of research strategy, and conceptual rigor.

[2]Major studies here include Böök (1953, 1960), Fremming (1951), Kallmann (1953, 1956, 1958), Shields and Slater (1961), Sjögren (1957), and Slater (1953).

SCHIZOPHRENIA AMONG RELATIVES OF SCHIZOPHRENICS

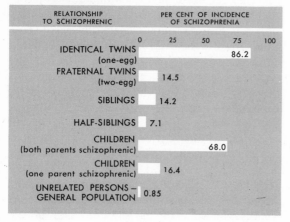

does not hold for other types of psychotic disorders but only for schizophrenia. Kallmann, who has long championed the cause of heredity in psychopathology, concluded that this distribution of schizophrenic rates is conclusive proof of the operation of genetic factors. His findings —which appear to be generally representative of the studies in this area—are summarized in the chart above. Kallmann's figures would indicate that:

1. The morbidity rates for all degrees of blood relationship are much higher than for unrelated persons—even half-siblings reveal an incidence over 8 times that of the general population.

2. The morbidity rates increase with increasing degrees of blood relationship—from 7.1 in half-siblings to 86.2 in identical twins.

3. The concordance rate for identical twins is very high and is approximately 6 times the rate for fraternal twins. Since twins of both types are usually raised in a similar environment, this difference in their rates would appear to be determined largely by genetic factors.

4. The concordance rate for fraternal twins and siblings is about the same—as is the similarity of their genetic endowment. Yet twins would be expected to share a more common environment than siblings in general. This again supports the argument for a genetic factor.

5. The morbidity rate for children with two schizophrenic parents is about 4 times that for children with one schizophrenic parent. Yet over

30 per cent of the offspring of two schizophrenics do not develop schizophrenia—an impossibility if schizophrenia were transmitted by a single recessive gene.

Neither Kallmann nor most other contemporary investigators now view schizophrenia as involving a simple recessive mode of inheritance. Rather they conclude that it must be transmitted by *genetic factors* in the form of "predisposition" —for example, that there may be some basic "error" in bodily metabolism which predisposes the individual to a schizophrenic reaction when placed under stress. In a favorable life situation with minimal stress, there is no reason to believe that a schizophrenic reaction will ever appear. In many cases, too, compensatory processes in other bodily systems may minimize the influence of the metabolic error so that it does not show up except under conditions of prolonged and extreme stress. As Kallmann has stated it:

"In evaluating the effect of genetic factors in psychopathological variations, it would be generally helpful to bear in mind that from a genetic standpoint, unusual behavior of any kind is viewed as an extremely complex and continuous chain of events in the individual's adaptive history and not as some inevitable manifestation of an inborn error of metabolism." (1958)

In short, the relationship between genetic endowment, development, and mental illness is highly complex and cannot be predicted from genetic formulations alone.

Despite the apparent forcefulness of genetic data, many investigators are inclined to minimize the concept of a hereditary predisposition to schizophrenia—at least in a large proportion of the cases. They point out that the life situation of an individual with a family background of schizophrenia is usually characterized by considerable stress, undesirable parental example, and pathological family interaction. Such conditions would be expected to predispose the individual psychologically to schizophrenia. They also emphasize the increasing array of evidence showing that early environmental influences as well as hereditary factors can lead to metabolic errors and neurophysiological pathology.

Finally, telling blows to the champions of genetic factors are directed toward limitations and flaws in their experimental procedures.

These criticisms have been well summarized and evaluated by Jackson (1960) and Gregory (1960). Both men have pointed to errors in the diagnosis of schizophrenia, in the determination of whether twins were identical or fraternal, and in the statistical formulae used in constructing morbidity tables. Gregory also commented on the puzzling problem that the "reproductive fitness" of schizophrenics is not greater than 0.70 —mainly as a result of diminished heterosexual aggressiveness, fewer marriages among schizophrenic males, and diminished fertility among schizophrenic females—whereas schizophrenia continues with apparently undiminished prevalence. This may result from a constant augmentation of the pool of pathological genes by mutation, or it may mean that some varieties of schizophrenia do not involve a hereditary factor.

Until research in human genetics clarifies this problem, it would appear that "the role of possible genetic factors in the development of schizophrenia and other 'functional' disorders will remain in the realm of speculation." (Gregory, 1960, p. 971) This conclusion is not intended to minimize the probable importance of genetic factors in the etiology of schizophrenia, but merely to emphasize that their specific role is at present unknown.

2. *Constitution.* Although constitutional differences in vulnerability to physical and mental disorders are usually presumed to result from faulty heredity, such differences may also arise from early environmental influences. As we have noted, toxins, viruses, ionizing radiation, and a wide range of other stresses during the mother's pregnancy may have profound and lasting influences on the development of the offspring. Similarly, a wide range of early postnatal influences may impair normal development. As in the case of faulty heredity, such environmental conditions may lead to arrested or atypical development and to continuing "errors of metabolism" which reduce the individual's adaptive resources. However, the precise role of such constitutional deficiencies in the development of schizophrenia and other functional psychoses remains to be clarified.

a) Physique. Since Kretschmer's (1925) contention that schizophrenics tend to be slender, considerable effort has been directed toward de-termining the importance of physique in the etiological pattern. The results of later investigators, such as Sheldon (1954), indicate that about two thirds of schizophrenics do in fact have a slender build, all types of physiques being represented among the remaining third. But the relation of physique to schizophrenia is difficult to evaluate. For one thing, schizophrenia occurs among a younger age group than is characteristic of other functional psychoses—a group generally more slender than older age groups. Also schizophrenics often reveal a long history of gradual withdrawal and introversion which is not conducive to muscular development.

In this connection we have already noted Sheldon's conclusion that children with slender builds are sensitive and prone to avoid the rough-and-tumble contacts of childhood, remaining on the sidelines and constituting a watchful but unsocialized periphery, and the corroborating finding by Davidson *et al.* (1957) that slender boys with below-average muscular development tend to display more anxiety and "showing off" behavior than boys with more fatty tissue or a stocky physique. The combination of sensitivity and anxiety may lead to the avoidance of normal social interaction and to the development of conditioned fear responses which impair normal socialization. In some instances, the net effect may be a predisposition to the development of schizophrenia under certain stressful conditions. However, there is insufficient evidence to indicate that most slender children suffer from inadequate socialization; nor do most slender individuals become schizophrenic. Again we are dealing with an interaction of factors whose specific importance is not clear and probably varies in different contexts. In any case, it seems doubtful that physique in and of itself is usually of key etiological significance.

b) Atypical development. Convincing evidence of constitutional factors in schizophrenia stems from the studies of childhood schizophrenia. We have noted that Bender (1953, 1955, 1961—in a study of over 600 schizophrenic children—emphasized the retarded and atypical development of the schizophrenic child from earliest infancy. In particular, she pointed to the immaturity and lack of integration of respiratory, autonomic, nervous, and other organ systems upon which normal behavior and development depend. As a consequence of such inadequate development, the schizophrenic child is often hypersensitive to sensory experiences, reveals disturbances in motor behavior, seems unable to develop a structural view of himself or the world around him, is unable to make adequate identification with role models, and does not develop the ego defenses essential for dealing with anxiety.

Such developmental irregularities may in turn lead to disturbances in parent-child relationships which further complicate the etiological picture. This point is well illustrated in Escalona's study of 17 psychotic children at the Children's Division of the Menninger Clinic. Escalona was impressed by the early atypical and pathological reactions of these children to ordinary maternal care and daily routine.

A baby who will not eat when food is offered, who cries when he is expected to sleep, who is incessantly active or pathologically lethargic, who reacts with panicky resistance to routine procedures such as bathing or being dressed, and who rarely provides for the mother the emotional gratification that comes from having the baby respond positively to her cannot help but be upsetting to even the most loving mother. Finding the usual methods of baby care unsuccessful, these mothers "try everything" and thus go to extremes in both strictness and indulgence—so that the child has a background of inconsistent management.

After years of more or less unsuccessful attempts to manage the child effectively, feelings of ambivalence and guilt inevitably develop in the mother. Meanwhile, the entire pattern creates an unfavorable psychological atmosphere in the home which tends to permeate other aspects of family interaction. (1948, adapted from pp. 127-128)

Thus whereas the disturbed parent-child relationship is commonly assumed to be of primary etiological significance, Escalona has demonstrated that this relationship may itself be the outgrowth of severe developmental irregularities.

It may be that the role of constitutional factors is different in childhood psychosis from what it is in psychotic reactions which develop later in life. Block *et al.* (1958) and Creak and Ini (1960) found evidence that this is so. Or the difference may be primarily one of degree.

Available data do not warrant any general conclusions here or support the view that early developmental irregularities are characteristic of most adolescents and adults who become schizophrenic casualties.

It is relevant here to note that as growth proceeds, there is often a tendency for constitutional deficiencies to be corrected or compensated for. Thus the various organ systems may later achieve better efficiency and integration. This is presumably reflected in the shift from a high incidence of EEG abnormality in childhood schizophrenics to a much lower incidence in older groups. Bender (1961) has pointed out that childhood schizophrenics often show a remission of symptoms during the rapid growth period of adolescence. Later, however, the stresses of young adulthood—such as job problems or childbirth—may again precipitate a schizophrenic break.

c) *Adaptive energy.* In studies of adult schizophrenics, most of the visceral organs and systems have come under scrutiny, but without any definitive results. One condition which has received consistent emphasis is an alleged *deficiency in adaptation energy,* which is assumed to reduce the individual's resources for coping with stress. In one study of 10 acute and 10 chronic schizophrenic patients, Beckett *et al.* (1963a) did find biochemical abnormalities in energy-producing systems, but after an intensive examination of the premorbid history of each patient, it was concluded that these biochemical abnormalities had resulted from a lack of the stimulation essential for the proper maturation of these biologic systems during infancy and childhood—for example, inadequate tactile stimulation by the mother or prevention of overt activity by the child in facing challenges.

Reported findings of autonomic imbalance and adrenal failure among schizophrenics have supported the concept of a "general-adaptation-syndrome" running its course from alarm through resistance to final exhaustion (Abood, 1960; Hoagland, 1954; Luby *et al.*, 1962; Rubin, 1962). Eventually, the adrenal glands may stop putting out the hormones needed by the organism for adapting to stress—resulting in behavioral disorganization. However, as Hoagland pointed out, "Our findings do not prove that the adrenal abnormalities cause the psychosis; they may be the result of it." (p. 76) In addition, most schizophrenics do not show adrenal failure.

In evaluating the evidence for constitutional factors in schizophrenia, it becomes apparent that a great deal of caution must be used. As Horwitt (1956) has pointed out:

"Year after year, papers appear which purport to distinguish between the state of schizophrenia and that of normalcy. The sum total of the differences reported would make the schizophrenic patient a sorry physical specimen indeed: his liver, brain, kidney, and circulatory functions are impaired; he is deficient in practically every vitamin; his hormones are out of balance, and his enzymes are askew. Fortunately many of these claims of metabolic abnormality are forgotten in time ... but it seems that each new generation ... has to be indoctrinated—or disillusioned—without benefit of the experiences of its predecessors." (p. 429)

It will be useful to keep this precaution in mind in our attempts to assess the role of neurophysiological processes in the functional psychoses.

3. *Stress and neurophysiology.* The search for constitutional factors in schizophrenia appears to be narrowing down to a study of brain structure and neurophysiological processes in brain functioning. It is thought that as a consequence of genetic and/or environmental conditions, certain individuals, when subjected to severe stress, may be predisposed to disturbances in basic neurophysiological processes—disturbances that lead to abnormal brain functioning.

a) Excitatory and inhibitory processes. The recent advances in brain research have intensified interest in the possibility of subtle deficiencies in brain structure and functioning. For example, some investigators believe that those who become schizophrenic may have a subtle but crucial imbalance in excitatory and inhibitory processes which predisposes them to behavioral disorganization in stressful situations. In extreme degree, such a constitutional imbalance is illustrated in monkeys, where the process of excitation predominates over that of inhibition —making these animals highly excitable and "unequilibrated" (Voronin, 1962).

This line of thought goes back to the early work of Pavlov which still largely dominates psychiatric thought in Russia (Kerbikov *et al.,* 1958; Wortis, 1962a). Pavlov thought that schizophre-

nia resulted from a state of partial inhibition resulting from a weakness of the nervous system. As a result of such inhibition, the brain supposedly responds equally to all stimuli and weak stimuli thus acquire the force of strong stimuli. As a consequence, the individual may have difficulty in distinguishing relevant from irrelevant stimuli while vague memories, fears, and fantasies may be confused with present reality. The individual becomes confused, can no longer distinguish clearly between fact and fantasy, and falls prey to hallucinations.

The view that hallucinations result from states of partial inhibition has been supported by pharmacological experiments demonstrating that cortical stimulants like caffeine temporarily abolish or diminish hallucinations while cortical depressants like bromides intensify them (Wortis, 1962b). It is argued that cortical inhibition could also involve vascular, visceral, endocrine, and other organ systems in the body and thus be responsible for observed abnormalities of response in these systems in schizophrenia.

Carrying this approach a step further, Meehl (1962) has suggested that one component of defective inhibition in schizophrenia may involve an imbalance between "aversive" and "pleasure" centers in the brain—particularly with respect to social interaction. As a consequence of unfortunate early experiences, the preschizophrenic may learn that to want something which depends on interpersonal relationships is to endanger himself. Presumably such experiences would strengthen the inhibitory functioning of the aversive centers with respect to all activities involving interaction with other people. If at the same time the brain centers which mediate pleasure were functionally weak, the long-term result would be an "aversive drift" —appearing clinically as exaggerated fear in regard to other people. This in turn would predispose the individual to withdrawal which might reach schizophrenic proportions under sufficiently stressful conditions. In this context, Meehl has pointed out that the aversiveness in schizophrenia involves mainly interpersonal areas—schizophrenics typically derive adequate pleasure in esthetic and cognitive experiences.

Since one neuron acts to either excite or inhibit another neuron, the study of the patterning of excitatory and inhibitory processes in the brain offers great promise for the better understanding of human behavior. Furthermore, as indicated in the chart on page 76, new electronic tools enabling the precise electrical stimulation of given parts of the brain are rapidly helping to clarify the functioning and interrelationships of various brain centers. Thus centers in the brain have been found which are concerned largely with regulating feelings of fear and anger, aggressive or submissive behavior, and emotional reactions to pain. But despite the wealth of new information already yielded by modern brain research, the precise role of excitatory and inhibitory processes and patterns in the functional psychoses still must wait for further clarification.

b) Endogenous hallucinogens. Other investigations of the role of neurophysiological processes in schizophrenia focus on the biochemistry of brain metabolism. Research has shown that some chemical agents can produce profound mental changes when present in the blood stream in even minute amounts. Intravenous injections of mescaline or lysergic acid (LSD), for example, lead to a temporary disorganization of thought processes and a variety of psychotic-like symptoms which are referred to as "model psychoses."

Such findings have encouraged investigators to look for some endogenous hallucinogen— some chemical substance arising within the body under stressful conditions which might account for the hallucinations in psychotic disorders:[1] A great deal of enthusiasm was engendered when a Swedish biochemist reported a new test for schizophrenia based on increased levels of *ceruloplasmin* in the blood stream (Akerfeldt, 1957). Subsequent investigations, however, demonstrated that this condition could be completely explained by a dietary insufficiency of ascorbic acid and was not related to the etiology of schizophrenia (Kety, 1960). Similarly, *serotonin,* a substance which exists in high concentration in the brain, has been assumed to be an important factor in brain metabolism, and it has been thought that disturbances in serotonin level might, in turn, lead to mental disturbances. Strong encouragement was given to this hypothesis when the antipsychotic drug *reserpine* was shown to cause a marked and persistent fall in the level of brain serotonin (Shore *et al.,* 1957). Later studies, however, failed to show the involvement of serotonin level in mental disorders.

Perhaps the most exciting finding was that made by Heath and his associates at the Tulane Medical School (Heath, 1960; Heath *et al.,* 1957; Heath *et al.,* 1958). Using two volunteer convicts from the Louisiana State Prison, these investigators were able to produce manifestations of schizophrenia by injecting *taraxein,* a substance obtained from the blood of schizophrenic patients. One subject developed a catatonic type reaction; the other, a paranoid type.

In a series of follow-up studies, taraxein was administered to additional nonpsychotic volunteers who all developed schizophrenic-like symptoms. The characteristic reaction was mental blocking with disorganization and fragmentation of thought processes. Many of the patients became autistic and displayed a lessening of animation in facial expression. Other common symptoms included delusions of reference, persecution, and grandeur; auditory hallucinations; and subjective complaints of depersonalization. The onset of the symptoms was gradual, reaching a peak between 15 and 40 minutes following the injection and then subsiding. In an additional experiment, rapid blood transfusions were made from schizophrenic to normal subjects; the latter developed mild schizophrenic-like symptoms which cleared up within an hour. On the basis of these findings, it was concluded that there is an inherited metabolic defect in schizophrenia which is activated by severe stress.

Unfortunately, the findings of Heath and his colleagues have not been confirmed by subsequent investigators. Despite the appealing simplicity of a theory of endogenous hallucinogens produced under severe stress in constitutionally predisposed individuals, the scientific evidence for this viewpoint remains to be established.

c) Sleep loss. In 1896 White gave the following picture of the effects of extreme sleep deprivation.

"One sort of treatment used for those accused of witchcraft was the 'tortura insomniae.' Under this practice,

---

[1]The biochemical effect might result from (a) excessive production or inadequate metabolism or detoxification of some substance normally in the blood stream, (b) insufficient production of some chemical essential for normal brain functioning, or (c) production of some qualitatively different substance found only in schizophrenic conditions.

SCHIZOPHRENIA AND DRUG-INDUCED "PSYCHOSES"

The similarities between the symptoms of schizophrenia and those produced by the psychotomimetic drugs (most commonly LSD-25, mescaline, and psilocybin) have led many investigators to speculate that their biochemical bases may be the same. But schizophrenia and drug-induced symptoms differ significantly, not only in many particular respects, but most importantly, in overall pattern.

	SCHIZOPHRENIC REACTIONS	DRUG-INDUCED PSYCHOSES
Mood	Daydreaming and extreme withdrawal from personal contacts, ranging from sullen reluctance to talk to actual muteness	Dreaming, introspective state, but preference for discussing visions and ruminations with someone
Communication	Speech vague, ambiguous, difficult to follow; no concern about inability to communicate; past tense common	Speech rambling or incoherent but usually related to reality; subjects try to communicate thoughts; present tense used
Irrationality	Great preoccupation with bodily functions; illnesses attributed to unreasonable causes (the devil, "enemies")	Great interest in the vast array of new sensations being experienced; symptoms attributed to reasonable causes
Hallucinations	Frequent hallucinations, usually auditory and extremely threatening; hallucinations very real and attempts to rationalize them rejected	Hallucinations predominantly visual; the rare auditory hallucinations not so personal or threatening; subjects attempt to explain them rationally
Delusions	Delusions common, usually of paranoid or grandiose pattern	Delusions rare; when occur, probably due to individual personality conflicts
Mannerisms	Bizarre mannerisms, postures, and even waxy inflexibility manifested by certain patients	Strange and bizarre mannerisms rare

Adapted from Hollister (1962) and Luby et al. (1962)

these half-crazed creatures were prevented, night after night and day after day, from sleeping or even resting. In this way temporary delusion became chronic insanity, mild cases became violent, torture and death ensued. . . ." (White, 1896, II, p. 119)[1]

Although White was describing the effects of prolonged sleep loss on people who presumably were already mentally ill, such deprivation has long been considered a form of severe torture.

Several contemporary investigators also suggest a relationship between schizophrenic reactions and sleep loss. Under conditions of extreme sleep deprivation, normal subjects have shown psychopathological changes including irritability, visual hallucinations, dissociative states, and paranoid thinking. Presumably, met-

abolic changes associated with sleep loss may afford a neurophysiological setting favorable to the development of psychosis in predisposed persons. Bliss *et al.* (1959) noted that sleep-deprived subjects were more sensitive to the hallucinogenic effects of lysergic acid and that some acute schizophrenic reactions were seemingly precipitated by loss of sleep. Additional evidence for this hypothesis was provided by Koranyi and Lehman (1960), who subjected 6 schizophrenic subjects to sleep deprivation and observed that progressive mental deterioration occurred after 72 hours. In fact, 5 of the 6 subjects again manifested their earlier acute symptoms.

[1]From: *A History of the Warfare of Science with Theology in Christendom* by Andrew D. White. Copyright 1896, D. Appleton and Company. Reprinted by permission of the publishers, Appleton-Century-Crofts, Inc.

In attempting to explain these findings, Luby *et al.* (1962) pointed out that under the stress of prolonged sleep deprivation there is an initial increase in energy output followed after about 100 hours by a decrease. This decrease is accompanied by a marked decline in emotional reactivity and an inability of the subject to marshal energy resources. Since the processing of external sensory input involves greater energy than attention to internal input, the sleep-deprived subject is likely to react predominantly to internal stimuli, such as fantasies. As a consequence, he tends to lose contact with reality and to show a disorganization of thought processes. One implication is that sleep loss resulting from emotional conflicts might lessen the individual's adjustive resources to the point where a stress he could normally withstand would become overwhelming.

Although the metabolic effects of sleep loss cannot be ignored, they appear to be one group of possible contributing factors rather than primary etiological agents. It has been demonstrated that drugs, fever, and other stresses which lower the adaptive resources of the organism may also precipitate a psychotic reaction in marginally adjusted individuals.

Other biochemical findings are of immediate interest. It has been shown that the cerebrospinal fluid of many schizophrenic patients contains unusual amounts of protein and other substances found in the spinal fluid of patients who have inflammatory and progressive diseases of the central nervous system (Chapman *et al.*, 1959, 1960). Continuing this line of exploration, Bogoch *et al.* (1962) found that recovery from functional psychoses was typically accompanied by changes in the protein content of the cerebrospinal fluid indicative of increased biochemical synthesis in brain metabolism. It may be pointed out, however, that the spinal fluid of normal persons also shows an increase in proteins after markedly augmented central nervous system activity and that some persons who recover from functional psychoses do not show concomitant chemical changes or actually show changes in the opposite direction.

In general, the data indicate that various neurophysiological and metabolic processes are altered in schizophrenia, but the etiological significance of these changes remains to be clarified.

The weeks and months of acute turmoil which ordinarily precede the diagnosis of the illness are likely to affect nutrition, sleep, activity patterns, and the entire metabolic functioning of the individual. In addition, few if any changes have proven to be specific to schizophrenia or any other particular reaction pattern. For example, many schizophrenic patients have been shown to have altered adrenocortical functioning, but these changes are not unique to schizophrenia, do not characterize all schizophrenics, and show a wide variation from hypofunction to hyperfunction (Roessler and Greenfield, 1961). In fact, Shagass and Schwartz (1962) have concluded that brain functioning probably reflects the current state of personality functioning rather than any predisposing factor.

From this point of view, it would appear unsafe to conclude that neurophysiology will provide a complete explanation for schizophrenia or other functional psychoses. Certain individuals may be constitutionally vulnerable to distortions in neurophysiological processes as a result of stress, but such disturbances in brain functioning are not likely to explain the total clinical picture. The personality make-up of the individual, the life stresses with which he is confronted, and the sociocultural context in which he lives all enter into the onset, nature, and outcome of the disorder.

Psychological factors.   Despite their fundamental organic bias, both Kraepelin and Bleuler believed in the importance of psychological factors in the development of schizophrenia. Bleuler in particular emphasized the role of frustration and conflict, concluding that conflicts caused what he referred to as a "splitting" of the personality.

Since the time of Bleuler, psychologists and psychiatrists have placed increasing emphasis on the early pathogenic experiences of children who later become schizophrenic. These experiences lead to immaturities and "weak spots" in personality make-up, to a lack of needed competencies, and to distortions in the individual's view of himself and his world. Such psychologically handicapped children then encounter serious difficulty in coping with the stresses of adolescence and adulthood. The following summary of Adolf Meyer's conclusions serves to illustrate this basic pattern:

In the process of personality development, the individual learns various methods of coping with his problems. Some of these methods involve dealing directly with life's problems and making the most effective adjustment to them that is possible. However, other adjustive reactions are in the nature of evasive substitutions—utilizing rationalization, projection, fantasy satisfactions, and emotional withdrawal and insulation. These evasive reactions inevitably lead to failure and self-devaluation which in turn makes their use even more necessary. Thus vicious habits of response become established which lead to a complete miscarriage of ego defense—instead of helping the individual to adjust successfully, they actually make such an adjustment impossible.

The individual who later develops schizophrenia usually manifests an early withdrawal from a world he interprets as frustrating and hostile. This withdrawal is often concealed behind what seems to be an exemplary childhood, but which on closer examination reveals adherence to meekness and formally good behavior in order to avoid fights and struggles. Instead of participating in an active and healthy way in the activities of childhood, the individual withdraws behind a façade of goodness and meekness. This withdrawal, of course, inevitably leads to failures and disappointments which in turn serve to encourage further withdrawal from the world of reality and foster the use of fantasy satisfactions to compensate for real life failures.

As this "good" child enters the adolescent period, he tends to be overly serious, painfully self-conscious, inhibited, and prone to prefer his own company. Often he is unduly preoccupied with various religious and philosophical issues. Normal interest in the opposite sex is lacking, and vivid ideas of the evilness of sexual behavior are usually only too apparent. As the adolescent enters the period of adulthood, with its demands for independence, responsibility, and family relationships, the youth's lack of adequate socialization and preparation for meeting these problems proves fatal. Instead of increased effort and a vigorous attack on the problems associated with assuming adult status, the youth finds the world unbearably hurtful and turns progressively inward to fantasy satisfactions. (Based on Christian, 1936; Lief, 1948)

Although the pattern described by Meyer does not characterize all cases of schizophrenia, it does serve to illustrate the background out of which many cases develop.

1. *Pathogenic family patterns.* The developmental picture of schizophrenia as a failure in socialization with the gradual accumulation of faulty attitudes and response patterns has been supplemented by increasing evidence of disturbed relationships in the families of schizophrenic patients.

a) Role of the mother. Many studies have been made of mothers of schizophrenics—particularly the mothers of male patients. Typically these mothers are characterized as rejecting, dominating, cold, overprotective, impervious to the feelings and needs of others. While verbally such a mother may seem accepting, basically she rejects the child. At the same time, she depends on him rather than on the father for her emotional satisfactions and feelings of completeness as a woman. Perhaps for this reason she tends to dominate, possessively overprotect, and smother the child, thus keeping him dependent and arresting his growth as a person. Often combined with this are rigid, moralistic attitudes toward sexual behavior which make her overreact with horror to any evidence of sexual impulses on the part of the child and lead to serious self-devaluation for him. In many instances, the mother is overtly seductive in her physical contacts with her son, thus augmenting his sexual conflicts.[1]

Such a relationship is usually indicative of a serious emotional disturbance on the part of the mother herself. Kaufman *et al.* (1960) reported that the mothers of 80 schizophrenic children and adolescents almost uniformly utilized psychotic-like defensive patterns in dealing with their own problems. Similarly, Alanen (1958) found that all but 16 of 100 mothers of schizophrenic patients in Finland suffered from a clear-cut neurosis or more serious psychopathology. Often the mother is hostile or condescending toward her husband and makes it clear to her son that she does not want him to be like his father—thus damaging the role of the father as a male model for the son's development.

In general, the mother-son relationship in schizophrenia appears to foster an immature, anxious youth who lacks a clear-cut sense of

---

[1]This picture is based on studies by Alanen (1958), Beck (1960), Clardy (1951), Fleck (1960), Fleck *et al.* (1963), Freeman and Grayson (1955), Garmezy *et al.* (1961), Gerard and Siegel (1950), Kaufman *et al.* (1960), Lidz (1958), Lidz *et al.* (1963), Meyers and Goldfarb (1962), Reichard and Tillmann (1950), Tietze (1949), and Wenar *et al.* (1962).

his own identity as a person, is handicapped by distorted views of himself and his world, and suffers from pervasive underlying feelings of inadequacy and helplessness.

b)   Role of the father.   Although the "schizophrenogenic" mother has long been a favorite target of investigators, the fathers have not escaped unscathed. Available studies have typically revealed a somewhat inadequate, indifferent, or passive father who appears detached and humorless. The father rivals the mother in his insensitivity to the feelings and needs of others. Often, too, he appears to be rejecting toward his son and seductive toward his daughter. In a study of the family histories of 568 male patients who developed schizophrenic reactions in the United States Navy, Wahl (1956) found a high incidence (50.3 per cent) of severe rejection and/or overprotection by one or both parents. Rejection was found to be much more common than overprotection and was more commonly manifested by fathers.

In families having a daughter who becomes schizophrenic, the father is often highly contemptuous and derogatory toward the mother while being seductive toward the daughter and making it clear that she is more important to him than his wife (Fleck et al., 1963). This tends to force the mother into competition with the daughter and devaluates the mother as a model for the daughter's development as a woman. In fact, the daughter may come to despise herself for any resemblances to her mother. Against this background, the daughter often moves into adolescence with an incestuous entanglement with her father which creates severe inner conflict and may eventually prove terrifying. Unfortunately, the mother's basic inadequacies make her unable to provide the healthy love and affection that might counteract these influences.

As a group, the fathers of schizophrenics also show numerous other psychopathological characteristics. Eisenberg (1957), in reviewing the records of 100 autistic children, concluded that 85 per cent of the fathers appeared to be autistic and to fit into the category of "ambulatory" schizophrenia. Similarly, Kaufman et al. (1960) found that both the fathers and the mothers of the schizophrenic patients studied by his group were emotionally disturbed and prone to the use of pathological defensive patterns in

their own behavior. Lidz et al. (1957) and Fleck (1960, 1963) also have reported a high incidence of psychopathology among the fathers of schizophrenic patients. They found that few if any of the fathers they studied filled the paternal role usually expected in middle- and upper-class families. Many exerted serious pathogenic influences upon the family structure and the rearing of children. Thus the father appears to contribute his share to the immaturities, distortions, and inadequacies in the personality make-up of the schizophrenic patient.

Such disturbed parent-child relationships are, of course, not exclusive to the background of schizophrenic patients. Nor are they invariably found. In one study of 20 autistic children, Block et al. (1958) failed to find pathogenic parent-child relations in the majority of cases. Here there is the possibility that constitutional factors may have played a determining role or that these children may have been overwhelmed by trauma which the parents could not prevent or alleviate but which was not the product of the parents' personalities. And where pathogenic patterns do occur, they vary considerably from case to case as well as with the socioeconomic level. For example, Myers and Roberts (1959) have pointed to the disorganization, neglect, chaos, insecurity, and brutality in the home backgrounds of schizophrenics coming from lower socioeconomic levels—conditions not so prevalent at other levels.

A number of investigators also have emphasized the fact that most parents of schizophrenic children have other children who are not schizophrenic. In attempting to explain this fact, Lidz et al. (1963) have noted that the pathological family setting may have different effects on different children as a result of their birth order, sex, changes in the family situation, or other factors. They also found that siblings of schizophrenics who made reasonably good adjustments tended to utilize two defensive maneuvers —"flight from the family," in which they used the defense mechanism of isolation to keep from having to face the full extent of intrafamilial difficulties, and "constriction of life activities" to situations where they could adjust adequately. However, constitutional differences between the children cannot be ignored in such cases. Goldfarb (1962) has suggested that constitutional factors may be the most important factors in cases where the family seems adequate, whereas the pathological family setting may be of crucial etiologic influence in other cases.

c) The family as a group. In assessing family influences in schizophrenia, investigators are increasingly studying the family as a group. Instead of focusing on mother-child or father-child relations, they are attempting to delineate the roles played by the various family members and the types and patterns of communication and interaction within the family—the total family system. This approach has led to a number of interesting findings.

Wynne *et al.* (1958), studying families of reactive schizophrenics from the standpoint of role theory, found that relationships among members of the family often had the appearance of being mutual, understanding, and open but in fact were not—a condition they termed *pseudomutuality*. They also found considerable rigidity in the family role structure, which tended to depersonalize the child and to block his growth toward maturity and self-direction. It was their conclusion that the personality structure of the reactive schizophrenic is to a significant extent derived from characteristics of the family social organization.

In a related study, Rychoff *et al.* (1959) also found rigid and stereotyped roles played by the family members—roles which reduced life events to simplified formulas somewhat like the roles in a play. Brodey has extended this analogy using a model based on the theater.

"The family is unlike the modern theatre. It is more like the morality play of medieval times. Actors take allegorical roles, positions that are stereotyped and confined—one is Good; another, Evil; a third Temptation." (1959)

Summarizing the data on some 50 schizophrenic families, Rosenbaum (1961) has suggested that the rigid and inflexible roles played by the family members permit a façade of continuing relatedness with each other and with the world and make the business of living seemingly understandable and controllable. But in these families the roles provided for the child are destructive to his personality growth.

Other investigators have drawn on communi-cation theory in their interpretation of interaction patterns in the families of schizophrenics—pointing to the conflicting and confusing nature of the intercommunications among members of such families. Bateson (1959, 1960) has used the term *double-bind* (mentioned in Chapter 4) to describe the transactions of members in the schizophrenic family. Here the parent presents to the child ideas, feelings, and demands that are mutually incompatible. For example, the mother may be verbally loving and accepting but emotionally anxious and rejecting. Or she may complain about the child's insufficient love and affection but freeze up or punish him when he approaches her affectionately. The mother subtly but effectively prohibits any comments on such paradoxes, and the father is usually too weak and impotent to intervene. In essence, the child is continually placed in situations where he cannot win. He cannot discriminate between his mother's conflicting messages and has no strong father to go to for clarification and reassurance.

Following a parallel line of thinking, Haley (1959, 1960) has pointed out that members of these families, when they interact, do not act in ways consistent with what they themselves say and continually disqualify each other's statements. Margaret Singer (1961) also found disqualifying communications in her analysis of families having a schizophrenic patient. Rashkis (1959) has pointed out that such unclear and inconsistent communications put the child into an acute approach-avoidance conflict which he cannot resolve and from which he cannot escape. It thus leads to increasing anxiety, with the usual accompanying tendency to overgeneralize and reduced ability to discriminate. The child becomes increasingly anxious and increasingly unable to organize his thinking, and the disorganization and inconsistent structure in his family setting come to be reflected in the disorganized thought processes of a schizophrenic reaction.

A third approach to the family organization of the schizophrenic patient emphasizes the marital incompatibility and emotional maladjustment of the parents and its effect on the children. Gerard and Siegel (1950) found open discord between 87 per cent of the parents of 71 male schizophrenics as compared to 13 per cent for a control group.

Bowen (1959, 1960), studying the backgrounds of 12 schizophrenics, noted the "striking emotional distance between the parents in all the families." (1959, p. 152) He referred to the emotional barrier which separated the parents as having the characteristics of an "emotional divorce." Although the parents in such families often maintained a façade of love—for example, making a big drama out of giving each other presents at Christmas—there was an underlying withdrawal accompanied by severe disappointment and often hostility. The patient's function had often been that of an unsuccessful mediator between the parents. In the case of the male patients, however, the most common pattern of all was an intense association between mother and son which excluded the father. Bowen also noted that as the years passed, the son was threatened by signs of the mother's aging or by other characteristics that might prevent her from being the strong person upon whom he was dependent, while the mother was threatened by any signs of personality growth that might prevent the son from being "her baby."

Of particular interest in the present context is the intensive study of the families of 14 schizophrenic patients by Lidz et al. (1957, 1958). These investigators failed to find a single family that was reasonably well integrated. Eight of the 14 couples lived in a state of severe chronic discord in which the continuation of the marriage was constantly threatened—a condition which the investigators called *marital schism*. A particularly malignant feature of these families was the chronic undermining of the worth of one marital partner by the other, which made it clear to the children that the parents did not respect or value each other. Each parent expressed fear that the child would resemble the other parent, and a child's resemblance to one parent was a source of concern and rejection by the other parent. The other 6 couples in this study had achieved a state of equilibrium in which the continuation of the marriage was not constantly threatened but in which the relationship was maintained at the expense of a basic distortion in family relationships—a pattern referred to as *marital skew*.

In some of the 14 families the serious psychopathology of one parent dominated the home; in others, the parents shared in their pathological outlook. There was a tendency for the wives to dominate the family and to relegate the husbands to an ineffectual role; in a minority of families, however, the husband was dominant to a pathological degree and demonstrated insatiable needs for admiration and indulgence. In over half of the cases, at least one parent was an ambulatory schizophrenic or was clearly paranoid. Still others were chronic alcoholics, severe obsessives, or passive-dependent "children" of their spouses. The fathers were considered as pathological as the mothers. Lidz et al. concluded that in these families there was a great deal of irrationality and distortion of reality—that the net effect on the child was to "provide training in irrationality."

In further studies of these and additional families with a schizophrenic offspring, Fleck (1960) and Lidz et al. (1963) pointed to other characteristics such as rigidity and isolation. Although the parents were often seemingly competent in their occupations, they were rigid, inflexible, and uncompromising in their family behavior and provided a home life quite deviant from the surrounding culture. In addition, the social life of these families was often quite limited, and this isolation tended to minimize the possibilities for corrective social experiences for the child.

These investigators also emphasized the finding that male schizophrenics usually came from skewed families with passive, ineffectual fathers and disturbed, engulfing mothers. Such a father failed to provide the son with a positive role model for guiding his development as a male—leaving the son somewhat undifferentiated from and dependent upon the engulfing mother, with his problems further augmented by incestuous entanglements. On the other hand, schizophrenic girls typically came from schismatic families with unempathic and emotionally distant mothers and narcissistic fathers who were often paranoid. Such a father was often seductive toward the daughter but contemptuous of his wife and disparaging of women in general. The daughter thus lacked a mother with whom she could identify or to whom she could go for help, while being subjected to the father's confusing combination of seductiveness and disparagement of women. It was observed that children growing up in such families tended to break down during young adulthood, when a sense of identity is essential for a more independent social role outside the family. To illustrate the effect of such family pathology in the transmission of irrationality and even in the learning of particular symptoms, Fleck cited the following case:

"[The patient] came to us from another hospital, to which he had been admitted following a serious suicide attempt. Although relatively compliant and cooperative at first, he soon became increasingly resistant to hospital routines, spoke less and less with anybody, neglected his appearance, grew a beard, and would not allow his hair to be cut, so that long locks soon framed his shoulders. Being unusually tall, he not only looked like the Messiah but was indeed preoccupied with strange mystical religions—seemingly of his own invention. As if this appearance were not bizarre enough in the setting of an unbelievably messy room in which he hoarded food, a typical daily scene showed him almost naked, sitting on his toilet, studying stock quotations in the *Wall Street Journal*. It may be noted in passing that he showed a typically schizophrenic phenomenon, exhibiting severe psychotic and delusional behavior, unable to have any comfortable human contact, while still able to select a stock portfolio for his therapist that he predicted correctly would increase 40 per cent on the market in a year's time—a coexistence of abnormal and normal high-order mentation never encountered in any known organic brain disorder.

"As we began to learn about the family background, it became clear that the patient conducted his hospital life in the same autocratic, pompous, and captious manner in which the father had governed the parental household. [The father] was an ingenious and successful foreign-born manufacturer, but at home he ruled his roost like an Eastern potentate, a role for which he also claimed divine sanction and inspiration via a special mystical cult that he shared only with a very few select friends. The patient would permit only a chosen few of the staff into his sanctum, just as the father had secluded himself in his bedroom during most of the time that he spent at home, with only his wife and the children's governess permitted to enter and attend to his needs. [The father], successful inventor and merchant, would sit there in his underclothes reading religious books by the hour. The entire household participated in the religious rites, the mother sharing his beliefs completely and continuing to do so even after his death, which according to the cult meant continuing life in a different form; the widow did not dare

to disavow his teachings, because she believed he would know of it.

"More than imitation and caricaturization of the father's behavior was involved. Both the patient and his only sister were emotionally deprived children who were isolated from the parents *and* from the surrounding community because the family milieu was so aberrant. Thus, when not mute, the patient often consented to communicate only in foreign languages, as if to emphasize his and the family's estrangement from the surroundings. He 'communicated' his sense of deprivation by hoarding food, and during one stage of his illness by devising a complicated airline system designed exclusively for transporting and distributing food supplies in such a way that his needs would be gratified from all over the world." (1960, pp. 337-338)

As Fleck pointed out, the case provides a striking example of the way in which the irrationality of family relationships may come to pervade the entire family as well as of the deviant patterns the child may learn in trying to adjust in such a family setting. To live satisfactorily outside the family, the patient would have had to learn a whole new set of adjustive patterns.

The general findings of these family studies have been summarized by Rosenbaum (1961):

"The *form* of the interactions of these families is that of an appearance of interrelatedness while in actuality very personal, often autistic perceptions and responses prevail. Roles are established which insure the appearance of certain classes of material and the disappearance of unwanted classes. The role structure is rigid and inflexible. The emotional lives of the members are constricted in the effort to maintain some private definition of 'love,' especially between mother and child, and to exclude any recognition of ambivalence, hate, and rejection. The relationships in the families are stereotyped and unchanging over time.

"The *means* by which such a state is maintained are by such maneuvers as the double-bind, reinterpretation of unacceptable perceptions through concertization, overgeneralizations, cliches, and encompassment by someone else. One finds parents distorting reality at any from the most gross and primitive levels of labeling a shared experience to a more sophisticated interpretation of a percept whose labels are agreed upon. Pervasive and large areas of gross family psychopathology are presented as being quite regular; the rest of the world is out of step." (p. 34)

Although Fleck (1960) and other investigators warn against assuming that all cases of schizophrenia are rooted in family interaction, Rosenbaum concludes from a review of the available evidence that "All the qualities of disordered thinking and interpersonal relations which have been described for the individual schizophrenic have recognized counterparts in his family." (1961, p. 28)

2. *Early psychic trauma and deprivation.* Schizophrenics have often had traumatic experiences during childhood. Wahl (1956) found that 41 per cent of 568 male schizophrenic patients in the United States Navy had lost a parent (usually the father) by death, divorce, or separation before the age of 15 years; 18 per cent had lost both mother and father before this age. These figures are approximately four times those for the general population.

Often such family trauma are reinforced by traumatic experiences occurring outside the family. The child may be rejected, made fun of, and beaten up by his peer group; he may be subject to sexual traumas which leave him guilt-ridden and devaluated; he may suffer painful injuries or illnesses requiring hospitalization and separation from his family; he may lack adequate food and other basic necessities of life. Bettelheim (1955) cited the case of a boy who was rejected by his mother and placed in an orphanage. Here he never learned the names of any of the other boys but referred to them as "big guys" and "little guys"—he lived in a terrifying world of shadowy figures who had the power to beat him up and hurt him without reason.

In a pioneering study of the psychoses of children and adolescents, Yerbury and Newell emphasized the total lack of security in human relationships, the severely disturbed home life, the beatings and brutal treatment which many of the children had experienced, and the hatred many of them bore their parents. They found that of the 56 psychotic cases

"Ten of them had been shocked by the deaths of parents to whom they had retained infantile attachments. Four children were so disoriented upon learning of their adoption that they could not reconcile themselves to the true situation. Four children had lived with mentally ill mothers who were finally hospitalized. Sex traumas were reported in 14 cases of children who were over-whelmed with guilt and fear regarding masturbation. Four boys had been seduced and exploited by homosexuals. Three children were horrified by incest in the home, and three girls had become pregnant. Five girls were obsessed with imaginary pregnancy, having had no sex instruction except from other girls. Six children had been tormented, beaten, tied, and confined by their companions so that they were terrified in the company of children, and felt safe only with adults." (1943, p. 605)

In contrast to a control group of normal children who had for the most part led happy and well-organized lives and whose problems centered around school difficulties and social strivings, the conflicts of the psychotic children centered around violent interpersonal relationships and sex experiences. The findings of this study were summarized in the chart on p. 271.

In the background of individuals who later became schizophrenic, there often appears to have been a continuity of early traumatic experiences which have made them view the world as a dangerous and hostile place; as a result they have become oversensitized, rigid, emotionally withdrawn, and lacking in warmth, spontaneity, and good socialization. Karl Menninger has supplied an excellent description of the results of such early trauma.

"Children injured in this way are apt to develop certain defenses. They cover up, as the slang expression puts it. They deny the injury which they have experienced or the pain which they are suffering. They erect a facade or front, 'All's well with me,' they seem to say. 'I am one of the fellows; I am just like everybody else. I am a normal person.' And indeed they act like normal persons, as much as they can. They go to the same schools, they complete the same work, they seek the same goals, they do the same things that all the rest of us do. Often they are noticeable only for a certain reticence, shyness, perhaps slight eccentricity. Just as often, they are not conspicuous at all. . . .

"What is underneath that front? One might say that the same sort of thing goes on in the emotional life that goes on when an abscess slowly develops beneath the surface of the body, for example in the lungs or in the liver. There has been an injury, an infection. Counteracting processes have been set up so that tenseness and pressure and potential pain are gathering. But all of this is concealed from the outsider. There is intense conflict and tension and anxiety and strong feelings of bitterness, resentment and hate toward those very people with whom the external relationships may be so perfectly normal. 'I hate them! They don't treat me right. They will never love me and I will never love them. I hate them and I could kill them all! But I must not let them know all this. I must cover it up, because they might read my thoughts and then they wouldn't like me and wouldn't be nice to me.'

"All this is covered up as long as possible—by trivial conversation, pleasant greetings, chat about the movies or the picnic and the next date, and the rest of the ordinary things of adolescent or early adult life. For the chief problem in the person who is going to develop what we call schizophrenia is, 'How can I control the bitterness and hatred I feel because of the unendurable sorrow and disappointment that life has brought to me?' His efforts to control it often show themselves in various kinds of withdrawal, lonewolfishness, seclusiveness, even mild suspiciousness, or just a quiet going of one's own way with disinterest in active social participation.

". . . the regimen under which they live has much to do with their successful adaptation. Given certain new stresses, the façade may break down and the underlying bitterness and conflict may break through. . . ." (1948, pp. 101-104)

Withdrawal from a dangerous world is not the only pattern that may emerge from early trauma. In some instances, the outcome seems to be what Arieti (1959b) calls a "stormy" personality. Here the individual does not settle on emotional insulation but tries aggressively to relate to people and to find a meaningful way of life. Without the armor of indifference, however, he tends to be highly vulnerable and his existence is usually an anxious one. Often his life is a series of crises, precipitated by minor setbacks and hurts which he magnifies out of all proportion. In other instances, the child develops a pattern of rebellion and somewhat disorganized paranoid ideation involving pathological lying, incorrigibility, unbridled aggression, running away, and various types of delinquent behavior (O'Neal and Robins, 1958a, 1958b). As we have noted, this pattern is often referred to as *pseudopsychopathic schizophrenia.*

In our discussion of the causes of abnormal behavior, we pointed to the importance of certain types of stimulation during early critical periods of development. Experiments in which animals have been subjected to impoverished or atypical environments during early growth periods have produced adult animals with reduced abilities to discriminate and solve problems and with abnormal socialization.

In a study of schizophrenic-like mechanisms in monkeys, Beckett *et al.* separated 20 infant rhesus monkeys from their mothers and placed them in individual cages in a room where they could see and hear—but not touch—each other. Ten of the infant monkeys were supplied with cloth surrogate "mothers" in their cages, while the other 10 were not.

Both groups of monkeys showed serious behavioral abnormalities in adulthood. In the surrogate mother group, abnormalities included clasping the head with the hands, rocking in autistic-like movements, repetitive stereotyped circling movements about the cage, chewing on their own arms or legs in response to fear or external threat, excessive masturbation, and lack of appropriate heterosexual behavior.

In the nonsurrogate mother group, the abnormal behavior was similar but more extreme, including sitting and staring fixedly into space, burying their heads in their arms and rocking, lack of appropriate heterosexual behavior, and beating their heads against the cage in self-destructive actions. (1963b, adapted from p. 837)

Here it is relevant to re-emphasize Gray's (1958) conclusion that in human beings as well as animals certain experiences are essential during early development for normal "imprinting" with respect to emotional and social behavior. Presumably, either a lack of certain types of experience or deviant experiences may lead to faulty imprinting which carries over into adult maladjustment. Certainly the parents of schizophrenic patients have often supplied both of these conditions.

Two additional considerations appear relevant in the present context. First, there may be a critical period for self-differentiation and integration—for getting the development of the self-structure under way. When this period is passed, it may be exceedingly difficult to correct the damage. This is suggested by severely autistic children, who manifest not only a chaotic self-image but an apparently impaired ability to develop an integrated self-structure. Secondly, there would appear to be a critical period during which the highly personalized images and thought processes of the child normally undergo "consensual validation" from parents. When the parents not only fail to exercise needed guidance and corrective influences during this period but also expose the child to their own distorted views of the world, the child is likely to develop a highly deviant frame of reference. Unfortunately, the evidence is insufficient to draw major conclusions here, but it would appear that many of the later emotional and social difficulties of the schizophrenic relate, at least in part, to the type of imprinting which has occurred in his earliest interactions with other people.

In general, it would appear that the effect of early traumas and deprivations depends upon the time of their occurrence, their severity, their duration, the constitutional make-up of the child, and the presence or absence of compensatory conditions in the child's life situation. It is evident, however, that psychological injury inflicted at an early age may continue to operate and influence the entire subsequent course of the individual's development (World Health Organization, 1959). This long-term effect may stem primarily from the pervasive effects of faulty imprinting or from sensitization to particular dangers, with a generalization of faulty attitudes toward these dangers and the development of unhealthy defenses against them.

3. *Lack of reality checks and vicious circles.* The basic assumptions of the preschizophrenic have grown out of unusually limited and atypical experiences, but, like all assumptions, they tend to be perpetuated and to shape all his perceptions, while his extreme sensitivity and continuing social withdrawal make it difficult for him to have corrective experiences. Normally an individual tries out various roles in the group and learns to discard, modify, or utilize them in accordance with his own abilities and the reactions of others. This eliminative process is diminished in the social development of the individual who becomes schizophrenic, with the result that he may have very unrealistic ideas about what types of social roles are open to him and it may be easy for him to fantasy himself as a great religious savior or some other remarkable or unusual person.

Similarly, his poorly differentiated and confused sense of self-identity makes him prone to distorted, fantasy-ridden assumptions about himself, while his dependence on parental dictates denies him the experience of self-direction and any feeling of control over his own destiny. He is an outer- rather than an inner-directed person and does not experience himself as an active agent in his own behavior. It is not surprising that he should be prone to the feeling that his thoughts and actions are alien to him and controlled by others.

We have previously noted that sensory deprivation tends to impair organized thinking and in extreme cases leads to confusion, delusions, and hallucinations. The schizophrenic's long-standing withdrawal from normal environmental interaction and preoccupation with his own inner conflicts and problems may lead to similar results by decreasing the amount of meaningful environmental stimulation and increasing the amount of "input" from memory and imagination (Ruesch, 1959; Sarvis, 1962).

As time goes on, his faulty frame of reference and lack of adequate competencies lead to an ever widening breach between himself and others, and his language and thought patterns become progressively more individualistic (Moran, 1953; Whiteman, 1954; Becker, 1962b). As Overstreet has described it, he becomes "an emotional stranger in a strange land, with his own inner problems and conflicts dictating what he sees in the world around him . . ." (1954, p. 83). Finally, to complete the vicious circle, comes the terrifying realization that he is "losing his mind"—that he has no control over his inner thoughts and impulses.

As the personality integration weakens and reality and ethical controls are lowered, individual impulses, ideas, and feelings appear to "split off" or gain "release" and to dominate thought and behavior in an exaggerated and illogical manner. In essence, there is a "loosening" and "fragmenting" of thought processes. As a consequence, the patient is no longer able to maintain habitual responses. Often he experiences a sense of depersonalization and of perplexity at the nature of his own thoughts: they seem to be something alien over which he has no control. Planansky and Johnston have particularly emphasized this point in relation to homosexual fantasies: "The perplexity which so typically accompanies homosexual preoccupation reveals that the patients perceive their alleged homosexuality as something alien; as if something unwanted, undesirable, and above all, not under their control was happening to them." (1962, p. 613)

The thought processes of schizophrenics have been likened to those in dreams, in which there is also a lowering of inner controls. There are many resemblances between schizophrenic ideation and dreams in terms of bizarre content, splitting of thought from affect, changes in time and space relationships, and gratification of fantasy desires, but the exaggerated ego defenses characteristic of the schizophrenic thought process do not appear to be a prevalent or essential part of dreams.

4. *Excessive stress.* The actual schizophrenic break may be precipitated either by some increased stress during puberty and young adulthood or by stresses occurring in later life. Often the precipitating stress is not apparent to others because it stems from the individual's evaluations rather than from objectively observable stress factors.

It is particularly in coping with the ordinary problems of adolescence and young adulthood —solving dependence-independence conflicts, handling hostility and sexual drives, establishing satisfying interpersonal relationships, assuming adult responsibilities, and building a meaningful way of life—that the sensitive, insecure, withdrawn personality seems to get into serious difficulties. Will has described the stress situation this way:

"There comes a time . . . (later adolescence and young adulthood) . . . at which one must declare himself; he must identify himself as a person apart from his family, establish intimacy with a friend or face loneliness, pattern his sexual behavior, and consider such matters as further formal education, marriage, work, and life in a community. All of these activities require increased self-identification, the ability to relate, and the revelation of self to others. The move toward intimacy involves increasing anxiety; the failure to make the move brings loneliness and the threat of unrelatedness. The extreme of either course is panic and the feeling of impending, if not actual, dissolution and death. Many of the phenomena observable during the development of this disorder reflect efforts to escape the intolerables of anxiety and aloneness." (1959, p. 217)

Lu (1962) has pointed out that the dependence-independence conflicts of the preschizophrenic are often intensified by contradictory parental demands and unrealistic levels of aspiration. While the parent or parents demand that the youth remain submissive, obedient, and dependent upon them, they also impose perfectionistic standards in regard to personal behavior and educational and occupational achievement. Thus the individual strives to do well in school and to be "good" as defined by his parents. In fact, many schizophrenics have previously been exemplary students—often being honor students and obtaining scholarships. The increased competition on higher educational levels may lead to academic difficulties and devaluating failures, but usually the crisis arises after the completion of formal training when strong pressure is exerted on the individual to assume occupational and other adult responsibilities. The preschizophrenic is poorly equipped to enter into vigorous social competition for jobs and adult status; rather, he tends to find the competitive aspects of adult life terrifying and disillusioning.

In the sexual sphere, the schizophrenic's problems are often complicated by highly moralistic attitudes toward sex and a failure to develop normal heterosexuality. Often he has had few close contacts with the other sex (it is not unusual to find schizophrenics over 30 years of age who have had few if any dates), and in many instances he has strong incestuous desires. Even if he has married and so has what appears to be a more adequate sexual pattern, the relationship is usually found on closer examination to be hopelessly unsatisfactory and conducive to feelings of repugnance and guilt. Because of this sexual immaturity, his sexual fantasies, like those of the early adolescent, may include a wide range of sexual objects, including members of the same sex. Since he tends to regard even heterosexual fantasies as immoral and unacceptable, it is not surprising that homosexual fantasies often lead to severe personality conflicts, self-devaluation, and in some instances the use of projection and other defense mechanisms that protect the self against these immoral inner desires.

We shall see in Chapter 9 that homosexual fantasies, as well as overt homosexual behavior, involve far more males than is ordinarily realized and usually do not lead to schizophrenia. They are dangerous only where the individual evaluates them as horribly immoral and repugnant. It is the resulting conflict and self-devaluation, rather than the homosexual fantasies or behavior, which are important in the etiology of mental illness.

In a similar way, the handling of hostility is a particularly stressful problem for such a "good" individual, because he usually considers it completely immoral and terribly dangerous. The hostility generated by feelings of hurt and frustration is often more than he can bear; yet as a consequence of his withdrawal from normal social participation, he typically lacks any adequate comprehension of the role of hostility in normal everyday social relations. He feels guilty and devaluated by his hostility toward family members or other persons and does not know how to express his hostility in socially acceptable ways. Also, he tends to be completely upset when he is the object of other people's hostility. Consequently, he usually tries to repress his hostility and to deny even to himself that he is the kind of person who has such unacceptable feelings and impulses. The author is reminded here of a schizophrenic patient who had been completely unable to express hostility. After several group therapy sessions, this patient proudly related to the group how for the first time in his life he had prevented a man from shoving in front of him in the cafeteria line.

For these many reasons, the preschizophrenic usually has serious difficulties in social adjustment. In a study of 89 schizophrenic patients treated at the Langley Porter Clinic, Ruesch *et al.* (1963) stated that "Most of these patients have been socially inadequate, have had strained human relationships, and have had difficulties in holding jobs, belonging to a group, or pursuing a vocation or profession." (p. 203)

Such an individual tends to withdraw from social participation, but this withdrawal does not necessarily reduce his need or desire for social approval, status, and love. It only reduces his chances of gratifying these desires by removing him from the normal stream of social development and preventing him from acquiring essential social competencies. So he finds it increasingly difficult to establish satisfying marital and other interpersonal relationships. At the same time, however, his strong dependence needs often make his relationships with "significant others" of especially critical importance. Thus the loss of a protective mother figure or even an unsatisfactory relationship with a superior at work may prove overwhelming.

Here it is of interest to note Aronson and Polgar's report (1962) of 13 soldiers who had served at least one year in the army before becoming schizophrenic and whose disorders were clearly precipitated by pathogenic relationships with important people in their immediate environment. They found that these soldiers had showed adequate and sometimes outstanding work performances as long as their supervisors made them feel accepted and at the same time demanded behavior in accordance with group norms, thus both providing support and setting limits. But when this relationship had been disrupted by the transfer of the patient or his supervisor, and the new supervisor had failed to set limits on the patient's behavior or imposed rigid performance expectations without providing emotional support, the soldier had developed an acute schizophrenic breakdown.

Finally, the preschizophrenic is confronted with the crucial problem of meaning (Burton, 1960; Becker, 1962b). He is deeply confused about who he is, what sort of world he lives in, and what an appropriate life pattern for him would be. It is common to hear a schizophrenic ask such questions as "Who am I?" "What is the meaning of it all?" and "Is there any future?" Typically, he feels alone and overwhelmed by a complex and hostile world which he does not understand—a world which seems to provide no meaning, hope, or incentive. The following excerpts from Curry's description of a 29-year-old female schizophrenic patient illustrate this picture:

"She seemed to have a different conception and experiencing of time (hopelessly entangled in the past) and of social space (tremendous gaps between individuals). Quite often she would describe her feelings of 'hopelessness,' 'emptiness,' 'the void,' and a general kind of despair and futurelessness.

"Hilda gave the impression of being crowded, squeezed into a very tiny corner of a universe, and fighting off oblivion. During our initial meeting, she lashed out angrily with questions of 'what' and 'how,' speculating rapidly and illogically.

"The world of this woman was a wasteland, a battlefield where the wreckage of interpersonal wars pressed her into isolation and suffocation. 'It is as if I'm a girl alone in an attic, with no air to breathe.' . . . [there] was only threat in her world—each human was at war with each other human. She could not get beyond this. Even in her intimate relations with men, there had been nothing: a tearfulness devoid of love and care.

"The structure of her existence was threat—impending attack, destruction. There was no orientation toward the future. . . . Each moment was but each moment, and like the first, long ago, filled with only emptiness. . . . In her distorted world there was only past, because she had had it; no future, because she could not make it. . . . What we called 'her psychosis' was her particular being-in-the-world, in all its pain and unauthenticity: a flight from true existence, a corruption of care. Gradually, she seemed to no longer need this world, having transcended it to, what she termed, 'beauty with eyes open.' " (1962, pp. 129-130, 133-135)

5. *Extreme defenses.* The schizophrenic process thus appears to function as a method of adjusting to an unbearably hurtful world, as the individual tries to protect himself against overwhelming feelings of frustration, helplessness, and worthlessness. It is not surprising that the behavior of the schizophrenic appears to be directed more toward avoiding further struggle and frustration than toward achieving rewards or gratifying needs (Myers and Roberts, 1959; Robinson, 1958; Rodnick and Garmezy, 1957). In fact, positive achievement may actually provoke anxiety, for it tends to reawaken hope and force the individual back into the dangerous and hostile world from which he has withdrawn (Winder, 1960).

a) Ego defensive value of symptoms. The ego defensive value of the schizophrenic symptoms is clearly apparent. Emotional blunting and distortion in schizophrenic reactions protect the patient from the hurt of disappointment and frustration. Regression enables him to lower his level of aspiration and to accept a position of dependence. Projection helps him to maintain some semblance of ego integrity by placing the blame for his difficulties on others and attributing his own unacceptable desires to them.

Wish-fulfilling fantasy enables him to achieve some measure of compensation for his feelings of frustration and self-devaluation. In various combinations and degrees, these mechanisms seem to constitute the basic defensive framework of schizophrenic reactions.

In the exaggerated use of fantasy and projection, we find the two mechanisms which are most apt to lead, in turn, to the development of delusions and hallucinations with their many further ego defensive values. Delusions of influence enable the patient to blame others for causing his own inadmissible thoughts and behavior. Fantasies of being the focus of widespread interest and attention help the patient to compensate for feelings of isolation and for lack of social recognition and status. Delusions of persecution explain away his failure to achieve a satisfactory adjustment in the real world. Delusions of grandeur and omnipotence may grow out of simple wishful thinking and may help to counteract feelings of inferiority and inadequacy by a sense of great personal worth and power.

Hallucinations in functional psychoses are related to delusions and have similar dynamic functions. They, too, are an outgrowth of wishful thinking, projection of unacceptable desires and impulses, and feelings of unbearable guilt. Some schizophrenic patients hallucinate conversations in which they hear God confer great powers upon them and assign them the mission of saving the world. They may be entrusted to make decisions on problems of justice, or to resolve international conflicts, or to bring a new code of morality to the world. Occasionally patients hallucinate sexual relations.

Acutely disturbed patients may be so upset by their emotional conflicts that their ideation becomes almost delirious, and with such acute turmoil, the ego defensive value of the delusions and hallucinations is greatly reduced or may come to be nonexistent. Thus intense conflict over immoral sexual desires may lead to hallucinations in which the patient hears voices accusing him of sexual misdeeds. He may even hear voices telling him to commit some immoral sexual act. In this context it may be noted that many schizophrenic breakdowns are precipitated by panic over the possibility of losing control over incestuous, homosexual, or homicidal impulses.

It should be emphasized that schizophrenic reactions appear to represent a total defensive strategy rather than simply a conglomeration of individual defenses. Unable to establish satisfying and meaningful relationships with the external world, the individual attempts to build meaning and self-identity in a highly personalized and symbolic inner world. But his key assumptions are continually being disconfirmed by discordant feedback from the outer world. An individual can handle a certain number of such experiences by ordinary defensive maneuvers such as denial and repression, but if there are too many for his adjustive capacity, he is faced with the alternative of desperate defensive measures or personality disintegration. Such defensive measures require a major reorganization in his frame of reference and lead to a process of conceptual restructuring which Jenkins (1952) has referred to as *psychotic reorganization*. In essence, the individual withdraws his emotional involvement from the real world and evolves a fairly stable system of false beliefs which enables him to distort and assimilate incongruent experiences without undergoing further self-devaluation. Even though this new defensive system may be highly illogical and far from satisfactory, it serves to relieve much of his inner tension and anxiety.

The stereotypy and other symbolic behavior that emerge with this restructuring can be understood in terms of the patient's particular mental processes and general reactive pattern. Thus the patient who thinks he is Christ may prostrate himself on the floor with his arms spread at right angles to form a cross, or dangerous obsessive desires may be counteracted by various magical rituals. Often, however, the symbolism is not easy to fathom.

As Arieti (1959b) has pointed out, the process of restructuring often involves the concretization of more vague and general assumptions. It is perhaps seen most clearly in the paranoid reaction type.

"Immediately prior to the outbreak of the psychosis, the patient experiences feelings of despair and inadequacy and an impression that the whole world is hostile toward him. Some of these feelings are abstract, all-pervading, indefinite, and imperceptible. They represent the culmination of his disastrous life history, par-ticularly in the presence of a challenge with which he knows he cannot cope. After the onset of the psychosis, the indefinite feelings become defined, the imperceptible becomes perceptible, the vague menace becomes a specific threat. It is no longer the whole horrible world which is against him: 'they' are against him. It is no longer a feeling of being under scrutiny, under the eyes of the world; no longer a mild sense of suspiciousness toward his unfriendly neighbors. The sense of suspiciousness becomes the conviction that 'they' follow him. We have thus a reduction of the conceptual and abstract to the concrete, the perceptual." (p. 476)

Now he is not a failure because of any personal deficiencies but because "they" are envious of his great ability and are working against him; similarly his incestuous or homosexual desires are not really part of him but result from his enemies pouring filth into his mind by means of electronic devices. But however well such psychotic defenses may serve to prevent further personality decompensation, the protection they provide is at the expense of severe and self-defeating reality distortion.

b)   Regression and deterioration.   Numerous investigators have emphasized the concept of regression to more primitive levels of behavior as newer and more highly differentiated patterns of behavior are disorganized. According to this approach, "secondary" thought processes, which follow the rules of logic and take into consideration the nature of external reality, are replaced by "primary" thought processes involving illogical ideas, fantasy, and magical thinking (Gill, 1959). Such primary thought processes presumably characterize the thinking of children. The child lives in a world which is partly fantasy and partly real, and he develops all manner of fantastic notions about the things and events around him. He talks to imaginary playmates, personifies inanimate objects, and attributes various powers to both. Not uncommonly, he feels that he is the center of the world and develops ideas of his own omnipotence. In some instances, he is convinced that adults and various supernatural beings can read his thoughts.

Many schizophrenics do at one time or another express ideas of omnipotence. This is illustrated by the patient who sits quietly in his chair with his index finger flexed in a certain way, afraid to change its position because he is sure that the world would suddenly be destroyed if he moved. Commonly, too, schizophrenics are convinced that other people can read their minds and know their thoughts. When questioned by a psychiatrist, the patient may look at him in amusement and consider the whole thing a farce since he obviously knows the patient's thoughts already without being told.

Various experimental findings have also been cited in support of the regression hypothesis in schizophrenia. In a review of these findings, Goldman (1962) has pointed out that the perceptual processes of the paranoid schizophrenic are fragmented and show a preoccupation with details comparable to performance of children 6 to 10 years of age. Hebephrenic and catatonic schizophrenics show the global, amorphous perceptual approach of the 3- to 5-year-old. He also noted the extreme lability of attention and the tendency of all stimuli to have equal potential so that they cannot be adequately discriminated in terms of their relevance to a given task. Each new stimulus tends to require attention and to disrupt the ongoing trend of thought. Goldman also found that the schizophrenic patients he studied showed a dedifferentiation of emotional processes to more global and less stable patterns, a reversion of thought processes to highly personalized and idiosyncratic thought, and a reversal of the usual trend toward interpersonal interaction and relatedness. In extreme form, regression is presumably manifested by the schizophrenic patient who assumes a fetal position, apparently symbolizing his desire to return to a helpless, irresponsible, dependent level.

Although schizophrenics commonly show a reversal of those patterns of perceiving, feeling, thinking, and acting which characterize the normal course of human development, it is apparent that the regressed adult is not simply a child again even though he may perceive, think, and feel in ways somewhat similar to those of a child. It is also relevant to note that the child, unlike the schizophrenic, can usually distinguish between his fantasies and the world of reality and that most children, despite their fantasies, imperfect logic, and lack of perspective are clearly not schizophrenic.

Related to the problem of schizophrenic decompensation and regression is the question of whether a permanent irreversible deterioration takes place in so-called deteriorated schizophrenics. Chapman *et al.* (1960) have suggested that changes in neurophysiological processes during prolonged periods of stress, mental disorganization, and faulty adaptation may lead to an irreversible impairment in brain functioning. It would appear, however, that this is not necessarily the case. In one early study, 100 unselected male schizophrenics with an illness duration of at least ten years were examined under sodium amytal. The investigator found that although apparent extreme disorganization was always present in cases presenting pronounced withdrawal symptoms, even the very disorganized patients could generalize and conceptualize rather freely when adequate rapport and cooperation had been established (Kant, 1943). More recent findings, utilizing standardized psychological tests, have also failed to find any evidence of irreversible mental deterioration (Foulds and Dixon, 1962; Lubin *et al.*, 1962; Griffith *et al.*, 1962).

6. *Psychodynamic differences between the types.* How do the dynamics in hebephrenic reactions differ from those in paranoid or catatonic reactions? The work of Boisen (1947), a psychiatrically trained chaplain who himself suffered an acute episode of catatonic schizophrenia, has been of great value here in giving us clues to the dynamic pattern typical of each group.

As we have seen, the preschizophrenic is characteristically a "good" boy who has accepted for himself the role his parents—and to some extent his teachers—have chosen for him. But increasingly he finds himself unable to achieve a sufficient degree of personality unification and self-actualization on the basis of this role. There are several different ways in which he may attempt to cope with his mounting feelings of personal failure and conflict.

In latent or ambulatory schizophrenic reactions the individual is forced to only a mild use of the various schizophrenic defenses in order to handle his inner needs and cope with reality. He manages to maintain his general reality orientation and to stabilize his defenses on a marginal level of adjustment. If the stress were to increase appreciably, he would decompensate further.

To: The football department and its members present and future
The University of New Mexico, Albuquerque, N. M.

I depend on correct, honest supplementation of this card by telepathy as a thing which will make clear the meaning of this card. There exists a Playing of The Great Things, the correct, the constructive, world or universe politics, out-in-the-open telepathy, etc. According to the Great Things this playing is the most feasible thing of all; but it is held from newspaper advertising and correct, honest public world recognition, its next step, by telepathic forces (it seems), physical dangers, and lack of money. Over 10,000 cards and letters on this subject have been sent to prominent groups and persons all over the world. Correct, honest contact with the honest, out-in-the-open world. This line of thought, talk, etc. rule. The plain and frank. Strangers. The Great Things and opposites idea. References: In the telepathic world the correct playings. Please save this card for a history record since it is rare and important for history.

SCHIZOPHRENIC WRITINGS

The personality decompensation in psychotic reactions—both organic and functional—is frequently manifested in the content and form of patients' letters and other spontaneous writings. These examples reveal clearly the "loosening" and deviation of thought and the distortion of affect so common in the actions of schizophrenics. In addition, they demonstrate different degrees of loss of contact with reality.

Above is a reproduction of a postcard sent by a paranoid schizophrenic. The handwritten example below is from a letter by an 18-year-old girl diagnosed as a paranoid

schizophrenic. Only the first and last parts of the letter are reproduced here. As will be apparent, the letter contained two quite different types of handwriting, indicating further the personality disintegration and emotional conflict the patient had undergone.

The handwritten selections are from samples of psychotic handwriting studied by Lewinson (1940) in an attempt to determine outstanding characteristics or disturbances in the writing of different types of psychotics. She found that abnormal rhythmic disturbances were typical, with rigidity or extreme irregularity in height, breadth, or depth, and that there were consistent differences in this regard between schizophrenic, paranoid, and manic-depressive patients.

"Dear Dad (15.) ~ Oct 9
.... Please come to
see me immediately
It's very urgent that
I see you as quickly
as possible
    Just now my
insides are rotting with
each meal & I have to
eat with very disagree-
able old hags

* * * * * * * *

But it's a matter of
life or death & if I
don't get any response
from you as yet I haven't
I swear by that Bible
I jump in front of a
car. That now in
need of fun I am
Goddam it Come up
as soon as possible Here are
the Fatal Day & the one
Red Letter day, is the one that
see do it on when released;
Last Chance! Danger
Oct 9, 10, 11, 12, 13 14 15 16,
be a corpse on 16th of the month
when I'm out Goodbye forever
Helen R

In simple schizophrenic reactions the individual withdraws from the struggle of life, becomes apathetic, and gives up the fight to achieve social status and esteem. Although the price of this withdrawal in terms of self-devaluation may occasionally be reflected in episodes of mental turmoil or impulsive behavior, the emotional insulation is generally effective, with only very gradual further disintegration. Of course, in simple schizophrenic reactions this decompensatory process may be stabilized, so that the individual becomes an apathetic drifter or remains a dependent, noncontributing member of the family without decompensating further to the point where hospitalization is required.

In hebephrenic reactions, the emotional withdrawal and personality disintegration reach their ultimate. The individual gives up all claim to social approval and status and seems to regress and disintegrate at the same time. The word-hash, silliness, regression, and other evidences of severe personality deterioration are considered part of this general hebephrenic fragmentation, growing out of the patient's discouragement, his loss of faith in himself, and his withdrawal from social contacts and reality.

There is evidence that in catatonic reactions, by contrast, the patient is engaged in a desperate struggle and is still stirred to the bottommost depths of his mental life in his attempt to solve his difficulties and maintain his ego integrity. Catatonic excitement is regarded as a frenzied attempt to deal with the threats to the ego, and catatonic stupor as a retreat during which the individual, behind his mask of passivity, is striving desperately to find some philosophy of life, some system of beliefs, some faith in himself and the world on which to build. Here malignant reactions have not become established as yet, and the individual though panic-stricken, is still fighting desperately to save himself and resist personality disintegration.

In the paranoid reaction, the patient tries to maintain feelings of personal worth and respect by misinterpreting the facts: he simply projects the blame for his difficulties upon others. Now it is all the other fellow's fault. He likes them but they don't like him. They are interfering with him and persecuting him. We shall presently see that in paranoia proper such delusional defenses hold up so well that the rest of the patient's personality remains relatively intact. In paranoid schizophrenia, however, even with the aid of these psychotic defenses the patient is so overwhelmed that he undergoes severe personality disorganization.

In the childhood reaction type, as we have seen, investigators have repeatedly emphasized developmental irregularities and disturbed parent-child relationships. Constitutional factors appear to play a more crucial role here than in the other reaction types, and atypical developmental factors are presumably reflected in abnormal brain functioning and an inability to develop a structured view of oneself and one's world. This, in turn, leads to marked anxiety and to the introduction of autism and other primitive ego defenses. As we have noted, disturbances in parent-child relationships may stem from problems created by either an atypical child or an emotionally disturbed mother or both. In some instances, there appears to be a mechanization or "frosting" in the mother-infant relationship which deprives the infant of the experience of a warm, loving relationship with another person.

Although it is useful to describe the differences in dynamic pattern between various forms of schizophrenic reactions, it should be emphasized that this is somewhat of an oversimplification. A given patient may exhibit features of any or all of the subtypes. In addition, the particular symptoms and defensive patterns of a given patient may change markedly with time. Thus the patient may initially show a paranoid-type reaction pattern which changes to a hebephrenic pattern after prolonged hospitalization.

Sociological factors. Schizophrenia occurs in all societies and in the same general forms (R. J. Campbell, 1958). As we have noted, however, it is evident that sociocultural factors influence the incidence, type of reaction, and particular symptoms that occur in a society.

Carothers (1953, 1959) has pointed out that while the overall incidence of functional psychosis appears to be considerably lower among Africans than among Europeans or Americans, schizophrenia is proportionately more common. Interestingly enough, however, the paranoid type of schizophrenia, which is the most frequent

PARANOID SCHIZOPHRENIC IN LITERATURE

Paranoid schizophrenia evidently occurs in all cultures, and sometimes it is the work of a novelist that gives us an especially clear picture of a particular case. For example, as Grant (1956) has pointed out, Kafka's novel *The Trial* paints a vivid picture of a man who lives in a world tinged with delusion and fantasy and who construes the most inconsequential and irrelevant events as "significant signs." It seems likely that this character, drawn so clearly, was derived from the personal experience of the author.

"[*The Trial*] begins with the arrest, for no reason he is aware of, of its central figure: 'Someone must have been telling lies about Joseph K. . . . .' The charge against him is undefined; he is simply informed that he is under arrest, but he is not detained. Called to an interrogation chamber, before an audience, he takes an aggressive attitude and makes accusations of unfair treatment; back of his arrest, he thinks, a 'great organization' is at work, by which the innocent are accused of guilt. K. observes the magistrate making a 'secret sign' to someone in the audience; he sees 'artifices'; he notes certain badges among the onlookers and concludes that they are in league with the magistrate and are there to spy upon him. He observes peculiar movements in the assembly, the people on the right side of the room behaving differently from those on the left. Strange and seemingly irrelevant incidents occur from time to time in the course of the narrative; e.g., K. is distracted, during his speech in the interrogation chamber, by an assault, apparently sexual, by a male spectator upon a 'washer-woman,' who turns out later to be connected with the court through her husband, and who promises him aid in his case. Other people, also, who would assumedly be unrelated to the action, are disclosed to have such 'connections,' including even some urchin-like girls at play in a tenement. In the same vein K. finds that various people whom he would have supposed were outsiders are familiar with his case; the news has travelled surprisingly. The concept of peculiar 'signs' appears again: there is a superstition that one may read, from the expression of a defendant's mouth, the outcome of his case; from the 'line' of his own lips, K. is told, people have judged that he will very soon be declared guilty; again, a man to whom he had spoken was shocked to read his own condemnation on K.'s mouth.

"Much of the novel is devoted to sustained preoccupation . . . with the details of litigation. . . . An important feature, in this context, is the explicit tokens that the guilt is subjective, and that the culprit's doom is inescapable.

K. himself asserts that the trial is a trial 'only . . . if I recognize it as such.' Following his first visit, he returns to the court without being ordered to do so. Though under arrest he is permitted to go about his usual business as a bank executive. There is no indication of force, or mention of physical punishment, imprisonment, etc. The case is a criminal one, but it 'is not a case before an ordinary court.' K. feels that he could formulate, himself, all the questions for his own cross-examination; in planning a written defense he considers giving an account of his life, with a moral appraisal of each important action. . . .

"It is equally clear that the final judgment will not be determined by the merits of the case. The court is arbitrary, capricious, and irritable. K. is advised that the 'first plea' of his case might determine everything, but also that it might be mislaid or even lost altogether. The defense will be difficult because the charge is unknown to the defense counsel as well as to the accused, though later it might be 'guessed at.' The right of defense itself, in fact, is merely tolerated, rather than legally recognized. The bringing of a charge is, in fact, equivalent to conviction of guilt, in the eyes of the court; one might as well plead innocence, K. is told, before a row of judges painted on canvas. Actual acquittal is almost unknown; there is 'ostensible' acquittal, but this may be followed by a second arrest, a second acquittal by a third arrest and so on.

"The unorthodox procedures of the court continue, through a rather eerie tableaux in an empty cathedral to a sinister climax; the novel ends when 2 callers walk K., unenlightened yet not unwilling, to a suburban quarry, and there thrust a knife into his heart.

"*The Trial* is notable for the unaccountable actions of its characters, and for bizarre unrealities presented with matter-of-fact and circumstantial realism. More important, the impression is strong that the interest, the *motivation* for a novel so obsessed with such a theme must be intimately related to something uniquely personal in its author. . . ." (Grant, 1956, pp. 143-144) type in the United States, is uncommon in Africa. More common in the clinical picture there is the confused ideation characteristic of the hebephrenic type. Carothers has attributed this to the lack of well-developed ego defense mechanisms among Africans, so that when decompensation does occur, a complete disorganization of the personality is more likely.

Field (1960) described the initial schizophrenic break among patients in rural Ghana as typically involving a state of panic and fear of imminent retribution for sin. He found that when the patient was brought to a shrine quickly for treatment, he usually calmed down and in a few days appeared recovered. But when there was a considerable delay before he reached the shrine, he presented a classical hebephrenic picture—inappropriately laughing, smiling, posturing, dancing, singing, replying to hallucinatory voices, standing still and mute, soiling, and smearing. Both delusions and hallucinations in these patients centered around magic and witchcraft. It seems likely that this clinical picture will change as rural Africans are exposed increasingly to urban living and Western civilization.

Apparently, the incidence of schizophrenia in primitive societies varies considerably. While it is proportionately high among rural Africans, it appears to be quite low among the aborigines of Formosa (Rin and Lin, 1962). It would also appear that societies undergoing rapid social change experience a disproportionately high rate of schizophrenia (World Health Organization, 1959).

Within our own society, there is a higher incidence of schizophrenia in the poorer areas of our large cities: Hollingshead and Redlich (1954) found schizophrenia to be eleven times as prevalent on the lowest socioeconomic level as on the upper level. Apparently, the social disorganization, insecurity, poverty, and harshness which characterize poorer neighborhoods intensify the personal problems of the individual and also provide a social environment in which no satisfactory conventional solutions are available. Myers and Roberts (1959) have also pointed out that lower-class patients typically come from homes in which they felt rejected and isolated, were often subjected to brutal treatment, and lacked adequate parental models

for patterning their behavior. This combination of conditions, involving both the family and the more general environment, appears to make adjustment especially difficult for the somewhat shy, withdrawn persons who later develop schizophrenia.

Schizophrenia also has shown a relatively high incidence among certain subgroups in our society.[1] For example, the rate is particularly high among nuns and is higher among the cloistered religious orders than among the more "active" groups (Jahrreiss, 1942; Kelley, 1958). It would appear that individuals with schizophrenic trends are often attracted to a life of meditation, withdrawn from everyday hustle and strife. However, as Kelley (1958) has pointed out, most sisters are in teaching orders and the stress of teaching may be an equally important factor. In a comprehensive study of psychotic disorders in Texas, Jaco (1960) found a relatively lower incidence of schizophrenic reactions among professional men but not among professional women. Women in professional and semiprofessional occupations showed a very high rate of schizophrenia as well as of other types of functional psychoses.[2]

In a comparison of Irish and Italian immigrants—including first, second, and third generations—who were schizophrenic first admissions to an urban mental hospital in New York, Opler (1959) found some interesting differences. The patients of Irish descent showed a much higher incidence of alcoholism, preoccupation with sin and guilt, and "fixity" in delusional systems. On the other hand, the patients of Italian descent revealed far more overt homosexuality, somatic complaints, rejecting attitudes toward authority, and problem behavior. Opler did not attempt to explain these differences systematically but pointed out that there is a far greater emphasis on the body in Italian culture and that in Irish families the central figure is usually the mother while in Italian families it is the father.

---

[1] Findings for several other subgroups in regard to psychoses in general were given on pages 268-270.

[2] It is of interest to note that psychotic disorders are almost three times as prevalent and schizophrenia about 18 times as prevalent among patients in the National Leprosarium in Carville, Louisiana, as in the general population. Manic-depressive reactions, involutional melancholia, and psychoneurotic disorders, by contrast, are rare (Lowinger, 1959). The meaning of these findings is not apparent, but the need for further research in this area is indicated.

In a study of first admissions to the Territorial (Mental) Hospital in Hawaii, Kimmich (1960) found that 52 per cent of the Japanese and 51 per cent of the Filipino first admissions were diagnosed as schizophrenics. Proportionately, this was much higher than for the Hawaiian and Caucasian groups. Most of the Japanese patients were of the paranoid type, showing outward conformity but powerful inner rebellion.

Vitols (1961) and other investigators have pointed to the proportionately higher incidence of Negro than white first admissions with schizophrenia in certain Southern states as well as in the state of New York. When socioeconomic conditions are taken into consideration, however, the racial differences would not appear to be significant. As Pasamanick has pointed out:

"The lower class population—Negro and white—living under adverse economic and social conditions and with less stable family ties is simply in no position to maintain, care for, and tolerate a disturbed and disturbingly ill individual. Such individuals are consequently institutionalized. This applies to lower class persons in general." (1962, p. 303)

Since a far greater proportion of the Negro population is found on lower socioeconomic levels, the Negroes as a group are less able than the white population to obtain medical supervision for the patient in the community or to send him to a private clinic. And of course the additional stress of adverse socioeconomic conditions takes a proportionately higher toll in adjustment difficulties.

Although the preceding studies afford some interesting "leads," the exact role of sociological factors in schizophrenia remains poorly understood. As Hardt (1959) has pointed out, however, the current trend is in the direction of emphasizing constitutional predisposition, early socialization experiences, and adult stresses and conflicts in the etiological pattern of schizophrenia.

Summary of dynamic (etiological) factors. In the course of our discussion, it has become apparent that the dynamics of schizophrenic reactions are by no means simple to fathom. The complex and diverse nature of this disorder is attested by the wide range of individual differences in clinical patterns—differences in constitutional make-up, family background, premorbid personality organization, precipitating stresses, defensive maneuvers, degrees of decompensation, duration of the disorder, eventual prognosis, and related considerations.

In general, it would appear that there is no one causal sequence in schizophrenia, but that there are several types of maladaptive reactions in schizophrenia—all of which have multiple causes. In some instances, biological factors seem of primary importance; in other instances, psychological or psychosocial factors appear to predominate in the etiological pattern. The relative importance of different factors evidently varies greatly from patient to patient. This summary viewpoint has been strongly emphasized by the World Health Organization Study Group on Schizophrenia (WHO, 1959) and is adhered to by most current investigators.

THERAPY AND PROGNOSIS

Sommer and Osmond have referred to the schizophrenic "no-society" to describe the extreme social isolation of schizophrenics in chronic wards where newer concepts of treatment have not been introduced. "Long-stay wards are inhabited by ghostly figures who, like the crew of the *Flying Dutchman,* are able to walk through one another without leaving a trace." (1962, p. 244) These investigators noted that more than eighty years ago Sir Francis Galton made a similar observation:

"There is yet a third peculiarity of the insane which is almost universal, that of gloomy segregation. Passengers nearing London by the Great West Railway must have frequently remarked upon the unusual appearance of the crowd of lunatics who take their exercise in the large green enclosures in front of the Hanwell Asylum. They almost all, without exception, walk apart in moody isolation, each in his own way, buried in his own thoughts." (1883, p. 67)

Certainly there are few other conditions where people live together for prolonged periods of time with so little spontaneous social interaction and relatedness.

Traditionally, the prognosis in schizophrenia has been unfavorable. Under the routine treatment prevalent before the introduction of modern medical, psychological, and sociological procedures, the rate of discharge approximated only 30 per cent. Now, with new treatment methods, half of all first admissions are discharged within 4 months, two thirds within 6 months, and 90 per cent within 1 year. Most of the remaining 10 per cent are discharged after a more extended period of treatment (Kennedy, 1963; Mandelbrote and Folkard, 1963; Ruesch *et al.*, 1963). At present, data on long-range readmission rates are not yet available. It appears, however, that with adequate treatment and follow-up programs, less than 20 per cent of all schizophrenic first admissions who are discharged from mental hospitals require readmission within a 1- to 3-year period.

The modern drugs—tranquilizers and energizers—have proven of great benefit in the treatment of schizophrenic patients. Commonly used drugs are (a) phenothiazines, such as chlorpromazine, which are used to control excitement, agitation, and thought disorders; (b) antidepressants, which are used to increase alertness and interest and to elevate mood; and (c) antianxiety drugs, which are used to decrease apprehension and tension and to promote sleep (Ruesch *et al.*, 1963). These drugs are frequently used in combination with each other and in some instances with electroshock therapy. Additional drugs may also be used to counteract the possible side effects of the phenothiazines. In the overall treatment and follow-up program, the phenothiazines are usually used for periods of months or even years, while the antidepressant and antianxiety drugs are usually used only for a short period of time and then intermittently during periods of special stress.

Acutely ill patients usually respond readily to drug treatment, showing marked alleviation of symptoms within a few weeks (Ruesch *et al.*, 1963; Lasky and Klett, 1962). The chronically ill patient usually responds more slowly, but his delusions and hallucinations are gradually eliminated or reduced to a point where he is no longer upset by them. For example, in paranoid schizophrenic reactions, the patient loses interest in his persecutors and begins to take more interest in his environment. "Voices" which have been a source of torment to him may still be heard but do not bother him any more.

In many cases—possibly 50 per cent or more—the effective use of various drugs enables the patient to be treated in an outpatient clinic or day hospital and thus avoids the necessity of hospitalization. Even recurring psychotic episodes can often be handled through medication, thus enabling the patient to function in his occupational, family, and community setting (Gross, 1960; Ayres, 1962).

By alleviating symptoms, ataractic drugs also make the patient more accessible to psychotherapy. This is of key importance since these drugs only treat symptoms. The schizophrenic whose delusions and hallucinations have disappeared through the influence of drugs remains schizophrenic in his basic personality structure. Psychotherapy is essential for helping him to overcome immaturities, correct distorted attitudes, and become a better integrated and more effective person. Since better socialization is often a primary therapeutic goal, group psychotherapy is particularly useful in providing the schizophrenic patient with a safe social environment for reality testing and for the development of understanding and skill in social relationships.

Recently, operant conditioning methods have been applied to the study and treatment of schizophrenic patients with promising results—particularly in childhood schizophrenia and with chronic "deteriorated" cases. Ferster and DeMyer (1962) have reported on extensive work with three severely disturbed autistic children in which they were able to widen the children's behavioral repertoire and bring much of their behavior under environmental control. The use of operant conditioning procedures in treating schizophrenic patients is described in the chart on page 599.

Sociotherapy, directed toward alleviating pathological family conditions, is receiving increasing emphasis as an essential part of the treatment program. As we have noted, this may involve therapy for the family as a unit. For hospitalized patients, an attempt is made to see that the whole climate is a therapeutic one (Scher, 1958; Wilmer, 1958; Jackson, 1962). In such a "therapeutic community"—with its emphasis upon the creation of a normal and meaningful world in which the patients participate actively in the regulation of their own activities—even isolated, withdrawn, chronic patients often show an increased awareness, interest, and interaction with their environment (Suess, 1958; Tourney *et al.*, 1960). For many patients, this is the starting point for their return to the community. Various therapeutic aids such as occupational and recreational therapy are also highly beneficial in giving the patient pleasant and meaningful contact with reality and acceptable outlets for emotional expression. These will be described further in Chapter 14.

Since an increasing number of schizophrenic patients are being discharged from mental hospitals as a consequence of more effective treatment procedures, increased attention has been given to rehabilitation planning with the patient's family and to outpatient clinics and other provisions in the community to help the patient in making a readjustment. In essence, the emphasis is now on short-term hospitalization and long-term follow-up in the community.

The prognosis in schizophrenia varies with the type of reaction, the particular patient, and the nature of the patient's home situation. Although cases having an insidious onset ("process" schizophrenia) typically have a longer hospital stay than cases with an acute onset ("reactive" schizophrenia), findings concerning long-range prognosis of the two groups are contradictory (Walker, 1962; Stephens and Astrup, 1963). Other things being equal, the prognosis is better for the catatonic, schizoaffective, and undifferentiated types than for the hebephrenic, simple, and childhood types. The paranoid type seems to fall somewhere in between. A number of studies have shown a correlation between early onset (in childhood or early adolescence) and an unfavorable outcome (Bender, 1955, 1961; Eisenberg, 1956; Masterson, 1958). Bender's follow-up studies on a group of 143 schizophrenic children showed that 89 per cent were still schizophrenic when examined in adulthood. There is also evidence that male schizophrenics coming from family backgrounds where the father is highly assertive have a more favorable prognosis than those from backgrounds where the mother is markedly assertive and the father tends to be submissive (Garmezy and Rodnick, 1959).

On an individual level, the prognosis appears to be unfavorable for patients who come from a severely pathological background, patients who show a long history of school and social adjustment difficulties prior to their schizophrenic breakdown, and patients who have had repeated schizophrenic episodes (Marks *et al.*, 1963; O'Neal and Robins, 1958b). The patient's social competence prior to his illness—as indicated by such factors as education, occupation, marital status, and interpersonal relationships—has also been shown to be of prognostic significance (Zigler and Phillips, 1960; Farina *et al.*, 1962).

A favorable home situation to which to return and willingness on the part of family members to participate in the overall treatment and rehabilitation program are often of crucial significance in determining the eventual outcome (Brown *et al.*, 1962; Klonoff, 1960; Zigler and Phillips, 1960; Masterson, 1958). Failure to follow prescribed medication after discharge from the hospital has been a frequent factor in rehospitalization (Ayres, 1962).

Although the prognosis for schizophrenic patients is now generally favorable, there still is no substitute for early detection and treatment—and preferably prevention. The following personality characteristics are possible danger signs during the periods of childhood and adolescence: (a) seclusiveness and preoccupation with one's own thoughts, (b) social withdrawal, with meekness and avoidance of healthy participation in social activities, (c) rigid personality, often with narrow interests, (d) unhealthy attitudes toward sexual behavior and serious difficulties in heterosexual adjustments, and (e) pervasive antisocial behavior, such as physical aggression, pathological lying, running away, and incorrigibility (O'Neal and Robins, 1958a, 1958b; Phillips, 1953; Thomas and Wilson, 1949). Contrary to popular opinion, shy, introverted children do not appear to be more likely than extroverts to develop schizophrenia (Michael *et al.*, 1957).

None of these characteristics necessarily ensures the later development of schizophrenic reactions, but all are psychologically handicapping. Consequently, their early detection and correction are important. By means of medical, psychological, and sociological diagnostic procedures—described in Chapter 13—pathological trends can be detected and corrective steps taken before such reactions become well established. Equally important is the detection and correction of pathogenic family patterns.

We have dealt with schizophrenia in some detail because it is the key problem in the functional psychoses from both a psychiatric and a social viewpoint. A great deal of research is being devoted to schizophrenic reactions; as more basic knowledge is accumulated, it should be possible to understand, effectively treat, and ultimately prevent this pervasive affliction of man.

Paranoid Reactions

The term *paranoia* has been in use a long time. The ancient Greeks and Romans used it to refer more or less indiscriminately to any mental disorder. Our present, more limited use of the term stems from the work of Kraepelin, who reserved it for cases showing systematized delusions without accompanying personality deterioration. Currently, two types of paranoid reactions are included under the general heading of paranoid disorders:

1. *Paranoia,* with an intricate, logical, systematized, and slowly developing delusional system centering primarily around delusions of persecution and/or grandeur. Aside from the delusions, the patient's personality remains relatively intact, with no evidence of serious personality disorganization.

2. *Paranoid state,* with transient paranoid delusions lacking the logical and systematic features of paranoia, but not manifesting the bizarre fragmentation and deterioration often found in schizophrenia. Hallucinations are common here.

Paranoid reactions are relatively rare in mental hospital populations, constituting less than 1 per cent of all first admissions. It was formerly thought that more men were affected, but the male-female ratio is about equal now. The average age at first admission is about 50 years, with most cases occurring between 25 and 65 years. The intellectual and economic level of the paranoiac is usually superior to that of the average patient.

Hospital statistics give a misleading picture of the actual incidence of paranoid reactions since many paranoiacs have sufficient judgment and self-control to avoid hospitalization. Many suspicious, exploited inventors, persecuted businessmen, fanatical reformers, self-styled prophets, and crank-letter writers belong in this category but escape hospitalization unless they become a serious public nuisance.

PARANOIA

Most of us on various occasions may wonder if we are not "jinxed," when it seems as if everything we do goes wrong and the cards seem to be "stacked against us." If we are generally somewhat suspicious and disposed to blame others for our difficulties, we may feel that most people are selfish and ruthless and that an honest man, no matter what his ability, does not have a fair chance. As a result, we may feel abused and become somewhat bitter and cynical. Many people go through life feeling underrated and frustrated and brooding over fancied and real injustices.

In paranoid reactions the picture is similar but considerably exaggerated. The individual feels that he is being singled out and taken advantage of, mistreated, plotted against, stolen from, spied upon, ignored, or otherwise mistreated by his "enemies." His delusional system usually centers around one major theme, such as financial matters, a job, an invention, an unfaithful wife, or other life affairs.[1] A person who is failing on the job may insist that his fellow workers and superiors have it in for him because they are jealous of his great ability and efficiency. As a result, he may quit his job and

---

[1]At one time it was customary to distinguish several types of paranoid reactions in accordance with the delusional ideas manifested—whether persecutory, grandiose, erotic, jealous, or litigious. But a classification in terms of delusional content has been found not to be very helpful because of the many directions in which delusions can develop.

go to work elsewhere, only to find friction developing again and his new job in jeopardy. Now he becomes convinced that the first company for whom he worked has written to his present employer and has turned everyone here against him, so that he has not been given a fair chance. With time, more and more of the environment is integrated into his delusional system as each additional experience is misconstrued and interpreted in the light of his delusional ideas.

Although the evidence the paranoiac advances to justify his claims may be extremely tenuous and inconclusive, he is unwilling to accept any other possible explanation and is impervious to reason. He may be convinced of his wife's unfaithfulness because on two separate occasions when he answered the phone the party at the other end hung up. Argument and logic are futile. In fact, any questioning of the patient's delusions usually only convinces him that his interrogator has sold out to his enemies.

Milner cited the case of a paranoiac, aged 33, who murdered his wife by battering her head with a hammer. Prior to the murder, he had become convinced that his wife was suffering from some strange disease and that she had purposely infected him because she wished him to die. He believed that this disease was due to a "cancer-consumption" germ. He attributed his conclusion in part to his wife's alleged sexual perversion and also gave the following reasons for his belief:

"1. His wife had insured him for a small sum immediately after marriage.

"2. A young man who had been friendly with his wife before their marriage died suddenly.

"3. A child who had lived in the same house as his wife's parents suffered from fits. (He also believed that his wife's parents were suffering from the same disease.)

"4. For several months before the crime his food had had a queer taste, and for a few weeks before the crime he had suffered from a pain in the chest and an unpleasant taste in the mouth." (1949, p. 130)

Although ideas of persecution predominate in paranoid reactions, many paranoiacs develop delusions of grandeur in which they endow themselves with superior or unique ability. Such "exalted" ideas usually center around Messianic missions, political or social reforms, or re-markable inventions. Religious paranoiacs may consider themselves appointed by God to save the world and may spend most of their time "preaching" and "crusading" to gain adherents to their new cult. Threats of fire and brimstone, burning hell, and similar persuasive devices are liberally employed. Many paranoiacs become attached to extremist political movements and are tireless and fanatical crusaders, although they often do their cause more harm than good by their self-righteousness and their condemnation of others.

Some paranoiacs develop remarkable inventions which they have endless trouble in patenting or selling. Gradually they become convinced that there is a plot afoot to steal their invention, or that enemies of the United States are working against them to prevent the country from receiving the benefits of their remarkable talents. Thus a patient may insist that international bankers or foreign agents are conniving to steal his invention and profit from it themselves. Hoffman cited the case of a patient who went to Washington to get presidential assistance in obtaining a patent for a flame thrower which, he claimed, could destroy all the enemies of the United States. He would patiently explain who he was. "There's God who is Number 1, and Jesus Christ who is Number 2, and me, I am Number 3." (1943, p. 574)

Aside from his delusional system, the paranoiac may appear perfectly normal in his conversation, emotionality, and conduct. Hallucinations and the other obvious signs of psychopathology are rarely found. This normal appearance, together with the logical and coherent way in which he presents his delusional ideas, may make him most convincing. In one case an engineer developed detailed plans for eliminating the fog in San Francisco and other large cities by means of a system of reflectors which would heat the air by solar radiation and cause the fog to lift. The company for whom he worked examined the plans and found them unsound. This upset him greatly and he resigned his position, stating that the other engineers in the company were not qualified to pass judgment on any really complex and advanced engineering projects like his. Instead of attempting to obtain other employment, he then devoted full time trying to find some other engineering firm who would have the vision and technical proficiency to see the great potentialities of his idea. He would present his plans convincingly but become highly suspicious and hostile when questions concerning their feasibility were raised. Eventually, he became convinced that there was a conspiracy among a large number of engineering firms to steal his plans and use them for their own profit. He reported his suspicions to the police, threatening to do something about the situation himself unless they took action. As a consequence of his threats, he was hospitalized for psychiatric observation and diagnosed as a paranoiac.

The delusional system is apt to be particularly convincing if one accepts the basic premise or premises upon which it is based. For example, where the delusional system develops around some actual injustice, it is difficult to distinguish between fact and fancy. As a result, the individual may convince his family, friends, and well-meaning public officials of the truth of his claims. However, his inability to see the facts in any other light, his typical lack of evidence for his far-reaching conclusions, and his suspicious and uncommunicative attitude when his delusional ideas are questioned usually give him away.

The following case history is a rather classical description of a mild paranoid reaction revealing the development of a logically patterned delusional system and the pertinent selection of environmental evidence in an attempt to involve more and more individuals in the supposed conspiracy. Despite her delusional system, however, the patient was not severely out of touch with reality, and there are many nonhospitalized cases in the community who reveal similar symptomatology to a more serious degree.

"This patient was an attractive 31-year-old nurse whose father was a chronic alcoholic and whose mother had died of influenza when she was five or six years of age. As a result the family was disrupted, she and her 4 sisters were separated, and she was raised by various neighbors and friends. She worked her way through high school, was granted financial help as a student nurse, and received her R. N. at the age of 21. She frequently boasted about her sexual prowess, but from her statements it was evident that she had never, at any time, felt the need for attempting to gratify her

sexual partners. On the other hand she may actually have been frigid. Her work history was also suggestive of maladjustment. During the eight years preceding her Army service, she had engaged in clinic nursing and private duty, but was unable to hold any position for more than a brief period of time, primarily because of what she termed 'professional differences of opinion about the way things should be done.'

"Shortly after the beginning of World War II, the patient was commissioned a second lieutenant in the Army Nurse Corps. From the beginning, she found it difficult to make professional and social adjustments with fellow nurses, was unable to get along with enlisted men under her supervision, and was frequently transferred from post to post, apparently because of difficulties arising from overzealousness on her part in carrying out in their detailed minutiae her own interpretation of ward regulations, as well as because of her egotistic overevaluation of the duties assigned her. According to one of her fellow nurses, 'She was too precise. Everything had to be in its exact place. She believed she was overcapable. She never had much psychiatry, but when she was assigned to the [psychiatric] section at our hospital, she believed she could change it completely. No one could get along with her.'

"After some two years of military service, the patient was transferred to the European Theater of Operations. Initially she made an excellent impression, but soon showed herself to be a perfectionist, a hypercritical and domineering personality who insisted on the immediate, precise, exact and detailed execution of orders. Within a 14-week period she was transferred on three separate occasions from post to post, and at each new post her manner and her attitude, despite her precise and meticulous efficiency, constituted a virtual demand that nurses, wardmen, patients, and medical officers conform to her exceedingly rigid ideas about the management of ward and even departmental routine.

"Nevertheless, she rationalized her failures so plausibly that many of her associates became sympathetic, believing her the victim of an unfortunate love affair. 'She never said a word, but we all knew it,' so one of her fellow nurses explained. During this same period, however, if one can believe statements which she herself seems to have circulated, she was in the midst of a love affair with an officer whose London flat had previously been owned by a Hollywood star who had equipped it with new and luxurious furnishings of every type.

"During the course of her last assignment, she received every possible help. She requested additional responsibility and was, therefore, assigned, as charge nurse, to the E.E.N.T. Clinic. Within a week she lodged a complaint with the commanding officer of the hospital, accusing the enlisted men of conspiring against her, the nurses of lying about her, and the officer in charge, of lack of co-operation. She was, therefore, transferred to one of the wards, where she expected wardmen, nurses and patients to execute her orders on the instant, in minute and exact detail, and where she violently berated them because of their inability to do so. A week later, the responsible medical officer requested that she be relieved from duty there. Instead, she discussed the problem with the chief nurse and promised to correct her attitude. Within four days, the patients as a group requested her removal. Two weeks later, the ward officer repeated his request. She was, therefore, given a five-day leave, and during her absence all ward personnel were contacted in an attempt to help her adjust when she returned to duty.

"During this period she became convinced that she was being persecuted. She grew tense and despondent, kept rigidly to herself, was unable to sleep in a room with a ticking clock, and frequently burst into tears. As she herself said, 'Some of the nurses deliberately went out of their way to annoy and criticize me. They wanted to make me trouble. That's why I was so upset.' On three separate occasions, she requested the appointment of a Board of Officers to investigate these alleged discriminatory acts. Finally she demanded that a Board of Officers be convened to determine her efficiency as a nurse. Instead, she was ordered to report to our hospital for psychiatric observation.

"On admission, few details of her military history were known. She seemed alert and co-operative, was well oriented in all three spheres, and was thought to be in complete contact. Extreme care, however, was necessary when addressing her. Even fellow patients would warn newcomers to the ward, 'Be careful what you say when she's around. She won't mean it, but she'll twist your statements without changing your words, and give them some meaning you never intended.' In addition, she was bitter about the unfair treatment she had received in the Army, wished to reform the Medical Department and the Army Nursing Corps, and indignantly repudiated the existence of any condition that could justify placing her under NP observation. As a result, she was at first thought to be an obsessive-compulsive personality with paranoid tendencies, and it was believed she could be returned to duty. While under observation, however, she became

unco-operative, aloof and seclusive. She preened constantly, and was exceedingly coquettish whenever men of any rank or grade appeared on the ward. . . . she was meticulous and precise, argumentative and domineering, hypercritical of others but upset by even the slightest hint of criticism directed against herself, and constantly antagonizing all with whom she came in contact. Rapport superficially appeared excellent, but few details could be obtained about her background. Her apparently frank and detailed answers, when analyzed, were seen to be verbose and digressive evasions.

"She was constantly complaining, 'These nurses dislike me because I'm so efficient. That's why they discriminated against me. . . . And the enlisted men didn't like taking orders from me. That's why they lied about me. . . . It doesn't seem credible but they actually got together in a sort of conspiracy [against me]. . . . And he [the officer in charge of the E.E.N.T. Clinic] backed them up: he deliberately misrepresented the facts.' And she adduced fact after fact which apparently supported this conclusion of hers.

"The diagnosis of 'paranoia, true type' was made, and she was returned to the United States, one month after admission to the hospital, a rigid and overzealous individual whose inelasticity had antagonized her associates and aroused severe emotional strain within herself, firmly convinced that she was being persecuted because of the necessary and badly needed work which she had much too efficiently performed. And by one of those fortuitous circumstances that nevertheless occur so frequently, she was received in the States as a patient in the very hospital to whose psychiatric section she had previously, for so brief a period of time, been assigned as ward nurse." (Rosen and Kiene, 1946, pp. 330-333)

Paranoiacs are not always as dangerous as we have been led to believe by popular fiction and drama, but there is always the chance that they will decide to take matters into their own hands and deal with their enemies in the only way that seems effective. In one instance, a paranoiac became convinced that the school board was discriminating against him and shot and killed most of the members of the board. In another case a paranoiac shot and killed a group of seven persons who he thought were following him. The number of husbands and wives who have been killed or injured by suspicious, persecuted mates is unknown but undoubtedly large. Even postmen have been accused and attacked.

PARANOID STATES

In paranoid states the delusions are less systematized; this category bridges the gap between paranoia proper and paranoid schizophrenia. There is often some evidence of disordered thought processes, as well as hallucinations and other psychopathological symptoms, but without the severe personality disorganization, thought fragmentation, and loss of contact with reality which are typical of paranoid schizophrenics.

In many cases these delusional systems develop rather suddenly, often following some particularly traumatic life experience. They are usually of short duration, clearing up spontaneously without psychotherapy. In some cases, however, they may become persistent and chronic. As in the case of the paranoiac proper, such individuals are often able to maintain their status in the community, although they are potentially dangerous.

The patient was a 33-year-old male accountant who had inherited a considerable fortune upon the death of his parents in a private plane crash. He had been married for about three years to a much younger and very attractive divorcée. The patient came voluntarily to a psychiatric clinic for assistance. He stated that he was very upset because his wife was planning to leave him to live with another man.

He then poured out a somewhat incoherent story in which he stated that his wife had first met this man at a cocktail party at the home of some friends and had met him repeatedly since then during the day at bars and motels. The latter information was made known to him because of a sixth sense he had which projected their clandestine meetings on a "screen in his head." He "had seen it all" and "knew exactly what they were up to." At this point the patient became very anxious and upset, and mumbled something about "love and marriage," "sacred vows," and the "better man." He was hospitalized for observation and treatment.

The wife was contacted and proved cooperative. She stated that her husband was impotent with her a good deal of the time and had always been jealous and suspicious. She said that she had met a man at a cocktail party to whom she had been greatly attracted and had casually mentioned to her husband that "Mr. —— seems like a very attractive man." She admitted that this had been "a great mistake." After this incident, her husband had made continual accusations of in-fidelity and had finally reached the point of insisting on inspecting her genitalia upon his return home from work "to see if she had been unfaithful during the day." She stated that their relationship had reached a point where she could not live with him any longer but feared it might be too dangerous to leave him.

GENERAL DYNAMICS

In paranoid reactions as in other functional psychoses, both the long-term developmental trends and the precipitating stress situation must be studied if we are to see the whole picture. Our immediate discussion of dynamic factors will deal primarily with paranoia; then we shall see to what extent the same considerations apply to paranoid states.

Biological factors. Although heredity and constitutional factors have received some attention in paranoid reactions, no conclusive evidence has been forthcoming. In a study of 148 patients who became paranoid after the age of 50, Funding (1961) found a high incidence of psychoses among their relatives (9.7 per cent) but a low incidence of paranoid reactions. He concluded that the genetic pattern in paranoid psychoses is not the same as that in schizophrenia or manic-depressive reactions.

Kretschmer (1925) maintained that paranoiacs were constitutionally of slender physique, but in a study of 8 cases in the armed forces, Rosen and Kiene (1946) found no predominance of any body type. Nor has any consistent medical evidence been found of head injury, focal infections, endocrine dysfunctions, or other general organic or brain pathology. In a post-mortem study of 200 cases of paranoid states, however, Pollak (1944) found an incidence of pathology of the endocrine glands which was four times higher than in nonparanoid psychotic reactions. He came to no final conclusion concerning either the time correlation or etiological significance of the morphologic findings in relation to the psychiatric symptoms. In the 8 patients studied by Rosen and Kiene, 2 had previously had cholecystectomies. More recent data concerning possible organic involvement in paranoid reactions or its significance in the total etiological pattern is not available.

Psychological factors. It is the psychological factors which seem to be of primary importance in the etiology of paranoid reactions.[1]

1. *Faulty personality development.* Schwartz (1963) has emphasized that whereas almost any personality type may retreat to autism and eventually to schizophrenia, paranoid reactions seem to be based on more specific predisposing psychological factors and seem to develop out of certain specific childhood trends. As children, most paranoiacs seem to have been aloof, suspicious, seclusive, stubborn, and resentful of punishment. When crossed, they became sullen and morose. Rarely did they show a history of normal play with other children or good socialization in terms of warm, affectionate relationships (Miller, 1941; Sarvis, 1962; Schwartz, 1963).

Often the family background is severely authoritarian or excessively dominating, suppressive, and critical (Bonner, 1951). Such a family has often been permeated with an air of superiority which was a cover-up for an underlying lack of self-acceptance and feelings of inferiority, creating for the child, in turn, the necessity of proving that he is superior. Inevitably his family background colors his feelings about people in general and his way of reacting to them. His inadequate socialization keeps him from understanding the motives and point of view of others and leads him to suspicious misinterpretation of their unintentional slights. Also he tends to enter into social relationships with a hostile, dominating attitude that drives others away. His inevitable social failures then further undermine his self-esteem and lead to deeper social isolation and mistrust of others.

In later personality development these early trends merge into a picture of self-important, rigid, arrogant individuals who long to dominate others and readily maintain their unrealistic self-picture by projecting the blame for difficulties onto others and seeing in others the weaknesses they cannot acknowledge in themselves. They are highly suspicious of the motives of other people and quick to sense insult or mistreatment. Such individuals lack a sense of humor, focus on their own assumptions, and are incapable of seeing things from any viewpoint but their own. Typically, they categorize people and ideas into "good" and "bad" and have difficulty in conceiving of something as having both good and bad qualities. Their goals and expectations are unrealistically high, and they refuse to make concessions in meeting life's problems by accepting more realistic goals. They expect to be praised and appreciated for even minor achievements and when such praise is not forthcoming, they sulk and withdraw from normal contacts. Although such individuals may have broad interests and appear normal in general behavior, they usually are unable to relate closely to other persons; they appear inaccessible, are overly aggressive, and maintain a somewhat superior air.

2. *Failure and inferiority.* The history of the paranoiac is replete with failures in critical life situations—social, occupational, and marital—stemming from his rigidity, his unrealistic goals, and his inability to get along with other people. Such failures jeopardize his picture of himself as being adequate, significant, and important and expose his easily wounded pride to what he interprets as the rejection, scorn, and ridicule of others.

His failure is made more difficult to cope with by his inability to understand the causes for it. Why should his efforts to improve the efficiency of his company—which people approve in principle—lead to such negative reactions from others? Why should people dislike him when he strives so hard to do the best possible job down to the very last detail? Unable to see himself or the situation objectively, he simply cannot understand how he tends to alienate others and elicit rebuffs and rejection.

Although the paranoiac's feelings of inferiority are masked behind his air of superiority and self-importance, they are manifested in many aspects of his behavior. Rosen and Kiene pointed out that clues in profusion were found in the pathetic craving of their patients for praise and recognition, in their hypersensitivity to criticism, in their exact and formal adherence to socially approved behavior, and in their conscientious and overzealous performance of the most minute occupational tasks.

In essence, then, the paranoid individual is confronted with failure experiences which in effect say, "People don't like you," "Something

---

[1] In the present discussion of psychological factors the author is indebted to the work of Salzman (1960) and Schwartz (1963).

is wrong with you," "You are inferior." But he is incapable of dealing with the stress situation in a task-oriented way—for example, trying to understand why people react to him as they do and making needed corrections in his attitudes and behavior. Instead, he tends to intensify his existing defenses. Thus he becomes more rigid, opinionated, and prone to blame others for his difficulties. He cannot admit weaknesses or mistakes but clings to the feeling that he is unique and has some important contribution to make to mankind. This defensive pattern —which relies heavily upon denial and projection—protects him from facing unbearable feelings of inferiority and worthlessness.

3. *Projection and the "pseudo-community."* Such a rigid, inadequately socialized, self-important, humorless individual as we have been describing may find that his defensive structure protects him reasonably well if his life situation remains relatively constant. With repeated hurtful failures, however, or some particularly devaluating experience, he may be forced to a further elaboration of his defensive structure.

At this point, his initial reaction may be one of puzzlement and uneasiness. Why was he denied a much deserved promotion? Why was it given to someone less experienced and obviously far less qualified than he? He becomes more vigilant, begins to scrutinize his environment, searches for hidden meanings, and asks leading questions. He ponders like a detective over the "clues" which he picks up, trying to fit them into some sort of meaningful picture.

Gradually the picture begins to crystallize. It becomes apparent that he is being singled out for some obscure reason, that other people are working against him, that he is being interfered with. In essence, he protects himself against the intolerable assumption "There is something wrong with me" with the projective defense "They are doing something to me." Now he has failed not because of any inferiority or lack on his part but because others are working against him. He is on the side of good and the progress of mankind while "they" are allied with the forces of evil. With this as his fundamental defensive premise, he then proceeds to distort and falsify the facts to fit it and gradually develops a logic-tight, fixed, delusional system.

Cameron (1959) has referred to this process as the building up of a paranoid "pseudo-community" in which the patient organizes the individuals around him (both real and imaginary) into a structured group whose purpose is to carry out some action against him. As this delusional system emerges, the patient often has the feeling that "Everything has become clear to me; I can see it all now." Everything comes to be interpreted in terms of this delusional system, and the most trivial events may take on an ominous meaning. If a new employee is hired by his company, the man was obviously sent by the organization to spy on him. If an employee under his supervision makes a mistake, it is done to discredit his competence as a supervisor. Even the most casual conversation of others may have a hidden and sinister meaning. This pseudo-community is not all embracing, however, in the sense that everybody is against him. It remains limited in scope to those stress areas— such as occupational failure—which present the greatest threat to his feelings of adequacy and worth. In other life areas not directly involved with his paranoid system, he may be quite rational and may function adequately. Over a period of time, of course, additional life areas and experiences may be incorporated into his delusional system.

In many cases the attention which the individual thinks he is receiving leads him to believe that he is a person of great importance. For why else would his enemies go to all this trouble? In one case, it was pointed out to the patient that if his enemies were persecuting him in the way he insisted they were, it would be costing them about $10,000 per day, which was obviously a ridiculous figure. The patient drew himself up proudly and replied, "Why shouldn't they? After all, I am the world's greatest atomic scientist." As might be expected, the particular content of the grandiose ideas that develop is closely related to the individual's education, vocation, and special interests. A paranoid person with strong religious convictions may develop the notion that he is a great religious savior, whereas the individual interested in science is more likely to envision himself as a great inventor.

The role of reaction sensitivity in the development of these delusional systems should be emphasized. Once the individual begins to sus-

A patient's feelings are often more evident from a painting or drawing than from what he says. Here a male patient with delusions of persecution sees himself a tiny lizard threatened on all sides by enormous feet, A. Symbolic representation of a paranoid is also seen in the rock drawn like a child's head on the bank of a torrent, B. Drawings by the paranoid patient are usually less abstract and confused than those of the schizophrenic, with more definitive form and content, and sometimes there is a foreign object in an otherwise naturalistic landscape—in this case the fetish shoe (Born, 1946).

pect that others are working against him, he carefully notes the slightest signs which point in the direction of his suspicions and ignores all evidence to the contrary. With this frame of reference it is of course quite easy in our highly competitive, somewhat ruthless world to find ample evidence that others are working against us. And the individual's very attitude leads him into a vicious circle, for his suspiciousness, distrust, and criticism of others drive his friends and well-wishers away and keep him in continual friction with other people, generating new incidents for him to grasp hold of and magnify. Often people do in fact have to conspire behind his back as to how best to keep peace and cope with his eccentricities.

4. *Sexual maladjustment.* As in the case of most psychopathological reactions, sexual as well as other life areas are typically involved. Often the paranoid individual has been brought up with rigid sexual morals and a self-righteous and prudish attitude toward all "immoral" be-

havior. He is apt to look upon himself as being above such morbid passions. Even normal sexual impulses then become disturbing to him, and he may resort to projection and other undesirable measures to defend himself against them.

Case histories of paranoiacs almost invariably show evidence of sexual maladjustment. Although all of the patients studied by Rosen and Kiene (1946) claimed normal heterosexual development, these investigators reported that only one of the patients had dared attempt the marriage relationship. Interestingly enough, this patient chose as her husband a chronic alcoholic eleven years her senior whom she divorced after four years of marriage. She was apparently sexually incompatible with this man, although whether because of frigidity on her part or sexually deviate practices on his was not clear. For not marrying, other patients gave such reasons as having had too many family responsibilities and never having met the right person. Most of the patients followed an exceedingly rigid moral code relative to sexual behavior and attempted to enforce this code upon others. The only patient who prided herself on her sexual prowess was so exhibitionistic and coquettish as to suggest that her activity was aimed at enhancing her self-esteem rather than at achieving sexual gratification. In fact, indications were that she may have actually been frigid.

Homosexual conflicts have frequently been emphasized in the origin of paranoid delusional systems. For example, the individual's accusation of infidelity against his wife may actually represent an ego defense against his own homosexual tendencies. In one case, the patient was sure that his wife had been unfaithful to him on numerous occasions because when salesmen came into their business establishment, he, the patient, had an erection. The patient could not accept his own erotic arousal and therefore projected the sexual desire to his wife, who now was charged with infidelity. This factor of homosexuality was strongly emphasized by Freud, who concluded that paranoia represents the individual's attempt to deal with homosexual tendencies which the ego is not prepared to acknowledge. Such homosexual tendencies are often projected to other men, who are seen by the individual as trying to seduce him and eventually are viewed as his persecutors.

There seems dubious justification for attributing a homosexual component to most cases of paranoia. Although anxiety-arousing homosexual impulses may play an important role in some cases, the dynamic core of the paranoid reaction appears to center around unbearable feelings of inferiority and inadequacy growing out of failure to achieve the aspirations and goals which the individual has adopted and considers his just due.

5. *Projection of guilt.* In certain paranoid delusional systems, guilt feelings over actual or contemplated unethical behavior appear to play an important role. Two dynamic considerations appear to be involved here: (a) the individual cannot tolerate the self-devaluation resulting from his failure to live up to his moral views and high opinion of himself, and (b) he justifies his own actions by projecting his unethical desires to others, who now are trying to take advantage of him.

It is not uncommon for a paranoid individual who has been unfaithful to his wife, or who has strongly wanted to be, to become suspicious of his wife's behavior and to come to the conclusion that she has been unfaithful to him. Now he no longer need feel guilty about his impulses or actions. In the novel *Treasure of Sierra Madre,* by Bruno Traven (1947), we have an excellent portrayal of the way this mechanism may work. One of the leading characters has strong impulses to kill his partner and steal the gold they have accumulated. Such thoughts are ethically unacceptable to him, however, so (unconsciously of course) he projects them onto his partner, becoming convinced that the partner is trying to murder him and steal the gold. In self-defense he then attacks his partner, leaves him presumably dead, and makes away with the gold himself.

6. *Paranoia and paranoid states compared.* The problem now arises as to the dynamic differences between paranoia and paranoid states. In paranoia we typically are dealing with a long-term defensive reaction to life stresses which eventuates in a rigid, internally logical, and unshakeable delusional system. This system protects the individual from overwhelming feelings of inferiority and unimportance and enables him to function adequately in life areas not involved in this system. In the paranoid state, the dynamics are similar, but the mechanism of projection is used on a much more elementary level without elaboration or systematization. Here the delusions are vaguer, more pervasive, and more in flux. Often they change spontaneously or can be changed by the questions of other people. In essence, this is a transitory psychotic reaction to some specific stress situation which has proved overwhelming for the individual. Paranoid trends and states often color the clinical picture in other types of psychopathological reactions.

Sociological factors. Paranoiacs tend to come from higher educational and socioeconomic levels. The significance of this fact for the development of paranoid reactions is not clear although the goals of their social group as a whole are so high as to be inevitably impossible of attainment for many members of the group. Yet most members of the group adopt these goals as their own and struggle against impossible odds in trying to measure up to their unrealistic standards.

THERAPY AND PROGNOSIS

Although paranoid states tend to clear up spontaneously after a few days or weeks, drugs may be used for alleviating the psychotic symptoms and shortening the duration of the disorder (Wortis, 1962b). The overall treatment program usually includes brief psychotherapy and in some cases sociotherapy.

For paranoia, the prognosis is far less favorable. In the early stages of paranoia, psychotherapy may be effective, particularly if the individual voluntarily seeks psychiatric assistance. In more fully developed cases, however, the delusional system is extremely resistant to change and all forms of treatment have so far proven inadequate. Occasional recoveries are reported, usually in conjunction with prolonged psychotherapy (Salzman, 1960; Schwartz, 1963), but despite such exceptions, paranoia is considered a chronic disorder in which the chances of recovery are slim.

Unfortunately, the hospitalization of these patients frequently presents a serious problem. Because of a lack of adequate facilities for long-range psychotherapy and the generally resentful attitude of the patient, hospitalization often seems more a punishment than a treatment procedure. A paranoiac is apt to regard himself as superior to other patients as well as to the doctors. Often he will complain that his family and the hospital staff have joined his enemies and will refuse to cooperate in treatment.

Eventually, hospitalization may "sober" the patient to the extent that he realizes that his failure to curb his actions and ideas will result in prolonged hospitalization. As a result, he may make a pretext of renouncing his delusions, admitting that he did hold such ideas but claiming that he now realizes they are absurd and has given them up. After his release, he is often more reserved in expressing his ideas and in annoying other people, but he is far from recovered.

Affective Psychotic Reactions

The psychotic reactions discussed so far have been mainly disorders of the thought processes with a certain amount of accompanying emotional blunting and distortion. We come now to psychotic reactions in which there is a severe disorder of mood with related thought disturbances. Two subgroups are listed under affective reactions: (a) *manic-depressive reactions,* and (b) *psychotic depressive reactions.* Another closely related reaction—*involutional psychotic reaction,* or *involutional melancholia* as it was formerly called—is classified separately and will be discussed in the section following this one.

MANIC-DEPRESSIVE REACTIONS

Descriptions of manic-depressive reactions are found among the early writings of the Egyptians, Hebrews, and Greeks. The great Greek physician Hippocrates classified all mental disorders into three general categories—mania, melancholia, and phrenitis—and his descriptions of mania and melancholia, based upon the clinical records of his patients, are strikingly similar to modern clinical symptomatology.

The sixth-century physician Alexander Trallianus was perhaps the first to recognize recurrent cycles of mania and melancholia in the same person, thus anticipating by several hundred years Bonet's (1684) "folie maniaco-mélancolique" and Falret's (1854) "folie circulaire." It remained for Kraepelin, however, to introduce, in 1899, the term *manic-depressive psychosis* and to clarify the clinical picture. Kraepelin described the disorder as a series of attacks of elation and depression, with periods of relative normality in between and a generally favorable prognosis. Kraepelin's clinical description was a major step forward in the delineation of this psychotic reaction.

Some patients evidence only manic reactions, others only depressive reactions; still others show both types of reaction, either alternating between the two or showing a combination of manic and depressive reactions at the same time.

Consequently, we may distinguish three major types of manic-depressive reactions: (a) manic reactions, (b) depressive reactions, and (c) circular and mixed reactions. Depressive reactions are by far the most common type.

The median age at time of first admission for manic-depressive reactions is approximately 44. The great majority of cases occur between the ages of 25 and 65, although such reactions may occur from early adolescence to old age. Anthony and Scott (1960) have reported an interesting case with onset at the age of 12, and first attacks have been observed even after the age of 85. The sex ratio is about 4 to 3, with women showing the higher rate.

Currently, manic-depressive cases constitute about 2 per cent of all first admissions to mental hospitals. This contrasts with a first admission rate of over 6 per cent in 1950. Although it would appear that manic-depressive reactions are decreasing in our society, it is more likely that a greater proportion of these patients—particularly depressed cases—are receiving treatment in psychiatric clinics and hence are not included in public hospital statistics. Grinker *et al.* (1961) have stated that depressive cases (including both neurotic and psychotic depressions) constitute 50 per cent of the first admissions to private hospitals and clinics.

General symptoms. The clinical picture in manic-depressive reactions is colored by the predominant emotional mood of the patient, which may be one of elation or depression. Against this affective background, there may be a variety of psychological and behavioral symptoms which are roughly appropriate to the prevailing mood. In manic reactions there are feelings of high optimism accompanied by a speeding up of thought processes and motor activities. The patient is loud and boisterous, appears to have unbounded energy and enthusiasm, and is involved in all sorts of activities. He shows impaired ability to concentrate, is easily distractible, and changes rapidly from one trend of thought and activity to another. Judgment is impaired and sexual restraints are lowered. Delusions of grandeur are common. The patient may envision himself as the ruler of the world, the most remarkable scientist who ever lived, or a great prophet who can solve the problems of all mankind.

In depressive reactions, the patient experiences a feeling of profound sadness and loneliness, and the whole world becomes joyless and gray. Nothing seems worth while any more, emptiness prevails, and only bad things are expected. Thought processes and behavior are slowed down. The patient speaks slowly in a monotonous voice. He limits himself to brief answers to questions. He rarely poses questions; he avoids people and has a listless facial expression and a stooping posture. Self-accusatory and hypochondriacal delusions are common. The patient may accuse himself of having committed various crimes, participated in immoral sexual acts, been selfish and callous with loved ones. He feels guilty of "unpardonable sins" and regards himself as basically worthless and not fit to live. He may be convinced that he has an incurable disease, that his internal organs have disappeared or are rotting away, that his body is undergoing peculiar changes. In older depressed patients, the delusional content often centers around ideas of poverty, of suffering from some terrible disease, and of being abandoned and doomed to die in loneliness and despair. The general mood of the depressed patient is well captured in the following excerpt from a poem by Joseph Cowen (1959):

> In the slave market of my melancholy mind
> I mount the auction block
> To sell myself to the highest bidder of misery.

Hallucinations are commonly found in severe manic-depressive reactions. They are usually somewhat fragmentary and may include a wide range of content. In an early study of 208 cases, Rennie and Fowler (1942) cited the following as being typical:

". . . conversed with God; heard sentences—'daughter is dead'; saw iceberg floating, bottle of carbolic in ceiling; . . . people talking through stomach; saw star on Christmas day; saw and heard dead mother; voices tell her not to eat, to walk backwards; sees something white—a vision; saw path of fire running up and down; saw and heard God and angels; saw snake coming to her; trees glitter like gold; saw dead father; animal faces in food; saw and heard animals; heard voices; voices—'they've got me now'; sees dead people and skulls (patient very superstitious); brother's and dead people's voices; God's voice; sees devil and Hell's flames; saw God; sees husband and coffin; hand pointing to cross; sees her babies in heaven; voice says: 'Do not stay with husband'. . . ." (p. 805)

About 75 per cent of depressed cases have suicidal ideas and some 10 to 15 per cent attempt suicide (Arieti, 1959a; Hastings, 1958). Occasionally, depressed patients commit infanticide or homicide—usually then taking or attempting to take their own lives (Easson and Steinhilber, 1961). Although manic patients may become hostile if interfered with and may physically assault others, they rarely kill anyone.

Manic-depressive reactions are of short duration as psychoses go. They come in the form of attacks which run their course with or without therapy; afterwards the patient usually returns to a state of normality and shows no evidence of mental deterioration. However, the attacks tend to recur, as shown in the chart on page 325. Even in the cases where no treatment is received, manic reactions usually run their course in about 3 months and depressive reactions in about 9 months, although attacks may be as short as a few days or as long as a year or more. Among adolescents and young adults, manic-depressive reactions are usually of brief duration (Toolan, 1962).

Manic reactions.   Manic reactions are characterized by varying degrees of elation and psychomotor overactivity.[1] Three degrees are commonly delineated, denoting the progression of behavior from mild to extreme degrees of manic excitement. Though these attacks differ in degree rather than kind, they merit separate consideration.

1.   *Hypomania.*   This is the mildest form of manic reaction and is characterized by moderate elation, flightiness, and overactivity. The patient states that he has never felt better or happier in his life. He has unbounded confidence in his ability and knowledge and will unhesitatingly express his opinion on any and all subjects. His thinking is speeded up and he may become particularly witty and entertaining. He seems tireless and gets practically no sleep, stating that he feels so well that he doesn't need any. During the day he engages in ceaseless activity, talking, visiting, keeping luncheon and other engagements, telephoning, writing, and working on various sure-fire schemes. Numerous appointments are made, postponed, and canceled. The mails frequently seem too slow to these patients, and they are fond of sending telegrams and special-delivery letters and making long-distance telephone calls.

The overall picture frequently appears at first to be one of an aggressive, brilliant, sociable individual who has many commendable enthusiasms and wonderful plans for the future. However, he soon becomes domineering, monopolizes the conversation, and shows difficulty in sticking to the subject. He is intolerant of criticism and may unsparingly denounce as a stupid fool anyone who dares to disagree with him or interfere with his plans. The details of his plans are seldom worked out; very few of them are ever put into action, and those few are not completed. However, the patient easily rationalizes his activities and concedes no mistakes. He spends money recklessly and in a short period of time may dissipate his entire savings. Moral restraint gives way, and he may engage in numerous promiscuous sexual acts and in alcoholic excesses.

Although these patients rarely show marked delusions or hallucinations, they show very poor judgment and usually lack insight into their condition. Any suggestion that they are ill and should be hospitalized is met with angry abuse. They are ready with a rebuttal to all charges made against them and threaten legal action against anyone who dares to touch them.

COMPARATIVE INCIDENCE
OF MANIC-DEPRESSIVE TYPES

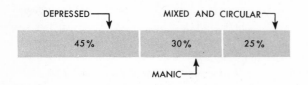

DEPRESSED   MIXED AND CIRCULAR

| 45% | 30% | 25% |

MANIC

---

[1]Actually, manic reactions are often impure in the sense that worry, sadness, and brooding often complicate the predominantly elated emotional mood. It is also common to find underlying depression close on the heels of elation. In fact, the manic attack is often considered a defense against depression.

The following conversation with a hypomanic patient reveals the elated mood and pressure toward activity typical of this reaction pattern. The patient was a woman of 46.

Dr.: Hello, how are you today?

Pt.: Fine, fine, and how are you, Doc? You're looking pretty good. I never felt better in my life. Could I go for a schnapps now? Say, you're new around here, I never saw you before—and not bad! How's about you and me stepping out tonight if I can get that sour old battleship of a nurse to give me back my dress. It's low cut and it'll wow 'em. Even in this old rag, all the doctors give me the eye. You know I'm a model. Yep, I was No. 1—used to dazzle them in New York, London and Paris. Hollywood has been angling with me for a contract.

Dr.: Is that what you did before you came here?

Pt.: I was a society queen . . . entertainer of kings and presidents. I've got five grown sons and I wore out three husbands getting them . . . about ready for a couple of more now. There's no woman like me, smart, brainy, beautiful and sexy. You can see I don't believe in playing myself down. If you are good and know you're good you have to speak out, and I know what I've got.

Dr.: Why are you in this hospital?

Pt.: That's just the trouble. My husbands never could understand me. I was too far above them. I need someone like me with savoir faire you know, somebody that can get around, intelligent, lots on the ball. Say, where can I get a schnapps around here—always like one before dinner. Someday I'll cook you a meal. I've got special recipes like you never ate before . . . sauces, wines, desserts. Boy, it's making me hungry. Say, have you got anything for me to do around here? I've been showing these slowpokes how to make up beds but I want something more in line with my talents.

Dr.: What would you like to do?

Pt.: Well, I'm thinking of organizing a show, singing, dancing, jokes. I can do it all myself but I want to know what you think about it. I'll bet there's some schnapps in the kitchen. I'll look around later. You know what we need here . . . a dance at night. I could play the piano, and teach them the latest steps. Wherever I go I'm the life of the party.

2. *Acute mania.* The symptoms in acute mania are similar to those in hypomania but are more pronounced. This condition may develop

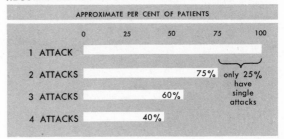

RECURRENCE OF MANIC-DEPRESSIVE ATTACKS

out of a hypomanic reaction or may develop suddenly with little or no warning except for a short period of insomnia, irritability, and restlessness. Elation and pressure of activity become more pronounced, and the patient may laugh boisterously and talk at the top of his voice. He becomes increasingly boastful, dictatorial, and overbearing, and may order everyone around as if he were a super-dictator.

Irritability is easily provoked and the patient's mood may change rapidly from gaiety to anger. Violent behavior is common and the patient may break up furniture, deface the walls, and even assault nurses and other patients. He is continually on the go, walking back and forth, gesturing to himself, singing, and banging on the walls and door demanding release. Even patients who have had the most rigid moral backgrounds will show a complete abandonment of moral restraint and may be obscene in their talk, expose themselves, and make sexual advances to those around them.

There is a wild flight of ideas, frequently leading to incoherent speech. The alternation in ideas may be so rapid that at one moment the patient may engage in erotic activities and the next deliver a profound religious dissertation. There may be some confusion and disorientation for time, place, and person, with a tendency to misidentify those about him.

Transient delusions and hallucinations may occur, in which the patient may have grandiose ideas of his wealth and abilities or in which he may hear voices and carry on conversations with persons whom he imagines to be present. Occasionally there may be short periods of relative calmness in which the individual shows some insight into his noisy behavior, and he may even apologize for it. In general, however, in-

A MANIC EPISODE

From a case study by Wiggins and Lyman (1944)

These pictures show the sequence of events during the first two days of a manic attack suffered by a 57-year-old Negro who had always been a hard worker, owned a farm, and was respected by the whole community. In his youth he had been converted during a revival meeting. Since the age of 35 he had been a deacon in his church. Often, when troubles had weighed heavy he had found relief singing and praying until his discouragement lifted. His first marriage had been happy, but a second marriage, following the death of his first wife, was very unhappy. In close succession the patient had suffered several emotional shocks and worries. An epileptic son was finally sent to the state hospital and died soon thereafter; the crops were bad and debts very heavy.

During this period he worked unusually hard and seemed to have an abnormal amount of energy, without ever being fatigued. When $500 arrived from his son's insurance, he interpreted it as coming from God as a first payment of his debts and was confident that the rest would come in the same way.

Then one day, while stripping tobacco, he suddenly jumped up shouting that the "spirit" had overtaken him. He said later that he had begun to get commands to jump up and roll over like a wheel, and then "to holler and praise the Lord and make a noise enough so He can hear you." He tried to get the others to follow his lead, and eventually fell down exhausted. He believed that he could stop the war if he could just get all the neighbors to take part in joint prayer.

He told the doctors later, "I was joy at heart—That is

why I couldn't stay still. I had to go talk with somebody and tell them how much joy."

The next morning he started out to walk to a neighbor's but was forcibly detained by his son, who carried him back and locked him in his room, where he busied himself reading a "doctors' book." The local doctor came, but had nothing to suggest.

When several days passed with no change, the family put the patient in the car and took him to the hospital, where he was happy and talkative and freely told the doctors his whole life history. His excitement was evident in the speed and intonation of his words, rather than in any bizarre behavior. There was little treatment beyond a quiet schedule. By the end of the first month there was a marked reduction in manic activity and after another month he had recovered, apparently completely.

He was sent home from the hospital soon thereafter and about three months after the onset of the attack, the whole family went through a re-enactment of the entire episode, under the supervision of one of the hospital staff. The patient reported that this re-enactment did much to relieve the fears he had been having in thinking back over his psychotic experience, and that now he could laugh at it although he still could not understand it. At an earlier stage such a re-enactment would undoubtedly have heightened his anxiety.

Throughout his life the patient had had three outlets of emotional expression—work, family, and religion. It is notable that in his manic episode he used the same outlets, particularly the latter, and, by feeling that he had won a superior place in God's favor, was able to achieve a feeling of authority over everyone else without challenging or rebelling against the rules of society.

sight and judgment are severely impaired, and periods of insight are shortly followed by a resumption of manic activity. The outstanding symptoms in acute manic reactions are the irritable and elated mood, the increased flight of irrational ideas, the rapid and frequent alternation in thought, and the extreme psychomotor overactivity.

The following brief description of an acute manic reaction will serve to illustrate some of the typical symptoms.

"On admission she slapped the nurse, addressed the house physician as God, made the sign of the cross, and laughed loudly when she was asked to don the hospital garb. This she promptly tore into shreds. She remained nude for several hours before she was restrained in bed. She sang at the top of her voice, screamed through the window, and leered at the patients promenading in the recreation yard. She was very untidy and incontinent, smearing her excreta about the floor and walls. Frequently she would utter the words, 'God, Thou Holy One,' cross herself, laugh, and then give vent to vile expletives while she carried out suggestive movements of the body. She yelled for water, and, when this was proffered, she threw the tin cup across the room." (Karnosh and Zucker, 1945, p. 78)

3. *Delirious mania.* In the most severe type of manic reaction the patient is confused, wildly excited, and violent. The condition may, develop out of hypomania or acute mania but more frequently appears suddenly and with very few warning signs. The patient is incoherent and severely disoriented. He has no appreciation of his surroundings and may have vivid auditory and visual hallucinations. It is impossible to converse with him or to hold his attention. He evidences the most extreme psychomotor overactivity, is violent and destructive, and spends his days and nights in restless pacing, singing, screaming, gesticulating, and incoherent shouting. His eyes may show a peculiar glare and his features may be contorted beyond recognition. One moment he may refuse food and the next devour everything he can get hold of. His behavior is obscene and entirely shameless, and personal habits completely deteriorate. He may smear his excreta on his person or about the walls. He is extremely dangerous to those about him and may seriously injure himself. In short, he fulfills the popular notion of a raving maniac.

In this condition the patient loses weight rapidly and may become utterly exhausted. A tremendous burden is placed on all bodily functions, and the chances of self-intoxication and infection by various diseases are very great.

The following scene, which took place in the courtyard of a state mental hospital before the advent of newer treatment procedures, illustrates the extreme excitement that may occur.

A manic patient had climbed upon the small platform in the middle of the yard and was delivering an impassioned lecture to a number of patients sitting on benches which surrounded the platform. Most of the audience were depressed patients who were hallucinated and muttering to themselves and not paying a bit of attention to the speaker. However, the speaker had an "assistant" in the form of a hypomanic patient who would move rapidly around the circle of benches shaking the occupants and exhorting them to pay attention to the speaker. If anyone started to leave, the assistant would plump him back in his seat in no uncertain terms. In the background were a number of apparently schizophrenic patients who were pacing a given number of steps back and forth, and beyond was the high wire fence which surrounded the yard.

The speaker herself was in a state of delirious mania. She had torn her clothing to shreds and was singing and shouting at the top of her voice. So rapidly did her thoughts move from one topic to another that her "speech" was almost a complete word hash, although occasional sentences such as "You goddam bitches" and "God loves everybody, do you hear?" could be made out. These points were illustrated by wild gestures, screaming climaxes, and outbursts of song. In the delivery of her talk, she moved restlessly back and forth on the platform, occasionally falling off the platform in her wild excitement. Her ankles and legs were bleeding from rubbing the edge of the platform during these falls, but she was completely oblivious to her injuries.

Fortunately, the degree of excitement in manic reactions can now be markedly reduced by means of various drugs—often in combination with electroshock—and scenes such as this need no longer occur.

Depressive reactions. The symptom picture in depressive reactions is essentially the opposite of that in manic reactions. Here, too, there are differences in degree.

1. *Simple depression.* The outstanding symptoms in simple depression are a loss of enthusiasm and a general slowing down of mental and physical activity. The patient feels dejected and discouraged. Work and other activities require tremendous effort and somehow do not seem worth bothering with anyway. Feelings of unworthiness, failure, sinfulness, and guilt dominate his sluggish thought processes. His loss of interest in things about him extends to eating and is usually reflected in loss of weight and digestive difficulties, such as constipation. Conversation is carried on in a monotone and questions are answered with a meager supply of words. In general, the patient prefers just to sit alone, contemplating his sins and seeing no hope for the future. As we have noted, suicidal preoccupation is common and actual suicidal attempts may be made.

Despite the mental and motor retardation, however, the patient shows no real clouding of consciousness or actual disorientation. His memory remains unimpaired and he is able to answer questions fairly satisfactorily if allowed sufficient time. Many of these patients have some insight into their condition and understand that they need treatment, although they may not admit that they are depressed but rather emphasize various bodily ailments such as headaches, fatigue, loss of appetite, constipation, and poor sleep. In fact, mild depressive cases are sometimes diagnosed as neurasthenia. In depressive reactions, however, the patient usually insists that his ailments and other difficulties are punishment for various mistakes and sins committed in the past. The following is a doctor's conversation with a young woman 25 years old who had been classified as a mild depressive.

Dr.: Good morning, how are you today?

Pt.: (Pause) Well, o.k. I guess, doctor. . . . I don't know, I just feel sort of discouraged.

Dr.: Is there anything in particular that worries you?

Pt.: I don't know, doctor . . . everything seems to be futile . . . nothing seems worth while any more. It seems as if all that was beautiful has lost its beauty. I guess I expected more than life has given. It just doesn't seem worth while going on. I can't seem to

This picture was made by a depressed patient who had little to say in words but liked to paint. Her therapist immediately recognized from this painting that the patient was thinking of suicide; the clue was not the many macabre figures, which are fairly common in mental patients' work, but the white bird-like figure slowly ascending. It was evident that the patient wanted to leave her morbid world and escape to heaven. As a result of this painting she was watched closely and in fact did attempt suicide unsuccessfully. Subsequently she recovered from her depression, was released, and succeeded in a responsible job.

make up my mind about anything. I guess I have what you would call the "blues."

Dr.: Can you tell me more about your feelings?

Pt.: Well . . . my family expected great things of me. I am supposed to be the outstanding member of the family . . . they think because I went through college everything should begin to pop and there's nothing to pop. I . . . really don't expect anything from anyone. Those whom I have trusted proved themselves less than friends should be.

Dr.: Oh?

Pt.: Yes, I once had a very good girl friend with whom I spent a good deal of time. She was very important to me . . . I thought she was my friend but now she treats me like a casual acquaintance (tears).

Dr.: Can you think of any reason for this?

Pt.: Yes, it's all my fault. I can't blame them—anybody that is . . . I am not worthy of them. I have sinned against nature. I am worthless . . . nobody can love me. I don't deserve friends or success. . . .

Dr.: You sinned against nature?

Pt.: Well . . . I am just no good. I am a failure. I was envious of other people. I didn't want them to have more than I had and when something bad happened to them I was glad. Now I am being repaid for my sins. All my flaws stand out and I am repugnant to everyone. (Sighs) I am a miserable failure. . . . There is no hope for me.

2. *Acute depression.* In acute depressive reactions the mental and physical retardation is increased. The patient becomes increasingly inactive, tends to isolate himself from others, does not speak of his own accord, and is extremely slow in his responses. Feelings of guilt and worthlessness become more pronounced and the patient becomes increasingly self-accusatory. He may hold himself responsible for plagues, floods, or economic depressions, and insist that he has committed all sorts of horrible sins which will bring disaster upon everyone. Delusions may take a hypochondriacal turn, and in keeping with his morbid mood, the patient may believe that his brain is being eaten away, that his "insides are slowly petrifying," or that his bowels are completely stopped up. One patient maintained that he had not had a bowel movement for over a month. The patient may refuse to eat because he has no stomach and is only a "living shell." He usually blames these ailments on early sex practices or other sins which have undermined his health and for which he is now being punished.

The patient's prognosis for himself is very unfavorable. He sees absolutely no hope for his case. Remedies are of no avail, and he can only anticipate a horrible end. Feelings of unreality and mild hallucinations occasionally occur, particularly in connection with ideas of sin, guilt, and disease. Of vital importance are persistent ideas of suicide, and the patient may show remarkable ingenuity and cunning in evading attendants and putting an end to his suffering. The patient in the following case was a man 47 years of age.

Dr.: Good morning, Mr. H., how are you today?

Pt.: (Long pause—looks up and then head drops back down and stares at floor.)

Dr.: I said good morning, Mr. H. Wouldn't you like to tell me how you feel today?

Pt.: (Pause—looks up again) . . . I feel . . . terrible . . . simply terrible.

Dr.: What seems to be your trouble?

Pt.: . . . There's just no way out of it . . . nothing but blind alleys . . . I have no appetite . . . nothing matters any more . . . it's hopeless . . . everything is hopeless.

Dr.: Can you tell me how your trouble started?

Pt.: I don't know . . . it seems like I have a lead weight in my stomach . . . I feel different . . . I am not like other people . . . my health is ruined . . . I wish I were dead.

Dr.: Your health is ruined?

Pt.: . . . Yes, my brain is being eaten away. I shouldn't have done it . . . If I had any will power I would kill myself . . . I don't deserve to live . . . I have ruined everything . . . and it's all my fault.

Dr.: It's all your fault?

Pt.: Yes . . . I have been unfaithful to my wife and now I am being punished . . . my health is ruined . . . there's no use going on . . . (sigh) . . . I have ruined everything . . . my family . . . and now myself . . . I bring misfortune to everyone . . . I am a moral leper . . . a serpent in the Garden of Eden . . . why don't I die . . . why don't you give me a pill and end it all before I bring catastrophe on everyone. . . .

Dr.: Don't you think we can help you?

Pt.: . . . (pause) . . . No one can help me . . . everybody tries to help me . . . but it is too late . . . (long pause, sigh) it's hopeless . . . I know that . . . it's hopeless. . . .

3. *Depressive stupor.* In the most severe degree of retardation and depression, the patient becomes almost completely unresponsive and inactive. He is usually bedridden and utterly indifferent to all that goes on around him. He refuses to speak or eat and has to be tube fed and have his eliminative processes taken care of. Confusion concerning time, place, and person is marked and there are vivid hallucinations and delusions, particularly involving grotesque fantasies about sin, death, and rebirth. During this period the patient is invariably constipated, has a foul breath, and suffers impairment in general physical health. The following brief description illustrates this severe depressive reaction.

The patient lay in bed, immobile, with a dull, depressed expression on his face. His eyes were sunken and downcast. Even when spoken to, he would not raise his eyes to look at the speaker. Usually he did not respond at all to questions, but sometimes, after apparently great effort, he would mumble something about the "Scourge of God." He appeared somewhat emaciated, his breath was foul, and he had to be given enemas to maintain elimination. Occasionally, with great effort, he made the sign of the cross with his right hand. The overall picture was one of extreme vegetative-like immobility and depression.

With the newer treatment methods—usually involving a combination of antidepressant drugs and electroshock—most depressive reactions can be rapidly ameliorated today, and few hospitalized patients remain severely depressed for an extended period of time.

Circular and mixed types. Although manic-depressive reactions have been considered historically as circular reactions, only some 15 to 25 per cent of these patients actually show an alternation between manic and depressive reactions. Usually when such an alternation occurs, there is a direct change from a manic to a depressive reaction or vice versa, but occasionally there is a transitional period or a period of normality between the two. For example, the patient may recover from a manic reaction and leave the hospital only to be readmitted several months or years later with a severe depression.

In mixed reactions, there may be various combinations of manic and depressive symptoms at the same time. For example, there may be a "manic stupor," in which the patient experiences marked feelings of elation, accompanied by a dearth of ideas and generally decreased psychomotor activity. There are also cases in which a severely depressed mood, with self-accusatory and other morbid ideas, is accompanied by marked mental and motor excitement in which the patient restlessly paces the floor, wrings his hands, and bewails his fate. Such a reaction differs from the agitated depressive reaction characteristically found in involutional psychoses (to be discussed in the next section) in that it is not so directly related to the problems and life situations of approaching old age as are involutional reactions. This distinction is well brought out in the following case.

The patient, a 24-year-old woman, had eloped two years previously with a young man of whom her parents disapproved. Following the elopement the parents disowned her and refused to have anything to do with her. The patient and her husband then travelled to California, where he obtained employment as a shipping clerk in a wholesale company.

The daughter and her parents did not correspond although the daughter had severe guilt feelings about letting her parents down—they had had great ambitions for her in college and had looked forward to her future marriage with a wealthy youth whose parents were old friends. During her first year in California, she became pregnant and just before the baby was to arrive wired her parents of the forthcoming event. Unfortunately, the baby died during birth and the handsome presents her parents sent for the baby only served to intensify her disappointment. However, this did serve to re-establish relations with her parents and they made immediate arrangements to drive to California to visit the patient and her husband. But on the way they were involved in a tragic automobile accident. The father was killed outright and the mother died on the way to the hospital.

Upon the receipt of this news, the patient became extremely depressed and attempted suicide by taking an overdose of sleeping tablets. Emergency medical attention saved her life but she remained depressed and was extremely anxious and tense, unable to sit still or concentrate on any topic except her parents' death. She blamed herself for it and paced the floor in great agitation, muttering to herself and bewailing her guilt. During this period the following conversation took place.

Dr.: You feel that you are to blame for your parents' death?

Pt.: Yes, oh why didn't I obey them. Now they are dead . . . I have killed them. They were wonderful to me and I have repaid them by disobedience and murder. I deserve to die too. Oh God! I have killed my baby and now my parents! I don't deserve to live . . . . I am no good, evil. I will be punished too . . . Oh God what have I done!

It was thought in this case that the patient had felt considerable hostility toward her parents following their rejection of her, as well as guilt for disobeying them. She had never been able to express this hostility even to her husband. Apparently it added considerably to her guilt feelings and played an important part in the severe guilt reaction and agitated depression which followed their death.

There are also, of course, manic-depressive patients whose symptom picture has a distinct schizophrenic coloring, but the marked distortion of reality common to the schizophrenic is not typically found in manic-depressive reactions.

General dynamics. In evaluating the predisposing and precipitating factors in manic-depressive reactions, we shall again find it profitable to consider possible factors on biological, psychological, and sociological levels.

1. *Biological factors.* Attempts to explain manic-depressive reactions on a biological level have run the familiar gamut from hereditary predisposition through constitutional factors to organic pathology.

Statistical findings indicate that the incidence of manic-depressive reactions is considerably higher among the relatives of manic-depressives than in the population at large. Slater (1944) found that approximately 15 per cent of the brothers, sisters, parents, and children of manic-depressives were also manic-depressives, while Kallmann's (1952, 1953) estimates are in the neighborhood of 25 per cent. These figures may be compared with an expectancy of 0.5 per cent for the general population. Similarly, Kallmann (1958) found the concordance rate for fraternal twins to be 26.5 per cent, while that for identical twins was 95.7 per cent. He also noted that schizophrenic and manic-depressive reactions do not occur in the same twin pair—that is, one twin does not develop a manic-depressive and the other a schizophrenic reaction. Kallmann concluded that the two reactions are genetically different; and that manic-depressive reactions involve a genetic defect in the neuro-hormonal mechanisms that control emotion.

Although such evidence for a hereditary predisposition to manic-depressive reactions cannot be ignored, it is subject to the same limitations we have mentioned before, since the factor of early environment has been left uncontrolled. The significance of heredity in the etiology of manic-depressive reactions is far from clear, and pending further clarification it is probably most profitable to think of heredity as an important interactional factor.

Many investigators have held that certain individuals have constitutional tendencies toward extreme emotional mood swings—some showing predominant feelings of well-being and elation, others discouragement and depression,

and still others alternating from one to the other. In a study of 18 manic-depressive children, J. D. Campbell (1952) found evidence of "cyclothymic make-up or disposition of the individual and his stock."

That many individuals show exaggerated mood swings at minor upsets cannot be denied, but whether such swings result from hereditary predisposition, acquired constitutional make-up, or learned psychological reaction patterns is another question. We have noted that in monkeys the processes of excitation predominate over the processes of inhibition, and that these animals are highly excitable and unequilibrated. In many other species, including man, there is a greater equilibration of excitatory and inhibitory processes, but in any species there are wide individual differences, probably stemming from both genetic and environmental factors. The neurophysiological nature of these differences and their role in manic-depressive reactions remain to be clarified.

Physique has also come in for its share of scrutiny as a possible predisposing constitutional factor. Kretschmer (1925) observed that manic-depressives tended to be short, stocky, thick-necked, vigorous individuals. Similarly, Sheldon *et al.* (1954) concluded that both mesomorphic (muscular, solid, athletic, energetic, aggressive) and endomorphic (stout, plump, soft, sentimental, pleasure-seeking, extrovertive) types are prone to the development of manic-depressive reactions when placed under excessive stress. Again, however, the question arises as to whether physique tends to foster the development of certain personality traits, or whether the personality traits foster the development of certain types of physique. It seems most likely that there is an interaction. In any event, manic-depressives are by no means all mesomorphs and endomorphs, and the role of physique in the etiological pattern of these reactions is far from clear.

Kraepelin considered this disorder to be toxic in nature, but although many later investigators have followed his lead, no underlying organic pathology has so far been demonstrated. Whatmore and Ellis (1959, 1962) did find that depressed patients showed hyperactivity of certain motor areas of the nervous system but pointed out that this might be a consequence

FACTS ABOUT SUICIDE

Incidence:

General

Over 200,000 attempts in the U.S. each year; some 25,000 successful; ranks 9th as cause of death. Largest number occur in spring, during morning, Monday or Tuesday. Most common methods: firearms, jumping from high places, sleeping pills, gas, poison, and hanging.

Age and sex

Three times as many men as women kill themselves, but women more often make half-hearted, unsuccessful attempts. Over half of persons who kill themselves are over 45. Divorced have highest rate, widowed and single next; 22 per cent lived alone.

Occupation

All occupations represented; incidence highest among professional groups, especially lawyers, dentists, and physicians; low among ministers.

Sociocultural

More common among urban than rural people. Low in certain strongly Catholic countries like Ireland; high in Japan and in some Iron Curtain countries. Less common during crises like war and earthquakes; more common during depressions.

Dynamics:

Physical illness

About 40 per cent of men and 20 per cent of women kill themselves because of ill health.

Mental illness

About 35 per cent kill themselves while temporarily insane, usually during a period of severe depression.

Guilt and hostility

Severe guilt feelings or intense hostility may be turned inward against self, making injury to self the only apparent solution to problems.

Losses

Individual may commit suicide after death of loved one he feels he cannot live without (usually mate after long, happy marriage) or after financial reverses, injuries, or other losses which require too great a change in way of life or intolerable lowering of status or self-evaluation.

Revenge

Suicide occasionally based on spite—to make others feel guilty; sometimes person only intends to scare others but succeeds by accident, as when overcome by gas fumes.

Prevention:

Recent studies have shown that the great majority of persons who attempt suicide make their intention known or give some cues in advance—for example, by threats, sudden increase in the consumption of alcohol or barbiturates, or a developing depression. One pilot clinic, the Los Angeles Suicide Prevention Center, is concerned with obtaining more data concerning potential suicides and with using this information for preventive purposes.

This chart is based on material from Blachly et al. (1963), Coe (1963), Dublin (1963), Farberow and Shneidman (1961), Stengel (1962), U.S. National Office of Vital Statistics (1962), and U.S. Public Health Service (1961).

rather than a cause of the disorder. Pavlov as well as more recent Russian investigators have assumed that manic reactions are states of excessive excitation and weakened inhibition of the higher brain centers, possibly involving chemical changes which lead to an increase in the transmission of nerve impulses and an "overloading" of the nervous system (Kerbikov *et al.,* 1958; Wortis, 1962a). Conversely, depressive states are presumed to involve an excessive inhibition of deeper subcortical formation. Again, however, it would appear relevant to refer to the conclusion of Shagass and Schwartz (1962) that alterations in cortical activity associated with various kinds of psychopathology may reflect the current state of personality functioning rather than some predisposing factor. This conclusion is supported by the fact that no clear-cut differences have yet been found between the brain waves of recovered manic-depressives and those of normals.

Currently, a good deal of research is being directed toward the study of biochemical changes in brain functioning in manic-depressive reactions. Bogoch *et al.* (1960) found distinctive changes in brain chemistry in manic, depressed, and schizophrenic patients. However, these investigators pointed out that biochemical patterns in brain functioning often vary considerably from one patient to another; they did not claim that changes in brain chemistry cause such disorders. Again the answers must await further research.

In general, it would appear probable that genetic and acquired constitutional factors do play a predisposing role in manic-depressive reactions, but the precise nature and importance of such factors remains to be clarified. Interestingly enough, there is some evidence that constitutional factors are more important in manic than in depressive reactions (James, 1961).

2. *Psychological factors.* Increasing emphasis has been placed on the role of psychological factors in manic-depressive reactions, and it is felt that these reactions—like paranoia and paranoid states—can best be explained in terms of the response of certain personality types to severe stress. This, of course, does not rule out the possibility that manic or depressive reactions may in turn lead to disturbances in neurophysi-

ological processes which contribute to the overall clinical picture.

As yet, we lack clear-cut studies showing the particular types of patterns of family interaction likely to lead to a personality predisposed to manic-depressive reactions. Study of a limited sample of patients (Gibson, 1958; Gibson *et al.,* 1959) indicates that manic-depressives come from home backgrounds marked by concern for social approval, striving for prestige, and an atmosphere of competitiveness and envy. Often there would appear to be rigid standards and severe punishment for misbehavior. One would also expect that exaggerated mood swings in the child would be fostered by similar emotional patterns in the parents. Since such emotional reactions would probably reduce anxiety, they would tend to persist as learned maladjustive response patterns.

Whatever their childhood background, available evidence indicates that manic patients, prior to their illness, have been ambitious, outgoing, energetic, sociable, often highly successful individuals. As contrasted with normals, they have placed a higher conscious value on achievement, have been very conventional in their attitudes, and have been deeply concerned about what others thought of them (Becker, 1960; Gibson *et al.,* 1959). Depressives share these characteristics but appear to have been more obsessive, anxious, and self-deprecatory, with an unusually rigid conscience development which prevented the overt expression of hostile impulses and made them particularly prone to guilt and self-blame (Grinker *et al.,* 1961). In a general sense, manic-depressives appear to have been "overly socialized" individuals who have internalized the conventional values of their society uncritically.

In the process of working with and studying manic-depressive patients, many investigators have been impressed with the high incidence of stressful life situations which apparently precipitated the psychotic breakdown. Rennie and Fowler (1942) found that approximately 80 per cent of their patients had had disturbing life situations which were dynamically related to the onset of the illness. Only 20 per cent of the cases seemed to have arisen relatively "out of the blue"—and these may have been based upon evaluations by the patient which were not apparent to an objective observer. In any event, manic-depressive disorders appear to be clearly stress-induced; they are not mysterious, constitutional, unmotivated reaction patterns.

Arieti (1959a) has concluded that the typical precipitating stresses in manic-depressive reactions can be put into three categories: (a) the death of a loved one—a person important to the patient, (b) failure in an important interpersonal relationship, usually with the spouse, and (c) a severe disappointment or setback in the work to which an individual has devoted his life. Arieti concluded that all of these precipitating conditions involve the loss of something of great value to the patient and represent abandonment, failure, and loss of meaning in his existence.

In understanding manic-depressive reactions to stress, it is helpful to remember that we all experience moods. We may feel particularly elated and self-confident at one time and vaguely anxious and depressed at another. In a pioneering study of euphoric and depressed moods in normal subjects, Johnson (1937) found striking differences in an individual's whole manner and approach to problems depending on whether he was in a euphoric mood or a depressed one. She found that in euphoric moods her subjects made more spontaneous and unnecessary conversation and reached decisions much more easily. In addition, they made more expansive movements in such psychomotor functions as writing. Depression, on the other hand, resulted in a very definite regression to childhood events in thought and memory, increased difficulty in making decisions, more cramped and smaller script and figures, and a judgment of distances as being greater than they actually were. Findings such as these in normal subjects help us to understand the effects of more exaggerated mood swings in manic-depressive reactions.

Although manic and depressive reactions appear to have certain background factors in common, they are two quite different ways of responding to excessive stress. Consequently, it is useful to consider their unique features as well as their similarities.

a) Manic patterns. Instead of turning inward to a private fantasy world like the schizophrenic, the manic tries to escape his difficulties by a "flight into reality." In less severe form, this type of reaction to stress is evidenced by the person who goes on a round of parties to try to forget a broken love affair, or tries to escape from anxiety by restless activity in which he occupies every moment with work, theaters, athletics, sex affairs, travel, and countless other crowded activities—all performed with professed gusto but actually with little true enjoyment.

In true manic reactions, the dynamics are similar but the pattern is exaggerated. The manic patient, with a tremendous expenditure of energy, tries to deny his failure and inadequacy and play a role of competence. He becomes more and more hyperactive in this role, undertaking endless activities. Although he never completes his projects, he is so busy with important plans and duties that he feels supremely competent and capable. He is stronger than any problem and the world is his. It is as if he overrides underlying doubts about himself and allays his anxiety by sheer weight of activity, reminding us of Shaffer's (1947) finding that soldiers felt less fear when some activity was possible, even activity that did nothing to lessen the actual danger they were facing.

Once this mode of coping with difficulties is adopted, it is maintained until it has spent itself in emotional exhaustion, for the only other alternative is an admission of defeat and inevitable depression. This is well brought out in the following case of a hypomanic patient.

"He dressed in flashy pajamas and loud bathrobes, and was otherwise immodest and careless about his personal appearance. He neglected his meals and rest hours, and was highly irregular, impulsive and distractible in his adaptations to ward routine. Without apparent intent to be annoying or disturbing he sang, whistled, told pointless off-color stories, visited indiscriminately and flirted crudely with the nurses and female patients. Superficially he appeared to be in high spirits, and yet one day when he was being gently chided over some particularly irresponsible act he suddenly slumped in a chair, covered his face with his hands, began sobbing, and cried, 'For Pete's sake, doc, let me be. Can't you see that I've just got to act happy?' This reversal of mood was transient and his seeming buoyancy returned in a few moments; nevertheless during a sodium amytal interview his defense euphoria again dropped away and he burst into frank sobbing as he clung to the physician's arm. He then confided that during the preceding year he had begun to suspect, with some reason, that his young second wife whom he 'loved to distraction' had tired of their marriage and had been unfaithful to him. He had accused her of this, but she had replied, almost indifferently, with an offer of divorce. His pride had been greatly wounded. . . ." (Masserman, 1961, pp. 66-67)

In manic reactions it would appear that sensory input overloading becomes an important contributing factor. The patient's thought processes are speeded up to a point where he can no longer "process" incoming information with any degree of efficiency and loses the capacity to discriminate between relevant and irrelevant incoming information. In a manner of speaking, "the programmer loses control of the computer" with a resultant lowering of inner integration and the appearance of maladaptive behavior.

b) Depressive patterns. Here, too, we find a stress situation that is too much for the patient, though he reacts differently. Instead of fighting, the depressive tends to blame himself for his difficulties and to feel that he is hopelessly inadequate and worthless. Apparently his rigid conscience leads to an intropunitive reaction to his life difficulties, and the hostility aroused by his frustrations and failures is turned inward toward the self rather than being directed toward the outside world, as in paranoid reactions:

"If such a person meets a situation representing to him an overwhelming loss or frustration, he is stymied, he is held up. Loss and frustration may be answered with the withdrawal of interest in the outside world and its objects so that such a person now pulls his tentacles in, severs himself from the outside, abandons the emotional investments and charges he has built up, becomes overwhelmed by the magnitude of the task or his failure and develops feelings of regret, feelings of catastrophe. As a result of the blockage and frustration of the drive in its outward push it will be withdrawn into the person and used to inhibit and to put the brake on any attempt of libidinous outreaching. Eventually it may be used for aggression against the self. . . ." (Weisz, 1947, pp. 214-215)

Several other considerations appear relevant to our understanding of depressive reactions. The depressive apparently gains some relief from his intolerable stress situation by admitting defeat and giving up the fight. Also the slowing down of thought processes may serve to decrease his suffering by reducing the sheer quantity of painful thoughts. However, the individual's feelings of relief are gained at the expense of his sense of adequacy and self-esteem and thus are accompanied by marked guilt and self-accusation. Like the soldier who panics and flees from combat, he may feel relieved to be out of an intolerable situation, but he also feels guilty and devaluated.

Masserman (1961) has pointed out that the depressive's symptoms may have symbolic and secondary gains. The patient's hypochondriacal notions may represent a thinly veiled reversion to narcissistic concern with his own body, and he may derive considerable secondary satisfaction from his self-centering of attention and interest. Even the patient's exaggerated self-accusations such as "I am the greatest sinner that ever lived and the whole world knows it" may not only express the patient's ideas of extreme guilt and unworthiness, but at the same time help to build up his feelings of self-esteem and importance.

The nature of the precipitating stress situation also appears to be important in depressive reactions. Freud and other psychoanalytic writers have emphasized the loss of a loved object—often the loss of one's mate through death or divorce. This loss results in a corresponding depletion in the self of the individual and leads to a natural reaction of mourning or depression. Freud theorized on the elaborate rituals—such as funeral rites—which society has established to ease the relinquishing of loved ones. As we have noted, normal grief and depression in such instances may be intensified to a pathological degree if the individual has felt hostility toward the loved person, which he regards as unacceptable and self-devaluating. The highly conscientious depressive may come to feel that his hostile wishes were responsible for the individual's death.

In this context it may be noted that depressed patients have often borne the brunt of the prestige strivings of their family. Although the patient has tried to live up to their expectations, he may also have harbored resentment as a result of the demands made upon him. Despite his efforts to repress such resentment as being unworthy, it may have appeared in hostile fantasies. Consequently, when something does happen to the loved person, he feels that he is somehow to blame for the disaster.

The significance of hostility and guilt feelings in depressive reactions is clearly brought out in cases where the individual actually is responsible for the death of the loved person. In a study of psychotic depressive reactions among soldiers who had accidentally killed a comrade, Beck and Valin (1953) found that the patients uniformly expressed a desire to be punished for their deeds. In a typical case, the patient hallucinated the voice of his dead buddy telling him to kill himself. In each case, the patient had felt strong hostility toward the buddy prior to the accident, and apparently this hostility was subsequently turned against himself in a self-punitive depressive reaction.

A second type of stress which appears to be of crucial significance in depressive reactions is the loss of meaning in one's existence (Szasz, 1961; Becker, 1962a). Field (1960) described depressed women in rural Ghana who travel to Ashanti religious shrines and there accuse themselves of vile witchcraft. To explain this phenomenon, Field pointed out that the Ashanti woman raises a large family with extreme care, is an excellent housekeeper, and is an efficient business manager. In short, she has a role to play which provides ample meaning in her life. But when she grows old and the children have left the family, the husband often takes on a younger bride on whom he lavishes his possessions and affection. Here the wife's life style, which had integrity and meaning, is suddenly undermined. Interestingly enough, however, the culture provides a ready rationalization which provides some continuity and meaning for her existence. The woman can simply acknowledge that all along she has really been a witch, and that she therefore deserves the evil that has befallen her. Thus society provides a transitional role which is intropunitive but which explains the sudden change in her life situation and paves the way for her new role as a discarded wife—which she will assume after her cure as a "witch" at the shrine.

Returning to our society, we can observe many instances in which the loss of a loved one forces drastic changes in the individual's life style which lead to a marked reduction in meaning. A woman who has helped her husband through college and worked hard to build a meaningful life with him may find his later interest in a younger woman both self-devaluating and destructive to her life pattern. As an individual grows older, the loss of contemporaries who have been significant in his life may lead to feelings of isolation and reduced meaning. Similarly, failures in occupational or other areas of great importance to the individual may deplete his life of meaning. The reaction to such loss of meaning tends to be discouragement, a reduction in effort, and depression. This is particularly true for individuals past middle age. For as Becker has said:

"The individual can be compared to a movie director who is saddled with a lifetime job of staging a plot, the outcome of which he never knows. Indeed, he never knows what will happen in the *very next* scene, but he must strive to give the whole thing credibility and self-consistency. This he can only accomplish by reworking the previous material as new events joggle his creation. When one gets down to the last twenty years of a life drama, it becomes more and more difficult to justify abrupt changes in continuity: there is too much preceding plot for it to be re-manipulated with ease. Whole portions cannot be re-interpreted with credibility, much less restaged. Hence, if the continuity is radically undermined, the individual grasps at whatever straws his ingenuity can muster." (1962a, p. 30)

For many individuals, there seem to be no such straws to grasp. Life seems to lose its meaning and there seems no valid reason for trying any more. In essence, "there is no use going on."

This picture is often intensified by our automatic tendency to consider failure in interpersonal relationships or occupational roles as the result of our own shortcomings. The depressive goes over his past with a microscope, picking out any possible sins of omission or commission and exaggerating their importance in relation to his present difficulties. Immoral sexual behavior, failure to observe religious convictions strictly, and any other unethical actions become quite naturally the focus of attention.

Even suppressed unethical impulses and

desires may be elaborated upon as if they had actually been carried out in action. Thus the patient may accuse himself of selfishness or unfaithfulness or hostile acts against loved ones which did not actually occur. These self-accusations seem to be attempts to explain and find some meaning in his predicament and at the same time achieve some measure of expiation and atonement. The latter mechanism may explain the otherwise mysterious phenomenon of spontaneous remission in depressive cases. Apparently there is a gradual working through of the individual's feeling of defeat and unworthiness, in which, by self-punishment, he pays the price for his failures and is then cleansed and ready to attempt another assault on his life situation. In fact, one major theory of the efficacy of shock therapy for depressive reactions is that it is interpreted as punishment by the patient so that he feels he is thereby cleansed of his sins.

c)   Patterns in mixed reactions.   In mixed reaction types, the dynamics are similar, although in agitated depressions there is usually an intensification of feelings of guilt and hostility toward the frustrating world. Even exaggerated self-condemnation does not defend the patient completely from his extreme guilt and resentment. As a result, the individual is restless, excited, apprehensive, fearful, and unable to relax. Often he complains of inexplicable feelings of hostility and violence. Suicide, as the only solution to such a life predicament, is of course always a serious danger.

3. *Sociological factors.* Rennie *et al.* (1957) and Hollingshead and Redlich (1958) found manic-depressive reactions as well as schizophrenia to be much more common among lower socioeconomic classes. These findings contrast with those of earlier investigators who found schizophrenia associated with lower-class membership but did not find this pattern for manic-depressive reactions (Faris and Dunham, 1939; Tietze *et al.*, 1941). In the Texas study, Jaco (1960) found manic-depressive psychoses distributed more equally throughout the population than schizophrenic disorders; he also found manic-depressive psychoses *relatively* more frequent among those of superior educational, occupational, and socioeconomic status. He found affective psychoses as a group

three times higher in urban than rural areas and higher among the divorced and separated than among the married or widowed.

From a broader socioeconomic perspective, the incidence of manic-depressive reactions appears to vary considerably among different societies. The rates appear to be high in New Zealand and Scotland, whereas they are low in Israel and various Oriental countries (Gold, 1951; Hes, 1960; New Zealand Department of Health, 1960; Scottish Home and Health Department, 1961). Among African natives generally, Carothers (1953, 1959) found manic reactions fairly common but depressive reactions relatively rare. Stainbrook (1953) found depressive reactions very rare also among lower-class psychotic patients in Bahia, Brazil.

Carothers has suggested how such differences in the incidence of depressive reactions might be explained in terms of sociocultural variations. Among Kenya Africans, for example, he stressed the fact that

Their behavior in all its major aspects is group-determined. Even religion is a matter of offerings and invocations in a group; it is not practiced individually and does not demand any particular attitude on the part of the individual. Similarly, grief is not borne in isolation, but appropriate rites are performed amid great public grieving. In these rites, the widow (or husband) of the deceased expresses her grief dramatically in ways prescribed by custom, and then resumes the tenor of her life as if no bereavement had occurred. Motives are social rather than individual; as a result, the individual feels none of the sense of personal aspiration and responsibility which is at the core of our Western attitudes toward our own behavior. Psychologically speaking, the Kenyan receives security because he is part of a larger organism and is not confronted with the problems of individual self-sufficiency, choice, and responsibility which may play such a large part in our culture. He does not set himself unrealistic goals, and he has no need to repress or feel guilty about "dangerous" desires. His culture actively discourages individual achievement of success, does not consider sexual behavior as evil, and is tolerant of occasional outbursts of aggressive hostility.

In addition, the Kenyan feels a great humbleness toward his natural environment, which is often harsh in the extreme. He always expects the worst, and hence can accept misfortunes with equanimity. Here too,

SPECIAL CHARACTERISTICS OF MENTAL DISORDERS FOUND IN KENYA AFRICANS

MENTAL DISORDER	SPECIAL CHARACTERISTICS IN KENYA AFRICANS	POSSIBLE EXPLANATION IN TERMS OF ASPECTS OF CULTURE
Psychoneuroses	Western-type anxiety reactions rare but "frenzied anxiety" common. Symptoms typically involve heart palpitations, cardiac pain, and shortness of breath	Anxiety felt to be outcome of bewitchment (and poisoning) which is threatening one's personal or procreative life. No feeling of personal responsibility or conflict over sex or hostility to foster Western-type anxiety reaction
	Phobic reactions—rare	Center around some known or unknown source of witchcraft—often involve fear that food is poisoned
	Obsessive-compulsive reactions seldom seen	Individual's status and role perfectly secure irrespective of accomplishment or ability. No need to develop own standards of conduct or cope with inner conflicts
	Conversion reactions common; include deafness, blindness, paralyses, and other symptoms formerly common in West	As in West, used as means of avoiding stressful situations
Schizophrenia	Most common psychotic reaction but predominantly of hebephrenic type—not paranoid type as in United States. Delusions unsystematized; paranoid reactions rare	Little need for ego defense mechanisms, hence none well developed and none to fall back on; when decompensation comes, complete personality disorganization thus more likely
Manic-depressive reactions	Manic reactions not uncommon but relative lack of depressive reactions	Apparently related to absence of feelings of individual responsibility or guilt
Involutional melancholia	No guilt; depression rare; tendency to develop persecutory ideas	Apparently related to absence of personal responsibility and lifelong habit of looking outward for causes of all misfortune
Old-age psychoses	No cases of cerebral arteriosclerosis. Fewer cases of senile psychoses than in West	Possibly due to lack of rush and tension, which foster high blood pressure and tendency toward arteriosclerosis. Fewer senile psychoses possibly result of shorter life span

Chart based on Carothers (1947, 1959) reports.

responsibility and blame are automatically placed on forces outside himself. Although he attempts to counteract misfortune and assure success in his ventures by performing appropriate rituals, the outcome is in the hands of the gods. He is not personally responsible and hence does not ordinarily experience self-devaluation or the need for ego-defensive measures. When excessive stress and decompensation do occur, there tends to be a complete disorganization of personality—as in the hebephrenic type of schizophrenia, which is the most common type of psychotic reaction. (Adapted from Carothers, 1947, 1951, 1953)

Needless to say, Carothers did not argue for the superiority of the Kenyan culture. Nor are we dealing with the cultural patterns of Kenya Africans as they exist today. Africa is in a major transition stage, and the preceding patterns have undoubtedly undergone change during the last decade. However, Carothers' description is of great value in helping us to understand the role of sociocultural factors in depressive reactions as well as other types of mental disorders.

Here it is of interest to note that in such depressive reactions as have been observed among Africans, the symptoms appear comparable to those in Western societies. As Field (1960) has pointed out, "patients suffering from severe depression are, the world over, unshakenly convinced of their own worthlessness and wickedness and irrationally accuse themselves of having committed every unforgivable sin." (p. 36)

Finally, we may briefly allude again to the finding that among 8000 Hutterites living in 70 collective settlements in the United States and Canada depressive reactions were found to be relatively common while schizophrenia and other forms of psychopathology were rare. In this group Eaton and Weil (1955) found over four times as many manic-depressive reactions (mainly of the depressive type) as schizophrenic disorders. This religious group encourages the submission of the individual to community expectations and emphasizes the principles of personal responsibility, guilt, and nonviolence. Eaton and Weil concluded that under excessive stress the Hutterites are more likely to be antiself than antisocial—and hence more likely to become depressed rather than to develop other types of psychotic reactions.

None of the preceding investigators minimize the possible role of genetic factors in influencing the incidence rates for manic-depressive reactions in different social groups, but it is apparent that sociocultural factors must also be considered as extremely important in the overall etiological pattern.

Therapy and prognosis. In the treatment of manic reactions, one of the immediate aims of therapy is to reduce the patient's overactivity. For this purpose various tranquilizing and antipsychotic drugs have proven effective. In refractory cases electroshock and prolonged narcosis may also be used. These forms of treatment do not necessarily shorten the length of the manic cycle, however, and a reduction in drug dosage too soon may lead to a reappearance of symptoms. Usually an important aspect of the treatment program is directing the patient's activities into constructive channels, perhaps by having him record his memoirs, write an autobiography, or engage in recreational therapy.

In the treatment of depressed patients, electroshock has proven of almost miraculous value. After a series of electroshock treatments the great majority of depressed patients once again become animated and relatively normal and approachable. Although by itself it leads to a rapid amelioration of symptoms, it is usually used in combination with antidepressant and antianxiety drugs which help to maintain the gains until the depression has run its course (Wortis, 1963; Ruesch et al., 1963).

With the reduction of symptoms in manic-depressive reactions, psychotherapy and sociotherapy become of great importance in helping the patient to stabilize his improvement and achieve a more satisfactory long-range adjustment. During hospitalization, proper nursing care is a vital aspect of treatment since depressed patients are frequently very ingenious in their efforts to put an end to their suffering. Despite the patient's seemingly earnest assurance that he will do nothing to harm himself, he may cut his wrists with a small fragment of glass or set fire to his clothing with a cleverly concealed match. Because of the ever present danger of such suicide attempts, family members should never try to care for depressed patients in the home.

Although manic-depressive reactions tend to recur and only about 1 out of 4 patients remains free from subsequent attacks, the general prognosis is favorable. Even without special treatment, the great majority of cases will recover within a year of first admission; with modern treatment procedures, the recovery rate approximates 100 per cent. However, factors such as age, a schizoid personality trend, or a highly unfavorable life situation may lead to more prolonged treatment or to the greater likelihood of an early recurrence of the psychotic reaction (Holt, 1960; Pollack, 1959). Interestingly enough, there appears to be no relation between recovery and hereditary "tainting."

PSYCHOTIC DEPRESSIVE REACTION

Psychotic depressive patients are severely depressed, with gross misinterpretation of reality and often delusions and hallucinations. This reaction differs from manic-depressive reactions, depressed type, principally in (a) absence of cyclical occurrence, and (b) more frequent presence of identifiable precipitating factors in the environment. When a neurotic "reactive depression" progresses to psychotic levels, it is classified here. The symptom picture is so similar to that of other depressive reactions described in this section that further discussion of this syndrome will be curtailed to avoid repetition.

Involutional Psychotic Reactions

Involutional psychoses are very similar to the agitated depression of the mixed type of manic-depressive reaction. They are differentiated from other depressive reactions by their initial occurrence in later life during the general involutional period of bodily and intellectual decline and also by the failure of these patients to show spontaneous recovery. This involutional period is usually considered to be from 40 to 55 years in women and from 50 to 65 in men. Involutional patients constitute about 4 per cent of all first admissions to mental hospitals. The average age at first admission approximates 57 years for men and 53 years for women. Involutional reactions occur slightly over twice as often among women as among men.

SYMPTOMS

Preliminary symptoms of this illness usually involve restlessness, insomnia, excessive worry about minor matters, and unprovoked spells of weeping. The patient is worried about the past and sees no hope for the future. As the more acute symptoms make their appearance, he becomes increasingly depressed and apprehensive and develops marked feelings of worthlessness and self-condemnation. Often he is preoccupied with some real or imagined misdemeanor

committed in the past for which he feels that he can never be forgiven and is eternally damned. He is in utmost despair and feels that there is absolutely no hope. He has committed the unpardonable sin.

These anxious and misery-laden feelings are usually accompanied by an increase in motor activity which may range from mere restlessness to extreme agitation in which the patient may pace the floor, weeping, wringing his hands, pulling his hair, biting his lips, and bemoaning his fate. Suicidal impulses are frequent.

Hypochondriacal delusions are common, and the patient may insist that his bowels are stopped up and will never move again, that his stomach is rotting away, that his body is all withered and dried up, that his brain has been eaten away, or that he has cancer or some other terrible disease. Feelings of unreality and nihilistic delusions frequently develop, and the patient may feel that he is living in a shadow world, that his wife and children are dead, and that nothing really exists.

Despite the patient's general depressed and anxious state, thought processes are not retarded, orientation is usually fairly good, and the patient may realize that he is ill and needs help. However, the danger of suicide remains great even in the patients who show considerable insight into their condition and plead for

SUMMARY CHART OF FUNCTIONAL PSYCHOSES

PSYCHOTIC DISORDER	GENERAL SYMPTOMS	PSYCHODYNAMICS (TENTATIVE)
Schizophrenic Reactions:		
Simple reaction	Reduction of external interests and attachments, impoverishment of interpersonal relationships, neglect of hygiene and appearance. Apathy and indifference common, but not conspicuous delusions or hallucinations.	Simple retreat from anxiety-arousing stress to lower level of psychobiological functioning involving emotional indifference and lowered aspiration.
Hebephrenic reaction	Shallow, inappropriate emotional responses, silliness, mannerisms, bizarre delusions, stereotypies, unpredictable hollow giggling.	Severe personality decompensation with fragmentation of thought processes, loss of faith in self and world, social withdrawal, and surrender to disintegration.
Catatonic reaction	Conspicuous motor behavior, with either generalized inhibition (stupor, mutism, negativism, waxy flexibility) or hyperactivity.	Individual momentarily overwhelmed by problems but struggling desperately to find some system of beliefs, some faith on which he can build.
Paranoid reaction	Delusions of grandeur and/or persecution; hallucinations, usually with constant attitude of suspiciousness and hostility. Sometimes expansive delusional system predominates, with delusions of omnipotence, remarkable talents, and high social status.	An attempt to maintain ego integrity by projecting blame for difficulties onto "enemies" and/or by compensating grandiose delusions. However, individual so overwhelmed by reality that delusions are not well systematized and personality disorganization is severe.
Childhood schizophrenia	Withdrawal, disorganization of thought processes, distorted emotional reactions and fantasy. Hyperactive, autistic.	Atypical psychological development with marked disturbances in parent-child relationships. Frequently evidence of constitutional abnormalities.

help. Prior to the advent of modern treatment procedures some 25 per cent of these patients died by their own hands (English and Finch, 1954).

Involutional reactions are of two main types, those characterized chiefly by depression and those centering around paranoid ideas. The depressed form, usually with accompanying agitation, is the more common.

The following case of a woman of 47 illustrates the feeling tone and thought content typical in involutional depressions.

Dr.: Hello—how do you feel today?

Pt.: Oh (moaning), why don't you just let me die! It would be better for everybody.

Dr.: What is the matter?

Pt.: Misery and death follow me around; everyone who gets close to me suffers. My mother and father, my children, and my husband suffered by my hand and died by my hand. (Gets up and paces back and forth.)

Dr.: Isn't the girl that visits you your daughter?

Pt.: She says she is my daughter, but my children are all dead—and it is my fault. I should die a horrible

Paranoid Reactions:

Paranoia	Systematized delusions of persecution and/or grandeur with rest of the personality remaining relatively intact. Rigid, self-important, suspicious personality.	Defense against self-devaluation resulting from feelings of failure; blame is projected on others. Imagined persecution seen as proof of own importance.
Paranoid state	Delusions of grandeur and/or persecution—not so well systematized as in paranoia but without bizarre fragmentation and deterioration of the paranoid schizophrenic. Hallucinations common.	Similar to above but less systematized and usually precipitated in predisposed individual by particular anxiety-arousing stress situation. Usually transient, with spontaneous recovery.

Affective Reactions:

Manic-depressive reaction	Exaggerated mood swings, with elation and overactivity or depression and underactivity or a combination or alternation of these. Bizarre, poorly systematized delusions and hallucinations.	Attempts to cope with anxiety-arousing feelings of failure by a "flight into reality" or by intropunitiveness, with self-recrimination and self-punishment to "undo" or "pay price" for failure.
Psychotic depressive reaction	Similar to depressive pattern above, but not cyclical.	Similar to depressive pattern above, with external precipitating factors more common.

Involutional Psychotic Reactions:

	Depression, usually with agitation, in absence of history of manic-depressive reaction. Two main types: those characterized chiefly by depression, with predominant mood of hopelessness, self-recrimination and guilt; and those centering around paranoid delusions.	Overreaction to feelings of failure to achieve goals and to approaching old age with no hope of future attainment. Allays anxiety in part by self-punitiveness but anxiety-arousing stress remains too great, leading to severe personality disorganization without spontaneous recovery.

death. God knows this and wants me to die. Why did I do it, there's nothing left for me but death. Nothing can be done for me—it's unforgivable, you should kill me. (Runs hands nervously through hair.)

Dr.: What did you do?

Pt.: I let them die and now I should die. I am only dirt, there is only dirt left in me. There is no reason for me to eat because I am only dirt—filthy, smelly dirt. I treated everyone like dirt and now I am dirt—the worst sort and everyone knows it.

Dr.: Don't the people treat you well here?

Pt.: They don't try to hurt me—but they will suffer like all the rest if they try to help me. They wouldn't try anyway—because they can see I am dirt turning to dirt. I am worthless and I can't do anything about it; no one can be my friend. They try to feed me. Can't they see that they can't feed dirt—earth into earth, that's the only place for me, and maybe I can atone for the evil I have caused.

Lanzkron (1961) has pointed out that involutional psychotics with paranoid delusions may commit acts of violence and should be hospitalized early. In a review of 8 cases admitted to a state hospital for the criminally insane after committing homicide, he noted that in every case there had been indications of the malignant nature of the patient's mental illness some time prior to the actual homicidal act.

GENERAL DYNAMICS

In involutional reactions the dynamics appear to be fairly well understood.

Biological factors. Many women at about the beginning of the involutional period experience various disturbances referred to as the menopause syndrome. The symptoms consist primarily of hot flashes, headaches, periods of dizziness, excessive sweating, nervous irritability, insomnia, and difficulty in concentrating. There may be mild depression and the clinical picture may resemble a mild neurosis, but the disturbance is transitory. It is apparently due to a decrease in ovarian hormone production, and treatment with ovarian hormone extracts is helpful.

Although the menopause syndrome and involutional psychosis may occasionally occur at the same time and the symptoms may be somewhat fused, the two conditions are distinct: involutional reactions are much more serious and do not respond to estrin treatment. Endocrine changes may play an interactive and aggravating role in involutional reactions, but they are not the primary causative factor.

In general, biological factors—hereditary predisposition, constitutional make-up, and organic pathology—have received little emphasis in studies of involutional reactions. It is interesting to note, however, that whereas schizophrenia has been reported as infrequent among the relatives of manic-depressive patients, it is found in approximately 5 per cent of the parents and siblings of patients with a diagnosis of involutional melancholia (Kallmann, 1953, 1959). As a consequence, Kallmann has concluded that involutional melancholia is more closely related to schizophrenia than to manic-depressive reactions. This viewpoint would appear to be supported by the observation that in cases of mixed symptomatology, paranoid delusions frequently persist after the depression has cleared up (Gregory, 1961).

Psychological factors. The primary emphasis in involutional reactions has been upon the reactions of a psychologically predisposed individual to the severe stresses of this life period. Although the precise nature of parent-child relations and patterns of family interaction of involutional patients have not yet been investigated, these patients are characterized as being compulsive in personality make-up (American Psychiatric Association, 1952). Frequently they reveal such traits as overconscientiousness, meticulousness, narrow social interests, overconformity, insecurity, perfectionism, and rigidity in everyday living habits (Gregory, 1961; Haggerty, 1941; Palmer, 1942). Paranoid-type patients have usually also been suspicious individuals who have always felt that everyone is out to take advantage of them. Women who have shown excessive jealousy, suspiciousness, and sexual frigidity are thought to be particularly prone to such upsets during the involutional period.

Many investigators, however, pay little heed to the frequency of these pre-psychotic personality factors, pointing out that many patients have been perfectly normal prior to the onset of the acute symptoms. In these cases, there is reason to believe that the picture of normality may have been somewhat superficial—many individuals are adept at concealing their actual feelings and present to others a false picture of personal maturity and stability.

Certainly an understanding of the stresses characteristic of the involutional period of life is of great importance in understanding the psychodynamics of involutional reactions. The involutional period marks the beginning of the period of general bodily and intellectual decline inevitably ending in senility and death. The individual finds himself unable to handle the work he used to handle; he tires easily, and sexual desire and power are materially lessened. The woman realizes that she can no longer bear children and that her beauty and physical attractiveness have greatly declined. It is often a period of loss and illness of loved ones when the patient too may have various physical ills such as prostate trouble or even seemingly minor complications such as adjusting to false teeth.

In a study of 379 involutional patients Tait and Burns (1951) found that the main precipitating factor was concern about the decline of the self. During this period many individuals realize for the first time that their life is almost over, that they will never have it to live again, and that they are committed to whatever success they have achieved and to whatever way of life they have adopted.

This mood is perhaps well caught in a patient's poem:

"My kin all dead, my childless home a hall
Of spells and spectres deforming the windowed sun,
Friends few and far, and passing one by one,
My body yoked here like an ox in stall
By long disease. . . ."

Each individual reacts to these stresses in his own way, depending upon his general personality organization and on the degree of success and independence he has achieved, his family attachments, and so on. Some people accept the inevitable with philosophical calm, perhaps tinged with a little sadness, and grow old gracefully; others begin the downward path as they climbed up, without much thought or awareness. Others, however, find this a most trying and difficult period. Even where the individual has been relatively well adjusted up to this point, a mild involutional reaction may be precipitated by the sudden realization that his life is about over and that he has failed to achieve his goals or gain the many values in life that he holds indispensable. This is particularly true if such general disappointment and frustration are accompanied by other precipitating factors such as financial losses, the death of a loved one on whom the patient feels dependent, business worries, or worry about health.

The dynamic patterns involved in both the depressed and the paranoid forms of involutional reactions are readily understandable and might almost be predicted. In response to the very real stresses at this time of life lonely, overconscientious, perfectionistic individuals easily become worried, anxious, and depressed. As past failures and disappointments loom large and as the future holds potentially less and less, the increased self-centering of interests and hypochondriacal concern provide a measure of substitute satisfaction. Then, as the involutional reaction becomes exaggerated, these hypochon-driacal factors may develop into definite delusions.[1]

Ideas of unreality probably develop out of this same self-centering of interests and the accompanying loss of interest in others and in the environment. It has been pointed out that to a large extent things feel real to us in proportion to the amount of interest we take in them; if we gradually become preoccupied with our own thoughts and difficulties, the external world can be expected to become progressively less real and to take on a somewhat shadowy aspect.

The patient's ideas of poverty are related to the general involutional picture in much the same way. As he feels more and more that he has failed to provide adequately for his security and status in later years, he becomes increasingly concerned with their importance. As he looks toward his bleak, dismal future, it is not surprising that part of the picture takes on the aspect of dire poverty and want, representing all that such a loss would mean to such a person in his old age—loneliness, lack of attention and respect, and, perhaps most vital of all, insecurity.

Delusions of sin grow naturally out of the individual's feelings of failure and self-recrimination. He begins to feel that he must not have deserved to succeed (for it is common in our culture to assume that a really good and deserving person who works hard is bound to be a success). It is then only another step to magnify the most trivial mistakes as cardinal and unpardonable sins and to distort them as a means of explaining his present predicament. And since he feels that he is being punished for these unpardonable sins, the future is hopeless and he looks forward only to imprisonment, torture, death, and eternal damnation. Small wonder that these patients need supervision to prevent suicide.

As with other depressives, the involutional patient probably gets some small satisfaction out of having committed his unpardonable sin, for this sets him off in a unique category. Also the excessive self-recrimination ensures some measure of expiation and atonement.

As we have seen, the manic-depressive is apparently only temporarily defeated: once he

[1]In Chapter 11 we shall take up in considerable detail the old-age psychoses, in which there are organic stresses in the form of brain degeneration, as well as the stresses arising out of the older person's life situation and personality.

has worked through the resulting self-condemnation and self-devaluation, he can return to the struggle of life. On the other hand, the depressive involutional patient, more rigid and perfectionistic, older, and facing what he evaluates as a hopeless future, has little incentive to get well.

In the paranoid form, the individual reacts to his disappointments and feelings of failure by becoming suspicious and projecting the blame for his difficulties onto others instead of blaming himself. Further discussion of this pattern is unnecessary since the dynamics are essentially the same as those in the paranoid state except that they take place in the context of the involutional period of life and its particular stresses.

Sociological factors. Differences in both the incidence and the symptom content of involutional reactions are found in different societies. Henderson and Gillespie (1950) have referred to the high incidence of involutional reactions in the rural areas of Scotland. Carothers (1947, 1959), on the other hand, found that involutional reactions constituted only 1.4 per cent of total admissions among Kenya Africans as contrasted with some 4 per cent in the United States. He also found almost no guilt in the Kenyan reactions, presumably because of the fact that their behavior is primarily group-determined rather than a matter of individual choice or personal responsibility. In general, however, it would appear that the symptoms of involutional reactions are pretty much the same the world over (Field, 1960).

In our society, Jaco (1960) found that the rate of involutional psychoses was over twice as high in urban as in rural areas in the state of Texas. He also found that the divorced and single had the highest rate and the widowed the lowest rate. Except for the lower rate for the widowed, these findings seem to be somewhat self-explanatory. However, the precise significance of sociocultural factors in involutional psychoses remains to be worked out.

THERAPY AND PROGNOSIS

The majority of involutional patients do not recover spontaneously, and prior to the advent of electroshock such reactions were usually of long duration. Many studies indicate that some 60 per cent of involutional patients recover with electroshock, and 80 to 90 per cent with electroshock plus psychotherapy (Bennett and Wilbur, 1944; Prados and Ruddick, 1947; Tait and Burns, 1951).

Although electroshock still appears to be the method of choice for obtaining a rapid alleviation of symptoms, it is usually combined now with antidepressant and various other drugs (Wortis, 1963). With combined medical, psychological, and sociological treatment procedures, it would appear that well over 90 per cent of involutional psychotics recover and make adequate life adjustments. The prognosis is somewhat less favorable for the paranoid than for the depressed type (Bigelow, 1959).

REFERENCES

The reference list includes not only the sources from which the author has drawn material, but acknowledgments of the permissions granted by authors and publishers to quote directly from their works.

ABOOD, L. G. A chemical approach to the problem of mental disease. In D. D. Jackson (Ed.), *The etiology of schizophrenia.* New York: Basic Books, 1960. Pp. 91-119.

AKERFELDT, S. Oxidation of N, N-Dimethyl-p-phenylenediamine by serum from patients with mental disease. *Science,* 1957, 125 (1), 117-119.

ALANEN, Y. O. The mothers of schizophrenic patients. *Acta psychiat. neurol. Kbh.,* 1958, 33 (Suppl. No. 124), 359.

ALLEN, E. B. Psychiatric disorders in forty male teachers. *J. nerv. ment. Dis.,* 1942, 45, 204-205.

American Psychiatric Association. *Diagnostic and statistical manual, mental disorders.* Washington: Author, 1952.

ANTHONY, J., & SCOTT, P. *J. child. Psychol. Psychiat.,* 1960, 1, 3.

ARIETI, S. Manic-depressive psychosis. In S. Arieti (Ed.), *American handbook of psychiatry.* New York: Basic Books, 1959a. Pp. 419-454.

ARIETI, S. Schizophrenia: the manifest symptomatology, the psychodynamic and formal mechanisms. In S. Arieti (Ed.), *American handbook of psychiatry.* Vol. 1. New York: Basic Books, 1959(b). Pp. 455-484.

ARONSON, J., & POLGAR, S. Pathogenic relationships in schizophrenia. *Amer. J. Psychiat.,* 1962, 119, 222-227.

AYRES, C. M. Causes of rehospitalization in schizophrenia (statistical study of complications of convalescence). *Dis. nerv. System*, 1962, 23, 469-477.

BATESON, G. Cultural problems posed by a study of schizophrenic process. In A. Auerback (Ed.), *Schizophrenia: an integrated approach*. New York: Ronald, 1959. Pp. 125-264.

BATESON, G. Minimal requirements for a theory of schizophrenia. *Arch. gen. Psychiat.*, 1960, 2, 477-491.

BECK, A. T., & VALIN, S. Psychotic depressive reactions in soldiers who accidentally killed their buddies. *Amer. J. Psychiat.*, 1953, 110, 347-353.

BECK, S. J. Families of schizophrenic and of well children: method, concepts, and some results. *Amer. J. Orthopsychiat.*, 1960, 30, 247-275.

BECKER, E. Toward a comprehensive theory of depression. A cross disciplinary appraisal of objects, games and meaning. *J. nerv. ment. Dis.*, 1962a, 135, 26-35.

BECKER, E. Toward a theory of schizophrenia. External objects and the creation of meaning. *Arch. gen. Psychiat.*, 1962b, 7, 170-181.

BECKER, J. Achievement related characteristics of manic-depressives. *J. abnorm. soc. Psychol.*, 1960, 60, 334-339.

BECKETT, P. G., FROHMAN, C. E., GOTTLIEB, J. S., MOWBRAY, J. B., & WOLF, R. C. Schizophrenic-like mechanisms in monkeys. *American Journal Psychiat.*, 1963b, 119, 835-842.

BECKETT, P. G., SENF, R., FROHMAN, C. E., & GOTTLIEB, J. S. Energy production and premorbid history in schizophrenia. *Arch. gen. Psychiat.*, 1963a, 8, 155-162.

BENDER, LAURETTA. Childhood schizophrenia; clinical study of one hundred schizophrenic children. *Amer. J. Orthopsychiat.*, 1947, 17, 40-56.

BENDER, LAURETTA. Childhood schizophrenia. *Psychiat. Quart.*, 1953, 27, 663-681.

BENDER, LAURETTA. Twenty years of clinical research on schizophrenic children, with special reference to those under 6 years of age. In G. Caplan (Ed.), *Emotional problems of early childhood*. New York: Basic Books, 1955. Pp. 503-515.

BENDER, LAURETTA. The brain and child behavior. *Arch. gen. Psychiat.*, 1961, 4, 531.

BENNETT, A. E., & WILBUR, C. B. Convulsive shock therapy in involutional states after complete failure with previous estrogenic treatment. *Amer. J. med. Sci.*, 1944, 208, 170-176.

BERNE, E. A psychiatric census of the South Pacific. *Amer. J. Psychiat.*, 1960, 117, 44-47.

BETTELHEIM, B. *Truants from life; the rehabilitation of emotionally disturbed children*. Glencoe, Ill.: The Free Press, 1955.

BIGELOW, N. The involutional psychoses. In S. Arieti (Ed.), *American handbook of psychiatry*. New York: Basic Books, 1959. Pp. 540-545.

BLACHLY, P., OSTERUS, H., & JOSALIN, R. Suicide in professional groups. *N. Eng. J. Med.*, 1963, 268, 1278-1282.

BLISS, E. L., CLARK, L. D., & WEST, C. D. Studies of sleep deprivation: relationship to schizophrenia. *AMA Arch. neurol. Psychiat.*, 1959, 81, 348-359.

BLOCK, JEANNE, PATTERSON, VIRGINIA, BLOCK, J., & JACKSON, D. D. A study of the parents of schizophrenic and neurotic children. *Psychiatry*, 1958, 21, 387-397.

BOGOCH, S., DUSSIK, K. T., FENDER, CHRISTA, & CONRAN, P. C. Longitudinal clinical and neurochemical studies on schizophrenic and manic-depressive psychoses. *Amer. J. Psychiat.*, 1960, 117, 409-420.

BOGOCH, S., BELVAL, P. C., DUSSIK, K. T., & CONRAN, P. C. Psychological and biochemical syntheses occurring during recovery from psychosis. *Amer. J. Psychiat.*, 1962, 119, 128-135.

BOISEN, A. T. Onset in acute schizophrenia. *Psychiatry*, 1947, 10, 159-166.

BONNER, H. The problem of diagnosis in paranoic disorders. *Amer. J. Psychiat.*, 1951, 107, 677-683.

BÖÖK, J. A. A genetic and neuropsychiatric investigation of a North Swedish population, with special regard to schizophrenia and mental deficiency. *Acta genet.*, 1953, 4, 1-100, 133-139, 345-414.

BÖÖK, J. A. Genetical aspects of schizophrenic psychoses. In D. D. Jackson (Ed.), *The etiology of schizophrenia*. New York: Basic Books, 1960. Pp. 23-36.

BORN, W. Artistic behavior of the mentally deranged; and Great Artists who suffered from mental disorders. *Ciba Symposia*, 1946, 8, 207-216, 225-232.

BOWEN, M. Family relationships in schizophrenia. In A. Auerback (Ed.), *Schizophrenia: an integrated approach*. New York: Ronald, 1959. Pp. 147-178.

BOWEN, M. A family concept of schizophrenia. In D. D. Jackson (Ed.), *The etiology of schizophrenia*. New York: Basic Books, 1960. Pp. 346-372.

BRODEY, W. M. Some family operations and schizophrenia. *AMA Arch. gen. Psychiat.*, 1959, 1, 379-402.

BROWN, G. W., MONCK, E. M., CARSTAIRS, G. M., & WING, J. K. Influence of family life on the course of schizophrenic illness. *Brit. J. prev. soc. Med.*, 1962, 16, 55-68.

BURTON, A. Schizophrenia and existence. *Psychiatry*, 1960, 23, 385-394.

CAMERON, N. Paranoid conditions and paranoia. In S. Arieti (Ed.), *American handbook of psychiatry*. New York: Basic Books, 1959. Pp. 508-539.

CAMPBELL, J. D. Manic-depressive psychosis in children. *J. nerv. ment. Dis.*, 1952, 116, 424-439.

CAMPBELL, R. J. The schizophrenias—current views: a report on the second International Congress for Psychiatry. *Psychiat. Quart.*, 1958, 32, 318-334.

CAROTHERS, J. C. A study of mental derangement in Africans, and an attempt to explain its peculiarities, more especially in relation to the African attitude of life. *J. ment. Sci.*, 1947, 93, 548-597. Reprinted by permission of G. W. T. H. Fleming, Editor-in-Chief.

CAROTHERS, J. C. Frontal lobe function and the African. *J. ment. Sci.*, 1951, 97, 12-48.

CAROTHERS, J. C. The African mind in health and disease. A study in ethnopsychiatry. Geneva: World Health Organization, 1953, No. 17.

CAROTHERS, J. C. Culture, psychiatry, and the written word. *Psychiatry*, 1959, 22, 307-320.

CHAPMAN, L. F., KUTT, H., & WOLFF, H. G. Evidence for disturbance in the metabolism of the central nervous system of patients with chronic schizophrenia. *Trans. Amer. neurol. Ass.*, 1959, 84, 82-85.

CHAPMAN, L. F., HINKLE, L. E., JR., & WOLFF, H. G. Human ecology, disease, and schizophrenia. *Amer. J. Psychiat.*, 1960, 117, 193-204.

CHRISTIAN, H. A. *Psychiatry for Practitioners*. New York: Oxford Univer. Press, 1936.

CLARDY, E. R. A study of the development and course of schizophrenia in children. *Psychiat. Quart.*, 1951, 25, 81-90.

COE, J. Suicides—a statistical and pathological report. *Minn. Med.*, 1963, 46, 22-29.

COLBERT, E. G., & KOEGLER, R. R. The childhood schizophrenic in adolescence. *Psychiat. Quart.*, 1961, 35, 693-701.

COWEN, J. R. Depression. *Psychiat. Quart.*, 1959, 33, 351.

CREAK, MILDRED, & INI, SYLVIA. Families of psychotic children. *J. child Psychol. Psychiat.*, 1960, 1, 156-175.

CURRY, A. E. The world of a schizophrenic woman. *Psychoanal. and psychoanal. Rev.*, 1962, 49, 129-135. Reprinted by permission of Editors and Publisher.

DAVIDSON, M. A., MC INNES, R. G., & PARNELL, R. W. The distribution of personality traits in seven-year-old children: a combined psychological, psychiatric, and somatotype study. *Brit. J. educ. Psychol.*, 1957, 27, 48-61.

DREGER, R. M., & MILLER, K. S. Comparative psychological studies of Negroes and whites in the United States. *Psychol. Bull.*, 1960, 57, 361-402.

DUBLIN, L. I. *Suicide. A sociological and statistical study.* New York: Ronald, 1963.

EASSON, W. M., & STEINHILBER, R. M. Murderous aggression by children and adolescents. *Arch. gen. Psychiat.*, 1961, 4, 1-9.

EATON, J. W., & WEIL, R. J. Some epidemiological findings in the Hutterite Mental Health Study. In *Interrelations between the social environment and psychiatric disorders.* New York: Milbank Memorial Fund, 1953. Pp. 222-234.

EATON, J. W., & WEIL, R. J. *Culture and mental disorders; a comparative study of the Hutterites and other populations.* Glencoe, Ill.: Free Press, 1955.

EISENBERG, L. The autistic child in adolescence. *Amer. J. Psychiat.*, 1956, 112, 607-612.

EISENBERG, L. The fathers of autistic children. *Amer. J. Orthopsychiat.*, 1957, 27, 715-724.

ENDERS, L. J., & FLINN, D. E. Clinical problems in aviation medicine. Schizophrenic reaction, paranoid type. *Aerospace Med.*, 1962, 33, 730-732.

ENGLISH, O., & FINCH, S. M. *Introduction to psychiatry.* New York: Norton, 1954.

ESCALONA, SIBYLLE. Some considerations regarding psychotherapy with psychotic children. *Bull. Menninger Clin.*, 1948, 12, 127-134. Reprinted by permission of the author and the *Bull. Menninger Clin.*

FARBEROW, N. L., & SHNEIDMAN, E. S. *The cry for help.* New York: McGraw-Hill, 1961.

FARINA, A., GARMEZY, N., ZALUSKY, M., & BECKER, J. Premorbid behavior and prognosis in female schizophrenic patients. *Journal consult. Psychol.*, 1962, 2, 56-60.

FARIS, R. E. L., & DUNHAM, W. *Mental disorders in urban areas.* Chicago: Univer. Chicago Press, 1939.

FERSTER, C. B., & DE MYER, M. K. A method for the experimental analysis of the behavior of autistic children. *Amer. J. Orthopsychiat.*, 1962, 32, 89-98.

FIELD, MARGARET J. *Search for security: an ethnopsychiatric study of rural Ghana.* Evanston: Northwestern Univer. Press, 1960.

FLECK, S. Family dynamics and origin of schizophrenia. *Psychosom. Med.*, 1960, 22, 333-344.

FLECK, S., LIDZ, T., & CORNELISON, ALICE R. Comparison of parent-child relationships of male and female schizophrenic patients. *Arch. gen. Psychiat.*, 1963, 8, 1-7.

FOULDS, G. A., & DIXON, P. The nature of intellectual deficit in schizophrenia. I. A comparison of schizophrenics and neurotics. *Brit. J. soc. clin. Psychol.*, 1962, 1, 7-19.

FREEMAN, R. V., & GRAYSON, H. M. Maternal attitudes in schizophrenia. *J. abnorm. soc. Psychol.*, 1955, 50, 45-52.

FREMMING, K. The expectations of mental infirmity in a sample of the Danish population. Occasional papers on eugenics, No. 7. London: Cassell & Co., 1951.

FRUMKIN, R. M., & FRUMKIN, MIRIAM Z. Religion, occupation, and major mental disorders. *J. human Relations*, 1957, 6 (1), 98-101.

FUNDING, T. Genetics of paranoid psychoses in later life. *Acta Psychiat. Scand.*, 1961, 37, 267-282.

FUSON, W. M. Occupations of functional psychotics. *Amer. J. Sociol.*, 1943, 48, 612-613.

GALTON, F. *Inquiries into human faculty and its development.* London: Macmillan, 1883.

GARMEZY, N., & RODNICK, E. H. Premorbid adjustment and performance in schizophrenia: implications for interpreting heterogeneity in schizophrenia. *J. nerv. ment. Dis.*, 1959, 129, 450-466.

GARMEZY, N., CLARKE, A. R., & STOCKNER, CAROL. Child rearing attitudes of mothers and fathers as reported by schizophrenic and normal patients. *J. abnorm. soc. Psychol.*, 1961, 63, 176-182.

GERARD, D. L., & SIEGEL, J. The family background of schizophrenia. *Psychiat. Quart.*, 1950, 24, 47-73.

GIBSON, R. W. The family background and early life experience of the manic-depressive patient: a comparison with the schizophrenic patients. *Psychiatry*, 1958, 21, 71-90.

GIBSON, R. W., COHEN, MABEL B., & COHEN, R.A. On the dynamics of the manic-depressive personality. *Amer. J. Psychiat.*, 1959, 115, 1101-1107.

GILL, M. The present state of psychoanalytic theory. *J. abnorm. soc. Psychol.*, 1959, 58, 1-8.

GOLD, H. R. Observations on cultural psychiatry during a world tour of mental hospitals. *Amer. J. Psychiat.*, 1951, 108, 462-468.

GOLDFARB, W. Families of schizophrenic children. *Res. Publ. Ass. Res. nerv. ment. Dis.*, 1962, 39, 256-269.

GOLDMAN, A. E. A comparative-developmental approach to schizophrenia. *Psychol. Bull.*, 1962, 59, 57-69.

GOOD, H. S. Fifteen days adrift on a raft; a clinical evaluation of five survivors. *Nav. med. Bull.*, 1943, 41, 367-373.

GRALNICK, A. Folie a deux—the psychosis of association; a review of 103 cases and the entire English literature, with case presentations. *Psychiat. Quart.*, 1942, 14, 230-263.

GRANT, V. W. Paranoid dynamics: a case study. *Amer. J. Psychiat.*, 1956, 113, 143-148.

GRAY, P. H. Theory and evidence of imprinting in human infants. *J. Psychol.*, 1958, 46, 155-166.

GREGORY, I. Genetic factors in schizophrenia. *Amer. J. Psychiat.*, 1960, 116, 961-972.

GREGORY, I. *Psychiatry, biological and social.* Philadelphia: W. B. Saunders, 1961.

GRIFFITH, R. M., ESTES, B. W., & ZEROF, S. A. Intellectual impairment in schizophrenia. *J. consult. Psychol.*, 1962, 26, 336-339.

GRINKER, R. R., AND OTHERS. *The phenomena of depressions.* New York: Harper, 1961.

GROSS, M. The impact of ataractic drugs on a mental hospital outpatient clinic. *Amer. J. Psychiat.*, 1960, 117, 444-447.

HAGGERTY, H. Pre-psychotic personality traits in women with involutional melancholia. *Smith Coll. Stud. soc. Work*, 1941, 12, 191-192.

HALEY, J. The family of the schizophrenic: a model system. *J. nerv. ment. Dis.*, 1959, 129, 357-374.

HALEY, J. Direct study of child-parent interactions: III. Observation of the family of the schizophrenic. *Amer. J. Orthopsychiat.*, 1960, 30, 460-467.

HARDT, R. H. The ecological distribution of patients admitted to mental hospitals from an urban area. *Psychiat. Quart.*, 1959, 33, 126-144.

HARDT, R. H., & FEINHANDLER, S. J. Social class and mental hospitalization prognosis. In T. Sarbin (Ed.), *Studies in behavior pathology.* New York: Holt, Rinehart & Winston, 1961. Pp. 326-332.

HASTINGS, D. W. Follow-up results in psychiatric illness. *Amer. J. Psychiat.*, 1958, 114, 1057-1066.

HEATH, R. G. A biochemical hypothesis on the etiology of schizophrenia. In D. D. Jackson (Ed.), *The etiology of schizophrenia.* New York: Basic Books, 1960.

HEATH, R. G., MARTENS, S., LEACH, B. E., COHEN, M., & ANGEL, C. Effect on behavior in humans with the administration of taraxein. *Amer. J. Psychiat.*, 1957, 114, 14-24.

HEATH, R. G., MARTENS, S., LEACH, B. E., COHEN, M., & FEIGLEY, C. A. Behavioral changes in nonpsychotic volunteers following the administration of taraxein, the substance obtained from serum of schizophrenic patients. *Amer. J. Psychiat.*, 1958, 114, 917-920.

HENDERSON, D., & GILLESPIE, R. D. *A textbook of psychiatry for students and practitioners.* New York: Oxford Univer. Press, 1950.

HES, J. P. Manic-depressive illness in Israel. *Amer. J. Psychiat.,* 1960, 116, 1082-1086.

HOAGLAND, H. Some considerations of the role of the adrenal cortex in the origin of the psychoses. *J. nerv. ment. Dis.,* 1954, 119, 75-76.

HOFFMAN, J. L. Psychotic visitors to government offices in the national capital. *Amer. J. Psychiat.,* 1943, 99, 571-575.

HOLLINGSHEAD, A. B., & REDLICH, F. C. Schizophrenia and social structure. *Amer. J. Psychiat.,* 1954, 110, 695-701.

HOLLINGSHEAD, A. B., & REDLICH, F. C. *Social class and mental illness.* New York: Wiley, 1958.

HOLLISTER, L. E. Drug-induced psychoses and schizophrenic reactions: a critical comparison. *Ann. N.Y. Acad. Sci.,* 1962, 96, 80-92.

HOLT, J. P., WRIGHT, E. R., & HECKER, A. O. Comparative clinical experience with five antidepressants. *Amer. J. Psychiat.,* 1960, 117, 533-538.

HORWITT, M. K. Fact and artifact in the biology of schizophrenia. *Science,* 1956, 124(3), 429-430.

HYDE, R. W., & KINGSLEY, D. V. Studies in medical sociology: 1. The relation of mental disorders to the community socio-economic level. *N. Eng. J. Med.,* 1944, 231, 543-548.

JACKSON, D. D. (Ed.). *The etiology of schizophrenia.* New York: Basic Books, 1960.

JACKSON, D. D. Schizophrenia. *Scientif. Amer.,* 1962, 207(2), 65-78.

JACO, E. G. *The social epidemiology of mental disorders.* New York: Russell Sage Found., 1960.

JAHRREISS, W. O. Some influences of catholic education and creed upon psychotic reactions. *Dis. nerv. System,* 1942, 3, 377-381.

JAMES, I. P. On depression. *Med. J. Austr.,* 1961, 48(2), 430-435.

JENKINS, R. L. The schizophrenic sequence: withdrawal, disorganization, psychotic reorganization. *Amer. J. Orthopsychiat.,* 1952, 22, 738-748.

JOHNSON, W. B. Euphoric and depressed moods in normal subjects, Part 1. *Charact. & Pers.,* 1937, 6, 212-216.

KALLMANN, F. J. Genetic aspects of psychoses. In *The biology of mental health and disease* (27th annual conference of the Milbank Memorial Fund). New York: Harper, 1952.

KALLMANN, F. J. *Heredity in health and mental disorder.* New York: Norton, 1953.

KALLMANN, F. J. The use of genetics in psychiatry. *J. ment. Sci.,* 1958, 104, 542-549.

KALLMANN, F. J. The genetics of mental illness. In S. Arieti (Ed.), *American handbook of psychiatry.* New York: Basic Books, 1959. Pp. 175-234.

KALLMANN, F. J., & ROTH, B. Genetic aspects of preadolescent schizophrenia. *Amer. J. Psychiat.,* 1956, 112, 599-606.

KANT, O. Clinical analysis of schizophrenic deterioration. *Psychiat. Quart.,* 1943, 17, 426-445.

KANT, O. Clinical investigation of simple schizophrenia. *Psychiat. Quart.,* 1948, 22, 141-151.

KARNOSH, L. J., & ZUCKER, E. M. *Handbook of Psychiatry.* St. Louis: Mosby, 1945.

KAUFMAN, I., FRANK, T., HEIMS, LORA, HERRICK, JOAN, REISER, D., & WILLER, L. Treatment implications of a new classification of parents of schizophrenic children. *Amer. J. Psychiat.,* 1960, 116, 920-924.

KAUFMAN, I., FRANK, T., FRIEND, J., HEIMS, LORA W., & WEISS, R. Success and failure in the treatment of childhood schizophrenia. *Amer. J. Psychiat.,* 1962, 118, 909-915.

KELLEY, SISTER M. WILLIAM. The incidence of hospitalized mental illness among religious sisters in the United States. *Amer. J. Psychiat.,* 1958, 115, 72-75.

KENNEDY, J. F. Special message on mental illness and mental retardation, Feb. 5, 1963. *Amer. Psychologist,* 1963, 18, 280-289.

KERBIKOV, O. V. *et al. Textbook of psychiatry.* Board of Educational Institutions of the USSR, 1958.

KETY, S. S. Recent biochemical theories of schizophrenia. In D. D. Jackson (Ed.), *The etiology of schizophrenia.* New York: Basic Books, 1960. Pp. 120-145.

KIMMICH, R. A. Ethnic aspects of schizophrenia in Hawaii. *Psychiatry,* 1960, 23, 97-102.

KLAF, F. S. Female homosexuality and paranoid schizophrenia. *Arch. gen. Psychiat.,* 1961, 4, 84-86.

KLAF, F. S., & DAVIS, C. A. Homosexuality and paranoid schizophrenia: a survey of 150 cases and controls. *Amer. J. Psychiat.,* 1960, 116, 1070-1075.

KLONOFF, H. A longitudinal study of schizophrenia. *Amer. J. Psychiat.,* 1960, 117, 348-353.

KORANYI, E. K., & LEHMANN, H. E. Experimental sleep deprivation in schizophrenic patients. *Arch. gen. Psychiat.,* 1960, 2, 534-544.

KRETSCHMER, E. *Physique and Character.* New York: Harcourt, Brace & World, 1925.

LANZKRON, J. Murder as a reaction to paranoid delusions in involutional psychosis and its prevention. *Amer. J. Psychiat.,* 1961, 118, 426-429.

LASKY, J. J., & KLETT, C. J. Comparative evaluation of six tranquilizers with 500 newly admitted male schizophrenics from 32 VA hospitals. *Amer. Psychologist,* 1962, 17, 322-323.

LEWINSON, THEA S. Dynamic disturbances in the handwriting of psychotics; with reference to schizophrenic, paranoid, and manic-depressive psychoses. *Amer. J. Psychiat.,* 1940-41, 98, 102-135.

LIDZ, T. Schizophrenia and the family. *Psychiatry,* 1958, 21, 21-27.

LIDZ, T., CORNELISON, ALICE R., FLECK, S., & TERRY, DOROTHY. Intrafamilial environment of the schizophrenic patient. I. The father. *Psychiatry,* 1957, 20, 329-342.

LIDZ, T., CORNELISON, ALICE R., TERRY, DOROTHY, & FLECK, S. Irrationality as a family tradition. *AMA Arch. neurol. Psychiat.,* 1958, 79, 305-316.

LIDZ, T., FLECK, S., ALANEN, Y. O., & CORNELISON, ALICE R. Schizophrenic patients and their siblings. *Psychiatry,* 1963, 26, 1-18.

LIEF, A. (ED.). *The commonsense psychiatry of Dr. Adolf Meyer.* New York: McGraw-Hill, 1948.

LOWINGER, P. Leprosy and psychosis. *Amer. J. Psychiat.,* 1959, 116, 32-37.

LU, Y. C. Contradictory parental expectations in schizophrenia: dependence and responsibility. *Arch. gen. Psychiat.,* 1962, 6, 219-234.

LUBIN, A., GIESEKING, C. F., & WILLIAMS, H. L. Direct measurement of cognitive deficit in schizophrenia. *J. consult. Psychol.,* 1962, 26, 139-143.

LUBY, E. D., GOTTLIEB, J. S., COHEN, B. D., ROSENBAUM, G., & DOMINO, E. F. Model psychoses and schizophrenia. *Amer. J. Psychiat.,* 1962, 119, 61-67.

LUBY, E. D., GRISELL, J. L., FROHMAN, C. E., LEES, HELEN, COHEN, B. D., & GOTTLIEB, J. S. Biochemical, psychological, and behavioral responses to sleep deprivation. *Ann. N.Y. Acad. Sci.,* 1962, 96, 71-78.

MALONEY, J. C. A study in neurotic conformity: the Japanese. *Complex,* 1951, 5, 26-32.

MANDELBROTE, B., & FOLKARD, S. The outcome of schizophrenia in relation to a developing community psychiatric service. *Ment. Hyg.,* 1963, 47, 43-56.

MARKS, J., STAUFFACHER, J. C., & LYLE, C. Predicting outcome in schizophrenia. *J. abnorm. soc. Psychol.,* 1963, 66, 117-127.

MASSERMAN, J. H. *Principles of dynamic psychiatry.* Philadelphia: W. B. Saunders, 1961.

MASTERSON, J. F. Prognosis in adolescent disorders. *Amer. J. Psychiat.*, 1958, 114, 1097-1103.

MEEHL, P. E. Schizotaxia, schizotypy, schizophrenia. *Amer. Psychologist*, 1962, 17, 827-838.

MENNINGER, K. Diagnosis and treatment of schizophrenia. *Bull. Menninger Clin.*, 1948, 12, 96-106.

MEYERS, D., & GOLDFARB, W. Psychiatric appraisals of parents and siblings of schizophrenic children. *Amer. J. Psychiat.*, 1962, 118, 902-908.

MICHAEL, C. M., MORRIS, D. P., & SOROKER, E. Follow-up studies of shy, withdrawn children. II. Relative incidence of schizophrenia. *Amer. J. Orthopsychiat.*, 1957, 27, 331-337.

MILLER, C. W. The paranoid syndrome. *Arch. Neurol. Psychiat.*, 1941, 45, 952-963.

MILNER, K. O. The environment as a factor in the aetiology of criminal paranoia. *J. ment. Sci.*, 1949, 95, 124-132. Reprinted by permission of G. W. T. H. Fleming, Editor-in-Chief.

MOORE, R. A., & SELZER, M. L. Male homosexuality, paranoia, and the schizophrenias. *Amer. J. Psychiat.*, 1963, 119, 743-747.

MORAN, L. J. Vocabulary knowledge and usage among normal and schizophrenic subjects. *Psychol. Monogr.*, 1953, 67, No. 40 (Whole No. 370).

MYERS, J. K., & ROBERTS, B. H. *Family and class dynamics in mental illness.* New York: Wiley, 1959.

New Zealand Department of Health. *Annual report of the medical statistician on the mental health statistics of New Zealand for the year 1960.* Wellington: Author, 1960.

O'NEAL, PATRICIA, & ROBINS, L. M. Childhood patterns predictive of adult schizophrenia: a 30 year follow-up study. *Amer. J. Psychiat*, 1958a, 115, 385-391.

O'NEAL, PATRICIA, & ROBINS, L. M. The relation of childhood behavior problems to adult psychiatric status: a 30 year follow-up study of 150 subjects. *Amer. J. Psychiat.*, 1958b, 114, 961-969.

OPLER, M. K. Cultural perspectives in research on schizophrenias: a history with examples. *Psychiat. Quart.*, 1959, 33, 506-524.

OVERSTREET, H. The mind alive. New York: Norton, 1954.

PAGE, J. D. Description of a psychotic reaction in 11th century Japan. *Amer. J. Psychiat.*, 1962, 119, 271-272. Based on novel by Murasaki Shikibu: *The Tale of Genji.* Trans. by Arthur Waley. New York: Random, 1960.

PALMER, H. D. Involutional psychoses: melancholia. *Pub. Hlth Rep.* (Suppl. No. 168), Washington, D. C., 1942, 118-124.

PASAMANICK, B. A survey of mental disease in an urban population. VII. An approach to total prevalence by race. *Amer. J. Psychiat.*, 1962, 119, 299-305.

PHILLIPS, L. Case history data and prognosis in schizophrenia. *J. nerv. ment. Dis.*, 1953, 117, 515-525.

PLANANSKY, K., & JOHNSTON, R. The incidence and relationship of homosexual and paranoid features in schizophrenia. *Journal ment. Sci.*, 1962, 108, 604-615.

POLLACK, B. Clinical findings in the use of tofranil in depressive and other psychiatric states. *Amer. J. Psychiat.*, 1959, 116, 312-317.

POLLACK, M. Comparison of childhood, adolescent, and adult schizophrenias. *Arch. gen. Psychiat.*, 1960, 2, 652-661.

POLLAK, O. J. Post-mortem studies in mental patients. Frequent findings in paranoid states. *Amer. J. clin. Pathol.*, 1944, 4, 289-300.

PRADOS, M., & RUDDICK, B. Depressions and anxiety states of the middle-aged man. *Psychiat. Quart.*, 1947, 21, 410-430.

RASHKIS, H. A. The psychology of schizophrenia. Conflict theory, learning theory, organization theory, early experience. *AMA Arch. gen. Psychiat.*, 1959, 1, 406-416.

REICHARD, SUZANNE, & TILLMAN, C. Patterns of parent-child relationships in schizophrenia. *Psychiatry*, 1950, 13, 247-257.

RENNIE, T. A. C. Prognosis in manic-depressive psychoses. *Amer. J. Psychiat.*, 1942, 98, 801-814.

RENNIE, T. A. C., SROLE, L., OPLER, M. K., & LANGNER, T. S. Urban life and mental health. *Amer. J. Psychiat.*, 1957, 113, 831-837.

RIN, H., & LIN, T. Y. Mental illness among Formosan aborigines as compared with the Chinese in Taiwan. *J. ment. Sci.*, 1962, 108, 134-146.

ROBINSON, NANCY L. M. Paired-associate learning by schizophrenic subjects under conditions of personal and impersonal reward and punishment. *Dissert. Abstr.*, 1958, 18, 1502.

RODNICK, E. H. Clinical psychology, psychopathology, and research on schizophrenia. In S. Koch (Ed.), *Psychology, a study of a science,* Vol. 5. New York: McGraw-Hill, 1963.

RODNICK, E., & GARMEZY, N. An experimental approach to the study of motivation in schizophrenia. In M. Jones (Ed.), *Nebraska symposium on motivation.* Lincoln: Univer. Nebraska Press, 1957. Pp. 104-184.

ROESSLER, R., & GREENFIELD, N. S. Incidence of somatic disease in psychiatric patients. *Psychosom. Med.*, 1961, 23, 413-419.

ROSEN, H., & KIENE, H. E. Paranoia and paranoiac reaction types. *Dis. nerv. System*, 1946, 7, 330-337. Reprinted by permission of the Physicians Postgraduate Press.

ROSENBAUM, C. P. Patient-family similarities in schizophrenia. *Arch. gen. Psychiat.*, 1961, 5, 120-126.

RUBIN, L. S. Autonomic dysfunction in psychoses. Adults and autistic children. *Arch. gen. Psychiat.*, 1962, 7, 1-14.

RUESCH, J. Psychotherapy with schizophrenics. In A. Auerback (Ed.), *Schizophrenia: an integrated approach.* New York: Ronald Press, 1959. Pp. 199-216.

RUESCH, J., BRODSKY, C., & FISCHER, A. The acute nervous breakdown. *Arch. gen. Psychiat.*, 1963, 8, 197-207.

RYCHOFF, I., DAY, JULIANA, & WYNNE, L. C. Maintenance of stereotyped roles in the families of schizophrenics. *AMA Arch. gen. Psychiat.*, 1959, 1, 93-98.

SALZMAN, L. Paranoid state—theory and therapy. *Arch. gen. Psychiat.*, 1960, 2, 679-693.

SARVIS, MARY A. Paranoid reactions: perceptual distortion as an etiological agent. *Arch. gen. Psychiat.*, 1962, 6, 157-162.

SCHEIER, I. H. Experimental results to date from the standpoint of the clinician. *Ann. N.Y. Acad. Sci.*, 1962, 93, 840-850.

SCHER, J. M. The structured ward: research method and hypothesis in a total treatment setting for schizophrenia. *Amer. Journal Orthopsychiat.*, 1958, 28, 291-299.

SCHWARTZ, D. A. A re-view of the "paranoid" concept. *Gen. Psychiat.*, 1963, 8, 349-361.

Scottish Home and Health Dept. *Scottish Health Statistics.* Edinburgh: Her Majesty's Stationery Office, 1961.

SHAFFER, L. Fear and courage in aerial combat. *J. consult. Psychol.*, 1947, 11, 137-143.

SHAGASS, C., & SCHWARTZ, M. Cerebral cortical reactivity in psychotic depression. *Arch. gen. Psychiat.*, 1962, 6, 235-242.

SHELDON, W. H., AND OTHERS. *Atlas of men: a guide for somatotyping the adult male at all ages.* New York: Harper, 1954.

SHERMAN, M. Hallucinations in children. *J. abnorm. soc. Psychol.*, 1924, 19, 165-170.

SHIELDS, J., & SLATER, E. Heredity and psychological abnormality. In H. J. Eysenck (Ed.), *Handbook of abnormal psychology.* New York: Basic Books, 1961. Pp. 298-343.

SHORE, P. A., PLETSCHER, A., TOMICH, E. G., CARLSSON, A., KUNTZMAN, R., & BRODIE, B. B. Role of brain serotonin in reserpine action. *Ann. N.Y. Acad. Sci.,* 1957, 66, 609-615.

SIMMONS, L. W. A sociologist's views on patient care. *Amer. J. Psychiat.,* 1960, 117, 385-392.

SINGER, MARGARET. Address delivered at Mt. Zion Hospital and Medical Center, San Francisco, Sept. 12, 1960. Reported in C. P. Rosenbaum, Patient-family similarities in schizophrenia. *Arch. gen. Psychiat.,* 1961, 5, 120-126.

SJÖGREN, T. The genetics of schizophrenia. In Synopses of the 2nd Int. Congr. Psychiat., Zurich, 1957. P. 129.

SLATER, E. *Psychotic and neurotic illnesses in twins.* London: Her Majesty's Stationery Office, 1953.

SLATER, E. T. O. Genetics in Psychiatry. *J. ment. Sci.,* 1944, 90, 17-35.

SOMMER, R., & OSMOND, H. The schizophrenic no-society. *Psychiatry,* 1962, 25, 244-255.

STAINBROOK, E. J. The schizophrenic, manic, and depressive behavioral reactions. *Ann. Amer. Acad. polit. Sci.,* 1953, 286, 45-54.

STENGEL, E. Recent research into suicide and attempted suicide. *Amer. J. Psychiat.,* 1962, 118, 725-727.

STEPHENS, J. H., & ASTRUP, CHRISTINA. Prognosis in "process" and "non-process" schizophrenia. *Amer. J. Psychiat.,* 1963, 119, 945-953.

SUESS, J. F. Milieu and activity therapy with chronically disturbed female patients. *Psychiat. Quart.,* 1958, 32, 1-12.

SZASZ, T. S. *The myth of mental illness: foundations of a theory of personal conduct.* New York: Harper, 1961.

TAIT, C. D., & BURNS, G. C. Involutional illnesses: a survey of 379 patients, including follow-up study of 114. *Amer. J. Psychiat.,* 1951, 108, 27-36.

THOMAS, G. C. G., & WILSON, D. C. The recognition of pre-schizophrenic states. *Va. med. Monogr.,* 1949, 76, 405-410.

TIETZE, C., LEMKAU, P., & COOPER, MARCIA. Schizophrenia, manic-depressive psychosis and social-economic status. *Amer. J. Sociol.,* 1941, 47, 167-175.

TIETZE, T. A study of mothers of schizophrenic patients. *Psychiatry,* 1949, 12, 55-65.

TOOLAN, J. M. Depression in children and adolescents. *Amer. J. Orthopsychiat.,* 1962, 32, 404-415.

TOURNEY, G., SENF, R., DUNHAM, H. W., GLEN, R. S., & GOTTLIEB, J. S. The effect of resocialization techniques on chronic schizophrenic patients. *Amer. J. Psychiat.,* 1960, 116, 993-1000.

TRAVEN, B. *The treasure of Sierra Madre.* New York: World, 1947.

U. S. National Office of Vital Statistics. Monthly vital statistics report, Vol. 10, No. 13, 1962.

U. S. Public Health Service. *Some facts about suicide.* (Publication No. 852). Washington, D. C.: U. S. Government Printing Office, 1961.

VITOLS, M. M. The significance of the higher incidence of schizophrenia in the Negro race in North Carolina. *N. C. med. J.,* 1961, 22 (4), 147-158.

VORONIN, L. G. Some results of comparative physiological investigations of higher nervous activity. *Psychol. Bull.,* 1962, 59, 161-195.

WAHL, C. W. Some antecedent factors in the family histories of 568 male schizophrenics of the United States Navy. *Amer. J. Psychiat.,* 1956, 113, 201-210.

WALKER, R. G. Some observations on the concept of "reactive" and "process" type schizophrenia. *J. clin. exp. Psychopath.,* 1962, 23, 7-10.

WEIL, ANNEMARIE P. Clinical data and dynamic consideration in certain cases of childhood schizophrenia. *Amer. J. Orthopsychiat.,* 1953, 23, 518-529.

WEISZ, S. Types of depressive reactions. *Dis. nerv. System,* 1947, 8, 212-216. Reprinted by permission of Physicians Postgraduate Press.

WENAR, C., HANDLON, M. W., & GARNER, ANN M. *Origins of psychosomatic and emotional disturbance. A study mother-child relationships.* New York: Paul B. Hoeber, 1962.

WHATMORE, G. B., & ELLIS, R. M., JR. Some neurophysiologic aspects of depressed states. *AMA Arch. gen. Psychiat.,* 1959, 1, 70-80.

WHATMORE, G. B., & ELLIS, R. M., JR. Further neurophysiologic aspects of depressed states. *Arch. gen. Psychiat.,* 1962, 6, 243-253.

WHITEMAN, M. The performance of schizophrenics on social concepts. *J. abnorm. soc. Psychol.,* 1954, 49, 266-271.

WIGGINS, E. J., & LYMAN, R. S. Manic psychosis in a Negro. *Amer. J. Psychiat.,* 1944, 100, 781-787.

WILL, O. A., JR. Human relatedness and the schizophrenic reaction. *Psychiatry,* 1959, 22, 205-223.

WILMER, H. A. *Social psychiatry in action.* Springfield, Ill.: Charles C. Thomas, 1958.

WINDER, C. L. Some psychological studies of schizophrenics. In D. D. Jackson (Ed.), *The etiology of schizophrenia.* New York: Basic Books, 1960. Pp. 191-247.

World Health Organization. Report of study group on schizophrenia. *Amer. J. Psychiat.,* 1959, 115, 865-872.

WORTIS, J. Pavlovianism and clinical psychiatry. In J. Wortis (Ed.), *Recent advances in biological psychiatry.* Vol. 4. N.Y.: Plenum Press, 1962a. Pp. 13-23.

WORTIS, J. Physiological treatment. *Amer. J. Psychiat.,* 1962b, 118, 595-599.

WORTIS, J. Psychopharmacology and physiological treatment. *Amer. J. Psychiat.,* 1963, 119, 621-626.

WYNNE, L. C., RYCKOFF, I. M., DAY, JULIANA, & HIRSCH, S. I. Pseudo-mutuality in the family relations of schizophrenia. *Psychiatry,* 1958, 21, 205-220.

YERBURY, E. C., & NEWELL, NANCY. Genetic and environmental factors in psychoses of children. *Amer. J. Psychiat.,* 1943, 100, 599-605.

ZIGLER, E., & PHILLIPS, L. Social competence and outcome in psychiatric disorder. *J. abnorm. soc. Psychol.,* 1960, 63, 264-271.

CHARACTER DISORDERS
(Personality Disorders)

chapter 9

In this chapter and the next we shall be considering reactions that stem primarily from faulty development rather than from decompensation under stress. They differ from the neuroses and the psychoses in that they tend to involve patterns of overt maladjustive behavior ("acting out") rather than mental or emotional symptoms, and the individual may even have little or no sense of distress. Occasionally head injury, epilepsy, or alcoholic intoxication plays a major role in this type of behavior, but in most cases there is no apparent organic pathology.

Personality or character disorders are currently classified under four subheadings: (a) special symptom reactions, such as stuttering and nail-biting; (b) personality pattern disturbances, which include several basic maladaptive personality types; (c) personality trait disturbances, in which the predominant feature is emotional immaturity; and (d) sociopathic personality disturbances, which include psychopathic and criminal behavior, sexual deviations, and addiction to alcohol and drugs. We shall discuss the first classification briefly, summarize the next two in chart form, and devote the rest of this chapter and the next to various socio-pathic patterns. The latter are by far the most serious in their consequences and the highest in incidence of the four groups. Fortunately, our understanding of these disorders has increased greatly in recent years, and the newer methods of treatment are proving increasingly effective.

Special Symptom Reactions

As its name suggests, this category is used where a specific single symptom is outstanding. For example, it is applicable to certain types of speech disorders which occur in the absence of organic pathology or other personality disorders. It would not be used for a speech impairment that was a symptom of conversion hysteria or for one that resulted from any organic defect such as cleft palate.

Reactions found here include stuttering, enuresis, tics, nail-biting, and compulsive gambling.

STUTTERING

Stuttering[1] involves a spasmodic blocking of certain speech sounds. It may vary from mild difficulty with the initial syllables of certain words to violent contortions and an inability to produce an initial sound at all. Typically there is a repetition of the initial syllable of some important word or phrase, as in "The b-b-b-boy took your letter" or "D-d-d-don't do that." Speech sounds which require the greatest articulatory effort, such as *b, d, s,* and *t,* are most often troublesome.

Most stutterers have many grimaces, head jerks, and bodily movements which accompany the repetition. In severe cases there may be rapid breathing, facial contortions, and a shaking of the whole body. The entire performance represents an "internal struggle" to speak. After this momentary disturbance, however, speech becomes smooth and fluent until the next stumbling block.

The stutterer's difficulty varies considerably from one situation to another. For example, most stutterers can speak normally or with fewer blocks when they are alone, when whispering or singing, and when they are with people considerably younger than themselves or with someone whom they consider to be their inferior. On the other hand, their stuttering increases in both severity and frequency in situations in which they feel inferior, embarrassed, or self-conscious. In one case, for example, a business executive rarely stuttered except in the presence of his supervisor.

Every age has had its quota of these speech sufferers. Some of the more illustrious names on the roster are Moses, Aristotle, Vergil, Demosthenes, Charles Lamb, Clara Barton, and Andrew Mellon. In the modern world, stuttering has been observed in diverse social contexts—among the Bantu of South Africa and the Polynesians of the South Pacific as well as among Oriental and Western groups (Aron, 1962; Lemert, 1962). In the United States alone there are about 1,800,000 stutterers, placing the incidence at about 1 per cent of our population. It is interesting to note that there are far more male than female stutterers. Estimates vary as to the actual sex ratio, but it would appear to be about 4 or 5 to 1. In 90 per cent of all cases the onset of stuttering occurs before the age of 6 years, with the greatest number of these between 2 and 4 years. The incidence of stuttering is considerably higher in middle- and upper-class families (Bloodstein, 1959; Despert, 1943; Johnson, 1961).

Dynamics. Stuttering has proved to be a most baffling disorder. Many explanations have been proposed.

1. *Hereditary predisposition.* Investigators adhering to this viewpoint usually assume two basic factors in the causation of stuttering—an inherited predisposition to the breakdown of speech functions under stress and some immediate stress factor that precipitates the speech dis-

---

[1]Stuttering is only one of the more common types of speech impairment which may be either organic or functional in origin.

order. Unquestionably there is a tendency for stuttering to be found in successive generations of the same family. In comparing a large group of children who stuttered with a matched group of nonstutterers, Johnson (1961) found that the children who stuttered had nine times as many parents or siblings—mostly fathers—who also stuttered. Although such findings do not prove the existence of a constitutional factor in stuttering, they certainly favor such a possibility. However, Johnson has pointed out that parents who are or have been stutterers are likely to overreact to the normal disfluent early speech of their children. This in turn would tend to make the child self-conscious and tense about his speech and could lead to actual stuttering. In general, current investigators emphasize family influences rather than genes in accounting for the fact that stuttering runs in families.

2.   *Neurological theories.*   Theories of stuttering have frequently emphasized brain damage resulting from birth injury or disease. Here it is presumed that even minimal brain damage might cause disturbances in the coordination of the motor functions of speech. In support of this viewpoint, it has been pointed out that many children have suffered from a severe infectious disease just prior to the onset of stuttering. For example, Goda (1961) has cited the case of a child who first developed stuttering following an attack of spinal meningitis at the age of 7 years 6 months. Prior to this illness his physical development and speech had been normal. For the great majority of stutterers, however, there is no evidence of brain damage. In fact, Williams (1953) has shown that the basic coordination of speech muscles is the same for both stutterers and nonstutterers. And the extensive work of Penfield and Roberts (1959) indicates that damage to cortical speech areas is much more likely to interfere with ideational processes involved in speech, such as the finding of the correct word, than to interfere with the motor coordination of speech sounds. The same would also appear to be true of damage to the brainstem, which plays a key integrative role in speech.

In the past, considerable emphasis was placed on the view that stuttering often resulted from forcing infants and children who were normally left-handed to use their right hand. This conclusion was based on the assumption that the cortical control of speech is normally located in the left cerebral hemisphere for right-handed persons and in the right hemisphere for left-handed persons. Presumably, the forced changing of handedness resulted in the disruption of cortical dominance and hence in incoordination of speech movements. Penfield and Roberts (1959), however, have shown that in the normal brain the left hemisphere controls speech for *both* right- and left-handed persons. And as Bloodstein (1959) has pointed out, stutterers as a group are not distinguished by being naturally left-handed nor has stuttering developed in the vast majority of children whose parents have changed their handedness.

3.   *Psychological theories.*   A wide range of psychological theories have been proposed to explain stuttering. Psychoanalytic theories have typically viewed stuttering as a state of arrested emotional development in which the libido has become fixed at the oral stage of development. Stuttering presumably gratifies an infantile oral need, and thus the stutterer unconsciously desires to stutter. Other theories have viewed stuttering as simply a bad habit or as a symptom of some severe emotional conflict.

For example, one theory holds that stuttering results from an approach-avoidance conflict (Sheehan, 1953; Sheehan *et al.*, 1962). According to this theory, the stutterer has somehow learned to fear the speech situation and wishes to avoid it; yet social necessity requires him to face it. Presumably he "blocks" when the two tendencies are equal in strength. Stuttering is then reinforced by reduction in fear which occurs once the stuttered word has been pronounced. Thus a vicious circle is formed in which (a) fear leads to moments of blocking in speech and (b) the actual act of stuttering terminates the specific incident and the accompanying reduction in fear tends to reinforce the stuttering. Sheehan has also suggested that the nature of the reinforcement in stuttering varies markedly from individual to individual. For example, in some cases the individual may gain tension reduction by feelings of shame and guilt, which follow the act of stuttering and punish him for his failure. Here the self-punishment is a form of atonement for his failure, and hence tends to be tension-reducing. It would also appear that stuttering tends to be reinforced with

BEFORE   DURING   AFTER

In a study investigating stuttering as an approach-avoidance conflict, stutterers were asked to draw whatever they felt most adequately represented their behavior before, during, and after a moment of stuttering. The drawings of one subject, reproduced above, clearly show his high tension just before and during the block and his relief afterward. Guilt, shame, dejection, and anger were also frequently expressed, and in many cases the feelings continued after the block (Sheehan et al., 1962).

experience as the individual comes to view himself as a stutterer—as "I am a stutterer" becomes a permanent part of his self-concept.

From his intensive studies of stuttering among children, Johnson (1959, 1961) has concluded that stuttering develops when the child has an overly critical listener during the early crucial period of his speech development. He has pointed out that concerned parents often mistake hesitancy and repetitiveness—a natural part of speech development in 3- and 4-year-olds—for the beginning of stuttering. The parents then worry about the child's speech, attempt to correct his mistakes, "tighten up" when he is speaking, and generally communicate their doubts and worries to the child. Their behavior causes the child to develop doubts and fears concerning his ability to express himself, and real stuttering begins. This pattern is then repeatedly reinforced by fears and actual speech difficulties in social situations. In essence, the normal nonfluency of the young child—which Johnson refers to as *primary stuttering*—is transformed into *secondary* or *actual stuttering*. Johnson's approach appears to be strongly supported by the fact that the child who gets by this early critical period of speech development without undue

difficulty is unlikely to become a stutterer at a later age. This approach also provides an explanation of how approach-avoidance conflicts in relation to speaking in social situations may be generated. Further research is needed to ascertain the full applicability of Johnson's viewpoint (Wingate, 1962).

All of us have probably experienced blocking of thought and speech in stage fright or in a situation where we have had to make unexpected introductions. In these situations it is probably safe to say that we were self-conscious and tense. Defective responses under these conditions are very common. We may generalize here and say that any factors (self-consciousness, tenseness, fear, parental concern) which increase the complexity of the situation beyond the speaker's power to cope with it will make for defective responses. These defective responses may be evidenced in the blocking of thought processes, in excessive perspiration and other physiological emotional changes, and in tremors and general motor incoordination, including the phenomena of stuttering.

Children in the process of learning the difficult motor coordinations involved in speech are especially vulnerable to such disrupting factors, but even in later life temporary stuttering is sometimes precipitated by severe stress which leads to an intense undermining of security and adequacy. For example, soldiers who have undergone prolonged or acute battle experience may begin to stutter. The vicious circle effect does not appear to operate here, however, and as the individual's overall psychological integration improves, his stuttering ceases and his speech becomes normal again.

Although most stutterers suffer from feelings of anxiety, self-consciousness, and inferiority in social situations, they do not appear to differ significantly from nonstutterers in personality make-up. In a review of the available research findings, Sheehan (1958) found that stutterers differed from nonstutterers only in showing a somewhat lower level of aspiration, which he considered to be an effect rather than a cause of stuttering.

Treatment and prognosis.   It is vitally important that the treatment of stuttering begin early. Early treatment may consist largely of eliminating environmental factors which are placing an excessive nervous strain on the child. Often stuttering can be arrested at this point by counseling the mother and helping her to put therapeutic suggestions into effect in the home. The family can help the child feel more secure and adequate and can avoid making an issue of his hesitations and repetitions in speaking (Johnson, 1961). In this way, the child can be helped to gain faith in himself as a speaker and to anticipate normal speech instead of failure.

Parents sometimes think stuttering is a bad habit that the child will outgrow. Available data indicate that this is not true—probably less than 10 per cent of the children who stutter overcome their difficulty without assistance.

Therapy in later life is usually much more difficult, for by then the vicious circle has extended from the home to schoolmates and friends. Frequently, too, the patient has adjusted himself to his stuttering and comes to view it as an undesirable but essential aspect of his personality—in the same way that a person might view an exceptionally large nose. The author knows a wealthy dentist who is a chronic stutterer but who says he has grown accustomed to his stuttering and that it doesn't bother him any more.

This unemotional acceptance is rarely seen during childhood and adolescence, however, when the stutterer has difficulty in obtaining the respect of others and in achieving group identification and may be made the butt of jokes. And too often, because of his incapacity, he is slighted in educational opportunities. He may not be given a chance to speak in class or to take public speaking. His stuttering may also be a severe handicap in his relations with the other sex. The following plea for help, written by a high-school boy, reveals the emotional intensity which may center around this handicap.

"I have stuttered since childhood, and it is spoiling my whole life. Is there any hope that I can overcome this affliction? Isn't there anything that can be done for boys like me?" (Greene, 1946, p. 120)

Current treatment of stuttering in adolescents and adults is aimed primarily at the development of a feeling of adequacy in speech situations. Specific practice in articulation and phonation to break up repetitive habits and ensure proper speech patterns may also be necessary. And with adults as well as children, it may be necessary to alleviate tension-producing factors in the environment before individual therapy can hope to succeed. Although tranquilizing drugs may reduce the stutterer's tension in social situations and hence alleviate his stuttering, they have not proved sufficient as the only form of treatment. Again an integrated biological, psychological, and sociological treatment program appears most likely to be effective.[1]

Although adequate statistics are lacking, it would appear that most stutterers can be either completely relieved of their symptoms or greatly helped by proper treatment. Subsequent psychic shocks or stresses, however, may lead to a reappearance of the stuttering. In a case which the author treated for over a year with successful results, the patient would have occasional quarrels with his wife, after which she would leave him and return temporarily to her mother. On each occasion the patient's stuttering returned. In stuttering, as in other forms of maladjustment, a long-range follow-up program is often essential to ensure the effectiveness of treatment.

---

[1] For a more detailed discussion of the treatment of stuttering, the reader is referred to Barbara (1962).

NAIL-BITING

At one time or another probably about a fifth of all children and adolescents bite their fingernails. The incidence of nail-biting appears to be higher than this among stutterers, children reared in institutions, and individuals confronted with stressful demands. The incidence of nail-biting is highest during the adolescent period and decreases thereafter. In a consecutive series of nearly 7000 naval recruits, L. A. Pennington (1945) found that about 1 male in 4 between the ages of 16 and 18 revealed this habit, whereas at the age of 30 the ratio had dropped to 1 in 9, and at 37 to only 1 in 12. Although about as many girls as boys bite their nails during childhood, males outnumber females at later ages, apparently because of the greater social disapproval of nail-biting among young women and the value of well-kept nails in attracting members of the other sex.

Nail-biting has been variously explained as (a) a substitute for masturbation, (b) a turning inward of hostility, (c) a fixation at the oral stage of development, and (d) a method of tension reduction. Nail-biters themselves most often explain their habit as resulting from a desire to keep busy, use up excess energy, and ease anxiety connected with stress (Coleman and McCalley, 1948b). The greater the felt tension, the more frequent and persistent the nail-biting. As a group, nail-biters are more anxious than non-nail-biters and more inclined toward intropunitiveness in the handling of hostility (Coleman and McCalley, 1948a; Coleman and Seret, 1950). The author has dealt with several cases in which the patients rarely bit their nails except when they felt extremely hostile toward their parents, usually as a result of parental overdomination. In general, it would appear that nail-biting represents either (a) a means of discharging anxiety in stressful situations by giving the individual "something to do," or (b) the discharge of hostility in an intropunitive and safe way. In either event, the nail-biting represents a learned means of tension reduction.

The treatment of nail-biting usually involves psychotherapy and need not be elaborated upon here. In many cases, tranquilizing drugs are also helpful, especially in getting the individual through some particularly difficult stress period.

It is generally agreed that the symptomatic treatment of nail-biting by restraint, bitter applications, and punishment is of little value.

TICS

A tic is a persistent, intermittent muscle twitch or spasm, usually limited to a localized muscle group. The term is used rather broadly to include blinking the eyes, twitching the mouth, licking the lips, shrugging the shoulders, twisting the neck, clearing the throat, blowing through the nostrils, grimacing, and many other motions. In some instances, as in clearing the throat, the individual may be aware of his tic. Usually, however, he performs the act so habitually that he is completely unaware of its occurrence. In fact, he may not even be aware that he has a tic unless someone brings it to his attention. Tics occur most frequently between the ages of 6 and 14 but also are fairly common among adults.

Although tics may have an organic basis, the great majority are psychological in origin, representing a means of reducing tension. In learning-theory terms, the tic is a learned habit which has been continually reinforced by its anxiety-reducing properties (Yates, 1960).

Many of us show nervous mannerisms or tics when we feel embarrassed or self-conscious in social situations. It is common for a public speaker to clear his throat repeatedly or to cough before he begins to speak. Ordinarily, this response is not carried over to social situations where he feels more confident and secure. In the case of the ticquer, however, the response tends to occur in a wide range of social situations and may even occur when he is alone if he feels under tension. Unfortunately, tics often lead to a further undermining of the individual's feelings of security and adequacy because they are so readily noticed and commented upon by others. A young man of the author's acquaintance was thinking of giving up teaching because he had been told by several well-meaning friends that he had a very noticeable twitching of the mouth which occurred persistently throughout his lectures. He had been unaware of this muscle twitch, and even after it was brought to his attention, he could not tell when it took place. However, he became acutely self-conscious during his lectures and continuously worried about the occurrence of his tic. As a result, his general level of tension increased and so did the frequency of the tic—a vicious circle had been established.

The treatment of tics involves psychotherapy directed toward more effective personality adjustment and toward the reduction of the patient's general tension level or of the tension associated with given situations. Here, too, tranquilizing drugs, which tend to reduce the tension level, are often an important treatment aid. Attempts to treat tics by a method of conditioned inhibition have had inconsistent results (Yates, 1960; Jones, 1960).

In some instances hypnosis has been used to change the tic from an easily noticed area to the foot or some other region where others cannot see it. Although such manipulations may be of practical value in some cases, they treat symptoms rather than the basic cause which led to the symptom. The latter requires appropriate psychotherapy.

ENURESIS

The term *enuresis* refers to the habitual involuntary discharge of urine after the age of three years. It may occur during the day but most commonly occurs during the night (bedwetting). The childhood enuretic characteristically urinates during deep sleep, while the adult enuretic does so in a light sleep (Ditman and Blinn, 1955; Pierce *et al.*, 1961). Among young adults, the enuresis frequently occurs in conjunction with dreams in which the patient imagines he is urinating in a toilet only to awaken and find he has wet the bed. Occasionally these dreams are sexual in nature, with the urination apparently closely related to sexual satisfaction. The enuresis may vary in incidence from regular nightly occurrences to occasional instances when the individual is under considerable stress. Commonly it occurs from two to five times a week.

There are an estimated 2 million or more enuretic children in the United States (Muellner, 1960; Tapia *et al.*, 1960). The number of enuretics among the adult population is not known but is probably higher than is generally suspected. Adler (1959) reported an incidence of about 1 per cent in military recruits and found that enuresis accounted for about one quarter of the neuropsychiatric discharges during recruit training. Since these men had already passed induction screening, the incidence among them was probably much lower than among the general population. It is generally believed that enuresis is considerably more common among males than among females. The incidence of enuresis declines markedly with age, and aside from cases involving organic pathology, the disorder seems to be relatively infrequent after the age of 30.

Dynamics. Enuresis may result from a variety of organic conditions including brain pathology and disturbances in the genitourinary system. The great majority of cases, however, appear to result from psychological rather than organic causes.

Among children, enuresis has been explained variously as (a) an indirect expression of anxiety, (b) an attempt to show a need for parental attention and help, (c) an expression of hostility, often unconscious, against the parents, (d) an indication of immaturity and emotional disturbance, and (e) the result of inadequate bladder capacity. Most investigators have emphasized disturbed family relationships and emotional maladjustment in the background of enuretic children—particularly conditions leading to sustained anxiety and/or hostility. For example, a child may regress to bed-wetting when a new baby enters the family and replaces him as the center of attention; or he may resort to bed-wetting to "get even" with his parents when he finds that such behavior is very annoying and upsetting to them. It may be pointed out, however, that it is often difficult to ascertain whether the emotional difficulties observed in enuretic children are a cause of, a consequence of, or independent of their enuresis. In addition, Tapia *et al.* (1960) found no significant differences in emotional adjustment between 83 enuretic children and a group of 824 children who were not enuretic. Relevant here, too, is Muellner's (1960) finding of a high incidence of restricted bladder capacity (in relation to age and stature) among enuretic children. It would thus appear that diverse etiological factors may be involved in childhood enuresis and that further research in this area is clearly indicated.

Although few recent investigations deal with the problem of enuresis among young adults, earlier studies clearly indicated its close association with other psychopathology. In a study of 150 enuretic patients, Levine (1943) found psychiatric abnormalities in 83 per cent. Similarly, Goldman and Bergman (1945), in a study of 137 adult male enuretics, reported that significant psychopathology was present in every case. Pierce and Lipcon (1956) found a close relationship between enuresis and sleepwalking, reporting that approximately 62 per cent of sleepwalkers are enuretics and that 27 per cent of enuretics are sleepwalkers. Particularly outstanding in all of these studies was the high incidence of emotional immaturity, psychoneurosis, and mental retardation. These findings are in general agreement with those of Hallgren (1956) who made an extensive study of enuretics in Stockholm, Sweden, and reported a high incidence of immaturity, emotional disturbances, and behavior abnormalities.

In connection with mental retardation, it is of interest to note that Thorne (1944) found a direct relationship between incidence of enuresis and degree of retardation: approximately 4 per cent of mild retardates were enuretic as compared with 13 per cent of moderate retardates and 84 per cent of those who were severely retarded. Among those of average or superior intelligence, however, there would appear to be no significant relationship between intelligence level and enuresis.

In general, adult enuretics seem to come from disturbed family backgrounds, to be emotionally immature, and to be of lower than average intelligence. Those who usually have adequate bladder control but have temporary enuretic episodes during periods of acute stress seem to be high in neurotic traits, while chronic enuretics appear high in sociopathic traits such as general inadequacy.

Treatment. The treatment of enuresis varies with the age, personality make-up, and life situation of the patient. In general, treatment methods fall into three categories: training procedures, drug therapy, and psychotherapy.

In the past, training procedures have depended heavily upon punitive measures and upon restricting the intake of fluids prior to bedtime. In one widely used method, an electrical device shocks the child when he urinates in his clothing or in bed. Although this method appears to be effective in many instances, several investigators have pointed out that its use with children who are emotionally upset or lack adequate bladder capacity is likely to lead to more problems than it solves (Adler, 1959; Muellner, 1960).

Using a less punitive conditioned response approach, Davidson and Douglass (1950) treated 20 cases ranging in age from 5 to 15 years with an electrified mattress that rang an alarm at the first few drops of urine—thus awakening the patient and eliciting a reflex inhibition of micturation. With this treatment, 14 cases were cured and 6 improved. These investigators also noted that enuresis had tended to impede emotional growth and social adjustment and that relief from this symptom led to positive personality changes. The results obtained by later investigators using similar conditioned response procedures range from 50 per cent cured and 24 per cent improved (Wickes, 1958) to 88 per cent cured and 5 per cent improved (Gillison and Skinner, 1958). Although some concern has been expressed about the relatively high number of relapses among patients treated by conditioned response methods, Jones (1960) has found that the large majority of patients who suffer relapses respond well to further treatment.

Considerable doubt has been cast on the popular technique of restricting fluid intake prior to bedtime. In fact, Nichols (1956) and Muellner (1960) have advocated the forcing of fluids during the day to enlarge bladder capacity and foster control of daytime urinary output. Both investigators have concluded that practice in holding urine during the day helps to achieve both daytime and nighttime bladder control. In treating a series of 30 enuretic children, Muellner utilized this method with 100 per cent success.

A number of drugs have been used in the treatment of enuresis. These include tranquilizers as well as drugs which tend to inhibit reflex bladder emptying. Although some measure of success has been reported—particularly in cases where earlier enuresis has reappeared under conditions of acute stress—it would appear that such drug treatment is at best an emergency or auxiliary measure (Adler, 1959; Jones, 1960; Muellner, 1960).

Although the potentialities of conditioned response and drug treatment of enuretics have not been fully explored, it would appear that psychotherapy and sociotherapy are often important aspects of the overall treatment program. With short-range psychotherapy Adler (1959) reported a remission rate of 85 per cent among military recruits who had regressed to enuretic behavior under the stress of military training. In chronic adult cases, however, the prognosis is less favorable. Such cases have often proved resistant to a variety of prior treatment procedures, and the enuresis is typically part of a more pervasive pattern of personality immaturity and maladjustment.

COMPULSIVE GAMBLING

There are an estimated 6,000,000 compulsive gamblers in the United States who lose some 20 billion dollars each year (Bloch, 1961; *Time,* 1961). Aside from the tremendous number of hours spent in gambling rather than productive activity, these individuals suffer from a disorder which disrupts their entire lives. Their compulsive gambling leads to neglect of their families, to difficulties in their work, and often to illegal methods of obtaining money with which to continue gambling. In general, it would appear that the compulsive gambler is higher than average in intelligence and has completed one or more years of college. He is usually married and often has a responsible managerial or professional position which provides a reasonably good income. Apparently far more men than women are compulsive gamblers.

Dynamics. Since very little research has been done in this area, the dynamics of compulsive gambling are not yet well understood. Often it would appear that the individual who later becomes a compulsive gambler wins a substantial sum of money the first time he is introduced to gambling. Somehow this leads him to the unrealistic belief that he can become rich through further gambling—that he can become a gambler rather than work for a living. Despite his awareness that the odds are against him and despite the fact that he never repeats his early performance, he continues to gamble fervently. In his efforts to finance his gambling, he often

dissipates family savings and borrows from friends and loan companies. Eventually, he may resort to embezzlement or other illegal means of obtaining money, feeling sure that his luck will change and that he will be able to repay what he has taken.

The question then arises as to the personality traits which appear to be associated with compulsive gambling. Psychoanalysts and other writers have described the gambler as being immature, hostile, passive-dependent, rebellious, obsessive, masochistic, magical in his thinking, and prone to acting out his impulses (Bergler, 1957; Bloch, 1961; Galdston, 1951; Greenson, 1947; Lindner, 1950). In a study of 30 men who had been compulsive gamblers and had become members of Gamblers Anonymous, Rosten (1961) found many of these traits to apply. His subjects proved to be rebellious, unconventional individuals who did not seem to understand fully the ethical norms of society. Half of the group described themselves as "hating regulations." Of the 30 men, 12 had served time in jail for embezzlement and other crimes directly connected with their gambling.

On a superficial level, the compulsive gambler tends to be quite sociable and is often socially facile and responsive. However, his social relationships are usually manipulative and shallow. In addition, his gambling activities tend to alienate him from family and friends. Whereas they view his gambling as unethical and disruptive, he is likely to see himself as a man taking "calculated risks" to build a lucrative business. Often he feels alone and resentful that others do not understand his activities. Apparently the only way he can vindicate his assumptions and life style is by further gambling. This, in turn, leads to further personal, financial, and often legal difficulties, and the problem is compounded. Increasingly, the only way out of his difficulties seems to be the way he got in—gambling.

Rosten also found compulsive gamblers unrealistic in their thinking and prone to seek highly stimulating situations. In the gambler's own words, he "loves excitement" and "needs action." For him life must be highly stimulating and risky to be really satisfying. Although these former compulsive gamblers admitted that they had known objectively the all-but-impossible odds they faced while gambling, they had felt that these odds did not apply to them. Often they had had unshakeable feelings that they were "special" and that "Tonight is my night." Typically they had also followed the so-called Monte Carlo fallacy that after so many losses, they were bound to win—that their turn was coming up and they would hit it big. Similarly, they had understood the consequences of illegal activity to secure funds with which to gamble but had not believed that they could lose and be unable to replace the funds they were taking. Many of these former gamblers discussed the extent to which they had "fooled" themselves by elaborate rationalizations. For example, one gambler described his previous rationalization as covering all contingencies: "When I was ahead, I could gamble because I was playing with others' money. When I was behind, I had to get even. When I was even, I hadn't lost any money." (Rosten, 1961, p. 67)

Since Rosten studied men who had stopped gambling, the question arises as to how his subjects differ from those who continue to gamble. He suggests the probability that the compulsive gambler who remains active is more egocentric, unconventional, unrealistic, and less insightful than the one who is able to stop. It is of interest to note that within a few months after they were studied, 13 of Rosten's 30 subjects either had returned to heavy gambling, had started to drink excessively, or had not been heard from and were presumed to be gambling again. Very little has been written about the compulsive woman gambler, and since Rosten's subjects were all men we can only speculate as to the extent to which his findings would generalize to women gamblers.

Treatment. Although the effectiveness of psychotherapy with compulsive gamblers has not been evaluated, it would appear to be the treatment of choice. Evidently membership in Gamblers Anonymous is also a valuable therapeutic aid. This organization was founded in 1957 in Los Angeles by two compulsive gamblers who found they could help each other control their gambling by talking about their past experiences. Since then groups have been formed in most major cities in the United States. The groups are modeled after Alcoholics Anonymous, and the only requirement for membership is an expressed desire to stop gambling. In group discussions members share their experiences and try to help each other gain insight into the irrationality of their gambling and realize the inevitable consequences if they continue to gamble. Members consider it their obligation to help each other when a member feels he cannot control himself or has a relapse. Gamblers Anonymous has no policy for influencing legislation with regard to gambling but emphasizes the view that each gambler must take personal responsibility for his actions.

In summary, these special symptom reactions are not ordinarily incapacitating, although they may be aggravated by minor stresses. Their treatment is similar to that for other disorders of psychological origin, with emphasis on the development of personal maturity and competence in dealing with the problems of living. Typically, even without psychotherapy, these individuals tend to improve somewhat as they grow older.

Antisocial (Psychopathic) Reaction[1]

Antisocial personalities are not classifiable as mentally retarded, neurotic, or psychotic. Their outstanding characteristic is a marked lack of ethical or moral development, with an inability to follow approved modes of behavior. They are frequently in trouble, profit little from experience or punishment, and maintain no real loyalties to any person, group, or code. Such individuals are often called *psychopathic* personalities.

The incidence of antisocial personality is difficult to estimate, for included here are a mixed group of individuals varying from unprincipled businessmen, shyster lawyers, quack doctors, high-pressure evangelists, and crooked politi-

---

[1]In the American Psychiatric Association classification, antisocial reaction, dyssocial reaction, sexual deviation, and addiction to alcohol or drugs are all listed as subcategories of the more general reaction type, *sociopathic personality disturbance.*

	Basic maladaptive personality types, often with physical abnormalities. Highly resistant to therapy; under stress likely to decompensate into regular psychosis.
Inadequate personality	General inadaptability, ineptness, poor judgment, lack of physical and emotional stamina, and social incompatibility. Inadequate response to intellectual, emotional, social, and physical demands.
Schizoid personality	Coldness, aloofness, avoidance of social contact or emotional closeness. Inability to express hostility, fearfulness; avoidance of competition; daydreams of omnipotence. Shy and withdrawn as children; at puberty become more introvertive, seclusive, often eccentric.
Cyclothymic personality	Extrovertive tendencies with alternating elation and sadness or persistent euphoria or depression without adequate external cause.

cians to imposters, rapists, and prostitutes. Few of these individuals find their way into mental hospitals: only about 1 per cent of all first admissions are so classified. A much larger number are in penal institutions, but the majority, although they are constantly in conflict with authority, manage to get by outside of institutions. This reaction is considered to be much more common among males than females.

SYMPTOMS

Antisocial personalities are typically intelligent, spontaneous, and very likable on first acquaintance. Yet they seem to live in a series of present moments without real consideration for past or future and with callous disregard for the happiness of others. Typically they are emotionally immature, irresponsible, impulsive, and lacking in judgment. They have an ability to rationalize their behavior so that to them at least it appears reasonable and justified.

Two 18-year-old youths went to visit a girl at her home. Finding no one there, they broke into the house, damaged a number of paintings and other furnishings, and stole a quantity of liquor and a television set.

They disposed of the latter to a mutual friend for a small sum of money. Upon their apprehension by the police, they at first denied the entire venture and then later insisted that it was all a "practical joke." They did not consider their behavior particularly inappropriate, nor did they think any sort of restitution for damage was called for.

Perhaps it will be profitable to summarize the wide range of symptoms which antisocial personalities may display. Not all of these are characteristic of a given case; rather they constitute symptoms which are considered indicative of this personality type (Cleckley, 1959; Darling, 1945; Heaton-Ward, 1963; Thorne, 1959; Wegrocki, 1961; Wirt *et al.*, 1962).

1. *Inadequate conscience development.* Inability to understand and accept ethical values, except on a verbal level. Marked discrepancy between level of intelligence and conscience development—"moral moron." Often deceives others by glib verbalizations about and seeming adherence to high standards of morality.

2. *Egocentric, impulsive, and irresponsible, with low frustration tolerance and poor judgment.* Prone to thrill seeking, deviant sexual patterns, and other unconventional behavior. Pathological liar with callous disregard for needs

PERSONALITY TRAIT DISTURBANCES

	Cases of personality immaturity or maldevelopment resulting in inability to maintain emotional equilibrium and independence under stress. Stress likely to bring regression rather than psychosis.
Emotionally unstable personality	Excitability and ineffectiveness in face of minor stress; fluctuating emotional attitudes which upset interpersonal relations and impair judgment. Poorly controlled hostility, guilt, and anxiety.
Passive-aggressive personality	Deep dependency, usually accompanied by morbid resentment. May take form of (a) passive dependence with helplessness, indecisiveness, need to cling to others; (b) passive aggressiveness with expression of aggression through pouting, stubbornness, procrastination, and passive obstructionism; or (c) active aggressiveness with irritability, tantrums, and destructiveness.
Compulsive personality	Rigidity, overinhibition, overconscientiousness; obsessive concern over conformity to standards; inability to relax.

and rights of others. Has learned to take from others rather than to earn what he wants.

3. *Hedonism combined with unrealistic goals.* Inability to forego immediate pleasures for future gains and long-range goals. Lives in the present without realistic consideration of past or future. External realities used for immediate personal gratification. Unable to withstand tedium and prone to frequent changing of jobs. However, marked discrepancy between actual status and ego ideal. Almost insatiable need to "be somebody" and "to have the best" but uses self-defeating means.

4. *Lack of anxiety or guilt.* Tends to act out tensions and anxieties rather than to worry them out. Often hostile, aggressive behavior toward others with little or no sense of guilt. Lack of anxiety and guilt combined with appearance of sincerity and candor may enable psychopath to avoid suspicion and detection for stealing and other illegal activities.

5. *Inability to profit from mistakes.* Tends not to learn from ordinary life experiences or punishment though may become adroit in manipulating and exploiting people and escaping punishment. Often behaves as if he is somehow immune from the consequences of his actions.

6. *Ability to put up a good front to impress*

and exploit others. Often a charming, likable personality with a disarming manner and an ability to win the liking and friendship of others. Typically good sense of humor and generally optimistic outlook. Prone to social climbing.

7. *Defective social relationships.* Usually cynical, unsympathetic, ungrateful, and remorseless in his dealings with others. No close friends or loyalty to other persons or groups. Unable to understand love from others or to give it in return.

8. *Rejection of constituted authority and discipline.* Behaves as if social regulations did not apply to him. Often shows considerable hostility toward constituted authority which may show itself in impulsive, hostile criminal acts. Frequently has history of difficulties with educational and/or law enforcement authorities. Many times drifts into criminal activities but is not typically a calculating professional criminal.

9. *Quick ability to rationalize and project the blame for his socially disapproved behavior.* Lacks insight into his own behavior. Lies readily even when it is obvious he will be found out.

10. *Irritating, disappointing, and distressing to others.* Is frequently a great burden upon family and friends and creates a great deal of unhappiness for others. Often promises to change but rarely does so permanently—incorrigible.

Many of these behavior patterns are also frequently found in varying degrees in neurotic and psychotic behavior. In the antisocial personality, however, they are more pronounced and occur apart from any definite neurosis or psychosis. Below is a letter written by a young inmate of a penal institution to a girl whom he had never seen, with utter disregard for his current circumstances, his past, and his probable future. It is a good example of the vivid imagination, wishful fantasy, impulsivity, and emotional immaturity and instability characteristic of the antisocial personality.

"DEAR JUNE,

"Of course you know my cousin, David! Well, I had a long talk with him about beautiful women. He said that you are the most beautiful thing on earth. The way he described you he made me think that I've known you all my life. You must be a second Jean Harlow. I've dreamed about you, from the very first day he told me. I'd give a million dollars to have you in my arms. Sometimes I think I am in love with you although I've never seen you. Maybe someday I will see you. June, my darling, I love you. I love you with all my heart and soul. Please believe me?

"June, my love, although I've never seen you I would like you to be my wife. I have lots of money and life would be a bowl of roses for you. I know that you will never regret it. Because I will make you the happiest woman on this earth. . . .

"I am six feet tall, weight is 190 lbs., light complexion, sharp and always in the chips. I can take you anywhere you desire. Money doesn't mean a thing to me. You can have anything your little soft, warm heart desires. I own a cafe on Seventh Avenue. Business is very successful. Money flows in like a bristling brook. I have an apartment and a . . . Chrysler convertible sedan, black with white-wall tires. Everything works by the push of a button. Life will be a luxurious one for you.

"In the winter, I vacation in Miami, Florida. In the summer, I go to Canada. If I can have you as my companion and later, my sweetheart and finally my wife, we both could enjoy these luxuries together.

Love,

(Signed) JAMES"

(Banay, 1943, p. 171)

One of the most interesting types of persons found in the category of antisocial personality is the impostor, whose achievements are often extremely dramatic and worthy of better causes. This is well brought out in the following case.

One of the boldest impostors of recent times was Ferdinand Waldo Demara, Jr. As an adolescent, he ran away from a rather tragic family situation and after unsuccessful attempts first to become a Trappist monk and then to teach school, he joined the army. Soon thereafter he went AWOL, joined the navy, and was assigned to duty on a destroyer during World War II. Here, by a ruse, he got hold of some navy stationery with which he managed to obtain the transcript of college grades of an officer who was on leave. He then "doctored" this transcript by substituting his own name and adding some courses; when photostated, it looked so impressive that he used it to apply for a commission. While waiting for his commission to come through, he amused himself by obtaining other records, including the full credentials of a Dr. French, who had received a Ph.D. degree in psychology from Harvard. Informed during a visit to Norfolk that he could expect his commission as soon as a routine security check was completed, he realized that such a check would surely expose him. Under cover of darkness, he left his navy clothes on the end of a pier with a note that "this was the only way out."

Now that Demara was "dead"—drowned in the oily waters off Norfolk—he became Dr. French. He obtained an appointment as Dean of Philosophy in a small Canadian college and taught courses in general, industrial, and abnormal psychology. Eventually, however, he had a disagreement with his superior and reluctantly left.

During this period he had become friends with a physician by the name of Joseph Cyr and had learned a considerable amount about the practice of medicine from him during the cold winter months when neither man had much to occupy his time. Interested in the possibility of getting a license to practice in the States, the trusting doctor had given Demara a complete packet including baptism and confirmation certificates, school records, and his license to practice medicine in Canada.

Using these credentials, Demara now obtained a commission as lieutenant in the Royal Canadian Navy. His first assignment was to take sick call each morning at the base. To help solve his problem of lack of knowledge in the field, he went to his superior officer and told him there had been a request for a rule-of-thumb guide for people in lumber camps, where physicians are not usually immediately available. His superior cooperatively compiled a small booklet which Demara then used faithfully as his guide. He also studied medical books and evidently picked up considerable additional medical knowledge. In any event, when later assigned as medical officer aboard a destroyer in the combat zone in Korea, he successfully performed a number of difficult operations. When his ship was sent to Japan for refitting, an eager young press information officer seized on Dr. Cyr's exploits and gave them the full treatment. His copy was released to the civilian press and the "miracle doctor" became world famous. But the publicity proved to be his undoing, for it led to queries to the real Dr. Joseph Cyr as to whether the physician mentioned in the press releases was a relative, and when Dr. Cyr saw the newspaper picture, he was shocked to find that it was his old friend.

Dropped from the Canadian Navy without fanfare —largely because he had managed to get a license to practice medicine in England and was now a licensed physician—Demara went through a difficult period. Wherever he went, he was soon recognized, and he lost job after job. He managed to work for a year at a state school for retarded children and did so well that he received a promotional transfer to a state hospital for the criminally insane. Here he found that the patients seemed to be attracted to him and that he was able to communicate with them. The experience began to bother him and he started to drink heavily and eventually resigned.

One morning after a prolonged drinking bout, he woke up in a Southern city and realized his drinking was getting out of hand. He joined the local chapter of Alcoholics Anonymous as Ben W. Jones, whose credentials he had acquired along the way. With the help of sympathetic friends in Alcoholics Anonymous and a few fraudulent references obtained by ingenious methods, he was hired as guard in a state penitentiary. Here he did a remarkable job, instituting a number of badly needed reforms in the maximal security block. Again he found himself able to communicate with the men, and he was promoted to assistant warden of maximal security. Ironically, one of his reform measures was to ask the townspeople to contribute old magazines, and before long one of the prisoners read the issue of *Life* which contained his picture and case history and recognized the new assistant warden.

Trying to get away lest he wind up as a prisoner in

the same penitentiary, Demara was jailed in a nearby state and given considerable publicity but eventually released. Some time later he telephoned the author from whose book this material is adapted to say, "I'm on the biggest caper of them all. Oh, I wish I could tell you." (Adapted from Crichton, 1959)

Nazi Field Marshal Goering, who was convicted as a war criminal and sentenced to death following the downfall of Germany in World War II, also showed many of the traits typical of the antisocial personality.

"Hermann Goering was a constitutional psychopath and his make-up was characterized by the plus and minus qualities of this dual type of personality. He was intelligent, forceful, persuasive, genial, colorful, ambitious, egotistical, uninhibited, unscrupulous, ruthless, bizarre, and exhibitionistic. He was described by Sir Neville Henderson as a blackguard but not a damn blackguard. He was known to the German people as 'Our Hermann' and as 'Iron Hermann.' Hess called him 'The Bull' and his party enemies called him 'The Blood Swiller.' When under treatment for morphinism at the asylum at Langbro, Sweden, he was considered 'an extremely dangerous asocial hysteric.'

"Goering had a better family background than most of his Nazi associates. His father had been Governor of German Southwest Africa and Resident Minister at Haiti. Hermann attended several boarding schools but he was bored and restless till he got to the Military Academy, where he settled down to his studies. He entered the army as an infantryman but he took flying lessons surreptitiously and got himself transferred to the Air Force against the wishes of his superior officers. He was a courageous and impetuous flyer and after the death of Richthofen he took charge of The Flying Circus.

"At the close of the First World War Goering went to Sweden where he worked as a mechanic and as a civil aviator. He married a wealthy woman and was able to return to Germany and enroll at the University of Munich. In Munich he met Hitler and joined the Nazi movement. His adventurous spirit persisted and he was wounded in the Munich Putsch. He fled to Austria and later to Italy. After the amnesty he returned to Germany and when Hitler came to power he joined him with number-two rank in the Nazi Party. He became President of the Reichstag, Premier of Prussia, Chief of the Prussian Police, Head of the State Secret Police, Chief Forester of the Reich, Air

Minister and Commander-in-Chief of the Air Force. He was made a General Field-marshall and later a Reichsmarshall.

"Goering's manner of living is described as 'Byzantine splendor' and as 'piratical splendor.' He built a pretentious country home near Berlin and furnished it magnificently with tapestries and paintings and antiques. He had a private zoo. He required his servants to address his wife as Hohe Frau, thus giving her the distinction of nobility. He felt that the Germans liked his display of luxury—that it gave food for their imagination and gave the people something to think about. Goering was given to exhibitionism and he had a passion for uniforms, gold braid, medals, and decorations. Because of his large collection of uniforms he was characterized as Public Clothes Horse No. 1. Facetiously it was said that he wore an admiral's uniform to take a bath. Among his uniforms was a mailed costume of the ancient Teutonic type. On a hunting expedition he once wore a bearskin and a Wagnerian headgear and he carried a spear. One writer says of Goering: 'My first impression was of being alone in a vast gold and blue room, with a man of average height, resembling a fat Caesar, standing at the end of the room beside his desk, girding an imperial robe about him, at his feet a sleeping lioness. Belasco couldn't have done a better job of the setting. . . . Back of Goering sunlight streamed golden through a long window between velvet draperies that matched his dressing gown. The nine-months-old lioness, Caesarin, crouched at his side in golden sunlight, in splendid contrast to the blue gown. Directly opposite me when I entered the room was a giant swastika done in blue and gold tile mosaic.' Goering's lion cubs, according to the writer, were a part of the theatrical setting and they were exchanged at the zoo when they grew too large for pets. They were always named Caesar or Caesarin. Goering would strut and swagger in private and public. In political rallies he made himself a flamboyant master of pomp and pageantry. He was an exhibitionist in the psychopathic pattern.

"Goering was coarse and gross. He was a Gargantuan eater and drinker. He was ribald in jest. He laughed uproariously when his pet lion urinated on a lady's dress. He once horrified his men and women guests at his country estate by having a bull and a cow mate before them. Personally he enjoyed the spectacle and declared that it was an old Teutonic custom.

" 'Our Hermann' was popular with the masses and they smiled goodnaturedly at his antics and self-display. He demanded that they make sacrifices in order to win victory and exhorted them to choose guns instead of butter. He patted his fat belly and said that he had lost forty pounds in the service of his country. The Germans appreciated his sense of humor.

"Despite this geniality Goering was unscrupulous. In furnishing and maintaining his home he bought whatever he wanted and challenged trades-people to send him a bill. When he was married he expressed his wishes regarding wedding presents in a manner which suggested intimidation. He received incomes from twenty or more public offices. . . . When he was captured by the Allies . . . he had an armored train of twenty cars loaded with art treasures which he had collected in conquered countries.

"Goering was unscrupulous in his exercise of authority. He was said to be courageous, hard, challenging and authoritative in the Prussian manner. He was described as an affable, hearty butcher. In connection with the persecution of Jews he declared, 'I define who is a Jew and who is not.' When he was made Chief of the Prussian Police he told his men to shoot first and inquire afterward. 'If you make a mistake, don't talk about it.' 'The faults which my officials commit are my faults; the bullets they fire are my bullets.' Goering regarded his bullets an an effective form of propaganda. He introduced the concentration camp and declared that it was not his duty to exercise justice, but to annihilate and exterminate. He reintroduced decapitation as an honest old German punishment. Goering is given credit for plotting the Reichstag Fire and for the planning and direction of the Blood Purge. Goering admitted that he had no conscience; his conscience was Adolf Hitler.

"Like many a psychopath Goering had a tender side. He was fond of animals, including his lion cubs. He declared that 'He who torments an animal hurts the feelings of the whole German people.' He introduced model game laws and one purpose of this legislation was to prevent suffering in wounded animals. In a jesting mood he told Sir Neville Henderson that if he was killed in the air raids on London he would send a special plane to drop a wreath at his funeral.

"Goering was often considered the most normal and the most conservative of the Nazi leaders. Like most psychopaths he would appear normal in his social relationships and he might seem genial and kindly with his humor and laughter. His pattern of behavior, however, identifies him as a constitutional psychopath and he presents a fair example of this personality disorder." (Bluemel, 1948, pp. 78-82)

DYNAMICS

Views regarding the dynamics of antisocial reactions vary widely. Some investigators believe they resulted from a constitutional deficiency; others attribute them to particular types of family and community patterns.

Biological factors.   A great deal of emphasis has been placed upon constitutional factors as a basis of antisocial personality, as evidenced by the various alternative names that have been coined for this reaction—such as "constitutional psychopathic inferior." Because the impulsivity, acting-out behavior, and intolerance of discipline tend to make their appearance early in life, several investigators have suggested an imbalance between inhibitory and excitatory processes in the nervous system as basic to the etiological pattern. For example, Stott (1962) has marshaled evidence indicating the possibility of congenital injuries which impair the higher inhibitory centers in the nervous system, thus making the psychopath more vulnerable to the breakdown of inner controls under stressful conditions. In a similar vein, Eysenck (1960) has concluded that the psychopath has a slower rate of conditioning than the normal individual. As a consequence, he presumably fails to acquire many of the conditioned reactions which form an essential part of normal socialization and is likely to be deficient in conscience development—he is not yet adequately socialized. However, Eysenck has pointed out that with time the necessary conditioned responses would occur, and the psychopath would achieve an adequate level of socialization.

Although such constitutional approaches appear plausible and account for many of the observed data concerning psychopaths, there is insufficient experimental evidence to justify far-reaching conclusions. There is no convincing evidence of a hereditary transmission of such alleged constitutional defects, and EEG studies have failed to reveal brain abnormalities in the great majority of cases (although such findings would not in themselves guarantee integrity of brain structure). In addition, however, mentally retarded and brain-damaged individuals who do reveal faulty brain structure are not usually psychopathic in their personality make-up. In general, it appears likely that brain anomalies—

when they do occur—are interactive factors rather than primary determinants.

Psychological factors.   As increasing experimental and clinical evidence has become available, many investigators have pointed out that the disruptive antisocial behavior of the psychopath typically seems to be defensive and retaliatory rather than simply disorganized or spontaneously disruptive as it might be with a constitutional defect. It is their contention that antisocial personalities learn to act out their conflicts and impulses instead of developing the neurotic pattern of worrying them out. Wilkins (1961) has pointed out that antisocial personalities, much like college professors or politicians (or anyone else), seem to have a "career" or life style. They can be viewed as following a consistent learned pattern of living which tends to be self-perpetuating. In fact, it appears to be especially resistant to change because of their ready rationalizations and projections and relative freedom from anxiety.

Although socioeconomic deprivation and delinquent gangs often appear to play a part in the development of antisocial personalities, patterns of family interaction appear to play the key etiologic role. It is probably for this reason that a high percentage of antisocial personalities come from middle- and upper-class families living in superior residential areas. In this context it is interesting to note the early findings of Heaver (1943) in a study of 40 male psychopathic personalities. He emphasized a type of early environmental conditioning provided by a mother who overindulges her son and a father who is highly successful, driving, critical, and distant. Following a somewhat similar dynamic orientation, Greenacre (1945) filled in a number of additional details which have been corroborated by more recent investigators. Greenacre emphasized frequent marked discrepancies and conflicts in the two parents' attitudes in regard to authority, independence, and goals of achievement. Often there is a stern, respected, and quite obsessional father, who is remote, preoccupied, and fear-inspiring in relation to his children, and an indulgent, pleasure-loving mother, who frequently is pretty but frivolous and often tacitly contemptuous of her husband's importance in the business world. Children are quick to sense these attitudes and conflicts.

Usually such parents are socially prominent and extremely dependent upon the approval and admiration of the other members of their community. As a result, it becomes of crucial importance to maintain the illusion of a happy family before the world, concealing any evidence of conflict, misery, bickering, and unhappiness and pretending that they do not exist. The children, too, become part of the show-window display, and a premium is put on formally good behavior and the pleasing of others. Thus develops in miniature the attitude which later is so characteristic of the antisocial personality—what seems to be is more valuable than what is. This attitude, together with either emotional impoverishment or emotional smothering, prevents the development of normal feelings of warmth or loyalty. Finally, the opportunistic need to be pleasing and to win social approval for their parents' sake seems to develop early in these children a superficial charm and great adroitness in handling people for purely selfish ends.

It is not surprising that under these circumstances a highly ambivalent attitude toward the parents and toward all authority tends to develop. The awe-inspiring, magic father is feared by the child, but at the same time there is an extension of the magic overevaluation to the child himself with a consequent feeling of exemption from the consequences of his behavior. And frequently the prominence of the father does in fact protect the child from the ordinary consequences of his behavior.

Because the remoteness and sternness of the father make more adequate and healthy identification with him impossible, a boy often remains in prolonged emotional subjugation to the mother and fails to develop a differentiated male sexual outlook. Consequently, homosexual behavior and other sexual deviations are easily adopted when environmental conditions promote them.

It is frequently said that the psychopath evidences no anxiety—that he has no guilt feelings. This is a matter of degree, however. Many psychopathic personalities do apparently suffer from guilt feelings which in extreme cases may lead to illegal behavior as a device to ensure punishment by society; by this means they alleviate their feelings of guilt about previous misbehavior. However, such feelings of guilt or anxiety do not change their behavior.

Although the above pattern of background factors seems to occur rather frequently in antisocial personalities, other types of family and environmental backgrounds are sometimes represented and should not be overlooked. In our discussion of delinquency and crime we shall have occasion to examine some of the other family patterns as well as more general sociocultural factors.

In summary, we may say it would appear that psychopathic personalities are a highly mixed group of individuals who seem to have in common the fact that they are impulsive, emotionally immature, irresponsible, and unethical and fail to make an adequate social adjustment. Their background frequently reveals possible constitutional or acquired brain abnormalities as well as environmental conditions which are not conducive to the development of adult patterns of emotional and ethical behavior.

TREATMENT AND PROGNOSIS

Because of prevailing confusion concerning the dynamics of antisocial personalities and the lack of adequate long-range treatment facilities, very little has been accomplished in the way of treatment (Maughs, 1961). Since these individuals are not psychotic, few of them receive help in mental hospitals. But even when treatment facilities are available, the therapeutic task is usually a difficult one. Organic factors which are impossible to correct may complicate the clinical picture, and the long developmental background makes the modification of antisocial behavior patterns difficult—especially in view of the fact that these individuals have little or no desire to be changed.

As a result, the prognosis for the recovery of antisocial personalities is not favorable. Early work by Banay (1945), however, demonstrated that with intensive therapy and constant supervision it was possible to bring many "hopeless" criminal psychopaths to a stability that made further criminal behavior unnecessary for them. Lindner (1945) reported good results through the use of hypnoanalysis. Thorne (1959), too, has pointed to successful results in a series of cases utilizing intensive long-range psychotherapy. Many antisocial personalities apparently improve after the age of 40, possibly due to a decrease in the strength of instinctual biological drives, to the gaining of some insight into their behavior, and to the accumulated effects of social conditioning. Often such individuals are referred to as "burned-out" psychopaths.

Recently a new therapeutic approach is being tried with ex-criminal drug addicts, most of whom are psychopathic personalities. It takes place in a therapeutic community known as *Synanon* and will be described in our later discussion of drug addiction. Any successful method of treatment must involve a compre-

hensive personality redintegration with an emphasis on the development of personal maturity, reality and ethical restraints, and personal responsibility. Such attitudes can be developed only under favorable conditions in a long-range therapy program. Even here results may be disappointing or relapses may occur.

In view of the unhappiness such individuals cause their immediate families and those who love them, however, as well as the general social damage they do, it would appear desirable and economical in the long run to spend more effort in developing effective treatment programs.

Dyssocial Reaction

Where individuals show no personality disorganization but are the product of a lifelong environment which has fostered social values in conflict with the usual codes of their society, they are classed as dyssocial personalities. Here we find gangsters, racketeers, and other professional criminals who usually emerge from criminal homes or neighborhood environments in which deviate codes of behavior and criminal models have served as the guides.

Dishay (1944) reported that about 10 per cent of the boys who appeared in the Children's Court in New York City were vicious, hardened, aggressive, habitual delinquents who espoused antisocial behavior as a career and the gang as a medium of protection, comfort, and training for effective operation. There is little reason to believe that this condition has changed appreciably since Dishay's study was made. Al Capone, Dil-

linger, and any number of other "public enemies" who have made criminal history in the United States, including the members of the much-publicized organization, Murder, Inc., could be used to illustrate this type of pathological personality. Such individuals are often capable of strong loyalties and typically do not show significant personality deviations aside from their adherence to the values and codes of their own predatory, criminal, or other social group.

Of course dyssocial individuals are not immune to mental disorders, and the increased stress of their life situation often shows up in symptoms of personality decompensation which, in some cases, may progress to neurotic or psychotic levels. In general, however, their background of training and their emotional insulation seem to protect them pretty well from ego disintegration, even with severe prison sentences.

The Problem of Delinquency and Crime

In our society crime is classified into three major categories: treason, felonies, and misdemeanors. Treason consists in giving aid and comfort to the enemy or in levying war against the United States. Felonies are serious crimes such as murder, forgery, robbery, burglary, and rape, which are punishable by death or imprisonment and

heavy fines. Misdemeanors are minor offenses such as disorderly conduct and vagrancy.

The incidence of crime in the United States is high in comparison with that in many other countries and is still on the increase. Statistics compiled by the Federal Bureau of Investigation (1961) reveal that there were 2,048,370 serious crimes reported in 1962.[1] This represents a new high in robbery, forcible rape, aggravated assault, and other felonies; a major crime was committed every 15 seconds.

In connection with these crimes, almost 4 per cent of the population were arrested in 1962. Approximately 80 per cent of both juvenile and adult offenders are male. As a consequence of apprehension and conviction for serious crimes, over 230,000 prisoners are in federal and state prisons (U.S. Bureau of Prisons, 1963). Besides there are some 40,000 inmates in schools for juvenile delinquents. During the past five years the crime rate has increased four times as fast as the general population.

JUVENILE DELINQUENCY

Juvenile delinquency is behavior on the part of boys or girls under 18 which society does not accept and which is generally judged to call for some kind of admonishment, punishment, or corrective measures. In many instances, delinquent behavior leads to arrest and court appearance on a delinquency charge; often, however, especially in the case of first offenders, the behavior is handled in other ways. Each year more than a million juveniles find themselves in serious trouble with the law and over 600,000 appear before juvenile courts. For 1962, persons under 18 years of age comprised 62 per cent of the arrests for auto theft, 51 per cent for larceny, 49 per cent for burglary, 25 per cent for robbery, 19 per cent for forcible rape, 13 per cent for aggravated assault, and 8 per cent for murder and nonnegligent manslaughter. In fact, for these crimes as a group, juveniles comprised 45 per cent of the total arrests.

Approximately 60 per cent of the juveniles arrested have prior police records. The increasing rate of juvenile delinquency and the sex ratio parallel those for adult crime. However, the arrests of girls, particularly for crimes against property, has shown a sharp increase. In general, male delinquents tend to commit crimes against property and to a lesser extent against the person, while girls most frequently commit sexual offenses, run away from home, and are found to be "incorrigible." Other offenses for both sexes include arson, vandalism, and narcotics.

Dynamics. Numerous conditions—singly and in combination—may be involved in the etiological pattern that leads to delinquent behavior. For present purposes, we shall attempt to summarize the role of four sets of conditions which appear to be of key importance.

1. *More pervasive pathology.* A number of investigators have attempted to "type" delinquents in relation to more pervasive patterns of pathology.

a) The organic delinquent. In a distinct minority of cases (probably about 1 per cent) brain pathology may result in lowered inhibitory controls and a tendency toward episodes of aggressive and violent behavior. These children are often hyperactive, impulsive, emotionally unstable, and unable to inhibit action when strongly stimulated. Often such children experience strong guilt feelings following their explosive outbursts. Whether or not such violent episodes occur may depend upon the acceptance or rejection of these children by parents and peer group members.

b) The mentally retarded delinquent. In a few cases (perhaps 5 per cent), low intelligence appears to be of etiological significance. Here the delinquent often does not know any better—he is unable to appreciate the significance of his actions or to foresee the probable consequences. This is particularly true of mentally retarded sexually delinquent girls (Wirt *et al.*, 1962). Occasionally, too, boys and girls of low intelligence fall prey to the suggestions of brighter sociopaths who dominate and exploit them. In some instances, mental retardation is associated with serious brain damage and leads to a combination of the features of both the organic and the mentally retarded delinquent.

c) The psychotic delinquent. In a limited number of cases (probably about 3 per cent), delinquent behavior is associated with a psychotic reaction. Often this involves a pattern of prolonged emotional and social withdrawal which culminates after long frustration in an explosive outburst of violent behavior (Bandura

---

[1]Since not all crimes are reported to the police the actual incidence is probably considerably higher—possibly over the three million mark. For example, there are an estimated million or more unreported criminal abortions performed each year in the United States (Calderone, 1960; Kummer and Leavy, 1961). Nearly 5000 women die each year as a consequence of these illegal operations.

and Walters, 1959). Here the delinquent act is the by-product of the personality disturbance rather than a reflection of a consistent antisocial orientation. Wirt *et al.* (1962) has found that a fair number of juvenile delinquents are descriptively schizoid rather than schizophrenic. That is, they are not actually psychotic but are distant from others and eccentric in their thoughts, showing flattened, unresponsive emotionality.

d) The neurotic delinquent. In more cases (an estimated 10 to 15 per cent), delinquent behavior appears to be directly associated with psychoneurotic disorders. Here the delinquent act often takes the form of a compulsion—such as "peeping," stealing things which the individual does not need, or firesetting. Typically, such compulsions are related to deviant sexual gratification in overly inhibited adolescents who have been indoctrinated in the belief that masturbation and other overt forms of sexual discharge are terribly evil and sinful. Often such individuals fight their inner impulses before the delinquent act and then feel extremely guilty afterwards. As Gibbens (1961) has pointed out, such neurotic disturbances appear to be on the decrease, possibly reflecting the fact that parents are no longer so prone to induce overinhibition in relation to sexual behavior.

e) The sociopathic delinquent. The great majority of persistent delinquents appear to share the traits which are typical of the antisocial personality. They are impulsive, defiant, resentful, guiltfree, incapable of establishing and maintaining close interpersonal ties, and unable to profit from their experiences in a constructive way. As a consequence of their lack of inner conscience and reality controls, they often engage in seemingly "senseless" delinquent acts which are not planned but occur on the "spur of the moment," in reaction to some momentary impulse. Thus they may steal a small sum of money which they do not need; or they may steal a car, drive it a few blocks, and then abandon it. In essence, these individuals are "unsocialized delinquents" who are largely at the mercy of their uncontrolled impulses.

f) The subcultural delinquent. Here the delinquent belongs to a subgroup whose values do not conform to those of the larger group. Thus what society considers to be a criminal act, the mores of the gang or subculture may not. As a consequence, the subculture often encourages the individual to engage in delinquent behavior and rewards him when he does so successfully. Often the members of delinquent gangs feel inadequate in and rejected by the larger society; they participate in gang activities as a means of gaining some measure of belongingness, approval, and status. In this context, we are typically dealing with social as well as individual pathology.

2. *Pathogenic family relationships.* Although various pathogenic family patterns have been emphasized in juvenile delinquency, the typical situation appears to be one in which the father plays a reduced role and fails to provide an adequate model for the growing child. This pattern may take a number of forms.

a) Broken homes. In a study of institutionalized delinquents in the state of Colorado, Barker and Adams (1962) found that only about one third of the boys and girls came from complete home settings—complete in the sense that they lived with both their original parents. In over one fourth of the homes the juvenile had lived with only the mother; an additional 12 per cent lived with the mother and a stepfather. Similarly, Morris *et al.* (1956) have pointed to the high incidence of multiple parental figures in the backgrounds of aggressively delinquent children.

In a few cases, early, prolonged parental deprivation seems to play a key role in producing "affectionless characters" and schizoid personalities who are poorly socialized and susceptible to involvement in delinquent activities. As Ainsworth (1962) has pointed out, however, follow-up studies of children who have suffered prolonged early deprivations show only a small incidence of delinquent outcomes. Apparently in most cases parental rejection, inconsistent discipline, broken homes, and other pathogenic family patterns are more important than early parental deprivation.

In the context of these findings in our society, it is interesting to note the findings of Bacon *et al.* (1963), who studied the incidence of crime in 48 nonliterate societies. These investigators found that in societies where the typical family restricts opportunities for the young boy to identify with his father, there is a much higher proportionate incidence of theft and personal crime.

b) "Parental absenteeism." In studies of

juvenile vandalism, Martin (1961) and other investigators have emphasized the feeling of *anomie*—of feeling unrelated to and hopelessly detached from family and society. Somehow lines of communication appear to be cut off, leading to a failure to learn appropriate social values and to a tendency to act out inner tensions in hostile, destructive behavior.

This feeling of rootlessness or unrelatedness may apply to young people who differ widely in age, intelligence, personality make-up, and socioeconomic status. A key source of this feeling appears to be "parental absenteeism"— which occurs not only in broken homes but with parents who are too absorbed in their own activities to provide the youth with needed support and encouragement during the many crisis periods involved in growing up.

c) Mother dominance. In a report to the World Health Organization, Gibbens (1961) has pointed to the common role of maternal dominance—in which the father, for work or other reasons, plays a reduced role in the family life and the mother takes over the function of providing both affection and discipline. During adolescence, the boy who has identified with his mother and relied heavily upon her as a role model presumably has difficulty in shaping a masculine self-concept. As a consequence, he tends to be rebellious and to engage in "proving" offenses—in which the primary motive is reassurance as to his own courage, independence, and virility.

d) Father rejection. Andry (1962) found that the preponderance of delinquent boys felt rejected by their father but loved by their mother, while nondelinquents felt equally loved by both parents. He also noted that though recognizing their fathers as head of the household, delinquent boys tended to obey them less.

In the background of a group of 26 aggressive, antisocial delinquent boys, Bandura and Walters (1959) delineated a pattern of father rejection combined with inconsistent handling of the boy by both parents. Normally the child learns to want to behave in ways which meet with parental approval; this desire is fundamental to his socialization. But if the child is rejected and treated inconsistently, he has little incentive to try to behave in approved ways. In addition, he lacks clear guides for controlling and directing his behavior. To complicate the pathogenic family picture further, the fathers typically used physically punitive methods of discipline, thus augmenting the hostility already felt by the boys toward their fathers as a result of rejection. The end result of such a pattern is a hostile, defiant, inadequately socialized boy who lacks normal inner controls and tends to act out his aggressive impulses.

Here it is of interest to note that parental rejection, combined with a sociopathic father, tends to produce early and prolonged delinquent behavior on the part of the son (McCord and McCord, 1959).

e) Sociopathic fathers. A number of investigators have pointed to the high incidence of sociopathic traits in the fathers of delinquent boys (Morris, 1956; O'Neal *et al.,* 1962; Glueck and Glueck, 1962; Bennett, 1961). These included alcoholism, brutality, antisocial attitudes, failure to provide, frequent absences from home, and other characteristics which made the father an inadequate and unacceptable model for the boy. In the case of girls, sociopathic fathers may contribute in various ways to delinquent behavior including covert encouragement of sexual promiscuity.

3. *The delinquent subculture.* Here we are concerned with conditions outside the home which tend to produce delinquency. Two conditions are of key significance.

a) The "social rejects." A new population element is making itself increasingly felt in our society. This is the growing population of 16- to 20-year-olds who lack the ability or motivation to do well in school but are unable to find acceptable jobs in the community. With the new emphasis on academic excellence in the United States, school pressures have become intolerable to them; and with increasing automation there are few jobs for which they can qualify. Whether they come from upper-, middle-, or lower-class homes, they have one crucial problem in common—they are not needed in our society. They are the victims of social progress, the "social rejects."

These youths frequently gather at night on street corners, in drive-ins, or in front of bowling alleys where they find some superficial psychological support and group identification. The latter is often enhanced by looking and dressing as much alike as possible. However, they can rarely communicate their deepest concerns to each other and tend to cover up with an air of bravado and various escapist activities, such as drinking, getting hopped up on pills, or engaging in promiscuous sexual relationships. Many of them sense and deeply resent their rejection by society. Their inner tensions are often revealed in serious delinquent acts, such as senseless beatings, vandalism, and party crashing, which may end in fighting, serious injuries, and the wanton destruction of property. Unable to find a meaningful or fulfilling role in our society, they lose their way.

b)   The delinquent gang.   There is ample research to show that the incidence of juvenile delinquency is much higher in the deteriorated areas of large urban centers. In these areas poverty and inadequate living conditions arouse frustration and discontent and foster hostile attitudes toward society. In such areas the child is exposed to many antisocial models, and it is difficult for parents to impart desirable values or to maintain control over the behavior of their children. And it is in such areas that teen-age gangs flourish. Fortunately, many of these gangs appear to provide a useful and constructive function in the socialization of the adolescent. It has been reported that only 35 teen-age gangs out of more than 200 such gangs in Chicago cause the police trouble (*Chicago American,* 1961). When such gangs become delinquent, however, they do extensive and lasting personal damage to the lives of their members as well as to those of their victims.

Investigators have found three more or less distinct types of delinquent subcultures among male adolescents in the lower-class areas of large urban centers (Vedder, 1963). One is essentially a "criminal subculture"—a type of gang which directs its activities toward theft, extortion, and other illegal means of obtaining income. A second is a "conflict subculture"—a type of gang in which violence predominates as a means of gaining status and group approval. A third is a "retreatist subculture"—a type of gang in which the use of drugs, promiscuous sexual relationships, and other illicit experiences are stressed.

Often such gangs appear to function as a haven for teen-agers who have an unclear sense of self-identity, feel rejected at home, and are confused and overwhelmed by the complex and seemingly indifferent society in which they live. In delinquent gangs they can find social approval and status while temporarily escaping from and defying the larger society around them. In the gang they also find a sense of self-identity and a ready-made value system. This value system, though often contradictory to that of society, may reflect more or less accurately the values of some small segment of society—such as a minority ethnic group in a given urban area. To survive in the hostile world which these gangs inhabit and to some extent create, loyalty to the group becomes a key essential of the "gang code." Many delinquent acts are ways of gaining or maintaining approved status in the gang.

Girls are often recruited into juvenile gangs and have membership—although often they play a subsidiary role. Frequently they are expected to submit to the sexual advances of the male members, and sometimes they assist the boys in gang fights or other illegal activities by carrying concealed weapons, acting as lookouts, or playing the role of decoys.

Juvenile authorities have expressed concern about the increasing number of girl gangs which have developed in recent years. Girl gangs provide much the same function for the confused, resentful, and defiant girls as male gangs do for the boys. In these gangs the girls create their "own world" for purposes of belongingness, protection, and defiance. In the gang they find acceptance, rules, loyalty, authority, discipline, and many of the other components which they cannot find or accept in the adult world around them. Many of these girl gangs are affiliated in varying degrees with male gangs while maintaining their own separate organizations. Fortunately, not all of these gangs constitute a delinquent subculture, but many of them do. Available statistics indicate that girls are involved in about 15 to 30 per cent of all delinquent gang activities that come to the attention of the police —assaults on other juveniles, automobile thefts, small gang raids, carrying deadly weapons, narcotics, and impulsive gang activity.

Whether the juvenile gang exercises a constructive or a destructive effect on the lives of its members, it is an extremely important influence. For once the individual joins a juvenile gang, it largely replaces the family as the principal agent of his further socialization—at least until he reaches adulthood.

4. *Precipitating events.* We have noted that many delinquent acts are based on the acting out of momentary impulses and that in other cases such behavior occurs as a part of the regular activities of a delinquent gang. Delinquent behavior may also be triggered by some relatively minor event, as when a fight between two youths triggers a riot among a gathering of youths from a given area.

In some instances traumatic events in the life of the boy or girl appear to act as precipitating events. In a study of 500 delinquent boys, Clarke (1961) found that in about a third of the cases it was possible to isolate highly stressful events preceding the delinquency—such as death of parents, disruption of family life, or discovery that they were adopted. These events had proved highly disorganizing and often had led to a period of poor school performance, truancy, brooding, and eventually delinquent behavior. Burks and Harrison (1962) have also emphasized the importance of stresses which directly threaten the youth's feelings of adequacy and worth as precipitating events in some cases of aggressive antisocial behavior. Such anxiety-arousing stresses lead to unbearable inner tension which the individual manages to relieve to some extent by his hostile acting-out behavior.

Three additional factors may be briefly mentioned in relation to the dynamics of delinquent behavior. First, the depiction of violence in television plays, movies, and comic strips does not appear to be an important factor in the increase in crimes of violence by juveniles (Gibbens, 1961). Such media may influence the nature of the violent act, but they do not supply the motivation for it. Second, it may be pointed out that the type of crime is often related to the motivation of the offender. Car stealing, for example, tends to be a crime of excitement and a means of gaining status and approval from delinquent peers; sexual delinquency is commonly associated with pervasive feelings of inadequacy and is a "proving" offense. Finally, there is evidence that a disproportionate number of delinquent boys have a mesomorphic (athletic) body build. Glueck and Glueck (1956) found that 60 per cent of 500 persistently delinquent boys from a disorganized urban area had a mesomorphic

physique as contrasted with 30 per cent for a matched nondelinquent control group. They interpreted this finding as indicating that mesomorphs tend to respond to environmental pressures differently from endomorphs and ectomorphs—for example, by a greater tendency toward aggressively acting out their tensions. Since gang activities often place a premium upon physical prowess, it is also possible that there is a selective factor operating here. In any event, the role of physique in juvenile delinquency merits further evaluation. However, it would appear to be a contributing rather than a key factor in the total etiological pattern.

Treatment and prognosis for delinquents. In view of the number of cases involved and the tremendous diversity of etiological factors, we can deal with the treatment of juvenile delinquency only in a very general way.

Perhaps the most important guiding principle is the coordination and effective utilization of all community personnel, agencies, and facilities which have a bearing on the problem—and this includes long-range social planning for the alleviation of slum conditions, the provision of adequate educational opportunities, and the delineation of a more meaningful role for adolescents in our society. Fortunately, our nation is well aware of the extent and seriousness of the problem. In 1961 the President's Committee on Juvenile Delinquency and Youth Crime was established to serve as a means of coordinating the work of the various youth-serving units within the Departments of Justice, Labor, and Health, Education, and Welfare. In the past, most programs for the control of delinquency might have been described as "mopping up operations"—a process of picking up the pieces after a crisis had arisen. The program of the President's Committee, by contrast, is aimed at demonstrating whether a comprehensive attack on the social causes of delinquency can result in a reduction of youth crime and delinquency and a better adjustment of the youth in high-delinquency areas. The emphasis is not on individual treatment of delinquents but on the establishment of social services that may effect a long-range change in the outlook, motivation, and employability of disadvantaged youths. One of the most notable demonstration projects now in process is the Mobilization for Youth project in New York City, a concerted, community-wide, multiple attack on youth crime, school failure, and lack of youth employment within a well-defined neighborhood.

Such measures, coupled with improvement in basic living conditions, parent education, and school health programs, should eventually accomplish a great deal toward the control and prevention of juvenile delinquency. However, there is still a shortage of trained personnel for dealing with delinquents, and our society has not yet come to grips with the admittedly difficult problem of helping adolescents to find a more meaningful and fulfilling role in our society.

On both an individual and a group level a key problem in dealing with troubled youths is that of opening lines of communication with them. Some of the most "hard-core" juvenile gangs have shown markedly improved behavior when social workers have managed to make contact with them and win their confidence and respect. Psychotherapy and sociotherapy can also be of great value, but the current available resources are hopelessly inadequate to deal with the overall problem. Juvenile institutions or training schools can be of great help for some youths who need to be taken out of their adverse environmental setting and given an opportunity to explore themselves and their world and find some sense of purpose and meaning in their existence. Unfortunately, crowded conditions and lack of trained personnel often defeat this goal.

From a more positive viewpoint, it may be emphasized that 80 per cent of our young people lead constructive lives and do not become involved in delinquent activities. It is also possible at present to identify many potential delinquents by means of a "social prediction score" worked out by Glueck and Glueck (1950, 1962). This score is based on an assessment of several characteristics, such as discipline and guidance, family cohesiveness, and child personality; it indicates the probability of future delinquency in children as young as six or seven years of age. Such information can be put to good use in the correction of pathogenic trends before they have proceeded to the point of actual delinquent behavior. And even where children do become delinquent, the outcome is usually not unfavorable. Although some delinquents do drift into lives of crime, the majority eventually marry, have families, and establish themselves in the community.

ADULT CRIME AND THE "NEW" CRIMINAL

Adult crime sometimes has its roots in juvenile delinquency but not always. Most juvenile delinquents do not become adult criminals, and many adult criminals do not show a prior history of juvenile delinquency. Adult crime overlaps with juvenile delinquency but it is an exceedingly complex problem in its own right.

Criminal acts occur in varying degrees of severity; they may range from an act which is committed once in a lifetime to a life style of criminal behavior. And a given type of crime does not always indicate the same type of psychopathology. Antisocial and dyssocial reactions constitute the largest single source of criminal behavior but by no means account for all of it. Arieff and Bowie (1947) needed 18 diagnostic categories to describe shoplifters referred by the Chicago Municipal Court for psychiatric investigation. Among the group were drug addicts, neurotics, psychopathic personalities, schizophrenics, alcoholics, and individuals suffering from senile brain degeneration. In a study of 300 check offenders, MacDonald (1959) found a high incidence of sociopathic personalities and chronic alcoholics and a lesser number of schizophrenics, manics, seniles, and mentally retarded individuals. Of 175 murderers, Guttmacher (1960) found that 105 were clearly nonpsychotic at the time of the murder, 53 were psychotic, and 17 were seriously abnormal. Included in the overall group were antisocial and dyssocial personalities, schizophrenics, alcoholics, and a wide range of other psychopathological types. Finally, most inmates of Sing Sing Prison can be put into one of five major groups, as shown in the chart on page 378. Of course, sometimes the same individual falls into more than one group.

As in juvenile delinquency, situational stresses and inner tensions often play a key role in precipitating criminal acts. Crimes committed by relatively normal individuals during periods of acute stress are not likely to be repeated. In general, social conditions contributing to deprivation,

A

B

THE TREATMENT OF DELINQUENTS

New Jersey has established a number of small residential treatment camps and centers to provide short-term treatment for selected youthful offenders. Some are pre-parole camps (A), which are bridges between release from the state reformatory and a return to the community. Others are centers to which first offenders or previous probation failures may go voluntarily as a condition of probation. In general, the programs avoid the regulations and security measures, the punitive atmosphere, and the complex, formal authoritarian social structure associated with correctional institutions. Their purpose is to turn delinquents into nondelinquents through establishment of a healthy, productive group situation in which peer pressures are toward cooperation and social responsibility. With encouragement and support, the boys are given an opportunity to examine their values and self-defeating techniques and to test out new and more satisfying modes of behavior.

The treatment centers have in common three major aspects: a work situation, guided group interaction, and community contacts. Days are filled with eight hours of work which may involve forestry projects (B), pheasant breeding and rearing (C), or other activities, plus housekeeping work at the center or camp. The purpose of this work is less to teach skills than to provide an experience analogous to one aspect of life in the free community.

The guided group interaction sessions are the core of the program (D). Sessions are held five nights a week with voluntary attendance. The boys choose the issues and

experiences to be discussed, while the therapist plays a critical, supportive, and guiding role. The potency of this approach is well displayed in the following summary of part of a group session.

"The group meeting started with a statement by Pete that he wanted to discuss some trouble that he had had with Joe. He said that he and Joe had not been very good friends for the past three weeks, and that Friday night, it had reached a climax, and that he wanted to bring it out in the open. When the leader asked the boys what they thought the difficulty was, Pete said Joe bothered him, and Joe said Pete 'picked on' him. . . . Pete said that Joe had always bothered him a little bit, and he resented having Joe about always wanting to do things for him or give him things. Pete then went on to give several specific illustrations and mentioned that on one occasion, Joe gave him a shirt, frequently supplied him with writing paper, and, at various times, offered him money. Pete said he had been willing to take the shirt and writing paper, but had never taken any money from Joe. Gus said that in doing this, Pete was only behaving with Joe the way he had behaved with girls in the past, taking things from them, and later on pushing them around. Steve said that Joe's demands on Pete were such that he couldn't be friendly in spite of the gifts. Pete said that he felt funny when he took the things, and while he didn't want to take things from Joe and feel indebted to him, he did because 'I liked to have them.' Later on, he described his feelings as wanting to be nice to Joe, but after a couple of days giving up and again 'picking on him' and doing things to get him angry.

C

D

"Joe said that much of what the boys said was true, that he did make a lot of demands on Pete and, above all, he wanted to feel that Pete would leave him alone or, what is more important, be on his side. Joe spontaneously told the boys that in giving Pete things, he was behaving toward him as he did toward his father. Joe stated that Pete, like his father, would 'pick on' him, say things to irritate him, and just as he gave his father money to leave him alone, he gave Pete gifts in the hopes that he would leave him alone. This admission on Joe's part surprised the other boys, and several of them stated that on different occasions they had noticed that when anyone picked on Joe, he would later do something for him or offer him some gifts. Gus said this was the only way Joe could make friends. . . . Joe said this was true, that both with his father and with others . . . he was willing to give them almost anything in the hopes that they would be friendly with him in their activities. . . . Joe said he resented very much having to give his father money, but it was easier than having him pick on you or having him fight with my mother.' Steve said that it looked as if Joe were behaving toward Pete as he did toward his father, and that he was having the same trouble as he did before.

"Pete said that it was important that he and Joe get this thing straightened out because they would both meet people on the outside who would resemble one another for them. Joe said he liked Pete, hoped he would be his friend, but at the same time resented him and his easy way of getting friends and how he was able to have the respect of all the boys without even trying. Larry said it

was all Joe's fault, that he was constantly creating trouble for himself, and, 'He has to learn that you can't push other people around.' Gus and Steve said they thought Joe did this because he never was sure that either Pete or Larry liked him. Pete said this was true because several times Joe had told them he didn't like them. Joe went on talking about how he had many similar feelings toward Pete that he had toward his father and several of his older brothers. In a pathetic manner, Joe described a lifetime of being 'picked on' by others, especially members of his family. He went on to tell the boys that he never felt sure that the others liked him, and since he did want them to like him, he would give them things.

"The boys were quite impressed by Joe's statement, and hastened to assure him that they liked him and would like him even more if he would 'stop his damn bragging.' " (Elias, 1958, pp. 11-12)

Community contacts include competitive sports and social activities, as well as frequent trips to surrounding towns for movies, refreshments, and church services. Sunday afternoons are free for visitors, and two weekend furloughs at home are granted—as a right, rather than a privilege. Such trips serve as a respite from the intensive camp program and offer chances for the boy to test what he is learning at the center and to start looking ahead to job or school opportunities; they also prevent the development of dependency on the institution.

(The pictures shown here were taken at the Pre-Parole Camp at High Point State Park and at the Ocean Residential Group Center.)

APPROXIMATE INCIDENCE OF PERSONALITY
TYPES IN SING SING PRISON

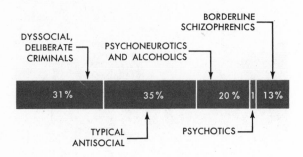

From Gaetaiello, 1963

instability, and conflict are conducive to criminal behavior. Excessive drinking often plays a part in the total etiological picture.

Yablonsky (1962, 1963) has pointed to the difference between the old "professional" criminal and the newer "psychic" type. The older criminal has traditionally been out to make money in the quickest and safest way possible. He was usually a resourceful felon who got his training in a criminal gang and had a clear code of "ethics." Typically, he specialized in a particular type of crime, such as robbery, forgery, or burglary. His particular method of committing the crime was usually somewhat unique and constituted what the police called his "modus operandi." For example, he might always tell the same story in attempting to cash forged checks or he might attempt to pass them only in crowded stores at a particular hour of the day. Often he made contacts with trusted people or belonged to a gang essential for the pursuit of his criminal work. In general, he attempted to avoid violence in the perpetration of his criminal acts, since such behavior would greatly increase the risk involved and the chances of detection and imprisonment. His crimes were well planned and even rehearsed as one might prepare for a military operation.

For a relatively simple type of criminal act, this pattern has been well described by Macdonald in his study of check offenders.

"The skilled bogus check writer plans his check passing carefully, limits it to a brief period in a large town and then moves quickly to another state where

he repeats his offenses when his funds are exhausted. The checks are printed with the title of a state or city government, a widely known or a nonexistent company. In the latter case a bank account may be opened but only a small deposit is made. The check may be labelled payroll and the value, which is printed with a protectograph, is for an irregular amount such as $88.72 to give the appearance of a payroll deduction for income tax. A large number of checks are passed late Friday afternoon and Saturday. When the bank discovers the fraud the following Monday, the check writer is already in another state." (1959, p. 439)

This type of criminal still exists, but new police methods of crime detection and changes in our social structure are depleting his numbers.

The "new" criminal is in many ways a different type of personality. Although interested in money, his crimes are perpetuated primarily for ego status and "kicks." A "kick" is derived from some taboo act which intensifies the present moment of experience and differentiates it as much as possible from the boring routine of daily life. Rather than belong to a criminal gang, the "new" criminal belongs to a violent gang; often he gets his "kicks" by senseless acts of violence. Typically his criminal act occurs in a spontaneous and unpremeditated way, and there is no evidence of prior contact between the assailant and his victim. The final consequence (often homicide) is not really anticipated. However, the brutal violence which he inflicts on some helpless victim "makes him feel good." As one youth told Yablonsky after a gang killing,

"If I would of got the knife, I would have stabbed him. That would of gave me more of a build-up. People would have respected me for what I've done and things like that. They would say, 'There goes a cold killer.' " (1963, p. 55)

When the "new" criminal does participate in planned criminal acts, he reveals a new style. The manipulative process of "how to win friends and influence people" has been filtered down to "how to beat a mark (victim)." Although he may be out to make money, his key target is to make himself "look sharp." With no commitment to goals beyond daily proving himself and seeking "kicks," the "new" criminal thus constitutes a major social menace.

A glance at the chart on page 378 will indicate clearly that for most imprisoned men, criminal behavior is only a part of a larger pattern of personality maladjustment. Thus the treatment and prevention of criminal behavior will have to involve the same procedures—hospitalization, medical and psychological therapy, social work, early detection and correction of unhealthy personality trends, correction of undesirable social conditions, and so on—which apply to abnormal behavior in general. Most investigators in this field feel that our criminal procedures have failed sadly and deplore the fact that law enforcement is still largely punitive and revengeful—that society is more concerned with exacting "an eye for an eye and a tooth for a tooth" than it is with the rehabilitation of the criminal. Unfortunately many people still hold the naïve belief that a criminal who is committed to prison should thereby realize the error of his ways and be completely cured of his criminal tendencies just by serving a term in jail. But this goal can be achieved only by long-range psychotherapy designed to meet the needs of the particular patient, coupled with an intelligent handling of the individual by society upon his release. Inasmuch as most prisoners eventually return to society, it is crucially important that we evaluate the actual effectiveness of our modern criminal procedures in preparing the criminal for a useful role in society. This would appear particularly true in view of the high rate of return to criminal behavior following release from prison—estimated to run between 40 and 70 per cent—and the obvious ineffectiveness of present penal procedures for treating the "new" criminal.

On the favorable side of the ledger is the fact that we are coming increasingly to view crime as a social and psychiatric problem and reformatories and prisons as places of detention during the all-important process of rehabilitation.[1]

Deviant Sexual Behavior

Although deviant sexual behavior frequently occurs in psychoses and other mental disorders, this category is used primarily in cases where sexual deviation grows out of faulty sexual development rather than appearing later as a product of personality decompensation.

The development of adult sexual behavior from the undifferentiated potentialities of the infant is a long and complex process, and the end results are by no means uniform. Each social group has its approved and disapproved sexual patterns and its sexual "deviates." In a few countries where American motion pictures are shown, the kissing scenes are looked upon as perversions. Among some peoples, polygamy, prostitution, and extramarital sexual relations are considered quite normal, whereas they are not approved by us. Even within our own culture, approved sexual behavior varies considerably from one socioeconomic level to another. For example, deep kissing, which is socially approved by upper-level groups, is often considered a perversion by those in lower educational and economic brackets. Thus *sexual deviation* is defined as any method of obtaining sexual satisfaction which is disapproved by the community, and the term encompasses a wide range of sexual behavior, from patterns which are relatively common and often socially ignored to more extreme deviations which are less common and strongly disapproved by society.

Because of our social taboos and regulations in this field, very little is known about our sexual patterns or the nature and extent of the sexual deviations which occur. The first comprehensive studies in this field were carried out by Kinsey and his colleagues (1948, 1949, 1953). Although they have been criticized for methodological flaws, they added considerably to our meager fund of information, and together with other available evidence indicate that certain deviations in sexual behavior are much more frequent

---

[1]We cannot here take up the problem of when an offender should be held criminally responsible for his acts and when he should be treated as a sick person. The following references may be useful to those interested in this problem: American Medical Association (1961), Guttmacher (1963), Lindman and McIntyre (1961), Nice (1962).

than had been generally supposed. Although our sexual patterns have undoubtedly shifted somewhat since these studies were made, many of their findings would still appear to be generally applicable and will be drawn on from time to time in the present discussion. Kinsey *et al.* (1949) reported that:

"In spite of the many centuries during which our culture has attempted to suppress all but one type of sexual activity, a not inconsiderable portion of all the sexual acts in which the human animal engages still fall into the category which the culture rates as 'perverse.' The specific data show that two thirds to three quarters of the males in our American culture, and some lesser number of the females, engage in at least some 'perverse' sexual behavior at some time between adolescence and old age. One half to two thirds of the males engage in such behavior with appreciable frequency during some period of their lives and a fair number engage in such behavior throughout their lives." (p. 28)

Since most of these deviations are not of a public nature, probably few of them are reported to the police. It is even estimated that in the case of public acts of deviation like exhibitionism and rape as many go unreported to the police as are reported (Dunham, 1951).

Of sex offenses reported to the police, extensive studies in Michigan and New Jersey indicated that only about 15 per cent led to convictions and only about 5 per cent to prison commitment (Dunham, 1951; Tappan *et al.,* 1950). These low figures are due to a number of factors, such as reports which prove to be false and the reluctance of victims to press charges in court for fear of adverse publicity. Also, the large number of exhibitionists and peepers (42.5 per cent of all sex offenders in the Michigan study) who are reported to the police are often considered minor offenders and nuisances and usually are given probation and suspended sentences by the judges. Even so, sexual offenses were found to constitute some 8 per cent of all crime convictions in the state of Michigan.

A breakdown of statistics with respect to the most frequent type of sexual deviations is somewhat difficult to make because of differences in legal and psychiatric terminology, reports vs.

convictions, and other considerations. It would appear, however, that peeping, exhibitionism, incest, rape (including statutory rape),[1] molesting of children, assaults with sex intent, and homosexuality are the most common offenses to come to the attention of the police (Tappan, 1957). Most of these sex crimes are committed by young, unmarried males, but the married, divorced, and separated are also represented in these categories. Aside from the girls brought before juvenile courts for sexual delinquency, few women are convicted of sexually deviate behavior. Where they are, it is usually for prostitution or for acts against children. Sixty per cent of the sex offenses reported to police in Michigan were directed against children seventeen years of age or younger, indicating one of the real dangers of the sexual offender in the community. Approximately one third of all sex offenders have a previous police record, although not necessarily for sexual offenses (Dunham, 1951; Brancale *et al.*, 1952; Pacht *et al.*, 1962). However, it has been found that males who were sex delinquents during adolescence are more likely to show sexual deviations as adults than are other types of juvenile delinquents.

GENERAL DYNAMICS

In our discussion of each of the deviations, we shall indicate the special factors which seem to play a part in the development of that particular disorder, but first it will be helpful to point out some of the general factors that are commonly involved in sexual deviations.

1. *Lowered controls associated with mental disorder.* Many of those arrested for sexual offenses are found to be suffering from a more general personality disturbance. In a study of 300 typical sex offenders in New Jersey, Brancale *et al.* (1952) found only 14 per cent to be psychologically "normal." Another 29 per cent were mildly neurotic; 35 per cent severely neurotic; 8 per cent borderline psychotic; 2 per cent psychotic; 5 per cent brain-damaged; 3 per cent psychopathic; and 4 per cent mentally

---

[1] *Statutory rape* is defined as sexual relations with a female under the age of consent, usually 18 years of age, even though the girl is matured and experienced and may voluntarily participate or even take the initiative in the relationship.

COMMON MISCONCEPTIONS CONCERNING SEXUAL OFFENDERS

"Sexual offenders are typically homicidal sex fiends."

Only about 5 per cent of all convicted sex offenders inflict physical injury upon their victims. Of course, this does not preclude extensive psychological damage. Homicide associated with sex crimes is rare, and the offender in such cases is usually insane as well as sexually deviant.

"Sexual offenders progress to more serious types of sex crimes."

Sex deviates usually persist in the type of behavior in which they have discovered satisfaction. Minor deviations may lose their "thrill" so that the offender progresses to major sex crimes in order to achieve satisfaction, but this pattern is the exception.

"Sexual offenders are 'oversexed.' "

Most of the sexual deviates arrested by the police are undersexed rather than oversexed. Typically, they have much misinformation about sexual functions and are more prudish than nondeviant individuals.

"Sexual offenders suffer from glandular imbalance."

Available evidence indicates that the direction of sexual discharge in humans is determined primarily by the kinds of experiences that the individual has had in his family situation and other interpersonal relations, not by hormonal secretions.

"Sexual offenders are usually repeaters."

Sex offenders have one of the lowest rates as repeaters. Less than 10 per cent of those convicted of sex crimes are arrested again for sexual offenses. Most of the repeaters are minor offenders such as peepers rather than criminals of serious menace.

This chart is based on material from Cabeen and Coleman (1962), Pacht et al. (1962), Tappan (1957), and Tappan et al. (1950).

---

deficient. Such pathological conditions often involve either the inadequate development or lowering of reality and ethical controls.

It is relevant to note here the typical relations of the various diagnostic categories to the types of deviate sexual behavior:[1] (a) The *antisocial personality* often engages in promiscuous sexual behavior, usually with the consent of the sexual partner. However, he may resort to threats, fraud, or force and frequently becomes involved in charges of seduction, sexual assault, and statutory or forcible rape. At times he may also participate in homosexual behavior. More deviant forms of sexual behavior are less frequently associated with psychopathic personalities. (b) The *neurotic* often shows inhibited attitudes toward sexual behavior and may manifest impotence or frigidity. Although he may attempt to compensate for underlying feelings of inadequacy and inferiority by guilt-ridden promiscuity, direct sexual assault is rare. When the neurotic becomes involved in deviate sexual behavior it is likely to involve such offenses as peeping, exhibitionism, and homosexuality. (c) Sexual behavior associated with the *functional psychoses* varies with the particular reaction type. The manic patient frequently engages in transient promiscuous sexual behavior and may expose himself or commit other lewd sexual acts. Occasionally he may attempt sexual assault. Severe inhibitions associated with schizophrenic and paranoid reactions usually act to prohibit homosexual and promiscuous heterosexual behavior. However, serious sexual deviations may be carried out by individuals who are overtly schizophrenic. Such deviations include

---

[1] This material is adapted in part from Cabeen and Coleman (1963), Gregory (1961), and Pacht et al., (1962).

rape or attempted rape, pedophilia, extreme fetishism, and bizarre acts of sadism. (d) *Inadequate and schizoid personalities* are often involved in offenses against children. These individuals show poor inner controls, are impulse-ridden, and lack any clear-cut sense of self-identity or self-direction. They are prone to verbalize their lack of responsibility for their behavior and often plead for somebody to provide direction for them. Usually their sexual offenses are directed against young girls, although young boys may also be involved. (e) The *mentally retarded* are apparently prone to promiscuous sexual behavior, particularly in the case of the female. In some instances, such individuals also exhibit themselves, and occasionally they are involved in sexual assault. However, the incidence of serious sexual deviations among mentally retarded individuals does not seem to be high. (f) Individuals suffering from *organic brain pathology* do not seem to follow any particular sexually deviate pattern. However, a relatively high proportion of cases of exhibitionism, incest, and acts against children appear to be associated with the lessening of cortical control in senile psychoses and other organic mental disorders associated with old age.

2. *Deviate sexual differentiation.* Sexual deviations are perhaps most often due to faulty differentiation and development in the long process of growing up and learning to find one's place in society. As we have noted, adult sexual behavior is the end result of a long process of development and differentiation, and the ultimate sexual patterns vary greatly, depending upon the training and experiences of the child. Homosexuality, for example, may be primarily the result of early seduction and training in homosexual patterns; frigidity may be the end result of a long process of repression and misinformation concerning the evils of sex. There is nothing inherent in the undifferentiated sexual potentialities of the infant which guarantees beforehand whether he will develop a "normal" heterosexual pattern or some other kind. There is an almost infinite variety both in the situations which are potentially stimulating sexually, and in the behavioral patterns that an individual may develop.

Among preadolescent and adolescent boys in particular, there are many conditions of both a sexual and a nonsexual nature which are erotically stimulating. Not only is there direct erotic arousal by slight physical stimulation of the genitalia, friction with clothing, bodily tensions, and so on, but for physiological and psychological reasons that are not entirely clear, any very strong emotional reactions of even pain or fear are often associated with sexual stimulation and even gratification. Included here are such things as accidents, fast car-driving, watching big fires, and being frightened. Sources of stimulation that are more specifically sexual include dancing and sex jokes; seeing burlesque shows, sex pictures, females in movies, and underclothing or other articles closely associated with females; and seeing animals in coitus.

Thus the young male shows a somewhat indiscriminate sexual reaction to a whole array of emotionally arousing situations. In some instances, where the experience is particularly intense or pleasurable, a conditioned response may be established which does not readily extinguish. With time, however, sexual stimulation ordinarily becomes delimited to a narrow range of specifically sexual conditions.

Kinsey *et al.* (1948) listed six chief sources of sexual discharge among American males: masturbation, nocturnal emissions, heterosexual petting, heterosexual intercourse, homosexual relations, and contact with animals. As we shall shortly see, there are also certain other sources of orgasm which are more rare and confined primarily to the more deviant patterns.

Some males derive 100 per cent of their sexual outlet from a single kind of sexual activity; others utilize several or even all of these more common outlets. According to Kinsey's findings, the average number of outlets used was between two and three, although this, of course, varied with different age groups and social levels. Also the particular sexual outlets utilized and the frequency of their usage were found to depend upon age, current possibilities for gratification, and individual variations in the strength of the sexual drive. Comparable findings were made in Kinsey's study of females with, however, a markedly lower general incidence of sexual behavior.

This concept of a "total sexual outlet," often comprising several modes of expression for full gratification, has several important implications for the understanding of sexual psychopathology which we shall elaborate in our future discussion. In passing, however, we may note that this concept helps to explain the puzzling fact that many exhibitionists and other sexual deviates are married and thus have "normal" sexual outlets in addition to their socially disapproved patterns. Here, too, we may think in terms of the *fixation* of sexual patterns on immature levels, as in the case of masturbation or promiscuous sexual behavior among young males, which interferes with normal heterosexual adjustment in marriage.

3. *Sexual frustration and other stresses.* Sexual behavior will depend not only on drives from within, but also on the rewards, frustrations, and problems presented by one's sociocultural environment, and on the standards, restraints, and evaluations made by the self.

Sexual behavior not only is based upon a strong physiological drive but is reinforced by the pleasure ordinarily accompanying sexual gratification. Consequently, sexual frustrations are often extremely difficult to face and may promote various deviate sexual practices designed to reduce sexual tensions and to yield some measure of gratification. In prisons and other institutions where the sexes are segregated, for example, the incidence of homosexual behavior is usually much higher than in normal life situations (Huffman, 1960). In other cases, frustration is provided by an individual's own feelings of sin and guilt associated with sexual matters. Thus the obstacles to normal discharge of sexual tension may be either internal or external, and in either case deviate patterns may develop instead. In a study of sexual offenders committed to Sing Sing Prison, Glueck (1956a) found a marked lack of knowledge about normal sexual behavior and childhood backgrounds characterized by a continuously traumatic, prohibiting, and inhibiting attitude toward sex. Those offenders showing the most marked sexual deviations gave a history of the greatest "modesty" and inhibition.

The influence of faulty family relationships in frustrating natural inclinations and encouraging substitute patterns can readily be seen in the occasional instances where parents are disappointed in having a boy and insist on raising him as a girl or encourage him in subtle ways to develop feminine traits. It has been pointed out that many individuals suffer from acute anxieties and worries prior to the commission of their sexual offense. Inner conflicts, frustrations, or the pressures of their life situation become unbearable, and as the breaking point is reached the individual acts out his inner tensions in an antisocial sexual offense. In the study and treatment of a group of lower-class sex offenders, Yalom (1961) has emphasized the extent to which hostility and resentment are acted out in sexual offenses.

4. *Relationship to victim.* In a study of cases taken from the files of the Detroit Police Department, Dunham (1951) has reported that the victim was known to the offender in about three fourths of the cases involving offenses against children, half the sexual assault cases, and a fourth of the cases of peeping and indecent exposure. Such findings raise the question of whether or not the victim may unconsciously encourage the sexual deviate. Although this may be far-fetched in most cases where a child is the victim, it may be an important consideration with adult victims and merits further investigation, especially in cases of homosexuality and other sexual offenses where the unconscious desires of the victim could lead to his giving cues to which the deviate responds with overt behavior.

The preceding factors are by no means the only ones to be considered in the dynamics of sexually deviate behavior. However, they do point to the importance of personality maladjustment, lack of information about normal sexual behavior, undesirable early conditioning, and the tendency to act out inner tensions in antisocial sexual offenses. We shall examine the role of endocrine and related physiological factors in connection with the types of sexual deviations in which they seem relevant.

TYPES OF DEVIATIONS

Sexual deviations may be separated into three general groups: (a) deviations involving excessive or deficient sexual activity or desire, such as impotence; (b) sexual behavior which involves a basically normal biological pattern but which takes place under antisocial conditions, such as promiscuity; and (c) sexual patterns which are considered abnormal in regard to the choice of sexual object, such as homosexuality.

The specific sexual deviations which will be discussed in the remainder of this chapter are the following[1]:

1. Impotence and frigidity
2. Satyriasis and nymphomania
3. Promiscuity and prostitution
4. Rape
5. Incest
6. Masturbation
7. Homosexuality and transvestitism
8. Pedophilia
9. Bestiality
10. Exhibitionism
11. Voyeurism (scotophilia, inspectionalism)
12. Fetishism
13. Necrophilia
14. Sadism
15. Masochism

Some of these so-called deviations, such as masturbation, are so common that "deviation" is hardly a proper term for them; they are included in our discussion only because of the social attitudes about them.

Impotence and frigidity. Impotence is an impairment in desire for sexual gratification in the male or an inability to achieve it. Although fatigue, worry, and various illnesses may temporarily impair sexual potency, prolonged or permanent impotence before the age of 55 is rather rare and is almost always the result of psychological conflicts. According to Kinsey's findings, only 27 per cent of the male population becomes impotent by the age of 70, and many of these cases are of psychological origin. There are, of course, occasional instances of injuries to the genitalia or diseases of the nervous system which may permanently affect erection or other genital functions. Even here, however, the importance of psychological factors is sometimes startling. Rowe and Lawrence (1928) have cited a case, for example, in which a patient's testes were bilaterally removed for medical reasons. The man temporarily lost his initiative and interest in work and became apathetic. However, he fell in love with a woman who understood his condition and reciprocated his love. He then found himself to be potent and his ambition and work efficiency returned.

The major psychological factors in impotence may be summarized as follows:

1. *Fear.* Such fear may relate to self-injury and possible loss of potency as a result of masturbatory activities, or it may relate to strong feelings of shyness and inferiority in approaching the opposite sex, or it may relate to possible detection and punishment. In a study of 50 impotent males ranging in age from 25 to 58 years, Senoussi *et al.* (1959) particularly emphasized fear centering around one's ability to play the male role and fear of rejection and humiliation by the female. The individual feels self-conscious and inadequate and anticipates failure, which his very attitude helps to bring about.

2. *Lack of emotional closeness to the sexual partner.* Here the individual may be in love with someone else so that strong feelings of unfaithfulness and guilt color his sexual behavior, or he may find his sexual partner physically repulsive, or there may be strong hostile or antagonistic feelings as a result of prior quarrels or conflicts. Occasionally, overattachment to the mother may lead to relatively unconscious feelings of unfaithfulness and hence to impaired potency.

3. *Latent or overt homosexuality.* Here erotic desires may be focused on members of the same sex with a corresponding loss of feeling or actual repulsion for members of the opposite sex.

Typically, sexual inadequacy leads to considerable worry and self-devaluation. Not infrequently such persons feel that something is profoundly wrong with them and that they can never achieve marital happiness. A vicious circle is started; the fears and doubts about one's adequacy make one less adequate.

Frigidity in the female is the counterpart of impotence in the male. Unlike impotence, however, frigidity is fairly common. It has been conservatively estimated that fully one third of all women are relatively or completely frigid—never experience orgasm. The primary causes of frigidity are psychological, and the frigidity apparently represents not an absence of sexual desire but a blocking, due to emotional conflicts.

In addition to the same factors often found in

---

[1]Other deviations include obscene phone calls, absorption in pornographic materials, gross lewdness, bigamy, adultery, seduction, and assault with sexual intent (the latter will be dealt with in terms of the specific deviate reaction of sadism).

the case of impotence (fear, lack of emotional closeness to the partner, and homosexuality), two other factors may be involved in frigidity. Where the partner is a "marital moron"—rough or unduly hasty or concerned only with his own gratification, the unpleasantness and disillusionment of romantic ideas may do serious psychic damage. Mann (1962) has pointed out that when the husband ejaculates prematurely, the wife may come to associate sexual excitement with tension and unfulfillment and may defensively suppress her own eroticism. Perhaps the most common factor of all, however, is undesirable early training in which sexual relations have been emphasized as lustful, bad, dirty, and evil. Under such conditions, inhibitions and attitudes are established which are not easily modified and which can lead to a great deal of emotional conflict during marriage.

Once a pattern of frigidity has been established, it may be extremely difficult or impossible to modify it. Particularly is this true in relation to a particular partner: it may be possible to achieve sexual satisfaction with someone else. However, this usually involves the establishment of a truly satisfactory emotional relationship with the new person and would not be expected from the indiscriminate practice of trying out new sexual partners as one would new shoes to see if there is a possible fit. For both impotence and frigidity, the only effective means of correction is usually the establishment of a stable, intimate, affectional relationship involving confidence, security, and love.

In discussing impotence and frigidity, it is frequently difficult to distinguish between impotent or frigid individuals and those who have a low sex drive and are sexually apathetic in general. In the former, however, investigation will usually reveal psychological factors which are leading to the inhibition or repression of sexual desire or to the inability of the individual to experience sexual gratification despite his desire to do so.

Satyriasis and nymphomania.   Satyriasis and nymphomania mean exaggerated or excessive sexual activity in men and women respectively. Such individuals may evidence intense and almost continuous sexual desire and center their entire lives around this activity.

In the light of current thinking, there is considerable question as to the meaningfulness of these terms. There are wide individual variations in the strength and frequency of sexual desire. The majority of males desires intercourse one to six times per week, but there are many individuals who engage in sexual relations several times a day over extended periods of time without apparent ill effects. Similarly, Terman (1938) found that a group of passionate wives experienced a desire for coitus averaging eight times as often as a group of nonpassionate wives. Consequently, it is extremely difficult to draw a meaningful line between normal sexual desire and what we may properly consider excessive or abnormal sexual desire.

If there is an answer to this problem, it would appear to lie in psychological rather than physiological considerations. Where the individual experiences an almost insatiable sexual desire and centers his behavior around sexual pleasures as (a) an escape from his problems, (b) a compensation for various frustrations, and (c) a means of bolstering feelings of masculinity or femininity and adequacy, then perhaps we may properly speak of his sexual behavior as excessive in degree. Such excessive sexual demands may take place within the framework of marriage or may involve a pattern of promiscuous or other deviant sexual behavior. In one case a 35-year-old business executive had maintained a pattern of 10 or more relations per week over a five-year period involving more than 300 girls. His thinking, interests, jokes, and general conversation were almost completely preoccupied with sexual themes, and he himself came voluntarily for clinical assistance. In his case the sexual activity was an unconscious attempt to prove his adequacy and masculinity.

Current brain research would also indicate that if the amygdala (a portion of the brain lying below the frontal lobes) is destroyed by disease or blocked off by surgery, the result is nymphomania in the female and satyriasis in the male. However, there is no experimental evidence to indicate that brain pathology is involved in the great majority of such cases. In most cases these reactions appear to represent compensatory satisfactions for life frustrations.

Promiscuity and prostitution.   Included here are premarital and extramarital relations and sexual delinquency.

Premarital and extramarital sexual relations

are inextricably bound up with social mores which not only are in a state of flux in our society, but vary from one socioeconomic level to another. Thus a full discussion of them is beyond our province. Kinsey *et al.* (1948, 1953) estimated, however, that 83 per cent of men and 50 per cent of women have intercourse before marriage and that 50 per cent of men and 27 per cent of women have extramarital relations at some time during marriage.

In the present discussion we shall confine ourselves to a consideration of certain dynamic aspects of sexual delinquency and prostitution. "Sexual delinquency" is used here to refer to transient promiscuous sexual relations which ordinarily end after the intercourse has taken place and typically involve girls under 18 years of age. Although the girls may receive clothes, meals, gifts, or even money, these relations are essentially of a noncommercial character and such returns do not constitute the conscious reason for resorting to promiscuous sexual behavior. Such behavior among young girls is considered a major social problem and an important factor in the spread of venereal disease.

Since the studies of sexual delinquency are hopelessly inadequate in relation to the amount of such activity that occurs, the dynamics involved are not completely understood. In terms of the information we do have, it appears that there are three major factors which enter into the etiology of sexual delinquency:

1. *Pathogenic family relationships.* An appreciable number of sexually delinquent girls come out of family backgrounds in which alcoholism and promiscuous sexual behavior on the part of parents has provided them with undesirable behavior patterns which they in turn imitate. A pathogenic family pattern appears to be particularly damaging in broken homes where the mother sets an example of promiscuity.

In many instances delinquent behavior arises out of a family background of rejection. Children under such circumstances often feel neglected, unwanted, and lonely. Broken homes, unhappy foster placements, and lack of adequate affection are propelling forces in converting neglected and deserted children into actual delinquents. To such girls the thrill of an "overnight romance" is often too much to withstand and offers an irresistible compensation in terms of feeling wanted, important, and loved. Once the pattern is begun, it is easy to slide into habitual delinquent behavior involving several such incidents a week with different men.

Some delinquent girls come from a family background of extreme strictness regarding sexual behavior and dates, which leads to considerable pent-up hostility and aggression. As a result, these girls swing to the opposite extreme of promiscuous sexual behavior, which represents a sort of defiance or lashing out against authority.

In this context it is interesting to note Gibbens' (1961) conclusion that girls suffer as much as boys from family tensions, but that girls tend to nurse their hurts and anxieties until adolescence when they are reflected rather suddenly in wayward or sexually promiscuous behavior. Promiscuity here is evidently an attempt to overcome frustrations and anxieties.

2. *The delinquent subculture.* We have previously noted that sexual delinquency is the most common offense among female juvenile delinquents. Often such behavior is associated with membership in a delinquent male gang in which such behavior is practiced. Each new member is expected to engage in promiscuous sexual behavior with various members of the group and is rapidly inducted into such practices—often in "initiation ceremonies." In less formal groups, the girl may feel under pressure to engage in such behavior in order to be accepted and not considered a "square."

Where the girl lacks information about normal sexual patterns and their desirability, it is relatively easy for her to be misled by peer group pressures. If she also feels basically inadequate and doubtful of her attractiveness, the factor of "proving" herself may be added to the total etiological pattern. In an early study of 267 habitually promiscuous girls referred to the City Clinic in San Francisco, it was found that although these girls had had sexual experiences far in advance of their years, their information regarding sexual matters and general physiology was extremely incomplete and inaccurate. Furthermore, over 60 per cent of them were relatively or completely frigid (Lion *et al.,* 1945).

3. *Sexual delinquency as a part of more pervasive psychopathology.* We have previously pointed out that sexual delinquency is not uncommon among mentally retarded girls who lack an understanding of the possible consequences of their behavior. Other types of psychopathology such as manic reactions, ambulatory schizophrenia, and antisocial reactions may also be of etiological significance in promiscuous sexual behavior. Here there is either a failure to develop normal inner controls or a lowering of these controls as a consequence of severe emotional maladjustment. In a study of 54 unwed mothers ranging in age from 15 to 39, Cattell (1954) found psychopathology in every case: 30 had character disorders, 17 were schizophrenic, and 7 were neurotic.

Since such diverse etiological patterns may be involved in the development of sexually promiscuous behavior, there is no one typical picture. The following case shows one type of pattern.

The patient's parents were divorced when she was seven. This event upset her because she was attached to her father and was forced to live with her mother. She felt rejected because her father remarried immediately after the divorce and seldom made any attempt to see her. During the following years while she was living with her mother and her maternal grandparents, she rarely saw him, and when she did her stepmother was so jealous of any attention she received from her father that the entire situation was very unpleasant.

The patient's mother was an undemonstrative, rigid, puritanical woman who became "soured" on men as a result of her divorce from the patient's father. To try to protect her daughter from being taken advantage of, she liberally indoctrinated her with the "evils" of sex and was very strict in the supervision of her dates. Even when the daughter was 16 years of age, the mother would not let her stay out on a date beyond 9:00 p.m. The patient stated that she never really liked her mother and bitterly resented her continual "meddling" and unreasonable supervision.

Shortly after her seventeenth birthday, the patient ran away from her home and by lying about her age managed to obtain a job as a hat-check girl in a night club in a large city. She states that she was so excited about this job that she could hardly sleep for several nights. It seemed to her that now she would have an opportunity to associate with really important and sophisticated people who knew how to live and were not bound by the iron rules of stupid mothers. Several days later she moved into a small apartment with another girl who had considerable influence upon her subsequent behavior.

Since the patient was quite pretty, she was frequently asked out, and eventually accepted a date with a very nice looking middle-aged "wolf" who got her drunk on their first date and more or less forced intercourse upon her. Although she did not enjoy the intercourse, he was interesting and glamorous in her eyes, bought her presents, and made her feel she was "really something." Since he seemed to expect sexual relations as a matter of course, and her roommate assured her that this was the right thing to do, she did not refuse him. She had visions of marrying him and settling down in a small honeymoon cottage with a flower garden and raising a family. When he soon tired of her and disappeared, she was terribly hurt.

Following this disappointment, she went out with a number of different men trying to "forget." Her roommate had advised her that the one sure way to forget one man was "in the arms of another" and she seems to have followed this advice rather faithfully. During this period she states that she did feel vaguely unhappy and guilty but that it was flattering to have so many men interested in her and to feel that she really "belonged" to the night-club set. Her room was always filled with flowers and candy and other presents and her roommate was most approving of her "progress." She states that she readily rationalized that such patterns were conventional among "sophisticated people." In the course of several months she had intercourse with some 30 men and was eventually brought to the attention of juvenile authorities because of her age.

Although promiscuity blends almost imperceptibly into prostitution, the latter is defined as the indiscriminate provision of sexual relations in return for money. When it is realized that many prostitutes can handle twenty or more men per night, it becomes obvious that organized prostitution is a highly lucrative business. However, it is so closely tied up with underworld activities and political vice that it is very difficult to get any clear-cut picture of its incidence or of the people who become prostitutes. So-called "houses" or "brothels" operate relatively openly in many areas, but in others intensive civic agitation has eliminated such places and the prostitutes who continue to operate do so more or less individually. The actual number of prostitutes in the United States is unknown but undoubtedly runs into many thousands. According to Kinsey's (1948) findings, about 69 per cent of the total white male population have some experience with prostitutes. Many of these are single experiences, however, and he estimated that prostitutes account for less than 5 per cent of the total sexual outlet of the male population. In countries where prostitution is governmentally controlled, it is a more widely utilized source of sexual discharge.

Although many of the etiological factors operating in promiscuity carry over into actual prostitution, the latter typically involves a more chronic picture of personality maladjustment and generally distorted life values. Interestingly enough, many prostitutes are married. In some manner, however, they seem to be able to reconcile their monetary sexual activities with their marital affections. In fact, Kinsey *et al.* (1953) found that many prostitutes will engage in oral-genital contacts for purposes of money, but consider such activities immoral and will not engage in them with their boy friends or husbands.

It has been presumed that the prostitute or call girl views her behavior strictly as a matter of business and financial remuneration and does not experience an orgasm or become emotionally aroused during a professional contact. However, there is evidence that this may not always be the case. Hollender has concluded from the intensive psychiatric treatment of several prostitutes that such behavior often "provides for human relatedness in a physical and nonpersonalized form when there is extreme difficulty in maintaining relatedness in an emotional and personalized form." (1961, p. 404) In essence, these girls wanted to be loved and to relate to others, but as a consequence of early experiences were terrified of close interpersonal relationships. Their choice of sexual partners was purposely unselective and represented both their need to relate and their defense against truly intimate interpersonal contacts.

As in the case of promiscuity, we again find a large percentage of mentally retarded girls, antisocial personalities, ambulatory schizophrenics, and other more serious psychopathological types among prostitutes. In some instances, the girl is forced into prostitution as a consequence of drug addiction—as the only means of obtaining sufficient money to maintain her supply of drugs. There are also "social levels" of prostitution ranging from street walkers to "high class" call girls who have a "select clientele." Many of the latter are not mentally ill in terms of any obvious symptoms. Often they are not only young and physically attractive but well-educated and sophisticated women. However, they somehow seem to convince themselves that prostitution is a perfectly acceptable business venture and preferable to being a secretary or working for a living. Usually, however, the meaningless and essentially empty nature of their existence becomes apparent to them over a period of time. Many of them eventually marry and attempt to establish a more meaningful life pattern. As Polly Adler (1953) summed it up in her book *A House Is Not a Home:* "Believe me, whoring is just a slow form of self-destruction."

There are, of course, male prostitutes—particularly for homosexuals—as well as female prostitutes, but they are relatively rare and are usually found only in large cities.

Rape. In rape, as in promiscuity and prostitution, sexual behavior is usually directed toward a normal sex object, but the behavior takes place under antisocial conditions. Over 16,000 cases of forcible rape reported in 1962 (Federal Bureau of Investigation, 1963). As we might expect, it is almost exclusively the male who is the offender. Most rapists are in their early twenties, and curiously enough, about half of them are married and living with their wives at the time of the offense.

In a study of 250 sex offenders in New York, offenses involving forcible rape were commonly found to be associated with antisocial personalities who had aggressive tendencies and past records of aggressive antisocial actions, though not always of a sexual nature (Apfelberg, 1944). Similarly Dunham (1951) found that almost half the offenders in cases of forcible rape in Michigan had previous police records. In a more recent psychological study of 100 rapists, Kopp (1962) again found a high incidence of antisocial personalities. He described them this way:

"This antisocial psychopath is a cold, seemingly unfeeling man who has always taken what he wanted from others without apparent concern for the feelings of his victims or for the consequences of his act. For him, rape is just another instance of aggressive taking, except that in this case he steals sexual satisfaction rather than money or property. When questioned about his offense, he often responds with callous sarcasm, completely devoid of guilt or concern. He may well simply respond with the statement, 'I wanted it so I took it.' The rape fits so well with his character structure and is so typical of his general behavior pattern that he can see nothing wrong with the act, and often goes on to rationalize that his victim probably enjoyed it. He wants no part of therapy unless he sees it as a means of manipulating his way out of incarceration. Needless to say, he is just as difficult to treat as those psychopaths who commit nonsexual offenses." (p. 66)

Although antisocial personalities constitute the largest group of offenders, forcible rape may also be associated with other psychopathology. Kopp (1962) has described the overly compliant offender who appears to fit the description of a passive-aggressive personality. His aggressive antisocial behavior is apparently related to a build-up of hostility and tension, and afterwards he feels guilty and much concerned about the well-being of his victim. The lowering of inner controls in manic reactions, schizophrenia, and other psychoses may also lead to physical assault and occasionally to forcible rape.

In a study of the wives of rapists, Palm and Abrahamsen (1954) found that they tended to be sexually seductive but rejecting, duplicating the type of relationship many of the rapists had had with their mothers. The deviate sexual act, then, could be interpreted as "a displaced attempt to force a seductive but rejecting mother into submission."

Often the rapist shows very little aesthetic preference in his choice of sex objects. Sometimes he simply decides that he will rape the next woman he sees, conditions permitting. East (1946) cited the case of an unprepossessing old maid over 70 years of age who was raped and then murdered by a man who was not mentally retarded, drunk, or suffering from a psychosis.

Rapists frequently inflict serious injuries upon their victims and sometimes even brutally murder them. It is not uncommon for women who struggle against their attackers to receive numerous physical injuries such as broken ribs, fractures, bruises of the breasts and abdomen, and various local injuries due to penetration. Occa-

sionally several offenders join together, as in the case of juvenile gangs, and rape the victim consecutively. The psychological as well as physical damage in such cases is apt to be considerable. Such experiences usually have disturbing effects upon the victim's marital relationships, often being upsetting to the husband as well as the wife. Particularly when the husband has been forced to watch the rape of his wife, their marital relationship may be severely disturbed. Because of the physical and psychological injury to rape victims, offenders are treated severely by society and are usually given long terms of imprisonment. The imprisonment itself seems to have little value aside from protecting society from further ravages by the offender while he is imprisoned, but until effective remedial procedures and trained personnel become available, society has little choice.

It may be noted that not all accusations of rape are valid. Occasionally women who have been seduced with promises of love and marriage and who subsequently find themselves pregnant and deserted have been known to make false accusations of rape which have resulted in imprisonment for the men involved (Tappan et al., 1950).

Incest. Culturally prohibited sexual relations between certain family members such as brother and sister or father and daughter are called incestuous. There may be many fantasies, particularly during the adolescent period, of sexual relations with brothers, sisters, mothers, or fathers, but actual incest is not common.

Although certain groups have approved various forms of incestuous relationships (at one time it was the established practice in Egypt for each king to marry his sister), most groups have definite prohibitions against incest. Such prohibitions have often been attributed to the recognition of dangers relative to inbreeding. However, the prevalent opinion among biologists at the present time is that these alleged dangers have been greatly exaggerated. Only when there are latent defects in the ancestral line do the marriages of close relatives result in defective offspring. Such inbreeding will not result in the introduction of any defects which are not already present in the stock.

Probably the most common form of incest in our society is between brothers and sisters. Such incestuous relations may occur in connection with low general family morals or as a result of mutual tendencies toward sexual exploration. Particularly where brothers and sisters share the same bedroom during the preadolescent or adolescent period there is a danger of sex experimentation. Occasionally older brothers and fathers force sexual relations upon younger female members of the family. This is freqeuntly a severely traumatic experience for the girl and may lead to the development of severe guilt feelings and an undesirable attitude toward sex. Even where the girl apparently tolerates the experience or actively participates in it at the time, later learned social inhibitions may lead to a re-evaluation of this activity and to severe self-devaluation.

Occasionally incestuous relationships, particularly between father and daughter, occur in connection with serious mental illness on the part of the parent; senile deterioration, manic reactions, alcoholism, and paresis are some of the conditions leading to such a lowering of moral restraints.

It is not uncommon in mental clinics to encounter patients who have severe conflicts over previous incestuous relationships or fantasy desires in this direction. Such conflicts are likely to be engendered in families where there are overly intimate general affectional relationships and the young adolescent is encouraged to behave as his mother's "little lover" or the daughter as the father's "girl." Where incestuous relationships actually occur, the aftereffects are in general more severe for the female.

The following case illustrates a rather severe reaction to incestuous relations:

The patient, a 20-year-old high-school graduate, had been subjected to incestuous sexual relations by an older brother from about the age of 12 to 15. She stated that during this period her family was extremely poor and she and her brother shared the same bedroom. Apparently also the moral level of the family left a great deal to be desired, for from the age of 15 to 17 her father forced sexual relations upon her as well.

During her last year in high school she took a course in mental hygiene during which the teacher discussed the harmfulness of incestuous relations with considerable emotionality, suggesting that the fathers participating in such activities should be summarily hanged. The patient reported that although she had had severe guilt feelings about her incestuous relationships, it was not until this talk that the full "evilness" of herself and her brother and father was brought home to her. For several days she contemplated suicide but finally gave up this idea.

Following this she could hardly stand the sight of her father—he appeared loathsome to her, "like a snake or something like that." She also stopped going out on dates, stating that she just didn't like men any more—they all seemed alike to her—and she didn't want to have anything further to do with them. After her graduation at 18, she obtained a job as a stenographer and moved into an apartment with an ex-classmate, also a stenographer. Her roommate was not pretty, had few dates, and spent most of her leisure time with the patient. Over a period of several months they became very fond of each other and enjoyed doing things and going places together. The patient stated that she did not know just how it happened, but one night after attending a party where they each had several drinks they found themselves kissing each other. This apparently led to a pattern of homosexual relations which continued over an 18-month period.

Then the patient met a homosexual youth at a party and they apparently became quite fond of each other. The patient states that they were good friends and could "feel at home in each other's company without getting involved in sex. Of course in the distant future we may try sexual relations and if this works out even get married." This apparently represented the patient's first attempt to return to a heterosexual pattern. It is interesting that it involved a homosexual partner. However, this first attempt almost failed, for her roommate became extremely jealous and reported to the patient that her boy friend was planning to get her pregnant as soon as possible so that he could force her to marry him. In the light of her previous relations with men, this news proved extremely traumatic to the patient and she became quite tense and disturbed. The following day she came voluntarily for psychological help.

Masturbation. Masturbation is defined as self-stimulation of the genitals for purposes of sexual pleasure. According to Kinsey's findings, 62 per cent of women and 92 per cent of men engage in masturbation at some time in their lives. It is the most common sexual outlet for men prior to marriage and the second most common outlet for women (heterosexual petting ranking first), usually giving way to coital relations after marriage. However, it may be resorted to whenever the individual is deprived of normal heterosexual opportunities, as when a man's wife is away or does not desire as frequent sexual relations as he. Most psychiatrists and psychologists consider it a normal sexual outlet in our society, which most people utilize to some extent on their way to adult heterosexual behavior. It seems of pathological significance only when it fails to yield to or interferes with the establishment of normal heterosexual relations or when feelings of fear and guilt centering around it lead to serious personality conflicts.

Partly as a result of the taboos and threats centering around masturbation, many millions of young people have lived in continual mental conflict over this problem. Many have been taught that masturbation is a vile habit that will undermine their health and possibly lead to insanity or have other terrible aftermaths. In fact, almost everything from weak eyes to impotence has at some time been attributed to masturbation. Mentally ill and mentally retarded persons have often been pointed to as horrible illustrations of the effects of masturbation, and at one time hospital authorities maintained a separate ward for patients whose insanity was presumably due to such practices. Such threatening information has often been presented in such a way as to make it appear that self-respecting people don't do such things and that all that is needed is a little self-control.

Often the youth fights against masturbating and promises himself that he won't give in again; then the sexual tension mounts, leading to failure of his resolve, and self-devaluation follows. Now he feels guilty and is convinced that he has no strength of character or he would not have masturbated. So he makes new and stronger resolutions and the whole cycle is repeated. It is difficult to imagine anything more admirably suited to permanent personality damage, for over a period of time a circular conflict of this type leads to strong feelings of guilt and inferiority, often complicated by intense fears concerning the possible physical or moral harm that he is doing to himself.

In addition, he may fear that the consequences of his despicable behavior may be detected by others. (One high-school physical education teacher told his students that masturbation could be detected "by the baggy appearance of the genitals.") And so the threat of social disapproval and scorn is added to the picture. Since such fears may seriously interfere not only with the individual's personal and social adjustment but with his subsequent marital adjustment, it is perhaps worth emphasizing that masturbation as practiced by the average adolescent has no known harmful physiological effects.

Under certain conditions masturbation may be considered pathological, but in such instances it is usually part of a larger picture of maladjustment. Children who feel unhappy, lonely, and unwanted may center too much of their activity around masturbatory practices in an attempt to compensate for their frustrations. Occasionally, masturbation may even be used as a form of negativistic or hostile behavior. This is well illustrated in a rather extreme case involving a group of about 25 boys in a sixth-grade class who openly masturbated en masse before their female teacher (Stirt, 1940). The boys came from underprivileged homes and psychiatric investigation revealed that their behavior involved a sort of mass protest based on feelings of frustration, hostility, and inadequacy.

Where individuals continue masturbation into adult life at the expense of normal heterosexual behavior, it is usually symptomatic of more serious underlying maladjustment. The individual may be extremely shy and fearful of the opposite sex; he may be a rather cold, withdrawn individual who finds an intimate relationship with another person disturbing; or he may consider masturbation the lesser of several sexual evils. A man may be in love with someone other than his wife, or he may find his wife physically unattractive and consequently prefer the more exciting and desirable persons depicted in his masturbatory fantasies. Often, of course, the fantasies that typically accompany masturbatory activities are of diagnostic value in determining the nature of the maladjustment. Men with strong homosexual inclinations may fantasy male figures and genitalia, while those whose sexual behavior centers around more deviant practices may fantasy being hurt or hurting others or exhibiting themselves, and so on.

Masturbation, then, may be of pathological significance as part of a larger picture of maladjustment. Ordinarily, however, it may be considered a normal phase through which most of us pass in the development of adult heterosexual behavior and one which may be reverted to under conditions of deprivation. Usually the only undesirable features are the worry, guilt, and self-devaluation which may be associated with it. Fortunately, more enlightened public attitudes have greatly reduced the devaluating inner conflicts which have so frequently centered around masturbation in the past.

Homosexuality. Here we are concerned with erotic relationships between members of the same sex. These relationships may vary from homosexual fantasies through kissing and mutual masturbation to fellatio, cunnilingus, and pederasty.

Contrary to public opinion, it is not possible to divide people into two clear-cut groups—homosexuals and heterosexuals. Rather these terms represent the extreme poles of a continuum, and in between we find many individuals whose experiences and psychic reactions combine both heterosexual and homosexual components, as the following statistics indicate (Kinsey *et al.*, 1948):

50 per cent of the adult male population has neither overt nor psychic experiences of a homosexual nature after the onset of adolescence.

13 per cent of all males react erotically to other males without having overt homosexual experiences after the onset of adolescence.

37 per cent of all males have homosexual experience to the point of orgasm after the onset of adolescence.

50 per cent of all males who remain unmarried to the age of 35 have had overt homosexual experience to the point of orgasm since the onset of adolescence.

18 per cent of all males reveal as much of the homosexual as the heterosexual in their histories.

8 per cent of males engage exclusively in homosexual activities for at least three years between the ages of 16 and 55.

4 per cent of males are exclusively homosexual from adolescence on.

Kinsey *et al.* (1953) found homosexual relationships far less common among women—28 per cent of the women as contrasted with 50 per cent of the men in his studies had made homosexual responses and of these only about a third as many had proceeded to the point of orgasm. Female homosexuals also had far fewer sexual partners and did not continue their homosexual activities over so long a time.

Homosexuality has existed throughout man's recorded history, and among some peoples it has been more or less tacitly accepted. In later Greece and Rome, for example, such practices were so common that homosexual prostitutes existed openly; "masculine" women were available for women and "effeminate" men for men. However, most groups have condemned homosexuality as socially undesirable; in our own society homosexuals are subject to arrest and imprisonment. This social attitude has been strongly maintained despite the fact that even those who are predominantly homosexual, with little or no heterosexual experience, may manifest no other evidences of serious personality deviation than we would expect to find in any random sample of the population (Hooker, 1957). Homosexuals may be of superior intelligence, well educated, and highly successful in their chosen occupations. Many of them have made outstanding contributions to our culture in music, art, and other fields. Not a few of the notable figures of history, including Alexander the Great, Michelangelo, and George Sand, are thought to have been homosexuals.

Problems of homosexuals. Inevitably it is difficult for homosexuals to make adequate occupational, sexual, and general social adjustments in the face of society's severe disapproval of their activities. Many live in continual fear of detection, loss of employment, and social disgrace even though they feel they have a right to their form of sexual adjustment. Others feel that their sexual desires are entirely wrong: they are in constant conflict within themselves. Especially where the homosexual is alone and not affiliated with any organized group of homosexuals, he tends to be continually at war with himself and to feel insecure, apprehensive, and lonely.

The following passage by a female homosexual is of considerable value in giving us insight into the problems faced by the homosexual individual:

"To those whose sex life is based on heterosexual relationships, the homosexual is a grotesque, shadowy creature—a person spoken of with scorn, pity or lasciviousness. The person so spoken of is often in the audience. If you are not one of us, it is impossible to realize our feelings when this occurs. It is incredible to us that a well educated girl could make the following remark: 'What do they look like? I wonder if I've ever seen one?' . . .

"What is it like to be this way?

"You are always lonely. It makes no difference how many friends you have or how nice they are. Between you and other women friends is a wall which they cannot see, but which is terribly apparent to you. This wall represents the differences in the workings of your minds.

"Between you and men friends is another difficult misunderstanding. Very few men desire platonic friendships, the only kind of which you are capable so far as they are concerned. The endless bitter disagreements with them cause many of us to renounce their companionship entirely. Very few men understand the need we have for their friendship and the aversion we feel for sexual love. Unable to find love or its most acceptable substitute, friendships, we frequently become psychiatric cases. You cannot keep a healthy state of mind if you are very lonely.

"The inability to represent an honest face to those you know eventually develops a certain deviousness which is injurious to whatever basic character you may possess. Always pretending to be something you are not, moral laws lose their significance. What is right and wrong for you when your every effort is toward establishing a relationship with another which is completely right to you, but appallingly wrong to others?

"How do homosexuals feel about one another?

"One of the saddest facts in this entire picture is that we seldom like one another. On the surface this appears ridiculous, but there are good reasons for it. . . ." (MacKinnon, 1947, p. 661)

Homosexual groups. Little is known about organized homosexual groups, but the preliminary study of Hooker (1962) on the "homosexual community" has added considerably to our knowledge. She has pointed out that there tend to be clusters of homosexuals in certain residential areas of large cities. Several of the apartment buildings on particular streets may be owned by and rented exclusively to homo-

sexuals, and most of the homes in a given area may be owned by homosexuals. As a group, the homosexual community constitutes somewhat of a subculture with unique customs, value systems, and communication techniques in terms of language, dress, and gesture.

Most of the activities of the homosexual community take place in friendship cliques, and only a small portion of the behavior is visible to the public. The visible portion is seen mainly in "gay" bars which function as social institutions where friends are met, news and gossip exchanged, invitations to parties issued, and warnings about current police activities given. In these bars sexual contacts are made—often through the exchange of long, meaningful looks. Typically, such contacts involve strangers who agree to meet at a certain time and place for sexual purposes. This relationship is usually transitory and subsequently each is likely to seek a new partner. A central feature of such relationships is the assumption that sexual gratification can be had without obligation or long-term commitments. When asked what it means to be "gay," one man answered:

"To be gay is to go to the bar, to make the scene, to look, and look, and look, to have a one night stand, to never really love or be loved, and to really know this, and to do this night after night, and year after year." (Hooker, 1962, p. 9)

The induction of a new recruit into such a homosexual group has been described by Hooker.

"The young man who may have had a few isolated homosexual experiences in adolescence, or indeed none at all, and who is taken to a 'gay' bar by a group of friends whose homosexuality is only vaguely suspected or unknown to him, may find the excitement and opportunities for sexual gratification appealing and thus begin active participation in the community life. Very often, the debut, referred to by homosexuals as 'coming out,' of a person who believes himself to be homosexual but who has struggled against it, will occur in a bar when he, for the first time, identifies himself publicly as a homosexual in the presence of other homosexuals by his appearance in the situation. If he has thought of himself as unique, or has thought of homosexuals as a strange and unusual lot, he may be agreeably astonished to discover large numbers of men who are physically attractive, personable, and 'masculine' appearing, so that his hesitancy in identifying himself as a homosexual is greatly reduced. Since he may meet a complete cross-section of occupational and socioeconomic levels in the bar, he becomes convinced that far from being a small minority, the 'gay' population is very extensive indeed. Once he has 'come out,' that is, identified himself as a homosexual to himself and to some others, the process of education proceeds with rapid pace. Eager and willing tutors—especially if he is young and attractive—teach him the special language, ways of recognizing vice-squad officers, varieties of sexual acts and social types. They also assist him in providing justifications for the homosexual way of life as legitimate, and help to reduce his feelings of guilt by providing him with new norms of sexual behavior in which monogamous fidelity to the sexual partner is rare." (1962, pp. 11-12)

Some homosexuals attempt to establish a more enduring relationship with another homosexual and engage in homosexual "marriages." Typically such "couples" also become members of homosexual friendship cliques. Most of these one-to-one relationships lead to disillusionment and are broken up after a period of months. Then the cycle begins anew with another partner. However, both the individual relationship and membership in the friendship clique appear to provide emotional support. The latter in particular provides the individual with the possibility of identification with a group, permits him momentarily to drop the mask of concealment which is often a heavy burden, and affords some release from tensions and anxieties associated with his homosexuality.

Where the homosexual has become affiliated with an organized homosexual group, there is a tendency for him to think of his problem as a group problem and therefore a social rather than an individual one. In such cases, there may be little feeling of fear or conflict, and the individual may accept his homosexual behavior as a perfectly natural form of sexual expression; he may even take pride in his homosexual behavior and consider himself "emancipated" from conventional heterosexual morality. However, many such individuals are overzealous in presenting rationalizations designed to demonstrate the superiority of homosexual behavior.

In addition to their other difficulties, adult homosexuals are sometimes the victims of youths who prey upon them for purposes of robbery or "sport" such as beating them up. And occasionally what starts out to be a "shakedown" ends up as a murder. In such instances, the youth usually has considerable latent homosexuality in his own make-up, and is motivated by unconscious homosexual desires as well as robbery. In the sequence of events the two usually go to the homosexual's apartment, where the youth is given a few drinks and then submits himself to some homosexual act. Much to his amazement, he finds the act pleasurable and in the tremendous anxiety aroused by this self-revelation of his own homosexual inclinations he may experience what is known as *homosexual panic:* he may become panic-stricken and blindly attack the homosexual with anything at hand.

Although there has been little research on the social aspects of male homosexual prostitution, two recent studies deal with this topic. Ross (1959) distinguished three types of male homosexual prostitutes: the bar-hustler, who frequents bars in search of homosexual clients; the street-hustler, who is usually a teen-age boy, and the call-boy, who does not solicit in public. Street-hustlers have the lowest prestige and look forward to careers as bar-hustlers when they are able to pass in bars as being of legal age. Ross found that the individuals of all three types regarded themselves as both prostitutes and homosexuals. Another investigator, however, found that teen-age street-hustlers did not regard themselves as homosexuals but considered hustling simply an acceptable substitute for other delinquent methods of getting money (Reiss, 1961). Usually the activity of these boys was learned from peers in a delinquent gang.

Homosexual patterns. Homosexual relationships involve various types of sexual patterns. A male homosexual may always take a female sexual role, or he may play a female role at one time and a male role at another. Similarly, a female homosexual may play a male role only or may alternate between male and female roles.

Considerable emphasis has been placed upon the "femininity" of male homosexuals and the "masculinity" of female homosexuals. For example, high-pitched voices, effeminate mannerisms, "swishing" in walking, artistic interests, and a

A transvestite in his male clothing (left), and in his female clothing (right). He came to a psychiatric clinic requesting that the physician give him a certificate stating he was a female. He was well developed and had a deep voice, normal male genitalia, and masculine physical proportions and distribution of hair, including beard. His IQ, obtained on an Otis test, was 95. He was married. There was no history of traumatic experience or sexual gland injury. He stated that since earliest childhood he had had cravings to be a girl. There were several other abnormalities besides his transvestitism, not typical of transvestites as a group. A Rorschach test indicated compulsive-neurotic tendencies, and he showed definite psychopathic trends. He was exhibitionistic, narcissistic, and displayed both sadism and masochism. He took ecstatic, fetishistic delight in the numerous trinkets he wore. There was an utter callousness and emotional frigidity, with pride in his way of life and rejection of any responsibility to society. (Summary of a case reported by Olkon, 1945)

tendency to enter so-called feminine occupations such as dress designing, hairdressing, music, and various entertainment fields have often been attributed to male homosexuals. Although many homosexuals do manifest such characteristics—and only homosexuals usually display them in extreme form—far more do not. Female homosexuals, in general, try to make themselves look as feminine and attractive as possible, and male homosexuals are found in military life, professional athletics, and other so-called "masculine" forms of endeavor, revealing no personality characteristics that can be identified as peculiarly effeminate. In fact, Hooker (1962) has pointed out that there is an emerging tendency in the homosexual world to avoid the appearance of being effeminate, so that the terms "active" or "passive" and "masculine or feminine role" are no longer applicable to most male homosexual behavior. Also, there are many homosexual relations which occur for purposes of immediate sexual discharge in which such role identification is reduced to a minimum.

A few homosexuals who identify themselves almost completely with members of the opposite sex are not only extremely "masculine" or "feminine" in their general personality make-up but even dress in the clothes of the other sex. For example, a male homosexual may wear lipstick, nail polish, high heels, and expensive clothes, including furs, and may otherwise appear as a very attractive and even beautiful woman. This is done not only so that he will appear more attractive to other men, but also because his female identification is so complete that he feels more comfortable and capable of achieving greater sexual pleasure in a feminine role. This condition is referred to as *transvestitism,* and such individuals usually show a long history of identification with the interests and attitudes of the other sex. Frequently they even request surgery to effect a change of sex.[1]

Constitutional factors. In general, there have been two opposed views concerning the etiology of homosexuality. The orthodox view has been that homosexuality has a constitutional basis in the form of direct genetic inheritance or physiological imbalance, such as an imbalance in sex hormones. Opposed to this is the newer psychosocial viewpoint, in which emphasis is placed on psychological and social rather than constitutional factors. This viewpoint is now favored by most psychiatrists and psychologists.

---

[1]It should be pointed out that not all transvestites engage in actual homosexual behavior and that in some instances transvestite behavior appears to be more in the nature of a fetish with strong homosexual overtones. Recent case histories of transvestites are reported by Lukianowicz (1960), V. M. Pennington (1960), Nielson (1960), and Grant (1960).

Constitutional approaches have in general emphasized the following points:

a)   Heredity.   Here the assumption is that homosexuality is transmitted via recessive genes. As evidence, the fact is cited that some families show a relatively high incidence of homosexuality running through two or more generations. More relevant are Kallmann's (1953) findings on a series of 95 pairs of male twins, of whom at least one member was exclusively or predominantly homosexual. In the case of the 44 twin pairs diagnosed as monozygotic (identical), both members of the twin pair were homosexual in every case. Interestingly, all denied homosexual acts with each other, and many claimed to have developed their homosexual patterns independently. By contrast, in the case of the remaining 51 twin pairs, who were diagnosed as dizygotic (fraternal), both members were homosexual in only 40 per cent of the cases. This indicated to Kallmann the importance of genetic factors, although he admitted the possibility of multiple causal factors in male homosexuality. In another study of only two pairs of identical twins, one male and the other female, the sexual roles were found to be divergent in each pair in the sense that one member of each pair was heterosexual (Rainer et al., 1960).

In the light of present evidence, genetic factors do not appear to be of crucial significance in homosexuality. And as Kinsey et al. pointed out, hereditary theories "must allow for the fact that some individuals change from exclusively heterosexual to exclusively homosexual patterns in the course of their lives or vice versa." (1948, p. 663)

b)   Chromosomal vs. anatomical sex.   A number of recent studies have been concerned with the possibility that there may be "chromosomal" differences between homosexuals and normals. It may be recalled that the normal male cell has one X and one Y chromosome; the normal female cell, two X chromosomes. But even though the genetic sex of the individual is determined at conception, the individual starts out with the potentiality for developing into either sex anatomically. In the normal individual, the sex organs of his chromosomal sex develop and the sex organs of the opposite sex are suppressed, although the residues of these undeveloped parts remain in his body. However,

various physiological events before or after birth can lead to a sex reversal (Bowman et al., 1960). Thus it is possible for an individual with two X chromosomes to develop anatomically as a male, and presumably such an individual would be prone to homosexuality. Several studies of the chromosomal patterns of homosexuals, however, have failed to produce evidence in support of this theory (Davidson and Winn, 1959; Gentele et al., 1960; Pare, 1956; Pritchard, 1962; Raboch and Nedoma, 1958).

c)   Hormone balance.   Early experiments with lower species demonstrated that the sexual behavior of male animals could be generalized to include homosexual activity by the administration of female sex hormones. This finding led to a considerable amount of research on the hormone balance in homosexuals, and a number of early studies did find imbalances. For example, Myerson and Neudstadt (1942) obtained disproportionate ratios in 25 of 29 homosexuals. As a consequence, many investigators concluded that homosexuality was the result of an abnormal androgen-estrogen ratio.

Later studies, however, have failed to support these early findings. Furthermore, even in the occasional instances where hormonal imbalances occur they do not appear to be of etiological significance since nonhomosexuals often show similar imbalances, individuals may shift from a homosexual to a heterosexual pattern or vice versa without a change in hormone balance, and treatment with sex hormones to change endocrine balance does not modify the direction of sexual behavior.

Although constitutional factors may play an interactional role in homosexuality, it would appear that on the human level sexual responsiveness is determined more by psychological factors than by hormone levels. Even in cases involving *hermaphroditism* (a condition in which the individual is possessed of well-developed genital organs of both sexes), where there is an anatomical basis for ambiguous sexuality, the pattern which develops cannot be understood solely in terms of constitutional factors.

Two sisters, aged 24 and 26 years, were to all appearances normal young women. They had feminine voices, smooth skin, no beard, well-developed breasts. They had been reared as girls, had feminine interests, and had never been sexually attracted by girls. However, medical examination revealed that one sister had a bifid scrotum with two well-descended testes, whereas fallopian tubes and ovaries were completely absent. She had married once, had later obtained a divorce, and was in love with another man. She insisted upon an operation to remove the male organs, following which she reported a reduction in sexual desire by about one-half. A subsequent marriage was successful. The other sister showed a similar medical and personal history. If these girls had been legally declared males, they would automatically have been homosexuals! (Summary of case from Witschi and Mengert, 1942)

Other studies of hermaphrodites have led to the conclusion that the sexual role assumed by the individual accords primarily with his masculine or feminine upbringing rather than with internal or external body characteristics. In deciding to which sex the individual should be assigned, the most important factor is considered to be the sex role established during the individual's period of growing up (Mann, 1962; Money *et al.*, 1955).

It is probably not surprising that many homosexuals themselves seize upon constitutional theories of homosexuality as justification of their behavior. For how, they argue, can a person with such a constitutional make-up be held responsible for his deviant sexuality?

Psychosocial factors. Psychological views are usually based on the concept of the gradual differentiation of sexual behavior, which, despite masturbatory activities and possible homosexual incidents, typically culminates in heterosexual behavior. As we have noted, there is no *a priori* assurance that such heterosexual behavior will develop without specific social encouragement, and in societies which have encouraged homosexuality, sexual development has been found to be readily directed toward such homosexual patterns. Among the major conditioning experiences which have been found to be conducive to the differentiation of sexual behavior in a homosexual rather than a heterosexual direction are the following:

a) Early homosexual experiences. A frequent factor is early seduction in childhood before sexual behavior is well differentiated in a heterosexual direction. East (1946) found seduction in early youth to be the most common single environmental factor in the background of 79 homosexuals. Similarly Bieber (1962) found that more than half of a group of 106 male homosexuals had had homosexual experiences by the age of 14, as compared with only one fifth of a control group of 100 heterosexuals.

It is doubtful that such early experiences determine the entire direction of later sexual development except in instances where they are reinforced by continual pleasurable repetition and serve to meet certain emotional needs, as well as providing sexual pleasure. In this connection it is interesting to note that Greco and Wright (1944), in a study of 10 chronically homosexual reform-school inmates and a control group of 10 normals, found that each of the homosexuals had had intimate association at an early age with a homosexual who had been a source of comfort to him at a time when he was in dire need of emotional and social security.

b) Pathogenic family pattern. Bieber (1962) also found a common pattern of family interaction in the background of homosexuals. Typically, the mother, frustrated by an unhappy marital relationship, establishes a "close-binding-intimate" relationship with the son which becomes seductive and romantic, stopping just short of physical contact. The son, overstimulated sexually, feels anxiety and guilt over his incestuous feelings, and the mother, aware of his feelings and fearful of exposing her own incestuous impulses, discourages overt signs of masculinity. The father, resenting the son as a rival, also makes it clear that the son's developing masculinity is offensive. Often the father shows preference for a daughter, and the son, in envy, wishes he were a girl. Bieber has described the end result as follows:

"By the time the H-son has reached the preadolescent period, he has suffered a diffuse personality disorder. Maternal overanxiety about health and injury, restriction of activities normative for the son's age and potential, interference with assertive behavior, demasculinizing attitudes and interference with sexuality—interpenetrating with paternal rejection, hostility, and lack of support—produce an excessively fearful child, pathologically dependent upon his mother and beset by feelings of inadequacy, impotence, and self-contempt. He is reluctant to participate in boyhood activities thought to be potentially physically injurious—usually grossly overestimated. His peer group responds with humiliating name-calling and often with physical attack which timidity tends to invite among children. His fear and shame of self, made worse by the derisive reactions of other boys, only drives him further away. . . .

"Failure in the peer group, and anxieties about a masculine, heterosexual presentation of self, pave the way for the prehomosexual's initiation into the less threatening atmosphere of homosexual society, its values, and way of life." (pp. 316-317)

Although Bieber found such family interactions most characteristic of the background of his homosexual patients, he also noted other patterns. In some instances, mothers were detached and hostile, while some fathers were overly protective. Some homosexuals were not excessively fearful in childhood and did not flinch from fighting; some even sought fights. However, these atypical cases still came from highly pathogenic family backgrounds and had come to fear a sustained heterosexual love relationship. Bieber concluded that a warm and supportive father who provides an adequate male model and a mother who approves her son's masculinity and understands his heterosexual responsiveness to her and other females promotes a masculine identification and precludes the possibility of a homosexual son. In this context it is interesting to note Dickey's (1961) finding that many homosexual males, despite their own aberrant sexual behavior, tended to idealize and identify with the typical heterosexual male role in our society.

c) Being reared as a member of the opposite sex. Occasionally a mother who has very much wanted a daughter will bring up her son as though he were a girl, keeping his hair long, dressing him in girls' clothes, and inculcating typically feminine attitudes and interests. The following case illustrates a pattern of identification with the other sex which was built up in this way.

"Mr. K. T., aged thirty-six years, liked to dress in women's clothes, and he came to the clinic with the request that he be operated on and have his genitalia removed and a vaginal-like orifice substituted. He was not psychotic, had a responsible position, and apparently adjusted well, except for his concern over the above-mentioned problem. His mother was very eager to have a girl-child, but had four boys, the last one being the patient. The mother, feeling disappointed, kept the patient away from the boys and dressed him like a girl. She gave him dolls to play with and taught him all the arts taught to a girl. This farce was kept up to the point that when he was six, he was sent to a girls' school dressed as a girl. When he was seven, 'I had the greatest disappointment of my life. My father took me to a barber and had my beautiful hair cut off. When I got home, both my mother and I cried. The next day I was sent to a boys' school, and I did not like to be dressed as a boy. My pants were rough, and the blouse was coarse, and I delighted in going home, taking off these clothes, and putting on my bloomers and dress, with its bows and ribbons.' " (Kraines, 1948, pp. 119-120)

This is a rather extreme example. In far more cases, the feminine attitudes and interests would be engendered in a more subtle way, so that the feminine identification might grow more or less unconsciously. The same factors apply, of course, in the case of a girl reared as a boy.

d) Traumatic social experiences. Where the boy or girl is ridiculed, rebuffed, and humiliated in his efforts to approach members of the opposite sex, he may turn toward homosexuality as a safer source of affection and sexual outlet. Early heterosexual experiences taking place under unfortunate conditions may have a comparable effect, as we saw in the case of the girl who had been subjected to incestuous relationships with her brother and her father.

In his study of 106 male homosexuals, Bieber (1962) has emphasized the effect of peer group rejection and humiliation. During childhood most of the patients he studied had been pathologically dependent on their mothers, oversensitive to physical injury, and fearful of exposing themselves to the jibes and humiliation of peer group members. Less than one fifth had participated in the usual games of boys; over one half had been isolated; one third had played mostly with girls. Such withdrawal from peer group participation is of course not conducive to developing normal male identification.

e) Castration anxiety. Psychoanalytic views have emphasized early male fears relating to castration which are reinforced by the shock of viewing female genitalia. Presumably the idea of being without a penis is too anxiety-arousing for some males, and they consequently go in search of a "girl with a penis." In this sense, the homosexual male is so set on the possession of a penis that he refuses to do without it even in his sexual partner. In females, according to psychoanalytic theory, the sight of the male sex organs may lead to fears of impending violation or to envy. Such fears and thoughts may interfere with sexual enjoyment and make sexual relations possible only when they can be achieved away from the presence of a male genital organ. But although fear of and aversion to male or female genitalia are often expressed by homosexuals, such attitudes would not appear to be crucial factors in the original determination of homosexuality. It would appear that such early anxieties, when they do occur, become important only when they are reinforced by other sources of anxiety which influence the entire course of psychosexual development.

f) *Prolonged heterosexual frustration.* In prisons, correctional institutions, and other situations where the sexes are segregated over long periods of time, there are marked increases in homosexual behavior. Huffman (1960) considers homosexual behavior so frequent in prisons as to be one of the "occupational hazards" of being an inmate. He has pointed out, however, that individuals engaging in homosexual acts in prison may not view themselves as homosexuals and often deny the existence of any homosexual tendency in themselves. Often they assume they are demonstrating their masculinity by seducing new inmates. Although such homosexual activities may be given up when heterosexual contacts again become available, inmates who serve long prison terms may become confused about their sexual role. After their release such individuals may seek out children or adolescents (Huffman, 1960).

Although homosexual behavior may occur in connection with, and may even be an important precipitating factor in, the development of conditions such as alcoholism, paranoid schizophrenia, and other psychopathology, there is no direct causal relationship in either direction between homosexuality and psychopathology. The homosexual is not typically mentally ill, nor are the mentally ill typically homosexual. Of course, homosexuals may become mentally ill. As we have seen, the general social conditions under which they have to live may place extreme pressures upon them and make effective personality adjustment most difficult. One can imagine how difficult it would be if such extreme social restrictions and threats were applied to heterosexual behavior, with homosexual patterns the only ones condoned by society.

Since the highly publicized case of Christine Jorgensen, a large number of physically normal male homosexuals have asked for surgery to remove their male genitals. Such surgery poses ethical, scientific, and legal problems. Worden and Marsh (1955) in a study of five such males, noted that these men seemed to feel that they were really women and had been given the body of a man by mistake. They considered themselves mistreated by a society that would not accept them as women, and they experienced intense conflicts about sex, which they perceived as threatening and unacceptable. But despite their desire to be changed physically to resemble women, they shared an "extremely shallow, immature and grossly distorted concept of what a woman is like socially, sexually, anatomically, and emotionally." Worden and Marsh concluded that the desire for surgery often represented an attempted "escape from . . . sexual impulses rather than a wish for a female sexual life." (p. 1297)

Treatment. The treatment of homosexuality is complicated by social considerations and is extremely difficult. Since society considers homosexuality undesirable and even criminal, and since the homosexual has such a difficult and precarious adjustment at best, it would appear desirable for him to change to heterosexual patterns if possible. But the majority are not readily amenable to treatment. Typically they believe that they were born as homosexuals or that familial factors operating early in their lives determined the outcome (Hooker, 1962). In either event, they feel it is a fate in which they have had no choice and over which they now have no control. However, some 25 to 30 per cent of the patients who receive psychotherapy show a change from homosexual to exclusively heterosexual patterns (Bieber, 1962; Freund, 1960). Not surprisingly, the prognosis is much more favorable for patients who are bisexual.

Some therapists feel that it is often more practical to encourage the homosexual to accept his homosexuality and to participate in homosexual groups than to try to change him, but the desirability and feasibility of such an approach remain to be ascertained. In any event, there is a growing conviction that the method of sending "vice squads" to track down homosexuals and imprison them neither helps the homosexual nor protects society.

Pedophilia. In pedophilia the sex object is a child or young adolescent. The sexual intimacy usually involves manipulation of the genitals of the child or partial or complete penetration. Occasionally the child is induced to manipulate the sex organs of the pedophiliac, or, in instances of homosexual relationships between an adult male and a young boy, to engage in mouth-genital contacts or in sodomy. Most pedophiliacs are men, although such practices occasionally involve women.

Offenders in this group are highly diverse in terms of age, educational background, and the general circumstances which surround their offenses. Most of the older offenders have been or are married, and many have children. In a study of 836 pedophiliac offenders in the state of New Jersey, Revitch and Weiss (1962) found that the older offenders tended to seek out immature children, while younger offenders were usually involved with adolescent girls between 12 and 15 years of age. The average age for pedophiliac offenders approximates 40 years. Aside from rapists, they are the group of sexual offenders most likely to use force to perpetrate their deviate behavior. This may take the form of verbal threats or physical restraint and may or may not result in physical injury to the child. In a study of 45 male offenders found guilty of offenses against girls of 7 to 10 years of age, Swenson and Grimes (1958) reported that physical violence was used in a fifth of the cases. In a study of pedophiliac offenders at Atascadero State Hospital in California, Frisbie (1959) found that over twice as many girls as boys were victims.

The etiological pattern in pedophilia varies considerably. In the case of young male offenders, however, we are usually dealing with individuals who feel markedly inadequate in their approach to the opposite sex and have an intense fear of rejection and humiliation. These inadequate and immature individuals focus their attention on children as a safer means of meeting their sexual needs and avoiding possible failure and self-devaluation. Kopp (1962) has pointed out that these men are usually unable to establish normal interpersonal relationships with people of their own age or to find a satisfying and self-sustaining role in the community. The findings of Glueck (1956b), Pacht *et al.* (1962), and Revitch and Weiss (1962) also indicate a very high incidence of ambulatory schizophrenics and schizoid personalities among this population of sex offenders.

Often these inadequate, schizoid individuals view their offenses more as idiosyncrasies than as serious problems and lack any clear sense of the inappropriateness of their behavior. Typically, they grasp at some seemingly rational explanation of their behavior. Thus an offender may insist that he was seduced by a sexually aggressive, precocious young girl or boy, or he may dismiss his deviant behavior as being entirely the result of overindulgence in alcohol. In many instances, the sex offense actually is committed under the influence of alcohol (Swenson and Grimes, 1958), but it is apparent that this does not provide an adequate explanation of the behavior, although alcohol may lower inner reality and ethical controls in an impulse-ridden and marginally adjusted individual.

The older group of pedophiliac offenders is more diverse and cannot be as readily characterized. In many instances, we appear to be dealing here with borderline psychotic individuals who are emotionally unstable, immature in their sexual differentiation, and subject to devaluating homosexual conflicts. Such offenders often avoid the full impact of their homosexuality while still giving it some gratification. In fact, most men who are arrested and institutionalized for homosexual offenses have molested or seduced underage boys (minors under the law) (Kopp, 1962).

In still other cases, we appear to be dealing with pervasive psychopathology which has weakened inner inhibitory controls, as in chronic alcoholism, paresis, and senile and arteriosclerotic brain degeneration. Pedophilia and exhibitionism are the most common sexual offenses committed by senile and arteriosclerotic patients. Here, of course, there may be a combination of lowered inner controls, regression, and fear of impotence. Kurland (1960) has pointed to similar factors in the case of schizophrenics who commit acts against children.

Society considers pedophilia a serious offense, and it is punishable in most states by confinement in prison or in mental hospitals for sexual offenders. Although confinement in prison probably does little to modify the behavior of the sexual deviate, it does protect society. Since pedophiliacs subject children to highly traumatic experiences and may physically injure them, imprisonment often is the only solution to this problem. However, an increasing number of pedophiliacs are being screened for treatability and given indeterminate sentences in state mental hospitals for sexual offenders. Here newer rehabilitative programs have proven highly effective. Unfortunately, legal prosecution of pedophiliacs involves a further ordeal for the child, and many cases of sexual assault on children undoubtedly go unreported (Henriques and Wells, 1961; Kurland, 1960). In such instances neither society nor the sex offender is helped.

In connection with the sexual offenses of older people, Kinsey *et al.* (1948) sounded a warning note. They pointed out that many small girls reflect the public hysteria over the prospect of "being touched by a strange person; and many a child who has no idea at all of the mechanics of intercourse interprets affection and simple caressing, from anyone except her own parents, as attempts at rape. In consequence, not a few older men serve time in penal institutions for attempting to engage in a sexual act which at their age would not interest most of them, and of which many of them are undoubtedly incapable." (p. 238) Revitch and Weiss (1962) have also pointed out that in many instances younger pedophiliac offenders undoubtedly are encouraged or even seduced by aggressive and seductive children or young adolescents. Here it is of interest to note that the great majority of victims and offenders know each other—most offenders are neighbors, friends of the family, or even family members.

Bestiality. In bestiality animals are used for the achievement of sexual excitation and gratification. The actual sexual pattern may involve masturbation by means of friction against the animal, fellatio, masturbation of the animal by the human subject, or actual sexual intercourse. Practically all large domesticated animals usually found on farms, such as dogs, calves, and sheep, are commonly involved. Occasionally ducks, chickens, and geese are also utilized. According to Kinsey *et al.* (1948), about 1 male in 12 or 14 of the general population has had sexual experience with animals. Among boys reared on farms about 17 per cent reported experiencing orgasm through animal contacts. Bestiality among girls and women is apparently much less common (Kinsey *et al.*, 1953).

Sexual contacts with animals were apparently a social problem even in ancient times, for there are well-established taboos in the Old Testament and in the Talmud against such practices. In some of these older codes, sexual relations with certain animals were permissible but contact with others was punishable by death. In general, however, society has frowned upon bestiality. In our own society, it occurs primarily in rural areas, where it is often learned from examples set by other boys or by experimentation after observing coitus among the animals themselves. Many people find it sexually stimulating to observe coitus among animals, and it is not surprising that many farm boys make some sort of identification with the male animal and attempt to replace him in such relations. Undoubtedly the lack of adequate heterosexual opportunities in many isolated farm areas also contributes to the substitution of animals for sexual purposes.

Where opportunities for normal heterosexual intercourse are not available, bestiality has usually been more or less condoned. However, it may be considered definitely pathological where the individual prefers sexual relations with animals when heterosexual outlets are available. This may occur as a result of the strong previous establishment of bestial patterns, or in some cases may reflect fear and inadequacy in approaching members of the opposite sex. Here, of course, the individual's fear of rejection and humiliation by the opposite sex is similar to that in pedophilia and, as we shall see, in exhibitionism and fetishism.

Exhibitionism. In exhibitionism sexual pleasure is achieved through exposure of the genitals in public or semipublic places, usually to members of the opposite sex or to children. Sometimes the demonstrations are accompanied by suggestive gestures or masturbatory activity, but more commonly there is only exposure.

The exposure may take place in some secluded location like a park or in a more public place, such as a department store, church, theater, or bus. In cities the exhibitionist often drives his car by schools or bus stops, exhibits himself while in the car, and then drives rapidly away. In many instances the exposure is repeated under fairly constant conditions, such as only in churches or buses, or in the same general vicinity and at the same time of day. Rickles (1942) cited the case of a patient who always exhibited himself at the top of the escalator of a large department store. The sex object too is usually fairly consistent for the same patient—ordinarily a stranger of the opposite sex, falling within a particular age range.

Exhibitionism is most common during the warm spring and summer months and occurs primarily among young adult males. Practically all occupational groups are represented, including engineers, teachers, students, salesmen, mechanics, and unskilled laborers. Among women the exhibition of the genitals is relatively rare, and those cases that do occur are less likely to be reported to the police than are offenses by male exhibitionists. Of course, many of the young males are not immediately reported, and not infrequently—especially in theaters—are encouraged by their victims.

A rather handsome 17-year-old boy had been seating himself beside girls and women in darkened theaters and then exhibiting himself and masturbating. He had been repeatedly successful in obtaining approving collaboration from the women before he finally made the mistake of exposing himself to a policewoman. Out of an estimated 25 to 30 exposures, he was reported only on three occasions.

Usually, however, the offender is reported. Although exhibitionists constitute the largest group of those apprehended by the police for sexual offenses, the actual dynamics involved are far from clear. The following aspects of exhibitionism may be noted (Hirning, 1947; Kinsey *et al.,* 1948; Kopp, 1962; Rickles, 1950):

1.   Over 99 per cent of preadolescent boys who engage in sex play, either of a homosexual or heterosexual nature, begin with the exhibition of the genitalia.

2.   Most exhibitionists seem to feel strongly that masturbation is sinful and evil and do not usually experience any pleasure from masturbation unless it is performed as a part of genital exhibition.

3.   The individual often struggles against the impulse to expose himself in much the same way that the adolescent struggles against the impulse to masturbate, but as the sexual tension rises, he feels compelled to carry out his exhibitionistic activities. And as in the case of masturbation, he often feels guilty and remorseful afterwards, particularly if he has achieved ejaculation.

4.   The suspense, excitement, and apprehension surrounding the exhibition of the genitals often intensify or reinforce its sexually stimulating aspects. In this connection it is interesting to note that indecent exposure is the only type of sexual crime which increases when the papers are playing up a "sex crime wave."

5.   Signs of being impressed or of emotional shock on the part of his victim are eagerly looked for by the exhibitionist. When the woman ignores his activities he is usually disappointed and abashed. But since many women react with disgust and obvious emotional shock, the exhibitionist is not usually disappointed.

6.   The typical exhibitionist is apparently a quiet, submissive, "nice" individual with strong feelings of inadequacy, inferiority, and insecurity in personal relations. He usually comes from a strict home environment, has adopted puritanical attitudes toward sex, and is often overly attached to a domineering mother.

7.   Although statistics indicate that approximately one half of the exhibitionists are married, they usually fail to achieve satisfactory sexual relations with their wives. Many state that they married only because of family pressure; many have married at a relatively late age.

There are apparently three major dynamic factors underlying exhibitionism. First, in many cases the exhibitionism seems to represent an immature approach to the opposite sex based upon inadequate information, puritanical attitudes toward masturbation and sexual relations, marked feelings of shyness and inferiority, and often overattachment to the mother.

A high-school teacher had exhibited himself for several months to a 30-year-old woman who lived next door. She finally reported him, and before arresting him the police took motion pictures of his activities from the woman's apartment. In order to get clearer pictures they raised the window. At this point the teacher thought he had finally made an impression and in turn raised his own window and intensified his masturbatory activities and suggestive gestures.

After his arrest he revealed a background of overattachment to a domineering mother and an inhibited, puritanical attitude toward sex. He had rarely gone out with girls and felt extremely shy and insecure in his approach to them. His strong bond to his mother undoubtedly contributed to his difficulties in heterosexual adjustment, making even his fantasies of sexual relations with other women seem like acts of unfaithfulness toward his mother. Yet his strong attitudes against masturbation gave him no adequate outlet for the discharge of his sexual tensions. As a result, he apparently blundered into his awkward, immature, and socially unacceptable form of sexual behavior.

This point is summarized by Karpman (1948):

"The exhibitionist, therefore, insofar as this particular activity is concerned, is an infantile individual. Otherwise, of course, he may be well educated, capable, efficient, and even highly moral, but with respect to this particular abnormality he is a child and is under the influence of wishes, impressions and emotional reactions which had their origin in his childhood." (p. 214)

Closely related to this background of immaturity and overattachment to the mother is the second major dynamic factor: doubts and fears about his masculinity. As a result of his strong female identification (with his mother), and together with the common fears and scruples about masturbatory activities, the exhibitionist has a strong need to demonstrate his masculinity and potency. Many patients readily express such ideas. Apfelberg *et al.* (1944), for example, cited the case of a patient who received sexual satisfaction only when he accompanied the exhibition of his genitals with a question to his victim as to whether she had ever seen such a large penis. On one occasion the woman, instead of evidencing shock and embarrassment, looked at him scornfully and assured him that she had. On this occasion the defendant stated that he received no sexual gratification. Such common expressions as "making her sit up and take notice" bear witness to the importance to these individuals of proving their "masculinity" and "potency."

Besides expressing immaturity or doubts about masculinity or both, exhibitionism may be only a part of more serious psychopathology. For example, Henninger (1941), in an analysis of 51 cases of indecent exposure, found 8 of them psychotic, 10 mentally retarded, 4 chronically alcoholic, and 3 psychopathic. The remaining 19 he classified as emotionally immature. It would appear here that conditions which lower restraints, weaken the individual's repressive forces, or lead to personality regression may eventuate in open exhibitionistic activities in predisposed personalities.

In very occasional cases another factor—hostility—enters in. Here the exhibitionistic activity appears to afford an outlet for hostile impulses towards members of the opposite sex or toward society in general. Instead of fire-setting, stealing, or other antisocial acts, the individual exhibits himself as a retaliation against rejections and frustrations which he attributes to others. In such cases, the exhibitionism may be accompanied by aggressive acts, and the victim may be knocked down or otherwise attacked. But this is rare. Ordinarily, as we have pointed out, the behavior is limited to the exposure of the genitalia, so that exhibitionists are not usually the dangerous psychopaths that many newspaper stories make them out to be. They usually respond well to psychotherapy designed to help them achieve more mature heterosexual adjustments. Punishment is usually useless and may be harmful.

Voyeurism. *Voyeurism, scotophilia,* and *inspectionalism* are synonymous terms referring to the achievement of sexual pleasure through clandestine peeping. Although children often engage in such behavior, it occurs as a sexual offense primarily among young males. These "peeping Toms," as they are commonly called, usually concentrate on females who are undressing or on couples engaging in sexual relations. Frequently they masturbate during the course of their peeping activities.

How do they develop this pattern? In the first place, viewing the body of a female seems to be quite generally sexually stimulating, as evidenced by the popularity of pictures and drawings of nude or seminude women and of burlesque shows, follies, and related types of entertainment. The common sayings "He feasted his eyes upon her" and "He raped her with his eyes" further attest to the "sexualization" of mere "looking" under certain conditions. In the second place, the hush-hush and mystery which surround sexual activities tend to increase curiosity and interest in them.

If a youth feels shy and inadequate in his relations with the other sex and has a good deal of curiosity concerning sexual activities, it is not too surprising if he accepts the partial goal of peeping. In this way he satisfies his curiosity and to some extent meets his sexual needs without the trauma of actually approaching a member of the opposite sex, and thus without the failure and lowered self-status which such an approach might involve. As a matter of fact, peeping activities often provide important compensatory feelings of power and superiority over the one being looked at, which may contribute materially to the maintenance of this pattern. Also, of course, the suspense and danger associated with the conditions of peeping may lead to emotional excitement and a reinforcement of the sexual stimulation.

Where older and sometimes married men engage in such peeping activities, the dynamics are quite similar, although the fantasy identification of the peeper with one or the other of the sexual partners may be quite important. Here we sometimes find older women as well as men being involved. In such instances the peeper is rarely well adjusted sexually in his own marital life.

A young married college student had an attic apartment which was extremely hot during the summer months. To enable him to attend school, his wife worked and came home at night tired and irritable and not in any mood for sexual relations. In addition, "the damned springs in the bed squeaked." In order "to

obtain some sexual gratification" the patient would peer through his binoculars at the room next door and occasionally saw the young couple there engaged in erotic scenes. This stimulated the patient greatly and he thereupon decided to extend his activities to a sorority house. However, during his second venture he was reported and apprehended by the police. This offender was quite immature for his age, rather puritanical in his attitude toward masturbation, and prone to rich but immature sexual fantasies.

Although a peeper observing the behavior of courting couples may become somewhat reckless in his secret pleasures and so may be detected and assaulted by his victims, such activity does not ordinarily have any serious criminal or unalterable antisocial aspects. In fact, many people probably have rather strong inclinations in the same direction, which are well checked by practical considerations and moral attitudes. Such immature behavior can usually be remedied by short-term psychotherapy without any serious consequences to the community. Occasionally, however, more serious consequences result from voyeuristic activities. For example, Yalom (1960) found a number of cases of peeping Toms who graduated from voyeurism to more serious sexual crimes such as attempted rape and arson. He cited the example of a youth who started with simple peeping, then began to make attention-getting noises .while peeping, progressed to accosting females verbally with the statement "My, you have big breasts," and finally attempted to rape a 45-year-old woman. The youth was 14 when his peeping began and 19 at the time of his arrest for attempted rape. In other extreme instances we find well-developed voyeuristic patterns in which the individual habitually frequents houses of prostitution where peepholes are provided. These cases are considered difficult to correct.

Fetishism.   In fetishism there is typically a centering of sexual interest on some body part or upon an inanimate object, such as an article of clothing. The range of fetishistic objects includes breasts, hair, ears, hands, underclothing, shoes, handkerchiefs, perfume, stockings, and similar objects associated with the opposite sex. The mode of using these articles for the achievement of sexual excitation and gratification varies considerably but commonly involves kissing, licking, fondling, tasting, or smelling the fetishistic object.

In order to obtain the required article, the fetishist may commit burglary, theft, or even assault. East (1946) related the case of a hair fetishist who was arrested for going up to a little girl on the street and cutting off some of her hair. At his residence five plaits of hair of different colors as well as 72 hair ribbons were found.

Probably the most commonly stolen articles are women's underthings. One young boy was found to have accumulated over a hundred pairs of panties from a lingerie shop before he was finally apprehended. In such cases the excitement and suspense of the criminal act itself typically reinforces the sexual stimulation, and in some cases actually constitute the fetish, with the article stolen being of little importance. For example, one youth admitted entering a large number of homes in which the entering itself usually sufficed for sexual purposes including actual orgasm. When this failed to produce satisfaction, he took some "token" such as money or jewelry.

The term *kleptomania* refers to compulsive stealing, usually of objects which are of no use to the individual but are typically associated with sexual gratification. The individual may steal a wide range of articles but commonly takes the more intimate items of women's wearing apparel, particularly panties and brassieres. In some cases the stolen objects are accumulated in a sort of collection; in others, the patient throws them away shortly after the act is completed.

The most common cases of kleptomania seem to involve various habitual forms of shoplifting by women and young boys and the stealing of wearing apparel from sorority houses and other women's establishments. As in other forms of fetishistic behavior, the excitement and suspense involved in stealing the fetishistic object contributes materially to the sexual excitation.

When finally apprehended, these individuals are usually quite penitent and embarrassed about their behavior and often are prone to deny even to themselves its sexual connotations. However, they admit that they seem unable to help themselves—that something forces them to perform the act. Where psychiatric treatment is

undertaken, such cases can usually be cleared up quite rapidly, but unfortunately such treatment is often unavailable.

Not infrequently, fetishistic behavior consists of masturbation in association with the fetishistic object. Here of course it is difficult to draw a line between fetishistic activities proper, and the use of pictures and other articles associated with a desired sexual object to increase the sexual excitation and satisfaction of masturbation. Utilization of such articles in masturbation is quite common and is not considered to be a serious deviation. However, where sexual gratification can take place adequately only in this way, we are probably justified in referring to the practice as fetishistic. For example, one 19-year-old youth could achieve sexual satisfaction only by entering a strange woman's bedroom and masturbating in connection with the wearing apparel and particularly the odors present. Bergler (1947) cited an unusual case in which the individual's sex life was almost completely absorbed by a fetishistic fascination for exhaust pipes of cars. Nor would just any exhaust pipe do; it had to be in perfect shape, that is to say, undented and undamaged, and it had to emit softly blowing gases. This became far more attractive to the patient than sexual behavior associated with females.

A more typical case concerns a man whose fetish was women's shoes and legs. He was arrested several times for loitering in public places like railroad stations and libraries watching women's legs. Finally he chanced on a novel solution to his problem. Posing as an agent for a hosiery firm, he hired a large room, advertised for models, and took moving pictures of a number of girls walking and seated with their legs displayed to best advantage. He then used these pictures to achieve sexual satisfaction and found that they continued to be adequate for the purpose (Grant, 1953).

In approaching the dynamics of fetishism, we can note that slight degrees of fetishism are frequently encountered in everyday life. Most men are perhaps stimulated by intimate articles of women's underclothing and by perfumes and odors associated with women. Some bobbysoxers have actually torn the clothing of a movie idol in order to possess some object intimately associated with him.

Many individuals are attracted sexually only by persons of a particular body build. Early childhood and adolescent crushes frequently lead to the association of certain traits of the desired person (such as red hair or dimples or long fingernails) with physical attraction, and in later life the individual may find himself sexually attracted to individuals possessing these same physical characteristics without realizing the specific basis for his attraction.

All these associations might seem mysterious if it were not for the fact that in the process of sexual development, as we have seen, almost any object or act may become associated with sexual excitation and satisfaction. In fetishism the first prerequisite seems to be a conditioning experience in which a particular object or bodily part is associated with sexual excitation. Such associations will become the preferred patterns of sexual gratification only if they are part of a larger picture of maladjustment. This typically includes what we may consider the second major ingredient in fetishism—fear of rejection and humiliation by members of the opposite sex. As in exhibitionism, we are apparently dealing with an immature individual who has deep feelings of inadequacy and fear in relation to the opposite sex, often intermixed with some measure of doubt as to his own masculinity. By his fetishistic practices the individual safeguards himself and also compensates somewhat for his feelings of inadequacy by mastery over the inanimate object, which comes to symbolize the desired sexual object and may become a substitute for it.

One additional fetishistic pattern which merits special consideration is that associated with firesetting (Gold, 1962). *Pyromania* or compulsive firesetting is frequently related to aberrant sexual behavior. It is interesting to note in this respect that "fire" and "passion" are often associated in popular songs and fiction. Typically the dynamics here involve some strong early emotional association with fire which was sexually stimulating plus the usual fear and inadequacy in approaching members of the opposite sex, leading to deviate channels of sexual discharge. A pyromaniac usually starts all his fires in the same way and feels forced to watch while the fire rages—at least for an initial period. This is accompanied by sexual excitation and orgasm and is often followed by feelings of guilt. One

youth was so helpful in putting out a major blaze that a deputy fire chief personally thanked him for his efforts. About a week later, at another serious conflagration, he was found again rendering major assistance. Questioning revealed that he had started both fires, and that in watching them burn he achieved full sexual gratification. He then felt extremely guilty and pitched in wholeheartedly to help put out the fire. Again, the excitement and suspense may add materially to the sexual stimulation. One apprehended arsonist who had set over 19 fires involving damage estimated at more than $2,000,000 stated that "It was the crowds more than the fires—those thousands of people. I can't explain it, but I got a tremendous bang out of it, like at a prize fight or bullfight."

Necrophilia. In necrophilia there is sexual excitation and gratification through viewing or actually having sexual relations with a female corpse. Although it has been recognized since antiquity as a sexual perversion, it is of relatively rare occurrence and is ordinarily associated with severe psychopathology. For the individual who has reason to pursue this subject, detailed case histories of necrophiliacs are cited by Brill (1941), Ehrenreich (1960), Klaf and Brown (1958), and Rapoport (1942).

Sadism. *Sadism* is a term derived from the name of the Marquis de Sade (1740-1814), who for sexual purposes, inflicted such inhuman cruelty on his victims that he was eventually committed as insane. Although the term has been broadened in its meaning so that it includes cruelty in general, we shall restrict our use of it to the achievement of sexual gratification through the infliction of pain upon the sexual partner. The pain may be inflicted physically, by such means as whipping, biting, and pinching, or verbally by means of humiliating remarks or criticism in front of others.

Sadistic sexual behavior ordinarily occurs on the part of the male. It may vary in intensity from mild fantasy, through pinching or whipping, to serious mutilation or even murder. In some cases the sadistic activities lead up to or terminate in actual sexual relations; in other cases full sexual gratification is obtained from the sadistic practice itself. A sadist may slash a girl with a razor or stick her with a needle, experiencing an orgasm during the process. A case showing the peculiar and extreme associations which may occur in sadistic behavior is that of a young man who entered a strange girl's apartment, forcefully held a chloroformed rag to her face until she lost consciousness, and then branded her on the thigh with a hot iron. She was not molested in any other way.

Sometimes sadistic activities are associated with fetishistic objects. East (1946) cited the case of a man who committed burglary in order to obtain possession of women's shoes, which he then slashed savagely with a knife. After being sent to prison he was found cutting the throats of women in the photographs which other prisoners kept in their cells. He admitted that he derived full sexual gratification from this procedure. Below is a more serious case of sadistic sexual murder.

"... a 35-year-old sexual psychopath who, under sadistic impulses, and partly under the influence of liquor, murdered his wife ... and two casually met women ... and mutilated their bodies.

"In childhood he gravitated toward the company of more or less delinquent boys; and at 13 was himself committed to the Essex County Training School in Mass., where he remained about two years. At 17 he joined the army, where a duty sergeant, 'who was a wolf,' pursued him for sexual purposes as he was 'young and pink cheeked.' For this reason, according to his account, he deserted after about four months.

"For many years he would experience, several times a year, a vague impulse to commit some violent act, especially on a woman. The danger of yielding to it seemed to him to be greatest when he was alone. Accordingly, he would seek immediately to place himself in the company of other men. He denied any homosexual leanings. His principal occupation has been that of a sailor. He stated that when other sailors, on reaching port, would go in quest of women, he would join only drinking groups.

"At twenty years he went to live with a young woman, and within three years, had two boys by her; finally married her, at the insistence of her parents. There was, however, constant maladjustment between them with repeated separations. One night ... about midnight, he visited his wife. They had a quarrel, he choked her to death and then mutilated her body by opening her abdomen to determine whether she was pregnant, as she had claimed.

"He then shipped as a seaman and eventually ...

arrived in San Francisco. [One] evening, he met Lena C. They engaged a room in a nearby hotel, sat around for about an hour, when he grabbed her by the throat, strangled her to death, and then mutilated her body by cutting off one of the breasts.

"He then shipped out of San Francisco, but returned about five years later, and ... met Irene C. in a beer hall. They had a number of drinks together and both were fairly intoxicated. He bought a bottle of whiskey and they went to a nearby hotel and engaged a room. The woman immediately undressed and went to bed. He did the same and found that she had 'passed out.' He tried to arouse her but she did not wake up. He grabbed her by the throat and choked her to death. He then mutilated her body by cutting out the vaginal tract, washed himself, and left the hotel.

"He had not had sexual intercourse with any of his victims, although he stated that he had gone with them each time for that purpose. ..." (Rosanoff, 1943, p. 493)

Various attempts have been made to explain the dynamics of sexual sadism. Among the more important factors which have been emphasized are:

1. Sexual sadism as merely one expression of a more general destructive and sadistic attitude toward others. Here the individual feels frustrated and rejected by others and seeks through hostile, destructive behavior to achieve compensatory feelings of power and importance and at the same time retaliation against the world for his mistreatment. Yalom (1961) has cited the case of a sexual offender who went out and seized women's breasts after arguments with his wife. His intent was to hurt the women and he studied their faces for expressions of pain. The act provided little sexual satisfaction and apparently represented an acting-out of intense hostility toward women. As might be expected, such individuals usually express their hate and sadistic tendencies in their whole general life orientation.

2. Sadistic behavior associated with intense attitudes toward sex as sinful and degrading. If an individual finds normal sexuality unacceptable, sadistic activities may protect him from seeing the full sexual implications of his behavior and at the same time express his contempt and punishment of the other person for engaging in sexual behavior. In one case a sadist achieved full sexual gratification by castrating young boys and killing and mutilating young girls; he rationalized his actions as the only way to save them from later immoral behavior (Wertham, 1949).

3. Sadistic behavior growing out of early experiences in which sexual excitation has been associated with the infliction of pain. Such associations may occur under a variety of conditions. In early sexual development, many children, in their sexual fantasies, visualize a violent attack of a man upon a woman. Such ideas are strengthened by stories, newspaper articles of sadistic assaults on females, and many everyday experiences in which the infliction of pain on an animal or other person gives rise to strong emotions and unintentionally to sexual excitation. We have noted elsewhere this connection between sexual stimulation and any strong emotional situation, especially during the adolescent period.

In some cases the sadistic behavior pattern becomes stabilized by means of various stereotyped rituals which must be carefully followed if the individual is to achieve satisfaction. But such patterns may lose their potency after a time, with the result that the individual may either give them up or be forced to resort to increasingly extreme sadistic practices in order to achieve sexual gratification.

4. Sadistic behavior growing out of castration anxiety. Sometimes the individual is trying to bolster lagging or inferior sexual potency, actual or feared. Many sadists are timid, feminine, undersexed individuals whose sadistic sexual behavior is apparently designed to arouse strong emotions in the sex object, which in turn arouse the sadist to a greater pitch of sexual excitement, thus making orgasm possible. The sadist receives little or no satisfaction if his victim remains passive and unresponsive to the painful stimuli. In fact, he quite frequently desires that the victim shall find the pain exciting and pleasurable, and he may even insist that his victim act pleasurably aroused even when being stuck with pins or otherwise hurt. In sadism based on castration anxiety even the killing of the sexual partner presumably would result not from the sadist's desire to cause pain and death, but from his desire to shed blood, which is a powerful emotional stimulant. In fact, the wound is usually in those parts of the body, like the neck or

abdomen, where a maximum of bleeding will occur. In addition, sexual stimulation is enhanced by suspense and excitement in the sadistic behavior. This is true even in more minor sadistic acts such as sticking a strange woman with a needle and then fleeing.

Closely tied in with castration anxiety are general feelings of inadequacy and fears of failure in approaching the opposite sex. A failure would result in humiliation and further self-devaluation; in order to protect his self-esteem and adequacy, the sadist presumably engages in the infliction of pain as a "safe" means of achieving sexual stimulation and gratification. As Fenichel (1945) put it, the sadist thereby feels, "I am the castrator, not the castrated one." In this way the individual gains strong compensatory feelings of power and superiority over the victim.

5. Sadistic sexual behavior as part of a larger picture of psychopathology. In schizophrenia, manic reactions, and other severe forms of psychopathology, sadistic sexual behavior and sadistic rituals may occur in psychologically predisposed persons as a result of the deviation of symbolic processes and the lowering of normal behavior restraints already discussed. Similarly, in certain types of antisocial personality where sexual excitement and the infliction of pain have become associated, the lack of inhibition and moral restraint typical of the antisocial personality may involve the individual in serious sadistic patterns.

It should be noted here, however, that rapists sometimes kill the only witness to the crimes, or criminals sometimes kill others in overcoming resistance or effecting their escape, and then mutilate the bodies in such a way as to make it appear that it is the work of a sadist or insane person. East (1946), for example, cited the case of a robber who murdered three prostitutes and then mutilated their bodies in such a way as to suggest that they were the victims of a sadist or insane person rather than a robber.

Masochism. In *masochism* the individual attains sexual pleasure through having pain inflicted on himself. The term is derived from the name of the Austrian novelist Leopold V. Sacher-Masoch (1836-1895), whose fictional characters dwelt lovingly on the sexual pleasure of pain. As in the case of sadism, the term *masochism* has been broadened beyond the field of sex to include pleasure derived from self-denial, from expiatory physical suffering such as that of religious flagellants, and from hardship and suffering in general. However, for our immediate purposes we shall restrict our discussion to the sexual aspects of masochistic behavior.

Masochistic activities may be confined to fantasies of ill treatment which are sexually stimulating or may involve a wide range of pain-inflicting activities such as binding, trampling, semistrangulation, spanking, switching, sticking with pins, and verbal abuse. East (1946) cited the case of a young woman who frequently cut herself about the arms, legs, and breasts, and inserted pins and needles under her skin. She felt relieved and experienced actual sexual pleasure from the pain and from seeing the blood from the incisions. Masochistic behavior is more common among women than men. This is presumably due to the fact that a certain degree of sexual submissiveness related to suffering is more characteristic of the female than of the male in our culture.

The dynamic factors underlying masochistic sexual behavior are essentially similar to those involved in sadistic sexual practices except that now the pattern involves the infliction of pain on the self instead of on others. Four patterns have been delineated:

1. Sexual masochism as one expression of a more general masochistic attitude toward life. Here the individual has presumably met overwhelming life frustrations by submerging himself in an orgy of misery and self-degradation which seemingly takes the sting out of specific life reverses. This may actually yield considerable satisfaction, based on our Christian belief in the virtues of suffering as a means of atonement and spiritual uplift. Often feelings of great self-righteousness and strength become associated with suffering and self-sacrifice.

Masochistic patterns are especially likely to occur where the individual has developed attitudes of shame, disgust, and guilt toward sexual behavior. In such instances the masochist apparently pays a penalty of suffering which then makes the experiencing of sexual pleasure permissible. That is, the masochist pays the price before rather than after the guilt-ridden behavior. Here, of course, the masochist does not necessarily wish to suffer cruelty but merely to pave the way for sexual pleasure.

2. Masochistic behavior growing out of early incidents in which the experiencing of pain has been associated with sexual excitation and pleasure, such as strong emotional situations, books, stories, and newspaper write-ups concerning masochistic behavior. In some instances mothers who have exaggerated the brutality and painfulness associated with their first sexual relations may deeply impress their daughters with the relation of pain to sexual pleasure. Subsequent experiences such as painful masturbation or defloration may serve to reinforce this early association.

Kraines (1948) described a case of a 27-year-old male that illustrates early association of pain and sexual pleasure. This patient could not have an orgasm unless he was beaten across the buttocks with a ruler. When the pain reached great intensity, an orgasm followed. Analysis of the case revealed that as a boy the patient had had a severe "crush" on a woman teacher. On one occasion she punished him for some minor misdeed by placing him across her lap and spanking him with a ruler. During this act the friction engendered by the teacher's knee against his genitals resulted in an orgasm. Kraines concluded that the patient's present masochistic desires were definitely traceable to this early incident.

In other cases the associative pattern may be more complex and may involve fears of abandonment, neglect, or rejection. Where children feel rejected by their parents, the only evidence of interest that they get from the parents may be when they are punished. Under such circumstances, punishment may come to be looked upon as evidence of love and affection, and later, in sexual relations, the girl may figuratively offer to submit to being hurt by her sex partner in order to increase her erotic feelings and her feelings of being loved and wanted. Persons with this background often tend to seek out sadistic individuals as marital partners, and clinical records indicate that they will undergo almost unbelievable pain and humiliation in order to assure themselves of their partner's love.

Many young people undergo experiences in which pain and sexual pleasure are associated, but most of them outgrow such associations in the course of heterosexual development. In the masochist, the association is reinforced and becomes deeply established.

3. Masochism as a means of increasing sexual pleasure. Masochistic sexual behavior on the part of women not infrequently represents an attempt to increase the emotional excitement of the sexual act and thus lead to maximal sexual satisfaction. This dynamic is indicated in a general sense in our common sayings of wishing to be "crushed in his arms" or "smothered with kisses." The erotic masochistic activities rarely result in severe injury; rather, they are in the nature of play-acting in which the abuse and pain are used as a source of forepleasure and building up of excitement through prohibited or deviant behavior. Usually, of course, there is a background even here of early attitudes relating sexual pleasure with pain.

4. Masochistic sexual behavior as a reaction formation to sadistic impulses. This pattern has been emphasized by psychoanalytic theorists. Presumably, learned ethical attitudes lead to the repression of sadistic impulses and to the formation of religious attitudes somewhat masochistic in nature. Such attitudes are then elaborated upon as a means of holding the repressed sadistic impulses in check. Thus the individual seems to crave situations in which he is hurt and humiliated and under certain conditions these attitudes carry over into the realm of sexual behavior. However, at times the repression may fail and the masochist may sadistically slay or mutilate his sexual partner.

The following is an unusual case showing the development of a masochistic pattern and its close relation to sadism:

"The patient is a thirty-nine-year-old lawyer. From early childhood, he has been obsessed by sexual ideas connected with the act of tickling. He remembers that once at the age of six or seven his older brother overpowered and tickled him. At the age of ten he read a short story which contained a detail dealing with titillation. In this story a boy was lying ill in bed and was tickled by two men who were paid to do so. They tickled his soles until he was shaken with spasms of laughter and finally lost consciousness. This story made a deep impression on the boy. It provided him with a powerful stimulus for autoeroticism. He mas-

turbated with the fantasy of a boy who was tickled by force, particularly on his bare soles. Whenever he played with young boys who were barefoot, he enjoyed tickling their soles. He often gave money and other gifts to young boys to induce them to overpower and tickle other young boys. Watching them perform this act excited him immensely. The greater the resistance of the overpowered boy, the greater the satisfaction. . . .

"His conscious trend was at first apparently homosexual; but at the age of fourteen he read a poem about an evil nymph who caught a beautiful girl in the forest and, according to her custom, tickled her to death. The poem was illustrated. The picture of the girl's torture took possession of the patient's mind and his fantasies gradually began to show a more heterosexual-sadistic character. . . .

"The patient's mother, a widow, owned a boarding house. Once the patient heard one of the tenants, a young girl, ask the patient's mother to tell a young man that she wasn't home for him that evening, casually adding that he frequently annoyed her by tickling her. The patient became very much excited. Later, when the young man visited her again, the patient often spent hours listening at the girl's door. He interpreted every spell of laughter and every exclamation as response to tickling, and enjoyed an intense sexual thrill at this occasion. . . .

"In his personal contact with girls, he was always cool and detached. He avoided conversation about sexual topics and the idea of a physical (genital) contact was repulsive to him. A few attempts at intercourse to which he was persuaded by friends ended with a complete failure. . . .

"Strange as it may seem, he succeeded in obtaining—for money—persons as partners and objects for his paraphilic enjoyment. But this type of prostitute was so expensive that he could not afford them for any length of time. Autoeroticism became therefore his only expedient. His fantasies varied. . . . The victim was often in the nude, invariably tied or made defenceless in some other way. Sometimes he visualized himself tied or crucified, with girls or men tickling his soles.

"When the patient was thirty-two years old, he met the woman who later became his wife. She instinctively recognized the patient's paraphilia, for she started to talk to him about her own erogenous zones and gave him descriptions of tickling scenes which aroused him intensely. Following such conversation, he was able to perform a normal intercourse with her.

"A short time later he married her. She was very cooperative and permitted him to use her in various improvised sadomasochistic scenes connected with titillation. She satisfied his most abstruse desires in this respect. His repulsion towards the woman's body gradually disappeared and a few years later a child was born.

"As time progressed, the patient, to his dismay, noticed that tickling his wife excited him less and less. Her vivid descriptions of her (fictitious) experiences with other partners began to grow duller and less effective. In her desire to help her husband, she tried to arrange scenes at her home, to offer the patient a substitute gratification. She invited friends to her house and then, in the course of the visit, without warning, she would start tickling them, while he was watching. Aroused, he would withdraw to the adjacent room and wait for her to join him in intercourse. During this period, this was the only way he could perform intercourse with his wife. Occasionally, the tickling scenes were arranged in a more elaborate way. The servant girl would rush in 'jokingly' and tie the unsuspecting visitor, then remove her shoes and stockings, so that the soles were exposed. The patient would observe the scene from the adjoining room through an open door.

"In the course of time all their friends stayed away. It became more and more difficult to obtain proper objects for his paraphilic fantasies. He studied books of all nations and tried to ferret out references to his paraphilia. Whatever he found, he copied or pasted into a book which he called his 'Tickle Book.'

"If he could not find anything suitable, such as stories, pictures, etc., he used his own imagination and described in glowing colors typical paraphilic scenes. He also recorded episodes told him by prostitutes. For this purpose he composed a questionnaire of 60 questions which he submitted to these women. He also ordered from artists paintings and drawings portraying such scenes; thus his collection grew larger and larger and his report ends with the paraphilia apparently confirmed in him as continuing to require one form or another of specific gratification." (Gutheil, 1947, p. 87)

In summary, the sexual drive, in seeking outlet, will apparently follow whatever pattern best suits the various considerations of practicality, previous experience and education, degree of maturity of the individual, moral restraints and attitudes of the individual and those around him, and so on. If there is healthy personality development and normal opportunity, a heterosexual pattern will probably develop; if not, the individual may rely on masturbation or homosexual contacts or on one of the other "deviant" patterns, the particular one depending both on his personality and on the experiences and training he has had. If masturbation is unacceptable to an individual, he is more apt to adopt a deviant sexual pattern.

The following case shows a progression of deviate behavior from relatively minor fetishistic patterns to sadistic murder. It is one in which inadequate and distorted sexual information played a major role and thus vividly illustrates the need for careful vigilance and early correction of deviations.

Some years ago, the police of one of our large cities were baffled by 3 sadistic murders which occurred with no evidence of monetary or other clear-cut motivation. On the wall of one apartment, in which an ex-Wave was brutally killed, there appeared in lipstick "For heaven's sake catch me before I kill more: I cannot control myself." In another killing, a child of six was kidnaped and her body dismembered and thrown into various sewers and drains. The kidnaper wrote and delivered a ransom note to the child's parents. No progress was made in this case until a policeman off duty captured a young man who was trying to make a getaway after an attempt at burglary. The boy would probably have been released on probation had it not been for an alert police official who noticed a resemblance between a curve flourish in the boy's signature and the ransom note. This boy, a 17-year-old university student, proved to be the perpetrator of these crimes.

The events leading up to these shocking murders by this youth have been carefully studied by psychiatrists and psychologists and the following points from the clinical report on this case are of considerable value in showing the dynamics in sexual sadism as well as in other sexual deviations. The boy was found to be of normal intelligence, not psychotic, and medically normal; electroencephalographic tracings were normal.

"When aged 9, the patient began to be interested in the 'feeling and color' and then 'the stealing' of women's underclothing. He began to take these at first from clothes lines, then from basements, and later from strange houses, the doors of which he found open or ajar. Dresses or other articles of woman's apparel made no appeal to him nor was he interested in the undergarments of his immediate family. Having secured a pair of woman's panties or drawers, he would take it to a basement or home, put it on, experience excitement and sexual completion. Most garments he then threw away, some he replaced, and some he hoarded.

"When 12 or 13 years of age, he secured the desired garments by going into houses through windows. This furnished more excitement. After three such expeditions, he took objects ('guns or money') other than underclothes; a change which was again an added stimulation. 'It seemed sort of foolish to break in and not take anything.' When he had thus changed his objective, the interest in underclothes largely evaporated and was replaced by the excitement experienced on 'making an entrance' through the window. Often he would struggle against his desire to leave his room at night, but when he did leave it was for the purpose of committing burglaries. He had sexual excitement or an erection at the sight of an open window at the place to be burglarized. Going through the window he had an emission."

Even after his admission to the university, this deviate behavior continued, although it apparently became increasingly difficult to achieve sexual gratification and it took several entrances to produce an emission. On one occasion he was startled in the act of burglarizing by a nurse whom he promptly struck and injured. This resulted in an orgasm and he left without striking her again and returned to his room at the university. On subsequent occasions when he was startled in the course of his burglarizing, he immediately killed. In one instance he had an erection on entering the house and then "The dog barked and the lady started hollering. She had on a night gown. She jumped up and hollered. Then I took the knife and stabbed her—through the throat—just to keep her quiet." Although this resulted in an orgasm he apparently had not intended to kill the woman. "It was the noise that set me off, I believe. I must have been in a high tension and the least bit of noise would disturb me in that manner."

"After an emission was the only time he felt he had done wrong . . . . [Then he suffered] from the pang of conscience. This compelling 'urge' had clearly a dynamic sexual origin . . . so we asked him had he never relieved this tension by manual manipulation. On one occasion he indignantly denied even the attempt . . . . Later he said he tried this method twice

without success. In the same manner, he at first denied ever having attempted any sex play with girls. Two days later with one of his rare shows of emotion he said, looking much ashamed, that twice, later correcting himself to eight times, he had touched girls 'on the breasts' and then pressed 'on the leg.' Always, having done this, he would immediately burst into tears and 'be upset and unable to sleep.' He forcibly denied ever having made any more intimate advances, except that he 'kissed them' sometimes. 'They wanted to kiss; I didn't.'

"It was clear that normal sex stimulation and experience were unpleasant, indeed 'repulsive,' to him, and these efforts afterwards created in him a negative emotional state. He found them improper in the conduct of others; he never spoke of them except in condemnation. . . ." (Adapted from Kennedy *et al.*, 1947)

TREATMENT AND PREVENTION OF SEXUAL DEVIATIONS

The specific treatment in sexual deviations, of course, depends upon the particular type of sexual disturbance and the general personality organization of the patient. The treatment of frigidity in a fairly normal and stable individual is of course considerably different from the treatment of homosexuality or pedophilia.

Drug therapy has proved useless in changing the direction of sexual outlet, although it may be used in reducing sex drive, especially in older men who have committed acts against children (Newkirk, 1961).

Cases of frigidity, impotence, fetishism, and homosexuality have been treated successfully by means of behavior therapy (Eysenck, 1960; Freund, 1960; Lazarus, 1963; Rachman, 1961; Stevenson and Wolpe, 1960). The assumption made in such therapy is that deviate sexual responses are maladaptive responses resulting from early conditioning which can best be changed by reconditioning. For example, impotence may be treated by conditioning experiences which reduce the patient's fear of rejection and humiliation by women. Conversely fetishism may be treated by establishing a conditioned aversion to the fetish. This tends to block the deviate sexual response and to permit the rechanneling of sexual behavior. In the treatment of homosexuality, Freund (1960) reported on an interesting conditioning program designed to inhibit homosexual behavior and stimulate heterosexual responses. The first phase of treatment consisted of the injection of an emetic mixture (causing vomiting). While the noxious effects were being experienced, the patient was shown slides of dressed and nude males. In the second phase of the treatment, testosterone was administered to increase sex drive and the patient was shown films of nude and seminude females. Follow-up studies 3 and 5 years after treatment indicated that about 25 per cent of 67 patients so treated showed permanent improvement. Differences in the selection of patients and evaluation of improvement, as well as other uncontrolled conditions, make it difficult to compare the results of behavior therapy with more traditional therapeutic approaches. According to preliminary findings, however, it would appear promising, at least in the treatment of certain types of patients.

The treatment of sexual deviations is essentially no different from the treatment of most other types of abnormal behavior. Typically, procedures are designed to help the patient gain insight into his motivations, change his basic attitudes, and work out more acceptable patterns of behavior. Kopp (1962), Yalom (1961), and other investigators have emphasized the value of group psychotherapy in achieving these treatment goals.

In addition to the problems connected with helping the sexual offender himself, there is also the problem of protecting society when the nature of the sexual disturbance requires such action. Often this protection is achieved in the form of a long jail sentence, which in the case of certain deviations, such as exhibitionism and homosexuality, is usually useless and may even be actually harmful. Of course in the case of more serious sexual offenses, such as sadism and pedophilia, there may be little choice but to remove the offender from society, for without adequate treatment there is always the chance that he may repeat his crimes or commit even worse ones.

Considerable public and psychiatric interest has been devoted of late to the results obtained by mental hospitals in the rehabilitation of sex offenders. In several states, individuals committing less serious offenses are sent to mental hospitals for treatment rather than to prison for punishment. The duration of their hospitalization depends upon their improvement: those who do not improve and are likely to repeat their sexual offenses are later sent to penal institutions, whereas those who show good improvement are put on probationary status and returned to the community. In this rehabilitation process, emphasis is placed on individual and group psychotherapy. Although many of these offenders do not respond sufficiently to this procedure to warrant their return to the community, the initial results are most encouraging and there is every reason to believe that improved methods of treatment will be developed.

Below is an account of an interesting and successful therapy program with 120 male sex offenders committed to a state mental hospital by the courts of Southern California (Cabeen and Coleman, 1961). Due to limitations of staff, group therapy was the only psychological treatment used aside from attempts to make the hospitalization itself a part of the treatment program.

"Within the framework of the general hospital rules, the sex offender group had its own program and governing body. They called it the Emotional Security Program (ESP). Every three months a Council of seven was elected by popular vote of all the 'patient body.' The Council served a variety of functions . . . they represented the patients and acted as liaison in dealing with the staff in matters of the patient's interests . . . they acted as a court in self-policing activities (relating to infractions of rules). A third major function of the Council was organizing and conducting the weekly ESP meetings. These meetings brought together the sex offender patients from all of the wards for a period of an hour and a half. Here reports were received from the different wards and group business or problems discussed. This was usually followed by some kind of a program. Sometimes it was very informal such as discussion of personal problems, dynamics, defenses, and principles of emotional health. Spontaneous participation from all the members was encouraged. The atmosphere was permissive and any feelings expressed were acceptable although often subject to analysis. A 'Question of the Week' was frequently used as a central theme around which to orient the interaction. At other times a more structured program was offered such as presentation and discussion of mental health films, psychodrama sessions, and talks by staff members. Other functions of the Council included new patient indoctrination activities and outside contacts with society. . . .

"When the sex offender first arrived he was oriented by an indoctrinator appointed by the Council who explained the program to him, including what he would expect and what he could do to help himself. Such an evaluation coming from another patient like himself often seemed more acceptable to him than if it had come from an authority figure.

"On the treatment wards the new patient found himself in a situation where all activities were therapeutically oriented and there was much discussion about 'problems.' Some of the discussion was between individuals and some was carried on in patient discussion groups. The patient discussion groups were spontaneous informal groups which met regularly to discuss emotional problems and difficulties. The group leader was usually a patient well advanced in his own therapy in a staff member's psychotherapy group. One of the important problems of such groups was to prepare patients for a formal psychotherapy group by learning to talk freely about their problems. The patient discussion groups were voluntary and all patients had equal opportunity to join one.

"The large majority of patients were actively engaged in working on their problems, and formed what might be called the in-group. As such they were accepted and enjoyed a certain status. Thus, the therapeutic attitude was reinforced by both individual and social reward. The small minority who denied having any problems or were resistant to therapy constituted what might be called an out-group, and were looked down upon by the rest as being immature or emotionally dishonest with themselves. In addition, their old defenses were easily penetrated or exposed by those who had been in the same position earlier but were working it through in psychotherapy. This unrewarding social position and the constant group pressure, in time, often broke through the resistance of some patients to facing their problems. Consequently, patients with initial defensive, resentful, or 'tough guy' attitudes were often able to accept therapy where they had been unable to do so under other conditions. . . ." (pp. 35-38)

"Visiting on the ward was permitted five days a week. Once a month there was a family day when the visiting was held in a large recreation yard and the children were allowed to visit. This enabled the patients to see their children, play with them, picnic and take part in other activities promoting the preservation of family ties. On the regular visits of the wives or parents there was often indication of therapeutic interaction taking place to the apparent advantage of both the patients and their visitors. . . . Mutual anxieties and problems of wives and parents were also discussed in occasional group meetings held for them by a psychiatric social worker.

"A final part of the sustained rehabilitation effort was the contact with society in general. The aim of this approach was two-fold. The first was an attempt to offset the feeling in the patients that they were outcasts from society and no one was interested in them. This was believed important in preserving and enhancing their identification with society and in increasing resistance to antisocial behavior. The second aim was to help inform or educate the public more completely about the sex offender and his treatment. One approach to maintaining contact with society was the invitation of representative citizens and officials to Emotional Security Program meetings. Many interested groups of individuals attended including state legislators, judges, attorneys, law enforcement officers, probation and parole officers, clergymen, educators, sociologists, penologists, physicians, and other professional groups, and many service organizations. Another approach to maintaining outside contacts and educating the public was the formation of an independent outside organization of expatients for mutual therapeutic support and dissemination of information." (pp. 40-41)

The potentialities of such hospitalization programs are attested by the fact that 79 of the 120 sex offenders were judged improved enough to return to society even though each had received only 1½ hours a week of formal psychotherapy, which consisted of group therapy with 6 to 8 other patients. A follow-up study indicated that only 3 of these 79 patients were arrested again for sex offenses after an average period of 17 months. Comparable findings were reported by Lieberman and Siegel (1957) for sex offenders treated in a mental hospital and by Pacht et al. (1962) for sex offenders given indeterminate sentences and treated in a prison setting.

Prognostic criteria for sexual offenders are still being worked out. In general, the degree and duration of deviation and the extent of accompanying psychopathology appear to be of prime prognostic significance. Brancale et al.

(1952) found that so-called normal sex offenders (those committing adultery or statutory rape) have a much better prognosis than other types of sex offenders. Inadequate and sexually inhibited neurotics who are prone to relatively minor sexual offenses such as exhibitionism probably come next. Hostile psychopaths who are prone to rape and more serious offenses and borderline psychotics who normally hold themselves in sexually but on occasion display outbursts of antisocial sexuality have a less favorable prognosis. Also included in the less favorable category are offenders who have well-differentiated and long-standing sexual deviations, as is the case with some homosexuals. Brancale *et al.* also found that offenders under 30 years of age were likely to be less deviant in their sex offenses and to have a better prognosis than those over 30. In general, these findings are supported by those of Cabeen and Coleman (1962), although the latter investigators did not find that older patients (excluding those with brain pathology) were poorer risks than younger ones.

With sexual deviation, as with other abnormal behavior, efforts at prevention are vital. On a general level, such efforts are directed toward the alleviation of pathogenic family patterns and the fostering of mature, healthy personalities. On a more specific level, prevention depends heavily on proper education concerning sexual behavior. It is evident from the preceding discussion that the majority of sexual deviates lack adequate information about sexual matters and have very little understanding of the importance and desirability of normal sexual patterns in marital relationships. Usually their education has been confined to vivid ideas of sinfulness and guilt which tend to make masturbation an unacceptable outlet for sexual tensions yet block normal heterosexual development and contacts. The result is, of course, a tendency to discharge sexual tensions in undesirable behavioral patterns. Fortunately, society is beginning to realize the importance of proper education and preparation for a healthy marital sexual adjustment.

We have now considered the special symptom disturbances, the personality pattern and personality trait disturbances (in chart form), and all the major categories of the sociopathic disturbances except alcoholism and drug addiction, which will be discussed in the next chapter.

REFERENCES

The reference list includes not only the sources from which the author has drawn material, but acknowledgments of the permissions granted by authors and publishers to quote directly from their works.

ADLER, H. M. Enuresis in recruits. *USAF Med. J.*, 1959, 10, 767-786.

AINSWORTH, MARY D. The effects of maternal deprivation: a review of findings and controversy in the context of research strategy. In World Health Organization, *Deprivation of maternal care: a reassessment of its effects.* Geneva: WHO, 1962. Pp. 97-165.

American Medical Association. *Conference on mental health services in the community,* Sept. 29-Oct. 1, 1961, Chicago. *Amer. J. Psychiat.*, 1962, 118, 636-637.

ANDRY, R. G. Paternal and maternal roles and delinquency. *WHO Publ. Hlth Paper,* 1962, 14, 31-44.

APFELBERG, B., SUGAR, C., & PFEFFER, A. Z. A psychiatric study of 250 sex offenders. *Amer. J. Psychiat.*, 1944, 100, 762-770.

ARIEFF, A. J., & BOWIE, CAROL G. Some psychiatric aspects of shoplifting. *J. clin. Psychopath.*, 1947, 7, 565-576.

ARON, MYRTLE L. The nature and incidence of stuttering among a Bantu group of school-going children. *J. speech hear. Dis.*, 1962, 27, 116-128.

BACON, MARGARET K., CHILD, I. L., & BARRY, H., III. A cross-cultural study of correlates of crime. *J. abnorm. soc. Psychol.*, 1963, 66, 291-300.

BANAY, R. S. Immaturity and crime. *Amer. J. Psychiat.*, 1943, 100, 170-177.

BANAY, R. S. *Wanted—an institute of criminal science.* Year-book of the National Probation Association, 1945.

BANDURA, A., & WALTER, R. H. *Adolescent aggression.* New York: Ronald, 1959.

BARBARA, D. (ED.) *The psychotherapy of stuttering.* Springfield, Ill.: Charles C. Thomas, 1962.

BARKER, G. H., & ADAMS, W. R. Comparison of the delinquencies of boys and girls. *J. crim. Law,* 1962, 53, 470-475.

BENNETT, IVY. *Delinquent and neurotic children: a comparative study.* New York: Basic Books, 1961.

BERGLER, E. Analysis of an unusual case of fetishism. *Bull. Menninger Clin.*, 1947, 2, 67-75.

BERGLER, E. *The psychology of gambling.* New York: Hill & Wang, 1957.

BIEBER, I., *et al. Homosexuality: a psychoanalytic study.* New York: Basic Books, 1962.

BLOCH, H. A. The dilemma of American gambling: crime or pastime? In H. A. Bloch (Ed.), *Crime in America.* New York: Philosophical Library, 1961. Pp. 333-351.

BLOODSTEIN, O. *A handbook on stuttering for professional workers.* Chicago: National Society for Crippled Children and Adults, 1959.

BLUEMEL, C. S. *War, politics, and insanity.* Denver: World Press, 1948. Reprinted by permission of Dr. Bluemel.

BOWMAN, K. M., ENGLE, BERNICE, & MERGENER, MARJORIE. Psychiatric and medicolegal implications of genetic and endocrinologic research in sex differentiation. *Amer. J. Psychiat.*, 1960, 117, 481-489.

BRANCALE, R., ELLIS, A., & DOORBAR, RUTH. Psychiatric and psychological investigations of convicted sex offenders: a summary report. *Amer. J. Psychiat.*, 1952, 109, 17-21.

BRILL, A. A. Necrophilia. *J. crim. Psychopath.*, 1941, 2, 51-73, 433.

BURKS, H. L., & HARRISON, S. I. Aggressive behavior as a means of avoiding depression. *Amer. J. Orthopsychiat.*, 1962, 32, 416-422.

CABEEN, C. W., & COLEMAN, J. C. Group therapy with sex offenders: description and evaluation of group therapy program in an institutional setting. *J. clin. Psychol.*, 1961, 17, 122-129.

CABEEN, C. W., & COLEMAN, J. C. The selection of sex-offender patients for group psychotherapy. *Int. J. group Psychother.*, 1962, 12 (3), 326-334.

CALDERONE, M. S. Illegal abortion as a public health problem. *Amer. J. Publ. Hlth,* 1960, 50, 948-954.

CATTELL, J. P. Psychodynamic and clinical observations in a group of unmarried mothers. *Amer. J. Psychiat.*, 1954, 111, 337-342.

Chicago American, Feb. 26th, 1961.

CLARKE, J. The precipitation of juvenile delinquency. *J. ment. Sci.*, 1961, 107, 1033-1034.

CLECKLEY, H. M. Psychopathic states. In S. Arieti (Ed.), *American handbook of psychiatry.* Vol. 1. New York: Basic Books, 1959. Pp. 567-588.

COLEMAN, J. C., & MC CALLEY, JEAN E. Nail-biting and mental health; a survey of the literature. *Ment. Hyg.*, 1948a, 32, 428-454.

COLEMAN, J. C., & MC CALLEY, JEAN E. Nail-biting among college students. *J. abnorm. soc. Psychol.*, 1948b, 43, 517-525.

COLEMAN, J. C., & SERET, C. The role of hostility in fingernail biting. *Psychol. Serv. Cent. J.*, 1950, 2, 238-244.

CRICHTON, R. *The great imposter.* New York: Random House, 1959.

DARLING, H. F. Definition of psychopathic personality. *J. nerv. ment. Dis.*, 1945, 10, 121-126.

DAVIDSON, J. R., & DOUGLASS, E. Nocturnal enuresis: special approach to treatment. *Brit. med. J.*, 1950, 1, 1345-1347.

DAVIDSON, W. M., & WINN, S. The relationship between genetic, nuclear and social sex. *Postgrad. med. J.*, 1959, 35, 494-500.

DITMAN, K. S., & BLINN, K. A. Sleep levels in enuresis. *Amer. J. Psychiat.*, 1943, 99, 881-885.

DICKEY, BRENDA A. Attitudes toward sex roles and feelings of adequacy in homosexual males. *J. consult. Psychol.*, 1961, 25, 116-122.

DISHAY, L. J. The challenge and solution of juvenile delinquency. *J. clin. Psychopath. Psychother.*, 1944, 6, 335-354.

DITMAN, K. S., & RLINN, K. A. Sleep levels in enuresis. *Amer. J. Psychiat.*, 1955, 111, 913-920.

DUNHAM, H. W. *Crucial issues in the treatment and control of sexual deviation in the community.* Lansing, Mich.: State Department of Mental Hlth, 1951.

EAST, W. N. Sexual offenders. *J. nerv. ment. Dis.*, 1946, 103, 626-666.

EHRENREICH, G. A. Headache, necrophilia, and murder: a brief hypnotherapeutic investigation of a single case. *Bull. Menninger Clin.*, 1960, 24, 273-287.

ELIAS, A. Highfields after five years. *Welf. Reporter,* 1958, 9, 3-21.

EYSENCK, H. J. *Behaviour therapy and the neuroses.* London: Pergamon Press, 1960.

Federal Bureau of Investigation. *Uniform crime reports, 1962.* Washington, D.C.: U.S. Government Printing Office, U.S. Department of Justice, 1963.

FENICHEL, O. *The psychoanalytic theory of neurosis.* New York: Norton, 1945.

FREUND, K. Some problems in the treatment of homosexuality. In H. J. Eysenck (Ed.), *Behaviour therapy and the neuroses.* London: Pergamon Press, 1960. Pp. 312-326.

FRISBIE, LOUISE V. Treated sex offenders and what they did. *Ment. Hygiene,* 1959, 43, 263-267.

GAETANIELLO, J. (Chief of Psychiatric Services, Sing Sing Prison, Ossining, New York) Personal communication. December 10, 1963.

GALDSTON, I. The psychodynamics of the triad, alcoholism,

gambling, and superstition. *Ment. Hyg.*, 1951, 35, 589-598.

GENTELE, H., LAGERHOLM, B., & LODIN, A. The chromosomal sex of male homosexuals. *Acta Dermatovener.*, 1960, 40, 470-473.

GIBBENS, T. C. N. Trends in juvenile delinquency. *WHO Publ. Hlth Paper*, 1961, 5, 56.

GILLISON, T. H., & SKINNER, J. L. Treatment of nocturnal enuresis by the electric alarm. *Brit. med. J.*, 1958, 2, 1268-1272.

GLUECK, B. C., JR. *Final report, research project for the study and treatment of persons convicted of crimes involving sexual aberrations.* New York: State Department of Mental Hygiene, 1956a.

GLUECK, B. C., JR. Psychodynamic patterns in the homosexual sex offender. *Amer. J. Psychiat.*, 1956b, 112, 584-590.

GLUECK, S., & GLUECK, ELEANOR T. *Unraveling juvenile delinquency.* Cambridge, Mass.: Harvard Univer. Press, The Commonwealth Fund, 1950.

GLUECK, S., & GLUECK, ELEANOR T. *Physique and delinquency.* New York: Harper, 1956.

GLUECK, S., & GLUECK, ELEANOR T. *Family environment delinquency.* Boston: Houghton Mifflin, 1962.

GODA, S. Stuttering manifestations following spinal meningitis. *J. speech hear. Dis.*, 1961, 26, 392-393.

GOLD, L. H. Psychiatric profile of the firesetter. *J. Sci.*, 1962, 7, 404.

GOLDMAN, G. S., & BERGMAN, M. S. A psychiatric and Rorschach study of adult male enuresis. *Amer. J. Orthopsychiat.*, 1945, 15, 160-166.

GRANT, V. W. A case study of fetishism. *J. abnorm. soc. Psychol.*, 1953, 48, 142-149.

GRANT, V. W. The cross-dresser: a case study. *J. nerv. ment. Dis.*, 1960, 131, 149-159.

GRECO, M. C., & WRIGHT, J. C. The correctional institution in the etiology of chronic homosexuality. *Amer. J. Orthopsychiat.*, 1944, 14, 295-308.

GREENACRE, PHYLLIS. Conscience in the psychopath. *Amer. J. Orthopsychiat.*, 1945, 15, 495-509.

GREENE, J. S. Hope for the stutterer. *Hygeia*, 1946, 24 (2), 120-121.

GREENSON, R. R. On gambling. *Amer. Imago*, 1947, 4, 61-77.

GREGORY, I. *Psychiatry, biological and social.* Philadelphia: W. B. Saunders, 1961.

GUTHEIL, E. A. A rare case of sadomasochism. *Amer. J. Psychother.*, 1947, 1, 87-92.

GUTTMACHER, M. S. *The mind of the murderer.* New York: Farrar, Straus, 1960.

GUTTMACHER, M. S. What can the psychiatrist contribute to the issue of criminal responsibility. *J. nerv. ment. Dis.*, 1963, 136, 103-117.

HALLGREN, B. Enuresis. *Acta Psychiat. Neurol. Scand.*, 1956, 31, 379-436.

HEATON-WARD, W. A. Psychopathic disorder. *Lancet*, 1963, 1, 121-123.

HEAVER, W. L. A study of forty male psychopathic personalities before, during, and after hospitalization. *Amer. J. Psychiat.*, 1943, 100, 342-346.

HENNINGER, J. M. Exhibitionism. *J. crim. Psychopath.*, 1941, 2, 357-366.

HENRIQUES, B., & WELLS, N. H. Sexual assaults on children. *Brit. med. J.*, 1961, 5267, 1628-1633.

HIRNING, L. C. Genital exhibitionism, an interpretive study. *J. clin. Psychopath.*, 1947, 8, 557-564.

HOLLENDER, M. H. Prostitution, the body, and human relatedness. *Int. J. Psychoanal.*, 1961, 42, 404-413.

HOOKER, EVELYN. The adjustment of the male overt homosexual. *J. proj. Tech.*, 1957, 21, 18-31.

HOOKER, EVELYN. The homosexual community. In *Proceedings of the XIV International congress of applied psychology.* Vol. II: *Personality research.* Copenhagen: Munksgaard, 1962.

HUFFMAN, A. V. Sex deviation in a prison community. *J. soc. Ther.*, 1960, 6, 170-181.

JOHNSON, W. *Stuttering and what you can do about it.* Minneapolis: Univer. of Minn. Press, 1961.

JOHNSON, W., et al. *The onset of stuttering.* Minneapolis: Univer. of Minn. Press, 1959.

JONES, H. G. Continuation of Yates' treatment of a tiqueur. In H. J. Eysenck (Ed.), *Behavior therapy and the neuroses.* London: Pergamon Press, 1960. Pp. 250-258.

KALLMANN, F. J. *Heredity in health and mental disorder.* New York: Norton, 1953.

KARPMAN, B. The psychopathology of exhibitionism. *J. clin. Psychopath.*, 1948, 9, 179-225.

KENNEDY, F., HOFFMAN, H. R., & HAINES, W. H. A study of William Heirens. *Amer. J. Psychiat.*, 1947, 104, 113-121.

KINSEY, A. C., POMEROY, W. B., & MARTIN, C. E. Sexual behavior in the human male. Philadelphia: W. B. Saunders, 1948.

KINSEY, A. C., POMEROY, W. B., & MARTIN, C. E. Concepts of normality and abnormality in sexual behavior. In P. H. Hoch, & J Zubin (Eds.), *Psychosexual development in health and disease.* New York: Grune & Stratton, 1949. Pp. 11-32.

KINSEY, A. C., POMEROY, W. B., & MARTIN, C. E. Sexual behavior in the human female. Philadelphia: W. B. Saunders, 1953.

KLAF, F. S., & BROWN, W. Necrophilia: brief review and case report. *Psychiat. Quart.*, 1958, 32, 645-652.

KOPP, S. B. The character structure of sex offenders. *Amer. J. Psychother.*, 1962, 16, 64-70.

KRAINES, S. H. *Therapy of the neuroses and psychoses.* (3rd ed.) Philadelphia: Lea & Febiger, 1948.

KUMMER, J. M., & LEAVY, Z. Criminal abortion. A consideration of ways to reduce incidence. *Calif. Med.*, 1961, 95, 170-175.

KURLAND, M. Pedophilia erotica. *J. nerv. ment. Dis.*, 1960, 131, 394-403.

LAZARUS, A. A. The treatment of chronic frigidity by systematic desensitization. *J. nerv. ment. Dis.*, 1963, 136, 272-278.

LEMERT, E. M. Stuttering and social structure in two Pacific societies. *J. speech hear. Dis.*, 1962, 27, 3-10.

LEVINE, A. Enuresis in the navy. *Amer. J. Psychiat.*, 1943, 100, 320-325.

LIEBERMAN, D., & SIEGEL, B. A. A program for 'sexual psychopaths' in a state mental hospital. *Amer. J. Psychiat.*, 1957, 113, 801-807.

LINDMAN, F. T., & MC INTYRE, D. M., JR. (Eds). *The mentally disabled and the law.* Chicago: Univer. Chicago Press, 1961.

LINDNER, R. M. Psychopathic personality and the concept of homeostasis. *J. clin. Psychopath. Psycother.*, 1945, 6, 517-521.

LINDNER, R. M. The psychodynamics of gambling. *Ann. Amer. Acad. polit. soc. Sci.*, 1950, 269, 93-107.

LION, E. G., JAMBOR, HELEN M., CORRIGAN, HAZEL G., & BRADWAY, KATHERINE P. *An experiment in the psychiatric treatment of promiscuous girls.* San Francisco: Department of Public Health, 1945.

LUKIANOWICZ, N. Two cases of transvestism. *Psychiat. Quart.*, 1960, 34, 517-537.

MC CORD, W., & MC CORD, JOAN. *Origins of crime.* New York: Columbia Univer. Press, 1959.

MAC DONALD, J. M. A psychiatric study of check offenders. *Amer. J. Psychiat.*, 1959, 116, 438-442.

MAC KINNON, JANE. The homosexual woman. *Amer. J. Psychiat.*, 1947, 102, 661-664.

MANN, E. C. Frigidity. *J. Mich. med. Soc.*, 1962, 61, 755-763.

MARTIN, J. M. *Juvenile vandalism: a study of its nature and prevention.* Springfield, Ill.: Charles Thomas, 1961.

MAUGHS, S. B. Current concepts of psychopathy. *Arch. crim. Psychodynam.*, 1961, 4, 550-557.

MONEY, J., HAMPSON, JOAN G., & HAMPSON, J. L. An examination of some basic sexual concepts: the evidence of human hermaphroditism. *Johns Hopkins Hosp. Bull.*, 1955, 97, 301-319.

MORRIS, H. H., JR., ESCOLL, P. J., & WEXLER, R. Aggressive behavior disorders of childhood: a follow-up study. *Amer. J. Psychiat.*, 1956, 112, 991-997.

MUELLNER, S. R. Development of urinary control in children: some aspects of the cause and treatment of primary enuresis. *J. Amer. med. Ass.*, 1960, 172, 1256-1261.

MYERSON, A., & NEUSTADT, R. The bisexuality of man. *J. Mt. Sinai Hosp.*, 1942, 9, 668-678.

NEWKIRK, P. R. The use of female sex hormones in therapy of male sex delinquents. *J. Neuropsychiat.*, 1961, 2, 163-165.

NICE, R. W. (Ed.) *Criminal psychology.* New York: Philosophical Library, 1962.

NICHOLS, L. A. Enuresis, its background and cure. *Lancet*, 1956, 271, 1336-1337.

NIELSON, P. E. A study in transsexualism. *Psychiat. Quart.*, 1960, 34, 203-235.

OLKON, D. *Essentials of neuropsychiatry.* Philadelphia: Lea & Febiger, 1945.

O'NEAL, PATRICIA, ROBINS, LEE N., KING, LUCY J., & SHAEFER, JEANETTE. Parental deviance and the genesis of sociopathic personality. *Amer. J. Psychiat.*, 1962, 118, 1114-1124.

PACHT, A. R., HALLECK, S. L., & EHRMANN, J. C. Diagnosis and treatment of the sexual offender: a nine-year study. *Amer. J. Psychiat.*, 1962, 118, 802-808.

PALM, ROSE, & ABRAHAMSEN, D. A Rorschach study of the wives of sex offenders. *J. nerv. ment. Dis.*, 1954, 119, 167-172.

PARE, C. M. B. Homosexuality and chromosomal sex. *J. psychosom. Res.*, 1956, 1, 247-251.

PENFIELD, W., & ROBERTS, L. *Speech and brain-mechanisms.* Princetown, N.J.: Princeton Univer. Press, 1959.

PENNINGTON, L. A. The incidence of nail-biting among adults. *Amer. J. Psychiat.*, 1945, 102, 241-244.

PENNINGTON, VERONICA M. Treatment in transvestism. *Amer. J. Psychiat.*, 1960, 117, 250-251.

PIERCE, C. M., & LIPCON, H. H. Clinical relationship of enuresis to sleepwalking and epilepsy. *AMA Arch. Neurol. Psychiat.*, 1956, 76, 310-316.

PIERCE, C. M., WHITMAN, R. M., MAAS, J. W., & GAY, M. L. Enuresis and dreaming: experimental studies. *Arch. gen. Psychiat.*, 1961, 4, 166-170.

PRITCHARD, M. Homosexuality and genetic sex. *J. ment. Sci.*, 1962, 108, 616-623.

RABOCH, JAN, & NEDOMA, KAREL. Sex chromatin and sexual behavior: a study of 36 men with female nuclear pattern and of 194 homosexuals. *Psychosom. Med.*, 1958, 20, 55-59.

RACHMAN, S. Sexual disorders and behavior therapy. *Amer. J. Psychiat.*, 1961, 118, 235-240.

RAINER, J. D., MESNIKOFF, A., KOLB, L. C., & CARR, A. Homosexuality and heterosexuality in identical twins. *Psychosom. Med.*, 1960, 22, 251-259.

RAPOPORT, J. A case of necrophilia. *J. crim. Psychopath.*, 1942, 4, 277-289.

REISS, A. J., JR. The social integration of queers and peers. *Soc. Probl.*, 1961, 9, 102-120.

REVITCH, E., & WEISS, ROSALEE G. The pedophiliac offender. *Dis. nerv. Sys.*, 1962, 23, 73-78.

RICKLES, N. K. Exhibitionism. *J. nerv. ment. Dis.*, 1942, 95, 11-17.

RICKLES, N. K. *Exhibitionism.* Philadelphia: J. P. Lippincott, 1950.

ROSANOFF, A. Thirty condemned men. *Amer. J. Psychiat.*, 1943, 99, 484-495.

ROSS, H. L. The 'hustler' in Chicago. *J. Stud. Res.*, 1959, 4, 13-19.

ROSTEN, R. A. Some personality characteristics of compulsive gamblers. Unpublished Dissertation, UCLA, 1961.

ROWE, A. W., & LAWRENCE, H. C. The male and female gonads. *Endocrinology*, 1928, 12, 591-662.

SENOUSSI, A. E., COLEMAN, D. R., & TAUBER, A. S. Factors in male impotence. *J. Psychol.*, 1959, 48, 3-46.

SHEEHAN, J. G. Theory and treatment of stuttering as an approach-avoidance conflict. *J. Psychol.*, 1953, 36, 27-49.

SHEEHAN, J. G. Projective studies of stuttering. *J. speech hear. Dis.*, 1958, 23, 18-25.

SHEEHAN, J. G., CORTESE, P. A., & HADLEY, R. G. Guilt, shame, and tension in graphic projections of stuttering. *J. speech hear. Dis.*, 1962, 27, 129-139.

STEVENSON, I., & WOLPE, J. Recovery from sexual deviations through overcoming non-sexual neurotic responses. *Amer. J. Psychiat.*, 1960, 116, 737-742.

STIRT, SONIA S. Overt mass masturbation in the classroom. *Amer. J. Orthopsychiat.*, 1940, 10, 801-804.

STOTT, D. H. Evidence for a congenital factor in maladjustment and delinquency. *Amer. J. Psychiat.*, 1962, 118, 781-794.

SWENSON, W. M., & GRIMES, B. P. Characteristics of sex offenders admitted to a Minnesota state hospital for pre-sentence psychiatric investigation. *Psychiat. Quart. Suppl.*, 1958, 32, 110-123.

TAPIA, F., JEKEL, J., & DOMKE, H. R. Enuresis: an emotional symptom? *J. nerv. ment. Dis.*, 1960, 130, 61-66.

TAPPAN, P. W. Sexual offenses and the treatment of sexual offenders in the United States. In L. Radzinowicz (Ed.), *English studies in criminal science.* Vol. 9. *Sexual offenses.* London: Macmillan, 1957. Pp. 500-516.

TAPPAN, P. W., *et al.* The habitual sex offender. Report of the State Commission, State of N. J., 1950 .

TERMAN, L. M. *Psychological factors in marital happiness.* New York: McGraw-Hill, 1938.

THORNE, F. C. The incidence of nocturnal enuresis after age five. *Amer. J. Psychiat.*, 1944, 100, 686-689.

THORNE, F. C. The etiology of sociopathic reactions. *Amer. J. Psychother.*, 1959, 13, 319-330.

Time. GAMBLERS ANONYMOUS. August 25, 1961. Pp. 48-49.

U. S. Bureau of Prisons. National prisoner statistics (a series). Washington, D. C.: Author, 1963.

VEDDER, C. B. *Juvenile offenders.* Springfield, Ill.: Charles C. Thomas, 1963.

WEGROCKI, H. J. Validity of the concept of psychopathic personality. *Arch. crim. Psychodyn.*, 1961, 4, 789-797.

WERTHAM, F. *The show of violence.* New York: Doubleday, 1949.

WICKES, I. G. Treatment of persistent enuresis with the electric buzzer. *Arch. Diseases Childhd*, 1958, 33, 160-164.

WILKINS, W. L. *The identification of character and behavior disorders in the military life.* U.S. Navy Medical Neuropsychiatric Research Unit, San Diego 52, California. Washington, D. C.: Navy Department, Bureau of Medicine and Surgery, 1961.

WILLIAMS, D. E. An evaluation of masseter muscle action potentials in stuttered and non-stuttered speech. *Speech Monogr.*, 1953, 20, 190-191.

WINGATE, M. E. Evaluation and stuttering, Part I: characteristics of young children. *J. speech hear. Dis.*, 1962, 27, 106-115.

WIRT, R. D., BRIGGS, P. F., & GOLDEN, J. Delinquency prone personalities III. The sociopathic personality: treatment. *Minnesota Med.*, 1962, 45, 289-295.

WITSCHI, E., & MENGERT, W. F. Endocrine studies on human hermaphrodites and their bearing on the interpretation of homosexuality. *J. clin. Endocrinol.*, 1942, 2, 279-286. Summarized by permission of the authors and Charles C. Thomas, publisher.

WORDEN, F. G., & MARSH, J. T. Psychological factors in men seeking sex transformation; preliminary report. *J. Amer. med. Ass.*, 1955, 157, 1292-1297.

YABLONSKY, L. Where is science taking us? *Saturday Rev.*, 1963, 46 (5), 54-56.

YALOM, I. D. Organic Brain diseases of senility. *Maryland St. med. J.*, 1960, 9, 781-787.

YALOM, I. D. Group therapy of incarcerated sexual deviants. *J. nerv. ment. Dis.*, 1961, 132, 158-170.

YATES, A. J. The application of learning theory to the treatment of tics. In H. J. Eysenck (Ed.), *Behaviour therapy and the neuroses.* London: Pergamon Press, 1960. Pp. 236-249.

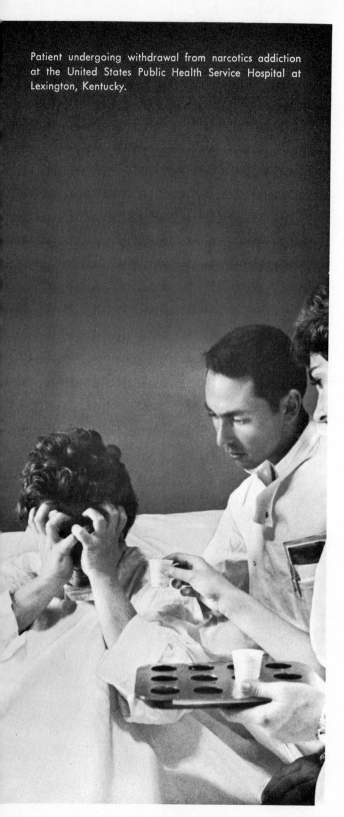

Patient undergoing withdrawal from narcotics addiction at the United States Public Health Service Hospital at Lexington, Kentucky.

ALCOHOLISM AND DRUG ADDICTION

chapter 10

ADDICTION TO ALCOHOL

ADDICTION TO DRUGS

Our contemporary problems of alcoholism and drug addiction are not new in the history of mankind. However, it has not been until recent years, with the direction of scientific attention to these problems, that they have come to be regarded as psychiatric disorders. In the past both alcoholism and drug addiction were usually considered "moral problems" resulting from moral weakness and lack of will power. But exhortation and other treatment approaches based on the theory of moral weakness proved singularly ineffective in changing the behavior of either alcoholics or drug addicts and thus, until recently, little progress was made in understanding the underlying dynamic factors or in developing effective methods of treatment.

Alcoholism and drug addiction are, in many respects, not yet understood, but their acceptance, investigation, and treatment as psychiatric problems have led to tremendous progress. We realize now that they represent merely two more of the many possible maladjustive ways in which an individual may react to stresses, internal or external, that are too severe for him to handle in "normal" adjustive ways.

Addiction to Alcohol

References to the excessive use of alcohol are found in many of man's earliest written records. As we have previously noted, Cambyses, king of Persia in the sixth century B.C., has the dubious distinction of being one of the first alcoholics on record and he seems to have been psychotic as well. Since his time, there have been many notable historical figures who have had their difficulties with the "demon rum."

INCIDENCE

It has been estimated that there are approximately 70 million users of alcohol in the United States; the cost of their alcohol consumption exceeds 10 billion dollars a year. The preponderance of such drinking is social and generally approved. Most users rarely if ever cause trouble for themselves or others. But some 5,000,000 people—roughly 6 per cent of the adult population—may be classified as alcoholics. Essentially, alcoholics are individuals whose alcohol consumption seriously impairs their life adjustment. Alcoholism is increasing at a rate of more than 200,000 new cases each year, and alcoholics constitute almost 15 per cent of the first admissions to mental hospitals.[1]

In our society the incidence of alcoholism appears to be higher on middle and upper socioeconomic levels. The popular notion of an alcoholic as an unshaven resident of "skid-row" is not accurate. This group constitutes only about 5 per cent of the alcoholic population. The average age for alcoholics is about 45, but alcoholism may occur during any life period from early childhood through old age. In our society alcoholism is rare before late adolescence. The cost of alcoholism to industry, as a consequence of absenteeism, lowered work efficiency, and accidents, is about 2 billion dollars yearly. Aside from undesirable psychological changes, one alcoholic in four shows physical complications due to prolonged excessive drinking. The lifespan of the alcoholic is about 12 years shorter than average. At present, alcoholism ranks as the fourth most prevalent disease in the United States. The problem of alcoholism is not confined to any particular race or group of people but is found among people all over the world. Its incidence, however, is far greater among certain peoples than among others. The Irish and French have a relatively high rate of alcoholism, while the Jews and Italians have a low rate. In the case of the Jews this is probably due to the existence of a powerful social tradition against the excessive use of alcohol (Snyder, 1955; Demone, 1963).

Social mores probably account also for the higher number of male than female alcoholics in general and for the different ratios found among different groups. In Scandinavia the ratio of male to female alcoholics is about 23 to 1; in Great Britain it is 2 to 1. In our own society the ratio is about 5 to 1. In general, women who drink excessively are more likely to be socially condemned and ostracized than men with similar drinking habits. Also, female alcoholics run the risk of sexual attack during periods of intoxication.

GENERAL EFFECTS OF ALCOHOLIC INTOXICATION

Contrary to popular beliefs, alcohol is not a stimulant but a depressant which attacks and numbs the higher brain centers, thus lessening their inhibiting control. As behavioral restraints decline, more primitive emotional responses appear; the drinker may indulge in the satisfaction of impulses he ordinarily holds in check. Some degree of motor incoordination soon becomes apparent, and the drinker's sense of discrimination and perception of cold, pain, and other discomforts are dulled. Typically he experiences

---

[1] Statistics in this section are based on the following sources: Block (1963), Brodie (1961), Chafetz *et al.* (1962), Demone (1962, 1963), Golin (1958), Gordon (1958), Gregory (1961), Jellinek (1960), U.S. Public Health Service (1963), Rainie (1959).

a sense of warmth, expansiveness, and well-being. In such a mood, unpleasant realities are screened out and the drinker's feelings of self-esteem and adequacy rise. Casual acquaintances become the best and most understanding friends in the world, and the drinker enters a generally pleasant world of unreality in which his worries are temporarily left behind. Thus he is stimulated emotionally while intellectual and motor functions are impaired.

When the alcohol content in the blood stream reaches 0.1 per cent, the individual is assumed to be intoxicated. Muscular coordination, speech, and vision are impaired, and thought processes are confused. When the blood alcohol reaches approximately 0.5 per cent, the whole neural balance is upset and the individual "passes out." Unconsciousness here apparently acts as a safety device, for concentrations above 0.55 per cent are usually lethal.

In general, it is the amount of alcohol actually concentrated in the bodily fluids, not how much liquor is drunk, which determines intoxication. However, the effects of alcohol vary with the individual—his personality, his physical condition, the amount of food in his stomach, and the duration of the drinking. The attitude of the drinker is important, too: although actual motor and intellectual abilities decline in direct ratio to the blood concentration of alcohol, many persons who consciously try can maintain adequate control over their behavior and evidence few outward signs of being intoxicated even after drinking relatively large amounts of alcohol. Despite such variations from one drinker to another, each usually reacts to alcoholic intoxication with a fairly consistent reaction pattern. Some drinkers become sad and mournful and pour out their troubles, others become drowsy and may go to sleep, while still others become suspicious, irritable, or pugnacious. Probably the great majority of excessive drinkers become subjectively euphoric and experience a marked sense of well-being, sociability, and adequacy.

The actual effect of alcohol upon the brain is not fully understood, but it does not seem to damage the tissue or cause injury by corrosion or irritation. Rather it seems to slow down the brain's functioning temporarily by a numbing or drugging action which progressively affects different parts of the brain—first the higher centers, involving judgment and inhibition, and later the centers that control motor coordination and the basic vegetative functions.

Many writers have maintained that alcohol is a systemic poison which has detrimental effects on various bodily organs. Actually, alcohol is a high-calorie food, which can be utilized by the body at the rate of about one ounce per hour. Amounts in excess of this remain in the blood stream until they can be oxidized. Some 10 per cent of the alcohol ingested is eliminated through breath, urine, and perspiration; the rest is completely utilized, though it may take several hours or even days. Alcohol in itself is no longer thought to have the detrimental effects on various body organs formerly ascribed to it. However, most alcoholic beverages contain a large number of congeners—components other than ethyl alcohol and water—that may have a toxic effect on certain body organs. In addition, individuals who drink excessively tend to depend increasingly upon alcohol as a major source of food and are likely to suffer from vitamin and nutritional deficiencies. As a consequence, prolonged excessive drinking is commonly associated with cirrhosis of the liver, brain damage, and a range of other organic ailments (Bennett et al., 1960; Chafetz et al., 1962; Fox, 1961). Important too is a lowering of overall resistance to disease. As we have noted, the life expectancy of alcoholics as a group is considerably reduced.

Although alcohol in itself does not seem to be a direct cause of organic pathology, except possibly in very extreme cases, excessive drinking does obviously produce abnormal behavior at the time of intoxication and hence may cause serious accidents, various types of irresponsibility which the individual later regrets, and untold suffering and unhappiness. A high percentage of all arrests in the United States are associated with excessive use of alcohol; approximately 15 per cent of the murders reported in 1962 were associated with drinking situations (U.S. Federal Bureau of Investigation, 1963). In addition, there are certain psychotic reactions which typically develop in individuals who have drunk excessively over long periods. These will be discussed in the following section, and then we shall attempt to unravel some of the causes of excessive drinking in our society and see what is being done to solve the problem.

PSYCHOSES ASSOCIATED WITH ALCOHOLISM

Psychoses associated with alcoholism can conveniently be divided into two types: acute reactions and chronic reactions.

Acute reactions. Acute psychotic reactions usually last only a short time and consist mainly of confusion, excitement, and delirium. There are four commonly recognized subtypes: (1) pathological intoxication, (2) delirium tremens, (3) acute alcoholic hallucinosis, and (4) Korsakoff's psychosis.

1. *Pathological intoxication* is an acute reaction which occurs in persons whose tolerance to alcohol is very low (such as epileptics or those of an unstable make-up) or in normal persons whose tolerance to alcohol is temporarily lessened by exhaustion, emotional stress, or other conditions. With even moderate amounts of alcohol, the patient may suddenly become hallucinated and disorientated, and may evidence a homicidal rage. During this confused state such patients sometimes commit crimes of violence. For example, Binswanger (1935) found that 26 of 174 patients of this type had been charged with crimes such as manslaughter, attempted murder, arson, burglary, or sexual assault. This confused, disoriented state is usually followed by a period of deep sleep, with complete amnesia afterwards. The following case history shows the pattern.

The patient was hospitalized following an altercation in a bar in which he attacked and injured a woman and her escort. On admission to the hospital he seemed very friendly and cooperative—in fact, almost servile in his desire to please those in authority. His personal history revealed that he had been involved in five such incidents during the previous two years.

Psychiatric evaluation revealed a family background torn with bickering and dissension. Both parents were stern disciplinarians and severely punished the patient for the most minor disapproved behavior. He was taught to feel that sex was very evil. In addition, they impressed upon him the importance of being "somebody" but rejected him in the family constellation. Thus he was burdened with a high level of aspiration while at the same time the parental rejection made it extremely difficult for him to feel adequate and worth while.

The patient manifested a high level of ambition but with unclear and unrealistic goals. He wanted to be "king of the hill," as he put it, but seemed vague as to just what this meant in terms of actual achievements. Although of superior intelligence, he had been handicapped by his lack of direction and his inability to maintain satisfactory interpersonal relations over a period of time. Apparently because he felt that both his parents and society had rejected him, he showed considerable repressed hostility. This hostility was not focused but rather was diffuse and directed toward people and the world in general. Although he revealed strong sexual desires toward women, his feelings were colored by sin, guilt, and hostility, which made a normal heterosexual adjustment impossible.

In the patient's previous altercations he had been arrested twice for disturbing the peace. In each case these incidents took place in bars where the patient, after a few drinks, would become aggressive, loud, and abusive, and would dare any and all to do anything about it. On several occasions he threw his drink in the face of someone close by, and on one occasion hit a bartender over the head with a bottle of scotch. His last escapade and arrest involved an attack upon a woman; this had apparently been provoked by her kissing her escort and making what the patient interpreted as sexual overtures in public. The patient approached the woman in a threatening manner, slapped her, knocked her escort out when he attempted to intervene, and then hit her several times with his fists before he was forcibly restrained by other customers. The patient was amnesic for the entire episode, apparently "coming to" on his way to the hospital.

It was felt in this case that the woman's behavior aroused unacceptable and therefore threatening sexual desires in the patient, against which he defended himself by becoming hostile and attacking her. The alcohol apparently served to lower the patient's normal behavioral restraints, permitting his hostility to be expressed in overt antisocial behavior.

2. *Delirium tremens* is probably the best known of the various alcoholic psychotic reactions. It is of fairly common occurrence among those who have drunk excessively for a long time (Block, 1962; Weeks and Lawrence, 1961). This reaction may follow a prolonged alcoholic debauch, it may occur during a period of abstinence in connection with a head injury or infection, or it may occur upon the withdrawal of alcohol after prolonged drinking.

The delirium is usually preceded by a period of restlessness and insomnia during which the patient may feel generally uneasy and apprehensive. Slight noises or a sudden moving object may cause considerable excitement and agitation. The full-blown symptoms include (a) disorientation for time and place, in which patients may mistake the hospital for a church or jail, friends are no longer recognized, and the doctor and hospital attendants may be mistaken for old acquaintances; (b) vivid hallucinations, particularly of small, fast-moving animals like snakes, rats, and roaches; (c) acute fear, in which these hallucinated animals may change in form, size, and color and terrify the patient; (d) extreme suggestibility, in which the patient can be made to see almost any form of animal if its presence is merely suggested to him or if he is asked what he sees on the wall; (e) marked coarse tremors of the hands, tongue, and lips (as indicated by the name of this disorder) and other symptoms including perspiration, a rapid and weak heartbeat and fever, a coated tongue, and a foul breath.

The hallucinatory animals the patient sees may cause him to cower, terrified, in a corner, or to stand up in his bed and desperately fight off the menacing creatures. This acute fear may extend beyond the various insects and animals which the patient sees to a general state of terror in which he feels that something horrible is going to happen to him. As a result, he may attempt suicide.

The delirium usually lasts from three to six days and is usually followed by a deep sleep. When the patient awakens, he has few symptoms, aside from possible slight remorse, but he frequently will have been rather badly scared and may not resume drinking for several weeks or months. Usually, however, there is eventual resumption and a return to the hospital with a new attack. The death rate in delirium tremens as a result of liver disease, heart failure, and other complications is relatively high—probably about 10 per cent (Tavel, 1962; Tavel et al., 1961).

The following is a brief description of a 43-year-old male delirium tremens patient.

The patient was brought forcibly to the psychiatric ward of a general hospital when he fired his shotgun at 3:30 A.M. while "trying to repel an invasion of cockroaches." On admission he was confused and disoriented and had terrifying hallucinations involving "millions and millions" of invading cockroaches. He leaped from his bed and cowered in terror against the wall, screaming for help and kicking and hitting frantically at his imaginary assailants. When an attendant came to his aid, he screamed for him to get back out of danger or he would be killed too. Before the attendant could reach him he dived headlong on his head, apparently trying to kill himself.

The patient's delirium lasted for a period of 3½ days, after which he returned to a state of apparent normality, apologized profusely for the trouble he had caused everyone, stated he would never touch another drop, and was discharged. However, on his way home he stopped at a bar, had too much to drink, and on emerging from the bar collapsed on the street. This time he sobered up in jail, again apologized for the trouble he had caused, was extremely remorseful, and was released with a small fine. His subsequent career is unknown.

In a study of 214 consecutive admissions to the Detroit Receiving Hospital, Krystal (1959) found that 82 per cent were men. Approximately one-fourth were married. The majority of patients were between 30 and 60 years of age and most of them suffered from infections or other concurrent illnesses in addition to delirium tremens. During the first day in the hospital 40 per cent of the patients had hallucinations, 58 per cent had marked tremors, and 60 per cent were uncontrollably anxious. Vomiting was noted in 40 per cent of the cases. All the patients revealed some degree of confusion and disorientation. On the second and third days of hospitalization these symptoms tended to abate, but a considerable number of patients showed even more marked anxiety, confusion, and tremors. The cause of the delirium tremens was judged to be a combination of severe physiological disturbance and emotional stress in an individual whose relation to reality was at best tenuous.

In many cases of delirium tremens and other acute psychotic reactions, there may be a residue of various psychotic symptoms after the immediate acute alcoholic reactions have been cleared up. In such cases it may be assumed that the alcoholism developed concomitantly with an underlying psychosis. This psychosis may be of a schizophrenic, manic, or other nature. In each case the psychosis develops in accordance with the underlying personality organization of the patient and is merely accentuated or precipitated by the alcoholic episode.

3. In *acute alcoholic hallucinosis,* the main symptoms are auditory hallucinations. At first the individual typically hears a voice coming from some one person and merely making certain simple statements. With time, however, the hallucinations usually extend to the voices of several people, who become critical and reproachful. The patient's innermost private weaknesses, particularly those of a sexual nature, are itemized and discussed, and various horrible punishments are then proposed by the voices. The patient may hear the clanking of chains, the sharpening of knives, pistol shots, or footsteps approaching in a threatening manner. Terror-stricken, he may scream for help or attempt suicide.

This condition may continue for several days or even weeks, during which time the patient is depressed but fairly well oriented and coherent, except for his hallucinations. After recovery, he usually shows considerable remorse and some insight into his previous behavior.

Investigators are less inclined than formerly to attribute this psychotic reaction directly to alcohol but now for the most part believe that it is based on an underlying mental disorder which is merely precipitated by the alcohol and could have been precipitated by drugs, illness, exhaustion, or other stresses. This was apparently the situation in the following case.

The patient was hospitalized after a suicidal attempt in which he slashed his wrists. He had been hospitalized once before after a similar incident in which he tried to hang himself with a bath towel. He was unmarried and lived alone.

The patient had been drinking excessively for a three-year period. He was not in the least particular about what he drank as long as it contained alcohol. For several days prior to his last suicidal attempt he had heard voices which accused him of all manner of "filthy sex acts." He was particularly outraged when they accused him of having committed homosexual acts with his mouth and of having had relations with animals. He complained of a terrible taste in his mouth

and imagined that his food had been poisoned as a means of punishing him for his sins. He was generally fearful and apprehensive and slept poorly.

After a stay of two weeks in the hospital, the patient made a good recovery and was discharged. At this time he seemed to have some insight into his difficulties, stating that he felt that his sexual problems had something to do with his suicidal attempt.

4. *Korsakoff's psychosis* was first described by the Russian psychiatrist Korsakoff in 1887. The outstanding symptom is a memory defect, particularly for recent events, which is concealed by falsification. A patient may be unable to recognize pictures, faces, rooms, and other objects as identical with those just seen, although they may appear to him as similar. Such patients increasingly tend to fill in gaps with reminiscences and fanciful tales which lead to unconnected and distorted associations. They may appear to be delirious, hallucinated, and disoriented for time and place, but ordinarily their confusion and disordered conduct are closely related to their attempts to fill in memory gaps. The memory disturbance seems to be associated with an inability to form new associations; thus new events are not retained and related to past events. This reaction usually occurs in older alcoholics, after many years of excessive drinking. Other symptoms include peripheral neuritis with tingling of the extremities, and in certain severe cases there may be abolition of the tendon reflexes and wrist and foot drop.

The symptoms in Korsakoff's psychosis are now considered to be due to vitamin B deficiency and other dietary inadequacies. A diet rich in vitamins and minerals generally restores the patient to more normal physical and mental health. However, some personality deterioration usually remains in the form of memory impairment, blunting of intellectual capacity, and a lowering of moral and ethical standards. These changes may be evidence of the psychological deterioration which frequently occurs in prolonged alcoholism rather than of any physiological toxic effects of the alcohol itself. In any event, post-mortem studies of the brains of persons who had died in the course of Korsakoff's psychosis reveal no gross organic lesions or damage such as might be expected if the symptoms were of organic origin.

Chronic alcoholic deterioration. The habitual use of excessive amounts of alcohol as a means of adjusting to life's problems is frequently accompanied by general personality deterioration, with a gradual intellectual and moral decline. Often there will be disturbances of memory, judgment, and ability to concentrate. The patient becomes coarsened and impulsive in behavior, takes less and less responsibility, loses pride in personal appearance and neglects his family, becomes touchy and irritable concerning his drinking, and will brook no interference. He is no longer able to correct his excessive drinking and engages in obvious rationalizations to justify his behavior. By lessening the drinker's inhibitions, alcohol may lead to attempts at deviant sexual patterns that outrage and antagonize the wife or husband. In his relations with outsiders the male patient is frequently fawning and servile; at home, however, he becomes a tyrant and makes life miserable for his wife and children.

Although initially he may be able to conceal his condition to some extent from others, this ability is gradually lost. His judgment is seriously impaired, he cannot maintain employment, and he becomes incapable of coping with changes or new demands that are made upon him. Gross physical symptoms—tremors, sluggish reaction of pupils, and extreme nausea—also make their appearance. In essence, he is a very sick human being—both psychologically and physically.

PHASES IN ALCOHOL ADDICTION

The alcohol addict is one who has lost control of his alcohol consumption. Heavy drinkers may consume as much as addicted individuals but still not exhibit this loss of control. When alcoholism progresses to the point of addiction, it tends to follow a predictable sequence. On the basis of a study of some 2000 alcoholics, Jellinek (1952) has outlined the series of stages commonly found in the development of addiction.

1. *The prealcoholic symptomatic phase.* The candidate for alcoholism starts out drinking in conventional social situations like other users of alcoholic beverages but soon experiences a rewarding relief in the drinking situa-

tion. This tension relief is strongly marked in his case either because his tensions are greater than those of other members of his group or because he has not learned to handle his tensions as effectively as others do. Initially he seeks this relief of tension through drinking only occasionally, but gradually his tolerance for tension decreases to such an extent that he resorts to alcohol almost daily. This transition from occasional relief-drinking to constant relief-drinking may take several months or as long as two years; it marks the prealcoholic phase.

2. *The prodromal phase.* This phase is marked by the sudden onset of blackouts during which the drinker may not show any signs of intoxication and may carry on a reasonable conversation or go through quite elaborate activities —but without a trace of memory the next day. Such amnesic episodes may occur to average drinkers when they drink excessively during a state of emotional or physical exhaustion, but their occurrence is very rare. Consequently, Jellinek considered this amnesia without loss of consciousness and even sometimes without intake of extremely large amounts of alcohol as marking a heightened susceptibility to alcohol in the prospective addict.

Certain correlated behaviors now make their appearance, among which are (a) surreptitious drinking, in which the drinker seeks occasions for having a few drinks unknown to others for fear that they will misjudge him if they notice he is drinking more than they are, (b) preoccupation with alcohol, which often takes the form of worrying about whether there will be sufficient drinks at a social gathering to which he is going —and perhaps having several drinks ahead of time in anticipation of a possible shortage, (c) avid drinking, in which the drinker now gulps the first one or two drinks, (d) guilt feelings about his drinking behavior, which he begins to realize is out of the ordinary, and (e) avoidance of references to alcohol in his conversation. During this period alcohol consumption is heavy but not yet conspicuous to others, and strong rationalizations concerning his drinking have not yet made their appearance. The individual may have some insight into his behavior and may fear the possible consequences—a fact which may make it possible to stop the incipient alcoholism at this stage.

PHASES OF ALCOHOL ADDICTION

This chart is based on a statistical analysis of the drinking histories of 2000 male alcohol addicts and shows the typical sequence in becoming addicted to alcohol. Not all symptoms occur in all cases, and the total time may vary from 7 to 25 years; the average for this group was 15 years.

The dots in the circle at the left represent men and women who are acquainted with each other and use small amounts of alcoholic beverages. Their use of alcohol is a kind of folkway that carries a small social reward. Most have come from the "average" population and get no special reward from alcohol. They make up about 95 per cent of all consumers of alcoholic beverages. But occasionally an individual enters the circle from a "marked" population; he suffers from neurotic trends or other personality inadequacies that make alcohol more rewarding to him than to the others, and he may also have an inborn or acquired constitutional liability. In complying with the drinking custom, he experiences considerable relief. So he looks for occasions to drink and may drink fairly heavily; his drinking is symptomatic of some underlying problem and continues until a new symptom appears—his first "blackout."

This marks the beginning of the prodromal phase, during which his drinking still may not be conspicuous and usually is limited to evenings and weekends. The crucial phase begins when the individual loses control over his drinking. Now he still can refrain from starting to drink, but controlled intake is no longer possible for him. During the crucial phase, intoxication becomes the rule but may still be limited to evenings. Solitary drinking begins, and the individual becomes more concerned about how his activities will affect his drinking than about how his drinking will affect his other activities. In the chronic phase, alcohol dominates his life. There is a decrease in physical tolerance and various psychic and physical symptoms may appear. The individual drinks to control his symptoms, but the drinking produces more symptoms. Rationalizations fail, and the individual may finally admit defeat and seek help.

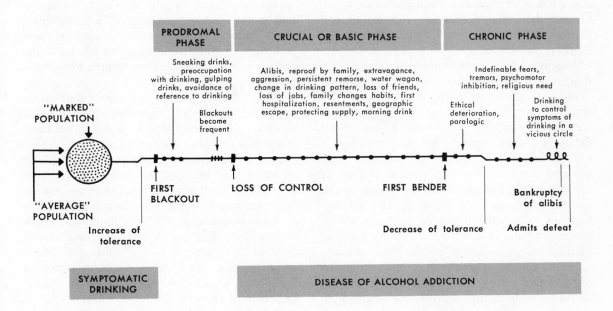

Redrawn from *The Phases of Alcohol Addiction in Males* by Dr. E. M. Jellinek.

3. *The crucial phase.* This stage is characterized by the loss of control over drinking, which means that any drinking of alcohol seems to start a chain reaction which continues until the individual is too intoxicated or too sick to ingest more. But although he has lost the ability to control his drinking once he has started, he still can control whether he will drink on any given occasion. This is evidenced by periods of abstinence or "going on the water wagon" following recovery from severe intoxication. During such periods the drinker seems to feel that he has lost his will power and that he can and must regain it. So when tensions rise and his natural remedy of "a drink" occurs to him, he promises himself that this time it will be only one or two drinks at most—but the results are always the same.

Almost simultaneously with the loss of control the alcoholic begins to rationalize his drinking behavior and produces the well-known alcoholic alibis. He finds explanations which convince him that he did not lose control—that he had a good reason for getting intoxicated. These rationalizations are primarily for himself, to permit him to continue his drinking, but they also serve to counter the social pressures which arise as the drinking becomes conspicuous and parents, wife, friends, and employer begin to reprove and warn him.

In spite of his rationalizations, there is a marked lowering of self-esteem, and the drinker may now attempt to compensate for this by extravagant expenditures and other grandiose behavior in which he projects the blame for his difficulties upon others and becomes hostile toward them. These defenses do not work well, however, and he has a persistent feeling of remorse which further increases his tension and is an added reason for drinking. The remorse together with social pressures usually leads to periods of total abstinence, but as his tensions increase, it may occur to him that perhaps his troubles arise from the kind of beverage he drinks and not from drinking per se. So now he may attempt to control his drinking by changing the pattern—drinking different beverages and setting up rules about not drinking before a certain hour of the day, in certain places only, and so on.

During this phase the alcoholic usually begins drinking in the afternoon and is intoxicated during the evening. The aftereffects of the evening's intoxication may cause some loss of time from his job, but he still struggles to maintain his employment and social standing although he has now begun a pattern of progressive withdrawal from his social environment.

The entire struggle puts the drinker under heavy strain and increases his hostility toward his environment. He begins to drop friends and quit jobs. Although in some cases, of course, he is abandoned by associates and dismissed by employers, he usually takes the initiative as an anticipatory defense. This process leads to increased isolation and to increased centering of his behavior around alcohol. He now becomes concerned primarily with how his activities may interfere with his drinking rather than with how his drinking may affect his activities. This leads in turn to a loss of outside interests, to marked self-pity, to a reinterpretation of his personal relationships, and to actual geographic escape or isolation from others.

The impact of these events, in turn, leads to a change in family patterns. His wife and children may withdraw from social activities to avoid the embarrassment he causes them, or they may become preoccupied with activities which take them away from the home. Such behavior, coupled with other events, leads the drinker to unreasonable resentments toward his family.

About this time, too, the alcoholic takes steps to protect his supply by laying in a large stock of alcoholic beverages which he hides in the most unthought-of places. Likewise, the neglect of proper nutrition begins to aggravate the effects of heavy drinking, and the first hospitalization for some alcoholic complaint may occur. Improper nutrition and other factors also tend to a marked decrease in sexual drive, which increases the hostility of the alcoholic toward his wife and gives rise to the well-known "alcoholic jealousy," in which the alcoholic blames his loss of sexual drive upon his wife's alleged extramarital affairs.

By now, remorse, resentment, the struggle between his responsibilities and his alcoholic needs, loss of self-esteem, and doubts and misleading rationalizations have so disorganized the alcoholic that he feels he cannot start the day without a drink to steady himself. This is the beginning of "regular matutinal drinking" and foreshadows the beginning of the chronic phase.

4. *The chronic phase.* The increasingly dominating role of alcohol and the struggle against this dominance progressively break down the drinker's resistance. He now finds himself intoxicated during the daytime on a weekday and continues in this state for several days until he is entirely incapacitated. This stage marks the onset of those prolonged periods of intoxication which are commonly known as "benders."

These drawn-out drinking bouts are usually associated with a marked impairment of thinking and ethical deterioration—processes which are reversible, however. At this time true alcoholic psychoses such as delirium tremens may occur although only 10 per cent or less of all alcoholics are affected in this way. The loss of morale is so severe by this time that the alcoholic drinks with persons far below his social level in preference to his usual associates—perhaps because he feels superior to them—and he will drink practically anything, including bay rum or rubbing alcohol, if his normal sources are not available.

Commonly noted at this time is a loss of alcohol tolerance: half of the previously required amount may be sufficient to produce an alcoholic stupor. Indefinable fears and tremors become persistent and are especially pronounced as soon as alcohol disappears from the organism. Consequently the alcoholic "controls" the symptoms by continuous drinking. Thus whereas initially the alcohol relieves symptoms of underlying personality conflict, eventually the drinking itself creates stresses and conflicts which the drinker also attempts to relieve by further drinking—a vicious circle.

In this chronic phase the alcoholic's rationalizations are beginning to fail as they are mercilessly tested against reality. And in many alcoholics—approximately 60 per cent—vague religious desires begin to develop. As the rationalization system finally gives way, the alcoholic admits defeat and becomes accessible to treatment although his obsessive drinking continues, for even though he at last feels the need of help, he does not know how to help himself.

DYNAMICS OF ALCOHOLISM

As we have noted, the problem of alcoholism has received unprecedented attention in recent years in both psychiatric and lay circles, and the older idea of alcoholism as primarily a moral problem has been once and for all dispelled. Alcoholism now is recognized as essentially a psychiatric problem with biological, psychological, and sociological aspects.

Physiological dependence. With prolonged excessive drinking, some individuals become physiologically addicted to alcohol. Here it may be pointed out that the individual who is not an alcoholic may develop a severe "hangover" after an excessive intake of alcohol. However, the nonalcoholic controls the toxic state by abstaining from the further excessive use of alcohol. The alcoholic, on the other hand, perpetuates the toxic condition by taking more alcohol to relieve the symptoms. Now when he attempts to stop drinking he experiences withdrawal symptoms. These withdrawal effects may involve relatively mild symptoms, such as a craving for alcohol, tremors, perspiration, and weakness; or severe symptoms such as nausea, vomiting, fever, tachycardia, convulsions, and hallucinations. Withdrawal symptoms show that cell metabolism has adapted itself to the presence of alcohol in the blood stream; this marks the development of physiological dependence upon alcohol.

The result is a vicious circle. The excessive drinking produced physiological dependence; physiological dependence now leads to a need or craving for alcohol as a means of warding off painful withdrawal symptoms. In learning-theory terms, each drink serves to reinforce alcohol-seeking behavior because it reduces drive; that is, it reduces the pain of the withdrawal symptoms. In essence, a recurrent cycle of alcohol-induced need is set up.

One question which has been raised in regard to physiological dependence is whether certain individuals show a constitutional vulnerability to such dependence. Is there a physiological predisposition to alcoholism—perhaps an unusual craving for alcohol once it has been experienced and hence a greater than average tendency to loss of control? Presumably such a craving could result from some genetic weakness.

It has been shown that alcoholism does tend

ALCOHOL ADDICTION AND RECOVERY

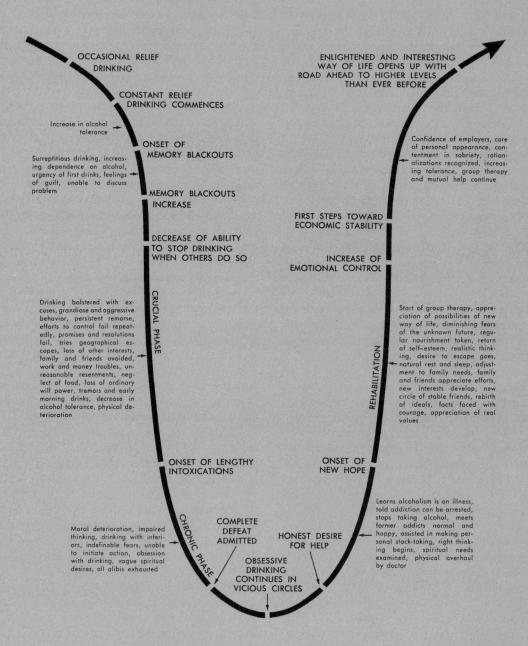

OCCASIONAL RELIEF
DRINKING

CONSTANT RELIEF
DRINKING COMMENCES

Increase in alcohol
tolerance

Surreptitious drinking, increasing dependence on alcohol, urgency of first drinks, feelings of guilt, unable to discuss problem

ONSET OF
MEMORY BLACKOUTS

MEMORY BLACKOUTS
INCREASE

DECREASE OF ABILITY
TO STOP DRINKING
WHEN OTHERS DO SO

CRUCIAL PHASE

Drinking bolstered with excuses, grandiose and aggressive behavior, persistent remorse, efforts to control fail repeatedly, promises and resolutions fail, tries geographical escapes, loss of other interests, family and friends avoided, work and money troubles, unreasonable resentments, neglect of food, loss of ordinary will power, tremors and early morning drinks, decrease in alcohol tolerance, physical deterioration

ONSET OF LENGTHY
INTOXICATIONS

CHRONIC PHASE

Moral deterioration, impaired thinking, drinking with inferiors, indefinable fears, unable to initiate action, obsession with drinking, vague spiritual desires, all alibis exhausted

COMPLETE
DEFEAT
ADMITTED

OBSESSIVE
DRINKING
CONTINUES IN
VICIOUS CIRCLES

HONEST DESIRE
FOR HELP

ONSET OF
NEW HOPE

Learns alcoholism is an illness, told addiction can be arrested, stops taking alcohol, meets former addicts normal and happy, assisted in making personal stock-taking, right thinking begins, spiritual needs examined, physical overhaul by doctor

REHABILITATION

Start of group therapy, appreciation of possibilities of new way of life, diminishing fears of the unknown future, regular nourishment taken, return of self-esteem, realistic thinking, desire to escape goes, natural rest and sleep, adjustment to family needs, family and friends appreciate efforts, new interests develop, new circle of stable friends, rebirth of ideals, facts faced with courage, appreciation of real values

INCREASE OF
EMOTIONAL CONTROL

FIRST STEPS TOWARD
ECONOMIC STABILITY

Confidence of employers, care of personal appearance, contentment in sobriety, rationalizations recognized, increasing tolerance, group therapy and mutual help continue

ENLIGHTENED AND INTERESTING
WAY OF LIFE OPENS UP WITH
ROAD AHEAD TO HIGHER LEVELS
THAN EVER BEFORE

Redrawn from Glatt (1957)

to run in families, but this would appear to result from social learning rather than hereditary tainting. In a crucial experiment, Roe *et al.* (1945) followed the case histories of 36 children who had been taken from severely alcoholic parents and placed in foster homes. The expectancy of their becoming alcoholics was no greater than that of a control group of 25 children who came from nonalcoholic parents.

The predisposition could be acquired rather than genetic. Whether there are acquired constitutional factors, such as endocrine imbalance, that increase vulnerability to physiological dependence is not known. The findings of Pelton *et al.* (1959) indicated that alcoholics may suffer from impaired adrenal function. However, it is difficult to unravel cause and effect, since studies usually follow a research design in which a group of alcoholics is compared with a group of nonalcoholics. What is needed are longitudinal studies that show whether there are metabolic differences preceding the alcoholism. In a recent study of this type, the results failed to show a relationship between metabolic disturbances in childhood and later alcoholism (McCord *et al.,* 1959).

Psychological dependence. Not only does the alcoholic become physiologically dependent on alcohol—he becomes psychologically dependent as well. Since excessive drinking impairs the total life adjustment of the individual—his physical health, his ability to obtain and keep a job, his marital relationship, his role as a parent, and his ability to establish and maintain satisfactory interpersonal relationships both inside and outside the family—the question arises as to what needs the alcohol meets which make the individual psychologically dependent on it.

Here it may be emphasized that alcohol is commonly used for a number of different purposes: (a) to counter disappointment and hurt, as in the case of divorce or a broken love affair; (b) to bolster one's courage, as in the case of acting a part in a play; (c) to alleviate feelings of isolation and aloneness, a reaction readily observable in bars; (d) to lower ethical restraints, thus enabling the individual to engage in infidelity or homosexual acts without feeling guilty; and (e) to blot out a sense of the meaninglessness of one's existence—a reaction that appears to be common to many lonely, neg-

lected, and frustrated housewives. In addition, alcohol leads to pleasurable feelings of adequacy, relief from worries, and sociability. Alcohol is thus a rapidly acting solvent of unpleasant reality, an ego booster, and a readily available source of pleasure. And since drinking is generally approved in our society, it is not surprising that it has come to be such a common pattern.

However, the problem remains as to why some individuals use alcohol in moderation while others drink excessively. Here the question is often raised as to psychological vulnerability. Is there an "alcoholic personality"—a type of personality organization which predisposes the individual to the use of alcohol rather than some other defensive pattern in coping with stress? Alcoholics do have many behavior traits in common, and their excessive drinking raises such similar problems for them that they often seem superficially alike. But despite numerous efforts, investigators have not found a specific personality constellation which is characteristic of alcoholics or which can be used to predict loss of control. About the only personality trait alcoholics appear to have in common is maladjustment—yet most maladjusted people who drink do not become alcoholics. Here it is of interest to note that almost all alcoholics remember their first drink, whereas only about 50 per cent of social drinkers remember it (Demone, 1963). Apparently, the first experience of drinking is of more significance to the individual who later becomes an alcoholic.

Despite the fact that studies have failed to show any alcoholic personality, many investigators consider alcoholics to be immature, passive-dependent persons with unrealistically high levels of aspiration and an inability to tolerate tension and failure. Such individuals often have the naïve opinion that whatever they want should be theirs for the asking; they do not fully appreciate the effort that is essential for genuine achievement. Typically they expect a good deal of praise and appreciation from others, are overly sensitive to criticism, and react to failure with marked feelings of hurt and inferiority. By the time the alcoholic comes to the attention of a clinic or hospital, he often shows as well a number of antisocial characteristics such as a tendency to rebel against conventional morality and a lack of responsibility (Gregory, 1961; Rosen, 1960).

Since personality deficiencies of alcoholics—like metabolic disturbances—may result from their illness, it is apparent that longitudinal studies are needed to delineate personality characteristics that may predispose the individual to alcoholism. Until such studies prove fruitful, we are left with the question of why a given individual, dealing with life stresses, resorts to the excessive use of alcohol rather than to neurotic or other defensive patterns.

One important lead in tracing the factors that predispose the individual to later alcoholism would appear to be that of parental example. Children tend to imitate their parents' modes of adjustment, and in adult life the children of alcoholics seem prone to use alcohol rather than some other defensive pattern in coping with severe stress. Here it may be pointed out that the alcoholic provides a highly undesirable model and that the home is typically unstable and torn with dissension. Often the nonalcoholic parent attempts to play the roles of both mother and father and fails to do either well. Almost inevitably the child of an alcoholic has problems in learning who he is, what is expected of him, and what to expect from others. And his range of coping techniques is likely to be more limited than that of the average child. In a study of 20 adolescent alcoholics referred to an alcoholism clinic in Boston, MacKay (1961) found a high incidence of alcoholic fathers and emphasized that the parental role models were persistently perceived by the young alcoholics as involving alcoholism. In attempting to deal with their own problems of feeling rejected, inadequate, and depressed, these adolescents apparently imitated the dominant parental mode of adjustment.

In any event, the potential alcoholic soon learns that with the aid of alcohol he can achieve gratifying feelings of adequacy and self-esteem and blissful relief from his anxiety and tensions. Unfortunately, as he comes to lean more and more on the temporarily satisfying process of drinking as a solution to his difficulties, he steadily regresses to a lower level of initiative, responsibility, and general adjustive functioning.

Sociocultural dependence. Alcohol is very much a part of our social world, and we have to deal with it in a social as well as an individual context. Most children are accustomed to seeing their parents and other adults drink, and the great majority of high school and college students drink alcoholic beverages (Demone, 1962). And of course the cocktail party has become a national institution. In fact, Chafetz *et al.* (1962) have pointed to the almost ritualistic role which alcohol has come to play in promoting gaiety, ease of conversation, and communication at adult gatherings. These investigators have also noted that as life becomes more complex and new sources of anxiety are introduced before old sources are eliminated, the individual must inevitably seek new and additional methods of reducing tension. In our society alcohol seems to play a prominent role in this respect. Thus in a general sense our culture has become dependent on alcohol as a social lubricant and a method of tension reduction.

A number of years ago Bales (1946) outlined three cultural factors which appear to play a part in determining the incidence of alcoholism in a given society: (a) the degree of stress and inner tension produced by the culture, (b) the attitudes toward drinking fostered by the culture, and (c) the degree to which the culture provides substitute means of satisfaction and ways of handling anxiety.

Evidence for the importance of the stress factor was supplied by Horton (1943) in an analysis of 56 primitive societies in which data were available concerning the basic level of security and the amount of alcohol consumed. The greater the insecurity or anxiety level of the culture, the greater the alcohol consumption, due allowance being made for the availability of alcohol. The effect of cultural attitudes toward drinking is well illustrated by the Moslems and the Mormons, whose religious values prohibit the use of alcohol, and by the Jews, who limit its use largely to religious rituals. The incidence of alcoholism among these groups is minimal. Finally, it becomes apparent that social customs determine whether alcohol is one of the modes of adjustment available and what alternatives there are to choose from.

Evidently differing cultural attitudes toward drinking—not just toward excessive drinking—are often important preventive or predisposing factors in alcoholism, and in considering reasons for drinking habits we need to look at both the general sociocultural traditions and the individual dynamics in a given case.

TREATMENT, PROGNOSIS, AND PREVENTION

Acute alcoholic intoxication can best be handled in a hospital setting. Drugs, such as chlorpromazine, have largely revolutionized the treatment of acute reactions (Block, 1962). Such drugs overcome motor excitement, nausea, and vomiting and alleviate tension and anxiety. The patient is able to retain fluids and nourishment, sleep restfully, and regain a normal physiological state with a minimum of withdrawal complications. Other special medical measures may be indicated, depending upon the condition of the particular patient.

After the patient has been deintoxicated, various medical deterrent measures are commonly utilized to prevent the continued use of alcohol. Before any effective overall treatment can be undertaken, the patient ordinarily must be taken off alcohol completely. For it appears that once a drinker has lost his tolerance for alcohol, he does not regain it regardless of the intervening period of sobriety (Brodie, 1961). Davies (1962) followed up 93 patients after treatment at Maudsley Hospital in London. After a period of 7 to 11 years, only 7 patients had developed the capacity to drink alcoholic beverages in a controlled way. Most investigators consider the risk of a relapse to be very great unless the patient maintains complete abstinence (Block, 1962; Brodie, 1961; Gregory, 1961). Thus the alcoholic can rarely return to being a "social drinker."

To help the patient refrain from further drinking, the physician may prescribe drugs—such as Antabuse—that cause an episode of intense illness if the individual drinks alcohol. The knowledge that this reaction will occur has strong deterrent value in preventing drinking. Another commonly used deterrent is conditioned-response therapy. The ancient Romans employed it by placing a live eel in a cup of wine. Forced to drink this unsavory cocktail, the alcoholic would presumably be disgusted and would be nauseated by wine thereafter. Today

this method is carried out by administering to the patient a drink of alcohol to which has been added some type of emetic. This results in severe retching and vomiting. With repetition, it acts as a strong deterrent to further drinking. Although tranquilizing drugs are commonly used in treating acute reactions, their effectiveness as a long-range replacement to reduce the need for alcohol has not been demonstrated.

Although deterrent therapy is a valuable treatment method, it is seldom advocated as the sole approach. In fact, part of its value lies in interrupting the alcoholic cycle for a period of time during which psychotherapy and sociotherapy may be undertaken. Both group and individual psychotherapy may be used to help the patient gain insight into his behavior and develop more effective coping techniques. Sociotherapy directed toward counseling the patient's wife or family and helping the patient make a readjustment in the community setting is also considered of crucial value. Usually attempts are made to maintain follow-up contact with the patient to prevent possible relapses.

Formerly it was considered essential that treatment take place in an institutional setting which removed the patient from his traumatic life situation and provided more control over his behavior—particularly his drinking. However, an increasing number of alcoholics are being treated in out-patient clinics. For patients who have been given jail sentences for drunkeness, or who do require hospitalization for psychotic reactions associated with alcohol, "half-way houses" are being established to bridge the gap between institutionalization and return to the community (Blacker, 1962).

A practical approach to the problem of alcoholism which has met with considerable success is that of *Alcoholics Anonymous*. This organization was started in 1935 by two individuals, Dr. Bob and Bill W. in Akron, Ohio. Bill W. recovered from alcoholism through a "fundamental spiritual change," and immediately sought out Dr. Bob, whom he helped to recover. Both in turn began to help other alcoholics; in 1939 an article on their efforts appeared in a national magazine and the A.A. movement spread rapidly. It has had such a remarkable growth that its facilities are now available in almost every city and town in the United States.

THE TREATMENT OF ALCOHOLISM

One kind of treatment for alcoholism is illustrated in the pictures above, which were taken at the Toronto clinic of the Alcoholism and Drug Research Foundation. In-patients at the clinic share comfortable bedrooms with three or four others. Some out-patients sleep at home but spend the day in the clinic. Patients meet twice daily in a group led by one of the clinic's therapists, and daily in a more informal gathering of patients and staff members. Staff social workers are on hand to help with job or family problems. There are interviews with a psychologist and individual contacts with staff members. Good meals, besides helping to create a pleasant environment, are especially important in view of the alcoholic's tendency to neglect his diet; milk and fruit juice are always available.

Most patients volunteer to help with odd jobs, such as raking leaves. Most of them also make use of the occupational therapy facilities. A range of recreational activities is provided, and free tickets to ball games and shows are often available. A local chapter of Alcoholics Anonymous holds meetings at the clinic.

After three to six weeks, the patient returns to his family and job. With the support furnished by membership in Alcoholics Anonymous and the opportunity to receive continued help on an out-patient basis, he faces the next step in his readjustment.

The Alcoholism and Drug Addiction Research Foundation

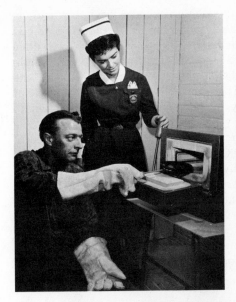

is financed largely by an annual government grant from the province of Ontario. It is organized to provide the province with services that may be divided into three broad categories: (a) research, both basic and applied; (b) education of the public and training of professional groups; (c) treatment, rehabilitation, and consultation. Much of the research is conducted by staff members working directly for the foundation. Through grants, the foundation also supports work at other institutions. Investigations are carried on in both the biological and the behavioral sciences. The education department holds seminars and workshops, provides consultants, and publishes materials of public and professional interest.

Treatment on both an in-patient and an out-patient basis is undertaken at the foundation's Toronto clinic; branch facilities in other Ontario communities provide out-patient care. Services in the clinics are free of charge. Most of the Toronto clinic's patients are in treatment for alcoholism, although patients addicted to narcotics and other drugs are also admitted. Patients may come on their own initiative or be referred to the clinic by physicians, family, friends, Alcoholics Anonymous, general hospitals, employers, or the courts. None of the treatment at the clinic is compulsory, though it is realized that a patient's wife or employer may have used some form of persuasion. An effort is made to keep rules to a minimum and to avoid creating a regulated, "institutional" atmosphere. Efforts are also made to provide counsel to the patient's family.

Essentially, Alcoholics Anonymous operates as a form of group psychotherapy. The meetings are devoted partly to social activities and partly to discussions of the problems of the alcoholic, usually with testimonials from members who have recovered. Although belief in a higher power is encouraged, and religious faith is an important factor in many cases, there are no specific religious affiliations. Membership may vary widely from those who are trying to find the inner strength to stop drinking to those who have attained sobriety for a long period of time. The atmosphere of the meeting is usually far from depressing and has a refreshing spiritual quality, with a genuine friendliness and concern of members for each other. Every attempt is made to integrate each individual into the group so that he feels himself an important member, participates in efforts to help other alcoholics, and enjoys social fellowship. It is hoped that in this way the new life, purpose, and sense of fellowship will become more important than isolation and superficial relationships at bars. In addition, the members provide emergency emotional support for each other during crisis periods, as when a member feels that he may be headed for a relapse. Thus by mutual support and reassurance through participation in a group with others who have shared similar experiences, many alcoholics acquire insight into their problems, a new sense of purpose, greater ego strength, and more effective coping techniques. And, of course, continued participation in the group helps to prevent a relapse.

With newer methods of treatment combining medical, psychological, and sociological procedures (typically including participation in A.A.), some 60 to 80 per cent of alcoholics can be helped to achieve permanent sobriety (Block, 1962, 1963; Fox, 1958; Rainie, 1959). However, the prognosis varies greatly from patient to patient. Gerard *et al.* (1962) found that about a third of 41 skid row patients had no desire to stop drinking because they were so depressed that they didn't care if they drank themselves to death. Many other patients were so physically ill or so far removed from conventional social interaction as to be beyond the range of outpatient treatment services.

Many other difficulties may stand in the way of effective treatment of the alcoholic. For one

thing, his alcoholism almost inevitably leads to serious disturbances in his overall life situation —with his family, friends, employer—and often to a police record. Usually his financial condition suffers, to the detriment of his wife and family. This, together with the other problems raised by his alcoholism, make a satisfactory marriage well-nigh impossible, and the deteriorated home situation then further aggravates his troubles. Often his alcoholism leads to separation or divorce and social isolation. In a study of 307 persons who were accepted for treatment at the Central Indiana Alcoholism Clinic, Weeks and Lawrence (1961) found that 173 were divorced or separated and an additional 68 were single or widowed. Only 66 were married. Most were "roomers" lacking residential and family stability. Yet their average age was only 46 years.

Not only does the alcoholic affect his family; the family also affects the alcoholic and his illness. Some studies indicate that many wives of alcoholics have personality weaknesses which led them to choose weak, dependent husbands. When the husband improves, the wife may decompensate. According to Whalen (1953) such wives often belittle their husbands and strive to prove their own superiority. In this context it is interesting to note Mitchell's (1959) finding that the alcoholic tends to view himself as possessing a sensitive nature which his mate does not appreciate, and to view her as prone to dominate him. In a study of 112 families with alcoholism, Lemert (1960) found that over 50 per cent of the wives had married men whose drinking problem was already well established. While the husband's drinking problem forced many of these wives to preempt the role of head of the family, in some instances this pattern preceded rather than followed the excessive drinking of the husband. In any event, some families help the alcoholic to recognize his need for treatment and give strong support to the treatment program; others discourage the patient from seeking treatment and are uncooperative if treatment is undertaken—thus helping to perpetuate the alcoholism.

The prevention of alcoholism is a particularly important problem in view of the widespread misery which it creates in our society, and also in view of the incompatability of excessive drinking with the operation of automobiles and with other aspects of technological life. In fact, automobile accidents constitute the single greatest cause of violent death among alcoholics (Ungerleider, 1958). Here it is of interest to note that about 6 per cent of high-school students who drink alcoholic beverages report drinking problems which include: (a) heterosexual misconduct—by their own definition, (b) fighting, (c) excessive emotionality, (d) talking too much, and (e) accidents (Demone, 1962). McKay (1963) found over 23 per cent of 622 delinquent boys (modal age about 15 years) to be heavy or addictive drinkers. Many investigators are hopeful that some biochemical means can be found to prevent alcoholism, but this remains a future possibility.

Since alcohol is so widely used in our society, a key aspect of prevention is education with respect to its use and an unbiased presentation of information concerning its dangers. The early detection and correction of unhealthy drinking patterns is also of crucial significance. To aid in the early detection of approaching alcoholism, the following warning signs have been suggested:

1. *Morning drinking.* One of the first danger signals for the frequent drinker occurs when he begins to drink in the morning as a means of reducing a hangover or because he wants a bracer to help him through the morning.

2. *Increasing consumption.* A key warning sign in the development of alcoholism is increasing consumption. This increase may be gradual, but the individual finds himself drinking more each month. Often he begins to worry about his drinking at this point.

3. *Extreme behavior.* When the individual, under the influence of alcohol, commits various acts which leave him feeling guilty and embarrassed the next day, his alcoholic indulgence is getting out of hand.

4. *Pulling blanks.* When the individual forgets what happened the night before, during his alcoholic bout, alcoholic indulgence is obviously becoming excessive. This does not usually occur until the excessive drinking has continued for some period of time.

A person showing the above pattern of warning signs is well on the road to becoming a chronic alcoholic, and the sooner corrective measures are undertaken the more favorable the prognosis.

Addiction to Drugs

From the earliest records, opium and certain other narcotic drugs such as hyoscyamus and hemlock are known to have been used by man. Early medical practitioners employed preparations containing opium for a multitude of physical and psychological ailments. Galen (130-201 A.D.) considered theriaca, whose principal ingredient was opium, as his favorite panacea:

"It resists poison and venomous bites, cures inveterate headache, vertigo, deafness, epilepsy, apoplexy, dimness of sight, loss of voice, asthma, coughs of all kinds, spitting of blood, tightness of breath, colic, the iliac poisons, jaundice, hardness of the spleen, stone, urinary complaints, fevers, dropsies, leprosies, the trouble to which women are subject, melancholy and all pestilences."

Even today, opium derivatives are still used for some of the above conditions.

It is essential to distinguish between drug *addiction* and drug *habituation*. Both involve repeated consumption of a natural or synthetic drug. Addiction is characterized by (a) an overpowering desire to continue taking the drug, (b) a tendency to increase the dosage, (c) psychological and physiological dependence on the drug, (d) detrimental effects to both the individual and society. In the case of habituation, however, (a) there is a desire but not a compulsion to continue taking the drug, (b) there is little tendency to increase the dosage, (c) there is some psychological but no physiological dependence, (d) any detrimental consequences affect the individual primarily (Seevers, 1962).

The drugs most commonly associated with addiction in the United States are the opium derivatives (morphine, heroin, paregoric, codeine), synthetic counterparts of these drugs, and the barbiturates (bromides, barbital, phenobarbital). Drugs associated with habituation are cocaine, which is derived from the coca shrub, derivatives of hemp (hashish, marijuana), the amphetamines such as benezedrine, and the tranquilizing drugs. Other drugs may be taken by teen-agers for "kicks" but they are not usually available in sufficient quantities to lead to either addiction or habituation. Our present discussion will focus on the use of narcotics (opium and its derivatives), although we shall briefly describe the effects of cocaine, marijuana, and the barbiturates.

The problem of drug addiction is still a severe one in certain Asian countries, and was formerly of considerable magnitude in the United States. In 1885, it was estimated that drug addiction in the United States involved from 1 to 4 per cent of the population (Gregory, 1961). However, public education and the strict control of drugs by federal and local authorities have greatly reduced this problem. Even so, there are an estimated 60,000 or more drug addicts in the United States, and, although there is no accurate information on the matter, it appears probable that addiction to the barbiturates may be considerably higher than this (Joint Committee, 1961; Cameron, 1963; Nyswander, 1959). Male addicts outnumber female addicts in the ratio of about 4 to 1. The great majority of opium addicts come from the lower socio-economic levels. Psychoses associated with drugs and other exogenous toxins constitute about 1 per cent of the first admissions to mental hospitals.

Drug addiction may occur at any age but seems to be potentially more dangerous to adolescents and young adults than to other age groups. Very few individuals become addicted after the age of fifty. This may be related to the fact that youth tends to seek adventure, excitement, and new thrills and does not always realize the dangers inherent in trying out drugs. For some, drugs also serve as an escape from difficult problems and as a means of achieving membership in an "in-group" among young people who lack feelings of belonging.

SYMPTOMS

The symptoms in drug addiction and habituation vary with the type of drug, the amount used, and the personality of the user. For this reason we shall consider the opiates, cocaine, marijuana, and the barbiturates separately.

Effects of opium.   Morphine and heroin, the principal derivatives of opium, are commonly introduced into the body by smoking or eating or by hypodermic injection. Immediate psychological effects typically include:

Lessening of voluntary movement
Decrease in sexual desire
Drowsiness, but with clarity of mind
Microscopic sense of time and distance
Relief of pain
Euphoria, with feelings of relaxation and contentment
Pleasant reverie or daydreaming

The nature of certain of these opium effects is amplified in De Quincey's description of his own opium dreams originally published in 1822.

"I seemed every night to descend, not metaphorically, but literally to descend, into chasms and sunless abysses, depths below depths, from which it seemed hopeless that I could ever reascend. . . . The sense of space, and in the end, the sense of time, were both powerfully affected. Buildings, landscapes, etc. were exhibited in proportions so vast as the bodily eye is not fitted to receive. Space swelled, and was amplified to an extent of unutterable infinity. . . . I sometimes seemed to have lived for 70 or 100 years in one night; nay, sometimes had feelings representative of a millennium passed in that time, or however, of a duration far beyond the limits of any human experience."— *Confessions of an English Opium Eater*

The pleasant effects last from 4 to 6 hours and are followed by a negative phase which produces a desire for more of the drug.

The use of opium derivatives over a period of time usually results in a psychological and physiological craving for the drug. The amount of time required to establish the drug habit varies, but it has been estimated that continual usage over a period of 30 days or longer is sufficient. The user now finds that he has become physiologically dependent upon the drug in the sense that he becomes physically ill when he does not take it. In addition, the user of opium derivatives gradually builds up a *tolerance* to the drugs so that larger and larger amounts are needed for the desired effects.

When addicts to opiates do not get a dose of the drug within 4 to 12 hours or longer after the previous dose, depending on the interval used by the addict, they start to experience what are called *withdrawal symptoms*. The character and severity of these depend on many factors, including the amount of the narcotic habitually used, the intervals between doses, the duration of the addiction, and especially the health and personality of the patient. The symptoms are usually quite severe within 48 hours.

The first symptoms to be noted are yawning, sneezing, sweating, and anorexia, followed by increased desire for the drug, restlessness, psychic depression and feelings of impending doom, irritability, muscular weakness, and an increased respiration rate. As time passes, these symptoms become more severe; in addition, there may be chilliness alternating with vasomotor disturbances of flushing and excessive sweating (this may result in marked pilomotor activity so that the skin of the addict resembles that of a plucked turkey), vomiting, diarrhea, abdominal cramps, pains in the back and extremities, severe headache, marked tremors. The patient refuses food and water, and this, coupled with the vomiting, sweating, and diarrhea, results in dehydration and in weight losses as great as 5 to 15 pounds in a day. Occasionally there may be delirium, hallucinations, and manic activity. Cardiovascular collapse may also occur and may result in the death of the patient. If morphine is administered at any point along the way, the subjective distress of the patient ends and physiological equanimity is restored in from 5 to 30 minutes.

If no morphine (or an equivalent synthetic drug) is given, the withdrawal symptoms reach their peak in from 72 to 96 hours and are definitely on the decline by the fifth day. Usually all symptoms of withdrawal have disappeared by the eighth day. As symptoms subside, the patient begins to eat and drink normally and rapidly regains his weight. After withdrawal symptoms have ceased, tolerance has disappeared and death may result from taking the former large doses of the drug. In fact, some patients undergo treatment so that they can begin all over again with smaller, less expensive dosages.

Occasionally an individual has enough self-control to use opiates without allowing them to interfere with his work and ruin his life. But this is rare, and the danger involved in the use of such drugs is very great, especially in the case of heroin, where tolerance may be rapidly built up so that large and therefore expensive amounts of the drug are soon required. For most patients it is extremely difficult to break the physiological and psychological dependency which opium derivatives build up. The addict increasingly centers his life around obtaining and using the drug, and so the addiction usually results in social regression or degradation due to the fact that he may be forced to lie and connive and steal and associate with undesirable companions and members of the underworld in order to maintain his dosage of drugs. Ethical and moral restraints are usually progressively lowered, and lack of an adequate diet leads to ill health and increased susceptibility to a variety of physical ailments. The typical clinical picture is one of progressive physical and psychological deterioration. In addition, the drug addict is usually ostracized by society, even after treatment, and often runs afoul of the law, since the illegal possession of narcotics is a criminal offense. If arrested, he is usually treated as a morally degenerate criminal and put in prison with hardened criminals.

As in the case of alcohol, opium derivatives have been blamed for a wide range of physical ills. Of course morphine is a toxin and in excessive amounts may make the user seriously ill or may even result in his death. In lesser amounts however, it does not appear in itself to impair physical health. Extensive clinical examinations of large numbers of patients who had been morphine addicts for from 5 to 20 years failed to reveal any harmful physical effects of the use of the drug (Pescor, 1944). The ill health and the general personality deterioration often found in opium addiction do not result directly from the pharmacological effects of the drug, but are typically the result of the sacrifice of money, proper diet, social position, and self-respect as the addict becomes more desperate in his efforts to procure the required daily dosage of the drugs.

In fact, in cases where drug addicts have the means to maintain both a well-balanced diet and an adequate supply of drugs without resorting to criminal behavior, they may maintain the drug habit over many years without any appreciable symptoms of either physical or mental illness. Many famous persons, including Edgar Allan Poe and De Quincey, have been narcotic addicts. In some instances even their closest associates were unaware of their drug habit (Goodman and Gilman, 1955). Some investigators have even stated that most alcoholics would be better off on narcotics if it were not for the greater social disapproval of these drugs by society. By "better off" they mean that the individual's general efficiency would not suffer so greatly.

As we shall see, however, most narcotics addiction in the United States is associated with serious personality disorders. The following case history gives a brief view of a teen-age heroin addict arrested by the police (Los Angeles Police Department, 1952).

"The boy was seventeen years of age. He had a pleasant way of talking, punctuating his remarks with an occasional smile. His excellent grammar and quiet manners indicated a good home and background. . . .

"Is this a 'dope fiend'? This is an inaccurate . . . term, but by all common standards and definitions the answer would be yes. Gene R_____, the boy in custody, is a confirmed heroin addict, a 'mainliner' injecting heroin directly into the main blood vessels of his arm. His body requires five 'pops' every day, costing him from $20 to $25 every twenty-four hours. He has managed to earn this amount by 'introducing' other teen-agers into the mysteries of marijuana smoking and, eventually, the use of heroin. The police report . . . lists five separate cases where good looking Gene R_____ has inflicted the dope habit upon 'girl friends,' all minors. Investigation indicates that four of these girls now pay for his, and their own, drug supply by means of prostitution.

". . . He does not have the 'furtive look,' the 'sallow complexion,' and other marks of the physical and mental deterioration that are expected of the heroin addict. Except to prospective teen-age 'customers,' he is not particularly dangerous. . . ." (pp. 3-4)

Effects of cocaine. Cocaine,[1] like the opiates, brings on a euphoric state lasting 4 to 6 hours, during which the addict experiences feelings of peace, contentment, and happy imagination. However, this blissful state may be preceded by headache, dizziness, and restlessness. In predisposed persons acute toxic psychotic symptoms may occur with frightening visual, auditory, and tactual hallucinations such as the "cocaine bug." Cocaine is sometimes used as a substitute for morphine.

Unlike the opiates, cocaine is a cortical stimulant, inducing sleeplessness and excitement as well as stimulating sexual processes. Consequently, individuals with perverted sexual patterns sometimes use it as a means of seduction.

Dependence on cocaine differs from morphine addiction in several important respects. With cocaine, there are no severe withdrawal symptoms when dosage stops. Tolerance is not increased and there is no specific physical craving for the drug. Consequently, it is not strictly accurate to speak of the use of cocaine as *drug addiction*. The individual may become psychologically habituated to it and dependent upon its use, but he does not become addicted in the sense of being physiologically dependent upon it. However, the World Health Organization lists it as a drug of addiction, presumably because of its detrimental effects on the individual and society.

With psychological dependence on cocaine, as with addiction to opiates, there is often a centering of behavior around procurement, with loss of social approval and self-respect and often with immoral sexual behavior. The following case shows this pattern.

The patient was a strikingly pretty, intelligent girl of 19 who had divorced her husband two years previously. She had married at the age of 16 and stated that she was terribly in love with her husband but that he turned out to be cruel and brutal to her. He would frequently take her to bars, where he would force her to drink while he spent the evening criticizing and berating her for no apparent reason. On several occasions he tried to force her to have sexual relations with his acquaintances under threat of bodily injury.

After six months of marriage she became pregnant.

---

[1]Cocaine was apparently discovered by the natives of Peru and Bolivia, who for centuries have chewed the leaves of the coca plant for stimulation to increase endurance. It has been considered a major social problem in the region.

Her husband, who did not wish to have any children, flew into a rage. He accused her of betraying him with other men, and hit her several times, finally knocking her into a stove with such force that she had a miscarriage.

The girl was too ashamed of her marriage failure (her parents had violently opposed the marriage and she had left home against their will) to return to her home. She moved away from her husband and got a job as a barmaid in the same bar where her husband had been accustomed to taking her. She was severely depressed, and several of his friends insisted on buying her drinks to cheer her up. This process continued for almost a year, during which she drank excessively but managed to hold her job.

Following this, she met a man in the bar where she worked who introduced her to cocaine, assuring her that it would cheer her up and get rid of her blues. At this time she was still feeling very depressed and sorry for herself and she thought she would try it out. She states that it both "hopped me up and gave me a feeling of peace and contentment." For a period of several months she purchased her supplies of cocaine from this same man until she became ill with appendicitis and was unable to pay the stiff price which he asked. Following an appendectomy, she was induced to share his apartment as a means of defraying her expenses and insuring the supply of cocaine which she had now become heavily dependent upon psychologically. She stated that she felt she could not work without it. During this period she had sexual relations with the man although she considered it immoral and had severe guilt feelings about it.

This pattern continued for several months until her "roommate" upped his prices on the cocaine on the excuse that it was getting more difficult to obtain and suggested to her that she might be able to earn enough money to pay for it if she were not so prudish about whom she slept with. At this time the full significance of where her behavior was leading seems to have dawned upon her and she came voluntarily for psychiatric assistance.

Effects of marijuana. Because there has been a good deal of publicity attendant upon the use of marijuana, it seems appropriate to include it briefly in our discussion. As with cocaine, the use of marijuana does not involve increased tolerance or withdrawal symptoms or the setting up of a specific physical craving.

Marijuana is a depressant which temporarily produces a euphoric state involving increased self-confidence and a pleasant feeling of relaxation, often with a sensation of drifting and floating away. Efficiency, both intellectual and motor, tends to be decreased, and time perception and intellectual and moral judgment may be impaired. Under the influence of marijuana the individual is frequently inclined to talk too much. It has often been stated that marijuana has a marked stimulating effect upon sexual processes, but apparently this aspect has been greatly exaggerated. The increased sexual activity which may take place under marijuana intoxication is apparently based primarily on a lowering of moral inhibitions and on increased feelings of self-confidence, which make the individual feel that the opposite sex is powerless to resist his charms. As a result, sexual advances may take place under conditions in which they might not otherwise occur.

The increase in feelings of adequacy probably accounts, also, for many of the incidents of reckless driving and other antisocial episodes in which some users of marijuana become involved. Similarly, occasional musicians resort to marijuana as a means of reducing monotony and improving their rhythm and speed. Although such individuals report that they feel they can play anything perfectly when so stimulated, their efficiency is actually reduced.

Marijuana, even when used over a long period of time, seems to have no harmful physical aftereffects in and of itself. However, the expense of maintaining a supply of the drug and the antisocial conditions under which such supplies are obtained may lead to an inadequate diet and to undesirable changes in ethical values. Marijuana tends to be somewhat unpredictable in its effects —a factor which prevents its use as a medicant. In many individuals it produces severely disturbed behavior akin to pathological intoxication in alcoholism. This may even include an acute psychotic reaction. No reliable statistics are available, but the use of marijuana is probably more widespread than is generally suspected.

Effects of barbiturates. Barbiturate drugs, commonly in the form of sleeping pills, are used in large quantities in the United States. These drugs involve the building of tolerance and physiological dependence and are true drugs of addiction. The individual who takes three or more barbiturate pills a night is considered likely to be addicted (Nyswander, 1959). However, there does not appear to be an overpowering desire to continue taking the drugs as in the case of the opiates. As a consequence, many individuals are able to maintain a minimal dosage of the drug over long periods of time for purposes of aiding sleep. Usually addiction occurs as a result of the gradual building up of tolerance and the tendency to take an increased dosage of the drug to get the required effect.

The predominant signs of excessive usage are cortical depression and impaired reasoning, orientation, and consciousness. Problem solving and decision making require great effort and the individual is aware that his thinking is "fuzzy." Prolonged excessive usage of barbiturates leads to brain damage and mental deterioration. In large amounts, barbiturates are lethal; they are often used by individuals who commit suicide.

Withdrawal symptoms are more dangerous, severe, and long-lasting than in cases of addiction to opiates (Gregory, 1961; Osnos, 1963). The patient becomes apprehensive and weak and manifests a coarse tremor of hands and face. Deep reflexes become hyperactive, and symptoms commonly include insomnia, nausea, vomiting, abdominal cramps, rapid heart rate, elevated blood pressure, and loss of weight. Between the sixteenth hour and the fifth day there may be grand-mal convulsions together with minor episodes of clonic twitching. An acute delirious psychosis often develops, which may include symptoms similar to those in delirium tremens. The withdrawal symptoms may continue for as long as four weeks, although they tend to abate by the end of the first week or ten days. Many narcotic addicts also use barbiturates, and their barbiturate addiction is often the principal medical problem from the standpoint of coping with withdrawal symptoms.

DYNAMICS

There is no dynamic picture that fits all drug habituation or addiction. Various ages, occupations, religions, races, and levels of intelligence are represented. In our present discussion, we shall confine ourselves primarily to addiction to narcotics. As we shall see, such addiction is usually a symptom of a larger pattern of personality maladjustment.

The following three-fold classification of narcotics addicts is a somewhat artificial but convenient means of ordering our discussion:

1. Addiction associated with character disorders and primarily involving teen-agers and young adults.
2. Addiction during physical illnesses where narcotics are used to relieve pain.
3. Addiction in professional personnel with access to narcotic drugs.

Addiction associated with character disorders and other pathology. Among neurotics and psychotics, narcotics addiction is relatively rare. When a neurotic turns to drugs, it is usually a symptom of mental illness plus an accident—the introduction to a narcotic drug. Typically there is a history of social inadequacy, and the narcotic appears to offer the individual a way of running away from anxieties and tensions by centering his life around a pleasant dream world. Here, of course, the pattern is somewhat similar to that of alcoholism. Among the very occasional psychotics who become drug addicts, the dynamic pattern is less complex and is apparently the result of lowered adaptive controls which open the way for the excessive use of alcohol or drugs as well as for other types of aberrant behavior.

The great majority of addicts are evidently suffering from character disorders. Most often they are immature, inadequate, passive-aggressive individuals. Typically these individuals explain their addiction as the consequence of curiosity or peer-group pressures which led them to get caught in the iron grip of physiological dependence. However, this explanation is not ordinarily tenable, for even after the physiological dependence is broken by treatment, most of them become addicted again. Thus we are dealing with maladjusted individuals who gain important satisfaction from the use of narcotics as a means of coping with unpleasant reality.

Teen-age narcotic addiction is often associated with membership in delinquent gangs where the use of narcotics is part of the gang culture. Often the first shot is given by the youth's "best friend," who is a member of the gang and himself already an addict. In a study of drug addiction in Chicago, Haines and McLaughlin (1952) found that the majority of the young addicts they observed had been introduced through social groups in which they felt pressure to conform.

Often the path to drug addiction follows a progression from other drugs to heroin, from which the youth is then unable to escape. The Los Angeles Police Department (1952) has stated, "The typical juvenile addict who comes to the attention of the police in this area has followed a familiar pattern—alcohol, marijuana or barbiturates (sometimes both), then heroin." (p. 16) Often the teen-ager is introduced to heroin while under the influence of marijuana.

Ausubel (1961) has delineated two types of teen-age addicts—the immature and the reactive. The immature addicts typically reveal deepseated personality problems, are peripheral rather than active members of delinquent gangs, and use narcotics more for their adjustive value than for "kicks." Reactive users, on the other hand, are often week-end "joy-poppers" who follow gang mores but rarely take the drug often enough or in sufficient quantity to develop physical dependence. After the age of 18, the reactive user tends to abandon both his predatory gang activities and his casual use of drugs in favor of more conventional concerns with occupation and family; the immature addict retreats further from normal adult adjustment into drug-induced euphoria.

With time, most immature addicts become withdrawn, lose interest in their friends (except those in the drug-addict group), and show little interest in sexual activity. They tend to abandon scholastic and athletic strivings and to show a marked reduction in competitive and aggressive behavior. Most of these young people apparently feel isolated, lack good masculine identification, and feel inadequate in the face of the demands of adulthood. Their feelings of belongingness are bolstered by identification with the addict group, while at the same time drugs represent both a means of revolt against constituted values and a means of alleviating their anxieties and tensions.

In a study of over 100 young male heroin addicts at the United States Public Health Service Hospital at Lexington, Kentucky, most of the patients reported that "within seconds after the intravenous injection of heroin or heroin and cocaine, they were 'hit' by a warm, glowing sensation, vaguely localized in the intestinal region, which gradually spread over the body and could be compared only to a sexual orgasm—a comparison volunteered by a number of the addicts" (Fort, 1954). These feelings were followed by a profound sense of relaxation and contentment. As Ausubel (1961) has pointed out, the euphoria produced by narcotics tends to have a uniquely efficient adjustive value for this group of addicts. It dulls their self-critical attitudes, provides immediate and effortless pleasure, and enables them to feel supremely contented with their immature adjustment to life.

In addition to the fact that we are dealing with maladjusted individuals who gain important satisfactions from the euphoria induced by narcotic drugs, it is also necessary to consider drug availability and community tolerance for drug addiction (Hill, 1962). Although our society in general is strongly disapproving, there are minority-group subcultures which tolerate or approve narcotics use. In fact, Ausubel (1961) has referred to the "new type" of drug addict—the slum-dwelling adolescent who is introduced to the use of narcotics through his associates in a closely-knit predatory gang, who has ready access to narcotic drugs, and who belongs to an underprivileged segment of the urban population which shows a high tolerance for narcotics addiction.

The specific home background of the young drug addict has not received a great deal of attention. One intensive study, however, found the father to be a shadowy figure or completely absent because of death or separation, while the mother was typically an unhappy woman who had very hostile feelings toward her children and tended to overpower, overprotect, and dominate them (Mason, 1958). In general, we would expect teen-age drug addicts who come from slum areas of large urban centers to show a high incidence of family instability and pathogenic family interaction in their backgrounds.

Addiction during physical illness. Many patients are given narcotic drugs, such as morphine, to relieve pain during illness or following surgery or serious injury. The vast majority of such patients never develop an addiction, and when their medication is discontinued, they do not again resort to the use of addicting drugs (Rasor, 1958). When physiological dependence has been established, it is usually broken by the gradual withdrawal of the drug. Addicts who blame their addiction on the use of drugs during an illness usually show personality deficiencies which predispose them to the use of drugs, such as immaturity, low frustration tolerance, and the ability to distort and evade reality by way of a flight into drug-induced fantasy.

Addiction in professional personnel with access to narcotic drugs.   Occasionally professional people entrusted with the use of narcotics, such as doctors and nurses, become addicted to these drugs. They may be tempted by curiosity, but more commonly their use of the drug would appear to be an attempt to ward off anxiety or depression induced by some environmental stress such as a divorce (Rasor, 1958). Often such individuals find themselves physiologically dependent upon the drug without quite understanding how it all came about. But these patients get little or no emotional satisfaction from the use of the drug; they are not psychologically dependent upon its use as a long-range means of escaping unpleasant reality. When their traumatic life situation has improved and their physiological dependence on the drug is broken, they feel no strong desire to continue its use. With the advent of the potent tranquilizing and antidepressant drugs, the addiction of professional personnel has become less common (Ausubel, 1961).

Drug addiction and crime.   Most young drug addicts show a history of delinquency in a group-supported and habitual form either prior to or simultaneously with their use of narcotic drugs. Even those who do not are usually forced into delinquent and criminal behavior in order to maintain their supply of drugs. In a study of 453 drug-addict patients discharged from the Public Health Service Hospital at Lexington, Kentucky, Duvall *et al.* (1963) found that approximately 70 per cent had one or more arrests during a five-year follow-up period. Two thirds of all arrests reported were for narcotics violations and most of the other arrests were for illegal acts resorted to by addicts to support their addiction. Most addicts, however, are not major criminals. They usually confine themselves to petty crimes, and very few commit crimes of violence. Usually

when they are well supplied with drugs, they feel too good to molest anyone, and when they are not, they feel too miserable to do so. This does not mean that the crimes that drug addicts do commit (stealing, prostitution, peddling narcotics, and so on) are not serious, but simply that addicts rarely plan and execute criminal acts in the same way as professional criminals.

It is true that certain habitual criminals become addicts or use drugs such as cocaine to assist them in performing their criminal acts. But such individuals might have used alcohol or other agents, and their use of drugs under these conditions is merely part of a larger pattern of criminal behavior, reflecting social or personal maladjustment in which the drug is not the primary cause of the crime.

There has been much talk about the importance of marijuana in contributing to juvenile delinquency and other antisocial conditions, but studies do not indicate that marijuana is a determining factor in either juvenile delinquency or major crimes (Bromberg and Rodgers, 1946; Mayor's Commission on Marijuana, n.d.). It may of course be a factor in reducing adaptive controls in an emotionally immature and already poorly integrated individual (Charen and Perelman, 1946; Gaskill, 1945). Probably the greatest danger of marijuana is that it is so often a stepping stone to heroin.[1]

TREATMENT AND PROGNOSIS

Treatment for drug addiction is similar to treatment for alcoholism and involves building up the patient both physically and psychologically and helping him make an adjustment in the community. Opium addiction also requires a special withdrawal treatment which is primarily a medical matter and is greatly feared by the patient. Actually, however, the withdrawal treatment is not abrupt but rather involves the administration of a synthetic drug which eases the withdrawal symptoms. Although the withdrawal symptoms are not eliminated entirely, they are

---

[1]There are a number of legal issues concerned with criminal sanctions for narcotic addicts who are apprehended for possession or selling of illegal drugs—such as questions of deterrence, responsibility, and intent. For a good discussion of such issues, the reader is referred to Cameron (1963).

rarely worse than a case of influenza (Osnos, 1963). During a relatively brief period, physiological dependence is broken. Adequate treatment requires hospitalization; the two major United States hospitals for treatment of drug addicts are located near Fort Worth, Texas, and Lexington, Kentucky.[1]

Although many addicts successfully complete a hospital treatment program, the prognosis in narcotics addiction is still generally unfavorable. In a follow-up of 1,881 patients who were discharged from the United States hospital at Lexington, Hunt and Odoroff (1962) found that 90 per cent of the patients became addicted again, and that more than 90 per cent of those becoming addicted again did so within 6 months after discharge from the hospital. Similarly Duvall *et al.* (1963), in their follow-up of 453 Lexington patients, found that more than 97 per cent had been addicted again at some time during the five-year follow-up period. However, by the end of the fifth year after discharge only an estimated 46 per cent of the study population was currently addicted; 49 per cent of the group were voluntarily or involuntarily abstinent. Those who were over 30 years of age at the time of discharge showed a significantly higher abstinence rate. Although there were fluctuations in the addiction status of patients during the follow-up period, the re-addiction rate decreased with the passage of time.

The general results of hospital treatment would appear to bear out the conclusion of Lowry (1956) that hospital treatment starts the patient on the road to recovery but cannot provide a lifetime immunity. Long-range psychotherapy and sociotherapy appear essential if the patient is to learn to face his problems and find an acceptable adult role and place in the community.

As in the case of Alcoholics Anonymous, there is an organization called Addicts Anonymous which helps recovered patients remain free of narcotics addiction. A relatively new treatment approach is that of Synanon, which is essentially a therapeutic community of ex-criminal addicts (Time, 1963; Yablonsky, 1963). This organization was originated by a former business executive, Charles E. Dederich, who had overcome an alcohol problem and was motivated to communicate to others the forces which had led to his recovery. A brilliant discussant and group leader, Dederich attracted a coterie of alcoholics and narcotics addicts who were stimulated by the group discussions he led. Many of these people had no roots; some moved into his residence, and others moved into nearby apartments. During 1958 Synanon House was established in Santa Monica, California. Its mutual self-help approach to narcotics addiction has achieved remarkable results.

Synanon patterns itself somewhat after Alcoholics Anonymous. All members are staff, and one of the greatest assets of Synanon is a breed of therapist who has three levels of experience that uniquely qualify him for helping drug offenders: (a) he has a history of drug addiction and criminal behavior, (b) he has experienced at Synanon the emotional stress involved in rejecting one way of life for another, and (c) he knows the Synanon social system. These ex-criminal addicts understand the newcomer and cannot be outmaneuvered by his rationalizations or manipulative behavior. This society creates for the offender a new social role which he can occupy as long as he wishes—the role of a therapist in helping other offenders break their addiction and find a more meaningful, constructive way of life.

In filling his role and finding legitimate social status in Synanon, the ex-offender necessarily learns to relate, communicate, and work with others. As these socialization processes take hold, he no longer finds it necessary to depend on narcotics or assume a deviant social role, and the way is paved for his gradual assumption of a constructive role in the community.

Some residents decide to make Synanon their life work. With the opening of new Synanons and the establishment of Synanon projects in federal and state prisons, this unique organization is having a marked effect on the treatment of criminals and of criminal narcotics offenders. At present, it appears to be one of the most feasible therapeutic systems for treating the "new" criminal, described in the preceding chapter.

---

[1]A narcotic addict who wishes hospitalization at the United States Public Health Service Hospital at Lexington, Ky., or at Fort Worth, Tex., for treatment as a voluntary patient can write to the Surgeon General of the United States, Public Health Service, Washington, D.C., who will see that he is furnished with the necessary blanks and instructions.

In his book on narcotics addiction in Britain and America, Schur (1962) pointed out another approach. He concluded that the United States must break with the punitive approach and experiment with outpatient medical treatment involving legalized dispensation of drugs by qualified physicians. In England, where the drug addict is treated as a sick person rather than a criminal and where physicians may prescribe minimum maintenance dosages of the drug in certain cases, the incidence of drug addiction is about one sixtieth of that in the United States (Bowman, 1958). However, Larimore and Brill (1962) have pointed out that the problem in Great Britain and the United States is essentially different in that the British have a strongly entrenched social attitude against the taking of dangerous drugs and the problem of drug addiction in Great Britain has never been a serious one.

Finally, it appears highly desirable to give serious consideration to the recommendations jointly agreed upon by the American Medical Association and the National Research Council (1962). These recommendations include:

1. Measures to permit the compulsory civil commitment of narcotics addicts for treatment in a drug-free environment.
2. Effective follow-up treatment in the community for addicts after withdrawal has been achieved.
3. Research designed to gain new knowledge about the rehabilitation of narcotics offenders and the prevention of narcotics addiction.

PREVENTION

Prevention of narcotics addiction requires the teamwork of federal and local agencies for controlling the illegal narcotics traffic, public education about the dangers and consequences of narcotics addiction, and a change in public attitude—from a view of the addict as a depraved and evil person to a view of him as an immature and sick person. Society's acceptance of drug addiction as a symptom of mental illness rather than as a sign of moral degeneracy would be tremendously beneficial to treatment. Long prison sentences and social ostracism are not conducive to rehabilitation of narcotics addicts.

REFERENCES

The reference list includes not only the sources from which the author has drawn material, but acknowledgments of the permissions granted by authors and publishers to quote directly from their works.

American Medical Association and National Research Council. Joint statement on narcotic addiction in the U.S. *Journal Indiana Med. Assoc.*, 55, 1056-1057, 1963.

AUSUBEL, D. P. Causes and types of narcotic addiction: a psychosocial view. *Psychiat. Quart.*, 1961, 35, 523-531.

BALES, R. F. Cultural differences in rates of alcoholism. *Quart. J. Stud. Alcohol*, 1946, 6, 480-499.

BENNETT, A. E., MOWERY, G. L., & FORT, J. T. Brain damage from chronic alcoholism: the diagnosis of intermediate stage of alcoholic brain disease. *Amer. J. Psychiat.*, 1960, 116, 705-711.

BINSWANGER, H. Klinische und charakterologische Untersuchungen an pathologisch Berauschten. *Z. f. ges. Neurol. Psychiat.*, 1935, 152, 703-737.

BLACKER, E. Half-way houses for problem drinkers. *N. H. Bull. Alcoholism*, 1962, 9 (1), 1-12.

BLOCK, M. A. Public health aspects of alcoholism. *N.J. St. J. Med.*, 1963, 63, 273-276.

BLOCK, MARGARET S. Medical treatment of alcoholism. In Council on Mental Health of the American Medical Association, Committee on Alcoholism, *Manual on alcoholism*. Chicago: Committee on Alcoholism, 1962, Pp. 7-33.

BOWMAN, K. M. Some problems of addiction. In P. Hoch, & J. Zubin (Eds.) *Psychopathology of communication*. New York: Grune & Stratton, 1958.

BRODIE, D. W. Alcoholism: an epidemiologic study of a common disease. *J. Ind. St. med. Ass.*, 1961, 54, 1142-1144.

BROMBERG, W., & RODGERS, T. C. Marihuana and aggressive crime. *Amer. J. Psychiat.*, 1946, 102, 825-827.

CAMERON, D. C. Addiction—current issues. *Amer. J. Psychiat.*, 1963, 120, 313-319.

CHAFETZ, M. E., DEMONE, H. W., JR., & SOLOMON, H. C. Alcoholism: its cause and prevention. *N. Y. J. Med.*, 1962, 62, 1614-1625.

CHAREN, S., & PERELMAN, L. Personality studies of marihuana addicts. *Amer. J. Psychiat.*, 1946, 102, 674-682.

DAVIES, D. L. Normal drinking in recovered alcohol addicts. *Quart. J. Stud. Alcohol*, 23, 94-104, 1962.

DEMONE, H. W., JR. Teenagers and alcohol. *N. H. Bull. Alcoholism*, 1962, 12 (2), 1-11.

DEMONE, H. W., JR. The sociology of alcoholism. *N. Hamp. Bull. Alcoholism*, 1963, 12 (4), 1-14.

DUVALL, H. J., LOCKE, B. Z., & BRILL, L. Followup study of narcotic drug addicts five years after hospitalization. *Publ. Hlth Rep.*, 1963, 78, 185-193.

Federal Bureau of Investigation. *Uniform crime reports, 1962.* U.S. Government Printing Office, U.S. Department of Justice, Washington, D.C.: 1963.

FORT, J. P., JR. Heroin addiction among young men. *Psychiatry*, 1954, 17, 251-259.

FOX, R. Antabuse as an adjunct to psychotherapy in alcoholism. *N. Y. J. Med.*, 1958, 58, 1540-1544.

FOX, J. H. An overview of alcoholism research. *Publ. Hlth Rep.*, 1961, 76, 223-230.

GASKILL, H. S. Marihuana—an intoxicant. *Amer. J. Psychiat.*, 1945, 102, 202-204.

GERARD, D. L., SAENGER, G., & WILE, RENÉE. The abstinent alcoholic. *Arch. gen. Psychiat.*, 1962, 6, 83-95.

GLATT, M. M. Group therapy in alcoholism. *Brit. J. Addiction*, 1957, 54 (2). Redrawn by permission.

GOLIN, M. Robber of five million brains. *J. Amer. med. Ass.*, 1958, 167, 1496-1503.

GORDON, J. E. The epidemiology of alcoholism. *N.Y. J. Med.*, 1958, 58, 1911-1920.

GREGORY, I. Alcoholism and drug addiction. *Minn. Med.*, 1961, 44, 445-453.

HAINES, W. H., & MC LAUGHLIN, J. J. Narcotic addicts in Chicago. *Amer. J. Psychiat.*, 1952, 108, 755-757.

HILL, H. E. The social deviant and initial addiction to narcotics and alcohol. *Quart. J. Stud. Alcohol*, 1962, 23, 562-582.

HORTON, D. The functions of alcohol in primitive societies: a cross-cultural study. *Quart. J. Stud. Alcohol*, 1943, 4, 199-320.

HUNT, G. H., & ODOROFF, M. E. Followup study of narcotic drug addicts after hospitalization. *Publ. Hlth Rep.*, 1962, 77, 41-54.

JELLINEK, E. M. Phases of alcohol addiction. *Quart. J. Stud. Alcohol*, 1952, 13, 673-678.

JELLINEK, E. M. *The disease concept of alcoholism.* New Haven, Conn.: Yale Center Alcohol Studies, 1960.

Joint Committee of American Bar Association and American Medical Association. *Drug addiction: crime or disease?* Bloomington, Ind.: Ind. Univer. Press, 1961.

KRYSTAL, H. The physiological basis of the treatment of delirium tremens. *Amer. J. Psychiat.*, 1959, 116, 137-147.

LARIMORE, G. W., & BRILL, H. Epidemiologic factors in drug addiction in England and the United States. *Publ. Hlth Rep.*, 1962, 77, 555-560.

LEMERT, E. M. The occurrence and sequence of events in the adjustment of families to alcoholism. *Quart. J. Stud. Alcohol*, 1960, 21, 679-697.

Los Angeles Police Department. *Youth and narcotics.* Reprinted by Los Angeles City School District, 1952, pp. 3-4.

LOWRY, J. V. Hospital treatment of the narcotic addict. *Fed. Probation*, 1956, 20, 45-51.

MC CORD, W., MC CORD, JOAN, & SUDEMAN, J. Some current theories of alcoholism: a longitudinal evaluation. *Quart. J. Stud. Alcohol*, 1959, 20, 727-749.

MAC KAY, J. R. Clinical observations on adolescent problem drinkers. *Quart. Journal Stud. Alcohol*, 1961, 22, 124-134.

MAC KAY, J. R. Problem drinking among juvenile delinquents. *N. H. Bull. Alcoholism*, 1963, 12 (3), 29-38.

MASON, P. The mother of the addict. *Psychiat. Quart. Suppl.*, 1958, 32, 189-199.

Mayor's Committee on Marihuana, New York. *The marihuana problem in the city of New York*, n. d.

MITCHELL, H. E. The interrelatedness of alcoholism and marital conflict: IV. Interpersonal perception theory applied to conflicted marriages in which alcoholism is and is not a problem. Symposium, 1958. *Amer. J. Orthopsychiat.*, 1959, 27, 547-559.

National Institute of Mental Health. *Patients in mental institutions, 1960: Part II; Public hospitals for the mentally ill.* 1963.

NYSWANDER, MARIE. Drug addictions. In S. Arieti (Ed.), *American handbook of psychiatry*, Vol. 1. New York: Basic Books, 1959. Pp. 614-622.

OSNOS, R. J. The treatment of narcotics addiction. *N. Y. J. Med.*, 1963, 63, 1182-1188.

PELTON, R. B., WILLIAMS, R. J., & ROGERS, L. L. Metabolic characteristics of alcoholics. I. Response to glucose stress. *Quart. J. Stud. Alcohol*, 1959, 20, 28-32.

PESCOR, M. J. A comparative statistical study of male and female drug addicts. *Amer. J. Psychiat.*, 1944, 100, 771-774.

RAINIE, R. C. Alcoholism, a local and national problem. *Postgrad. Med.*, 1959, 26, 841-847.

RASOR, R. W. Narcotic addicts: personality characteristics and hospital treatment. In P. H. Hoch, & J. Zubin (Eds.) *Psychopathology of communication.* New York: Grune & Stratton, 1958.

Research Council on the Problems of Alcohol. *The scientific approach to the problems of chronic alcoholism.* New York: Author, n. d.

ROE, A., BURKS, B., & MITTELMANN, B. Adult adjustment of foster children of alcoholic and psychotic parentage and the influence of the foster home. *Mem. Section on Alcohol Studies,* No. 3. New Haven: Yale Univer. Press, 1945.

ROSEN, A. C. A comparative study of alcoholic and psychiatric patients with the MMPI. *Quart. J. Stud. Alcohol,* 1960, 21, 253-266.

SCHUR, E. M. *Narcotic addiction in Britain and America.* Bloomington, Ind.: Ind. Univer. Press, 1962.

SEEVERS, M. H. Medical perspectives on habituation and addiction. *J. Amer. Med. Assoc.,* 181, 92-98, 1962.

SNYDER, C. R. Studies of drinking in Jewish culture. IV. Culture and sobriety: a study of drinking patterns and sociocultural factors related to sobriety among Jews. *Quart. J. Stud. Alcohol,* 1955, 16, 101-117.

TAVEL, M. E. A new look at an old syndrome: delirium tremens. *Arch. int. Med.,* 1962, 109, 129-134.

TAVEL, M. E., DAVIDSON, W., & BATTERTON, T. D. A critical analysis of mortality associated with delirium tremens. *Amer. J. med. Sci.,* 1961, 242, 18-29.

Time. Mutual aid in prison. 1963, 81 (9), 45.

UNGERLEIDER, J. T. Alcohol, convulsions and tranquilizers: a clinical and electroencephalographic study. *J. nerv. ment. Dis.,* 1958, 127, 518-527.

WEEKS, G. C., & LAWRENCE, F. E. Characteristics of patients at the Central Indiana alcoholism clinic. *J. Ind. med. Ass.,* 1961, 54, 1506-1511.

WHALEN, THELMA. Wives of alcoholics. Four types observed in a family service agency. *Quart. J. Stud. Alcohol,* 1953, 14, 632-641.

YABLONSKY, L. Where is science taking us? *Saturday Rev.,* 1963, 46 (5), 54-56.

DISORDERS ASSOCIATED WITH BRAIN PATHOLOGY

part four

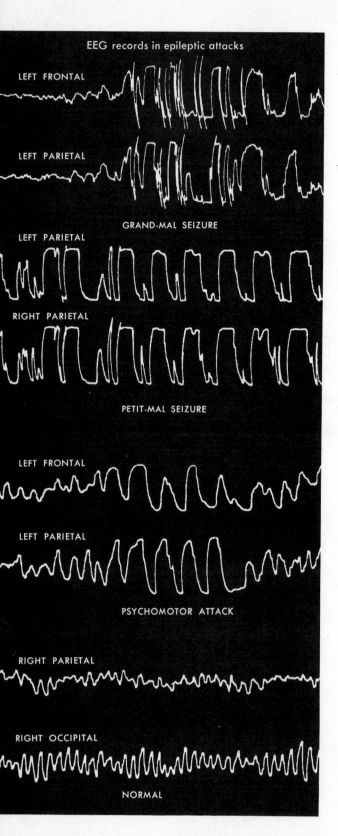

EEG records in epileptic attacks

LEFT FRONTAL

LEFT PARIETAL

GRAND-MAL SEIZURE

LEFT PARIETAL

RIGHT PARIETAL

PETIT-MAL SEIZURE

LEFT FRONTAL

LEFT PARIETAL

PSYCHOMOTOR ATTACK

RIGHT PARIETAL

RIGHT OCCIPITAL

NORMAL

ACUTE AND CHRONIC BRAIN DISORDERS

chapter 11

DISORDERS ASSOCIATED WITH INFECTION

DISORDERS WITH BRAIN TUMORS

DISORDERS WITH HEAD INJURY

DISORDERS WITH TOXINS AND METABOLIC DISTURBANCES

DISORDERS OF UNKNOWN ORIGIN

ABNORMAL BEHAVIOR ASSOCIATED WITH EPILEPSY

PSYCHOSES OF THE AGED

There are a number of diseases and other conditions which affect the central nervous system and give rise to behavioral disturbances. These may simply involve an impairment of function, or they may be associated with a wide range of mental disorders, depending upon (a) the nature and extent of the neural damage, (b) the premorbid personality of the patient, and (c) the general life situation to which the patient must return.

Of these, the second and third are often fully as important as the first. In fact, the severity of the mental disorder correlates with the degree of previous emotional instability and immaturity as well as with the amount of neural damage. There are many cases involving severe brain damage in which mental change is astonishingly slight. In other cases mild brain damage leads to a psychotic reaction. These variations are to be explained by the previously emphasized fact that the individual reacts to all stress, whether organic or psychological, as a holistic, functional unit. A well-integrated person can withstand brain damage or any other stress better than a rigid, immature, or otherwise psychologically handicapped individual. Similarly, the patient who has a favorable home and general life situation to return to is likely to have a much more favorable prognosis than the patient for whom hospitalization may be an actual relief from life's worries and stresses.

Thus in general the clinical symptoms in organic reactions are much the same as those which the patient would have developed in response to any other precipitating stress—he may become hypochondriacal, depressive, or paranoid or develop any of the other neurotic or psychotic patterns.

However, since the nervous system represents the essential basis for the integration of behavior, there are limits to the amount of neural damage that an individual can tolerate or compensate for without manifesting symptoms of disorder. Where the brain damage is extensive, there are certain symptoms that stem directly from the impaired functioning of the nervous system and are present as a basic syndrome whether or not neurotic or psychotic reactions appear. Such symptoms may be mild, moderate, or severe, depending on the nature and extent of the brain damage, but typically include:

1. Impairment of orientation
2. Impairment of memory
3. Impairment of learning, comprehension, and judgment
4. Lability and shallowness of affect, with general emotional oversensitivity and arousal of laughter or tears with minor provocation
5. Deterioration in conduct, with carelessness in personal appearance and lowering of inner reality and ethical controls

Frequently, too, there are sensorimotor disturbances, such as aphasia, paralysis, and incoordination.

There are an estimated 15,000,000 people in the United States suffering from neurological disorders. Fortunately, the great majority of these cases do not involve serious psychopathology. Even so, mental disorders associated with brain pathology constitute over one third of all first admissions to mental hospitals.

Organic brain disorders are classified as *acute* or *chronic*. The primary consideration here is

reversibility of the brain pathology: an acute disorder is likely to be temporary and reversible whereas a chronic one is chronic because of permanent damage to the nervous system. This classification is not a hard and fast one, however, because often an acute condition leaves some residual damage resulting in chronic disorder, and a chronic condition may have occasional acute episodes. Also, the same factors may produce either temporary or permanent damage. But despite these limitations, a general picture can be given of acute and chronic brain disorders.

Acute brain disorders result from diffuse impairment of brain tissue function accompanying high fevers, nutritional deficiencies, drug intoxication, or any of a variety of other conditions. Symptoms range from mild mood changes to acute delirium and may be complicated by delusions, hallucinations, and other personality disturbances. With extensive brain pathology or upset of brain cell metabolism, physiological rather than psychological factors may play the dominant role. In some cases, the brain tissue impairment, by lowering cortical controls, releases a latent personality disturbance which then may persist. In a few cases symptoms which appear to result from brain damage actually reflect the fluctuations of a mental illness unrelated to it.

The prognosis in acute brain disorders is by definition good, and such conditions *do* generally clear up. With older patients, however, or in cases of severe exposure to a toxic agent, there may be residual brain damage. The acute brain disorder and delirious excitement may also aggravate some physical disease or even result in the patient's death.

In the chronic brain disorders, the permanent destruction of brain tissue is reflected in some degree of impairment of higher integrative functions. This may involve disturbances of memory, learning, comprehension, reasoning, judgment, orientation, and affect. In general, the greater the amount of tissue loss, the greater the impairment of function (Chapman and Wolff, 1959). Various mental disorders—neuroses, psychoses, or character disorders—may be either precipitated by the brain disorder or superimposed upon it.

As we have seen, there is an attempt on both

biological and psychological levels to compensate for damage or loss. Unfortunately, the regenerative capacities of the central nervous system are limited. Cell bodies and nonmyelinated neural pathways do not have the power of regeneration, which means that their destruction is permanent. However, the central nervous system abounds in back-up apparatus. If a given circuit is knocked out, others may take over, and functions lost as a result of brain damage may often be relearned. Thus functional disabilities even following an irreversible brain lesion do not ordinarily remain constant. The degree of recovery may be relatively complete, or it may be limited; it may proceed rapidly or slowly. And, of course, there are limits to both the plasticity and the relearning ability of the brain, so that extensive brain damage may lead to a permanent loss of function.

On a psychological level, compensation for impaired intellectual functioning often takes the form of expansive, grandiose reactions, which apparently serve to protect the individual from facing his lowered capacities and making appropriate re-evaluations of himself. This process is undoubtedly fostered by his lowered critical and intellectual abilities. Where he is marginally adjusted to begin with or is overwhelmed by the changes in his life situation brought about by the brain damage, the stage is set for personality decompensation.

As will be apparent from the complete classification given on the back endsheets, both acute and chronic brain disorders have a number of subcategories based on the various factors that can result in brain pathology. Because the same factor may often bring on either acute or chronic reactions, many of the same subcategories appear in both groups. To avoid repetition we will not try to discuss each one separately but will devote the remainder of this chapter to a consideration of some of the more common causes of brain pathology and the related mental disorders that may develop.

Disorders Associated with Infection

Mental disorders may appear in connection with brain infections resulting from bacteria or viruses which invade the brain and damage or destroy nerve tissue.

Among the major infectious diseases of the brain are cerebral syphilis, epidemic encephalitis, and cerebrospinal meningitis.[1]

CEREBRAL SYPHILIS

Syphilitic infection of the brain is associated with three somewhat distinct syndromes—*general paresis, juvenile paresis,* and *meningovascular syphilis.* An understanding of these syndromes must begin with an understanding of syphilis, an infectious disease which has taken an incalculable toll in human lives and happiness. Unless properly treated, syphilis eventually disables and then kills its victims.

Apparently syphilis appeared on the stage of history with dramatic suddenness only a few centuries ago and spread within a few years as a great plague over the known world (Pusey, 1933). Many medical historians contend that syphilis was introduced into Europe by the members of Columbus' crew, who presumably contracted it from the women of the West Indies. In fact, Kemble (1936) has pointed out that Columbus himself may have been infected. During his second voyage, in 1494, Columbus began having attacks of fever, possibly indicating the secondary stage of syphilis. During his third voyage, in 1498, he developed "a severe attack of gout" which was widespread and not confined to one or two of the smaller joints as gout usually is. During this voyage also, the first signs of mental disorder made their appearance. He began to hear voices and to regard himself as an "ambassador of God." On his last voyage, in 1504, Columbus was so ill that he had to be carried ashore. His whole body was dropsical from the chest downward, his limbs were paralyzed, and

---

[1]Various other infectious diseases such as scarlet fever, measles, and smallpox may involve temporary delirium or other transitory psychotic symptoms.

his brain affected—all symptoms of the terminal stages of syphilis.

Whatever the origin, syphilis spread like a tornado throughout Europe and became known as *The Great Pox* (Parran 1937; Pusey 1933). In 1496 the disease appeared in Paris and the number of victims became so great that the government was forced to pass an emergency decree forbidding a syphilitic to leave his home until completely cured.[1] In Edinburgh during the same year, all afflicted inhabitants were ordered into banishment on an island near Leith.

The numerous armies of mercenaries and adventurers of that period no doubt contributed materially to the rapid spread of the disease. Apparently also this early strain of syphilis was both extremely contagious and unusually virulent and attacked its victims with a violence almost unknown today.[2] High fever, delirium, violent headaches, horrible sores, and bone ulcers were typical even during the early stages of the disease. By 1498 the disease had spread to England. Vasco da Gama and his pioneering Portuguese are credited with carrying it around the Cape of Good Hope, and an outbreak occurred in India in 1498, spreading eastward to China by the year 1505.

During this early period there was no name for the disease. Each suffering nation blamed it upon some other nation. The Italians called it the *French* or *Spanish disease,* the English called it the *French pox* and so on. It finally received its specific name when in 1530 an Italian physician, Fracastorius, wrote a long poem about the disease in which the leading character, a shepherd named Syphilis, was stricken with it because of an insult to Apollo. The poem became tremendously popular, and *syphilis* became the accepted name for the dread disease.

Although many early theories of treatment contained some germs of truth, the physicians of those days could offer little help, and it was several hundred years before any major advances were made in the conquest of syphilis. In Chapter 2 we sketched the several steps by which the deadly spirochete that causes syphilis was discovered, blood tests developed, and methods of treatment worked out.

The spirochete of syphilis may gain entrance to the body through minute breaks or scratches in the skin or directly through mucous mem-

branes such as the lining of the mouth or the genital tract. Even though the mucous membrane is intact, the spirochete can wriggle through it in an hour or so. Syphilis is typically spread from person to person during sexual intercourse, although in exceptional cases it may be contracted through kissing or from direct contact with open syphilitic sores or lesions. It may also be transmitted from mother to child during fetal development; in this case it is referred to as *congenital syphilis.*

Once they have breached the outer defenses of the body, the spirochetes begin their systematic destruction of the body in four fairly well-defined stages.

First stage. Immediately after the spirochetes gain entrance to the body, they begin to multiply rapidly. From 10 to 40 days later, a sore called a *hard chancre* appears at the point of infection, which usually takes the form either of a pimple that feels hard to the touch or of an open ulcerated sore. In some instances it may be so insignificant that the patient is unaware of its existence. Even if untreated, this sore disappears in from four to six weeks, often leaving the victim with the mistaken notion that it was really only a minor irritation or that he is now cured.

Second stage. Following the chancre by some three to six weeks is the appearance of a copper-colored skin rash which may be mild and transitory or more severe, covering the entire body. This skin eruption may look like measles or smallpox and originally gave rise to the term *Great Pox* to differentiate this disease from *smallpox.* The rash may or may not be accompanied by fever, headaches, indigestion, loss of appetite, loss of hair in spots over the scalp, and other symptoms not usually thought of in connection with syphilis.

Third stage. This is known as the latent period, for in most cases all symptoms disappear. Again the victim is apt to think he is cured and so either avoid or discontinue treatment. During this period, however, the spirochetes are attacking various internal bodily organs and, if

---

[1] A "cure" probably meant the temporary remission or disappearance of symptoms—common during the third stage of syphilis—which the people of that period mistook for recovery.

[2] Undoubtedly the severity of this disease was also due in part to the lack of resistance or partial immunity usually acquired in the case of older diseases.

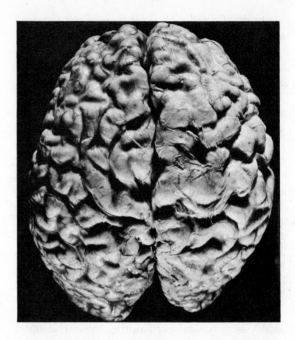

General paresis results when the spirochetes invade the cerebral cortex (left). A post-mortem examination typically reveals thickening of the meninges surrounding the brain and atrophy of the convolutions, especially in the frontal and temporal lobes (right).

untreated, cause permanent degeneration. The spirochetes may attack the bone marrow, the spleen, the lymph glands, or any tissue or organ of the body. Blood vessels and nerve cells seem to be favorite targets.

Fourth stage.   In this last stage we see the accumulated damage produced during the latent period. Ten, twenty, and even thirty years after the initial infection, the degenerative work of the spirochete may become apparent in a sudden heart attack, failure of vision (formerly 15 per cent of all blindness in the United States was due to syphilis), loss of motor coordination in walking, or mental disturbances. Syphilis is often called the "great imitator" because of the wide range of organic disease symptoms that it may produce. The most frequent and fatal forms of late syphilis are those in which the spirochete invades the walls of heart and blood vessels and the nervous system. It is the latter with which we are primarily concerned in our study of abnormal psychology.

General paresis.   General paresis is a mental disorder caused by the progressive infiltra-

tion and destruction of brain tissue by the spirochetes of syphilis. It has also been variously called *general paralysis of the insane, dementia paralytica,* and *paresis.* Approximately 3 per cent of untreated syphilitics eventually develop general paresis (Gibson, 1960; U.S. Public Health Service, 1961). The first symptoms usually appear about 10 years after the primary infection, although the incubation period may be as short as 2 years or as long as 40. Unless the patient receives treatment, the outcome is always fatal, death usually occurring within a period of 2 to 3 years after the initial symptoms. The average age of onset is approximately 50 years for both men and women, although the disease may occur early or in extreme old age. The number of new cases of general paresis has decreased markedly in the last decade, and general paresis now accounts for less than 1 per cent of all first admissions to mental hospitals.

General paresis is associated with a wide range of organic and psychological symptoms. During the early phase of the disorder, the patient typically becomes careless and inattentive and makes mistakes in his work. At first he may notice his mistakes but attributes them to being overly tired; later, he does not even notice them. Personal habits may show some deterioration, and the once-neat person may become slovenly. Comprehension and judgment suffer, and the patient may show a tendency to evade important problems, or he may react to them with smug indifference. Accompanying these symptoms is a blunting of affect, so that the patient does not share in the joys, sorrows, or anxieties of loved ones. He seems unable to realize the seriousness of his behavior and may become irritable or resort to ready rationalizations if his behavior is questioned. Overly sentimental behavior is typical and may involve promiscuous sexual patterns.

As the disorder progresses, a number of well-delineated physical symptoms make their appearance. The pupils are irregular in size and the pupillary reflex to light is either sluggish or entirely absent. Typically, speech functions become badly disturbed, with considerable stuttering and slurring of words. A phrase which invariably gives trouble and is of diagnostic significance is "Methodist Episcopal." This may be mispronounced in a number of ways, such as "Meodist Epispal" or "Methdist Pispal." Writing is similarly disturbed, with tremulous lines and the omission or transposition of syllables. Frequently, the patient has a rather vacant, dissipated look, with a silly grin. Where the spirochetes have also damaged neural pathways within the spinal cord, there may be difficulty in motor coordination. Such patients typically have a shuffling, unsteady walk referred to as *locomotor ataxia*. In addition, there may be tremors of the face, lips, and fingers and an absence of tendon reflexes, such as the knee jerk. During this period convulsive seizures may also make their appearance.

Paralleling these physical symptoms is a general personality deterioration. The patient is unmannerly, tactless, unconcerned with his appearance, and immoral in his behavior. Memory defects, which may be noticeable in the early phases of the illness, become more obvious. The patient may be unable to remember what he did even a few minutes before. He may ask when dinner will be served only a few minutes after he has finished eating it. This memory impairment extends to remote events, and the patient tends to fill in memory losses by various fabrications. As his intellectual processes are increasingly impaired, he becomes unable to comprehend the simplest problems and may optimistically squander his money on harebrained schemes or become involved in a variety of immoral and antisocial acts.

This entire picture of personality deterioration is usually colored by emotional reactions in the form of either marked euphoria, depression, or apathy. Thus three categories are commonly used to distinguish clinical types of paretics—*expansive, depressed,* and *demented* —although these types are by no means always distinct, and depressed patients frequently change categories by becoming euphoric. As the disease enters the terminal period, the extensive brain damage leads to a similar picture for all three types in which the patient leads a vegetative life, expresses no interest in anything, becomes inarticulate in speech, and can no longer care for himself. Convulsive seizures usually become common. Finally, a terminal infection or breakdown of bodily machinery leads to death.

1. *Expansive type.* Some paretics become extremely euphoric and expansive. If such a patient is asked how he feels, he may answer "Just wonderful! Everything is just perfect!" He often shows an overevaluation of himself in the form of delusions of grandeur. He may state that he is the richest and most powerful man in the world. When asked if he had a million dollars, one patient euphorically admitted he had billions of dollars as well as an abundance of other material possessions such as "about a million of the latest model Cadillacs, millions of wonder homes, and the best race horses in the country."

Such patients, with optimistic abandon, may plan gigantic projects involving huge sums of money. One patient had plans to build a superhighway from New York to China that would be at least a hundred miles wide. They seem utterly unable to realize the ludicrous nature of their claims and look forward to the outcome of every idea, and for that matter the entire future, with the utmost optimism. As might be expected, delusional ideas here are poorly systematized. When their ideas are questioned, patients may become irritable, but more often they dismiss criticisms as inconsequential.

The following description of a paretic patient will serve to illustrate the typical symptoms in expansive cases.

"C. W. flew planes from the United States to North Africa. His route began in Florida, passed through Natal, Ascension Island, and terminated in Dakar. His earlier health record was excellent, save for some 'difficulty' in his early twenties. Now, at 38, he was strong, well liked, and an expert pilot in the ferry command. He had completed a dozen or more trips.

"As he flew his plane eastward on his last journey, C. W. was unusually gay. 'It's a great world,' he sang. 'My rich aunt in Oklahoma is going to leave me $30,000,000.'

"During the periods of relief by his co-pilot, he talked loudly and became chummy with other members of the crew. As a matter of fact, he offered to loan the navigator $50,000. Landing safely in Dakar, his high spirits continued. Then his friends found him buying several 'diamonds' from an Arab street merchant, spending most of his cash for this purpose.

" 'Boy,' he exclaimed, 'I got a swell bargain! Six diamonds for $100 cash now and $100 more on my next trip! I sure fooled that Arab; he's never going to collect the rest from me.'

" 'How do you know the diamonds are genuine?' he was asked.

" 'I tested them,' he boasted. 'I struck one with a hammer and it proved hard; diamonds are hard.'

"Upon the return journey, C. W. continued the story of his expected wealth and the sum grew with the distance of travel.

" 'It's $40,000,000 I am getting and I expect to share some of it with you guys,' he announced. When his co-pilot received this astounding information with doubt and anxiety, C. W. could not understand it. When the co-pilot asked him to rest, he assured him that his body was perfect, that he didn't need rest. Then he added that he could fly the plane without gas, which he tried to prove by doing some fancy maneuvers in the sky.

" 'Funny,' he said later, 'no one seemed to believe me. Even when I offered them a million each they weren't happy, but looked at each other in such a puzzled way. It made me laugh, how they begged me to rest and how worried they looked when I refused. I was the boss and I showed them.'

"When the plane landed in Brazil by a miracle, C. W. was examined by a physician, forced into another plane and brought to Florida. Upon examination he was talkative, eyes gleaming, exuberant with statements of wealth and power. 'I am now one of the richest men in the world,' he said. 'I'll give you $5,000,000 to start a hospital. My eyes are jewels, diamonds, emeralds,' . . ." (Fetterman, 1949, pp. 267-268)

2. *Depressed type.* Some patients react to the progressive organic damage by becoming discouraged and depressed. Such patients usually have some insight into their failing functions and general life situation, though this insight is usually lost as the disorder progresses. Depressed patients frequently develop bizarre hypochondriacal delusions—they may become convinced that they have no brain, or that their bowels are completely stopped up, or that they are dead. Although suicidal attempts among such patients are not uncommon, the intellectual deterioration usually results only in rather childish, unsuccessful attempts.

Occasionally, depressed patients show considerable anxiety and agitation. Even though their mood is predominantly one of depression, they may have episodes of expansiveness. In general, depressed patients become expansive as their personality deterioration becomes increasingly severe.

The following brief conversation with a depressed female paretic, 42 years of age, serves further to illustrate these symptoms.

Dr.: How are you today, Miss——?
Pt.: Not so good doctor . . . (pause)
Dr.: What seems to be your difficulty?
Pt.: My brain has been eaten away. . . . I am no longer living, just a dead shell (shakes head despondently).
Dr.: How do you account for this trouble?
Pt.: I don't know doctor. . . . I have ruined my life . . . my brain is gone . . . there is no hope . . . (stares at floor) . . . my heart has stopped beating . . . I am only a dead shell . . . it's all over now. . . .

3. *Demented or simple type.* Strictly speaking, all patients show gradual intellectual and personality deterioration and hence are demented. However, this term is usually used to indicate cases where there is no pronounced euphoria or depression, and where the symptom picture consists chiefly of apathy, memory impairment, and general personality deterioration. Often the clinical picture here is similar to that in schizophrenia, with a gradual withdrawal from the environment, accompanied by delusions and hallucinations, usually of a simple nature. The simple type is the most common of the psychotic reactions associated with general paresis. The following case is typical of simple paresis.

"A woman of twenty-six was brought to the hospital because she had become lost when she attempted to return home from a neighboring grocery store. About seven months before the patient's admission her husband noticed that she was becoming careless of her personal appearance and neglectful of her household duties. She often forgot to prepare the family meals, or in an apparent preoccupation would burn the food. She seemed to have little appreciation of time and would not recognize when to get up or to go to bed. The patient would sit idly about the house staring uncomprehendingly into space.

"At the hospital the patient entered the admission office with an unsteady gait. There, by way of greeting, the physician inquired, 'How are you today?' to which she replied in a monotonous, tremulous tone, 'N-yes-s, I was-s op-er-a-ted on for 'pen-pendici-ci-tis.' She never made any spontaneous remarks and when, a few days after her admission, she was asked if she were sad or happy she stared vacantly at the physician and with a fatuous smile answered, 'Yeah.' The patient would sit about the ward for hours, taking no interest in its activities. Sometimes she would hold a book in her lap, aimlessly turning the leaves, never reading but often pointing out pictures like a small child and showing satisfaction when she found a new one to demonstrate. Neurological examination showed dilated pupils that reacted but slightly to light and on convergence. There was a coarse tremor of lips and facial muscles on attempt to speak. The protruded tongue showed a coarse tremor. All deep tendon reflexes were hyperactive. The Wassermann reaction was strongly positive on both blood serum and cerebrospinal fluid." (Noyes and Kolb, 1963, p. 210)

Although the various physical symptoms, together with deterioration of behavior in a previously well-adjusted individual, may be indicative of general paresis, the final diagnosis must rest upon the actual presence of the spirochete in the patient's blood stream and nervous system, usually demonstrable by means of blood and spinal-fluid tests.

The onset of symptoms in general paresis usually extends over several months or even years, but in some instances symptoms appear with dramatic suddenness in the course of a few days. Frequently, the early signs of the disorder are not recognized by family and friends until an acute episode of some sort occurs. The family of one patient noticed nothing particularly wrong until the patient one day went to a bar instead of to his office and there became noisy and expansive. Actually, for several months there had been less obvious symptoms, including forgetfulness of business appointments and peculiar color combinations in dress, but no one had noticed anything seriously amiss.

Although much is now known about general paresis, a number of questions still puzzle investigators. Why does less than one of 30 untreated syphilitics develop general paresis? Why do a higher percentage of whites than Negroes develop general paresis after syphilitic infection? Why do far more male than female syphilitics develop general paresis? And why is the relative incidence of general paresis much higher in some countries than in others? Some investigators hold that the syphilitic spirochetes attack the most vulnerable organs of the patient's body and that general paresis develops in patients whose brain tissue has an especially low resistance to syphilis. Other investigators have suggested that different strains of spirochetes may account for many of these differences. But the final answers to these questions are not yet available.

Juvenile paresis. Juvenile paresis results from congenital syphilis and is a condition of general paresis occurring in childhood or adolescence. Although no longer a major problem in the United States, congenital syphilis is still relatively common in certain other countries and contributes to a high infant mortality rate as well as to various afflictions other than juvenile paresis.

The symptoms in juvenile paresis are similar to those in general paresis and involve a picture of progressive mental and physical deterioration, including progressive impairment of memory, comprehension, and judgment. Motor incoordination, speech disturbances, and convulsions are common. The juvenile paretic usually has no insight into his condition and is apt to show a relatively simple deterioration without pronounced emotional coloring or marked psychological compensation.

The symptoms may appear at any time after birth, although ordinarily there are no noticeable symptoms until the child approaches puberty at about the age of 10 to 12. In some cases, however, retarded physical development, mental retardation, and convulsions make their appearance prior to the onset of the typical paretic syndrome (Bruetsch, 1959). In juvenile paresis, the course of the disorder is longer than in adult paresis, averaging about 5 years between the appearance of initial symptoms and termination in death.

The following is a description of a 15-year-old boy diagnosed as a juvenile paretic.

The patient was referred to the hospital by a school doctor after the boy had become rather "droopy" in class and began to talk in a rather funny and thick-tongued manner. On admission to the hospital the boy was slightly unsteady in his walk, his pupils were widely dilated and did not show a normal pupillary reflex to light. His emotional mood seemed to alternate from one of depression and apathy to one of mild euphoria. He soiled himself, was careless in his personal appearance, and exposed himself indiscriminately to males and females alike. The following conversation took place during a period of mild euphoria:

Dr.: How are you feeling today, Bob?
Pt.: Jus wonful, jus wonful (silly, fatuous grin).
Dr.: Can you say Methodist Episcopal Church?
Pt.: Mesdus Episfal Chursh.
Dr.: How are your studies progressing at school?
Pt.: Jus fine, jus fine, purfect.

Failure to maintain proper safeguards against congenital syphilis may result in heart damage or other organic disorders as well as in juvenile paresis. Formerly, syphilis accounted for more than half of all blindness in children at birth. It was also the largest cause of still-births and the primary reason for the deaths of many infants during the first weeks of life (Parran, 1937).

Historically, Henry VIII of England has often been cited to illustrate the tragic results of congenital syphilis. The first of his wives, Catherine of Aragon, bore four children, all of whom were stillborn or died immediately after birth. A fifth child, a daughter, finally survived to reign later as "Bloody Mary." Mary herself showed many signs of congenital syphilis— her face was prematurely old and scarred; her hair thin and straggling; her head square, with a grotesquely protruding forehead; and her sight extremely bad. Her sudden death at the age of 42 was presumably due to syphilitic complications. Of Henry's six wives, Anne of Cleves, whose marriage was never consummated, was thought by the medical historian Kemble (1936) to be the only one who might have shown a negative Wassermann test.

Meningovascular syphilis. Meningovascular syphilis differs from general paresis in that the syphilitic damage initially centers in the blood vessels and meninges of the brain rather than in the neural tissue. This form of cerebral syphilis is relatively rare and constitutes considerably less than 1 per cent of all first admissions to mental hospitals.

The symptoms in meningovascular syphilis differ from those in general paresis in that there is rarely any marked deterioration of conduct. Typical are persistent headaches, dizziness, blurring or doubling of vision; often there is insomnia and nausea. Lethargy, confusion, and difficulty in concentration are common. Physical symptoms of diagnostic value include disturbed pupillary reactions to light and accentuated knee-jerk reflex. Speech and writing usually are not markedly affected but convulsive seizures are common.

During the early stages of meningovascular syphilis the actual amount of brain damage is usually less than in general paresis, and the personality deterioration is correspondingly less. In advanced cases, the brain damage, symptom picture, and dynamics are comparable for the two disorders.

Treatment and prognosis for cerebral syphilis. Prior to the advent of malaria fever treatment and more recently the use of penicillin, the outcome in cerebral syphilis was invariably progressive deterioration and death. Although malaria fever treatment appears to be as effective as penicillin, it is more difficult to perform and more hazardous. Consequently, penicillin is now considered the method of choice (Gibson, 1960). For certain cases a combination of penicillin and malaria therapy may be used (Fleischl, 1960).

It is, of course, important that detection and treatment of cerebral syphilis be accomplished as early as possible. Unfortunately, routine medical diagnostic techniques do not always reveal the presence of syphilitic infection of the brain. The Wassermann blood test appears to be positive in about 80 per cent of the cases and the spinal fluid test in about 65 per cent (Bruetsch, 1959). Beerman *et al.* (1962) have reviewed newer diagnostic approaches for detecting syphilis in cases that cannot be diagnosed by conventional methods.

The specific prognosis in cases receiving medical treatment depends to a large extent upon the amount of cerebral damage that has taken place before treatment is started. If the damage is not extensive, the adaptive capacities of the individual—both neurological and psychological—may leave only a small residue of impairment of brain function. Unfortunately, in many cases treatment is not undertaken until the disease has produced extensive and irreparable brain damage. Here about all that can be hoped is to arrest further inroads of the deadly spirochete. In such cases, the intellectual picture may show considerable improvement, but the patient never approaches his previous level of intellectual ability. For treated paretics as a group, the following rough estimates of outcome may be made:

1. Some 20 to 30 per cent of the patients show good recovery and can resume their former occupation and activities.
2. Another 30 to 40 per cent show some improvement but usually require a transfer to less complex occupational duties as a consequence of residual intellectual or personality impairment.
3. 15 to 25 per cent show no improvement.
4. 10 per cent die during the course of treatment (or within a 10-year period following the instigation of treatment).

On the other hand, when treatment is started early, approximately 80 per cent of general paretics show a sufficient remission of symptoms to return to their original or other type of employment (Hahn *et al.*, 1958, 1959). As with other mental disorders, psychotherapy and sociotherapy may be essential aspects of the total treatment program.

Prevention of cerebral syphilis. The only fully adequate approach to cerebral syphilis is, of course, the prevention of syphilitic infection or early detection and treatment where infection has taken place. Although we now have the medical means to eradicate syphilis, it remains a major health problem in our society because its roots are social as well as medical. In fact, in recent years there has been an upsurge in the incidence of syphilis. In 1961, there were 18,781 new cases of infectious syphilis reported in the United States, representing a three-fold increase in the four years since 1957 (U.S. Public Health Service, 1962).[1] Over half of the reported cases of syphilis involve teen-agers and young adults under 25 years of age.

The majority of cases go unreported, and the true incidence of new cases in 1961 was estimated to be at least 60,000. In addition, it was estimated that there was a reservoir of 1,200,000 untreated syphilitics in the United States. Unless these cases are found and treated, some 180,000 may be expected to develop disabling manifestations, including some 91,000 cases of cardiovascular syphilis and 53,000 cases of paresis and meningovascular syphilis (Brown, 1960).

One key problem in the control and prevention of syphilis is finding and treating all infected cases. Toward this end it has become common practice for patients with infectious syphilis to be interviewed for sex contacts. Every effort is then made to locate these individuals and screen them for possible syphilitic infection. In one study in a major urban center only 11 patients out of 292 reported as having primary or secondary syphilis were unable or unwilling to identify at least one person with whom they had had sexual contact. Of the 159 males who revealed the identity of sex-

---

[1] The recent upsurge in the incidence of syphilis led the Surgeon General, Public Health Service, to appoint a special Task Force to review the syphilis problem and to recommend a course of action to eradicate syphilis as a public health problem (U.S. Public Health Service, 1962).

RESULTS OF ADDING CLUSTER TESTING   (8-month period)

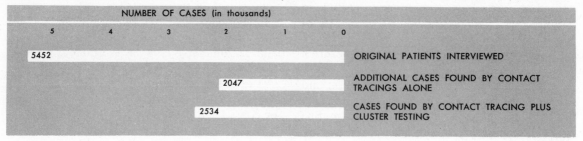

NUMBER OF CASES (in thousands)

5	4	3	2	1	0	
5452						ORIGINAL PATIENTS INTERVIEWED
			2047			ADDITIONAL CASES FOUND BY CONTACT TRACINGS ALONE
		2534				CASES FOUND BY CONTACT TRACING PLUS CLUSTER TESTING

ual partners, 49 named exclusively female sexual partners, 21 named both male and female sexual partners, and the remaining 89 named only male sexual contacts. The latter group named 551 different persons as sexual partners, of whom 93 were later found to have syphilis. The group who had had exclusively heterosexual relations identified 137 sexual partners, of whom 29 were found to have syphilis (Tarr and Lugar, 1960).

To improve on the efficiency of case-finding, the Task Force appointed by the Surgeon General advocated the extension of interviews to include not only sex contacts of patients but also friends and acquaintances, whose sexual behavior is assumed to be similar to that of the patient. This is called cluster testing, and the results of such interviewing of 5452 patients with primary and secondary syphilis are shown in the chart above.

Despite the recent upsurge in the incidence of syphilis in the United States, there have been widespread advances in the control and prevention of syphilis on both national and international levels. In the United States, facilities are provided for the free diagnosis and treatment of syphilis; most states require examinations before marriage; and public educational campaigns are vigorously supported by federal, state, and local civic, religious, and educational agencies. The schools in particular play an important role in imparting realistic attitudes and adequate information concerning the nature, development, and disastrous effects of untreated syphilis. This is particularly necessary in view of the fact that promiscuous sexual behavior among teen-agers has become a major source of infection and spread of syphilis (Beerman *et al.,* 1962; U.S. Public Health

Service, 1962). With the cooperation of national and international agencies, better education, and more adequate facilities for diagnosis and treatment, there is every reason to believe that syphilis can be eliminated as a public health problem.

EPIDEMIC ENCEPHALITIS

Epidemic encephalitis[1] is an inflammation of the brain tissue caused by a filterable virus. As in the case of the syphilitic spirochete, this virus causes diffuse degenerative changes accompanied by a variety of personality disorders. In the acute phase of the disease the patient is typically lethargic and appears to be sleeping all of the time. For this reason the condition was once called *encephalitis lethargica* and is now popularly known as *sleeping sickness.*

This disease was apparently uncommon prior to an epidemic in Europe and the United States following World War I and now again is relatively rare. However, an acute epidemic among children was reported in Lucknow, India in 1958 (Bajpai *et al.,* 1960), and it remains a serious problem in certain parts of Africa. Epidemic encephalitis accounts for only some 0.1 per cent of first admissions to our mental hospitals. Although no age group is immune, it is more common among children and young adults.

Symptoms and dynamics. The onset and acute symptoms in epidemic encephalitis may take many forms, but usually the clinical pic-

---

[1]*Encephalitis* means inflammation of the brain. There are a number of types of encephalitis in addition to epidemic or lethargic encephalitis (Jervis, 1959).

ture is one of fever, drowsiness or stupor, and ocular or pupillary disturbances. The patient sleeps constantly, although he can usually be awakened long enough to answer questions or to take nourishment.

Another common form of the disease, which occasionally follows the drowsy or stuporous state, is characterized primarily by symptoms of a hyperkinetic type. Here the clinical picture centers around insomnia, restlessness and agitation, irritability, excitability, and choreiform movements. In some cases, the latter symptoms are complicated by delirium, disorientation, and hallucinations. Although many patients appear to make a satisfactory recovery, neurological and psychological disturbances may follow encephalitis.

1. *Aftereffects in adults.* A common aftereffect of this disease in adults is *Parkinson's disease,* which will be described later in the present chapter.

Among other common physical aftereffects of epidemic encephalitis are twitches of the face, arm, and hand muscles and various pupillary and ocular disturbances. Included in the latter category are the "oculo-gyric crises" in which the eyes suddenly turn upward in a spasm and remain that way for several minutes. Another ocular symptom of diagnostic significance is loss of the blink reflex, which results in a staring and masklike facial expression.

The aftereffects of epidemic encephalitis in adults do not in themselves seriously impair intelligence nor do they ordinarily result in psychological maladjustments. However, the patient may react to the neurological aftereffects and the resultant changes in his life situation with a variety of neurotic or psychotic symptoms. The most common psychotic reaction appears to be an agitated depression in which the patient is anxious and restless and at the same time discouraged and dejected. In other cases the patient may become expansive or apathetic and withdrawn. Occasional adult patients become impulsive and aggressive in their behavior (Brill, 1959). They appear to have good insight into their behavior and the capacity for self-criticism but are unable to control their inner impulses. The patient is "master of what he says" but the "slave of what he does." The actual relation of such behavior to the brain damage resulting from epidemic encephalitis is not known.

2. *Aftereffects in children.* The aftereffects of this disease are ordinarily much more serious in children than in adults. Children who were previously well behaved and cheerful often become restless, aggressive, cruel, impudent, and generally unmanageable. They seem to lose their self-control and to be under a continual pressure of restless activity. Often they will state that they do not want to behave as they do, but that they cannot seem to help themselves. Without provocation they may impulsively engage in destructive, homicidal, sexually aberrant, and other delinquent behavior. As a result, such children usually require hospitalization. Other typical symptoms are hypersalivation, motor incoordination, and bizarreness of posture, such as leaning conspicuously backward or forward when walking. The precise relation of the symptoms to the neurological damage is not known. Among children under five years of age, mental development may be severely retarded and the child may not attain his normal intellectual status. Jervis (1959) has reported that encephalitis accounts for some 5 per cent of all institutionalized cases of mental retardation. In general, the older the child at the time of onset of the disease, the less the mental impairment.

In cases where the child becomes impulsive, aggressive, and hyperactive in postencephalitic behavior, most investigators have emphasized the etiological role of residual brain damage, which impairs inner controls and the organization of thought processes. Bender (1948, 1961) has particularly emphasized the inability of these children to organize and interpret perceptual experiences in a meaningful way. It becomes difficult or impossible for these children to develop consistent environmental and self assumptions in terms of which to evaluate subsequent experience and direct their behavior. As a result, these children presumably feel vaguely apprehensive and anxious and driven to manipulate their environment in order to try and establish some sort of order and meaning, which are prerequisites to feelings of adequacy and security. In this sense they are driven to reality testing—incessantly displayed in their drive toward objects and persons—

while at the same time they are further frustrated by their inability to learn or profit normally from such experiences. This persistent and uncoordinated drive toward mastering reality, together with their diffuse anxiety, tends to their ultimately destroying and devouring objects and to a vicious circle of catastrophic activity.

The following case brings out many of the symptoms typically found in severe postencephalitic behavior disorders among children and is interesting with respect to Bender's theory.

"Harold is a boy of fifteen years whose behavior is so unpredictably and dangerously impulsive that his family cannot keep him at home. He must always live in an institution.

"He presents a strange, almost uncannily freakish appearance. He is short and squat in stature and has a short squarish head that is oversized for his body. He walks with an awkward, shambling gait, a little like a monkey. As you watch him, he sidles toward another child in a gingerly, apparently affectionate manner. Suddenly he grasps the child's finger and bends it backward mercilessly; then he slinks impishly away, laughing and chuckling. In a moment he raises his bitten nails to his mouth and stares at the cloudless sky as though abruptly transported, and mutters some incoherent remark about a 'terrible storm coming that will break all the limbs of the trees.' A few minutes later with tears streaming from his eyes he presents an appearance of genuine remorse. He puts his arms around the same child's neck and suddenly chokes the child painfully with a tremendous hug. When a teacher pries him away he tries to bite her hand. He murmurs to the teacher: 'I hurt you, didn't I? Can you whip? Whip me.' Perhaps a while later he may be seen to shuffle stealthily toward the same teacher and whisper to her in a childlike manner: 'I like you.' Then quick as a flash he may poke his finger into her eye and cry again: 'Can you whip? Whip me.'

"He did not thrive well in his childhood, for he was beset with many illnesses. His physical and mental development was markedly retarded. He failed to adjust himself to school and at home became uncontrollably provocative and destructive. Very much distraught, the parents resorted to beatings to discipline him, but they were of no avail.

"His mental age is about eight years (I.Q. 60). Emotionally he is very unstable; often he unaccountably

bursts into tears. The most striking aspects of his behavior are his uncontrolled impulsive cruelties and his perverted craving to suffer pain himself. Like the rest of us, he wants love and affection, but he seeks it in a strange way. He torments and hurts others so they may do the same to him. He appears to derive an erotic pleasure from the pain which he provokes from others in lieu of love. To such injuries he adds those which he inflicts upon himself.

"This is a strange boy indeed. His disordered behavior is the consequence of an inflammatory illness of the brain, encephalitis, which complicated a contagious disease in infancy." (Menninger, 1946, pp. 41-42)[1]

Treatment and prognosis. Ordinarily epidemic encephalitis can be arrested by antibiotics which kill the invading virus, and most children make a complete recovery. However, some children die during the acute phase (probably 10 per cent or more), and still others recover but reveal various neurological and psychological aftereffects. Death or irreparable brain damage is likely where treatment is delayed or not undertaken.

Once the chronic syndrome has been established, the prognosis has traditionally been considered unfavorable (Brill, 1959). However, Levy (1959) has reported favorable results on 100 patients described by parents as hyperactive, unpredictable, destructive, and unable to learn by experience. Since they were able to live at home, however, they were presumably not extreme cases. Following a daily administration of benzedrine sulfate, an amphetamine drug, there was diminished hyperactivity, increased concentration and attention, and reduced aggressive behavior, which, in turn, led to improved scholastic performance for those attending school and to more favorable attitudes of parents and teachers toward the patients. Levy concluded that postencephalitic behavior disorder is definitely an organic condition and can be treated successfully by medication. The full potentialities of specialized medical, psychological, and educational pro-

---

[1]For a more detailed description of types of encephalitis and postencephalitic syndromes the reader is referred to Fairweather (1947), who made an extensive investigation of 275 cases, to Bajpai *et al*. (1960), who has reported on 301 children suffering from acute epidemic encephalitis in Lucknow, India, and to Aguilar (1959), who has summarized the history of this disease.

cedures for these children are still largely unexplored though encouraging results have been achieved even in severe cases.

MENINGITIS

Although there were outbreaks of meningitis in Europe during the nineteenth century, it is relatively rare in the United States and considerably less than 1 per cent of all first admissions to mental hospitals are so diagnosed at present. Formerly, however, about 2 per cent of the institutionalized cases of mental deficiency were attributed to meningitis in early childhood, and during World War II more United States military personnel died of meningitis and bacteremia than of any other infectious diseases (Eigler *et al.,* 1961).

The disease is caused by bacteria, which attack and cause an inflammation of the meninges, or membranes covering the brain cortex.

In some instances the infection spreads from the meninges into the underlying brain tissue. The disease is highly virulent with a mortality rate of about 30 per cent (Eigler *et al.,* 1961).

During the acute phase, the patient may manifest a wide range of symptoms characteristic of central nervous system involvement— coma, delirium, emotional lability, convulsions, and disturbances of motility. Upon recovery from the acute episode, various neurological aftereffects may remain, among the more common of which are muscle weakness and blurring of vision. Meningitis does not appear to result in any residual pattern of psychological symptoms. Only where the disease serves to precipitate a neurosis or psychosis in an already predisposed individual are the psychological symptoms of great significance. The aftereffects of meningitis may be more serious in the case of children, where, as we have noted, damage to the brain may affect development of mental capacity (Johnson, 1960).

Disorders with Brain Tumors

In the writings of Felix Plater (1536-1614) we find the following rather remarkable account of "A Case of Stupor due to a Tumour in the Brain, Circular like a Gland":

"Caspar Bone Curtius, a noble knight, began to show signs of 'mental alienation' which continued through a period of two years until at last he became quite stupefied, did not act rationally, did not take food unless forced to do so, nor did he go to bed unless compelled, at table he just lay on his arms and went to sleep, he did not speak when questioned even when admonished, and if he did it was useless. Pituita dropped from his nose copiously and frequently: this condition continued for about six months, and finally he died. . . . At the post mortem when the skull was opened and the lobes of the brain separated, a remarkable globular tumor was found on the upper surface of the Corpus Callosum, resembling a gland fleshly, hard and fungus-like, about the size of a medium sized apple, invested with its own membranes and having its own veins, lying free and without any connection with the brain itself. . . . This tumour, by its mass, produced

pressure on the brain and its vessels, which causes stupor, torpor, and finally death. Some doctors who had seen this case earlier attributed it to sorcery, others just to the humors, but by opening the skull we made clear the abstruse and hidden cause." (1664)

A tumor is a new growth involving an abnormal enlargement of body tissue. Such tumors or new growths are most apt to occur in the breast, the uterus, the prostate, or the intestinal tract, although they are not uncommonly found in the central nervous system. In adults, brain tumors occur with the greatest frequency during the forties and fifties.

Some of these tumors are malignant in that they destroy the tissue in which they arise; others are not destructive except by reason of the pressure that they exert. Since the skull is an unyielding container, a relatively small tumor in the brain may cause marked pressure and thus may interfere seriously with normal brain functioning.

Autopsies in general and mental hospitals

have revealed brain tumors in about 1 per cent of the general population and 2 to 4 per cent of mental hospital patients (German, 1959; Patton and Sheppard, 1956; Wilson, 1940). Yet psychoses associated with brain tumors constitute less than 0.1 per cent of all first admissions to mental hospitals. Apparently many brain tumors do not produce recognizable symptoms.

SYMPTOMS AND DYNAMICS

The clinical picture which develops in cases of brain tumor is extremely varied and is determined largely by (a) the location, size, and rapidity of growth of the tumor, and (b) the premorbid personality of the patient.

The brain tumor itself may result in both localized and general symptoms. Damage to a particular part of the brain may result in localized disturbances of sensory or motor functions. General symptoms appear when the tumor becomes large enough to result in greatly increased intracranial pressure. Common early symptoms here are persistent headache, vomiting, memory impairment or confusion, listlessness, and "choked disc"—a phenomenon due to swelling of the optic nerve· when cerebrospinal fluid is forced into it by intracranial pressure.[1]

As the tumor progresses and the intracranial pressure increases, there may be clouding of consciousness, disorientation for time and place, carelessness in personal habits, irritability, convulsive seizures, vomiting, sensorimotor losses, hallucinations, apathy, and a general impairment of intellectual functions. Terminal stages are similar to other types of severe brain damage, in which the patient is reduced to a vegetative stupor and eventual death.

The range of symptoms which may occur in brain tumor cases has been clarified by Levin (1949) in an intensive study of 22 cases admitted to the Boston Psychopathic Hospital. These patients ranged in age from 22 to 65 years, the majority (73 per cent) falling between the ages of 40 and 60 years. There were 11 males and 11 females. Prior to hospitalization the range of symptoms shown by these patients included those listed at the top of the next column.

SYMPTOMS PRIOR TO HOSPITALIZATION	NUMBER OF CASES
Memory impairment or confusion	13
Depression	9
Seizures	8
Headaches	8
Complaints of visual impairment	6
Drowsiness	6
Irritability	6
Indifference	5
Restlessness	4
Complaint of generalized weakness	4
Loss of sense of responsibility	3
Syncopal attacks	2
Paranoid ideas	2
Fearfulness	2
Tendency to be combative	2
Euphoria	2
Aphasia	2
Hypochondriacal tendencies	2

The interval between the onset of the symptoms and hospitalization varied from 1 week to 6 years with an average interval of 17 months. In most cases, symptoms were evident 6 months or longer prior to admission.

The patient's emotional reaction to the organic damage and to the resulting intellectual impairment depends to a large extent upon his premorbid personality and his degree of insight into his condition. Initially, the patient may merely be overly irritable, drowsy, and mildly depressed. As the disorder progresses, however, he may have some insight into the seriousness of his condition and become severely depressed, anxious, and apprehensive.

Patients who have less insight into their condition usually react to the brain damage and their failing functions by becoming expansive and euphoric. Such patients seem unconcerned about their illness and may joke and laugh in a most unrestrained and hilarious manner. Such reactions are apparently compensatory and are especially frequent in advanced stages when there is considerable brain damage or pressure.

Serious tumors, especially those with psychiatric complications, are most common in

[1]For more details concerning symptomatology in brain-tumor cases the reader is referred to Gal (1958), German (1959), McTaggard *et al.* (1961), Mulder (1959), Segelow and Davis (1961), Sherman (1961).

the frontal, temporal, and parietal lobes (McTaggard *et al.,* 1961; Soniat, 1951). Frontal-lobe tumors often produce subtle peculiarities, such as inability to concentrate, personal carelessness, a loss of inhibitions, and absentmindedness that later becomes a memory defect. Often, too, the patient becomes silly and prone to punning and general jocularity.

Tumors involving the special sensory areas in the brain may result in hallucinations of sight, hearing, taste, and smell. It has been estimated that about one half of the patients with brain tumors evidence hallucinations some time during the course of their illness. Visual hallucinations predominate and may involve dazzling, vividly colored flashes of light, as well as various kinds and sizes of animals and other objects. In temporal-lobe tumors "Lilliputian hallucinations" are sometimes found in which the patient sees small figures that he usually knows are not real. Such hallucinations apparently result from irritation of the visual pathways passing through the temporal lobe.

Similarly, irritation of the olfactory pathways may result in the perception of peculiar odors, such as rubber burning, for which there is no external stimulus. Auditory hallucinations may include buzzing, ringing, roaring, and occasionally voices and conversations.

The following excerpt from the case history of a 55-year-old patient shows some of the milder symptoms commonly found in frontal-lobe tumors.

Several months prior to his hospitalization, the patient had complained to his wife about frequent and severe headaches which he attributed to tension over difficulties in getting along with his supervisor at work. About three months after the headaches appeared, the patient began to have occasional vomiting spells which he also attributed to tension and an "upset stomach." Despite his wife's insistence, he refused to have a medical checkup. Shortly after this, his wife noticed that the patient "seemed preoccupied and absentminded a good deal of the time." He also became somewhat careless in his personal appearance and slovenly in his eating habits. On several occasions he became emotionally upset over trivial matters; sometimes he would joke about unhumorous topics, such as the death of someone in an automobile accident.

Some nine months after the appearance of his head-

aches, the patient's wife was called in for a conference with his supervisor. The supervisor stated that her husband "didn't seem to be himself" and was becoming increasingly indifferent about the quality of his work. He had talked to the patient but "didn't seem to get through." He suggested that she encourage her husband to see a psychiatrist.

The wife agreed to carry out this suggestion, but the patient refused to see a psychiatrist or to admit that his personality had changed. Two evenings later, however, he had a convulsive seizure. His wife called a physician who had the patient hospitalized for observation. A thorough medical checkup revealed the presence of a growth in the right frontal lobe. Surgery proved successful and the patient made a good recovery and was eventually able to resume his former employment.

Although such personality change is so common in brain-tumor cases that it has in the past been attributed directly to the tumor, we now realize that these symptoms are neither inevitable nor to be thought of as due solely to the tumor. We have stressed repeatedly that adjustive reactions must always be thought of as a function of both the stress situation (including biological, psychological, and sociological stresses) and the personality of the individual —his stability and level of stress tolerance. The greater an individual's maturity and stability, the greater the stresses which he can successfully withstand. Nowhere is this more clearly brought out than in the tremendous range of reactions which we see in patients suffering from definite, observable, measurable stress in the form of brain pathology.

A most dramatic example of the importance of the patient's pre-illness personality in determining the effects of brain pathology is related by John Gunther (1949) in a story of his son Johnny's refusal to give in to a brain tumor.

Johnny was sixteen and in his junior year at preparatory school when the tumor was discovered. There had been none of the common warning signs of dizziness, vomiting, chills, tremors, or double vision. A stiff neck led to examination and eventual diagnosis of tumor. An operation was performed immediately, at which time it was discovered that the tumor was in the right occipital parietal lobe and was about the size of an orange. It was not encapsulated and only about half of it could be removed. The skull was left open, so that if the tumor continued to grow, the pressure would be outward rather than inward against the brain. X-ray treatments were begun. Throughout this ordeal Johnny remained cheerful, belittling his discomfort and increasing weakness and trying to ease his parents' worry. He was concerned about the school work he was missing and scrupulously followed the doctors' orders in the minutest detail in an effort to hasten his recovery. His courage and good humor continued through the course of exhausting X-ray treatments, though he later confided that he had been so worried about them that he had been unable to sleep at night.

About a month after the operation he was allowed to leave the hospital and spent a busy summer studying, working in his laboratory-workshop, calculating the mathematical odds in poker, making barbecues, and playing with his boat, between trips to the hospital for check-ups every ten days and for care in successive crises. He invited several school friends to visit him, but feared that his inability to join them in active sports was spoiling their fun. He also showed great concern over the inconvenience and burden of expense he was causing his parents.

The tumor began growing again very soon and was diagnosed as a fatal malignant glioma. By this time his field of vision had become considerably restricted.

Other types of treatment were tried, with some success: first, intravenous injections of mustard gas, which is a poison that kills cells with abnormally fast growth, and which had never before been attempted in a brain case. Johnny felt stronger, and in August, with the help of a friend, he successfully worked out a new process for the liquefaction of ammonia, following an experiment he had designed in theory. Johnny was confident that he would be able to return to school.

The end of August he was worse again. He was very weak, his white blood count was below 1000, and there were capillary breakdowns resulting in huge bruises on chest and arms. A special fatless and saltless diet was tried, supplemented by over thirty pills daily to supply needed minerals and vitamins. Again his condition improved, although by this time his visual field was so limited that he could not see the whole chess board at one glance, and he could hardly move the fingers of his left hand or walk without swaying.

Realizing that he could not return to school that fall, Johnny set out to make up the work by tutoring. Two tutors were called in and Johnny carefully mapped out his course of study. He knew exactly what he wanted to cover in each session. Before long he insisted on taking a test for which his tutor thought he was not ready and successfully passed it.

Shortly thereafter, an abscess developed and Johnny became tired and feverish until the abscess opened spontaneously and was successfully drained. Following this, there were several months of definite improvement. Johnny worked tirelessly, determined to catch up with his class and pass college entrance exams. Although he began to have attacks of amnesia and the tumor began to grow again, he caught up in one course after another—with grades in the 90's—and in mid-April took the college board exams, a six-hour ordeal following an hour of standing in line.

By the end of April the tumor, now diagnosed as glioma multiforme, was growing so rapidly that a second major operation was necessary. This time the surgeon penetrated 11 centimeters without even reaching healthy brain tissue. Two weeks later Johnny went home, feeling a little better and able to joke with his family and friends. He refused to admit that it was becoming increasingly hard for him to fix his belt and shoelaces. Walking was very difficult.

Late in May he graduated with his class, walking very slowly down the center of the long aisle and grasping the diploma in his weak left hand despite the efforts of the president of the board to place it in his right. Less than a month after this summation of his long struggle, there was a cerebral hemorrhage, and Johnny died, without pain or fear. All through those fourteen months he had never lost his sweetness, selflessness, courage, or humor.

TREATMENT AND PROGNOSIS

Treatment of brain-tumor cases is primarily a surgical matter and thus is outside the scope of our present discussion. However, it may be noted that the degree of recovery of the patient in such cases depends both upon the size and location of the growth and on the amount of brain tissue which may have to be removed with the tumor. In some cases there seems to be full recovery while in others there may be a residue of symptoms such as partial paralysis and a reduction in intellectual level. Where tumors are well advanced and require extensive surgery, the mortality rate is high.

The following case, summarized from a report by Brickner reveals a postoperative reduction in general intellectual capacity and the overcompensatory reaction of the patient to his changed life situation.

The patient was a man of 40 who had been a successful broker on the New York Stock Exchange. During the operation to remove his tumor, large portions of the frontal lobes of the brain were removed on both sides. As a result the patient's general adjustive capacities— including comprehension, judgment, restraint, memory, and learning capacity—were markedly lowered.

Much of his behavior was childish and abusive. He would refuse to wash his face in the morning or to get undressed in the evening. On occasion he would walk into a room where a card game was going on and would say, "You're all a lousy bunch of players. Do you want to start something?"

The following excerpt from Brickner's extensive case record on this man will serve to show his impaired intellectual capacity and his grandiose overcompensating reaction. . . .

B.: One thing your illness lost you is the knowledge that you're not perfect.

A.: It's a damned good thing to lose.

B.: Do you really believe in your heart that you are perfect?

A.: Yes. Of course we all have faults. I have faults like everyone else.

B.: Name some of your faults.

A.: I don't think I have any.

B.: You just said you had.

A.: Well, they wouldn't *predominate* on the Exchange.

B.: I mean personal faults.

A.: Yes, I have personal faults. I never give a man an opportunity to do what he wants to do on the Exchange, if I know it.

B.: Is that a fault?

A.: That's being a good broker.

B.: Can you name a personal fault? Do you really believe you're perfect?

A.: You bet I do—pretty near perfect—they don't come much more perfect than I am." (1936, pp. 47-48)

Ordinarily the prognosis in brain-tumor cases depends heavily upon how early and how accurately the condition is diagnosed and whether treatment is undertaken. German (1959) has stated that about 40 per cent of all brain tumors are potentially curable and about 20 per cent are capable of palliation for periods of five or more years, while the remainder are fatal within a short period of time. Unfortunately, in many cases benign (noncancerous) tumors grow slowly and for a time do not produce any of the tell-tale symptoms.

Apparently the brain can accommodate itself to slowly expanding tumors for some period of time. Here the first symptoms, psychiatric or organic, may follow some severe emotional trauma (Sandler, 1960). In such instances psychiatric symptoms may closely resemble neurotic or psychotic symptomatology, and the disorder may be mistakenly diagnosed as functional rather than organic in nature. However, physicians are alert to the possibility of brain tumors in psychiatric as well as general medical cases, and an early diagnosis can often be made by means of EEG and other neurological procedures. Unfortunately, there are no known methods for preventing the development of brain tumors.

Disorders with Head Injury

Since ancient times, brain injuries have provided a rich source of material for medical and popular speculation concerning mental functions. Hippocrates pointed out that injuries to the head could cause sensory and motor disorders, and Galen included head injuries among the major causes of mental disorders.

Perhaps the most famous historical case is the celebrated American crowbar case reported by Dr. J. M. Harlow in 1868. Since it is of both historical and descriptive significance, it merits a few details:

"The accident occurred in Cavendish, Vt. on the line of the Rutland and Burlington Railroad, at that time being built, on the 13th of September, 1848, and was occasioned by the premature explosion of a blast, when this iron, known to blasters as a tamping iron, and which I now show you, was shot through the face and head.

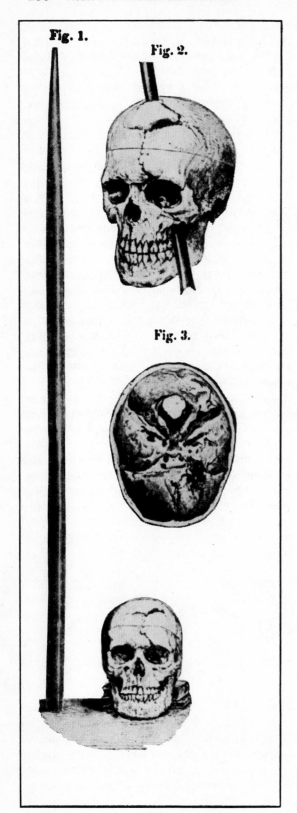

Fig. 1.

Fig. 2.

Fig. 3.

Harlow illustrated his famous crowbar case by these drawings, showing (1) the comparative sizes of the cranium and the tamping iron which passed through it; (2) a view of the cranium showing just where the iron passed through, and also a large section of the skull which was entirely torn away and later replaced; and (3) an upward view from inside the skull, giving the position and relative size of the hole that was made and showing a deposit of new bone partially closing it over.

"The subject of it was Phineas P. Gage, a perfectly healthy, strong and active young man, twenty-five years of age . . . Gage was foreman of a gang of men employed in excavating rock, for the road way . . . .

"The missile entered by its pointed end, the left side of the face, immediately anterior to the angle of the lower jaw, and passing obliquely upwards, and obliquely backwards, emerged in the median line, at the back part of the frontal bone, near the coronal suture. . . . The iron which thus traversed the head, is round and rendered comparatively smooth by use, and is three feet seven inches in length, one and one fourth inches in its largest diameter, and weighs thirteen and one fourth pounds. . . .

"The patient was thrown upon his back by the explosion, and gave a few convulsive motions of the extremities, but spoke in a few minutes. His men (with whom he was a great favorite) took him in their arms and carried him to the road, only a few rods distant, and put him into an ox cart, in which he rode, supported in a sitting posture, fully three quarters of a mile to his hotel. He got out of the cart himself, with a little assistance from his men, and an hour afterwards (with what I could aid him by taking hold of his left arm) walked up a long flight of stairs, and got upon the bed in the room where he was dressed. He seemed perfectly conscious, but was becoming exhausted from the hemorrhage, which by this time, was quite profuse, the blood pouring from the lacerated sinus in the top of his head, and also finding its way into the stomach, which ejected it as often as every fifteen or twenty minutes. He bore his sufferings with firmness, and directed my attention to the hole in his cheek, saying, 'the iron entered there and passed through my head.'" (1868, pp. 330, 331, 332)

Some time later Dr. Harlow made the following report.

"His physical health is good, and I am inclined to say that he has recovered. Has no pain in head, but says it has a queer feeling which he is not able to describe. Applied for his situation as foreman, but is undecided whether to work or travel. His contractors, who regarded him as the most efficient and capable foreman in their employ previous to his injury considered the change in his mind so marked that they could not give him his place again. The equilibrium or balance, so to speak, between his intellectual faculties and animal propensities, seems to have been destroyed. He is fitful, irreverent, indulging at times in the grossest profanity (which was not previously his custom), manifesting but little deference for his fellows, impatient of restraint or advice when it conflicts with his desires, at times pertinaciously obstinate, yet capricious and vacillating, devising many plans of future operations, which are no sooner arranged than they are abandoned in turn for others appearing more feasible. A child in his intellectual capacity and manifestations, he has the animal passions of a strong man. Previous to his injury, though untrained in the schools, he possessed a well-balanced mind, and was looked upon by those who knew him as a shrewd, smart business man, very energetic and persistent in executing all of his plans of operation. In this regard his mind is radically changed, so decidedly that his friends and acquaintances said he was 'no longer Gage.' " (pp. 339-340)

Such changes in personality following frontal-lobe damage have been noted by laymen as well as doctors. In his book *Arctic Adventure,* Freuchen describes an old Eskimo, Agpaleq, whose gun exploded in his hand while he was shooting caribou and resulted in extensive destruction of the brain. The left frontal lobe was badly shattered in the accident and about a cupful of brain matter was lost.

"They cleaned out more with a spoon, after which Alequisaq sewed the skin together. . . . Agpaleq's recovery was slow, but almost complete. The accident resulted in peculiarity of habits rather than invalidism. During the remainder of his life he could sleep for a week or more at a time, and remain awake an equal length of time. When asleep, it was almost impossible for him to be awakened, and it became quite the custom for his neighbors to walk into his house and help themselves to whatever they might desire, including his wife. Agpaleq slept soundly through it all and never knew what practical jokes were played on him.

"He also became almost unbearably dirty, soiled himself and never cared. Prior to the accident he had been neat and clean, but afterward he was always smeared with grease or blood or both. His hands were filthy, his toes rotted away and filled the house with the most noisome stench. He could still hunt in his kayak, for he retained his heels and half of his feet, and was useful until the time of his death." (1935, p. 57)

Head injuries occur frequently in modern life, particularly as a result of falls, blows, and automobile and other accidents. It has been estimated that about 1,500,000 persons suffer head injuries in automobile accidents alone each year (Brosin, 1959). Not infrequently bullets or other objects actually penetrate the cranium. Yet few patients with brain injuries find their way into mental hospitals. Only some 0.6 per cent of all first admissions to mental hospitals belong to this category. This is due to the fact that most brain injuries, even when they result in a temporary loss of consciousness, are relatively minor and clear up rapidly without residual psychiatric complications.

It is pertinent to point out here that most of us have received a blow on the head at one time or another, and in giving the case history of a mental patient, relatives often remember some such incident to which they attribute his difficulties. Patients, too, are apt to search their own childhood for evidence of having fallen on their heads or having been hit on the head. Apparently, blaming the alleged head injury for the difficulties is a convenient method of escaping the "disgrace" of a functional mental illness and at the same time avoiding any hereditary stigma to the family. Consequently, it may be emphasized that only when the brain injury is very severe is it apt to leave any residual handicapping symptoms.

GENERAL SYMPTOMS AND DYNAMICS

Head injuries usually give rise to immediate acute reactions, the severity of which depends on the degree and type of injury. These acute reactions may then clear up entirely or develop into chronic disorders.

Acute traumatic[1] disorders. Fortunately the brain is an extraordinarily well-protected organ; even so, however, a hard blow on the head may result in a skull fracture in which portions of bone press upon or are driven into the brain tissue. Even without a fracture, the force of the blow may result in small, pinpoint hemorrhages throughout the brain or in the rupturing of larger blood vessels in the brain.

The patient who is rendered unconscious by a head injury usually passes through stages of stupor and confusion on his way to recovering clear consciousness (Symonds, 1962). This recovery of consciousness may be complete in the course of minutes, or it may take hours or days. In rare cases, the patient may live for extended periods of time without regaining consciousness. The specific symptoms, of course, depend largely upon the nature of the brain injury.

1. *Cerebral concussion* typically involves a mild head injury which disrupts circulatory and other brain functions and results in a slight clouding or momentary loss of consciousness. On regaining consciousness, the patient may be somewhat confused and disoriented, has a loss of memory for the accident, and suffers from a headache. Severe psychological symptoms rarely occur here, and the patient usually makes a rapid recovery within a few hours or days. However, partial or total amnesia for the circumstances of the accident usually remains. This simple concussion syndrome is illustrated in the case of a football star who was knocked out in a head-on collision with an opposing player. He regained consciousness while being carried off the field but was disoriented and confused and called signals as if he were still in the game. About an hour after his arrival at the hospital, the mental confusion cleared up and he seemed normal except for complaints of a terrible headache and an inability to remember just what had happened.

2. *Cerebral contusion* may occur if violence to the head is so severe that the brain, normally anchored in a fixed position, is shifted within the skull and is pushed or compressed against the opposite side. In this sudden movement of the brain there may be an actual bruising of the surface of the brain against the cranium. Here, in addition to the symptoms seen following a concussion, there may be pro-

longed unconsciousness for hours or even days, followed by a train of more serious symptoms which may include delirium. When the patient regains clarity of mind, he usually complains of severe headaches, sensitivity to noise and light, and dizziness, nausea, and weakness. Even though these symptoms may, in the main, clear up in a few days or weeks, certain symptoms such as irritability may persist for a prolonged period of time. There may also be an impairment of intellectual and motor functions which remains after the acute symptoms have cleared up.

Cerebral contusion is illustrated by the following case of a flier who was injured during a crash landing of his plane.

When taken to the hospital he was unconscious. Some eight hours after the accident he returned to consciousness but was confused and mildly delirious. There was a gradual return to clarity over a period of the next two days, accompanied by complaints of headache, dizziness, and nausea, especially if he moved. He was also hypersensitive to noise and light. He was able to leave the hospital within a week but complained for several months of headaches and inability to tolerate noise.

3. *Cerebral laceration* is an actual rupture or tearing of the brain tissue. This often results in skull-fracture cases when a portion of the bone is driven into the brain tissue. It may also result from injury by bullets or other objects which actually penetrate the cranium or from the internal laceration of the brain, as, for example, in cases of severe contusion.

The immediate symptoms of cerebral laceration are similar to those in contusion—unconsciousness followed by confusion or delirium and a gradual return to clarity of mind. In addition to persistent headaches and related symptoms, there may be a residual impairment of intellectual and motor functions. This was illustrated in the crowbar case reported by Dr. Harlow, quoted on pages 467-469.

During the coma that follows severe cerebral injury—including contusion and laceration—pulse, temperature, and blood pressure are af-

---

[1]The word *trauma* here refers to a physical wound or injury. We have previously used the term to refer to psychological wounds or shocks. This need not be confusing if we remember that stress may be biological or psychological.

fected and the patient's survival is uncertain. The duration of the coma is determined primarily by the extent of the injury. In severe cases, the patient may be unconscious for days or even weeks. If he survives, the coma is usually followed by delirium in which he may manifest acute excitement and confusion, disorientation, hallucinations, and generally anxious, restless, and noisy activity. Often he talks incessantly in a disconnected fashion, with no insight into his disturbed condition. Gradually, the confusion clears up and the patient regains his contact with reality. The severity and duration of residual symptoms will depend primarily upon (a) the nature and extent of the cerebral damage, and (b) the premorbid personality make-up of the patient.

Some degree of bleeding, or *intracerebral hemorrhage,* occurs in most cases of head injury. In severe head injuries there is usually gross bleeding or hemorrhaging at the site of the damage. When the hemorrhaging involves small spots of bleeding—often microscopic sleeves of red cells encircling tiny blood vessels —the condition is referred to as *petechial hemorrhages.* There is some evidence of petechial hemorrhages in most brain injuries, but in fatal cases they are usually multiple or generalized throughout the brain. Professional boxers are likely to suffer such petechial hemorrhaging from repeated blows to the head; they may develop a form of encephalopathy (area or areas of permanently damaged brain tissue) from the accumulated damage of such injuries (Noyes, 1958). As a result, they may suffer from impaired memory, inability to concentrate, involuntary movements, and other symptoms—a condition popularly referred to as being "punch drunk."

Chronic or post-traumatic disorders. Although many patients make a remarkably good recovery, even after severe brain injury, others show various residual *post-concussional* or *post-contusional* symptoms (O'Connell, 1961). Common aftereffects of moderate brain injury are chronic headaches, anxiety, irritability, dizziness, easy fatigability, and impaired memory and concentration. Where the brain damage is extensive, the patient's general intellectual level may be markedly reduced, especially where there have been severe frontal-

lobe lesions (Norrman and Svahn, 1961). In addition, various specific neurological and psychological defects may follow localized brain damage: occipital-lobe lesions may impair vision, parietal-lobe lesions may result in sensory aphasia, and so on. Some 2 to 4 per cent of head-injury cases develop post-traumatic epilepsy, usually within two years of the head injury but sometimes much later (Gibson, 1959). In general, the longer the period between the injury and the first convulsive seizure, the more likely they are to persist.

In a minority of brain-injury cases—some 2 to 3 per cent—there are personality changes such as those described in the historic cases of Phineas Gage and Agpaleq (O'Connell, 1961). Among older people and individuals who have suffered extensive damage to the frontal lobes, the symptom picture may be complicated by markedly impaired memory for recent events and confabulation, in which the patient fills in gaps of memory with what he considers plausible events. This clinical picture is referred to as the *Korsakoff syndrome,* or the *amnesia-confabulatory syndrome.* In our discussion of psychoses associated with alcoholism, we described the Korsakoff syndrome.

Among children, post-traumatic personality disorders vary considerably in symptomatology. In a distinct minority of cases the symptom picture is similar to that following certain cases of encephalitis—with hyperkinetic behavior, distractibility, lability of mood, and marked aggressiveness. Small (1962) reported that 9 children out of 131 seen in a clinic for cerebral palsy showed this "hyperkinetic behavior syndrome."

Post-traumatic personality changes are often difficult to evaluate in terms of the actual role of the organic brain injury. There are no well-defined criteria to indicate the extent to which such personality changes are caused directly by the brain injury and the extent to which they represent secondary reactions of the personality to the injury. It is significant, however, that such changes are much more likely to occur among marginally adjusted personalities than among well-adjusted ones, and that an analysis of the premorbid personality of the patient often sheds considerable light on the post-traumatic personality changes (Auerbach *et al.,* 1960; Brosin, 1959; Merritt, 1943). For example, Weinstein (1961) found that patients who related to others in a "narrow and rigid" fashion and followed stereotyped social roles were especially likely to develop post-concussion symptoms. In a study of 500 cases of cranio-cerebral injury evacuated to an army neurologic center, Aita and Reitan (1948) found that in the few cases where a psychosis developed later on, the actual brain injury played a secondary role, serving merely as an aggravating factor. In a long-range follow-up study of 232 men who had sustained penetrating brain wounds—gunshot or shell fragment injuries—Teuber (1960) found that motivation was an important factor but noted that cerebral injury may directly affect the neural structures that subserve motivation.

"One of the saddest cases in our group of 232 brain-injured men is that of a former motorcycle policeman who suffered a deep biparietal wound while fighting on the Anzio beachhead. In contrast to most of the other patients in our group, he was in coma for several weeks, and there were persistent neurologic signs pointing at midbrain involvement. He recovered, that is, he survived, but only to lead a completely passive existence, markedly different from his premorbid zestful and energetic life. Outstanding among his troubles were severe retention defects and marked difficulties with spatial orientation—so marked that he, the former motorcycle policeman, could not travel alone. Whenever he comes to our laboratory, he is accompanied by his wife, since by himself he invariably gets lost in the traffic." (1960, p. 324)

Teuber concluded from his studies that "a patient's pre-injury motives and attitudes can modify post-injury loss, but these effects are more marked with smaller lesions, and may be overridden by large lesions, or lesions strategically placed, which interfere with the patient's ability to act on his motives or to remember them." (p. 324)

TREATMENT AND PROGNOSIS

Immediate treatment for brain damage is primarily a medical matter and does not concern us in the present context except in so far as prompt treatment may prevent further injury. In severe cases immediate medical treatment may have to be supplemented by long-range re-education and rehabilitation although some patients are so impaired intellectually that they cannot ever adjust outside of an institutional environment. In less severe cases, aphasia and other special defects may have to be handled through re-education and rehabilitation. This may include preparation for acceptance of a lower level of occupational and social functioning. Psychotherapy and other treatment aids are often of vital importance in such cases.

Prognoses in brain-injury cases are hard to make, because they depend upon two factors which are often hard to gauge: (a) the exact nature and extent of the injury, and (b) the way the patient is going to react to the injury and to changes in his life situation. The majority of patients suffering from mild concussion recover within a short period of time. In moderate brain injuries, a sizable number of patients recover promptly, a somewhat larger number suffer from headaches and other symptoms for prolonged periods of time, and a few patients develop chronic incapacitating symptoms (Auerbach *et al.,* 1960). O'Connell (1961) has estimated that about 55 per cent of such patients show post-concussional symptoms after 6 months and 40 per cent after 18 months.

In severe brain-injury cases, the prognosis is less favorable. But here again, patients with stable, well-integrated personalities are often able to make a satisfactory adjustment, even when considerable amounts of brain tissue have been destroyed. In many cases, there is improvement with time, due largely to re-education and to the taking over of new functions by intact brain areas.

In general the following factors indicate a favorable prognosis: (a) a short period of unconsciousness, (b) nonstrategic location of the brain lesion, (c) a well-integrated premorbid personality, (d) motivation to recover or make the most of residual capacities, and (e) a favorable life situation to which to return.[1]

---

[1]For more detail on the clinical symptomatology and prognosis in brain-injury cases see Auerbach *et al.* (1960), Bender (1961), Brosin (1959), Gibson (1959), Jarvie (1960), O'Connell (1961), Symonds (1962), Teuber (1960), and Weinstein and Kahn (1961).

Various other complicating factors may also have a direct bearing upon the outcome of brain injuries. Children recover better than adults, although serious brain injury may, of course, leave the child mentally retarded. Patients who are also victims of alcoholism, drug addiction, arteriosclerosis, or any of a wide range of other organic conditions have an unfavorable outlook. Alcoholics in particular are prone to head injuries and other accidents and do not show good resiliency from the standpoint of recovery. Severe emotional conflicts not only appear to predispose an individual to accidents but also seem to delay recovery. Although malingering is thought to be rare in brain-injury cases, compensation may be a factor in the exaggeration and maintenance of symptoms.

Disorders with Toxins and Metabolic Disturbances

Disturbances in cerebral functions may result from several types of toxins and a wide range of metabolic disorders—including nutritive deficiencies, endocrine imbalances, and the stress of surgery or childbirth.

TOXIC DELIRIA (PSYCHOSES)

The most common form of toxic psychosis is that of delirium accompanying infectious diseases such as diphtheria, pneumonia, and typhoid fever. Toxic deliria may also result from other diseases, such as uremia and pernicious anemia, from extreme exhaustion, and from the ingestion of various drugs, metals, and gases (Wamsley and Flinn, 1961; West, 1962). In these disorders there usually is an acute onset of the disturbance with delirium and coma.

The early symptoms of delirium usually consist of restlessness, uneasiness, and increased sensitiveness to noise and light. The patient's sleep may be troubled by frightening dreams. As the delirium progresses, consciousness becomes clouded and the patient becomes confused and disoriented for time and later for place and person (Levin, 1960). During this phase, attention and concentration are severely diminished, and the patient is unable to remember or interpret properly what he sees and hears. Often he has visual illusions or hallucinations which may be interwoven with unsystematized delusions.

Although some patients become emotionally elated and euphoric, the typical emotional reaction is fear and apprehension. The fears relate especially to the misinterpretation of sounds, which the patient perceives as threatening to his safety. A footstep may be a murderer stealthily approaching to kill him.

Often the patient's repressed desires and general fears and worries are well represented in the content of his delirious wanderings. One delirious patient who was ordinarily extremely inhibited in her sexual attitudes used obscene language in her overt but confused overtures to the attending physician.

As the delirium becomes more acute, the picture becomes one of increasing confusion, apprehension, and agitation. Often there are periods of drowsiness or coma alternating with the delirium. The degree of the delirium will, of course, depend to a large extent upon the severity of the patient's illness—the degree of toxic disturbance. However, persons who have poorly integrated personalities or who are marginally adjusted may become delirious with mild fevers, whereas better-adjusted persons may be able to maintain their psychological integration even in the face of dangerous elevations in bodily temperature and other very severe illness.

Unless the toxic condition is very severe or prolonged, there usually is little or no actual damage to the neurons in the brain, and the psychopathology is temporary and clears up rapidly. Typically, disorientation for time, place, and person clears up first and hallucinations later (Levin, 1960). If a toxic psychosis continues, as occasionally happens to a woman after childbirth, it indicates a personality which was ready to break under any additional strain. The organic stress here has merely precipitated a functional disorder.

Since a number of internal and external toxic agents tend to produce somewhat similar disturbances, we shall confine our present discussion to a brief review of some of the more common types. However, it may be pointed out that the initial and final phases of a toxic psychosis vary somewhat with the nature of the toxic agent and that the same toxin can lead to different symptomatology depending upon the make-up of the individual affected (Henderson, 1962; Simson, 1960).

Drug intoxication. Toxic reactions associated with alcohol and certain other drugs were considered in Chapter 10. In excessive amounts, a wide range of drugs may produce toxic deliria. Bromide intoxication is a useful illustration. As bromide accumulates in the system from an excessive dosage, the patient becomes sluggish, dull, forgetful, and irritable, but remains oriented and rational. He is said to be suffering from simple bromide intoxication and seldom reaches a mental hospital. When the serum bromide reaches a high level of toxicity, however, the patient becomes confused, disoriented, apprehensive, and hallucinated— evidencing a delirium which does not differ markedly from that caused by other toxic agents (Levin, 1959, 1960).

Recovery in bromide delirium is usually gradual involving a period of several days or even weeks, depending primarily on the degree of intoxication and the rate of elimination of the drug from the body (Henderson, 1962).

Not long ago bromides were prescribed somewhat indiscriminately for nervous and mental disorders, and cases of bromide intoxication were common. As physicians became aware of the toxic effects of bromides, such cases have become relatively rare (Levin, 1960).

Deliria with febrile illness (fever). Influenza, pneumonia, typhoid and typhus fever, malaria, rheumatic fever, smallpox, and scarlet fever are the diseases most apt to bring on acute delirious reactions. The symptoms here are similar to those in other toxic deleria.

Postoperative disturbances. Psychotic reactions may follow general operations as a result of loss of blood, tissue trauma, and psychological tensions.[1] In the majority of cases, these are manic-depressive or schizophrenic reactions precipitated in predisposed personalities by the increased stress accompanying hospitalization and surgery; an appreciable number, however, are of a toxic-delirious type.

Elderly patients in particular are susceptible to delirious reactions. Many elderly patients have already suffered damage to the brain from previous cerebrovascular accidents or have varying degrees of cerebral arteriosclerosis, resulting in a diminished blood supply to the brain. Such conditions produce a more precarious physiological balance in brain metabolism and heightened susceptibility to cerebral anoxia—lowered oxygen supply to the brain —which may accompany major surgery (Scott, 1960).

Postoperative delirium is characterized by irritability, restlessness, confusion, apprehension, hallucinations, and severe stupor or coma. As the patient's physical condition improves, he usually shows a rapid recovery, although in severe cases irreversible brain damage may have occurred. The final outcome in such cases depends on preoperative constitutional and personality factors, the stressfulness and duration of hospitalization, and the nature and extent of brain damage. The specific type of operation may also be relevant here. Cohen and Ehrens (1953) have noted the frequent occurrence of mental disturbances following cataract operations, attributing it to the long period after the operation when the eyes must remain covered. Reactivation of earlier trauma or memories relating to the death of loved ones during surgery may also play a part in some cases.

Lead poisoning. A variety of metals, such as lead, mercury, and manganese may be ingested or have fumes that may be inhaled, resulting in toxic reactions.

Lead poisoning is more commonly seen among children than among adults; usually it results from the ingestion of material from paint, water pipes, sprays, toys, and crayons (White and Fowler, 1960). Lead poisoning

---

[1]It was formerly estimated that one psychosis occurs in every 400 general operations (Figarra and Lionella, 1950). Probably this number has been reduced somewhat with improvements in surgical procedures.

has long been a hazard in certain trades, but today workers are carefully guarded from it. Early mild symptoms typically include fatigue, weakness, listlessness, and extreme irritability. Children may develop vomiting, fearfulness, and crying for no apparent reason. In more severe cases the patient may become delirious and show restlessness, confusion, insomnia, alimentary disturbances, anxiety, hallucinations, tremors, and convulsions. Where the delirium is followed by coma, death may ensue (Henderson, 1962).

Lead poisoning may result in extensive cortical damage. In these cases there may be residual symptoms in the form of lowered mental capacity and progressive all-round deterioration. Typical symptoms here include irritability, lack of emotional control, forgetfulness, confabulation, and impaired judgment. Among children, convulsive seizures and mental retardation commonly follow chronic lead poisoning (Cohen, 1959; White and Fowler, 1960).

Carbon-monoxide exposure. Carbon monoxide is the best known of the gases which may lead to delirium and other neuropsychiatric symptoms. This gas results from the incomplete combustion of petroleum or coal products. Inhalation of carbon monoxide in large amounts reduces the blood's capacity to take up oxygen and results in a state of *anoxemia* which impairs the functioning of the nerve cells in the brain.

In severe cases of carbon-monoxide exposure, the patient dies from asphyxiation. In cases of severe inhalation which are not fatal, the patient usually manifests a state of delirium or coma (Henderson, 1962). The acute confusional state may clear in a few days and the patient usually makes a satisfactory recovery. In about 1 case in 500 of acute exposure, severe brain damage occurs (Morgan, 1955). The typical residual symptoms in such cases are similar to those in lead poisoning and include confusion, apathy, memory impairment, loss of initiative, and a general lowering of mental functions. There may also be convulsions, tremors, and partial blindness.

Exhaustion delirium. Here we find acute confusion or delirium without any infection or fever. Although not common, such reactions may occur under conditions of extreme physi-

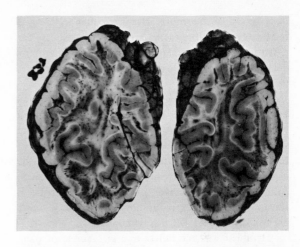

Above are sections of the brain of a patient who had suffered hemorrhagic encephalitis after carbon monoxide poisoning.

cal exertion. Often there is a combination of physical exhaustion and starvation, as in the case of individuals who become lost in remote forest and desert areas and run out of food and water.

The onset here usually includes insomnia, mild confusion, some clouding of consciousness, perplexity, vague fears, and fleeting hallucinations and delusions. The individual may see and hear rescuers, or he may see a lake, or tables loaded with food. Gradually his perceptions of his surroundings become increasingly distorted.

Sometimes the increasing confusion may be punctuated by a period of comparative clarity in which the patient finds that he has been wandering in circles. This toxic-exhaustive state may continue for several days or even weeks, but usually clears up rapidly once the patient is given proper food and rest.

Admiral Byrd's record of his stay alone at the Bolling Advance Weather Base during the Antarctic winter night is a graphic and fascinating account of the thoughts and behavior of a man struggling desperately to survive in the face of cold, loneliness, monoxide poisoning, and exhaustion. The following brief excerpts are of dynamic interest.

"The next day, June 1, was a Friday. A black Friday for me. I awakened from a dream of horrors to find that I could hardly move. I realized that all I could reasonably hope for was to prolong my existence for a few days by hoarding my remaining strength; by doing the necessary things very slowly and with great deliberation.

"My first need was warmth and food. The fire had been out 12 hours; I had not eaten in 36. Performing every act in slow motion, I edged out of the bunk and worked into my clothes. Faintness seized me as I touched the floor, and for many minutes I sat in the chair just staring at the candle. Then I gained enough strength to light the stove. The flame burned red and smoky from faulty combustion. This fire was my enemy, but I could not live without it.

"My thirst was the tallest tree in a forest of pain. The tunnel where I cut ice to melt for water was a hundred miles away, but I started out. Soon I slipped and fell. My ice quarry was too far. I licked the tunnel wall until my tongue burned, and then scraped up half a bucket of dirty snow from the floor. It was still a soggy mass when I tried to drink. My hands were shaking and it spilled all over me. Then I vomited all that I had drunk. On the verge of fainting, I crawled up on my bunk to rest.

"Death had confronted me many times . . . . Now death was a stranger sitting in a darkened room, secure in the knowledge that he would be there when I was gone.

"Great waves of fear swept through me and settled deep within . . . .

"Afterwards, lying in the sleeping bag, I tried to analyze the possibilities. For five interminable days I had been lost on a great plateau of pain where all the passes were barred. I had suffered and struggled, hoped and stopped hoping. . . . Now I asked myself, What are your assets? What might be done that has not already been done?

"The first necessity was that to survive I must husband my strength. Second, to avoid further poisoning, I must use the stove sparingly and the gasoline pressure lamp—my one good light—not at all. And to build up my strength I must sleep and eat.

"But if I depended on this routine alone, I should go mad from the hourly reminders of my own futility. Something more—the will to endure these hardships— was necessary. That must come from deep inside me. But how? By taking control of my thoughts and dwelling only on those which would make for peace. A discordant mind, black with confusion and despair, would finish me off as thoroughly as the cold." (1938, pp. 175-190)

Experimental studies with volunteer subjects indicate that exhaustion delirium may also occur as the result of prolonged sleep deprivation. Early symptoms include attention lapses, visual disturbances leading to illusions, and a growing sense of drowsiness, weariness, and lack of interest in the outside world. By the fifth night there are usually prolonged and vivid hallucinatory experiences which the subject initially questions but eventually accepts as real. As the sleep deprivation continues,

"periods of overt confusion and clouding of consciousness are seen. Disorientation becomes more frequent and prolonged; first for time, then for place, then for person, and finally, for self. Gross delusional thinking, usually paranoid, becomes increasingly prominent. By night the subject gives a picture resembling a case of toxic deliria, with lucid intervals growing fewer and shorter. . . .

"The total impression is of a progressive disorganization of ego structure. . . ." (West *et al.*, 1962, p. 69)[1]

NUTRITIONAL DEFICIENCIES

Nutritional deficiencies have been shown to underlie certain types of neuropsychiatric disorders.

Vitamin and mineral deficiencies. Deficiencies in the vitamin B complex seem to be the type most commonly involved in the production of neuropsychiatric disorders. Perhaps the best known of these deficiencies is "beri-beri" which once plagued people in the Far East who lived primarily on a diet of polished rice, deficient in vitamin B_1 (thiamine). "Beri-beri" means "I cannot" and is an apt description of the lassitude, weakened muscles, intestinal distress, depression, and lowered "will to do" which follow a deficiency in vitamin B_1.

Pellagra and pernicious anemia are other conditions associated with deficiencies in vitamin B. Pellagra is characterized by skin lesions, gastrointestinal disturbances, and a variety of mental symptoms including fatigue, insomnia, apprehension, anxiety, and inability to concentrate. More severe symptoms, which occur

---

[1] Additional sources here include Brauchi and West (1959), Luby *et al.* (1962), Tyler (1955), West *et al.* (1962), Williams *et al.* (1959).

in some 5 to 10 per cent of pellagra victims, may involve delirium with confusion, disorientation, and hallucinations (Brožek and Grande, 1960; Henderson, 1962). In pernicious anemia, mental symptoms appear to depend heavily upon the personality make-up of the patient and hence may be quite diverse, ranging from slight disturbances of mood or mental slowness to severe depression, agitation, confusion, and delirium. In both pellagra and pernicious anemia the administration of appropriate B-complex vitamins, together with general nutritional therapy, typically leads to a reversal of the pathological metabolic changes and to a clearing up of the mental symptoms.

In an early experiment, Brožek et al. (1946) studied the personality changes in eight normal young men maintained 161 days on a partially restricted intake of B-complex vitamins, followed by 23 days of acute deficiency and 10 days of thiamine supplementation. Little or no evidence of personality change was observed during the period of partial restriction, but consistent and striking deterioration occurred during the acute deficiency with depression, loss of spontaneity, increased tension, hysteria, hypochondriasis, and increased emotionality. Adding thiamine to the diet produced rapid recovery. In a more recent experiment, Caster (1957) subjected 10 normal young males to a severe restriction of vitamin B_1 for 168 days. The resulting symptoms of acute deprivation were comparable to those observed in the preceding experiment.

A number of minerals—such as sodium chloride, copper, and calcium—are required for normal brain metabolism. Heat cramps are a well-known symptom of salt (sodium chloride) deficiency. Acute or chronic conditions associated with a low concentration of salt in the blood may lead to a variety of mental symptoms: prominent are lassitude, apathy, apprehension, and depression (Brožek and Grande, 1960). We shall shortly examine the effects of iodine deficiency. Many other vitamins and minerals, though less directly related to mental symptoms, are essential for bodily health and the maintenance of normal resistance to organic and psychological stress.

Semistarvation. Semistarvation occurs when there is a severe restriction of calorie intake over a prolonged period of time. It is characteristic during famines and is a common condition for malnourished peoples in certain parts of the world. Throughout man's history it has been the most important type of nutritional deficiency.

A number of observations have been made on behavior under conditions of "natural starvation," stemming in the main from famines following the aftermath of wars and from the meager diet of prisoner-of-war and concentration-camp inmates. Observations of advanced stages of semistarvation during famines in Leningrad and other Russian cities during World War II emphasized a number of neurological, physical, and mental changes (Brožek and Grande, 1960). Asthenia was considered the principal mental syndrome, characterized by a slowing of thought processes, impaired ability to concentrate and sustain mental effort, a lowering of higher-level interests and feelings, increased irritability, and apathy with a tendency to daydreaming. Psychotic reactions were rare and occurred mostly in cases where caloric deficiency was complicated by infection, trauma, and related conditions. Writing on the basis of his experience in German POW camps, Leyton (1946) reported similar symptoms and also emphasized a marked reduction in sexual desire, lowered standards of cleanliness, loss of pride in personal appearance, and deterioration of moral standards.

In Chapter 3 we noted the study on semistarvation carried out by Keys et al. (1950) on a group of 36 young conscientious objectors who volunteered for the experiment. These subjects underwent a 24-week semistarvation period during which they were maintained on a diet characteristic of European famine areas near the end of World War II. Physical changes included a 25 per cent loss in body weight, a 40 per cent decrease in basal metabolism, and a 30 per cent reduction in body strength. The men became haggard, emaciated, subject to fainting attacks, and fatigued by the slightest exertion. Sexual urges and affectional responses decreased markedly. The outstanding mental symptoms were apathy, depression, loss of sense of humor, irritability, uncooperativeness, loss of pride in personal appearance, preoccupation with thoughts of food, and seriously impaired ability to concentrate on anything else. Most of the men worried about their declining intelligence and other functions, and their self-confidence was replaced by feelings of inferiority. So striking were these personality changes that Keys and his colleagues adopted the term *semistarvation neurosis.*

Unfortunately, many people in the world today still suffer from malnutrition, including vitamin and mineral deficiencies, and it can be readily seen that their condition has serious implications both on individual and social levels. Even in the United States, where food is plentiful, many people unnecessarily lower their resistance to both biological and psychological stress as a consequence of unbalanced and inadequate diets.

Dehydration. The symptoms of dehydration in man are seen in patients suffering from cholera or extensive burns and in the behavior of shipwreck survivors and persons lost in the desert.

Aside from intense thirst, early symptoms of dehydration include apathy, impatience, and sleepiness. As the dehydration continues, the power to concentrate is diminished and temperamental traits appear to be exaggerated. Thus people prone to be serious may become sombre, while those prone to be cheerful may exhibit a somewhat hollow vivacity (Black *et al.,* 1944). At this point, thirst becomes a dominant subjective symptom and may completely overshadow the discomforts of hunger, cold, and fatigue and the pain of wounds or injuries (Critchley, 1943). When the dehydration exceeds 10 per cent of the original body weight, more serious symptoms develop, including delirium, spasticity, and inability to walk (Brožek and Grande, 1960). Perception is severely impaired and blindness and deafness may develop. In the terminal stages, stupor and unconsciousness dominate the clinical picture. It is believed that no one can survive a 20 per cent deficit in the water content of the body.

ENDOCRINE DISTURBANCES

The endocrine glands manufacture chemical substances known as *hormones* which are essential for normal physical and psychological development and functioning. Consequently, underactivity or overactivity of any endocrine gland may have marked effects upon psychological functions, including a lowering of general stress tolerance.

Endocrine disturbances may also lead to physical anomalies which, in turn, contribute to adjustive difficulties. Hyperfunction of the pituitary gland during childhood, for example, may result in extreme growth in which the child may attain a height well above 7 feet. Although the intelligence of such a "giant" is not affected, his stature is apt to lead to severe adjustment problems. Similarly, pituitary midgets, bearded ladies, extremely fat persons, and other endocrine "freaks" are subjected to curiosity, ridicule, and other abnormal conditions which tend to make self-acceptance and normal personality development extremely difficult. Fortunately, medical advances in the diagnosis and treatment of such conditions have greatly reduced their incidence.

In the following discussion of thyroid and adrenal dysfunctions—the most common of the endocrine disorders associated with severe psychological disturbances—three points are well worth remembering: (a) endocrine dysfunction may contribute to psychopathology as well as result from such pathology, (b) malfunction of any gland may have widespread effects on the functioning of other glands and other bodily organs and systems, and (c) glandular dysfunction may vary considerably in degree and its effects differ widely depending upon the age, sex, and general personality make-up of the individual. It should also be re-emphasized that the endocrine system is normally under the general control of the central nervous system.

Thyroid dysfunction. The best understood of the endocrine glands is the thyroid, which regulates bodily metabolism. Either oversecretion or undersecretion of the thyroid hormone *thyroxin* will produce definite signs of physical and/or mental pathology.

Oversecretion (*hyperthyroidism*) accelerates the metabolic processes of the body and leads to loss of weight, tremors, tenseness, insomnia, and emotional excitability. Psychotic manifestations of moderate intensity have been found in about 20 per cent of hyperthyroid patients. These cases account for about 1 per 1000 of hospitalized mental patients (Bursten, 1961). Psychotic symptoms in these cases commonly include severe anxiety, apprehension, agitation, and transitory delusions and hallucinations. In some instances, there is delirium; in other cases, there is a predominantly schizophrenic or other psychotic syndrome. Personality factors appear to play an important role in determining the overall clinical picture.

The following case was diagnosed as a psychotic reaction precipitated by hyperthyroidism.

The patient was a 44-year-old single white woman admitted to the psychiatric ward of a general hospital for observation. A few days before her admission she had become belligerent and antagonistic and had gone on a spending spree ordering $100 worth of flowers and hiring a dance hall. She believed she possessed $50,000.

On admission, the patient was found to be hyperactive evidencing a press of speech with many ideas flowing in rapid succession but in poor logical sequence. The symptom picture suggested a manic reaction but the examiners commented on her flattened affect and felt that the patient was basically a paranoid schizophrenic.

Medical diagnosis was positive for hyperthyroidism and treatment was instituted which led to a rapid clinical remission of this condition. However, mental symptoms persisted—particularly those of a paranoid schizophrenic type.

The patient was sent to a state mental hospital where no further thyroid treatment was prescribed. Her admission diagnosis was paranoid schizophrenia. Subsequent electroshock and drug treatment led to a gradual clearing of her delusions and hallucinations, and she was discharged. (Adapted from Bursten, 1961, p. 270)

In his evaluation of this case Bursten considered it possible that a "manic veneer" related to her thyrotoxic condition and increased metabolism was superimposed on a schizophrenic process. With the control of the hyperthyroidism the manic behavior subsided and the underlying paranoid schizophrenic reaction became manifest.

Not only does the personality of the patient appear to play a prominent role in the way he reacts to hyperthyroidism, but long-continued or repeated emotional stress may precipitate thyrotoxicosis in a predisposed subject. However, Gibson (1962) has pointed out that the emphasis here is on "predisposed." In a critical review of available studies, Gibson failed to find convincing evidence that emotional stress produces chronic pathological changes in thyroid activity in individuals who lack a genetic or other constitutional predisposition.

The treatment of hyperthyroid patients has been almost exclusively a medical matter involving such methods as (a) iodine or radio-iodine therapy, which produces a variable degree of remission in some 95 per cent of thyrotoxic patients; (b) goitrogenic compounds, which inhibit the synthesis of thyroid hormone and thus reduce the amount of its secretion; and (c) thyroidectomy, which involves the surgical removal of part of the thyroid gland itself (Gimlette, 1959; Leiser, 1961). In the majority of cases these medical procedures correct the hyperthyroidism, but patients with psychotic symptoms may require additional treatment.

Pronounced thyroid deficiency in adulthood *(hypothyroidism),* typically associated with an iodine deficiency, leads to a condition called *myxedema.* Here metabolism is slowed down and the patient typically puts on weight, becomes sluggish in action and thought, shows memory defects for recent events, and is generally listless and sleepy (Reitan, 1953). Both the personality of the patient and the degree of hypothyroidism appear to play important roles in determining the symptom picture. In marginally adjusted individuals the myxedema may serve to precipitate an underlying mental disorder. With severe hypothyroidism many patients show reactions similar to those in hyperthyroidism, with nervousness, restlessness, anxiety, and irritability. In some patients these symptoms progress to actual delirium, which is the most common psychotic reaction associated with myxedema (Browning *et al.*, 1954; Pitts and Guze, 1961; Sanders, 1962). Although personality factors may enter in, such delirious reactions are based primarily on disturbances in brain metabolism stemming from the severe hypothyroidism (Pitts and Guze, 1961). Fortunately, thyroid medication is highly effective

ABNORMALITIES ASSOCIATED WITH ENDOCRINE DYSFUNCTION

PINEAL (functions still unknown)

PITUITARY (regulates growth)
DYSFUNCTIONS:
Gigantism—excessive pituitary hormone during growth period, with extreme growth to height of 7 to 9 feet. Intelligence and affect not appreciably modified.
Midgetism—deficient pituitary hormone in early life, preventing normal growth, but body correctly proportioned; intelligence, affect not appreciably modified.
Acromegaly—excessive pituitary hormone in adulthood, with thickening and elongating of bodily extremities, especially hands, feet, and jaw.

THYROID (regulates rate of bodily metabolism)
DYSFUNCTIONS:
Cretinism—thyroid deficiency in infancy, with physical and mental dwarfing, heavy features.
Myxedema—thyroid deficiency in adulthood, with overweight, puffed physical features, general sluggishness.
Oversecretion—accelerated metabolic processes, tremors, tenseness, emotional excitability, weight loss; psychotic symptoms including delusions and hallucinations may occur.

PARATHYROID (regulates calcium and phosphate metabolism)
DYSFUNCTIONS:
Tetany—due to removal or destruction of parathyroids; muscular twitches, tremors, cramps, convulsions.

THYMUS (related to body's immunities)

ADRENALS (medulla secretes hormones making extra energy available for emergencies; cortex hormones influence secondary sex characteristics and help regulate metabolism)
DYSFUNCTIONS:
Addison's disease—deficiency of cortin from adrenal cortex, with increased fatigability, loss of appetite, anemia, listlessness, irritability, darkening of skin.
Puberty praecox—oversecretion of adrenal androgens in childhood, leading to early development of secondary sex characteristics.
Cushing's syndrome—excessive secretion of cortisone, with muscle weakness, reduced sex drive, fatigability, and disfiguring bodily changes.
Failure of adrenals—apparent breakdown following prolonged emotional mobilization.

GONADS (determine sex drive and development of secondary sex characteristics)
DYSFUNCTIONS:
Eunuchism—castration of male before puberty, with development of secondary sexual characteristics of female (musculature, bodily proportions, etc.). varying degrees of deficiency on gonadal hormones during childhood result in failure to develop secondary sex characteristics and lack of sexual interest and drive.
Menopause or climacteric—marked reduction of gonadal hormone production; usually during late forties in women, often with irritability, restlessness, hot flashes, mental depression, and insomnia.

in this disorder, and together with improved methods of diagnosis has made serious hypothyroid conditions extremely rare. (The relation of mental retardation to hypothyroidism during the prenatal period or early infancy will be taken up in Chapter 12.)

Adrenal dysfunction. The adrenals are paired glands consisting of an outer layer called the *adrenal cortex* and an inner core called the *adrenal medulla*. The adrenal medulla secretes the hormones adrenaline and noradrenaline (epinephrine and norepinephrine) when the individual is under strong emotion. In Chapter 4 we noted that such emotional reactions may be useful in emergency situations but that when they are prolonged or become chronic, they can lead to a breakdown in adrenal function. The relation of such a breakdown of function to mental disorders remains to be clarified.

The cortex of the adrenal glands functions in the regulation of salt and water metabolism, in pigment metabolism, in the elaboration of steroid sex hormones, and in some aspects of carbohydrate metabolism.

Undersecretion or deficiency of the adrenal cortex results in *Addison's disease* (named after the physician who first described the disease in 1855). This disorder is characterized by a variety of metabolic disturbances, including a lowering of blood pressure, body temperature, and basal metabolism and a darkening of the skin. The accompanying mental symptoms typically include lack of vigor, easy fatigability, depressed sexual functions, headaches, irritability, lassitude, and lack of ambition. More severe mental disturbances in Addison's diseases are rare and appear to be related to the personality of the patient although there is evidence that disturbed brain metabolism plays a dominant role in some psychotic cases (McCulloch and Calverley, 1961; Smith, 1958).

In the following case, the patient showed clear schizophrenic symptoms.

The patient was an 18-year-old male manifesting his first attack of mental illness. He was admitted to a mental hospital with complaints of tension, irritability, and the conviction that he was being doped. His illness had developed over a period of about 5 months without known precipitating events.

A psychological examination revealed psychomotor retardation, poverty of thought, and inappropriate smiling. Thought content centered about the notion that the lights outside the hospital were related to Sputnik and that the physicians were poisoning him with tablets. The patient was not hallucinated and was oriented as to time and also knew the year and month but not the exact date.

The medical examination was normal except that the EEG was slightly slow in the anterior and temporal lobes. The patient's personal history revealed that from the age of eight, he had had spells of nausea, vomiting, and extreme weakness accompanied by a "yellowing" of the skin. These spells lasted from 2 to 7 days with spontaneous remission. The patient had received no medical treatment for them.

Because of gradual improvement following hospitalization, supportive psychotherapy was decided upon as the method of treatment. After the first week, however, the patient showed rapid deterioration with grimacing, muteness, and the maintenance of postures for hours when left alone. These symptoms were sometimes interrupted by outbursts of destructiveness and combativeness. As a consequence, electroshock treatments were given, and the patient showed marked improvement. Thorazine was prescribed but had to be discontinued as a consequence of undesirable side effects involving the swelling of the hands, wrists, and oropharynx. Eight days after the onset of the swelling, bronzing of the skin was noted and shortly thereafter the patient developed nausea, vomiting, abdominal pain, and hypotension. Laboratory findings proved consistent with hypoadrenalism.

As the signs and symptoms of Addison's disease progressed, the patient's condition again deteriorated —the patient becoming withdrawn and tense and demonstrating blocking of thought processes and strong emotional ambivalence. Cortisone treatment was instituted, and within 48 hours the symptom picture cleared up. The patient was placed on a maintenance dosage of 12.5 mgm. of cortisone daily, and examination one year after discharge revealed no symptoms of either Addison's disease or schizophrenia.

The precise relation of Addison's disease to the mental reaction could not be ascertained, but the institution of hormonal therapy was closely followed by a remission of the schizophrenia symptoms. (Adapted from Wolff and Huston, 1959, pp. 365-368)

Hypersecretion of the adrenal cortex may lead to a number of rare and dramatic changes in secondary sex characteristics (Moon, 1961).

An oversecretion of adrenal estrogens in the male tends to the development of female characteristics—a condition referred to as *feminism*. On the other hand, an oversecretion of adrenal androgens in the female results in a deepening of voice, shrinking of breasts, growth of beard, and other masculine changes—a condition referred to as *virilism*. In young boys, the oversecretion of adrenal androgens accelerates puberty. The latter condition is referred to as *puberty praecox,* and children subject to it may develop adult stature and reach sexual maturity at a very early age. Although the mental development of such boys does not keep pace with their accelerated physical and sexual development, they are usually extensively and aggressively interested in sexual matters.

In cases of tumor or abnormal growth of the adrenal cortices, there may be an excessive secretion of cortisone leading to serious alterations in sugar, protein, and other metabolic functions. The resulting clinical picture is referred to as *Cushing's syndrome*.[1] Typical symptoms include muscle weakness, easy fatigability, reduced sex drive, headache, and a number of disfiguring bodily changes such as obesity, changes in skin color and texture, and spinal deformity (Trethowan and Cobb, 1952). In some cases, there is an excessive growth of body hair. Cushing's syndrome is relatively rare, occurring most often among young women. Reactive emotional disturbances are common among such patients.

Extensive bodily changes associated with hypersecretion of the adrenal cortices—particularly changes of a disfiguring nature—complicate the individual's life adjustment and thus may eventuate indirectly in a wide range of psychopathological reactions. Among adults the pre-illness personality is a key factor in determining the patient's reaction to the disease (Rome and Robinson, 1959). The clinical picture not only varies markedly from one patient to another but often varies in the same patient in the course of the disease.

Treatment in adrenal dysfunction is primarily a medical matter. Cortisone and hydrocortisone as well as various drugs which suppress corticoid secretions are heavily relied upon. In cases of tumor and related conditions, surgery may be indicated. With early detection and treatment, the prognosis in adrenal disorders is usually highly favorable. As in other endocrine disorders, however, the psychiatric complications may not subside with the clearing up of the adrenal dysfunction and additional therapy may be required.

A brief summary of the immediate symptoms associated with the dysfunction of the thyroid, adrenals, and other endocrine glands is shown on page 480.

PSYCHOSES ASSOCIATED WITH CHILD-BIRTH (POSTPARTUM PSYCHOSES)

It has been estimated that psychotic reactions occur in connection with at least 1 of every 400 pregnancies—either before or after childbirth.[2] About 10 to 15 per cent of these psychotic reactions occur during pregnancy, 60 per cent during the first month after childbirth, and the others during the next 8 months. Interestingly enough, few of these reactions occur during the first 48 hours after the birth of the child. About 5 to 8 per cent of all female admissions to mental hospitals stem from mental illness associated with childbirth.

Symptoms. Most investigators agree that postpartum psychoses do not differ essentially from psychoses occurring under other circumstances except that preoccupation with rejection, hostility, or harm toward the newborn infant or the husband or both are common. Schizophrenic and depressive reactions appear to account for the great majority of these psychoses. Schizophrenic reactions appear to occur in individuals prone to such reactions under severe stress:

"The majority of such patients have a typical history of aloofness and introversion and may remain emotionally bound to their parents. The wife has often not achieved psychosexual maturity or a full emotional relation with her husband. During pregnancy such a

---

[1] Cushing's syndrome may also be induced by the administration of potent adrenal cortical steroids in the treatment of other diseases (Rome and Robinson, 1959). Here the symptoms typically clear up rapidly when the patient is taken off the drug.

[2] Statistics and other factual information here are drawn from Kroger (1962), Markham (1961), Poffenbarger *et al.* (1961), Pugh *et al.* (1963), Thomas and Gordon (1959), Weiner and Steinhilber (1961).

patient is often morose, irritable and flighty, and these symptoms may progress to a schizophrenic episode before term. After delivery, the patient appears odd, preoccupied and uncertain in her behavior and verbal productions. Frequently, indifference or open antagonism is expressed toward child and husband. Not uncommonly, the schizophrenic breakdown is acute, with confusion, apprehension, perplexity, paranoid delusions; and auditory hallucinations. Often the patient symbolically reveals her attitude toward the child by fearing or dreaming that he has been lost, kidnapped, or killed, or by denying her marriage and pregnancy. Features reminiscent of a toxic delirious state may cloud the diagnosis during the first few days." (Weiner and Steinhilber, 1961)

Psychotic depressive reactions are to be distinguished from milder depressions known colloquially as the "maternity blues" or the "disenchantment syndrome" which commonly occur upon the mother's return home with the baby and are characterized by weeping, apathy, and fatigue. However, such mild reactions may progress almost imperceptibly to deep depression characterized by lethargy, psychomotor retardation, dejection, self-accusations of sin and unworthiness, and a marked sense of futility. The mother may express a lack of interest in the infant or have fears that it may be harmed. Such severe depressions constitute a hazard to the lives of both mother and child: suicide, infanticide, or both may occur.

Manic reactions appear to be infrequent following childbirth, but involutional-type depressions with elements of depression, agitation, and suspiciousness may occur. Occasionally, delirious reactions are precipitated by infection, hemorrhage, exhaustion, or toxemia—particularly in marginally adjusted individuals. Here there is a clouding of consciousness, hallucinatory states, and some degree of confusion and disorientation. Formerly toxic-exhaustive psychoses were common following childbirth, but the introduction of antibiotics and improved obstetrical procedures has made these reactions relatively rare.

Dynamics. The stress in postpartum psychoses has numerous organic and psychological elements. Organic factors include metabolic reorganization incident to the pregnancy, the pain of delivery, and possible hemorrhage, lacera-

tions, and infections. Further metabolic readjustment occurs with lactation. Psychological stresses depend heavily upon the attitude of the mother toward pregnancy and childbirth; in some instances, there is worry about the normality of the baby or about negative attitudes of the father to having a child. Often the new mother feels "trapped" and experiences strong guilt feelings because she does not enjoy her baby as society expects mothers to do.

The stress of childbirth, however, in and of itself is not the primary cause of psychotic decompensation except possibly in rare cases of toxic delirium. In most cases, the pregnancy, childbirth, and adjustments attendant on assuming the role of a mother serve as precipitating factors in an already unstable personality or one particularly vulnerable to this particular stress situation. In fact, psychotic reactions indistinguishable from typical postpartum psychoses occasionally follow the adoption of a child (Tetlow, 1955).

In a study of 100 cases of puerperal psychoses, White et al. (1957) emphasized the following factors: (a) unstable marriage; (b) immaturity of patient; (c) long-standing maladjustment of patient; (d) unstable family history; (e) lack of desire for baby on part of wife or husband; (f) extra responsibility, particularly financial, imposed on patient by birth of baby; (g) physical illness of mother or baby, including extreme fatigue resulting from caring for a sick baby; and (h) an unfavorable home situation after delivery, such as poor living conditions and marital friction. The latter point deserves emphasis since an immature, neurotic reaction on the part of the husband to his wife's pregnancy and to his own later fatherhood may markedly augment the stressfulness of the entire situation for the wife.

Factors evidently not significantly related to such psychoses include the mother's age, the fact of bearing a child, the legitimacy of the offspring, and the normality of the baby (Poffenbarger et al., 1961; Thomas and Gordon, 1959; Weiner and Steinhilber, 1961). Nor is there conclusive evidence that the marked endocrine changes during pregnancy and the early postpartum days are key factors (Weiner and Steinhilber, 1961). Occasionally, the pregnancy complicates an already ongoing psychotic episode and in a few cases is itself the result of heightened eroticism and indiscretion associated with a mental disorder.

Prognosis.   In most cases, the prognosis is favorable. Some 90 per cent of these patients recover from the psychotic episode within a relatively short period of time (Martin, 1958; Poffenbarger *et al.*, 1961; Weiner and Steinhilber, 1961; White *et al.*, 1957). Although many patients were formerly advised to avoid another pregnancy for two or three years, such counseling now is more carefully weighed in relation to the particular patient. In a follow-up study of 41 women who became pregnant subsequent to a postpartum psychosis, Poffenbarger *et al.* (1961) reported that only half (21) had a recurrence of their illness, usually with symptoms similar to those of their prior psychotic episode. Other studies have found only about 1 in 5 suffering a second episode (Martin, 1958; White *et al.*, 1957).

Prevention.   At present, preventive measures in postpartum psychoses depend primarily on good obstetric care, on preparing the mother psychologically for the birth of the child, and on alleviating any factors in the family situation which may be placing additional stress on her. As in other mental disorders, early detection and correction are of vital importance. Weiner and Steinhilber (1961) have identified several warning signs: (a) a history of mental illness or personality traits that may make the patient more vulnerable; (b) an unfavorable attitude of the patient toward her pregnancy; for example, rejection of the fetus may take the form of irresponsible behavior directed toward producing a miscarriage, or of excessive drinking or resentment toward her husband and her expected role as mother; (c) an unfavorable attitude of the husband toward his wife's pregnancy and/or serious marital conflicts; (d) early symptoms of psychological difficulties and progressive personality change, such as insomnia, anxiety, irritability, agitation, and depression.

Weiner and Steinhilber have suggested that individual discussion with the obstetrician and group discussions in prepartum clinics may help greatly in allaying fears and anxieties and preparing the expectant mother for childbirth and for her later role as mother. Often discussions with the husband are of great value in helping him to accept and prepare for his role as father.

Disorders of Unknown Origin

There are several rare disorders resulting from progressive degenerative diseases of the nervous system, in which the origin of the disease remains essentially unknown at the present time despite considerable research. Among the better known of these are *Parkinson's disease, Huntington's chorea, Alzheimer's disease,* and *Pick's disease.*

PARKINSON'S DISEASE

Parkinson's disease, also known as *paralysis agitans* and *shaking palsy,* is a chronic, progressive disease of the central nervous system involving particularly the thalamus, basal ganglia, and reticular activating system. The true incidence of Parkinson's disease is unknown although estimates center around 600,000.[1] Al-

though no one is immune, Parkinson's disease rarely occurs until after the age of 30, with the great majority of cases falling in the age range of 50 to 70. The average age of onset is approximately 60 years.

This disorder is characterized by rigidity and spontaneous tremors of various muscles, usually beginning in one arm and gradually spreading to the leg on the same side of the body, then to the neck and face, and lastly to the limbs on the other side. With time, the face becomes rigid and masklike, with speech drawling and indistinct. Often there is a tendency to lean forward in walking, with the result that the individual appears to be running in order to keep from

[1]Statistics and other factual information here are drawn from Campbell (1963), Constable (1960), Doshay (1960), Gillingham (1961), Mettler and Crandell (1959), National Health Education Committee (1961), Poskanzer and Schwab (1961), Spellman (1962).

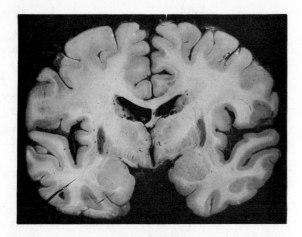

Above is a section of the brain of a 73-year-old man who had suffered from Parkinson's disease. He had had a two-year history of progressive weakness in his legs and a tendency to fall. He had a tremor in both hands, general rigidity and weakness, and slurred, unintelligible speech but normal reflexes and no disorientation or mental deterioration.

falling forward. Unless the progression of the disease is halted, the patient eventually becomes completely helpless and dependent on others.

Although the neurological manifestations are intensified with time, with increasing rigidity and tremors of the hands, arms, lower limbs, lips, and tongue, intelligence is little affected and there may not be pronounced mental symptoms. Usually, however, the patient gradually withdraws from social intercourse, becomes apathetic, indifferent, and unable to concentrate, and shows a general lessening of intellectual interest, activity, and flexibility (V.A.-D.V.A. Study Group, 1960; Mettler and Crandell, 1959). These symptoms apparently result primarily from the patient's reaction to his disease rather than directly from the neurological pathology itself. Typically, the psychological symptoms become more pronounced with the progression of the disease.

Although James Parkinson described this disorder quite accurately as long ago as 1817, its cause is still unknown. Occasionally parkinsonian symptoms have been observed after epidemic encephalitis, carbon monoxide exposure, manganese poisoning, and brain tumors. Here the parkinsonian symptoms are part of a more com-

prehensive clinical picture in which there is extensive known damage to the brain. Consequently, such cases are not considered to represent "true" Parkinson's disease, which involves more limited and focal neural degeneration. In some cases, too, parkinsonian symptoms are induced by tranquilizing drugs, but here the symptoms typically clear up as soon as the drug is discontinued.

At present, two forms of so-called "true" Parkinson's disease are distinguished—the *idiopathic* and the *arteriosclerotic*. The arteriosclerotic type starts later and is likely to be bilateral from the beginning, but there is apparently no essential difference between the two types in basic etiology or final neuropathology (Doshay, 1960).

Parkinson's disease is not generally considered to be hereditary in nature, although some investigators, noting a much higher incidence in certain families have concluded that inherited metabolic defects are key etiologic factors in some 5 to 16 per cent of cases (Spellman, 1962). Other investigators blame a virus, pointing to the fact that a predilection for a particular area of the nervous system is characteristic of virus infections (Poskanzer and Schwab, 1961). Such a virus might still be present and active in cells of the central nervous system or might have caused damage during early life, leading to a premature aging and degeneration of certain brain cells.

Most investigators attribute Parkinson's disease to an acquired deficiency in brain metabolism. They believe that inadequate circulation and the accumulation of waste products in the brain leads, with increasing age, to the damaging of certain brain cells, particularly in the thalamus, basal ganglia, and reticular activating system. The defective functioning of these cells, in turn, results in the malfunctioning of the feedback circuits in the thalamus and other brain areas which modify and influence the activity of the motor cortex. With progressive pathology, the disease runs its tragic course.

Although this hypothesis appears highly plausible, the precise nature of the metabolic defect remains to be ascertained. Nor does this theory explain the fact that not all cases of Parkinson's disease seem to have impaired circulation, or the fact that only a minority of patients

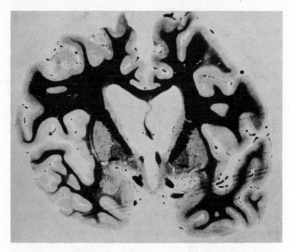

The typical atrophy of the cortex and basal ganglia found in Huntington's chorea is shown in this slide.

with cerebral arteriosclerosis develop the Parkinsonian syndrome. It is also relevant to note that emotional stress and physical exhaustion frequently precipitate the initial symptoms and that, as in many other diseases, anxiety and stress make the symptoms worse (Travis, 1961). Only further research can clarify the etiological picture.

No completely effective treatment has been worked out for Parkinson's disease. Drug treatment may relieve the rigidity and tremors for a period of time, but eventually the disease overwhelms the drug and continues its progression. At present, the most promising treatment method appears to be surgery to destroy the defective brain cells or to remove or deactivate a small part of the thalamus which relays information to the brain's motor center (Masland, 1962). Psychotherapy and sociotherapy may also be important elements in the overall treatment program. With early detection and treatment, the prognosis for Parkinson's disease is considered relatively favorable. In some 90 per cent of cases, the rigidity and tremor can be abolished or greatly reduced and the progression of the disease can be stayed, giving the patient many more years of useful life. Thus another disease once considered hopeless is now within our power to arrest and in some cases even cure.

HUNTINGTON'S CHOREA

Huntington's chorea is a rare degenerative disease of the nervous system; it was first differentiated and described by the American neurologist George Huntington in 1872. The incidence rate is about 5 persons per 100,000 of the general population (Pearson *et al.,* 1955; Pleydell, 1954). Cases have been reported among all races and in all parts of the world (Bigelow *et al.,* 1959). The disease usually occurs in adults between the ages of 30 and 50 and is characterized by a chronic, progressive chorea[1] with mental deterioration ending in dementia and eventually death.

Symptoms. The major physical symptoms include uncontrollable movements which become increasingly widespread, continuous, and violent as the disease progresses (Bellamy, 1961). These choreic movements usually begin with the facial muscles, with grimacing, nodding the head, moving the jaws, and smacking the tongue and lips, and gradually spread to the trunk and limbs, with continuous stretching, jerking, and grasping movements. The patient manifests a bizarre, jerking, irregular gait; speech is slow, indistinct, and explosive. The involuntary movements become more marked when the patient is excited, tend to diminish when he is quiet and disappear during sleep.

Interestingly enough, behavior deterioration often becomes apparent several years before the neurological manifestations appear. In a study of 21 cases at the Dorothea Dix Hospital in North Carolina, Bellamy (1961) found that in 6 patients the first indications of the disease had been behavior problems characterized by such symptoms as violence, depression, confusion, vagrancy, prostitution, paranoid thinking, and suicidal ideas and attempts. The remaining 15 patients had been admitted with definite neurologic signs but also had showed a long history of prior personality changes extending back from 2 to 12 years. By the time of admission, typical symptoms included depression, hyperactivity, great irritability, poverty of thought and affect, memory failure, and defective attention and judgment.

Although there may be pronounced emotional apathy, suicidal attempts, depression, and

---

[1]Involuntary, irregular, twitching, jerking movements.

other serious symptoms, there is usually no delusional or hallucinatory development during early phases unless the disease serves to precipitate a psychosis in an already psychologically predisposed individual. Later, with the dementia, there may be hallucinations and delusions of a simple, silly type. Terminally, the patients become extremely difficult management problems, with totally uncontrollable movements and severe mental deterioration.

Dynamics. The exact cause of the extensive and progressive neural degeneration in Huntington's chorea is unknown, but the disease is attributable to defective genetic inheritance. It runs in families and is the only psychiatric disorder which follows a simple Mendelian ratio. A dominant gene carries it, and 50 per cent of the children of a gene-carrying parent will be affected (Bellamy, 1961; Gregory, 1960). However, it may be noted that isolated cases of Huntington's chorea have occurred in children of apparently normal parents with no familial history of the disease—apparently as a result of a gene mutation (Bigelow *et al.*, 1959).

The actual brain pathology in Huntington's chorea consists mainly of atrophy or degeneration of the small ganglion cells of the corpus striatum. Other degenerative brain changes in Huntington's chorea vary markedly from case to case but may be extensive (Facon *et al.*, 1957). In a post-mortem study of 21 cases, McCaughey (1961) found that when cortical degeneration occurred, it closely resembled the degeneration found in simple senile atrophy.

Treatment and prognosis. At the present time there is no effective treatment for Huntington's chorea, although a variety of drugs and neurosurgical procedures may alleviate the uncontrollable movements to some extent (Bellamy, 1961). Typically, the course of the disease is one of progressive physical and mental deterioration over a period of 10 to 20 years.

In view of the hereditary basis of the disorder, prevention is primarily a matter of eugenics. Bellamy (1961) has concluded that if all affected individuals were to have no children, Huntington's chorea would disappear in one generation. A complicating factor here is that the symptoms do not usually manifest themselves until about the age of 37, and the individual presently has no way of knowing for sure whether he carries the trait or not. By the time a diagnosis is made, he may have married and had children. As newer findings in genetics are applied to Huntington's chorea, the exact genetic defect involved in this disorder probably will be identified. From a study of gene and chromosome structure, it should then be possible to make an early determination of whether or not a given individual is affected.

ALZHEIMER'S DISEASE

A third rare disease of unknown origin is Alzheimer's disease, named for the German psychiatrist who first described it in 1907. King (1960) has reported that 48 cases diagnosed as Alzheimer's disease were admitted to the Warren State Hospital in Pennsylvania during a 20-year period, as compared to 1138 cases of senile brain disease—a ratio of about 25 to 1. However, the actual incidence is not known.

Alzheimer's disease differs from senile dementia primarily in terms of (a) earlier age of onset—usually in the forties and fifties, (b) rapid progression, with especially severe brain damage and mental deterioration during the early stages of the illness, and (c) frequent development of aphasias and apraxias, in which articulation of words becomes severely impaired and the words may be slurred and mixed up.

The course of the disease can be conveniently divided into three stages (Ferraro, 1959a; Henderson and Batchelor, 1962; Wheelan, 1959):

1. A stage of defective perception and comprehension, gradual loss of memory, impaired reasoning, difficulties in concentration, and impaired efficiency, extending to mistakes in simple everyday tasks. Often the patient blames others for his growing incapacity and develops transient, unsystematized delusions of reference and persecution.

2. As the disease progresses, intellectual impairment becomes obvious in all areas. Memory is particularly impaired, and confabulations may be used to fill in the memory gaps. In general, the patient's mood is one of depression, apprehension, and irritability. Emotional apathy and euphoria are occasionally encountered but are rare. Often the patient cries or laughs compulsively and there usually are indications of a

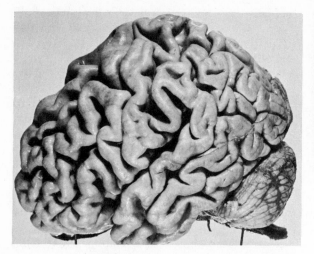
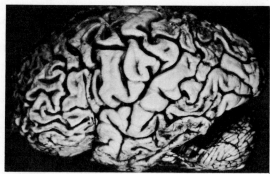

On the left is the brain of a 58-year-old man with Alzheimer's disease, showing general cortical atrophy. He had had a gradual onset of memory defect, nervousness, and impaired judgment, leading to hospitalization. On arrival at the hospital he showed poor memory for recent events, incoherence and perseveration of speech, alexia, and agraphia. He died shortly thereafter. On the right is the brain of a 24-year-old patient with Pick's disease, showing greatest cortical damage in the frontal lobes and in parts of the temporal and parietal lobes. The first symptoms had been emotional apathy and a reduction in spontaneous speech and activity. There was rapid progressive deterioration, with impairment of abstract thinking and the appearance of aphasia, agnosia, echolalia, rapid gait, and general rigidity. The patient's mother and older brother had suffered from the same disorder.

general hyperactivity which takes various forms, such as general restlessness, aimless wandering around, repetition of acts, and purposeless movements. Language difficulties which may have begun earlier now become pronounced, and the patient also becomes unable to read or write.

3. During the third or terminal stage of this disease, the patient becomes disoriented for time, place, and person and is unable to recognize his wife or other close relatives. There also is a general impairment of coordination and bodily emaciation and enfeeblement. Eventually, the patient becomes bedridden and reduced to a vegetative existence. Here there is little to distinguish his condition from that seen in the terminal stages of other organic brain disorders.

The neurological changes typically involve severe cortical atrophy involving the entire brain but often are most pronounced in the frontal lobes. A characteristic change is the degeneration of nerve cells and their replacement by neurofibrillary tangles—the so-called *Alzheimer neurofibrillar disease*. Senile plaques are typi-

cally found but usually in the occipital and parietal lobes rather than in the frontal lobes as in senile dementia (Ferraro, 1959a).

Although we have emphasized the characteristic syndrome in Alzheimer's disease, wide variations in symptoms occur from one patient to another. Although occasional remissions are noted, the disease typically runs a rapid course ending in death in from 2 to 10 years, the average being about 4 years. The reason for the early and rapid neural degeneration is not known. Most investigators tend to emphasize an inherited or acquired metabolic defect (Ferraro, 1959a; Korey *et al.*, 1961; Wheelan, 1959). Treatment is limited mainly to routine medical measures and custodial care.

PICK'S DISEASE

Pick's disease, even more rare than Alzheimer's disease, was first described by Arnold Pick of Prague in papers published in 1892. It is a degenerative disease of the nervous system usually having its onset between 45 and 50 years of age. Women are apparently more subject to the disease than men in the ratio of about 3 to 2 (Ferraro, 1959a).

The onset of the disorder is slow and insidious, involving difficulty in thinking and concentration, slight memory defects, easy fatigability, and often character changes with a lowering of moral inhibitions and an inability to adjust to new situations. When called upon to account for their unusual behavior, patients usually minimize or rationalize their conduct. At first, there is a rather circumscribed atrophy of the frontal and temporal lobes (Ferraro, 1959a; Henderson and Batchelor, 1962). Then, as the atrophy becomes more severe, the mental deterioration becomes progressively greater and typically includes apathy and disorientation as well as severely impaired judgment and other intellectual

functions. Focal cortical lesions may lead to aphasia and apraxia as well as other relatively specific symptoms, depending on the site and extent of the lesion.

In contrast to the tendency toward overactivity, emotional distress, and agitation in Alzheimer's disease, there usually are tendencies toward apathy and loss of initiative in Pick's disease. In addition, memory defect occurs later and is less pronounced as compared with the more global and rapid deterioration in Alzheimer's disease.

At present, the cause of Pick's disease is unknown although in some instances it tends to run in families and appears to be based on faulty genetic inheritance (Ferraro, 1959a; Schenk, 1959). The disease usually runs a fatal course within a period of 2 to 7 years. Currently, treatment is primarily a matter of routine medical and custodial care.

Abnormal Behavior Associated with Epilepsy

Epilepsy has the longest medical history of any disease (Hoch and Knight, 1947). Thousands of years ago it was called "the sacred disease" because it was believed to be the result of a divine visitation. In other eras it was blamed on a devil or an evil spirit which supposedly had entered the brain. Some authorities have concluded that the holes found in the skulls of ancient cave men and of the early Incas were bored so that this devil could get out (Silverman, 1948).

In the course of subsequent history, numerous other names and theories have been proposed. It has variously been called "the falling disease," "fits," "seizures," and "epilepsy." The latter term is derived from the Greek word for *seizure* and is now the accepted name. A myriad of theories ranging from astrology through sex have been advanced to account for epilepsy, and practically every substance in the world capable of passing through the gullet of man has at one time or another been considered effective in its treatment.

Many famous historical figures have been subject to epileptic attacks, including Hercules, Jul-

ius Caesar, Mohammed, Charles V, Napoleon, Lord Byron, Guy de Maupassant, and Van Gogh. Dostoievski's *The Idiot* and a number of other classic and modern works have dealt with the epileptic and his problems. Writing in 95 B.C., Lucretius gives us a vivid picture of an epileptic seizure and a clue to the then prevalent view of its causation.

"Oft too some wretch, before our startled sight,
Struck as with lightning, by some keen disease
Drops sudden:—by the dread attack o'er powered
He foams, he groans, he trembles, and he faints;
Now rigid, now convulsed, his laboring lungs
Heave quick, and quivers each exhausted limb,
Spread through the frame, so deep and dire disease
Perturbs his spirit; as the briny main
Foams through each wave beneath the tempest's ire.
But when, at length, the morbid cause declines,
And the fermenting humors from the heart
Flow back—with staggering foot the man first treads,
Led gradual on to intellect and strength."

The true incidence of epilepsy in the United States today is unknown, although estimates place the number of persons subject to epileptic seizures at about 1,500,000 to 2,000,000.[1] During both World Wars approximately 5 out of every 1000 draftees between 20 and 40 years of age were rejected for military service because of some form of convulsive disorder, and the figure is probably about the same for current draftees. The World Health Organization (1957) mentions a rate of 0.4 to 0.5 per cent for children of school age. It is thus apparent that epilepsy is a disorder of considerable magnitude.

Epilepsy may affect any individual and may have its onset at any age. All races appear equally subject to this disorder, and it is about equally prevalent among males and females. Although found among all age groups, it is more common among children than adults. The age of onset of over half the cases of known epilepsy is under 15 years (Committee on Child Health, 1958). Most individuals with epileptic seizures are of normal intelligence, and the incidence of epilepsy among the mentally retarded (with the exception of severe retardates) is about the same as that among the general population. Nor are epileptic seizures associated with progressive brain damage and mental deterioration except in rare instances.

Despite the relatively high incidence of epilepsy in the general population, only about 1.4 per cent of first admissions to mental hospitals involve psychoses associated with convulsive disorders, and even here the role of epilepsy in the mental disorder is usually unclear.

SYMPTOMS

Epilepsy is a disorder of the nervous system characterized by disturbances in the rhythm of electrical discharges from the brain.[2] It is typically associated with sudden and recurring episodes of clouding or loss of consciousness. The particular episode or seizure may take a variety of forms depending on the nature of the precipitating stimulus, the region of the brain where the disturbance begins, and the severity and spread of the discharge. Symptoms range from a slight lapse of awareness to loss of consciousness with severe convulsions; in one form there is a clouding of consciousness accompanied by automatic

behavior for which the individual is later amnesic. In about half the patients, the seizures are preceded by some kind of warning, known as the *aura*. This may take the form of dizziness, discomfort in the abdomen, a feeling of apprehension, or an "unpleasant smell" or other sensory, motor, or psychic symptom. The aura is really a part of the seizure and usually lasts only a few seconds—ordinarily not long enough to give the patient time for preparation.

Types of epilepsy.   Although epileptic seizures are infinitely varied in form, they may, for practical purposes, be classified into four main types. Typical EEG patterns for these types are shown on page 450.

1.   *Grand mal: "great illness."*   This is the most prevalent and spectacular form of epileptic seizure and occurs in some 60 per cent of epileptic patients. Its outstanding features are loss of consciousness and convulsive muscular activity. During a grand-mal attack, the patient loses consciousness, and breathing is suspended. His muscles become rigid with jaws clenched, arms extended, and legs outstretched, and he pitches forward or slumps to the ground. He may cry out or groan, although he later remembers no pain. His face may become dusky, then pale, and he may bite his tongue and lose control of his sphincter.

With the return of air to the lungs his movements, instead of being rigid (tonic) become jerking (clonic). Now he begins muscular spasms with his head striking the ground, his arms thrust repeatedly outward, his legs jerking up and down, his jaws opening and closing and creating a bubbly foam in the mouth. Usually in about a minute the convulsive movements slow, the muscles gradually relax, and the patient begins to return to normality. Some patients return to consciousness rather rapidly after the attack is ended; others fall into a deep sleep which may last for a few minutes or several hours.

There may be several attacks a day, or they may be as infrequent as one a year. Although the attack is a strenuous physical workout, it does not ordinarily result in permanent physical

---

[1]Statistics here are based on Banay (1961), Campbell (1963), Lennox (1960), National Epilepsy League (1962), National Health Education Committee (1961).

[2]Seizures classified as *epilepsy* and unrelated to other diseases are referred to medically as *cerebral dysrhythmia*.

or mental damage. The exception is *status epilepticus* in which attacks follow one another continuously without the patient's regaining consciousness in between. However, such attacks can usually be stopped by medical means to prevent complete exhaustion.

Patients subject to grand-mal seizures frequently injure themselves by biting their tongues, and cutting, burning, or bruising themselves. Although the patient's falling seldom results in more than minor injury, it may be serious where the patient is climbing stairs or is in some other relatively dangerous position when the seizure occurs. For example, one patient broke her neck falling against the edge of a bathtub.

2. *Petit mal: "small illness."* In petit-mal epilepsy there is usually diminution rather than a complete loss of consciousness. The patient stops whatever he is doing, stares vacantly ahead or toward the floor, and then in a few seconds resumes his previous activity. Often there is a rhythmic twitching of eyelids or eyebrows, and if the patient is holding a fork or spoon, he may drop it. But sometimes the patient is not even aware of the attack. Less common forms of petit mal include *akinetic* seizures involving episodes of sudden muscular collapse ranging from head nodding to falling, and *myoclonic* seizures in which there are brief involuntary muscular contractions of the arms or other bodily parts. In these forms of petit mal there may or may not be a lapse of consciousness.

Petit-mal seizures tend to be frequent, typically occurring several times per day. These seizures usually begin in childhood or adolescence and are rare after the age of 20. They are more frequent among girls than among boys. Unlike patients suffering from grand-mal seizures, petit-mal patients rarely have an advance warning or aura (Lennox, 1960). In some instances, petit-mal attacks occur in addition to or develop into grand-mal seizures.

3. *Jacksonian.* This type of epileptic seizure, first described by the neurologist Hughlings Jackson, is much like a modified grand-mal attack. The attack begins in one region of the body with a muscle twitching or spasm or with a sensory disturbance, such as numbness, tingling, or burning. These muscular or sensory disturbances then spread over the entire side of the body on which they originate. Often the patient remains conscious during the initial phase of the attack, and then loses consciousness as the attack spreads. In many cases, the attacks terminate in generalized convulsive seizures. Apparently in these seizures the attack arises from focal involvement in the brain areas controlling the particular movements or sensory functions where the first symptoms of the attack appear. Although the typical Jacksonian "march" of motion or sensation is rare in children, a seizure occurring in adolescence or adulthood may have its origin in a brain lesion sustained in early life (Lennox, 1960).

4. *Psychomotor.* The principal feature of these attacks is a psychic disturbance, which varies greatly from one patient to another. There is a lapse or clouding of consciousness, but activity continues and the patient appears to be conscious. Attacks usually last a few seconds or minutes, but in rare cases they last for several days. During his attacks the patient may perform either routine tasks or some unusual or antisocial act.

Psychomotor attacks occur in about 10 per cent of children experiencing epileptic seizures and in about one third of adult epileptics (Holowach *et al.*, 1961; National Epilepsy League, 1962). For reasons which are not clear, they occur more frequently among males than among females. Fortunately, only a few of these patients have attacks of a violent homicidal type, but during these attacks they may mutilate themselves or injure other people. The Flemish painter Van Gogh was subject to periods of irrational behavior for which he was later amnesic. On one occasion he cut off one of his ears, wrapped it in a sack, and presented it to a prostitute (Born, 1946). In a more serious case, a brain-injured soldier subject to psychomotor epilepsy reported a dream in which he found himself trying to ward off attackers. Actually during this incident he had beaten his 3-year-old daughter to death. The child's skull had been fractured and her right hip broken, but the patient was completely amnesic for the entire tragic episode, except for the dream.

Banay has emphasized the fact that some bizarre and seemingly senseless crimes of violence are associated with brain pathology such as that found in psychomotor epilepsy. For example, he has cited the case of an epileptic boy of 14

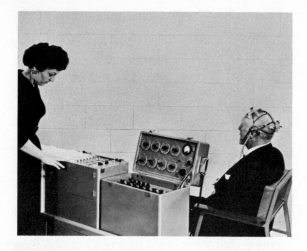

The recording of spontaneous electrical activity in the brain, in the form of an electroencephalogram (EEG) has become common practice. Separate readings are taken from each of the four lobes in both hemispheres of the brain. Abnormal tracings are valuable clues to brain pathology.

". . . who murdered with exceptional brutality. Precociously husky and muscular, he was visiting an aunt, 23 years old, the mother of two children and pregnant, to watch television. When the young woman complained of feeling unwell and asked the boy to leave, he was overcome by a 'sudden urge' as he rose to go. He struck her in the face and when she fell kicked her about the face and head. He struck her again with a soda bottle, brought a metal spray gun from the next room and struck her with that. He then beat her with a lamp, obtained a large knife from the kitchen and stabbed her in the neck. Still in furor, he wound a lamp cord around her neck and was dragging her to the kitchen, intent on stringing her body on a water pipe, when a knock on the door alarmed him and he fled through a window. The boy had a history of two serious head injuries and of blackouts attributable to them. His only previous offense had been car thefts, carried out in frivolous disregard of the likelihood of detection. He was clinically found to be an epileptic as a consequence of brain injury." (1961, pp. 875-876)

Here it may be re-emphasized that most psychomotor epileptics are not dangerous to others. Turner and Merlis (1962) found that only 5 out of 337 epileptics who had committed illegal acts had probably committed such acts during seizures. Even in these cases they considered the matter to still be an "open question." However, it is of interest to note that in each of these five cases the behavior had involved extreme violence.

Many epileptic patients experience more than one type of seizure; estimates range from 25 to 40 per cent (Duggins, n.d.; National Epilepsy League, 1962). In such cases, petit-mal or Jacksonian seizures are often associated with grandmal seizures.

Many investigators also list various *autonomic* seizures as a type of epilepsy. Such autonomic seizures involve recurrent attacks of sweating, heart palpitation, vomiting, abdominal pain, or other symptoms indicating a disturbance in the functioning of the autonomic nervous system. The relationship of such attacks to "true epilepsy" is not clear although central nervous system defects may apparently be involved in some cases.

Mental deterioration or psychotic reactions. In rare cases, epileptics show progressive deterioration or associated psychotic reactions, but apparently the psychopathology results primarily from the reaction of the patient to his affliction rather than from anything inherently deteriorative in the epilepsy itself. For example, in a group of 85 epileptics whose frequent seizures necessitated their institutionalization, Falk *et al.* (1945) found that only three became psychotic and none showed mental deterioration over a nine-year period. Those who show deterioration are also likely to show more frequent seizures, poor response to medication, and a greater incidence of generalized EEG abnormalities accompanied by superimposed focal abnormalities (Chaudry and Pond, 1961). A minority of children with epilepsy also suffer from cerebral palsy, mental retardation, or other structural defects or injuries to the brain which further increase their adjustive burden. If their difficulties are further augmented by an unfavorable emotional climate in the family and community, both serious maladjustment and deterioration are more likely to occur (Committee on Child Health, 1958).

The following case, diagnosed as *epileptic deterioration*, is one in which a psychotic deteriorative reaction did appear in connection with epileptic seizures. The patient was 37 years old at the time of his hospitalization.

The patient suffered a gunshot wound in the head during a hunting trip. Two years later he began to have Jacksonian seizures beginning in the left hand. Although he was treated with dilantin and other drugs over a period of some five years, he continued to have attacks about twice a week. During the next two years his attacks, which had formerly been confined to Jacksonian seizures, became complicated by grand-mal seizures as well. The patient was unable to work and used up all of his savings.

He was hospitalized at the suggestion of his wife, who stated that he had become extremely irritable and depressed and that she was afraid that he would either injure her or kill himself or both. On admission to the hospital, he was belligerent and uncooperative and accused the other patients of stealing his money. Although he had attended two years of college prior to his injury, intelligence testing now indicated borderline intellectual functioning. He manifested a variety of hypochondriacal complaints and delusions, among which was the attitude that sex had ruined his life and had resulted in his brain being "destroyed." From time to time he became extremely anxious, agitated, and depressed.

Despite medical therapy, the patient's course in the hospital was downhill during the two years that he was observed. He became increasingly narcissistic and self-centered in his activities and paid no attention to other patients on the ward or to personal hygiene. Often he appeared confused and sometimes he spelled words instead of pronouncing them when he talked. When his wife visited him, he would sometimes appear somewhat silly and jocular, as if trying to compensate for his situation and indicate to her that he was getting along fine; on other occasions he appeared depressed, apathetic, and withdrawn. In general, the clinical picture appeared to be a mixed picture of psychotic withdrawal in the face of his changed life situation and organic deterioration from extensive brain damage.

DYNAMICS

Numerous theories have been advanced regarding the causation and dynamics in epileptic attacks, and here, as in the case of other disorders, our ideas have changed radically as our knowledge has increased.

Biological factors. Hysterics and other mentally ill patients may simulate epileptic seizures, but apparently in true epilepsy some underlying brain condition is always involved, as evidenced by the fact that distinctive brain waves of a pathological variety have been found not only for epileptics in general but even for the four different types. The precise nature of this brain condition is not known although neurophysiological studies point to nerve cell instability probably associated with structural or metabolic defects which result in excessive or deficient neuronal firing (Friedlander, 1962).

New techniques of medical diagnosis—such as the implantation of minute electrodes in brain areas suspected of being the origin of abnormal discharges—have made it possible to find identifiable brain pathology in a majority of epileptic cases. This pathology may be the result of infections, fever, malformation, tumor, vascular disturbances, degenerative diseases, or brain injuries occurring before, during, or after birth. Seizures associated with such brain damage are referred to as *symptomatic* epilepsy. In cases where brain damage cannot be demonstrated, the epilepsy is referred to as *idiopathic* (of unknown origin). Here the seizures are usually attributed to some unidentified metabolic deficiency of brain cells. In such cases, which are preponderantly of the grand-mal type, EEG findings typically show a diffuse cerebral dysrhythmia. Actually, anyone can have seizures, and at least 10 per cent of the normal population also reveal brain-wave abnormalities that presumably make them more susceptible to seizures than persons with normal brain-wave patterns (Duggins, n.d.; National Epilepsy League, 1962).

Although some sort of organic brain pathology appears to be the primary cause of seizures, there is usually some secondary or precipitating cause as well. Many varieties of sensory, intellectual, and emotional stimuli seem capable of provoking seizures in predisposed individuals. Such stimuli are often highly specific to the given patient involved. For example, in some patients "photic" convulsive seizures may be induced by the flicker of incorrectly operating television sets (Blattner, 1961); in others, musical notes of a given frequency may precipitate seizures (Joynt et al., 1962); in still others, attacks may be precipitated by particular intellectual demands or

CHANGING CONDITIONS RELATED TO ONSET OF EPILEPSY	
AGE OF ONSET OF SEIZURES	**MOST COMMON CAUSES**
Infancy and childhood (before 10 years)	Congenital structural defects of brain, birth injuries, early postnatal infections
Adolescence and young adulthood (12-35)	Head injuries, sequelae of birth injuries, benign tumors (high percentage idiopathic cases make first appearance at adolescence)
Middle age (35-55)	Tumors, head injuries, vascular disease
Later maturity (55-70)	Circulatory defects and vascular pathology (lesions produced by abnormalities of blood vessels), tumors, degenerative diseases of brain
After age of 70	Circulatory or vascular disorders, tumors (onset rare in this period)

by emotional stress. The actual neurological processes relating the precipitating stimuli to the induced seizures are not known, although the "irritation theory" has long been popular. Here it is presumed that underlying instability makes these nerve-cells hypersensitive to certain types of stimulation or irritation, thus leading to excessive or deficient neuronal discharges and epileptic symptoms.

Traditionally, the predisposition to epilepsy in idiopathic cases has been attributed to hereditary factors. Here investigators have pointed to the fact that a family history of epilepsy is over three times as common among epileptics as among the general population (Eisner *et al.*, 1959; Harvald, 1954; Lennox, 1960; Metrakos and Metrakos, 1961) and that there is a much higher concordance of idiopathic epilepsy for monozygotic than for dizygotic twins (Friedlander, 1963; Lennox, 1960; Marshall *et al.*, 1962). These statistics apply primarily to grandmal seizures, however, and it is now thought that the predisposition in idiopathic epilepsy may be either inherited or acquired and that in most cases it is probably of mixed origin. Even in symptomatic epilepsy, where organic brain pathology can be demonstrated, there still may

also have been a genetic predisposition to epilepsy. Apparently, there is more likelihood of a genetic predisposition in cases where symptomatic seizures begin early in life than where the seizures start after brain damage in adult life (Holowach *et al.*, 1961).

Psychological factors. The search for psychological factors in epilepsy has centered around three problems: (a) the possible role of psychological stress in precipitating epileptic seizures, (b) the question of whether or not there is an "epileptic personality," and (c) the reaction of the epileptic patient to his affliction and to any changes it may effect in his life situation.

Most investigators now agree that psychological conflicts and frustrations can precipitate seizures in many persons organically predisposed to epilepsy. Thus the frequency of actual seizures is often determined in part by the personality·adjustment and life situation of the particular patient. This relationship was well demonstrated by Kupper (1945) in his study of a patient whose attacks had started some six years earlier following an emotional upset. With the patient under hypnosis, convulsive seizures were induced when the therapist discovered and suggested the psychic conflict. Interestingly enough, no other means of stimulation was effective in producing a seizure. Kupper concluded that this patient had had a predisposing constitutional background which had produced no symptoms until a particular psychic conflict precipitated them.

In many cases, there would appear to be an emotional threshold which must be passed before a convulsive or other type of seizure takes place. Apparently the psychological stress—often thought to be the problem of handling intense hostility—acts as a trigger in precipitating disorderly discharges of brain cells. Considerable speculation has also centered around the hypothesis that epileptic convulsions are tension-reducing mechanisms which represent an explosive discharge of the lower brain centers, resulting in the lowering of emotional tensions. There is a wealth of practical clinical observations to support this view.

An epileptic patient was referred to a psychiatrist, who, by means of drugs, freed him from attacks for a period of some four weeks. At this time the psychiatrist went on a vacation, and psychotherapy was temporarily suspended. The patient shortly began to feel terribly tense, anxious, and depressed and felt that if he could only have a seizure he would be all right again.

Some investigators, following this hypothesis, are inclined to look upon psychomotor epilepsy as a psychic equivalent and substitute for the epileptic convulsion. The psychomotor activities presumably are tension-reducing, however abnormal and unadaptive. Additional evidence is needed before this viewpoint can be either accepted or rejected.

Numerous attempts to delineate an "epileptic personality" have been unsuccessful (Strauss, 1959; Tizard, 1962). Epilepsy does not necessarily cause maladjustment nor are certain types of personalities especially susceptible to epileptic seizures. But although no personality type or specific pattern of reaction characterizes the majority of epileptic patients, the brain condition and/or additional stresses of the patient's life situation appear to take their toll in a higher incidence of personality maladjustment than is found among physically normal individuals.[1]

There is also some evidence that the nature of the personality maladjustment among epileptics may vary with the type of epilepsy.

Many children who experience these episodes become self-conscious and ill at ease in social situations and show other signs of adjustive difficulties. Their difficulties may, of course, be augmented by overly protective or rejecting parents. As young adults, they may continue to face unequal competition and frustrating restrictions—social nonacceptance, problems in getting married, restricted educational channels, and limited job opportunities—which augment the stresses of modern living.

Not surprisingly, some epileptics react to these additional stresses in unhealthy ways. Risch and Henry (1960) have pointed out that many severe cases are fearful and lacking in confidence, viewing themselves as unemployable, discriminated against, socially rejected, and stigmatized. As chronic epileptic patients grow older, there also appear to be frequent tendencies toward circumstantiality, egocentricity, irritability, and projection of blame (Guller, 1960; Sinclair-Gieben, 1961; Strauss, 1959). But these personality traits are not limited to epileptics and may stem in part from their brain pathology.

It has also been pointed out that children suffering from symptomatic epilepsy, particularly involving lesions of the temporal lobe, often are hyperactive, irritable, and aggressive (Holowach *et al.,* 1961; Lovit, 1961; Strauss, 1959; Walker, 1961). As we have previously noted, these symptoms are often found in brain-injured children whether they are subject to seizures or not.

---

[1]The reader is referred to Tizard (1962), who has reviewed much of the available research data in this area, and to Guerrant *et al.* (1962), who found a high incidence of emotional disturbances in a group of 32 psychomotor and 26 idiopathic grand-mal adult outpatient cases at the Langley Porter Neuropsychiatric Institute in San Francisco. Additional references include Chaudry and Pond (1961), Hill (1961), Holowach *et al.* (1961), Lovit (1961), Lennox (1960), Sinclair-Gieben (1961), Strauss (1959). Here it may be pointed out that three factors suggest caution in interpreting findings with respect to personality maladjustment among epileptics since (a) some studies report on institutionalized epileptics, and some on patients attending outpatient clinics; (b) some studies report on patients whose seizures are controlled by medication and some mix controlled, partially controlled, and uncontrolled cases; and finally (c) the type and amount of medication taken may influence the psychological assessment—due allowance must be made for the possible effects of medication on intellectual and affective processes.

Sociological factors. All races seem to be about equally subject to epilepsy although definitive studies on predominant types for given racial groups have not been made. In all probability, differences would be limited to symptomatic epilepsy and hence would reflect acquired brain damage rather than inherited "racial" characteristics. There is some evidence that epilepsy may be somewhat more common on lower socioeconomic levels.

There is no question but that superstition, stigma, restrictions, and the seizures themselves often block or handicap the epileptic in meeting many of life's problems. In many states persons with epilepsy are forbidden to drive cars; epilepsy often proves a handicap in competition for desired mates; and many epileptics find it difficult to obtain employment. This picture is beginning to change, however, with the better control of seizures through the use of new drugs, with new research demonstrating successful performance by epileptics, and with improved public understanding of the nature of epilepsy. Some states now permit an epileptic to drive a car when his physician certifies that he is under treatment and that his seizures are controlled— for example, if he has not had a seizure for two years or longer. Keip *et al.* (1961) have reported that the accident rate of these epileptic drivers in Ohio is only one sixth that of the driver population as a whole. It has also been estimated that with newer methods of treatment 80 per cent of adult epileptics are capable of regular productive employment in a wide range of jobs (Juul-Jensen, 1961; Udel, 1960). Thus the centuries-old discrimination against epileptics as well as other handicapped persons is gradually giving way.

TREATMENT AND PROGNOSIS

In 1911, Dr. Alfred Hauptman introduced the use of phenobarbital in treating epileptics and met with some success. Then, in 1937, Putnam and Merritt (1938), after trying many combinations of drugs related to phenobarbital, discovered dilantin. Since then, other effective drugs have come into use and new ones are in the investigational stage. Certain of the newer drugs tend to be particularly effective for certain types of seizures (Fine, 1961; Forster, 1960; Friedlander, 1963). Phenurone, for example, is used only for psychomotor cases; while tridione has proven particularly effective in the treatment of petit mal. Often dilantin is combined with other drugs.

Although drug treatment is the cornerstone in the management of seizures, surgery is coming into increasing use. It is used especially with patients who do not respond to drugs and in cases where the site of the brain lesion is such that its excision or partial excision will not produce a crippling neurological defect.

The proper orientation of the patient to his disorder and assistance with educational, marital, and occupational problems are often essential elements in the overall treatment program. Problems of self-pity, shame, and withdrawal from social contacts may need to be worked through. And as one might expect, a well-ordered regimen of living, with avoidance of undue fatigue, alcoholic excesses, and other conditions which reduce overall physical fitness, is considered especially important for epileptics.

With combined medical and psychological therapy, seizures can now be completely controlled in some 50 to 60 per cent of cases, and the number and severity of attacks can be markedly reduced in another 30 per cent (Forster, 1960; National Epilepsy League, 1962). The prognosis varies considerably, however, for the various types of epilepsy and for various patients. In general, grand-mal and petit-mal seizures respond to treatment best, with Jacksonian and psychomotor following in that order. In psychomotor epilepsy, it has been estimated that only about one third will become seizure-free (Holowach, 1961; Kiorboe, 1961). Fortunately, epileptic seizures beginning in early life tend to diminish with time—particularly in the case of petit mal—and many patients can gradually discontinue their medication after being seizure-free for many years. Often the EEG is of help in deciding whether a patient who has not had a seizure for several years should continue with his medication.

Many studies have found epileptics as a group quite capable of normal academic work, social adjustment, and work performance. In one early study of 95 University of Michigan students subject to epilepsy, Himler and Raphael (1945) found that 70 per cent were capable of doing creditable college work. In a follow-up of 63 of these same students they found, on the whole, excellent adjustment:

54 had made entirely satisfactory personal adjustments
3 had chronic neurotic reactions
4 showed basic personality instabilities
2 were deteriorated, one with paranoid symptoms

In a more recent follow-up of the case records of 1284 consecutive epileptic patients seen in the Mayo Clinic, it was found that (Mulder, 1959):

19 per cent made "superior" adjustment
68 per cent were self-supporting
9 per cent were partially dependent
4 per cent were totally dependent

These outcomes, interestingly enough, showed no correlation with type, frequency, or duration of seizures.

Even in older persons the prognosis in epilepsy is good except in the case of certain neoplastic (tumorous) or degenerative brain diseases. Undoubtedly, as new and more effective drugs are introduced, the prognosis in epilepsy will become even more favorable.

PREVENTION

Adequate preventive measures have not yet been developed for epilepsy. As already indicated, however, the handicapping effects of seizures can now usually be prevented entirely or greatly minimized by (a) early detection and prompt adequate treatment, including the avoidance of extreme psychological stress and a well-ordered regimen of living, and (b) reduction of the social, economic, and emotional pressures on persons subject to seizures. Unfortunately, a large number of epileptics still do not receive adequate medical treatment and hence are the victims of unnecessary seizures (National Epilepsy League, 1962).

There is considerable evidence to support the contention of some investigators that for the benefit of possible offspring two persons with epileptic brain waves should not marry regardless of whether or not they have actual attacks. Here medical counseling is recommended to help such individuals gain a realistic picture of genetic considerations. And as new research findings in genetics become available, it may be hoped that medical scientists will be able to develop preventive procedures for certain types of epilepsy.

Psychoses of the Aged

"But worse than any loss of limb is the failing mind, which forgets the names of slaves, and cannot recognize the face of the old friend who dined with him last night, nor those of the children whom he has begotten and brought up." (Juvenal, n.d.) Such references to mental disturbances in the aged and to the more dramatic aspects of apoplexy are found in the earliest scientific and literary works. Shakespeare's King Lear has been considered an example of senile dementia, and in *Gulliver's Travels* there is a famous passage picturing the progressive physical and mental decline in senility.

Today, with our increasing longevity, these disorders have become increasingly important. Through the prolongation of life by medical science, the United States is approaching a far greater older population, both absolutely and relatively, than any other country has ever had in all history, and we can expect this trend to continue. Already there are five times more people in this country over 65 than there were in 1900, while the total population has increased less than threefold. At mid-century, figures showed 10 million people in the United States over 65; in 1960, the number had increased to almost 16 million. By 1980, it is expected to approximate 25 million—some 10 per cent of the anticipated total population (Hunt, 1960; Parsons, 1960; Pollack *et al.,* 1960; White House Conference on Aging, 1961). In 1960, the average life expectancy in the United States approximated 70 years, and as medical advances continue to conquer killing diseases, a life span of 90 to 100 years may not be far distant (American Medical Association Committee on Aging, 1960). This is in striking contrast to the life expectancy of some 23 years in the days of the Roman Empire.

The shift in the age make-up of our population has given rise to a great many psychological, sociological, and medical problems, which are receiving more attention as their importance is being realized. We might suspect that among these problems would be an increase in the mental disorders of old age, and such is the case. Between 1940 and 1960 the number of mental hospital patients 60 years and over increased about five times as fast as the overall hospital population. Psychoses associated with old age now constitute about 25 per cent of all first admissions to mental hospitals. Recently there has been a slight decrease in first admissions of patients over 65 to mental hospitals, but this apparently reflects the use of nursing homes and other facilities for the care and treatment of the aged rather than any decrease in the number of mentally ill older patients (Pollack et al., 1960). It has been estimated that some 30 to 50 per cent of the 500,000 or more older persons residing in nursing homes or homes for the aged are mentally ill (Goldfarb, 1962; Hoch and Zubin, 1961). In addition, many senile and arteriosclerotic patients with pronounced mental symptoms still live in the community. The mental disorders of old age have thus become a major mental health problem in our society.

PROBLEMS OF AGING

Just why men age is a problem of great theoretical and practical interest. In general, there are two major contemporary views. The older and more conventional view is that the physiological aging of the body is quite as natural and inherent a process as is growth. It occurs in later life after the fundamental biological functions have been fulfilled, and is considered an irreversible process and an inherent characteristic of the germ plasm itself.

The second, more recent view of aging suggests that the gradual degenerative or involutional processes are due to infections, toxins, traumas, ionizing radiations, and other conditions which have impaired the general functional and regenerative capacities of the body cells. From this point of view, aging and death result from the body's failure to eliminate waste products and repair damage and from a garbling of the DNA code. We can hasten this process through exposure to irradiation, faulty nutrition, neglect of symptoms of illness, and excessive stress (Selye and Prioreschi, 1960; White House Conference, 1961). Or we can retard it, within limits, by good health practices—both physical and psychological. Some authorities speculate that as new research leads to a better understanding of the factors in aging and to means of preventing or retarding the aging process, man may live 150 years or more.

Irrespective of which theory we accept, the present fact remains that man does age, and a crucial problem becomes that of distinguishing between normal changes with age and pathological ones. We are concerned here with biological, psychological, and sociological changes associated with abnormal behavior.

Normal changes in old age. Biological aging brings a decline in muscular strength and coordination, lowered energy reserves, a decrease in perceptual acuity, reduced ability to withstand stress, greater susceptibility to disease and slower recovery, and changes in physical appearance.[1] Old age is also associated with many bodily infirmities. Joints become less flexible, bones lose their dense structure and are more easily fractured, muscles tend to atrophy and to become hypertonic, the skin becomes wrinkled and loses its elasticity, the hair becomes thinner and gray, and internal organs undergo a gradual atrophy. The vascular and nervous systems are among the first to suffer from the aging process. The brain becomes smaller and there is some degree of atrophy and a decrease in the number of neurons (Himwich, 1962). Fatty deposits form in the cerebral arteries, and there is a hardening of the cerebral arteries, leading eventually to impaired cerebral circulation (Leake, 1962).

An increasing body of research indicates that certain psychological changes usually accompany

---

[1] It may be pointed out here that some individuals age much more rapidly than others and that aging may occur more rapidly in some bodily systems than in others. Himwich (1962) has pointed out that endocrine and other physiological functions in healthy older people may be on a par with those of much younger individuals.

physiological regression. Prominent among these changes are an increase in the time required for various psychomotor tasks; an impairment of memory, particularly for recent events; a reduction in the rate of new learning; lowered ability to integrate new information with old and to organize appropriate responses; a decrease in flexibility and creativity in problem solving; and a somewhat lowered capacity for coping with psychological stress (Birren, 1960; Wechsler, 1961; White House Conference, 1961). However, most psychological changes occur gradually and are not seriously handicapping, and not all changes are in a downward direction. Experience and wisdom are cumulative and give older persons the advantage in many situations.

Both biological and psychological aging may be hastened or retarded depending on the motives, attitudes, flexibility, and other personality traits of the individual and the stresses in his life situation. Those who remain intellectually active and vitally interested in the events of the world about them may continue into advanced age with little perceptible loss in intellectual functions. Goethe completed *Faust* after the age of 80; Judge Learned Hand completed 50 years of service in 1959 at the age of 87; Amos Alonzo Stagg, the grand old man of American football, was still coaching at the age of 100; and it has been said that Winston Churchill, one of the greatest men of recent times, would have been considered little more than a prominent failure had his career ended at 65 (Bowman and Engle, 1960; Holle, 1960). Many other prominent literary, scientific, and political figures have been productive well past the age of 80.

In addition to biological and psychological aging, there is also what may be called sociological aging—changes in the position of the individual as a member of his family and of society. These changes typically include retirement from work, completed parental roles, death of husband or wife, reduced income, and a considerable increase in leisure time. Concomitant with these are changes in the individual's self-concept and social role as well as in the images, attitudes, and expectations which society expresses toward him. Some aspects of sociological aging have positive as well as negative values, but all require adjustment on the part of the individual.

Where the individual looks upon retirement as an opportunity to expand his life space and otherwise deals flexibly and effectively with the stresses confronting him, he may find old age an interesting and satisfying portion of his life. All too often, however, the older person is not adequately prepared for later maturity and feels devaluated, alone, and alienated from the world about him.

Mental illness in old age. The two major psychotic disorders of older people are those associated with *senile brain disease* (involving cerebral atrophy and degeneration) and *cerebral arteriosclerosis* (involving either blocking or ruptures in the cerebral arteries). These two disorders account for approximately 80 per cent of the mental disorders of old age (Marks, 1961). Both are classified as chronic brain syndromes because it has long been held that the degenerative senile and arteriosclerotic changes in the brain are the direct cause of the psychotic symptoms. It is now recognized, however, that there is little correlation between the degree of neurological damage and the severity of the mental disorder for the great majority of cases.

It should be pointed out that mental illness among the aged is by no means restricted to these two chronic brain syndromes. Longstanding neurotic patterns may continue into old age or new ones may appear for the first time in response to the increased stress of this life period. Anxiety states, hypochondriacal reactions, and depressive reactions are especially common. Any of the functional psychoses may also develop among older persons. Psychotic depressive reactions are the most common, followed by paranoid states (Williams and Jaco, 1958; Straker, 1963).

In many cases, of course, it is difficult to separate functional symptoms from organic components. But although neurotic or functional psychotic reactions occurring among the aged may be complicated by brain damage, the dynamic patterns are essentially the same as those discussed previously.

SENILE BRAIN DISEASE

In senile brain disease (senile dementia) the degenerative brain changes of old age are accompanied by a clinical picture of progressive

SYMPTOMS IN OLD-AGE PSYCHOSES

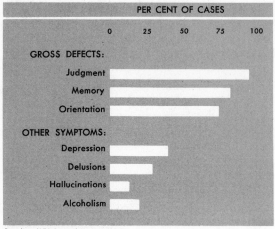

Based on Whittier and Korenyi (1961)

This chart summarizes the symptom picture in 540 male patients 60 and over admitted for the first time to a state hospital. Neurological abnormality was evident in only 27 per cent of the cases. About half of these patients died within the first year.

mental deterioration. Senile psychoses constitute about 8 per cent of the first admissions to mental hospitals. Women slightly outnumber men, which might be expected in view of the longer life span of women. The average age of first admission is about 75 years for both sexes, although the onset of the disorder may be any time from the 60's to the 90's. Since many senile patients are cared for at home for some time before the family decides on hospitalization, the mean age of onset of the disorder is lower than the mean age of first admissions would indicate.

The onset of senile dementia is ordinarily gradual, involving a slow physical and mental letdown. In some cases, a physical ailment or some other situational stress is a dividing point, but usually the patient passes into a psychotic state almost imperceptibly, so that it is impossible to date the onset of the disorder precisely. The symptom pattern varies greatly from one patient to another, depending upon the premorbid personality of the patient, the nature and extent of the brain degeneration, and the particular stresses in his life situation.

General symptoms. Faulty reactions on the part of the older person often begin with a gradual withdrawal into himself, a narrowing of so-

cial and other interests, a lessening of mental alertness and adaptability, and a reduction in tolerance to new ideas and to changes in routine. Often there is a self-centering of thoughts and activities and a preoccupation with the bodily functions of eating, digestion, and excretion. As these various changes—typical in lesser degree of most older people—become severe, additional symptoms such as periods of confusion and impairment of memory for recent events make their appearance.

Often the patient suffers from insomnia and is restless during the night. He may get up in the small hours and putter aimlessly about the house. In some instances, he wanders away from home and is unable to find his way back. Not infrequently, such patients become suspicious of the motives and activities of those about them, and these suspicions may be elaborated into paranoid states.

Some patients become very untidy and careless in personal habits, although this particular kind of deterioration is usually a later manifestation. Patients are often easily aroused to either cheerfulness or tears; anxious and agitated states are frequent, but deep depressions are uncommon. Impairment of judgment and a decrease in control of sexual impulses sometimes lead to dishonest or immoral behavior; the latter may take the form of molesting children.

As the psychosis develops, the memory impairment becomes more pronounced, although the patient may be able to remember events of childhood when later events have been forgotten. This is probably closely related to the tendency of the senile patient to live in the past, indulging in reminiscences concerning childhood events and other occurrences of long ago. He may tell the same stories over and over again. Fabrications and loss of accurate temporal relationships are common; for example, the patient may think that a childhood event happened yesterday. He may have difficulty in remembering how many children he has, or whether he is married or not; he may ask for a mother or father who has been dead for many years. He has trouble remembering the names of new acquaintances and sometimes even members of the family, and often cannot remember where he has left various objects. There is increasing impairment of comprehension, with some degree of confusion and eventually defective self-identity and disorientation for time and place. Speech becomes rambling, circumstantial, and often incoherent; delusions, hallucinations, and delirious episodes may gradually make their appearance.

Specific symptoms such as restlessness, agitation, and delirious states may come and go from day to day so that the clinical picture is by no means a uniform one until the terminal stages when the patient is reduced to a vegetative level. There is also, of course, a great deal of individual variation in the rapidity of progression of the disorder, and in some instances there may be a reversal of psychotic symptomatology and a partial or even good recovery.

Types of senile dementia. A clear-cut division between various types of senile dementia is not only difficult to make but somewhat artificial. For convenience, however, senile reactions have been divided into five groups.

1. *Simple deterioration.* This is, as the name suggests, a relatively uncomplicated exaggeration of the "normal" changes of old age. The patient gradually loses contact with the environment and develops the typical symptoms of poor memory, tendency to reminisce, intolerance of change, disorientation, restlessness, insomnia, and failure of judgment. This is the most common of the senile psychotic reactions, constituting about 50 per cent of the entire group.

The following case is typical of simple deterioration.

The patient had been a successful engineer and had retired some seven years prior to his hospitalization. During the past five years he had shown a progressive loss of interest in his surroundings and during the last year had become increasingly "childish." His wife and eldest son had brought him to the hospital because they felt they could no longer care for him in their home, particularly because of the grandchildren. They stated that the patient had become careless in his eating and other personal habits, was restless and prone to wandering about at night, and couldn't seem to remember anything that had happened during the day but was garrulous concerning events of his childhood and middle years.

After admission to the hospital, the patient seemed to deteriorate rapidly. He could rarely remember what had happened a few minutes before, although his mem-

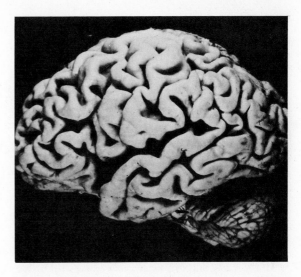

This is the brain of a 79-year-old man who had been hospitalized with a diagnosis of senile dementia; his symptoms included marked confusion, memory defects, especially for recent events, slight aphasia, paranoid ideation, and agitated depression. The cortex shows extensive, diffuse atrophy with a narrowing of the convolutions and a widening of the fissures throughout.

ory for remote events of his childhood remained good. When he was visited by his wife and children, he did not recognize them, but mistook them for old friends, nor could he recall anything about the visit a few minutes after they had departed. The following brief conversation with the patient, which took place after he had been in the hospital for nine months, and about three months prior to his death, shows his disorientation for time and person:

Dr.: How are you today, Mr.——?

Pt.: Oh . . . hello . . . (looks at doctor in rather puzzled way as if trying to make out who he is).

Dr.: Do you know where you are now?

Pt.: Why yes . . . I am at home. I must paint the house this summer. It has needed painting for a long time but it seems like I just keep putting it off.

Dr.: Can you tell me the day today?

Pt.: Isn't today Sunday . . . why, yes, the children are coming over for dinner today. We always have dinner for the whole family on Sunday. My wife was here just a minute ago but I guess she has gone back into the kitchen.

2. *Paranoid reaction.* In this type of senile psychosis the main characteristic is a gradual formation of delusions, usually of a persecutory, erotic, or grandiose nature, and usually accompanied by related hallucinations. For example, the patient may develop the notion that his relatives have turned against him and are trying to rob and kill him. His suspicions are confirmed by the noxious gases which he smells in his room, or by the poison he tastes in his food. Fortunately, such delusions are poorly systematized and rarely lead to overt homicidal attacks on his alleged persecutors. Grandiose delusions are usually minor in degree and may be obviously wish-fulfilling in nature. For example, Rothschild (1944) has cited the case of an 84-year-old unmarried woman who had the delusion that she was married and the mother of two children.

In the early stages, the memory loss and other manifestations of senile degeneration are usually not so pronounced as in other types of senile reactions. Confusion and other disturbances of consciousness are not common and often the patient remains oriented for time, place, and person.

The following case is typical of paranoid senile reactions.

The patient, a woman of 74, had been referred to a hospital after the death of her husband because she became uncooperative and was convinced that her relatives were trying to steal the insurance money which her husband had left her. In the hospital she complained that the other women had joined together against her and were trying to steal her belongings. She frequently refused to eat, on the grounds that the food tasted funny and had probably been poisoned. She grew increasingly irritable and disoriented for time and person. She avidly scanned magazines in the ward reading room but could not remember anything that she had looked at. The following conversation reveals some of her symptoms:

Dr.: Do you find that magazine interesting?

Pt.: Why do you care? Can't you see I'm busy?

Dr.: Would you mind telling me something about what you are reading?

Pt.: It's none of your business . . . I am reading about my relatives. They want me to die so that they can steal my money.

Dr.: Do you have any evidence of this?

Pt.: Yes, plenty. They poison my food and they have turned the other women against me. They are all out to get my money. They even stole my sweater.

Dr.: Can you tell me what you had for breakfast?

Pt.: . . . (Pause) I didn't eat breakfast . . . it was poisoned and I refused to eat it. They are all against me.

These paranoid reactions are largely determined by the pre-psychotic personality of the patient and tend to develop in individuals who have been suspicious and somewhat paranoid in their make-up. Existing personality tendencies are apparently intensified by the senile degenerative changes and the stresses of the senile period. Approximately 30 per cent of psychoses associated with senile brain disease take a paranoid form.

3. *The presbyophrenic type.* This senile psychosis is characterized by fabrication, a jovial, amiable mood, and marked impairment of memory. Such patients may appear superficially alert, and may talk volubly in a rambling, confused manner in which gaps in present memory are filled in with events that occurred twenty or thirty years before. They usually show a peculiar restlessness or excitability and engage in continual aimless activity. A patient may fold and unfold pieces of cloth as if he were ironing, or he may collect various discarded objects with a great show of importance.

The presbyophrenic type of senile reaction apparently occurs most frequently in individuals who have been lively, aggressive, jovial, and extrovertive in their younger days. It constitutes less than 10 per cent of the entire group of senile psychotics. Traditionally, the presbyophrenic type has had an unfavorable prognosis, since these patients tend to exhaust themselves very rapidly.

The following conversation illustrates the jovial mood, impaired memory, and fabrication usually seen in these patients.

Dr.: How do you feel today, Mr. ——?

Pt.: Just fine, doctor. Just fine. Isn't that funny, doctor, I was just thinking about you. How are you today?

Dr.: Very well, thank you. How is your work progressing?

Pt.: Fine, doctor, just fine. I'm always busy here. I can't stand to sit and do nothing. When I first came here I was kind of worried because I didn't know exactly what was expected of me, but now that I have charge of the hospital laundry, it keeps me jumping.

Dr.: Are you well paid for your work?

Pt.: Oh, yes, doctor. Why, just the other day I got another raise. That shows how important my work is . . . the fifth raise in two years . . . not bad, doctor, eh?

Dr.: How long have you been working in the laundry?

Pt.: Well, let's see, doctor . . . I would say about 10 years . . . I had just graduated from high school . . . made good grades, you know, but jobs were scarce and I had to start at the bottom. I'm a hard worker though and now I am the superintendent. You can't keep a good man down, they always say.

4. *Delirious and confused types.* In these cases there is a severe mental clouding in which the patient becomes extremely restless, combative, resistive, and incoherent. He recognizes no one and is completely disoriented for time and place. Such delirious states are often precipitated in old people by acute illness or by traumas such as a broken leg or hip. Although transient delirious episodes often occur in senile dementia, chronic confusion and delirium are uncommon except in terminal states; they account for less than 10 per cent of senile reactions.

5. *Depressed and agitated types.* Here the patient is severely depressed and agitated and usually suffers from hypochondriacal and nihilistic delusions. Often he expresses morbid ideas about cancer, syphilis, and other diseases. Delusions of poverty are also common, and he may feel that he is headed for the poorhouse, that nobody wants him, and that he is a senseless burden on his children and just generally "in the way." In some cases, the patient becomes self-accusatory and develops delusions of great sin. In many respects the symptoms resemble those in involutional reactions, and as in other psychotic depressions the possibility of suicide must be guarded against. This type constitutes less than 10 per cent of senile reactions.

In general, the deterioration in senile dementia can be expected to continue its downward course over a period of months or years. Eventually, the patient becomes severely deteriorated, oblivious of his surroundings, bedridden, and reduced to a vegetative existence. Resistance to disease is lowered, and death usually results from pneumonia or some other infection.

ARTERIOSCLEROTIC BRAIN DISEASE

Psychoses with cerebral arteriosclerosis are similar to senile psychoses, but there are certain differences in both anatomical and behavioral symptoms. The vascular pathology in cerebral arteriosclerosis involves a "hardening" of the arteries of the brain.[1] Large patches of fatty and calcified material known as *senile plaques* accumulate at particular points in the inside layers of the blood vessels and gradually close down the arterial channel. Circulation becomes sluggish or may be blocked altogether by (a) the accumulation of deposits; (b) *cerebral thrombosis,* in which a blood clot forms at a site where fatty and calcified materials have accumulated and blocks the vessel; or (c) an *embolism,* in which a fragment of hardened material is sloughed off the inside wall of the vessel and carried to a narrow spot where it blocks the flow of blood. There may then be a rupture in the blood vessel, with hemorrhage and intracranial bleeding.

Either blockage or rupture with hemorrhage may occur in large or small blood vessels anywhere in the brain. Of course, damage to a large vessel will do more harm than damage to a small one. When the narrowing or eventual blockage is gradual and involves small blood vessels, cerebral nutrition is impaired and there are areas of softening as the brain tissue degenerates. Such areas of softening are found in some 90 per cent of patients suffering from arteriosclerotic brain disease (Rothschild, 1956; Yalom, 1960).

Frequently, there is a sudden blockage or rupture in a small blood vessel, resulting in various transient physical and mental symptoms referred to as a *small stroke.* A series of such small strokes may lead to cumulative brain damage.

When the blockage or rupture involves a large vessel, the individual suffers a major stroke (*cerebral vascular accident—CVA*). Here there is both focal and generalized impairment of brain function, resulting in coma or an acute confu-

---

[1]Cerebral arteriosclerosis, as used here, includes *atherosclerosis,* a disease primarily of the large arteries characterized by plaquelike intimal deposits (Dawber, 1962; Moses, 1963). Some investigators prefer to use specific terms such as *atherosclerosis, medial sclerosis,* and *arteriolar sclerosis* rather than the more general term *arteriosclerosis,* which includes all these conditions.

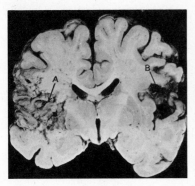 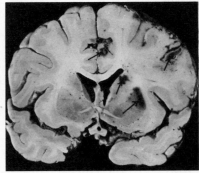 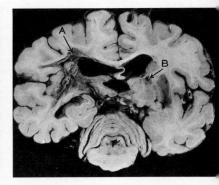

On the left, above, is a section through the frontal lobes of a patient who had suffered cerebral arterial thrombosis. The area marked by A shows a recent softening correlated with a recent stroke that had been followed by two months of paralysis on one side. The area marked by B correlated with a stroke 17 years earlier which had been associated with aphasia; here the softening has been transformed into a cavity. In the case illustrated in the center, scattered emboli had plugged up several arterial branches, leading to many tiny hemorrhages and widespread local damage. At the right is a section from the brain of a man who died at 43 after suffering from hypertension and two strokes that had resulted in some paralysis on both sides, emotional lability, and convulsions. His brain shows a severe degree of atherosclerosis.

sional state. If the patient survives, the acute symptoms may largely clear, but usually he suffers from some degree of residual brain damage.

It is estimated that about 2,000,000 persons in this country are handicapped or incapacitated by cerebral vascular disease (Marks, 1961; National Health Education Committee, 1960). The incidence of psychiatric complications in these cases is not known. However, psychoses associated with cerebral arteriosclerosis account for about 15 per cent of all first admissions to mental hospitals—ranking second only to schizophrenia in incidence. Although arteriosclerotic brain disease may occur in young adulthood or middle age, it usually has its onset after 55 years of age. The average age at first admission approximates 74 years for both sexes. There are slightly more male than female first admissions. Although cerebral arteriosclerosis appears to be most common among persons on lower socioeconomic levels, it occurs in all economic groups.

As in other chronic brain disorders, the symptoms in cerebral arteriosclerosis vary considerably depending on the nature and extent of the brain damage and the patient's premorbid personality and life situation. In general, patients suffering from arteriosclerotic brain disease do not show the profound physical and mental de-

terioration found in the senile patient. Frequently they have considerable insight into their condition, which serves to increase their worries.

In slightly over half of the cases of arteriosclerotic brain disease, the symptoms appear suddenly (Yalom, 1960). Here patients are usually admitted to a mental hospital in an acute confusional state resulting from a cerebral vascular accident.[1] Such patients show marked clouding of consciousness, disorientation for time, place, and person, incoherence, and often hemiplegia (paralysis of one side of the body). In a large series of cases having an acute onset, Rothschild (1956) reported such paralysis in about 50 per cent. Convulsive seizures are also relatively common and may precede the acute attack, occur at the same time, or appear at a later point in the illness. In severe cases the patient may die without a clearing of his confusional state, or there may be a total loss of consciousness ending in death.

Acute confusional states may last for days, weeks, or even months with an eventual remission of the acute symptoms. In these cases, there may be varying degrees of residual brain damage

[1] Each year more than a million people suffer strokes, many of them fatal (Campbell, 1963). Cerebral vascular accidents are the third major cause of death in the United States, ranking only behind heart disease and cancer.

and impairment in physical and mental functions. Often the patient is able to compensate for his brain damage, particularly with the help of special rehabilitative measures designed to alleviate physical handicaps and clear up possible aphasic conditions. Sometimes, however, there is a progressive loss of mental efficiency accompanied by other psychiatric symptoms, such as emotional lability, irritability, and hypochondriacal concern over bodily functions.[1]

Despite fluctuations and improvement in symptoms from time to time, the progression of the disease involves increasing personality deterioration. Additional strokes may leave the patient permanently paralyzed and bedridden. Death usually occurs from pneumonia, heart attack, or an extensive cerebral vascular accident within 3 to 5 years.

When the onset of the disorder is gradual, early symptoms may include complaints of weakness, fatigue, dizziness, headache, depression, memory defect, periods of confusion, and lowered efficiency in work. Often there is a slowing up of activity and a loss of zest in living. There may be a considerable delay between the appearance of such symptoms and the hospitalization of the patient.

By the time of hospitalization the clinical picture usually is similar to that in senile dementia. The memory defect has now increased although it may be somewhat uneven—for example, it may be more severe when the patient is tired or under emotional stress. Emotional lability becomes pronounced and the patient may be easily moved to tears or highly irritable, with a tendency to "flare up" at the slightest provocation. Usually the flare-up is brief and the patient ends with tears and repentance. Increased irritability may be accompanied by suspiciousness and poorly organized delusions of persecution. By this time, there is also a more pronounced impairment of concentration and general intellectual functioning. Interest in the outside world and in others is markedly reduced as are the individual's initiative and work capacity. Judgment is impaired and in some instances there is a lowering of moral controls, with a tendency to sexual offenses involving children. Frequently, there are feelings of depression associated with some insight into failing physical and mental powers. As in cases with an acute

onset, there may be marked fluctuations in the clinical picture, but the general course of the disease is in the direction of increasing deterioration and eventual death.

Clinical aspects of senile and cerebral arteriosclerotic psychotic reactions are so much alike that a differential diagnosis is frequently very difficult to make. In some cases, there is a mixture of the two disorders—a senile reaction may be superimposed upon an arteriosclerotic condition or vice versa. However, mixed reactions are not nearly so common as might be expected, and usually one condition or the other predominates (Ferraro, 1959b; Rothschild, 1956).

Among the clinically distinguishing features of these two disorders are the following: (a) senile psychoses are usually gradual and progressive and last longer, while cerebral arteriosclerosis reactions are more apt to be ushered in by a cerebral vascular accident and to run a brief and stormy course ending in death; (b) in senile dementia there is usually more pronounced intellectual impairment and paranoid patterns are more common; (c) symptoms common in the arteriosclerotic group but less often seen in senile dementia are headaches, dizziness, convulsive seizures, depression, and strong emotional outbursts; and finally (d) the symptoms in cerebral arteriosclerotic reactions typically show more pronounced fluctuations. But although these differences are observable in early and intermediate stages, all patients become very much alike with progressive intellectual deterioration.

DYNAMICS IN OLD-AGE PSYCHOSES

Early psychiatrists, in accord with the trend of the times, seized upon the obvious damage to the brain as the only factor of importance in the causation of both senile and cerebral arteriosclerotic reactions. But with the increased interest and attention devoted in recent years to the mental disorders in old age, these early beliefs

---

[1] In small strokes there may be other transient symptoms, such as acute indigestion, burning and bad taste in the mouth, changes in handwriting, and unsteadiness in gait. Although a small stroke may lead to a more serious one, many patients experience a series of small strokes, resulting in gradual personality changes and mental deterioration (Travis, 1961; Yalom, 1960).

have undergone considerable revision. Although cerebral damage alone, when sufficiently extensive, may produce marked mental symptoms, it has become evident that in most cases the anatomic changes are only one set of interactive factors in a total picture in which the personality organization of the individual and the stresses in his life situation are also of key importance. And since specific brain pathology, personality makeup, and stress factors vary from patient to patient, we find a somewhat different etiological pattern in each case.

Biological factors. In any psychotic disorder there is always a search for possible hereditary and constitutional predisposing factors. A number of early studies have shown a high incidence of senile and arteriosclerotic brain disease, as well as other types of psychopathology, in the family backgrounds of these patients (Mayer-Gross, 1944; Post, 1944). Such findings have led some investigators to attribute the group of old-age psychoses to a single dominant genetic factor, while other investigators, taking a more cautious approach, have suggested that two genetic factors are involved, one controlling aging and the other producing the pathology.

In a comprehensive review of available findings—including his own extensive study on aging in twins—Kallmann (1961) has concluded that it is unrealistic to search for a dominant genetic factor as the primary cause of the psychoses of old age. He has suggested that the primary causative agent is a longstanding deficit in adjustive plasticity complicated by vascular and metabolic changes in the brain. This, of course, does not exclude the influence of genetic factors on the rapidity of physiological aging.

A number of investigators have emphasized the effects of senile and arteriosclerotic degenerative changes on brain metabolism. In cases involving cerebral vascular accidents, gross disturbances in circulatory and metabolic processes are apparent, and we have noted the confusional states and other symptoms that may result. However, in mental disorders having a gradual onset, much remains to be learned about the role of metabolic factors. At one time, lowered oxygen consumption, presumably resulting from circulatory deficiency, received considerable attention. But Himwich (1962) has pointed out that although the oxygen consumption of the brain does decrease with age, this is not caused ordinarily by limitation of the blood supply to the brain but rather by a reduction in brain size resulting from the atrophy and diminution of neurons—a condition characteristic of aging in general but exaggerated in senile dementia. It has also been pointed out that many patients suffering from cerebral arteriosclerosis suffer concomitant arteriosclerosis of the coronary arteries, which may further impair cerebral circulation (Marks, 1961; Slaney and Ashton, 1962). But although serious disturbances in brain metabolism and functioning do occur when there is a critical restriction of cerebral blood flow, arterial disease of this magnitude is not commonly found on post-mortem examination of elderly patients suffering from old-age psychoses (Riggs and Wahal, 1962).

Metabolic disturbances associated with nutritional and endocrine deficiencies have also come under scrutiny. In a few cases, deficiency in vitamin B_{12} appears to lead to confusional states and other symptoms commonly found in senile dementia (Droller and Dossett, 1959). Usually the clinical condition of these patients clears dramatically with vitamin therapy. Setel (1959) found protein depletion and negative nitrogen balance in 32 geriatric patients (aged 62-89) who were studied for 8 to 10 months. These deficiencies were mild to moderate in degree, however, and would not appear to be crucial factors in mental illness. It is true, of course, that the stress situation of the older person may lead to depression and reduced food intake, resulting in vitamin and other nutritional deficiencies which lessen his overall adjustive resources.

Malfunction of the endocrine glands has been held suspect in old-age psychoses, but metabolic disturbances due to hormone deficiencies are apparently rare (American Geriatric Society Panel Discussion, 1962). However, Shipley (1962) has pointed out that many women suffer estrogen deficiency after the menopause; he has recommended long-term replacement therapy.

Although the exact effects of arteriosclerotic and senile brain degeneration on brain metabolism and behavior need further clarification, recent research advances have delineated certain factors contributing to the arteriosclerotic condition itself. Hypertension, psychological stress, and a diet high in saturated fat appear to be crucial factors—particularly when occurring in combination with each other (Dawber and Kannel, 1962; Groom, 1961; Moses, 1963; Stamler, 1962).[1] Here it is interesting to note that occupational stress was the single most important factor distinguishing a group of 100 younger patients suffering from coronary heart disease from a normal control group (Russek and Zohman, 1958). However, the stress situation *per se* may not be so crucial as the way the individual perceives and reacts to it. In a large-scale clinical study of executive and nonexecutive personnel followed over a 5-year period, no increase in the incidence of hypertensive or arteriosclerotic disease was observed in the executive group—presumably indicating that most executives learn to handle occupational stresses effectively (Lee and Schneider, 1958).

From all the available evidence, we can conclude that in the great majority of older patients there is little correlation between the degree of dementia and either EEG abnormality or the extent of brain pathology (Gal, 1959; Turton and Warren, 1960). The same damage which is associated with a psychosis in one patient may yield no psychotic symptoms in another; some patients with only mild mental symptoms reveal extensive cerebral damage while others with minimal cerebral damage show severe psychopathology. Again it is apparent that changes in psychological symptoms do not necessarily parallel neuroanatomic alterations, and that we must view the organism in a broader perspective. As Arnhoff (1961) has pointed out, it is an oversimplification to view man as a machine in which the wearing out of components results in specific psychological deficiencies.

With progressive cerebral impairment, of course, the role of personality factors recedes as a determinant of behavior and the residual brain capacity shapes the response in greater measure. This point is well brought out by Ullman and Gruen in summarizing their findings with 84 patients who had suffered strokes and showed mild, moderate, or severe degrees of cerebral deficit.

"Patients who have experienced mild strokes with little or no residual mental impairment react to the stress in their own idiosyncratic fashion. Some will integrate the experience successfully; others will become enmeshed in psychopathological maneuvers of varying

severity. In patients with moderate or severe brain damage, the situation is quite different. Here the unique features of the stroke are highlighted, the chief of these being that the very organ governing the adaptation to stress is itself impaired. The resulting clinical picture has to be evaluated now, not only in terms of what the experience means to the patient, but also in terms of the capacity the patient has for evaluating the situation." (1961, p. 1009)

Psychological factors. It has been said that next to dying, our recognition that we are aging may be the most profound shock we experience in our lifetime. Every day in the United States more than 3,000 persons cross the invisible barrier of age 65 and by custom and law are "benched" for the remainder of the game. They are "older persons" or "senior citizens." How these individuals react to their changed status and to the difficult stresses of this age period depends heavily on their personality make-up as well as on the challenges and frustrations of their life situation. As important as actual brain changes are, the psychoses of old age depend heavily—and often primarily—upon psychological factors.

1. *The role of the pre-psychotic personality.* Several studies have shown that individuals who are handicapped psychologically by undesirable personality traits are especially vulnerable to psychoses in old age. Obsessional trends, rigidity of outlook, obstinacy, compulsiveness, eccentricity, narrowness of interests, seclusiveness, suspiciousness, social inadequacy, and poor adaptability are some of the traits that have been emphasized in the background of such patients (Leake, 1962; Post, 1944; Rothschild, 1956; Sheps, 1960; Wagner, 1944). Even negative attitudes toward growing old can be serious adjustment handicaps.

In an interesting attempt to delineate personality characteristics relating to normal and pathological aging, Riesman (1954) has described three personality types:

a) The *autonomous,* who seem to bear within themselves the psychological sources of self-renewal; here there are an aliveness of spirit, a dedication to an idea, and continuing productiv-

[1]Fishbein (1962) pointed out that present research findings are based upon limited samples and that it is difficult to assess the significance of a given factor since combinations of factors are both characteristic and more predictive.

ity which tend to act as preservatives against physiological aging and changes in their stress situation.

b) The *adjusted,* who are basically rigid and lacking in adaptability but are kept going by their power and prestige or by a routine environment which is protective and well structured in relation to their needs. If their life situation changes drastically, they become psychiatric casualties.

c) The *anomic,* who do not have either clear inner values and resources to help them or the protection of a supportive life situation. These individuals deteriorate very rapidly. Riesman calls them the prematurely weary and resigned. Although Riesman's classification appears to be an oversimplification, it does serve to emphasize the influence of previous personality traits and modes of adaptation on an individual's adjustment to the stresses of old age.

2. *The special stresses of old age.* An older person faces numerous very real fears and insecurities that have not plagued him in his more hale and hearty earlier years. In fact, the unfavorable environmental circumstances of older people are often more hazardous to mental health than are organic brain changes. Even well-integrated personalities may break down under the combined assault of the cerebral changes and severe situational stress.

a) Retirement and reduced income. Retirement is often the brand that marks a man as a member of the "old age" group. It can be quite demoralizing if it is forced upon him. Repeated studies have shown that most persons of 65 are productive workers and that many would prefer to keep on working when they reach retirement age (AMA Committee on Aging, 1960).

Most men depend heavily upon their work for status, for self-identity, for satisfying interpersonal relationships, and for meaning in their lives (Goodstein, 1962). Retirement ordinarily does not meet these needs, and there is often a tendency to react with the feeling that one's usefulness and worth are at an end and that one's life is really over—a reaction conducive to rapid physical and mental deterioration.

Retirement usually leads also to a marked reduction in income, which further augments the older person's adjustive burden. In 1960, three out of five individuals over 65 had a total income

of less than $1000 per year; and about half of all older couples had an income of less than $2500 per year (U.S. Senate Subcommittee, 1960). Many older citizens drift to rented rooms or small apartments in run-down areas where there is a depressing skid-row atmosphere (U.S. Senate Subcommittee, 1960). Obviously such conditions are not conducive to mental health.

b) Fear of invalidism and death. The gradual physical deterioration of one's body and the increased possibility of falling prey to some chronic and debilitating disease lead to increased preoccupation with bodily functions and worry over failing health—symptoms characteristic of older people. Such concern is likely to be aggravated when the individual has a history of medical difficulties which are likely to be aggravated by the aging process. Whereas a young person usually expects to make a complete recovery from sickness, many illnesses among older people become chronic and the individual has to adjust to living with them. When chronic illness and failing health lead to invalidism and dependence on others, the individual faces a difficult situation.

In a study of 534 patients (aged 60 and over) admitted for the first time to the psychiatric ward of a general hospital in San Francisco, a strikingly high incidence of serious physical disease was found: 70 per cent required daily care just for physical disability, and in more than 40 per cent of the cases, serious mental symptoms had been precipitated by acute physiological disorders (Bowman and Engle, 1960).

The discovery that one has a disease is often traumatic. Even a mild stroke may be a frightening experience, as illustrated in the following statement by a patient.

"When I got dressed I knew something was funny—I could not get my hand in my sleeve. As I got out of the cab I fell and acted as though drunk. I noticed my speech was wrong, I knew I had a stroke. I was frightened." (Ullman and Gruen, 1961, p. 1006)

Knowledge that one has had a severe stroke or heart attack is likely to give rise to many fears and apprehensions.

With aging and physical deterioration, the individual is confronted with the inescapable fact of his own impending death. Some older people react with equanimity, often stemming from deep religious faith in the meaningfulness of man's existence and in the certainty of a life hereafter. Others die as they have lived, with little concern for life or human existence. In fact, they may welcome death as a solution to unsolvable problems and a meaningless life. This is sometimes true also of older people who have lost their friends and loved ones and feel that they have "outlived their time." However, for many people the realization that their life is drawing to a close is a highly stressful experience for which they have no adequate ego defenses (Cappon, 1959).

c)   Isolation and loneliness. As the individual grows older, he is faced with the inevitable loss of loved ones, friends, and contemporaries. The death of one's mate, with whom he may have shared many years of close companionship, is often a particularly difficult adjustment problem. This is especially true for women, who tend to outlive their spouses by some 7 years (Bowman and Engle, 1962). Other factors, too, may contribute to social isolation. Children grow up, marry, and move away; impairment of vision or hearing and various chronic ailments may make social interaction more difficult; attitudes of self-pity and an inward centering of interests may alienate family and friends alike. In many instances, the older person also becomes increasingly rigid and intolerant in his outlook and is unable to make effective use of the opportunities for meaningful social interaction that still remain to him.

As Busse (1960) has pointed out, however, isolation and loneliness are not just matters of inability to interact with loved ones or to make new friends. In a larger view, they involve the inability to work productively and to feel oneself a vital and essential part of the human enterprise. In essence, the forces of isolation progressively destroy the older person's linkages with his world, reducing the meaningfulness of his existence and increasingly forcing him back into himself.

This viewpoint is well illustrated by the case of a 79-year-old professional man who was admitted to a mental hospital for treatment as a result of a severe state of anxiety, depression, and indecision. The rather unusual course of this case follows.

The patient's disorder was apparently precipitated by his retirement from the firm for which he had worked for over 40 years. In the course of his hospitalization, the patient evidenced little improvement until the hospital received a letter from his firm inquiring about his condition. They were experiencing difficulty without him and needed his help. Upon receipt of the news the patient showed marked improvement. He was given a leave of absence and returned to his old job. A follow-up study a year later revealed that he was handling his responsibilities with unimpaired judgment, appeared younger, showed good stamina, and reported regularly to work at the age of 80.

d)   Reduction in sexual functions and physical attractiveness. The findings of Kinsey *et al.* (1948) indicate that there is a gradual decrease in sexual activities with increasing age rather than any abrupt cessation, and that many people maintain reasonably satisfactory patterns of sexual gratification into extreme old age. In a more recent study of 74 men, mostly college graduates, with an average age of 71, Freeman (1961) reported that 25 per cent had been impotent by age 60 and that most of the others reported a sharp drop in sex activity at age 65. However, 86 per cent of the total of 74 men called their lifetime sex experience excellent or good. Although there would appear to be marked individual differences in the way individuals react to a loss or reduction in sexual functions, many older people are concerned about the termination of one of their main sources of physical and emotional satisfaction. In many cases, increasing preoccupation with eating, sleeping, defecation, and other bodily functions apparently represents in part a compensatory source of pleasure for the diminution or loss of sexual gratification.

The aging person also has to adjust to his decreasing physical attractiveness on both a sexual and a general level. This is often a particularly difficult adjustment for persons whose feelings of femininity or masculinity are closely tied up with their physical attractiveness to members of the opposite sex. In a culture as conscious of age and beauty as ours, the progressive loss of physical attractiveness in old age requires changes in one's body image and self-concept which are difficult for most of us to make.

e)   Forces tending to self-devaluation. As

we have noted, there are many forces tending to self-devaluation with increasing age—forced retirement and lowered income, feelings that one's usefulness and worth are greatly diminished, awareness of one's progressive decline in physical ability and attractiveness, and constant reminders of our society's emphasis on youth. Often the experience of the older generation has little relevance to the problems of their children, and the older person is deprived of active participation and decision making in both occupational and family settings. Not infrequently, children assume a patronizing and protective attitude toward the aging parent and in other ways tend to deprive him of dignity, responsibility, and a feeling of importance in the scheme of things. Many parents are treated as unwanted burdens, and their children may secretly wish that they would die to relieve them of financial and other responsibilities.

It is thus not surprising that many of our senior citizens are inadvertently pushed into the role of simply "being an old person" with all this implies in terms of self-devaluation and self-deterioration (Bloom, 1961). As Combs and Snygg (1959) have pointed out:

"Some elderly people seem limited by their perceptions of self. Seeing themselves as unable, unacceptable, or useless, they behave as though they were, though they may be enjoying perfectly good health." (p. 217)

In such instances, there are strong tendencies for the individual to turn inward, to reduce his involvement in the world around him, and to reminisce about and live increasingly in the past. Often his own lack of attention and interest helps to account for his poor memory for recent events, and if he feels he is unwanted, it is a short step to becoming irritable and suspicious of others' motives and feelings. If, finally, he looks back on his life as full of failures and mistakes or feels unable to carry through on needed work before he dies, it can readily be seen how feelings of hopelessness, apathy, and depression may develop.

Sociological factors. The significance of sociocultural factors in senile and arteriosclerotic brain disease is a matter of considerable speculation. In a pioneering study, Carothers (1947) found a high rate of senile psychoses among Kenya Africans but no psychoses with cerebral arteriosclerosis, possibly because their culture was relatively free from the tensions conducive to high blood pressure. Other cross-cultural studies show varying rates of senile and arteriosclerotic brain disease, probably influenced in part by differences in diagnostic procedures.

Within our own society, statistics indicate that for both senile dementia and arteriosclerotic brain disease the urban rate of first admissions to mental hospitals is approximately twice as high as the rural rate. But we do not know how far this indicates that urban living, with its faster pace, noise, crowds, and excitement, is more conducive to the development of these disorders and how far it simply means that more patients are cared for at home in rural areas. The picture is also complicated by the factor that in rural areas the older person enjoys higher social status, is able to work productively for a longer period, and is subjected to fewer stresses for which he is poorly prepared.

In our great urban centers the problem of old age has caught us largely unprepared. We have not provided in our society ample conditions for utilizing the experience and wisdom of our older people or even conditions necessary for them to continue their life span in reasonably respected and useful positions. As we have noted, old age does not bring increasing respect in our culture, as it does in some, but usually quite the opposite. In fact, Williams and Jaco (1958) have used the concept of "role obsolescence" to refer to society's attitude that the older person has outlived his mode of usefulness to the group.

Even the individual's self-acceptance tends to diminish during the period between 50 and 59 years of age (Bloom, 1961). This is probably in part a reflection of the negative stereotype of old age which the individual tends to share with the rest of society, and in part the result of growing doubts and anxieties about his actual adequacy and security. Most companies refuse to hire people over 45; should anything happen to his present position, the chances of his finding satisfactory employment would be minimal. Also he is rapidly approaching the period of enforced retirement and lowered income. All in all, he finds himself facing many severe new stresses during a life period when his adjustive resources and reserves are reduced.

THERAPY, PROGNOSIS, AND PREVENTION

Whether or not to hospitalize the aged mentally ill patient is often a problem. Particularly is this true in mild conditions where the patient may be able to attend an outpatient clinic and remain in his own home. Many authorities regard hospitalization as a last resource, feeling that the sudden change in environment and manner of living is too hard on the older patient and may lead to a feeling of hopelessness and complete letdown.

On the other hand, patients manifesting such symptoms as confusion, violent and noisy behavior, depression, antisocial behavior, and disorientation for time, place, and person usually require hospitalization. This is often true also for patients who have a tendency to roam and get lost or who present serious nursing problems, such as extremely untidy elimination habits or unwillingness to eat. Frequently, the final decision is not only a medical one but also is based upon the lack of adequate facilities in the home. In any event, there seems to be a growing tendency to send aged patients to nursing homes and mental hospitals.

At the present time, therapy for the older patient leaves much to be desired. This inadequacy results partly from a lack of facilities and trained personnel, partly from the fact that adequate care is expensive, and partly from a lack of understanding concerning the mental disorders of later life. Most investigators now take the position that impairment of mental or physiological functioning or both requires a comprehensive program, including medical, psychiatric, and sociological treatment as indicated by the needs of the given patient (Kahn *et al.,* 1960).

Medical treatment ranges from surgical and other specialized medical procedures to dietary and related measures designed to improve the physical health of the patient. Tranquilizing drugs have proved of marked value in controlling emotional disturbances in aged patients regardless of whether these are mainly functional or organic (Bowman and Engle, 1962; Hoch and Zubin, 1961). These drugs are not effective, however, in ameliorating the mental deterioration found in advanced cases of senile and arteriosclerotic brain disease. For patients suffering from the residual effects of strokes—such as paralysis and aphasia—specialized physical, physiological, and educational retraining procedures are utilized.

Much remains to be learned about the value of various psychotherapeutic procedures with the aged. Psychoanalysis is almost never used with aged patients; on the whole they have been regarded as being too rigid and deeply structured in their personality make-up to be subject to change. Freud himself did not believe that older people could be psychoanalyzed successfully.

It cannot be denied that the aging organism has a diminished capacity to repair itself, and with brain damage there is further reduced adaptability. Nevertheless, psychotherapy is being used increasingly with geriatric patients, particularly supportive individual therapy and group therapy. Rosenthal (1959) has reported successful results with 30 older patients who were, in the main, treated like younger patients. Similarly, Butler (1960) has reported favorable preliminary results with intensive psychotherapy over a 9-month period with 12 patients aged 75 to 95. A number of more recent studies have supported these findings (Bowman, 1962; Straker, 1963) and definitely indicate the need for additional research to delineate the limitations and values of individual and group psychotherapy with older patients.

Sociotherapy with these geriatric patients is directed toward creating an environment in which the older patient can function successfully. In a hospital setting or nursing home this includes the provision of comfortable surroundings and stimulating, worth-while activities which encourage the older patient to utilize the capacities which remain to him. The psychiatric social worker also works with the family in an attempt to help them understand the nature of the patient's illness and be supportive in showing that they care. Where the patient is convalescing at home, follow-up visits by the psychiatric social worker may be of great value in helping both the patient and the family to adjust.

Brain damage in aged patients often leads to an inability to deal adequately with new stimuli and to feelings of strangeness toward and fear of their environment (Sheps, 1958). As a consequence, many older patients strive to limit their environment in such a way that they can cope with it; often, too, they tend to alter their perceptions of the environment to make it seem more familiar and hence manageable (Sheps, 1958; Weinstein and Kahn, 1959). Thus the provision of an environment to which the aged person can adjust without grossly exaggerated defensive measures can be of great therapeutic value.

A number of investigators have suggested the need for studying the effects of intensive treatment in the earliest stages of the disorder—particularly in cases having a gradual onset. In one study, half of a group of patients given intensive treatment recovered sufficiently to leave the hospital later as compared with less than 10 per cent of a control group given the usual geriatric treatment (Sklar and O'Neill, 1961). Unfortunately, most patients come to mental hospitals in relatively advanced states without having had even a minimal amount of psychiatric assistance.

The prognosis in cases of senile and arteriosclerotic psychoses is not favorable, for the cerebral damage and other clinical symptoms seem to be irreversible, once the psychosis is well under way. About three quarters of patients hospitalized for old-age psychoses die within the first five years (Malzberg, 1958). As already indicated, however, the prognosis is not completely hopeless, and even without a complete recovery, many patients can be returned to their homes in a more manageable state (Manson and Engquist, 1962).

Interestingly enough, both the greatest number of deaths and the greatest number of improvements occur during the first year after admission. Apparently, if the patient fails to show rather immediate improvement, there is little expectation that he will improve later on.

Although the prognosis varies greatly among older patients with chronic brain disorders, the following factors would appear favorable in import on first admission: (a) well-integrated premorbid personality, (b) limited rather than severe mental deterioration, (c) mild rather than severe cerebral vascular accidents, (d) cerebral thrombosis rather than cerebral hemorrhage, (e) freedom from (or mild rather than severe) overweight or hypertension, (f) average or better intelligence, (g) superior education and technical competence, and (h) a favorable life situation to which to return.[1] As might be expected,

fewer patients in the age group over 75 years are released from mental hospitals than in the 65 to 74 age group (Pollack, 1961). As in other mental disorders, an integrated medical, psychological, and sociological treatment program is essential for maximal results and the early detection and treatment of pathological trends—organic and psychological—are of vital importance.

In 1921, Dr. Lillian J. Martin (1851-1943), at the age of 70, made a historic contribution to the theory and practice of preventing mental disorders in old age by establishing an old-age clinic in San Francisco (Lawton, 1942). She saw the need for making the day-to-day living of older people more stimulating in order to combat their tendency to reverie and mental deterioration. In her clinic each client was inducted into some kind of group activity. The chief groups were educational, social, economic, political, religious, and aesthetic.

Since this pioneering effort, many clinics and guidance centers have been established where older people are helped to understand their problems, accept and use their decreased abilities, and improve social relations with their contemporaries—thus bolstering feelings of worth and usefulness in a world which is thrusting them aside. By developing new interests, making new friends, and filling their time with constructive, companionable activities, older people are helped to satisfy basic needs that are just as real at 70 as at 7. For older persons who need psychiatric assistance but do not require hospitalization, out-patient psychiatric facilities have been established in most major urban centers.

During the past decade society has become increasingly aware of the problems confronting its senior citizens. Federal, state, and local groups are focusing attention on all aspects of the aging problem.[2] The National Institute of Mental Health, for example, maintains a laboratory of clinical science for appraising the physiological, psychological, and sociological characteristics of elderly symptom-free men (Leake,

---

[1] These criteria are based largely on Bowman (1961), Kahn *et al.* (1961), Marks (1961), Parsons (1960).

[2] See, for example, reports of White House Conference on Aging (1961), U.S. Senate Subcommittee on Problems of the Aged and Aging (1960), American Medical Association Committee on Aging (1960), and American Psychopathological Association (1961).

1962). Other scientists in medicine, psychology, and sociology are investigating the pathological as well as normal aspects of aging. In communities, centers and clinics for assisting older people with retirement and other problems are increasing in number as are facilities for the inpatient care of those who are physically or mentally ill. Specially designed housing developments for the elderly are springing up in many areas, although it is too early to assess the impact such facilities will have on mental illness.

Among the favorable results of this increased attention to the problems of aging has been a gradual change in attitude toward our older people, a realization that people over 65 make up a great reservoir of experience, ability, and skill which society needs to utilize to a much greater extent, and a conviction that society should create conditions which enable the older person to live out his life with some measure of dignity, hope, and feeling of involvement in the human enterprise.[1]

But although society can do much to improve the status of the older person, the individual also needs to prepare himself for the problems typical of old age. He needs to face realistically the fact that he *is* getting older and plan ahead for an active and useful life in his later years— a life that will take full advantage of the opportunities that are afforded to him. Of course, many of the adjustments of old age are highly specific to the life situation of the given individual and hence cannot be fully anticipated, but at any age it is important to maintain mental flexibility and adaptability, establish new and satisfying interpersonal relationships, and continue to grow and fulfill one's potential. Fortunately, tendencies toward integration and growth continue into the old age period. Parsons (1960) concluded from his studies at the New England Age Center that "If basic needs are met, older people continue to try to do what seems 'worth-while.' " In short, old age is by no means incompatible with a meaningful and fulfilling mode of life.

---

[1]For further reading on the problems and opportunities of later maturity, see Birren (1962), Tibbitts (1962), and Burgess (1962).

REFERENCES

The reference list includes not only the sources from which the author has drawn material, but acknowledgments of the permissions granted by authors and publishers to quote directly from their works.

AGUILAR, MARY J. Chronic viral encephalitis as a pathogenetic factor in epilepsy. *Amer. J. med. Sci.*, 1959, 238, 354-362.

AITA, J. A., & REITAN, R. M. Psychotic reactions in the late recovery period following brain injury. *Amer. J. Psychiat.*, 1948, 105, 161-169.

American Geriatric Society. Endocrine regulatory mechanisms as people age (panel discussion). *J. Amer. Geriat. Soc.*, 1962, 10, 1-34.

American Medical Association. Committee on Aging. *Report on regional conferences on aging.* Chicago: Author, 1960.

American Psychopathological Association. Aging. In P. H. Hoch & J. Zubin (Eds.), *Psychopathology of aging.* New York: Grune & Stratton, 1961.

American Public Health Association. Committee on Child Health. Services for children with epilepsy. New York: Author, 1958.

ARNHOFF, F. N. Concepts of aging. In P. H. Hoch & J. Zubin (Eds.), *Psychopathology of aging.* New York: Grune & Stratton, 1961. Pp. 136-148.

AUERBACH, A., SCHEFLEN, A., REINHART, R., & SCHOLZ, CAROL. The psychophysiologic sequelae of head injuries. *Amer. J. Psychiat.*, 1960, 117, 499-505.

BAJPAI, P. C., DIKSHIT, S. K., SHARMA, J. C., & GUPTA, N. P. Acute epidemic encephalitis in children: a clinical study. *J. Indian med. Ass.*, 1960, 35, 1-13.

BANAY, R. S. Criminal genesis and the degrees of responsibility in epilepsies. *Amer. J. Psychiat.*, 1961, 117, 873-876.

BEAN, W. B., HODGES, R. E., & DAUM, K. Pantothenic acid deficiency induced in human subjects. *J. clin. Invest.*, 1955, 34, 1073-1084.

BEERMAN, H., NICHOLAS, L., SCHAMBERG, I. L., & GREENBERG, M. S. Syphilis. *Arch. int. Med.*, 1962, 109, 323-344.

BELLAMY, W. E., JR. Huntington's chorea. *N. C. med. J.*, 1961, 22, 409-412.

BENDER, LAURETTA. Genesis of hostility in children. *Amer. J. Psychiat.*, 1948, 105, 241-245.

BENDER, LAURETTA. The brain and child behavior. *Arch. gen. Psychiat.*, 1961, 4, 531.

BIGELOW, N., ROIZIN, L., & KAUFMAN, MAIRS A. Psychoses with Huntington's chorea. In S. Arieti (Ed.), *American handbook of psychiatry*, Vol. 2. New York: Basic Books, 1959. Pp. 1248-1259.

BIRREN, J. E. (Ed.) *Handbook of aging and the individual: psychological and biological aspects.* Chicago: Univer. Chicago Press, 1960.

BLACK, D. A. K., MC CANCE, R. A., & YOUNG, W. F. Study of dehydration by means of balance experiments. *J. Physiol.*, 1944, 102, 406-414.

BLATTNER, R. J. Photic seizures—television-induced. *J. Pediat.*, 1961, 58, 746-749.

BLOOM, K. L. Age and the self concept. *Amer. J. Psychiat.*, 1961, 118, 534-538.

BORN, W. Great artists who suffered from mental disorders. *Ciba Symposia*, 1946, 7, 223-233.

BOWMAN, K. M., & ENGLE, BERNICE. Geriatrics. *Amer. J. Psychiat.*, 1960, 116, 629-630.

BOWMAN, K. M., & ENGLE, BERNICE. Geriatrics. *Amer. J. Psychiat.*, 1962, 118, 621-623.

BRAUCHI, J. T., & WEST, L. J. Sleep deprivation. *J. Amer. med. Ass.*, 1959, 171, 11-14.

BRICKNER, R. M. *The intellectual functions of the frontal lobes.* New York: Macmillan, 1936.

BRILL, H. Postencephalitic psychiatric conditions. In S. Arieti (Ed.), *American handbook of psychiatry*, Vol. 2. New York: Basic Books, 1959. Pp. 1163-1174.

BROSIN, H. W. Psychiatric conditions following head injury. In S. Arieti (Ed.), *American handbook of psychiatry*, Vol. 2. New York: Basic Books, 1959. Pp. 1175-1202.

BROWN, W. J. Current status of syphilis in the United States. *Pub. Hlth. Rep.*, 1960, 75, 990-993.

BROWNING, T. B., ATKINS, R. W., & WEINER, H. Cerebral metabolic disturbances in hypothyroidism. *AMA Arch. int. Med.*, 1954, 93, 938.

BROŽEK, J., & GRANDE, F. Abnormalities of neural function in the presence of inadequate nutrition. In J. Field (Ed.), *Handbook of physiology; section 1, neurophysiology*, Vol. 3. Baltimore, Md.: Williams & Wilkins, 1960. Pp. 1891-1910.

BROŽEK, J., GUETZKOW, H., & KEYS, A. A study of personality of normal young men maintained on restricted intakes of vitamins of the B complex. *Psychosom. Med.*, 1946, 8, 98-109.

BRUETSCH, W. L. Neurosyphilitic conditions. In S. Arieti (Ed.), *American handbook of psychiatry*, Vol. 2. New York: Basic Books, 1959. Pp. 1003-1020.

BURGESS, E. W. *Aging in western societies.* Chicago: Univer. Chicago Press, 1960.

BURSTEN, B. Psychosis associated with thyrotoxicosis. *Arch. gen. Psychiat.*, 1961, 4, 267-273.

BUSSE, E. W. Mental disorders of the aging. In W. M. Johnson (Ed.), *The older patient.* New York: Harper, 1960. Pp. 513-542.

BUTLER, R. N. Intensive psychotherapy for the hospitalized aged. *Geriatrics*, 1960, 15, 644-653.

BYRD, R. E. *Alone.* New York: Putnam, 1938.

CAMPBELL, R. Circuits of the senses. *Life*, 1963, 54, 64-76.

CAPPON, D. The dying. *Psychiat. Quart.*, 1959, 33, 466-489.

CAROTHERS, J. C. A study of mental derangement in Africans, and an attempt to explain its peculiarities, more especially in relation to the African attitude to life. *J. ment. Sci.*, 1947, 93, 548-597. Reprinted by permission of G. W. T. H. Fleming, Editor-in-Chief.

CASTER, W. O. Addendum to J. Brožek article: some biochemical data. *Amer. J. clin. Nutrition*, 1957, 5, 119-120.

CHAPMAN, L. F., & WOLFF, H. G. The cerebral hemispheres and the highest integrative functions of man. *Arch. Neurol.*, 1959, 1, 357-424.

CHAUDRY, M. R., & POND, D. A. Mental deterioration in epileptic children. *J. Neurol. Neurosurg. Psychiat.*, 1961, 24, 213-219.

COHEN, G. J., & EHRENS, W. H. Chronic lead poisoning. *J. Pediat.*, 1959, 52, 271-284.

COHEN, S. The toxic psychoses and allied states. *Amer. J. Med.*, 1953, 15, 813-828.

COMBS, A. W., & SNYGG, D. *Individual behavior.* (rev. ed.) New York: Harper, 1959.

Committee on Child Health. American Public Health Association. *Services for children with epilepsy.* New York: Author, 1958.

CONSTABLE, K. Parkinson's disease; its challenge and outlook. *J. Amer. Med. wom. Ass.*, 1960, 15, 757-760.

CRITCHLEY, M. *Shipwreck-survivors; a medical study.* London: Churchill, 1943.

DAWBER, T. R., & KANNEL, W. B. Atherosclerosis and you: pathogenic implications from epidemiologic observations. *J. Amer. ger. Soc.*, 1962, 10, 805-821.

DOSHAY, L. J. Parkinson's disease. *J. Amer. med. Ass.*, 1960, 174, 1962-1965.

DROLLER, H., & DOSSETT, J. Vitamin B^{12} levels in senile dementia and confusional states. *Geriatrics*, 1959, 14, 367-373.

DUGGINS, VIRGINIA A. *Epilepsy, its causes, effects, and treatment.* Washington, D. C.: Epilepsy Found., Federal Ass. for Epilepsy, Inc., n. d.

EIGLER, J. O., WELLMAN, W. E., ROOKE, E. D., KEITH, H. M., & SVIEN, H. J. Bacterial meningitis—I. General review (294 cases). *Proceedings Staff Meeting Mayo Clin.*, 1961, 36, 357-365.

EISNER, V., PAULI, L. L., & LIVINGSTON, S. Hereditary aspects of epilepsy. *Bull. Johns Hopkins Hosp.*, 1959, 105, 245-271.

FAÇON, E., STERIADE, M., CORTEZ, P., & VOINESCO, S. Contributions anatomocliniques à l'étude de la chorée de Huntington. *Acta neurol. psychiat. belg.*, 1957, 57, 898-912.

FAIRWEATHER, D. S. Psychiatric aspects of the post-encephalitic syndrome. *J. ment. Sci.*, 1947, 92, 201-254.

FALK, R., PENROSE, L. S., & CLARK, E. A. The search for intellectual deterioration among epileptics. *Amer. J. ment. Def.*, 1945, 49, 469-471.

FERRARO, A. Presenile psychoses. In S. Arieti (Ed.), *American handbook of psychiatry*, Vol. 2. New York: Basic Books, 1959a. Pp. 1046-1077.

FETTERMAN, J. L. *Practical lessons in psychiatry.* Springfield, Ill.: Charles C. Thomas, 1949.

FIGARRA, B. J., & LIONELLA, J. Postoperative psychosis. *J. Int. Coll. Surgeons*, 1950, 14, 111.

FINE, R. B. The pharmacological treatment of epilepsy. *Scot. med. J.*, 1961, 6, 273-275.

FISHBEIN, M. Statistics and the epidemiology of arteriosclerosis. *Postgrad. Med.*, 1962, 31, 311-312.

FLEISCHL, H. Effect of massive doses of penicillin on aging patients with general paresis. *J. Amer. geriat. Soc.*, 1960, 8, 855-857.

FORSTER, F. M. Drugs most effective in the control of epilepsy. *Postgrad. Med.*, 1960, 27, 711-715.

FREEMAN, J. T. Sexual capacities in the aging male. *Geriatrics*, 1961, 16, 37-43.

FREUCHEN, P. *Arctic adventure.* New York: Rinehart, 1935.

FRIEDLANDER, W. J. Epilepsy. *Amer. J. Psychiat.*, 1962, 118, 623-627. Refers to Symposium on Basic Mechanisms of the Epileptic Discharge. *Epilepsia*, 1961, 2 (whole issue.)

FRIEDLANDER, W. J. Epilepsy. *Amer. J. Psychiat.*, 1963, 119, 654-659.

GAL, P. Mental symptoms in cases of tumor of temporal lobe. *Amer. J. Psychiat.*, 1958, 115, 157-160.

GAL, P. Mental disorders of advanced years. *Geriatrics*, 1959, 14, 224-228.

GERMAN, W. J. Initial symptomatology in brain tumors. *Conn. Med.*, 1959, 23, 636-637.

GIBSON, J. Mental effects of head injury. *Canad. Nurse*, 1959, 55, 118-119.

GIBSON, J. General paralysis. *Canad. Nurse*, 1960, 55, 118-119.

GIBSON, J. Emotions and the thyroid gland: A critical appraisal. *J. psychosom. Res.*, 1962, 6, 93-116.

GILBERT, G. J., & GLASER, G. H. Neurologic manifestations of chronic carbon monoxide poisoning. *N. E. J. Med.*, 1959, 261, 1217-1220.

GILLINGHAM, F. J. Parkinsonism. *J. chron. Dis.*, 1961, 13, 215-220.

GIMLETTE, T. M. The muscular lesion in hyperthyroidism. *Brit. med. J.*, 1959, 2, 1143-1146.

GOLDFARB, A. I. Prevalence of psychiatric disorders in metropolitan old age and nursing homes. *J. Amer. geriat. Soc.*, 1962, 10, 77-84.

GOODSTEIN, K. *After effects of bain injuries in war.* New York: Grune and Stratton, 1942.

GREGORY, I. Genetic factors in schizophrenia. *Amer. J. Psychiat.*, 1960, 116, 961-972.

GROOM, D. Population studies of atherosclerosis. *Ann. int. Med.*, 1961, 55, 51-62.

GUERRANT, J., et al. *Personality in epilepsy.* Springfield, Ill.: Charles C. Thomas, 1962.

GULLER, BARBARA. *Schweizer Arch. Neurol. Neurochirurg. Psychiat.*, 1960, 86, 218.

GUNTHER, J. *Death be not proud.* New York: Harper, 1949.

HAHN, R. D., et al. The results of treatment in 1,086 general paralytics the majority of whom were followed for more than five years. *J. chron. Dis.*, 1958, 7, 209-227.

HAHN, R. D., WEBSTER, B., WEICKHARDT, G., THOMAS, E., TIMBERLAKE, W., SOLOMON, H., STOKES, J. H., MOORE, J. E., HEYMAN, A., GAMMON, G., GLEESON, G. A., CURTIS, A. C., & CUTLER, J. C. Penicillin treatment of general paresis (dementia paralytica). *AMA Arch. Neurol. Psychiat.*, 1959, 81, 557-590.

HARLOW, J. M. Recovery from the passage of an iron bar through the head. *Publ. Mass. med. Soc.*, 1868, 2, 327.

HENDERSON, D. K. *Textbook of pyschiatry for students and practitioners.* (9th ed.) London: Oxford Univer. Press, 1962.

HENDERSON, D., & BATCHELOR, I. R. C. *Textbook of psychiatry.* London: Oxford Univer. Press, 1962.

HILL, D. The clinical and electroencephalographic diagnosis of temporal-lobe epilepsy. *Scot. med. J.*, 1961, 6, 258-263.

HIMLER, L. E., & RAPHAEL, T. A follow-up study on 95 college students with epilepsy, Ann Arbor, Michigan. *Amer. J. Psychiat.*, 1945, 101, 760-763.

HIMWICH, H. E. Research in medical aspects of aging. *Geriatrics*, 1962, 17, 89-97.

HOCH, P. H., & KNIGHT, R. P. *Epilepsy.* New York: Grune & Stratton, 1947.

HOCH, P. H., & ZUBIN, J. (Eds.) *Psychopathology of aging.* (Proceedings of 51st annual meeting of the American Psychopathological Association, Feb. 1961) New York: Grune & Stratton, 1961.

HOLLE, H. A. The basic challenge today: a realistic attitude toward aging. In American Medical Association Committee on Aging, *Report on regional conferences on aging.* Chicago: American Medical Association, 1960.

HOLOWACH, JEAN., RENDA, Y. A., & WAPNER, I. Psychomotor seizures in childhood. *J. Pediatrics*, 1961, 59, 339-346.

JARVIE, H. Problem-solving deficits following wounds of the brain. *J. ment. Sci.*, 1960, 106, 1377-1382.

JERVIS, G. A. The mental deficiencies. In S. Arieti (Ed.), *American handbook of psychiatry*, Vol. 2. New York: Basic Books, 1959. Pp. 1289-1316.

JOHNSON, EVA M. A study of psychological findings of one hundred children recovering from purulent meningitis. *J. clin. Psychol.*, 1960, 16, 55-58.

JOYNT, R. J., GREEN, D., & GREEN, RENÉE. Musicogenic epilepsy. *J. Amer. med. Ass.*, 1962, 179, 501-504.

JUUL-JENSEN, P. Vocational training of epileptics. *Epilepsia*, 1961, 2, 197-206.

JUVENAL. *Satires.* G. G. Ramsay (tr.) Cambridge, Mass.: Harvard Univer. Press, n. d.

KAHN, R. L., GOLDFARB, A. I., POLLACK, M., & GERBER, I. E. The relationship of mental and physical status in institutionalized aged persons. *Amer. J. Psychiat.*, 1960, 117, 120-124.

KAHN, R. L., POLLACK, M., & GOLDFARB, A. Factors related to individual differences in mental status of institutionalized aged. In P. H. Hoch, & J. Zubin (Eds.), *Psychopathology of aging.* New York: Grune & Stratton, 1961. Pp. 104-113.

KALLMANN, F. J. Genetic factors in aging: comparative and longitudinal observations on a senescent twin population. In P. H. Hoch & J. Zubin (Eds.), *Psychopathology of aging.* New York: Grune & Stratton, 1961. Pp. 227-247.

KEIP, J. C., et al. The epileptic automobile driver in Ohio. *Ohio med. J.*, 1961, 57, 1127-1131.

KEMBLE, J. *Idols and invalids.* New York: Doubleday, 1936.

KEYS, A., BROŽEK, J., HENSCHEL, A., MICKELSON, O., & TAYLOR, H. L. *The biology of human starvation.* Minneapolis: Univer. Minn. Press, 1950.

KING, P. D. A statistical comparison of senile brain disease and Alzheimer's disease. *J. clin. exp. Psychopath.*, 1960, 21, 31-33.

KINSEY, A. C., POMEROY, W. B., & MARTIN, C. E. *Sexual behavior in the human male.* Philadelphia: Saunders, 1948.

KIORBOE, E. The prognosis of epilepsy. *Acta Psychiat. Scand.*, 1961, 36 (Supplement 150), 166-178.

KOREY, S. R., SCHEINBERG, L., TERRY, R., & STEIN, A. Studies in presenile dementia. *Trans. Amer. neurol. Ass.*, 1961, 86, 99-102.

KROGER, W. S. (Ed.) *Psychosomatic obstetrics, gynecology and endocrinology.* Springfield, Ill.: Charles C. Thomas, 1962.

KUPPER, H. I. Psychic concomitants in wartime injuries. *Psychosom. Med.*, 1945, 7, 15-21.

LAWTON, G. *Psychological guidance to older persons.* Washington, D. C.: Public Health Reports, Supplement No. 168, 1942.

LEAKE, C. D. Section on aging: National Institute of Mental Health. *Geriatrics*, 1962, 17, 3.

LEE, R. E., & SCHNEIDER, R. F. Hypertension and arteriosclerosis in executive and nonexecutive personnel. *J. Amer. Med. Ass.*, 1958, 167, 1447-1450.

LEISER, A. E. Endocrine disorders in the aged. *Texas J. Med.*, 1961, 57, 825-828.

LENNOX, W. G., & LENNOX, MARGARET A. *Epilepsy and related disorders*, Vol. 1. Boston: Little, Brown, 1960.

LEVIN, S. Brain tumors in mental hospital patients. *Amer. J. Pyschiat.*, 1949, 105, 897-900.

LEVIN, M. Bromide hallucinosis. *Arch. gen. Psychiat.*, 1960, 2, 429-433.

LEVY, S. Post-encephalitic behavior disorders—a forgotten entity: A report of 100 cases. *Amer. J. Psychiat.*, 1959, 115, 1062-1067.

LEYTON, G. B. The effects of slow starvation. *Lancet*, 1946, 251, 73-79.

LOVIT, I. M. Childhood epilepsy. *Scot. med. J.*, 1961, 6, 270-272.

LUBY, E. D., GRISELL, J. L., FROHMAN, C. E., LEES, H., COHEN, B. D., & GOTTLIEB, J. S. Biochemical, psychological, and behavioral responses to sleep deprivation. *Ann. N.Y. Acad. Sci.*, 1962, 96, 71-79.

MC CAUGHEY, W. T. The pathologic spectrum of Huntington's chorea. *J. nerv. ment. Dis.*, 1961, 133, 91-103.

MC CULLOCH, T. A., & CALVERLEY, M. O. Addison's disease with psychosis. *Canad. med. Ass. J.*, 1961, 85, 31-33.

MC TAGGART, A. N., ANDERMANN, F., & BOS, C. A survey of cerebral tumors presented at a psychiatric institution. *Canad. Psychiat. Ass. J.*, 1961, 6, 333-338.

MALZBERG, B. Cohort studies of mental disease in New York State, 1943-1949. *Ment. Hyg.*, 1957, 41, 250-269, 420-444.

MANSON, M. P., & ENGQUIST, C. L. Post-hospital adjustments of a geriatric-psychiatric group. *J. Amer. Geriat. Soc.*, 1962, 10, 60-76.

MARKHAM, S. A comparative evaluation of psychotic and nonpsychotic reactions to childbirth. *Amer. J. Orthopsychiat.*, 1961, 31, 565-578.

MARKS, H. H. Characteristics and trends of cerebral vascular disease. In P. H. Hoch, & J. Zubin (Eds.), *Psychopathology of aging.* New York: Grune & Stratton, 1961. Pp. 69-99.

MARSHALL, A. G., HUTCHINSON, E. O., & HONISETT, J. Heredity in common diseases. *Brit. med. J.,* 1962, 1, 1-6.

MARTIN, M. E. Puerperal mental illness: a follow-up study of 75 cases. *Brit. med. J.,* 1958, 2, 733-777.

MASLAND, R. L. as reported in J. R. Moskin, Urgent search for a cure. *Look,* July 17, 1962, 26, 73.

MAYER-GROSS, W. Arteriosclerotic, senile, and presenile psychoses. *J. ment. Sci.,* 1944, 90, 316-327.

MENNINGER, K. *The human mind.* New York: Knopf, 1946.

MERRITT, H. H. Head injury: review of the literature (concluded). *War Med.,* 1943, 4, 187-215.

METRAKOS, K., & METRAKOS, J. D. Genetics of convulsive disorders: II. Genetic and electroencephalographic studies in centrencephalic epilepsy. *Neurology,* 1961, 11, 474-483.

METTLER, F. A., & CRANDELL, A. Relation between parkinsonism and psychiatric disorder. *J. nerv. ment. Dis.,* 1959, 129, 551-563.

MOON, H. E. (Ed.) *The adrenal cortex.* New York: Harper, 1961.

MORGAN, J. L. Carbon monoxide poisoning—a danger of farm and home. *Industr. Med. Surgery,* 1955, 24, 302-306.

MOSES, C. *Atherosclerosis.* Philadelphia: Lea & Febiger, 1963.

MULDER, D. W. Psychoses with brain tumors and other chronic neurologic disorders. In S. Arieti (Ed.), *American handbook of psychiatry,* Vol. 2. New York: Basic Books, 1959. Pp. 1144-1162.

National Epilepsy League. Special issue of *Horizon,* May 1962, 1-8.

National Health Education Committee. *Facts on the major killing and crippling diseases in the United States today.* New York: Author, 1961.

NORRMAN, B., & SVAHN, K. A follow-up study of severe brain injuries. *Acta Psychiat. Scand.,* 1961, 37, 236-264.

NOYES, A. P. *Modern clinical psychiatry.* (2nd ed.) Philadelphia: W. B. Saunders, 1939.

NOYES, A. P., & KOLB, L. C. *Modern clinical psychiatry* (6th ed.) Philadelphia: W. B. Saunders, 1963.

O'CONNELL, B. Postcontusional syndrome. *J. Foren. Med.,* 1961, 8, 122-130.

PARRAN, T. *Shadow on the land.* New York: Reynal & Hitchcock, 1937.

PARSONS, T. Toward a healthy maturity. *J. Hlth human Behav.,* 1960, 1, 163-173.

PATTON, R. B., & SHEPPARD, J. A. Intracranial tumors found at autopsy in mental patients. *Amer. J. Psychiat.,* 1956, 113, 319-324.

PEARSON, J. S., *et al.* Symposium on Huntington's chorea; an education approach to the social problem of Huntington's chorea. *Proceedings Staff Meeting Mayo Clin.,* 1955, 30, 349-357.

PITTS, F. N., JR., & GUZE, S. B. Psychiatric disorders and myxedema. *Amer. J. Psychiat.,* 1961, 118, 142-147.

PLEYDELL, M. J. Huntington's chorea in Northamptonshire. *Brit. med. J.,* 1954, 2, 1121-1128.

POFFENBARGER, R. S., *et al.* The picture puzzle of the postpartum psychosis. *J. chron. Dis.,* 1961, 13, 161-173.

POLLACK, E., LOCKE, B., & KRAMER, M. Trends in hospitalization and patterns of care of the aged mentally ill. In P. H. Hoch & J. Zubin (Eds.), *Psychopathology of aging.* New York: Grune & Stratton, 1961. Pp. 21-56.

POSKANZER, D. C., & SCHWAB, R. S. Studies in the epidemiology of Parkinson's disease predicting its disappearance as a major clinic entity by 1980. *Trans. Amer. neurol. Ass.,* 1961, 86, 234-235.

POST, F. Some problems arising from a study of mental patients over the age of sixty years. *J. ment. Sci.,* 1944, 90, 554-565.

PUGH, T. F., JERATH, B. K., SCHMIDT, W. M., & REED, R. B. Rates of mental disease related to child-bearing. *N.E. J. Med.,* 1963, 268, 1224-1228.

PUSEY, W. A. *The history and epidemiology of syphilis.* Springfield: Charles C. Thomas, 1933.

PUTNAM, T. J., & MERRITT, H. H. SDH in treatment of convulsive disorders. *J. Amer. med. Ass.,* 1938, 3, 1068-1073.

REITAN, R. M. Intellectual functions in myxedema. *AMA Arch. Neurol. Psychiat.,* 1953, 69, 436-449.

RIESMAN, D. Some clinical and cultural aspects of the aging process. *Individualism reconsidered,* and other essays. Glencoe, Ill.: Fress Press, 1954.

RIGGS, HELENA E., & WAHAL, KRISHNA M. Role of cardiovascular insufficiency in intellectual deterioration in senium. *Geriatrics,* 1962, 17, 26-30.

RISCH, F., & HENRY, J. J. Epilepsy explored in California study. *J. Rehabilit.,* 1960, 26, 13-15.

ROME, H. P., & ROBINSON, D. B. Psychiatric conditions associated with metabolic, endocrine, and nutritional disorders. In S. Arieti (Ed.), *Handbook of psychiatry,* Vol. 2. New York: Basic Books, 1959. Pp. 1260-1288.

ROSENTHAL, HATTIE R. Psychotherapy for the aging. *Amer. J. Psychother.,* 1959, 13, 55-65.

ROTHSCHILD, D. The role of the premorbid personality in arteriosclerotic psychoses. *Amer. J. Psychiat.,* 1944, 100, 501-505.

ROTHSCHILD, D. Senile psychoses and psychoses with cerebral arteriosclerosis. In O. J. Kaplan (Ed.), *Mental disorders in later life.* (2nd ed.) Stanford: Stanford Univer. Press, 1956.

RUSSEK, H. I., & ZOHMAN, B. L. Relative significance of heredity, diet, and occupational stress in coronary heart disease of young adults. *Amer. J. med. Sci.,* 1958, 235, 266-277.

SANDERS, V. Neurologic manifestations of myxedema. *N.E. J. Med.,* 1962, 266, 547-552, 559-602.

SANDLER, S. A. Psychiatric symptoms in brain tumors. *J. med. Soc. N. J.,* 1960, 57, 471-474.

SCHENK, V. W. Re-examination of a family with Pick's disease. *Annu. human Genet.,* 1959, 23, 325-333.

SEGELOV, J. N., & DAVIS, R. Towards earlier diagnosis of brain tumours. *Med. J. Aust.,* 1961, 48 (2), 1-6.

SELYE, H., & PRIORESCHI, P. Stress theory of aging. In N. W. Shock (Ed.), *Aging: some social and biological aspects.* Washington, D. C.: Amer. Ass. Advancement Sci. (Publication No. 65), 1960. Pp. 261-272.

SETTEL, E. Engymatic factors in protein malnutrition of the geriatric patient. *J. Amer. geriat. Soc.,* 1959, 7, 416-421.

SHEPS, J. Paranoid mechanisms in the aged. *Psychiatry,* 1958, 21, 399-404.

SHEPS, J. Factors in the rejection of the aged by society. *Psychosomatics,* 1960, 1, 84-85.

SHERMAN, I. J. Symptoms and signs in 100 cases of verified brain tumor. *Conn. Med.,* 1961, 25, 484-485.

SHIPLEY, R. A. The gonads and aging. *J. Amer. geriat. Soc.,* 1962, 10, 26-34.

SILVERMAN, M. We can lick epilepsy. *Saturday Evening Post,* 1948, 220 (29), 22-23.

SIMSON, T. P. Infection psychoses. *Publ. Hlth Rep.,* 1960, 75, 451-456.

SINCLAIR-GIEBEN, A. H. The psychiatric aspects of epilepsy. *Scot. med. J.,* 1961, 6, 264-269.

SKLAR, J., & O'NEILL, F. J. Experiments in intensive treatment in a geriatric ward. In P. H. Hoch, & J. Zubin (Eds.), *Psychopathology of aging.* New York: Grune & Stratton, 1961. Pp. 266-273.

SLANEY, G., & ASHTON, F. Cerebral dysfunction due to extracranial atherosclerosis. *Brit. J. clin. Pract.*, 1962, 16, 687-697.

SMALL, J. G. A psychiatric survey of brain-injured children. *Arch. gen. Psychiat.*, 1962, 7, 120-124.

SMITH, G. M. *Canad. Psychiat. Ass. J.*, 1958, 3, 145.

SONIAT, T. L. L. Psychiatric symptoms associated with intracranial neoplasms. *Amer. J. Psychiat.*, 1951, 108, 19-22.

SPELLMAN, G. G. Report of familial cases of Parkinsonism. *J. Amer. med. Ass.*, 1962, 179, 372-374.

STAMLER, J. Breakthrough against hypertensive and atherosclerotic diseases. *Geriatrics*, 1962, 17, 31-40.

STRAKER, M. Prognosis for psychiatric illness in the aged. *Amer. J. Psychiat.*, 1963, 119, 1069-1075.

STRAUSS, H. Epileptic disorders. In S. Arieti (Ed.), *American handbook of psychiatry*, Vol. 2. New York: Basic Books, 1959. Pp. 1109-1143.

SYMONDS, C. Concussion and its sequelae. *Lancet*, 1962, 1, 1-5.

TARR, J. D., & LUGAR, R. R. Early infectious syphilis. Male homosexual relations as a mode of spread. *Calif. Med.*, 1960, 93, 35-37.

TETLOW, C. Psychoses of childbearing. *J. ment. Sci.*, 1955, 101, 629-639.

TEUBER, H.-L. In EISENBERG, L., KNOTT, J. R., PASAMANICK, B., KNOBLOCH, HILDA, THOMPSON, W. R., BENTON, A. L., & TEUBER, H.-L. Brain behavior. Session II. Symposium, 1959. *Amer. J. Orthopsychiat.*, 1960, 30, 292-329.

THOMAS, C. L., & GORDON, J. E. Psychosis after childbirth: ecological aspects of a single impact stress. *Amer. J. med. Sci.*, 1959, 238, 363-388.

TIBBITTS, C. (Ed.) *Handbook of social gerontology: societal aspects of aging.* Chicago: Univer. Chicago Press, 1960.

TIZARD, BARBARA. The personality of epileptics: a discussion of the evidence. *Psychol. Bull.*, 1962, 59, 196-210.

TRAVIS, GEORGIA. *Chronic disease and disability [a basic medical social guide].* Berkeley: Univer. Calif. Press, 1961.

TRETHOWAN, W. H., & COBB, S. Neuropsychiatric aspects of Cushing's Syndrome. *AMA Arch. Neurol. Psychiat.*, 1952, 67, 283-309.

TURNER, W. J., & MERLIS, S. Clinical correlations between electroencephalography and anti-social behavior. *Med. Times*, 1962, 90, 505-511.

TURTON, E. C., & WARREN, P. K. Dementia: a clinical and EEG study of 274 patients over the age of 60. *J. ment. Sci.*, 1960, 106, 1493-1500.

TYLER, D. B. Psychological changes during experimental sleep deprivation. *Dis. nerv. Sys.*, 1955, 16, 293-299.

UDEL, M. M. The work performance of epileptics in industry. *Arch. environment. Hlth*, 1960, 1, 257-264.

ULLMAN, M., & GRUEN, A. Behavioral changes in patients with strokes. *Amer. J. Psychiat.*, 1961, 117, 1004-1009.

U. S. Public Health Service. *Syphilis—modern diagnosis and management.* (Publication No. 743). Washington, D. C.: U.S. Government Printing Office, 1961.

U. S. Public Health Service. The eradication of syphilis; a Task Force Report to the Surgeon General on syphilis control in the United States, 1962.

U. S. Senate. Committee on Labor and Public Welfare. Aged in mental hospitals; report by the subcommittee on problems of the aged and aging. Committee Print, 1960.

V. A.-D. V. A. Study Group. Part IV. Parkinson's disease. Some psychological and psychiatric studies. *Med. Serv. J. Canad.*, 1960, 16, 536-542.

WAGNER, M. Mental hazards in old age. *Family*, 1944, 25, 132-137.

WALKER, A. E. Murder or epilepsy? *J. nerv. ment. Dis.*, 1961, 133, 430-437.

WAMSLEY, J. R., & FLINN, D. E. Toxic psychosis. *Aerospace Med.*, 1961, 32, 1148-1150.

WECHSLER, D. Intelligence, memory and the aging process. In P. H. Hoch, & J. Zubin (Eds.), *Psychopathology of aging.* New York: Grune & Stratton, 1961. Pp. 152-159.

WEINER, A., & STEINHILBER, R. The postpartum psychoses. *J. Int. Coll. Surgeons*, 1961, 36, 490-499.

WEINSTEIN, E. A. Psychiatric aspects of head injury. *N.Y. J. Med.*, 1961, 61, 1879-1883.

WEINSTEIN, E. A., & KAHN, R. L. Patterns of sexual behavior following brain injury. *Psychiatry*, 1961, 24, 69-78

WEST, L. J., JANSZEN, H. H., LESTER, B. K., & CORNELISÖON, F. S., JR. The psychoses of sleep deprivation. *Ann. N. Y. Acad. Sci.*, 1962, 96, 66-70.

WHEELAN, L. Familial Alzheimer's disease. *Annu. human Genet.*, 1959, 23, 300-310.

White House Conference on Aging. The Nation and its older people, report of White House Conference on Aging, Jan. 9-12, 1961. Washington, D. C.: Author, 1961.

WHITE, H. H., & FOWLER, F. D. Chronic lead encephalopathy. A diagnostic consideration in mental retardation. *Pediatrics*, 1960, 25, 309-315.

WHITE, M. A., PROUT, C. T., FIXSEN, C., & FOUNDEUR, M. Obstetrician's role in postpartum mental illness. *J. Amer. med. Ass.*, 1957, 165, 138-143.

WHITTIER, J. R., & KORENYI, C. Selected characters in aged patients: a study of mental hospital admissions. *Comprehen. Psychiat.*, 1961, 2, 113-120.

WILLIAMS, W. S., & JACO, E. G. An evaluation of functional psychoses in old age. *Amer. J. Psychiat.*, 1958, 114, 910-916.

WILLIAMS, H. L., LUBIN, A., & GOODNOW, J. J. Impaired performance with acute sleep loss. *Psychol. Monogr.*, 1959, 75 (14), (Whole No. 484).

WILSON, S. A. K. *Neurology*, Vol. 2. Baltimore: Williams & Wilkins, 1940.

WOLFF, H. D., & HUSTON, P. E. Schizophrenia associated with Addison's disease. *Amer. J. Psychiat.*, 1959, 116, 365-367.

World Health Organization. Juvenile epilepsy, report of a study group. Geneva: Author, 1957.

YALOM, I. D. Organic brain diseases of senility. *Maryland state med. J.*, 1960, 9, 781-787.

MENTAL RETARDATION

chapter 12

At Marbridge Foundation near Austin, Texas, mentally retarded boys prepare to become competent, useful, and reliable urban or rural citizens. Classes include woodworking, home repairs, auto mechanics, and agricultural activities.

DIAGNOSIS AND CLASSIFICATION

CAUSES AND MENTAL RETARDATION (ETIOLOGY)

COMMON CLINICAL TYPES OF RETARDATION

MENTAL RETARDATION AND ABNORMAL BEHAVIOR

TREATMENT AND PROGNOSIS

PREVENTION OF MENTAL RETARDATION

In every age of history, in all cultures, in every stratum of society there have always been individuals who have manifested subnormal intellectual functioning. Many of these individuals do not have the ability to manage their affairs with ordinary prudence, are incapable of profiting from ordinary schooling, and are unable to maintain themselves in the community. Some cannot grasp even simple concepts. All these conditions are part of what has been variously termed *feeble-mindedness, mental deficiency, mental subnormality,* and *mental retardation.*[1]

There are an estimated 5,500,000 mentally retarded children and adults in the United States.[2] This constitutes about 3 per cent of the population. Actual figures, of course, depend on the exact criteria used and the "cut-off" point adopted. Current draft figures indicate that about 4.5 per cent of all men examined for military service are being rejected for mental retardation. Several epidemiologic investigations indicate a higher proportion of mental retardation among males than females.

Prior to 1847, when the Walter Fernald State

School in Massachusetts was established, no suitable residential facilities for the care or training of the mentally retarded were available. Since that time many state and private institutions have been established. The 1960 directory published by the American Association on Mental Deficiency lists 108 state and 289 private residential institutions and homes in the United States (AAMD, 1960). Today about 215,000 mental retardates (approximately 4 per cent of the mentally retarded population) are in such institutions. A small additional number are cared for in state mental hospitals. The great majority remain in the community.

Diagnosis and Classification

The American Association on Mental Deficiency (founded in 1876) has defined *mental retardation* as "subaverage general intellectual functioning which originates during the development period and is associated with impairment in adaptive behavior" (Heber, 1961, p. 499). By this definition, *mental retardation* implies a deficiency or defect in actual mental equipment and adjustive resources.

The IQ provides a rough measure of the individual's relative brightness and level of intellectual functioning and is widely used for diagnosing the intelligence dimension of mental deficiency. In fact, most states now have laws providing that individuals with IQ's below 70 can be classified as mentally retarded and committed to institutions.

There has been much criticism, however, of the practice of making diagnosis and/or commitment on the basis of IQ alone. For one thing, it is extremely difficult in many cases to make an accurate assessment of intellectual level (Delp, 1961; Fisher, 1962). This is particularly true in the case of brain-damaged children. Often these children possess genuine ability but have difficulty in making adequate responses because of spasticity, athetosis, defective hearing or vision, or other impairments.

Even more important, the criterion of adaptive behavior is not revealed in an IQ—particularly in the case of individuals with only mild or moderate retardation. Some people with IQ's in the low 50's and 60's can support themselves and get along creditably in the community. This is particularly true of those who have received the advantages of training in state or private schools. Consequently, even when an individual's IQ is as low as 50, he may or may not need custodial care, depending on the level of his emotional, vocational, and social adjustments. Certainly, when an individual's IQ is in the 60's and he is making an adequate adjustment in the community, there seems little point in labeling him as a mental retardate. Thus *mental retardation,* like *insanity,* is essentially a legal term; it means inability, intellectually and in other ways, to take care of oneself.

The President's Panel on Mental Retardation (1962) recommended a fourfold classification of mental retardation based on measured intelligence and adaptive behavior. It follows closely that of the American Association on Mental Deficiency but omits the *borderline* category.

Mild (IQ approximately 50 to 70). This category comprises by far the largest group of the mentally retarded—about 5,000,000 persons. In adult life, these individuals attain intellectual levels somewhat comparable to that of the average 8- to 11-year-old child. Their social ad-

---

[1]For over 100 years in the United States, *feeble-mindedness* was used to refer to subaverage intellectual functioning. This in turn gave way to the term *mental deficiency* and more recently to the term *mental retardation.* However, some investigators believe that neither term is adequate, suggesting that *mental deficiency* should be used for cases with demonstrable brain damage or pathology and that *mental retardation* should be confined to cases suffering from severe sociocultural deficiencies which presumably have retarded the individual's potential intellectual development. In 1954, the World Health Organization proposed the term *mental subnormality* as an overall term to refer to subaverage intellectual functioning, but this term has never received wide usage. Currently, *mental retardation* appears to be the preferred term (Gardner and Nisonger, 1962; Heber, 1961).

[2]Statistics based on Benda *et al.* (1963), Exceptional Children's Foundation (1962), Group for the Advancement of Psychiatry (1959), Heber (1959), Kennedy (1963), Menninger (1948), Nisonger (1962), U.S. Public Health Service (1963).

justment often approximates that of the adolescent, although they tend to lack the normal adolescent's imagination, inventiveness, and judgment. Ordinarily they do not show signs of brain pathology or other physical anomalies. Often they require some measure of supervision due to limited ability to foresee the consequences of their actions. With early diagnosis, parental assistance, and special educational programs, the majority of this group can adjust socially, master simple academic and occupational skills, and become self-supporting citizens.

Moderate (IQ approximately 35-50). This group comprises some 300,000 to 350,000 persons. In adult life these individuals attain intellectual levels similar to that of the average 4- to 7-year-old child. Some of the brighter members of this group can be taught to read and write a little, and some manage to achieve a fair command of language. Their learning rate is relatively slow, however, and the level of complexity of concepts with which they can deal is extremely limited. Physically, they appear clumsy and ungainly, and they usually suffer from physical abnormalities or deformities and poor motor coordination. Typically, they present an affable, dull, and somewhat vacuous personality picture. Infrequently, they are hostile and aggressive.

In general, with early diagnosis, parental help, and adequate opportunities for training, most of the moderately retarded can achieve partial independence in daily self-care, acceptable behavior, and economic usefulness in a family or other sheltered environment. Whether or not they require institutionalization usually depends on their general level of adaptive behavior.

Severe (IQ 20-35) and *profound* (IQ below 20). There are an estimated 60,000 to 90,000 severely and profoundly retarded persons in the United States—mostly children and adolescents. Individuals classified as severely retarded never attain an intellectual level greater than that of the average 3-year-old child. Most of this group are markedly deficient in adaptive behavior and are unable to master any but the most simple tasks. Useful speech, if it develops at all, is on a rudimentary level. Sensory defects and motor handicaps are prevalent, along with retarded growth, physical anomalies, and high susceptibility to disease. Although some of the brighter members of the severely retarded group can profit from specialized training, they will be dependent all their lives on the care and supervision of others. Cases of profound mental retardation require the care given to an infant.

While mild mental retardates may be somewhat slow in learning to talk and in other aspects of development, they usually show no obvious symptoms which set them apart from other children. As a result, their condition usually is not revealed until difficulties in school learning lead to a diagnostic evaluation. On the other hand, moderate, severe, and profound cases of mental retardation usually are diagnosed in infancy as a consequence of physical malformations, grossly delayed habit training, and other obvious symptoms of abnormality (Suczek, 1961). Some of these children evidence general mental retardation while others show disabilities in only specific aspects of behavior. Brain damage may result in relatively subtle defects or disorganizations of sensory, motor, or integrative behavior.

Causes of Mental Retardation (Etiology)

It was formerly thought that mental retardation —as distinct from the mental impairment associated with chronic functional psychoses and the blocking of intellectual functions by emotional conflicts—was a simple matter of heredity. Then, as the brain pathology underlying certain types of mental retardation became apparent, a

twofold classification in relation to etiology was introduced: (a) *primary* or *endogenous,* presumably resulting from heredity, and (b) *secondary* or *exogenous,* resulting from known brain pathology. This classification was widely accepted until 1959, when the American Association on Mental Deficiency published an official classification and terminology manual (Heber, 1959).[1] This manual combines the 100 or more specific causes into 8 major groups.[2]

1. *Sociocultural factors.* Adverse social, economic, and cultural factors appear to play a major role in the etiology of mental retardation. Although mental retardation strikes children from all socioeconomic levels, it is much more frequent in city tenements and rural slums where there are heavy concentrations of poorly educated families with low incomes. It has been shown that 10 to 30 per cent of school-age children in some slum areas are mentally retarded as contrasted with 1 to 2 per cent in the more prosperous neighborhoods of the same cities (President's Panel, 1962). Families deprived of the basic necessities of life—and of opportunity and motivation—contribute a disproportionately high number of the nation's mentally retarded children. There is a selective factor operating here too, of course: parents with low intelligence are likely to be concentrated at the bottom of the economic heap. But it is now realized that this does not begin to explain the high incidence of mental retardation among children in slum areas.

Severe environmental deprivation during infancy and childhood may retard the child's intellectual development even when his potential at birth is within a normal range (Group for the Advancement of Psychiatry, 1959). This conclusion is supported by recent research findings which show that young children who have been living in impoverished environments and functioning at a retarded intellectual level often show marked improvement when placed in a more stimulating learning situation (Nisonger, 1962; Kennedy, 1963). In fact, many of these children approach normal levels of intellectual functioning. Unless severely depriving environmental conditions are corrected early, however, permanent intellectual impairment may occur.

2. *Genetic-chromosomal factors.* Mental retardation tends to run in families. This is particularly true of mild retardation, which presumably results from the action of multiple genes. However, poverty also tends to run in families, and early exposure to a culturally deprived environment may also be a primary or concomitant etiological agent in these cases. As we shall see, genetic factors stand out more clearly

in the determination of certain rare biochemical disorders associated with moderate and severe degrees of mental retardation. Here mutant genes prevent or alter basic biochemical reactions essential for the normal development and functioning of the brain.

Recent advances in the field of genetics have also shown that a number of relatively rare types of mental retardation are associated with chromosomal anomalies. The most common clinical condition of this type is *mongolism.* It has been estimated that about 1 per cent of institutionalized mentally retarded males and a somewhat smaller percentage of females have abnormal numbers of sex chromosomes (Mosier *et al.,* 1960; Stimson, 1961; Maclean and Mitchell, 1962). The abnormal chromosome pattern in a case of mongolism was shown in Chapter 4.

3. *Biochemical (metabolic) disorders.* There are some 25 rare biochemical diseases associated with mental retardation. Often these diseases appear to result from mutant genes. Perhaps the best known of these is *phenylketonuria* (PKU). This disorder occurs in infants who lack an enzyme needed to break down phenylalanine, an amino acid found in protein foods. Other clinical syndromes here include *galactosemia,* which involves an inability to metabolize galactose; *maple syrup urine disease,* a disorder of metabolism of chain amino acids; and *familial goiterous cretinism,* which results from a defect in thyroid synthesis.

4. *Infections.* Mental retardation may be associated with a wide range of conditions due to infection. The fetus of a mother with certain virus diseases, such as German measles, may suffer brain damage; apparently damage is greatest when the viral infection occurs during the first eight weeks of pregnancy. The fetus of a

---

[1]This manual was modified slightly in 1961 but the etiologic groups remain the same (Heber, 1961).

[2]In the present discussion, we have modified these etiologic groups somewhat for instructional purposes. In addition to the manual mentioned, the following references were utilized in our present outline of the major groups of causative factors: Coffey and Jessop (1959), Conen *et al.* (1962), De Haas *et al.* (1961), Forssman and Lehmann (1962), German *et al.* (1962), Gillis (1962), Graham *et al.* (1962), Heber (1959, 1961), Jancar (1961), Kennedy (1963), Kirkman and Riley (1959), Maclean and Mitchell (1962), Nishimura (1962), Robinson (1961), Rundle (1962), Schwartz (1961), Siegel and Greenberg (1960-1961), D. W. Smith *et al.* (1962), Stimson (1961), Tarjan *et al.* (1960), Wright and Tarjan (1958), Yacorzynski *et al.* (1960).

mother with syphilis may suffer infection and varying degrees of brain damage. Brain damage may also result from infections occurring after birth, as in the case of epidemic encephalitis. Mental retardation resulting from such infectious diseases is rare in the United States today.

5. *Toxic agents.* A number of toxic agents, such as carbon monoxide and lead, may lead to brain damage during fetal development or after birth. In some instances, immunological agents, such as antitetanus serum or typhoid vaccine, may result in brain damage. Similarly, certain drugs administered to the mother during pregnancy may lead to congenital malformations, or an overdose of drugs administered to the infant may lead to toxicity and brain damage. In rare cases, brain damage results from incompatibility in blood types between mother and fetus— Rh and ABO incompatibility. Fortunately, early diagnosis and blood transfusions can now minimize the effects of this disorder.

6. *Trauma or physical agents.* Formerly, it was estimated that from 6 to 10 per cent of the cases of mental retardation resulted from birth injuries (Doll *et al.,* 1932). With modern obstetrical methods, this figure has undoubtedly been greatly reduced. However, difficulties in labor due to malposition of the fetus or other complications may still damage the infant's brain at birth. Bleeding within the brain is probably the most common result of such birth trauma. *Anoxia* stemming from delayed breathing of the newborn infant or other causes is another type of birth trauma which may damage the brain. Anoxia may also occur after birth as a result of cardiac arrest associated with operations, heart attacks, or near drownings. Serious postnatal head injuries, too, may result in permanent brain damage, although these injuries are not so frequent as is often assumed by parents, who may find it comforting to be able to attribute their child's retardation to accidental injury instead of to either faulty heredity or any possible failure on their part.

7. *Ionizing radiation.* Recently a great deal of scientific attention has been focused on the damaging effects of irradiation on the sex cells and other bodily cells and tissues. On the basis of figures published by the United States Federal Radiation Council (1962), it has been estimated that as a result of weapons testing through 1962 there may ultimately be over 16 million cases of gross physical or mental defects from fall-out and carbon-14 (Pauling, 1962). These figures apply to the world population. Ionizing irradiation may act on the fertilized ovum directly or may produce gene mutations in the sex cells of either or both parents which, in turn, lead to defective offspring.

8. *Other causes.* Follow-up studies indicate that infants born prematurely, weighing less than 1500 grams at birth, reveal a high incidence of neurological disorders including mental retardation (Kennedy, 1963; Knobloch *et al.,* 1956). In fact, very small premature babies are 10 times more likely to be mentally retarded. A limited number of cases of retardation are associated with brain tumors and other new growths which either damage the brain tissue directly or lead to increased cranial pressure and concomitant brain damage. In many kinds of mental retardation, there are uncertain or unknown prenatal causes. These include a wide range of abnormalities in brain structure, such as malformation of the gyri, congenital *hydrocephalus,* and *microcephaly.* A number of types of postnatal brain pathology, usually of a degenerative type, also result from uncertain or unknown causes. In occasional cases, severe and prolonged emotional disturbances dating from an early age appear to block the normal growth and integration of intellectual functions—leading to mental retardation.

The preceding groups of causes are useful in giving some idea of the range and scope of causes of mental retardation. In general, mild retardation, most prevalent at the lower end of the socioeconomic scale, is most commonly associated with severe environmental deprivation; moderate, severe, or profound retardation, distributed more evenly throughout the population, is more commonly associated with infections, trauma, metabolic diseases, chromosomal irregularities, ionizing radiation, and other pathological conditions. The various etiological factors may operate singly or in various combinations; and they may operate before, during, or after birth. In a given case it is often difficult or impossible to ascertain the precise causal pattern though medical science can now identify precise causes in 15 to 25 per cent of all cases.

Common Clinical Types of Retardation

In addition to the classification by level (mild, moderate, severe, profound), there are recognizable clinical types of mental retardation. Several of the more common ones will be described in this section. Others are summarized on page 530.

CULTURAL-FAMILIAL
MENTAL RETARDATION

Traditionally, this category has included those cases of mild mental retardation with no apparent indication of brain pathology and with evidence of similar mental retardation in one or more siblings (if there are siblings). In the main, these cases have been assumed to be due to low-quality or defective genes and to represent the lower end of the normal distribution of intelligence in the general population. The only tangible evidence to support this genetic hypothesis, however, has been the tendency of mild mental retardation to run in families. Actually the precise mode of genetic transmission of intelligence is not yet understood, and as we have noted, the tendency for a disorder to run in families does not prove genetic origin.

Increasing emphasis is being placed upon sociocultural rather than genetic factors in the etiology of mild mental retardation. Whether or not they carry a genetic defect, the majority of these children come from homes representing the lower economic, educational, and cultural segments of the population.

Many of the parents of these children are mentally retarded themselves or otherwise inadequate as parents. In a study of 205 institutionalized mild mental retardates—ages 5 to 16 years with no clear-cut neurological symptoms —Benda *et al.* (1963) found that in 30 per cent of the families, one or both parents and at least one sibling were mentally retarded. Sixty per cent of the children came from homes which were rated as functionally inadequate in that the parent or parents were incapable of providing for the child; and 50 per cent of the children

came from homes in which there was only one parent in the family unit. Only 49 families—less than one fourth—were both intact and functionally adequate. Relevant also is the finding that 70 per cent of the retardates came from families having an income from unskilled or semiskilled occupations. Admittedly, one would expect to find a higher incidence of family pathology in the background of mild retardates who are institutionalized than in the mild retardate population in general. However, the results of Benda's study are thought-provoking.

It may also be pointed out that many women each year—an estimated 455,000 in 138 large cities in the United States—lack the funds to pay for adequate health care during pregnancy and following the birth of the baby; and in public hospitals, between 20 and 60 per cent of the mothers receive inadequate prenatal care or none at all and little in the way of follow-up care (Kennedy, 1963). As one might expect, the infant mortality rate and complications of birth are much higher among this population— and so is the incidence of mental retardation among the offspring. Often the effects on the child appear to be subtle rather than gross in nature. As the President's Panel noted:

"A variety of unfavorable health factors, including lack of prenatal care, poor nutrition, deficient postnatal care, and similar unfavorable factors, may produce damage to the brain or to the body which cannot be generally measured with present techniques but which will constitute a drag on physical and neurological development." (1962, p. 8).

In general, it would appear that we are dealing with a cluster of factors—lack of proper maternal health care, environmental deprivation, and lack of intellectual stimulation—all of which tend to characterize the more disadvantaged classes of our society. This, of course, does not preclude the possible role of genetic factors either as primary determinants or as codeterminants with environmental factors. However, the precise role of genetic factors in the etiology of mild mental retardation is far from clear and probably varies for different cases.

The school failure of the mild mental retardate, combined with an inadequate family and environmental background, may lead to acting-out behavior—such as truancy or offenses against property, persons, or morals. However, except in cases of persistent delinquent behavior and/or parental inability to care for the child, retardates in the cultural-familial category rarely require institutionalization.

Where adequate educational facilities are available, children in this group are usually placed in special classes where they typically are able to master simple occupational skills and to achieve an adequate level of socially adaptive behavior. Following the school years they usually make an acceptable adjustment in the community and their identity as mentally retarded is lost.

MONGOLISM

Mongolism is the most common of the clinical types with moderate and severe retardation. It is often referred to as *Down's syndrome* after Clifford Down, who first described it in 1866. The term *mongolism* is also used because of the slant eyes characteristic of individuals in this group. Approximately 1 in every 500 births is a mongoloid, which means that about 23 mongoloid babies are born daily into American families (Benda, 1960; Boggs, 1962). The total number of mongoloids in the United States is not known, although it is probably well over 100,000. Mongoloids constitute some 10 to 20 per cent of institutionalized mental retardates (Tarjan *et al.*, 1960).

The mongoloid child has almond-shaped, slanting eyes, with the skin of the eyelids abnormally thick. Lips are thin and appear fissured and dry, with the tongue also showing deep fissures. Teeth are usually small and misshapen; the nose is flat; hair is generally sparse, fine, and straight. Hands and feet are broad and clumsy, and the mongoloid is usually awkward in both gross and fine motor coordination. He has characteristic fingerprints, with L-shaped loops rather than the usual whorls. One other outstanding char-

acteristic of the mongoloid is his deep voice, which is often helpful in making a diagnosis.

Mongoloids are particularly susceptible to circulatory, gastrointestinal, and respiratory disorders. In approximately 10 per cent of the cases, there is an associated congenital heart defect (Heber, 1959). As a consequence of these factors, their life expectancy is considerably reduced (Collman and Stoller, 1963). However, antibiotics, better medical care, and a more healthful and stimulating environment are increasing the life expectancy of many of the victims of this disorder.

Although the term *mongolian idiot* has been widely used in the past, it is misleading because most of these children show only moderate mental retardation. In one study of 77 mongoloid children evaluated during a 3-year period at a state clinic, Wunsch (1957) found that about 75 per cent of the children could be classified as moderately retarded and 4 per cent as mildly retarded. Despite their limitations, most of these children can learn self-help skills, acceptable social behavior, and routine manual skills which enable them to be of assistance in a family or institutional setting. The social adjustment of mongoloid children is often helped by their tendency to be affectionate and relatively docile, although these traits are by no means universal. Wunsch found that about 51 per cent of the children in his study exhibited such docile-affectionate behavior, while about 14 per cent exhibited persistent aggressive-hostile behavior.

Traditionally, the cause of mongolism was assumed to be faulty heredity. A number of studies demonstrated, however, that more than one case of mongolism in a family was very infrequent, occurring in less than 1 family in 100 (Southwick, 1939). As a consequence, a number of investigators turned to the study of metabolic factors and concluded that mongolism was probably due to some sort of glandular imbalance, most likely involving the pituitary gland (Benda and Farrell, 1954; Benda, 1956). Then, in 1959, the French scientists Lejeune, Turpin, and Gauthier found 47 chromosomes in several mongoloid cases, and research centered on possible chromosomal anomalies.

Subsequent studies have shown that about 95 per cent of mongoloids have 47 chromosomes instead of the normal complement of 46 (Robinson, 1961). Typically, it would seem, mongoloids are trisomic for chromosome 21, although in some instances there appears to be a trisomy of chromosome 22 or other chromosome groups (Forssman and Lehmann, 1962). The 5 per cent who do not have 47 chromosomes are explained by anomalies elsewhere in the chromosome structure. In a review of the studies, Conen *et al.* (1962) concluded that varying types of chromosomal anomalies may make it possible for an individual to show physical and mental development ranging from nearly normal to clearly mongoloid. Interestingly, there appears to be little if any correlation between the number of physical symptoms of mongolism and the degree of mental retardation (Tarjan *et al.*, 1961; Dunsdon *et al.*, 1960).

The reason for the characteristic nondisjunction (failure to separate) of chromosome 21 during gametogenesis is not clear. Recessive genes or gene mutations occurring in one parent are probably critical determinants in some of the cases (Hamerton *et al.*, 1961). In the majority of cases, however, it would appear that a mutation of genes occurs in the egg cell just after fertilization or that something goes wrong in the mechanics of the growth process (Forssman and Lehmann, 1962). The latter hypothesis is supported by the fact that the incidence of mongoloid babies increases markedly with the age of mothers, particularly for mothers over 35. Bleyer (1937), analyzing 2822 cases, found that more than 50 per cent of mothers were over the age of 35 when their mongoloid child was born—more than 10 years beyond the average maternal age. It would thus appear that the probability of nondisjunction of chromosome 21 is influenced by metabolic factors; it is also possible, however, that the older the mother, the greater the probability that she has been exposed to ionizing radiation, resulting in gene mutations. Further research is needed to clarify the picture.

Whatever the cause of the chromosomal anomaly, the end result is the distortion in the growth process which is characteristic for this clinical syndrome. Once it occurs, mongolism is irreversible. There is no known effective treatment, nor have preventive measures been worked out, although Benda (1960) has recommended a program of extra precautions during pregnancy

At the left is a 27-month-old cretin, first diagnosed as a mongoloid. Note the large head, normally set eyes, short, depressed nose, normal mouth, and short neck. The same child is shown at the right at the age of six after 4 years of thyroid treatment. Her IQ had risen from 74 to 115.

to guard against glandular or dietary deficiencies. The desirability of avoiding unnecessary ionizing radiation has also received emphasis. Of course, it may be practical eventually to identify adults who have an abnormal number of chromosomes—or even specific defective genes—and to apprise them of the danger they run in having children. Also, as Hamerton *et al.* (1961) have suggested, chromosome studies may be used to detect parents with a high risk of having a second mongoloid child.

CRETINISM

Cretinism provides a dramatic illustration of mental retardation resulting from endocrine imbalance. In this condition, the thyroid either has failed to develop properly or has undergone degeneration or injury; in either case, the infant suffers from a deficiency in thyroid secretion. Brain damage resulting from this insufficiency is most marked during the prenatal and perinatal periods—during early periods of rapid growth (Pickering and Fisher, 1958).

In the valleys of central Switzerland and other geographical areas of the world where iodine is deficient in the soil, and therefore in food grown on it, cretinism was formerly a common affliction. Pregnant mothers in such areas often gave birth to infants with defective thyroid glands which remained undeveloped or atrophied later.

Because cretinism was observed to run in families in such areas, it was once thought to be a hereditary disorder. In 1891, however, Dr. George Murray published his discovery that the injection of thyroid gland extract was beneficial in cases of *myxedema*—a disorder resulting from thyroid deficiency in adult life and characterized by mental dullness. This discovery, in turn, led to the treatment of cretinism with thyroid gland extract and to the realization that this condition, too, was the result of thyroid deficiency.

Although most cases of cretinism result from lack of iodine in the diet, later studies have shown that genetic defects leading to a clinical condition of hypothyroidism may be of key etiological significance in some cases (Stanbury, 1960). Thyroid deficiency may also occur as the result of birth injuries (involving bleeding into the thyroid) or in connection with infectious diseases such as measles, whooping cough, or diphtheria. The resulting clinical picture will depend on the age at which the thyroid deficiency occurs, as well as on the degree and duration of the deficiency.

As a result of public health measures—on both national and international levels—including the use of iodized salt and the early detection and correction of thyroid deficiencies, severe cases of cretinism have become relatively rare. In the United States, cretins now constitute considerably less than 5 per cent of the institutionalized mentally retarded population.

Typical descriptions of cretins involve cases in which there has been a severe thyroid deficiency from an early age—often before birth. Such a cretin has a dwarflike, thick-set body and short, stubby extremities. When standing, his height is usually just a little over three feet. His shortness is accentuated by his slightly bent legs and a curvature of the spine. He walks with a shuffling gait that is easily recognizable. His head is large, with abundant black, wiry hair; his eyelids are thick, giving him a sleepy appearance; his skin is dry and thickened and cold to the touch. Other pronounced physical symptoms include a broad, flat nose, large and flabby ears, a protruding abdomen, and failure to mature sexually. The cretin reveals a bland personality make-up, and his thought processes tend to be sluggish. Most cretins fall within the severe and moderate categories of mental retardation, depending upon the extent of brain damage. In cases with less pronounced physical signs of cretinism, the mental retardation is usually less severe in degree.

Early treatment in cases of thyroid deficiency can produce striking results, and there are many instances of children restored to normal intellectual and personality levels. The success of treatment depends upon the age at onset of the disorder and its degree and duration: the prognosis is less favorable with early onset (for example, during the prenatal period) and with increasing duration, particularly in the severe cases. Smith *et al.* (1957) have shown that early treatment is essential and that patients not treated until after the first year of life may have permanently impaired intelligence. In long-standing cases, thyroid treatment may have some ameliorating effects, but the damage to the nervous system and to general physical development is beyond repair.

MICROCEPHALY

The term *microcephaly* means "small-headedness." It refers to a type of mental retardation resulting from impaired development of the brain and a consequent failure of the cranium to attain normal size. In an early study, Greenfield and Wolfson (1935) reported that post-mortem examination of the brains of microcephalics showed development arrested at the fourth or fifth month of fetal life in practically all cases examined. Fortunately, this condition is extremely rare.

The most obvious characteristic of the microcephalic is his small head, which rarely exceeds a circumference of 17 inches, as compared with the normal of approximately 22 inches. Penrose (1954) also described microcephalics as being invariably short in stature but having relatively normal musculature and sex organs. Beyond these characteristics, microcephalics differ considerably from each other in appearance, although there is a tendency for the skull to be cone-shaped, with a recession of the chin and forehead (Tredgold, 1952). Although microcephalics have traditionally been thought to be inclined toward hyperactivity and restlessness, but good-

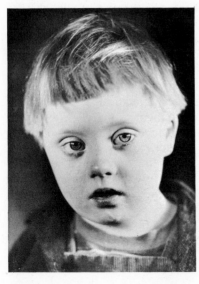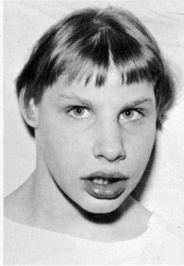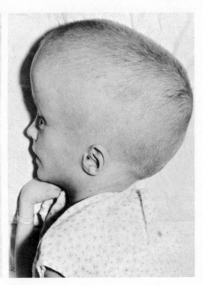

These children show three of the clinical types of mental retardation. At the left is a 6-year-old mongoloid boy with the characteristic round head, slanting eyes with thick eyelids, small mouth with fissured lips, and short neck. In the center is a microcephalic girl with the usual cone-shaped skull and receding chin and forehead. On the right is a hydrocephalic boy whose face is of normal size in contrast with the greatly enlarged back part of his head.

natured and easy to get along with, Brandon *et al.* (1959) failed to find any consistent qualities of temperament in a group he studied. Microcephalics fall in the profound, severe, and moderate categories of mental retardation. The majority show little language development and are extremely limited in mental capacity.

Microcephaly may result from a variety of causes (Cowie, 1960). So-called true or primary microcephaly has been considered by several investigators to be transmitted via a single recessive gene (Böök *et al.,* 1953; Heber, 1959; Koch, 1959). The evidence here is rather meager, however, and the precise nature of the genetic defect or defects remains to be clarified. Whether or not there is a characteristic chromosomal anomaly in microcephaly is not known.

It is known now that microcephaly may also result from a wide range of nongenetic factors which impair brain development, including intrauterine infections and pelvic irradiation of the mother during the early months of pregnancy (Cowie, 1960). A number of cases of microcephaly in Hiroshima resulting from the explo-

sion of the atom bomb were observed by Plummer (1952). The effects were more marked the nearer the pregnant mothers were to the center of the explosion.

Since diverse etiological factors may be involved, Cowie (1960) has questioned the value of the term *microcephaly,* pointing out that it tends to connote a disease entity and thus is misleading. She also pointed out that there are pygmies—such as those found in the rain forests of Africa—whose heads are small but proportional to the rest of their bodies. Here microcephaly, as we define it, is not a meaningful term. And in our general population, a considerable variation in head size is considered within the normal range.

Despite the apparent validity of these objections, microcephaly appears to be a useful category for describing certain types of mental retardates, although specific etiology should also be indicated when it is known. As yet, no medical treatment has been developed which is effective once the faulty brain development has occurred.

Both these sisters were afflicted with PKU, but the youngest one, at the left, was immediately placed on a special diet and the course of the disease was arrested.

HYDROCEPHALUS

Hydrocephalus is a relatively rare condition which results from the accumulation of an abnormal amount of cerebrospinal fluid within the cranium, causing damage to the brain tissues and enlargement of the cranium.

In a small number of congenital cases, hydrocephalus is present at birth or the head begins to enlarge soon after birth, presumably as a result of a prenatal disturbance in the formation, absorption, or circulation of cerebrospinal fluid (Heber, 1959). More frequently, the disorder develops in infancy or early childhood in association with intracranial neoplasms or acute inflammatory brain disease, such as chronic meningitis or encephalitis. Here the condition seems to result from a blocking in the cerebrospinal pathways and excessive accumulation of fluid in certain brain areas rather than from a failure in the mechanisms for forming or absorbing the fluid (Laurence, 1960).

The clinical picture in hydrocephalus depends upon the extent of neural damage, which, in turn, depends upon the age of onset, the duration, and the severity of the disorder. In chronic cases, the chief symptom is the gradual increase in size of the upper part of the head out of all proportion to the face and the rest of the body. Although the face remains relatively normal, the protruding skull gives the appearance one might expect in a race of super geniuses. The

expansibility of the skull helps minimize the destructive pressure on the brain, but serious brain damage does occur, leading to intellectual impairment and other effects such as convulsions and impairment or loss of sight and hearing. The degree of intellectual impairment varies; in advanced cases, the child manifests severe or profound mental retardation.

A good deal of attention has been directed to the surgical treatment of hydrocephalus, and with early diagnosis and treatment this condition can usually be arrested with a minimum of brain damage (Laurence, 1960). Unfortunately, some cases do not respond to treatment and in "expanding" hydrocephalus there is a progressive physical and mental deterioration ending in the death of the patient.

PHENYLKETONURIA (PKU)

Phenylketonuria is a rare metabolic disorder occurring once in 10,000 to 25,000 births (De Prospo, 1962; Nisonger, 1962). The baby appears normal at birth but lacks an enzyme needed to break down phenylalanine, an amino acid found in protein foods. When this condition is undetected, the phenylalanine builds up in the blood and damages the brain. The disorder usually becomes apparent between 6 and 12 months after birth, although symptoms such as vomiting, a peculiar odor, infantile eczema, and seizures may become apparent during the early weeks of life (Partington, 1961). Often the first symptoms noticed are signs of mental retardation, which may be moderate to severe, depending upon the degree to which the disease has progressed.

The discovery of PKU was made in 1934 when a Norwegian mother sought to learn the reason for her child's mental retardation and peculiar musty odor. She consulted with many physicians to no avail until Dr. Asbjorn Folling found phenylpyruvic acid in the urine and concluded that the child had a disorder of phenylalanine metabolism (W. Centerwall and S. Centerwall, 1961).

Most older PKU patients show severe mental retardation, although a few cases fall in the moderate or mild range (Hsia, 1959; Fishler, 1962). Motor incoordination and other neurological manifestations relating to the severe degree of brain damage are also common (Rubinstein, 1962). Testing of institutionalized mentally retarded populations has shown that about one half to one per cent of all institutionalized mental retardates have this disorder (W. Centerwall *et al.,* 1960).

Phenylketonuria is assumed to be transmitted via a recessive gene, and 1 person in 70 is thought to be a carrier (Hsia, 1959; Kalter, 1962). Various tests have been devised for early detection, and the infant with a positive diagnosis is placed on a special diet low in phenylalanine (W. Centerwall *et al.,* 1960). With early diagnosis and treatment, the brain damage may be minimal or prevented altogether.

Mental Retardation and Abnormal Behavior

Often mental retardates show behavioral irregularities or mental disorders in addition to their retardation. It will therefore be profitable to examine the role of mental retardation in the total picture.

MENTAL RETARDATION AND DELINQUENCY

Popular opinion, based on outdated psychological findings, has the view that mental retardates are especially prone to delinquent and criminal behavior. Indeed, one of the major reasons why institutionalization was first recommended for the mentally retarded was to protect society from their supposed "criminal propensities."

More recent psychological evidence has conclusively demonstrated that mental retardation is neither the specific cause nor the outstanding factor in crime and delinquency (Blatt, 1960). Although a higher than proportionate percentage of delinquent children come from the ranks of the mentally retarded, particularly from those of borderline intelligence, delinquency is not caused by mental retardation *per se;* it is usually the result of mental retardation combined with other factors, such as undesirable home conditions, school failure, early school drop-out, difficulty in finding and retaining employment, undesirable peer group affiliations, and inadequate social planning for post-school life for the mental retardate (J. O. Smith, 1962).

Undiagnosed mental retardates living in society at large often have demands put upon them which they cannot possibly meet, and maladjustment is the almost inevitable result. In some instances, this maladjustment takes the form of acting-out, delinquent behavior. Occasionally, too, brain-damaged children show uncontrollable outbursts of primitive hostile behavior, but such cases are a distinct minority. When properly taught and cared for, the great majority of mentally retarded children do not show a greater tendency toward delinquency than the general population. Of course, mentally retarded children are less able to foresee the probable consequences of their behavior and are more easily led than the normal child. As a consequence, they often get into trouble unintentionally or by following the lead of others.

Although mental retardation does not appear to play a determining role in the actual occurrence of delinquent behavior, it does play a role in determining the *type* of delinquency the person will show if he becomes delinquent. Among mentally retarded boys, truancy, petty stealing, and minor aggressive acts appear to be the most common delinquent patterns while among mentally retarded girls, sex offenses are the most common delinquency problem (Tarjan *et al.,* 1961). Since even adult mental retardates do not have the ability to plan and carry out complex criminal activities, their crimes usually follow similar patterns.

MENTAL RETARDATION AND MENTAL ILLNESS

Mental retardates may develop psychotic or other types of mental disorders. This is hardly surprising since, as a group, they suffer many

OTHER DISORDERS COMMONLY ASSOCIATED WITH MENTAL RETARDATION[1]

CLINICAL TYPE	SYMPTOMS	CAUSES
Gargoylism	Large head, protruding forehead, bushy eyebrows, saddle-shaped nose, thick lips, large tongue. Received name from gross and grotesque features of afflicted individuals.	Disorder of lipoid metabolism carried by single recessive gene.
No. 18 trisomy syndrome	Characterized by peculiar pattern of multiple congenital anomalies. The most common are low-set malformed ears, flexion of fingers, small mandible, and heart defects.	Autosomal anomaly of chromosome 18.
Tay-Sach's disease	Common symptoms include hypertonicity, listlessness, blindness, progressive spastic paralysis, convulsions, and death by the third year.	Disorder of lipoid metabolism.
Turner's syndrome	Characterized by webbing of the neck, increased carrying angle of forearm, and sexual infantilism.	Sex chromosome anomaly.
Klinefelter's syndrome	Symptoms vary from case to case; only constant finding is presence of small testes after puberty.	Sex chromosome anomaly.
Niemann-Pick disease	Usually has onset in infancy with loss of weight, dehydration, and progressive paralysis.	Disorder of lipoid metabolism.
Dwarfism	Facial features are drawn and sunken, hair thin or absent, skin atrophic and wrinkled. Appearance is that of premature senility.	Unknown etiology; presumably due to multiple genetic defects.
Macrocephaly	Increase in size and weight of brain, enlargement of skull, visual impairment, convulsions, and other neurological symptoms resulting from abnormal growth of glia cells which form supporting structure for brain tissue.	Unknown.

[1]The information in this chart is taken from the following sources: Brante (1957), Holub and Grumbach (1959), Haddad and Wilkins (1959), Herndon (1954), Rundle (1962), Shapiro and Ridler (1960), D. W. Smith et al. (1962), Stimson (1961).

difficult stresses—such as inability to understand the complexities of the world around them and failure to meet the educational and other demands that are often placed upon them. Many mildly retarded individuals are acutely aware of their intellectual inadequacy and suffer from severe feelings of inferiority.

When the mentally retarded do develop manic-depressive, schizophrenic, or other psychotic reactions, the symptom picture is usually somewhat different from that of persons of normal intelligence who develop such mental disorders. In general, there are fewer symptoms and the content of the symptoms is less sophisticated. For example, paranoid delusional symptoms are less complex and systematized. It would also appear that psychotic symptoms among mental retardates tend to be more transient and that spontaneous recoveries and relapses are frequent.

Sometimes brain-damaged children who are not schizophrenic show symptoms similar to those of schizophrenic children—for example, repetitive and stereotyped motions, bizarre body movements, distorted space and time orientations, aggressive temper displays, and perseverative behavior (Baer, 1961; Cleland, 1962). For this reason, there is sometimes a problem in the differential diagnosis of mental retardation and schizophrenia. However, mental retardates evidencing such behavior are usually of the severe type and various neurological involvements are generally apparent. In a minority of cases, mental retardates manifest the hyperactive, emotionally volatile, antisocial behavior which we have described in certain cases of postencephalitic behavior and other types of brain damage. In general, research findings indicate more psychological disorganization among brain-injured re-

tardates than among those suffering from developmental defects (Suczek, 1961).

Adequate statistics concerning the incidence of mental disorders among the mentally retarded population are not available. Some years ago Angus (1948) reported that 28 per cent of one year's admissions to a special school for the mentally retarded were psychotic. In a more recent study of a group of 159 mentally retarded children aged 3 to 6, Webster (1963) found a high incidence of emotional maladjustment. Thirty-five per cent were rated as mildly disturbed, 48 per cent as moderately disturbed, and 17 per cent as severely disturbed. He did not find a single child who was "simply retarded," and he concluded that the mental retardation syndrome "regularly includes significant disturbances in emotional development. . . . " (p. 39)

However, his sample cannot be considered characteristic of the mentally retarded as a group, and there is some question as to whether other investigators would agree with his criteria of emotionally "disturbed." Often, too, children are simply classified as mentally retarded and there is no attempt to make a secondary psychiatric diagnosis. In a study of 279 children below 10 years of age who were admitted to a state institution for the mentally retarded, Tarjan *et al.* (1961) noted that 63 per cent manifested a withdrawn personality, but no secondary diagnosis was made. Over half of these children had IQ's below 20, making precise assessment almost impossible.

Despite a lack of adequate statistics, it would appear safe to assume that the incidence of mental disorders is higher among the mentally retarded than among the general population, but the nature and the magnitude of the difference remain to be determined.

Treatment and Prognosis

State institutions for the mentally retarded are often desperately overcrowded and a family may have to wait several months before their child can be admitted, whereas most private institutions are beyond the means of the average family. Fortunately, as we have seen, most retard-

ates do not need to be institutionalized, and there have been several breakthroughs in treatment for retardates both in and out of institutions. Thyroid medication for cretinism, surgical treatment for hydrocephalus, and special diets for PKU have already been mentioned. It should be emphasized, however, that in every case early diagnosis is of vital importance if therapy is to be of maximal value. Once serious brain damage has occurred, there is no effective medical treatment.

In many cases, drugs have proved helpful but by no means a cure. In many cases tranquilizing drugs have proved useful in controlling hyperactive and disturbed behavior among brain-damaged children (Kanjilal and Matheson, 1962; Pilkington, 1962; Sharpe, 1962; Timberlake *et al.*, 1957). In an investigation of the effects of reserpine on 200 mentally retarded children who were either overactive, abusive and destructive, or withdrawn, Timberlake *et al.* (1957) reported improved social behavior in 65 per cent of the cases. It should be noted, however, that there is a great deal of variation among mental retardates in their reaction to tranquilizing drugs.

In addition to drug treatment, both individual and group psychotherapy have been utilized with mental retardates with varying success (Windle, 1962). This approach, too, is directed more toward ameliorating behavior problems and helping the child utilize his capacities better than toward dealing with the mental retardation proper.

The mentally retarded child is not only a medical problem but a family, psychological, educational, and socioeconomic problem as well. The family, the school, the neighborhood, the legal system, and community facilities all influence his adjustment for better or for worse. Basically, of course, he has the same needs as other children: he needs love, acceptance, physical care, a sense of adequacy and worth, guidance, and an education commensurate with his mental capacity. Many aspects of these needs can be met by the family unit and by facilities available to all members of the community. Other aspects may require various types of specialized or additional measures.

Sometimes disappointed parents, insecure and guilt-ridden because of imagined responsibility for the child's condition, demand behavior and intellectual achievement beyond the child's abilities; other parents take an overly protective approach in their efforts to shield the child from any challenging situation, thus interfering with the development of whatever capacities he may have. Contrary to popular opinion, recent research indicates that parents do not ordinarily reject their mentally retarded child; such a child may, however, place a considerable strain on the family as a group (Dimichael, 1961; Saenger, 1960). Social workers have come to place strong emphasis on counseling aimed at helping parents understand and accept the child's shortcomings and make plans appropriate to his capacity.

Educators have become increasingly aware of their responsibility to the mentally retarded child, and many public schools now have special classes and programs for the mentally retarded (Gardner and Nisonger, 1962; Wrightstone, 1961). Classes for mild retardates concentrate on a functional program which usually emphasizes social skills, budgeting and money matters, and the development of simple occupational skills. Such programs have been successful in helping mild retardates to become independent, productive members of their community. These children are also capable of some degree of achievement in academic subjects such as reading and arithmetic. Classes for moderately and severely retarded children have more limited objectives but strive to help the child to develop self-care and other skills which will enable him to function adequately and be of assistance in either a family or an institutional setting. In some cases simple job skills can be learned.

Much remains to be learned about the most effective educational procedures to use with the mentally retarded, but specially trained teachers utilizing new materials and techniques have produced encouraging results (Davy, 1962; Woolman and Davy, 1963). The best use of new technological media for educating the mentally retarded have not been fully delineated, but preliminary findings give every reason to believe that they will be of great value (Rothstein, 1961; Price, 1963). Similarly, exploratory studies utilizing operant conditioning methods with severe mental retardates have shown encouraging results in the development of basic self-care and related skills (Barnett *et al.*, 1960). Aside from the humanitarian value of providing the mentally retarded child with appropriate training and educational opportunities, it has been estimated that saving just one mentally retarded child from a life of institutionalization saves the

A

B

C

D

Although new, improved facilities are being built and the present emphasis is on smaller, community-centered units, Dixon State School for the mentally retarded at Dixon, Illinois, is still typical of many institutions throughout the United States. It is understaffed and badly overcrowded, with 5000 retardates living in wards designed for 3200. Yet despite discouraging handicaps, much is being accomplished. Classes for the mildly retarded (A) teach academic skills up to the fifth-grade level and prepare many of these young people to become self-supporting citizens. Classes for moderately retarded children (B) teach largely self-care and acceptable social skills which will enable these youngsters to function usefully in their homes or in other sheltered situations. For older retardates (C), occupational therapy provides both recreation and training in useful skills. Recreation and sports are as valuable for retardates as for anyone else, and such activities at Dixon include a choir, a baton-twirling group, weekly dancing, sports like boxing and volley ball, and a drum and bugle corps of which all are rightly proud (D).

taxpayers somewhere around $100,000 (S. Centerwall and W. Centerwall, 1960).[1]

One problem which often elicits a great deal of anxiety on the part of parents is whether or not to institutionalize their mentally retarded child.[2] In general, children who are institutionalized fall into two groups: (a) infants and children with severe mental retardation and associated physical impairments who enter the institution at an early age, and (b) adolescents who usually have no physical impairments but show mild mental retardation and fail to adjust socially, eventually requiring institutionalization for delinquent or other acting-out behavior (Tarjan *et al.*, 1961). The families in the first group come from all socioeconomic levels, whereas a significantly higher percentage of the families in the second group come from lower educational and occupational strata.

S. Centerwall and W. Centerwall (1960) compared 32 mongoloid children reared at home for at least two and a half years after birth with a control group who had been placed in an institution shortly after birth. They found that the children reared at home were superior in physical development, had higher measurable IQ's, and functioned at a higher intellectual level. It has also been shown that female retardates placed in an institution have a more negative self-attitude and see themselves as of less value than do those who remain at home (Guthrie, 1963). As a consequence of such considerations, institutionalization is not recommended where the child makes a satisfactory adjustment at home and in any special training school that he may attend during the day. Unfortunately, many mental retardates do not have families in a position to care for them.

For children who have grown up in a family setting, institutionalization, with its separation from home and family, is often a traumatic experience—particularly for children with moderate and mild mental retardation. After a transitional period, however, most mentally retarded children adjust well in modern institutional settings where they live and compete with children in their own ability range and have the advantage of specialized educational, medical, and other services.

For mental retardates who become ready to attempt an adjustment in the community and

have no families to whom they can return, a program of foster-home placement has been developed recently in several cities. Such placements, of course, require considerable supervision and the careful education of the foster parents with respect to the needs and limitations of the mentally retarded child. For adolescents and young adults suffering from moderate to mild degrees of mental retardation, the use of "sheltered workshops" in the community appear to be of value both to mental retardates making the transition from institutional to community life and to many mental retardates residing with their families (Beasley, 1961; Gardner and Nisonger, 1962; Niehn, 1958). In such sheltered workshops mental retardates who cannot compete successfully in modern industry can learn and perform simple occupational tasks under supervision. With the assistance of their families, they may thus find it possible to live reasonably satisfying and constructive adult lives in the community.

In addition to other resources available to the mentally retarded, the United States Vocational Rehabilitation Administration and various state and private agencies provide diverse types of assistance to mental retardates, including medical, psychological, and social-vocational assessment; specialized training in vocational skills; selective placement and follow-up in employment; and counseling with personal problems. In line with other mental health efforts, a concerted effort is being made to establish community-centered agencies that will provide a coordinated and continuous program of services to meet the needs of the mentally retarded.

The prognosis for an individual case is often difficult to assess. As we have noted, the great majority of mild retardates make successful family and community adjustments, and even 75 per cent or more of moderate and severe cases can live in family settings (Nisonger, 1962). Windle (1962) has emphasized the following prognostic criteria: (a) Older retardates (young adulthood to some as yet unspecified age) are more likely than younger ones to succeed on

---

[1] A detailed discussion of learning theory and mental retardation, public school programs for the mentally retarded, and educational programs in state institutions for the mentally retarded is contained in Rothstein (1961).

[2] For a more detailed discussion of the factors precipitating institutionalization of retarded children, see Group for the Advancement of Psychiatry (1959), Saenger (1960).

vocational and home leave. (b) Retardates institutionalized between 10 and 20 years of age are more likely to be released and to make successful community adjustments than are those institutionalized at earlier or later ages. (c) Retardates with familial or undifferentiated diagnoses are more likely to be released than those with specific disorders. (d) Mild retardates are more likely to be released than moderate or severe cases. (e) Delinquent behavior before institutionalization is not clear in its prognostic significance, but bad behavior within the institution is prognostically unfavorable. (f) The sanction of the institution in releasing the retardate is highly important in predicting success on release. (g) The more favorable the home situation to which the patient is released, the better

his chance of making a successful adjustment. The sex of the mental retardate does not appear to be of prognostic significance.

In discussing treatment and prognosis in mental retardation, it is essential to emphasize the need for society to be concerned with the long-range life adjustment of the mental retardate as well as with his immediate schooling. Increasing automation is making it extremely difficult for these persons to compete on the labor market, and often they need help in adjusting to the problems of our technical, complex, and rapidly changing society. The eventual outcome for most mild mental retardates thus appears to depend heavily upon the type of community program which society is willing to provide for this handicapped segment of our population.

Prevention of Mental Retardation

The problem of preventing mental retardation involves the question of genetic factors as well as a wide range of biochemical, neurophysiological, and psychocultural conditions. Inevitably, it is an interdisciplinary problem concerned with human development in general.

Until recently the most hopeful approach to the prevention of mental retardation has been the emphasis on routine health measures for the pregnant mother, precautions against the possibility of intrauterine or birth damage, and the use of various diagnostic measures to ensure the early detection and, where possible, correction of abnormalities. With such health measures and a normal and stimulating environment after birth, many cases of mental retardation which were once thought to be hereditary and inevitable have been and can be prevented.

In the past decade, two new frontiers have opened up in the field of prevention—one in genetics, the other in sociocultural approaches. Work in genetics has shown the role of chromosomal abnormalities in faulty development, and tests have been developed to identify parents who have some chromosomal anomalies, thus making it possible to counsel them concerning the danger they run in having children. As yet,

such tests have not come into routine use, but in the not too distant future, chromosomal examinations may be required of people planning to marry, in much the same way that blood tests for syphilis are now required.

Perhaps of even greater potential significance have been recent studies showing the biochemical basis for gene action (Stimson, 1961). Geneticists have shown that genes direct the manufacture of chemicals called *enzymes* which act as catalysts for the thousands of metabolic reactions essential for life and development. A defect in a given gene may prevent or alter basic biochemical reactions essential for normal brain development and functioning. Apparently, multiple as well as single gene defects may be involved in a given developmental abnormality, and an individual may have an "overdose" as well as an "underdose" of certain genes. If scientists can detect the missing enzyme or genetic defect in time, they may be able to correct it by artificial means and thus prevent or minimize damage to the offspring. As we have noted, this has, in fact, been accomplished in the case of PKU, where the baby has defective genes which fail to provide for a liver enzyme that normally converts phenylalanine into tyrosine and energy.

In essence, this discovery means that modern science is no longer completely powerless against genetic diseases.

The second horizon in prevention involves the alleviation of sociocultural conditions which deprive children of the necessary stimulation, motivation, and opportunity for normal learning and mental development. As the late President Kennedy pointed out:

"Studies have demonstrated that large numbers of children in urban and rural slums, including preschool children, lack the stimulus necessary for proper development in their intelligence. Even when there is no organic impairment, prolonged neglect and a lack of stimulus and opportunity for learning can result in the failure of young minds to develop. Other studies have shown that, if proper opportunities for learning are provided early enough, many of these deprived children can and will learn and achieve as much as children from more favored neighborhoods. The self-perpetuating intellectual blight should not be allowed to continue." (1963, p. 286)

As much more research is done on genetic and chromosomal anomalies, on the biochemistry and neurophysiology of life processes, on the vicissitudes of intrauterine life, on the effect of ionizing radiation on sex and somatic cells, on neurological effects of viral infections during infancy and early childhood, and on the precise effects of various specific sociocultural conditions on intellectual development, there is every reason to believe that our knowledge of mental retardation and our ability to prevent it will greatly increase. Even at present, however, it has been estimated that more than half of all cases of mental retardation could be prevented if we would apply our existing knowledge in a "broad spectrum" approach—directed at both the specific causes which medical science has identified and the broader adverse social, economic, and cultural conditions which are so highly correlated with the incidence of mental retardation (Kennedy, 1963).

The President's Message (Kennedy, 1963), based on the report submitted by the Panel on Mental Retardation, has directed the nation's attention to the tragic and costly problem of mental retardation in the United States. In the years immediately ahead, we can expect to see a concerted all-out attack on the problem of mental retardation. The following "keys to future progress" are being emphasized:

1. *Prevention.* High priority is given to prevention of mental retardation through the application of existing knowledge. General health, welfare, education, and urban renewal programs should contribute to the overall effort. More adequate medical care for the mother and baby, improved nutrition, specialized educational programs, and greater social and economic opportunities are expected to reduce mental retardation to the low incidence that has been achieved in some other countries.

2. *Community services.* The need for a new and comprehensive approach to facilities and services for the mentally retarded is stressed, with the emphasis being placed on community-centered agencies that will provide a coordinated range of diagnostic, health, educational, employment, rehabilitation, welfare, and related services. This phase of the program includes the training of needed personnel.

3. *Research.* Emphasis is placed on the facilitation and acceleration of research on all phases of the problem: etiology, educational procedures, social effects on the family, psychological effects on the individual, and the changing role and functions of community and state services and agencies.

The "broad spectrum" approach seems realistic in terms of both immediate practical action and long-range research and should lead to marked progress in understanding, diagnosis, treatment, and prevention of the age-old problem of mental retardation.

In Parts Three and Four we have examined the many syndromes of abnormal behavior identified in the APA classification of mental disorders. Part Five will be devoted to theories and methods of diagnosis and therapy and to a "progress report" on current organized efforts for mental health.

REFERENCES

The reference list includes not only the sources from which the author has drawn material, but acknowledgments of the permissions granted by authors and publishers to quote directly from their works.

American Association on Mental Deficiency. *Listings of state and private training school and homes for the retarded.* Willimantic, Conn.: Author, 1960.

ANGUS, L. R. Schizophrenia and schizoid conditions in students in a special school. *Amer. J. ment. Def.,* 1948, 53, 227-238.

BAER, P. E. Problems in the differential diagnosis of brain damage and childhood schizophrenia. *Amer. J. Orthopsychiat.,* 1961, 31, 728-737.

BEASLEY, D. Sheltered workshops. *J. N. Zeal. INCPA, Inc.,* 1961.

BENDA, C. E. Mongolism: a comprehensive review. *Arch. Pediat.,* 1956, 73, 391-407.

BENDA, C. E. *The child with mongolism.* New York: Grune & Stratton, 1960.

BENDA, C. E., & FARRELL, M. Metabolic studies in mongolism: discussion. *Amer. J. Psychiat.,* 1954, 111, 144-145.

BENDA, C. E., *et al.* Personality factors in mild mental retardation. Part I. Family background and sociocultural patterns. *Amer. J. ment. Def.,* 1963, 68, 24-40.

BLATT, B. Some persistently recurring assumptions concerning the mentally subnormal. *Train. Sch. Bull.,* 1960, 57, 48-59.

BLEYER, A. Theoretical and clinical aspects of mongolism. *J. Mo. med. Ass.,* 1937, 34, 222-227.

BOGGS, E. Mongolism: new discoveries every month. *Child. ltd.,* 1962, 10, 6-9.

BÖÖK, J. A., SCHUT, J. W., & REED, S. C. A clinical and genetical study of microcephaly. *Amer. J. ment. Def.,* 1953, 57, 637-660.

BRANDON, M. W. G., KIRMAN, B. H., & WILLIAMS, C. E. Microcephaly. *J. ment. Sci.,* 1959, 105, 721-747.

CENTERWALL, S. A., & CENTERWALL, W. R. Study of children with mongolism reared in the home compared to those reared away from the home. *Pediatrics,* 1960, 25, 678-685.

CENTERWALL, W. R., & CENTERWALL, S. A. Phenylketonuria (Folling's disease): the story of its discovery. *J. Hist. Med.,* 1961, 16, 292-296.

CENTERWALL, W. R., *et al.* Phenylketonuria: screening programs and testing methods. *Amer. J. Publ. Hlth,* 1960, 50, 1667-1677.

CLELAND, C. C. Severe retardation: program suggestions. *Train. Sch. Bull.,* 1962, 59, 31-37.

COFFEY, V. P., & JESSOP, W. J. Maternal influenza and congenital deformities: a prospective study. *Lancet,* 1959, 7109, 935-938.

COLLMAN, R. D., & STOLLER, A. A life table for mongols in Victoria, Australia. *J. ment. Def. Res.,* 1962, 7, 53-59.

CONEN, P. E., BELL, A. G., & RANCE, C. P. A review of chromosome studies in the diagnosis of mongolism. *J. Pediat.,* 1962, 60, 533-539.

COWIE, VICTORIA. The genetics and sub-classification of microcephaly. *J. ment. Def. Res.,* 1960, 4, 42-47.

DAVY, RUTH A. Adaptation of progressive-choice method for teaching reading to retarded children. *Amer. J ment. Def.,* 1962, 67, 274-280.

DE HAAS, K. J., QUINN, K. V., & PRYLES, C. V. Enforced delay at delivery and its relationship to brain damage and mental deficiency. *Amer. J. ment. Def.,* 1961, 65, 610-614.

DELP, H. Psychological evaluation: some problems and suggestions. In J. Rothstein (Ed.), *Mental retardation.* New York: Holt, Rinehart, & Winston, 1961.

DE PROSPO, C. J. News and notes. *Amer. J. ment. Def.,* 1962, 67, 113-136.

DIMICHAEL, S. G. Social and economic effects of mental retardation. In J. Rothstein (Ed.), *Mental retardation.* New York: Holt, Rinehart, & Winston, 1961. Pp. 101-112.

DOLL, E. A., PHELPS, W. N., & MELCHER, R. T. *Mental deficiency due to birth injuries.* New York: Macmillan, 1932.

DUNSDON, M. I., CARTER, C. O., & HUNTLEY, R. M. Upper end of range of intelligence in mongolism. *Lancet,* 1960, 1, 565-568.

ELLIS, N. R., BARNETT, C. D., & PRYER, MARGARET W. Operant behavior in mental defectives: exploratory studies. *J. exp. anal. Behav.,* 1960, 3, 63-69.

Exceptional Children's Foundation. *A lot of little figures.* Los Angeles: Author, 1962.

FISHER, G. M. Further evidence of the invalidity of the Wechsler Adult Intelligence Scale for the assessment of intelligence of mental retardates. *J. ment. Def. Res.,* 1962, 6, 41-43.

FISHLER, K. Mental development in children with phenylketonuria. *Amer. Psychologist,* 1962, 17, 311.

FORSSMAN, H., & LEHMANN, ORLA. Chromosome studies in eleven families with mongolism in more than one member. *Acta Pediat. (Upps),* 1962, 51, 180-188.

GARDNER, W. J., & NISONGER, H. W. A manual on program development in mental retardation. *Amer. J. ment. Def.,* 1962, 66 (4, Monogr. Suppl.), 192 p.

GERMAN, J. L. 3RD, RANKIN, J. K., HARRISON, P. A., DONOVAN, D. J., HOGAN, W. J., & BEARN, A. G. Autosomal trisomy of a group 16-18 chromosome. *J. Pediat.,* 1962, 60, 498.

GILLIS, S. *The year book of pediatrics, 1961-62.* Chicago: Year Book Publishers, 1961.

GRAHAM, FRANCES K., ERNHART, CLARIE B., THURSTON, D., & CRAFT, MARGUERITE. Development three years after perinatal anoxia and other potentially damaging newborn experiences. *Psychol. Monogr.,* 1962, 76 (3, Whole No. 522). 53 pp.

GREENFIELD, J. C., & WOLFSON, J. M. Microcephalia vera. *AMA Arch. Neurol. Psychiat.,* 1935, 33, 1296-1316.

Group for the Advancement of Psychiatry. Report. No. 43. *Basic considerations in mental retardation: a preliminary report.* New York: Publications Office, 1959.

GUTHRIE, G. M., BUTLER, A. & GORLOW, L. Personality differences between institutionalized and non-institutionalized retardates. *Amer. J. ment. Def.,* 1963, 67, 543-548.

HADDAD, H. M., & WILKINS, L. Congenital anomalies associated with gonadal aplasia. Review of 55 cases. *Pediatrics,* 1959, 23, 885-902.

HAMERTON, J. L., BRIGGS, S. M., GIANNELLI, F., & CARTER, C. O. Chromosome studies in detection of parents with high risk of second child with Down's syndrome (mongolism). *Lancet,* 1961, 2, 788-791.

HEBER, R. A manual on terminology and classification in mental retardation. *Amer. J. ment. Def.,* 1959, (Sept.) 64, Monogr. Suppl. No. 2.

HEBER, R. Modifications in the manual on terminology and classification in mental retardation. *Amer. J. ment. Def.,* 1961, 65, 499-500.

HERNDEN, C. N. Genetics of lipidosis. *Ass. Res. nerv. ment. Dis., Proc.,* 1954, 33, 239-258.

HOLUB, D. A., GRUMBACH, M. M., & JAILER, J. W. Seminiferous tubule dysgenesis (Klinefelter's syndrome) in identical twins. *J. clin. Endocrinol. Metabolism,* 1958, 18, 1359-1368.

HSIA, D. Y. *Inborn errors of metabolism.* Chicago: Year Book, 1959.

JANCAR, J. Postencephalitic endocrine disorders with mental subnormality. *J. ment. Def. Res.*, 1961, 5, 115-123.

KALTER, H. Paper delivered at symposium on phenylketonuria. Institute for post-graduate education, Cincinnati, Nov. 16, 1961. Reported Ross Laboratories: *Currents in Publ. Hlth*, 1962, 2.

KANJILAL, G. C., & MATHESON, B. A trial of tetrabenazine ("nitoman") in disturbed mentally subnormal patients. *J. ment. Sci.*, 1962, 118, 225-228.

KENNEDY, J. F. Message from the President of the United States relative to mental illness and mental retardation. *Amer. Psychologist*, 1963, 18, 280-289.

KIRKMAN, H. N., & RILEY, H. D., JR. Posthemorrhagic anemia and shock in the newborn due to hemorrhage during delivery: report of 8 cases. *Pediatrics*, 1959, 24, 92-96.

KNOBLOCH, HILDA. Neuropsychiatric sequelae of prematurity: a longitudinal study. *J. Amer. med. Ass.*, 1956, 161, 581-585.

KOCH, G. Genetics of microcephaly in man. *Acta Genet. Med. Gemellol.*, (Roma), 1959, 8, 75.

LAURENCE, K. M. Hydrocephalus and disability. *Cerebral Palsy Bull.*, 1960, 2, 170-179.

MACLEAN, N., & MITCHELL, J. M. A survey of sex chromosome abnormalities among 4,514 mental defectives. *Lancet*, 1962, 1, 293-296.

MENNINGER, W. C. *Facts and statistics of significance for psychiatry*. Austin, Tex.: Hogg Found., Univer. Texas, 1948.

MOSIER, H. D., SCOTT, L. W., & COTTER, L. H. The frequency of the positive sex-chromatin pattern in males with mental deficiency. *Pediatrics*, 1960, 25, 291-297.

NIEHN, B. Study of sheltered workshops for the mentally retarded. *Train. Sch. Bull.*, 1958, 54, 67-71.

NISHIMURA, H. Current knowledge on the cause of congenital anomalies. *Jap. J. child Psych.*, 1962, 3, 1-16.

NISONGER, H. W. Changing concepts in mental retardation. *Amer. J. ment. Def.*, 1962, 67, 4-13.

PARTINGTON, M. W. The early symptoms of phenylketonuria. *Pediatrics*, 1961, 27, 465-473.

PAULING, L. Genetic effects of weapons tests. *Bull. atom. Scientists*, 1962, 18 (10), 15-18.

PENROSE, L. S. *Biology of mental defect* (2nd ed.) New York: Grune & Stratton, 1963.

PICKERING, D. E., & FISHER, D. A. Therapeutic concepts relative to hypothyroidism in childhood. *J. chron. Dis.*, 1958, 7, 242-263.

PILKINGTON, T. L. A report on "tofranil" in mental deficiency. *Amer. J. ment. Def.*, 1962, 66, 729-732.

President's Panel on Mental Retardation. *A proposed program for national action to combat mental retardation*, Oct. 1962. Washington, D. C.: U. S. Government Printing Office, 1963.

PRICE, J. E. Automated teaching programs with mentally retarded students. *Amer. J. ment. Def.*, 1963, 68, 69-72.

ROBINSON, A. The human chromosomes. *Amer. J. Dis. Child.*, 1961, 101, 379-398.

ROTHSTEIN, J. H. (Ed.) *Mental retardation*. New York: Holt, Rinehart & Winston, 1961.

RUBINSTEIN, J. Paper delivered at symposium on phenylketonuria. Institute for post-graduate education, Cincinnati, Nov. 16, 1961. Reported Ross Laboratories: *Currents in Publ. Hlth*, 1962, 2.

RUNDLE, A. T. Etiological factors in mental retardation: I. Biochemical II. Endocrinological. *Amer. J. ment. Def.*, 1962, 67, 61-68, 68-77.

SAENGER, G. *Factors influencing the institutionalization of mentally retarded individuals in New York City*. Albany: N. Y. St. Interdepartmental Health Resources Board, 1960.

SCHWARTZ, P. *Birth injuries of the newborn*. New York: Hafner, 1961.

SHAPIRO, A., & RIDLER, M. A. The incidence of Klinefelter's syndrome in a mental deficiency hospital. *J. ment. Def. Res.*, 1960, 4, 48-50.

SHARPE, D. S. A controlled trial of trifluoperazine in the treatment of the mentally subnormal patient. *J. ment. Sci.*, 1962, 108, 220-224.

SIEGEL, M., & GREENBERG, M. Fetal death, malformation and prematurity after maternal rubella; results of a prospective study, 1949-1958. *Yearbk. Pediat.*, 1960-61 series, 11-12.

SMITH, D. W., BLIZZARD, R. M., & WILKINS, L. The mental prognosis in hypothyroidism in infancy and childhood. *Pediatrics*, 1957, 19, 1011-1020.

SMITH, D. W., PATAU, K., THERMAN, E., & INHORN, S. L. The no. 18 trisomy syndrome. *J. Pediat.*, 1962, 60, 513-527.

SMITH, J. O. Criminality and mental retardation. *Train. Sch. Bull.*, 1962, 59 (3), 74-80.

SOUTHWICK, W. E. Time and stage in development at which factors operate to produce mongolism. *Amer. J. Dis. Child.*, 1939, 117, 68-69.

STANBURY, J. B., WYNGAARDEN, J. B., & FREDRICKSON, D. S. (Eds.) *The metabolic basis of inherited disease*. New York: McGraw-Hill, 1960.

STIMSON, C. W. Human cytogenetics and its clinical application to mental retardation. *Amer. J. ment. Def.*, 1961, 65, 713-725.

SUCZEK, R. The assessment and treatment of children with brain injury. In J. Rothstein (Ed.), *Mental retardation*. New York: Holt, Rinehart, & Winston, 1961. Pp. 125-135.

TARJAN, G., DINGMAN, H. F., & MILLER, C. R. Statistical expectations of selected handicaps in the mentally retarded. *Amer. J. ment. Def.*, 1960, 65, 335-341.

TARJAN, G., WRIGHT, S. W., DINGMAN, H. F., & EYMAN, R. K. Natural history of mental deficiency in a state hospital. *Amer. J. Dis. Child.*, 1961, 101, 195-205.

TIMBERLAKE, W. H. T., BELMONT, ELIZABETH H., & OGONIK, J. The effect of reserpine on 200 mentally retarded children. *Amer. J. ment. Def.*, 1957, 62, 61-66.

TREDGOLD, A. F., & TREDGOLD, R. F. *Textbook of mental deficiency*. London: Baillière, Tindall & Cox, 1952.

U. S. Federal Radiation Council. *Health implications of fallout from nuclear weapons testing through 1961*. Washington, D. C.: Author, 1962.

U. S. Public Health Service. *Patients in mental institutions, 1960. Part II. Public hospitals for the mentally ill*. Washington, D. C.: Public Health Service Publication No. 963, 1963.

VAN BOGAERT, L., et al. (Eds.) *Cerebral lipidosis*. Springfield, Ill.: Charles C. Thomas, 1957.

WEBSTER, T. G. Problems of emotional development in young retarded children. *Amer. J. Psychiat.*, 1963, 120, 37-43.

WINDLE, C. Prognosis of mental subnormals. *Amer. J. ment. Def.*, 1962, 66 (5, Monogr. Suppl.), 180 p.

WOOLMAN, M., & DAVY, RUTH. *Developing symbolic skills in the mentally retarded*. Washington, D. C.: Institute of Educational Research, Inc., 1963.

WRIGHT, S. W., TARJAN, G., LIPPMAN, R. W., & PERRY, T. L. Etiologic factors in mental deficiency. *Amer. J. Dis. Child.*, 1958, 95, 541-562.

WRIGHTSTONE, G. Some philosophies of education for the mentally retarded. In J. Rothstein (Ed.), *Mental retardation*. New York: Holt, Rinehart, & Winston, 1961.

WUNSCH, W. L. Some characteristics of mongoloids evaluated in a clinic for children with retarded mental development. *Amer. J. ment. Def.*, 1957, 62, 122-130.

YACORZYNSKI, G. K., & TUCKER, BEATRICE E. What price intelligence? *Amer. Psychologist*, 1960, 15, 201-203.

MODERN METHODS OF DIAGNOSIS, UNDERSTANDING, TREATMENT, AND PREVENTION

part five

DIAGNOSIS

chapter 13

When a patient arrives at a mental hospital or comes to an outside agency or clinic for psychiatric help, the first step is usually a diagnosis of the case.[1] In diagnosis we are primarily concerned with determining the precise nature of the patient's illness. This means not just applying a label for the disorder, but obtaining as complete a view as possible of the symptom picture and evaluating the role of biological, psychological, and sociological factors in the development and present dynamics of the disorder.

To keep a record of the diagnostic information obtained, the treatment program undertaken, and the subsequent progress of the patient, psychiatric agencies use case-history or case-record forms. Such a form usually includes entries for:

I   Identifying data (name, address, age, sex)
II   Nature of problem
III   Personal history
IV   Medical examination
V   Psychological assessment
VI   Sociological evaluation
VII   Diagnosis or classification
VIII   Treatment program and results
IX   Termination or discharge data
X   Follow-up

More and more modern clinics and mental hospitals are using electronic equipment for maintaining their case records. Such equipment makes it readily possible to retrieve case data and analyze the information for research purposes.

We have already suggested that there are several important objectives associated with the accumulation of diagnostic information. These may be summarized as follows:

1. To obtain a summary view of the symptom picture
2. To understand the development and present dynamics of the disorder
3. To classify the patient
4. To provide a sound basis for treatment
5. To give a partial basis for prognosis

Here it may be emphasized that psychiatric treatment involves a considerable amount of far-reaching decision making—for example, concerning the necessity for hospitalization, the use of drugs, the role of psychotherapy, and related aspects of the overall treatment program. These decisions may be made with or without the participation of the patient, depending upon the nature and severity of his mental illness. In either event, such decisions are most likely to be scientifically sound and practicable if they are based on accurate diagnostic evaluation.

The objectives of diagnosis will, of course, vary somewhat with the particular agency, the type of patient, and various other considerations. If the purpose is to determine whether or not the individual should be committed to an institution, the general nature and severity of his disorder may be of primary interest. If the diagnostic data is to be used for purposes of formulating a treatment program, then the focus may be on developing a working "model" of the patient in relation to his life situation. After a period of treatment, a diagnostic evaluation may be undertaken to ascertain how much progress has been made and to provide a basis for planning subsequent treatment. In cases where the individual is applying for disability insurance, diagnostic techniques may be used primarily for determining the actual type and degree of the patient's incapacity for normal adjustment.[2]

It will thus be readily apparent that classification of the patient—fitting him into some diagnostic category such as *schizophrenia*—is only one of the major purposes of diagnosis. As a matter of fact, classifications are often difficult to make, sometimes misleading, and not infrequently incorrect. They are useful, however, in making it possible for us to evaluate the effectiveness of a particular type of therapy with a particular disorder, since the procedure insures that those referring to "paranoid schizophrenic," for example, are talking of patients with roughly the same type of disorder. Without some standard, generally agreed-on classification procedure, the personnel in one clinic or hospital would be unable to make use of findings from other clinics or hospitals, and our progress in the understanding and treatment of mental disorders would be very much slower.

Collection of Diagnostic Information

Modern diagnosis involves evaluation from several points of view and is achieved through the coordinated activities of a "psychiatric team" consisting of a psychiatrist, a clinical psychologist, a psychiatric social worker, and such other specialized personnel as conditions warrant. Such a team is designed to yield the following types of information.

1. *Medical data.* Included here are a general picture of the patient's present physical state, with emphasis on any pathological conditions which may be causative factors in his illness. The data are obtained by means of thorough medical and neurological examinations.

2. *Psychological data.* Included here are reports concerning the patient's symptoms and complaints, intellectual resources, frame of ref-

---

[1] In certain cases emergency medical measures take precedence, but ordinarily the treatment program is based on a comprehensive diagnostic evaluation.

[2] Approximately 1,500,000 former workers receive monthly benefits under the disability insurance program of the Social Security Act (Lerner, 1963). In addition to medical evaluation, psychological examinations are frequently required for evaluating intellectual and/or emotional impairment or disturbances.

erence, conflicts and other perceived stresses, adjustive patterns, and general personality make-up. The data are obtained through observation, interviews with the patient, psychological tests, and other assessment procedures.

3. *Sociological data.* Included here is information concerning the patient's home condition; marital, occupational, and social adjustment; financial status; and general life situation. Where possible, the record also includes information about the patient's developmental, health, school, family, and social history. The data are usually obtained from the referral source, the patient, and the patient's family by the psychiatric social worker.

The comprehensiveness of the diagnostic evaluation will, of course, vary with the needs of the particular case and the facilities of the treatment agency. For each of the three types of evaluation there are several procedures which may be used. These will be our concern throughout the present chapter, with emphasis on the psychological assessment.

THE MEDICAL EVALUATION

We have seen that a wide range of organic pathology may be associated with mental illness, and the primary purpose of the physical and neurological examination is to detect any such conditions which may have a bearing on the present disorder. The examination itself is a highly specialized procedure which is handled by the psychiatrist and other medical specialists. It includes an evaluation of metabolic and cardiovascular functions, blood and spinal-fluid tests for syphilis, EEG and other tests for brain damage or pathology, and a wide range of other assessment data. These findings serve as the basis for improving the general physical health of the patient and for planning any necessary medical therapy.

The following items, taken from a medical examination form, illustrate the type of information that is typically obtained in such examinations:

Physical examination:
 Blood pressure ....
 Heart ....

 Lungs ....
 Abdomen ....
 Glands ....
Neurological examination:
 Pupils ....
 Gait ....
 Reflexes ....
 Sensations ....
 EEG ....

One rather specialized medical diagnostic technique already referred to in connection with epilepsy is electroencephalography. This involves the recording of the minute electrical charges or "brain waves" which accompany the metabolic activities of the brain. By means of electrodes placed over different areas of the brain, the functioning of these areas may be investigated. Depending upon the particular brain area involved, these tracings are referred to as *occipital EEG, frontal EEG,* and so on. Records made by placing the electrodes on the surface of the scalp are referred to as *electroencephalograms;* those obtained by placing the electrodes in direct contact with exposed areas of the brain are called *electrograms.* Electroencephalograms of four types of brain waves have been distinguished in terms of their frequency and amplitude:

1. Alpha waves: large, rhythmic, smooth waves averaging about 10 per second.
2. Beta waves: more rapid, somewhat irregular waves averaging approximately 25 per second.
3. Gamma waves: very low amplitude waves with frequencies of 35 to 45 per second.
4. Delta waves: slow waves of relatively large amplitude having frequencies of 8 or less per second.

Brain pathology is reflected in various abnormal rhythms, irregularities, and frequencies of brain-wave patterns which are called *dysrhythmias.*

Advances in medicine and allied sciences are contributing many new diagnostic procedures which are of great value in certain psychiatric cases (Merritt, 1963; Coughlan, 1963). New and relatively mild surgical procedures have been developed for locating brain lesions causing convulsive seizures—for use primarily in cases which do not respond to medication. Brain tumors, atrophy of the brain, and disturbances in cerebral circulation can be diagnosed by means of EEG findings and various specialized techniques such as pneumoencephalography and myelography. Radioactive isotopes have also proven of value in delineating certain disturbances in the nervous system, and various biochemical tests have been developed for detecting a wide range of rare metabolic diseases as well as opiate addiction and other conditions. The plotting of "chromosomal maps" has provided highly useful information concerning certain types of mental retardation.

PSYCHOLOGICAL ASSESSMENT

The psychological assessment represents a systematic attempt to construct a working psychological "image" or "model" of the patient. It is based upon samples of the patient's behavior which are intended to be representative of his present functioning and which can be used as a partial basis for predicting his potentialities for change. Various assessment procedures may be utilized.

Observation of general behavior. Where possible, a description of the patient's behavior may be made in his life setting as well as in the clinic or hospital. With children, for example, the patient may be observed at school, in his peer groups, and in his home. Here the purpose may be to obtain a sampling of the patient's behavior in ordinary situations in order to understand his difficulties and adjustive reactions.

Usually there is a brief description of the patient's behavior (orientation, affect, and general characteristics) on admission to a clinic or hospital. In a hospital setting, more detailed observations are then made on the ward. Here the primary purpose may be to obtain a concise description of the salient aspects of the patient's behavior—appearance, speech, emotional behavior, orientation, delusions or hallucinations, insight, attitudes, sexual behavior, suicidal tendencies, and so on. To facilitate these observations, rating scales are usually used. These are so designed as to enable the recorder to indicate not only the presence or absence of a trait but also the prominence of it. The following rating-scale items will serve to illustrate both the kinds of descriptive data obtained here and the five-

point-scale questions commonly used in recording such observations.

Appearance:

1. Extremely untidy and slovenly. No attention to personal hygiene unless forced. Clothes soiled with feces, food, or dirt.

2. Slovenly about appearance but will change clothes and clean up when requested.

3. Average attention to personal hygiene. Reasonably clean and neat without supervision.

4. Very tidy and clean. Spends much time in personal hygiene.

5. Excessively concerned about cleanliness. Spends excessive amount of time washing, maintaining clothes, and ensuring immaculate appearance.

Sexual behavior:

1. Sexually assaultive. Aggressively approaches males or females with sexual intent.

2. Sexually soliciting. Exposes genitals with sexual intent, makes overt sexual advances to other patients or staff, masturbates openly.

3. No overt sexual behavior. Not preoccupied with discussion of sexual matters.

4. Avoids sex topics. Made uneasy by discussion of sex, becomes disturbed if approached sexually by others.

5. Excessive prudishness about sex. Considers all sexual matters filthy; condemns sexual behavior in others; becomes panic-stricken if approached sexually.

Observations of the patient's behavior may be made not only for initial assessment purposes but also for checking on the course or outcome of treatment procedures.

Interviewing. The interview is probably the oldest method for assessing the personality traits of another person. For centuries, men have assumed that they could "size up" another person by talking to him for a period of time.

Interviewing usually involves a face-to-face conversation between two people, conducted in such a way that one person (the psychiatrist, for example) can obtain information from and evaluate the other (the patient). This description is an oversimplification of the wide range and complexity of processes that may be involved in interview situations. For example, the interview may vary from a simple set of questions designed to gather certain information— as in an *intake* or *case history* interview—to a *stress* interview, designed to see how the patient functions intellectually and emotionally in a difficult situation. And, of course, there is the complex *therapeutic* interview, which may involve both assessment and psychotherapy.

While interview assessment techniques are widely used, they are subject to many sources of error. The patient may be uncooperative; he may be more anxious to present himself in a good light than to impart needed information about his problems; or he may respond in terms of what he thinks the interviewer wants to hear rather than in terms of what he actually feels or thinks. Sometimes differences in social class between the interviewer and the patient or theoretical bias on the part of the interviewer influence the kind and extent of information that is obtained. In order to minimize such sources of error or distortion, interview assessment is usually carefully structured in terms of goals, content to be explored, and the type of relationship the interviewer attempts to establish with the patient. Here, too, the use of rating scales may help focus and structure the interview.

One such rating scale is the Inpatient Multidimensional Psychiatric Scale. Categories of symptoms identified by this scale through factor analysis were listed in the chart on page 267. In using this scale, the rater evaluates the patient after an interview of about 40 minutes. The rating scale itself contains questions such as the following:

"Compared to the normal person, to what degree does he exhibit . . . an attitude of self-importance, superiority, or conceit?

"Cues: Speech is pompous or stilted; boasts of his accomplishments and demands and expects special privileges." (Lorr 1962, p. 855)

Most of the ratings are made on a 9-point scale from "not at all" through "moderate" to "extreme." This scale has proved useful not only in diagnosis but also in evaluating the results of chemotherapy.

Psychological tests. Psychological tests are specialized diagnostic procedures for determining the patient's intellectual capacity, motivations, conflicts, ego defenses, environmental and self-evaluations, interests and aptitudes, and general personality organization. Such tests are of particular value in revealing the psychological dynamics of the patient's illness. In addition, special psychological tests are utilized in the diagnosis of brain pathology.

1. *Intelligence tests.* There is a wide range of intelligence or capacity tests from which the clinician can select. The Wechsler Intelligence Scale for Children (WISC) and the Stanford-Binet Intelligence Scale are widely used in the measurement of the intellectual capacity of children. Probably the most commonly used clinical instrument for the measurement of adult capacity is the Wechsler Adult Intelligence Scale (WAIS). It covers both verbal and performance materials and consists of ten subtests with one alternate subtest. A brief description of three of the subtests—two verbal and one performance—will serve to illustrate the type of functions the WAIS measures:

General information. This subtest consists of questions designed to tap the patient's range of information on material that the average person with average opportunity would ordinarily acquire. Sample questions are:

"What are the colors in the American flag?

"How many weeks are there in a year?

"Who wrote *Hamlet?*

"What is ethnology?" (Wechsler, 1955, pp. 33-35)

General comprehension. This subtest consists of questions designed to measure the "common sense" of the subject and his judgment, as revealed in situations described to him. Sample questions are:

"What is the thing to do if you find an envelope in the street, that is sealed and addressed and has a new stamp?

"What should you do if, while sitting in the movies, you were the first person to see smoke and fire?

"Why should we keep away from bad company?

"If you were lost in the forest in the daytime, how would you go about finding your way out?" (p. 36)

Picture completion. This subtest consists of 21 cards showing pictures, each with a part missing. The task for the subject is to indicate what is missing. The test is designed to measure the individual's ability to differentiate essential elements from nonessentials.

Analysis of scores on the various subtests reveals the patient's present level of intellectual functioning and may indicate any impairment due to mental illness or brain damage. In addition, the evaluation of the actual responses of the subject, together with his behavior in the test situation, reveals much relevant diagnostic information about his personality make-up and ethical attitudes. For example, to the question "What is the thing to do if you find an envelope in the street, that is sealed and addressed and has a new stamp?" one patient answered, "I would open it to see if there was any money in it." In other instances the subject may be unduly upset by mistakes, continually apprehensive for fear he is not doing well, or vacillating and indecisive in his responses; or he may manifest other reactions which reveal a great deal about himself.

2. *Personality tests.* There are a great many tests designed to measure various aspects of the personality organization of the patient. In considering these personality tests, it is convenient to group them into two categories—nonprojective tests and projective ones.

a) Nonprojective tests. Tests of this type typically utilize the questionnaire, self-inventory, or rating-scale technique of measurement. One of the major clinical nonprojective tests is the Minnesota Multiphasic Personality Inventory. The MMPI consists of 550 test items covering topics from physical condition to moral and social attitudes. The subject checks those that apply to him. Sample items are:

"___I sometimes keep on at a thing until others lose their patience with me."
"___Bad words, often terrible words, come into my mind and I cannot get rid of them."
"___I often feel as if things were not real."
"___Someone has it in for me."
(Hathaway and McKinley, 1951, p. 28)

The number of items that a subject marks in the same way that schizophrenics, hysterics, or other types of patients have been found to answer them indicates his tendencies in any of those directions. This test also has a built-in "lie" scale and "defensiveness" scale which helps the examiner evaluate the validity of the patient's responses to the test items.

A second major nonprojective approach is the "Q sort." Here a large number of statements are prepared concerning various traits, behavior patterns, or situations. The patient may then be asked to sort these statements into piles graded from highly typical of him to highly untypical. For example, a statement may read: "Is highly anxious and tense most of the time," or "Views sex as evil and strives to inhibit his sexual impulses," or "Thinks most of his difficulties stem from his unhappy marital situation." In some instances someone else may do a sorting after interviewing or otherwise getting to know the patient. A variety of statistical techniques can then be used to evaluate the results of the sorting.

b) Projective tests. Projective tests are less "structured" than nonprojective tests, relying upon various ambiguous stimuli such as inkblots, rather than upon specific test questions and answers. Here the subject is forced to organize and interpret the ambiguous material and in the process reveals a good deal about his own conflicts, level of aspiration, intellectual level, adjustive techniques, and other aspects of his personality make-up. Thus projective tests place greater emphasis upon the ways in which experience and adjustive reactions are patterned by the inner attitudes and general ego structure of the subject. Prominent among the many projective tests now common in clinical use are the Rorschach Test, the Thematic Apperception Test, the Make A Picture Story Test, and the sentence completion tests.

The Rorschach Test is named after the Swiss psychiatrist Hermann Rorschach, who first started experimental use of inkblots in personality diagnosis in 1911. The test consists of ten symmetrical inkblot pictures to which the subject responds in succession. The subject is instructed as follows:

"People see all sorts of things in these inkblot pictures; now tell me what you see, what it might be for you, what it makes you think of." (Klopfer and Davidson, 1962, p. 28)

The scoring and interpretation of the subject's responses require a highly skilled clinician and in competent hands will reveal much about the subject's general personality structure—the way he deals with his inner drives, his introversive and extroversive tendencies, and so on. The following excerpts are taken from the responses of a patient to the sample inkblot

shown here. From his responses and findings from several other tests he was diagnosed as an antisocial personality with strong hostility.

"This looks like two men with genital organs exposed. They have had a terrible fight and blood has splashed up against the wall. They have knives or sharp instruments in their hands and have just cut up a body. They have already taken out the lungs and other organs. The body is dismembered . . . nothing remains but a shell . . . the pelvic region. They were fighting as to who will complete the final dismemberment . . . like two vultures swooping down . . ."

Another, more recently developed inkblot test is the Holtzman Inkblot Technique. This test offers two alternate forms of 45 cards each, with considerable variety among the inkblots. More objective scoring is possible, and percentile norms are available for several clinical groups.

The Thematic Apperception Test (TAT) was introduced in 1935 by its coauthors Morgan and Murray of the Harvard Psychological Clinic. It consists of a series of pictures about which the subject is instructed to make up stories. Again the usual instructions accompanying the test reveal much about its nature:

"This is a test of imagination, one form of intelligence. I am going to show you some pictures, one at a time; and your task will be to make up as dramatic a story as you can for each. Tell what has led up to the event shown in the picture, describe what is happening at the moment, what the characters are feeling and thinking; and then give the outcome. Speak your thoughts as they come to your mind. Do you understand? Since you have fifty minutes for ten pictures, you can devote about five minutes to each story. Here is the first picture." (Murray, 1943, p. 3)

Stories collected in this way—in terms of the heroes, the types of plots, the outcomes, the characters with whom the subject identifies himself, and so on—often reveal a great deal about his conflicts, attitudes, level of aspiration, and related aspects of his personality.

The following story made up around the picture reproduced below illustrates the type of material that may be obtained on the TAT and shows the actual conflict with which this patient was trying to cope.

"This old lady is quite upset because her daughter has been going out and making a tramp out of herself. She is remonstrating with her daughter and warning her of the trouble she will get into if she doesn't change. The old lady used to be quite pretty but her husband died, and she had to work so hard supporting herself and

One of the series of pictures shown to the subject in the Thematic Apperception Test. There also is a set of pictures for use in testing children.

At the left are shown one of the stage settings and several of the cutout figures employed in the MAPS test. The patient uses several backgrounds in the course of the examination, making up a story for each. On the right is the picture being described in the case reported by Fantel and Shneidman below.

her daughter that it aged her before her time. Since she was working such long hours she could not keep an eye on her daughter who grew up self-willed and adventurous. The daughter is eager for life. She wants to be gay and carefree and have fun and go out with men. But her mother's continual warnings upset her. She doesn't let her mother know this and she is too self-willed to let it affect her behavior. But she wishes her mother would stop bothering her and go away . . . not really away, but just mind her own business."

In the Make A Picture Story Test (MAPS) developed by Shneidman (1952), there are many cutout figures—males, females, animals, legendary and fictitious figures such as Superman, and silhouettes, and 22 varied backdrops which form a sort of stage—living rooms, bathrooms, bedrooms, camp, street scene, cemetery, life raft, and so on. Any figure can be placed on any background, and as the subject is given the different backgrounds, he selects one or more of the figures and populates the background pictures, telling a story of the situation he is depicting.

The following story, told in relation to the picture above was given by a 22-year-old patient who since childhood had had numerous sado-masochistic compulsions such as looking into the sun and putting his tongue on frozen metal, as well as strong desires to mutilate himself and other members of his family.

"Young girl walking through woods . . . a young man going in the opposite direction along a parallel path separated by thirty feet. He notices her. She fails to see him. He follows her and attempts to make advances. She is very receptive at first without realizing his exact intentions. He attempts to caress her. She struggles to free herself. He proceeds to abuse her physically inflicting severe pain. Tearing clothes from her body and attacks her. She—he treated her more roughly than he intended to and she collapses from the ordeal and dies from the attack. He realizes this immediately afterward. Conceals the body . . . . Very upset and makes his way out of woods onto highway. Feeling he is being watched continuously. By whom he does not know. . . . This is his first but not his last attempt. His environment and feelings are too strong for him to control at times." (Who might this be?) "That represents myself." (Fantel and Shneidman, 1947, pp. 7-8)

In summarizing this patient's MAPS test records Fantel and Shneidman concluded that although there was a psychotic coloring with paranoid tendencies, the main picture was "of a severely disturbed neurotic, preoccupied with masturbatory guilt and sexual fantasies involving rape, voyeurism, and sadism . . ." (p. 8)

Another projective procedure which has proven highly useful in personality assessment is the sentence completion test. Actually there are a number of such tests designed for children, adolescents, and adults. The material consists of the beginnings of sentences which the patient is asked to complete. For example:

1. I wish ....
2. A mother ....
3. People ....
4. The worst ....
5. I hate ....
6. Girls ....
7. My father ....
8. I could kill somebody who ....
9. Sex is ....
10. I plan ....

The attempt here is to tap questions that are meaningful to the patient and that deal with common trouble spots for individuals who are experiencing difficulties. Since sentence completion tests are more structured than the Rorschach and most other projective tests, items can be selected that pinpoint areas the examiner feels should be explored.

A somewhat different type of projective test is the Kahn Test of Symbol Arrangement (Kahn, 1955; Kahn and Giffin, 1960). In this test the subject is asked to tell what symbols—such as a heart or an anchor—mean to him and to arrange them in different patterns. Since the symbols used have rather definite meanings to most people in our society, the subject's verbal account and arrangements can reveal much about

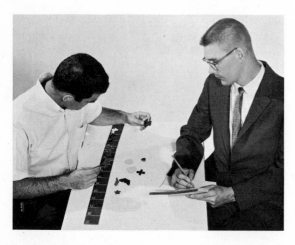

A subject working on one part of the Kahn Test of Symbol Arrangement.

his personality to a skilled clinician. This test has several advantages, including an administration time of only 15 minutes and a scoring time of only 3 minutes. In addition, it can be used by persons without extensive psychological training. It has proved particularly effective as a basis for categorizing patients into broad psychiatric classes. For example, by interpreting the symbol patterns of 48 patients, a member of an Air Force neuropsychiatric team was able to classify four fifths of them correctly as schizophrenics, neurotics, persons with character disorders, or persons with organic psychoses (Murphy *et al.*, 1957). As might be expected, indications of schizophrenia are particularly clear-cut, since schizophrenics are especially prone to a distortion of symbolic thinking.

3. *Other diagnostic tests.* Many other psychological tests are available for clinical use to reveal the patient's abilities, interests, aptitudes, temperament, anxiety level, self-concept, value assumptions, and other aspects of the patient's personality organization. There are also several highly specialized tests which help in the diagnosis of brain pathology.[1]

The tests chosen are those best suited to the needs of a particular case. Often the test battery includes WAIS, MMPI, Rorschach, TAT or MAPS, and the Kahn Test of Symbol Arrangement. Where the patient lacks occupational skills or is having difficulty in occupational adjustment, tests of aptitude, interest, and ability are often of great help. Typically tests are used in combination with other procedures.[2]

Often the examiner's observations concerning the patient's behavior during the evaluation add materially to the overall assessment data. It goes without saying that in contacts with a patient it is vitally important that the psychologist or clinician maintain a sympathetic and understanding attitude designed to gain the patient's confidence and cooperation. The nature of the rapport he can establish has a direct bearing on the ac-

[1]Many books and articles deal with psychological assessment procedures. Useful references here include Buros (1959), Rabin and Haworth (1960), and Sundberg and Tyler (1962).

[2]In psychological assessment, a distinction is often made between the *idiographic* and the *nomothetic* approaches. Essentially, the former involves an intensive study of one individual, whereas the latter involves a study of many individuals in an effort to identify principles that apply to people generally.

The Scenotest being administered here by Dr. Gerchild von Staabs, the psychiatrist who developed it, is a diagnostic and therapeutic device for use with emotionally disturbed children. The young patients are encouraged to arrange and play out scenes with characters chosen from a large assortment of flexible dolls, animals, and furniture. The boy shown here had been referred because of theft and truancy; in the scene at the left (played early in therapy) he is showing a mother preoccupied with a younger child (his baby brother) while a grandmother tells stories to older children, perhaps indicating the boy's wish that all children be given equal attention. As therapy proceeded and the boy came to feel more loved and more fairly treated, the truancy and thefts stopped. Near the end of therapy, he acted the scene at the right, in which two dogs are racing; the bigger one wins, but the little one gets a consolation prize.

curacy and value of the psychological evaluation.

Psychological tests are, as yet, far from perfect tools.[1] Many of them leave much to be desired in terms of validity and reliability, and often they tend to focus attention on variables within the patient at the expense of important factors in his life situation. Their value depends heavily on the competence of the clinician who interprets them. In general, however, they have proved superior to other assessment procedures —including interviewing—and they tend to minimize the personal prejudices and psychological blindspots of the examiner. Often, too, they reveal pathological trends which are not shown by other assessment procedures. In a general sense, psychological tests are useful to clinical psychologists in revealing pathology in much the same way that chemical tests, such as the Wassermann, are useful to physicians. In both cases, pathology may be revealed in patients who appear to be quite normal.

Operant conditioning. Another major diagnostic approach is the use of operant conditioning as an assessment procedure. Here the individual is placed in a controlled situation where he is rewarded when he performs a certain task —such as pressing a lever—in response to given stimuli. For example, the hearing ability of an emotionally disturbed autistic child might be

[1]It may be emphasized that continual research is going on in an attempt to improve the range, validity, and reliability of psychological assessment procedures and that such procedures are used for research in personality dynamics as well as for diagnostic purposes. For further information, the reader is referred to Beck (1962), Dreikurs (1963), Ebel (1961), Flanagan and Schmid (1959), Harrower *et al.* (1960), Kagan and Lesser (1961), Little and Shneidman (1959), Meehl (1960), Overall and Gorham (1962), Sundberg and Tyler (1962).

measured by conditioning the child to press a lever when he hears a tone. His reward might be watching a doll dance. If he presses the lever when the tone is not on, the doll does not dance; thus he receives no reinforcement. After the response has been established, the tone is gradually reduced in intensity until the child can no longer hear it. Similarly, the child's intelligence may be tested by conditioning him to press a lever to receive a reward when two objects shown him have certain characteristics in common. For example, the two objects may be animals or buildings. In this way, the ability of the child to perceive similarities or form new concepts can be assessed.[1]

Operant conditioning methods can also be used with adults when other assessment procedures are not workable or to supplement other assessment measures. As compared with normals, the mentally ill tend to be very erratic in their activities, showing long periods of no response punctuated with sporadic bursts of activity called for by the conditioning task.

Although we shall not attempt to deal with them in our present discussion, a number of other psychological assessment procedures have proved of value. Particularly worthy of mention are role playing and activity assessment in real or simulated stress situations.

SOCIOLOGICAL EVALUATION

We are interested not only in the personality dynamics of the patient but also in his total life situation—the nature of the stresses with which he is confronted, the quality of his significant interpersonal relationships, and his role behavior in the various groups to which he belongs. An unhappy marriage, a divorce, occupational dissatisfaction, unpleasant parental relations, minority group membership, an interrupted education, a slum environment, a sense of living a meaningless, unfulfilled life—any one or a combination of several of these factors can be of vital importance in the development and dynamics of his disorder. Without such data concerning the patient's general life situation, any understanding of his disorder is incomplete, and the planning of effective therapy may be severely handicapped. Much of this data may be obtained in the course of psy-

chological assessment, but whenever possible, a psychiatric social worker visits the home, talks to members of the patient's family, and observes the nature of the family interaction.

The following summary of the family situation of a 23-year-old female alcoholic shows the value of a sociological evaluation.

The mother is the dominant figure in the family constellation and rules the family with an iron hand. She married her husband for his money, which he subsequently lost. Since that time she has earned the family living and is contemptuous and scornful in her relations with him. She does not sleep in the same bedroom with him and refuses to have anything to do with him physically. The mother has transferred her affection to the daughter, whom she has overly protected and dominated and for whom she has ambitions which represent the vicarious gratification of her own frustrated hopes. She has always made the daughter's clothes and done her best to make her a show piece. She is extremely critical to the point of actual jealousy of the young men who have taken an interest in her daughter and has made it so unpleasant that most of them have stopped calling. The only suitor that she encourages for her daughter is Bob ———, the son of a wealthy and socially prominent family, who is very passive and weak and resembles her husband in many respects. The daughter "can't stand" this fellow, but at her mother's insistence has been going "steady" with him. He is a fairly heavy drinker, and it was through associating with him that she first started drinking about two years ago. For the past six months her mother has been putting increasing pressure upon the daughter to marry Bob. She points out all that she has done for her, states that she is dying of cancer (which is probably not true), and that the least her daughter can do for her is to marry the right person. The daughter turned to her father for assistance, but he is completely dependent upon the mother and suggested that she "better do what mother says." The mother is unable to understand her daughter's excessive drinking but feels that her daughter has let her down and continually tells the daughter so.

Sundberg and Tyler (1962) have pointed out that the process of assessing the situational factors in a clinical case involves four steps:

---

[1]For additional details about these methods of assessment, the reader is referred to Bijou (1958), Ferster and DeMyer (1962), and Lindsley (1954).

(a) identifying the significant interactive systems —the family and other primary groups that are of key significance in the patient's life; (b) studying the characteristics of each of these systems or groups—including the roles of the major participants, the rules and patterns of interaction, and the nature of the communication that goes on within the system; (c) comparing the characteristics of the patient and the system—including the role or roles he typically plays, the extent to which his perception of the situation corresponds to others' perceptions of it, and whether he possesses the competencies essential for the tasks he is expected to carry out; and

(d) determining how best to utilize situational resources or what changes should be made in the system or patient or both. Although the clinician does not ignore the larger organizations and communities to which the patient belongs, the situational assessment usually focusses on the immediate interpersonal drama.

Despite its great importance, we are only now beginning to develop a psychopathology of family and community life. It is essential that the dimensions of our diagnostic thinking not be limited to the individual but include his family and community setting and the interactions in which he takes part.

Integration of Diagnostic Information

Once the diagnostic information is gathered, the task remains of interpreting its meaning and integrating it into a coherent "working model" of the individual in relation to his life situation. This working model is then used as a basis for decisions about treatment.

THE STAFF CONFERENCE

In a clinic or hospital setting, the diagnostic material obtained is usually evaluated and integrated in a staff conference attended by the psychiatrist, the clinical psychologist, the psychiatric social worker, and other personnel concerned with the treatment of the patient. By a pooling of the various diagnostic findings, it is possible to see whether they agree with and complement each other or whether there are discrepancies that need further investigation. At this time a diagnostic label (classification) is decided upon and coordinated plans for therapy worked out. The findings of each member of the staff, as well as the joint recommendations, are then entered in the patient's case record, so that it is always possible to check back and see why a certain course of action was undertaken, how accurate the original diagnosis was, and how wise the recommendations were. In this way clinical theory can constantly be checked against the actual results of a given course of treatment.

Although we have been primarily concerned with the diagnostic evaluation of mental patients upon their initial contact with a clinic or mental hospital, diagnostic procedures are by no means confined to this area. Psychological and sociological assessment procedures are widely used in educational, occupational, and marital counseling. Diagnostic procedures may also be used for preventive purposes. In much the same way that routine medical check-ups are of great value in detecting and correcting early organic pathology, psychological tests may be used to detect unhealthy trends in personality development long before the subject's behavior becomes manifestly abnormal. In addition, such tests may be used periodically during the course of treatment to check on progress and to see if changes in the treatment program are indicated. Similarly, sociological assessment procedures can be used to ensure the early recognition of pathogenic marital or other group interactions as well as the maladjustive behavior of individual members.

Thus our diagnostic tools are our "eyes" in the difficult and complex attempt to help mental patients back toward a normal adjustment. By means of them we can see where we are, plan where we want to go and the best way to get there, and check our progress. Without these "eyes," the potential usefulness of even the best of therapeutic tools would be diminished.

Here it may be emphasized that much relevant

diagnostic material may be obtained in the course of psychotherapy. This material may be utilized as a supplement to diagnostic data previously obtained and as a check on their accuracy. In some instances, the entire psychological assessment is made during psychotherapy.

USE OF ELECTRONIC DEVICES

We have mentioned the use of electronic devices in record keeping. Here it is relevant to mention the future possibilities of computers and other electronic devices in contributing to or actually making the diagnostic evaluation. In the field of medicine, computers can be helpful in diagnosing conditions about which a great deal of knowledge exists. After data are collected on a given patient by electronic devices, the computer can compare them with tables of symptoms, laboratory tests, and other relevant information in the computer's memory. The computer can also provide the physician with the latest information concerning the treatment of patients suffering from this disorder or even indicate an appropriate treatment program for a given patient.

On a psychological level, electronic devices may also be used to collect certain types of information from the patient which can be supplemented by additional information from the examiner. The computer can then search its enormous memory and supply the clinician with a tentative diagnosis as well as with pertinent data on similar cases. Here again, the computer may assist in formulating an appropriate treatment program by indicating the procedures which have proven most effective in treating similar cases. Similarly, on a sociological level, the computer may be given a sample of the interactions among family members and then may make an evaluation of the nature of the communication, emotions, and roles involved. The computer may even suggest changes in the behavior of given members or in organizational structure that might improve the functional effectiveness of the family group and provide greater satisfactions and growth opportunities for its members.

Computers may also be used for the simula-

tion of human thought processes—particularly in terms of learning, problem solving, and decision making (Tomkins and Messick, 1963). Given sufficient information, it may eventually be possible for the computer to simulate accurately the thought processes of the mentally ill patient—thus assisting in understanding, diagnosis, and prediction. In fact, Colby (1963) has described the computer simulation of a neurotic process. The early detection of pathological trends by means of computer technology may even be helpful in preventing mental disorders. Wooldridge (1963) has pointed to the tremendous potentialities inherent in the convergence of the disciplines of computer and brain research.

The full possibilities of the computer for collecting and processing diagnostic data and for planning—and perhaps even carrying out—treatment remain to be ascertained. Many scientific as well as ethical problems have yet to be resolved, but computers and other electronic devices are beginning to make their imprint in psychiatry and clinical psychology as well as in general medicine, and the importance of their role in diagnosis, treatment, and prevention is likely to increase greatly in the not-too-distant future.

In sketching the tremendous potentialities of computers, one may wonder if the human clinician may not be largely, if not entirely, eliminated. Potentially, the computer can certainly collect and process data more effectively than the clinician. It is reassuring to note, however, that the computer is unlikely to be able to interact with the patient in the same way that the clinician does—at least in the foreseeable future (Holtzman, 1960). And this interaction is a key aspect of modern psychotherapy.

Occasionally the question is raised as to whether diagnostic evaluations are necessary or worth the effort involved. Some therapists feel that the patient's personality structure will be revealed in the course of psychotherapy and that extensive preliminary testing is unnecessary (Bugental, 1963; Meehl, 1960; Rogers, 1961). Since a full diagnostic evaluation requires several hours, this point of view cannot be summarily dismissed. As Sundberg and Tyler (1962) have pointed out, however, ". . . it is not a question of *whether* one should use assessment, but how best to use it. Assessment is the process of getting to know the patient in some fashion. Whenever any patient is handled clinically, sound decisions have to be made. They should be made on as scientific and practicable a basis as possible." (p. 277)

A great deal of research is currently being devoted to a study of the accuracy and effectiveness of various assessment procedures. The findings from this research should lead to continuous improvement of diagnostic evaluations as a basis for planning effective treatment programs.

REFERENCES

The reference list includes not only the sources from which the author has drawn material, but acknowledgments of the permissions granted by authors and publishers to quote directly from their works.

BECK, A. T. Reliability of psychiatric diagnoses: I. A critique of systematic studies. *Amer. J. Psychiat.*, 1962, 119, 210-216.

BECK, A. T., WARD, C. H., MENDELSON, M., MOCK, J. E., & ERBAUGH, J. K. Reliability of psychiatric diagnosis: 2. A study of consistency of clinical judgments and ratings. *Amer. J. Psychiat.*, 1962, 119, 351-357.

BIJOU, S. W. A child study laboratory on wheels. *Child Developm.*, 1958, 29, 425-427.

BUROS, O. K. (Ed.) *Fifth mental measurements yearbook.* Highland Park, N.J.: Gryphon, 1959.

COLBY, K. M. Computer simultation of a neurotic process. In S. S. Tomkins & S. Messick (Eds.), *Computer simulation of personality:* frontier of psychological theory. New York: Wiley, 1963. Pp. 166-180.

COUGHLAN, R. Control of the brain. Part I. Behavior by electronics. *Life*, 1963, 54, 90-92.

DREIKURS, R. Psychodynamic diagnosis in psychiatry. *Amer. J. Psychiat.*, 1963, 119, 1046-1048.

EBEL, R. L. Must all tests be valid? *Amer. Psychologist*, 1961, 16, 640-647.

FANTEL, E., & SHNEIDMAN, E. S. Psychodrama and the make a picture story (MAPS test). *Rorschach Res. Exch. & J. proj. Tech.*, 1947, 11, 42-67.

FERSTER, C. B., & DE MYER, MARIAN K. A method for the experimental analysis of the behavior of autistic children. *Amer. J. Orthopsychiat.*, 1962, 32, 89-98.

FLANAGAN, J. C., & SCHMID, F. W. The critical incident approach to the study of psychopathology. *J. clin. Psychol.*, 1959, 15, 136-139.

HARROWER, MOLLY, VORHAUS, PAULINE, ROMAN, M., & BAUMAN, G. *Creative variations in the projective techniques.* Springfield, Ill.: Charles C. Thomas, 1960.

HATHAWAY, S. R., & MC KINLEY, J. C. *The Minnesota multiphasic personality inventory.* Rev. ed. New York: Psychol. Corp., 1951.

HOLTZMAN, W. H. Can the computer supplant the clinician? *J. clin. Psychol.*, 1960, 16, 119-122.

KAGAN, J., & LESSER, G. S. (Eds.) *Contemporary issues in thematic apperceptive methods.* Springfield, Ill.: Charles C. Thomas, 1961.

KAHN, T. C. Personality projection on culturally structured symbols. *J. proj. Techn.*, 1955, 19, 431-442.

KAHN, T. C., & GIFFEN, M. B. *Psychological techniques in diagnosis and evaluation.* New York: Pergamon Press, 1960.

KLOPFER, B., & DAVIDSON, HELEN H. *The Rorschach technique: an introductory manual.* New York: Harcourt, Brace, & World, Inc., 1962.

LERNER, J. The role of the psychologist in the disability evaluation of emotional and intellectual impairment under the Social Security Act. *Amer. Psychologist*, 1963, 18, 252-256.

LINDSLEY, O. R. *Studies in behavior therapy: status report III.* Waltham, Mass.: Metropolitan State Hospital, 1954.

LITTLE, K. B., & SHNEIDMAN, E. S. Congruencies among interpretations of psychological test and anamnestic data. *Psychol. Monogr.*, 1959, 73, No. 6 (Whole No. 476).

LORR, M. Measurement of the major psychotic syndromes. *Ann. N. Y. Acad. Sci.*, 1962, 93, 851-856.

MEEHL, P. The cognitive activity of the clinician. *Amer. Psychologist*, 1960, 15, 19-27.

MERRITT, B. H. Recent advances in neurology significant to psychiatry. *Amer. J. Psychiat.*, 1963, 120, 454-457.

MURPHY, P. D., FERRIMAN, M. R., & BOLINGER, R. W. The Kahn Test of Symbol Arrangement as an aid to psychodiagnosis. *J. consult. Psychol.*, 1957, 21, 503-505.

MURRAY, H. A. *Thematic apperception test.* Cambridge, Mass.: Harvard Univer. Press, 1943. Reprinted by permission of the publishers.

RABIN, A. I., & HAWORTH, MARY R. (Eds.) *Projective techniques with children.* New York: Grune & Stratton, 1960.

ROGERS, C. R. *On becoming a person:* a therapist's view of psychotherapy. Boston: Houghton Mifflin, 1961.

SHNEIDMAN, E. S. *Manual for the Make a Picture Story method.* Proj. Tech. Monogr., 1952, No. 2.

SUNDBERG, N. D., & TYLER, LEONA E. *Clinical psychology.* New York: Appleton-Century-Crofts, 1962.

TOMKINS, S. S., & MESSICK, S. (Eds.) *Computer simulation of personality.* New York: Wiley, 1963.

WECHSLER, D. *Manual for the Wechsler Adult Intelligence Scale.* New York: The Psychological Corporation, 1955.

WOOLDRIDGE, D. E. *The machinery of the brain.* New York: McGraw-Hill, 1963.

THERAPY

chapter 14

The treatment of the mental patient includes a wide range of medical, psychological, and sociological procedures. In severe cases it involves the coordinated teamwork of psychiatrists, clinical psychologists, psychiatric social workers, psychiatric nurses, attendants, occupational and recreational therapists, and other specialized personnel. Increasing emphasis is being put on getting the patient out of the hospital and back into the community as soon as possible.

Although all treatment is directed toward improving the adjustment of the mental patient, specific aims of necessity vary somewhat with the patient and with the therapeutic facilities which are available. In advanced cases of paresis, for example, where a great deal of organic brain damage has taken place, it would be relatively useless to undertake a prolonged program of psychotherapy, and too often in the case of chronic antisocial personalities, time and personnel limitations prohibit any but the most superficial psychological treatment. However, within the limitations of the patient's potentialities and life situation and the available facilities, all therapy has the following aims:

1. *Physical improvement:* this includes the correction or alleviation of any organic pathology and the improvement of general physical condition.

2. *Psychological improvement:* this includes the modification of faulty assumptions and reaction patterns, the development of more effective coping techniques, and the opening of pathways toward greater maturity and continuing self-actualization.

3. *Sociological improvement:* this includes the correction of any existing conditions in the life situation of the patient which make it impossible or difficult for him to achieve an adequate personality adjustment.

It is inevitable in a science so new that there should still be considerable difference of opinion in theory and practice in this field. Although the major "schools" have come much closer to each other in recent years, there remain certain cleavages which should be understood by the student. Likewise, he should gain some knowledge of the many specific therapeutic aids and techniques which have been developed and the several *dimensions* of therapy, for even with the most complete agreement among practitioners, all patients would not be treated in the same way. To be effective, the treatment program must be formulated in relation to the needs and characteristics of the given patient.

Accordingly, the present chapter will be devoted to a consideration of the medical, psychological, and sociological treatment procedures which are currently in use.

Medical Therapy

Medical therapy of the mental patient may, of course, embrace practically any branch of medicine, depending upon the needs of the particular patient. Tranquilizers may be used for excited patients, special diets for emaciated patients, brain surgery for tumor cases, and so on. However, there are certain special medical procedures which have been used primarily with psychiatric patients. Among these are (a) shock therapy, (b) psychosurgery, and (c) chemotherapy.

SHOCK THERAPY

The advent of the so-called shock therapies opened a new era in the physiological treatment of psychotic patients. The major procedures here are insulin shock[1] and electroshock therapy. As we shall see, these procedures have been largely supplanted by the newer drug therapies.

Insulin shock therapy. The new era of shock therapies was introduced by the work of Sakel (1937), who presented the first report of his work on insulin shock from the University of Vienna in 1933. His procedure involved the production of a prolonged coma through the reduction of the sugar content of the blood by means of large doses of insulin. Following the coma the patient often had a lucid period which increased in length with subsequent treatments and during which psychotherapy could be successfully undertaken. The loss of consciousness in insulin therapy is presumably caused by the fact that the brain cells are deprived of glucose—their principal fuel—with a consequent decrease in the metabolic processes of the brain.

Insulin shock therapy was considered of particular value in the treatment of paranoid schizophrenia, being of lesser value in the catatonic type and of least value in the simple and hebephrenic forms. An acute onset of symptoms, short duration of illness, and a relatively stable premorbid personality have also been considered prognostically favorable in the insulin shock treatment. Statistics on the recovery of insulin-treated patients vary considerably, but typically some 60 to 70 per cent of schizophrenic patients receiving a course of insulin shock treatment have either recovered or improved (Bond and Rivers, 1944; Kalinowsky and Hoch, 1946; Paster and Holtzman, 1947).

The fatality rate in insulin shock treatment has been less than 1 per cent. A person's tolerance is somewhat variable and hence difficult

---

[1] Insulin shock is also called ICT—insulin coma therapy.

to gauge accurately, and the most common complication here is the inadvertent production of a prolonged and irreversible stupor. Insulin shock therapy is contraindicated where there are acute infections, severe cardiovascular disease, diabetes mellitus, pulmonary tuberculosis, or other serious organic disorders (Kolb and Noyes, 1963).

Although insulin shock was formerly used extensively in the treatment of schizophrenia, it has been largely replaced by the newer drug therapies and is rarely used at the present time. In a comparative study of a large case population, McNeill and Madzwick (1961) found that trifluoperazine produced better results than insulin shock on all counts. It is of interest to note that insulin shock treatment appears to have been used far more widely in Russia for the treatment of schizophrenic patients than in the United States (Wortis, 1961b). There too, however, its use appears to be declining.

Metrazol therapy. In 1935 Von Meduna, a Budapest psychiatrist, introduced a new shock treatment for schizophrenics. He had observed that there seemed to be a much lower incidence of epilepsy among schizophrenic patients than in the population as a whole and that the schizophrenic symptoms tended to disappear temporarily following the convulsions in those patients who did have epilepsy. Accordingly, he set out to produce artificial epileptic-like convulsions in his schizophrenic patients. He first tried camphor and oil, but this did not work out well because he was unable to predict when the convulsion was going to occur. Sometimes the convulsions appeared in the middle of the night following the treatment and sometimes they failed to occur for two or three days. In his search for a more predictable convulsion-producing drug, Von Meduna hit upon metrazol.

However, metrazol produced a high incidence of fatalities as well as fractures and patients experienced intense feelings of fear and apprehension prior to the loss of consciousness. As a consequence, it was considered a "barbaric" form of treatment. Fortunately it was destined to be replaced very shortly by electroshock.

Electroshock therapy (EST). In 1938, two Italians, Cerletti and Bini, introduced the use of electroshock for the artificial production of convulsive seizures in mental patients.

1. *Procedure.* The patient is placed on a well-padded bed and his shoulders and limbs are held lightly by nurses and attendants to prevent injury during the convulsion. A resilient mouth gag is placed between his teeth and held in place by an attendant to prevent him from biting his tongue. Anectine or other muscle relaxants are ordinarily used to "soften" the seizure and reduce the danger of fractures or dislocations. Electrodes are fastened to the patient's head. Then a current ranging from 70 to 130 volts is applied for a period of 0.1 to 0.5 seconds. Since the electric current travels faster than the nerve impulse, the patient feels no pain. The ensuing convulsion usually lasts from 30 to 60 seconds and is similar to the grand-mal seizure in epilepsy. There is a sudden flexion of the body, usually accompanied by a cry, followed by a tonic phase in which the patient is rigid, and then a clonic phase with generalized convulsions and jerking contractions of the extremities. The tonic phase usually lasts about 10 seconds and the clonic phase about 30 seconds.

Following the convulsion, the patient remains unconscious for about 10 to 30 minutes. On regaining consciousness, he usually appears semistuporous, drowsy, and confused and not infrequently complains of a headache and generalized aches and pains. However, he has no memory of the "shock" or the ensuing convulsion.

Typically, this treatment is continued 2 to 3 times a week, although in acutely disturbed patients who otherwise would be threatened by exhaustion 2 treatments a day may be given for several days. The duration of treatment depends primarily upon the results obtained. In depressive reactions, maximum benefit may be achieved in 5 to 10 treatments. In patients who are improving slowly but definitely, treatments may continue to 20 or more. Sargant (1961) has pointed to the importance of spacing out electroshock treatments as far as possible and of using as few treatments as possible to avoid unpleasant memory upsets.

Although electroshock patients commonly show a post-shock period of memory defect in which they seem somewhat confused about many past events, their learning ability is not impaired, and the memory defect clears up in a short time. Often patients fear electroshock therapy and have bizarre notions of what it is likely to do to them. Actually, fatalities are very rare, though fractures, dislocations, and other complications do occasionally occur. In rare instances, electroshock precipitates psychomotor excitement or other psychotic manifestations (Chapman, 1960). In general, it is considered a safe treatment for a wide range of patients. It is contraindicated in cases of cardiac decompensation and certain other serious organic ailments (Noyes and Kolb, 1963).

Research is currently in progress on a new technique of applying current only to the nondominant lobe of the brain. Studies of over 2000 treatments indicate this to be as effective as the standard bilateral method while producing a significant reduction in post-convulsive confusion and amnesia (Cannicott, 1963). It has also been noted that when electroshock is combined with antidepressant and/or tranquilizing drugs, the number and frequency of treatments can often be greatly reduced—sometimes to only 2 or 3 in all (Sargant, 1961; Witenborn *et al.,* 1961).

2. *Results of treatment.* Electroshock treatment has proved highly effective in the treatment of neurotic and psychotic depressive reactions. Even in involutional melancholia, a recovery rate of 90 per cent or more is obtained with only a short course of treatments. Prior to the advent of electroshock therapy, involutional melancholia often lasted for years. Undoubtedly the rapid alleviation of depressive symptoms by means of electroshock has saved many depressed patients from committing suicide.

Electroshock is less effective in the treatment of manic reactions. The use of frequent treatments for a period of 2 or 3 days may result in the alleviation or remission of manic symptoms, but this improvement is apt to be unstable. The effectiveness of electroconvulsive treatment in schizophrenia has been a subject of considerable controversy. Apparently the best results are obtained in catatonic patients and in other cases evidencing an acute onset of symptoms and strong emotional coloring. For simple and hebephrenic types, electroshock has proved of little value. Electroshock has also been found to be ineffective and contraindicated in neurotic reactions with the exception of neurotic depressive reactions.

Despite the great contribution electroshock treatment has made to the treatment of mental disorders—particularly depressive reactions—it is gradually being replaced by antidepressant drugs (Witenborn *et al.,* 1961; Wortis, 1962, 1963). However, it still appears to be a potent treatment for the rapid alleviation of depressive symptoms, and it is still relied upon for treating depressive patients who do not respond to drug medication.

PSYCHOSURGERY

Among the most widely publicized innovations in the treatment of psychogenic mental disorders was brain surgery. The assumption underlying such psychosurgery was that the cutting of nerve pathways between the prefrontal lobes of the brain and the hypothalamus (an important center of emotion) would reduce the emotional torment of disturbing thoughts and hallucinations.

Brain surgery in the treatment of functional psychoses was first reported in 1936 by Moniz, a former professor of neurology at the University of Lisbon. During the ensuing twenty years, thousands of operations along similar lines were carried out with a wide range of mental patients, including schizophrenics, involutional melancholics, antisocial personalities, manic-depressives, and even some neurotics.

Procedure. The surgical procedures involved are primarily medical matters and will not concern us in detail. The original procedure used by Moniz consisted in cutting two openings in the skull, one on each side above the temple, and then cutting through a measured section of the nerve fibers connecting the frontal lobes with the thalamus. This operation is referred to as *prefrontal lobotomy* or *leucotomy.* Since 1936, modifications and improvements have been made in surgical technique, particularly by Freeman and Watts, 1942, who played the major role in introducing psychosurgery in the United States.

One of these modifications is called *transorbital lobotomy.* It consists of driving a sharp, slender instrument through the bony part of the eye socket into the frontal lobe of the brain. The instrument is then swung through an arc of thirty degrees and withdrawn. Within an hour or more, many patients so treated are able to get out of bed and perform simple activities. Two additional modifications are *topectomy*, in which certain parts of the frontal lobes are actually removed, and *thalectomy*, in which an electric needle is lowered into the thalamus and a searing current turned on. The effect of this is presumably similar to that of a lobotomy without the irreparable damage to the frontal lobes. Still another technique utilizes high frequency sound waves to produce graded subcortical lesions (Lindstrom, 1954).

Results. The post-operative effects of psychosurgery have varied widely, as might be expected in view of the differing techniques and the many types of mental disorders which have been involved. In many cases there have been temporary or permanent organic complications, including convulsions, aphasia, increased appetite, and rectal or vesical incontinence. Mortality has ranged from 1 to 4 per cent (Greenblatt and Myerson, 1949).

The specific effects of lobotomies upon the personality of the patient vary somewhat with different surgical procedures, due to the fact that somewhat different areas and amounts of frontal-lobe tissue may be involved in the section. However, there are certain generalities which seem to be in order concerning the post-lobotomy personality. If successful, the operation checks the terrific emotional tension and anxiety characteristic of most pre-operative patients, although the price for this decreased tension is a loss in personality depth and a shallowness of affect. In varying degrees the patient is likely to become complacent, cheerful, and indifferent to the feelings and opinions of others. Often he seems to be cut off from the past and to lack awareness of himself as he was previously. In essence, he loses the feeling that he is the same person he was yesterday and will be tomorrow. As a consequence, his past life seems to mean little to him and fails to provide an adequate basis for his present or future behavior. Although the patient's intellectual ability is reduced, it is not usually impaired to a serious degree. In a general sense, he seems to emerge from the operation with a childish, immature personality which may or may not mature with time and experience. Over a period

of time, many patients appear to develop a fairly mature post-operative personality.

Although these general personality changes are typical of what may be expected, there are many variations. In some instances the emotional drive of the patient is markedly reduced so that he tends to lead a very passive, almost vegetative existence. In one instance involving a homicidal patient who was chronically overactive and would impulsively attack anyone within range, the lobotomy had no apparent effect upon the patient's fundamental attitudes. She still wanted to kill everyone, but now she lacked the emotional drive to carry out her inclinations. She would raise her arm as if to hit the doctor, and then it would drop down in a listless fashion to her side. On the other hand, the symptoms of some patients become more pronounced, perhaps because they are no longer so well restrained by the inhibiting control of the higher brain centers. Freeman and Watts (1944) cited the case of an insurance salesman, with a history of several nervous breakdowns and suicidal attempts in the course of some 25 years. After psychosurgery he was relieved of his nervous tension and suicidal notions, but he became so aggressive and hostile that he lost his job and his family was broken up.

Conclusions as to the effectiveness of lobotomies with respect to different types of mental disorders vary considerably. Moniz thought that his operations on schizophrenic patients turned out to be failures because the basic symptoms of the schizophrenics did not disappear, although there were changes in patients' ward behavior that made many of them more manageable. According to present findings, not much more can be expected. Here it may be pointed out that reports of "good" and "fair" improvement following psychosurgery are often misleading. For example, Freeman and Watts (1944) have used the terms "good," "fair," and "poor" with respect to improvement, but "good improvement" may include cases in which the psychotic thought content remains fundamentally unchanged although the patient's affective response to his delusions and hallucinations is markedly reduced. Similarly, Freeman (1963) has reported that 35 per cent of schizophrenic patients operated on in state hospitals were "at home" 10 years later. However, where the patient has to be cared for at home and is unable to resume his former life activities, the degree of improvement involved is debatable.

Results with psychopathic personalities are contradictory, some workers reporting success, others failure. Linneman (1952) has reported failure in the treatment of habitual criminals by lobotomy. Although the figures for involutional patients, manic-depressives, and neurotics appear favorable from the standpoint of alleviating their mental illness symptoms, the desirability of using such drastic procedures to treat these conditions is highly questionable.

Antagonism against the indiscriminate use of psychosurgery was well summarized in an early report by the Group for the Advancement of Psychiatry.

". . . It is an operation, performed in the name of therapy, steadily advised with greater frequency not only for intractable psychoses, but also for a wide variety of psychological disturbances. It is now being used for neuroses and in some clinics even for the treatment of war neuroses. It is often done hastily, without adequate previous study, without the previous use of rational therapeutic measures and it is performed before an opportunity is afforded for possibility of spontaneous remissions. It represents a mechanistic attitude toward psychiatry which is a throwback to our pre-psychodynamic days, which in itself would not be of great concern if it were successful and did not harm the patient. It is a man-made, self-destructive procedure that specifically destroys several human functions which have been slowly evolved and that especially separate us from other animals. If the operation is of importance as a therapeutic procedure in certain selected cases, it becomes all the more important for us to establish definite clinical indications and controls so that its usefulness will not be diluted by utilization in situations where it can do little good and much harm." (1948, p. 2)

Although psychosurgery still has its proponents, it has come to be considered a method of last resort in chronic, violently disturbed patients who have not responded to other forms of treatment. For once psychosurgery has been performed, it cannot be undone, and its results are highly uncertain and often undesirable. In a 5- to 10-year follow-up study of 1000 prefrontal lobotomy cases, Barahal (1958) has pointed to the relatively high death rate, the frequency of post-operative convulsive seizures, and undesirable personality changes. Fortunately, advances in chemotherapy have led to a drastic reduction in the use of psychosurgery.

CHEMOTHERAPY

The present huge and growing market for psychotherapeutic drugs[1] began slightly over a decade ago with the introduction of two major tranquilizers—reserpine and chlorpromazine. The dramatic effect of these drugs in the alleviation of various mental disorders led to a great deal of research in the development and evaluation of new drugs for the treatment of mental illness. At the present time, a wide range of such drugs are available and new ones are continually making their appearance. In general, these drugs fall into two categories: *tranquilizers* and *energizers*.

Tranquilizers. For centuries the root of the plant rauwolfia (snakeroot) has been used in India for the treatment of a wide variety of mental disorders. In 1943, mention was made in the *Indian Medical Gazette* of improvement in manic reactions, schizophrenia, and other mental disorders following the use of *reserpine,* a drug derived from rauwolfia.

The psychiatric use of reserpine began in this country about 1954 after it was found to be of value in treating hypertension and to have a calming effect on mental patients (Kline, 1954). Although useful for a variety of mental disorders, reserpine appears to have found its greatest use for schizophrenia—particularly in calming disturbed, overactive, excited patients. Barsa and Kline (1955) treated 200 chronically disturbed psychotic patients—mostly schizophrenics—with reserpine and found some degree of improvement in 86 per cent of the cases. Braun (1960) has also reported the successful use of reserpine with schizophrenic patients who had failed to respond to chlorpromazine, electroshock, and insulin shock therapy.

---

[1]Drugs which produce changes in any psychological process are called *psychoactive drugs* or *psychochemicals*. Those which have therapeutic value in the treatment of mental disorders are often referred to as *ataractic* or *psychotherapeutic drugs*. The study of psychoactive drugs is the province of the field of *psychopharmacology*.

Reserpine has been found to shorten manic reactions (Watt, 1958) and also to be effective in calming the irritable, quarrelsome, hostile senile patient and the overactive disturbed or brain-injured child (Noyes and Kolb, 1963).

Reserpine appears to have a definite antipsychotic action (especially, antidelusional and antihallucinatory) and to have value as a sedative in diminishing anxiety and tension (Barsa, 1960). Despite its value, however, resperine sometimes causes undesirable side effects such as low blood pressure, ulcers, weakness, nightmares, nasal congestion, and depression (Merlis and Turner, 1961; Wortis, 1963; Evarts and Butler, 1959). Depression is of particular significance since in some instances it has led to suicide (Kramer, 1958; Noyes and Kolb, 1963). Also, more recent studies suggest that the effects of reserpine upon pathological behavior are not as great as those of chlorpromazine and other phenothiazine drugs. Consequently, it has largely been replaced by these newer drugs.

The synthetic drug *chlorpromazine* was first used to treat psychotic reactions in 1952. Its greatest effectiveness appears to be in the control of excitement, agitation, and disorders of thought in schizophrenic patients (Casey *et al.* 1960; Lasky and Klett, 1962; Ruesch, *et al.*, 1963; Winkelman, 1957). Often the acutely disturbed patient calms down (stops rushing about the ward, shouting and screaming or molesting others) within 48 hours after the beginning of treatment. Within the first 2 weeks, hallucinations and delusional ideas are frequently alleviated or abolished entirely (Noyes and Kolb, 1963). Interestingly enough, delusional ideas appear to be more resistant than hallucinations to this treatment (Winkelman, 1957). Chronically ill schizophrenic patients usually respond more slowly than others, but in many instances delusions and hallucinations are either gradually eliminated or reduced to the point where they no longer upset the patient (Casey *et al.,* 1960; Denber and Bird, 1957). Chlorpromazine also has a favorable effect on resistiveness, personal hygiene, and emotional withdrawal in schizophrenic patients. In a comprehensive study of the treatment of 1523 acute and chronic schizophrenic patients treated with chlorpromazine, Denber and Bird (1957) reported improvement in 81.8 per cent of the cases.

The sedative and antipsychotic value of chlorpromazine has also been demonstrated in the treatment of other mental disorders. Gatski (1955) found chlorpromazine to be of great value in the treatment of emotionally disturbed and chronically disruptive children, making them calmer and more cooperative. In this study, the children's tension and restlessness returned when placebos were substituted for the chlorpromazine. Chlorpromazine has also proved beneficial in quieting manic patients and in alleviating the difficult control problem posed by restless and agitated patients suffering from degenerative brain changes in old age (Klein and Fink, 1962; Noyes and Kolb, 1963). In both acute and chronic alcoholism, chlorpromazine is a useful therapeutic adjunct (Block, 1962; Cummins and Friend, 1954). It is of particular value in controlling motor excitement in acute alcoholism and fostering a return to physiological normalcy with a minimum of withdrawal symptoms. Although less commonly used in psychoneurotic disorders, chlorpromazine is effective in the treatment of severe neurotic anxiety reactions (Winkelman, 1957; Ruesch *et al.,* 1963).

Chlorpromazine is considered a relatively safe drug when administered properly, but it sometimes has various undesirable side effects, such as jaundice, dermatitis, or convulsive seizures (Anderson and Sanchez-Longo, 1961; Hippius and Korenke, 1960; Noyes and Kolb, 1963). Usually such difficulties clear up rapidly with an adjustment in drug dosage or discontinuation of treatment. However, there also are certain subtle complications which may arise in chlorpromazine therapy and are worthy of note here. For example, chlorpromazine does not mix well with alcohol and for ambulatory patients may create problems involving traffic offenses (Wortis, 1961a). A peculiar susceptibility to heat stroke among adolescents under chlorpromazine therapy has been described (Merkin and Hogan, 1960); and an increased tendency to both accidents and illness among older patients has been reported (Olson and Peterson, 1959).

Since the advent of chlorpromazine, a number of other phenothiazine derivatives such as perphenazine (Trilafon) have been tested and placed in clinical usage. In general, their effectiveness appears to be about the same as that of chlorpromazine, but they differ somewhat in side effects (Casey *et al.,* 1960).

Besides the major tranquilizing drugs, such as chlorpromazine, several "minor" tranquilizing, or antianxiety, drugs have been introduced. These drugs are used for reducing tension and anxiety in normal individuals, as well as for neurotics and psychotics. Perhaps the best known of these is *meprobamate* (marketed as Miltown or Equanil). *Librium* has also been widely used and has proved its effectiveness for a variety of neurotic and milder disorders (Azima *et al.,* 1962; Barron, 1961; Jones, 1962; Wortis, 1963). It is a derivative of *chlordiazepoxide*—a drug which was found to have a unique taming effect on vicious agitated monkeys, dingo dogs, and wild animals. These drugs are essentially mild tranquilizers which reduce anxiety and tension and promote sleep. They have little or no antipsychotic action.

Although these drugs are considered to have minimal side effects, they are not without their complications. The meprobamates may induce addiction, and patients may experience severe withdrawal symptoms—including insomnia, tremors, hallucinations, and convulsions—if the medication is stopped suddenly (Ewing and Haizlip, 1959; Stough, 1958). In relatively heavy dosage, Librium may induce drowsiness and in rare instances it appears to induce strange "absences" or sleep attacks which can cause accidents (Merlis and Turner, 1961; Wortis, 1963).

A combination of reserpine and chlorpromazine or other tranquilizing drugs is often more effective than the use of one alone. We shall shortly note the advantages of using drugs in various combinations—including tranquilizers and energizers in the treatment of particular mental disorders.

Energizers. Although the tranquilizing drugs were highly beneficial for many mental patients, they were found to be ineffective and often contraindicated in depressive reactions. Such patients seemed to need a "mood elevator"—to be energized rather than tranquilized.

As medical researchers were considering this problem, a new antituberculosis drug called *iproniazid* was being tested which proved to have a very curious side effect. Tuberculosis patients treated with the drug became gay, optimistic,

and zestful—often to the extent of not getting enough rest. The euphoric effect of iproniazid came to the attention of Dr. Nathan S. Kline of New York's huge Rockland State Mental Hospital. He tried the drug on patients suffering from depression and found that in most cases their gloom lifted (Kline, 1958). Further tests proved iproniazid to be an effective antidepressant, but unfortunately it had dangerous physiological side effects which prohibited its use.

The discovery of the antidepressant effects of iproniazid, however, led to the study of other *monoamine oxidase inhibitors* (MAO inhibitors), and several chemical analogues of iproniazid were found which were effective antidepressants with minimal side effects. Among the more widely used of these have been *phenelzine* (Nardil) and *isocarboxazid* (Marplan). In the treatment of 77 patients suffering from neurotic or psychotic depressions, Agin (1963) found that approximately 82 per cent responded to therapy with phenelzine and that the results were excellent in 70 per cent of the cases. Neurotic and psychotic depressions responded equally well. The response was evident within 5 to 15 days and side effects—such as headache, insomnia, and constipation—were mild and easily controlled. Similarly, English (1961) reported the rehabilitation of 88 per cent of 228 depressed patients with phenelzine and 91 per cent of 195 depressed patients with isocarboxazid. In both groups of patients, a tranquilizer was also given to control mood elevation and prevent excitement and overactivity. In a placebo control group, 35 per cent were rehabilitated. The median improvement time for isocarboxazid was 8 days. In a preliminary study of another MAO inhibitor called MO-109, Bucci and Saunders (1961) found effective results with 22 of 25 depressed patients. This is an interesting finding since most of these patients were schizophrenics manifesting autism and flatness of affect as well as depression, and in the past schizo-affective reactions have not responded well to antidepressant drugs (Greenblatt *et al.,* 1962; Woods and Lewis, 1962). Further research is needed to establish fully the range of use and effectiveness of these drugs.

About the same time that the MAO inhibitors were being introduced, Kuhn (1957) published his first results with a new drug *imipramine*

(Tofranil) which he had found to have strong antidepressant qualities. Since then, studies have shown it to be effective in some 70 to 80 per cent of patients with clear-cut depressive reactions (Keup, 1962; Klein and Fink, 1962; Oltman and Friedman, 1961). It is less effective in depressions complicated by schizophrenia or organic brain pathology (Greenblatt *et al.,* 1962; Overall *et al.,* 1962). Comparable results have been reported for *amitripthyline* (Elavil), another non-MAO inhibitor and close relative of Tofranil (Oltman and Friedman, 1961; Pressman and Weiss, 1961). In the studies of both Tofranil and Elavil, side effects were minimal. Sometimes patients who fail to improve with one drug do so with another.

In general, it would appear that the major antidepressant drugs are effective in producing moderate improvement to remission of symptoms in 70 to 80 per cent of relatively clear-cut depressive reactions. Although their precise effects are not fully understood, these drugs appear to have an antidepressant, a stimulating, and an antipsychotic action (Barsa, 1960; Holt *et al.,* 1960).

The use of antidepressant drugs has greatly reduced the need for electroshock in the treatment of depressive reactions. In fact, Agin (1963) has concluded that electroshock should be used only when the threat of suicide is acute or an immediate improvement is required. Even this apparent limitation may be overcome by the use of so-called potentiating drugs or the development of more potent antidepressants. For example, using an MAO inhibitor and intravenous 5-HTP, Kline and Sacks (1963) reported that 18 of 20 patients with clear-cut depressive reactions responded with definite or marked improvement within 24 hours. If further research supports these findings, it is to be anticipated that electroshock will be largely discontinued except in selected cases.

Other drugs. A wide range of other drugs has been investigated from both a therapeutic and a general experimental viewpoint. We shall not attempt a survey of these drugs, but it may be pointed out that many of them are highly specific in their action. For example, axacyclonol (Frenquel) has elicited considerable interest because of its almost specific antihallucinatory effect (Gerle, 1960).[1]

Use of drugs in combination. In the preceding discussion, we have assessed the effectiveness of various tranquilizing and energizing drugs singly. In actual clinical practice drugs are often used in combination to ensure maximal effectiveness. As we noted in our discussion of schizophrenia, among the most commonly used drugs are the:

Major tranquilizers (phenothiazines, such as chlorpromazine, trifluoperazine—drugs which control excitement, agitation, and thought disturbances.

Antianxiety drugs (for example, meprobamate, chlordiazepoxide)—"minor" tranquilizers which decrease apprehension and tension.

Antidepressants (for example, isocarboxazid, imipramine)—drugs which elevate mood and increase alertness and interest in the environment.

The problem of matching drug and dosage to meet the needs of a given patient is a difficult one. Both the drugs and the dosages vary for different patients. Medication may be changed as the patient's reactions are observed. For example, if the patient does not respond, the medication may be changed; or if he does respond, the dosage may be lowered over a period of time. In many cases, patients are kept on "maintenance" dosages of given drugs after their acute symptoms have subsided.

Despite variations dictated by the need of the patient, Ruesch *et al.* (1963) has pointed out that in depressive reactions it is often helpful to combine either a phenothiazine or an antianxiety drug with an energizer. In the treatment of schizophrenia, the alleviation of the patient's acute symptoms by a phenothiazine may be followed by depressive symptoms which can then be alleviated by a combination of an energizer with the phenothiazine. Since a great many patients are both acutely anxious and depressed at the same time, the simultaneous use of a tranquilizer and an energizer often proves beneficial. In the treatment of 460 neuropsychiatric patients involving a wide range of diagnostic types —including schizophrenia, manic-depressive

---

[1] An excellent review of the major new drugs which appear of therapeutic value may be found in Wortis (1961a, 1962, 1963, 1964). In this discussion, since our focus is on drugs for therapeutic purposes, we have made to attempt to cover the "nerve gases" and other psychic disorganizers developed for military use.

reactions, involutional depressive reactions, and anxiety reactions—Pennington (1962) found that approximately 60 per cent were greatly improved by the combined use of chlorpromazine, meprobamate, and an energizer. Pennington also noted a decrease in side effects in multiple drug medication, partially attributable to the fact that a lower dosage of given drugs can often be used when they are combined with others. As we have previously noted, the use of drugs may be combined with electroshock when the patient does not respond adequately to drug treatment alone.

Effectiveness of chemotherapy. Although it is difficult to assess the effectiveness of chemotherapy, it would appear to be a major breakthrough in the treatment of mental disorders. The newer tranquilizing and energizing drugs have made it possible for many patients to function in the community who would otherwise require hospitalization; they have led to the earlier discharge of patients who do require hospitalization; they have reduced the severity of symptoms and made locked wards and restraint largely a thing of the past; and they have outmoded more drastic forms of treatment, such as psychosurgery. One of their greatest values has been in making many patients more accessible to psychotherapy. All in all, they have led to a much more favorable hospital climate for patients and staff alike.

But chemotherapy is not a cure-all. Psychotherapeutic drugs are welcome adjuncts to the total treatment program, but it would appear unrealistic to assume that mental disorders based on the gradual development of faulty frames of reference and response patterns could be perma-nently cleared up by such limited methods. As many investigators have pointed out, tranquilizers and energizers tend to "mask" symptoms rather than to come to grips with the actual causes of mental disorders. In many instances, drug therapy provides a reduction in tension and anxiety and an increase in overall stress tolerance that enable the patient to resume or maintain his life activities, but although he may be regarded as "recovered," it would appear essential in most cases to include psychotherapy and sociotherapy in the total treatment program if such gains are to be maintained or improved upon. Unfortunately, many patients delay psychotherapy or try to avoid it by means of drugs.

In evaluating studies of chemotherapy, we also need to be on the lookout for a lack of adequate experimental controls, a careless use of the term "improved," and failure of the patient to maintain improvement after the termination of medication. Disregard for these and other factors have sometimes made published results somewhat misleading. It is also relevant to note that, with the possible exception of reserpine, there is no information on the effects of tranquilizing and energizing drugs over sustained periods of time.

From a more positive viewpoint, it would appear that continued advances in brain research and psychopharmacology will eventually enable man to understand the complexities of brain functioning and to deliver the right doses of chemicals to the right locations when disturbances do occur—whether these disturbances result from organic or psychological factors. But the problem of finding a meaningful and fulfilling way of life will remain.

Psychotherapy

Psychotherapy is directed toward helping the patient to achieve a more adequate personality adjustment; thus it may involve varying degrees of personality change or restructuring. The particular goals and procedures adopted for their achievement will depend upon the resources and needs of the patient and the therapeutic facilities available.

That psychotherapy, as practiced today, is not something completely new or strange or far removed from the ken of all of us has been well brought out by Alexander:

". . . Everyone who tries to console a despondent friend, calm down a panicky child in a sense practices psychotherapy. He tries by psychological means to restore the disturbed emotional equilibrium of another person. Even these commonsense, everyday methods are based on the understanding of the nature of the disturbance, although on an intuitive and not a scientific understanding. Talking over with a person an acute harassing experience is based on the instinctive knowledge of the curative effect of abreaction. Giving advice and assuming a firm attitude again is based on the instinctive knowledge that the panicky and confused individual needs emotional support which we can give him by allowing him to lean on us. We also know intuitively that a person who is overwhelmed by a threatening situation cannot use his reasoning faculties effectively and therefore we try to calm him down by giving him support. At the same time discussing with him the objective situation, we lend him our own reasoning faculties. Doing all this, we then practice a combination of supportive and insight therapy. . . . Methodical psychotherapy to a large degree is nothing but a systematic, conscious application of methods by which we influence our fellow men in our daily life. The most important difference is that intuitive knowledge is replaced by the well established general principles of psychodynamics." (1946, p. 110)

Psychotherapy with seriously disturbed patients usually takes place in a hospital or inpatient clinic setting. The various psychotherapeutic procedures we shall be discussing, however, are by no means confined to in-patients. Most patients who receive psychotherapy for neuroses, alcoholism, or character disorders do so on an out-patient basis—either in an outpatient clinic or with psychiatrists or clinical psychologists in private practice.

GOALS OF PSYCHOTHERAPY

In general, psychotherapy aims toward personality growth in the direction of maturity, competence, and self-actualization. This usually involves the achievement of one or more of the following specific goals: (a) increased insight into one's problems and behavior, (b) a better delineation of one's self-identity, (c) resolution of handicapping or disabling conflicts, (d) changing of undesirable habits or reaction patterns, (e) improved interpersonal or other competencies, (f) the modification of inaccurate assumptions about one's self and one's world, and

(g) the opening of a pathway to a more meaningful and fulfilling existence.

These goals are by no means easy to achieve. Often the patient's distorted environmental perspective and unhealthy self-concept are the end products of faulty parent-child relationships reinforced by many years of life experiences. In other instances, the patient's life situation is such that any adequate occupational, marital, or social adjustment is well-nigh hopeless even with the best psychotherapy. It would be too much to expect that the psychotherapist could step in, and in a few hours of interview undo the entire past history of the patient and prepare him to meet a difficult life situation in a fully adequate manner. It is not to be expected that all psychotherapy can succeed.

However, the psychotherapist does have certain assets on his side. The most important of these is the inner drive of the patient toward integrity and health. Although this inner drive is often obscured in more disturbed patients, the majority of mental patients are anxious, unhappy, and discouraged, and eager to cooperate in any program that holds some hope for improvement in their personality adjustment. Some degree of commitment on the part of the patient—a decision to try—is essential if psychotherapy is to have much chance of succeeding.

The second major asset of the psychotherapist is the unique personal relationship which he establishes with the patient. We shall discuss the therapeutic nature of this relationship in more detail shortly, and for the moment want to point out only that it is a friendly and permissive relationship which enables the patient to bring up and discuss his deepest conflicts and problems without fear of censure or retaliation.

TYPICAL STEPS IN PSYCHOTHERAPY

Although there are a number of different systematic views of psychotherapy, such as psychoanalysis and client-centered therapy, as well as a wide range of therapeutic techniques from which the psychotherapist can choose, there are certain events or stages through which psychotherapy usually progresses. These are:

Creation of a therapeutic atmosphere and relationship. This includes the provision of a room or office that is reasonably quiet and otherwise suitable for interview or discussion purposes. Typically, as we have suggested, the therapist maintains a friendly and accepting attitude which is conducive to the establishment of confidence on the part of the patient, so that he can feel secure in bringing up his real problems. In addition, it is the therapist's function to plan or "structure" the therapeutic situation in terms of time, expense, responsibility, and so on. In general, the patient and therapist sit facing each other and the therapy is conducted via discussion or interview. In some instances, the therapist and patient sit side by side, or the patient reclines on a couch facing away from the therapist.

The personal relationship between the patient and the therapist is fully as important as anything that is said or done. Often it is the patient's first experience of being in a permissive and accepting atmosphere in which he feels that he is truly understood and can safely express his innermost thoughts and feelings. This feeling of confidence and harmony which is established between the therapist and the patient is referred to as *rapport*.

Emotional release (catharsis). In the permissive atmosphere of the therapeutic situation, the patient brings up his problems and expresses the hostility, fear, guilt, and other emotions that center around them. Often, as he "talks out" his problems, hostility or fear or other feelings of which he was totally unaware will come to the surface. This "release"—verbal expression—of true emotional feeling is considered essential to effective psychotherapy; it paves the way for the development of insight and positive action toward the solution of his problems. For until the patient "gets these feelings off his chest" the tension and conflict connected with them operate as blocks to any learning of new, more adjustive attitudes.

To assist in the "uncovering" of emotional conflicts and the release of the tensions connected with them, various techniques such as questioning, interpretation, free association, and hypnosis may be used for "probing." These will all be discussed in some detail during the present chapter.

Insight. As the patient's emotional conflicts are brought out into the open where he can see them for what they are, he spontaneously gains a good deal of understanding into his motivations and behavior. For the first time, for example, he may realize that his level of aspiration is unrealistically high and that this is what keeps him continually feeling inadequate and inferior. His developing understanding or "insight" may be augmented by appropriate "interpretations" by the therapist and provides the basis for positive action. Most therapists consider self-understanding highly important for successful therapy, but with some approaches, such as behavior therapy, insight is ordinarily regarded as unnecessary.

Personality change. As the patient gains insight into his problems and the faulty ways in which he has been trying to solve them, he is in a position to make indicated changes in his behavior and to attempt more appropriate adjustive measures. These changes may be minor or major in scope and may involve assumptions, habits, social roles, and many other aspects of the patient's behavior. In some instances, the patient may be helped to replace a faulty habit with a more efficient one; in other instances, he becomes more aware of the assumptions which guide his behavior and hence better able to make effective use of his opportunities for choice; and in still other instances, he is helped to make major changes in assumptions or reaction patterns. Often the first steps consist of "positive action" of a minor sort, such as learning to express hostility in socially acceptable ways rather than keeping it bottled up. These positive actions gradually lead to increased competence and self-confidence. In essence, the entire process of personality change focuses around new learning and is often referred to as "emotional re-education."

Termination. When the patient has "worked through" his conflicts or made substantial progress toward resolving his problems, the time comes for the termination of the therapy. This is ordinarily not difficult inasmuch as the patient now feels more confident and able to get along on his own. However, it is important to leave the way open for the patient to return any time he feels the need.

Thus the sequence of events in psychotherapy, regardless of the particular systematic approach, typically involves the establishment of a therapeutic situation, emotional release, insight into the uncovered material, and positive actions or corrective emotional experiences necessary to replace old reaction patterns. Whether this abreaction and the corrective learning experience take place through narcosis interviews, or on a couch during free association, or in direct discussion between patient and therapist, or with the aid of hypnosis or role playing, and whether the patient is seen one hour a day, five days a week, as in psychoanalysis, or once a week, as in various eclectic therapies—all these are technical details which can best be determined by the nature of the individual case. In some cases the development of insight, with resolution of conflicts and emotional re-education, may be a very slow and laborious process which must be achieved in small steps. In patients with greater ego strength or less severe conflicts, the therapeutic process may go ahead rapidly.

In our review of psychotherapy, we shall find considerable variation in points of view, specific goals, and therapeutic procedures. The basic steps, however, are much the same for most of the systematic approaches.

KEY DIMENSIONS OF PSYCHOTHERAPY

Up to this point we have noted the aims and the typical stages of the psychotherapeutic process. We shall shortly consider various specific techniques and systematic approaches. Before going on, however, let us glance briefly at certain other dimensions or characteristics of psychotherapy which will help to provide us with an overall view of this rather complex field.

Individual vs. group. Where the therapist treats one patient at a time, the procedure is referred to as individual therapy. Its effectiveness depends primarily upon the patient-therapist relationship. In group therapy, the therapist handles several patients at the same time. Here the patient is treated through the medium of the group, and the relationship of the patient to other members of the group as well as to the therapist is of great importance in determining the effects of the therapy.

In general, individual therapy is more effective in working through deep conflict material, such as conflicts centering around homosexuality, while group therapy has proved of particular value in socialization. Feelings of isolation are removed through the mutual sharing of problems in which each member realizes that others have difficulties similar to his, and there is a mutual support and assistance in working through these common problems. Furthermore, the group relationship provides each member with opportunities for social reality testing and the development of more efficient techniques in interpersonal relations. Often a combination of individual and group psychotherapy is the most effective therapeutic procedure.

Brief vs. long-term. The historical leader among modern psychotherapeutic approaches—standard psychoanalysis—attempts a major restructuralization of the personality. Typically this requires therapy sessions five times a week over a period of several years. However desirable such ambitious *long-term* psychotherapy may be, it does restrict the benefits of psychotherapy to a relatively small number of patients who can afford the time and money. As a result, various *brief* or *goal-limited* forms of treatment have now been worked out to make psychotherapy available to larger numbers of people who are in need of it. These goal-limited approaches are designed to benefit the patient as much as possible in a shorter period of time. To achieve this aim, they restrict the therapy to those conflicts or problems whose resolution will most aid the patient's immediate personality adjustment. These briefer approaches include both individual and group psychotherapy and both analytically[1] and nonanalytically oriented approaches.

Goal-limited therapy has proved of particular value in mental hospitals and clinics where the lack of adequate personnel and the small amount of time available for psychotherapy for each patient restrict more intensive, long-range therapy to a very few cases. It may be emphasized here that goal-limited therapy is not restricted to "symptomatic" or "surface" therapy but may also be used in the working through of "deep" conflicts.

Surface vs. depth. In so-called surface therapy, there is no attempt to go deeply into the patient's underlying conflicts. Rather an attempt is made to reassure the patient and to reinforce

---

[1] "Analytical" is commonly used synonymously with "psychoanalytical."

his present ego defenses. In many crowded mental hospitals and clinics, surface therapy is about all the psychotherapy the patient ever gets. There are times, however, when surface therapy is all a patient needs. Usually this involves cases where the patient's ego strength and adjustive adequacy are fairly good but where overwhelming stress has made him a psychiatric casualty—where the excessive stress rather than any deep pathological trend within the personality is the main cause of the difficulty. Surface therapy may also be indicated in cases where the individual is severely limited in adjustive resources—as in many cases of senile brain degeneration—and in cases where the individual has acquired a conditioned maladaptive response which can be dealt with by reconditioning techniques.

In depth therapy, the uncovering and working through of deep conflictual material or highly traumatic and painful experiences is attempted. This may be achieved in either goal-limited or long-term psychotherapy.

Conative vs. cognitive. It is often useful in psychotherapy to distinguish between what might be termed conative and cognitive aspects of the patient's behavior—between desires and emotions on the one hand and intellectual knowledge and competencies on the other. In some cases, the alleviation of anxiety or other emotions centering around traumatic experiences is the primary focus of therapy; in other cases, the focus is on inaccurate assumptions which the individual has acquired about himself and his world.

These two aspects of psychotherapy are not mutually exclusive, of course. Emotional trauma may be alleviated if the patient can view the traumatic experience in a different light—for example, as something in the past and a type of experience with which many people have to cope. Similarly, many of our assumptions have strong emotional charges and cannot be changed without modifying the emotions attached to them. For example, the patient who can trace his lack of self-confidence to overly critical parents may have insight into the false image he has of himself and know, intellectually, that he is actually superior in ability; but still he feels inadequate and lacks self-confidence. The early emotional conditioning has done its work well. Therapy must make him *feel* differently about himself if it is to be successful in helping him to

change his self-concept and become a more effective person.

In some instances, insight is all a patient needs to be able to begin reshaping his assumptions, but therapy is rarely so simple, and in most cases both conative and cognitive factors must be considered.

Directive vs. nondirective. There are wide differences among therapists with respect to the amount of responsibility they place upon the patient and the degree of responsibility they themselves assume for the direction of the therapy. In what is termed "directive" therapy, the therapist takes an "active" role in the therapy situation. This usually includes taking the lead in attempting to uncover the patient's underlying conflicts, interpreting to the patient what is revealed, and guiding him toward positive actions designed to effect personality changes. The use of directive therapy is illustrated in the following excerpt from a case record:[1]

Pt.: "I tried to ignore all these things. At 19 I was so infatuated with the girl, yet so scared, that I could not approach her. The feeling was so strong that it seemed to bottle itself up. Thus it was all or nothing with me. So far it has been nothing. With the present girl, when I feel so strongly about her, I feel I must do *something* about it. I do nothing. I am afraid of the devil."

Th.: "It does not look as though you have sold yourself to the devil after all."

Pt.: "If it broke out, I would go wild."

Th.: "And that is?"

Pt.: "Possibly I might hurt the girl in some way. The thought occurs to me that in this frenzy I might kill the girl."

Th.: "How would you kill her?"

Pt.: "I might strangle her, with my hands round her neck."

Th.: "What is it that you are strangling?"

Pt.: "I am strangling my own feelings—my own feelings of a great desire for sexual intercourse with her."

Th.: "So the girl stands for your desire which you are so afraid of, just as the devil stood for it. In this phantasy of strangling the girl you are dramatizing the struggle that is within your own mind."

[1]Reprinted from *A Casebook of a Medical Psychologist* by Charles Berg by permission of W. W. Norton & Company, Inc. and George Allen & Unwin, Ltd. Copyright 1948 by W. W. Norton & Company, Inc.

In so-called nondirective therapy, the therapist is less active and the major share of the responsibility for the therapy rests with the patient. Here the therapist merely provides a friendly and permissive atmosphere which enables the patient to feel secure and accepted and to bring up his innermost thoughts and feelings without fear of censure or retaliation. Rather than "probing" and interpreting, the therapist confines his efforts to helping the patient to clarify his underlying feelings and attitudes as they emerge in the therapy situation. This clarification is usually achieved by means of "reflecting" rather than interpreting the feelings and attitudes expressed by the patient. The following excerpt from the case record of a patient treated nondirectively will help to indicate the difference between nondirective and directive approaches.

Pt.: I am afraid I am falling in love with her . . . and I can't study or do anything when I don't see her . . . and yet I know she would not be faithful to me . . . I just don't know which way to turn.

Th.: You want to continue seeing Frances but you are afraid you will be hurt.

Pt.: Yes, I look forward so much to seeing her and I don't think I could get along without her . . . I can't study or anything when I don't see her . . . but, well she likes to run around and I know she has sexual relations with other fellows . . . and . . . well this upsets me . . . I can't stand the thought of her making love to someone else. If she would only settle down with me, but . . . well I am afraid she won't.

Th.: You feel that everything would work out if she only loved you, but you are afraid . . .

Pt.: Afraid to even try I guess . . . she does insist that she loves me . . . but . . . well . . .

In actual practice directive and nondirective approaches represent two poles of a continuum and few therapists are either completely directive or completely nondirective. Usually it is a matter of emphasis, leaving room for considerable flexibility in terms of the needs of the particular patient. In general, nondirective emphasis has proved most effective in the handling of patients with fairly stable personalities who are having difficulty in coping with particular immediate problems, whereas directive emphasis has proved most appropriate in the handling of

more disturbed and severely ill mental patients. Later in the chapter we shall examine in considerable detail the theory behind both the directive and the nondirective approaches and the ways in which they are employed by the major "schools."

Flexibility vs. inflexibility.   There are some therapists who faithfully follow a particular systematic approach, such as psychoanalysis, adhering closely to the dynamic concepts and therapeutic techniques advocated by that approach. In fact, some therapists have even maintained that directive and nondirective approaches are incompatible and that a therapist should confine himself to the use of one or the other. But the great majority of psychotherapists can be best described as eclectic—that is, they utilize various concepts and procedures from psychoanalysis and other approaches as the needs of a given patient warrant. This does not mean that standard psychoanalysis or nondirective therapy is not entirely appropriate for certain patients. However, to attempt to apply one of these approaches to all persons in need of psychotherapy would be a wasteful venture. Obviously, an approach confined largely to the nondirective clarification of feeling and attitude would likely prove futile in the treatment of a chronic schizophrenic who is delusional and hallucinated.

Those therapists who confine themselves to a certain procedure usually carefully select patients who can best profit from it. For example, a 60-year-old schizophrenic would not ordinarily be chosen for psychoanalysis. Other therapists accept a more heterogeneous group of patients and modify their therapeutic procedures as best fits the needs of each case.

Segregated vs. total push.   A great deal of psychotherapy takes place in what might be called a "segregated" fashion. The patient may receive an hour of psychotherapy several times a week in an attempt to help him work through his conflicts and achieve healthier techniques of adjustment, but little effort is made to relate the therapy to his life situation or to coordinate it with his other activities. In contrast to this is what may be called "total push" or "milieu" therapy, where the entire life situation and all the activities of the patient are brought directly into the therapeutic plan. In a hospital setting, this would involve the coordination of all of the patient's activities from the time he gets up in the morning until he goes to bed at night through the careful planning and participation of the hospital staff—psychiatrists, psychologists, nurses, ward attendants, occupational therapists, and others who come into contact with the patient. For the patient who feels unwanted and unworthy of esteem from others, it means creating an atmosphere of warmth and love. Psychotherapy may be supplemented by various other patterns of interpersonal relationships, ranging from planned recreational activities to group therapy with the patient and his family. The results with total push therapy have been most gratifying, and at the major psychiatric clinics and hospitals in the United States, every activity in the hospital setting as well as various aspects of the patient's life situation are brought—in so far as possible—into the therapy program.

PSYCHOTHERAPEUTIC PROCEDURES

Early in therapy—of whatever kind—the therapist attempts to identify the component tasks to be mastered in achieving his final goals. The component tasks—and the specific procedures for tackling them—are then sequenced in such a way as to ensure optimal progress toward the final goal. In essence, a complicated learning outcome—such as "feeling more adequate in social situations"—is broken down into successive subtasks which insure continuous progress and positive reinforcement in relation to the final goal. Unfortunately, the programming of therapy is not a simple matter. Caution must be exercised to avoid the premature formulation of therapeutic goals, and often changes in plans must be made as the therapy continues.

Inasmuch as entire books have been written about many of the specific psychotherapeutic techniques and their uses, we shall content ourselves here with a brief summary of the more important ones.[1] They may be used in almost any combination, depending on the needs of the individual patient. In acute conditions such as those we discussed in Chapter 5 where previously well-adjusted individuals are overwhelmed by especially severe stresses, the therapist may select techniques chiefly designed to help reduce the intensity of the disturbing emotions by supportive measures and emotional re-

lease. Where the difficulty involves a more chronic personality maladjustment, techniques may be utilized which are effective in working through underlying conflicts or in modifying assumptions concerning value, reality, and possibility. The needs and resources of the patient and the therapeutic goals which are established usually determine the nature of the psychotherapeutic procedures which are selected.

Interview therapy. In any type of therapy, but especially in interview therapy, communication is a crucial process. Often the patient finds it difficult to express himself and does so in a halting and confused way, or sometimes in quite indirect ways. Usually he does not himself understand the thoughts and feelings he is struggling to express. As in the case described on the front endsheet, the therapist may need to be highly perceptive in order to understand what the patient is trying to tell him. However, a feeling of being understood tends to encourage the patient to try to communicate more of his experience; conversely, a feeling that the therapist does not understand or is not trying to understand is likely to terminate the therapy.

Often individuals who have never participated in psychotherapy wonder what the patient talks about and how the therapist manages to guide the direction of conversation along therapeutic channels. Actually there are a variety of techniques at the disposal of the therapist which he can use in attempting to achieve emotional release, develop insight, and promote emotional re-education in a patient. Among the most important of these techniques are the following.

1. *Reflection.* We have already noted the use of reflection in helping the patient to clarify his underlying feelings and attitudes. In essence, this technique consists in repeating the attitudes and feelings expressed by the patient. In this way the therapist acts as a sort of mirror in which the patient is enabled to see the attitudes and feelings that he has expressed for what they are. This is not a simple technique to use: considerable training and skill are needed to recognize the real attitudes and feelings of the patient.

[1]More detailed discussions of psychotherapeutic techniques can be found in Brammer and Shostrom (1960), Edelson (1963), Eysenck (1960), Frank (1961), Ingham and Love (1954), Masserman (1963), Rogers (1961), Snyder (1963), Sundberg and Tyler (1962), Watkins (1954, 1960), Wolberg (1954), Wolf and Schwartz (1962).

Should the therapist make repeated errors, the patient may feel misunderstood and may discontinue the therapy or become uncooperative. The excerpt from a nondirective therapy session cited on page 568 shows the use of reflection in clarifying the patient's feelings about himself and his problem. It also shows the need for perceptiveness and skill by the therapist in picking out what should be mirrored and what should be disregarded.

2. *Interpretation.*   The technique of interpretation consists essentially in pointing out to the patient what his underlying motivations and attitudes are, as revealed in the course of therapy. It is one of the most difficult of all therapeutic techniques to use effectively. Premature or traumatic interpretations may effectively block further progress. For example, the therapist may be convinced after the first session that the patient's conflict centers around hostility aroused by an overly possessive and domineering mother. But if at this point he makes such an interpretation, the patient is likely to reject it, insisting that his mother is a wonderful woman and that his only feelings toward her are those of love. Thus interpretations must be made only as the patient becomes ready to accept and profit from them. Where their timing is appropriate, such interpretations may lead to the relaxing of ego defenses and thus enable the patient to get a little closer to underlying conflicts and problems. This apparently comes about through the supporting influence of the therapist, which makes the patient feel more secure, and by the perception that his conflicts are not as dangerous or threatening as his elaborate ego defenses would imply.

Another common error in the use of interpretation has been the naïve assumption that intellectual insight into our problems will lead automatically to a change in our emotional attitudes and behavior—that as soon as the patient understands the reasons for his difficulties, he will voluntarily modify his behavior. Psychotherapists operating on this assumption have devoted their energies to diagnosing the patient's difficulties and interpreting their findings to him. The danger inherent in this procedure has been summarized by Murphy and Weinreb in a discussion of the training of psychotherapists in a Veterans Administration Hospital.

"By far, the most common problem was the universal tendency of the resident to interpret the patient's symptoms to him unwisely, too frequently and too deeply, thus endeavoring to substitute intellectual insight for the self-revelation which is the true goal with any effective analytic psychotherapy. There would accordingly be created unsurmountable barriers and problems in resistance with which they did not have the technical ability to cope. The tendency to confront the patient with the doctor's understanding is an evidence of psychotherapeutic anxiety. . . . The defensiveness of their behavior is frequently manifested by authoritative interpretations and a pinning down of their patients with keen, if futile logic. Hostile reactions by patients to this form of approach are then mistaken for therapeutic triumphs in relieving latent hostility." (1948, p. 102)

Thus effective interpretation is not a simple matter and requires considerable perceptiveness and restraint on the part of the therapist. If a patient feels inferior and anxious much of the time, it will not suffice to point out to him that this stems from an insecure mother and unfavorable comparisons with an older brother. Such an intellectualized interpretation may be quite accurate, but the patient goes on feeling anxious and inferior. Modern psychotherapy has come to place increasing emphasis upon helping the patient himself to identify, clarify, and accept his feelings.

3. *Associative anamnesis.*   Deutsch (1949) worked out an interview technique which he has called *associative anamnesis.* Its purpose is to keep the therapeutic approach centered around certain conflicts or problems which the therapist has decided are the core ones that most need to be worked through. It is a complicated technique and provides the basic procedure for a goal-limited psychotherapeutic approach which he termed "sector therapy." With this method, the therapist unobtrusively but effectively controls the direction of the therapy by selecting and repeating certain key words or phrases in the patient's statements. For example, suppose the patient states that he has "always hated women." At this point the therapist may feel it desirable to explore the patient's past in this respect, but instead of asking him to go back and tell him about his childhood, he merely repeats the word "always," which then forces the patient into the past smoothly and without an interruption in his chain of associations. On the other hand, if he repeats the word "hated," the patient's associations are directed toward the clarification of his feelings and attitudes in relation to "hating women."

4. *Questions.* There are many occasions when the clarification of feeling and the promotion of insight are best served by direct questions and requests to the patient to elaborate on the meaning of his statement. By means of such questions as "How did you feel?" or "What were your thoughts?" or "Would you mind explaining what you mean?" the therapist can effectively control the direction of the therapy discussion.

As in the case of interpretation, questions must be used appropriately if they are to prove effective. Premature probing, morbid curiosity on the part of the therapist, and the unearthing of unnecessary details may seriously interfere with effective therapy.

5. *Reinforcement.* The therapist can also influence the direction of interview therapy by the way in which he responds to statements of the patient. Here the therapist essentially reinforces certain types of responses of the patient by showing approval. Thus when the patient makes a statement concerning his deeper feelings, the therapist may nod his head or simply lean forward in a more attentive manner. In response to other types of material which he wishes to elicit from the patient he may smile or say "good." Since the approval of the therapist is usually important to the patient, it is not surprising that the patient can be guided by such reinforcement effects even though he may not be aware of what is taking place.[1]

Still other interview techniques, which we can mention only briefly, are silence and confrontation. Often a patient is somewhat uncomfortable during periods of silence and will volunteer additional information to fill in the "space." In confrontation, the patient may be confronted with the probable consequences of his present undesirable behavior patterns; or he may be confronted with problems of meaning, purpose, and value and challenged to find answers.

Group therapy. During and immediately after World War II group therapy was used be-

cause enough therapists for individual therapy were not available. It was found to be so effective that the same methods were applied to civilian cases, and group therapy is now considered one of our most important therapeutic approaches.

Group therapy differs from individual therapy primarily in simulating social reality—that is, the group situation with its social give-and-take is much more like real life. For this reason it has proved particularly valuable in the more effective socialization of the patient—helping him to realize that others have difficulties similar to his, giving him a chance to become a member of and identify with a group. In group therapy he finds support and assistance in working through his problems, improves his techniques of interpersonal relations through the group opportunities for social reality testing, and loses his feeling of isolation. In the hands of a skilled therapist, this process eventuates in increased insight and clarification of the self-picture, the resolution of disabling conflicts, greater self-acceptance, and general personality growth.

Several types of group therapy may be utilized. *Play* or *release therapy* is used mainly with children and includes puppet shows, fingerpainting, and similar creative activities that provide emotional release and re-education. *Didactic group therapy* consists of more or less formal lectures and discussion conducted by the psychiatrist or psychologist in a sort of classroom approach. Unfortunately, this approach has been found generally ineffective and is rarely used now except for certain specialized groups of patients. Tuberculosis patients, for example, might profit from such a formal, intellectualized discussion of the organic nature of their illness. *Inspirational group therapy* stresses group identification, the sharing of experiences, and positive group emotions—as in Alcoholics Anonymous. *Interview group therapy* involves the discussion approach already described in our review of individual therapy techniques. Here the patients discuss their problems and all members of the group are encouraged to participate. In *family therapy* two or more family members are treated as a group. In the present context we are interested primarily in interview group therapy and family therapy.

---

[1]Reinforcement as a technique for guiding interview therapy is well discussed by Frank (1961).

1. *Interview group therapy.* For effective group therapy the patients selected should have a definite desire to improve their adjustment, and the group should not be either too heterogeneous or too homogeneous. Group members who differ widely in age, intelligence, and severity of illness may not have enough in common with each other, whereas patients who are too homogeneous do not have the maturing experience of working in a broader social context, nor do they seem to maintain adequate group interaction. Ordinarily patients sit in a semicircle—sometimes around a table. Typically sessions last for an hour and a half and are held once or twice a week for several months. The optimal number for most groups is 6 to 8 members.

In conducting interview group therapy, the therapist may utilize practically any of the individual techniques which we have reviewed, such as reflecting, interpreting, and asking questions. Among the primary functions of the therapist are (a) the establishment and maintenance of a therapeutic atmosphere, (b) the encouragement and direction of group interaction, and (c) the maintenance of systematic records of the sessions, which can then be used for purposes of clinical evaluation. Often, too, such records are used for research. One of the problems faced by the group therapist is that of focusing on the nature of the group interaction rather than on the problems and dynamics of individual patients. Although some therapists attempt to maintain a particular systematic approach, most are eclectic, varying their approach to suit the needs of the group.

The group interaction is a fascinating process to watch. There is a give and take of hostility, warmth, fear, support, rejection, and the myriad other social aspects of group behavior. Again, as in individual therapy, the interaction may take place on a relatively superficial surface level or it may involve the working through of deep emotional conflicts of the various members of the group. In general, the course of therapy is similar to that in individual therapy, going from the expression of hostility and negative feelings through emotional insight to positive actions and growth.

The following are excerpts from the first session of one group, together with interpretive comments.

"*Therapist* (enters after men assemble): Hello men. (Members respond with various greetings.) Let's introduce ourselves first of all, and then perhaps talk a bit about ourselves. Jack, would you like to begin?

Jack: We introduced ourselves, Doc, before you got here. So I guess that's taken care of. (Pause) Well—my problem is asthma. I've had it since I was four and no one knows what it's all about. It left me once when I was given some shots, and I thought that was it. But when I was in the Army I really began to have attacks. I got in school here and finally wound up in the Clinic. There are emotional factors, I guess. One damned thing, though, I'm far from being an emotionally adjusted person!

Albert: What do you mean—who is well adjusted? And how do you know he is?

Jack: Well—you fellows all look well adjusted, and it seems kind of foolish to shoot the bull this way! (At this point regarding the therapist with evident resentment.)

Oliver: You guys call me Oliver in here. My name is Jack, but the other Jack spoke first. (To Jack) I'd really like to correct you. I don't think this is shooting the bull or that being able to talk even is well adjusted. I think that's my problem—that I talk too easily and too much. I think it's worse than your problem. With me it's an attention-getting device, and I do it because I'm anxious.

Jack: (*To Albert*) What do you think about this?

Albert: I don't think either of you is right. Why is Oliver so easy and free, and why are you at the opposite end of the chain? What is normal?

Oliver: I'm not happy unless I'm getting attention. You sounded kind of disgusted there, Al. Well, I dream of suicide every night and of an obituary, and I have no intention of doing it. It's just attention-getting.

Jack: I still say this is just bull!

Therapist: A few moments ago when you said that, you seemed resentful toward me.

Jack (laughingly): Yeah—I guess maybe I was. I don't know why, though.

(Although up to this point the therapist has been mostly silent, one does not feel he maintains this quiet arbitrarily or punitively. After the introductory remarks, the patients pursue their own patterns. They mention some of their symptoms, disagree with each other, and one dares to show some hostility by glancing at the therapist resentfully. Yet, when this display first happens, the therapist accepts it without comment.

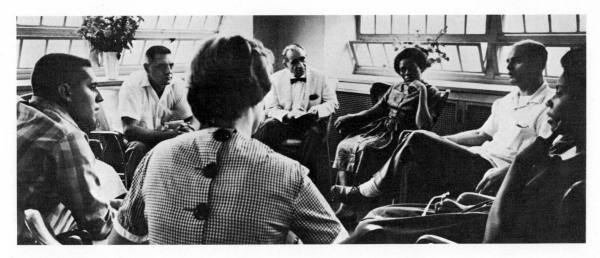

In group therapy, patients sit informally in a circle or around a table. Individual members of the group listen to what others have to say and take part to whatever extent they wish.

Later, rather casually, he suggests the possibility of resentment. When Jack's tension is released a little by laughter, the therapist again lapses into silence. . . .)

Joel: You can call me Red—everyone does. Say, are all you guys maladjusted? One thing worries me— you fellows are all so darned normal!

Oliver: Another thing that is really my problem is that I'm accident-prone. I get into accidents about once a year—really serious ones.

Jack: You're farther along the scale, maybe, than I am, but in the Army I used to have problems too, very much like that.

Mark: I guess I'm afraid of people. My object is never to be the big wheel. I suppose they found out I had high blood pressure, and that's why they sent me up here to the Clinic. I don't know just why I have it, though. In the Navy I was in the Personnel Bureau. I was a conference reporter in one of the 'red rooms.'

Jack (laughingly): We're in the wrong room, boys. Let's move.

(The patients compare notes and see their resemblances and their differences. This spontaneous contrast and clarification results in group identity, a feeling one for the other in the permissive presence of the therapist. A less mature therapist easily could seize upon Oliver's admission of being accident-prone for interpretation, could point it up as a possible indication of a need to be self-punishing; or he could use Mark's comments in regard to his war assignment to show need for status.

Instead, although undoubtedly aware of the inferential possibilities, the therapist permits the patients to explore further their self-directiveness.)" (Hinckley and Hermann, 1951, pp. 22-24.)

In groups that are functioning effectively, the members usually find their group membership and interaction an interesting and satisfying experience and look forward to the sessions. An example of group therapy with delinquents was described on pages 376-377.

2. *Family therapy.* A special form of group therapy fast gaining in popularity is family therapy. We have repeatedly emphasized the importance of the family in personality development and adjustment. It is not surprising that increasing attention is being directed toward treatment of the family group as a unit in order to provide conditions conducive to better mental health and effectiveness for the patient. Marital partners are commonly treated together in psychotherapy, and in many instances parents and children are also treated as a group. New approaches are being tried out in this field, and in some cases where one member of the family requires hospitalization, the entire family may live on the ward and receive treatment as a group. This does not, of course, preclude additional individual psychotherapy.

As we have noted, a pathogenic family group

In the Community Child Guidance Centers in Chicago, several mothers learn from each others' problems. First, the mother describes the problem as she sees it or reports on events since the previous session (left). Then she goes out of the room while the counselor talks to the children (right), after which she talks further with the mother. A report is also made of the children's behavior in the playroom. Three or four cases may be discussed at a given session.

commonly manifests problems in communication, role expectations, values, and other aspects of family organization and interaction which may seriously reduce the satisfactions achieved by the family members or even lead to the mental illness of one or more family members. Family therapy is thus directed toward helping individual members to express their feelings and "gripes," to develop a better understanding of each other and of the family, and to. find more effective ways of relating to each other and solving their common problems.

In this context it is interesting to note Ackerman's conclusion that the first member of a family to seek psychological assistance is often "an emissary in disguise of an emotionally warped family group." (1958, p. 104) This "primary patient" may or may not be severely disturbed emotionally.

The following is an excerpt from the fourth session with a family in which the parents had been unsuccessfully using moralizing to try to curb their son's rebelliousness.

"*Mr. Clay:* I think that it has been a little easier week this time. I don't know how Dick is coming out on his school problems, but I think that it has been a

little better, partly because he has had his own way.

Dick: The teachers sent me five times to the office this week. That's an improvement.

Mr. Clay: Improvement? Do you mean that you've gone to the office more times? How many times? Once a day?

Dick: No, I went three times in one day. Twice. One time in two different days.

Mr. Clay: The average has been worse than that?

Dick: It's usually been about two times every day.

Mr. Clay: Do they come from the same or different teachers?

Dick: Oh, it's usually the same one. I have my ideas and I'm not going to back down. If you do back down you are a lost soul. You've got to have your own head.

Mr. Clay: You have a point there. But sooner or later you back up against something you can't control and then what are you going to do?

Dick: I'm going to just push right forward.

Mr. Clay: You can't sometimes.

Dick: Hmmm.

Mr. Clay: I wonder what the answer is. It seems to me that everyone is going to have to knuckle down some place sometime. It's just a matter of when and how quick.

Mrs. Clay: It has been awful easy for me to have a

high standard in life. I have it for myself as well as others, but I think that I am coming to realize that I can't influence others—that if I keep my standard for myself that then I'll have to let others choose their standards. I think I have been getting a little more peace in my mind and realizing that I am responsible to God for myself and to train others, but the results are not my— —

Dick (interrupts): Mother, this isn't church. Good night!

Mr. Clay: Well, those things have to be said.

Dick: She can do it in church—not here. A bunch of preaching!

Mr. Clay: Most people have to learn the hard way. But they'd like you to learn some other way than the hard way, but I kind of think that you are going to have to learn the hard way, however hard it is. If you're going to fall, you'll just have to fall.

Mrs. Clay: Well, I've just wanted to prevent that, but I don't think that can be done.

Therapist: Is it that you feel irritated with Dick or that you feel that the children need to learn on their own?

Mr. Clay: I kind of feel, maybe I'm sounding off here against Dick, but that's not necessarily the case, that not the last couple of years but previous to that he didn't get all that was coming to him, not only him but the rest of us in this room. Their discipline wasn't as tough as it might have been. And now that it is starting to tighten up again, they are kind of behind the eightball and they don't know what to do about it. They don't want to give in—they have had their own way for a while—and now the fun begins.

Therapist: How do you feel about this, Dick?

Dick: I'm not backing down.

Therapist: That seems to be your theme, doesn't it?

Dick: Boy, there's going to be something that's really going to come up. Someone is going to have to work hard. I'm not going to back down.

Therapist: It's important for you to keep your own head all the way.

Dick: Yeah.

Mr. Clay: I think Dick has said exactly what his major trouble is, if you call that a trouble—Dick doesn't think so—he thinks it's a good point. Well, nobody can be boss all the time—there isn't any question. That is the reason I say that everybody is going to have to lower their head and get it bloody sometime in order to learn that they can't run the whole show. The sooner we realize it, the better off we are. I don't mean that they should cow-tow to everybody, but at the same time sooner or later they are going to run up against somebody that's not going to fool with that kind of stuff. If it's on the job, they may get canned, and if it's other places there are other results.

Therapist: I wonder what Dick could tell us to help us to feel how it feels to have to fight to keep from being pushed around.

Dick: When I was in school did I tell you how I got to the office?

Therapist: How?

Dick: Well, we were—yeah, I'll tell about yesterday. There was a party at school. A friend and I, we were passing out the punch and I was doing okay. One of the other guys started talking to me and he was talking and we got to laughing about something. The teacher got mad and after the party was all over he said, 'Would you mind going to the office?' So we went to the office and he said, 'I don't want you guys to make a fool of us anymore.' I said, 'Well, if I knew I was making a fool of you I'd of made a big one.' And then at the time I said that he came over to me and said, 'If you are going to say any more I'll bend you over.' So I went back and sat down. As soon as we got out I said, 'The next time I go to the office I'll bend *him* over,' and I think he heard me—I'm pretty sure he did." (Sundberg and Tyler, 1962.)

Psychodrama and role playing. Psychodrama was developed in 1921 by a young Viennese physician, J. L. Moreno, who observed the changes that occurred in people when they spontaneously acted out their personality problems. Psychodrama takes place on a stage which may be specially designed. The chief actors are the protagonist (the patient), the director (the chief therapist), the auxiliary egos (other patients or assistant therapists), and the audience. The particular situation utilized is suggested either by the therapist or by the patient. Immediately before the session the situation is briefly outlined—for example, that the patient's wife has told him that she is in love with someone else and is leaving him. This plot merely serves to set the general drama situation, and the patient acts out the scene spontaneously. Auxiliary egos are assigned roles that support the action. One of their chief functions is to help bring out the feelings and problems of the patient. The goal in psychodrama is to help the patient achieve emotional catharsis and be-

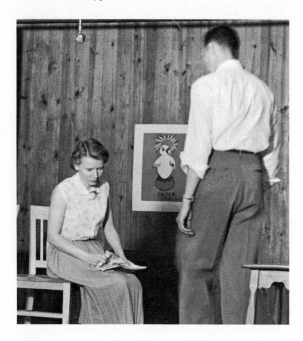

A psychodrama session may take place on an actual stage, as shown here, and may involve varying real or imaginary "props," including other actors. The patient can "let himself go" without fear of disapproval or retaliation and thus may express feelings long held in and perhaps not even known to himself. In family group psychodrama members may play their own roles or each others'.

come a more adequate, spontaneous, and creative person. There are many techniques for developing the psychodrama production, and the director-therapist may be didactic and directive or may serve merely as a catalyst—as his clinical judgment dictates (Moreno, 1959).

In the process of psychodrama, the patient reveals a great deal about his personality organization—his motives, problems, and typical ego defenses. Of great therapeutic significance is the cathartic effect upon the patient of acting out roles relating to his past traumatic experiences and present problems. Here he may express his fears, his resentments, his feelings of jealousy, his guilt and self-recrimination, his feelings of inadequacy, and desires that he cannot display in everyday life. This material may be used in later individual therapy sessions with the director-therapist.

Another important value of psychodrama lies in the training patients receive in spontaneity, both in re-meeting old situations and working them through more appropriately and in facing new ones that arise during the dramatic re-enactment with the supporting cast. Learning to express oneself easily and spontaneously and to meet new situations effectively as they arise in the course of psychodrama frees the individual from emotional blocks, develops insight into and appreciation of the feelings and behavior of others, and promotes adequacy and flexibility in social skills.

An interesting variation on psychodrama procedures is the introduction of hypnosis. Some therapists feel that hypnosis is particularly valuable here in removing most resistances to dramatics and in reproducing traumatic incidents and emotional scenes with an intensity and vividness that is not usually achieved in the waking state. This uncovering and catharsis are then followed up by interview therapy sessions designed to increase insight and emotional reeducation.

A less formal technique which has developed out of the psychodrama approach is "role playing." Here a dramatic situation is chosen and the roles assigned to two or more patients. In a hospital or clinic setting, four types of situations are common, each having a somewhat different therapeutic goal.

1. Reality situations designed to prepare the individual for the type of situation he may meet when he leaves the hospital—perhaps how to handle the stigma attached to mental patients when they are applying for a job after release from the hospital.

2. Situations designed to encourage group spirit and identification and better patient-personnel understanding. For example, Haber and his colleagues dealt with the problem of ward attendants and nurses not reporting infractions of hospital rules because of friendly feelings for the patients and not wanting to be branded as "stool pigeons."

"An aide (played by a patient) greeted a patient just returned from a pass and idly inspected a new portable radio the patient was carrying. He opened the back of the compartment and found a bottle of whiskey." (1949, p. 27)

In the ensuing discussion of this problem, the group without exception approved reporting this incident, thus assuring the aides and nurses that the fulfillment of their duty would be understood.

3. Situations directed toward the release of pent-up emotions. The patient may act out what he would have liked to say to the ward doctor when the latter turned him down for a weekend pass, or he may re-enact an upsetting emotional scene with his wife.

4. Situations directed toward the resolution of conflicts and the achievement of greater adequacy. For example, an overprotected son shows how he would tell his possessive, widowed mother (played by another patient) that he would like to leave home, get a job on his own, and get married.

Through such opportunities for social reality testing, the patient gains insight into the motivations and problems of others as well as into his own and develops more satisfactory interpersonal relationships. In the same way, role playing among the members of a family in family group therapy can give all the members greater understanding of each other's feelings and a new objectivity about their own accustomed role in family interactions.

Role playing may also be used with similar goals in individual therapy. It appears to be particularly helpful in forcing the patient to concretize his problem and in developing new coping techniques for dealing with specific types of stress situations.

Conditioning. A number of conditioning techniques are being experimented with in the treatment of mental disorders on the theory that maladaptive responses, being learned, can be unlearned or otherwise changed through usual conditioning methods. These involve chiefly environmental manipulation in which the patient is presented with stimulus conditions and appropriate "reinforcers" designed to elicit and strengthen particular desired responses. An attempt is thus made to change specific behavior directly, without regard to psychodynamic factors. Though any therapist may "reinforce" certain kinds of verbal responses in an interview situation by showing interest and approval of some statements and not others, therapy based on conditioning techniques is limited to behavior therapists. Thus further discussion of the several

This patient has been told under hypnosis that she is a little girl 5 years old and has been directed to write her name and draw a picture of a man.

specific conditioning techniques used will be deferred until our discussion of behavior therapy as a major modern systematic approach. (See page 596).

Any of the conditioning procedures forces the therapist to specify the particular response he is trying to elicit or eliminate and also to specify the means he intends to use for achieving these adaptive behaviors. This is a major advantage in clarifying the nature and outcome of procedures in psychotherapy.

Use of hypnosis. Hypnosis was known among the ancient Egyptians and other peoples, but its modern use in psychotherapy is credited to Mesmer, whom we have previously mentioned in our historical introduction. Since Mesmer's work, there have been periodic rises and falls in its popularity. Hypnosis played an important role in the work of Liébeault and Bernheim, who found that it could be used to modify conversion (hysterical) symptoms even without any understanding of their etiology.

As Freud discovered later, however, the use of hypnosis to remove symptoms was only temporarily effective. The symptoms would return

 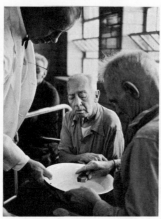  

REMOTIVATION

The phenomenon of a watery handprint disappearing before the heat of a lighted match, the remembrance of a long-forgotten line from a poem by Sandburg, the sudden recognition of the once-familiar contours of the earth's surface—these are but a sampling of the "wonders" being rediscovered and reacted to by severely withdrawn schizophrenic patients who were once considered hopelessly unreachable. Responsible for such reawakenings is *Remotivation,* a technique of group interaction that can be administered by a psychiatric aid or attendant. Thus one of its important features is that it makes better use of the hospital staff already on hand and makes help available to chronic patients who have too often had little or no treatment in our big overcrowded, understaffed mental hospitals.

The theory behind the technique is simple—that there is always an "unwounded area" of the mind of a mental patient, which, if discovered, can be used as a key to unlock the door to his solitary world. Basic to the technique are carefully planned group conversations that cover a wide variety of topics not related to the patient's illnesses. Usually a series of meetings is held, conducted by a trained aid-leader and attended by 10 to 15 of his patients. These meetings follow a five-step program which was developed by the technique's originator, the late Dorothy Hoskins Smith.

1 *A climate of acceptance* is created by the aid or attendant as he warmly greets each patient at the beginning of each session by shaking hands, addressing him by name, and adding some favorable comment about the patient's appearance.

2 The *bridge to reality* is built by the reading of lively, rhythmical poetry to the patients. Eventually many of them supply missing lines to old favorites or "spell" the aide-leader by reading parts of the poems to the rest of the group.

3 *Sharing the world we live in* involves discussing the particular topic of the day—which may be anything from baseball to the reaction of water to heat or perhaps a comparison of bascule and draw bridges. The only limitation on the choice of subject is that it not be of an inflammatory nature, such as sex, politics, religion, or marital relations. Five or six sessions may go by before a subject comes up that reaches the attention of a particular patient, but eventually the "right" subject does come up for most patients. Typical topics and activities—and the rapt attention and participation of the patients—are illustrated in the pictures above.

4 An *appreciation of the work of the world* often follows the third step naturally. Within the range of subjects discussed during the meetings, there is usually a reminder of a past occupation or hobby, which the patient can be encouraged to rediscover.

5 *A climate of appreciation* is established at the end of each session as the aid-leader thanks each patient for coming, makes some personal comment about his participation, and mentions something about the plans for the next session.

again or crop up in some other form. Hence Freud discontinued the use of hypnosis in psychotherapy. Later experimental research into hypnosis has led to a better understanding of its dynamics and to a renewed interest in its psychotherapeutic potentialities.[1]

Essentially, hypnosis is a highly suggestible state into which a willing subject is induced by a skilled therapist (Leuba, 1960). In the hypnotic state, the subject concentrates exclusively on the situation, actual or symbolic, to which the therapist directs his attention.

1. *Induction of hypnosis.* There are many techniques for the induction of hypnosis which may be used flexibly according to the signs of approaching hypnosis manifested by the subject. In general, these techniques have the following factors in common: (a) enlisting the cooperation of the subject and allaying any fears he may have concerning hypnosis, (b) having the subject assume a comfortable position and relax completely, (c) narrowing and focusing the subject's attention—for example, having him fix his gaze on the eyes of the therapist or upon some bright object, and (d) directing the subject's activities by means of reinforced suggestions. This is typically based upon the sheer repetition of suggestions and the use of normal bodily reactions as if they have come about at the direction of the therapist, creating the impression on the part of the subject that he is obeying the suggestions of the therapist and thus increasing his suggestibility to further directions. For example, the subject may be directed to look upward toward a light and after a short period of time be told that his eyelids feel slightly heavy. This is a normal reaction to the strain of looking upward but the subject interprets it as due to the directions of the therapist, and the way is thus paved for the acceptance of additional suggestions.

Of course, not all persons can be hypnotized and there are varying degrees in the depth of hypnosis produced. The latter may vary from light hypnosis, in which the subject becomes distinctly drowsy and tends to follow simple directions, to deep hypnosis, in which complete anesthesia may be produced and the subject may open his eyes and move about without any disturbance of the hypnotic state.

2. *Hypnotic behavior.* There are many interesting phenomena which can be produced under hypnosis, such as cataleptic rigidity (in which the subject can be made to stiffen his body and can be suspended across two chairs like a board), anesthesia (wherein a bodily part or even the entire body can be made insensible to feeling so that surgical operations may be performed upon the subject without his experiencing any pain), and amnesia for the hypnotic trance (which is usually spontaneous). However, we are primarily concerned with certain phenomena which relate more directly to the use of hypnosis in psychotherapy. Among these are:

a) Recall of buried memories. Traumatic experiences which are repressed from consciousness may be recovered under hypnosis. In combat-exhaustion cases in World War II, hypnosis was occasionally used for having the amnesic patients relive their battle experience. In this way they could discharge the emotional tensions associated with it and permit it to be assimilated into the ego structure. The "shock" reactions of civilian life may be similarly handled, as well as various traumatic experiences of childhood and adolescence which may be tending to the maintenance of distorted environmental and self attitudes.

b) Age regression. Closely related to memory recall is age regression, in which the subject may be told that he has become a six-year-old child again and will subsequently act, talk, and think very much as he did at the age of six years. In regressing a subject back through successive ages even his handwriting will become increasingly childish. Age regression has been found of particular value in going back to the time just preceding the onset of certain symptoms such as phobias and uncovering the particular events which precipitated the symptoms. Thus age regression may be of value in recovering buried trauma in order to relieve the symptoms associated with it.

Lecron and Bordeaux (1947) have reported a case which well illustrates age regression under hypnosis.

---

[1]For additional information with respect to hypnosis, the reader is referred to Barber (1961a, 1961b), Brenman and Gill (1947), Dorcus (1957), Erickson (1939). Estabrooks (1962), Moss *et al.* (1962), Orne (1962), Shor (1962), Sutcliffe (1961), Wolberg (1945).

"Betty R——, a forty-two-year-old spinster, had come to us with a neurosis of long standing, one of the symptoms of which was a compulsive necessity to clear her throat every few moments. This was not only extremely annoying and embarrassing, but had compelled her to give up a promising career as a singer and become an office worker—employment which she despised. During hypnoanalysis, an effort was made to locate the cause for this particular symptom. Questioning brought a statement that it had first developed eighteen years earlier, and she was sure she was twenty-four years old at the time.

"Placed in a deep trance, she was successfully regressed to that age, but it was found that the throat distress was still present. She was then instructed to regress still further to a time left indefinite but just before the genesis of the trouble, whereupon she stated that she was twenty-two and her throat no longer bothered her. She was then told to reexperience whatever strong emotional event had occurred at that time, whereupon she told of attending a picnic with her fiancé, whom she loved deeply and was to marry within a few days. They picnicked at a lake on which they went canoeing, and she told of the craft tipping over and their struggles in the water. She was unable to swim, but the young man saved her by pulling her to the overturned canoe, to which she clung until rescued by others. Not a good swimmer himself and exhausted by his efforts, he had gone down and was drowned. All was described with great emotional discharge, and finally she seemed to be choking as though swallowing water. After she had become calmer she cried, 'I love him so, I can't stand losing him, I just can't swallow it; it sticks in my throat!' Then she added, 'Why, that's the reason I clear my throat!' She was returned to the present and the trance was ended. Subsequently, with further insight and reeducation the symptom disappeared and she found herself better adjusted to life." (pp. 211-212)

Sometimes therapy consists in systematically going back and successively working through, with the aid of the therapist, many early experiences which are of significance in the development of the patient's mental disorder. Through this process the patient is able to view these experiences in a new, more mature way, leading to healthy modifications in existing attitudes and ego structure. This procedure, which is referred to as *hypnoanalysis,* requires a highly skilled therapist.

c) Dream induction. By means of hypnosis, dreams can be made to occur during the hypnotic trance or later during the normal waking state. Such dreams or hallucinations may be valuable in uncovering repressed conflicts or in desensitizing the patient to prior emotional trauma. Moss (1960) has reported the case of an art instructor who had a chronic phobia of dogs.

Through the use of hypnotic age regression, the phobia was traced to a highly traumatic experience when she was 4 years old which was associated with the dog her family then had. To facilitate the process of desensitization and relearning, "the patient was given the posthypnotic suggestion that between therapy sessions, whenever she was alone and desired to re-establish her acquaintance with Rover, the dog of her early childhood, she could experience a positive visual hallucination of him. . . ." It was further emphasized that she had complete control of the relationship and could "allow the dog as close as (she) desired or keep him as distant as (her) fear dictated." (p. 268)

The patient reported that she had been able to experience Rover's presence quite vividly and laughingly referred to him as "my little black Harvey." She stated that her feelings toward him had changed from those of fear to something more "like two old friends who have quarreled and don't quite know how to make up." (p. 269)

The patient was then given the post-hypnotic suggestion that she would continue to work toward overcoming her irrational fear in the following way:

"Of course, it will not be possible for you to keep Rover indefinitely. As you pointed out today, it would be so nice to have Rover really there. I think you can have Rover *really there* in a sense that down through the years Rover has always been there in every dog that you met, particularly in little, frisky dogs. Each dog has been Rover as you looked at him with your little-girl eyes. If you work hard at becoming friends with Rover, your fear will leave you and you will quite naturally develop a greater acceptance of all dogs. As time goes on you will develop the idea of having a real Rover for you to enjoy and especially for Jane, who needs and wants a Rover of her own." (p. 269)

A short time thereafter the patient reported that she was completely free of her phobia and later phoned that she had purchased a black cocker spaniel puppy for her daughter Jane.

d) Post-hypnotic suggestions. Perhaps the most widely used of all hypnotic procedures in psychotherapy is that of post-hypnotic suggestions, whereby suggestions made in the hypnotic trance are carried over into the waking state although the patient is not aware of their source. For example, by means of post-hypnotic suggestion, the patient may be told that he will not stutter after he awakens or that he will no longer desire to smoke or drink. When properly handled, such hypnotic suggestions carry over effectively into the waking state, but unfortunately their duration may be short. That is, the individual will again experience a desire to smoke or drink in a few hours or days unless the suggestion is continually reinforced.

Most direct post-hypnotic suggestions do nothing to remove the conditions that cause the stuttering or the drinking, and the eventual relapse of the patient may undermine his confidence in himself and in the therapy because it represents one more failure. Even so, the immediate alleviation of symptoms is often an important aspect of therapy. It may give the patient a considerable boost in morale, and thus pave the way for other measures aimed at modifying the existing ego structure and removing the causes for the symptoms.

In completing our discussion of hypnosis, a warning note should perhaps be sounded concerning the possible dangers of hypnosis in the hands of untrained persons. Amateur hypnosis serves no useful purpose and may injure the subject as well as involve the hypnotist in an unpleasant situation.

Narcosynthesis. Although it has long been known that patients under the influence of alcohol and during the induction phases of an anesthetic will reveal personal conflicts, repressed motivations, and other usually unrecognized facets of the personality, the English psychiatrist Horsley (1943) was one of the first, in the 1930's, to make systematic use of the drowsiness produced by the intravenous injection of barbiturate drugs for the diagnosis and treatment of mental disorders. He called this method "narcoanalysis."

During World War II, Grinker and Spiegel used a modification of this method for the treatment of combat-exhaustion cases who had undergone severely traumatic battle experiences. With this technique, the patient usually reclines comfortably on a cot and is given an intravenous injection of enough sodium amytal or sodium pentothal to make him groggy and suggestible but not unconscious. The patient is then told that he is again in the front lines, with specific details added depending upon the amount of known history. The patient then typically launches into a vivid account of his battle experience accompanied by intense emotional expression and appropriate motor activity.

One of the cases reported by Grinker and Spiegel was described in some detail in Chapter 5—that of an infantry officer who was both mute and amnesic until the experiences he had repressed were brought to the surface in a narcosis interview. The intensity of emotion which may be displayed as the patient relives his traumatic experience during the narcosis interview has been emphasized by Grinker and Spiegel.

"The terror exhibited in the moments of supreme danger, such as the imminent explosion of shells, the death of a friend before the patient's eyes, the absence of cover under a heavy dive-bombing attack, is electrifying to watch. The body becomes increasingly tense and rigid; the eyes widen and the pupils dilate, while the skin becomes covered with fine perspiration. The hands move about convulsively, seeking a weapon, or a friend to share the danger. The breathing becomes incredibly rapid and shallow. The intensity of the emotion sometimes becomes unbearable; and frequently at the height of the reaction, there is a collapse and the patient falls back in bed and remains quiet for a few minutes, usually to resume the story at a more neutral point. Some patients return over and over again to one short, traumatic scene, living it through repeatedly, as if, like a needle traveling around a cracked record, they could not get past this point." (1945, p. 80)

By reliving the traumatic battle experience, the patient discharges much of the emotional tension associated with it; with the help of the therapist he becomes able to view his experience in a less traumatic light and to assimilate or "synthesize" it into his ego structure.

Narcosynthesis has been applied to civilian mental disorders with varying degrees of success. It would appear most useful in the treatment of transient personality reactions to extremely traumatic experiences—the course of treatment being comparable to that in combat reactions. However, in the hands of a skilled therapist, narcosis interviews may be effective in the release of pent-up emotions, in recovering lost memories, as in neurotic dissociative reactions, in removing the paralyses or other symptoms in conversion reactions, and in the uncovering and working through of deep conflictual material. The therapist may also leave suggestions with the patient during the narcosis interview which, like post-hypnotic suggestions, tend to be carried out in his later waking state. Both during and following the narcosis interview the therapist aids the patient by means of suggestion, interpretation, and other techniques to re-evaluate and assimilate the traumatic and conflictual material that has been revealed.

In the use of both hypnosis and narcosis in civilian cases, Murphy and Weinreb again have sounded a warning note in referring to the training of psychotherapists in a Veterans Administration Hospital.

"As an alternative to the residents who 'enlighten' their patients by engaging them in intellectual skirmishes, we have had the revivalist type who were not happy unless down on their knees wrestling with the unconscious for the patient's ego. This type liked hypnosis and amytal interviews, preferably highly emotional ones, and hoped that the abreaction of some dark secret moments in the patient's past would effect a miraculous cure. . . . When their 'cures' relapsed, it was felt that either psychotherapy was a hopeless proposition or that there must have been one more secret episode in the patient's past that had been missed." (1948, p. 102)

LSD experience.   The three main hallucinogens—lysergic acid diethylamide (LSD-25), psilocybin, and mescaline—have been used not only experimentally to induce "model psychoses" but also in psychotherapy. The most widely used of these hallucinogens is LSD, which has effects comparable to the other two drugs but requires less dosage and is largely free of undesirable side effects such as nausea.

The psychological effect which the drug has on the patient seems to depend to a large extent upon his prior "mental set" and the environmental setting in which the therapy occurs. When the subject expects to have a rewarding experience, has confidence in the therapist, and regards the therapeutic setting as pleasant, the experience is likely to be a constructive one. As the drug takes effect, the most important psychic manifestation is a tremendous intensification of visual perception. Objects seem to become clearer, sharper, and brighter and to become endowed with dimensions which the subject has never perceived before. Thus he may lose himself in the rapt contemplation of a flower or some other object and feel that at last he understands its essential nature.

With a deepening of the drug's effects, he may experience delusions and hallucinations, some of which may be frightening and unpleasant. Often the patient relives scenes from his childhood with the feeling that he is having the same emotions he had then. Yet while participating in these experiences, he usually remains lucid and has a feeling of being a detached observer of his own behavior.

Another phenomenon has been called *"humanity identification"*—in which the individual experiences love, loneliness, or grief as he thinks it has been experienced by all people in all history. Several of the effects of LSD and other drugs were summarized in the chart on page 291. The reaction to LSD continues for several hours and then gradually fades. Usually within 8 to 10 hours the subject returns to normal. Curiously enough, these effects arise from an invisible speck of chemical weighing approximately 1/200,000 of an ounce (Coughlan, 1963).

In psychotherapy, LSD appears to be of value in several ways. It tends to foster feelings of confidence and rapport between the patient and the therapist; it can be used to facilitate the uncovering of repressed memories and enables the patient to relive them with their original emotional content; it enables the patient to see himself and his problems in a more detached and objective way; it increases the patient's ability to communicate his thoughts and feelings to the therapist; and finally, it often appears to have an integrative effect in which the individual achieves increased self-acceptance and freedom

PSYCHOTHERAPEUTIC AIDS

There are a number of procedures which have proved of considerable psychotherapeutic value but which usually serve as adjuncts or aids to the general therapeutic process. Actually, virtually all the life activities and interpersonal relationships of the patient have some effect on his personality functioning and may be systematically utilized for therapeutic purposes.

EDUCATIONAL THERAPY:

Bibliotherapy

Books, pamphlets, and other reading material are often of considerable assistance in helping the patient to realize that others have problems similar to his and in increasing his self-understanding. The reading material is usually selected in terms of the needs and intellectual abilities of the patient.

Audio-visual aids

An increasing number of very fine psychiatric films show the factors underlying the development of unhealthy reaction patterns in a vivid and dramatic way that is particularly useful in promoting insight and some measure of emotional re-education. Such films are commonly used in a group setting but may also be used with individual patients.

Formal educational procedures

Many social skills are taught, such as dancing, dressing in good taste, managing finances, bowling or playing tennis, and so on. Many hospitals have classes in English, mathematics, and other subjects which the patients can take for high-school credit; college credits may often be earned by extension courses.

OCCUPATIONAL AND RECREATIONAL THERAPY:

Occupational therapy

Occupational therapy may go beyond crafts or hobbies to constructive work which contributes to the operation of the hospital; in such work the patient has the satisfaction of knowing that he is playing a useful role in the community.

Social events

Many hospitals have a regular calendar of social events including dances, teas, and theatrical productions—the latter put on sometimes by touring movie and theatrical people and sometimes by the patients themselves. These events help the patients to meet others and to feel less isolated.

Athletics

Regularly scheduled athletic events for patient participation include softball, basketball, baseball, and other team sports. Where such facilities are available, a program of appropriate athletic activities is usually worked out to meet the needs of each patient. In team competition on a friendly basis, the patient also has practice in handling wins and losses and in meeting competitive situations.

Music therapy

Patients are given opportunities for both listening to music and playing an instrument. Traditional music and folk songs have been found especially effective in fostering group cohesion, emotional release, and better personality integration.

Art productions

Fingerpainting, clay sculpturing, and other art media serve in the release of feelings and provide the patient with the sense of pride and accomplishment that comes from personal expression in creative activity.

from inner conflict. The therapist, of course, plays a key role in guiding the patient through the LSD experience and maximizing its therapeutic potentialities for the given patient. However, the drug itself often seems to help the patient gain increased insight into his self-concept and life style; to alter his frame of reference and to see alternative solutions to his problems; and to achieve better personality integration and a more meaningful life pattern in which he tends to feel less isolated and more "a part of the infinite." Thus it is somewhat like a religious experience. In fact, various primitive peoples have used similar drugs to enhance the meaningfulness of religious rites.

Although the use of LSD in psychotherapy is still in an experimental stage, it has been found effective in the treatment of many chronic alcoholics and character disorder cases which are highly resistant to ordinary psychotherapy.[1] In the treatment of 61 alcoholics with poor prognosis, MacLean et al. (1961) reported that 30 patients were much improved and 16 showed some improvement. The following case was cited as being illustrative:

"Case No. 2. This 44-year-old salesman of high normal intelligence used alcohol to excess for over 15 years. He had previously managed to achieve 10 months of sobriety in A.A. but had 'slipped' into a heavy drinking pattern again. He was becoming morose and extremely tense.

"After the ingestion of 400 gamma of LSD-25 the patient felt adverse effects in the form of increasing tension. Gradually he went through a process of concentrated self-analysis. He said, 'This experience has given me quite an awakening and a real good look at myself. It seemed to clear a lot of garbage away. I can see and appreciate things about myself I never knew existed before.' Seventeen months after therapy the patient said, 'Although I know the experience is not a cure-all it does make you see ways of enjoying life and accepting the idea that alcohol is not a necessity.' The patient also felt that although he had enjoyed sobriety for nearly a year and a half, yet it was necessary to 'work on oneself' every day in the way of continual adjustment. Result: much improved." (p. 42)

Unfortunately, LSD is apparently contraindicated in the treatment of psychotics and other patients with a highly unstable personality make-up (Dahlberg, 1963). The loss of reality ties during the LSD experience is often a frightening experience even to individuals with relatively good ego strength; to a marginally adjusted individual, it may induce extreme terror and personality disorganization. As Chwelos et al. (1959) have pointed out: "In this state the person is keenly aware of the possibility of slipping into a psychotic state or to madness that appears an ever present possibility, and he feels that he is walking a razor's edge, gaining slowly in confidence as he goes." (p. 586) Further research is needed to delineate the neurophysiological changes resulting from LSD and to ascertain its full potentialities and limitations in psychotherapy.

Other psychotherapeutic procedures. Strangely enough, little is known about one of the most potent of all therapeutic factors—*love*. Particularly with psychotic patients who have withdrawn from a world viewed as hostile and frustrating, or who have inner conflicts of a guilt-arousing nature, love is a potent therapeutic weapon. Love from others raises the self-evaluation of the patient and helps him to accept himself as a worth-while person; it modifies the withdrawn patient's environmental evaluation so that he becomes able to relate to the therapist and bring up his conflicts and difficulties. The need of many of these patients for unqualified love, their longing for affection and acceptance, is often so great that until this need is partially met they can only be fearful, withdrawn, broken individuals.

We are, of course, using "love" here in a general affectional sense, not in a sexual sense. In many clinics "tender loving care" is specifically prescribed for certain patients—meaning that all persons dealing with the patient are to show him unqualified acceptance and warmth. Not all patients need or can accept affection of this sort, but the beneficial effect of love on some sensitive, withdrawn patients is often dramatic to observe.

Other psychotherapeutic procedures—free association, dream analysis, and the handling of transference—will be discussed in connection with psychoanalytic therapy.

---

[1] Further relevant studies here include Belden and Hitchen (1960, 1963), Chwelos et al. (1959), Cohen and Eisner (1959), MacLean et al. (1961), Smith (1958).

Major Systematic Approaches to Psychotherapy

There are a number of systematic approaches to psychotherapy which differ in goals and procedures because they reflect different theoretical orientations. The focus of our present discussion will be on the methods of therapy rather than the theories underlying them; a summary of several of the current theories of personality will be found in the Appendix.

As we saw in our historical introduction, individual differences in the therapeutic approaches of different therapists are gradually coming to obliterate systematic or "school" differences. Thus there is often a great deal of variation from one psychoanalyst to another in the use of concepts and techniques. Of course, there are still cliques who follow closely what they consider to be the "party line," but in general, the trend is toward the acceptance or rejection of concepts in the light of their experimental evaluation and toward flexibility in the planning of therapy around the needs of the individual patient.

CLIENT-CENTERED (NONDIRECTIVE) PSYCHOTHERAPY

It is convenient to begin our discussion of systematic approaches to psychotherapy with the so-called "client-centered" or "nondirective" approach formulated by Carl Rogers (1942, 1951, 1959, 1961) to which we have already alluded. This approach relies heavily upon the individual's drive toward integration, health, and self-actualization—a drive which has presumably been blocked by faulty assumptions and emotional conflicts. Therapy is thus primarily aimed at the removal of such blocks and the freeing of the individual to accept his unique self and to grow and change in his own natural way. Basic to the client-centered approach is the view that human nature is basically good and that each individual has the capacity for constructive self-directed change. As a consequence, the patient bears much of the responsibility for

the course and outcome of therapy. Client-centered therapy has been utilized mainly with relatively stable persons who have the intellectual capacity and personality integration requisite for working out their problems with a minimum of guidance from the therapist.

Rogers has considered the therapeutic process itself to be relatively orderly and predictable, typically following five steps:

1. *The client comes for help.* This is considered an important step in the therapy situation, for the individual has, as it were, taken himself in hand and on his own initiative taken the first step toward finding a solution to his problems. Thus Rogers has concluded that nondirective counseling is likely to be most effective where the patient is under sufficient psychological distress from his conflicts to wish to do something about them and take active steps in that direction.

During the first interview with the patient the therapeutic situation is defined. The counselor makes it clear that he does not have all the answers but that the therapy situation will provide a place where the patient can work out his own solutions.

2. *Expression of feeling.* By his permissive and accepting attitude, the therapist encourages the free expression of feelings, and now the negative emotions that have been bottled up inside the patient are permitted at last to come out into the open. In a case reported by Rogers, an 18-year-old client says:

"I know I'm not so hot, and I'm afraid they'll find it out. That's why I do these things. . . . They're going to find out some day that I'm not so hot. I'm just trying to put that day off as long as possible. . . . If you knew me as I know myself—." (1961, p. 167)

As these negative feelings come spilling into the open, it is the therapist's function to recognize, accept, and clarify them and assumptions underlying the patient's problems. This is done in such a way that the client can recognize his feelings and assumptions for what they are and no longer keep hiding them even from himself.

When the patient's negative feelings have been fully expressed, they are followed by faint and tentative expressions of positive feelings. Thus the patient who has felt devaluated and ashamed of himself as a person states:

"But now I'm adamantly refusing to do things from the old viewpoint. . . . It's as if I'm convinced that someone said, 'The way you will *have* to be is to be *ashamed* of yourself—so *be* that way!' And I accepted it for a long, long time, saying 'OK, that's me!' And now I'm standing up against that. . . ." (Rogers, 1961, p. 169)

These positive feelings likewise are recognized, clarified, and accepted without praise or blame in such a way that the patient can accept them, too, as part of himself without the need to feel defensive about them.

3. *Development of insight.* Gradually this increased recognition and acceptance of the real self leads to the development of insight or understanding. Rogers has likened the process to "removing colored glasses" from the patient's eyes. At first his perception of himself and his situation is distorted by emotional attitudes that keep him under tension and stress. As his feelings are released and clarified, however, he learns to see himself and his environment in a truer perspective. Among the most important elements of insight emphasized by Rogers are (a) the experiencing, understanding, and acceptance of aspects of himself which he has previously repressed, (b) a clearer understanding of the causes behind his behavior and improved integration, and (c) a clarification of possible courses of positive action.

4. *Positive steps.* Intermingled with and following the gradual development of insight is the clarification of possible decisions and possible courses of action. Often this is infused with a rather hopeless attitude in which the client sees his situation and himself more clearly but still does not know what to do about it. As the possible courses of action become clarified, however, the client begins tentatively to consider various steps that he must take. Again it is the function of the counselor to recognize and clarify and not to attempt to lead the client.

"An extremely withdrawn high-school boy, who has expressed his fear and hatred of others and has also come to recognize his deeply buried desire to have friends, spends a whole hour giving all the reasons why he would be too terrified to accept a social invitation he has had. He even leaves the office saying he will probably not go. He is not urged. It is sympathetically recognized that such action would take a great deal of courage, and that while he wishes he had such fortitude, he may not be able to take such a step. He goes to the party, and is enormously helped in his self-confidence." (Rogers, 1942, p. 41)

Although the first positive steps worked out by the client may not be dramatic, they are stepping stones in the right direction and with time, as these minor positive actions bring satisfaction and increased feelings of adequacy and self-assurance, the client moves toward positive growth and development.

5. *Ending the contacts.* As the client graduates from fearful and tentatively undertaken positive actions to an increasingly confident integration of positive and self-directed actions, there is a feeling of decreasing need for help and a recognition on the part of the client that the therapeutic relationship must end. The decision to terminate, like the earlier decisions to attempt positive actions, comes from the client. By terminating the contacts under his own initiative, he has taken the final step toward independence. For he has now assumed a full measure of responsibility for his own life.

This general sketch of nondirective psychotherapy serves to show its general nature. Its most marked differences from other systematic approaches are (a) the high level of responsibility for the direction and fruition of the therapy which is placed upon the client; (b) the restriction of the therapist's role primarily to the acceptance, reflection, and clarification of feeling; (c) a minimizing of the transference between therapist and patient, thus making it not necessary to handle complicated transference relationships; (d) a de-emphasis on diagnostic psychological tests, which are regarded as ordinarily unnecessary and as merely taking up time that could be more profitably devoted to working directly with the patient's problems; and (e) the setting of the pace by the client, presumably a safeguard in that he will discuss and work through his conflicts as his ego strength permits and not be pushed into revelations that would be too traumatic.

The following portion of a second interview with a young woman will serve to illustrate further the general nature of client-centered psychotherapy.

"Alice: I was thinking about this business of standards. I somehow developed a sort of a knack, I guess, or —well—habit—of trying to make people feel at ease around me, or to make things go along smoothly. I don't know whether that goes back to early childhood, or—I mean, to our family situation where there was a large family, and so many differences of opinion and all that there always had to be some appeaser around (laughing) and seeing into the reasons for disagreeing and being sorta the oil that smoothed the waters. Well, that is a role that I have taken for a long time. And—I—it's gotten so it really—I mean, before this sort of thing came up I realized that as a person in a social situation or something—I could help things to go along nicely and appear to be having a good time. And I'd see where someone else needed more punch, or where someone didn't have a partner, or where somebody was bored with that person, and something—somebody was standing in a corner, and I could go out and meet them. And sometimes I'd surprise myself by arguing against what I really thought when I saw that the person in charge would be quite unhappy about it if I didn't. In other words, I just wasn't ever—I mean, I didn't find myself ever being set and definite about things. I could see what I thought might be interjected to make people feel happy, and I'd do that.

Counselor: In other words, what you did was always in the direction of trying to keep things smooth and to make other people feel better and to smooth the situation.

Alice: Yes I think that's what it was. Now the reason why I did it probably was—I mean, not that I was a good little Samaritan going around making other people happy, but that was probably the role that felt easiest for me to play. I'd been doing it around home so much. I just didn't stand up for my own convictions, until I don't know whether I have any convictions to stand up for.

Counselor: You feel that for a long time you've been playing the role of kind of smoothing out the frictions or differences or what not . . .

Alice: M-hm.

Counselor: Rather than having any opinion or reaction of your own in the situation. Is that it?

Alice: That's it. Or that I haven't been really honestly being myself, or actually knowing what my real self is, and that I've been just playing a sort of false role. Whatever role no one else was playing, and that needed to be played at the time, I'd try to fill it in.

Counselor: Whatever kind of person that was needed to kinda help out that situation you'd be that kind of person rather than being anything original or deeply your own.

Alice: I think so. I remember one summer. We used to go to the YWCA camp in the summers. And our family lived way out near the edge of town. We went with the school groups that went at a certain time during the summer. Well, we didn't know those children very well, because we didn't see them except on Sundays when we went to church. So going to camp wasn't an awfully satisfying experience because I felt quite strange among the children. Well, this summer—I'd been to camp once before—and I think I'd decided that I was going to be one of the popular girls at camp. So I went to camp with these children that I didn't know too well. And I don't remember what I did that summer; but anyway, I came home voted the most popular camper. What I do remember, though, is when I got ready to go to camp I—and I don't know how old I was then —I was not thirteen, I don't suppose; maybe twelve or thirteen, I don't know quite how old; I just decided I was going to be the most popular girl at camp. So I went to camp with that decision, and I did the things that needed to be done. Whatever they were, I'm sure I don't—I mean, it was probably a lot of drudgery too; like making other people's beds and doing other things like that—I'm sure. But anyway I went through a set campaign and came home and was actually chosen the most popular girl at camp (laughing). And it seems that what I've done is do things like that instead of developing a real self.

Counselor: In other words it's been kind of a planful campaign in each case rather than because you really felt that way or really wanted to be that kind of person. Is that it?

Alice: Well, yes. I think so. It seems that it's more— that it's not realistic, or it's not honest, or not— it's not sincere, maybe." (Rogers, 1951, pp. 152-154)

Essentially client-centered psychotherapy focuses on *"the process of becoming a person"* —with a heavy emphasis on self-understanding and acceptance, "openness" to both inner and outer experience, effective self-direction, and continued self-growth. Therapists relying primarily upon a nondirective approach to therapy feel that the achievement of insight and positive action through the initiative of the patient is of more value than if the initiative is taken by the therapist. It is thought to be a more effective growth experience for the patient—one that utilizes his own potentialities for growth to a greater extent and thus one that will assist him to become able to cope successfully not only with his present problems but with those that come up later. Therapists who tend to more directive approaches agree that the patient's inner potentialities for growth should be relied upon and utilized as fully as possible, but feel this growth process can often be facilitated by appropriate interpretations and other more directive procedures.

Client-centered therapists have contributed a great deal of valuable research information concerning the processes and outcomes of psychotherapy. Their contributions have profoundly influenced the thinking of many contemporary theorists and therapists.

ANALYTIC (PSYCHOANALYTIC) PSYCHOTHERAPY

In Chapter 2 we noted the influence of psychoanalysis on the development of modern psychological and psychiatric thought and its permeation of other fields such as anthropology, sociology, and literature. Criticisms of psychoanalysis have, however, remained rather persistent, and the average clinician working in the field has often found it extremely difficult to think his way through the maze of controversy surrounding psychoanalytic concepts and procedures.

Modern analytic psychotherapy stems from the work of Freud. It is an intensive, long-term procedure for uncovering repressed memories, motivations, and conflicts and helping the patient to resolve them in the light of adult realities. Essentially, it aims at increased insight and integration, improved personal effectiveness, and freedom for personal growth.

1. *Free association and the unconscious.* Freud concluded that all of us repress certain painful or anxiety-arousing experiences, desires, and conflicts. As a consequence, we are often unaware of the real basis for our thoughts and behavior. In psychoanalytic therapy the principal procedure for uncovering such repressed material is free association. The patient, usually reclining comfortably on a couch with the therapist sitting behind him, is encouraged to let his mind wander freely and give a running account of his thoughts, feelings, and desires regardless of how personal or painful it may be to him to do so. This free and uninhibited flow of associations leads to the gradual uncovering of underlying conflicts and to emotional catharsis. Then, by means of appropriate interpretations to the patient as to what his free associations have revealed, the therapist helps the patient to achieve increased insight into these underlying motivations and conflicts of which he has been unaware.

The following is an excerpt from an analytic session with a thirty-five-year-old female patient who had been troubled the preceding five years by nausea when she dined in the presence of a man. The therapist considered these typical of her associations early in therapy.

"This . . . is like a first date, because I get the same sort of sick nauseated feeling . . . Mother certainly has a queer daughter . . . Once when I was four years old and sick she brought me a doll . . . I'm not so sure of things when I'm out with a man . . . I won't keep this up if it makes me feel nauseated . . . Why did even thinking of B (patient's lover) make me sick to my stomach? . . . I hope I'll be able to come tomorrow." (Masserman, 1961, p. 221)

When the patient nears traumatic material, there may be a sudden blocking of associations or a shifting of thought and ideas—a clear indication to the therapist that the patient is skirting some underlying conflict which he is trying, usually unconsciously, to avoid facing. This tendency to maintain existing ego defenses and avoid the uncovering of anxiety-arousing material is referred to as *resistance* and is a common occurrence in psychotherapy. The patient's resistance may lead to rejection of the therapist's interpretations, to coming late or failing to keep appointments, or even to the termination of therapy. Thus the proper analysis and handling of resistance becomes of crucial importance in psychoanalytic therapy.

2. *Dream analysis.* Another important procedure for uncovering unconscious motivation is dream analysis. When the patient is asleep, repressive defenses are lowered and forbidden desires and feelings may find an outlet in dreams. For this reason dreams have been referred to as the "royal road to the unconscious." But some repressed desires are so anxiety-arousing that even in dreams they are not revealed openly. Thus a dream has two contents: the *manifest* content, which is the dream as it appears to the dreamer, and the *latent* content, which is the symbolic meaning of the manifest content. For example, an old witch (manifest content) might symbolically represent the patient's wife or mother (latent content). Free association in regard to the manifest content gradually brings to light the symbolic meaning or latent content. This is illustrated in an example reported by Berg (1948). The patient, a young university lecturer who had strong feelings of being rejected and inferior to others, related the following dream:[1]

"I came into the dining-room to talk to my father while he was having supper. I was sitting there playing with my cat. The cat was asking for a long finger biscuit, which she likes. I was going to give it to her but my father said she mustn't have it as it was not good for her.

"I said 'very well' and put the tin away. The cat was annoyed, and it bit my shoe and scratched me. My father had finished his meal. I went upstairs to a bed that was much too high for me to be comfortable in. I felt very depressed." (p. 106)

Subsequently, during her associations of thought, some of the symbolism in the dream was brought out. In the course of her associations of thought, she said:

"Father would not let me wear pretty clothes and go to parties when I was a girl. He seemed to have forgotten that girls get married. Career was everything to him; I had to do exams all the time. There was never any lovemaking, nor indeed any pleasure, in my young life. The bed that was too high is my job which is too exalted and uncomfortable for me."

Dr. A. A. Brill and a patient during a therapy session. In psychoanalytic therapy the patient commonly reclines on a couch and does not look at the therapist.

Berg sums up the meaning as follows:

"Thus her father rejects and refuses her sexual life (the desires of the pussy) while gratifying his own (he finished his meal). Conflict and injury results (the cat bit and scratched her). She ignores this and goes to a high, uncomfortable bed (her academic career) and feels depressed (and inferior)." (pp. 106-107)

The preceding discussion is not intended to cover the dynamics of dreams, but merely to indicate the general nature of dream interpretation and its possible value as a psychotherapeutic technique. It should be pointed out in passing that not all dreams are amenable to interpretation and that the meaning of a dream is not usually evident to the dreamer. Even the therapist may not recognize its meaning in the personality dynamics of the patient.

3. *Analysis of transference.* As the patient and therapist interact in the process of psychotherapy, the relationship between them may become a complex and emotionally involved one. Often the patient carries over and

[1]Reprinted from *A Case Book of a Medical Psychologist* by Charles Berg by permission of W. W. Norton & Company, Inc. and George Allen & Unwin, Ltd. Copyright 1948 by W. W. Norton & Company, Inc.

applies to the therapist attitudes he has formed in his relations with people in the past. Thus he may develop toward the therapist attitudes and feelings he had as a child toward his father. In some instances, a female patient may view the therapist as an "ideal husband and lover." These emotional reactions of the patient are largely irrational from the point of view of the realities of the current situation.

To the psychoanalyst, the handling of transference is a crucial part of the therapeutic process, and he regards transference as an important therapeutic tool despite its irrationality. For example, suppose the patient identifies the therapist with his father, who was a distant and rejecting authority figure in real life. By recognizing the transference relationship, the therapist may provide the patient with what he particularly needs—the experience of having a "good" father. It thus becomes possible for the patient to work through his conflicts in regard to his own father and to overcome feelings of self-devaluation stemming from his father's rejection. In essence, the pathological effects of an unsatisfactory early relationship are counteracted by working through a similar emotional conflict in a more healthy setting. The patient's reliving of his pathogenic past in a sense re-creates his real-life neurosis, and for this reason the experience is referred to as a *transference neurosis*.

It is not possible here to consider at greater length the complexities of transference relationships, but it should be stressed that such relationships by no means always follow simple positive (love, admiration) or negative (hostility, envy) patterns. Often the patient is ambivalent and in conflict—distrusting the therapist and feeling hostile toward him as a symbol of authority, but at the same time seeking acceptance and love. Also, the problems of transference are by no means confined to the patient, for the therapist, too, may have various irrational feelings toward the patient. This is known as *counter-transference* and must be recognized and handled properly by the therapist. Here it is important that the therapist have an understanding of his own motivations, conflicts, and "weak spots" if these powerful forces are to be channeled wisely.

Although most psychotherapists recognize transference as a reality and realize the importance of utilizing it for therapeutic purposes, it is the psychoanalysts who place greatest emphasis on the transference situation as the essential medium for successful therapy.

4. *Emotional re-education.* Particularly during the early stages, psychoanalysis is concerned with uncovering unconscious desires and conflicts and helping the patient to change his attitudes toward them and integrate them into his conscious functioning. However, the new insights achieved by the patient do not automatically transfer to his marital and other life relationships. There is much to be discussed and worked through even after the patient has achieved a better integration of the conscious and unconscious dimensions of his personality. In addition, a deep transference relationship may require a considerable period of time to be resolved satisfactorily. However, as the therapy progresses toward its terminal phases, it is increasingly directed toward positive actions which further the emotional re-education and personal growth of the patient.

Modern psychoanalytic therapy has undergone various modifications from traditional psychoanalysis but remains aimed at changes in ego structure through insight and emotional reorganization. Some analysts still adhere strictly to standard long-term psychoanalysis, involving the application of free association, dream interpretation, and transference neurosis to the uncovering and working through of the patient's major emotional conflicts. Others have worked out various modifications in technique designed to shorten the time required and meet the needs of particular types of patients. Thus analytically oriented therapy has become available to a larger number of patients, and whereas it was once restricted primarily to neurotic patients, it is now used for a variety of mental disorders. Both individual and group psychotherapy may be analytically oriented.

The following material[1] is taken from an early analytic interview with a woman in her middle thirties who was suffering from an obsessive-compulsive neurosis. At the beginning the patient had no understanding of the sym-

---

[1]Reprinted from *A Case Book of a Medical Psychologist* by Charles Berg by permission of W. W. Norton & Company, Inc. and George Allen & Unwin, Ltd., Copyright 1948 by W. W. Norton & Company, Inc.

bolism in her fears and impulses or of the connection between her obsessive thoughts and her real desires. (Patient and Analyst are designated by "P" and "A.")

"P.: I was perfectly well and happy, Doctor, until three years ago when I had an attack of influenza. During that illness, while I was feverish, I had several bad dreams. It was a few months after this that I developed a number of nervous symptoms, which in the course of several months settled down to these absurd impulses and fears, which have remained with me ever since, and against which all my efforts to fight and kill have proved unavailing.

The first symptoms included extreme lassitude: I could hardly walk upstairs. I used to get palpitations of the heart and dreadful headaches at the back of my head. Insomnia followed: then more terrifying dreams. I would awake at night with a desire to scream. I thought I was going mad. I read something in a book about leprosy, and then I could not get that *word* out of my head.

I had a terrifying dream:

I was going to . . . . . Station in a taxi and passed a man with his hands out begging. He was headless, and I knew he had leprosy.

Another dream I had was that my employer was staring at me with a strange look in his eyes, and I felt he was going to harm me.

This dream also has had a lasting effect, because now if he comes behind me I get an awful frightened feeling. It is absurd, but I cannot get rid of it.

Then there was a third dream:

I dreamed he had his back to me, and he was bending over doing something, and I stabbed him in the back.

The sequel to this dream has been my most persistent symptom. I shortly developed a sort of desire or impulse to stab him in the back, and of course, an ever-present fear of doing so. I dare not even see a pair of scissors lying about at the office. It is most odd, as I am really *very* fond of this man.

I have always had such a clear and efficient mind that it seems to me a most brutal tragedy that I should be afflicted with these symptoms, 'leprosy' and wanting to kill. A doctor that I saw years ago put it down to sex repression, but that is not true. Besides fear of going mad, I now have ideas of suicide.

Now I have been sent to you as a last resort, but to be candid, I have no faith in this psychological treatment. I believe it is all nonsense but I have now

had these symptoms for nearly three years, and something has got to be done about them.

A.: Is there any satisfaction of your nature or impulses which you were enjoying three years ago, and which you have since been deprived of?

P.: I don't think so. The only thing that happened three years ago was that I gave up my own flat and went to live with my father and stepmother.

That reminds me that at first it was my father that I 'wanted' to stab. But it soon became my employer. In phantasy I have pictured myself killing him, stabbing him in the back with the bread knife. He was bending over, and I actually visualized myself raising my arm, bending over him, and stabbing him! This picture keeps recurring. Occasionally it gives place to the thought of suicide. Then I would picture myself looking in the glass and cutting my throat.

A.: Have you any grievance against your father or your employer?

P.: As a child I idolized my father until I came to realize that he made mother very unhappy. I thought indirectly, he might have been the cause of her early death. Then I hated him. But now the impulses are not about him, but about my employer, who has always been very good to me. I have been perfectly happy with this employer for the past fourteen years until this trouble started three years ago. We have always been so much in tune with each other.

He runs his own business, and says that its success is entirely due to me, my efficiency and the help I have been to him. Of course, I have helped him with every ounce of energy and ability I possess, for I have loved him ever since I was twenty-two.

But that can't have anything to do with my illness, and I would rather not talk about it, if you don't mind.

(Here the therapist again explained that free association of thought was her part of the work and that nothing that crossed her mind should be withheld from him—that complete frankness was essential to the success of the treatment.)

P.: Oh, well, if you must have it, I will tell you. I didn't break his marriage up. It was already cold and dead before I met him. I was quite willing for his wife to divorce him, but she would not. She said: 'If you want to become his mistress, you stew in it.' This was years ago, when I was only twenty-two. I felt he was the only man I could love in my life. We have been very happy all these years, until the onset of this wretched illness.

A.: Is there any satisfaction that you were getting before three years ago, which has since been lost to you?

P.: Well, of course, as I have told you, I had my own flat up to that time, and he could visit me freely and stay as long as he pleased. Since I have gone to live with my father and stepmother we naturally only meet at business and there is not much opportunity for love-making, nor is it so satisfactory. But I don't see what that has got to do with my symptoms, except that, as you have pointed out, there seems to be a time-coincidence. Now I am afraid of the future, afraid of losing my mind. It has been a good intelligent mind up to now. I am indignant that these impulses and phobias and this horrible word should keep intruding.

A.: Perhaps you have always opposed your impulses and feelings very strongly.

P.: Well, I know I have always had strong feelings—strong feelings of repugnance towards nasty things; and I know I am capable of strong feelings of love. Love means sacrifice, caring for people. I have felt of this man on some occasions that I love him so much I could eat him.

A.: And now perhaps you are saying: 'I love him so much I could stab him.'

P.: Oh, no! That is nonsense!

A.: Unless it is that you are saying: 'I hate him so much I could stab him.'

P.: I know I have had very strong hatreds for certain things, but I can't believe that I have ever hated him.

I dislike animals. I can't bear them to touch me. I can't bear hair or furs. I had the idea once that leprosy was carried by furs, and I don't believe I have ever got over that idea. . . . I have never been able to wear furs. I can't handle them or touch them.

A.: What else do you dislike handling?

P.: Soil, worms, spiders. I have always been fussy about touching things that were not quite clean. The idea gives me a nasty feeling, a cold horror, and that word 'leprosy' comes to my mind. I could never stroke a kitten, and if an animal brushes against me I go hot and cold with fear, like I go hot and cold with fear at those thoughts I have had. Can it be connected with the fact that when I was very much younger I disliked anybody touching me. . . .

I used to get a similar feeling of fear, a sort of cold horror, with one or two men I met in my youth up to the age of twenty-two. I think of a beastly type of man. I think of men who take advantage of you when they are dancing with you. If either of these men even touched my arm when he was dancing with me I would get a feeling of cold horror, like I get at the thought of 'leprosy.' One of these men also had a nasty habit of holding me too close, and he stroked my arm in a horribly suggestive way.

A.: What would it suggest?

P.: Oh, something nasty—intercourse, I suppose.

A.: What does the curved back that you want to stab suggest to you?

P.: A curved knife: the long curved packing needle that I once thought of stabbing my lover with. Oh, doctor, you make me think of most horrible things. I can't tell you what I thought of them.

When I was about nineteen, I went to see a film about venereal disease. I was white as a ghost after it. I felt everything was pretty dreadful. Dirt and sin and sex are all the same—like venereal disease, and now I come to think of it that is the feeling I get when I think of 'leprosy.'

I was horrified at all such things, and I was very much 'don't-touch-me' at that time. And yet it was just about then that I was so much in love with this man that I gave way to him. My father had wanted me to marry somebody he thought suitable, but the thought nearly drove me mad. I couldn't have borne him—even to touch my elbow, and yet I willingly gave way to this man.

He was already married. I don't think I really wanted intercourse, even with him. I don't think I should ever have wanted sexual intercourse on my own account. But I loved him so much I couldn't have refused him anything. I couldn't love him like that mentally without wanting to be kissed and fondled. I did like it when he first kissed me. But I didn't like the other part at first. I didn't see why he wanted to bring sex into it.

Although I learnt sometimes to appreciate that too, even now more frequently than not my feelings are against it. But, of course, I still could not refuse him anything. It is often against my feelings, and yet it is my nature never to refuse him.

A.: What association of thought do you get to these feelings?

P.: The memory of those horrid men I have spoken about, who touched my arm suggestively. I remember now how I was forced at an early age to kiss my father against my inclination. I hated it.

A.: So now at last we have the hate we were looking for. What association do you get to this?

P.: The cold horror. The feeling I get when I think of 'leprosy.' That headless man in the dream. Some atrocity being committed. Dirtiness, sexual intercourse. The impulse to stab. And the fear I have of it.

A.: So your resistance to being touched, which was so evident in the dancing experiences before you were twenty-two, has not disappeared. It seems to be there still, in spite of your love of this man. While, on account of your love, you allow him to do what he pleases to you, you at the same time frequently retain your old revulsion, the feeling of cold horror, and the idea of 'leprosy,' which, it seems, is another name for venereal disease. Although you cooperate with him in doing violence to your resistance, it seems that your resistance returns with a vengeance after the act. And then you wish to stab him *or it* in the back." (Berg, pp. 47-51)

In the course of her analysis, this patient was able by means of free association, aided by the questions and interpretations of the analyst, to gain insight into her repressed feelings and conflicts, to modify certain emotional attitudes, and to gain release from the symptoms that had been so frightening and disabling.

Psychoanalytic therapy has been criticized on a number of grounds. Some critics disagree with the psychoanalytic personality theory upon which it rests—particularly questioning the emphasis on the unconscious and on the influence of early experience. Others question its methods, especially its reliance upon free association and the transference relationship. And still other critics point to the time and expense involved—psychoanalytic therapy usually requires several thousand dollars and two to three years of frequent therapeutic sessions—whereas there is little scientific evidence as to its actual results. It may be re-emphasized, however, that for better or for worse, psychoanalytic theory and therapy have profoundly influenced our contemporary thinking about human nature and behavior.

EXISTENTIAL PSYCHOTHERAPY

Existential philosophies and approaches to psychotherapy were prominent in Europe for some time before they became generally known in the United States. Since existential psychotherapy does not follow any standard procedure, it seems most profitable to examine certain fundamental concepts on which this form of therapy appears to rest.

As indicated by its name, existentialism emphasizes first of all the importance of existence itself—man is in a situation. As Tillich (1952) has described it: "Where there is an Existential point of view there is the problem of the human situation experienced by the individual." (p. 130) And existential philosophers are very much concerned about the predicament of modern man. They emphasize the breakdown of traditional faith, the depersonalization of man in our mass culture, and the loss of meaning in human existence.

Despite his predicament, however, man is viewed as being essentially free. Unlike other living creatures, man has the ability to be conscious of himself as a self, to be reflective, and to question his own existence. He is aware that it is he who is in a situation and that he can do something about his problems through *his choices.* Man's freedom is highly valued and confronts him with the responsibility for *being* —for deciding what kind of a person he shall be, for defining and actualizing himself. If he is to fulfill himself, he must have the courage. to break away from old patterns, to seek new and potentially more fulfilling pathways, to make choices, and to tolerate anxiety.

Central to being is the problem of meaning. This is primarily a matter of finding satisfying values. Frankl (1955) has distinguished three sets of values: (a) *creative values,* which relate to the achievement of tasks, (b) *experiential values,* which adhere in experiencing the good, the true, and the beautiful and in understanding and loving another human being, and (c) *attitudinal values,* which involve courage and the facing of inevitable suffering without flinching. Since some of these values can be realized regardless of how hopeless the objective situation of the individual may appear, it is always possible to find some meaning in one's existence. However, each individual is unique; each must find the pattern of values capable of giving meaning to his life. This is not viewed as a matter of moral nihilism, for all people are faced with the task of learning to live constructively with themselves and with others. Hence one would expect to find an underlying continuity in value patterns. In addition, existentialism strongly emphasizes the individual's responsibility to his fellow man. Life is viewed as an *obligation,* and the most important consideration is not what one hopes to get from it, but what one can contribute to it. One's definitions of *self* and *actualization* can be meaningful only if they involve socially constructive values and choices—the individual needs to relate positively to and participate with other human beings.

Non-being is the opposite of being. In ultimate form, it is death, which is the inescapable fate of all human beings and adds a dimension of urgency to the existence of the individual. However, non-being can also occur in lesser degree. The outer-directed man escapes being by blind conformity and immersion in the group; the neurotic lives in a narrow and shrunken life space; and the psychotic loses outer reality. In each case, the individual pays a heavy price in the blocking of his own growth and the failure to live a full life. In addition, he experiences futility, guilt, and anxiety, for to flee from one's freedom and obligation to life is to be inauthentic, to show bad faith, and to live in despair.

Although existential therapists do not follow any prescribed procedures, it is apparent that they are concerned with values and with helping the individual to work out a meaningful and fulfilling self-definition and way of life. In their approach they tend to place heavy emphasis upon the uniqueness of the individual and upon trying to understand his way of "being-in-the-world." In essence, the existential therapist is concerned with the aspects of the individual's life style which are causing his symptoms and with helping him to make changes in the direction of self-actualization and a fuller experience of his existence. In this endeavor, most existential therapists also stress the importance of *confrontation*—challenging the individual directly with questions concerning the meaning and purpose of his existence—and the *encounter*—the relationship which is established between two interacting human beings in the therapeutic situation.[1]

The following is taken from the case of Hilda,

a 29-year-old white female patient diagnosed as "chronic undifferentiated schizophrenia." This was the third time she had been hospitalized for mental illness.[2]

"I first met her in an admission ward's patient meeting. She was asking questions about her anxiety and her unconscious. Obviously familiar with psychiatric terminology and keenly able to penetrate the facades of others, she proceeded to create quite a widespread negative reaction to herself. She was given thorazine and other medications, situational therapies, periods of intensive group therapy, and she had two interviews a week with me for four-and-a-half months.

"Prior to this current hospitalization she had been unemployed; had 'floated around and almost starved.' Her relationships with females were negative and hostile; with men, always rather 'shady,' mistress types of things.' She expressed feelings of failure, inadequacy, anger and dread. She was loud, boisterous, brutally frank and blistering to anyone who 'crossed' her. . . .

"The questions that interested me most were: What was her world? What was she to herself? I decided to attempt to meet her in her world, hoping to achieve some understanding of her—she had had the gamut of traditional types of treatment. I knew that I would have to encounter her where she was before she would be able to accept me as a helping person, who was—in essence—criticizing her way of being. My 'treatment goal' was, therefore, to encounter her in her own world, which seemed to be constructed upon a series of negative reflections which made unauthentic being in the world the only existence possible for her. I further sought to explore and understand her system, so that I might attempt to lead her, or point her, toward the possibility of orienting herself to the hopeful timelessness of a true future, instead of to the futile finiteness of her factual past. . . .

"Hilda continued her group participation—missing one meeting in ninety-two—and twice-a-week sessions with me. These individual sessions were started for purposes of discussing her intra-group functioning. She was angrily defensive against the other women; they were each something that she was not. She attacked everyone in the group, on the ward, and argued

---

[1]For additional details of existential psychotherapy, the reader is referred to Frankl (1955), May *et al.* (1958), May (1961, 1963), Pervin (1960), Sarte (1953).

[2]This is a fuller account of the case cited on pages 302-303.

long, complicated and illogical points. She would scream, condemn, swear and use the most exquisite histrionics to make her presence known. Needless to say, her aggressive, hostile tactics alienated everyone. It was as if she wanted herself to know that she was 'there,' and she knew only this method. After a two month period of trying to establish her identity in the group (by her methods) and reviewing with me, she began to talk quite freely about herself, but referring to herself in a detached way:

" '. . . That action of going along with the group by Mr. C. made Hilda feel deathly alone and rejected, even by Mr. C., and that was the ultimate in being hurt . . . For some reason Hilda is getting her typewriter fixed tonight. She even wrote a letter to her boss . . . I'm talking about Hilda as if she were not me . . .'

"We then began to explore, in earnest, 'the world of Hilda,' as she termed it, and I followed where she led. She proved to be unsure of where she had been or where she was. As she grew more and more related to me, I began to ask her: 'Where are you?' It was not very long before she stopped saying 'in the nuttery . . .'; and started telling me things which made me wonder if she were not trying to give me something; trying to tell me about Hilda. She began to disorganize but could write:

" 'I'm glad I'm young in heart. You're at this time my strongest contact with reality. You are it. This "epistle" represents my "search for reality." Ha, ha. Let's call it that: one fool's search . . .'

"She began to stay up all night, for days on end, pounding away at the typewriter; and, when others could not stand the sound of typing, she would scribble out notes haphazardly in long-hand, or huge, almost illegible printing, saying:

" '. . . It is as if I'm a girl alone in an attic. With no air to breath, or only at certain times . . .'

"Finally, she evaluated my relationship to her:

" '. . . I wanted to give you my illness . . . but you don't want it. You want me to just lose it and work it out of my system, but I'm giving it to you in written form instead . . . Keep watching the light up there above San Francisco like a beacon! Guide me, please guide me out of this . . . I'm mesmerized today . . . Now I'm going ashore, the bridge will be my vehicle . . .'

"Shortly after this 'prophecy,' she became so disorganized that I could not read her writings, nor follow her arguments. However, I tried, spending time with her almost every day. She was put on an in-creased dosage of Thorazine but still managed to get to group meetings and to our interviews. Even in her disorganization, she clung to her relationship with me, and managed to write:

" '. . . I must listen when you talk, I'm not always there . . .'

"She had encountered me, perhaps long before I became fully aware of it. The idea of love—love without purpose—was emerging from deep within her. On 800 milligrams of tranquilizer, she gradually became less disorganized. With a burst of unbelievable energy, she began to plan for a 'future'; took hospital jobs, as she said, 'fighting to stay awake.'

"When the patients on her ward elected her president of the government group, she got up and ran out of the room, crying violently. I felt that I had lost; she had recoiled from letting herself be liked. But she returned to the room, accepting the role of president. Later she was to write:

" 'Well here I am with time on my hands, you in my heart and getting well on my mind . . . I'm very selfish about getting well. I've been hurt and hindered enough. I must not keep confusing hurt with masochism because that is what I do. It is too bad I ever heard of all those terms. They have been very seductive . . . You can keep your glorious terms, I'll take romance—a continual romance with life, good or bad . . . Love, to me, is beauty with eyes open, ears open, head open . . .'

"She was in the midst of turning from her futureless, pseudo-world of distortions to the world of possibility, in which one could find hope and meaning; in which one could establish an authentic relationship!

"One of the last things she wrote, before she gave up writing, was a poem which began:

Glorious night all is right
No time for flight too tired to fight . . .

and ended:

I'm awake I'm awake
A happy wake for a former fake . . .

"Hilda remained on leave for one year, received her discharge and managed extremely well for approximately another year. She experienced a slight relapse and was rehospitalized elsewhere for about three months. After this, she once again returned to the community." (Curry, 1962, pp. 129-135)

Existential therapy has been criticized for its lack of systematic and scientific grounding, for the varying approaches and emphases of its different proponents, and for its lack of clarity and completeness. Despite its inadequacies, however, many existential concepts—the uniqueness of man, his freedom and responsibility, his quest for meaning and fulfillment, and the conflict between being and non-being—have received serious consideration by many social scientists in our country.

BEHAVIOR THERAPY

Behavior therapy stems from the work of Pavlov and is based on the assumption that maladaptive behavior results from (a) *deficient conditioned reactions*—the failure of the individual to acquire needed adaptive responses, as a consequence of either defective conditioning powers or lack of opportunity to learn, or (b) *surplus conditioned reactions*—maladaptive anxiety reactions which have been learned under certain conditions and have generalized to other situations. Therapy, in turn, becomes an attempt to provide corrective conditioning experiences in which missing responses will be learned and adaptive responses will be substituted for maladaptive ones. The techniques used are many, including simple classical conditioning, operant conditioning, aversive conditioning, and reciprocal inhibition.[1]

Simple classical conditioning involves the associating of two stimuli formerly not seen as related. A simple application has been used in the treatment of enuresis. For example, an electrical device may be used which rings a bell when the child begins to urinate in his sleep. With successive experiences the sensations from bladder distention which immediately precede the sound of the bell are sufficient to awaken the child. Thus the child is conditioned to awaken at the stimulus of bladder distention and his enuresis is eliminated.

Operant conditioning involves the manipulation of various "reinforces" to elicit and strengthen desired responses. Food is considered to be a powerful reinforcer; it has been used therapeutically to strengthen a wide range of adaptive behaviors. The improvement in certain types of responses brought about by the manipulation of food also tends to generalize to social responses, producing an increase in social interaction among patients. The chart on page

599 describes an application of this technique with chronic schizophrenics.

A variation of operant conditioning called *approximation* has been used extensively in the training of animals. Initially the trainer rewards all responses that roughly approximate the desired behavior. As learning progresses, he reinforces only the closer approximations. Inappropriate responses are dropped, and highly complex tasks may be mastered. Using this technique in therapy, the therapist may at first show approval of certain general role behaviors and then gradually limit his approval to the closer approximations of the specific role behavior which is the therapeutic objective.

Aversion conditioning involves the modification of behavior patterns through punishment—an undesired pattern comes to be associated with pain or punishment rather than with pleasure or reward. We have already seen this principle utilized in the treatment of alcoholism by means of drugs which make the patient intensely nauseated if he drinks alcohol. The knowledge that this painful reaction will occur has strong deterrent value in preventing further drinking.

In Chapter 9 we cited the use of this technique in treating homosexuality. Freund (1960) treated 67 male homosexuals by giving them an emetic mixture and then showing them slides of dressed and undressed men. One treatment was given each day up to a maximum of 24. This constituted the aversion conditioning. In the second phase of treatment, the patients were given male sex hormones and then shown films of nude or seminude women.

Although the results of this treatment approach have been questioned, the attempt points the way for further research with aversion conditioning. Greater success has been reported in the treatment of fetishism and transvestism (Raymond, 1960; Lavin *et al.,* 1961).

Sometimes maladaptive responses can be eliminated through simple nonreinforcement. For instance, a man with a phobia of air travel might lose his irrational fear by first getting used to sitting in an airliner on the ground, later sitting in the plane while it taxied around the

[1] An excellent review of the theory and practice of behavior therapy is given in Eysenck (1960, 1963). Several relevant articles dealing with operant conditioning and behavior therapy may be found in Bachrach (1962).

airport, and finally taking a short flight with other passengers.

Often, however, neurotic anxiety persists despite nonreinforcement, and desensitization is not achieved through mere exposure. In such cases, deconditioning may be achieved through specific training in making a response incompatible with the anxiety reaction in the presence of anxiety-evoking stimuli. This is based on the principle of reciprocal inhibition, and the procedure grew out of the studies on induction and elimination of experimental neuroses in animals, as described on pages 234-235. In the case of animals, it was found possible to get rid of the neurotic anxiety by feeding the animal repeatedly in the presence of a weak form of the conditioned stimulus. As the anxiety responses lessened, increasingly strong stimulus situations were presented until finally no anxiety was aroused in any of the situations in which anxiety had originally been conditioned. We also reported in Chapter 2 the early experiment of Mary Cover Jones (1924) in which a child's fear of furry animals was lost when a rabbit in a cage was brought into the room while the child was eating and gradually brought closer and closer.

With human patients, other anxiety-inhibiting responses, such as relaxation, may be substituted for eating. The technique of desensitization used by Joseph Wolpe (1958, 1960, 1961) in the treatment of neuroses was mentioned in Chapter 6 and merits further description here.

During the first six therapy sessions patients are given intensive training in relaxation by learning first to contract and then to relax the deep muscle systems of the body. Meanwhile the therapist is working out a hierarchy of the patient's anxieties by means of responses to a personality questionnaire, an analysis of the case history, and probings about situations which arouse anxiety even in the absence of objective threat. Desensitization sessions are then begun. These may be conducted under hypnosis to foster complete relaxation, or drugs may be used to aid in relaxation. Once relaxation has been achieved, the patient is told to imagine the weakest item on his anxiety hierarchy while remaining completely relaxed. Gradually, from session to session, he then works his way up the hierarchy. Often a par-

ticular item may require several repetitions to ensure desensitization. The duration of a given scene is usually about five seconds. Since the scenes are imaginary, the therapist can control the dosage of phobic stimulation and the amount of anxiety elicited by his choice of scene and by how long he lets it run. One patient may recover in 6 sessions while another may require 100 or more.

Below is the hierarchy of anxieties established for one patient. Three main themes have been identified: fear of hostility, fear of death, and fear of her symptoms. In each group the most disturbing items are at the top of the list.

"A. Fear of hostility
   1. Devaluating remarks by husband
   2. Devaluating remarks by friends
   3. Sarcasm from husband or friends
   4. Nagging
   5. Addressing a group
   6. Being at a social gathering of more than four people (the more the worse)
   7. Applying for a job
   8. Being excluded from a group activity
   9. Anybody with a patronizing attitude

"B. Fear of death and its accoutrements
   1. First husband in his coffin
   2. At a burial
   3. Seeing a burial assemblage from afar
   4. Obituary notice of young person dying of heart attack
   5. Driving past a cemetery
   6. Seeing a funeral (the nearer the worse)
   7. Passing a funeral home
   8. Obituary notice of old person (worse if died of heart disease)
   9. Inside a hospital
   10. Seeing a hospital
   11. Seeing an ambulance

"C. Fear of symptoms (despite *knowing* them to be insignificant)
   1. Extrasystoles
   2. Shooting pains in chest and abdomen
   3. Pains in left shoulder and back
   4. Pain on top of head
   5. Buzzing in ears
   6. Tremor of hands
   7. Numbness or pain in fingertips
   8. Dyspnea after exertion (shortness of breath)
   9. Pain in left hand (old injury)"

The following is an excerpt from the seventeenth desensitization session with this patient.

"At this session she was hypnotized in the same way as in the first session, but, as would be expected, the procedure took much less time. When she was deeply relaxed, I spoke as follows: 'I am going to present a number of scenes to your imagination which you will imagine very clearly. It goes without saying that, if by any chance any scene should disturb you, you will indicate it by raising your left hand. First, I want you to imagine that you are standing at a street corner and a funeral procession passes you. You may have some feelings of sadness, but apart from this you are absolutely calm. (Brief pause.) Stop the scene. (Pause of about 4 seconds.) Now I want you to imagine the same scene of the funeral passing in the street before you. (Pause of 6 or 7 seconds.) Now just relax. Think of nothing but your muscles. (Pause of about 15 seconds.) Now I want you to imagine the same scene of the funeral again. (Pause of about 8 seconds.) Stop imagining that scene and just relax. If the last presentation of that scene disturbed you even to the slightest degree I want you now to raise your left hand. (Hand does not rise.) Good.'" (1958, pp. 145-146)

In subsequent sessions sources of anxiety higher up on the patient's anxiety hierarchy were gradually worked through by means of this relaxation procedure.

In behavior therapy procedures like interpretation, role playing, and other more usual techniques may also be utilized. However, these procedures are supplemental to the basic approach of inhibiting and extinguishing the undesirable response patterns and establishing more appropriate ones.

Wolpe (1958) has reported highly successful results in the treatment of a wide range of neurotic reactions with reciprocal inhibition. Of 210 cases of various types, he reported that 39 per cent were apparently cured, 50.5 per cent much improved, and 7.2 per cent slightly or moderately improved. Only 3.3 per cent were unimproved. Follow-up information indicated that the gains were largely maintained. In a later study of 39 patients manifesting phobias and allied neurotic anxiety reactions, he reported successful results with 35 cases in a mean of 11.2 sessions. No relapses and no new symptoms were found in a six-month to four-year follow-up study of 20 of the 35 successfully treated patients (Wolpe, 1961). Several other investigators have reported comparable results, particularly in the treatment of phobic reactions (Rachman, 1959; Lang and Lazovik, 1963).[1] It is possible that special selective factors in the choice of patients may have influenced the results in some cases.

Despite reports of successful results in the treatment of a wide range of mental disorders, behavior therapy has not been widely utilized. This would appear to be due in part to the complexities of human behavior and the difficulties inherent in isolating given stimulus-response patterns for modification and in part to the behavior therapist's concentration on the alleviation of symptoms without concern for faulty assumptions or other determinants of the maladaptive behavior. As Eysenck has stated it: "Get rid of the symptom and you have eliminated the neurosis." (1960, p. 9) Apparently, most contemporary psychotherapists do not agree that the treatment of mental disorders is usually such a simple process.

THERAPY AS CHANGE IN ASSUMPTIONS AND "PLANS"

In our previous discussion we have emphasized the view that the individual guides his behavior in terms of three sets of assumptions about himself and his world—assumptions concerning fact, value, and possibility. These assumptions may be accurate or they may be seriously distorted. But accurate or inaccurate, they determine an individual's *life style* and the *plans* that he makes. The goals he strives for, the types of relationships he tries to establish with others, and the meaning he finds in his existence all depend on his underlying pattern of assumptions.

Following this viewpoint, a number of therapists conceive of psychotherapy as a process of helping the patient to change his faulty assumptions and plans. In this sense, psychotherapy is not so much a change of habits as a change

[1]Lazarus (1963) has clearly delineated the successful use of systematic desensitization in the treatment of chronic frigidity.

CONDITIONING TECHNIQUES FOR PSYCHOTIC PATIENTS

A series of experiments at the Saskatchewan hospital by Ayllon and Haughton (1962) have demonstrated that with only food as a reinforcer, even chronic schizophrenic patients who had for years refused to eat unless fed by nurses not only resumed feeding themselves but maintained an adequate diet and normal weight. Many had shown poor reality contact or even active delusions about food, such as that it was poisoned or that God was forbidding them to eat.

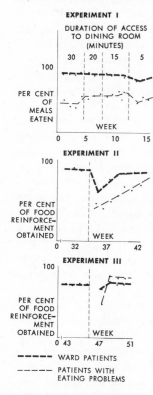

EXPERIMENT I

DURATION OF ACCESS TO DINING ROOM (MINUTES)

30 | 20 | 15 | 5

PER CENT OF MEALS EATEN

WEEK

EXPERIMENT II

PER CENT OF FOOD REINFORCEMENT OBTAINED

WEEK

EXPERIMENT III

PER CENT OF FOOD REINFORCEMENT OBTAINED

WEEK

- - - - WARD PATIENTS
- - - - PATIENTS WITH EATING PROBLEMS

I **Subjects:** 32 chronic patients, mostly schizophrenic. 7 chosen because of long-standing refusal to eat without help.
Procedure: At mealtime a nurse announced the meal and opened the dining room door. After 30 minutes (later 20, 15, and finally 5 minutes) the door was shut and patients could not enter. The time limit was not announced. All coaxing, reminding, escorting, and other help was discontinued, and the nurses were kept away from the patients.
Results: All patients eventually went to the dining room in the allotted time and ate unassisted, usually by the third day.
The graphs show the per cent of meals eaten by those with eating problems as compared to the others in this and the two later experiments.

II **Subjects:** Same as before plus 6 new subjects with feeding problems.
Procedure: Same as before plus a motor response. Each patient was given a penny and told to drop it in can at dining room door. Entrance refused otherwise.
Results: Temporary drop in meals eaten, with nearly complete recovery. Final difference between new subjects and ward patients less than 10 per cent.

III **Subjects:** Seven new patients with feeding problems plus all former subjects except 2.
Procedure: Same as preceding experiment plus a social response. Pennies now obtainable only if 2 patients simultaneously pushed buttons. Verbal clues given during 1st week.
Results: All patients learned sequence except one who found coins elsewhere and was permitted to use them to enter the dining room.

The investigators concluded that food is sufficient to control the eating behavior of schizophrenics and even to teach additional motor and social responses whereas coaxing, sympathy, and other forms of social reinforcement will actually produce and maintain eating problems.

Another use of conditioning techniques with psychotics is illustrated by the device shown at the right, developed by Dr. Stewart Armitage of the Veterans Administration Hospital at Battle Creek, Michigan. When the patient moves the lever the "right" way, a green light flashes and he may pull one of 3 other levers to get candy or cigarettes or see a picture flashed on a screen. Patients progress from 1-lever problems to 2-lever problems and then to team problems. Schizophrenic patients long regarded as "unreachable" not only have solved these problems but have shown improvement in their whole orientation.

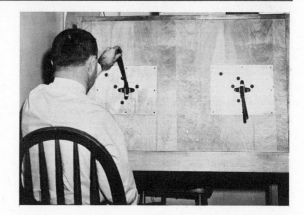

in one's style of life. Both client-centered psychotherapy and existential therapy are strongly oriented in this direction, but both are somewhat less directive in changing the patient's assumptions and plans than the therapies which we shall review briefly here.

Alfred Adler—a Viennese psychiatrist who was an early disciple of Freud but later broke away to develop his own personality theory—was probably the first therapist to focus psychotherapy on making changes in the patient's life style. Adler concluded that the individual's conscious and unconscious goals, the means he uses in achieving them, and his techniques for coping with problems of living lead to a relatively consistent life style. For the maladjusted individual, this life style is likely to be interwoven with inaccurate assumptions which lead to neurotic or other difficulties. In essence, the therapist's task then becomes one of understanding the patient's life style, discovering the mistaken assumptions which are causing difficulty, and helping the patient to make changes which will lead to more effective relationships with others and a generally more fulfilling existence.

Following a similar approach, Ellis (1958) has developed *rational psychotherapy*. This approach emphasizes the view that the patient's difficulties stem from certain inaccurate assumptions that are sustained by "self-talk"—a sort of self-dialogue in which the patient continually affirms his own faulty assumptions. For example, the patient may continually tell himself that it is essential to be approved by everyone, that it is tragic not to be highly successful, or that one should be thoroughly self-confident and adequate. Essentially the task of the therapist then becomes one of unmasking the patient's self-defeating verbalizations by (a) bringing them to the patient's attention or consciousness, (b) showing the patient how they are causing and maintaining his difficulties, and (c) helping the patient to change his faulty assumptions and to verbalize more constructive ones to himself. The therapist also encourages the patient to put his new ideas into action even though the process may be painful.

One of the most systematized approaches to psychotherapy as a change in assumptions is the "assertion-structured" therapy of Phillips (1956). In this approach, the patient's difficul-

ties are analyzed in terms of a four-point model: *assertion, disconfirmation, tension, redundancy*. In dealing with the problems of living and attempting to meet his needs, the individual makes certain assertions or assumptions. If these assertions are reasonably accurate, the individual is likely to make an adequate adjustment. However, if his assertions are incorrect, a vicious circle gets under way. For the assertion he is making about a particular problem is disconfirmed; this leads to tension and a defensive tendency to reiterate the assertion more strongly than ever. In referring to children's problems, Phillips cited the following pattern as typical:

"1. *Assertion*. Child's expectations are for constant attention, accord, interest; he expects to get his way; expects to have others give in to him in the interest of his comfort and his immediate demands.

2. *Disconfirmation*. The school and other out-of-the-home environments cannot treat the child in this way; therefore they act to disconfirm the child's expectations. These social facts conflict with the expectations themselves.

3. *Tension*. At school or in other atypical situations (i.e., not typically like the home setting) tensions develop from this conflict.

4. *Redundancy*. Child redoubles efforts to get attention, refuses to make academic effort, becomes a behavior problem owing to tension and partly to his fighting back at disconfirming experiences. The child now falls behind in school work in real and formidable ways; this failure, in turn, becomes more disconfirming to him and his original assertions. Thus the vicious circle proceeds; and until it is entered into in effective ways, it continues." (pp. 31-32)

To break this vicious circle, Phillips has emphasized the importance of reducing the patient's negative feelings and fear of alternative solutions so that he has greater flexibility and can move in any positive direction that he perceives as open to him. For the child, this may involve helping him to see that sharing and cooperating may meet his needs more effectively.

A number of other investigators and therapists have developed systematic approaches that deal with faulty assumptions and life plans. The *"psychobiology"* of Adolf Meyer (1958) attempts to re-educate the patient along common sense and practical lines. In his *fixed role* therapy, Kelly (1955) has stressed the view that psychotherapy should be directed toward freeing the patient from his particular system of assumptions or constructs so that he can achieve increased flexibility and try out different views and roles. Finally, we may mention the interesting concept of psychotherapy as a *change in plans* developed by Miller, Galanter, and Pribram (1960). Here the individual is seen as considering possible plans for dealing with problems and meeting his needs in the light of his assumptions concerning himself and his world. Thus he may plan to go to college, to invest in real estate, or to get married and raise a family. Some plans are abandoned and others executed as circumstances seem to warrant. Often plans are shared with others, and we can even talk about the plans of a nation as well as a family or individual. Difficulties seem to arise when (a) the individual is unable to decide what to do—he seems to be completely planless, (b) he cannot choose between two or more plans which are in basic conflict with each other, or (c) the plans which have guided his life seem no longer valid or feasible. Here therapy becomes primarily a matter of exploring the patient's plans and helping him make indicated modifications or formulate new plans which will enable him to function more effectively.

Perhaps the greatest problem faced by therapeutic approaches which emphasize changes in assumptions and plans is the problem of value judgments. How can a therapist be sure that one assumption or course of action is more desirable than another? Some therapists tend to avoid this problem by assuming that any change in an unworkable assumption or plan will improve the patient's adjustment; other therapists tend, consciously or unconsciously, to use their own value systems for guiding the patient; still others view the therapy situation as providing the patient with an opportunity to explore his own values and reach his own decisions.

Nor is the problem of values limited to the approaches whose central focus is a change in assumptions. There is ample research evidence to show that the therapist's value system influences his patients whether he wants it to or not—at least in successful therapy (Krasner, 1963). We need much more research on the actual effects of given values on an individual's mental health and self-actualization. Fortunately, we are seeing a strong revival of interest in values among psychologists and a much greater awareness of the need to be concerned about the value orientation of therapists.

There are a number of other systematic approaches to psychotherapy in addition to those we have reviewed. One is Jungian analysis, in which the therapist may utilize free association, dream analysis, interpretation, transference, and other procedures. Particular emphasis is placed on the patient's search for meaning and on his development as a unique, creative self. This form of therapy is based on the complex personality theory of Carl Jung, which is summarized in the Appendix. Another approach is that of Sullivan (1953, 1956). Here mental illness is viewed largely as a failure in one's relationship with "significant others," and treatment is oriented toward improvement of such relationships. In concluding our immediate review of systematic approaches to psychotherapy, it may be re-emphasized that many therapists take an eclectic approach both in their theoretical orientation and in their work with patients.

Evaluation of Psychotherapy

In view of the fact that hundreds of thousands of men, women, and children undergo psychotherapy each year, it is surprising how little scientific knowledge we have concerning the processes and outcomes of psychotherapy.

It has proven virtually impossible to compare the effectiveness of various systematic forms of psychotherapy because of differences in types of patients, choice of goals, duration of therapy, and ways of evaluating "improvement." Some investigators have even questioned whether any form of psychotherapy is effective. Certainly it would appear that what happens to the patient will depend to a large extent upon the therapist

METHODS OF ADMISSION TO STATE MENTAL HOSPITALS IN CALIFORNIA

Voluntary
admission

Patient—or guardian of a minor—applies directly to nearest state mental hospital. Later, if discharge is requested, patient must be released within a week of written request.

Health officer
admission

Any relative or friend of a person believed to be mentally ill may report this fact to local health officer who may make such investigation as he deems necessary. If it appears to health officer that hospitalization is in best interests of person, he may make application to a state hospital. Such application must be accompanied by certificates from two physicians who have examined patient within three days of the date of the certificate, and such application must be presented to superintendent of the hospital within 7 days of its date. This method cannot be used if patient or any relative or friend protests prior to patient's admission. After admission, patient or anyone on his behalf can at any time demand court hearing regarding continued hospitalization.

Temporary
90-day
admission

Superintendent may admit patient for a period not to exceed 90 days who is believed to be mentally ill and who does not object to such admission. Application on his behalf may be made by family, relative, friend with whom he resides, guardian, health or welfare officer of the community, or the head of a hospital, sanitarium, or other institution in which the person may be. The application must be accompanied by certificates of two physicians. At any time after admission, the patient or anyone on his behalf may give notice in writing to the superintendent of his desire to leave the hospital. The patient shall then be discharged within 15 days after receipt of this notice, or if the superintendent feels the patient needs further hospitalization, a court hearing is initiated.

Involuntary
admission

Anyone may initiate court action for placement of mentally ill person who appears to be either (a) in need of supervision, treatment, care, or restraint, or (b) dangerous to himself or others. If after examination two physicians certify that patient is mentally ill, the judge may sign an order (a) for person to be cared for and detained in a licensed sanitarium or hospital for care of the mentally ill, (b) that person be committed to a Veterans Administration or other agency of the United States Government, or (c) that person be committed to the Department of Mental Hygiene for placement in a state hospital designated by the court.

Emergency
admission

When person becomes so mentally ill as to be likely to injure himself or others or requires immediate treatment or restraint, a peace officer or other designated person may take person into custody. Person may be admitted and detained in quarters provided by any county or state hospital upon application in writing by the officer stating the conditions of the case and his conviction that person is mentally ill. Patient must be released within 72 hours unless he seeks voluntary admission or unless admittance is sought under health officer method or a petition is filed. In latter case, patient goes through regular court procedures.

Chart based on Morrison (1963).

to whom he goes. For example, a psychoanalyst is likely to be concerned primarily with the integration of conscious and unconscious forces in the personality; the client-centered therapist with self-growth; the existential therapist with values; and the behavior therapist with habit change. Although these goals are by no means incompatible, they certainly are not identical. And it would appear that both the processes involved in therapy and the outcomes are likely to vary with the different goals.[1]

A better understanding of the exact effects of therapy can come only with more research. In general, research in psychotherapy can be divided into two classes: (a) *outcome research,* focusing on assessing the specific effects of psychotherapy and (b) *process research,* focusing on what actually happens in the course of psychotherapy. Both types of research are designed to provide information which will help us to understand psychotherapy better and increase its effectiveness.

There is an increasing tendency to view psychotherapy as one form of "behavior control." This means that we must be concerned not only with identifying and learning to apply the most effective techniques but also with developing societal safeguards against the misuse of these techniques—controlling the controller. We shall comment further in Chapter 15 on the problem of behavior control. For the moment it must suffice to point out that this problem arises on biological and sociological as well as psychological levels of treatment.

Sociotherapy

Sociotherapy refers primarily to some modification of the environment in order to provide a life situation in which the patient has a reasonable chance of making a successful adjustment. In the treatment of children with behavior problems, this often involves the treatment of the parents rather than the child; in some cases it means a foster-home placement for the child. Sociotherapy with adults may involve assistance with child-rearing or with marital or other life problems. Usually sociotherapy is carried out by the psychiatric social worker, often with the aid of various welfare and community service agencies.

When one family member is hospitalized, an emotional strain and additional responsibilities are often placed on other family members. Here the assistance of the psychiatric social worker may range from individual or family therapy to obtaining help in resolving financial difficulties. A second type of problem involves the transition of the mental patient from the hospital to the community. As the hospital treatment of mental patients becomes increasingly effective, this aspect of the total treatment program is receiving increasing emphasis. Often a key type of assistance rendered by the psychiatric social worker is that of smoothing the way for the patient's return home by discussing with the family what to expect of the patient and how to react to him. The psychiatric social worker also may help the patient to find employment or may help the employer to understand the patient's illness and recovery.

A third type of problem involves the followup of the mental patient after his return to the community. With periodic visits by the psychiatric social worker many patients who might otherwise still require hospitalization are helped to adjust satisfactorily in the community. When stresses begin to build up and become too threatening, they know they can turn to the psychiatric social worker for help over the crisis period. The continuity provided by being able to discuss their problems with someone they know and have confidence in is often highly important in the patient's successful adjustment in the community.

Obviously, the psychiatric social worker plays an important role in the total treatment program and requires extensive training in personality dynamics, in family and other types of group interaction, and in the use of available commu-

---

[1] For a further discussion of the scientific and ethical issues in psychotherapy, the reader is referred to Braun (1961), Krasner (1962), and Sundberg and Tyler (1962).

nity resources, as well as in psychotherapy proper. The following case is illustrative of the importance of sociotherapy in treating mental patients.

A 48-year-old mother would travel some 30 miles by bus after work on Friday evening to meet her son at the hospital. The son, a 22-year-old patient diagnosed as a paranoid schizophrenic, would then accompany his mother home for the weekend and return to the hospital on Monday morning.[1] He was perfectly capable of going home by himself, but his mother insisted that he remain at the hospital until she could get there, which was usually after 9 o'clock in the evening. By the time they got home, it was well after 12:00 and the mother would be worn out. She would then be sick the next day and continually remind her son how she had gotten sick looking after him, insisting that the least he could do would be to remain with her during his weekend visit. In this way he was unable to go out on dates or otherwise do anything that he wanted to do and on his return to the hospital on Monday morning he was hostile and severely disturbed. Thus his weekends at home were undoing practically all that had been accomplished with him

in psychotherapy the preceding week. It was not until a psychiatric social worker counseled the mother and managed over a period of time to modify her attitudes and behavior that the patient began to show consistent improvement.

Newer approaches in sociotherapy are also being directed at treating the patient in his ongoing life situation and modifying the broader social systems of which the individual is a part. In Chapter 5 we noted the emphasis in modern military organizations on making soldiers' working, living, and fighting conditions as favorable as possible and on the early recognition and treatment of maladjustments while the soldier is still a member of his unit. We have also noted that in recent years social workers have been working directly with delinquent gangs in an attempt to exert a corrective influence. Mental hospitals and other types of treatment facilities have come to realize the importance of establishing environmental conditions that will themselves be therapeutic. The mental hospital as a therapeutic community will be discussed in the next section.

Mental Hospital and Clinic

The principal facilities for the treatment of mental disorders consist of in-patient facilities such as mental hospitals and out-patient facilities such as mental health clinics. Since the great majority of mental patients are treated in such facilities—rather than by psychiatrists or clinical psychologists in private practice—it will be of value to review briefly their nature and their role in the overall handling of mental disorders.

HOSPITALIZATION AS THERAPY

The modern mental hospital is a far different place from the old custodial institutions where patients often lived under almost unbelievable conditions. Even as late as 1949 many patients in state hospitals were kept naked, half-starved, shackled to their beds or otherwise restrained, and crammed together in filth-infested wards

meant for less than half the number of patients in them (Deutsch, 1949). Conditions are much improved, but low funds still keep some state hospitals from offering much more than custodial care.

In our present discussion of hospitalization as therapy, we are referring to modern mental hospitals which are well equipped and well staffed. These hospitals have demonstrated that intensive treatment can restore most mental patients to the community within a relatively short period of time.

The mental hospital as a therapeutic community. In the modern mental hospital every effort is made to make the patient's whole environment one which is favorable to recovery. From this point of view, the hospital becomes

---

[1]Not uncommon in milder cases, regardless of classification, either in terms of a weekend pass or a "TV" (trial visit).

a *therapeutic community* in which all the on-going activities of the hospital are brought into the total therapeutic effort. In a sense, the whole hospital becomes the "doctor."

In the therapeutic community, as few restraints as possible are placed on the freedom of the patient, and open wards which permit the patient the use of grounds and premises are the rule. "Patient government" is utilized to permit the patients some decision making in ward management and other appropriate activities, thus conferring "citizenship" on them and giving them a sense of responsibility for managing their own affairs. Often the patient is permitted considerable freedom in planning his activities during the day so that he plays an important role in his own therapy. The interaction among patients—as in discussion groups, drama projects, and social events—is planned in such a way as to be of therapeutic benefit to the patients involved. All hospital personnel are oriented toward treating the patients as individuals meriting consideration and courtesy. In essence, responsibility is placed upon all hospital personnel for creating a "milieu" which fosters the recovery of the patient. A number of studies have shown the influence of the staff attitudes and the overall emotional and social climate of the facility upon patients.

Curiously enough, in establishing a therapeutic community or total treatment "milieu," the hospital staff has to be on guard against building a little world for the patients which they will not want to leave. To avoid this, mental hospitals try to establish as close ties as possible with the community and to maintain a "recovery expectant" attitude.

It is usually desirable to maintain the patient in his normal life situation and avoid hospitalization altogether whenever possible. However, hospitalization can be of great therapeutic value for some patients in removing them from highly stressful life situations and providing them with an opportunity to work out their problems in a supervised and sheltered environment.

The treatment sequence. The sequence of events in the hospitalization and treatment of a mental patient involves several steps:

1. *Admission.* The methods of admission to state mental hospitals are outlined in the chart on page 602. Often the patient is ac-

On their road back to mental health, patients need chances to take responsibility and use imagination and judgment on things that count. Here patients at St. Elizabeth's Hospital in Washington, D. C., are shown discussing their parts in a coast-to-coast TV program in which they dramatized some of the problems of mental illness.

companied by a relative and asks voluntarily for hospitalization. He can make this request with the understanding that he may leave the hospital if he decides that he does not want to remain. As a consequence, some patients are discharged at their own request even though the hospital staff does not feel that they are ready. This type of discharge is referred to as "AMA"—against medical advice. To commit a patient to a mental hospital against his will requires the certification of two physicians to the effect that he is dangerous to himself or others. Often the term "dangerous" is stretched here to admit persons who need psychiatric aid and would themselves suffer if left in the community. After the individual has become a patient, he may be discharged as soon as his condition warrants.

On admission, the patient is usually assigned to a nurse or ward attendant who helps to orient him to the hospital environment. This includes assigning him to a room and bed and

---

[1]Additional information concerning the concept of the therapeutic community may be found in Denber (1960), Jones (1961), and Rapaport (1963).

A

C

B

Many kinds of special treatment centers have been developed in recent years. They have in common an imaginative experimentation with new methods and an attempt to prepare their patients for active and responsible participation in the community. A home for disturbed and delinquent boys at Dobbs Ferry, New York, has an Indian Village (A), built by the boys themselves, where boys can develop strength and skill and find recognition for resourcefulness and legitimate kinds of adventure. A special day school for schizophrenic children in Woodbury, New York (B), helps children to establish social interaction and other contacts with reality; the school also offers instruction in usual school subjects. A still different approach is the program for adolescent therapy offered at the Psychiatric Treatment Center in New York (C). Here traditional psychotherapy is combined with a new technique known as "program therapy" in which therapist and adolescent patient establish an unusual degree of rapport through outings, shared sports, and other meaningful activities.

bringing him into contact with the psychiatrist who will be in charge of his treatment.

2. *Diagnosis and treatment.* As soon as possible after admission, the patient is given a complete medical and psychological examination. This is supplemented by life history and sociological assessment date. When the patient has adapted to the world within the ward—his

room, fellow patients, nurse, and psychiatrist— he is encouraged to discuss some of his problems with the psychiatrist or psychologist assigned as his therapist. This information together with the results of medical, psychological, and sociological evaluation is then integrated during a staff conference at which the patient may be assigned to a particular psychiatric classification—such as schizophrenia—and co-ordinated plans for a program of therapy are formulated.

Both emergency and long-range therapy may be planned, depending on the facilities and personnel available as well as on the needs of the individual patient. If he is severely disturbed, he may be put at once on drug medication aimed at alleviating certain target symptoms such as depression or agitation. Long-range therapy may include a combination of any of the various medical, psychological, and sociological procedures which we have discussed.

Often the individual who has never been in a mental hospital has the impression that most mental patients are disoriented and agitated and must be kept in locked wards. Although some patients are severely disturbed, particularly on admission, the great majority appear like normal people. In fact, it is sometimes hard for a visitor to be sure whether he is talking to a patient, a ward attendant, a psychologist, or a psychiatrist. Despite their difficulties, most mental patients are aware of who they are, where they are, and how they are being treated.

3. *Discharge, transition, and follow-up.* As the time of discharge approaches—when the patient no longer needs hospital supervision—plans are made for his return to the community. As we have noted, the psychiatric social worker may assist the patient in making the transition back to family and community and may maintain supportive follow-up contacts. In fact, the current trend is toward short-term hospitalization and long-term follow-up.

In some cases, the return to family and community involves a transitional phase in which the patient is discharged from the hospital to a "half-way house" or to a "day hospital."[1] In these clinic settings, the patient receives less supervision than he would in the mental hospital but more than he would staying at home. Usually such patients are still in treatment and are not expected to resume full domestic or occupational responsibilities.

After the patient returns to the community, he often is urged to maintain follow-up contacts with the mental hospital or a mental health clinic in his area. In many cases, he also is encouraged to maintain active membership in expatient groups such as Recovery, Inc. which are appropriate in relation to the nature of his previous illness.

THE MENTAL HEALTH CLINIC

One of the most outstanding achievements of the mental health movement in the last decade has been the growth of mental health clinics. Such clinics are defined as "outpatient mental health service units with a psychiatrist in attendance at regularly scheduled hours who takes the medical responsibility for all clinic patients" (National Institute of Mental Health, 1957, National Association for Mental Health, 1962). Assisted by federal aid, in most instances, we now have some 2000 such clinics. These clinics utilize a team approach—psychiatrists, psychologists, and psychiatric social workers work together and offer a wide range of treatment services. For example, patients may be helped with problems concerning child guidance, marital adjustment, excessive drinking, anxiety, feelings of depression, and other difficulties.

Some of these clinics deal exclusively with the problems of children, others with the problems of adults, and still others have no age limitations for patients. An estimated 665,000 patients were served by the 1568 mental health clinics in operation in 1961 (Bahn *et al.*, 1963). Patients under 18 years of age and over 18 were about equally represented. Boys outnumbered girls in the ratio of almost 2 to 1, but among adults there was only a slight excess of male in relation to female patients. The largest diagnostic category for children was transient situational personality disorders (Norman *et al.*, 1962). For adults, personality (character) disorders, psychoneurotic disorders, and psychotic disorders predominated in that order. The average number of interview hours per patient approximated 4. Fewer than 10 per cent of all patients received 25 interviews or more.

Mental health clinics operate at both ends of the "continuum"—providing treatment short of hospitalization for many patients and helping the ex-patient to adjust in the community after his release from the hospital.

[1] For further details the reader is referred to Wechsler (1961) and Joint Commission (1961).

Trends in the Treatment of Mental Disorders

In the course of our discussion of therapy, we have described a variety of medical, psychological, and sociological treatment procedures and the importance of integrating them in the overall treatment program. We have also emphasized the increasing reliance upon tranquilizing and energizing drugs as basic to most treatment programs and the trend toward treating social systems of which the patient is a part—such as the family—as well as the patient. Where hospitalization is necessary, we have also noted the trend toward getting the patient out of the hospital and back into the community as rapidly as possible.

Several additional trends are of significance:

1. The establishment of *day* and *night* hospitals as alternatives to hospitalization. These are relatively recent innovations in the United States and are expected to become more common, especially as services in psychiatric wards of general hospitals.

2. The location of mental health services in the community where the patients reside. Increasingly, psychiatric wards are being established in general hospitals in the community. Having facilities available locally makes possible earlier detection and treatment of incipient mental illness; it fosters a better understanding of the patient and his situation by the staff of the clinic; it permits a continuum of services from diagnosis through treatment and aftercare.

3. The development of new and promising *aftercare programs.* In 1960 approximately 170,000 patients were discharged from public mental hospitals, but during the same year, there were slightly over 90,000 readmissions. The rapid discharge of mental patients and the high rate of readmissions indicate the need for increased emphasis upon transitional and aftercare programs to insure the patient's successful readjustment in the community. In addition to the use of mental health clinics to assist ex-patients on a more systematic basis, a number of experimental programs are being tried out, including foster-family care, "half-way houses," and various types of ex-patient organizations.

4. The increasing reliance upon *research.* Although much more research on treatment is needed, we have noted the new emphasis upon *process* as well as *outcome* research. Recently, the federal government has given increased financial support to research in the whole mental health field including the area of treatment.

5. Finally, we may point to the increasing concern of the general public as well as of governmental bodies with mental health problems —a concern that encompasses both treatment and prevention of mental illness. The many ways in which this concern has been translated into programs for action will be the subject of our final chapter.

REFERENCES

The reference list includes not only the sources from which the author has drawn material, but acknowledgments of the permissions granted by authors and publishers to quote directly from their works.

ACKERMAN, N. W. *The psychodynamics of family life; diagnosis and treatment of family relationships.* New York: Basic Books, 1958.

AGIN, H. V. Phenelzine in the treatment of depression. *Amer. J. Psychiat.,* 1963, 119, 1173-1174.

ALEXANDER, F. Individual psychotherapy. *Psychosom. Med.,* 1946, 8, 110-115.

ALTSCHULER, M. Massive doses of trifluoperazine in the treatment of compulsive rituals. *Amer. J. Psychiat.,* 1962, 119, 367-368.

ANDERSON, J. H., & SANCHEZ-LONGO, L. P. The complications and side effects of the phenothiazine ataraxics. A review of 178 clinical series of 10 phenothiazine derivates. *Bol. Asoc. Med. Rico,* 1961, 53, 123-151.

AYLLON, T., & HAUGHTON, E. Control of the behavior of schizophrenic patients by food. *J. exp. Analysis Behav.,* 1962, 5, 343-352. Graphs redrawn with permission.

AYLLON, T., & MICHAEL, J. The psychiatric nurse as a behavioral engineer. *J. exp. Anal. Behav.*, 1959, 2, 323-334.

BACHRACH, A. J. (Ed.) *Experimental foundations of clinical psychology.* New York: Basic Books, 1962.

BAHN, ANITA K., NORMAN, VIVIAN B., HENCH, CATHERINE L., MC CARTY, CAROL L., & RIPPY, MARY A. Gains in outpatient psychiatric clinic services, 1961. *Ment. Hyg.*, 1963, 47, 177-188.

BARAHAL, H. S. 1000 prefrontal lobotomies: five-to-ten-year follow-up study. *Psychiat. Quart.*, 1958, 32, 653-678.

BARBER, T. X. Physiological effects of "hypnosis." *Psychol. Bull.*, 1961, 58, 390-419.

BARBER, T. X. Antisocial and criminal acts induced by hypnosis. *Arch. gen. Psychiat.*, 1961, 5, 301-312.

BARRON, A. R., RUDY, L. H., & SMITH, J. A. Effect of drugs on "poor" treatment cases. *Dis. nerv. System*, 1961, 22, 692.

BARSA, J. A. Combination drug therapy in psychiatry. *Amer. J. Psychiat.*, 1960, 117, 448-449.

BARSA, J. A., & KLINE, N. S. Treatment of 200 disturbed psychotics with teserpine. *J. Amer. med. Ass.*, 1955, 18, 110-113.

BELDEN, E., & HITCHEN, R. The identification and treatment of an early deprivation syndrome in alcoholics by means of LSD-25. *Amer. J. Psychiat.*, 1963, 119, 985-986.

BERG, C. *The case book of a medical psychologist.* New York: Norton, 1948.

BLOCK, MARGARET S. Medical treatment of alcoholism. In Council on Mental Health of the Amer. Med. Ass., Committee on Alcoholism, *Manual on alcoholism.* Chicago: Committee on Alcoholism, 1962. Pp. 7-33.

BOND, E. D., & RIVERS, T. D. Insulin shock therapy after seven years. *Amer. J. Psychiat.*, 1944, 101, 62.

BRAMMER, L. M., & SHOSTROM, E. L. *Therapeutic psychology.* New York: Prentice-Hall, 1960.

BRAUN, J. R. *Clinical psychology in transition.* Cleveland: Howard Allen, Inc., 1961.

BRAUN, M. Reserpine as a therapeutic agent in schizophrenia. *Amer. J. Psychiat.*, 1960, 116, 744-745.

BRENMAN, M., & GILL, M. *Hypnotherapy.* New York: International Univer. Press, 1947.

BUCCI, L., & SAUNDERS, J. C. A psychopharmacological evaluation of 2-diethyl-aminoethyl-para-aminobenzoate (procaine). *J. Neuropsychiat.*, 1960, 1, 276.

BUCCI, L., & SAUNDERS, J. C. A unique monamine oxidase inhibitor for depression. *Amer. J. Psychiat.*, 1961, 118, 255-256.

CANNICOTT, S. M. Technique of unilateral electro-convulsive therapy. *Amer. J. Psychiat.*, 1963, 120, 477-480.

CASEY, J. F., LASKY, J. J., KLETT, C. J., & HOLLISTER, L. E. Treatment of schizophrenic reactions with phenothiazine derivatives: a comparative study of chlorpromazine, triflupromazine, mepazine, prochlorperazine, perphenazine, and phenobarbital. *Amer. J. Psychiat.*, 1960, 117, 97-105.

CHAPMAN, A. H. Psychiatrogenic illness. *Amer. J. Psychiat.*, 1960, 116, 873-877.

CHILDERS, R. T., JR. Selective effectiveness of chlorpromazine and trifluoperazine in schizophrenia. *Dis. nerv. System*, 1962, 23, 156-157.

CHWELOS, N., BLEWETT, D. B., SMITH, C. M., & HOFFER, A. Use of d-lysergic diethylamide in the treatment of alcoholism. *Quart. J. Stud. Alcohol*, 1959, 20, 577-590.

COHEN, S., & EISNER, B. G. Use of lysergic acid diethylamide in a psychotherapeutic setting. *AMA Arch. Neurol. Psychiat.*, 1959, 81, 615.

COUGHLAN, R. Control of the brain, Part II. The chemical mind-changers. *Life*, 1963, 54 (11), 81-82.

CUMMINS, J. F., & FRIEND, D. G. Use of chlorpromazine in chronic alcoholics. *Amer. J. med. Sci.*, 1954, 227, 561-564.

CURRY, A. E. The world of a schizophrenic woman. *Psychoanal. and psychoanal. Rev.*, 1962, 49, 129-135. Reprinted by permission of Editors and Publisher.

DAHLBERG, C. C. Pharmacologic facilitation of psychoanalytic therapy. In J. Masserman (Ed.), *Current psychiatric therapies*, Vol. III. New York: Grune & Stratton, 1963. Pp. 91-97.

DENBER, H. C. B. (Ed.) *Research conference on the therapeutic community.* Springfield, Ill.: Charles C. Thomas, 1960.

DENBER, H. C. B., & BIRD, ETTA G. Chlorpromazine in the treatment of mental illness. IV. *Amer. J. Psychiat.*, 1957, 113, 972-978.

DEUTSCH, A. *The mentally ill in America.* Columbia Univer. Press, 1949.

DORCUS, R. M. *Hypnosis and its therapeutic application.* New York: McGraw-Hill, 1956.

EDELSON, M. *The termination of intensive psychotherapy.* Springfield, Ill.: Charles C. Thomas, 1963.

ELLIS, A. Rational psychotherapy. *J. gen. Psychol.*, 1958, 59, 35-49.

ENGLISH, D. C. A comparative study of antidepressants in balanced therapy. *Amer. J. Psychiat.*, 1961, 117, 865-872.

ERICKSON, M. H. Experimental demonstrations of the psychopathology of everyday life. *Psychoanalyt. Quart.*, 1939, 8, 338-353.

ESTABROOKS, G. H. *Hypnosis. Current problems.* New York: Harper, 1962.

EVARTS, E. V., & BUTLER, R. N. A review of the effects of chlorpromazine and reserpine in patients with mental disorders. In J. O. Cole & R. W. Gerard (Eds.), *Psychopharmacology problems in evaluation.* Washington, D. C.: National Academy Science and National Res. Council, 1958. Pp. 64-77.

EWING, J. A., & HAIZLIP, T. M. A controlled study of the habit forming propensities of meprobamate. *Amer. J. Psychiat.*, 1958, 114, 835.

EYSENCK, H. J. (Ed.) *Behaviour therapy and the neuroses.* London: Pergamon Press, 1960.

EYSENCK, H. J. Behaviour therapy, spontaneous remission and transference in neurotics. *Amer. J. Psychiat.*, 1963, 119, 867-871.

FRANK, J. D. *Persuasion and healing.* Baltimore: Johns Hopkins Univer. Press, 1961.

FRANKL, V. E. *The doctor and the soul.* New York: Knopf, 1955.

FRANKL, V. E. Existential dynamics and neurotic escapisms. *J. existen. Psychiat.*, 1963, 4, 27-42.

FREEMAN, W. Psychosurgery. *Amer. J. Psychiat.*, 1963, 119, 626-628.

FREEMAN, W., & WATTS, J. W. Psychosurgery: an evaluation of 200 cases over seven years. *J. ment. Sci.*, 1944, 379, 532-537.

FREUND, K. Some problems in the treatment of homosexuality. In H. J. Eysenck (Ed.), *Behaviour therapy and the neuroses.* London: Pergamon Press, 1960.

GATSKI, R. L. Chlorpromazine in the treatment of emotionally maladjusted children. *J. Amer. med. Ass.*, 1955, 157, 1298-1300.

GERLE, B. Clinical trials of R 1625. *Acta Neurol. belg.*, 1960, 60, 70.

GOLDBERG, M. A. A new procedure for the administration of carbon dioxide. *J. clin. exp. Psychopath.*, 1958, 19, 309-311.

GREENBLATT, M., & MYERSON, P. G. Medical progress, psychosurgery, *N. E. J. Med.*, 1949, 240, 1006-1017.

GREENBLATT, M., GROSSER, G. H., & WECHSLER, H. A comparative study of selected antidepressant medications and EST. *Amer. J. Psychiat.*, 1962, 119, 144-153.

GRINKER, R., & SPIEGEL, J. P. *War neuroses.* Philadelphia: Blakiston, 1945.

Group for the Advancement of Psychiatry (Dr. William Menninger, Chairman), *Res. Prefrontal Lobotomy, Report No. 6,* June 1948, 1-9.

HABER, S., PALEY, A., & BOLCKM, A. S. Treatment of problem drinkers at Winter Veterans Administration Hospital. *Bull. Menninger Clin.,* 1949, 13, 24-30.

HINCKLEY, R. G., & HERMANN, LYDIA. *Group treatment in psychotherapy.* Minneapolis: Univer. Minn. Press, 1951.

HIPPIUS, H., & KORENKE, H. D. [Therapeutically undesirable effects of modern psychopharmacological agents. II Monsamino oxidase inhibitors.] *Internist,* (Berl.), 1960, 1, 461-465.

HOLT, J. P., WRIGHT, E. R., & HECKER, A. O. Comparative clinical experience with five antidepressants. *Amer. J. Psychiat.,* 1960, 117, 533-536.

HORSLEY, J. S. *Narco-analysis.* London: Humphrey Milford, 1943.

INGHAM, H. V., & LOVE, LENORE R. *The process of psychotherapy.* New York: McGraw-Hill, 1954.

Joint Commission on Mental Illness and Health. *Action for mental health: final report of the Joint Commission on Mental Illness and Health.* New York: National Rehabilitation Association, 1961.

JONES, M. Intra and extramural community psychiatry. *Amer. J. Psychiat.,* 1961, 117, 784-787.

JONES, MARY C. A laboratory study of fear; the case of Peter. *Pedagog. Sem.,* 1924, 31, 308-315.

JONES, T. H. Chlordiazepoxide (librium) and the geratric patient. *J. Amer. Geriat.,* 1962, 10, 259-263.

KALINOWSKY, L. B., & HOCH, P. H. *Shock treatments and other somatic procedures in psychiatry.* New York: Grune & Stratton, 1946.

KELLY, G. A. *The psychology of personal constructs.* Vol. 1. *A theory of personality.* Vol. II. *Clinical diagnosis and therapy.* New York: Norton, 1955.

KENNEDY, J. F. Message from the President of the United States relative to mental illness and mental retardation. *Amer. Psychologist,* 1963, 18, 280-289.

KEUP, W., *et al.* Inpatient treatment of depressive states with Tofrānil (imipramine hydrochloride). *Amer. J. Psychiat.,* 1959, 116, 257-258.

KLEIN, D., & FINK, M. Psychiatric reaction patterns to imipramine. *Amer. J. Psychiat.,* 1962, 119, 432-438.

KLINE, N. S. Use of *Rauwolfia sepentina* in neuropsychiatric conditions. *Ann. N. Y. Acad. Sci.,* 1954, 54, 107-132.

KLINE, N. S. Clinical experience with iproniazid (marsilid). *J. clin. exp. Psychopath.,* 1958, 19, Suppl. 1, 72-78; discussion, 78-79.

KLINE, N. S., & SACKS, W. Relief of depression within one day using an MAO inhibitor and intravenous 5-HTP. *Amer. J. Psychiat.,* 1963, 120, 274-275.

KRAMER, M. Public health and social problems in the use of tranquilizing drugs. In J. O. Cole, & R. W. Gerard (Eds.), *Psychopharmacology problems in evaluation.* Washington, D. C.: National Academy Science and National Res. Council, 1958. Pp. 108-135.

KRASNER, L. Behavior control and social responsibility. *Amer. Psychologist,* 1962, 17, 199-204.

KRASNER, L. Reinforcement, verbal behavior and psychotherapy. *Amer. J. Orthopsychiat.,* 1963, 33, 601-613.

KUHN, R. The treatment of depressive states with G 22355 (imipramine hydrochloride). *Amer. J. Psychiat.,* 1958, 115, 459-464.

LANG, P. J., & LAZOVIK, A. D. Experimental desensitization of a phobia. *J. abnorm. soc. Psychol.,* 1963, 66, 519-525.

LASKY, J. J., & KLETT, C. J. Comparative evaluation of six tranquilizers with 500 newly admitted male schizophrenics from 32 VA hospitals. *Amer. Psychologist,* 1962, 17, 322-323.

LAVIN, N. I., THORPE, J. G., BARKER, J. C., BLAKEMORE, C. B.,
& CONWAY, C. G. Behavior therapy in a case of transvestism. *J. nerv. ment. Dis.,* 1961, 133, 346-353.

LAZARUS, A. A. The elimination of children's phobias by deconditioning. In H. J. Eysenck (Ed.), *Behaviour and the neuroses.* London: Pergamon Press, 1960. Pp. 114-122.

LAZARUS, A. A. The treatment of chronic frigidity by systematic desensitization. *J. nerv. ment. Dis.,* 1963, 136, 272-278.

LECRON, L. M., & BORDEAUX, JEAN. *Hypnotism today.* New York: Grune & Stratton, 1947.

LEUBA, C. Theories of hypnosis: a critique and a proposal. *Amer. J. clin. Hypnosis,* 1960, 3, 43-48.

LINDSTROM, P. A. Prefrontal ultrasonic irradiation—a substitute for lobotomy. AMA *Arch. Neurol. Psychiat.,* 1954, 72, 399-425.

LINNEMAN, E. J. *Nordisk Med.* (Stockholm, Sweden), 1952, 48, 1257.

MAC LEAN, J. R., MAC DONALD, D. C., BYRNE, U. P., & HUBBARD, A. M. The use of LSD-25 in the treatment of alcoholism and other psychiatric problems. *Quart. J. Stud. Alcohol.,* 1961, 22, 34-45.

MC NEILL, D. L., & MADGWICK, J. R. A comparison of results in schizophrenics treated with (1) insulin, (2) trifluoperazine ("stelazine") *J. ment. Sci.,* 1961, 107, 297-299.

MASSERMAN, J. *Principles of dynamic psychiatry.* Philadelphia: W. B. Saunders, 1961.

MASSERMAN, J. H. (Ed.) *Current psychiatric therapies.* New York: Grune & Stratton, 1963.

MAY, R. (Ed.) *Existential psychology.* New York: Random House, 1961.

MAY, R. Existential theory and therapy. In J. Masserman (Ed.), *Current psychiatric therapies.* Vol. 3. New York: Grune & Stratton, 1963. Pp. 74-81.

MAY, R., *et al.* (Eds.) *Existence: a new dimension in psychiatry and psychology.* New York: Basic Books, 1958.

MERKIN, M., & HOGAN, E. M. Chlorpromazine (thorazine) "light exhaustion" in adolescents. *Amer. J. Psychiat.,* 1960, 116, 926.

MERLIS, S., & TURNER, W. J. Drug evaluation and practical psychiatric therapeutics. *J. Amer. med. Ass.,* 1961, 177, 38-42.

MEYER, A. *The commonsense psychiatry of Dr. Adolf Meyer.* A. Lief (Ed.) New York: McGraw-Hill Book Co., 1948.

MILLER, G. A., GALANTER, E., & PRIBRAM, K. H. *Plans and the structure of behavior.* New York: Holt, Rinehart & Winston, 1960.

MORENO, J. L. Psychodrama. In S. Arieti (Ed.), *American handbook of psychiatry.* Vol. II. New York: Basic Books, 1959. Pp. 1375-1396.

MORRISON, A. C. *Welfare and institutions code and laws relating to social welfare, State of California.* Sacramento, Calif.: Documents Section, Printing Division, 1963.

MOSS, C. S. Brief successful psychotherapy of a chronic phobic reaction. *J. abnorm. soc. Psychol.,* 1960, 60, 266-270.

MOSS, C. S., LOGAN, J. C., & LYNCH, DOROTHY. Present status of psychological research and training in hypnosis: a developing professional problem. *Amer. Psychologist,* 1962, 17, 542-549.

MURPHY, W. F., & WEINRUB, J. Problems in teaching short term psychotherapy. *Dis. nerv. System,* 1948, 9, 101-104. Reprinted by permission of Physicians Postgraduate Press.

National Association for Mental Health. *Directory 1961, outpatient psychiatric clinics and other mental health resources in the U. S. and territories.* New York: Author, 1962.

National Institute of Mental Health. *A manual on record-*

keeping and statistical reporting for mental health clinics. Washington, D. C.: U. S. Government Printing Office, 1957.

NORMAN, V. B., ROSEN, B. M., & BAHN, A. K. Psychiatric clinic outpatients in the United States, 1959. *Ment. Hyg.,* 1962, 46, 321-343.

NOYES, A. P., & KOLB, L. C. *Modern clinical psychiatry.* (6th ed.) Philadelphia: W. B. Saunders, 1963.

OLSON, G. W., & PETERSON, D. B. The development of intercurrent disease and injury in the tranquilized psychiatric patient. *Amer. J. Psychiat.,* 1959, 116, 459-460.

OLTMAN, JANE E., & FRIEDMAN, S. Comparison of marplan and tofranil in the treatment of depressive states. *Amer. J. Psychiat.,* 1961, 117, 929-930.

ORNE, M. T. Implications for psychotherapy derived from current research on the nature of hypnosis. *Amer. J. Psychiat.,* 1962, 118, 1097-1103.

OVERALL, J. E., HOLLISTER, L. E., POKORNY, A. D., CASEY, J. F., & KATZ, G. Drug therapy in depressions. Controlled evaluation of imipramine, isocarboxazide, dextroamphetamine-amobarbital, and placebo. *Clin. Pharmacol. Therapeut.,* 1962, 3, 16-22.

PASTER, S., & HOLTZMAN, S. A study of 1000 psychotic veterans treated with insulin and electric shock therapy. *Ann. Rep.,* 1947, VAMTG, Kennedy Hospital, Memphis, Tennessee.

PENNINGTON, VERONICA M. Combined psychopharmaceutical treatment in 460 neuropsychiatric patients. *Amer. J. Psychiat.,* 1962, 118, 935-937.

PERVIN, L. A. Existentialism, psychology, and psychotherapy. *Amer. Psychologist,* 1960, 15, 305-309.

PHILLIPS, E. L. *Psychotherapy. A modern theory and practice.* New York: Prentice-Hall, 1956.

POST, F. The impact of modern drug treatment on old age schizophrenia. *Gerontol. Clin.,* 1962, 4, 137-146.

PRESSMAN, M. D., & WEISS, L. B. Experiences with Elavil: treatment of fifty-one cases of depression. *Amer. J. Psychiat.,* 1961, 118, 74-75.

RACHMAN, S. The treatment of anxiety and phobic reactions by systematic desensitization psychotherapy. *J. abnorm. soc. Psychol.,* 1959, 58, 259-263.

RAPAPORT, R. N. Principles for developing a therapeutic community. In J. Masserman (Ed.), *Current psychiatric therapies,* 1963. New York: Grune & Stratton, 1963. Pp. 244-256.

RAYMOND, M. J. Case of fetishism treated by aversion therapy. In H. J. Eysenck (Ed.), *Behaviour therapy and the neuroses.* London: Pergamon Press, 1960.

ROGERS, C. *Counseling and psychotherapy.* New York: Grune & Stratton, 1942.

ROGERS, C. *Client-centered therapy.* Boston: Houghton Mifflin, 1951.

ROGERS, C. A theory of therapy, personality, and interpersonal relationships, as developed in the client-centered framework. In S. Koch (Ed.), *Psychology: a study of a science.* Vol. III. *Formulations of the person and the social center.* New York: McGraw-Hill, 1959. Pp. 184-258.

ROGERS, C. R. *On becoming a person: a client's view of psychotherapy.* Boston: Houghton Mifflin, 1961.

RUESCH, J., BRODSKY, C., & FISCHER, A. The acute nervous breakdown. *Arch. gen. Psychiat.,* 1963, 8, 197-207.

SAKEL, M. A new treatment of schizophrenia. *Amer. J. Psychiat.,* 1937, 93, 829.

SARGANT, W. The physical treatment of depression: their indications and proper use. *J. Neuropsychiat.,* 1961, 2 (Suppl. 1), 1-10.

SARTRE, J. P. *Existential psychoanalysis.* Hazel E. Barnes (Tr.) New York: Philosophical Library, 1953.

SHOR, R. E. Three dimensions of hypnotic depth. *Int. J. clin. exp. Hypnosis,* 1962, 10 (1), 23-38.

SMITH, C. M. A new adjunct to the treatment of alcoholism: the hallucinogenic drugs. *Quart. J. Stud. Alcohol,* 1958, 19, 406-417.

SNYDER, W. U. *Dependency in psychotherapy.* New York: Macmillan, 1963.

SULLIVAN, H. S. In Helen S. Perry, & Mary L. Gawel (Eds.), *The interpersonal theory of psychiatry.* New York: Norton, 1953.

SULLIVAN, H. S. In Helen S. Perry, et al. (Eds.), *Clinical studies in psychiatry.* New York: Norton, 1956.

SUNDBERG, N. D., & TYLER, LEONA E. *Clinical psychology.* New York: Appleton-Century-Crofts, 1962.

SUTCLIFFE, J. P. "Credulous" and "skeptical" views of hypnotic phenomena: experiments on esthesia, hallucination, and delusion. *J. abnorm. soc. Psychol.,* 1961, 62, 189-200.

TILLICH, P. *Courage to be.* New Haven: Yale Univer. Press, 1952.

WATKINS, J. G. Psychotherapy: an overview. In L. A. Pennington & I. A. Berg (Eds.), *An introduction to clinical psychology* (2nd ed.). New York: Ronald, 1954. Pp. 483-501.

WATKINS, J. G. *General psychotherapy; an outline and study guide.* Springfield, Ill.: Charles C. Thomas, 1960.

WATT, D. C. The effect of reserpine on the duration of manic attacks. *J. Neurol. Neurosurg. Psychiat.,* 1958, 21, 297-300.

WECHSLER, H. Transitional residences for former mental patients: a survey of halfway houses and related rehabilitation facilities. *Ment. Hyg.,* 1961, 45, 65-76.

WINKELMAN, N. W., JR. An appraisal of chlorpromazine. *Amer. J Psychiat.,* 1957, 113, 961-971.

WITTENBORN, J. R., PLANTE, M., BURGESS, F., & LIVERMORE, N. The efficacy of electroconvulsive therapy, iproniazid and placebo in the treatment of young depressed women. *J. nerv. ment. Dis.,* 1961, 133, 316-332.

WOLBERG, L. R. *Hypnoanalysis.* New York: Grune & Stratton, 1945.

WOLBERG, L. R. *Technique of psychotherapy.* New York: Grune & Stratton, 1954.

WOLF, A., & SCHWARTZ, E. K. *Psychoanalysis in groups.* New York: Grune & Stratton, 1962.

WOLPE, J. *Psychotherapy by reciprocal inhibition.* Stanford: Stanford Univer. Press, 1958.

WOLPE, J. Reciprocal inhibition as the main basis of psychotherapeutic effects. In H. J. Eysenck (Ed.), *Behaviour therapy and the neuroses.* London: Pergamon Press, 1960. Pp. 88-113.

WOLPE, J. The systematic desensitization treatment of neuroses. *J. nerv. ment. Dis.,* 1961, 132, 189-203.

WOODS, L. W., & LEWIS, D. J. Use of phenelzine (Nardil) in a general hospital setting. *Canad. med. Ass. J.,* 1961, 84, 212-213.

WORTIS, J. Physiological treatment. *Amer. J. Psychiat.,* 1961a, 117, 595-600.

WORTIS, J. A psychiatric study tour of the U.S.S.R. *J. ment. Sci.,* 1961b, 107, 119-156.

WORTIS, J. Psychopharmacology and physiological treatment. *Amer. J. Psychiat.,* 1964, 120, 643-648.

WORTIS, J. Physiological treatment. *Amer. J. Psychiat.,* 1962, 118, 595-599.

WORTIS, J. Psychopharmacology and physiological treatment. *Amer. J. Psychiat.,* 1963, 119, 621-626.

ACTION
FOR MENTAL
HEALTH

chapter 15

PERSPECTIVES ON PREVENTION

ORGANIZED EFFORTS FOR MENTAL HEALTH
   IN THE UNITED STATES

INTERNATIONAL MEASURES FOR MENTAL HEALTH

THE PRESENT ROLE OF PSYCHIATRY

THE INDIVIDUAL'S CONTRIBUTION

As modern psychiatry has become an established and sophisticated clinical science, it has directed its efforts toward prevention as well as understanding, diagnosis, and treatment.[1] Just as medical science has developed vaccines and antitoxins to prevent smallpox and diphtheria, so modern psychiatry is attempting to formulate principles that can help us to ensure mental health.

What we have said of the causation of abnormal behavior has, of course, direct implications for its prevention. Conditions known to play a part in psychopathology must be alleviated. We know, for example, that specific metabolic deficiencies underlie certain types of mental retardation, some of which can be detected and corrected before serious brain damage has occurred. Unfortunately, we lack sufficient knowledge concerning the etiology of the functional psychoses and certain other mental disorders to be equally positive and specific in preventing them.

[1]The term *psychiatry* is used in this chapter not to denote a medical specialty but more broadly as a term embracing insights and procedures from three essential fields: the biological sciences, clinical and experimental psychology, and the social-sociological sciences.

In this, our final chapter, we shall examine the possibilities for preventing mental disorders, the nature and scope of organized efforts for mental health (including both treatment and prevention), and the contribution which the individual can make to the overall effort to alleviate and eventually prevent the ravages of mental illness.

Perspectives on Prevention

In the prevention of mental illness we are confronted with two key tasks: (a) to seek out and eradicate the causes of mental disorders, and (b) to establish conditions which foster positive mental health. Preventive measures thus run the gamut from programs directed toward specific and known causal agents to programs aimed at more general social advances.

Since etiological factors have been examined in Chapter 4 and in our subsequent discussion of specific disorders, we shall not focus on them here. Rather, we shall be concerned with measures which appear conducive to mental health —in the light of what we now know about personality, stress, and adjustive reactions.

BIOLOGICAL PREVENTIVE MEASURES

Proposed biological preventive measures have usually involved two rather different approaches: (a) emphasis on adequate maternity services— including prenatal care—and the later physical health of the individual, and (b) attempts to manipulate genetic factors so as to get a healthier individual to start with.

General health measures. The importance of adequate maternity services—including a continuity of medical service from the time of conception—has received increasing emphasis as a preventive measure. This includes adequate obstetric service and follow-up care. Preparation of the mother and father for parenthood is also important: childbirth usually has a great deal of emotional significance to both parents, and there may be psychological as well as medical problems. Sometimes pregnancy and childbirth disturb family equilibrium or complicate an already disturbed situation. Unfavorable factors in the life situation may need to be changed if the home setting is to foster healthy family relations and provide a supportive environment for both children and parents.

Clearly, it is important to maintain our optimal physical vigor and health as a means of increasing resistance to all types of stress. Increasing importance is being placed on periodic medical examinations throughout life to insure the early detection of organic pathology.

In the course of our discussion of mental disorders we have emphasized the importance of tranquilizing and energizing drugs in the treatment of mental disorders. In many instances, these drugs can also be of preventive value in helping the individual through difficult stress periods or in halting or reversing actual personality decompensation. Again it may be emphasized that psychotherapy and sociotherapy should ordinarily accompany drug therapy if underlying etiological factors are to be effectively dealt with and the patient helped to a better long-range adjustment.

The emerging role of genetics. For many years there have been advocates of eugenic measures to prevent the birth of children to parents with allegedly adverse hereditary make-up. Some states have legalized the sterilization of the mentally retarded, and the advocates of controlled breeding would like to see such measures extended to antisocial personalities, schizophrenics, and individuals with other types of mental disorders. Certainly it is reasonable to emphasize the importance of good heredity and a good start in life. For the future of the species there are possible advantages in exercising some control over who provides society with the bulk of its children. Unfortunately, however, the role of heredity in schizophrenia, character disorders, and the neuroses is so poorly defined that the value of applying genetic regulations would be extremely questionable except on the grounds that individuals with such disorders would probably not be most highly qualified for rearing children. In addition, the moral problems involved in attempts on the part of society to determine who is and who is not qualified to have children are, of course, tremendous.

With the recent breakthroughs in modern genetics, which we have described in Chapter 4, it has been possible to show the role of chromosomal aberrations in a wide range of congenital malformations and hereditary diseases as well as certain types of mental retardation. As we have noted, it is now possible to make a "chromosomal map" for a prospective parent which is useful in predicting the likelihood of certain types of organic pathology in his offspring. Although such maps are not useful for predicting nonorganic mental disorders, they nevertheless represent an important step in the direction of genetic preventive measures.

The development of techniques for studying the actual structure of the genes which make up the chromosomes has opened new vistas in prevention. For by learning the molecular structure of each gene, it will become possible to distinguish between normal and mutant genes. This information can then be used to delineate the role of mutant genes in many diseases, and the present controversy over the role of genetic factors in various types of mental disorders will be resolved. And with the deciphering of the genetic code, it may eventually even become possible for man to correct faulty genes, thus providing him with fantastic new power to correct and prevent hereditary pathology.

PSYCHOLOGICAL PREVENTIVE MEASURES

We have defined normality as the optimal development and functioning of the individual consistent with the long-term well-being and progress of the group. From the standpoint of preventing abnormal behavior, this definition implies the development of adequate, well-integrated persons who have sound attitudes and values and a high degree of stress tolerance.

Psychological preventive measures involve assistance during crucial stress periods in the individual's life as well as the fostering of healthy personality development. Here we may reiterate the importance of meeting basic psychological needs. The person who is least vulnerable to stress is the one who feels—and is—basically adequate, who has deep feelings of belonging and relatedness, and who sees hope and meaning in his life.

Healthy personality development. Ideas about child-rearing have changed greatly in recent years, but there appears to be general agreement with respect to the following measures for preventing faulty psychological development among infants and preschool children: (a) an uninterrupted relation with a responsive, empathic mother or her substitute, (b) flexibility in feeding schedules, toilet training, and lessons in social living, (c) freedom commensurate with maturity such that necessary limits are set on behavior but undue restrictions are not placed on reality testing, (d) consistent guidance and support, including desirable adult models for the child and extra support during crucial periods, and (e) most important, a loving atmosphere in which the child is respected as an individual and made to feel that he is an important member of the group but no more important than others.

Throughout this volume we have seen repeatedly what a large part faulty parent-child relationships and pathogenic patterns of family interaction can play in the development of abnormal behavior; thus one of our most essential tasks for psychological prevention is parent education. Partly, of course, this will mean supplying information about children's needs and developmental patterns, but information is only the first step. Parents have their own needs and limitations, and in many cases the pathogenic family patterns they establish are a reflection not of ignorance but of their own insecurities, tensions, hostilities, and other difficulties. Parent education will thus often involve parent and family counseling to foster the establishment of a climate in the home which is conducive to the mental health of all family members.

Although healthy development during infancy and childhood goes far to ensure later mental health, it is not a lifetime guarantee. Difficulties can and often do arise during the later periods of adolescence, adulthood, and old age. We have already dealt with the vicissitudes of these life periods and need not elaborate upon them here except to point out that during childhood and adolescence, the school plays a crucial role in the continued personality development of the individuals entrusted to its care. It cannot claim to have responsibility for only intellectual development because it cannot help but influence many other facets of the child's development whether it wishes to or not. It can only try to make its influence a constructive one.

Development of essential competencies. We have noted that the failure to achieve adequate emotional, social, and intellectual competencies is an important factor in the etiology of mental disorders. Since competence in learning, problem solving, and decision making are usually well covered in elementary psychology texts, we shall limit our present discussion to a brief review of emotional and social competencies.

One of the most vital dimensions of personal experience is the emotional or affective dimension. In the course of our everyday activities we all are likely to experience fear, joy, sadness, anger, and anxiety. Each one of us has developed a characteristic pattern of emotional reactivity that is an important part of his life style and may contribute to or detract from his mental health and effectiveness. In the present context, we can do little more than point to some of the key components of emotional competence.

1. *Adequate depth of feeling.* Some people apparently experience a great depth of feeling, reacting to the ups and downs of living with intense emotion. Others seem to be insulated from any strong feelings. Although wide differences in emotional feelings are evidently within a normal range, emotional competence would appear to require a sufficient depth of feeling to insure vigorous participation in living.

2. *Adequate expression and control.* Some people's emotional reactions are out of proportion to the situation with the result that they squander their resources on trivial events. Others hold such a tight rein on their emotions that they give no direct or overt expression to their feelings; sometimes they are afraid of such feelings and cannot even acknowledge having them. Emotional competence requires both the ability to express emotions in spontaneous and appropriate ways and the ability to control emotional expression according to the requirements of the situation.

3. *Ability to function with emotions.* Al-though adequate preparation for stressful situations can do much to allay destructive emotions, fear and other negative emotions are normal in certain situations. Rather than try to repress or fight such feelings, it is often important to function adequately despite them. Thus the brave soldier is not the one who experiences no fear, but the one who carries out his duties despite his fear.

4. *Ability to cope with problem emotions.* Fear, anxiety, hostility, grief, and love are problem emotions. Fear often paralyzes constructive action; hostility frequently leads to strong guilt feelings or to aggressive or defensive acts that only make the situation worse; love involves a calculated risk which some people find difficult to accept. Therefore, it is important to understand the nature and normal role of such emotions in our behavior and prevent them from disrupting our long-range purposes.

5. *Encouragement of positive emotions.* Positive emotions such as love and humor are highly constructive influences in our lives, while negative emotions such as fear and anger are potentially destructive influences. As we have seen, this does not mean that fear and anger have no role in normal behavior, but only that positive emotions should predominate. This is important at any life period but especially during the developmental years.

To a large extent, the satisfactions we gain in living depend upon the types of interpersonal relationships that we are able to establish— particularly with the significant people in our lives. Success in attracting a desired mate, achieving a happy marriage, gaining occupational advancement, and making lasting friends depends heavily upon our social competence. We lack adequate scientific knowledge of the factors involved in social competence, but the following appear to be important:

1. *A recognition of mutual rights, needs, and responsibilities.* Perhaps the first step in developing good interpersonal relationships is the recognition that they are *inter*relationships involving mutual rights, needs, and responsibilities. A mutually satisfying relationship is not consistent with trying to "influence" or "manipulate" others in order to meet one's own needs at their expense.

2. *An understanding of self and others.*

Often people have an erroneous view of their own "stimulus value." A man may see himself as a witty conversationalist, while others think he dwells on trivialities and talks too much. Perception of others is equally crucial. A man who views others as basically stupid, selfish, and dishonest is likely to have difficulty in establishing satisfactory relationships with them.

3. *Adequate structuring.* Personal relationships, especially close ones, need to be defined clearly in terms of limits, responsibilities, and roles. For example, a young engaged couple face the problem of structuring in terms of permissible limits of affection, of behavior with other members of the opposite sex, of honesty in their dealings with each other, and of mutual effort in maintaining their relationship. If they have different expectations and standards as to their roles and responsibilities, they will soon find themselves in conflict. If a relationship is not structured consciously, by mutual understanding, its structure will develop by chance and may not turn out to be what either party would wish.

4. *Common purposes.* It is difficult or impossible to establish satisfactory relationships with others if one's goals or purposes are in conflict with theirs. This is often apparent in unhappy marriages, where the marital partners disagree about having children or about their basic goals and values. Often interpersonal relationships can be improved by exploring areas where there is commonality of purpose rather than concentrating on the conflicting goals and interests.

5. *Accepting the other person while disapproving what he does.* Accepting another person does not mean approving of everything he does. For example, in dealing with a child who has stolen something, it is important to make it clear that he still is accepted and respected as a person even though this particular kind of behavior has to stop. Often a similar attitude is of value in dealing with adults.

6. *Personal integrity.* It is important to be sensitive to the needs of others and to the requirements of given situations in order to avoid unnecessary friction, but it is equally important to deal honestly with others and to take a stand on issues one feels are important. It is unlikely that good interpersonal relationships can be established by means of deceit or by the sacrifice of one's own values.

7. *Expression of praise and appreciation.* Everyone likes to receive sincere praise and appreciation and to feel approved by others. Being praised tends to produce positive feelings toward others and motivation toward increased effort, whereas being criticized is likely to induce discouragement, hostility, and defensiveness.

Marital and occupational adjustments.   One of the life adjustments which is often a crucial influence on the mental health of the individual is that of marriage. A compatible marriage is based upon the meaningful sharing of experiences and the formation of deep emotional bonds. Such a marriage helps both partners to feel adequate, wanted, needed, socially approved, secure, and complete—to a degree which cannot be achieved in any other human relationship. Where a compatible marriage is made even more meaningful and worth while through children, a strong family unit is built which contributes to the parents' sense of accomplishment and satisfaction in living.

Unfortunately, many modern marriages are contracted without adequate preparation and lead to bitterness, disillusionment, and unhappiness. One out of every four marriages ends in divorce; of the marriages that endure, it is estimated that one out of three continues in the face of deep frustration and dissatisfaction. Such statistics indicate situations in which a potential bulwark against mental disorder has become a source of stress and self-devaluation. As we have noted, the children in these families experience emotional trauma and instability instead of a secure, loving home base and suffer also through divided loyalties and a lack of adequate models.

A number of studies have emphasized the following factors in unhappy marriages: (a) emotional immaturity of either or both partners, with unrealistic and often "idealistic" attitudes toward marriage and little conception of its duties and responsibilities, (b) incompatability due to differences in age, intelligence, religion, values, and other factors, (c) lack of common goals and purposes relating to such matters as having children, what money should be spent for, and leisure time activities, (d) sexual incompatibility, often resulting from a lack of either emotional closeness or physical attraction, and (e) adverse environmental factors such as interfering in-laws and substandard living conditions.

Although there are no prior guarantees for a happy marriage, the following factors have been found to be important in preventing marital maladjustment and divorce: (a) specific preparation for marriage in terms of mutual understanding of the duties and functions of each member, as well as agreement on basic values and purposes; (b) a determination by both marital partners to make marriage work despite obstacles, and (c) early psychological attention to a marriage which is "sick" or a marital partner with serious personality problems. Where such services are available, premarital counseling may be of great value in helping engaged couples plan for their marriage and anticipate the difficulties they are likely to encounter.

Since we have discussed the importance of unemployment and occupational dissatisfaction in Chapter 4, we will not elaborate here on these sources of stress. Freedom from serious economic worry, a sense of self-respect and accomplishment, hope for the future—all of these underlie happy family life and all depend upon a healthy occupational adjustment.

Support during crucial stress periods. At one time or another most of us have to face highly stressful situations—perhaps a divorce, the death of a loved one, unfairness or deceit by someone we have trusted, loss of employment, or a serious operation. During such periods the emotional support of family members and perhaps trained outsiders can be of crucial importance in preventing a breakdown.

Additional emotional support is often particularly important during childhood. The World Health Organization has pointed out, for example, that the emotional trauma a child may suffer from hospitalization can cause more harm than is generally realized (1962). A WHO Study Group has agreed that if possible a sick child should not have the anxieties of separation from his family added to those of physical illness. Often the child has little conception of time and can readily feel that he has been abandoned. When hospitalization is necessary, the mother should try to remain with the child in the hospital at least for a period and ideally during the child's entire stay.

Many times during the course of growing up a child needs extra emotional support to help him over hurdles. We have previously noted that the most common problem of children attending mental health clinics involves transient situational reactions to special stresses.

Adults as well as children need support during critical stress periods. The deep trauma of an unwanted divorce, for example, is a crushing experience for many adults. In therapy many divorced people describe their feelings as "the crumbling of their whole world." Psychiatric assistance during such a critical period can do much to help the individual work through the experience without being completely overwhelmed by it. And when he has reached a point in the process of recovery where he realizes that life must go on and that he must rebuild again, psychiatric assistance may keep him from a "marriage on the rebound" and also help him learn to be a more adequate mate later in a new marriage.

Extra emotional support is often important in dealing with less stressful events also—particularly when such events represent "the final straw" to the person involved. Even minor setbacks may be extremely upsetting to an individual who is already deeply worried and discouraged about other problems.

Support during critical periods may also take the form of supplying missing ingredients needed for normal development. For example, members of the Big Brothers of America help many boys who are without a father. Such boys badly need the companionship, guidance, and supervision of a mature male during their formative years. Working under supervision, a member acts as a "semi-foster" father—taking the boy to sports events and working with him in various constructive activities. To ensure continuity, such "big brother" relationships are maintained over a period of time.

The importance of values and meaning. The statement that "man does not live by bread alone" is generally accepted in our society. It is not always easy, however, to find this "something more" than bread in the midst of so much world conflict and rapid social change. Many people, unable to find any enduring faith, conclude that life is ultimately futile and meaningless. They find themselves living in this age of anxiety without any values in which they have faith or any unifying philosophy of life. The inability to find such values and meanings provides a fertile ground for mental disorders.

Although different persons find meaning and reward in different areas of life—some in family life, some in social service, some in intellectual or professional work—there are certain basic assumptions that mentally healthy people seem to hold in common. Listed below are some of the values widely held by rational and healthy people in our own society. We are not arguing here for the universality—or even the validity—of these assumptions. We are merely pointing out that, in our society at least, they seem to be closely connected with mental health and social usefulness.

1. A belief in the importance and worth of each individual.

2. A belief that social progress is both possible and worth while.

3. A belief in the value of the "truth" that we try to approach by means of modern scientific techniques, and in its usefulness for social progress.

4. A belief that democracy, with its respect for the individual, provides the most congenial atmosphere for the pursuit of truth as well as for the happiness and progress of both the individual and the group.

5. An acceptance of individual responsibility for carrying forward the social progress made by preceding generations.

6. A belief in mankind as a functional part of the universe, with potentialities for evolution that can be fulfilled.

7. A belief that brotherly love and other fundamental tenets of Christianity and other great religious philosophies are not only compatible with an effective modern, democratic society but actually indispensable to it.

Such beliefs, if actually operative in a person's life and not just a set of intellectual principles, provide a basic value orientation which pervades his relationships and activities and makes him feel a significant part of the human enterprise. They give his life direction and momentum; he is not easily overwhelmed by the stresses of living. This basic value orientation, of course, is filled in and expanded by the emotional and intellectual experiences of the individual.

SOCIOLOGICAL PREVENTIVE MEASURES

As we have come to realize more clearly the importance of "social pathology" in the production of abnormal behavior in individuals, increasing attention has been focused on sociological preventive measures. In such measures, in essence, "society itself is the patient."

Although certain broad sociological preventive measures are being undertaken—such as the provision of housing projects to eradicate slums, the expansion of community-based mental health facilities, and urban planning to meet better the needs of residents—the current emphasis is on research directed toward a better understanding of the sociological causes of mental disorders. The research now under way on local, national, and international levels offers hope that someday we shall be able to pinpoint and correct the sociological causes of mental disorder much as we can now pinpoint and correct the poor sanitary conditions that lead to epidemics. Two types of programs on the sociological level are of immediate interest.

Epidemiology. Study of the incidence, distribution, and etiology of disease in a community is referred to as *epidemiology*.[1] Science has found that most contagious physical diseases can be brought under control once their distribution and modes of communication in the community are discovered. In Chapter 11 we noted an instance of an epidemiological approach in which the incidence and communication of syphilis in a major urban area were studied by tracing the sexual contacts of patients obtaining treatment for syphilis. Epidemiological studies are also helping to bring to light many of the factors involved in mental disorders.

1. *Research on the incidence and distribution of mental disorders.* The incidence and distribution of mental disorders in our society have not yet been thoroughly studied. We have noted several studies of the survey or "ecological" type in which the patterns of abnormal behavior have been described with respect to the geographical areas of large cities. We have also mentioned studies based upon draft and Armed Forces data and census statistics, as well as

---

[1] A description of the scope of epidemiology in psychiatry is to be found in the *WHO Chronicle* (1963).

studies indicating that both type and amount of abnormal behavior vary with socioeconomic level. These studies have revealed much interesting and valuable information. For example, as we saw in Chapter 8, Jaco's comprehensive study of psychotic disorders in Texas (1960) revealed a very high incidence of schizophrenia and other functional psychoses among women in professional and semiprofessinoal occupations. Similarly, studies based on Selective Service data have shown an increasing incidence of mental disorders from higher socioeconomic levels to lower ones, a finding which has also been supported by surveys of mental disorders in major urban centers (Srole *et al.*, 1962).

Although such findings do not indicate much about the origin of mental disorders, they do help identify "trouble spots" where research and preventive action should be concentrated.

2. *Research on the social origins of abnormal behavior.* Many studies have demonstrated the influence of the social setting on the content and orientation of personality development. Studies of widely differing cultures have shown that characteristic personality configurations often develop in a given society, or in subgroups within a society (such as social class and ethnic subgroups) and that such basic configurations differ from one society to another. For example, in one society a paranoid suspiciousness may be a common characteristic; in another a self-effacing noncompetitiveness may be typical; in still another, the common pattern may be passivity with occasional violent outbursts.

Similar study of various relatively homogeneous subgroups in our own society has also been revealing. Here we may again mention the study of Eaton and Weil (1955) of 8000 Hutterites living in 70 collective settlements in the United States and Canada. In these communal groups property is held in common and community life is highly social: the members not only work together but eat together in community dining rooms. This religious group encourages the submission of the individual to community standards and expectations and emphasizes the principles of personal responsibility, guilt, and nonviolence. Under excessive stress, the members of these Hutterite communities are four times as likely to develop depressive reactions as they are to develop schizophrenia.

Currently, epidemiological studies are in process or being planned to deal with the psychological effects of such problems as (a) modern technology and increasing automation in our own society, (b) the stress and anxiety resulting from helplessness against the threat of nuclear war, (c) the world "population explosion," and (d) the major social and cultural changes among peoples who are experiencing new political independence and rapid industrialization. With respect to the effects of rapid social change, the following statement from the *WHO Chronicle* is relevant.

"Societies have a threshold of tolerance for rate of change which, if exceeded, must lead to some measure of social disorganization. Past experience has shown how great an effect industrial and technological changes may have on mental health, through their impact on family life and their disruption of old patterns of living. In this field, the immediate task is to find out more about the effects, prevention and control of social disintegration, and the reactions of individuals and groups to rapidly changing circumstances." (1962, pp. 176)

3. *Evaluative research.* Many of our procedures have grown up pragmatically and been continued from habit and inertia. If the effort that is put into the treatment and prevention of mental disorders is to be maximally effective, we need continual research evaluation of current practice. As already indicated, this must include research on possible unwanted side-effects of treatments and long-term as well as short-term evaluation of results.

Similarly, research evaluation of the mental health programs carried on by public and private organizations—nationally and locally—would provide guidelines for increased efficiency in the use of mental health resources. The same is true for the work of clinical psychologists and psychiatrists in private practice.

The planning of preventive measures. In the twentieth century, responsibility for planning preventive measures falls increasingly on our social institutions. Gone is the relative self-sufficiency of a hundred years ago and with it the old idea that each individual should be able singlehandedly to make a successful adjustment to life. With our greater interdependency has come greater mutual responsibility for each

PRESENT RESEARCH AND SERVICE PROGRAM OF THE NATIONAL INSTITUTE OF MENTAL HEALTH

Research

Research on all phases of mental illness is carried on by the National Institute of Mental Health at (a) the Public Health Service Clinical Center in Bethesda, Maryland; (b) the William A. White Pavilion in Washington, D.C., operated jointly by the Institute and Saint Elizabeth's Hospital; and (c) the Institute's Addiction Research Center at the Public Health Service Hospital, Lexington, Kentucky. In addition to its broad program of clinical investigation and laboratory research, the Institute plans and conducts biostatistical studies of mental illness and awards research grants to independent investigators. It has also established (a) a Psychopharmacology Research Center, (b) a system of research fellowships and research career awards, and (c) a series of grants for the construction of research facilities.

Training

The Training Branch program makes teaching grants to universities and training centers for the purpose of expanding existing training programs and developing new ones. It awards trainee stipends in psychiatry, psychology, social work, psychiatric nursing, and community mental health to qualified graduate students selected by universities and other training centers. Grants are also given to schools of medicine, public health, and nursing to help them augment the mental health content of their curricula. Relatively new programs of support include those for (a) developing interdisciplinary mental health training, (b) training biological and social scientists in aspects of mental illness, (c) training mental health personnel in research techniques or social science skills; and (d) giving psychiatric training to general practitioners. On a pilot basis, the Training Branch has supported a program to give appropriate psychiatric information to ministers, lawyers, teachers, and other professional groups.

Community services

Grants-in-aid are made to states and territories for the development of state and local mental health programs. Money is allocated on the basis of population, extent of the problem, and financial need, but every dollar of federal funds must be matched with a dollar of state and local funds. The responsibility for receiving and administering the federal grants is vested in an agency designated by the state as its "mental health authority." In addition, the Community Services Branch of the Institute and mental health consultants in the regional offices of the Department of Health, Education, and Welfare provide state mental health and mental hospital authorities with professional and technical assistance in the form of consultation, surveys of a state's mental health problems, conferences, and help in setting up demonstration projects to try out and evaluate new mental health techniques. A new service, established in 1956, is the provision of support through mental health project grants, which are given for experiments, demonstrations, experimental studies, or administrative research that might lead to better methods of caring for, treating, and rehabilitating the mentally ill.

Program development

Finding new techniques for studying and attacking mental health problems not yet explored is primarily the work of the Professional Services Branch; its proposals are then integrated into the Institute's operating program.

Public education

A broad educational program, utilizing all the communications media, is carried out by the Publications and Reports Section of the Institute.

Chart based on material from U.S. Public Health Service (1960, 1962).

other's welfare and greater need for careful joint planning in the best interests of all. An intelligent society will take all possible steps to establish a general sociocultural climate which not only permits healthy personality growth and functioning but is actively conducive to it. In the next section we will examine the various organized efforts now being made in this direction.

Organized Efforts For Mental Health in the United States

With increasing public awareness of the magnitude and severity of our contemporary mental health problem, a large number of governmental, professional, and lay organizations have begun a concerted attack on mental disorders —directed toward better understanding, more effective treatment, and long-term prevention.

THE GOVERNMENT AND MENTAL HEALTH

The care of the mentally ill traditionally has been—and still is—primarily the responsibility of state and local agencies. Until recent years, in fact, the involvement of the federal government in the mental health field has been relatively slight. During World War II, however, the extent of mental disorders in the United States was illuminated by the large number of young men—two out of every seven recruits— who were rejected for military service for psychiatric reasons. Aware of the need for more research, training, and services in the field of mental health, Congress in 1946 passed its first comprehensive mental health bill, the *National Mental Health Act,* which laid the basis for the government's present mental health program.

Emergence of a national program. The Act of 1946 provided for the establishment of a National Institute of Mental Health (NIMH)— in or near Washington, D. C.—to serve as a central psychiatric research and training center and as headquarters for the administration of a grant-in-aid program. The grant-in-aid feature was designed to foster research and training elsewhere in the nation and to help state and local communities establish and improve their community mental health services. New powers were conferred on NIMH in 1956, when Congress, under Title V of the *Health Amendments Act,* authorized the Institute to provide support for "mental health project grants"—a term used to identify experimental studies, demonstrations, pilot projects, surveys, conferences, and research on techniques designed to improve methods of diagnosis, treatment, and aftercare of the mentally ill. The present program of the NIMH is outlined in the chart on page 620, although some changes are anticipated as a result of recent legislation. The method by which research grants are made is shown in the illustration on page 622.

The NIMH is one of several Institutes of Health established by the federal government, the latest of which is the National Institute of Child Health and Human Development, which was authorized by the 87th Congress (1961-3). This new institute has already embarked on its task of training medical, psychological, and other professional personnel and pursuing research into the causes of mental retardation and other mental disorders and the most effective ways of treating them.

Much of the work that the NIMH is doing is also complemented by that of other federal agencies. The Veterans Administration has long been a leader in the treatment of the mentally ill, has provided funds and facilities for the training of psychiatrists and clinical psychologists, and has pioneered programs for the more effective handling of mental patients. Other federal agencies which have effective programs in the mental health field are the Children's Bu-

HOW A RESEARCH GRANT IS MADE

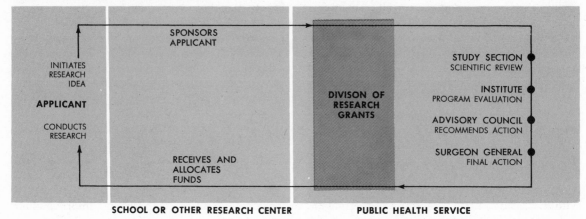

SPONSORS
APPLICANT

INITIATES
RESEARCH
IDEA

APPLICANT

CONDUCTS
RESEARCH

RECEIVES AND
ALLOCATES
FUNDS

DIVISON OF
RESEARCH
GRANTS

STUDY SECTION
SCIENTIFIC REVIEW

INSTITUTE
PROGRAM EVALUATION

ADVISORY COUNCIL
RECOMMENDS ACTION

SURGEON GENERAL
FINAL ACTION

SCHOOL OR OTHER RESEARCH CENTER   **PUBLIC HEALTH SERVICE**

Redrawn from U.S. Public Health Service (1960)

reau, the Office of Vocational Rehabilitation Administration, and the Department of Defense.

An event of national significance was the release of the final report of the Joint Commission on Mental Illness and Health (1961)[1] which had received from Congress in 1955 a mandate to survey resources and to make recommendations for combating mental illness in the United States. Some of its many findings and recommendations are shown in the chart on page 623. In February 1963 President Kennedy sent to Congress a special message relative to mental illness and mental retardation based in large part upon the recommendations made by the Joint Commission in which he outlined a national program for mental health and a related program to combat mental retardation (Kennedy, 1963). (The retardation program was mentioned in Chapter 12.) These recommendations are now being partially implemented.

A central concept in the new mental health program is that of comprehensive community care—the provision of local facilities for all aspects of mental health. Such provision makes possible a better understanding of the patient's needs in the context of his life situation, a more favorable atmosphere for his recovery, and a continuum of treatment services throughout all phases of his illness without the necessity for him to leave his own community for treatment in a different locality. It was the feeling of the Joint Commission that the first priority in the immediate future should be put on the treatment

of existing mental illness rather than on prevention, though it was anticipated that present preventive efforts would be continued and gradually expanded.

State and local programs. Although the federal government provides considerable leadership and financial aid for mental health purposes, actual state and local mental health programs are formulated and run by the states and localities themselves. The states establish, maintain, and supervise their own mental institutions, and some have set up separate departments of mental health. A number of states have also pioneered in the development of mental health clinics, in rehabilitation services for ex-patients in the community, and in the treatment of alcoholism, drug addiction, and other special mental health problems.

A recent trend has been the development of "Community Mental Health Services Acts," by which states provide grants-in-aids to localities for the development and expansion of local mental health services, including psychiatric clinics, rehabilitation services to ex-patients, and consultant services to schools, courts, and welfare agencies. The focus of service in these programs is the provision of facilities where the people who need them are located—in the local communities.

[1]The Joint Commission was composed of representatives from 31 medical, psychiatric, psychological, scientific, and related professional and voluntary organizations and 6 government agencies. Its membership also included 45 individuals interested in mental illness.

SUMMARY OF THE JOINT COMMISSION'S RECOMMENDATIONS

Pursuit of
new knowledge

Extension and expansion of present NIMH research grant program with emphasis on diversification, on basic as opposed to applied research, on long-term projects, on greater allocations for risk capital, on financial incentives for young scientists in mental health careers, on expansion of support of program research in established institutions, on help in establishing of new research centers, and on investment in new facilities for research where such facilities are lacking or in short supply.

Better use of
present knowledge
and experience

Manpower—a fuller utilization of volunteers and the partially trained, with a clear delineation of what jobs must be done by professionals and what jobs can be done by other personnel with consultation, guidance, or short-term or on-the-job training.

Community services for troubled people—more psychiatric training and consultation available for clergymen, physicians, pediatricians, teachers, probation workers, and others so that they can provide counseling before a serious breakdown occurs.

Immediate professional care at onset of a mental breakdown—professional psychiatric attention in the community and more flexible commitment laws, with voluntary admission preferred.

Intensive treatment for acutely ill mental patients—by fully trained professionals whether in community clinics, psychiatric units of general hospitals, or intensive psychiatric treatment centers, such as state-run community-based hospitals of less than 1000 beds. All new state hospital construction should be of these smaller intensive treatment centers. Major mental illness is regarded as the core problem and main unfinished business; it should have the first call on fully trained members of the mental health professions.

Care of chronic mental patients—those with chronic diseases, including mental illness, to be cared for in chronic disease centers—in many cases what are now the larger state mental hospitals.

Aftercare, intermediate care, and rehabilitation services—to be developed through many kinds of resources, including day and night hospitals, aftercare clinics, nursing services, foster-family care, convalescent homes, rehabilitation centers, work services, and ex-patient groups.

Costs

Expenditures for public mental patient services should be doubled in 5 years, tripled in 10. This will be possible only if the federal government carries a share of the cost of local and state services. Federal subsidies should encourage states to follow the example set by VA mental hospitals. Local responsibility would be fostered by the criteria such as the following, to be set for the awarding of federal grants: acknowledgment of responsibility for adequate treatment as well as custody and for treatment without hospitalization where indicated, acceptance of all who need treatment regardless of place of legal residence, differentiation of personnel required for intensive treatment centers and facilities for the chronically ill, operation of open mental health hospitals as mental health centers and as part of an integrated community service with emphasis on out-patient and aftercare as well as in-patient service. Training programs for all types of personnel would be encouraged; ultimately states should be required to spend 2.5 per cent of their mental patient service funds for such training and another 2.5 per cent for research.

The Joint Commission believes there should be greater recognition of the fact that mental illness, though resulting from natural causes like physical illness, does often arouse rejection, lack of sympathy, or outright revulsion. It recommends public education aimed at a clearer picture of what mental illness is, of its physiological, psychological, and social causes, and of the improved prospects of recovery or improvement.

PROFESSIONAL ORGANIZATIONS CONCERNED WITH MENTAL HEALTH

American Psychological Association (APA)	An association of professionally trained psychologists. Its purpose is to advance psychology as a science, as a profession, and as a means of promoting human welfare. It has 20 divisions concerned with various specialized interests within the field of psychology.
American Psychiatric Association (APA)	An association of medically trained psychiatrists. Its purpose is to further study of the nature, treatment, and prevention of mental disorders; to help set, improve, and maintain standards of practice and service in mental hospitals, clinics, general hospital psychiatric units, and institutions for the mentally retarded; to further psychiatric research and education; and to foster enlightened views with regard to the social and legal aspects of mental illness.
American Medical Association (AMA)	An association of those physicians who are members of constituent state medical associations. Its concern with mental illness as a general health problem led it to join with the American Psychiatric Association in urging Congress to authorize establishment of the Joint Commission on Mental Illness and Health. Its Council on Mental Health has developed a program designed to further the physician's knowledge of psychiatric principles and to encourage his participation in efforts to establish effective community mental health programs.
American Psychoanalytic Association (APA)	An association of analytically trained psychiatrists. It sets standards for the training of psychoanalysts, supervises and maintains standards in 17 training Institutes affiliated with the association, conducts research on the contribution that psychoanalysis can make to social problems and the prevention of mental illness.
American Association on Mental Deficiency (AAMD)	An interdisciplinary association of doctors, educators, administrators, social workers, psychologists, psychiatrists, and others interested in mental retardation. It works with the American Psychiatric Association in setting standards for hospitals and schools for the mentally retarded.
Group for the Advancement of Psychiatry (GAP)	An invitational association of limited membership (approximately 185 psychiatrists at any one time). Members are organized into small working-group committees for the purpose of studying and reporting on various aspects of psychiatry and on the applications of current knowledge. Its influential, action-directed reports are often developed through consultation and collaboration with experts from many other disciplines.
Association for the Advancement of Psychiatry (AAP)	An association of analytic and nonanalytic psychiatrists interested in exchanging views on psychotherapy and related fields. It sponsors seminars for advanced training and is especially interested in evaluating the results of psychotherapies.

Through the combination of federal grants with state funds, a wide range of vital mental health activities has been made possible. Surveys of mental health needs and facilities have been carried out. Psychiatric clinics have been expanded in number and scope and provisions made for needed increases in staff. Funds have been made available for research and for the evaluation of new approaches to mental health problems. Training grants have increased the number of professional personnel in psychiatry, clinical psychology, psychiatric social work, and related mental health areas. In addition, extensive educational campaigns have been conducted for the general public and for professional workers concerned with mental health.

American Orthopsychiatric Association (AOA)	An organization of psychiatrists, psychologists, social workers, sociologists, and members of other disciplines working in a collaborative approach to the study and treatment of human behavior, primarily in the clinical setting.
American Group Psychotherapy Association (AGPA)	An association of psychiatrists, psychologists, and psychiatric social workers. Its purpose is to advance group psychotherapy and to coordinate and clarify its theory and practice.
American Sociological Association	An association of sociologists, social scientists, and other professional persons interested in research, teaching, and application of sociology. Its sections on Social Psychology, Medical Sociology, and Criminology have special pertinence to mental health.
National Association of Social Workers (NASW)	An association of professionally trained social workers. Its purpose is to promote the quality and effectiveness of social work by setting standards, conducting research, improving professional education, and interpreting the field of social work to the community. Its special committees on Group Work, School Social Work, Psychiatric Social Work, and Community Organization are particularly pertinent to mental health and hospital programs.
American Occupational Therapy Association (AOTA)	A professional society of registered occupational therapists administering medically supervised activities to physically or mentally ill persons. It maintains standards of education and training, makes surveys and recommendations on request, and works with its state associations in the preparation and certification of occupational therapy volunteer assistants.
National Rehabilitation Association (NRA)	An association of physicians, counselors, therapists, and others (including organizations) concerned with rehabilitation of the physically and mentally handicapped. Reviews existing services and makes recommendations for improved rehabilitation programs.
American Nurses Association (ANA)	An association of registered professional nurses concerned with high standards of professional practice. Two of its clinical conference groups (one on Psychiatric Nursing Practice and one on Maternal and Child Health Nursing) have special mental health concerns. A Coordinating Council unites its program with that of the National League for Nursing, a voluntary organization of professional, semiprofessional, and lay persons and of institutions and organizations; the National League is the principal standard-setting group in the nursing field.

PROFESSIONAL AND VOLUNTARY MENTAL HEALTH ORGANIZATIONS

Much of the government's increasing interest and activity in the mental health field can be attributed to persistent urging by informed citizens and members of the mental health professions for the improvement of services to the mentally and emotionally ill. This urging is, indeed, one of the major activities of the various professional and voluntary mental health organizations, whose nationwide memberships and state and local divisions work, often against discouraging apathy, to advance the cause of mental health and stimulate action on behalf of the mentally ill.

The Role of Professional Organizations.
Largely responsible for the establishment of
high professional and ethical standards in the
various fields in or related to mental health are
the professional organizations of psychologists,
psychiatrists, and others who wish to advance
and improve their fields of specialization, to exchange information, and to further their own
various educational and service contributions.
Professional organizations in the mental health
field are of many types (the most important ones
are listed in the chart on pages 624-625). Some
are limited to persons in one field of specialization only; others are interdisciplinary. Some admit institutions and agencies to membership as
well as individuals. Some have open membership to all qualified personnel; others can be
joined only on invitation. Some have general
purposes; others perform a particular type of
service.

Despite their differences, these professional
organizations have certain elements in common.
They all hold periodic meetings, symposia,
workshops, refresher courses, etc. for the exchange of information, especially on new research and study in their fields. They all issue
publications (usually professional journals, but
sometimes special reports and monographs) as
a means of continuing the education of their
members and acquainting them (as well as members of other professional groups and sometimes
the general public) with recent trends and findings in their fields. And they all sponsor programs of public education as a means of advancing the interests of their professions, of drawing
attention to their professional undertakings, and
of attracting students to careers in their professional fields.

One of the most important functions of many
professional organizations, however, as already
suggested, is that of setting and maintaining
standards within their respective fields. These
functions may include (a) the establishment
and review of training qualifications for professional workers; (b) the setting of standards for
and the inspection and approval or accreditation of graduate and undergraduate training
programs; (c) standard-setting and approval
of service operations (such as the inspection
and accreditation of hospital, clinical or counseling programs), and (d) the holding of inquiries into cases of reported unethical or non-
professional conduct.

Composed as they are of trained and qualified
personnel only, professional mental health organizations are in a unique position to give technical advice on mental health facilities and programs not only on the national level (through
their national association) but also on the state
and local levels (through their state and local
subunits). Many have established legislative
services to advise their members of proposed
legislation affecting their interests and to work
toward improvement of mental health services.
Increasingly they are establishing closer liaison
with one another as well as with both government agencies and voluntary and service agencies concerned with mental health. Some of them
(the American Psychological Association and
the American Psychiatric Association, for instance) have established joint committees to
clarify their relations with each other, to work
toward greater interprofessional solidarity, and
to combine forces with one another on matters
of shared concern.

**The Role of the Voluntary Mental Health
Agency.** While the professional person and
organization can give expert technical advice in
regard to mental health needs and facilities, real
progress in improving services may lag unless an
informed and action-minded citizenry insists
upon a greater public and private investment
on behalf of mental health and the mentally ill.
In the health field generally, the main job of
stimulating such citizen support and getting
action falls to "voluntary health agencies," so-
called because they are made up of concerned
individuals—both lay and professional—who
have voluntarily associated for the specific purpose of advancing their cause. The voluntary
health agency is a uniquely American approach
to social progress and reform, and usually relies on popular donations. Besides appeals to
the public conscience through mass education
and informational activities, its program invariably consists of support to research, promotion
of services to the afflicted, and use of volunteers.
Of the many voluntary health agencies in the
United States, two are especially concerned with
mental disability: the National Association for
Mental Health (NAMH) and the National
Association for Retarded Children (NARC).

The best-known voluntary mental health agency—and the only such organization devoting itself exclusively to the fight against mental illness—is the National Association for Mental Health, formed in 1950 by the merger of the National Committee for Mental Hygiene, the National Mental Health Foundation, and the Psychiatric Foundation and further expanded in 1962 by its amalgamation with the National Organization for Mentally Ill Children. Through its national governing body and over 800 state and local affiliates, the NAMH works for the improvement of conditions and services in mental hospitals; helps to recruit, train, and place volunteers for service in hospital, rehabilitation, and aftercare programs; assists the returned patient in making a readjustment to the community; works for enlightened mental health legislation and new service facilities; encourages study of new methods for the care, treatment, and education of mentally ill children; helps the relatives and families of mentally ill persons to understand the patient and their role in his recovery; fosters the establishment of such community mental health services as psychiatric units in general hospitals, mental health clinics for children and adults, and counseling and guidance services in schools, business firms, and courts; provides information and referral services to individuals and community agencies; and conducts special educational programs and institutes.

In addition, the NAMH carries on two separate but related research programs: (a) it sponsors its own program of basic and applied research, and (b) it administers and cosponsors a special grant for research on schizophrenia. Its publications are aimed at helping people to recognize and understand mental illness, overcome their misconceptions and prejudice about mental illness, and achieve better mental health. It also carries on a special "Mental Health Careers Program" for students.

In many of its efforts, the NAMH works jointly with professional organizations and government agencies. It helps them sponsor the inspection and rating of mental hospitals and is concerned with current legislation and administrative practices. With the American Psychiatric Association it has formed a Joint Information Service for the provision of accurate scientific and statistical data; it is a cosponsor with NIMH of the annual Mental Health Week observed throughout the nation.

With a program and organization similar to that of the NAMH, the National Association for Retarded Children works to reduce the incidence of mental retardation; to seek community and residential treatment centers and services for the retarded; and to carry on a program of public education aimed at better citizen understanding of the problems of the retardate and citizen support for modern legislation on his behalf. It stimulates and fosters diverse scientific research into methods of diagnosis, evaluation, education, and rehabilitation, and works with professional and government organizations in helping to recruit and train professional workers and to encourage the development of sound programs of community action. On the local level, it is especially interested in forming groups of parents of retarded children, to help such parents understand, accept, and deal with their children's limited capabilities.

The New Role of the Mental Health Volunteer. The mental health movement has gained a great deal of strength from volunteer workers. They are, of course, the foundation and main support of the programs and services of mental health associations. But volunteers also perform a great many services to the mentally ill under other auspices, such as the Red Cross Gray Ladies, women's clubs, men's clubs, veterans' organizations, parent-teacher associations, and other civic-minded groups. Some groups, such as the League for Women Voters, have made major contributions by studying legislation dealing with mental health activities and conducting public educational programs on the issues involved. Others, such as the Council for Jewish Women, have been particularly active in helping to establish new facilities for treating or rehabilitating ex-mental patients. And still others have concentrated their help on providing personal services to both in-patients and out-patients of mental hospitals and clinics.

Once confined to performing relatively menial tasks in the hospital setting, the volunteer has recently taken on new "professionalized" duties. With special training, volunteers are now making many kinds of contributions to the hospitals' activities programs: they give bridge or chess

Student volunteers who go regularly each week to work, play, or talk with mental patients can form continuing relationships with lonely patients that can be of value to all concerned. The volunteer shown here is one of a group of six who worked over several months to prepare long-term patients for leaving the hospital by introducing them to noninstitutional activities. There was a 94 per cent discharge rate among the patients worked with by this group of volunteers.

lessons to patients, conduct garden club projects, put on social events, help with patient music or drama groups, hold good grooming classes and patient fashion shows, and conduct patient art exhibits. Besides the direct help they give to the patients, the volunteers provide both the hospital and its patients with important ties to the community and the "outside" world. In addition, the volunteers play a highly important role in interpreting the institution and its program to the public.

With the shortage of psychiatrists and other professional personnel in the mental health field, volunteers have quite recently been cast into a new role of more than peripheral therapeutic value to the patient and are even taking an active part in his treatment program. First participated in by college students, this new activity focuses on the formation of a close and meaningful one-to-one relationship between a volunteer and a single patient (Holzberg, 1963; Joint Commission, 1961). Typically, the student (or other volunteer) spends an hour each week with the patient (often a chronic case who has little or no contact with anyone outside the hospital) and a second hour each week in a group dis-

cussion with a professional member of the hospital's staff and other persons participating in the project. In the discussion hour, the volunteer is counseled on how best to establish a relationship that will work toward the patient's recovery.

While the volunteers in such programs do not perform miracles, they have demonstrated that relatively untrained people can, with proper supervision, make a worth-while contribution to the patient's treatment. And the success of the projects (often called "student volunteer programs," "companion programs," or "adopt-a-patient programs") has led to their being extended to helping not only chronic patients but also emotionally disturbed children and adolescents. High-school students as well as couples acting as volunteer parents are being recruited into similar projects.

NONPSYCHIATRIC AGENCIES WITH MENTAL HEALTH FUNCTIONS

In addition to the agencies whose purpose is service to the mentally ill, there are a number of other agencies in most communities whose main purpose is not psychiatric, but who nevertheless have widespread effects on the mental health of those they serve, either by strengthening the individual's physical or psychological resources or by lessening the stresses of his life situation. These agencies include family casework agencies, child welfare services of many kinds, and the many kinds of recreation and group-work agencies, including the various character building organizations. Churches and schools, besides their respective religious and educational functions, often do much to help meet people's psychological and social needs and sometimes provide the only counseling and guidance services available. An enlightened probation service can do much to turn minor offenders away from further lawbreaking and toward greater social responsibility.

Frequently the nonpsychiatric agencies are useful in identifying mentally ill persons and referring them to treatment agencies. All too often, however, the treatment services in the community are in such short supply that disturbed individuals get no treatment other than what they receive from these nonpsychiatric agencies. Indeed, it has been suggested that until psychiatric help becomes more universally available, most of the mental health problems of large segments of the population, especially among the lower economic classes, will be the responsibility of nonpsychiatric agencies and that the primary job of mental health people should be to offer such agencies as much consultation, training, supervision, and other kinds of direct and indirect support as possible (Ryan, 1963).

International Measures For Mental Health

Mental health is a major problem not only in the United States but in the rest of the world as well. Indeed, many of the unfavorable conditions in this country with regard to treatment of the mentally ill are magnified throughout most of the world.

The actual incidence of mental disorders in the world can be only roughly estimated, but it is known to be tremendous. The need for treatment facilities is correspondingly great. Whereas the more than 185,000,000 people in the United States have a total—quite insufficient—of about 13,000 psychiatrists and some 750,000 psychiatric beds, the ratio is far more inadequate in many other countries. India and China, with enormous populations, have only a handful of psychiatrists and extremely limited hospital facilities for the treatment of mental disorders. All underdeveloped countries have similar deficiencies in the number of psychiatrists, clinical psychologists, psychiatric social workers, psychiatric nurses, and other personnel.

The question has arisen as to whether we or any other advanced industrialized nation can achieve mental health in isolation from the rest of the world, however great our efforts. Mental disorders, wars, international tensions, and similar troubles are interrelated, and what happens to the rest of the world affects us also, both directly and indirectly. The possibility of nuclear war breeds anxiety over the future in the minds of all of us, and our military defenses absorb vast funds and energy which otherwise might be turned to health, education, and other constructive pursuits.

Although world-wide tensions and conflicts lessen the effectiveness of our own mental health activities, by the same token every measure undertaken on an international scale to treat and prevent mental disorders and improve the conditions of mankind makes its contribution to our nation's programs for mental health. Without slackening our efforts at home, we will find it increasingly essential to participate—even take the lead—in international measures promoting mental health.

It was this attitude which served to bring about several international organizations at the end of World War II. We shall discuss here the World Health Organization and UNESCO (both agencies set up by the United Nations) and the World Federation for Mental Health.

THE WORLD HEALTH ORGANIZATION (WHO)

It is the general function of the World Health Organization to formulate recommendations concerning physical and mental health to be carried out by member states of the United Nations. Brock Chisholm, the first Director-General, said: "The desperate need of the human race at this most precarious stage of its development is for understanding of man and for the development of methods by which he can learn to live in peace with his kind." (1948, p. 543) Dr. Chisholm then called for study of the psychological evils that stand in the way of physical and mental well-being.

A WHO Expert Committee on Mental Health had its first meeting in 1949 to formulate the principles that should govern the acitvities of WHO in the mental health field. In view of the tremendous needs and the shortage of psychiatric personnel and facilities throughout the world, the Committee considered that it would be impossible to provide therapeutic facilities for all the needy people of the world within the forseeable future. As a consequence, the Committee placed great emphasis upon the promotion of the general welfare and physical health of peoples as well as upon the development and application of mental health resources as rapidly as conditions would permit.

The Committee has conducted studies and issued Expert Committee reports on such topics as alcoholism, drug addiction, maternal deprivation, mental hospital organization, the psychiatric aspects of delinquency and crime, and the development of community health facilities. WHO has assisted with the development of psychiatric facilities in member states by making consultants available, providing training grants, and sponsoring conferences, both world-wide and local in scope. Since its inception, WHO has made and is continuing to make many significant contributions to world mental health.

WHO has headquarters in Geneva and Regional Offices for Africa, the Americas, South-East Asia, Europe, the Eastern Mediterranean, and the Western Pacific. Hence its activities extend into areas with diverse physical environments, types of social organization, and psychiatric facilities. In its work, WHO does not try to impose a predetermined plan on this diversity; rather it works toward "discovering, or uncovering, the basic needs of member states or of whole regions and delineating those areas where effort may be most usefully expended." (WHO, 1962, p. 78) In helping member states with consultative or other assistance, WHO also strives to make its services available over a period of several years to insure continuity and success for the programs which are undertaken.

THE UNITED NATIONS EDUCATIONAL, SCIENTIFIC, AND CULTURAL ORGANIZATION (UNESCO)

The constitution of UNESCO contains a statement which seems to strike many people with the force of a conversion: "Since wars begin in the minds of men, it is in the minds of men that the defenses of peace must be constructed." UNESCO seeks "to contribute to peace and security by promoting collaboration among the nations through education, science, and culture in order to further universal respect for justice, for the rule of law and for the human rights and fundamental freedoms which are affirmed for the peoples of the world, without distinction of race, sex, language, or religion, by the Charter of the United Nations."

Probably the most elaborate international undertaking involving psychiatric perspectives and aiming at better mental health was the UNESCO Project on International Tensions. The Project was under the Social Sciences Department of UNESCO. It was outlined and specific tasks were assigned to cooperating personnel at two general conferences, at Mexico City in 1947 and at Beirut in 1948. Since then, studies have been carried out in all parts of the world, and the results have been published in numerous books and articles. Major works include *Tensions That Cause Wars,* edited by Dr. Hadley Cantril; *Tensions Affecting International Understanding,* by Dr. Otto Klineburg; *Democracy in a World of Tensions,* edited by Dr. Richard McKeon; *How Nations See Each Other,* by Drs. Hadley Cantril and William Buchanan; and *In the Minds of Men* by Dr. Gardner Murphy.

UNESCO has sponsored many other studies and projects which are relevant to mental health.

Only a few of them can be mentioned here:

1. Studies on differences in national cultures, including studies of national "stereotypes" —ready-made conceptions of what people of different countries are like.

2. Studies of attitude formation and change, particularly with regard to international prejudice, including studies of the effectiveness of exchange fellowships in combating prejudice. Included here, too, are a series of studies showing how harmful racial discrimination is to the total structure of any society where it is practiced.

3. Investigation of the influences of modern technology on attitudes, changes in living patterns, and relationships among people and groups.

4. Studies of the relationship between population problems and international understanding.

5. Encouragement of the introduction of mental health concepts into teaching practice and their application to problems of leisure.

Currently UNESCO has a number of long-range projects under way. It has undertaken four regional educational programs to help alleviate the problem of illiteracy, which still affects about two fifths of the world's population. More recently, at the request of the United Nations General Assembly, the project has been expanded to include a world literacy campaign (*UNESCO Chronicle,* 1963). A second major project is a ten-year effort to increase understanding and appreciation of both eastern and western cultural values among all peoples.

Perhaps the most appropriate conclusion to such a brief description of the multitudinous activities of WHO and UNESCO on behalf of mental health is the early warning given by Dr. Klineberg:

"Our goal is, of course, research leading to action. There is a real and obvious danger in action which is premature. There is an equal danger in delaying action until it is too late. Our major difficulty lies in steering the proper course somewhere in between." (1949, p. 10)

The problem of world mental health is obviously a highly complex one, and the application of effective measures on an international level is a most difficult task.

THE WORLD FEDERATION FOR MENTAL HEALTH

In 1948, at an International Congress on Mental Health held in London, the World Federation for Mental Health was established. The Federation consists of a group of nongovernmental organizations and individuals concerned with the promotion of mental health throughout the world. Its establishment represented an important step toward furthering cooperation between governmental and nongovernmental mental health efforts at the international level, and more than forty different countries are represented in its membership. The Federation has been granted consultative status by both WHO and UNESCO and assists the UN agencies by collecting information on mental health conditions all over the world. It has undertaken various studies, including world-wide studies of childhood mental health and of the relation of mental health to developing industrialization. In addition, it seeks to aid underdeveloped countries through consultation with local health groups and to broaden their vision of the advances that are now within their reach.

The twelfth and thirteenth Annual Meetings of the World Federation for Mental Health— both of which fell within the World Mental Health Year 1959-1960—were devoted to *Planning for Mental Health* and *Action for Mental Health,* respectively. The scientific papers presented at these conferences cover a wide range of topics and plans in the mental health field; they have been published in one volume, *Planning and Action for Mental Health.*

We have now seen something of the veritable maze of local, national, and international measures for mental health. It is the first time in history that mental health problems have been viewed as having discoverable causes and as amenable to scientific methods of treatment— and it is the first time that this global problem has been subjected to a systematic attack. Many now believe with Julian Huxley that through the tools science is giving us, "human life could gradually be transformed from a competitive struggle against blind fate into a great collective enterprise, consciously undertaken...for greater fulfillment through the better realization of human possibilities." (1959, p. 409)

The Present Role of Psychiatry

In the present volume we have assessed the nature and extent of the tremendous problem of abnormal behavior in modern life and have examined the armaments that have gradually been built up to combat it. We have discussed the development of our modern views of abnormal behavior and have seen that at long last mental disorders and social pathology have been generally recognized as phenomena which follow natural laws and are therefore subject to scientific investigation and control. In the light of available scientific evidence we have outlined what appear to be the essential dynamics of personality adjustment and have reviewed the neuroses, psychoses, and other mental disorders. We have briefly indicated the theories and methods of modern diagnosis and treatment and some of the measures which appear relevant to prevention. In the course of our discussion we have tried to clarify and emphasize fundamental points of agreement in this whole field. In concluding our discussion of abnormal behavior, there are certain points relating to the present status of modern psychiatry and its future potentialities which are of interest to us all.

LIMITATIONS IN
MENTAL HEALTH EFFORTS

Despite the progress that psychiatry has achieved in the last half-century in the understanding, diagnosis, and treatment of mental disorders, many limitations still exist. Standards are far from being met and in many cases the standards themselves are open to question.

Personnel limitations. At the present time the number of psychiatrists in the United States approximates 13,000, whereas more than twice that number may be considered a minimum figure for meeting mental health needs adequately. In 1960, state mental hospitals had only about 60 per cent of the number of physicians (including psychiatrists) called for by the minimum standards set by the American Psychiatric

Association. Thus whereas the American Psychiatric Association calls for one physician for every 30 patients for "admission and intensive treatment services" and one physician per 150 patients for "continued treatment services," many physicians in state hospitals are responsible for a far greater number of patients.

Although personnel shortages are found in all branches of psychiatry, the deficiency is greatest in the field of child psychiatry. In 1960, there were only 165 qualified child psychiatrists in the United States, according to certification records of the American Board of Psychiatry and Neurology.

In differing degrees, clinical psychologists, psychiatric social workers, and other specialized personnel required for the treatment of mental disorders are all in short supply. In 1960 the American Psychological Association listed only 2376 clinical psychologists (Tyron, 1963). Its standards call for one clinical psychologist per 100 patients for "admission and intensive treatment services" and one per 500 patients for "continued treatment services." Since clinical psychologists play a key role in both psychological assessment and psychotherapy, their shortage may become more acute as the number of mental health facilities increases.

There is an acute shortage of psychiatric social workers in public mental hospitals and mental health clinics. In 1960, only about 40 per cent of the number needed in mental hospitals were available (National Association for Mental Health, 1962a). Similarly, the current annual output of psychiatric nurses approximates 1000 while it is estimated that at least 4000 are needed (Joint Commission, 1961).

Although efforts are being made to overcome these personnel shortages, the training of professional persons is a time-consuming process. In the meantime, many mental patients must go without adequate treatment.

Limitations in mental hospital and clinic facilities. There are over 500 mental hospitals in the United States, with a capacity of

MINIMUM PERSONNEL RATIOS FOR PUBLIC MENTAL HOSPITALS

Concepts and types of treatment are changing, and as the Joint Commission's recommendations for reorganization of treatment facilities are increasingly implemented, new standards will need to be set on new bases.

	ADMISSION AND INTENSIVE TREATMENT	CONTINUED TREATMENT SERVICES	GERIATRIC SERVICES
Physicians (including psychiatrists)	1 per 30 patients	1 per 150 patients	1 per 150 patients
Clinical psychologists	1 per 100 patients	1 per 500 patients	——
Registered nurses	1 per 5 patients	1 per 40 patients	1 per 20 patients
Registered occupational therapists	1 per 100 patients	1 per 500 patients	1 per 250 patients
Attendants	1 per 4 patients	1 per 6 patients	1 per 4 patients
Social workers	1 per 80 new admissions 1 per 60 convalescent or family-care patients 1 supervisor for every 5 case workers		

American Psychiatric Association (1958)

over 750,000 beds.[1] A large percentage of these beds, however, are in buildings which are obsolete and badly deteriorated. In addition, the trend toward smaller in-patient facilities located in the communities from which the patient come will necessitate major changes in the overall hospitalization program.

Although in-patient hospital care has improved greatly in the last decade, there still are wide differences in the quality of care provided for the mentally ill. Some mental hospitals have up-to-date treatment programs and are organized to utilize the latest psychiatric knowledge. Others have changed little in the past fifty years and continue to operate principally in terms of custodial care, often with overcrowded wards, appalling filth, idleness for their inmates, and other conditions more likely to aggravate the patient's illness than to foster his recovery. The Joint Commission found the large majority of state mental hospitals still operating primarily on the principle of custodial care—due in large part to a lack of adequate funds (Joint Commission, 1961).

Since most severely ill mental patients must turn to the public mental hospitals for help, the inadequacies of many existing treatment facilities are a regrettable and expensive social evil. And for individuals who have committed criminal offenses and been sent to "correctional institutions"—such as prisons and juvenile detention facilities—no therapy at all is usually available. Yet many of these persons suffer from character disorders, neuroses, and other conditions which warrant psychiatric treatment.

In April of 1961 there were an estimated 1568 mental health clinics in the United States, as contrasted with 1429 in 1959 and 1234 in 1954 (Bahn *et al.*, 1963). Despite this progress, considerably more facilities are needed to meet the goal of one full-time clinic for each 50,000 population, set by the Joint Commission on Mental Illness and Health (1961). In general, it would appear that these out-patient clinics offer a higher quality of service to their patients than do public mental hospitals. But many communities do not have such clinics, and in

[1]In recent years there has been a slight reduction in patient population in many state mental hospitals. Unfortunately, this reduction indicates a movement out of state hospitals and into other facilities—such as psychiatric wards in general hospitals—rather than a reduction in the total patient loads (Joint Commission, 1961).

other communities the clinics are not adequately staffed to deal with nearly all the requests for help that come to them. Unfortunately, this means that a large number of emotionally disturbed children and adults who need immediate therapy do not receive it (Joint Commission, 1961).

Similarly, there is a pressing need for additional day and night mental hospitals, which would enable many mental patients who are now in state mental hospitals to remain in their communities—and often to maintain their occupational responsibilities. A major trend in this connection is the increasing establishment and use of psychiatric wards in general hospitals. With additional community health facilities and emphasis on early detection and treatment, there could be a reduction in the long run in the number of persons requiring hospitalization.

Lack of adequate research.   In relation to the magnitude and social importance of mental disorders in our society, research in the area of mental health is very inadequately financed. In fact, we spend over 150 times as much money each year on alcohol as we do on research in mental health—almost 11 billion dollars as compared with about 68 million in

1959 (National Committee Against Mental Illness, 1961). Yet it is safe to say that the effectiveness of modern psychiatry will inevitably depend upon the extensiveness and soundness of the research upon which its theory and practice are based.

The lack of adequate research has severely handicapped psychiatry in its attempts to gain a greater understanding of psychopathology. For example, we really know very little as yet about the development of schizophrenia, and this gap in our knowldege is conducive to all sorts of theoretical speculation and verbal controversy which, however stimulating, will be of questionable value until the hypotheses are subjected to experimental support or negation. Similarly, the effectiveness of psychological treatment procedures—on both individual and group levels—is still inadequately understood and assessed. As a result, there are wide differences of opinion about a number of unsolved problems and issues—about how much time should be devoted to psychotherapy; about what types of psychotherapy are best suited to specific disorders; about what happens to the patient's psychological processes during the course of psychotherapy; and even about how effective any psychotherapy actually is. Until adequate

RESULTS OF CUTTING HOSPITAL MEDICAL STAFF

1951-1953 BIENNIUM	1953-1955 BIENNIUM
11 MD (including psychiatrists)	ONLY 6 MD (including psychiatrists)
84 PER CENT DISCHARGE RATE (during first year after admission)	60 PER CENT DISCHARGE RATE (during first year after admission)
174 PROBABLE LIFE PATIENTS	421 PROBABLE LIFE PATIENTS
$4,872,000 (cost for 174 life patients at $28,000 total per patient)	$11,788,000 (cost for 421 life patients at $28,000 total per patient)

"Economy" may not be economy at all in the long run. Hastings State Hospital, in Nebraska, with 11 physicians, including psychiatrists, had achieved a discharge rate of 85 per cent and in a 2-year period acquired only 184 chronic patients. But when insufficient funds forced a cutback to only 6 physicians, their discharge rate in the next 2 years dropped to only 60 per cent, and they acquired 421 chronic patients who, requiring the hiring of 73 additional attendants, more than canceled the saving from the psychiatric cutback and gave the state the prospect of a lifetime bill of $11,788,000.

and coordinated research supplies us with needed concepts and evaluations, the full potentialities of modern psychiatry cannot, of course, be achieved.

Though funds for research are short of what they should be, they are far greater than in the past and are steadily increasing. The renewed emphasis on research has led to a habitually critical and evaluative attitude toward concepts and procedures—an extremely healthy attitude for the advancement of psychiatric theory and practice. At the same time, the general public has become aware of the value of psychological help when problems become overwhelming or when life seems futile and unsatisfactory. This awareness is resulting in the treatment of emotional difficulties in the early stages (when they are easier to correct); and it has led to greater public support for improved treatment, training, and research.

PSYCHIATRY AND SOCIAL ILLS

The progress made in the field of psychiatry through the coordinated efforts of psychiatrists, clinical psychologists, social workers, anthropologists, and other professional personnel has not been easily attained. Only in recent years have psychiatrists been begrudgingly accorded recognition by their medical colleagues, and clinical psychologists have received little if any better treatment from either psychiatrists or fellow psychologists. However, as the knowledge gained from the study and treatment of mental disorders has proved itself of value in diverse areas of military and civilian life, psychiatry has won its professional status, and today there is considerable speculation as to the possible role it may be able to play in the alleviation of social ills. Can psychiatric knowledge be of value in the eradication of racial intolerance? Can it help in the setting up of worth-while social goals which are compatible with the potentialities and needs of man and will lead to a maximum of both social progress and human fulfillment? Can it help us maintain our democratic way of life and prevent a devastating global war? In the same way that general medicine has raised the physical health standards of the nation, can psychiatry raise our standards of mental health?

These are, of course, difficult and controversial questions. Many clinicians frown upon such hopes; they insist that psychiatry is primarily concerned with the understanding and treatment of mental disorders and not with the problems of social progress. It is difficult to see, however, how physical medicine could have reached its present level of efficiency if it had concerned itself only with the diagnosis and treatment of individuals and not with preventive methods involving public education and social action. Thus many today would agree with the noted psychiatrist William Menninger in his conviction that psychiatry *can* guide us in undertaking preventive measures that will contribute to the alleviation of the world's ills.

Like other knowledge, psychiatric knowledge can be used for good or evil. At the present time we live in a paradoxical world where scientific advances have actually endangered our very existence. The modern age has produced the most incredible developments in the physical and biological sciences—rocket power, communication satellites, the harnessing of atomic energy, electronic computers, antibiotic drugs, "mind-changing" drugs, and countless other wonders. Unfortunately, these tremendous advances in the physical and biological sciences have not been matched by equal progress in the social sciences, and the lag may well prove fatal to modern man.

Modern science has given man fantastic potentialities for the shaping and control of human behavior. It is now theoretically possible to decide what type of man we want—passive and cooperative, aggressive and competitive, apathetic and emotionless, or happy and carefree—and to proceed to create him in this image. It is not impossible, technically, to equip a human being with a transistor set and control certain of his actions from a distance by stimulating given parts of the brain. Ensuring that such scientifically available means of human control will not be misused presents a serious problem for modern man.

If social sciences are to attempt to keep pace with progress in other sciences and to assist in the solution of the social ills and common problems of mankind, modern psychiatry can, potentially at least, play a very important role. As research shows us which assumptions about man and the world lead to effective and fulfilling behavior and which ones lead to maladaptive behavior and futility, such findings can be incorporated into daily living. By way of analogy, we can point to the scientific finding that poor sanitation favors disease. Those who first championed this theory were faced with vigorous dissent and even ridicule. Now, however, society has adapted itself and incorporated this knowledge into its very structure through health departments and related services.

Throughout the centuries, there have been men who sketched out their dreams—and fears—of the future. Each has drawn his picture from elements of his own times, magnifying some features, eliminating others. Each new philosophical and scientific advance has indicated some kind of Utopia, and we have Plato's "phil-

osopher kings," the socialist Utopia of H. G. Wells, the "scientific" community of Skinner's *Walden Two,* the mock authoritarian perfection of George Orwell's 1984, and many others to read about and ponder. Although such fantasies are often unrealistic, they serve to point out hidden premises, dangers, and potentialities inherent in scientific and political advances.

Today we feel that as our scientific knowledge grows we shall increasingly have it within our power to establish conditions which will foster healthy personality development and social progress. This emphatically does not mean that man will or should become the planned product of a scientific society, but rather that science can be used to create conditions that will foster his growth and fulfillment as a unique human being with the prerogatives of freedom and choice.

The Individual's Contribution

When students become aware of the tremendous scope of the mental health problem and the still relatively inadequate facilities for meeting it, they often ask "What can I do?" Because of the frequency of this question, and because of the magnitude of the problem facing us nationally and internationally, it may be appropriate to suggest for interested students a few of the lines of action that they can profitably take.

Professionally, of course, there are many opportunities open to college graduates in the field of mental health, broadly conceived. Social work, psychiatric nursing, clinical psychology, and psychiatry itself—all are rewarding, both in monetary and spiritual terms.[1] And as we have seen, the personnel shortage is great in all these fields.

A citizen can find many ways to be of direct service if he is familiar with national and international mental health objectives and programs and takes pains to be cognizant of his community's special needs and problems. Whatever his occupation—a student, teacher, lawyer, homemaker, businessman, or trade-unionist—his interests are at stake, directly and indirectly. Besides accepting some measure of responsibility for the mental health of others through the

quality of his own interpersonal relationships, there are several constructive courses of action open to him, including (a) serving as a volunteer in a local mental hospital, clinic, or youth organization, (b) joining with other members of his community in work toward enlightened public education, racial tolerance, religious freedom, and responsible government, (c) becoming acquainted with the crucial issue of using science to control man vs. using science to create conditions conducive to man's fulfillment as a human being and then using whatever influence he has toward the latter objective, and (d) supporting and helping others to understand the need for expanded mental health facilities—including direct services, training, and research.

All of us are also concerned with mental health for very personal reasons: we want to overcome the harassing problems of modern living and find our share of happiness, "peace of mind," and self-fulfillment. To do so, we may sometimes need the courage to admit that our problems are too much for us. When existence seems futile and meaningless or the going becomes too difficult, the mature persons seeks competent psychological assistance in much the

[1]See page 654 for more specific information.

same way that we would go to a physician for appendicitis. (See page 655)

Finally, all of us can help by reminding ourselves of the following basic truths, which have been emphasized in the course of the present book.

1. From time to time everyone has difficulties in dealing with the problems of living.

2. Psychiatric assistance can be of great help with such problems and is available via many public and private clinics and other agencies.

3. Mental illness is not a disgrace. It can happen to anyone if the stress is sufficiently severe or prolonged.

4. The early detection and correction of pathological trends is of great importance in preventing the development of chronic mental as well as physical disorders.

5. Social preventive measures based upon scientific findings are the most effective long-range approach to the solution of both group and individual mental health problems.

To remind ourselves of these truths is essential because statistics show that almost all of us will, in our lifetimes, have to deal with mental illness in ourselves or in those close to us. The close interdependence among us and the loss to us all, individually and collectively, when any one of us fails to achieve his potential are eloquently expressed in the famous lines of John Donne:

"No man is an island, entire of itself; every man is a piece of the Continent, a part of the main; if a clod be washed away by the sea, Europe is the less, as well as if a promontory were, as well as if a manor of thy friends or of thine own were. Any man's death diminishes me, because I am involved in mankind. And therefore never send to know for whom the bell tolls. It tolls for thee."

REFERENCES

The reference list includes not only the sources from which the author has drawn material, but acknowledgments of the permissions granted by authors and publishers to quote directly from their works.

American Psychiatric Association. *Standards for psychiatric hospitals and clinics,* rev. ed. Washington, D. C.: Author, 1958.

BAHN, ANITA K., NORMAN, VIVIAN B., HENCH, CATHERINE L., MC CARTY, CAROL L., & RIPPY, MARY A. Gains in outpatient psychiatric clinic services, 1961. *Ment. Hyg.,* 1963, 47, 177-188.

CHISHOLM, B. The future of psychiatry. *Amer. J. Psychiat.,* 1948, 104, 543.

EATON, J. W., & WEIL, R. J. *Culture and mental disorders; a comparative study of the Hutterites and other populations.* Glencoe, Ill.: Free Press, 1955.

HOLZBERG, J. D. The companion program: implementing the manpower recommendations of the joint commission on mental illness and health. *Amer. Psychologist,* 1963, 18, 224-226.

HUXLEY, J. The future of man. *Bull. atom. Scientists,* 1959, 15, 402-409.

JACO, E. G. *The social epidemiology of mental disorders.* New York: Russell Sage Found., 1960.

Joint Commission on Mental Illness and Health. *Action for mental health: final report of the Joint Commission on Mental Illness and Health.* New York: National Rehabilitation Association, 1961.

KENNEDY, J. F. Message from the President of the United States relative to mental illness and mental retardation. *Amer. Psychologist,* 1963, 18, 280-289.

KLINEBERG, O. The UNESCO project on international tensions: a challenge to the sciences of man. *Int. soc. Sci. Bull.,* UNESCO, 1949, 1, 1-2.

NEWELL, A. & SIMON, H. A. Computer simulation of human thinking. In T. W. Costello & S. S. Zalkind (Eds.), *Psychology in administration.* New York: Prentice-Hall, 1963. Pp. 359-371.

National Committee Against Mental Illness. *What are the facts about mental illness?* Washington, D. C.: Author, 1961.

RYAN, W. Urban mental health services and responsibilities of mental health professionals. *Ment. Hyg.,* 1963, 47, 365-371.

SROLE, I., LANGER, T. S., MICHAEL, S., OPLER, M. K., & RENNIE, T. A. C. *Mental health in the metropolis: the midtown Manhattan study,* Vol. 1. New York: McGraw-Hill, 1962.

TRYON, R. C. Psychology in flux: the academic-professional bipolarity. *Amer. Psychologist,* 1963, 18, 134-143.

UNESCO. Preparation of a world literacy campaign. *UNESCO Chronicle,* 1963, 9 (1), 28-29.

U. S. Public Health Service. *National Institute of Mental Health.* (Public Health Service Publication No. 20, rev.) Washington, D. C.: U. S. Government Printing Office, 1960.

U. S. Public Health Service. *The national mental health program and the states.* (Public Health Service Publication No. 629, rev.) Washington, D. C.: U. S. Government Printing Office, 1962.

World Health Organization. WHO and Mental Health. The development of psychiatric services. *WHO Chronicle,* 1962, 16, 75-84.

World Health Organization. WHO and Mental Health. Mental health and the public health service. *WHO Chronicle,* 1962, 16, 124-129.

World Health Organization. WHO and Mental Health. Some problems of prevention and treatment. *WHO Chronicle,* 1962, 16, 171-181.

World Health Organization. WHO and Mental Health. The scope of epidemiology in psychiatry. *WHO Chronicle,* 1963, 17, 3-9.

appendix

It is often confusing to the student to discover the diverse ways in which personality may be conceptualized. Personality theory is relatively young and incomplete, and there are a number of viewpoints of varying degrees of comprehensiveness. Some have been developed primarily on the basis of laboratory experimentation, some come from clinical observations and research, some are derived from the conceptual tools of mathematics, and some are based on philosophical concepts.

The present discussion cannot attempt to review the entire range of personality theories. We shall confine ourselves to six theories that are especially relevant to a study of psychopathology and fairly representative of contemporary theories.

PSYCHOANALYTIC THEORY

Psychoanalysis is a comprehensive and intricate personality theory as well as a therapeutic method. Freud's originality and his concern with the dynamic interaction of psychic forces led him to a view of man's nature and behavior that has greatly influenced modern thought.

Psychosexual development. Freud viewed personality development as the organization and expression of basic sexual energy, or *libido*. This development he saw as taking place in five stages.

Oral stage. During the first year of life, the mouth is the principal erogenous zone; the infant's greatest source of gratification is assumed to be sucking.

Anal stage. From ages two to three, the membranes of the anal region presumably provide the major source of pleasurable stimulation.

Phallic stage. From age three to age five or six, self-manipulation of the genitals provides the major source of pleasurable sensation.

Latency stage. From the sixth to the twelfth year, sexual motivations presumably recede in importance. The child becomes preoccupied with developmental skills and activities.

Genital stage. After puberty, the deepest feelings of pleasure come from heterosexual relations. Ideally, the genital stage culminates in marriage, sexual relations with a loved mate, and child rearing.

Freud assumed that the events of infancy and early childhood are major determinants of adult personality; thus he saw the first three stages as especially significant in their relation to adult behavior. For example, an individual who did not receive sufficient gratification during the oral period may attempt to compensate by eating excessively in adulthood. In such cases, a portion of the libido is said to be *fixated* at an earlier level of development.

In general, each stage of development poses demands which must be met and arouses conflicts which must be resolved if the individual is to attain maturity. One of the most important conflicts arises during the phallic stage, when the pleasures of masturbation and accompanying fantasy pave the way for the *Oedipus complex*. Oedipus, according to Greek mythology, unknowingly killed his father and married his mother. Each young boy, Freud thought, symbolically relives the Oedipus drama. He has incestuous cravings for his mother and views his father as a hated rival. However, he fears the wrath of his dominant father, and fears especially that his father may harm him by removing his penis. This *castration anxiety* forces the boy to repress his sexual desires for the mother and his hostility toward the father. Eventually the boy identifies with his father and comes to have only harmless tender affection for his mother.

The female Oedipus complex is more intricate, but is based essentially on the view that the girl wants to possess her father and replace her mother. For either sex, resolution is crucial if the young adult is to develop satisfactory heterosexual relationships.

Instincts.   In Freud's view, man is motivated by inborn instincts. Some instincts, such as hunger, thirst, and sex, are constructive; they are directed toward individual survival and the propagation of the species. These *life* instincts are opposed by the *death* instincts, which are more obscure in their functioning. They are postulated as the source of hostile aggression and self-destructive behavior. In fact, Freud concluded that each person has an unconscious wish to die and that "the goal of all life is death." (Freud, 1955, p. 38)

Id, ego, and superego.   The instincts are contained in a subsystem of the personality, the *id*. The id is present at birth and knows nothing of reality or morality. It seeks only to gratify instinctual drives, to enjoy the pleasure that results when tension aroused by body needs is discharged. For this reason it is said to operate according to the *pleasure principle*. The id seeks this gratification of needs by means of the *primary process:* it forms a mental image of the object desired. The primary process is evident in dreams, wishful thinking, and hallucinations. This attempt to satisfy the instinctual demand by producing a mental image is called *wish-fulfillment*.

Since the source of instinct is in some body need, the images supplied by the primary process cannot fill these physiological needs. The body's need for water cannot be satisfied by imagining water. Thus some part of the organism must carry out transactions with the real world. The organism must perceive, solve problems, organize and store knowledge, and initiate acts appropriate for achieving goals in the external world. A second subsystem of the personality, the *ego*, develops to perform these functions. Because the ego's primary role is to deal effectively with reality, the ego is said to obey the *reality principle*. Its reality-oriented operations constitute the *secondary process*.

The *superego* is the last system of the personality to emerge. It develops initially from the learning or introjection of the values of society. As the individual matures, the superego is also influenced by the individual's own critical examination of his values. The superego includes what we call *conscience;* it is concerned with whether a thought or act is good or bad, right or wrong.

In general, then, the personality can be viewed as a composite of biological aspects, represented by the id; psychological aspects, represented by the ego; and social aspects, represented by the superego. Man's basic nature is irrational and selfish. Only social prohibitions (including his internalization of social rules) restrain his instinctive strivings.

Anxiety and defense mechanisms.   Freud distinguished three types of anxiety. *Reality* anxiety stems from dangers or threats in the external world. *Neurotic* anxiety arises when id impulses threaten to break through ego controls and cause behavior for which the individual will be punished. *Moral* anxiety arises when the individual does something or even contemplates doing something that arouses feelings of guilt.

Anxiety warns of impending danger, and drives the individual to do something about the situation. Often the individual can cope with anxiety by rational action, but when this does not suffice, the ego is forced to use irrational measures. These measures are referred to as *defense mechanisms;* they were discussed at some length in Chapter 3.

All defense mechanisms are alike in two ways: they deny or distort reality, and they operate on an unconscious level so that the individual is not aware of what is happening. Defense mechanisms are used to some extent by everyone, but their use in extreme, exaggerated form disrupts personality integration and causes *regression*.

Regression is a retreat to a lower level of psychosexual development. In the course of regression, the individual goes from the secondary process to the primary process—from reality-oriented behavior, controlled by the rational processes of the ego, to irrational behavior determined by the instinctual processes of the id. Schizophrenia, for example, is considered a regression to the most primitive level of development, the oral stage. Thus personality abnormalities may have their origin not only in the fixations already discussed, but also in excessive stress and decompensation.

The unconscious and psychotherapy.   Freud thought that the conscious represents a relatively small area of the mind. The unconscious, like the submerged part of an iceberg, is much the larger portion. In the vast domain of the unconscious are the images, desires, feelings, and ideas that have been either forgotten or repressed. The assumption is that objectionable memories, wishes, and impulses are less disruptive to the ego and arouse less anxiety when they have been excluded from consciousness. These repressed feelings may continue to influence our behavior, however, and we are often unaware of the real basis for our thoughts, beliefs, and actions.

Once material has been repressed, the ego has to keep it under close guard to prevent it from re-entering consciousness, an activity called *resistance*. The ego must be assured that the trauma which led to the repression is no longer dangerous before the material can be permitted to enter consciousness. Repressed material may be very active and may find an outlet in dreams when ego controls are lowered.

To circumvent repression and to unearth and deal with the irrational and unhealthy thoughts and impulses in the unconscious, Freud developed the techniques of free association and dream analysis which are basic to psychoanalytic therapy. In Chapter 14, the goals and procedures in psychoanalytic therapy are discussed in some detail.

Psychoanalytic theory has been criticized for placing too much emphasis on the role of sex in human behavior, for being unduly pessimistic concerning man's basic nature, for failing to consider motives toward fulfillment as well as maintenance, for a lack of adequate scientific evidence for many of its assumptions, and on various other grounds. Whatever the weaknesses or inaccuracies in psychoanalytic theory, the concepts of developmental stages and their crucial importance for adult behavior, of the interplay of intrapsychic forces (id, ego, and superego), and of anxiety and defenses against anxiety have been incorporated in practically all modern psychological theory.

JUNG'S ANALYTIC THEORY

The Swiss psychiatrist Carl Jung, initially a devout admirer of Freud, dissented from psychoanalytic theory in various respects. Eventually the friendship of the two men was completely severed, and Jung formulated a personality theory of his own. Jung's *analytic psychology,* though less systematized than psychoanalysis, is a comprehensive one.

The libido and development. Jung used the term *libido* to refer to the general energy of life. Sexuality is only one manifestation of libido. Libidinal energy is used first for meeting biological needs; when these needs are met, it becomes available for cultural, social, and creative pursuits.

As the individual matures, his libidinal energy may follow different channels. Jung suggested dividing the life span into three phases corresponding roughly to the direction of libidinal energy. During the first five years of life, the libido is invested in the development of basic competencies, such as walking and talking, that are essential for survival. After age five the libido is oriented more toward sexual goals—a pattern that reaches its height during adolescence. Jung considered incestuous longings important during this period, but did not believe that they reach the proportions of the classic Oedipus complex except when the child is overprotected.

This second developmental stage continues through young adulthood with marriage and the acceptance of vocational, marital, and parental responsibilities. During this period the individual is energetic, outgoing, impulsive, and passionate. In the late thirties or early forties a radical change occurs as libidinal energy gradually changes direction toward spiritual and philosophical goals. In this transition to the third phase, the person is transformed from an energetic, extrovertive, and biologically oriented individual to one more introvertive and spiritually oriented.

These stages characterize broadly the direction of libido, but, as we shall see, libidinal energy during any period may take various forms.

The personal and the collective unconscious. Jung saw the mind as composed of three areas: the conscious, the personal unconscious, and the collective unconscious. The conscious mind, or *ego,* is made up of perceptions, thoughts, memories, attitudes, and feelings. It is a kind of primitive self, essential for psychological integration. The individual regards it as the center of his existence, and it accounts for his feelings of identity and continuity. Jung considered the conscious mind essential in adapting to the environment, but felt it had been overemphasized at the expense of the unconscious.

The *personal unconscious* consists of experiences that have been forgotten, suppressed, or repressed, and experiences too weak to have made a conscious impression in the first place. It includes fantasies, such as dreams, which stem from forgotten or repressed experiences. Of particular significance are *complexes*—constellations of thoughts, feelings, and attitudes that form relatively autonomous systems—though complexes do not occur only in the personal unconscious. These complexes may represent focal points in the individual's personality in terms of particular motives and experiences, as in the case of a "power" complex; or they may represent contradictory attitudes, roles, and motives within the personality. In extreme form, the latter may result in so-called multiple personality.

The *collective unconscious* is the "deposit of ancestral experience from untold millions of years, the echo of prehistoric world events to which each century adds an infinitesimally small amount of variation and differentiation." (Jung, 1928, p. 162) These ancestral experiences or "racial" memories are inherited in the brain structure in the form of "primordial images" or "archetypes." An *archetype* is a universal image or idea which contains a large element of emotion and is elicited by some aspect of the individual's life situation. Thus the archetype of the mother—the primordial image of the Eternal Mother who supplies love, nutrition, and care—is normally elicited by the child's own mother. The archetypal images are limited in number: they correspond to the fundamental and typical human situations which characterize man's existence. Such "collective" memories were used by Jung to account for similarities in folklore, mores, symbols, and other aspects of culture found among diverse peoples throughout the world.

Everything within the unconscious seeks outward manifestation. Material from the racial unconscious is represented in fantasies, images, and dreams, and only as this material becomes accessible to the conscious mind can the individual achieve integration and wholeness.

The persona, anima and animus, shadow.   The theatrical masks once worn by actors were called in Latin *personae*. In Jung's use, the persona is the face we show the world, the social mask we adopt. It is determined largely by the social roles we play. Such social roles are heavily based on social expectations and customs and appear essential for social living. However, Jung pointed out that when the ego identifies too strongly with the persona, the individual becomes more conscious of the role he is playing than of himself. Although he may be a fine and dedicated lawyer, he forgets how to be a human being; he is cut off from his personal and racial unconscious.

Jung viewed man as bisexual: the male secretes both male and female hormones and so does the female, and on a psychological level both sexes manifest masculine and feminine behavior. Each male has in his psyche an *anima,* the unconscious feminine aspects of his being; each female has her *animus,* the unconscious male aspects of her being. The anima and animus are archetypes that stem from the racial experiences of man and woman living together. In the course of human history man has become feminized by living with woman, and woman has become masculinized by living with man.

The masculine archetype emphasizes mastery and competence and the feminine archetype emphasizes receptivity, loving, and nurturing. However, archetypal images may also include other components—the archetypal image of woman may include the Virgin, the Eternal Mother, the Witch, the Harlot, the Temptress, and the Spiritual Guide. Similarly, the archetypal images of man may include the Hero, the Defender, the Adventurer, the Seducer, and the Knight Errant. In short, man's anima is his collective or universal picture of woman's, and woman's animus her collective view of man, as both have appeared through the centuries of human experience.

When a man is aware of the nature of his anima, it helps him to be creative and to understand and relate to woman; when a woman is conscious of the nature of her animus, it helps her to deal more objectively with problems and to understand and relate to man. On the other hand, when the anima or animus remains unconscious, these archetypes have distinct dangers. For example, when a man projects his unconscious anima upon a woman, it results in an illusion or mirage which conceals the woman who is there. Obviously, such unrealistic projections may lead to conflict and disillusionment.

Another danger of these archetypes when they remain unconscious is that the man may react with resentment and strive to deny the feminine aspects of his own psyche with the result that his anima tends to dominate his unconscious, or he may unknowingly give himself over so completely to his anima that his masculine potential is impaired. Similarly, since the woman's animus tends toward reason and other masculine characteristics, its unconscious manifestations may take the form of dogmatic ideas, opinions, and insinuations which tend to disrupt relationships with others. Here it may be re-emphasized that manifestations of the anima or animus which remain unconscious are unavailable to the ego and cannot be controlled or directed. Hence they are irrational. Great effort is often required to bring them to the level of conscious recognition.

The *shadow* in Jung's theory represents the dark side, the primitive animal instincts inherited in man's evolution from lower forms of life. Socially reprehensible thoughts and feelings that enter consciousness stem from the shadow and are usually repressed into the unconscious. The shadow is also the opposite of whatever the individual has emphasized in his ego-consciousness or actual living. Thus the man who attempts an overmasculine adaptation at the expense of his anima will have proportionately strong and submerged elements of femininity in his unconscious shadow.

Personality types: attitudes and functions.   As the individual relates to the surrounding world, the libido takes two general directions. One direction, which Jung called *introversion,* is toward the inner, subjective world; the other direction, *extroversion,* is toward the outer world. Jung described the introvert as ruminative, imaginative, more interested in ideas and values than in people. The extrovert, in contrast, is outgoing, sociable, pragmatic, interested in people and things.

These two directions of the libido are fundamental attitudes of the personality and exert an important influence on interpersonal relations and on our general pattern of living. One attitude is usually conscious and dominant, but the individual has within himself, subordinate and unconscious, the counterpart of the predominant attitude.

To the introvertive and extrovertive attitudes which characterize the general orientation of the individual to the world, Jung adds four *functions*—sensation, thinking, feeling, and intuition—which represent the ways the individual perceives and deals with information and experience. Sensing is the perceptual function and yields concrete information about the outer world or ourselves; thinking enables us to interpret or recognize the meaning of what is perceived; feeling involves value judgments as to whether the object or situation perceived is desirable or undesirable; and intuition points to the possibilities inherent in a situation. By means of these four functions, Jung thought it possible to "orient ourselves with respect to the immediate world as completely as when we locate a place geographically by latitude and longitude." (1933, p. 107)

Ideally, each function would be equally developed and all four would work in harmony. In reality, one function is usually more highly developed than the others and is called the *superior* function; the next most highly developed function acts in an *auxiliary* capacity to the dominant function. The two less developed functions are largely relegated to the unconscious but may express themselves in dreams and fantasies. Thinking and sensation are considered masculine traits and usually go together, while feeling and intuition are considered feminine traits and also tend to go together. Thus a person may be described as a sensation-thinking type or a feeling-intuitive type. When a particular function is too far overdeveloped at the expense of the other functions, the personality is thrown off balance. For example, when thinking is carried too far without support from other functions the individual becomes pedantic and preoccupied with pure "facts" at the expense of the feeling and intuitive aspects of his make-up.

Attitudes and functions are interrelated in that the functions take place within a personality whose psychological orientation is introvertive or extrovertive. This orientation largely determines how the dominant functions operate. For example, the intuitive-feeling extrovert may become the visionary prophet who leads a nation, while as an introvert he might become a spiritual leader.

Integration and self.   For Jung, the self is not something that unfolds in the course of growing up but rather something that must be achieved, and that achievement can come only by great effort. It is the ultimate goal of life, which most people seek but few reach.

Before the self can emerge, the various components of personality must become fully differentiated. For this reason, the self can become evident only after middle age. When the person reaches middle age, he attempts to change the center of his personality from the conscious ego to a point midway between the conscious and the unconscious. In the mature personality, the self thus replaces the more primitive and vague ego or "child-self." The self provides the personality with unity, equilibrium, and stability and thus represents the fullest development and harmonious blending of all aspects of the personality.

The differentiation of the various components of personality, such as the persona and the anima, is the *individuation process*. As components become differentiated, they are integrated into a new unity by the *transcendent function*. Thus the individual tends toward growth and wholeness. However, various obstacles may block the normal *progression* of personality development and lead to *regression*—to a withdrawal of energy from the outer world and its displacement to the unconscious. This is not necessarily bad; the individual may surmount the obstacle by using the reservoir of knowledge and wisdom in his personal and collective unconscious, knowledge that may have been ignored or repressed. But when, because of regression, a personality component is neglected and fails to develop, the integration of the personality is disrupted and neuroses or other psychopathology may result. In dealing with obstacles and arrested development, Jung emphasized the significance of *symbols* created by the unconscious—and manifesting themselves in dreams, fantasies, and art productions—as guides to the nature of the problem.

It is not easy to harness the constructive powers of the unconscious and to achieve selfhood. Not only must the components of the personality be differentiated and integrated, but the individual must also listen to the "inner voice" of his unconscious, use its constructive aspects, and cope with its darker side. He must have the courage to separate himself from group convention and go his own way in isolation, making the moral decision to become a person in his own right. Thus the full development of the personality—of the self—is an achievement of heroic proportions and one not attained by the great mass of mankind, who live out their lives in the safe confines of social convention. Only as the individual achieves selfhood does he find wholeness and fulfillment.

Although analytic theory has been criticized as being too mystical and as lacking scientific grounding, integration, and completeness, Jung is considered one of the most profound thinkers of modern times. Perhaps the most distinctive features of analytic theory are its emphasis on the collective unconscious in the evolution of personality and behavior, on the development of opposite traits and tendencies within the personality, and on the difficulties involved in achieving selfhood. Jung also placed strong emphasis upon spiritual values, upon man's capacity for moral choice, and upon the forward progression and purposefulness of human existence—both on individual and group levels.

ROGERS' SELF THEORY

Most contemporary personality theories make some provision for the role of *self* as a unifying force in human behavior. The most clearly worked out and systematized self theory is the client-centered psychology of Carl Rogers, which is based largely on his pioneering research into the nature of the psychotherapeutic process itself. Both as a therapist and a theorist, Rogers has emphasized the importance of the self as the unifying and directing force in behavior and has stressed man's potential for self-definition and self-actualization.

Basic propositions.   Rogers has formulated his personality theory in a set of propositions. Perhaps the most effective way to introduce his theory is to cite his 19 basic propositions.

1.   "Every individual exists in a continually changing world of experience of which he is the center." This world of experience may be called the *perceptual* or *phenomenal field*. It is private; only the individual himself can know it in any genuine sense.

2.   "The organism reacts to the field as it is experienced and perceived. This perceptual field is, for the individual, 'reality.'" The individual behaves not according to some objective reality, but rather according to his own unique perceptions of himself and his world.

3.   "The organism reacts as an organized whole to this phenomenal field." One of the most basic characteristics of a living creature is its tendency to respond as an organized unit or totality and to maintain its integration.

4.   "The organism has one basic tendency and striving—to actualize, maintain, and enhance the experiencing organism." Specific needs, both organic and psychological, are seen as components of a single, general tendency to survive and grow.

5.   "Behavior is basically the goal-directed attempt of the organism to satisfy its needs as experienced, in the field as perceived." To maintain and actualize himself, the individual must meet specific needs. His ways of meeting these needs depend upon his unique perceptual field.

6.   "Emotion accompanies and in general facilitates such goal-directed behavior, the kind of emotion being related to the seeking versus the consummatory aspects of the behavior, and the intensity of the emotion being related to the perceived significance of the behavior for the maintenance and enhancement of the organism." Emotions, whether pleasant or unpleasant, usually direct the individual toward action that maintains or enhances him. Thus emotion, when not excessive, is beneficial rather than disruptive.

7.   "The best vantage point for understanding behavior is from the internal frame of reference of the individual himself." Since the individual reacts to the field that he perceives, the best way to understand his behavior is to try to see his world as he sees it.

8.   "A portion of the total perceptual field gradually becomes differentiated as the self." The term "self" refers to the experience of the "I," "me," "myself," and to the awareness of being and functioning.

9.   "As a result of interaction with the environment, and particularly as a result of evaluational interaction with others, the structure of the self is formed —an organized, fluid, but consistent conceptual pattern of perceptions of characteristics and relationships of the 'I' or the 'me,' together with values attached to these concepts." The self-structure includes the individual's perceptions of his characteristics and abilities; his concepts of himself in relation to others and to the environment; his goals and ideals; and the values—the liking or disliking—attached to experience, objects, his perceptions, and his goals.

10.   "The values attached to experiences, and the values which are a part of the self-structure, in some instances are values experienced directly by the organism, and in some instances are values introjected or taken over from others, but perceived in distorted fashion, *as if* they had been experienced directly." The child appears to value experiences he perceives as enhancing himself and to place a negative value on experiences that seem to threaten him, but his valuations may be influenced by parental values which are introjected and accepted as if they were his own.

11.   "As experiences occur in the life of the individual, they are either (a) symbolized, perceived, and organized into some relationship to the self, (b) ignored because there is no perceived relationship to the self-structure, (c) denied symbolization or given a distorted symbolization because the experience is inconsistent with the structure of the self." Perception is selective. Experience is accepted when it relates to the individual's needs and is consistent with his self-structure. It may be denied or distorted when it is incongruent with self-structure.

12.   "Most of the ways of behaving which are adopted by the organism are those which are consistent with the concept of self." The individual attempts to meet his needs in ways that are consistent with his view of his abilities and his value patterns. He acts in ways appropriate for the type of person he regards himself as being.

13.   "Behavior may, in some instances, be brought about by organic experiences and needs which have not been symbolized. Such behavior may be inconsistent with the structure of the self, but in such instances the behavior is not 'owned' by the individual." In an emergency situation the individual may react automatically and efficiently, but may do things that surprise him and may feel that he is not in control of his actions. Similarly, "immoral" sexual impulses may break through inner controls and cause behavior which the individual disowns because "I wasn't myself."

14.   "Psychological maladjustment exists when the organism denies to awareness significant sensory and visceral experiences, which consequently are not symbolized and organized into the gestalt of the self-structure. When this situation exists, there is a basic or potential psychological tension." When inner or outer experiences, such as sexual desires or information that is incongruent with the self-structure, are denied admission to consciousness, conscious control of behavior becomes more difficult. If the individual senses the discrepancy in himself he becomes anxious and unsure of his direction and feels he is not united or integrated.

15. "Psychological adjustment exists when the concept of the self is such that all the sensory and visceral experiences of the organism are, or may be, assimilated on a symbolic level into a consistent relationship with the concept of self." For adjustment, the self-concept must be roughly congruent with all the experiences of the organism. Conscious acceptance of impulses and perceptions increases the possibility of self-control and self-growth.

16. "Any experience which is inconsistent with the organization or structure of self may be perceived as a threat, and the more of these perceptions there are, the more rigidly the self-structure is organized to maintain itself." The self erects defenses against threatening experiences by denying or distorting them. These threatening experiences are a part of reality, and when they are not admitted to consciousness they cannot help to shape the self-concept. Thus the self-concept becomes increasingly incongruent with reality. The increasing conflict between self and reality leads to anxiety and even greater use of defensive measures. If the self cannot defend itself successfully against threat, the result is psychological breakdown and disintegration.

17. "Under certain conditions, involving primarily complete absence of any threat to the self-structure, experiences which are inconsistent with it may be perceived, and examined, and the structure of self revised to assimilate and include such experiences." This proposition is basic to client-centered therapy. When the client feels completely accepted he is able to bring his unconscious, unsymbolized, incongruent experiences into awareness. Gradually he is able to symbolize and assimilate such threatening experiences.

18. "When the individual perceives and accepts into one consistent and integrated system all his sensory and visceral experiences, then he is necessarily more understanding of others and is more accepting of others as separate individuals." The person who must continually protect himself against threatening experiences tends to view all experiences as potential threats and to be constantly on the defensive with others. He may react to such presumed threats with hostility inappropriate to the external realities.

19. "As the individual perceives and accepts into his self-structure more of his organic experiences, he finds that he is replacing his present value *system*— based so largely upon introjections which have been distortedly symbolized—with a continuing organismic valuing *process*." In client-centered therapy the individual gradually frees himself from the tyranny of what others think he "should" do and be. In place of the rigid value system he has introjected, he learns to have confidence in his ability to place valuations upon his

experiences and to establish his own values. Since each individual has the same basic nature and needs, the value systems worked out by different persons will have much in common but each person needs to work out his own and experience it as his own.

Breakdown and reintegration. The basic propositions just cited are seen as applying to every person to a greater or lesser extent. Personality disorganization and reintegration, however, occur only in certain individuals under certain conditions.

When there is a high degree of incongruence between the concept of self and one's actual experience, and when some event occurs in such a manner as to make the incongruence highly obvious, the individual's defenses cannot operate successfully. Anxiety is experienced in an amount proportional to the extent of self-structure under threat. Since defense is unsuccessful, the unexpected experience is accurately symbolized in consciousness, and the unity of the self-structure is ruptured by the resulting experience of incongruence, resulting in a state of *disorganization*. This process of breakdown might occur, for example, in an individual who viewed himself as highly courageous and brave and thought that people who showed fear were cowards. Confronted with extreme physical danger, he might experience fear, and the incongruence between his concept of himself and this experience of himself might lead to a breakdown of organized behavior.

After such acute disorganization has occurred, the individual attempts to reduce the painful incongruence. He may deny the fear experience, saying that he actually was not fearful. He may distort the experience— for example, he may insist that someone else was controlling his thoughts and feelings. Or he may devaluate himself, altering his self-concept to include the theme that he is a coward.

If a healthy reintegration is to occur, threatening experiences must be accurately symbolized in consciousness and must be assimilated into the self-structure without undue self-devaluation. Such reintegration is facilitated when the individual receives unconditional positive regard and empathic understanding from another person: he can then increase his own self-regard, lower his defenses, explore and accurately symbolize threatening experiences, and integrate them into his self-concept.

The fully functioning person. The fully functioning person is one whose psychological functioning is optimal and whose movement is toward further self-actualization. In essence this involves "becoming a person"—becoming one's true self. Rogers views this as a continual process. The fully functioning person is constantly changing and developing.

The process of becoming can take place only when the individual feels accepted, safe, and free to explore his innermost thoughts and feelings. Creating this situation is a goal of client-centered therapy. Such an atmosphere facilitates constructive changes in the individual.

Getting behind the mask.   The individual gradually drops the false fronts, masks, or social roles with which he has faced life. He tries to discover something more basic and more truly himself.

The experiencing of feeling.   Unknown elements of the self are discovered. The individual explores attitudes and feelings that he has not let himself experience because they were not consistent with his concept of himself.

The discovery of self in experience.   The individual's deep and often vivid experiencing of the elements within himself is painful when these elements are incongruent with his view of himself. But when such elements are accepted as part of the self, the result is a feeling of unity and harmony underlying one's attitudes and feelings. The real self is discovered in experience, as the individual gets behind the mask with which he has been deceiving himself.

To the extent that such constructive changes occur, the individual will be more nearly a fully functioning person. He will show certain characteristics consistent with his formation and acceptance of a more "realistic" self-concept.

Openness to experience.   All experience about the self, whether arising within the individual or from outside, can be perceived accurately and accepted. In so far as the individual's experience of himself is congruent with his concept of himself, the defensive processes of denial and distortion are unnecessary.

Trust in one's organism.   The individual now places trust in himself. He relies on his own ability to evaluate situations and to choose the actions most appropriate to satisfaction and actualization.

An internal locus of evaluation.   The individual realizes that he must choose, that he must take the responsibility for his existence. He looks less to others for approval or disapproval, for values and standards, and for decisions and guidance.

Willingness to be a process.   The individual accepts himself as continually in the process of becoming. Instead of striving to be a finished product, he continually tries to discover and actualize new aspects of himself in the course of living.

The fully functioning person is one who frees himself from dependence on a social role, or conformity to the expectations of others, or cynical denial of deeper feelings, or a front of intellectual rationality. He becomes an existing, experiencing, emerging, growing, unique person.

Interpersonal relations.   Rogers has formulated a view of interpersonal relations which stems primarily from his view of the therapeutic process. Each individual needs positive regard—acceptance, liking, warmth, empathy, and respect—from other people who are significant to him. Such positive regard from others helps the individual to accept and be himself.

It reduces his need to be defensive and to conceal his true feelings behind a mask. In accepting himself, the individual tends to develop feelings of positive regard for others; this feeling, in turn, facilitates the communication of real feelings and the development of a healthy and satisfying relationship. Conversely, when the members of a relationship do not have positive regard for one another, both members become more defensive, and more rigid in their perceptions. They merely act in social roles; their communication becomes superficial. The relationship is unsatisfying and tends to deteriorate; meanwhile, it fosters psychological maladjustment in both persons.

In essence, Rogers' view is that satisfying and growth-promoting interpersonal relationships are based on the same conditions of acceptance and freedom that are found in the therapeutic relationship. He applies this view of interpersonal relations to problems of family life, education, leadership, and group conflict.

Rogers' personality theory has been criticized as unrealistic in its view of a benign, unfolding inner self which only needs freedom and acceptance for its emergence. Some critics believe his view fails to give due consideration to the effect of the social and cultural environment in determining the particular potentials we attempt to actualize and the nature of the self that develops. In any case, Rogers' formulations have given rise to a great deal of psychological research and have profoundly influenced the thinking of many contemporary psychologists and psychiatrists.

EXISTENTIALISM

One response to the loss of traditional values and beliefs in Western society has been the development of existentialism—a view of man and his role which derives largely from European philosophers.[1] Existential theory is not a clear or complete personality theory but is important in emphasizing the uniqueness of the individual, his consciousness of self, his freedom of choice, his quest for values and meaning, and his responsibility for determining whether his existence has meaning.

Since we have dealt with a number of basic existential concepts in our consideration of psychotherapy in Chapter 14, we shall limit our present discussion to a brief review of these and certain additional concepts from existential theory.

Being and non-being.   From the existential viewpoint, man's basic motivation is to find the best pos-

---

[1]Among the European philosophers who have made major contributions to existential theory are Søren Kierkegaard, Friedrich Nietzsche, Martin Heidegger, and Jean Paul Sartre. It may be pointed out that existential theory has also been influenced by a number of American philosophers, psychologists, and psychiatrists, including Paul Tillich, Rollo May, Erich Fromm, Abraham Maslow, Gordon Allport, and Carl Rogers.

sible way of life, to actualize his potentialities, and to fulfill himself as a human being. However, in an age of profound cultural change, traditional mores and beliefs are no longer adequate guides to the good life. As a result, modern man suffers from confusion and deep spiritual and emotional strain.

Essentially, man can resolve his dilemma in one of two ways: (a) by giving up his quest and finding some satisfaction in blind conformity and submergence in the group, or (b) by striving for increased self-definition in the reality of his own existence—his own experience of *being*. Being is a matter of commitment to increased self-awareness and definition, to the development of one's unique potentialities, to sensitivity to the realities of one's world, to finding the way of life for which one is best suited, and to accepting the responsibility for making choices and directing one's destiny.

Non-being is the opposite of being. In ultimate form it is death, which is the inescapable fate of all human beings. At each moment, the individual threads his way along the sharp edge of possible annihilation; never can he escape the fact that death will arrive at some unknown time and place. But to realize what it means to exist, he must also grasp the possibility of non-existence. Thus existence takes on urgency, and the awareness of inevitable death adds a new dimension to immediate experience. It is the awareness of inevitable death that leads to *existential anxiety*—to deep concern over whether one is living a meaningful life.

Freedom, choice, and courage. For the existentialists, man is essentially free. Unlike other animals, man is conscious of himself as a self and has the ability to reflect and to question his own existence. He is aware that it is he who is faced by problems and that he can do something about them through *his* choices based upon *his* experience of being. Man's freedom is highly valued, but it confronts him with the problems of choice and responsibility and thus often becomes an agonizing burden. The anxiety it arouses, however, normally acts as a driving force in his search for new possibilities and his exploration of the unknown.

But freedom also gives man the power to choose non-being over being. He can take his own life and negate being; or he can give up the fullness of being by conformism or neurotic solutions.

Making the most of one's life does not occur by chance. It requires a willing decision or affirmation by the individual, and it often requires the courage to break away from old patterns and seek new and more fulfilling pathways and the ability to translate new insights into consistent action. Thus the good life involves a moral commitment to make the most of one's self and one's opportunities—to become an actualized human being.

Meaning, value, obligation. A central human characteristic is a will-to-meaning. This is primarily a matter of finding satisfying values and is a highly individual matter. For the values that give one life meaning may be quite different from those which provide meaning for another. Each person must find his own pattern of values.

As a consequence of its emphasis upon individual value patterns, existentialism has been accused of moral nihilism. Critics argue that people would work out radically different sets of values in the process of defining and actualizing themselves and that this would make organized society impossible. Existential philosophers maintain that this line of reasoning is unjustified because of the basic unity of mankind. All people are faced with the task of learning to live constructively with themselves and with others. Hence, there will be an underlying continuity in the value patterns chosen by different individuals.

Existentialism places strong emphasis upon the individual's *obligation* to his fellow man. The most important consideration is not what one can hope to get from life but what one can contribute to it. One's life can be fulfilling only if it involves socially constructive values and choices.

Anxiety, guilt, and despair. Anxiety is elicited by threats to one's being—to living as fully as possible, to self-definition and actualization. Such threats to existence may stem from outer or inner sources.

Existential philosophers are very concerned about the social predicament of modern man. They emphasize the breakdown of traditional faith, the depersonalization of man in our mass culture, and the loss of meaning in human existence. They view modern man as alienated and estranged—as a stranger to God, to himself, and to other men. Thus they see the social context of contemporary life as one which leads to existential anxiety. Anxiety is also seen as stemming from inner conflicts between being and non-being. For example, the individual may be confronted with the anxiety-arousing choice of maintaining his present life pattern with the security it offers or exploring a new possibility which appears to offer greater self-fulfillment but also involves greater uncertainty.

Often the individual lacks the courage to follow the path to greater self-definition and actualization and so denies new possibilities for being. The neurotic may cling to his pathological life pattern; the outer-directed man may escape the anxiety of being by blind conformity and immersion in the group. In each case, however, the individual pays a heavy price in the blocking of his own growth and fulfillment. To the extent that he fails to realize his potentialities for being he is a failure and feels *guilty*. To flee from one's freedom and obligation to life is to be unauthentic, to show "bad faith," to live in *despair*.

Existential therapy. We reviewed existential therapy in Chapter 14 and need note here only that in such therapy the patient moves from feelings of confusion about who he is and feelings of being controlled by others to a rewarding sense of freedom to define himself as a person and to choose his own path of existence. In this process, he gradually feels less chained to his past or limited by his present and becomes more aware of possibilities for the present and future.

Existential theory has been criticized on a number of grounds. Some psychologists and psychiatrists believe that it consists of a cluster of speculative assumptions which may or may not be valid; others point to an alleged overemphasis on the uniqueness of the individual which may discourage the hope that science can ever understand and predict individual human behavior. Still others consider existentialism a retreat from the realities of science into inner soul searching and ultimate frustration and irrationality. Whatever its limitations, however, many existential concepts—the uniqueness of the individual, his freedom and responsibility, the conflict between being and non-being, and man's quest for values, meaning, and self-fulfillment—merit serious consideration in any attempt at an adequate theory of "humanness."

S-R THEORY

Following the lead of Pavlov and Watson, many investigators have used conditioning techniques to study learning in man and the lower animals. In consequence, a large body of knowledge concerning such learning has been accumulated. Many psychologists and psychiatrists are beginning to apply this knowledge to the study and treatment of mental illness. Basic to this approach is the assumption that behavior, whether normal or abnormal, is at least in part a product of learning and subject to learning principles. These investigators tend to regard *learning* as synonymous with *conditioning.*

Stimulus-response theory (S-R theory) is actually a cluster of theories including the somewhat different theoretical viewpoints formulated by such men as Guthrie, Hull, Spence, and Skinner. There is no single S-R theory. However, S-R theorists do have a common goal—that of accounting for the acquisition, retention, and modification of behavior patterns that occur with experience. They commonly emphasize *stimuli* and *responses,* rather than "mediating" processes such as perceiving, interpreting, and reasoning. This emphasis is designed to avoid introspection and intuition, which are seen as pitfalls implicit in psychoanalytic and other personality theories. As yet, S-R theory is far from a unified or complete personality theory.

Fundamental concepts. A number of basic concepts are essential for an understanding of S-R theory. We shall list and briefly define some of these concepts.

Drive means motivation. Primary drives, such as hunger, are innate; they relate directly to the meeting of physiological needs. Emotions are also considered primary drives. Secondary drives, such as the need for social approval, are drives learned in the social context in which the individual develops.

Cues are stimuli that indicate the appropriate direction for activity. The same stimulus may both arouse the organism to action and serve as a cue. For example, the smell of food may both activate the organism and indicate where the food may be found. In general, however, drives activate the organism and cues direct the response. Lower organisms are limited by their perceptual and nervous systems in the range of cues which they can distinguish, and this limits their ability to learn and adapt to the environment.

Response is behavior directed toward reducing drive. It may involve thinking, feeling, or acting. Responses may be adaptive or maladaptive, and some are more readily elicited than others. In general, the strength and persistence of a response is directly related to drive strength.

Reinforcement influences the relation between a stimulus and a response. Positive reinforcement, or reward, reduces drive; drive reduction strengthens the connection, or "bond," between stimulus and response. To say the S-R bond is strengthened is to say that next time the same stimulus appears, the same response is more likely to occur. Negative reinforcement, or punishment, reduces the probability that an established response will occur the next time the stimulus appears.

Extinction occurs when a response is punished or unrewarded. An organism tends to stop making responses that are not positively reinforced. The old response is not destroyed, but rather tends to become dormant or inhibited.

Stimulus generalization is the tendency for a response associated with a cue to become associated with similar but different cues. Thus fear of a dog may generalize to other dogs or even other small quadrupeds—it might be aroused by cats, for example. The more similar the cue situations, the greater the tendency to generalization.

Discrimination occurs when the organism learns to distinguish between different cue situations. If the cues are similar, the first tendency is toward stimulus generalization; the organism tends to respond the same way to both situations. If his response is rewarded only in one of the situations, he learns to make the response only in that situation—he learns to discriminate between the different situations.

Habits are relatively enduring cue-response associations. Habits operate automatically; hence they free conscious attention for problems that require thought.

Cue-producing responses are the higher thought processes, such as reasoning, which may intervene between cue and final response. Thoughts constitute responses, but they also act as cues in eliciting further responses. Of particular importance here is the use of language, which facilitates generalization and discrimination and makes possible a far more flexible adaptation to the environment.

Personality development and maladaptive learning. Personality develops through the continual interaction of the growing individual with his environment. In this process, the child learns the assumptions he makes about his world and himself, acquires a pattern of motives, develops various competencies, and learns to respond to stimulus events in given ways. The individual is continually reacting to and being changed by stimuli; his reactions, in turn, change stimulus situations in ways that may influence his subsequent behavior.

What the individual learns depends on his innate and acquired equipment, his level of maturation, and the stimulation and reinforcement which the environment provides. Some environments foster the development of certain behavior patterns, while others foster different patterns. Whether or not a given kind of behavior is learned depends heavily on both environmental stimulation and reinforcement. Thus the mother, the family constellation, and the general sociocultural environment are of great significance in determining the direction and quality of the individual's development.

The environment may fail to provide the stimulation essential for needed learning, or it may provide stimulation which fosters unhealthy or maladaptive learning. A child growing up in an impoverished interpersonal and cultural environment may be deprived of needed stimulation for healthy personality growth, and a child brought up by parents who display maladaptive response patterns is likely to imitate and acquire these patterns in dealing with his own problems.

The child may also undergo specific traumatic experiences—such as being bitten by a vicious dog—which lead to undesirable learning. Traumatic experiences elicit intense anxiety, and experiments have shown that conditioned responses acquired in anxiety-arousing situations are highly resistant to extinction. Such responses also tend to generalize more readily to similar or related stimuli. Thus a child's conditioned fear response to dogs is likely to be difficult to extinguish and may generalize to other furry animals. Watson's experiment with little Albert, described in Chapter 2, demonstrates how such maladaptive fear responses or phobias can be established. Also important in this context is the possibility that individuals differ in conditionability. Some learning theorists have maintained that emotionally labile children are more likely to develop conditioned fear reactions, anxieties, and phobias.

Preverbal learning is especially critical for later development. Learning that occurs before language is acquired is not "labeled" or "recorded" in such a way that it can be recalled, and thus may be considered a part of the unconscious. When cues produce conscious thoughts as intermediate responses, the thought process can produce a final response that takes into account all the important factors in the situation. But when a cue-response bond is unconscious, the response, if it occurs, is less subject to modification and adjustment. Other cues in the situation do not influence it. Since the individual is thus reacting to only a part of the total situation, his response is likely to be inappropriate and maladaptive.

Even after language is acquired, the child may undergo experiences, such as taboo sexual experiences, which involve learning but are recorded inaccurately or in such a way that they cannot be readily recalled because of a lack of language facility in this area. In addition, experiences which were formerly conscious may be suppressed or repressed and thus forced out of awareness.

Conflict. Conflict occurs when a stimulus situation arouses competing response tendencies. One important kind of conflict results when approach and avoidance tendencies compete. An individual, for example, might have at once strong desires for sexual activity and powerful fears about the consequences of such activity. Or he might wish to marry, yet fear the loss of his independence.

Dollard and Miller (1950) have formulated five assumptions as a basis for analyzing approach-avoidance conflicts: (a) The tendency to approach a desired goal becomes stronger as the individual nears the goal—this is called the *approach gradient.* (b) The tendency to avoid a negative goal becomes stronger as the individual nears the goal—this is called the *avoidance gradient.* (c) The avoidance gradient is steeper than the approach gradient—that is, avoidance tendencies increase at a greater rate than approach tendencies as the individual nears the goal. Thus as the marriage date approaches, an ambivalent individual will become increasingly reluctant to go through with the marriage. (d) An increase in the drive associated with approach or avoidance will raise that gradient. (e) The stronger of the two competing responses is the one which will occur. These assumptions have proven highly useful in explaining conflictful behavior.

In assessing the importance of conflict in maladaptive behavior, it may be pointed out that conflicts developing in early life may be unlabeled and unconscious, as may also conflicts which have been suppressed or repressed. Hence they may lead to irrational behavior. Where conflicts are conscious but the alternatives are of equal value, the individual is likely to hesitate and vacillate in his responses; where conflict produces severe stress, he may become disorganized and "break down." We have observed this in the "experimental neuroses" of animals whose feeding responses competed with conditioned avoidance tendencies (see Chapter 6).

Drive level and irrationality. Mednick (1958) and other learning theorists have concluded that heightened drive increases the strength of any response tendencies that may be aroused by a given stimulus. In general, the hungrier, the more anxious, or the more angry the organism, the greater the drive strength, and the swifter and stronger the response.

Where the situation is a relatively simple one in which the habitual response aroused is adaptive, no particular problem occurs. But in complex situations, a marked increase in drive may evoke irrelevant and inappropriate habit tendencies with which the correct response must compete. Thus the thinking of persons with a high drive level may be disrupted by the intrusion of irrelevant thought units.

When a high drive level is further increased by anxiety, stimulus generalization increases and the ability to discriminate decreases. Thus stimulus events similar to the one producing the initial problem also elicit anxiety, because they are not perceived as different. This, in turn, increases anxiety, and the spiral of stimulus generalization and increased anxiety mounts. Now the high level of drive keeps thoughts racing through the individual's mind, and many of these thoughts are irrelevant or silly. The individual may feel that he is "going crazy." At this point, his ability to discriminate among stimulus events and response possibilities is seriously impaired and his behavior becomes highly irrational.

This spiraling of increased drive level and irrationality may be reversed if the individual is able to work out some adaptive solution to his problem. Often tranquilizing drugs are of value in reducing anxiety and stimulus generalization, thus increasing the individual's ability to discriminate. In other instances the individual may resort to exaggerated and deviant defensive maneuvers, such as the development of delusions.

Behavior therapy. The application of learning theory principles in the treatment of mental illness has been termed *behavior therapy*. The general assumption underlying this form of therapy is that maladaptive responses, having been learned, can be modified or unlearned. Treatment depends on manipulating stimulus variables in ways that induce specific forms of behavioral change. First, the S-R bonds that are causing anxiety or difficulties in adjustment must be identified. These may be labeled and their origin and effects may be explained to the patient. Reconditioning or counter-conditioning is then used to provide the patient with a new and more adaptive response to the stimulus that originally caused difficulty. Similarly, conditioning methods may be used to reinforce attitudes, actions, and feelings that contribute to more effective adaptation. Behavior therapy was discussed in Chapter 14.

S-R theory has been criticized for overemphasizing the role of instinctual drives in determining behavior, for being reluctant to come to grips with complex cognitive processes such as the concept of self, and for overemphasis on the role of conditioning and environmental stimuli in human behavior. Learning theorists tend to view man as a somewhat automatized victim of his past conditionings—as one whose behavior can be modified only by the manipulation of external stimuli. Man is thus seen as basically devoid of choice or free will. This point of view is at odds with personality theories which view man as a creative, striving, evaluating creature with the capacity for reflection and rational self-direction under normal conditions.

Many S-R concepts have influenced and been used by personality theorists. Several investigators have also attempted a rapprochement between S-R theory and psychoanalysis. The success of these attempts remains to be ascertained; in any case S-R theory, because of its simplicity, precision, and objectivity, exercises a great deal of influence on contemporary psychology.

TRAIT AND FACTOR THEORY

In our everyday efforts to understand and predict behavior, we often characterize people in terms of traits—as honest or dishonest, ambitious or lazy, rational or irrational, well adjusted or maladjusted. Trait theory grew out of attempts to measure the differences among individuals in such characteristics. It represents a systematic effort to identify and measure common personality characteristics or traits which underlie and determine individual behavior.

Traits derived mathematically by the statistical procedure of factor analysis are called *factors*. For our present purposes, we shall use the terms *factor* and *trait* interchangeably.

Trait theorists thus try to understand the individual by comparing him with others on many dimensions of variation. This is called a *nomothetic* approach, as opposed to the more usual clinical *idiographic* approach of making the individual's unique personality structure the unit of observation.

Some properties of traits and factors. To understand trait theory, we need to examine several of the properties of traits.

Scalability. Many traits, such as intelligence, are scalable. Different individuals have different degrees of the trait. Other traits, such as having a phobia, are not scalable. The individual either has it or does not.

Polarity. Unipolar traits, such as athletic ability, extend from a theoretical zero point to a great amount. Bipolar traits, such as introversion-extroversion, extend from one pole through a zero point to an opposite pole.

Consistency of position. The degree to which a person possesses a trait determines his trait position relative to others. In many cases this trait position is assumed to be relatively constant.

Durability. In some cases, in addition to temporary minor fluctuations in trait position, there are long-term changes from one life period to another.

Universality. Some traits are common to all members of the population and are called *universal* traits in that population. Other traits are found in certain groups but not in all; still other traits are relatively unique to given individuals.

Generality. Some traits, such as intelligence and self-confidence, are manifested in many aspects of behavior; these are called *general* traits. Other traits, such as shyness, may be manifested only in a specific type of situation.

Inclusiveness. Some traits include others. The more inclusive the trait, the greater its significance. Thus intelligence is an inclusive trait while perceptual speed is a much less inclusive, or relatively noninclusive, trait.

Independence versus correlation. Some traits, such as nervousness, sensitivity, and emotional excitability, are interrelated, or positively correlated with each other. Other traits, such as the ability to spell words, are relatively independent of each other.

Personality structure. In an intensive survey, Allport and Odbert (1936) found almost 18,000 terms which have been used to describe human traits. If traits are to prove useful in describing personality structure, it is essential to select from this tremendous number of traits a manageable number that will serve the purpose. At the same time, it is essential that no significant characteristic of the personality be slighted or omitted.

Factor analytic procedures have been of great help in this task since they make it possible to identify patterns of traits that go together—that are interrelated—and to delineate the limited number of primary traits or factors that underlie such patterns. Thus it becomes possible theoretically to describe personality in terms of a limited number of relatively independent factors. Cattell (1958) has pointed out that when measurements of a large number of traits of young adults are subjected to factor analysis, their personality structure can be viewed in terms of some 16 to 20 basic factors. Three of these factors are briefly described here for illustrative purposes:

Cyclothymia—schizothymia. This factor shows itself at one pole in carefree, emotionally expressive, outgoing behavior, and at the other pole in rigid, aloof, cold attitudes.

Ego strength—neurotic tendency. This factor is evidenced at one pole by emotional maturity, stability, and realism, and at the other pole by general emotionality, ego defenses, dissatisfaction, neuortic symptoms.

Radicalism—conservatism. Although first found in studies of political and religious attitudes, this factor has been shown to be a more general personality or temperament factor. An individual tends to be consistently radical or conservative in most life areas.

Guilford (1959) has suggested that such personality factors can be divided into two broad groups—*hormetic* and *temperament* factors. The word *hormetic* is of Greek origin and means "to have a purpose" or "to strive," and hormetic factors are direct motivational aspects of personality—measurable needs, interests, and attitudes. Temperament factors describe the *manner* in which the individual typically operates. In terms of temperament traits, for example, an individual might be deliberate or impulsive, nervous or composed.

Psychopathology. A number of investigators (Eysenck, 1961; Guilford, 1959) have contributed to our understanding of psychopathology by applying the methods of factor analysis to the study of mental illness. Cattell (1961) has shown that certain traditional clinical syndromes can be differentiated and described in terms of factor profiles derived from personality questionnaires. He found, for example, that individuals judged clinically to be neurotic depressives were high on such factors as cyclothymia and guilt proneness and low on ego strength. He also noted that individual differences in neurotic reactions can be described in the factor analytic framework by identifying the influence of each factor component on the total neurosis score.

Trait theory as a problem for research. The reader may have begun to feel that trait theory consists of lists of static characteristics rather than dynamic explanations of behavior. This is in part a misleading impression resulting from the brevity of our discussion. Nevertheless, identifying traits and arranging them hierarchically is basically a matter of description and classification. So it is important to understand why trait theory puts so much emphasis on delineating traits.

In general, the trait theorist would argue that in studying any phenomenon, progress depends on discovering its significant properties. Thus, for example, the motion of objects in a vacuum depends on mass, acceleration, and force, whereas individual objects have many other properties, such as color, shape, chemical composition, and specific gravity, which are not significant in this context. Inevitably any personality theorist emphasizes some aspects of personality as of primary importance in determining behavior and assigns other aspects a lesser role. But factor theorists especially are doubtful that relatively intuitive and unsystematic analyses will suffice in the identifying of these critical central aspects.

What factor analysts are trying to do is to identify the basic personality dimensions in an objective and systematic way. Trait and factor theories may in the end include many personality aspects that have been emphasized in other theories. Other once-accepted aspects may be dropped or merged or subsumed under aspects found to be more basic. And new aspects may be discovered.

When the major dimensions have been at least tentatively identified, and the lesser aspects of the personality subsumed under them, the groundwork will be laid for further investigation. Are the basic dimensions in one cultural group the same as those in another? Given a set of significant traits, how do they interact to direct behavior? Does a given trait depend on the biological nature of the individual, or is it learned in his interaction with the environment? In what ways does a trait change or develop with time?

Whether the technique of factor analysis is in fact suitable for the purpose of identifying the basic personality dimensions common to all individuals in a group is questioned by many, but the arguments on this point are beyond the scope of the present discussion. Even more basic is the question of whether there *are* such basic dimensions common to all members of a group which are responsible for determining the behavior of all the members of the group.

There is also the problem of whether trait theory can take adequate account of individuality. An individual's scores on tests are statements of how he *differs* from other people, of his relative standing on the various dimensions measured. Thus describing him in terms of these scores is describing him in terms of a series of comparisons with other people rather than focusing on *him* as the unit of observation. Can such a listing pinpoint the essence of his individuality, his particular organization of motives, attitudes, assumptions, and feelings? Or can adding together elements measured separately give an accurate or complete representation of the functioning whole?

Whatever its long-term potentialities and limitations, factor analytic approaches have pointed up the need for a more explicit formulation of concepts and for more adequate standards of measurement in psychopathology. Trait and factor theories provide a useful framework for understanding the uniformities and differences among people.

CONCLUSION

In our review of personality theory, we have arbitrarily limited ourselves to certain contemporary theories which are relevant to psychopathology and representative of personality theory in general. As a consequence, we have not dealt with a number of theories which have made important contributions to contemporary psychology. Particularly obvious is the omission of the socially oriented personality theories of Adler, Fromm, and Sullivan. We have, however, referred to various concepts from these theories in our discussion of abnormal behavior—Adler's unifying concept of "life style," Fromm's concept of the alienation of man in a vast impersonal society, and Sullivan's emphasis upon viewing the individual's interpersonal situation as well as the individual.

Another approach to personality theory requires mention, although it is primarily a method of studying personality rather than a systematic theory. This is the computer simulation of personality, which makes use of high-speed electronic computers—popularly referred to as "giant brains." In a preliminary way, attempts have been made to simulate with computers the processes of human learning and problem solving. Similar attempts are being made to simulate other parameters of personality, such as motivation; Colby (1963) has even attempted the computer simulation of a neurotic process. In fact, there is some hope that use of computers will help overcome the familiar dilemma of psychologists in feeling that they must choose between significant problems and rigorous methods. Newell and Simon (1963) see the complex electronic devices and feedback mechanisms of the computer as providing a means for clarifying concepts of adaptive behavior like goal-seeking, thus encouraging problem-oriented psychologists to give more precise operational meaning to concepts that have been vague, while technique-oriented psychologists will be encouraged to tackle problems that have previously seemed too complex for their tools.

Finally, it should be pointed out that existing personality theories are continually being modified by new scientific findings and theoretical formulations. Although contemporary clinical psychologists and psychiatrists may favor different viewpoints, they have all been influenced to a greater or lesser extent by the theories we have reviewed, and probably most look forward to an increasing convergence in point of view.

REFERENCES

ALLPORT, G. W., & ODBERT, H. S. Trait-names: a psycholexical study. *Psychol. Monogr.*, 1936 (Whole No. 211).

CATTELL, R. B. The structure of intellect, temperament and personality. In F. L. Ruch, *Psychology and Life* (5th ed.). Chicago: Scott, Foresman, 1958.

CATTELL, R. B., & SCHEIER, I. H. *The meaning and measurement of neuroticism and anxiety.* New York: Ronald, 1961.

COLBY, K. M. Computer simulation of a neurotic process. In S. S. Tomkins & Z. Messick (Eds.), *Computer simulation of personality: frontier of psychological theory.* New York: John Wiley & Sons, Inc., 1963. Pp. 166-180.

DOLLARD, J., & MILLER, N. E. *Personality and psychotherapy: an analysis in terms of learning, thinking, and culture.* New York: McGraw-Hill, 1950.

EYSENCK, H. J. (Ed.) *Handbook of abnormal Psychology.* New York: Basic Books, 1961.

FREUD, S. Beyond the pleasure principle. In J. Strachey (Ed.), *The standard edition of the complete psychological works.* Vol. XVIII. London: Hogarth, 1955.

GUILFORD, J. P. *Personality.* New York: McGraw-Hill, 1959.

JUNG, C. G. *Modern man in search of a soul.* New York: Harcourt, Brace & World, 1933.

JUNG, C. G. *Psychology and religion.* New Haven: Yale Univer. Press, 1938.

MEDNICK, S. A. A learning theory approach to research in schizophrenia. *Psychol. Bull.,* 1958, 55, 316-325.

NEWELL, A., & SIMON, H. A. Computer simulation of human thinking. In T. W. Costello & S. S. Zalkind (Eds.), *Psychology in administration.* New York: Prentice-Hall, 1963. Pp. 359-371.

Abnormal Psychology in Modern Literature

Modern psychology has had a pervasive influence on modern fiction, drama, and criticism. In addition, the publication of case histories and other books written for the thoughtful layman has led to the creation of some new "literary" forms inspired by the subject itself. The following books, a selection of "classic" and popular fiction, drama, autobiography, case studies, and nonfiction, are offered only to introduce the student to the vast and growing body of writings concerned with abnormal behavior and with the influence of psychiatric theory on modern life and letters.

Fiction

Bowen, Elizabeth. *Death of the Heart.*
New York: Alfred A. Knopf, 1939.

This moving account of the conflict between sensitivity and insensitivity tells of a warm, imaginative child who experiences loneliness and emotional shock when brought to live in the cold and selfish milieu of her half sister's home. The book is written without clinical terms but with great psychological insight.

Dawson, Jennifer. *The Ha-Ha.*
Boston: Little, Brown and Company, 1961.

More than just another macabre account of madness, this short novel tells of a schizophrenic who, almost well, suffers a relapse and must try again to salvage her "self" to escape extinguishment.

Dostoevski, Feodor. *The Idiot.*
New York: Modern Library, no date.

Dostoevski, of all novelists, was endowed with a profound psychological insight and with an intuitive understanding of multiple and uncertain human motivation. Virtually his entire output could be included in this list; *The Idiot* is chosen for its almost clinical discussion of epilepsy, a malady from which the author suffered.

Faulkner, William. *The Sound and the Fury* and *As I Lay Dying.*
New York: Modern Library, no date.

Sometimes regarded as being among Faulkner's masterpieces, these novels are of the "stream of consciousness" school, the stories being told through the minds of the characters. The first concerns the dissolution of the old southern Compson family and is partly narrated by the mentally retarded son, Benjamin. The second is a psychological foray into the emotional abnormalities of another subnormal family.

Fitzgerald, F. Scott. *Tender Is the Night.*
New York: Charles Scribner's Sons, 1960.

A neurotic wife "uses" her psychiatrist-husband to advance her own cure and so drains him of his energy that his own ability to cope with life is demolished. More an account of poorly supported illusions than a psychiatric appraisal of life, the novel grew out of Fitzgerald's own declining morale during his wife's several breakdowns and final commitment as an "incurable" schizophrenic.

Frame, Janet. *Faces in the Water.*
New York: George Braziller, Inc., 1961.

Written by an ex-mental patient with a gift for literary expression, this novel unforgettably depicts the thoughts and fears of a hospitalized patient.

Golding, William. *Lord of the Flies.*
New York: Coward-McCann, Inc., 1962.

A group of boys, evacuated from England and then wrecked on an uninhabited island, try to establish a civilized society. A nightmarish commentary on what the author sees as the primitive nature of man.

James, Henry. *The Portrait of a Lady.*
New York: Modern Library, no date.

In this (as in his other major works) James—the brother of psychologist William James—writes from a psychological viewpoint. The story concerns the growing self-awareness of Isabel Archer, who, given the chance to do whatever she will with her life, becomes a pawn to other people's meddlesome intrusions.

Kafka, Franz. *The Trial* (rev. ed.).
New York: Alfred A. Knopf, Inc., 1957.

This novel gives the subjective thoughts and outlook of a paranoid personality. The story centers around the arrest and trial of an "innocent" man for a "crime" which is never explained to him. Shows the paranoid's tendency to interpret all events as unwarranted and mysterious persecution.

Keilson, Hans. *The Death of the Adversary.*
New York: Orion Press, 1962.

Written by a German-Jewish psychoanalyst now living in Holland, this novel discusses the phenomenon of hate with profound sympathy and understanding of both victim and aggressor.

Kesey, Ken. *One Flew over the Cuckoo's Nest.*
New York: The Viking Press, 1962.

A novel contrasting patients' struggles for survival in a mental hospital with an equally compelling symbolic struggle between tyranny and the tyrannized.

Lawrence, D. H. *Sons and Lovers.*
New York: Modern Library, no date.

Written before Lawrence had any real acquaintance with Freud's work (which he later rejected as being "too scientific"), this novel is nevertheless considered a classic and penetrating study of the "Oedipus complex."

Paton, Alan. *Cry, the Beloved Country.*
New York: Charles Scribner's Sons, 1948.

An unusual novel of race relations and crime, distinguished by clear understanding of psychological motives and of the environmental background of behavior. Although set in South Africa, the novel is full of insights for Americans.

Salinger, J. D. *The Catcher in the Rye.*
New York: Modern Library, no date.

Account of the inner life of a 16-year-old boy during a 3-day leave from school; a poignant revelation of adolescent turmoil.

Drama

Miller, Arthur. *Death of a Salesman.*
New York: The Viking Press, 1949.

A Pulitzer Prize play about the psychological and economic struggles of a lower middle-class American family in which two sons are growing up with an overprotective mother and an intensely ambitious, competitive father.

O'Neill, Eugene. *Long Day's Journey into Night.*
New Haven, Connecticut: Yale University Press, 1956.

Published after the author's death, this autobiographical play unfolds more as a case history of the tortured O'Neill family than as genuine dramatic tragedy. Nevertheless, it is an absorbing psychological experience as each character searches his own past to supply the background for his misery and is forced to face himself, without self-deception, for the first time in his life.

Strindberg, August. *A Dream Play* (from Strindberg's *Five Plays,* translated by Elizabeth Sprigge).
Garden City, New York: Doubleday (Anchor paperback edition), 1960.

In this play, Strindberg, whose own life was characterized by emotional and mental disturbance, tried to imitate the "disconnected, but apparently logical" form of the dream. (Other plays of Strindberg, found in this or other anthologies, are also of interest to students of abnormal psychology.)

Nonfiction

Beers, Clifford W. *A Mind That Found Itself* (rev. ed.).
Garden City, New York: Doubleday and Co., 1948.

This book is the "classic" of all ex-mental patient autobiographies.

Bettelheim, Bruno. *The Informed Heart: Autonomy in a Mass Age.*
New York: Free Press of Glencoe, 1960.

A noted psychiatrist, imprisoned in a concentration camp during the Hitler regime, reviews the dissolution of personality in the coercive environment of camp life and sees some of the same dangers in a depersonalized mass society.

Bosselman, Beulah Chamberlain. *Self-Destruction: A Study of the Suicidal Impulse.*
Springfield, Illinois: Charles C. Thomas, 1958.

A psychiatric study of the suicidal impulse showing, through text and case histories, the many ways in which self-destructiveness may be expressed.

Evans, Jean. *Three Men: An Experiment in the Biography of Emotion.*
New York: Alfred A. Knopf, Inc., 1954.

A convincing presentation of the motivations, problems, and adjustive difficulties of three living men. (Names of people and places changed.)

Fromm, Erich. *The Art of Loving.*
New York: Harper and Brothers, Publishers, 1956.

A psychoanalyst investigates the nature of love, the barriers that contemporary society create to hinder its achievement, and its possibilities as an answer to the problem of human existence.

Hoffman, Frederick J. *Freudianism and the Literary Mind* (2nd ed.).
Baton Rouge, Louisiana: Louisiana State University Press, 1957.

A scholarly and objective investigation of Freud's influence on such modern writers as James Joyce, D. H. Lawrence, Franz Kafka, Thomas Mann, Sherwood Anderson, F. Scott Fitzgerald, Conrad Aiken, Dylan Thomas, Ludwig Lewisohn, Henry Miller, and others.

Lindner, Robert. *The Fifty-Minute Hour: A Collection of True Psychoanalytic Tales.*
New York: Holt, Rinehart and Winston, Inc., 1955.

Written by a psychoanalyst who was also a good storyteller, these five case histories present a fascinating collection of case types: a compulsive glutton, a homicidal schizophrenic, a dependent personality, a leader in a Fascist movement, and a scientist whose mind has escaped into outer space.

Marcuse, Herbert: *Eros and Civilization: A Philosophical Inquiry into Freud.*
Boston: The Beacon Press, Inc., 1955.

A political scientist considers psychoanalytic theory for its political and sociological implications. The style is heavy, but the book's insights make for a fresh and sensitive contribution to the problem of man in a political society.

Information for
Study and Action

The following information may be helpful to students who, either now or in later years, may wish to follow independently some of the lines of interest suggested by this book.

Information

Before undertaking independent study or action in the field of mental health or in some specialized field related to mental health, it will be helpful to write for a publications list from the appropriate organizations. Publications issued may include books of either technical or general interest, bibliographies, and free or low-cost pamphlets.

National Association for Mental Health, Inc.
10 Columbus Circle, New York 19, New York
Offers materials on mental illness, mental hospitals, problems of children and adolescents, preparation for marriage, aging, and community action. The same materials are usually available also from state and local mental health associations.

National Institute of Mental Health
Bethesda 14, Maryland
Offers general mental health information and publications on alcoholism, mental health of children, community mental health, drugs, hospitals and institutions, mental health legislation, NIMH program activities, and psychiatry and rehabilitation. Other publications on similar subjects may be available from your state's mental health authority.

Mental Health Materials Center, Inc.
104 East 25th Street, New York 10, New York
Handles publications on mental health, family life, and human relations issued by the American Psychiatric Association, the American Public Health Association, the Child Study Association of America, the Group for the Advancement of Psychiatry, and the National Council on the Aging.

The National Council on Alcoholism, Inc.
2 East 103rd Street, New York 29, New York

Rutgers Center of Alcohol Studies
Rutgers University, New Brunswick, New Jersey

The Alcoholism and Drug Addiction Research Foundation
24 Harbord Street, Toronto 5, Ontario, Canada
When writing, specify whether you want information on alcoholism or drug addiction and whether your interest is personal, general, or professional.

Department of Health, Education, and Welfare
Washington 25, D.C.
Children's Bureau offers publications on child care, handicapped children, gifted children, unprotected adoption, retardation, and delinquency. Special Staff on Aging offers annotated bibliography and other materials on aging. Vocational Rehabilitation Administra-
tion offers information on rehabilitation services for physically and mentally disabled persons.

American Society of Criminology
c/o Mr. Donal E. J. MacNamara
New York Institute of Criminology
115-117 West 42nd Street, New York 36, New York
Offers bibliographical materials on criminal psychopathology, narcotics addiction, alcoholism, juvenile delinquency, and other subjects of related interest in the field of criminology.

National Council on Crime and Delinquency
44 East 23rd Street, New York 10, New York
Offers a reading list on delinquency and crime; publications range over child welfare, adolescence, sociology, and mental illness.

National Epilepsy League
203 N. Wabash Avenue, Chicago 1, Illinois

National Society for Crippled Children and Adults
2023 West Ogden Avenue, Chicago 12, Illinois
Offers publications catalog and other materials on wide range of subjects connected with disabling conditions, both physical and mental.

American Association on Mental Deficiency
P. O. Box 96, Willimantic, Connecticut

National Association for Retarded Children
386 Park Avenue South, New York 16, New York

Association for Family Living
32 West Randolph Street, Chicago 1, Illinois
Offers pamphlet list on subjects related to child care, adolescence, sex education, and courtship and marriage. List includes publishers' names and addresses for pamphlets issued by organizations other than the association itself.

Family Service Association of America
44 East 23rd Street, New York 10, New York
Although many of its publications are of professional interest only, some have general interest for students of child development and family living.

The American Institute of Family Relations
5287 Sunset Boulevard, Los Angeles 27, California
Offers list of publications issued by the Institute on preparation for marriage and family life.

Volunteer work

Information about volunteer work in community mental health programs can be obtained from the National Association for Mental Health or from any of its state or local affiliates. Information on volunteer work in mental hospitals, clinics, or rehabilitation facilities may be had from state and local mental health associations, from the directors of volunteers of a local mental hospital or other mental health facility, or from the volunteer bureau of a local community welfare council. Additional information on opportunities for volunteer work in psychiatric settings may be obtained by writing to:

Consultant in Psychiatric Rehabilitation
American Occupational Therapy Association
250 West 57th Street, New York 19, New York.

Mental health careers

Both the National Association for Mental Health and the National Institute of Mental Health prepare and distribute special information on mental health careers. Still more career information, especially in regard to training requirements for specific professions, can be had by writing the following sources.

Clinical or Counseling Psychology:

Education and Training Board
American Psychological Association
1333 16th Street, N.W., Washington 6, D.C.

Psychiatric Nursing:

Committee on Careers, National League for Nursing
10 Columbus Circle, New York 19, New York

Psychiatric and Family Service Social Work:

National Commission for Social Work Careers
345 East 46th Street, New York 17, New York

Personnel Department
Family Service Association of America
44 East 23rd Street, New York 10, New York

Occupational Therapy:

American Occupational Therapy Association
250 West 57th Street, New York 19, New York

Psychiatry:

American Psychiatric Association
1700 18th Street, N.W., Washington 9, D.C.

Psychoanalysis:

Mrs. Helen Fischer, Executive Secretary
American Psychoanalytic Association
One East 57th Street, New York 22, New York

Sources of psychiatric help

Some students may wish to consult qualified psychotherapists, either during college or in later years. In college, they may obtain the names of qualified therapists from student deans or counselors or from professors of abnormal or clinical psychology. In many communities, unfortunately, psychotherapeutic facilities are extremely limited, especially for those of average income.

1. Psychiatrists and clinical psychologists in private practice often have waiting lists, and private therapy may be comparatively expensive; this is particularly true of psychonalysis, which often lasts two or more years and may cost several thousand dollars. Most psychologists and psychiatrists, however, offer briefer intensive therapy.

2. For those who cannot afford psychotherapists in private practice, low-cost clinics are a possible recourse.

Facilities are extremely limited, however, especially outside the larger cities.

3. An excellent possibility for those of average income, or for those who are not sure that extended psychiatric or psychoanalytic treatment is necessary, is the local family service agency. These agencies are a source of help on social and emotional problems for both individuals and families. They can also, if necessary and possible, make referrals to other community facilities, such as psychotherapists, psychiatric clinics, or child-guidance clinics.

The student may also find the following organizations helpful in suggesting sources of qualified psychotherapeutic help.

American Psychiatric Association
1700 18th Street, N.W., Washington 9, D.C.
Will give names and addresses of qualified local psychiatrists, if any.

Board of Professional Affairs
American Psychological Association
1333 16th Street, N.W., Washington 6, D.C.
Will give names and addresses of qualified local clinical or counseling psychologists, if any.

Mrs. Helen Fischer, Executive Secretary
American Psychoanalytic Association
One East 57th Street, New York 22, New York
Will give names and addresses of qualified local psychoanalysts, if any. Will also provide information on location of training institutes affiliated with the Association, at which patients may be able to obtain low-cost psychoanalysis or therapy based on psychoanalytic principles.

Family Service Association of America
44 East 23rd Street, New York 10, New York
Will give addresses of local family service agencies which operate an information service for people seeking help with emotional and family problems.

Veterans Administration
Washington 25, D.C.
Will provide information on psychiatric services available to former members of the U.S. armed forces.

American Institute of Family Relations
5287 Sunset Boulevard, Los Angeles 27, California
Will give names of competent and qualified marriage counselors in or near your own community.

In addition, information and referral sources are often a part of the program of local and state mental health associations. Many useful suggestions on selecting a source of help may also be found in "How to Choose a Psychiatrist," by Frederick C. Redlich, M.D., and Maya Pines, published in *Harper's Magazine,* March 1960.

Glossary

Abnormal. Pathological deviation from the norm or usual; behavior that is detrimental to the individual and/or the group.

Abreaction. Expression of pent-up emotions.

Abulia. Impairment of ability to initiate voluntary action and make decisions.

Achondroplasic dwarfism. Peculiar type of dwarfism caused by defective development of ends of long bones.

Acromegaly. Progressive disease associated with hyperfunction of the pituitary; characterized by permanent enlargement of the skeleton, hands, feet, and face.

Acrophobia. Morbid fear of high places.

Acting-out. Manifesting conflicts in overt behavior rather than controlling them via suppression or other defenses; characteristic of antisocial personalities.

Activation. Energy mobilization.

Acute situational maladjustment. Superficial maladjustment to newly experienced life situations which are especially difficult or trying.

Adaptability. Flexibility in meeting changed circumstances or demands.

Addicts Anonymous. An organization of ex-drug addicts similar to Alcoholics Anonymous.

Addison's disease. Disease of the adrenal glands characterized by an anemic, emaciated condition and a brownish coloration of the skin.

Adjustive behavior. Behavior by which the individual attempts to deal with stress and meet his needs; also, efforts to maintain harmonious relationships with the environment.

Adjustment. Outcome of the individual's efforts to deal with stress and meet his needs.

Adrenal androgens. Hormones, secreted by the adrenal cortex, which regulate the development of secondary sex characteristics, particularly those associated with masculinity.

Adrenal cortex. Outer layer of the adrenal glands; secretes the adrenal androgens and other hormones.

Adrenal glands. Endocrine glands located at the upper end of the kidneys; consist of inner adrenal medulla and outer adrenal cortex.

Adrenaline. Hormone secreted by the adrenal medulla during strong emotion; causes such bodily changes as an increase in blood sugar and a rise in blood pressure. Also called *epinephrine*.

Affect. Any experience of emotion or feeling.

Affective reaction. Psychosis characterized by severe disturbance of mood or feeling.

Aggression. Response to frustration by attacking either the source of frustration or a substitute.

Agitation. Marked restlessness and psychomotor excitement.

Agnosia. Loss or impairment of ability to recognize familiar objects.

Agoraphobia. Morbid fear of large, open places.

Agraphia. Loss or impairment of ability to express ideas in writing.

Akinesia. Loss or impairment of motor functions.

Alarm reaction. First stage of the general-adaption-syndrome, characterized by the mobilization of defenses to cope with a stressful situation.

Alcoholics Anonymous. Organization composed of ex-alcoholics for treatment of alcoholism via personal, religious, and social rehabilitation.

Alcoholism. Abnormal behavior associated with chronic excessive use of alcohol.

Alienation. Lack or loss of relationships to others.

Alzheimer's disease. A presenile dementia.

Ambivalence. Simultaneous existence of contradictory emotional attitudes toward the same person, e.g., love and hate.

Ambivert. Personality type intermediate between introvert and extrovert.

Amblyopia. Visual weakness or dimness without associated organic pathology of the eye structure.

Ambulatory schizophrenic. Mild schizophrenic who is not hospitalized and continues to live and function in the community.

Amentia. Inferior mental capacity originating before or shortly after birth.

Amnesia. Total or partial loss of memory.

Amygdala. Area in the brain whose destruction results in excessive sexual behavior.

Amytal. See **Sodium amytal.**

Anal eroticism. Fixation of libido at anal phase of development with persistence of attempts to maintain pleasurable sensations arising in anal region and with "anal character traits" of obsessive orderliness, cleanliness, miserliness. (Psychoanalytic term.)

Analgesia. Loss or impairment of pain sensibility.

Analytic psychology. The school or system of psychology developed by Carl Jung.

Anamnesis. The personal and family history of a case, as given by the patient.

Androgen. Hormone which regulates development of male sexual characteristics.

Anesthesia. Loss or impairment of sensitivity (usually to touch but often applied to sensitivity to pain and other senses as well).

Anomie. Without relationship or feeling of belonging.

Anorexia (nervosa). Loss or severe diminishment of appetite.

Anoxia. Lack of sufficient oxygen.

Anterograde amnesia. Loss of memory for events following trauma or shock.

Antianxiety drugs. Drugs which are used primarily for alleviating anxiety.

Antidepressant drugs. Drugs which are used primarily to elevate mood and relieve depression.

Antisocial (psychopathic) personality. A type of personality disorder characterized by such traits as impulsivity, inability to profit from experience, and unethical behavior.

Anxiety. A state of emotional tension characterized by apprehension and fearfulness; psychic pain.

Anxiety reaction (anxiety neurosis, anxiety hysteria). A psychoneurotic disorder characterized by persistent morbid anxiety, often punctuated by acute anxiety attacks.

Aphasia. Loss or impairment of ability to communicate and understand language symbols—involving loss of power of expression by speech, writing, or signs, or loss of ability to comprehend written or spoken language—resulting from brain injury or disease.

Aphonia. Loss or marked impairment of voice without associated or organic pathology.

Apoplexy (stroke). Sudden diminution or loss of consciousness with possible paralysis due to brain hemorrhage.

Argyll-Robertson pupil or **sign.** Failure of the pupillary reflex to light, a diagnostic sign in general paresis.

Arteriosclerosis. Degenerative thickening and hardening of the walls of the arteries, occurring usually in old age.

Ascending reticular system. System of ascending nerve fibers which carry impulses from the subcortical areas of the brain to the cerebral cortex.

Astasia-abasia. Inability to stand or walk without the legs wobbling about and collapsing, although the patient has normal control of legs while sitting or lying down; no associated organic pathology.

Astereognosis. Loss or marked impairment of ability to identify objects by the sense of touch.

Asthenic reaction (neurasthenia). A psychoneurotic reaction characterized by feelings of listlessness, lack of enthusiasm, and physical and mental fatigue.

Astraphobia. Morbid fear of lightning, thunder, and storms.

Ataractic drugs. Drugs having therapeutic value with mental patients.

Ataxia. Muscular incoordination, particularly of the arms and legs. See **Locomotor ataxia.**

Athetosis. Recurring involuntary, tentacle-like movements of the hands and feet, usually associated with brain pathology.

Atonicity. Lack of normal muscle tone.

Atrophy. Wasting away or shrinking of a bodily organ.

Attitude. A consistent, learned, emotionalized predisposition to respond in a particular way to a given object, person, or situation.

Aura. Subjective sensations, such as a peculiar odor, preceding an epileptic seizure.

Autistic thinking. Imaginary gratification of desires in fantasy as contrasted with realistic attempts to gratify them.

Autochthonous idea. Idea which appears independent of the individual's train of thought and which he usually regards as foreign and thrust upon him.

Autoeroticism. Masturbation; self-gratification of sexual desires without another person.

Autointoxication. Poisoning by some uneliminated toxin generated within the body.

Automatic writing. Writing without full conscious awareness or control.

Automation. The use of machines to control machines.

Automatism. Performance of repetitious acts of a nonhabitual and nonreflex nature without conscious intent or supervision.

Autonomic nervous system. The section of the nervous system that regulates the internal organs; consists primarily of ganglia connected with the brain stem and spinal cord and may be subdivided into the sympathetic and parasympathetic systems.

Autonomy. Self-reliance; the sense of being an individual in one's own right.

Autosome. Any chromosome other than those determining sex.

Aversive center. Nerve center in brain particularly reactive to noxious stimuli or involved in noxious experience.

Avoidance conditioning. Form of conditioning in which the animal learns to behave in a certain way in order to avoid an unpleasant stimulus.

Bedlam. Popular corruption of the name of the early London asylum of St. Mary of Bethlehem.

Behavior control. Shaping and manipulation of behavior by drugs, persuasion, and other techniques.

Behavior therapy. Psychotherapy based upon conditioned responses and other concepts of behaviorism; primarily directed toward habit change.

Behaviorism. A systematic approach or school of psychology which regards objective, observable manifestations such as motor and glandular responses as the key to an understanding of human behavior. Consciousness, feeling, and other "subjective" phenomena are disregarded as unnecessary or regarded as mediating processes between stimulus and response.

Benign. Of a mild, self-limiting, recoverable nature; not malignant.

Bestiality. Sexual relations with animals.

Biochemical disorders. Disorders involving disturbances in metabolic processes.

Biogenic. Originating in biological processes.

Blocking. Involuntary inhibition of recall, ideation, or communication (including sudden stoppage of speech).

Brain pathology. Diseased or disordered condition of the brain.

Brain potentials (waves). Minute electrical oscillations given off by the cerebral cortex.

Brainwashing. Intensive form of propaganda conducted under highly stressful conditions, as in a prisoner-of-war camp.

Cardiovascular. Pertaining to the heart and blood vessels.

Castrating. Refers to any source of injury to or deprivation of the genitals, or, more broadly, to a threat to the masculinity or femininity of the individual.

Castration complex (castration anxiety). In psychoanalytic theory, fears, centering around injury or deprivation of the genitals as punishment for forbidden sexual desires. Often used more broadly to include interference with self-actualization, particularly with respect to masculine and feminine roles.

Catalepsy. A condition in which the muscles are waxy and semirigid, tending to maintain the limbs in any position in which they are placed.

Catastrophic reaction. Severe disintegration of personality organization under excessive stress.

Catatonia. Schizophrenic reaction characterized by alternation between stupor and excitement.

Catharsis. Discharge of emotional tension associated with repressed traumatic material by "talking it out."

Cathexis. Investment of an object, idea, or action with special significance or affect for the individual.

Censorship. In psychoanalytic theory, the functioning of the ego and superego in preventing dangerous impulses or desires from entering consciousness.

Cerebral arteriosclerosis. See **Arteriosclerosis.**

Cerebral thrombosis. The formation of a clot or thrombus in the vascular system of the brain.

Cerebral vascular accident (CVA). Breaking of a blood vessel in the brain.

Cerebrotonic. Type of personality correlated with the ectomorphic body build, with predominance of intellective processes.

Character disorders. Personality disorders characterized by developmental defects of a pathological type rather than decompensation under excessive stress.

Chemotherapy. Use of drugs in the treatment of mental disorders.

Chlorpromazine. One of the major tranquilizing drugs.

Chorea. A pathological condition characterized by jerky, irregular, involuntary movements. See also **Huntington's chorea.**

Chromosomal map. Photograph showing number and arrangement of chromosomes for a given individual.

Chromosomes. Small bodies found in the cells; contain the genes which determine hereditary traits.

Chronic. Long, persistent, more or less permanent.

Circumstantiality. A characteristic of conversation involving the use of many irrelevant details.

Claustrophobia. Morbid fear of small, narrow, or enclosed places.

Client-centered psychotherapy. A nondirective approach to psychotherapy developed chiefly by Carl Rogers and based on his personality theory.

Climacteric. The life period from 42 to 50 associated with the menopause in women and various related glandular and bodily changes in men.

Clinical picture. The total available diagnostic picture of the patient including symptoms, stresses, dynamics, and so on.

Clonus. Rapid, oscillatory movements in which muscular rigidity and relaxation rapidly follow each other; occurs following tonic phase in grand-mal epilepsy.

Cognitive dissonance. Condition existing when new information is contradictory to one's assumptions.

Cognitive processes. Those processes by means of which an individual becomes aware of objects and situations or represents them to himself. Include learning, reasoning, remembering, imagining, problem solving, and decision making.

Coitus. Sexual intercourse.

Collective unconscious. Term used by Carl Jung to refer to that portion of the unconscious which he considered common to all mankind.

Coma. Profound stupor with unconsciousness.

Combat reaction. Transient personality decompensation resulting from the acute stress of battle experience. Also called *combat exhaustion* and *traumatic reaction to combat.*

Compensation. The ego defense mechanism by means of which an undesirable trait is covered up by exaggerating a desirable trait. May also refer to the correction of an organic deficit by increased functioning of another organ.

Complex. Group of emotionally toned attitudes, desires, or memories which are partially or totally repressed.

Compromise reaction. A response to frustration in which the individual partially relinquishes his original goal; often involves a lowering of his level of aspiration or the acceptance of substitute goals.

Compulsion. Irresistible tendency to perform some act even though the individual realizes it is irrational.

Conative. Striving or purposive; related to motivation.

Conceived values. The individual's conception of the ideal values.

Concussion. Severe impact to the skull causing rupturing of small blood vessels in the brain.

Conditioned inhibition. Process by which an organism or individual is conditioned not to respond to some stimulus which formerly produced a response.

Conditioning. A basic form of learning in which a given stimulus comes to be associated with another stimulus or with a response.

Confabulation. The filling in of memory gaps with false and often irrelevant details.

Conflict. Stress characterized by incompatible desires, needs, or environmental demands.

Congenital. Existing at birth or before birth but not necessarily hereditary.

Conscience (superego). The functioning of an individual's system of moral values in the approval or disapproval of his own thoughts and actions.

Consciousness. State of being aware.

Constitution. The relatively constant biological make-up of the individual, resulting from the interaction of heredity and environment.

Continuous reinforcement. Reward or reinforcement given regularly after each correct response.

Conversion reaction (hysteria). Ego-defensive process by which emotional conflicts are "converted" into physical-illness symptoms; a neurotic reaction.

Convulsion. Pathological, involuntary, muscular contractions.

Coprophilia. Morbid interest in feces.

Correlational studies. Studies dealing with the extent to which two or more variables co-vary.

Counseling psychology. Branch of psychology in which the psychologist tries to help another person solve certain adjustment problems, usually pertaining to education, marriage, or occupation.

Counter transference. Arousal by the patient of the analyst's repressed feelings; symbolic libidinal relationships, partly unconscious, of the psychoanalyst with the analytic patient.

Covert. Concealed, disguised, not directly observable.

Crazy. Mentally disordered (term not used in scientific circles).

Cretinism. Mental and physical disorder associated with thyroid deficiency at an early age; usually involves low intelligence.

Critical period. Period in maturation when the organism is physiologically "prepared" to learn in response to a given type of stimulation. Also used to refer to a period of acute stress.

Cunnilingus. Use of the tongue or mouth in erotic play with female genitals.

Cycloid. Personality type characterized by marked mood alternations between elation and depression.

Cyclothymic personality. Individual characterized by frequently alternating moods of elation and sadness stimulated apparently by internal rather than external events.

Cytogenetics. Science dealing with the study of the structure and functions of genes and chromosomes.

Day hospital. A community-based mental hospital where the patients are treated during the day, returning to their homes at night.

Decompensation. Ego or personality disorganization under excessive stress.

Deconditioning. The extinction of a learned habit by means of conditioning techniques.

Defense mechanism. See **Ego defense mechanism.**

Delinquency. Antisocial or illegal behavior by a minor.

Delirium. State of mental confusion characterized by clouding of consciousness, disorientation, restlessness, excitement, and often hallucinations.

Delirium tremens. Acute delirium associated with prolonged alcoholism; characterized by great anxiety, tremors, and hallucinations.

Dementia. Severe mental disorder involving impairment of mental ability; not congenital.

Dementia praecox. Older term for schizophrenia.

Denial of reality. Ego defense mechanism by means of which the individual protects himself from unpleasant aspects of reality by refusing to perceive them.

Deoxyribonucleic acid (DNA). Principle component of the genes.

Dependent variable. In an experiment, the factor which the hypothesis predicts will change with changes in the independent variable.

Depersonalization. Loss of sense of personal identity, often with a feeling of being something or someone else.

Depression. Emotional state of dejection, gloomy ruminations, feelings of worthlessness and guilt, and usually apprehension.

Dereistic thinking. Thinking (including fantasy) in which the individual ignores reality and logical organization; often applied to "irrational" schizophrenic fantasies.

Desensitization. Therapeutic process by means of which reactions to traumatic experiences are reduced in intensity by repeatedly exposing the individual to them in mild form, either in reality or in fantasy.

Desire. To wish for or want some object or condition related to psychobiological needs.

Deterioration. Degeneration of mental abilities due to brain pathology (sometimes used more broadly to include any impairment of intellectual functions, whether of functional or organic origin).

Deviant behavior. Behavior which deviates markedly from the average or norm; usually pathological in nature as used in abnormal psychology.

Deviant logic. Thinking sequences often found in psychotic behavior in which conclusions are drawn that are not logically compatible with the premises or evidence.

Diagnosis. Determination of the nature and extent of a specific disease.

Didactic group therapy. Group therapy consisting of more or less formal group lectures and discussions.

Diplopia. Double vision; seeing one object as two.

Directive therapy. Type of therapeutic approach in which the therapist supplies direct answers to problems and takes much of the responsibility for the progression of therapy.

Diseases of adaptation. Stomach ulcers and other disease conditions resulting from the stresses of life.

Disintegration. Loss of organization or integration in any organized system.

Disorganization. Lack of orderly relations.

Disorientation. Mental confusion with respect to time, place, or person.

Displacement. Transfer of an emotional attitude or symbolic meaning from one object or concept to another. As an ego defense mechanism, the redirection of emotional charges to less dangerous objects, e.g., hostility aroused by one's boss may be taken out on one's wife.

Dissociation. Separation or "isolation" of mental processes in such a way that they become split off from the main personality or lose their normal thought-affect relationships.

Dissociative reaction. Psychoneurotic reaction characterized by amnesia, fugue, somnambulism, or multiple personality.

Dissonant cognitions. See **cognitive dissonance.**

Dizygotic. Twins from two ova; fraternal twins.

Don Juan. Legendary roué, seducer, and profligate.

Double-bind. Situation in which an individual will be disapproved for performing a given act and equally disapproved if he does not perform it.

Down's syndrome. Type of mental retardation also known as *mongolism.*

Dream analysis. Psychotherapeutic technique involving the interpretation of the patient's dreams.

Drive. Motive power behind behavior.

Drug addiction. Continual use of and physiological dependence upon habit-forming drugs.

Drug habituation. Psychological but not physiological dependence on a drug.

Drug therapy. See **Chemotherapy.**

Dual personality. See **Multiple personality.**

Dynamic. Pattern of interactive factors underlying a particular event or condition.

Dynamism (ego defense mechanism). Device used to protect ego integrity.

Dysfunction. Impairment or disturbance in the functioning of an organ.

Dysgraphia. Impaired ability to write because of ataxia, tremors, or similar conditions.

Dysrhythmia. Disturbance in rhythm.

Dyssocial reaction. Criminal behavior involving distorted value systems but good ego strength.

Echolalia. Meaningless repetition of words by the patient, usually of whatever is said to him.

Echopraxia. Automatic imitation by the patient of another person's movements or mannerisms.

Eclectic therapy. Psychotherapy based on elements of various theories or procedures.

Ecology. Study of mutual relations between organisms and their physical environment.

Economy, principle of. Theory that the individual meets stress in the simplest way possible (in terms of his evaluation of the stress situation and of his own capacities).

Edema. Watery swelling of tissues.

Ego. The self; the integrating core of the personality which mediates between needs and reality.

Ego defense mechanism (reaction). Type of reaction designed to maintain the individual's feelings of adequacy and worth rather than to cope directly with the stress situation; usually unconscious and reality distorting.

Ego-ideal. The person or "self" the individual thinks he could and should be.

Ego involvement. Perception of a situation in terms of its potential effect on the individual.

Ego structure. The attitudes, defensive reactions, and other aspects of the ego or self which form the integrating core of the personality.

Egocentric. Preoccupied with one's own concerns and relatively insensitive to the concerns of others.

Electra complex. In psychoanalytic theory, an excessive emotional attachment (love) of the daughter for the father.

Electroencephalograph (EEG). Instrument for recording brain potentials.

Electroencephalography. The recording of electrical brain waves.

Electroshock treatment. Use of electricity to produce convulsions and unconsciousness; most widely used form of convulsive therapy.

Embolism. Lodgment of an embolus in a blood vessel too small to permit its passage.

Emotion. Complex state of feeling involving conscious experience, internal and overt responses, and power to motivate the organism to action.

Emotional immaturity. Failure to develop normal adult degrees of independence and self-reliance, with consequent use of immature adjustive patterns and inability to maintain equilibrium under stresses which most people can meet satisfactorily.

Emotional instability reaction. Immature reaction to minor stress, characterized by excitability and ineffectiveness.

Emotional insulation. Ego defense mechanism in which the individual reduces the tensions of need and anxiety by withdrawing into a shell of passivity.

Emotional reinforcement. The reinforcement of adjustive patterns via the mobilized energy and drive of various emotional reactions.

Empathy. Ability to understand and to some extent share the state of mind of another person.

Encephalitis. Inflammation of the brain.

Encephalitis lethargica. Sleeping sickness.

Encephalography. Examination of the brain and mapping of the result.

Endocrine glands. Ductless glands which secrete hormones directly into the lymph or blood stream.

Endogenous. Originating from or due to internal causes.

Energizer. Drug which has a stimulating effect.

Enuresis. Bed-wetting; involuntary discharge of urine.

Environmental evaluation. Way in which the individual views the world—its dangers, pleasures, etc.

Enzyme. Complex organic substance which aids in such processes as digestion.

Epidemic encephalitis. Disease of the brain believed to be caused by a filterable virus.

Epidemiology. Study of the distribution of physical or mental disorders.

Epilepsy. Chronic disease characterized by disturbances in consciousness and/or convulsive seizures. See **Grand mal, Petit mal, Psychomotor epilepsy, Jacksonian epilepsy.**

Epileptic furor. See **Psychomotor epilepsy.**

Equilibrium. Balance.

Erogenous zones. Those parts of the body which when stimulated give rise to sexual feelings, e.g., lips, breasts, sex organs.

Erotic. Pertaining to sexual stimulation and gratification.

Estrogens. Female hormones produced by the ovaries.

Ethnic group. Group of people who are treated as distinctive in terms of culture and group patterns.

Etiology. Causation; the systematic study of the causes of disorders.

Eugenics. Science concerned with conditions that affect inborn or hereditary qualities of a race or group in direction of either improvement or degeneracy.

Eunuch. Castrated male.

Euphoria. Exaggerated feeling of well-being and contentment.

Excitation. Process whereby activity is elicited in a nerve.

Excitement. Generalized emotional state.

Exhibitionism. Public display or exposure of genitals for conscious or unconscious purpose of sexual excitement and pleasure.

Existential anxiety. Anxiety concerning one's ability to find a satisfying and fulfilling way of life.

Existential psychotherapy. Therapy based on existential concepts, emphasizing the development of a sense of self-direction and meaning in one's existence.

Existentialism. View of man which emphasizes man's responsibility for himself and for becoming the kind of person he should be.

Exogenous. Originating from or due to external causes.

Exophthalmic goiter (Graves' disease). Disorder of the thyroid characterized by enlargement of this gland, protrusion of the eyeballs, and various mental symptoms.

Exorcism. Various techniques practiced in ancient and medieval times for casting the "evil spirit" out of the mentally ill, based on the concept that mental illness was caused by demons or evil spirits.

Experimental neurosis. Neurosis-like behavior in animals produced when they are forced to make discriminations or adjustments which are beyond their range of adjustive adequacy.

External frustration. Environmental obstacle to goals and need satisfactions.

Extrapunitive. Characterized by a tendency to evaluate the source of frustrations as external and to direct hostility outward.

Extrovert. Personality type characterized by interests directed toward the external environment of people and things rather than toward inner experiences and oneself; outgoing, sociable.

Fabrication. Relating imaginary events as if they were true without intent to deceive; confabulation.

Familial. Pertaining to characteristics which tend to run in families and have a higher incidence in certain families than in the general population.

Family group therapy. Treatment of the family or key family members as a group rather than treatment of the patient apart from his family setting.

Fantasy. Daydream; also, an ego defense mechanism by means of which the individual escapes from the world of reality and gratifies his desires in fantasy achievements.

Feeling. The pleasure and pain dimension of emotion or bodily functions.

Fellatio. Insertion of penis into the mouth for purposes of sexual gratification.

Festinating gait. Incoordinated, hurried, uncertain walk in *paralysis agitans.*

Fetishism. Sexual deviation in which the individual achieves sexual gratification by means of an object (hair, handkerchief, panties) which symbolizes the person to whom it belongs.

Fetus. Embryo after the sixth week following conception.

Fixation. Unreasonable or exaggerated attachment to some person or arresting of emotional development on a childhood or adolescent level.

Flight into illness. Escaping from some unpleasant situation or problem by simulating the symptoms of some organic ailment and/or becoming convinced that one is ill.

Flight of ideas. Rapid succession of ideas without logical association or continuity.

Focal lesion. Lesion in a particular area of the brain.

Folie à deux. A psychotic interpersonal relationship involving two people; e.g., husband and wife both become psychotic with similar symptomatology.

Fornication. Extramarital sexual relations.

Fraternal twins. Dizygotic twins; fertilized by separate germ cells, thus not having same genetic inheritance. May be of the same or opposite sex.

Free association. Uninhibited expression of ideas as they enter consciousness during therapy.

Free-floating anxiety. Anxiety not referable to any specific situation or cause.

Frigidity. Lack of or reduced sexual desire in a woman; inability to experience sexual pleasure or gratification.

Fröhlich's syndrome. Disease of anterior lobe of pituitary occurring during adolescence, resulting in obesity and arrested development of sex glands.

Frontal lobe. Portion of the brain active in reasoning and other higher thought processes.

Frustration. Thwarting of a need or desire.

Frustration tolerance. See **Stress tolerance.**

Fugue. Dissociative reaction in which the individual leaves his present life situation and establishes a somewhat different mode of life in another locale. Although he is amnesic for his past life, his other abilities are unimpaired and he appears normal to those around him.

Functional. Having no demonstrable organic basis or etiology; psychogenic.

Functional psychosis. Psychosis precipitated primarily by psychological stress.

Furor. Transitory outbursts of excitement or anger during which the individual may be quite dangerous.

Galectosemia. Type of mental retardation due to metabolic deficiency.

Gamblers Anonymous. Voluntary organization of ex-gamblers patterned along the lines of Alcoholics Anonymous.

Gamete. Male or female germ cell; contains only half the number of chromosomes found in other cells of the body.

Ganser syndrome. The simulation of confusion, disorientation, or other supposed psychotic behavior, especially among prisoners; may involve malingering or neurotic behavior or a mixture of both.

"Gay." Slang term referring to homosexuals.

Gene. Element of germ plasm found in the chromosomes; responsible for the transmission of hereditary characteristics.

General-adaptation-syndrome. Reaction of the individual to excessive stress; consists of the alarm reaction, the stage of resistance, and the stage of exhaustion.

Generalized other. An individual's abstracted concept of others.

Genetic code. Means by which DNA controls the sequence and structure of proteins manufactured within each cell and also makes exact duplicates of itself.

Genetics. Science of heredity.

Genitalia. Organs of reproduction, especially the external organs.

Geriatrics. Science of the diseases and treatment of the aged.

Germ cells. Reproductive cells (male sperm and female ovum) which unite to produce a new individual.

Gerontology. Science dealing with the study of old age.

Gestalt psychology. School of psychology which emphasizes patterns rather than elements or connections, taking the view that the whole is more than the sum of its parts.

Gigantism. Abnormally tall stature resulting from hyperfunctioning of the pituitary.

Glioma. Tumor.

Globus hystericus. Choking sensation in the throat; once a common complaint in hysterical (conversion) reactions.

Glove anesthesia. Area of anesthesia approximating the area of hand and wrist that would be covered by a glove. Formerly common in hysterical (conversion) reactions.

Goal. Object or condition for which an individual strives.

Gonads. Testes or ovaries.

Grand mal. Major convulsive attack with loss of consciousness in epilepsy.

Graves' disease. See **Exophthalmic goiter.**

Group therapy. Psychotherapy with two or more patients at the same time.

Guilt. Unpleasant feeling of sinfulness arising from behavior or desires contrary to one's ethical principles. Involves both self-devaluation and apprehension growing out of fears of punishment.

Gynephobia. Morbid fear of women.

Habit. Any product of learning, whether it is a customary or transitory mode of response.

Hallucination. Sense perception for which there is no appropriate external stimulus.

Hallucinogens. Drugs or chemicals capable of producing hallucinations.

Hebephrenic reaction. Type of schizophrenic reaction characterized by marked shallowness and distortion of affect and silly, inappropriate behavior.

Hedonism. Doctrine that pleasure is the primary good or value in life.

Hemi-. Prefix meaning *half.*

Hemiplegia. Paralysis of one lateral half of the body.

Hemophobia. Pathological fear of blood. Also *hematophobia.*

Hereditary potential. Individual's genetic potentialities for development.

Heredity. Genetic transmission of characteristics from parents to their children.

Hermaphrodite. Anatomical sexual abnormality in which an individual has well-developed sex organs of both sexes.

Heterosexuality. Sexual interest in a member of the opposite sex.

Hierarchy of needs. The concept that needs arrange themselves in a hierarchy in terms of importance or "prepotence," from the most basic biological needs to those psychological needs concerned with self-actualization.

Holistic. A systematic approach to science involving the study of the whole or total configuration; the view of man as a unified psychobiological organism inextricably immersed in a physical and sociocultural environment.

Homeostasis. Tendency of organisms to maintain conditions making possible a constant level of physiological functioning.

Homosexuality. Sexual interest in or overt sexual activity with members of one's own sex.

Hostility. Emotional reaction or drive toward the destruction or damage of an object interpreted as a source of frustration or threat.

Huntington's chorea. Incurable disease, presumably of hereditary origin, which is manifested in jerking, twitching movements and mental deterioration.

Hutchinson's teeth. Notched or peg-shaped teeth typically found in congenital syphilis.

Hydrocephalus. Enlargement of the cranium from the pressure of spinal fluid.

Hydrotherapy. Use of hot or cold baths, ice packs, etc., in treatment.

Hyper-. Prefix meaning *increased*.

Hyperalgesia. Increased sensitivity to pain.

Hyperesthesia. Increased touch sensitivity.

Half-way house. Treatment facility assisting in transition of patient from mental hospital to the community; usually of the in-patient type.

Hyperkinesis. Excessive or exaggerated muscular activity.

Hypermnesia. Unusual retentiveness of memory or clarity of memory images.

Hypersensitivity. Oversensitivity.

Hypertension. High blood pressure.

Hypesthesia. Decreased sensitivity, especially to touch.

Hypnagogic. Pertaining to drowsiness or a sleep-like or trance-like state.

Hypnoanalysis. Analytic psychotherapy carried out under hypnosis.

Hypnosis. Trance-like mental state induced in a cooperative subject by suggestion.

Hypnotherapy. Use of hypnosis in psychotherapy.

Hypnotic regression. Process by which a subject is brought to relive, under hypnosis, early forgotten or repressed experiences.

Hypo-. Prefix meaning *decreased*.

Hypochondriasis. Neurotic reaction characterized by excessive concern about one's health in the absence of related organic pathology.

Hypokinesis. Decreased motor activity.

Hypomania. Mild form of manic excitement in manic-depressive reactions.

Hypothalamus. Key structure at the base of the brain; important in temperature regulation, emotion, and motivation.

Hypothesis. Statement or proposition, usually based on observation, which is tested in an experiment; may be denied or supported by experimental results but never conclusively proved.

Hysteria. Older term used to include conversion and dissociative neurotic reactions; involves the appearance of symptoms of organic illness in the absence of any related organic pathology.

Id. In psychoanalytic terminology, the reservoir of instinctual drives; the deepest, most inaccessible, and most primitive stratum of the mind.

Identical twins. Monozygotic twins; developed from a single fertilized egg.

Identification. Ego defense mechanism in which the individual identifies himself with some person or institution, usually of an illustrious nature.

Idiographic. Approach to personality study which emphasizes the unique aspects of the individual personality.

Idiopathic. Of unknown causation; inherent in the constitutional make-up of the individual.

Idiot. Older term referring to severe and profound degrees of mental retardation (I.Q. below 24).

Illusion. Misinterpretation of sensory data; false perception.

Imbecile. Older term, no longer used in the U.S., referring to moderate to severe degrees of mental deficiency (I.Q. of 25-49).

Immaturity reaction. Subcategory of the APA classification which includes individuals who are emotionally immature and therefore unable to maintain their equilibrium and independence under stress.

Impotence. Inability of male to achieve orgasm.

Imprinting. Form of learning in very young animals which determines the exact course an instinctive behavior pattern will take; e.g., a duckling learns to follow the first moving object it sees.

Impulse. Tendency to action.

Impulsiveness. Tendency to act without thinking.

Impunitive. Tending toward a conciliatory attitude rather than blaming either self or others.

Inadequate personality. Individual who is neither physically nor mentally grossly deficient, but who manifests inadequate responses to intellectual, emotional, social, and physical demands; e.g., ineptness, poor judgment, lack of adaptability.

Incest. Sexual relations between close relatives such as father and daughter or brother and sister.

Incompetent. Legal designation of an individual as incapable of managing his affairs with ordinary prudence because of mental illness or deficiency.

Independent variable. Factor whose effects are being examined in an experiment; it is manipulated in some way while the other variables are held constant.

Individuation. Pattern of development from the general to the specific; characteristic of human maturation.

Infantilism. Persistence of infantile emotional attitudes and patterns into adult life.

Inferiority complex. Strong feelings of inadequacy and insecurity which color an individual's entire adjustive efforts.

Inhibition. Conscious restraint of impulse or desire.

Innate. Inborn.

Inner controls. Reality, value, and possibility assumptions which serve to inhibit dangerous or undesirable behavior; could also apply to conditioned avoidance reactions.

In-patient. Hospitalized mental patient.

Insanity. Legal term for mental disorder, implying lack of responsibility for one's acts and inability to manage one's affairs.

Insight. Clinically, the individual's understanding of his illness or of the motivations underlying his behavior; in general psychology, the sudden grasp or understanding of meaningful relationships in a situation.

Instinct. Inborn tendency to particular behavior pattern under certain conditions in absence of learning; characteristic of species.

Instrumental conditioning. Type of conditioning in which the subject learns to make a predetermined response, such as pressing a lever, in order to obtain a reward.

Insulin shock therapy (insulin coma therapy—ICT).

Treatment of psychiatric disorders by the production of hypoglycemic states by injection of insulin.

Integration. Organization of parts (psychological, biological functions) to make a functional whole.

Integrity. The acceptance of oneself and the living up to one's moral values.

Intellectualization. Ego defense mechanism by which the individual achieves some measure of insulation from emotional hurt by cutting off or distorting the emotional charge which normally accompanies hurtful situations.

Internal frustration. Barrier to goals and need satisfactions arising from personal limitations or attitudes of the individual.

Intrapsychic conflict. Inner conflict; e.g., between values.

Introjection. Incorporation of qualities or values of another person or group into one's own ego structure with a tendency to identify with them and to be affected by what happens to them.

Intropunitive. Responding to frustration by tending to blame oneself.

Introvert. Personality type characterized by the direction of interest toward oneself and one's inner world of experiences.

Invert. Homosexual.

Involutional melancholia (Involutional psychotic reaction). Depressive psychotic reaction characterized by depression, agitation, and apprehension.

Ionizing radiation. Form of radiation, such as an X-ray, that causes the formation of ions in substances through which it passes. Often used in the treatment of cancer. Major cause of gene mutations.

Isoimmunization. Incompatibility of blood type between mother and fetus.

Isolation. Ego defense mechanism by means of which contradictory attitudes or feelings which normally accompany particular attitudes are kept apart, thus preventing conflict or hurt.

Jacksonian epilepsy. Muscle spasms usually restricted to a small group of muscles or to one half of the body, although occasionally the entire body may become involved. Consciousness is usually retained.

Juvenile delinquency. Legally prohibited behavior committed by minors.

Juvenile paresis. General paresis in children; usually of congenital origin.

Kleptomania. An irresistible compulsion to steal, usually without any use for the article stolen.

Korsakoff's psychosis. Psychosis usually associated with chronic alcoholism and characterized by disorientation, gross memory defects, confabulation, and polyneuritis.

Lability. Instability, particularly with regard to affect.

Latent. Inactive or dormant.

Latent content. In psychoanalytic theory, repressed wishes that are indirectly expressed in the manifest content of dreams.

Lesbianism. Homosexuality in women.

Lesion, neural. Injury in specific area of brain or nervous system.

Leucotomy. Brain operation, involving the severing of association pathways in the frontal lobes of the brain, in which the instruments are inserted transorbitally.

Level of aspiration. Standard by which the individual judges success or failure of his behavior.

Levels of defense. Biological, psychological, or sociological adjustive reactions.

Libido. In general psychoanalytic terminology, the instinctual drives of the id. In a narrow sense, the drive for sexual gratification.

Life history method. Technique of psychological observation in which the development of particular forms of behavior is traced by means of records of the subject's past or present behavior.

Life style. The general pattern of assumptions, motives, cognitive styles, and coping techniques that characterize the behavior of a given individual and give it consistency.

Lobectomy. Excision or removal of parts of the prefrontal lobes; formerly used in treatment of certain severe cases of mental illness.

Lobotomy. Brain operation involving the severing of pathways in the frontal lobes of the brain; used in treatment of certain severe cases of mental illness.

Locomotor ataxia. Muscular incoordination usually resulting from syphilitic damage to the spinal-cord pathways.

Logic-tight compartments. Form of intellectualization in which contradictory desires or attitudes are "sealed off" in separate areas of consciousness.

Logotherapy. School of existential analysis which focuses upon the individual's need to see meaning in his life.

Low adaptation energy. Low constitutional energy.

Lues. Syphilis.

Lunacy. Legal term roughly synonymous with insanity. The term originates from the Latin word *luna* (moon); the moon was presumed to be the cause of certain types of mental illness.

Lycanthropy. The delusion of being a wolf.

Lysergic acid diethylamide (LSD-25). A very potent hallucinogen which is being used on a limited basis in some forms of psychotherapy.

Macrocephalic. Having an abnormally large cranium.

Macropsia. Abnormal condition in which objects are perceived as larger than they really are.

Madness. Nontechnical synonym for mental illness.

Maladaptive. Characteristic of a response which makes it inappropriate in dealing with stress.

Maladjustment. A more or less enduring failure of adjustment; lack of harmony with self or environment.

Malinger. To fake illness or disability symptoms consciously.

-mania. Suffix denoting a compulsive or morbid preoccupation with some impulse or activity; e.g., compulsive stealing is called kleptomania.

Manic-depressive reaction. Group of psychotic reactions characterized by prolonged periods of excitement and overactivity (manic), or by periods of depression and underactivity (depressive), or by alternation or mixture of the two.

Manifest content. In psychoanalytic theory, the apparent meaning of a dream; masks the latent content.

Mannerism. Recurring stereotyped gesture, posture, or movement.

Marasmus. Gradual withering of tissues; may result from inadequate mothering in infancy.

Marijuana. Drug derived from the plant *cannabis indica;* used in cigarettes called "reefers."

Masochism. Sexual deviation in which an individual obtains sexual gratification from having pain inflicted upon him.

Mass madness. Group outbreak of conversion reactions (hysteria).

Masturbation. Self-stimulation of genitals for sexual gratification.

Maternal deprivation. Lack of adequate care and stimulation by the mother or mother surrogate.

Maturation. Process of development and body change resulting from heredity rather than learning.

Maturity, emotional. Degree to which an individual manifests behavior appropriate to his age and intelligence levels.

Mechanism. Device (e.g., rationalization) by which an individual unconsciously attempts to protect his ego integrity.

Mechanization (frosting). Lack of adequate material love; coldness in mother-infant or parent-child relationships.

Megalomania. Delusions of grandeur.

Melancholia. Mental disorder characterized by extreme depression.

Meninges. Membranes which envelop the brain and spinal cord.

Meningitis. Inflammation of the meninges.

Mental age (MA). An individual's degree of mental development as measured against standardized norms.

Mental deficiency. Synonym for mental retardation; the latter term is now preferred.

Mental disease. Mental disorder associated with an organic disease of the nervous system.

Mental disorder. Mental illness; psychopathology.

Mental hygiene. Scientific field primarily concerned with healthy personality development and the prevention of psychiatric disorders.

Mental retardation. Low intelligence which renders the individual to some degree ineffective in handling his affairs.

Mescaline. One of the hallucinogenic drugs.

Mesmerism. Theories of "animal magnetism" (hypnosis) formulated by Anton Mesmer.

Metabolic psychoses. Psychotic reactions associated with metabolic disturbances.

Metrazol therapy. Administration of metrazol to produce epileptiform convulsions, formerly used in the treatment of certain psychotic reactions.

Microcephaly. Abnormal smallness of the head with associated mental retardation.

Micropsia. Perception of objects as smaller than they actually are.

Migraine. Psychosomatic disorder characterized by recurrent severe headaches, often with visual disturbances and nausea.

Milieu. The immediate environment, physical or social or both; sometimes used to include the internal state of an organism.

Military psychology. Field of psychology that deals with psychological problems in the armed forces.

Model psychoses. Psychotic-like states produced by various hallucinogenic drugs such as LSD.

Modus operandi. Manner or mode of behavior; a criminal's typical pattern of performing his crimes.

Mongolism. Type of mental retardation; associated with chromosomal irregularities.

Monomania. Compulsive preoccupation with one idea or activity.

Monoplegia. Paralysis of one arm or leg.

Monozygotic twins. Identical twins, developed from one fertilized egg.

Mood. Emotional state of relatively long duration; usually less intense than a simple emotion.

Moral moron. One who fails to develop adequate moral values.

Morbid. Unhealthy, pathological.

Moron. Term formerly used to refer to mild degrees of mental retardation.

Motivation. Often used as a synonym for drive or activation; implies that the organism's actions are partly determined in direction and strength by its own inner nature.

Motivational sequence. Need-goal-means-satisfaction sequence.

Motive. Internal condition which directs action toward some goal; term usually used to include both the drive and the goal to which it is directed.

Multiple personality. Type of dissociative reaction characterized by the development of two or more relatively independent personality systems in the same individual.

Mutation. Sudden change in the composition of a gene, usually causing harmful or abnormal characteristics to appear in the offspring.

Mutism. Refusal or inability to speak.

Mysophobia. Morbid fear of germs or contamination.

Myxedema. Disorder due to thyroid deficiency in adult life, characterized by mental dullness.

Narcissism. Self-love.

Narcolepsy. Abnormal reaction characterized by transient, compulsive states of sleepiness.

Narcotherapy (narcoanalysis, narcosynthesis). Carrying on psychotherapy while the patient is under the influence of a narcotic drug, such as sodium amytal or pentothal.

Narcotic drugs. Drugs such as morphine which lead to physiological dependence and increased tolerance.

Necrophilia. Morbid sexual interest in corpses.

Need. Biological or psychological condition whose gratification is necessary for the maintenance of homeostasis or for self-actualization.

Need-satisfaction sequences. Behavior leading to the gratification of needs, with accompanying pleasure or satisfaction.

Negativism. Form of aggressive withdrawal which involves refusing to cooperate or obey commands, or doing the exact opposite of what has been requested.

Neobehaviorism. General point of view that emphasizes the central position of *response* in psychology.

Neo-Freudians. Modern psychoanalysts who believe that therapy must be aimed at understanding the patient's present situation as well as his childhood experiences and unconscious mental processes.

Neologism. Word coined by a patient.

Neoplasm. Tumor.

Nervous breakdown. Refers broadly to lowered integration and inability to deal adequately with one's life situation.

Nervousness. State of emotional tension, restlessness, and hypersensitivity.

Neurasthenia. Older term for asthenic reaction, a neurotic reaction characterized by chronic mental and physical fatigue and listlessness.

Neurologist. Holder of an M.D. degree who specializes in the treatment of diseases or injuries of the brain and nervous system.

Neuron. Individual nerve cell.

Neuropsychiatry. Broadly speaking, the scientific field concerned with the diagnosis, treatment, and prevention of psychiatric disorders.

Neurosis (psychoneurosis). Mild functional personality disorder in which there is no gross personality disorganization and in which the patient does not ordinarily require hospitalization. Synonymous with *psychoneurotic disorder, neurotic disorder.*

Neurosyphilis. Syphilis affecting the central nervous system.

Neurotic-depressive reaction. Psychoneurotic reaction characterized by marked, persistent dejection and discouragement.

Night hospital. Mental hospital in which an individual may receive treatment during all or part of the night while carrying on his usual occupation in the daytime.

Nihilistic delusion. Fixed belief that everything is unreal, that nothing really exists.

Nomadism. Withdrawal reaction in which the individual continually attempts to escape frustration by moving from place to place or job to job.

Nomothetic. Approach to personality study which emphasizes those psychological elements presumed to be common to all individuals.

Nondirective therapy. An approach to psychotherapy in which the therapist refrains from advice or direction of the therapy. See also **Client-centered psychotherapy.**

Normal. Conforming to the usual or norm.

Norms. Standard based on measurement of a large group of persons; used for comparing the scores of an individual with those of others in a defined group.

Nosology. Naming and classification of diseases.

Nurture. Environmental surroundings or care of the young.

Nyctophobia. Morbid fear of darkness.

Nymphomania. Excessive sexual desire in females.

Obsession. Persistent idea or thought which the individual recognizes as irrational but cannot get rid of.

Obsessive-compulsive reaction. Psychoneurotic reaction characterized by persistent irrational thoughts and impulses.

Occupational therapy. Use of occupational training or activity in psychotherapy.

Ochlophobia. Morbid fear of crowds.

Oedipus complex. In psychoanalytic theory, excessive emotional attachment, involving conscious or unconscious incestuous desires, of the son for his mother.

Operant conditioning. Form of learning in which the correct response is reinforced and becomes more likely to occur.

Opium. Narcotic drug which leads to physiological dependence and the building up of tolerance; derivatives are morphine, heroin, paregoric, and codeine.

Oral eroticism. Pleasurable sensations centering in lips and mouth; related to early pleasure arising out of nursing.

Organic psychosis. Psychosis associated with organic brain pathology.

Organic viewpoint. Theory that all mental disorders have an organic basis.

Orientation. Individual's ability to comprehend the environment with reference to time, place, and person.

Orthopsychiatry. Field of psychiatry primarily concerned with unhealthy personality trends and the maladjustments of children.

Outcome research. Research concerned with the effects of treatment or other procedures upon behavior.

Out-patient. An ambulatory patient who visit a hospital clinic for examination and treatment, as distinct from a hospitalized patient.

Out-patient clinic. Clinic where patients are treated on a nonhospitalized basis.

Ovaries. Female gonads (sex glands).

Overcompensation. Marked exaggeration of compensatory activities in an effort to cover up weakness or inferiority. See **Compensation.**

Overloading. Subjecting to excessive stress; also refers to forcing the organism to handle or "process" an excessive amount of information.

Overprotection. Shielding a child to the extent that he becomes too dependent on the parent.

Overt behavior. Activities which can be observed by an outsider.

Ovum. Female gamete or germ cell.

Panic. Severe personality disorganization involving intense anxiety and usually either paralyzed immobility or blind flight.

Paralysis agitans. See **Parkinson's disease.**

Paramnesia. False memory in which the individual "remembers" events that did not occur.

Paranoia. Disorder characterized by slowly developing, logical, well-systematized delusions of persecution and/or grandeur.

Paranoid personality. Individual showing abortive paranoid reaction characterized by projection (as a defense mechanism), suspiciousness, envy, extreme jealousy, and stubbornness.

Paranoid state. Disorder characterized by transient, poorly systematized delusions of persecution and/or grandeur.

Paraplegia. Paralysis of the legs and lower part of the body.

Parasympathetic division. Division of the autonomic nervous system which controls most of the ordinary vital functions, such as digestion.

Parergasic. Pertaining to psychotic disorders characterized by incongruities, oddities, mannerisms, etc.

Paresis. General paresis; an organic psychosis caused by syphilitic infection of the brain.

Paresthesia. Pathological cutaneous sensations, such as the feeling that bugs are crawling under the skin.

Parkinson's disease (Paralysis agitans). Progressive disease characterized by a masklike, expressionless face and various neurological symptoms.

Parorexia. Appetite or craving for peculiar or inappropriate foods.

Partial reinforcement. In conditioning, reinforcement that is given intermittantly rather than on every trial.

Passive-aggressive reaction. Immaturity reaction in which aggressiveness is expressed by such passive measures as pouting, stubbornness, procrastination, inefficiency, and passive destruction.

Passive-dependency reaction. Immaturity reaction characterized by helplessness, indecesiveness, and a tendency to cling to others for protection and support.

Pathogenesis. Origin and course of development of a disease.

Pathogenic. Pertaining to conditions which lead to pathology.

Pathological intoxication. Severe cerebral and behavioral disturbance in an individual whose tolerance to alcohol is extremely low.

Pathological personality types. Individuals who are neither neurotic nor psychotic but manage to maintain a borderline adjustment which might be likened to an abortive stage in the development of a more severe mental disorder.

Pathology. Diseased or abnormal physical or mental condition; also the science which deals with such conditions.

Pederasty. Sexual intercourse between males via the anus.

Pedophilia. Sexual deviation in which an adult engages in or desires sexual relations with a child.

Peer group. Social group of equivalent age and status.

Pellagra. A vitamin deficiency disease.

Penis-envy. The desire of the female for male sex organs and status.

Pentothal interview. See **Narcotherapy.**

Perceptual defense. Selective perception; the unconscious screening out of unpleasant or threatening perceptions.

Peripheral nervous system. Nerve fibers passing between the central nervous system and the sense organs, muscles, and glands.

Perseveration. Persistent continuation of a line of thought or activity once it is under way. Clinically, inappropriate repetition.

Personality. The unique pattern of traits which characterizes the individual.

Personality pattern disturbance. Any of several personality types that can rarely be basically altered by therapy and tend to decompensate to psychosis under stress; includes inadequate personality, schizoid personality, cyclothymic personality, and paranoid personality.

Personality trait disturbance. Emotional immaturity with inability to maintain emotional equilibrium and independence under even minor stress; includes emotionally unstable personality, passive-aggressive personality, compulsive personality, and related personality trait disturbances.

Perversion. Deviation from normal.

Pervert. A sexual deviate.

Petit mal. Relatively mild form of epilepsy involving a temporary partial lapse of consciousness.

Phallic symbol. Any object which resembles the erect male sex organ.

Phantasy. See **Fantasy.**

Phenylketonuria (PKU). Type of mental retardation resulting from a metabolic deficiency.

Phobia. Irrational fear; the individual may realize its irrationality but nevertheless be unable to dispel it.

Phobic reaction. Psychoneurotic reaction characterized by various irrational fears.

Photophobia. Morbid fear of strong light.

Physiology. Study of the functioning of living organisms and their parts.

Pick's disease. Form of presenile dementia.

Pineal gland. Small gland at the base of the brain whose function is unknown.

Pituitary gland. Endocrine gland associated directly with growth.

Placebo. Inactive substance administered in place of an active drug.

Play therapy. Use of play activities in psychotherapy with children. The counterpart for adults is recreational therapy.

Pleasure centers. Areas of the brain where stimulation is known or presumed to be pleasurable in nature. Also called *reward centers.*

Pleasure principle. In psychoanalysis, the demand that an instinctual need be immediately gratified regardless of reality.

Polyneuritis. Disease of the peripheral nerves.

Possessed. Ancient term for mental illness, based on the belief that the patient was "possessed" by an evil spirit.

Post-hypnotic suggestion. Suggestion given during hypnosis to be carried out by the subject after he is brought out of hypnosis.

Precipitating cause. The particular stress which precipitates a disorder.

Predisposing cause. Factor which lowers the individual's stress tolerance and paves the way for the appearance of a disorder.

Predisposition. Likelihood that an individual will develop certain symptoms under given stress conditions.

Prefrontal lobectomy. See **Lobectomy.**

Prefrontal lobes. Forward part of the frontal lobes of the brain.

Prefrontal lobotomy. See **Lobotomy.**

Prejudice. Emotionally toned conception favorable or unfavorable to some person, group, or idea.

Prenatal. Before birth.

Pressure. Demand made on an organism.

Primary cause. Cause without which a disorder would not have occurred.

Primary mental abilities. Relatively independent abilities, such as verbal comprehension and numerical ability, which make up "general intelligence."

Primary reinforcement. Reward which directly satisfies some need of the organism.

Privileged communication. Freedom from the obligation to report to the authorities information concerning legal guilt revealed by a client or patient; enjoyed by lawyers, by clergymen, and in some states by physicians.

Prodrome. Early or warning symptom of a disease.

Prognosis. Prediction as to the probable course and outcome of a disorder.

Projection. Ego defense mechanism in which the individual places the blame for his difficulties upon others or attributes to others his own unethical desires and impulses.

Projective technique. Any psychological technique for the diagnosis of personality organization utilizing relatively unstructured stimuli which reveal the individual's basic attitudes, conflicts, and so on.

Promiscuity. Nonselective sexual intercourse.

Prostitution. Sexual intercourse for financial gain.

Pseudocommunity. Delusional social environment developed by a paranoiac.

Pseudocyesis. False pregnancy; a hysterical (conversion) reaction.

Pseudolalia. Meaningless sounds made by some psychotics.

Psychasthenic reaction. See **Obsessive-compulsive reaction.**

Psychiatric evaluation. Medical, psychological, and sociological data used in the diagnosis of mental disorders.

Psychiatric nursing. Field of nursing primarily concerned with mental disorders.

Psychiatric social work. Field of social work primarily concerned with the mentally ill.

Psychiatrist. Medical doctor who specializes in the diagnosis and treatment of mental disorders.

Psychiatry. Field of medicine dealing with the understanding, diagnosis, treatment, and prevention of mental disorders.

Psychic pain. Synonym for *anxiety.*

Psychoanalysis. A comprehensive, systematic approach to human behavior whose broad outlines were laid down by Sigmund Freud. It comprises a theory of personality development and functioning, psychotherapeutic techniques, and research techniques for the investigation of personality functions.

Psychobiology. Broad, eclectic approach to human behavior fostered by Adolf Meyer, emphasizing the pluralistic determinants of behavior and the necessity for maintaining a holistic approach.

Psychodrama. Psychotherapeutic technique worked out by J. L. Moreno in which the acting of various roles is a cardinal part of the therapy.

Psychogenic. Of psychological origin; originating in the psychological functioning of the individual.

Psychological assessment. Psychometric and other personality and behavior assessment data used in the diagnosis of mental disorders.

Psychological feedback. Knowledge of results process whereby the individual gains information concerning the correctness of his responses.

Psychological need. Need emerging out of environmental interactions, e.g., the need for social approval.

Psychological test. Standardized procedure designed to measure the subject's performance on a specified task.

Psychology. Science of human behavior.

Psychomotor. Involving both psychological and physical activity.

Psychomotor epilepsy. State of disturbed consciousness in which the individual may perform various actions, sometimes of a homicidal nature, for which he is later amnesic.

Psychoneurosis. See **Neurosis.**

Psychopathic personality. Older term used to refer to a variety of immature and pathological personality types now included under the general heading of

Character and Behavior Disorders in the Army classification. See also **Antisocial personality.**

Psychopathology. Field of science dealing with the causes and nature of abnormal behavior.

Psychophysiologic disorder. Physical symptoms resulting from the continued emotional mobilization during sustained stress; often involves actual tissue damage. Also called *psychosomatic disorder.*

Psychosis. Severe personality disorder involving loss of contact with reality and usually characterized by delusions and hallucinations. Hospitalization is ordinarily required.

Psychosocial development. Development of the individual in his relationships to others.

Psychosomatic disorder. See **Psychophysiologic disorder.**

Psychosurgery. Any of the various techniques of brain surgery for the treatment of mental disorders.

Psychotherapy. Treatment of personality maladjustment by psychological techniques.

Psychotic. Pertaining to a psychosis.

Puberty praecox. Oversecretion of adrenal hormones in childhood, resulting in pathologically early sexual maturity.

Puberty. Stage of physical development when reproduction first becomes possible.

Pyromania. Compulsion to set fires.

Pyrophobia. Morbid fear of fire.

Random sample. Sample drawn in such a way that each member of the population has an equal chance of being selected.

Randomization. Selection of experimental groups by chance or at random in the hope of eliminating any selective factor which might affect the results of the experiment.

Rape. To force sexual relations upon another person.

Rapport. Interpersonal relationship characterized by a spirit of cooperation, confidence, and harmony.

Rating scale. Device for evaluating oneself or someone else in regard to specific traits.

Rational psychotherapy. Psychotherapeutic technique developed by Albert Ellis by which the patient is encouraged to substitute rational for irrational ideas in an inner dialog.

Rationalization. Ego defense mechanism in which the individual thinks up "good" reasons to justify what he has done, is doing, or intends to do.

Reaction formation. Ego defense mechanism in which dangerous desires and impulses are prevented from entering consciousness or from being carried out in action by the fostering of opposed types of behavior and attitude.

Reaction sensitivity. Sensitization or tendency to perceive certain elements of a total situation, as a result of acquired attitudes and previous experience.

Reactive depression (neurotic depressive reaction). Continued depression in the face of loss or environmental setback.

Reality assumptions. Assumptions which relate to the gratification of needs in the light of environmental possibilities, limitations, and dangers.

Reality principle. Awareness of the demands of the environment and adjustment of behavior to meet these demands.

Reality testing. Behavior aimed at testing or exploring the nature of the individual's social and physical environment; often used more specifically to refer to the testing of the limits of permissiveness of his social environment.

Recessive gene. Gene which is effective only when paired with an identical gene.

Reciprocal inhibition psychotherapy. Conditioning approach to habit change utilizing systematic desensitization.

Recidivism. Recurrence of delinquency or criminal behavior despite punishment or treatment.

Recompensation. Increase in integration or inner organization. Opposite of *decompensation.*

Redintegration. Condition in which an element of an experience serves to re-establish the whole.

Referral. Sending or recommending an individual for psychiatric diagnosis or treatment.

Regression. Ego defense mechanism in which the individual retreats to the use of less mature responses in attempting to cope with stress and maintain ego integrity.

Reinforcement. In conditioning, the process of rewarding the learner for making adequate responses.

Reliability. Degree to which a test or measuring device produces the same result each time it is used to measure the same thing.

Remission. Marked improvement or recovery appearing in the course of a mental illness; may or may not be permanent.

Repression. Ego defense mechanism by means of which dangerous desires and intolerable memories are kept out of consciousness.

Reserpine. One of the major tranquilizing drugs.

Resistance. Tendency to maintain symptoms and resist treatment or uncovering of repressed material.

Retroactive inhibition. Difficulty in remembering due to interference by activity which has occurred since the learning.

Retrograde amnesia. Loss of memory for events prior to the patient's accident or injury.

Reward centers. See **Pleasure centers.**

Rigid control. Ego defense mechanism involving reliance upon inner restraints, such as inhibition, suppression, repression, and reaction formation.

Role. See **Social role.**

Role obsolescence. Condition pertaining when the social role of a given individual is no longer of importance to the social group.

Role playing. Form of psychotherapy in which the individual acts out a social role other than his own or tries out a new role for himself.

Romberg sign. Tendency to sway when eyes are closed and the feet are placed close together; diagnostic sign in locomotor ataxia.

Sadism. Sexual deviation in which sexual gratification is obtained by the infliction of pain upon others.

St. Vitus' dance. Hysterical chorea of common occurrence during the Middle Ages.

Sample. Group upon which measurements are taken; should normally be representative of the population about which an inference is to be made.

Satyriasis. Excessive sexual desire in males.

Scapegoating. Displacement of aggression onto some object, person, or group other than the source of frustration.

Schizoid personality. Abortive schizophrenic reaction characterized by unsociability, seclusiveness, serious-mindedness, and often eccentricity.

Schizophrenia. Major psychotic disorder characterized by emotional blunting and distortion, disturbances in thought processes, and a withdrawal from reality.

Scotophilia. Sexual deviation in which the individual obtains full sexual gratification from "peeping" or observing others, particularly in the nude or in the act of intercourse. Also called *voyeurism* or *inspectionalism.*

Secondary cause. Factor which contributes to a mental illness but which in and of itself would not have produced it, as distinct from a *primary cause,* without which the disorder would not have occurred.

Secondary reinforcement. Reward which does not directly satisfy any need but has come to be satisfying in itself, usually because of previous association with some primary reinforcement.

Sector therapy. Type of goal-limited psychotherapy, worked out by Felix Deutsch, utilizing "associative anamnesis" as a therapeutic technique for keeping the therapy focused on a particular problem area.

Security. Maintenance of conditions necessary to need gratification.

Self (ego). The integrating core of the personality which mediates between needs and reality.

Self-actualization. Development of one's potentialities; synonym for *self-fulfillment.*

Self-concept. The individual's assumptions about his identity and worth as a person.

Self-devaluation. Lowered feelings of worth and self-esteem.

Self-differentiation. Degree to which the individual achieves a sense of unique identity apart from the group.

Self-esteem. Feeling of personal worth.

Self-evaluation. Way in which the individual views himself—his worth, adequacy, etc.

Self-ideal. See **Ego-ideal.**

Self-recrimination. Self-condemnation and blame.

Self theory. Personality theory which utilizes the self-concept as the integrating core of personality organization and functioning.

Senile. Pertaining to old age.

Sensory deprivation. Restriction of sensory stimulation below the level required for normal functioning of the central nervous system.

Sentence-completion test. Form of projective technique utilizing incomplete sentences which the subject is to complete.

Sequelae. Symptoms remaining as the aftermath of a disorder.

Sexual deviate. Individual who manifests homosexuality, pedophilia, fetishism, or other sexually pathological behavior.

Shaping. Form of instrumental conditioning used in training animals; at first, all responses resembling the desired one are reinforced, then only the closest approximations, until finally the desired response is attained. Also called *approximation.*

Sheltered workshops. Workshops where mentally retarded or otherwise handicapped individuals can engage in constructive work in the community.

"Shock" reaction. Transient personality decompensation in the face of sudden acute stress.

Shock therapy. Use of insulin, metrazol, or electroshock as methods of treatment in mental disorders.

Siblings. Offspring of the same parents.

Situational test. Test which measures performance in a simulated life situation.

Social feedback. Exchange of error-reducing information among members of a group.

Social pathology. Abnormal patterns of social organization, attitudes, or behavior; undesirable social conditions which tend to the production of individual pathology.

Social role. The particular function and place of an individual in a group.

Socioeconomic status. Position on the social and economic scale in the community, as determined largely by income and occupational level.

Sociogenic. Having its roots in sociocultural conditions or causes.

Sociopathic personality disturbance. Inability to conform to prevailing social standards; lack of social responsibility.

Sociotherapy. Treatment of interpersonal aspects of the patient's life situation.

Sodium amytal, Sodium pentothal. Barbiturate drugs sometimes used in psychotherapy to produce a state of relaxation and suggestibility.

Sodomy. Sexual intercourse via the anus.

Somatic. Pertaining to the body.

Somatotype. Physique or build of a person, as assessed by various theories relating temperament to physical characteristics.

Somnambulism. Sleepwalking.

Sour grapes mechanism. Form of rationalization in which the individual denies the hurt of frustration by concluding that what he wanted is not worth having after all.

Spasm. Intense, involuntary, usually painful contraction of a muscle or group of muscles.

Spasticity. Marked hypertonicity or continual overcontraction of muscles, causing stiffness, awkwardness, and motor incoordination.

Sperm. Male gamete or germ cell.

Spontaneous recovery. Spontaneous remission. Also, in conditioning, the return of a conditioned response which has once been extinguished.

Spontaneous remission. Recovery of a mental patient without treatment or with minimal treatment.

S-R psychologists. Psychologists who emphasize the role of stimulus-response (S-R) connections in learning, also called *associationists.*

Stage of exhaustion. Third and final stage in the general-adaptation-syndrome, in which the organism is no longer able to resist continuing stress; may result in death.

Stage of resistance. Second stage of the general-adaptation-syndrome.

Startle reaction. Sudden involuntary motor reaction to unexpected stimuli, especially to mild stimuli, as a result of a state of hypersensitivity.

Stereotype. A preconceived, prejudiced picture of the members of some particular group.

Stereotypy. Persistent and inappropriate repetition of phrases, gestures, or acts.

Stimulus generalization. The spread of a conditioned response to some stimulus similar to, but not identical with, the conditioned stimulus.

Stress. Any conditions impinging on the organism which require adjustive reactions.

Stress interview. Interview of a subject or patient under simulated stress conditions.

Stress tolerance (frustration tolerance). Nature, degree, and duration of stress which an individual can tolerate without undergoing serious personality decompensation.

Stupor. Condition of lethargy and unresponsiveness, with partial or complete unconsciousness.

Stuttering (stammering). Speech disorder characterized by blocking and repetition of initial sounds of words.

Subconscious. Pertaining to mental activities of which the individual is not aware; term no longer in common use.

Subcortical structures. Structures of the brain lying under the cortex.

Sublimation. Ego defense mechanism by means of which frustrated sexual energy is partially channeled into substitutive activities.

Substitution. Acceptance of substitute goals or satisfactions in place of those originally sought after or desired.

Superego. Conscience; ethical or moral dimensions (attitudes) of personality.

Suppression. Conscious forcing of desires or thoughts out of consciousness; conscious inhibition of desires or impulses.

Surrogate. Substitute parental figure.

Symbol. Image, object, or activity that is used to represent something else.

Symbolism. Representation of one idea or object by another.

Sympathetic division. Division of the autonomic nervous system which is active in emergency conditions of extreme cold, violent effort, and emotions.

Sympathism. Ego defense mechanism by means of which one gains the sympathy of others by telling them about one's "bad breaks" and difficulties.

Synanon. Voluntary group organization for the rehabilitation of ex-criminal drug addicts.

Syncope. Temporary loss of consciousness resulting from cerebral anemia.

Syndrome. Group or pattern of symptoms which occur together in a disorder and represent the typical picture of the disorder.

Syphilophobia. Morbid fear of syphilis.

Tabes dorsalis. See **Locomotor ataxia.**

Tachycardia. Rapid pulse.

Tarantism. Type of hysterical dancing occurring in epidemic form during the Middle Ages.

Task-oriented reaction. Realistic rather than ego-defensive approach to stress.

Temporal lobe. Portion of the brain located just beneath the temples.

Tension. Condition arising out of the mobilization of psychobiological resources to meet a threat; physically, involves an increase in muscle tonus and other emergency changes; psychologically, is characterized by feelings of strain, uneasiness, and anxiety.

Testosterone. Male sex hormone.

Therapeutic. Pertaining to treatment or healing.

Therapeutic community. The hospital environment used for therapeutic purposes.

Therapy. Treatment; application of various treatment techniques.

Threat. Imagined or expected danger to the self.

Thyroid glands. Endocrine glands in the neck which affect body metabolism, intelligence, and physical growth.

Thyrotoxic. Pertains to oversecretion of thyroxin.

Thyroxin. Hormone secreted by the thyroid glands.

Tic. Intermittent twitching or jerking, usually of facial muscles.

Tonic. Pertaining to muscle tension or contraction; muscle tone.

Topectomy. Type of brain surgery used in the treatment of certain cases of chronic mental illness which do not respond to other types of therapy; involves the removal of circumscribed areas of brain tissue.

Total push. Type of therapy in which all treatment procedures—medical, psychological, sociological—are coordinated into a total therapeutic attack.

Toxemia. Pathological condition resulting from poison in the blood.

Toxic. Poisonous.

Toxic deliria (psychoses). Severe disturbances in cerebral functions resulting from toxins.

Trait. Any persisting characteristic of an individual.

Trance. Sleeplike state in which the range of consciousness is limited and voluntary activities are suspended; a deep hypnotic state.

Tranquilizer. Drug which calms and soothes the patient; a sedative.

Transference. Identification, usually unconscious, of some person in the individual's immediate environment with some important person in his past life. In therapy, the identification of the therapist with someone in the patient's past.

Transient situational personality disorders. Acute symptom response to an overwhelming situation in a basically stable personality.

Transorbital lobotomy. See **Lobotomy.**

Transvestism. Persistent desire to dress in garments of the opposite sex and feeling of discomfort when dressed in clothing of one's own sex; persistent association of sexual excitement with dressing in clothes of the opposite sex. Also called *transvestitism.*

Trauma. Wound or injury, may be either biological or psychological in nature.

Traumatic. Pertaining to a wound or injury.

Traumatic neurosis. See **"Shock" reaction.**

Tremor. Continuous, involuntary muscular trembling or spasm, limited to a small area.

Trephine (trepan). Instrument for perforating the skull.

Tube feeding. Feeding patients by inserting a flexible tube through the nostrils into the throat and pouring liquids directly into the esophagus.

Twilight state. State of disordered consciousness in which the individual performs purposeful acts for which he is later amnesic. See **Psychomotor epilepsy.**

Unconscious. Lack of awareness; in Freudian theory, that portion of the psyche which is a storehouse of repressed or forgotten memories and desires which are not directly accessible to consciousness but may be brought into consciousness when ego restraints are removed, as in hypnosis.

Unconscious motivation. Motivations for an individual's behavior of which he is unaware.

Undoing. Ego defense mechanism by means of which the individual performs activities designed to atone for his misdeeds, thereby, in a sense, "undoing" them.

Vacillate. To waver or fluctuate between two or more alternatives.

Validity. Extent to which a measuring instrument actually measures what it was designed to measure.

Value assumption. Any assumption as to the nature of "right" and "wrong" or "good" and "bad."

Vasomotor. Pertaining to the walls of the blood vessels.

Vegetative. Withdrawn or deteriorated to the point where the individual leads a passive, vegetable-like existence.

Verbigeration. Prolonged and monotonous repetition of meaningless words and phrases.

Vertigo. Dizziness.

Vicarious living. Attempt to evade efforts toward self-fulfillment by repressing one's own individuality and identifying with some hero or ideal.

Vicious circle. Chain reaction in which the individual resorts to an unhealthy defensive reaction in trying to solve his problems, which only serves to complicate his problems and make them more difficult to solve.

Virilism. Accentuation of masculine secondary sex characteristics, especially in a woman or young boy, caused by overactivity of the adrenal cortex.

Viscera. Internal organs.

Voyeurism. See **Scotophilia.**

War neuroses. See **Combat reaction.**

Wassermann test. Serum test used in the diagnosis of syphilis.

Withdrawal. Intellectual, emotional, or physical retreat.

Withdrawal symptoms. Wide range of symptoms evidenced by addicts when the drug on which they are physiologically dependent is not available.

Word hash. Jumbled or incoherent use of words by psychotic or disoriented patients.

Working through. Confronting and dealing with a problem situation until satisfactory adjustments are achieved and firmly established; a growth experience in the direction of maturity.

Worry. Persistent, undue concern about past behavior or about anticipated dangers in the present or future.

X-chromosome. Sex-determining chromosome found in all female gametes and half of all male gametes; union of two gametes with X-chromosomes produces female offspring.

Y-chromosome. Sex-determining chromosome found in half of all male gametes; uniting with the X-chromosome always provided by the female gamete produces male offspring.

Zoophilia. Abnormal degree of affection for animals or a particular animal.

Zoophobia. Morbid fear of animals.

Zygote. Cell formed by the union of the male and female gametes.

Acknowledgments

The illustration program of *Abnormal Psychology and Modern Life* was made possible through the cooperation of many psychologists, psychiatrists, and special sources. Certain illustrations are acknowledged in some detail on the pages on which they appear; sources for others are given in the reference sections. All other sources are acknowledged below. To all, the author and the publisher wish to express their appreciation.

The excerpt from *The Cocktail Party* by T. S. Eliot, which appears on p. 244, is reprinted by permission of the publishers, Harcourt, Brace & World, Inc., New York, and Faber and Faber, Ltd., London.

The illustrations appearing on the front endsheets were reproduced from *The Door of Serenity* by Dr. Ainslie Meares. They were made available by Dr. Meares and were reprinted by permission of Charles Thomas Co., Springfield, Illinois, and Faber and Faber, Ltd., London.

The charts and graphs are the work of John Mayahara.

2 Chicago Tribune photo

4 The Bettmann Archive, Inc.

7 The Bettmann Archive, Inc.

10 Chicago Tribune photo

24 The Bettmann Archive, Inc. (Meyer).
Photo from European Picture Service, by Douglas Glass (Jung).
Culver Pictures, Inc. (Freud, Pavlov, Kraepelin).

30 The Bettmann Archive, Inc. (left).
Culver Pictures, Inc. (upper right).
Radio Times Hulton Picture Library (lower right).

31 Radio Times Hulton Picture Library.
The Bettmann Archive, Inc. (center and right).

34 The Bettmann Archive, Inc. (left and bottom right).
Culver Pictures, Inc. (upper right).
The Bettmann Archive, Inc.

35 & 47 The Bettman Archive, Inc.

36 From *A History of Medical Psychology*, by Gregory Zilboorg and W. Henry, W. W. Norton, 1941, used by permission.

40 The Bettmann Archive, Inc. (center and upper and lower right).
Radio Times Hulton Picture Library (left).

41 Culver Pictures, Inc. (lower.)
The Bettman Archive, Inc. (upper).

60 Photo by Pinney, Monkmeyer Press Photo Service.

66-67 From the film *Shyness,* courtesy of National Film Board of Canada.

76 Courtesy of Dr. Neal E. Miller and the American Psychological Association.

86-87 From the film *The Quiet One* released by Joseph Burstyn Film Enterprises, Inc.

89 Courtesy of Dr. Philip L. Harriman and the *American Journal of Psychiatry*.

102 Courtesy of Dr. John Romano, Dr. Jules Masserman, and the W. B. Saunders Company.

110 From the film *Stress,* National Film Board of Canada.

116 Photo by Landwehr, Monkmeyer Press Photo Service.

120 Redrawn with permission from "Chromosomes and Disease" by A. G. Bearn and James L. German II, *Scientific American,* November 1961.

127 Courtesy of University of Oregon Medical School and *Medicine at Work* published by the Pharmaceutical Manufacturers Association.

131 Courtesy of Dr. Harry F. Harlow.

137 Courtesy of Dr. Albert Bandura and the American Psychological Association.

138 From the film *Angry Boy,* courtesy of Mental Health Film Board.

148 From the film *Overdependency,* courtesy of National Film Board of Canada.

150 Courtesy of National Rehabilitation Association, photo by Boston University Photo Service.

166 United Press International.

175 From the film *Let There Be Light,* U.S. Signal Corps.

180 Wide World Photo.

192 Courtesy of *Today's Health,* published by the American Medical Association.

206 Courtesy of Dr. Percy G. Hamlin and the *Military Surgeon.*

234-235 Photos courtesy of Dr. Jules Masserman.

242-243 From the film *Overdependency,* courtesy of National Film Board of Canada.

248 Adapted from "Life Stress and Bodily Disease" by Harold G. Wolff, in *Contributions Toward Medical Psychology,* edited by Arthur Weider. Copyright 1953, The Ronald Press Company.

262 Reproduced from *Depth Psychology and Salvation* by Wilfried Daim, Frederick Ungar Publishing Co., New York, 1963, with permission.

280 Photo from Black Star by Joe Pazen (upper).

Courtesy of Dr. Strecker and Dr. Ebaugh, and the Blakiston Company (lower).

284 Photos from Black Star, by St. Louis Post Dispatch.

306 Courtesy of Thea Stein Lewinson and the *American Journal of Psychiatry.*

320 Radio Times Hulton Picture Library (left). After A. Hrdlicka, "Art and Literature in the Mentally Abnormal." *American Journal of Insanity,* LV (1899) (right).

329 From *Art and Mental Health* by Edward Adamson, Director of Art, Netherne Psychiatric Hospital, England. Reprinted with permission.

352 Reproduced from "The Delinquent and the Law" by Ruth and Edward Brocher, *Public Affairs Pamphlet No. 337.* Courtesy of Public Affairs Committee, Inc., New York.

355 Redrawn from "Guilt, Shame, and Tension in Graphic Projections of Stuttering," by Dr. Joseph G. Sheehan, Mr. Peter A. Cortese, and Dr. Robert G. Hadley, *The Journal of Speech and Hearing Disorders,* 1962, Vol. 27, No. 2.

376-377 Photos courtesy of Commissioner Lloyd W. McCorkle, Department of Institutions and Agencies, and Director Albert C. Wagner, Division of Correction and Parole, State of New Jersey.

395 Courtesy of Dr. David Olkon and Lea and Febiger and Company.

420 Photo by Larry Keighley. Reprinted by permission of *The Saturday Evening Post* and the U.S. Public Health Service Hospital, Washington.

427 Courtesy National Council on Alcoholism.

430 Courtesy National Council on Alcoholism.

434-435 Photos by Gilbert A. Milne & Co. Courtesy of Dr. H. David Archibald and the Alcoholism and Drug Addiction Foundation, Toronto 5, Ontario.

454 Courtesy of Dr. H. Houston Merritt. Reproduced with permission from *Neurosyphilis* by Dr. Merritt, Dr. Adams, and Dr. Solomon.

468 Courtesy of the *American Journal of Psychiatry.*

475 & 486 Courtesy of Dr. H. Houston Merritt. Reproduced with permission from *A Textbook of Neurology,* 3rd ed., 1963, by H. Houston Merritt, Lea & Febiger, Publishers.

485, 488, 501 & 504 Courtesy of Dr. Nathan Malamud. Reproduced with permission from *Atlas of Neuropathology* by Nathan Malamud, University of California Press.

492 From *Living with Epileptic Seizures* by Samuel Livingston. Charles C. Thomas, Publisher. Reproduced by permission.

518 Courtesy of the Marbridge Foundation.

525 Courtesy of Dr. Clemens E. Benda. Reproduced with permission from "Aspects of Endocrine Disorders in Mental Retardation" by C. E. Benda in *Proceedings of Second International Congress on Mental Retardation,* Vienna, 1961, Part 1, pp. 278-294. (S. Karger, Basel, New York, 1963.)

527 Courtesy of Dr. Clemens E. Benda. (left). Courtesy of Dixon State School, Dixon, Illinois (center, right).

528 Courtesy of the National Association for Retarded Children, Inc.

533 Courtesy of Dixon State School, Dixon, Illinois.

540 Photo from Magnum Photos, Inc., by I. Morath.

546 Courtesy of Hans Huber, Publisher, Berne. From *Psychodiagnostik* by Hermann Rorschack (Distributors for the U.S., Grune & Stratton, Inc., New York) (upper left). Courtesy of Dr. Henry Murray and the Harvard University Press (lower right).

547 Courtesy of Dr. Edwin S. Shneidman for *The Make A Picture Story (MAPS) Test.* New York: The Psychological Corporation, 1949.

548 Official USAF Photos, Aerospace Medical Division, USAF Hospital, Lackland AFB, Texas.

549 Courtesy of Dr. Gerhild von Staabs.

554 Courtesy of Smith Kline & French Laboratories.

573 Courtesy of The National Association for Mental Health, Inc. (Not actual patients)

574 Courtesy of the Community Child Guidance Centers, Chicago. Counselor Miss Eleanore Redwin, Alfred Adler Institute. Photos by Don Stebbins.

576 Courtesy of the National Institute of Mental Health Public Service, in cooperation with St. Elizabeth's Hospital, Washington, D.C.

577 Radio Times Hulton Picture Library.

578 Courtesy Smith Kline & French Laboratories.

589 Time Inc.

599 Courtesy of Dr. Stewart G. Armitage.

605 Wide World Photos, Inc.

606 Wide World Photos, Inc. (upper left). An Arthur Leipzig photo (right). Photo by Gus Pasquarella (lower left).

612 Courtesy of The National Association for Mental Health, Inc.

628 Courtesy of the American Friends Service Committee, photo by Matt Herron.

634 Redrawn by permission from Public Affairs Pamphlet No. 228, *New Medicines for the Mind: Their Meaning and Promise,* By Gilbert Cant. Public Affairs Committee, Inc., New York.

Name Index

Subject Index

CLASSIFICATION OF ABNORMAL REACTION PATTERNS

Disorders of psychogenic origin or without clearly defined physical cause or structural change in brain

Transient Situational Personality Disorders

Acute symptom response to an overwhelming situation in basically stable personality.

- Gross stress reaction—reactions to combat or to civilian catastrophes.
- Adjustment reaction of infancy—undue apathy, excitability, feeding or sleeping difficulties of psychogenic origin.
- Adjustment reaction of childhood—habit disturbances (nail-biting), conduct disturbances (truancy), neurotic traits (tics).
- Adjustment reaction of adolescence—transient reactions due to adolescent conflicts.
- Adult situational reaction—maladjustment to difficult situation.
- Adjustment reaction of later life—reactions to environmental demands of later life.

Psychoneurotic Disorders (Neuroses)

Chief characteristic is anxiety, directly felt or unconsciously controlled by use of various psychological defense mechanisms. No gross disorganization of personality or loss of contact with reality.

- Anxiety reaction—diffuse anxiety often punctuated by acute anxiety attacks.
- Dissociative reaction—fugue, amnesia, multiple personality, somnambolism.
- Conversion reaction—anxiety converted into functional symptoms of illness.
- Phobic reaction—persistent fears despite individual's realization that they are irrational.
- Obsessive-compulsive reaction—persistent, irrational thoughts and impulses.
- Depressive reaction—extreme dejection over environmental setback or loss.
- Psychoneurotic reaction, other.

Psychophysiologic Autonomic and Visceral Disorders ("Psychosomatic Disorders")

Structural change following chronic, exaggerated physiological expression of emotion; the emotion is repressed and discharged through viscera.

- Skin reaction, such as atopic dermatitis.
- Musculoskeletal reaction, as tension headaches.
- Respiratory reaction, as hiccoughs.
- Cardiovascular reaction, as hypertension.
- Hemic and lymphatic reaction, as diffuse changes in blood systems.
- Gastrointestinal reaction, as chronic gastritis.
- Genitourinary reaction, as menstrual disturbances.
- Endocrine reaction, as obesity.
- Nervous system reaction, as general fatigue.
- Reaction of organs of special sense, as physical changes in retinae or eardrums.

Psychotic Disorders (Functional Psychoses)

Personality disintegration with disorientation for time, place, and/or person. Hospitalization ordinarily required.

- Schizophrenic reactions—a group of psychotic reactions involving withdrawal from reality, disturbances in thought processes, and emotional blunting and distortion.
    1 Simple type—apathy and indifference without conspicuous delusions or hallucinations.
    2 Hebephrenic type—severe disorganization with silliness, mannerisms, delusions, hallucinations.
    3 Catatonic type—conspicuous motor behavior with excessive motor activity and excitement or generalized inhibition and stupor.
    4 Paranoid type—poorly systematized delusions; often hostility and aggression.
    5 Acute indifferentiated type—sudden schizophrenic reaction which may clear up or develop into other definable type.
    6 Chronic undifferentiated type—chronic, mixed symptomatology not fitting other types.
    7 Schizo-affective type—admixture of schizophrenic and affective reactions.
    8 Childhood type—schizophrenic reactions occurring before puberty.